Microsoft® Exchange Server 2010

Best Practices

Siegfried Jagott and Joel Stidley
with the Microsoft Exchange Server Team

PUBLISHED BY
Microsoft Press
A Division of Microsoft Corporation
One Microsoft Way
Redmond, Washington 98052-6399

Library of Congress Control Number: 2010929323

Printed and bound in the United States of America.

1 2 3 4 5 6 7 8 9 WCT 5 4 3 2 1 0

A CIP catalogue record for this book is available from the British Library.

Microsoft Press books are available through booksellers and distributors worldwide. For further information about international editions, contact your local Microsoft Corporation office or contact Microsoft Press International directly at fax (425) 936-7329. Visit our Web site at www.microsoft.com/mspress. Send comments to mspinput@microsoft.com.

Acquisitions Editor: Martin DelRe
Developmental Editor: Karen Szall
Project Editor: Carol Vu
Editorial Production: Christian Holdener, S4Carlisle Publishing Services
Technical Reviewers: Tony Redmond and Scott Schnoll; Technical Review services provided by Content Master, a member of CM Group, Ltd.
Cover: Tom Draper Design

Body Part No. X17-00144

I dedicate this book to my mum, Johanna, for all the support and love she gave to me throughout my whole life. Without her effort I would not be where I am today.

—Siegfried Jagott

To my wife, Andrea. Without her patience, love, and support I would not be able to take on new and exciting challenges.

—Joel Stidley

Contents at a Glance

Contents

PART III UPGRADING TO EXCHANGE SERVER 2010

About the Sidebars

This book includes sidebars that provide you with real-world experience and insights from Microsoft Exchange product group members as well as well known Exchange subject matter experts. Each sidebar covers a specific topic of expertise and reflects the opinion of the sidebar contributor, not necessarily the opinion of Microsoft or the authors of this book.

Sidebars in this book are categorized into the following distinguishing sidebar elements:

- **Notes from the Field** Insights and experiences from Microsoft consultants, technical support professionals, partners, and early adopter customers.
- **Inside Track** Insider information or tips from Microsoft program managers, technical product managers, developers, and testers.
- **Lessons Learned** Examples of things that did not go well or what not to do. Learn from others so that you don't repeat their mistakes.
- **Trade-Offs** Best practices are rarely absolute. We point out key decisions that you should be weighing.

Chapter 1

Chapter 2

Chapter 3

Chapter 4

Chapter 5

Chapter 6

Chapter 7

Chapter 8

Chapter 9

Chapter 10

Chapter 11

Chapter 12

Chapter 13

Chapter 14

Chapter 15

Chapter 16

Chapter 17

Foreword

Every day we rely more and more on electronic mail to handle our most basic communication needs. Our reliance leads us to require dependability. To ensure an efficient transition from an older system to Exchange 2010, you must determine how to integrate a myriad of systems. Your users will demand compatibility and high levels of uptime, and managers will demand lower costs in terms of servers and storage. I have spent 15 years at Microsoft working with teams to enhance the end-user experience. I've never been as excited about the work we've done as I am now with the release of Exchange 2010. With Exchange 2010, our development team was dedicated to building a brand-new release that effectively took a deliberate approach to building new features, refining existing features, and making sure at every step that we stayed true to our goals of delivering an awesome release of Exchange. The breadth and depth of the technologies Microsoft Exchange 2010 finally delivers is astounding. Exchange 2010 provides new features such as Exchange Control Panel (ECP), Domain on the Middle Tier (DoMT), High Availability (HA), and Role-Based Access Control (RBAC). Federated sharing, archiving, and lower storage cost options are knocking down barriers that have traditionally stopped customers from deploying or meeting user needs. Any one of the features I just mentioned would be interesting on its own, but the combination is truly compelling.

Exchange is easy to install, but to get the most out of it you need to explore the many features and capabilities that more than 20 million lines of code bring to it. You want to understand the software in detail, and the authors of this book have the experience to show you all of the features and components. The authors have done an awesome job getting the details right and have taken great care in bringing you what I think is the best book on the subject. Recently there has been talk about books like this being out of date as soon as they go to press, or that getting information from the Internet is the new way to learn. To this I say, "Nonsense!" With this book, you will gain from the authors' vast experience with a topic that is vast in scope. How did the authors get such in-depth, detailed experience with a product released in November of 2009? That level of detail—including best practices for deployment—requires time and teamwork, and that is where the Technology Adoption Program (TAP) comes into play.

Microsoft's Technology Adoption Program is designed to validate new versions of Exchange by having customers test and run production deployments of pre-release builds of the next version of Exchange. This gives participants the opportunity to provide real-time design feedback to the Exchange product development team. Microsoft deployed the first production Exchange 2010 server on April 16, 2007, and in January of 2008 released bits to TAP customers and partners for review. Shortly thereafter, the authors and other customers were running Exchange 2010 in their production deployments. When Microsoft officially shipped Exchange 2010 on November 9, 2009, TAP partners had already deployed more than 200,000 mailboxes into production! Through this preliminary process, the authors participated in every step of the final design, gaining valuable experience with each TAP release for deployment. During this TAP deployment phase, all TAPs work together with Microsoft to find the best product and best ways to deploy. Here is what one TAP had to say about this process:

> *"We have learned a lot through this process, and not only about Exchange 2010. By interacting with other TAP members and the product group on a daily basis we have been able to remove the blinders we sometimes wear from administering the same system day in and day out. This has allowed us to consider alternate approaches we could take to improve our system overall and to identify where some of our own shortcomings are. I've seen things posted I've never even thought of before and hope that our contributions have done the same . . ."*

Individually and collectively the authors who wrote this book have been working with Exchange 2010 for as long as many senior developers at Microsoft. They have done an awesome job of providing readers with the ins and outs of the full range of features of Exchange 2010, which will help you get the most out of the product. Exchange administrators will find the experienced, hands-on approach of this book invaluable in designing and deploying Exchange 2010. You wouldn't want a book that only skimmed and introduced new features. Fortunately for you, this book is based on the experience of years of successful deployments in complex environments and a teamwork approach to the final design process. Microsoft and TAPs have built a product that we are truly proud of, and this book brings you the right way to walk through it. This book definitely belongs on the shelf of every serious Exchange administrator and IT manager.

David Espinoza

Senior Program Manager, Exchange Ship Team

Microsoft Corporation

May 2010

I love the idea of a best practice book. The initial challenge is to capture the knowledge of real-life designs and deployments that underpin best practice. The next challenge is to validate that the claimed best practice is actually valuable. The final challenge is to focus on a best practice that has enduring value rather than the tenets that flame into existence sparked by a notion of someone at a conference or other event and expire just as quickly when everyone realizes that the proposition being advanced isn't such a good idea after all. Active Directory designs for Exchange are an example of best practice that has changed since 1999. The initial designs for large corporations all seemed to favor the "minimal root domain and geographic sub-domains" design at a time when we assumed that a domain was a security boundary and that it was good to segment administration across sub-domains. Of course, at that time we were influenced by PC LAN networks and couldn't quite comprehend how Active Directory would evolve to accommodate the range of design options that are available and in use today. Of course, saying what best practice is for Active Directory is another question. The answer is that there is no best practice, but there are solid guiding principles that any designer needs to understand and respect before deployment.

I think the same is true for Exchange Server. Best practice is transient and changes from version to version. It also changes over the lifetime of a version as the Exchange community comes to grips with the product and understands the strengths and weaknesses of the software. Microsoft also contributes to the evolution of best practice by publishing a wealth of information through Microsoft TechNet and other sites, including the Exchange development group's blog. Microsoft also changes best practice as they issue roll-up updates and service packs to address product flaws and sometimes even introduce new functionality (and maybe reinforce the old adage that no one should ever deploy a Microsoft server application until the first service pack is available).

Even though I regard best practice as transient, I still think that it is possible to set out solid guiding principles that help system designers and administrators to figure out how to make Exchange work for their organization. Well-organized books like this render a great service to the Exchange community by laying out Exchange 2010 in a practical manner that's based on insight and experience. I guess this could be called best practice, and that's certainly what the title says, but I prefer to think of the knowledge contained here as the guiding principles that every administrator should be acquainted with before deploying Exchange. You won't find a magic bullet here, nor will you find a recipe that you can simply adopt for a deployment. Instead, the chapters unfold to deliver a comprehensive guide to Exchange 2010 in an informative and easy-to-follow manner. Even better, because this book was written well after Exchange 2010 was released, it doesn't suffer from the "must be first to market" syndrome that afflicts so many technical books and leads to guesses and inaccuracies because the book's content is based on beta code. And as we all know, beta code isn't necessarily what is delivered to customers.

I've enjoyed reading this book and I think it will be valuable to anyone who wants to get to know Exchange 2010. Use it to establish your own foundation but don't forget that best practice evolves over time so be prepared to evolve your own knowledge by keeping up to date with developments.

Tony Redmond

Exchange MVP

May 2010

Acknowledgments

We wanted this book to be something special, something that reflects our passion and dedication to Microsoft Exchange. Our goal was to write a book for Exchange geeks by Exchange geeks. We also didn't want to write something that fell short of our expectations. To accomplish this lofty goal we required input, assistance, and support from a long list of people. This may sound like an award acceptance speech, but it is true. Although only two authors are named on the cover of this book, without a dedicated group of contributors, reviewers, and supporters this book would not exist.

First, we want to thank Stanley Riemer for believing in the project and helping get us the project approved and started. We regret not being able to work with you on this book and we hope to be able to work with you again soon. We also would like to thank Andy Schan and Jeffrey Rosen for being able to fill the void that Stanley left on our project. Without their assistance the project would have never been completed.

Many other people assisted during this project, but a few people in particular from the Exchange product group stand out for their support, patience, and insight—especially as changes were made to the product: Kristian Andaker, Ed Banti, Matthias Leibmann, Alexander Nikolayev, Greg Taylor, Paul Wimmer, Gary Cooper, and Brian Desmond.

In addition to these people, we also want to thank the following teams and companies for their dedicated support and input: everyone on the Microsoft Exchange 2010 TAP List, Siemens Workplace Architecture Team, the Exchange administrators at Axel Springer Media AG, and the supportive people at the Microsoft Enterprise Engineering Center in Redmond.

The three most critical pieces of a successful technical book are its technical accuracy, its grammatical accuracy, and the support of its editing staff. For technical accuracy, we were fortunate to have had two of the most thorough and knowledgeable people in the Exchange server ecosystem to provide technical guidance for the book: Tony Redmond and Scott Schnoll. They provided candid reviews that helped improve the content both technically and logistically. This is a better book thanks to each of them. We also want to thank David Espinoza and Tony Redmond for their kind words and the keen insight they provided in the Foreword for this book.

Although it may be shocking to hear, we as authors do not have perfect grammar, and one of our pet peeves is reading a book with blatant grammatical errors. Thankfully, we had Becka McKay to help ensure that the book's grammatical excellence met the highest standards. She was able to mold our sometimes narrowly focused word choices and improved not only the way the book sounds but also its accuracy and clarity.

The support we received from the editorial staff at Microsoft Press has been unmatched by any of our previous experiences. This book started with Martin DelRe, the acquisitions editor, bootstrapping the project about a year and a half prior to its publication. This happened during the final throes of the Exchange 2010 development process, yet he was still able to wrangle some key players in the Exchange product group to help out. This is a testament both to Martin's ability to get things done as well as to the product group's willingness to assist on this project. Shortly after we got started, Karen Szall, the book's developmental editor, was brought on board. She was critical in helping shape the look and feel of the book, and she also answered our unending barrage of questions and encouraged us to start writing. After Karen provided the momentum, we had the privilege of working with Carol Vu, the book's project editor. Carol was able to keep track of multiple versions of each chapter, deadlines whooshing by, and a variety of other forms of drama all without breaking a sweat. A lesser project editor would have had a panic attack long ago. We'd also like to thank Christian Holdener for managing this seemingly unending project and Maureen Johnson for being able to sift through the pages and pages of technojargon to make an index that is actually useful to our readers.

We want to extend special thanks to the Exchange product group members and Exchange experts who spend long hours of their free time reading our draft chapters to make sure we produced the highest-quality content possible. We gratefully salute the following people who were part of the review process: Alessandro Goncalves, Alexander Nikolayev, Andrew Sullivan, Ankur Kothari, Arno Zwegers, Charlie Chung, Christian Schindler, Colin Lee, Dave Chomas, David Espinoza, Ed Banti, Erik Szewczyk, Evan Dodds, Gary Cooper, Greg Taylor, Henrik Walther, Ilse Van Criekinge, Joe Cirillo, John Glynn, Kamal Janardhan, Korneel Bullens, Kristian Andåker, Kumar Venkateswar, Matthias Leibmann, Nagesh Mahadev, Paul Wimmer, Ross Smith IV, Steve McIntyre, Thierry Demorre, Tim McMichael, Todd Hawkins, Todd Luttinen, and Yesim Koman.

Finally, we would like to thank all of the sidebar contributors; these people really helped add a more comprehensive view of the subject and added depth to many topics. We're proud of the number of practical sidebars in the book, and our thanks go to their creators: Alessandro Goncalves, Alexander Nikolayev, Andreas Bode, Andreas Essing, Andrew Ehrensing, Ankur Kothari, Arno Zwegers, Brian Day,

Brian Desmond, Carsten Allendoerfer, Charlie Chung, Christian Schindler, Colin Lee, Devin L. Ganger, Ed Banti, Ed Wilson, Erick Szewczyk, Gary A. Cooper, Greg Taylor, Henrik Walther, Jeff Mealiffe, Joe Cirillo, John P. Glynn, Jon Webster, Korneel Bullens, Kristian Andaker, Lars Riehn, Manfred Kornagel, Markus Bellmann, Matthias Leibmann, Nicolai Wagner, Paul Wimmer, Robin Thomas, Ross Smith IV, Sascha Schmatz, Steve McIntyre, Thierry Demorre, Todd Hawkins, Todd Luttinen, Tony Redmond, and Ulf Hansen.

We thank you for taking the time to read our book; we hope that everyone's effort comes across and that you find the book both interesting and beneficial.

Introduction

Welcome to *Microsoft Exchange Server 2010 Best Practices*, a book that was developed together with the Microsoft Exchange product group to provide in-depth information about Exchange and best practices based on real-life experiences with the product in use in different environments. Numerous sidebars are also included that detail experiences from skilled industry professionals such as Certified Exchange Masters and Exchange Most Valuable Professionals (MVPs).

> ***NOTE*** **The book is largely based on the original version of Exchange Server 2010 released in October 2009 together with information about the changes that you can expect in Service Pack 1. Because Service Pack 1 was not yet released when the book was finished, we based our experience in the book on information available from the Microsoft Exchange product group and on a pre-release build of Service Pack 1. To make sure we only cover features that will be in the release of Service Pack 1, we addressed only the most notable changes.**

In November of 2008 Joel was updating an Exchange 2007 book when the two of us began chatting about writing a book on Exchange 2010. Having worked on several books already, we did not want to write the usual "click-here-and-do-this" type of Exchange book. We wanted to do something special, something that reflected our passion for and dedication to Exchange. The idea of working together along with the Microsoft Exchange 2010 product group to produce a book that could document years of experience from so many knowledgeable people thrilled all of us.

From beginning to end, this book took about 17 months to complete, and took a great deal of effort by a lot of hard-working and intelligent people. We hope that this effort comes across to you and that you find this book a worthwhile part of your Exchange library.

Who Is This Book For?

Microsoft Exchange Server 2010 Best Practices is for experienced Messaging architects, Exchange administrators, support professionals, and engineers, especially those who are working in medium to large enterprise organizations and also have at least one year of experience in administering, deploying, managing, monitoring, upgrading, migrating, and designing Exchange Server.

IT professionals who work in smaller companies also will benefit from the recommendations and sidebars presented in this book as well as many of the tips and tricks.

To get the most benefit from this book, prior to reading it you should at least be able to do the following:

- Design and deploy an Exchange messaging enterprise according to business requirements.
- Understand Active Directory concepts, especially how sites and services provide its essential structure.
- Understand the Windows permission model.
- Have good experience with the networking protocol TCP/IP v4 and the messaging protocol SMTP.
- Understand Windows PKI infrastructures and digital certificates.

You should also understand the basics of Exchange Server 2010, including the differences between each of the Exchange server roles (experience gained with Exchange 2007 is valuable here), and you should have experience with using the Exchange Management Console (EMC) and the Exchange Management Shell (EMS). The book does not focus on the "how to" and thus does not include step-by-step guides for each and every setting. This book builds on the knowledge and experience needed to successfully pass the Microsoft 70-663 exam, Pro: Designing and Deploying Messaging Solutions with Microsoft Exchange Server 2010.

The target audience for *Microsoft Exchange Server 2010 Best Practices* is interested in insights and in looking beyond the common administrative tasks performed in Exchange 2010 as well as those who want to unveil the full functionality of the product.

This book is a 300-level technical book; however, the planning and managing chapter will also be very useful to IT managers seeking guidance on understanding technical concepts for managing Exchange projects.

How Is This Book Organized?

This book is organized into four parts:

- Part I: Preparing for Exchange Server 2010
- Part II: Designing Exchange Server 2010
- Part III: Upgrading to Exchange 2010
- Part IV: Deploying and Managing Exchange Server 2010

The first part of this book consists of three chapters that focus on preparing your organization for Exchange Server 2010. Chapter 1, "Introducing Exchange Server 2010," provides an introduction to Exchange Server 2010, including high-level information about Exchange and Windows PowerShell. Chapter 2, "Exchange Deployment Projects," provides a project-oriented approach to Exchange Server implementation as well as information about the imaginary company scenarios that are used throughout the book. Chapter 3, "Exchange Environmental Considerations," then provides information about other areas, such as Active Directory, that you need to consider to have a successful Exchange implementation.

The second part of this book considers areas that are required for designing an Exchange Server 2010 implementation. In Chapter 4, "Client Access in Exchange 2010," you learn about the Client Access Server role of Exchange 2010. Chapter 5, "Routing and Transport," explains how message routing works and how you plan for the Hub Transport server role. Chapter 6, "Mailbox Services," considers the Mailbox server role and explains the database changes introduced in Exchange 2010. Chapter 7, "Edge Transport and Messaging Security," considers the details of the Edge Transport server role and, in addition to discussing messaging security, also covers antivirus and anti-spam functionality. Chapter 8, "Automated Message Processing, Compliance, and Archiving," covers the Exchange compliance and archiving features and also explains how you can perform automated message processing. Chapter 9, "Unified Messaging," explains Exchange Unified Messaging or how to access your mailbox using voice as well as OCS 2007 R2 interoperability with Exchange. Chapter 10, "Federated Sharing," describes how to connect two Exchange Organizations using Federated Sharing. Chapter 11, "Designing High Availability," introduces you to the concept of Database Availability Groups (DAGs) and how DAGs can be implemented to provide high availability for your messaging service as well discussing other availability aspects such as network load balancing. Chapter 12, "Backup, Restore, and Disaster Recovery," takes you through backing up and restoring your Exchange servers, databases, and features to mitigate the need for restores. Chapter 13, "Hardware Planning for Exchange Server 2010," concludes the design part of this book by providing guidance about hardware planning for your Exchange servers.

The third part of this book consists of Chapter 14, "Transitioning from Exchange 2003 and Exchange 2007," which considers how you can approach the upgrade of your existing Exchange 2003 or Exchange 2007 installation to Exchange Server 2010 and what important factors you need to consider beforehand.

The fourth part of this book considers deploying and managing Exchange Server 2010. Chapter 15, "Preparing for and Deploying Exchange Server 2010," describes how to prepare Active Directory and the servers for Exchange 2010, how you check your environment to make sure all Exchange requirements are covered, and how you install Exchange 2010 both manually and automatically. Chapter 16, "Managing Exchange," discusses how to manage Exchange Server 2010. Finally, Chapter 17, "Operating and Troubleshooting Exchange Server 2010," provides information about operating and troubleshooting your Exchange 2010 server environment.

How to Read This Book

This book is written as a reference, and each chapter was written to stand on its own, so you do not need to read the chapters in order—you can jump between the chapters that interest you. However, we'd like to point out some chapters that provide an excellent start and are used for other areas in the book as well.

Almost every chapter in the book uses sample scenarios that are introduced in detail in Chapter 2. These fictional scenarios are used as real-world examples and to provide illustrations of how the ideas presented in a chapter could be implemented in practice. Chapter 3 provides the basis for reading about Exchange environmental areas such as networks, operating systems, and certificates. We strongly recommend reading these chapters—they also provide an excellent overview and best practices around the topic you might want to investigate.

What This Book Is Not

In *Microsoft Exchange Server 2010 Best Practices*, we assume that you have a good understanding of Exchange Server 2010 and Windows PowerShell 2.0. For this reason, this book does not teach the basics of every feature nor does it include a how-to section for common administrative tasks.

This book is also not a preparation guide for Exam 70-662: TS: Microsoft Exchange Server 2010, Configuring, or Exam 70-663: Pro: Designing and Deploying Messaging Solutions with Microsoft Exchange Server 2010, even though when you apply the knowledge and experience covered in this book, it will help you to pass these exams.

In general, the book does not include detailed steps for every configuration setting but tries to provide a foundation so that you can make your own decisions for what would be optimal in your environment. It does not dictate one specific way to configure Exchange 2010; instead, it provides the options available and the factors that should influence your decisions. Thus this book is not a guide for how to configure your Exchange servers; it is meant to improve your already configured environment or help you add new features such as Unified Messaging.

System Requirements

This book is designed to be used with the following Exchange 2010 software requirements:

- Windows Server 2008 or Windows Server 2008 R2
- 1 GB of RAM
- x64 architecture-based computer with Intel or AMD processor that supports 64 bit
- 1.2 GB of available disk space
- Display monitor capable of 800 × 600 resolution

The following list details the minimum system requirements needed to run the content in the book's companion Web site:

- Windows XP with the latest service pack installed and the latest updates from Microsoft Update Service
- Display monitor capable of 1024 × 768 resolution
- CD-ROM drive
- Microsoft Mouse or compatible pointing device

The Companion Web Site

This book features a companion Web site that makes available additional information to you such as job aids, quick reference guides, and additional Exchange 2010 resources. We have included these elements to help you plan and manage your Exchange 2010 organization and apply the book's recommended best practices. The companion Web site includes the following:

- **Job Aids** Additional documents on most of the chapters that help you to collect and structure your work through the book.
- **Quick Reference Guides** Such as the Exchange 2010 Best Practices Quick Reference Guide, which is an overview of all best practice recommendations in the book, and the Exchange 2010 Additional Reference Guide, a collection of all Internet links referenced in the book.
- **TechNet Exchange 2010 Resources** Additional links that might be useful when reading the book.

You can download these files from the companion Web site, located at *http://go.microsoft.com/fwlink/?LinkId=193963.*

Full documentation of the contents and structure of the companion Web site can be found in the Readme.txt file in the download.

Support for This Book

Every effort has been made to ensure the accuracy of this book. As corrections or changes are collected, they will be added to a Microsoft Knowledge Base article accessible via the Microsoft Help and Support site. Microsoft Press provides support for books, including instructions for finding Knowledge Base articles, at the following Web site: *http://www.microsoft.com/learning/support/books/*.

If you have questions regarding the book that are not answered by visiting the site above or viewing a Knowledge Base article, send them to Microsoft Press via e-mail to *mspinput@microsoft.com*. Please note that Microsoft software product support is not offered through these addresses.

We Want to Hear from You

We welcome your feedback about this book. Please share your comments and ideas via the following short survey: *http://www.microsoft.com/learning/booksurvey*. Your participation will help Microsoft Press create books that better meet your needs and your standards.

> **NOTE** We hope that you will give us detailed feedback via our survey. If you have questions about our publishing program, upcoming titles, or Microsoft Press in general, we encourage you to interact with us via Twitter at *http://twitter.com/MicrosoftPress*. For support issues, use only the e-mail address shown above.

PART I

Preparing for Exchange Server 2010

CHAPTER 1

Introducing Exchange Server 2010

This chapter introduces you to Exchange Server 2010, the most successful messaging system available today. Because Exchange 2010 is now the third generation of this messaging product, you will read about what happened in the previous versions and why—in addition to developing new features and functionality—certain functionality was abandoned because of changes and evolving customer demands that occurred over time in the IT landscape.

The overview section introduces several tools that you need to use to manage Exchange 2010, provides an overview of the Exchange server roles, describes the functionality that has been removed, the options that exist to mitigate now defunct functionality, and the difference between Exchange On-Premise and Exchange Online.

This book includes functionality available only with Exchange 2010 Service Pack 1 (SP1), so a section will provide you with an overview of the changes that have been introduced by SP1 and in what chapters you can read detailed information about them.

Understanding Exchange 2010 editions and licensing, which is important for planning your organization's license requirements, is also described, and a Windows PowerShell 2.0 introduction with some useful cmdlets you need to remember while reading this book completes the chapter.

The History of Exchange Server

Exchange Server has been in use since 1996, but it did not start with the product you know today. Exchange Server has changed and evolved quite a lot to reflect the change in IT since its introduction. In Exchange's early days, hard disk space was expensive—thus, single-instance storage was implemented in the Exchange store. Today hard disk space is cheap and a different technological focus is important.

Throughout the years many Exchange versions have been released, and Table 1-1 provides an overview of all versions from the first release to Exchange 2010.

TABLE 1-1 Exchange Versions Overview

VERSION	CODE NAME(S)	RELEASE DATE (RTM)	GENERATION
Exchange 4.0	Spitfire (early 1990's), Mercury, Touchdown	March 31, 1996	First generation
Exchange 5.0	—	February 27, 1997	
Exchange 5.5	Osmium or Oz	November 5, 1997	
Exchange 2000	Platinum or Pt	July 31, 2000	Second generation
Exchange 2003	Exchange.Net, Titanium or Ti	June 30, 2003	
Exchange 2007	E12	December 8, 2006	Third generation
Exchange 2010	E14	October 8, 2009	

The Years Before Exchange

In the early 1990s, many messaging systems were on the market. Messaging systems favored by large companies, such as Siemens's MailX, Digital Equipment's ALL-IN-1, IBM PROFS, and PC LAN-based systems such as Lotus Notes, Lotus cc:Mail, and Novell GroupWise. The two standard protocol standards in messaging were X.400 and the Internet standard SMTP. Back then, X.400 was more common; SMTP was only gaining popularity because of the growth of the Internet community.

With Microsoft Mail, Microsoft offered a file-based messaging system that stored all messages in a file share where users accessed their mailboxes using the LAN. A Microsoft Mail server installation was called a Post Office and it needed a Message Transfer Agent (MTA) to be able to send messages between Microsoft Mail Post Offices. Limited versions of Microsoft Mail were also included in Windows 95 and Windows NT 4.0 that excluded the ability to route messages between Post Offices.

Microsoft Mail made its initial appearance in 1988. At that time, its network stack was designed for AppleTalk Networks. The last version, Microsoft Mail v3.5, included a multitasking MTA and was only released because the release of Exchange Server was delayed.

Do you know why the Messaging Application Programming Interface (MAPI) was developed? The problem was that at the time, Microsoft used different messaging systems: Internally they used their Xenix Mail System and externally they sold Microsoft Mail. Thus there was a need to develop a protocol to connect different messaging systems to each other, and thus MAPI was born. MAPI is actually an API, but many people refer to MAPI as a protocol the very same way as they refer to POP3. You can find more information about MAPI at *http://en.wikipedia.org/wiki/MAPI*.

NOTES FROM THE FIELD

Exchange 4.0 Beta: Codename Touchdown

Andreas Essing
Director Microsoft Services, Siemens AG, Germany

I had the first contact with Touchdown (project name of Exchange) in 1994. During that time, we were actually working on getting a "Microsoft consulting business" within SIETEC Consulting (a subsidiary of Siemens Nixdorf) up and running. This approach was not very successful until Microsoft delivered Exchange after two years of waiting.

Between 1994 and 1996 we had several opportunities to test the software, starting with TR 2 (the second test release of Touchdown). I remember one phone call from a Microsoft representative who proudly told me that a message could be delivered between two Exchange servers. We had computers with 32 MB of main memory, Windows NT 3.1 Server, and the Exchange client running on Windows NT Workstation or on Windows for Workgroups 3.11. I still remember the Public folder Chess Application, an example of how to create an e-mail application using Exchange.

In late 1996, we also had the chance to test the Exchange Web Connector (delivered on two diskettes). This was the first time we could access the mailbox via a browser. Outlook was still in development, and the Exchange product group was not very convinced by Outlook, which was developed by the Office product group at Microsoft.

Exchange Server Before Active Directory

The first generation of Exchange Servers had their own Directory Service integrated in the product and did not use a directory service provided with the operating system, such as Active Directory. Exchange 4.0, 5.0, and 5.5 formed this Exchange generation.

NOTES FROM THE FIELD

Migrating from Microsoft Mail 3.5 to Exchange 4.0

Gary A. Cooper
Senior Systems Architect, Horizons Consulting Inc., United States

I began working with Exchange 4.0 early in the beta cycle (I don't recall the specific version) at a customer organization. We had moved much of their organization globally to Microsoft Mail (from nine other e-mail systems) and had tested Exchange 4.0 in a lab environment for months. However, we did have a significant issue (otherwise known as a bug) that we ran into when we deployed Exchange 4.0 RTM into production. At that multinational company, which had about 90,000 seats, we deployed the initial Exchange 4.0 servers in each of three regional data centers and began directory synchronization between them during the Thanksgiving 1996 holiday weekend. Unfortunately, the MTA service would crash after about a third of the directory sync completed. After internal attempts to troubleshoot the issue, we opened a support case with Microsoft PSS, who worked around the clock to determine and resolve the core issue causing the crash. They eventually determined that the bug was involved in how the MTA service periodically exported the MTA0 readable file to disk. To get our directory sync completed, two developers came into the office in Redmond, WA, at two o'clock in the morning on a holiday weekend to build us a "Buddy Build" of the MTA code DLLs that did not write the MTA0 file to disk, thus bypassing the bug. Later, we received an official hotfix that resolved the core issue.

Exchange 4.0

Exchange Server 4.0 (codenamed Spitfire, Mercury, and finally Touchdown) was the initial release of the Exchange Server product and was a X.400-based messaging system including the first version of the Extensible Storage Engine (ESE) database, a database technology that was optimized for e-mail including single-instance storage functionality so that messages were only stored once in a database, even if they existed in multiple mailboxes. Microsoft saw the need to move away from a file-based messaging system to a database to save disk space as well as increase performance. Today you can still save approximately 25 percent of your disk space if you move from a file-based to a database-based messaging system such as Exchange. However, Microsoft limited the mailbox database size to 16 GB, which later became a key issue.

To develop Exchange 4.0, Microsoft bought the technology from a few other companies:

- **X.400 MTA or Transport** This part came from a company called DC of Enfield in the UK. Their code was scattered across literally hundreds of small modules that collectively formed the X.400 MTA.
- **X.500 (Directory)** This came from a 3Com code base that was originally developed for Cairo, which was an object-oriented file system that was supposed to be included in Windows NT 4.0.
- **Information Store** Microsoft's original plan for SQL Server was to use a database called Jet Blue. However, Microsoft bought database technology from Sybase and used it to develop the SQL product instead. The Exchange team adopted the Jet Blue database, otherwise known as the Extensible Storage Engine, and has used it ever since.

Exchange 4.0 made its appearance on March 31, 1996—39 months late. Not based on the same codebase but newly developed from scratch, Exchange 4.0 was the official successor of Microsoft Mail and thus also continued to use the version numbering. The last version of Microsoft Mail was 3.5, so Exchange Server used 4.0 as its first version. A different story behind the version number is that Lotus Notes (it was still called Notes and not Lotus Domino back in those days) had just released their 4.0 version in January 1996 and because of marketing concerns Exchange Server needed to have an equal version number.

In addition to the mailbox database, Exchange 4.0 included Public Folders, which were targeted to bring groupware functionality to Exchange and directly compete with the Lotus Notes replicated database model for applications. Microsoft also provided the 16-bit Visual Basic–like Electronic Forms Designer to easily and quickly develop form-based applications that used Public Folders for storage and replication. However, the form-based applications did not scale as expected in large environments, so many companies did not continue to develop applications but instead used Public Folders in a basic way to share messages, calendar information, and contacts.

Exchange 4.0 included an internal, X.500-based directory structure that Microsoft later used as the foundation for Active Directory. It had a centralized administrator console called Exchange Administrator (ADMIN.EXE) and also addressed the requirement to support more users on a single server, which went up to 500 mailboxes.

NOTE **A basic Exchange 4.0 server hardware back in 1996 was a 486 processor with 66 MHz, 64 MB of memory, and a 4-GB hard disk.**

Exchange 4.0 shipped with its own client, Exchange Client 4.0 (code-named Capone client) and an application for calendaring called Microsoft Schedule+ 7. You can still see the legacy in the System Public Folder called Schedule + Free/Busy, which includes the free/busy times for Outlook 2003 clients and before.

NOTES FROM THE FIELD

The Release of Exchange 4.0 as Experienced in Germany

Lars Riehn
Chief Executive Officer, InfoWAN Datenkommunikation GmbH, Germany

I remember the CeBIT computer fair in Germany back in 1996—this was also my first CeBIT after leaving Microsoft and founding infoWAN. Microsoft released Exchange 4.0 during CeBIT. Luckily, we had a beta on our demo computers and could show Exchange live. It was great to get all the visitors wanting to see what Exchange and e-mail were all about. Yes, in those days we still had to answer questions like "What is e-mail?", "Why do I need e-mail?", and "Will employees really use e-mail?" These days I am having a déjà vu experience with OCS as the same argument occurs about its method of communication.

At that CeBIT, we went to a cocktail reception at the Lotus Notes booth. When I told people that I started a company purely focused on Microsoft Exchange and related technologies, everyone thought I was crazy and would go bankrupt in a year. They were sure Exchange would disappear and Lotus Notes would gain 100 percent of the market share. Today, infoWAN is still going strong and the success of Exchange in the market speaks for itself.

I grew up with X.400 as a nice standard for e-mail. At the time, Exchange was still built around X.400 at the core and X.400 Connectors were the right way to connect Exchange Servers beyond the LAN. Yes, X.400 was somewhat complex, but I liked it. And I feel that with X.400 we would have a much smaller problem with spam today.

Here are my favorite longstanding myths for Exchange:

1. Microsoft will change the Exchange database to use SQL.
2. Microsoft will stop developing new versions of Exchange.
3. Public Folders will disappear.

Exchange 5.0

Exchange Server 5.0, which did not have any codenames, introduced support for Windows NT 4.0 operating system and support for technologies such as LDAP v2 and SMTP.

For Microsoft, it was obvious that the dominance of the Internet technologies would keep growing, so they included all sorts of Internet protocols such as SMTP (with the Internet Mail Connector on a separate disk), NNTP (called Internet News Connector), and POP3.

This move was initiated when Bill Gates wrote his famous "everything to the Internet" memo that forced all Microsoft engineering groups to consider how to build Internet support into their products as quickly as possible. Exchange's reaction was also to introduce the first Web-based e-mail client, Exchange Web Access (EWA), which later was renamed Outlook Web Access and then Outlook Web App (OWA). Exchange 5.0 was released to manufacturing on February 27, 1997.

Exchange Client 5.0 and Microsoft Schedule+ 7.5 were included as client software but in mid-1997 Microsoft Outlook 8.0 made its first appearance, combining both clients into a single program. It was immediately successful.

NOTES FROM THE FIELD

When OWA Was Invented

Tony Redmond
Exchange MVP

The original version of OWA was delivered in Exchange 5.0 after Bill Gates got the Internet religion. The browser to server communications layer was based on MAPI and didn't scale at all, nor did it deliver a tenth of the functionality that exists in OWA today. As I recall, the "access" part of the name indicated the original belief that all you would ever want to do is access your mailbox from the Web—all real work would be done through Outlook.

Exchange 5.5

Exchange 5.5 (codename Osmium or OZ) was released to manufacturing on November 5, 1997, just half a year after the release of Exchange 5.0. Exchange 5.5 implemented support for symmetric multiprocessing and was available for two different processor generations, Intel and DEC's Alpha processor. Even though the Alpha processor was more powerful, the fact that Exchange was never compiled to take advantage of the Alpha's 64-bit processor meant that it was an unpopular platform and never achieved commercial success.

The maximum database size was increased from 16 GB to 16 TB (or as Microsoft called it back then, the unlimited store), which also brought two Exchange server licenses types: Standard and Enterprise. Standard had a 16-GB database limitation and Enterprise had 16 TB. In addition, Exchange 5.5 also introduced support for two-node failover clustering.

The SMTP connector was renamed Internet Mail Service (IMS) and was integrated into the core Exchange server—there was no need to install extra disks anymore. NNTP was also renamed to Internet News Service (INS). IMAP4 and LDAP v3 support was added. Other connectors available in the product were X.400 connector, Site Connector, and Microsoft Mail Connector.

Exchange 5.5 also had a special version: Exchange 5.5 Defense Messaging System (DMS). This was the same core Exchange 5.5 that relied on X.400 connectors as its basis with a few registry keys turned on and a specially developed client for the U.S. Department of Defense.

One of the biggest problems of Exchange 5.5 in large environments was the limitation of having only 202 Exchange sites if you wanted to connect the sites and share a single Exchange Address Book. My company back then counted roughly 1,000 Exchange 5.5 sites and thus was not able to connect them together.

Exchange 5.5 was a very robust, trustworthy messaging system. Many companies stayed on Exchange 5.5 for a long time because they did not see the urgent need to move on. The Exchange Administrator, as shown in Figure 1-1, was also well understood by most Exchange administrators. From the client support perspective, Exchange 5.5 fully relied on Outlook v8.03 as its message client and thus Exchange Client and Schedule+ were abandoned.

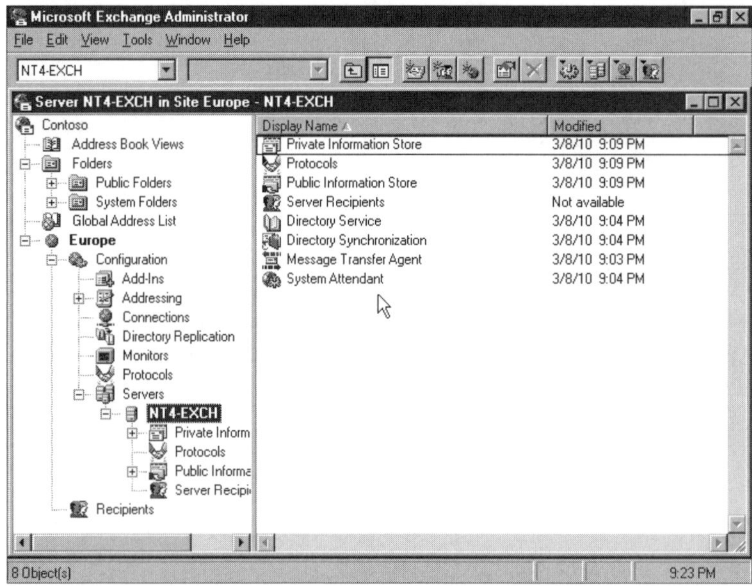

FIGURE 1-1 Exchange Administrator in Exchange 5.5

Exchange Server 2000 and 2003

The second Exchange server generation used Active Directory as its directory service and extended Exchange's functionality beyond e-mail by adding Conferencing Services and Instant Messaging. Exchange Server 2000 and 2003 belong to the second Exchange server generation.

Exchange 2000

Exchange Server 2000 was the first application that fully depended on Microsoft's new directory service, Active Directory. Exchange 2000 (codenamed Platinum or Pt) was released to manufacturing on August 31, 2000, and is version 6.0. It required Windows Server 2000 as the operating system and thus no longer supported Windows NT 4.0. The Exchange Administrator program was exchanged with the Exchange System Manager (ESM) that was based on the Microsoft Management Console (MMC) framework.

On the Exchange database level, the concept of Storage Groups was implemented, providing the functionality to host multiple Mailbox Stores (now called mailbox databases) in a Storage Group. One Exchange server was now able to host as many as 20 databases. Cluster support was extended from two to four nodes.

Multiple Public Folder hierarchies were also introduced. Unfortunately, MAPI (the dominant client protocol) and API did not support more than one hierarchy; thus this feature was bound to die quickly.

Exchange 2000 moved from an X.400 Message Transport Agent (MTA) to an SMTP MTA. The SMTP connectors (until then known as IMS) became virtual SMTP servers linked into the new transport engine. This was a pretty fundamental move for the product.

For migration, the Active Directory Connector (ADC) was included that connected an Exchange 5.5 directory service to Active Directory for smoothly moving users over to Exchange 2000.

Exchange 2000 also introduced the first Exchange Instant Messaging (later moved to Live Communication Server, or LCS, which was then renamed to Office Communication Server 2007, or OCS 2007, as it is known today). The Exchange Conferencing Server was another new feature, but both products were removed from Exchange in the next version.

NOTES FROM THE FIELD

Right-Click in Exchange System Manager

Tony Redmond
Exchange MVP

In a keynote I delivered at the Microsoft Exchange Conference in 2000, I discussed the introduction of right-click functionality in the management console. I received some applause from the 4,000 people in the hall and replied that I wasn't responsible for the feature but that "I'd be happy to share the clap with the engineers." About two nanoseconds later I realized what I had said and so did the audience, which dissolved in laughter. For months afterwards, I received messages from engineers in the Exchange development group who politely inquired about my experience. I can't think of how many MPEG clips of my unfortunate comments I received too!

Exchange 2000 also introduced the concept of Administrative Groups and Routing Groups to separate the scope of administration from the message routing scope. Thus administrators could provide mail administrators with exactly the right permissions for managing their servers without interfering with the organization's routing connectors. However, the administrative model had some faults that prevented large, dispersed companies that needed a split-administrative model from rolling out Exchange 2000.

With Routing Groups came the concept of intelligent routing, called *Link State updates,* that was used until Exchange 2003. Exchange matured further by using the LocalSystem account to run its services instead of maintaining its own administration accounts whose smooth operation could easily be disrupted by simple actions such as passwords expiring.

Exchange 2003

Exchange Server 2003's first codename was Exchange .NET—it had fallen into the .NET phase of Microsoft when almost all products had that suffix, but later the codename was changed to Titanium, or Ti. It was released on June 30, 2003, as version 6.5 and it further built on the foundation established by Exchange 2000. It was the first Exchange version based on Active Directory widely accepted by customers; many large companies migrated their Exchange 5.5 environments to Exchange 2003.

Exchange 2003 ran on Windows 2000 Server or Windows Server 2003. Besides adding stability and robustness, it introduced a couple of key client access features to Exchange: the first was the introduction of cached Exchange mode with Outlook 2003 to provide better use of bandwidth, especially for remote clients; the second was the ability to connect Outlook clients using RPC over HTTPs to remove the requirement to use VPN connections to access the Exchange server. Using RCP over HTTPs (later renamed Outlook Anywhere) only requires an HTTP connection to synchronize e-mail.

In Exchange 2003, the functionality provided by Microsoft Mobile Information Server 2001 and 2002 were integrated into Exchange to provide ActiveSync support for mobile clients—namely Windows Mobile 5 or later devices directly out of the product. Initially client devices were configured to sync on a regular schedule with the option of SMS notification for new messages (also known as AUTDv1). The "push-mail" feature using DirectPush technology (also known as AUTDv2) was implemented with Exchange 2003 Service Pack 2.

Exchange 2003 Service Pack 2 also introduced a new database size limit of 75 GB, even in the Standard Edition of Exchange. The maximum database size limit in Enterprise remained 16 TB.

Anti-spam and antivirus protection was gaining awareness, so Exchange 2003 SP1 introduced the Intelligent Messaging Filter (IMF) to scan and reject spam messages. A more sophisticated anti-virus API was also added to provide a better foundation for third-party antivirus solutions to protect the system. Figure 1-2 illustrates the Exchange System Manager that was used to manage Exchange in Exchange Server 2003.

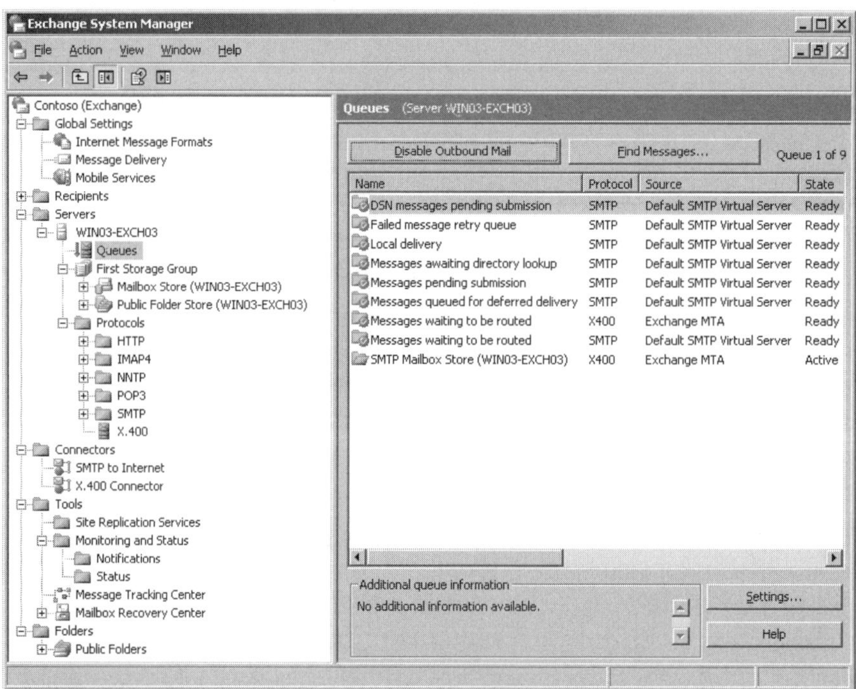

FIGURE 1-2 Exchange System Manager in Exchange 2003

Exchange Server 2007 and Beyond

Exchange Server 2007 can be seen as the third generation of Exchange server. It was rebuilt from the ground up, and not only required a 64-bit processor architecture, but was also the first version of Exchange in which the Exchange Management Console (EMC)—successor of the Exchange System Manager—no longer included all configuration options. Configuring many of the advanced configuration options required Windows PowerShell.

Windows PowerShell in and of itself was the biggest step from moving to Exchange 2007. Exchange administrators were required to learn some scripting before they could use Windows PowerShell. However, it soon became one of the major success factors because administrators could automate administrative tasks quickly and easily. The Exchange Management Console was based on Windows PowerShell, which is still the case in Exchange 2010. Every option you select in the EMC triggers an associated Windows PowerShell cmdlet in the background.

Exchange 2007 also introduced five server roles: Mailbox, Client Access Server, Hub Transport, Edge Transport, and Unified Messaging. Specialized Exchange server roles can be added and removed when needed and also install only the code that is needed for whatever server roles run on a computer, not everything as required by previous Exchange versions. Exchange 2007 changed again the concept of message routing and removed Routing Groups to rely fully on the Active Directory site model and use Active Directory sites and site links for internal routing purposes. The X.400 Connector was retired, and storage groups were modified to support continuous replication. Up to 50 databases could be created on a single server.

From the failover clustering perspective, Exchange 2007 added log file shipping technology and laid the foundation for the Database Availability Group functionality in Exchange 2010. Thus, in addition to implementing the traditional single-copy cluster (SCC) that required a shared disk, such as that provided by a storage area network (SAN) system, it also supported cluster continuous replication (CCR) and local continuous replication (LCR) as a means to provide failover clustering with replicating transaction log data to be replayed to update a database copy on another server (CCR) or disk (LCR). Exchange 2007 SP1 introduced standby continuous replication (SCR) to replicate a message database to a remote Exchange server.

Exchange 2007 de-emphasized Public Folders by removing their support from the EMC with the original version, but because of customer feedback they implemented Public Folder management back in a separate console launched from the EMC toolbox with Exchange 2007 SP1. Exchange 2007 also laid the basis to move away from Public Folders by implementing Autodiscovery and Availability service used by Outlook 2007 and later clients.

Bringing voice to the mailbox was another change that Microsoft implemented into the core of Exchange 2007. The Unified Messaging server role was added to provide users with the ability to access their mailboxes using voice and also served as a voice mail system for Office Communication Server 2007 R2.

From the client perspective, for the first time in Exchange history Exchange Server 2007 no longer included a message client apart from the OWA.

Overview of Exchange Server 2010

Exchange Server 2010 is one of the most functional messaging systems on the market, and the most popular messaging system used in organizations. To maintain competitiveness and to continue the development of technology began in Exchange 2007, Exchange 2010 brought several new features and functionality to the market.

Management Consoles

Exchange 2010 includes a couple of management consoles that help you to perform administrative tasks or manage Exchange's configuration.

Exchange Management Console

The EMC is the main administrative console for configuring and managing Exchange, as shown in Figure 1-3. It shows the most important settings of the Exchange configuration and allows you to modify them if you have permissions.

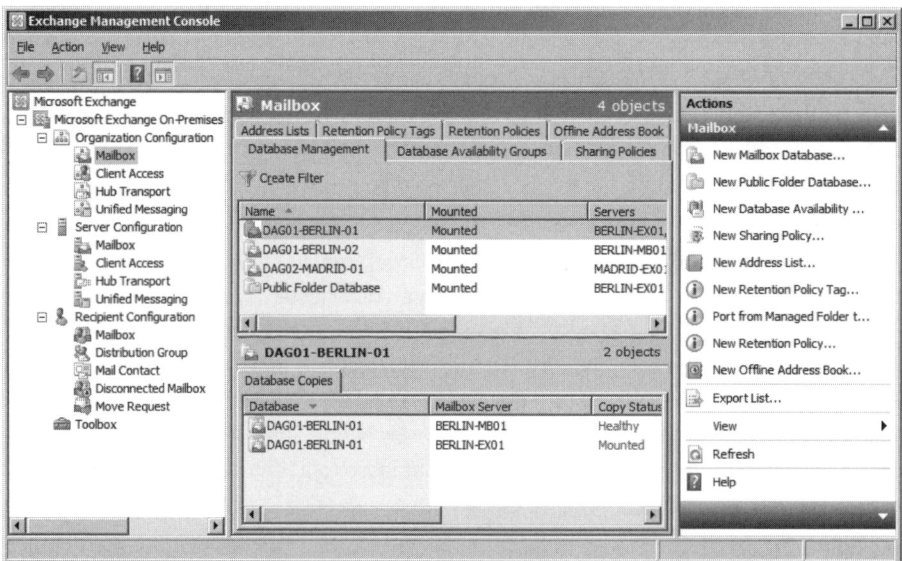

FIGURE 1-3 The EMC

The EMC includes the following main areas that help you to manage Exchange:

- **Exchange Configuration** Includes organization-wide configuration that applies not only to a single Exchange server but can also affect all servers. For example you configure Database Availability Groups (DAGs) and mailbox databases are configured on this level.
- **Server Configuration** Allows you to view and modify server-based settings that apply only to an individual server—such as server-specific OWA or POP3 settings—or assign a Dial-Plan to a Unified Messaging server.

- **Recipient Configuration** Here you do all recipient-related tasks such as enabling a mailbox or creating a distribution list or a contact.
- **Toolbox** Includes various tools that help you to configure, monitor, and troubleshoot your Exchange organization, such as Queue Viewer and Best Practices Analyzer.

SHOW EXCHANGE MANAGEMENT SHELL COMMAND

The Show Exchange Management Shell command button is a very useful but not widely known improvement to the EMC in Exchange 2010. It is located in the bottom-left corner of the dialog boxes used to reveal and set properties on Exchange objects, as shown in Figure 1-4. When you click this button a window opens, showing the Windows PowerShell command that Exchange will execute when you click OK or Apply.

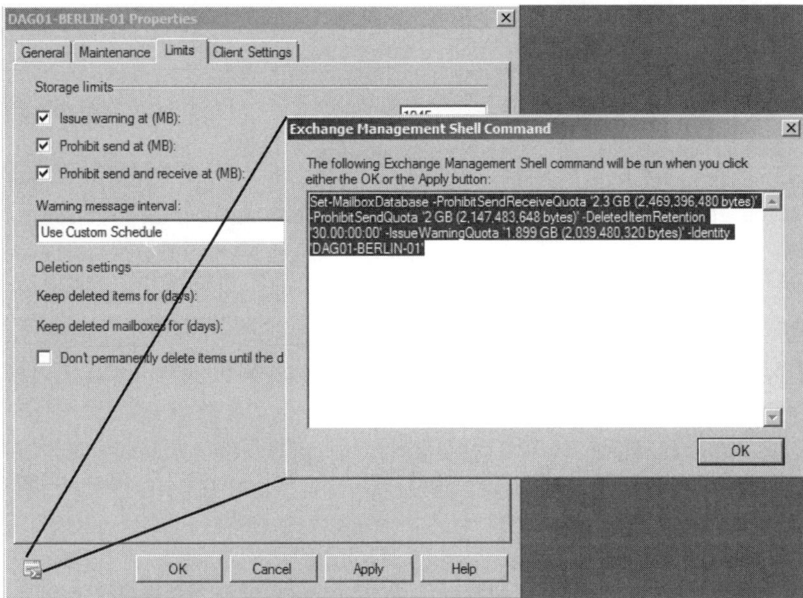

FIGURE 1-4 Show EMS command button

> ***NOTE*** **As a best practice it is recommended that you take a look at the cmdlets that are executed in EMC quite frequently at the beginning to familiarize yourself with the syntax and to remember the cmdlet when you need it in EMS.**

EXCHANGE MANAGEMENT SHELL COMMAND LOG

Another tool new to the EMC in Exchange 2010 is the Exchange Management Shell Command Log, which records all shell commands that you run in EMC. As shown in Figure 1-5, you can start command logging, which provides you with detailed information about the commands that you've run. You also have the option of exporting the commands to a CSV file.

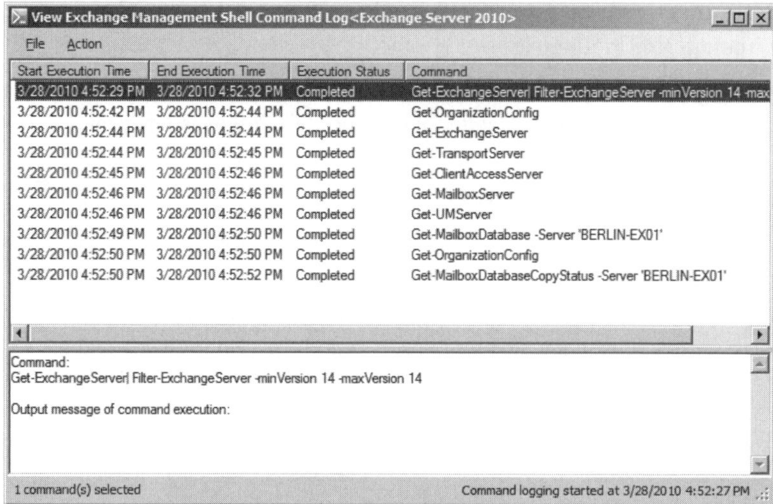

FIGURE 1-5 View Exchange Management Shell Command Log

You can access the View Exchange Management Command Log by right-clicking an object such as Mailbox in the left pane of EMC and then clicking View and selecting View Exchange Management Log.

Exchange Management Shell

The EMS is a task-based, tailored command-line shell on top of the Windows PowerShell scripting language that can ease the way you do administration.

Using the EMS, as shown in Figure 1-6, you can perform every task that can be done in the EMC and additional tasks that are not available in EMC such as configuring the port of a POP3 connection.

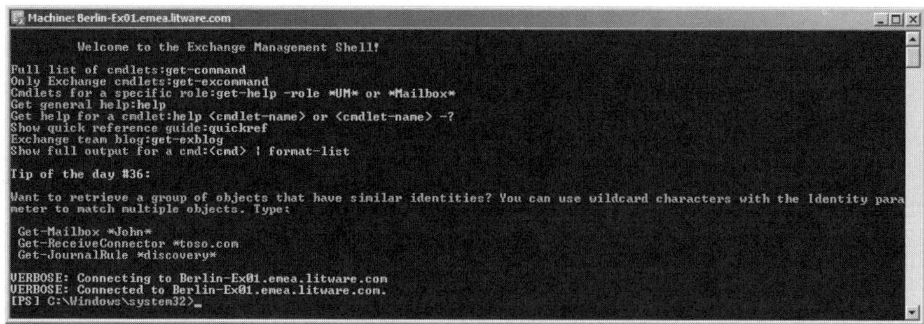

FIGURE 1-6 The EMS

All of your Exchange administrators should be trained to understand the basics of the EMS and how to create batch scripts that ease their daily business lives. Although EMS will be used mainly by administrators, any Exchange user who is enabled for PowerShell (the default setting) can use EMS, provided that she has access to a workstation that has EMS installed. Role-Based Access Control (RBAC) limits the set of cmdlets that a user can see or run to those included in the role(s) assigned to the user.

> ***IMPORTANT*** **Some cmdlets require elevated permissions, so if you're not working with the administrator account but with a normal user account it is a best practice to start EMS with Run As Administrator.**

Exchange Control Panel

With the Exchange Control Panel (ECP), Exchange 2010 now provides a Web-based management console that can be used by administrators and end users to perform common management tasks for Exchange 2010. ECP uses the RBAC permissions model of Exchange 2010; thus you can only see the functionality that you have permissions to access. It can be accessed using the URL *https://<CASserver>/ECP*, OWA, or from Outlook 2010 and opens in the Web browser as shown in Figure 1-7.

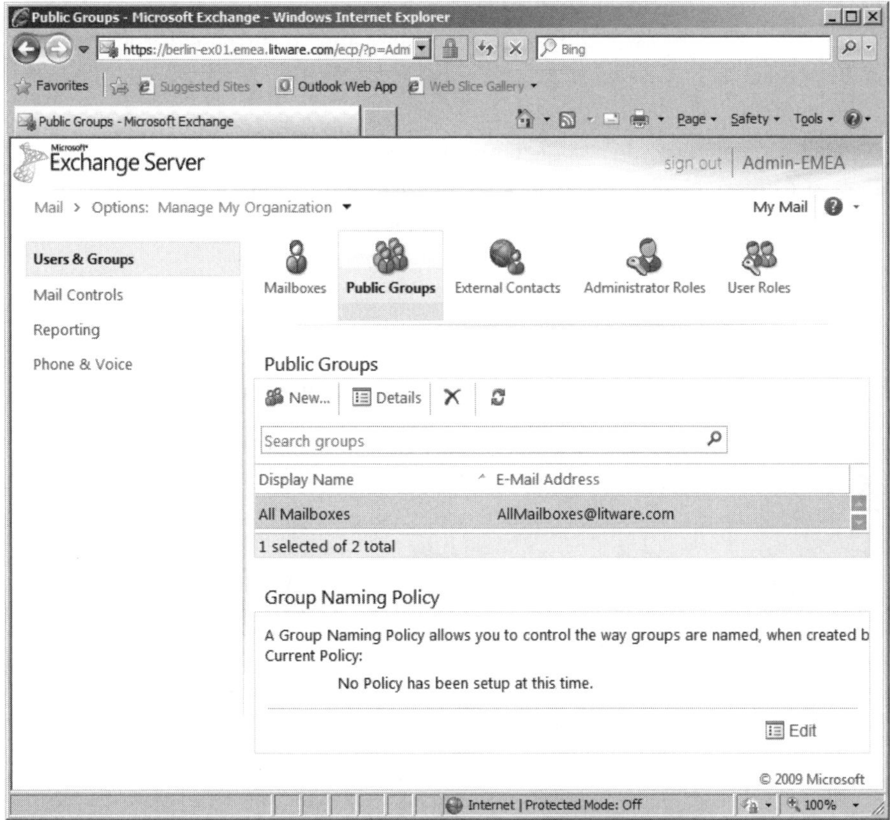

FIGURE 1-7 Exchange Control Panel

In ECP you can perform several User & Groups–related tasks, such as modifying mailbox properties and creating distribution groups now called *public groups*. You can configure Mail Controls such as Transport or Journal Rules, you can perform Reporting tasks such as searching Delivery Reports and view or export Auditing Reports, and you can perform Phone & Voice–related tasks such as quarantining a device and configuring an ActiveSync Policy.

You can find more information about the ECP in Chapter 4, "Client Access in Exchange 2010."

> **NOTE** A new functionality in Exchange 2010 SP1 is that you do not need a mailbox-enabled account to be able to use ECP. This is a particularly helpful change in environments where you use separate accounts for administrative tasks.

Exchange Server Roles

Exchange 2010 is quite a massive product that includes many facets of messaging included in a single product. It includes a sophisticated messaging routing engine that is capable of processing very large volumes of e-mail while applying anti-spam, antivirus, and compliance checks; it supports a very wide range of client protocols from the simple, such as POP3, to the highly functional, such as MAPI; and it accommodates varying hardware designs from a simple multi-role server to designs based on the new Database Availability Group (DAG) feature to deliver high availability.

Including all the functionality in a single product would just blow the requirements on hardware, so Microsoft implemented server roles, allowing you to choose to install only the roles you require. Figure 1-8 shows all available Exchange Server roles.

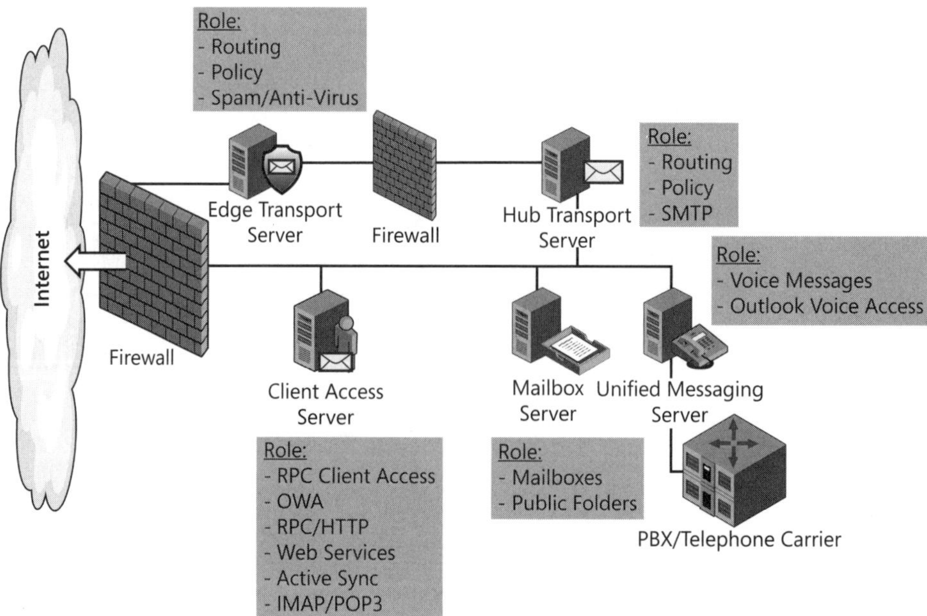

FIGURE 1-8 Exchange 2010 Server Roles Overview

The Client Access Server role is responsible for serving client connections: Outlook, OWA, Outlook Anywhere, Exchange ActiveSync, Exchange Web Services (EWS), and POP3 and IMAP4 protocols. It pipelines end user–based communication to mailbox server role and is responsible for additional services such as Autodiscover, availability, and Exchange Web Services (EWS). Chapter 4 provides an in-depth overview of the Client Access Server role.

Mailbox databases—and thus the mailbox data—are stored on the Mailbox server role. The public folder database is also on the Mailbox server role. The mailbox role includes DAGs to make the server role fault-tolerant. You'll find more information about the Mailbox role in Chapter 6, "Mailbox Services."

All message routing is done by the Hub Transport server role, which is responsible for delivering messages to the correct destination mailbox server and routing messages to the perimeter outside such as the Internet. Chapter 5, "Routing and Transport," provides you with the necessary information about the Hub Transport role.

Similar to the Hub Transport, the Edge Transport server role is also responsible for messaging routing purposes, but is a special server role that can be placed in a perimeter zone to send and receive messages from the Internet. Because of this situation, it also includes anti-spam and antivirus functionality to protect your internal environment. You can get more information about the Edge Transport role in Chapter 7, "Edge Transport and Messaging Security."

The Unified Messaging (UM) server role combines voice and e-mail messaging in the Exchange Server store, and it integrates telephony networks into Exchange. This role allows you to use Exchange as your voice mail system for your OCS 2007 R2 implementation. Chapter 9, "Unified Messaging," includes all information about the UM role.

NOTE **One of the best Exchange 2010 resources available for understanding all Exchange roles including the features is the Exchange 2010 Architecture Poster, which is scheduled for public availability in August 2010 at *http://go.microsoft.com/?linkid=9729251*. You should definitely have a copy of it pinned to the wall in your working environment where you can review the details daily.**

Feature Changes from Exchange 2003 and 2007

As with every new version of software, features and functionality of previous versions will be retired. As technology continuously advances and changes, the Microsoft product group has to balance adding new functionality, maintaining existing functionality, and removing outdated functionality for Exchange 2010.

Of course, you can retain Exchange 2003 or 2007 functionality by keeping a legacy Exchange server to use only for that functionality, but it's always an in-between step. Therefore, if you're currently running Exchange 2003 or 2007 it is important to clearly understand your current messaging environment in terms of used features and what protocols your applications use. This will prevent you from unpleasant surprises such as an application that stops working because you moved the mailbox to Exchange 2010.

Table 1-2 lists all Exchange 2003 features that are no longer available and explains their replacement functionality available in Exchange 2010.

TABLE 1-2 Replaced and Retired Features of Exchange 2003

EXCHANGE 2003 FEATURES	EXCHANGE 2010 REPLACEMENT
Administrative groups	RBAC permission model.
Routing groups Link state routing	Active Directory site-based routing model.
Recovery storage group	Recovery database.
Routing objects Event service	No replacement.
Intelligent Message Filter	Anti-spam agents available in Edge or Hub Transport.
Microsoft Exchange Connector for Novell GroupWise and migration tools Microsoft Exchange Connector for Lotus Notes	No replacement—use a third-party migration tool for migration.
Network News Transfer Protocol (NNTP) X.400 message transfer agent (MTA) Exchange Installable File System (ExIFS)	No replacement.
Exchange extensions in Active Directory Users and Computers (ADUC)	Recipient management is exclusive to EMC or Windows PowerShell.
Exchange Server Mailbox Merge wizard (ExMerge.exe) Clean Mailbox tool	Use the *Export-Mailbox* cmdlet in Exchange 2010 RTM or the *New-MailboxExportRequest* cmdlet in SP1.
Exchange Profile Redirector tool (ExProfRe)	No replacement.
Recipient Update Service	No separate service available; use EMS for the same functionality.
Monitoring and status node	Exchange 2010 Management Pack for SCOM.
Message Tracking Center	Use Message Tracking or Tracking Log Explorer tools.
Mailbox Recovery Center	Use the *Restore-Mailbox* cmdlet.
Mailbox Management Service	Retention Policies or Messaging records management (MRM).
Migration Wizard	Use the Local Move Request and Remove Move Request wizards.

EXCHANGE 2003 FEATURES	EXCHANGE 2010 REPLACEMENT
Non-MAPI top-level hierarchies in a public folder store NNTP access to Public folders IMAP4 access to Public folders	No replacement.
CDO 1.2.1 MAPI32 CDOEX (CDO 3.0) Exchange WebDAV ExOLEDB Store events	Protocols no longer available; use EWS or EWS Managed API.

Even though Exchange 2007 looks very similar to Exchange 2010, there have been quite a few changes, as listed in Table 1-3.

TABLE 1-3 Replaced and Retired Features of Exchange 2007

EXCHANGE 2007 FEATURES	EXCHANGE 2010 REPLACEMENT
Cluster continuous replication (CCR) Standby continuous replication (SCR) Single copy cluster (SCC)	Database availability groups (DAGs).
Local continuous replication (LCR)	No replacement.
Storage groups	Every database has its own set of transaction logs.
Extensible Storage Engine (ESE) streaming backup APIs	VSS plug-in for Windows Server Backup.
DSProxy	RPC Client Access and Address Book service.
Exchange WebDAV	Protocols no longer available; use EWS or EWS Managed API.
Move-Mailbox cmdlet	Use Local Move Request and Remove Move Request wizards.
Setup /recoverCMS	Setup /m:RecoverServer.
OWA Document access	No replacement.
OWA Web Parts	Not implemented in Exchange 2010 RTM, again available with Exchange 2010 SP1.
Microsoft Transporter Suite for Lotus Domino or IMAP/POP3 migration	No replacement—use third-party migration tool for migration.
Exchange UM Test Phone	Can still be used with Exchange 2010 RTM, but must be replaced in SP1 with the UM Troubleshooting Tool.

NOTE If your company requires the preservation of specific features or functionalities of legacy Exchange versions, you should plan to keep an Exchange server of the required version in operation to ensure continued access to the functionality. However, you should not underestimate the additional effort this creates, such as the need to migrate in a two-step approach from Lotus Domino to Exchange 2007 and then to Exchange 2010.

Exchange On-Premise versus Exchange Online

A traditional Exchange installation requires hardware that is placed in your datacenters, the purchase of software licenses so that the product is allowed to run, and administrators that manage the servers. For some time there has been a push for on-demand service provisioning, where users only pay for the service they use, not for the complete cost basis to establish and deliver the service.

In early 2006, Microsoft introduced the idea of Software as a Service (SaaS) to provide application services on-demand and called their in-the-cloud messaging service Exchange Online. To distinguish between Exchange Online and the installation you run in your own company, Exchange 2010 uses the term *Exchange On-Premise* (or on-prem) because the servers run on your premises. Today's version of Exchange Online is based on Exchange 2010. The two service options available for Exchange differ in the following ways:

- **Exchange On-Premises** This version is generally dedicated to the customer, Exchange servers are placed in a datacenter for the customer (on the customer's premises), and licensing is a fixed price including both hardware and software licensing.
- **Exchange Online** This service is provided as multi-tenant or hosting service, generalized and highly standardized for many customers. Licensing is on-demand, meaning that you pay only for the mailboxes you use. The Exchange servers are placed in a common datacenter and you connect to it over the Internet using a secure connection.

Microsoft provides Exchange Online service as part of the Business Productivity Online Services (BPOS) line.

Exchange Server 2010 is the first version of Exchange that provides a real hybrid approach to Exchange Online services. It was fully designed to allow you to host your sensitive users on-premises and move the rest to the cloud, or in this case, to Exchange Online. Coexistence between the users is achieved by Exchange 2010's new feature, Federation Service, which allows sharing mailbox information such as free/busy times with another company, as shown in Figure 1-9.

All Exchange 2010 Management Consoles such as EMC are capable of managing both an on-premises and an online setup. Thus, running an Exchange organization that operates as a hybrid service can be a real option for your company to reduce the costs of mailboxes. Features include moving mailboxes from on-premises to Exchange Online while the user of the mailbox is logged in and on a scheduled basis, as well as the ECP, which supports self-service control for users. Of course, Microsoft is not the only company that delivers hosted Exchange 2010. Some companies have hosted Exchange for 10 years or more and have much experience

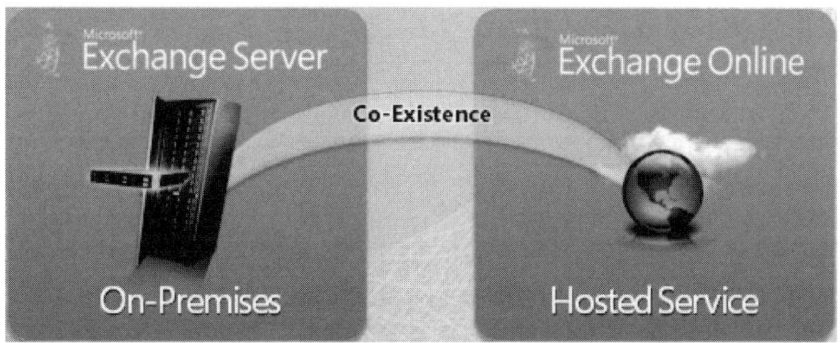

FIGURE 1-9 Exchange 2010 in a hybrid environment

in this space. The difference to Exchange Online is that the Microsoft develops a product to operate as smoothly in a hosted environment as it does in an on-premises deployment.

This book focuses on Exchange On-Premises, but Chapter 10, "Federated Sharing," provides information on how to connect another Exchange organization to your Exchange environment, including information on how to connect Exchange to Exchange Online.

For more information about Exchange Online, see *http://www.microsoft.com/online/exchange-online.mspx*.

NOTES FROM THE FIELD

Europe's Issues with Exchange Online

Manfred Kornagel
Principal Consultant, Siemens AG, Germany

Exchange Online offers you full integration in an existing Exchange System and greatly reduces the operating costs for your messaging system, especially in the areas of administration, maintenance, and upgrade. On the other hand, you have to make sure that the link between your offices and Exchange Online is redundant so that network problems will not interfere with your messaging system.

One of the most critical areas I see currently in Europe is security. Because Exchange Online hosts the mailboxes in centralized datacenters throughout Europe, one in Dublin and one in Amsterdam, the county's laws might not allow storing company-related data in a foreign country. This is the situation as of 2010; remember that Microsoft may have other datacenters in place in Europe in the coming years. It can also be company policy not to store any sensitive data outside the company, which would prevent migrating fully to Exchange Online.

However, the big opportunity I see here is with regard to hybrid implementations, in which you mix Exchange 2010 and Exchange Online. You move your non-critical mailboxes to the cloud and keep your important or business-critical mailboxes on-premises.

Exchange Server 2010 Service Pack 1

Exchange Server 2010 Service Pack 1 (SP1) is scheduled to be released in third quarter 2010. Traditionally, service packs have been bug fixes and security updates. Of course, SP1 still includes all Exchange 2010 RTM Update Rollups and several other bug fixes, but also includes additional functionality and some new features.

SP1 also comes with a schema update that requires you to plan the update accordingly. Table 1-4 provides an overview of what is newly added by SP1 and in which chapter of this book you can find more information.

TABLE 1-4 Exchange 2010 Service Pack 1 New Features

EXCHANGE 2010 SERVICE PACK 1	CHAPTER
Schema and Domain Update ■ SP1 requires you to update the Active Directory schema and every domain.	Chapter 3
Outlook Web App (OWA) ■ Outlook UI includes improvements with the goal of better user experience on different screen sizes, such as on netbooks. ■ Outlook Themes allow you to select different layout styles for OWA. ■ Calendar print allows you to select a calendar view and print it accordingly. ■ Support adding inline images while composing new e-mail. ■ Long-running operations do not block user experience. ■ Auto-save drafts while composing new e-mail. Exchange Control Panel (ECP) ■ Accounts used no longer need to be mailbox-enabled. ■ RBAC management has been improved. ■ Calendar sharing permission management for the end user is included. ■ Create and configure transport and journaling rules. ■ Manage Exchange ActiveSync Policies and ActiveSync Access Settings. ■ Manage quarantined devices and Device Access Rules. ■ Manage RBAC Roles Groups and User Roles (covered in more detail in Chapter 16). ■ Create and manage resource mailboxes and security groups. ■ Create and manage Allow/Block/Quarantine policies. Exchange Web Services (EWS) ■ Includes support for certificate authentication.	Chapter 4

EXCHANGE 2010 SERVICE PACK 1	CHAPTER
RPC Client Access ■ Includes enhanced monitoring and diagnostic tools. ■ Supports cross-premises and datacenter scenarios. Throttling ■ Can now be turned on/off. ■ Includes delay throttling for users. ■ Protects CAS and Active Directory from being overwhelmed by a single user. AutoDiscover ■ Includes enhanced monitoring. Exchange ActiveSync (EAS) ■ Photos are not only available from local contracts, but also from GALs. They are also cached locally and thus available offline. ■ Enhanced EAS throttling support such as configure that a user can only connect a single device. ■ Block/Quarantine notification to mobile device. ■ Includes Simple Rights Management Messaging.	
Delivery Class Throttling ■ Classifies a message based on certain characteristics and assigns it a delivery class. Throttling will investigate messages when they are sent by individual users and add a cost to each message based on message size, number of recipients, and frequency. This cost factor allows assigning a delivery class to the messages.	Chapter 5
Log growth monitoring ■ Monitor and track how quickly the log is growing.	Chapter 6
No changes to Edge Transport, anti-spam, and antivirus in SP1	Chapter 7
Discovery Search ■ Includes improved discovery search functionality such as being able to view the size of a search before adding it to the discovery search mailbox. Archive Mailbox ■ Archive mailboxes can be in any database in the organization. You can move the archive mailboxes to a desired database. ■ Move archive mailboxes between Exchange organizations and cross-premises, such as Exchange Online. ■ Outlook 2007 also supports archive mailboxes (requires Outlook 2007 security update released in Q3/2010).	Chapter 8

EXCHANGE 2010 SERVICE PACK 1	CHAPTER
Managed Folders ■ De-emphasized in Exchange Server 2010 and only managed through EMS in SP1 (not available in EMC in SP1). Retention Policy, or MRM 2.0 ■ You can use the EMC GUI to configure and manage retention polices and retention tags; in RTM, you could only manage these via Windows PowerShell. IRM/RMS ■ **IRM-enabled Active Sync SP1** Builds IRM into ActiveSync, allowing non-Windows Mobile EAS clients to protect and consume IRM-protected content. ■ **RMS support for Web-ready document view** SP1 provides the ability to access attachments that are IRM-protected using Web Ready Document Viewing.	
Unified Messaging ■ More OVA configuration settings are available in ECP, such as choice of ordering. ■ Calls Name Display support if your PBX provides caller names to UM. ■ UM users can belong to two UM Dial Plans. ■ Voicemail Preview includes more languages such as European Spanish and was increased in accuracy. ■ New UM Troubleshooting Tool is based on the *Test-ExchangeUMCallFlow* cmdlet to test UM connectivity. ■ UM Reporting includes Call Statistics and User Call Logs reports that no longer require SCOM 2007 but are accessible from ECP. ■ Mailbox move from Exchange 2007 or cross-premises includes UM Dial Plan move. Instant messaging integration in OWA ■ Instant messaging integration is no longer configured in the web.config file but uses the *Set-OwaVirtualDirectory* cmdlet. ■ OWA now supports alerts such as instant messaging invites.	Chapter 9
No changes to Federation in SP1	Chapter 10
Database Availability Groups (DAGs) ■ Static IP for DAGs. ■ Granular replication. ■ Failover performance improvements. ■ Support for a two-node DAG in Datacenter Activation Coordination mode.	Chapter 11

EXCHANGE 2010 SERVICE PACK 1	CHAPTER
■ Outlook cross-site database failover experience such as being able to enable or disable cross-site direct connect. ■ Additional scripts such as a script to distribute active database copies across servers. ■ Faster failovers with improved post-failover client experience.	
No changes to Backup and Restore in SP1	Chapter 12
Performance and Scalability planning ■ Loadgen. ■ Capacity Planning and Performance Reporting Toolkit. ■ EPA for 2010.	Chapter 13
Move Mailbox ■ Improvement such as converting mailboxes to/from linked mailbox, archive, cross-forest support, and so on.	Chapter 14
Setup ■ All software requirements can be installed automatically. ■ Support to implement split permissions.	Chapter 15
Active Sync ■ Manage Active Sync devices using ECP. Group Management ■ Naming Policy for group naming restrictions Manage Security Groups using ECP. ■ Hide Groups from GAL using ECP. ■ Define a default OU for group creation. ■ Ability to configure Hierarchical Address Books (HABs). Role-Based Access Control (RBAC) ■ Split permissions between Domain administrators and Exchange administrators so an Exchange admin is not able to grant itself Domain Admin rights. ■ Support for scoping based on database level. ■ Manage RBAC Roles Groups and User Roles with ECP. *New-MailboxExportRequest* cmdlet ■ Uses an internal PST writer library and thus doesn't require Outlook to be installed on any Exchange server as the *Export-Mailbox* cmdlet required. Follows the asynchronous model of mailbox moves: you place a request and it will be processed by MRS that writes a PST file. ■ Replaces the *Export-Mailbox* cmdlet.	Chapter 16

EXCHANGE 2010 SERVICE PACK 1	CHAPTER
Public Folder Troubleshooting ■ Repair Public Folder database cmdlets.	Chapter 17
Message Tracking ■ Cross-premises message tracking.	
Client Access Server Troubleshooting ■ Reset Client Access Server virtual directory.	
Mail flow monitoring ■ Cross-premises mail flow monitoring functionality.	

Exchange 2010 Editions and Licensing

An area that is often underestimated but also important when planning your Exchange server deployments is which editions of Exchange Server 2010 you will use and what type of licenses you will buy for your users. This topic is especially important because planning thoroughly can save you money.

The most common license types are Server Editions and Client Access Licenses (CALs). However, in Exchange 2010 you can also purchase an Exchange 2010 External Connector License, which allows an unlimited number of clients to access an Exchange server in scenarios where the number of CALs is uncertain. This type is limited to non-employees such as partners or suppliers.

You can access more information about licensing for Exchange Server 2010 (on-premises) at *http://go.microsoft.com/fwlink/?LinkId=181503*.

Exchange Server 2010 Editions

As in previous Exchange versions, two server editions are available: Standard and Enterprise. Both editions are licensed by a product key, which mean you can switch a Standard edition to an Enterprise edition when you enter a valid license product key.

Although the Exchange Server 2010 Standard edition is targeted for smaller companies, it also can be used for specific server roles such as Hub Transport or Unified Messaging server roles, as well as in small branch offices. The Enterprise edition supports up to 100 mounted databases at the same time and thus is targeted to large companies. Table 1-5 provides an overview of each edition's offerings.

TABLE 1-5 Exchange Server 2010 Edition Offerings

FEATURE	STANDARD EDITION	ENTERPRISE EDITION
Mounted Mailbox Databases	Maximum 5 databases	Maximum 100 databases
Passive Database Copies	257 databases	257 databases
Database Size Limit	16 TB	16 TB
Default Database Size Limit	1 TB but can be changed with registry key	16 TB (16,000 GB)
Database Availability Groups (requires Windows Server 2008 Enterprise edition)	Included (limited by mounted databases)	Included
Unified Messaging	Included	Included

The major difference between the Standard edition and the Enterprise edition is the number of mounted mailbox databases on that server. You also can create DAGs with an Exchange 2010 Standard edition, but remember that you need a Windows Server 2008 Enterprise edition as an operating system to get the cluster features needed for DAGs.

As a guideline, you can use Standard editions for all server roles and you need only to plan for Enterprise editions at mailbox servers that will have more than five databases mounted at the same time. This licensing model allows you also to start with a Standard edition, and when you require it purchase an Enterprise edition.

NOTE **If you ever wondered what happens when the trial edition expires in Exchange 2010, the quick answer is nothing, except that you will see some extra nag screens to remind you that your Exchange servers need to be licensed. You will stay on your Standard edition license and the expiration of the trial edition will have no functional impact. However, remember that you will not get any support from Microsoft for a trial edition.**

Exchange Server 2010 Client Access Licenses

Exchange Server 2010 comes with two CAL editions that are also called Standard and Enterprise. The difference from the server editions is that the CAL is an additive license, so you always need to buy a Standard CAL and then add an Enterprise CAL to gain advanced functionality, such as voice mail.

Both CAL editions can run against either server edition; thus, a Standard CAL can run against an Enterprise edition server and vice versa. Table 1-6 shows an overview of what each CAL edition offers.

TABLE 1-6 Exchange Server 2010 Client Access Licenses

FEATURE	STANDARD CAL	ENTERPRISE CAL
E-mail, shared calendaring, contacts, tasks	X	X
Advanced Active Sync Policies		X
Journaling on per-user or per-distribution list basis	(per database only)	X
Unified Messaging (voice mail, for example)		X
Custom Retention Policies		X
Archive Mailbox		X
Multi-Mailbox Search and Legal Hold		X
Information Protection and Control (IPC): journal decryption, transport protection rules, Outlook protection rules, IRM Search		X
Advanced anti-spam including Forefront Protection 2010 for Exchange Server		X

IMPORTANT **If you're planning on using Information Rights Management features of Exchange 2010, you need to purchase additional Windows 2008 Rights Management Server (RMS) CALs for each user or device that uses it!**

Exchange Organizational Health

EMC includes an option to generate an Organizational Health report to provide an overview of your Exchange organization including licensing information as well as a summary of the Exchange servers and recipients. You can use this information to verify that your Exchange Editions and Licenses are purchased correctly. Figure 1-10 shows a sample report.

Organizational Health scans the following sets of users to determine the CAL calculation:

- Unified Messaging Users
- Managed Custom Folder Users
- Advanced ActiveSync Policy Users
- Archived Mailbox Users
- Retention Policy Users
- Searchable Users
- Journaling Users

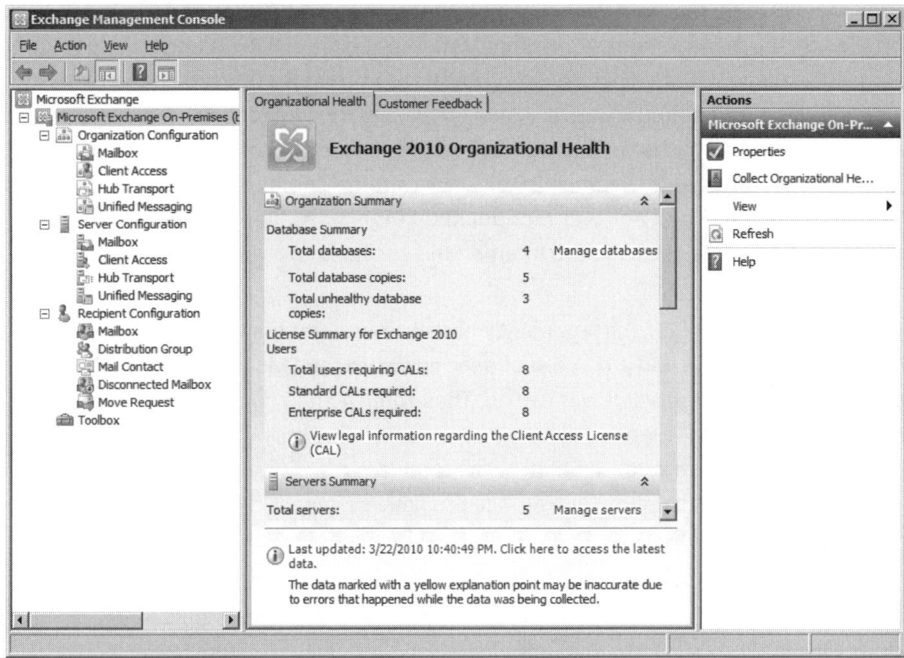

FIGURE 1-10 Viewing Organizational Health in EMC

Windows PowerShell and Exchange 2010

One of the biggest changes since the move to Active Directory in Exchange 2000 was the move to Windows PowerShell as the basis for automating management tasks in Exchange 2007. Windows PowerShell is a command-line interface created to provide a scriptable and programmable management interface.

Building on the success of Exchange 2007 and Windows PowerShell, Exchange 2010 integrates tightly with Windows PowerShell 2.0 and Windows Remote Management 3.0 (WinRM) to create a Roles-Based Access Control system that provides a secure and scalable scripting solution. WinRM provides an implementation of WS-Management (WSMan). It allows for remote management by listening for management connections using IIS primarily on TCP/IP port 80. By default, communication is only allowed when it is encrypted using the Negotiate or Kerberos Security Service Provider.

The Role-Based Access Control (RBAC) security is a feature built upon Windows PowerShell 2.0. This allows a role to be created and then used to filter the cmdlets and parameters that are available for viewing and executing.

> **NOTE** RBAC in Windows PowerShell 2.0 allows you only to see the cmdlets you have permissions for. For example, even though you are member of the Organizational Management role group, you cannot see the *New-MailboxExportRequest* cmdlet, which requires the Mailbox Import Export role.

In Exchange 2007 the Windows PowerShell runspace and the Exchange snap-in have to be installed on the management workstation and also require full RPC connectivity to the managed Exchange servers. This proved problematic in complex domain and network environments. This also required that every management station needed the Exchange binaries installed and maintained anytime updates were released. As mentioned earlier, with Exchange 2010 and Windows PowerShell 2.0 all administrative communication is now handled over TCP/IP port 80 or 443 and not over random RPC TCP/IP ports. Because these ports are commonly open to provide access to the Internet, this provides encrypted communications more easily through a firewall.

Although the Exchange 2007 management framework brought many great functions with Windows PowerShell, it had a number of deficiencies. In the EMS in Exchange 2007 the cmdlets execute on the server it was run on. Therefore you had no ability to throttle or control the resources that these cmdlets would consume. In Windows PowerShell 2.0 communication is handled through WSMan, which provides the ability to throttle connections to reduce the likelihood that an administrator can negatively impact client performance by performing too many administrative tasks against the Exchange server.

> ***NOTE*** **When you remotely connect to an Exchange server, you do not immediately see which server you're connected to. To determine which Exchange server you're connected to, use the *Get-PSSession | fl ComputerName* cmdlet.**

The main difference between Exchange 2007 with Windows PowerShell 1.0 and Exchange 2010 with Windows PowerShell 2.0 is that the Exchange snap-in is not loaded locally when you open the EMS. Instead, Windows PowerShell connects to the closest Exchange 2010 server using WinRM, performs authentication checks, and then creates a remote session for you. Figure 1-11 shows the process used for logging into EMS in Exchange 2010.

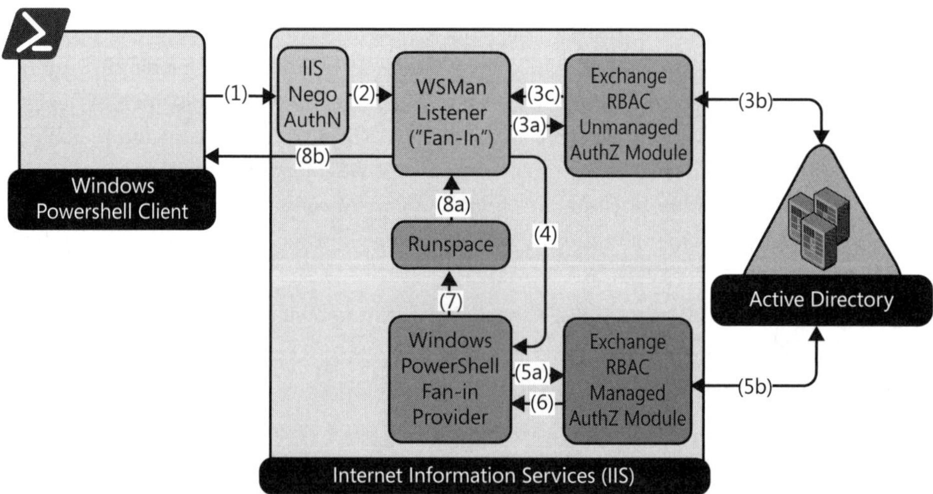

FIGURE 1-11 EMS Process

When you run EMS, the following process happens in the background before you can use it:

1. When EMS is opened a new remote Windows PowerShell session is established with IIS on the remote server. IIS will authenticate the user at this time.
2. The WSMan virtual directory (or Windows PowerShell vdir) is contacted on the server and given the authenticated user's information.
3. The Exchange RBAC Unmanaged Authorization module is contacted to verify that the logon process can continue. It then contacts Active Directory to authorize the user. If successful, WSMan is instructed to continue the process. If authorization is unsuccessful, WSMan is instructed to terminate the process.
4. WSMan passes the user principal information to the Windows PowerShell fan-in provider. A fan-in provider allows many connections to a single service. The PowerShell Fan-in provider allows IIS to call Windows PowerShell.
5. Windows PowerShell hands off the user principal information to the registered authorization module (the Exchange RBAC Managed Authorization module), which analyzes the connecting user's RBAC definitions against Active Directory, and then builds the initial session state for handoff back to Windows PowerShell. The initial session state contains the cmdlets and parameters that will be exposed to the connecting user.
6. The Exchange RBAC Managed Authorization Modules sends this information back to Windows PowerShell via their initial session state interfaces.
7. A client runspace is created on the server within the IIS worker process and PowerShell configures implicit remoting proxies to be handed back to the client.
8. The runspace is returned and imported using the *Import-PSSession* operation on the client.

> **NOTE** If you have the Exchange Management tools installed, you can attempt to manually load the Exchange snap-ins in a local Windows PowerShell session; however, this is not supported. For information about manually connecting a remote EMS to an Exchange server see *http://technet.microsoft.com/en-us/library/dd297932.aspx.*

Windows PowerShell is also available for other products, not only Exchange. These include Microsoft products such as System Center Operations Manager, Systems Center Virtual Machine Manager, System Center Data Protection Manager, Microsoft SQL Server 2008, and many features in Windows Server 2008 R2. Other third-party products also have embraced Windows PowerShell as a management interface for their products. This momentum provides added incentive to learn about and become proficient in using Windows PowerShell so as to more easily manage all of these products.

IMPORTANT Learning to master Windows PowerShell is outside the scope of this book. However, a basic understanding of Windows PowerShell and how it works is required to understand portions of this book. For additional information about Windows PowerShell scripting visit the Microsoft TechNet Script Center at *http://technet.microsoft.com/scriptcenter.*

Windows PowerShell Basics

For those who have made the plunge into Windows PowerShell by using it in Exchange Server 2007, thankfully little has changed in how it functions on the surface even with all of the changes underneath. If you have not had any experience with Windows PowerShell prior to Exchange 2010, a basic overview will help you navigate the remainder of this book.

Windows PowerShell is an object-based operating environment built to provide a simple yet powerful administrative interface. Each Windows PowerShell action is known as a cmdlet. These cmdlet names always start with a verb, then have a hyphen followed by a noun. For example, to retrieve information about a mailbox you may run the *Get-Mailbox* cmdlet.

Some of the common verbs used in Exchange cmdlets are:

- *Add* This verb places an object in an already created object. For example, *Add-DistributionGroupMember* adds a mail-enabled object into a distribution group.
- *Get* This verb retrieves information—it will not change any settings. For example, the *Get-Mailbox* cmdlet retrieves information about one or more mailboxes.
- *New* This verb creates a new instance of an object or task. For example, *New-Mailbox* creates a new mailbox.
- *Remove* This verb deletes an object or removes it from another object. For example, *Remove-DistributionGroup* removes the specified distribution group.
- *Set* This verb makes a configuration change. For example, *Set-Mailbox* will change the configuration of a specific mailbox.

The noun portion of the cmdlet (the part to the right of the hyphen) has a number of options and is the target of the verb. For example, you can *New-*, *Get-*, *Remove-*, and *Set-* the Mailbox noun.

This verb-noun pairing makes it easy to discover cmdlets that match the action you want to take. If you need to create a new database, you know you need to find a cmdlet that starts with *New-* and that contains *MailboxDatabase*. Thus to create a new mailbox database you need to use *New-MailboxDatabase*.

Each cmdlet also has a variety of parameters that are used to control the actions the cmdlet performs. For example, the *Set-Mailbox* cmdlet has a number of parameters, including *Identity*, *DisplayName*, *HiddenFromAddressListEnabled*, *IssueWarningQuota*, *LitigationHoldEnabled*, and so forth.

You can use more than 100 parameters with the *Set-Mailbox* cmdlet. For example, to set Joel's mailbox warning quota to 2 GB you run the *Set-Mailbox -Identity Joel*

-IssueWarningQuota 2GB cmdlet. The *Identity* parameter in each cmdlet is the object that you want to perform the object against. In the previous example *Identity* was the alias for the mailbox we wanted to adjust. A positional parameter means that PowerShell expects a value for the parameter at a specific place in the cmdlet syntax.

For most cmdlets the *Identity* parameter is expected in the first position and does not need to be identified. To illustrate we could modify the previous example to omit the reference to the Identity parameter to the *Set-Mailbox Joel -IssueWarningQuota 2GB* cmdlet and get the same result.

Using *Get-Help*

Each Exchange cmdlet also has help information available. The cmdlet that retrieves help for other cmdlets is *Get-Help*. To obtain help about *Get-MailboxDatabase* run *Get-Help Set-MailboxDatabase*, as shown in Figure 1-12.

```
Machine: Dallas-MB01B.contoso.com
[PS] C:\Windows\system32>Get-Help Get-MailboxDatabase

NAME
    Get-MailboxDatabase

SYNOPSIS
    Use the Get-MailboxDatabase cmdlet to retrieve one or more mailbox database objects from a server or organization.


SYNTAX
    Get-MailboxDatabase [-Identity <DatabaseIdParameter>] [-DomainController <Fqdn>] [-DumpsterStatistics <SwitchParame
    ter>] [-IncludePreExchange2010 <SwitchParameter>] [-Status <SwitchParameter>] [<CommonParameters>]

    Get-MailboxDatabase -Server <ServerIdParameter> [-DomainController <Fqdn>] [-DumpsterStatistics <SwitchParameter>]
    [-IncludePreExchange2010 <SwitchParameter>] [-Status <SwitchParameter>] [<CommonParameters>]


DESCRIPTION
    If you use the Get-MailboxDatabase cmdlet with no parameters, it gets information about all mailbox databases in th
    e Exchange organization.
    If you use the Get-MailboxDatabase cmdlet with the Server parameter, it gets information about all mailbox database
    s on the server that you specify.
    You need to be assigned permissions before you can run this cmdlet. Although all parameters for this cmdlet are lis
    ted in this topic, you may not have access to some parameters if they're not included in the permissions assigned t
    o you. To see what permissions you need, see the "Mailbox Database permissions" section in the Mailbox Permissions
    topic.


RELATED LINKS
    Online Version http://technet.microsoft.com/EN-US/library/e12bd6d3-3793-49cb-9ab6-948d42dd409e(EXCHG.140).aspx

REMARKS
    To see the examples, type: "get-help Get-MailboxDatabase -examples".
    For more information, type: "get-help Get-MailboxDatabase -detailed".
    For technical information, type: "get-help Get-MailboxDatabase -full".
```

FIGURE 1-12 Using the *Get-Help* cmdlet

As shown, some common parameters are available when getting information about Exchange cmdlets: *-examples*, *-detailed*, and *-full*.

The *-examples* parameter only displays examples for using the cmdlet. The *-detailed* parameter shows a more detailed version of the default help, and *-full* provides the full help content.

> **NOTE** If your administrative workstation has Internet access you can also specify the *-online* parameter to view the latest version of help online.

Using *Get-Command*

With hundreds of possible cmdlets, narrowing your search for the appropriate cmdlet can be a little overwhelming. Thankfully, the *Get-Command* cmdlet can be used to find commands or cmdlets. For example, if you want to search for all commands that include the word *Restore*, just run the *Get-Command *Restore** cmdlet.

You can also use the *Get-Command* cmdlet and specify the *-Verb* or *-Noun* parameter. To retrieve a list of all cmdlets that include *Database* in them you can run the *Get-Command -Noun *Database** cmdlet as shown in Figure 1-13. The *Get-Command* cmdlet will return any registered cmdlet. To narrow your search to only Exchange cmdlets, you can use the *Get-ExCommand* cmdlet in the same way you use the *Get-Command* cmdlet.

```
Machine: Dallas-MB01B.contoso.com
[PS] C:\Windows\system32>Get-Command -noun *Database*

CommandType     Name                                           Definition
-----------     ----                                           ----------
Function        Add-DatabaseAvailabilityGroupServer            ...
Function        Add-MailboxDatabaseCopy                        ...
Function        Clean-MailboxDatabase                          ...
Function        Dismount-Database                              ...
Function        Get-DatabaseAvailabilityGroup                  ...
Function        Get-DatabaseAvailabilityGroupNetwork           ...
Function        Get-MailboxDatabase                            ...
Function        Get-MailboxDatabaseCopyStatus                  ...
Function        Get-PublicFolderDatabase                       ...
Function        Mount-Database                                 ...
Function        Move-ActiveMailboxDatabase                     ...
Function        Move-DatabasePath                              ...
Function        New-DatabaseAvailabilityGroup                  ...
Function        New-DatabaseAvailabilityGroupNetwork           ...
Function        New-MailboxDatabase                            ...
Function        New-PublicFolderDatabase                       ...
Function        Remove-DatabaseAvailabilityGroup               ...
Function        Remove-DatabaseAvailabilityGroupNetwork        ...
Function        Remove-DatabaseAvailabilityGroupServer         ...
Function        Remove-MailboxDatabase                         ...
Function        Remove-MailboxDatabaseCopy                     ...
Function        Remove-PublicFolderDatabase                    ...
Function        Restore-DatabaseAvailabilityGroup              ...
Function        Resume-MailboxDatabaseCopy                     ...
Function        Set-DatabaseAvailabilityGroup                  ...
Function        Set-DatabaseAvailabilityGroupNetwork           ...
Function        Set-MailboxDatabase                            ...
Function        Set-MailboxDatabaseCopy                        ...
Function        Set-PublicFolderDatabase                       ...
Function        Start-DatabaseAvailabilityGroup                ...
Function        Stop-DatabaseAvailabilityGroup                 ...
Function        Suspend-MailboxDatabaseCopy                    ...
Function        Update-MailboxDatabaseCopy                     ...
```

FIGURE 1-13 Using the *Get-Command* cmdlet

Using Cmdlet Aliases and Tab Completion

To make working within Windows PowerShell easier you can create aliases for cmdlets. One of the default aliases is *dir*, which is an alias for *Get-ChildItem*. To view currently assigned aliases you can run *Get-Alias*. To create an alias of *nm* for the *New-Mailbox* cmdlet, run the *New-Alias nm New-Mailbox* cmdlet.

Another time-saving feature of Windows PowerShell is tab completion. You can start typing a cmdlet and press the Tab key and it will finish typing the cmdlet name for you. Tab completion is also available for cmdlet parameters.

Using Pipelines

One of the features that puts the "power" in Windows PowerShell is the ability to pipeline information between cmdlets. In many other shells, such as those used by Linux, pipelining is done by passing strings from one command to another. Because Windows PowerShell is based on .NET, the information passed between cmdlets in a Windows PowerShell pipeline is objects with attributes that can be retrieved and modified. To pass the object collection from the output of one cmdlet into the next cmdlet, all you need to do is separate the cmdlets with the pipeline operator, the pipe character (|).

A simple use of a pipeline operation is to take the output of the *Get-Mailbox* cmdlet and format the output as a table. The cmdlet used to format the output as a table is the *Format-Table* cmdlet, which has a commonly used alias of *fl*. To use this cmdlet to format the output of the *Get-Mailbox* cmdlet, run *Get-Mailbox | Format-Table* as shown in Figure 1-14.

```
Machine: Dallas-MB01B.contoso.com
[PS] C:\Windows\system32>Get-Mailbox | Format-Table

Name                      Alias                ServerName         ProhibitSendQuota
----                      -----                ----------         -----------------
Administrator             Administrator        dallas-ex01        unlimited
DiscoverySearchMailbox... DiscoverySearchMa... dallas-ex01        50 GB (53,687,091,200 bytes)
Kim Abercrombie           KimA                 dallas-ex01        unlimited
Hazem Abolrous            HazemA               dallas-ex01        unlimited
Luka Abrus                LukaA                dallas-ex01        unlimited
Ahmad Abu-Dayah           AhmadA               dallas-ex01        unlimited
Humberto Acevedo          HumbertoA            dallas-ex01        unlimited
Gustavo Achong            GustavoA             dallas-ex01        unlimited
Pilar Ackerman            PilarA               dallas-ex01        unlimited
Gudmundur Adalsteinsson   GudmundurA           dallas-ex01        unlimited
Terry Adams               TerryA               dallas-ex01        unlimited
Michael Affronti          MichaelA             dallas-ex01        unlimited
Manoj Agarwal             ManojA               dallas-ex01        unlimited
Nupur Agarwal             NupurA               dallas-ex01        unlimited
```

FIGURE 1-14 Using a pipeline to format the output of *Get-Mailbox*

A pipeline can consist of any number of chained cmdlets. For example, to sort the content from the previous example based on the *Name* property you can run *Get-Mailbox | Sort-Object Name | Format-Table*, as shown in Figure 1-15.

```
Machine: Dallas-MB01B.contoso.com
[PS] C:\Windows\system32>Get-Mailbox | Sort-Object Name | Format-Table

Name                      Alias                ServerName         ProhibitSendQuota
----                      -----                ----------         -----------------
Aaron Alex Selig          AaronAlexS           dallas-ex01        unlimited
Abu Obeida Bakhach        AbuObeidaB           dallas-ex01        unlimited
Adam Barr                 AdamB                dallas-ex01        unlimited
Adam Trukawka             AdamT                dallas-ex01        unlimited
Administrator             Administrator        dallas-ex01        unlimited
Adrian Lannin             AdrianL              dallas-ex01        unlimited
Ahmad Abu-Dayah           AhmadA               dallas-ex01        unlimited
Ajay Solanki              AjayS                dallas-ex01        unlimited
Alan Shen                 AlanS                dallas-ex01        unlimited
Aldis Vilums              AldisV               dallas-ex01        unlimited
Alex J. Simmons           AlexJ.S              dallas-ex01        unlimited
Alexandre Silva           AlexandreS           dallas-ex01        unlimited
Alicia Thornber           AliciaT              dallas-ex01        unlimited
Alistair Speirs           AlistairS            dallas-ex01        unlimited
```

FIGURE 1-15 Using a pipeline to sort and format the output of *Get-Mailbox*

The *Format-Table* cmdlet can be used to show specific columns in the table if they are specified. To display only the *Name* and *ServerName* fields in the previous example, you would run *Get-Mailbox | Sort-Object Name | Format-Table Name,ServerName*. Another command formatting cmdlet is *Format-List*. You can use the *Format-List* cmdlet, which has an alias of *fl*, to format the output in a list format. Piping an object to *Format-List* will list each item and all of its properties. In a table format only a few columns can be shown; however, piping the list to *Format-List* will provide a detailed list that can be reviewed. Pipelining opens up endless opportunity to perform complex administrative tasks for a command line.

Scripting

Windows PowerShell is not only a command shell, but also includes a full scripting language, including support for logic, loops, variables, functions, and error handling. Scripts can be saved in files with a .PS1 file extension and then run from the command line. However, to prevent malicious scripts from being accidentally run, the security policy is set to not allow unsigned scripts to run. In a controlled environment where you are confident that malicious scripts are not present, you can change the security policy using the *Set-ExecutionPolicy* cmdlet. The valid parameters matching the execution policies available are as follows:

- **AllSigned** This policy requires that all scripts and configuration files are signed by a trusted publisher.
- **Bypass** This policy blocks nothing and the user sees no warnings or prompts when he runs the script.
- **RemoteSigned** This policy requires that all scripts and configuration files downloaded from the Internet be signed by a trusted publisher.
- **Restricted** This policy does not load configuration files or run scripts.
- **Undefined** This policy removes the currently assigned execution policy from the current scope as long as it has not been set through Group Policy.
- **Unrestricted** This policy loads all configuration files and runs all scripts. If you run an unsigned script that was downloaded from the Internet, you are prompted for permission before it runs.

INSIDE TRACK

Windows PowerShell 2.0 Best Practices

Ed Wilson

Author of Windows PowerShell 2.0 Best Practices, Microsoft Scripting Guy, US East Region

When working with Windows PowerShell, it is helpful to keep in mind what I call the *script progression*. Things that are acceptable when working from the Windows PowerShell console are certainly not good form when writing a script. One of the features that make working with Windows PowerShell in an interactive fashion useful is the ability to use a shortcut name, or alias. Aliases reduce the typing burden by allowing you to type a short name instead of a very long name. Instead of typing **Get-Process**, you can type **gps.** Instead of typing **Foreach-Object**, you can type **%.** While making Windows PowerShell easier to use, this technique does nothing for readability.

More than just readability, however, the use of aliases in a script can lead to inconsistent results. This is because it is possible to delete or to change the definition of an alias—even aliases that ship with Windows PowerShell. If someone changes the definition of an alias to another cmdlet that uses the same signature, no error will be generated when the alias is called, but the results of the script will be completely different. Therefore, as a best practice use aliases on the Windows PowerShell console, but avoid them in your scripts.

Another technique that is useful on the Windows PowerShell console command line is the use of positional parameters. A positional parameter occurs when you leave out the name of the parameter, and just include a value for the parameter. For example, the following command starts notepad:

```
Start-Process notepad
```

If you want to stop the notepad process, you might assume you could use this command:

```
Stop-Process notepad
```

However, that command generates an error because of the difference between the positional arguments. In the *Start-Process* cmdlet, the default parameter is *–filepath*, not *name* as you might suspect. When you do not supply any parameters, Windows PowerShell looks for a program named notepad in the search path, retrieves the one it comes up with, and launches the program. The default parameter for the *Stop-Process* cmdlet, however, is *–id,* not *–name*. When you do not supply any parameters for the *Stop-Process* cmdlet, Windows PowerShell expects a process ID, not a program name. When writing a script, you want to clarify what the script is doing, in case the script becomes modified in the future to accept command-line arguments.

Speaking of command-line arguments, I consider it a best practice to incorporate some kind of command-line help, if the script accepts parameters or arguments. You want your users to be able to run the script directly from the command line—you don't want to require them to open the script and look at the contents to figure out what the arguments are and what values are acceptable. The best way to provide this help is to use the Windows PowerShell 2.0 help tags and integrate the script with the *Get-Help* cmdlet. However, creating a parameter named *help* and then performing a quick check for the presence of the parameter is sufficient to provide help to a user.

The key to all of this is to realize that what is acceptable when using Windows PowerShell from the command line is not the same standard to use when you begin scripting. In the case of enterprise scripts that will be shared with others in your organization, the standard increases proportionality, and you should be looking at advanced functions and perhaps modules to contain your code. However, even in a simple straight-line script you should avoid aliases and positional parameters.

For more information about using Windows PowerShell, see the Hey Scripting Guy blog at *http://blogs.technet.com/heyscriptingguy*, where I write about a wide range of scripting topics, discussing everything from automating Microsoft Office to using Windows PowerShell to working with Active Directory.

Additional Resources

- Messaging Application Programming Interface: *http://en.wikipedia.org/wiki/MAPI*
- Exchange 2010 Architecture Poster (scheduled availability in August 2010): *http://go.microsoft.com/?linkid=9729251*
- Microsoft Exchange Online: *http://www.microsoft.com/online/exchange-online.mspx*
- On-Premise Licensing for Exchange Server 2010: *http://go.microsoft.com/fwlink/?LinkId=181503*
- Microsoft TechNet Script Center: *http://technet.microsoft.com/scriptcenter*
- Hey Scripting Guy Blog: *http://blogs.technet.com/heyscriptingguy*

CHAPTER 2

Exchange Deployment Projects

As an information technology (IT) professional, you might groan after reading the title of this chapter. And you might be tempted to flip through the remaining pages of this chapter to see whether any tables or pictures catch your interest. Before you choose that course, consider that no matter how technically astute you are, you will undoubtedly be able to improve how you handle deployment and migration projects. You will also have better business relationships with non-technical people in your company if you have a firm grasp on how to best manage an Exchange deployment project. If you have been involved in any sort of enterprise-level messaging deployment, you can attest to the fact that these projects are extremely complicated, they can very easily go badly, and any improvement is welcome.

Most non-technical people and the people that manage the technical people require that IT projects be run a lot like other projects at the company. You know—with deadlines, project plans, and all that nonsense that most technical people couldn't care less about. However, being able to work with these non-technical people and make them happy will no doubt make the project progress better and improve your overall employment opportunities.

If you are a project manager and reading through this chapter, you may think that an enterprise messaging project is just like any other project. Although the basic steps are the same, there are areas that make a messaging project different than other projects. For example, few IT projects touch so many aspects of a business. From the users' computers, to the network configuration, to the line of business applications, very few areas will be unaffected. This means that messaging projects, for one, are very visible and require political savvy, technical prowess, meticulous organization, and a drive to get things done to be successful. Even a seasoned project manager can benefit greatly from reviewing and more thoroughly understanding how messaging deployment projects differ from other enterprise IT projects.

The complexity of IT operations has driven many companies, especially those with large or forward-looking IT departments, to adopt an operational framework, such as ones based on the Microsoft Operations Framework (MOF) or Information Technology Infrastructure Library (ITIL). These frameworks are just that, a frame that can be used to form the way the company plans, delivers, operates, and manages IT services. They are not full lists of rigid rules and plans that fit every situation. Most often, consultants are hired to help adjust and implement the framework to meet the needs of each specific business. As such, this chapter considers using the MOF for Microsoft Exchange Server 2010 deployment projects to establish a common set of terms and to form the basic deployment and life-cycle process.

NOTE To learn more about MOF, visit *http://www.microsoft.com/mof*. To learn more about ITIL, visit *http://www.itil-officialsite.com/AboutITIL/WhatisITIL.asp*.

Exchange Deployment Project Framework

MOF has three phases: Plan, Deliver, and Operate. However, there is another operational layer or process called *Manage,* as shown in Figure 2-1. Although the names of the phases summarize simply what each phase includes, many details and processes underlie each, and when combined they form the complete picture of MOF.

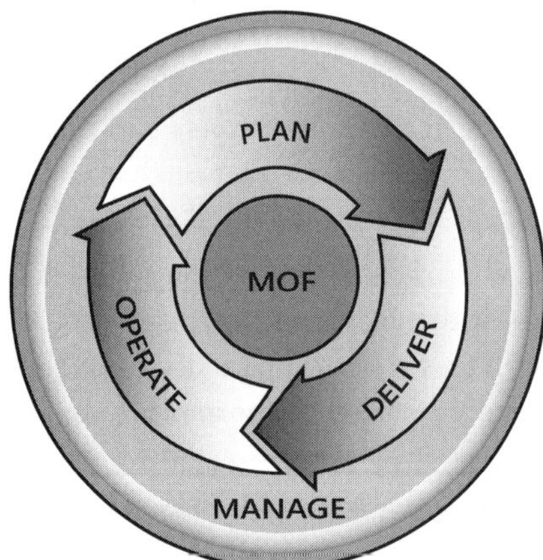

FIGURE 2-1 The MOF life cycle

The Plan Phase includes developing the overall strategy for the company. The Deliver Phase includes developing and implementing strategic projects. The Operate Phase includes maintaining the deployed systems. The Manage Phase is a continual process that drives improvements to each of the operational phases.

Planning Exchange Deployment Projects

Although this isn't an MOF training book, this chapter will apply the basic phases to an Exchange Server 2010 deployment and provide additional detail where needed. In the next several sections of this chapter, each of these phases is discussed as it relates to deploying Exchange Server 2010. Use this chapter as a baseline to create your own best practices as you discover what works best for your organization.

Plan

The Plan Phase is twofold and is usually completed with the participation of the business owners, executives, and the technical architects, as these resources are needed to guide the direction of any IT projects in the company. First, the Plan Phase consists of assessing the capacity management of the current solution and then planning for future capacity and needs. Second, this phase deals with creating a business and technology strategy around the IT solutions leveraged by the company.

The Plan Phase can be likened to purchasing an automobile. You first recognize the need to purchase a new car when your current car no longer meets your needs. The next step is to determine what your budget is, which features and functionality you require, and when you will purchase the automobile. Likewise, in the Plan Phase the decision makers identify the need for change and then choose the high-level functionality needed as well as when the project should be completed. The output of this phase will include the IT mission statements and budgetary information.

A number of questions need to be answered during the Plan Phase. These questions can be separated into business and technical questions.

Business Questions

Although the exact questions will vary for each business and over the course of time, the following list will help start this process

- What are the organization's strategic business objectives?

  The strategic objective and initiatives include projects and market trends that affect the company today as well as those that may affect the company over the next few years. Documenting these objectives is crucial to creating an IT vision that meets the needs of the entire company. Have a goal to list at least three short-term and three long-term objectives. These objectives might include market trends such as increased pressure to improve customer service response time, or they might include being able to achieve certification. A long-term goal might be for the company to become publically traded or to become competitive in a new market that may require new regulations. Having this information will shape the functionality, features, hardware, and third-party software that should be evaluated to meet these needs.

- What are the budgetary goals for these types of projects?

  As with any project, there is a limitation on the resources available. These resources might be monetary, personnel-related, or even limited by time. Identify this information before starting any project. Surprises of constrained resources later in a project can doom the project to failure. One budgetary goal may be to reduce overall hardware and software costs for a particular solution or perhaps to minimize operational costs by minimizing the amount of staff required to maintain the messaging solution.

- Are there any internal business roadblocks that could cause delays or objectives to the business requirements?
- Do any internal business processes or departments need extra attention to ensure the success of the project?

  As these departments and processes are identified as risks, the risks should either be accepted or mitigation plans should be documented and put into place.

- Which tasks should be handled by current IT staff, consultants, or other outsourced resources?

  Some functions might not be strategic to the business, or might require specialized training or skills; therefore, they might be outsourced to a consulting company or to a service provider. Services such as Unified Messaging administration or anti-spam services may fall into this category.

- What are the business reasons for adopting the particular technology? Are there business drivers for the migration or for the new implementation or technology?

  Often there are driving factors, such as improved productivity or reduced overall cost, that drive adoption of new technology. In this case, are there return on investment (ROI) or total cost of ownership (TCO) metrics that must be met? Or does older software and hardware need to be retired to avoid ongoing maintenance costs and support issues?

- What industry-specific system requirements are needed?

  Many industries today have specific requirements around regulations and compliancy, including Health Insurance Portability and Accountability Act (HIPAA), Payment Card Industry Data Security Standard (PCI DSS), Sarbanes-Oxley Act (SOX), and others. Because these requirements can drastically change the overall design specifications of the environment, they need to be identified and captured in the vision of any IT project.

Technical Questions

The following list includes some of the technical questions that should be answered during the Plan Phase.

- What are the most important technology goals and objectives for your organization?

  The messaging environment is usually one of the core services of the business. As such, the decisions made during the deployment can help or hinder the ability to meet strategic business goals. List the main goals, which may include improved collaboration, improved availability, improved remote user experience, legal discovery, and Unified Messaging. These features may also include any of the other native Exchange Server 2010 features or any third-party services that can interface with Exchange Server 2010.

- What are the service-level requirements the messaging system and related services should meet?

  Identifying the service-level requirements will affect the redundancy built into the system, the types of service agreements needed for dependent hardware, and organization-level agreements between departments to ensure that the system meets these requirements. All of these can add up to complications and expense. If the requirements and optional goals are clearly defined, you can avoid undue cost and frustration further into the project.

- What are the functional requirements for the messaging system?

  Most likely the strategic requirements for the current e-mail system will not have changed significantly for a new release. Users will no doubt need to send e-mail messages to other users on the messaging system as well as to the Internet. While defining the functional requirements, it is a great time to capture functionality that might be required for things such as anti-spam, Unified Messaging, or even instances where certain users need to be blocked from being able to print or forward specific e-mail types. The functional requirements will be used in designing a test environment, a test plan, and eventually the production deployment. To make sure these requirements are thorough, reach out to the customers, the business stakeholders, and the end users. You can do this informally by speaking with a subset of people or even by sending out surveys.

- Which IT skills and resources are strategic to the organization?

  When deciding which groups will be responsible for delivering and operating the messaging service, skill sets and priorities also need to be evaluated. Perhaps specific projects are more critical to the business and should be handled by internal staff, whereas other projects might be outsourced.

  When deploying new software and services, all involved staff will no doubt need additional training. If new features will be utilized or new challenges addressed, staff may need even specialized training to understand how these features are delivered, operated, and managed in the business environment. Governmental regulations might also require a change to operational procedures. To avoid potential problems, complete training early to ensure that the appropriate staff knows how to meet those regulations.

Also consider the track record of the IT staff in projects with a similar scope as well as the current workload of the staff. In some cases, a project may require additional dedicated resources with specialized skills. This is especially true with regard to deployments because many corporate IT departments do not have staff that regularly completes messaging deployments. Additional highly skilled resources may also need to be considered if the project needs to be completed in a short time frame. Otherwise, you'll need to allocate additional time to bring the current IT staff up to speed and able to perform the deployment tasks.

- Which tools and third-party applications need to be included in the design?

  As part of the strategic requirements, it is important to decide up front which strategic tools and applications need to be integrated or included in the solution. Adding in core applications later in the process could require design changes or cause compatibility issues. When you work on a large project that will involve many changes, avoid any inclination to implement many changes at once. At other times a single change will require other changes to be completed and properly orchestrated. Before moving forward, you need to make business decisions about how to control the amount of change—whether that change will affect only the basic essential upgrades (servers and clients) or will also include new applications and services.

- How many users need to be included and where are they located?

  Determining the number and location of users that will be affected by a messaging project will help determine the scope of the project and the scalability needs of the messaging system. Understanding the network configuration and available bandwidth for each of these sites is essential to help determine the resources available as well as what will be required at each location.

At the end of the Plan Phase, a document should be created that summarizes the general business and technology goals and strategy for the company. This document should include the business justification, the project scope, and the success criteria for the project. This document might also include a project vision scope that will drive and focus the project. This information should be signed off on by the technical and business leadership that will ultimately be responsible for delivering the solution.

Deliver

After the business and technology strategy has been defined to meet the project goals, the delivery of the project can begin. Numerous methodologies can be used for this stage and may vary from business to business. No matter which methodology you use, the effort you put into this stage will allow for easier and smoother future steps.

Returning to the earlier automobile purchase analogy, the Deliver Phase is where you identify the vehicles that meet your needs, test-drive the cars, select the final car, and then complete the necessary paperwork to purchase the car. Likewise, the Deliver Phase is where the products and methodology are selected and then executed to meet the criteria set out in the Plan Phase. MOF includes five main steps in this phase: Envision, Project Planning, Build, Stabilize, and Deploy. These are the main functions covered in the Deliver Phase in the chapter. However, to ensure clarity of the process, these steps are broken down further into nine discrete steps:

- Envision
  - Step 1: Envision: Identify business and technical requirements.
  - Step 2: Assess.
  - Step 3: Evaluate the new solution(s) and potential designs.
  - Step 4: Build a proof of concept.
  - Step 5: Create a design.
- Project Planning
  - Step 6: Develop the deployment and obtain buyoff.
- Build/Stabilize
  - Step 7: Implement a pilot. Begin pilot, adjust the plan, and complete deployment.
- Deploy
  - Step 8: Deploy.
  - Step 9: Post-implementation review.

Envision

The first part of the Deliver Phase is to identify the business and technical goals defined in the Plan Phase that apply to the messaging project so as to define a project vision and the scope. Completing this step successfully is a lot more difficult than it might seem. Doing the legwork properly at the beginning should ensure not only that you meet current and future business requirements, but that you also get the support you need to complete the project with the right resources. Essentially, this vision should match up with the business's short-, medium-, and long-term goals as well as include optional requirements, and changes that the business is considering or could benefit from.

Because every business is different, no single best practice answer says you should complete this step one way or the other. Therefore, in most instances the best plan is to go through a list of those tough questions and try to get the answers. This is not to say that all the questions will be answered, or that all questions will be identified to fit the requirements of your business. What is important is that conversations occur and thought goes into gathering the requirements. During this phase, you must also describe how this vision will impact all levels and tasks of users in the organization. This vision will be used to create a design and an internal marketing plan.

A vision statement summarizes the project goals either as a catchy slogan or as a more developed paragraph or list of tenets that help focus the project. Often, the vision statement is passed down from the Plan Phase and used to drive the rest of the project including creating a full vision for the project. To create a vision for a specific project, it is sometimes helpful to consult standard lists of items that IT organizations typically focus on improving, such as:

- Service and Organizational Level Agreements (SLAs or OLAs)

  Are the current agreements sufficient? Are the current agreements obtainable? Will new hardware and software allow for improving system availability?

- Operational costs

  Many studies have shown that ongoing operational costs make up the majority of a system's cost. These costs often include staffing, power and cooling, and maintaining the hardware and software.

- Network costs

  The location of the servers and clients and the amount, size, and frequency of messages that flow into and through the system will affect the design and cost of the network.

- Backup and restore cost and performance improvements

  New techniques and features are available that may reduce the amount of data that needs to be backed up. Exchange Server 2010 opens the doors for sweeping changes to the backup philosophy and processes. These options should be evaluated.

- Improved provisioning processes (for example, HR Systems)

  The process of creating users and managing information and groups can be both time-consuming and inaccurate. Some companies automate these processes by allowing the human resources system to create and maintain user information rather than requiring manual administrative efforts to ensure that user information is accurate.

- Exchange enhancement that enables larger mailboxes

  One of the major enhancements made to Exchange Server 2010 is the ability to provide large mailboxes much more cost effectively than previous versions of Exchange Server.

- Reducing licensing costs

  A portion of the initial cost of every messaging solution is the software licensing. The complexity of many of the licensing options requires that you take care to properly estimate the number and type of licenses needed to complete the project.

- Return on investment (ROI) and budgetary considerations

  Most projects require extensive budgetary considerations. With additional costs or budgetary approval a return on this additional cost is going to need to be justified. Part of the vision of the project may be to not only roll out the new software but also realize quantifiable benefits for doing so.

- Data retention and isolation

  Many companies now fall under regulations, many of which affect e-mail configuration. These include HIPPA, SOX, the Gramm-Leach-Bliley Act, and others. If your company is bound by these regulations, take time to understand how to comply with them. It is best to meet with your company's auditors to ensure that the regulations are fully understood before a vision is created.

- Auditing and compliance requirements

  Again, regulations often require that access to data be tracked and logged. Certifications such as the Payment Card Industry Data Security Standard (PCI DSS) also require that event and access logs be archived and be accessible for set periods of time for review.

- Message archiving requirements

  Message retention is fast becoming a requirement in today's business world. This puts the IT decision makers in a position of trying to optimizing the message environment while keeping the required amount of e-mail. Even when not required for regulatory reasons, legal departments often request that messages be archived. Determining the detailed functionality required for an archiving solution will help you determine whether the native features are adequate or if additional products will be required to meet those needs.

- Antivirus and anti-spam functionality

  Although anti-spam functionality is built in to Exchange Server and has improved dramatically over the last few releases, thwarting sophisticated spammers can be very difficult and is never foolproof. Some businesses choose to not take on this challenge and use hosted services such as the Microsoft Exchange Hosted Anti-spam service. When it comes to antivirus solutions, a number of available antivirus products may fit in with the business requirements, especially if a variety of antivirus vendors are being used elsewhere in the company or have other features that might be required.

- Client access

  What clients will be used to connect to the e-mail system? Will kiosks be allowed to connect to Outlook Web App and open files? Or will any ActiveSync-capable mobile device be able to retrieve e-mail? Will other non-ActiveSync mobile devices be supported? As mobile devices have proliferated over the last few years it is often no longer a question whether mobile support will be provided—the question is which devices will be supported. As these clients are identified, what type of support will be offered for them, if any?

- Security requirements

  In some instances additional security is needed to meet regulations or best practices. This starts with a good deployment plan for appropriate network security configuration, antivirus software, and applying software updates. This can also require segmentation of duties by the operational staff. If this is the case, what are the specific roles that need to be defined and implemented in the environment?

- Line-of-business application integration

  Are there applications integrated into the messaging system that are critical to the business? These applications need to be tested with the new messaging system because changes in the software may require updates, adjustments, or other workarounds to the third-party application to be able to work with the new deployment configuration.

- Performance planning

  Determining the appropriate hardware and the expected application performance metrics is required to ensure satisfactory performance for end users. Because each environment is different, information gathered from actual usage on the current messaging environment will yield the most accurate inputs for creating a performance plan. When migrating between versions of Exchange or between messaging environments, usage patterns will change. End users will behave differently depending on the features available and limitations imposed. These behavior changes can make it difficult to estimate usage ahead of time. During any migration it is important to understand that you plan for estimated performance and thus latitude may be needed to account for variance.

- Capacity planning and management

  After the messaging system is deployed, the natural business cycle will lead to changes in the environment. These could be fluctuations in mailbox size or number. As these usage patterns change, so should the configuration of the messaging system. To best plan for this, critical metrics should be gathered periodically to trend these changes and then action should be taken to adjust for these changes. This should include a plan to scale up and down in line with business initiatives. For example, if a business has a seasonal need for additional capacity, the plan may include adding additional servers to handle the seasonal load.

NOTES FROM THE FIELD

Gathering Business Requirements

John P. Glynn
Principal Consultant, Microsoft Consulting Services, US/Central Region

One of the top reasons for failure of a project implementation is not satisfactorily meeting the expectations of the customer. Requirements need to be completely discovered, examined, and agreed upon. A successful implementation project will have agreed-upon requirements and freeze feature usage early in the planning phase. One of the often forgotten areas of discovery is around actual business requirements. As technologists, we tend to instantly jump to conclusions around what the business wants or needs and look to what cool technology features we can implement. This also underscores the importance of having a solid executive sponsor who can assist in ensuring that the business needs are being represented in the plan. This sponsor can also help reduce the tendency for the project scope to creep as a result of changing requirements mid-project.

Though the IT department tends to have a pretty good foothold on what the business requirements in the organization might entail, take the time to set up meetings with strategic decision makers in the business groups. Understand what

their strategic initiatives involve and have conversations around how the features of the solution can assist them in meeting their business objectives. One method for defining the business requirements is to create a feature or service map. These maps define how product or service features pertain to specific business groups and their strategic initiatives.

Assess

To know where you are going you first need to know where you are. Before creating and implementing a design it is necessary to gather and firm up documentation on what, if anything, is currently deployed, how it is configured, and how it is used. Over the months and years as usage patterns change and configuration changes are made, a messaging system evolves. Design documents are often created only during deployments or when major changes happen. Because of this it is important to verify this documentation prior to embarking on a new messaging project. In the absence of an existing change and configuration management history log, the system and server configuration, message routing, anti-spam configuration, and third-party application settings should be collected. It is likely that each of these components will be configured to meet operational needs. Some of these applications might also have been adopted or developed either to solve a deficiency in the messaging environment or developed in a way that interfaces in an unsupported or deprecated way.

IMPORTANT **It is essential to identify the how, what, why, where, and when at the beginning of the process to ensure the fidelity of the final design. Finding new integrated applications and requirements later during the Deploy Phase will no doubt cause unplanned delays and expense.**

Care should be taken to objectively identify how well the system has been performing and how well it is meeting the user needs. Because these issues can be emotionally charged, information should be collected and tallied. Even if the feedback from users is negative, it still may be important feedback that can be addressed with training or with a change in the configuration.

Identify any application that is dependent on the existing e-mail system. Because Exchange Server 2010 touches so many other services and components of the infrastructure, it is important to gather information about the infrastructure so that educated decisions can be made on how to deploy Exchange and its related services:

- Identify and prioritize currently deployed applications by how crucial they are to business functionality.

  Many businesses have a number of applications that integrate with their messaging systems. These may be monitoring systems that send e-mail notifications or software that does customer relationship management (CRM).

- Identify the clients that are currently in use.

  Identify the clients that are being used to access e-mail. For example, which versions of Outlook are deployed? Are there any non-Microsoft clients such as Apple Macintosh or Linux-based client computers? Are there POP3 or IMAP4 clients (such as Outlook Express or Outlook)? Which mobile devices are being used, and which will be supported going forward? Is there a need to support additional clients more effectively?

- Document service-level and organizational-level agreements in place.

  Identify any service- and organizational-level agreements currently in place and determine how they are being enforced.

- Inventory the hardware currently in use.

  Identify the hardware that is in place and determine whether any of it could be redeployed in an updated solution. Many companies will also make sure that any hardware is still under a maintenance agreement or that parts are on hand in case of a failure.

- Document the network infrastructure design.

  Gather any available network configuration and utilization documentation. It is important to understand the path that e-mail messages and client traffic will take and whether bandwidth is available to handle current and predicted traffic.

- Identify where the messaging servers are currently located, the number and size of local mailboxes and public folder replicas, and the number and average size of the e-mail messages sent and received.

  Consider also gathering performance information for each of these servers, which will help to identify any sizing concerns that might need to be addressed or identify locations that may be consolidated.

- Identify the Active Directory Domain Services (AD DS) configuration.

  Exchange Server relies heavily on AD DS–specific information about the domain and forest functional levels, as well as site and link configuration. When noting the current configuration, also note any barriers to changing the configuration to better support the Exchange server deployment.

- Update any messaging configuration documentation to ensure that all data needed to complete a project plan is available.

  If your business has a previous version of Exchange deployed, consider using Exchange Best Practices Analyzer to document the current configuration and to ensure that all critical issues have been addressed.

- Identify the people involved in managing Exchange and all of the dependent services.

  Managing Exchange touches so many different departments and disciplines in larger organizations, including AD DS, security services, storage, server, and networking. If multiple people or departments control these services be sure to identify each of them and whether they have any special requirements—such as a separate change control process—to ensure that these issues are planned for rather than being a surprise when deadlines are looming. Issues between departments and business units can kill a project faster than almost any other single factor.

- Perform a risk assessment.

  No doubt your current deployment has issues and risks, so be sure to identify them. Often risks include non-redundant services such as power or Internet connectivity. They can also include insufficient training, or lack of spare hardware.

- Document the executive escalation path.

  Often problems during the deployment require an executive decision or guidance to overcome hurdles or resolve resource conflicts.

After this information is identified, a vision and the objectives and scope for the project can be generated. These business requirements can then be matched up with the current messaging system to identify any deficiencies.

NOTES FROM THE FIELD

Assessing a Current Exchange Deployment

Joseph Cirillo
Senior Engineer, MCA:M Horizons Consulting, Inc.

To best prepare for a successful messaging system deployment, it is critical to conduct a full discovery and audit of the current messaging infrastructure, its dependencies and systems reliant on it. This simple exercise will allow you to abstract the complexity of the current system into manageable parts to help determine the purpose and function of the transitioned messaging system it is to perform.

The information gathered from the audit should consist of, but not be limited to, the following items, each of which will contribute to the design of the deployed infrastructure.

- **Business requirements**
  - **Long-term vision**
  - **Service level agreement**
  - **Legal and compliance**
  - **Security**
  - **Performance**
  - **Business continuity**
  - **Availability**
  - **Scalability**
  - **Client access methods**

- Technical requirements
  - Geographic information
  - Network
  - Protocols
  - DNS structure
  - Active Directory topology
  - Active Directory components
  - Current messaging topology
  - Current messaging components
  - Boundaries of the current Exchange system
  - Third-party applications that interface with the messaging system
  - Administrative model
  - Operations structure and tasks
  - Client versions
  - Naming standards
  - Hardware
  - Storage
  - Monitoring and reporting
  - Disaster recovery
  - Firewall

If the current messaging system is a legacy version of Exchange, I make use of the LDIFDE.exe command-line utility to export the current Exchange configuration to a file by executing the following command from a server class domain-joined machine:

```
ldifde -f ExchConfig.txt -d "CN=<Organization Name>,CN=Microsoft Exchange,
CN=Services,CN=Configuration,<Domain Naming Context>" -p SubTree
```

The output file ("ExchangeConfig.txt") contains a complete snapshot of every Active Directory object and attribute currently set by the legacy Exchange system. This information can assist in the discovery and audit process, as well as provide insight to items that may need to be cleaned up prior to deploying Exchange 2010.

An example of a cleanup item can be any object that references a deleted object. For example, by performing a search for the text "0ADEL," I found the following Mailbox Database using an invalid Public Folder database that has been deleted:

```
dn: CN=MB 1-1,CN=StorageGroup1,CN=InformationStore,CN=MailServer02,CN=
Servers,CN=St. Louis,CN=Administrative Groups,CN=ExchangeOrg,CN=Microsoft
Exchange,CN=Services,CN=Configuration,DC=domain,DC=org
```

Another example of a useful piece of information to gather is the versions of Exchange currently operating in the organization:

```
dn: CN=ServerName,CN=Servers,CN=St. Louis,CN=Administrative Groups,CN=
ExchangeOrg,CN=Microsoft Exchange,CN=Services,CN=Configuration,DC=domain,
DC=org
versionNumber: 7638
```

A final example of a necessary piece of information to gather would be to list all the current Exchange recipient policies and the SMTP domain(s) they currently support. This output can be used to compose a complete list of SMTP domains currently supported in the organization.

```
"dn: CN=Inbound Domains-Authoritative,CN=Recipient Policies,CN=ExchangeOrg,
CN=Microsoft Exchange,CN=Services,CN=Configuration,DC=domain,DC=org"
gatewayProxy: SMTP:@contoso.com
gatewayProxy: SMTP:@wingtips.com
```

Evaluate the Solution

With a grasp of the vision of the project and the assessment of what is currently in place, you can begin the evaluation of products, configurations, and services to meet the project needs. This step includes evaluating the new Exchange Server 2010 features and identifying which ones fit your needs. This is also the time to identify third-party products and configuration changes that might be necessary to deploy Exchange in your environment to meet the business requirements. Evaluation includes learning about the options available. This can be done by attending seminars, reading documentation and other material, and meeting with vendors.

Evaluate possible migration strategies. If migrating from an Exchange Server 2003 or Exchange Server 2007 messaging environment, specific steps and requirements need to be completed to be successful. On the other hand, if you are migrating from another messaging product, additional work is needed to test migration options and to identify any limitations or additional requirements and training necessary for using that migration tool or technique.

Many projects falter when not enough time is spent understanding all of the options and tactics available for deploying, configuring, migrating, and operating the messaging system. You should also use this time to reevaluate whether all the necessary personnel will be available for the project or if additional resources will be needed to assist with specific applications, hardware, facilities, or utilities.

As different portions are evaluated for inclusion in the project, it is important to cover not only the software but also the server hardware, network configuration, storage hardware, antivirus software or services, Unified Messaging system, mobility options, migration tools, and archival and compliance software to make sure they can work together.

To make sure these features work as expected in your environment, you might need to create a proof-of-concept deployment. This is done in an isolated lab where testing of the features can occur without affecting your production systems. To appropriately perform testing, the lab environment should mimic the pertinent details of the production environment.

Proof of Concept

Traditionally, there are at least two places a proof of concept can be done. Some people would expect to see a proof of concept after the design has been created. Others, as is shown in this book, place the proof of concept where all the parts expected in the design are tested together in an isolated environment. At that time all of the questions and issues are tested to prove that they not only work in concept but also in reality. Testing should involve all of the activities done by end users and administrators, similar to what is done during user acceptance testing when a change is made during a change window. This allows the full range of functionality to be tested.

Load testing should also be done at least on a small scale to gauge how much hardware will be needed during the production rollout. If standard user and administrator tests are not already defined, gather a list of these tests by polling the appropriate people in your organization. Documenting a standard set of tests will ensure that the required results are gathered. If changes are made to the standard list of tests later in the process, these tests will need to be run again.

This does not mean you should simply set up a full production environment in your lab. You do, however, want to set up a representative sample of your production environment. You should plan your testing so that you can use the equipment you have to maximum advantage and proceed in a logical and controlled manner. Start by testing features that are mission-critical to your organization.

NOTE Testing is a checkpoint against progress. Progress should always be verified by testing.

Test migration scenarios that are relevant to your environment. Although migration documentation may seem straightforward, adjustments often need to be made to fit each environment to give the users the best possible experience.

The phases of a proof of concept are shown in Table 2-1.

TABLE 2-1 Proof of Concept

Prepare	Verifying functionality is critical in the test environment. This testing allows time to verify assumptions, verify functionality, and create a detailed and accurate deployment design. This is also a good time to learn more about the product. To prepare for this work, gather all of the software, hardware, and configuration guides that are being considered for use in the design.

Deploy Proof of Concept	Deploy an isolated test environment that is as close as possible to the expected production environment and allows testing to be completed. Testing in this phase should include potential migration scenarios.
Test	Perform the test scenarios and note the detailed results. Be sure to note any changes to the test scenarios because of new or changed features.
Review Test Results	After the testing is completed, the issues and potential changes should be reviewed. The reasons for any unexpected results should also be captured. For instance, did the test fail because a feature or function didn't work as expected, or were there limits reached? The review should categorize each issue's criticality and then each issue should be addressed by changing the design, opening support cases with the appropriate vendors, or adjusting the current process to accommodate the new functionality. Any user behavioral changes should be documented and later clearly communicated to the affected users.

Create a Design

This is the step where you start to put all of the pieces together with the information that has been gathered and tested to generate a design that will be used to develop the processes and procedures around it. Although a single person may drive this process, creating a design involves all of the disciplines involved up to this point and may require several iterations to be created and reviewed by a group of people to have a satisfactory design.

Designing a new solution requires the creation of a detailed plan for how to configure and install Exchange Server 2010. Describe the different types of users, what software they will use, how they will connect, and the network configuration. Also detail the messaging and third-party features that will be implemented and how they will be deployed. All of these elements must align with the scope and vision of the deployment project.

The major phases of the Create a Design step are shown in Table 2-2.

TABLE 2-2 Creating a Design

Define Client Standards	Many organizations will choose to upgrade or refresh client configurations. A standard supported definition should include the operating system configuration, antivirus configuration, Microsoft Outlook version. For Outlook Web App users, the standards might include the configuration and versions of browsers that will be allowed. Coordinating client upgrades during the deployment phase may require additional resources; however, it will provide end users with an optimal experience and they'll be able to use all of the new features.

Define Network and Security Designs	The Exchange Server 2010 deployment plan also needs to include the network and security plan. The flow of e-mail messages and connectivity to the clients requires properly designed connectivity. Also, the security of the solution needs to be considered to protect such a vital portion of the business communication. Security options may include message- and transport-level encryption, firewalls, intrusion detection and prevention, auditing, and activity logging to apply best practices and meet regulatory requirements.
Define Antivirus and Anti-spam Design	E-mail is an attack vector for many viruses, spammers, and phishing schemes that have become very lucrative for criminals in recent years. There is increased pressure to protect the corporate e-mail system and the end users from these sorts of threats. Antivirus and anti-spam designs will include the products that will be used, where they will be deployed, and whether these services will be outsourced or handled in-house.
Define Application Compatibility and Integration	Exchange Server 2010 is the foundation for messaging and collaboration in the corporation; therefore, many businesses have adopted or developed processes and products that integrate with Exchange. These include line-of-business applications, unified communications products, and workflow applications. Because there are significant changes in how Exchange Server 2010 works, thorough testing during the Proof of Concept phase and working with the vendor is important to ensure that the applications work after the migration.
Define Infrastructure Changes	In many instances changes will need to be made to optimize the network and storage configuration for the Exchange Server 2010 deployment. Ensure that the network and storage administrators understand the requirements of Exchange Server 2010 features so that these groups can raise any concerns and define any changes required. Changes also may be required for other portions of the network or the current messaging infrastructure; these all need to be identified and planned at this time.
Define and Remediate Risks	When changes are being made—especially to important systems—there is always some form of risk. Risk is introduced when mailboxes are moved, when engineers complete a task for the first time, and when restores have not been tested. One of the key areas that can introduce the most risk is an unrealistic schedule, or one that doesn't build in time for risk mitigation. Attempting to complete too much work in a single window of time often leads to rushed work and inadequate testing and verification. This also reduces the likelihood that a back-out plan can be executed should a failure require it to be executed.

Develop Communication Plan	Communication between team members, stakeholders, and end users is essential to a well-run project. If key people do not have the information they need to prepare and deal with the deployment project, these individuals are likely to either fail completing their portion of the plan or become frustrated. Some of these issues can be mitigated by following good change-management practices; however, additional diligence in communication should be planned for the deployment. Communication with other groups that may be affected by changes, such as the network or storage groups, will also ensure that issues that arise can be handled quickly, and reduces the likelihood that overlapping changes or initiatives could introduce risk. For example, the network team may be planning to replace the infrastructure firewalls and may require additional time to configure new services. Good intra-group communication can identify this planned change early on to ensure that testing schedules can be worked out to minimize the risk it will introduce.
Develop Marketing and Training Plan	To build anticipation for the new features and functionality of the new messaging system, it is important to market them to the end users. This marketing should then be followed up in conjunction with the deployment with training. This includes hands-on training for the administrators as well as the end users.
Define Detailed Architecture	Creating a messaging architecture requires coordinating a variety of technologies and disciplines. To succeed, all the parts must function together when the project is complete. The architectural design needs to include all of these components to ensure that the project is successful.
Define Migration Process	The design should include the migration process, which defines how the design will be implemented and how the users will be migrated to the new design. Often this portion is neglected and left to be figured out during the deployment process. However, it is a best practice to define it at this stage because it affects how the end user interfaces with the messaging system. The migration process needs to be fully tested and the steps fully documented. It is important that the migration process follow the goals set forth. In some cases the end-user impact, such as manual reconfiguration of clients or manual migration of e-mail data is acceptable. However, the end user may be expecting a fully automated process. These goals will drive the process documentation and perhaps tools needed by the migration team to be able to meet the business requirements.

Develop a Deployment Plan

Developing the deployment plan takes all of the results of previous phases such as the design and the proof of concept and creates a project plan so that the work is completed.

Creating an effective project plan takes more than technical acumen. It also requires project management and business skills. Identify changes that need to be made to get from the current solution to the new solution and identify stakeholders and project resources. The major phases of this step are shown in Table 2-3.

TABLE 2-3 Develop a Deployment Plan

Create Design Milestones	Using the created design, develop project milestones that can be broken up into discrete steps, including the pilot. Each of these steps should also include an estimate of the required resources needed to complete them.
Obtain Project Resources	The messaging environment interfaces with many points within in an organization .This requires many people and skillsets to be involved in the project. In small implementation projects, one person might fill several roles; in large implementation projects, several people might be assigned to each role. Make sure to engage these resources early and schedule the required time so that other projects do not interfere with or compete with the Exchange Server 2010 deployment project.
Define Education and Training Requirements and Communications Plan	Users will need to be trained on any new interfaces and actions. Adequately preparing users for any changes is one of the most often overlooked steps; however, it is one of the most important steps to ensure end-user satisfaction with the project. Communications that need to be defined include the notifications sent to end users on milestones that affect them. The plan also defines when and how to keep project members and executives informed of the project status.
Obtain Executive Buy-in	Present the solution and preliminary plan to the executive sponsors and get feedback. Make any necessary adjustments based on the feedback, and ultimately get the executives to buy off on the project and provide the needed momentum for the project. Without their unwavering support, you are unlikely to be successful in your project.

As previously mentioned, it is essential to get the appropriate resources engaged in the project. Plan carefully so that you do not accidentally overlook a particular group. Table 2-4 lists some potential team members that you might consider for your Exchange deployment project.

TABLE 2-4 Deployment Team Members

TECHNICAL ARCHITECTS	TECHNICAL TEAM MEMBERS	NONTECHNICAL TEAM MEMBERS
■ Consultants ■ Directory Architect ■ Messaging Architect ■ Network Architect ■ Security Architect ■ Storage Architect	■ Active Directory Administrator ■ Change Management Administrator ■ Deployment Engineer ■ Desktop Administrator ■ Messaging Administrator ■ Network Administrator ■ Helpdesk Administrator ■ Technical Evangelists	■ Business Decision Makers or Departmental Heads ■ Pilot and Pre-Pilot Users ■ Project Manager or Program Manager ■ Testing or Quality Assurance Team ■ User Education ■ End Users

A number of people who are not directly involved in the project also need to receive updates or reports on the progress throughout the project:

- Executive sponsor (if the sponsor is not your product manager)
- Chief Executive Officer/Managing Director (unless your product manager or management sponsor is performing this function)

NOTES FROM THE FIELD

Escalations

John P. Glynn
Principal Consultant, Microsoft Consulting Services, US/Central Region

During any project it is likely that something (people, process, or technology) will become a roadblock in your project's critical success path. One hopes that these issues will be overcome through regularly scheduled project status meetings. However, it is crucial that early on in the project—during the planning phase—an escalation path be identified and created. Be sure to get executive sponsorship of the path. The escalation path is the project's lifeline when time or resource roadblocks are encountered. Knowing when and whom to escalate to could be the difference between an on-time, on-budget project implementation and one that drags out forever.

Through properly defined risks you will have already identified several spots in your project when escalations might be needed. Also be on the lookout for and identify areas that have had negative implications on other projects in the past, such as resource issues with dependency teams, purchasing processes, or the amount of time needed to get a server physically racked and installed on the datacenter floor. Try to bring these known issues to the first level of your escalation path very early in the process, look for the signs that you are about to encounter them, and look for date slips and resource contention.

When should you escalate? At the risk of raising a false alarm, you should escalate early and often to ensure that the issue gets all the proper attention that is needed. Without escalation the chances of project recovery are very slim. To cross some of the silos within an organization, escalation to executives is often required. Be sure the executives along the escalation path understand the importance of the issue and its impact on the time and cost of the project.

Implement a Pilot

The pilot begins after you have created a workable and approved design and a project plan that was proven in the test environment. The pilot is where the basic configuration is completed and a subset of users is migrated to verify functionality and the migration process. This process offers the ability to test and then adjust the project plan, and helps reduce the risk of encountering unexpected problems during the full deployment.

The pilot also is an opportunity to get feedback from the users about how well specific features and the deployment process are working. To be effective, this feedback needs to be reviewed and used to resolve any issues or to document workarounds. The pilot deployment should be used to validate that all of the planning and design work is correct and to provide an opportunity to modify the plans so that the main rollout can go as smoothly as possible. The pilot process can be likened to a software beta test, in which you test the deployment and then gather feedback and bugs. As a best practice, consider implementing a second pilot after the first pilot's changes are incorporated. This reduces the likelihood that new problems were introduced and provides an additional opportunity to find problems.

The number of pilot iterations that you do will depend on the complexity of the deployment and the level of risk that will be tolerated during the deployment. Pilots should be broken into phases so that only portions of the deployment are tested in each pilot iteration. For example, the first pilot might only validate the Exchange Server 2010 Edge Transport's ability to handle a portion of e-mail traffic. Or one of the pilot phases may have to deal with users that only access e-mail using Outlook Web App (OWA—previously known as Outlook Web Access). This also helps reduce exposure during the pilot and focuses on which components are being tested.

The amount of feedback and issues discovered during the pilot will help you to determine the resources needed to handle new issues during the production rollout. It is also important during this time to gauge the pace that you will be able to achieve during the production rollout. When mailboxes are moved or clients are upgraded, a limited number of migrations or upgrades can be done in a given time period, and a limited amount of resources can handle any issues that arise during the deployment.

The major steps of the Pilot Phase are shown in Table 2-5.

TABLE 2-5 Pilot Phase

Pilot Planning	The pilot is a miniature deployment and thus needs to be approached with the same diligence. During this planning exercise the portions of the design that are to be tested need to be defined and separated into discrete portions that can be tested without interfering with the production messaging users. This stage is also when the department and key personnel that should be included or represented in the pilot are identified. The key people in the information technology, human resources, accounting, or other departments may have requirements that need to be met and thus should be validated during the pilot. Creating a plan for the pilot helps to ensure that each portion is documented, which in turn helps to ensure that feedback is gathered from each portion so that it can be repeated or adjusted during the production deployment.
Implement the Core Exchange 2010 Infrastructure	Implementing the core architecture is the first step in the Pilot deployment. This includes putting mail services in place, building servers, and performing user acceptance testing to ensure that the Exchange infrastructure is ready for the pilot deployment.
Pilot Deployment	When all of the appropriate change controls have been implemented, the deployment can begin. During the deployment it is helpful if those completing the work are diligent about taking notes on each step they take, especially if a step does not match the steps documented. The pilot is the last appropriate time to tweak processes and documentation. It is essential to have resources that are meticulous so that any issues can be worked out. Another overlooked step in the pilot deployment is testing the back-out plan. Ensuring that the back-out plan works during the pilot is much more manageable than testing and ultimately trying to adjust the plan during the production deployment. Finally, the plan should include what denotes a success for each portion of the pilot. These success criteria might be a list of tasks that need to be completed successfully, or a specific threshold of issues or problems that cannot be exceeded.

Evaluate the Pilot Process	The pilot team needs to diligently watch and evaluate the pilot progress to identify any issues and fix them as they pop up. These issues might be identified by the pilot users, the deployment team, or a monitoring system such as Systems Center Operations Manager. The issues should be properly tracked in a ticketing system to ensure that they are resolved. To elicit feedback from the users, it is important to not only make it easy for the users to give feedback but also to ask specific questions. This can be done in person or through simple online surveys. If the users don't find it easy to give feedback, they often will not and the pilot team loses out on being able to fix important issues before the production deployment.
Pilot Evaluation	After the pilot project is complete, the objectives and success criteria must be reviewed. At this stage the decision is made to make more adjustments, to continue to the Deployment Phase, or to stop the project.

Execute Deployment

As a result of the work done in the pilot, albeit with a much larger scope, the complete deployment plan is created. During the pilot process a lot of the details and issues were worked out; now a very detailed plan can be created. The Pilot Phase can be likened to the dress rehearsal and the Deployment Phase is the main performance in front of a sold-out audience. With all of the visibility of a deployment, diligence is needed to make sure that all of the contributors know what they need to do and when they need to do it.

The deployment plan will include a detailed rollout schedule and plan for each portion of the deployment. This includes server deployment, user training, desktop configuration changes, software deployment, and mailbox moves. The goal is to complete the deployment and then smoothly transition the solution into production and into the Operate Phase. The obvious goal is to deploy Exchange Server 2010 with as little disruption to the business as possible.

The major portions of the Deployment Phase are shown in Table 2-6.

IMPORTANT **Ensure that during deployment the users have an advocate on the deployment team so that user feedback and issues can be addressed or fixed. This can be done with regular reviews of support cases opened with the help desk, surveys, or meetings.**

TABLE 2-6 Deployment Phase

Create Migration Plan and Schedule	The information gathered in the pilot should give a good indication of the number of migrations that can be successfully completed in a session. Create a schedule for migrations, with additional time for contingency, back-out, and verification in each session. Problems can arise during all portions of the migration. It is better to schedule more time than is needed for a migration session and be done early than it is to have insufficient time to fully complete the migration. Complete the migration for administrative and support staff early in the migration deployment so that they can gain experience and assist other users during the deployment.
Complete Deployment Communication and Training	Notify the stakeholders and end users about the deployment project and of any client-side changes before you make changes that affect the end users. If user training is required, make sure the training occurs before any changes are made. In cases where administrator and support staff require training make sure it is completed early in the deployment.
Implement the Exchange 2010 infrastructure	The first step in the actual deployment is implementing any additional architecture that wasn't deployed during the pilot. This includes putting in place additional servers and performing user acceptance testing to ensure that the Exchange infrastructure is ready for the deployment.
Perform Migration	Migrating the services and mailboxes over should follow the plan laid out. Adjustments should be made carefully during this phase to reduce the likelihood of changes causing additional issues. This does not mean that adjustments cannot be made that will benefit the deployment, just that change management procedures should be followed.

Postimplementation Review

After implementation is complete and ready to be pushed into the Operate Phase, an implementation review should be done. This review should be completed with the input of all the major stakeholders as well as the end users to get a complete and objective picture of how the deployment went.

The primary goal of this review is to get executive buyoff indicating that all documented and undocumented requirements were met for the deployment. Providing a summary of the requirements and how each was met to the executive sponsors will help provide them with a report card of the project.

The other goals of this review are to document the changes necessary to have a stable and complete deployment, document the lessons learned for the next deployment, and ensure that all of the requirements have been met or addressed. A best practice is to provide detailed documentation of any changes to the design or process. All of these aspects are important because support of the solution will often be provided by another group when the solution transitions into the Operate Phase. To support the solution, that group needs accurate and complete information.

Now that the implementation has been successful, the entire messaging system needs to be transitioned into the Operate Phase.

Operate

The end goal of the Plan and Deliver Phases is to have the services end up in the Operate Phase. The Operate Phase is where the services are maintained at or above the level for which the services were designed and delivered. If you were purchasing a car, this phase would be likened to receiving the car and driving it from day to day. While you own the car you must rotate the tires, change the oil, and perform standard maintenance. You monitor to make sure that anytime a warning indicator alerts you to a problem you have it repaired by a professional. Likewise in the Operate Phase, the solution is in service and performing its functions. Regular maintenance is completed and monitoring is done to catch any issues as they arise so that they can be fixed. The main functions in the Operate Phase are summarized in Table 2-7.

TABLE 2-7 Operate Phase Functions

Operations	The Operations team ensures that all of the Exchange services are available. This team may also perform routine administrative functions such as user administration, SMTP queue maintenance, database health monitoring, and other proactive maintenance duties.
Service Monitoring and Control	The Service Monitoring and Control function monitors the Exchange services to ensure system health. If problems arise or are detected, this team—usually with automated tools—alerts other teams to take action to rectify the problem. More than just rudimentary service availability, the goal of this function is to provide enough information to determine service issue patterns. The function also provides metrics to ensure that service-level and organizational-level agreements are being met. Finding a balance between providing detailed timely alerts and not overloading operations staff can be difficult. Obviously, the quicker an issue can be resolved, the better the customer experience will be. However, false alerts and erroneous information can cause operations and customer service staff to ignore this information and not act appropriately.

Customer Service	Customer service is the entry point and interface between the customer and the entire Operate Phase. This team will record, categorize, resolve, and close customer support requests.
Problem Management	The Problem Management team is responsible for identifying the root cause and fixing ongoing and recurring problems. This includes documenting workarounds or remediation steps for reoccurring problems.

Manage

As the messaging deployment slides into the Operate Phase, often many of the people involved with the deployment transition into other projects and roles as well. This requires that another component comes into place to oversee that the solution is maintained and continues to meet the business's needs. This is where the MOF Manage layer comes into play. The Manage layer is a continuous process that aims to ensure that all of the phases run smoothly and by design. Once again this can be likened to a car purchase in that the government makes sure that the automobile manufacturer obeys certain laws, and that the car is driven safely, operated by licensed drivers, and maintains certain safety standards.

The Manage Phase of MOF is continuous and consists of several functions, as shown in Table 2-8.

TABLE 2-8 Manage Phase Functions

Governance, Risk, and Compliance	The purpose of this group is to establish well-documented governance for all IT-related groups. This requires the group to review and control risks. For ongoing diligence the group must also self-audit to ensure that they are maintaining this level of performance.
Change and Configuration Management	The purpose of this group is to ensure that the change and configuration procedures are documented. This group also manages the process of introducing change into the environment, as well as the configuration management database. A configuration baseline is created and periodic audits are completed to verify that the baseline configuration is maintained. The baseline configuration includes the operating system version, the updates applied, and even application configuration options. The goal of this group is to control the risks of negative change. Due diligence can be ensured by requiring changes to be fully tested.
Process Improvement and Management	Those responsible for this function keenly understand the key principles for organizing and running IT systems. They define roles and accountabilities and ensure that the appropriate resources are assigned responsibilities and roles to ensure that the processes are followed.

Putting a Project Together

With all of the phases, frameworks, and checklists it can still take time and practice to refine the process that works for your organization and for your specific project type. As you work through a project, be sure to keep diligent notes on the progress and what does and does not work, so that a different approach can be taken next time around. Rather than identifying and fixing the problem, often these problems are repeated each time. By using this chapter as a baseline for best practices and then adding your own each time you are involved with a project, you will be able to hone the process.

Case Studies Used in This Book

This section provides a basis for the rest of the book by introducing the three main case studies that will be used.

Contoso

The first deployment example that is used in this book is Contoso, which is a basic centralized deployment. The company has several remote retail locations and sales offices. All of the employees access and use their e-mail, which is hosted at corporate headquarters in Seattle. These types of deployments are usually done where the sites are adequately connected to support the users at each site, and there is a small centralized IT department.

Contoso is currently running Exchange Server 2003 and has 750 mailboxes. The company chose to transition to Exchange Server 2010 for the improved OWA interface for e-mail and to replace aging hardware. Because the IT staff at Contoso does not have a great deal of experience with migrations, they will be augmenting their team with consultants. Contoso does not currently have any solution in place for legal discovery of e-mail messages and will be implementing the built-in Exchange Server 2010 tools. Because most client computers are still running Microsoft Windows XP and Office Outlook 2003, the clients will be refreshed during the transition. Table 2-9 summarizes this information.

TABLE 2-9 Contoso Summary

GATHERED INFORMATION	DETAIL
Users	750
Deployment Type	Centralized Single permission model
Transitioning From	Server: ■ Seattle: One Exchange Server 2003 ■ Clients ■ Microsoft Windows XP and Office Outlook 2003
Key Requirements	Require consultants to assist in migration Need simple legal discovery tools

GATHERED INFORMATION	DETAIL
Mailbox Availability SLA Target	99 percent
Active Directory Configuration	Contoso.com
Locations	One main office, four remote offices

The company locations are configured as shown in Figure 2-2.

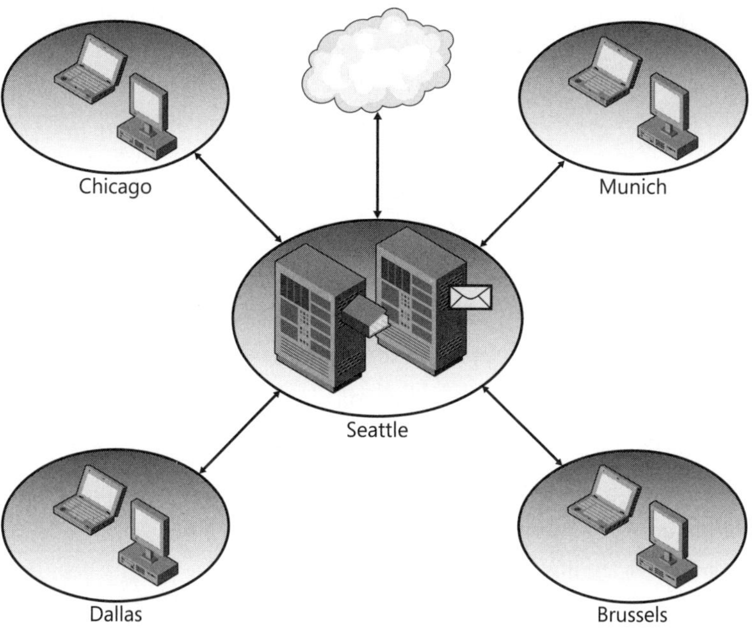

FIGURE 2-2 Contoso logical view

Fabrikam

The second example deployment is Fabrikam, which has four large sites that host the current Exchange Server 2007 computers. High availability is important to Fabrikam and the business has chosen to transition their 7,000-user deployment into a site-resilient Exchange Server 2010 solution.

Fabrikam has had a number of issues with unsolicited e-mail and has chosen to outsource their anti-spam and antivirus tasks to a third party. Fabrikam has recently completed a transition to Exchange Server 2007. With such a deep, in-house knowledge of transition, the company has decided to now transition to Exchange Server 2010. All of the client computers are either Windows Vista with Office Outlook 2007 or Apple Macintosh clients using an IMAP4-based client. The Windows-based clients will not be upgraded during the transition; however, the Apple Macintosh computers will need to be upgraded to use Exchange Web Services or use OWA to benefit fully. Table 2-10 summarizes this information.

TABLE 2-10 Fabrikam Summary

GATHERED INFORMATION	DETAIL
Users	7,000
Deployment Type	Semi-distributed Split permission model
Transitioning From	Servers: ■ Exchange Server 2007 ■ Miami: Two combination Hub Transport and Client Access Servers, one UM server and one Single Copy Cluster Mailbox Server ■ Denver: Two combination Hub Transport and Client Access servers and one Single Copy Cluster Mailbox Server Clients: ■ Windows Vista and Office Outlook 2007 ■ Apple Macintosh with IMAP4-based clients
Key Requirements	Will outsource anti-spam and antivirus Develop a site resilient solution
Mailbox Availability SLA Target	99.9 percent
Active Directory Configuration	Fabrikam.com
Locations	Two main offices, four branch offices

The company locations are configured as shown in Figure 2-3.

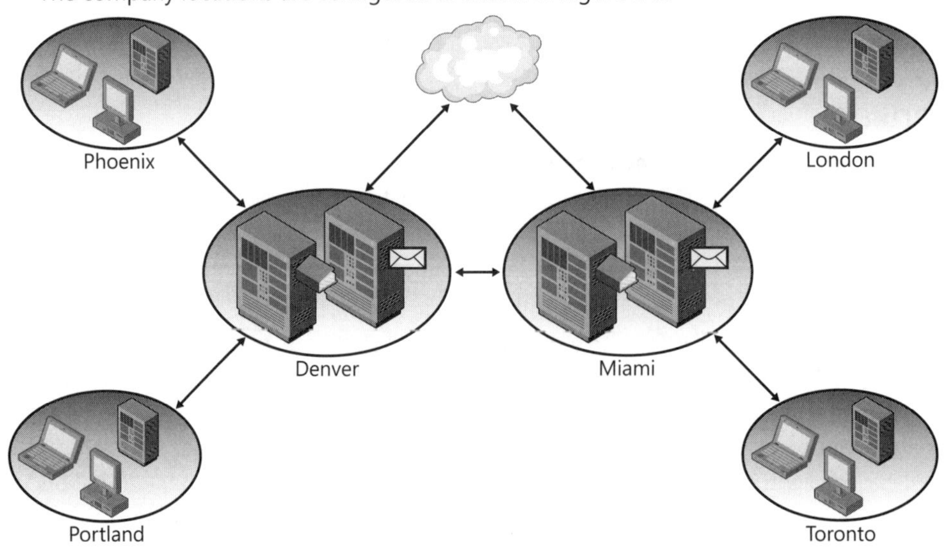

FIGURE 2-3 Fabrikam logical view

Litware

The third deployment example in this book is Litware Inc. This global company has numerous and diverse sites. The company has an empty domain root to control permissions across the domains. They have Exchange Server 2007 computers deployed in nine sites, in three different Active Directory domains in the same forest, to handle the company's 50,000 mailboxes. As a larger multinational company, Litware is very concerned with security so they will be handling all aspects of their messaging system transition in-house. The company's IT department has deployed Edge Transport servers in both Fresno, California, and Berlin, Germany. Litware will be using multisite failover and integrating Exchange Server 2010 into their Office Communications Service 2007 R2 deployment. Table 2-11 summarizes this information.

TABLE 2-11 Litware Inc. Summary

GATHERED INFORMATION	DETAIL
Users	50,000
Deployment Type	Regionally distributed
Transitioning From	Servers: ■ Exchange Server 2007 ■ Fresno: Four Edge Transport servers, four Hub Transport and four Client Access Servers, one UM server, and four cluster continuous replication environments ■ Berlin: Three Edge Transport servers, three Hub Transport servers, three Client Access servers, one Unified Messaging server, and two cluster continuous replication environments ■ Tokyo: Two servers with both the Hub Transport and Client Access roles installed and one cluster continuous replication environments ■ Anaheim, Delhi, Houston, Kobe, Prague, and Madrid: One Exchange Server with all roles installed Clients: ■ Windows XP and Office Outlook 2007
Key Requirements	Will not outsource any services
Mailbox Availability SLA Target	99.99 percent

GATHERED INFORMATION	DETAIL
Active Directory Configuration	litwareinc.com (root) emea.litwareinc.com na.litwareinc.com apac.litwareinc.com
Locations	Three regional offices, six branch offices

The company locations are configured as shown in Figure 2-4.

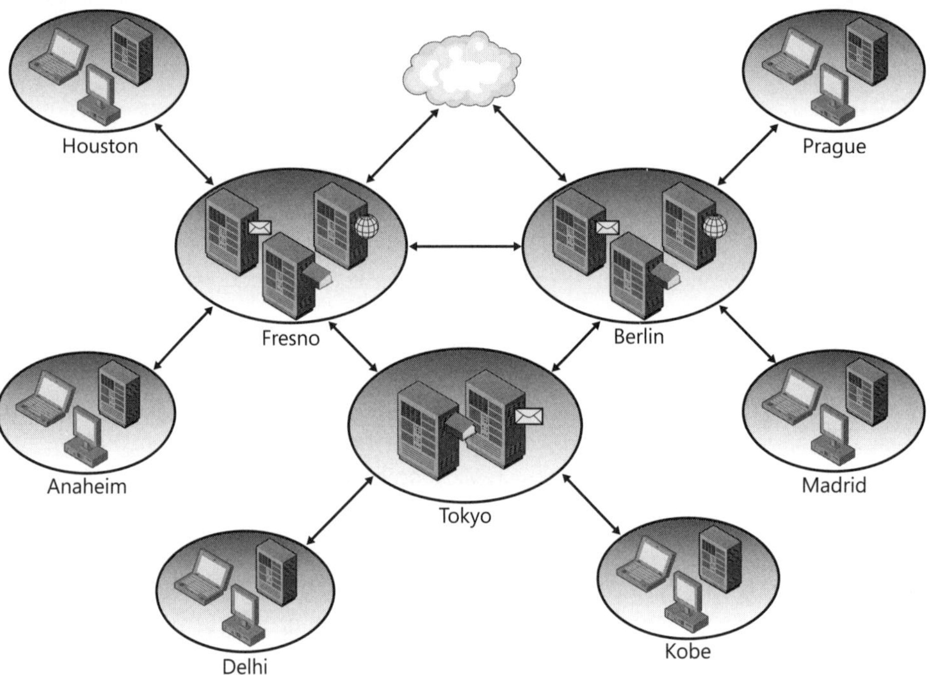

FIGURE 2-4 Litware Logical View

In future chapters, you will see each of the scenarios and the final configuration of each Exchange Server 2010 deployment in greater detail.

Additional Resources

- More information about ITIL: *http://www.itil-officialsite.com/AboutITIL/WhatisITIL.asp*
- MOF download and related information and resources: *http://www.microsoft.com/mof*

CHAPTER 3

Exchange Environmental Considerations

This chapter describes all the basic components surrounding Exchange Server 2010 that need to be considered to plan a solid Exchange implementation. These components provide the basis to build Exchange on a solid foundation and to identify potential issues.

It provides a basis for other chapters in this book by describing some of the technologies that will be discussed later. For example, this chapter includes a discussion on namespace design as well as a review of certificate requirements, which are then taken to the next level in Chapter 4, "Client Access in Exchange 2010." Of particular importance when using this book is the "Planning Naming Conventions" section, which explains the names that are used throughout the entire book.

Evaluating Network Topology

Evaluating the network topology through which Exchange Server 2010 will communicate is crucial during the Delivery Phase, Step 2: Assess, as described in Chapter 2, "Exchange Deployment Projects." Often, making changes in the network infrastructure can take a considerable amount of time because the Exchange team isn't necessarily responsible for making changes to the network, and communication and negotiation are often required before network changes can be made, especially in large organizations that support heterogeneous operating systems.

Identifying any required changes and making sure that the execution of the change can occur without any difficulties early in the design process can save time later when you are implementing Exchange Server 2010.

This section provides an overview of the network-related requirements for Exchange 2010.

Reviewing Current and Planned Network Topology

The first step is to collect all information about your internal network, the perimeter network, and its external collections as thoroughly as possible from a variety of sources. These sources include the following:

- **Physical network topology** Verify that TCP/IP is used everywhere, which Internet Protocol is used (IPv4 and/or IPv6), how IP addresses are allocated for servers, and that IP subnets are used according to location.
- **Internal physical network connections or links** This includes LAN and WAN links, router, and so on.
- **External physical network connections** This includes the Internet, partner companies, and so on.
- **Interconnection of physical network connections** This includes hub-and-spoke, ring or star, and point-to-point.
- **Physical network speed** Divide between guaranteed bandwidth, available bandwidth, and latency for each identified network link.
- **Network protection that might interfere** This includes firewalls that protect physical links or network link encryption devices that reduce the link speed.
- **Firewall port availability to both external and internal systems.**
- **Server name resolution used in locations or between locations (DNS/WINS name resolution).**
- **Defined namespaces in DNS** This is described in the "Planning Namespace" section later in this chapter.
- **Perimeter network servers** Including any servers that are located in a perimeter network, especially any server that provides SMTP-relay functionality.

Be sure to identify any known changes that will occur to the network configuration during the interim between the planning phase and the deployment phase so that the impact of the change can be assessed just prior to deployment and the proper adjustments made.

NOTE In large organizations, gathering this information might be quite a time-consuming effort—you may have to meet with many disparate network teams to get a thorough understanding of the network specific details. If you want to evaluate a global network infrastructure that includes many sites or locations, make sure you understand the company structure, the businesses that Exchange will serve, and how these businesses are supplied with IT currently. Having these discussions will provide you with much insight into the current network topology and help identify any problems and potential issues that you should consider when planning the messaging design.

Domain Name System (DNS)

This section is about the technical foundation on domain name system (DNS). It does not include any discussion about namespace planning. The aspects of namespace planning and disjoint namespace or single label domains are described in the "Planning Namespace" section later in this chapter.

DNS and Active Directory

Microsoft Windows uses the DNS standard as the primary name registration and resolution service for Active Directory. For that reason it is a basic requirement that all clients and servers must be able to reliably resolve DNS queries for a given resource in the appropriate namespace.

DNS provides a hierarchically distributed and scalable database where hosts can automatically update their records. These dynamic records can be fully integrated into Active Directory when using Active Directory–integrated DNS zones.

NOTE In Exchange Server 2003 or earlier, the Windows Internet Name Service (WINS) was required to support multi-domain environments. This is no longer required for Exchange Server 2010.

The following list provides best practices for DNS settings when implementing Exchange Server 2010 in your Active Directory:

- Use the DNS Server service that is part of Windows Server. This provides you with features such as Dynamic Update and Active Directory–integrated DNS zones. For example, domain controllers register their network service types in DNS so that other computers in the forest can access them.

- If you cannot use the Windows DNS Server for Active Directory and Exchange, make sure the DNS server supports SRV resource records and allows dynamic updates of Locator DNS resource records (SRV and A records). If your company uses BIND, make sure you use BIND 8.x or later.
- Store all DNS zones as Active Directory–integrated in Active Directory to gain the benefit of having DNS and Active Directory replicated by a single mechanism. This prevents the need to use different tools for troubleshooting.
- Configure Dynamic Updates as Secure, thus only allowing authorized clients to register their host name and IP address.
- Only configure Forward Lookups Zones, which are required by Exchange 2010. You do not need to configure Reverse Lookup Zones because they are not used by Windows 2008 or Exchange 2010.

More information can be found in the whitepaper "DNS Requirements for Installing Active Directory" at *http://technet.microsoft.com/en-us/library/cc739159(WS.10).aspx.*

NOTES FROM THE FIELD

DNS Dynamic Updates

John P Glynn
Principal Consultant, Microsoft Consulting Services, US/Central Region

Active Directory is a key dependency for Exchange; without it Exchange does not and will not properly function. Active Directory is based on the DNS service. Without DNS, many components of Active Directory, Exchange, and client interaction fail to function properly. When a domain controller is installed on a domain, a series of records is created. These DNS records contain service location records for Kerberos, LDAP, GC, site-specific information, and a domain record that is a unique GUID.

Exchange servers utilize these DNS records to locate authentication or other specific services. Exchange will use Active Directory site-specific service location records for services such as: locating the closest Global Catalog servers to utilize for name resolution, locating domain controllers to utilize for Exchange configuration information, and routing messages between remote Exchange servers. Exchange servers as well as workstations that run the Exchange management tools rely heavily on Kerberos for authentication. Therefore, it is equally important that the Exchange server A records are registered within DNS correctly as well.

As a best practice, implement DNS with dynamic updates enabled. I have been in a few environments where transient Exchange and client issues were tracked to missing or invalid SRV records. Some of the specific issues that I have seen include the following:

- Invalid host record for the Exchange Server—the connection suffix of the server did not match the DNS record causing Kerberos authentication failure.
- The domain GUID records for the domain were incorrectly entered under the _msdcs zone, causing improper identification of domain controllers for the Active Directory domain.
- Slowness issues resulting from missing site location records, causing Exchange to possibly grab a Global Catalog located at a distant site—thus communication needs to flow across WAN links. This might be because some or all of the following records are missing or incorrect in DNS: _ldap._tcp._sitename._sites._gc._msdcs.domain.com.

Most modern DNS implementations in use today support dynamic updates. As a best practice it is advisable to allow only secure updates, which prevents rogue systems from injecting invalid entries into your DNS zones.

A few environments refused to globally enable dynamic updates on their zones. We were able to convince the team to allow only domain controllers to dynamically update their records. Exchange server records were created manually. However, A records are familiar to DNS administrators and less likely to be incorrect. As with any manual process, it can be incorrectly created, so always double-check. If this is not possible, try to convince the DNS team to temporarily enable dynamic updates during the DCPROMO process and the subsequent reboot to allow the domain controllers to dynamically create/update all of the necessary records. Obviously this requires more process overhead, but in the long run it will save on issues, outages, and hours of troubleshooting caused by incorrectly configured DNS records.

Several tools are available to validate records and the functionality of DNS, such as DNSLint, DCDiag, and netdiag. Other standard tools include nslookup, ipconfig, and nltest.

DNS Records Used by Exchange 2010

DNS provides a number of critical functions for Exchange 2010. This section provides an overview of the most important records in DNS.

A RECORDS

A records or *Host records* provide a host name to IP address mapping. Host records are required for each domain controller and other hosts that need to be accessible to Exchange Servers or client computers. Host records use IPv4 (A records).

Here is an example of an A record:

```
berlin-dc01.litware.com. IN A 10.10.0.10.
```

SRV RECORDS

All Exchange 2010 servers use DNS to locate a valid domain controller or global catalog. By default, each time a domain controller starts the Netlogon service, it updates DNS with *service (SRV) records* that describe it as a domain controller and global catalog server, if applicable.

SRV resource records are DNS records. These records identify servers that provide specific services on the network. For example, an SRV resource record can contain information to help clients locate a domain controller in a specific domain or site. For that reason, the SRV records for domain controllers and global catalog servers are registered with several different variations to allow Exchange servers locating a suitable domain controller or global catalog during the Active Directory discovery process.

One option is to register DNS records by site name, which enables computers running Exchange Server to find domain controllers and global catalog servers in the local Active Directory site. Exchange Server always favors the selection of a domain controller and/or global catalog from the same site that Exchange is installed into.

Here is an example of an SRV record:

```
_ldap._tcp.litware.com. IN SRV 0 100 389 berlin-DC01.litware.com.
```

MX RECORDS

A *Mail Exchanger (MX) record* is a resource record that allows servers to locate other servers to deliver Internet e-mail using the Simple Mail Transfer Protocol (SMTP). An MX record identifies the SMTP server that will accept inbound messages for a specific DNS domain. Each MX record contains a host name and a preference value. When you deploy multiple SMTP servers that are accessible from the Internet, you can assign equal preference values to each MX record to enable round-robin between the SMTP servers. You also can specify a lower preference value for one of the MX records. All messages are routed through the SMTP server that has the lower-preference-value MX record, unless that server is not available.

Here is an example of an MX record:

```
litware.com MX 10 fresno-ht01.na.litware.com.
```

NOTE You don't need MX records for Hub Transport servers that are involved in internal mail routing. That is only required for external SMTP routing—for example, to the Internet.

More information about MX records and how they are used for SMTP message routing can be found in Chapter 5, "Routing and Transport."

SPF RECORDS

Exchange Server 2010 uses *Sender Policy Framework (SPF) records* to support Sender ID spam filtering. If you want to use this feature, you need to configure the SPF records in DNS. This is described in more detail in Chapter 7, "Edge Transport and Messaging Security."

Split DNS

Split DNS or split-brain DNS is about setting up separate DNS zones so that DNS requests that come from the Internet will resolve to different IP addresses than requests coming from your internal workstations or servers. In other words, as shown in Figure 3-1, if the Internet client resolves mail.litware.com, it will receive an IP address that is associated with an external firewall solution that is sitting in the perimeter network. The internal client will get an IP address associated with the internal Client Access server array.

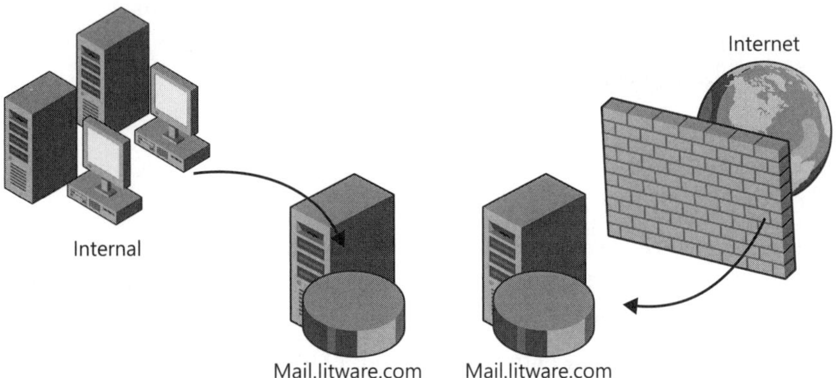

FIGURE 3-1 How split DNS works

The benefit of using split DNS is that it helps control client access. Internal clients use the internal systems instead of the external systems. In other words, internal users' sessions aren't handled by the firewall application and you do not expose internal IP addresses or host names to the Internet.

You can also limit access to specific hosts that are part of the perimeter network or force users to take a specific communication route. For this reason it is a best practice to implement split DNS in every Exchange organization that has server roles exposed to the Internet.

Fixed IP Address vs. Dynamic IP Address

It's important to know whether your company has an Internet provider that provides your company with fixed IP addresses or if you're using dynamic IP addresses to access the Internet. If your servers that have some relationship to external communication, such as Edge Transport servers, have fixed IP addresses and your DNS entries (MX or A records) are registered accordingly, you're working with the best practices approach.

However, a fixed IP address might be a cost issue, especially in small companies. Thus some companies might want to implement Exchange 2010 based on an Internet provider that only provides a dynamic IP address. If you're in this situation, you should consider a Dynamic DNS service that lets you register your dynamic IP address to their DNS service. However, make sure the dynamic DNS service includes the following:

- Your IP addresses should automatically register in DNS when the IP address changes. Your router and/or Dynamic DNS service provider need to support this.
- IP updates should be replicated in DNS real time to make sure the change is known to the Internet immediately.
- For external SMTP servers to know how to send messages to your domain, the DNS record for your domain should include an MX record.
- The Dynamic DNS service should provide you with an SMTP relay host to send messages to the Internet. If you directly send messages, your server is quite likely to be detected as spam because of your changing IP addresses. Many SMTP servers consider dynamic IP addresses as not trustworthy and thus don't accept messages from them.

If you consider these points, you'll have no problem operating Exchange Server 2010 when using a dynamic IP address.

Internet Protocol (IPv4 and IPv6)

Internet Protocol Version 4 (IPv4) is commonly available and the basis for communication between any device on the Internet. The successor of IPv4 is called Internet Protocol Version 6 (IPv6), as defined in RFC 2460 in 1996.

IPv6 was developed to correct many of the shortcomings of IPv4, such as the limited pool of available IP addresses and the lack of extensibility. Because IPv6 addresses are 128 bits long (compared to IPv4 addresses, which are 32 bits long), there are enough IPv6 addresses available for every living insect, animal, and person on earth.

Unfortunately, IPv6 is not an extension of IPv4 but a completely new protocol. Therefore, an IPv4 network can't communicate directly with an IPv6 network and vice versa. Any network device, such as a router, needs to be able to understand IPv6; otherwise, IPv6 causes communication problems.

IPv6 for Windows

The client and server software needs to support IPv6 to use it. The following Microsoft server operating systems support IPv6:

- Windows Server 2003 (IPv4 is installed and enabled; IPv6 is not installed by default.)
- Windows Server 2008 (IPv4 and IPv6 are installed and enabled by default.)
- Windows Server 2008 R2 (IPv4 and IPv6 are installed and enabled by default.)

> ***IMPORTANT*** **Microsoft also recommends that you do not turn off IPv6 in a clustered environment because Windows Server 2008 R2 Clustering uses IPv6 for internal communication.**

Not only does the server need to support IPv6, but also the client operating system. The following Microsoft client operating systems support IPv6:

- Windows XP Service Pack 1(SP1) or later (IPv4 is installed and enabled; IPv6 is not installed by default.)
- Windows Vista (IPv4 and IPv6 are installed and enabled by default.)
- Windows 7 (IPv4 and IPv6 are installed and enabled by default.)
- For more information about IPv6, see the IPv6 for Microsoft Windows FAQ at *http://go.microsoft.com/fwlink/?LinkId=147465*.

NOTES FROM THE FIELD

Hardware Provider Recommended to Disable IPv6 for Windows Server 2008

For a recent project I consulted my server hardware provider, who recommended turning off IPv6 because their network interface card (NIC) drivers caused problems especially when using NIC Teaming. The operating system was Windows Server 2008; thus we used the following registry key to disable IPv6 from all LAN interfaces, connections, and tunnel interfaces:

```
HKEY_LOCAL_MACHINE\SYSTEM\CurrentControlSet\Services\Tcpip6\Parameters\
DisabledComponents set to 0xFFFFFFFF (DWORD type)
```

After a reboot, even IPCONFIG.exe no longer showed IPv6 addresses. You can find more information on how to disable IPv6 at *http://support.microsoft.com/kb/929852/*.

Windows Failover Clustering on Windows Server 2008 R2 requires IPv6 and the Exchange 2010 Database Availability Group uses some elements of Windows Failover Clustering. However, Exchange 2010 does not use IPv6 within a DAG. This does not mean that you can disable IPv6. Even though the DAG neither depends on nor uses IPv6, disabling IPv6 completely for Windows Server 2008 R2 is not a tested scenario and could therefore result in unpredictable consequences for a DAG.

IPv6 for Exchange Server 2010

Because Exchange Server 2010 runs on Windows Server 2008 or R2, you might think that it automatically supports IPv6. However, you should consider a few things before planning for IPv6 and Exchange 2010. The following Exchange Server roles can cause issues when using IPv6 addresses:

- **Hub or Edge Transport** Features such as IP Allow List Providers or Sender reputation do not support IPv6 because they require static IP addresses.
- **Unified Messaging** All features do not support IPv6 but need IPv4 to work correctly.
- **Client Access Server** Autodiscover and EWS Web services endpoints because you cannot configure an IIS binding for an IPv6 address—WCF throws a Watson exception if you try to configure it.
- **Database Availability Group (DAG)** Even though you cannot define an IPv6 DAG IP address, IPv6 is supported. When static IPv4 addresses are specified for a DAG, it only uses IPv4. When no static IPv4 address is specified, Exchange use DHCP for the IPv4 addresses and also creates IPv6 address resources.

Exchange Server uses the Windows network stack to process any request. Each request depends upon two things:

- Name resolution (when initiating the request)
- Packet type (when receiving a request)

First, the name resolution will determine how to initiate the request to another computer based on which address (IPv4 or IPv6) is resolved first. When the name resolution comes back with an IPv6 address, this address is used to initiate the request.

Second, packet types do not mix IP versions midstream. If the request comes in as IPv4, the response will also use IPv4, and the same is true for IPv6. As for unfulfilled requests, they should be handled before name resolution is completed and would otherwise fail after name resolution in the same way other transient network failures occur. For features that don't support IPv6, Exchange causes the request to fail so that the client initiates another request using IPv4. Thus an IPv6 request, even to the Unified Messaging role, does not cause a problem but is just ignored.

NOTE The official Microsoft support statement for IPv6 is that Exchange Server 2010 running on Windows Server 2008 or R2 requires an IPv4 address. Exchange Server 2010 is not supported in a pure IPv6 environment where you disable the IPv4 protocol.

Understanding Client Load Patterns

Another important aspect that should be understood when planning for Exchange 2010 is the current client load patterns—namely the traffic between Outlook clients (or other mail clients) and the Exchange server.

The scope of this task depends on what your current mail clients are. If most of your clients use POP3 or IMAP4 clients, the load on an Exchange server is significantly lower and you can plan for many more users on a single server.

If you're using a MAPI-based client, such as Microsoft Outlook 2003 or Outlook 2007, you need to analyze which profile your average users fall into to understand the impact of the traffic to the Exchange server. You can use the information available from your monitoring system, such as Microsoft System Center Operations Manager if available. Alternatively you can use Windows Performance Monitor to collect the performance information of your clients. Consider using the following performance counters:

- Messages sent/received per day
- Average message size
- Messages read per day
- Messages deleted per day
- Outlook Web Access logon and logoff per day

Consider collecting the client data from each Exchange server or mail server (when coming from a non–Exchange System) for at least a couple of days (at peak times, not on weekends) to have a representative aggregation of performance data.

NOTES FROM THE FIELD

Identifying Current Client Load

Andy Schan
Senior Consultant, Schan Consulting Inc., Canada

To work out the current client load, my last couple of projects had Quest MessageStats in place, so I sat down with the MessageStats data and Microsoft Excel and crunched the numbers for the last couple of quarters to come up with a profile of their typical users.

To come up with a useful client load picture for scaling the new environment, I typically make assumptions similar to the following:

- 10-hour workdays
- 5-day workweeks, Monday–Friday
- Messages/day/user derived from the data are all sent during normal working hours

I also use the messaging data for the previous calendar year quarter and derive message/day data from that, to ensure that I'm seeing a reasonably accurate picture of the average client activity in the environment and to minimize any effects from brief periods of increased activity. I may also go back two quarters, if the previous quarter includes quiet periods such as summer vacation or Christmas holidays.

I focused on figuring out messaging activity (number of messages/day sent and received, calendaring activity, and so on) rather than actual bits over the wire, which changes once you get them to cached mode and a newer version of Outlook. Together with the data from the client, I used the following Microsoft whitepaper to assess the load: "Outlook Anywhere Scalability with Outlook 2007, Outlook 2003, and Exchange 2007" at *http://technet.microsoft.com/en-us/library/cc540453(EXCHG.80).aspx.*

After you collect the results, you can compare the data with Table 3-1 to identify how to classify your client profile according to Microsoft's most common client profiles.

TABLE 3-1 Common Client Profiles

TASK/PROFILE	LIGHT	MEDIUM	HEAVY	VERY HEAVY
Sent per day	5	10	20	30
Received per day	20	40	80	120
Average message size	50k	50k	50k	50k
Messages read per day	20	40	80	120
Messages deleted per day	10	20	40	60
Outlook Web Access logon and logoff per day	2	2	2	2

When you have identified your typical client load pattern, you should plan to implement a load-generating tool such as Exchange Load Generator 2010 to verify your Exchange server hardware performance. Exchange Load Generator 2010 (64 bit) is available at *http://www.microsoft.com/downloads/details.aspx?displaylang=en&FamilyID=cf464be7-7e52-48cd-b852-ccfc915b29ef.*

You'll find more details on how to plan your Exchange hardware and how to use the Exchange Load Generator in Chapter 13, "Hardware Planning for Exchange Server 2010."

Perimeter Network

Communication to the Internet or external network is also important. You'll find information about the required firewall ports or protocols that need to be configured later in this chapter in the "Planning Network Port Requirements" section. This discussion does not cover other security options, such as IPsec or VPN, that allow clients on the Internet to directly connect to their internal network.

The recommended deployment for Exchange Server 2010 Internet access includes two firewalls or routers in a back-to-back firewall scenario, which enables you to implement a perimeter network between the two. An external firewall faces the Internet and protects the perimeter network. You then deploy an internal firewall between the perimeter and your internal corporate network.

In the perimeter network you place any Internet-facing server, such as the Edge Transport role of Exchange Server 2010. Microsoft does not support any topologies that put firewalls between a Client Access, Hub Transport, Unified Messaging, and a Mailbox (MBX) server. Putting these roles between a firewall could cause issues because they use dynamic ports that could be blocked unintentionally by the firewall. The only Exchange 2010 role supported for deployment in a perimeter network—and with a firewall server separating it from other Exchange servers it talks to—is the Edge Transport role.

IMPORTANT **The Edge Transport server role should never be a member of your internal domain, but should be a stand-alone server or member of an available perimeter Active Directory forest.**

The most common servers that are placed in the perimeter to support Internet access are:

- A smart host to route SMTP messages between the internal and external network, such as Edge Transport server role or any other smart host.
- A reverse proxy or application-layer firewall that supports client-related traffic such as Autodiscover, Outlook Web App (OWA, previously known as Outlook Web Access), Outlook Anywhere, ActiveSync, POP3, IMAP4, SMTP, and so on to the internal network. Microsoft Forefront TMG and Microsoft ISA Server 2006 are example application-layer firewalls. However, don't underestimate the scalability challenges for software-based reverse proxy servers. Any implementation that needs to handle more than 100,000 concurrent connections on an ongoing basis should focus on a hardware solution.

NOTE You should not deploy the Client Access Server role in a perimeter network to reduce the attack surface of your internal forest. Because the Exchange computer account of the Client Access Server role has elevated privileges, it can be used by an attacker to destroy your Active Directory. Instead, use an application-layer firewall such as Microsoft Forefront Threat Management Gateway (TMG) to publish the Client Access server services to the Internet.

If you do not use an application-layer firewall from Microsoft, consider the following key areas for choosing a firewall application of highest security standard:

- **Pre-authenticate traffic** To prevent unauthenticated traffic from entering the corporate network.
- **Packet inspection** Application-layer firewalls allow for identification of known protocol attacks prior to entering the corporate network.
- **Intrusion Detection System (IDS)** Simplifies identification of attacks on the system. If attacks occur internally, chances are they will be successful and difficult to detect because they may look like typical traffic, whereas if the proxy starts requesting RPC to other servers, or tries to get through the firewall, it is blocked and logged.
- **Fixed Ports/IP Addresses** Only specific ports and IP addresses are allowed into the corporate environment.
- **Group Membership allowance** Provides the capability to allow only specific groups to access specific applications; for instance, my current customer does not allow hourly workers to access mail externally.
- **Load balancing** Arrays of reverse proxy servers can distribute network traffic for a single URL.

As a best practice, always implement a reverse proxy or application-layer firewall if you want to provide Internet access to your Exchange servers. However, some companies, especially in the small to medium sector, do not implement any kind of security between their servers and the Internet. If you do not implement an application-layer firewall, consider the following recommendations:

- Deploy a firewall between the internal and external network and open only the ports or protocols you need.
- Implement a server certificate for all your Exchange servers. (This can be a single certificate that includes the required domain names, as described in the "Planning Certificates" section of this chapter.)
- Require SSL to encrypt client communication (for Outlook client traffic).
- Require TLS for SMTP and SSL if you enable POP3 or IMAP4.
- Make sure that any operation requires authentication.
- Implement Forms-based authentication for Outlook Web App.

This provides you with at least minimum security but still might expose some of your user data to the Internet. However, it's better than nothing.

Avoiding Pitfalls by Providing Technical Recommendations

The following list provides ways to avoid potential pitfalls on the network topology side. Any problems must be rectified before Exchange Server 2010 can be installed at the location.

- Make sure that the physical network speed of sites that will host Exchange Server 2010 has at least 64 Kb per second of bandwidth available.
- Exchange Server 2010 does not support a pure TCP/IP v6 (IPv6) environment. If you've already implemented pure IPv6 addresses anywhere in your company, make sure that they also support IPv4 addresses; otherwise, the clients might encounter errors in communicating with Exchange Server 2010.
- IP subnets should map to the locations of the company and should be non-overlapping between locations. However, sometimes single locations have multiple IP subnets, which is fine. If IP subnets are spanned between multiple physical locations, make sure the WAN link between them matches LAN link speed—10 megabits per second (Mbps) or more.
- Make sure your Active Directory sites match IP subnets for each location.
- DNS must be used for network name resolution.
- Active Directory uses service (SRV) resource records in DNS to register a list of domain controllers for client use. If you do not use Windows Server 2008 DNS Service for Active Directory, make sure that your DNS server software supports the resource records!
- To receive messages from the Internet, an appropriate mail exchanger (MX) resource record in DNS is required for the company's domain name.

NOTES FROM THE FIELD

Additional Beneficial Server Settings

Joe Cirillo
Senior Engineer and Architect, Horizons Consulting, US/Central Region

Microsoft has always provided some invaluable guidance regarding the installation and automation of Exchange. Over the years, I have found some additional settings I like to confirm or set to help ease administration or to further ensure that the installation will occur without error.

Network Interface Card Naming Standard

I always try to reduce ambiguity for any objects that I interface with. Because I often refer to the settings on the NIC when troubleshooting, I like to provide an easy-to-follow naming standard for the NICs. This is particularly helpful when multiple NICs are configured, as required when using the Exchange Server 2010 Database Availability Group.

Confirm that the adapter binding order is correct

Because the server host name in the registry will bind to the first interface in the adapter/bindings list, the binding order must be set properly.

I have seen connectivity issues caused by improperly configured bindings. Anytime you make changes to the network configuration (such as adding protocols, adapters, modems, or services), the binding order can potentially change. Be sure to check the binding order on server install and anytime you make changes to the network configuration.

Confirm that Windows Remote Registry Service is running

Exchange Server requires access to the local registry to retrieve various settings. One example is the Exchange Setup program. The Exchange Setup program uses DNS to obtain the fully qualified domain name (FQDN) of the local computer to access the registry. If the Windows Remote Registry Service is not running, setup will be unable to access the registry, causing the installation of Exchange to fail.

Confirm that Date, Time, and Time Zone are set properly

Exchange gets its date and time information from the operating system. Windows Directory servers need to have their time synchronized for Kerberos authentication to work correctly. Kerberos works by exchanging time-stamped authenticator identification tokens. By default, directory servers have a maximum tolerance for computer clock synchronization of five minutes. This is known as clock skew. Clock skew is the range of time allowed for a server to accept Kerberos tickets from a client. If the clock skew is greater than five minutes, Kerberos authentication fails, which results in cascading authentication failures for Exchange Server.

If an Exchange server's time is out of sync with the Domain Controller time, issues will occur such as Exchange services failing to start or client connections being rejected. To prevent issues caused by time skew, make certain of the following:

- The Exchange server has network connectivity with the Domain Controller.
- The Exchange server time is synchronized with either the Domain Controller time or the time server that is used by the Domain Controller.

Desktop Background

Setting the Desktop Background to display useful information is also useful for eliminating ambiguity when logging onto a server. It is very inefficient to have to click through several diagnostic windows just to find that you logged on to the wrong server, or to find information such as the IP address or operating system version. If you manage multiple computers you will benefit greatly by displaying relevant information about the Windows server on the desktop's background. You can find the BgInfo tool at *http://technet.microsoft.com/en-us/sysinternals/bb897557.aspx*.

Import any Trusted Root Authorities onto the local computer

Depending on how you are managing certificates (such as by using a stand-alone Certificate Authority, enterprise Certificate Authority, or third-party Certificate Authority), you may need to add the certificate for a foreign Certificate Authority to the Trusted Root Certification Authorities container on the local computer. If this is necessary, be sure to add the certificate for the foreign Certificate Authority to every server you install to ensure consistency in your build and to avoid communication errors between servers.

Any e-mail client connecting to the Exchange Server's secure sites must trust the Exchange Server's site certificates. Before it can successfully negotiate a secure SSL/TLS link with the Exchange Server, the e-mail client must trust the Certificate Authority (CA) issuing the Web site certificate to the Exchange Server's services. If the certificates issued by the foreign CA will be used by client-facing Exchange services (such as Outlook Web App or Outlook Anywhere), be sure to also add the certificate of the foreign CA to the Trusted Root Certification Authorities container on any user workstation or mobile device.

Evaluating and Planning for Active Directory

Active Directory is the integrated, distributed directory service included with Windows Server operating systems. Many applications, such as Exchange Server 2010, integrate with Active Directory. This creates a link between user accounts and applications, which enables single sign-on for applications. Additionally, the Active Directory replication capabilities enable distributed applications to replicate application-configuration data.

How Exchange 2010 Uses Active Directory

The Active Directory database is divided into logical partitions—namely the schema partition, the configuration partition, and a domain partition for every domain.

Windows Server 2008 and R2 includes a tool called *Repadmin* that can be used to list all Active Directory partitions available. Figure 3-2 shows the result from the Litware Scenario using the command *Repadmin /showrepl.*

As shown in the figure, Active Directory is made out of the configuration, schema, application, and domain partitions.

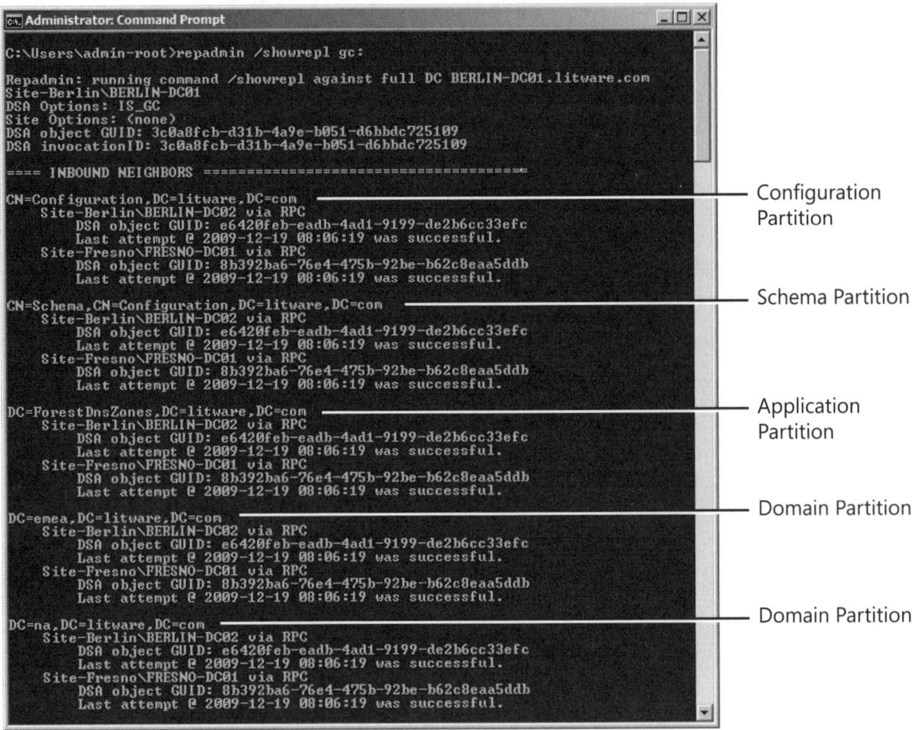

FIGURE 3-2 Using Repadmin to look at Active Directory partitions

> ***NOTE*** Additional information about Active Directory Partitions can be found in "Active Directory Logical Structure and Data Storage" at *http://go.microsoft.com/fwlink/?LinkId=179859.*

The Schema Partition

Before Exchange Server 2010 can store information in Active Directory, the schema partition needs to be modified so that Exchange-related objects (such as connector or mailbox information) and attributes (such as an Exchange Mailbox server or a user object) are defined in the Active Directory schema. The schema partition stores the general layout of all Active Directory objects and its attributes. It includes two types of information:

- **Schema classes** The objects that can be created
- **Schema attributes** The properties that can be used for each object

NOTE Each and every domain controller and global catalog server in Active Directory contains a complete replica of the schema partition. Thus it is important to plan the Exchange Server 2010 schema extension accordingly—you cannot remove a schema extension.

INSIDE TRACK

How to Safely Extend the Schema

Ross Smith IV
Senior Program Manager, Exchange Server Product Group, Microsoft Corporation

Schema extensions are permanent. Care should be taken to ensure that a schema extension is successful because a failed schema extension may mean rebuilding the forest. The preferred way to mitigate the impact of a failed schema extension is to isolate the schema master by disabling its ability to replicate changes to other domain controllers in the forest.

This is accomplished by executing the command *repadmin /options +DISABLE_OUTBOUND_REPL*. When outbound replication has been halted on the schema master, you can then proceed with extending the schema. If the schema extension is successful, you can re-enable outbound replication and allow the changes to propagate throughout the forest. If, on the other hand, the schema extension fails, you simply shut down the schema master server, wipe it, and seize the schema master role on another domain controller.

Because Exchange depends on Active Directory, each released Exchange version implemented different schema versions. To identify the current Exchange schema version, the schema attribute *ms-Exchange-Schema-Version-Pt* was added. In the attribute, you can identify the schema version by looking at the *rangeUpper* attribute and identify the Exchange version according to Table 3-2.

TABLE 3-2 Exchange Schema Version Numbers

RANGEUPPER NUMBER	EXCHANGE VERSION
14622	Exchange Server 2010 or Exchange Server 2007 SP2
11116	Exchange Server 2007 SP1
10628	Exchange Server 2007

RANGEUPPER NUMBER	EXCHANGE VERSION
6870	Exchange Server 2003
4406	Exchange Server 2000 SP3
4397	Exchange Server 2000

In Figure 3-3 you can see that the Exchange Schema version is currently Exchange Server 2010 or Exchange Server 2007 Service Pack 2.

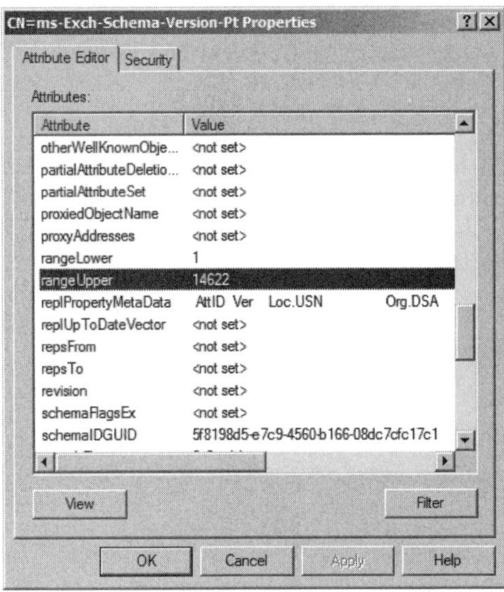

FIGURE 3-3 Checking the Exchange schema version in ADSI Edit

Using the *rangeUpper* attribute you can also identify whether a schema update was replicated successfully to the local domain controller. By connecting to the DC and then verifying that the attribute has the current value, you can be sure that the schema update has replicated.

> ***IMPORTANT*** **It is true that the Exchange Server 2010 schema extension also includes the Exchange 2003 and 2007 schema extensions. However, if you plan to ever install an Exchange 2003 or 2007 server into the organization after Exchange 2010 is deployed, you must install the older Exchange Server version as the first server and install Exchange Server 2010 afterwards. Exchange Server 2007 should include the Mailbox, Client Access Server, and Hub Transport roles. Once you have installed Exchange Server 2010, you will not be able to install Exchange 2003 or 2007 anymore!**

The Configuration Partition

The configuration partition contains configuration information for the Active Directory forest. Additionally, some distributed applications and other services store information in the configuration partition. This information in the configuration partition replicates through the entire forest so that each domain controller and global catalog has a replica of it.

The configuration partition stores each type of configuration information in separate containers. A *container* is an Active Directory object similar to an organizational unit (OU) that you use to organize other objects.

Exchange Server 2010 stores information such as global settings, address lists, connections, and so on to the configuration partition. Figure 3-4 shows you how to look at the information Exchange Server 2010 stores in the configuration partition. You can see it either using ADSI Edit or Active Directory Sites and Services. (You'll need to enable the Show Services Node.) You also need to be a member of the Organizational Management group or the View-Only Management group; thus, you must have Exchange Organizational permissions to expand below the Exchange Organization level.

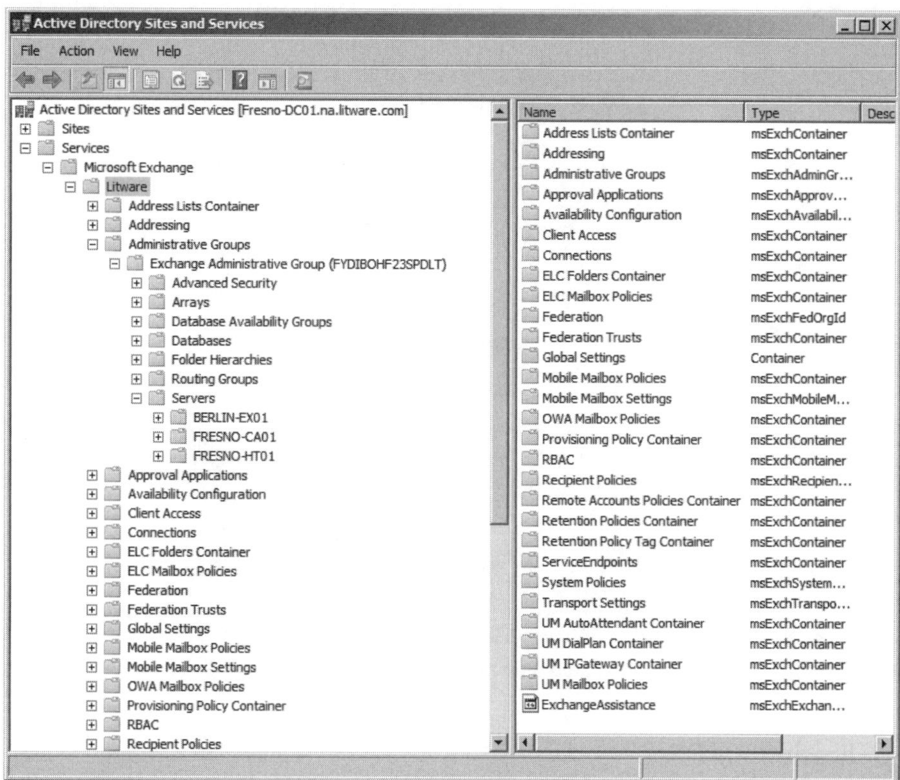

FIGURE 3-4 Exchange configuration in the configuration container

The Domain Partition

The domain partition holds domain-related information in containers as well as OUs. It includes information about users, groups, and computers in that domain. The domain partition is stored on every domain controller of that specific domain. Every global catalog server has a subset of information from every domain partition in the forest, as well as a complete copy of its own domain's objects. For example, a global catalog server in a different domain will contain information on the individual user, such as the user's display name or its SMTP addresses, but not its password.

For every Exchange-prepared domain (meaning that the Exchange Setup /PrepareDomain has been run for the domain) Exchange Server 2010 creates an OU called Microsoft Exchange System Objects in which it will store Exchange-related system objects such as the mailbox database's mailbox and public folder proxy objects.

You can verify that a domain was Exchange Domain–Prepared by looking at the *ObjectVersion* attribute on the Microsoft Exchange System Objects OU in that domain. For Exchange 2010 RTM it should read 12639, as shown in Figure 3-5.

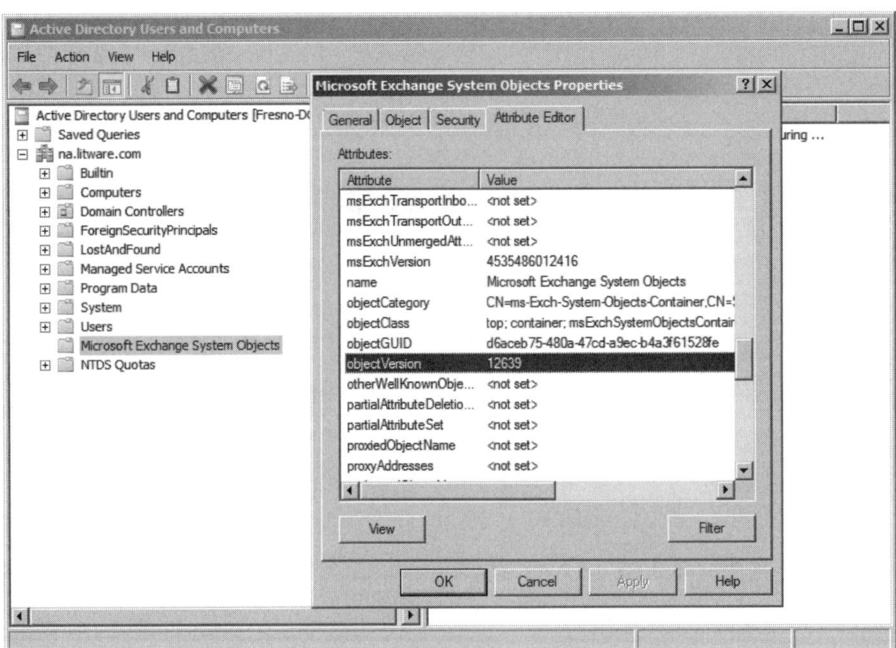

FIGURE 3-5 Identifying an Exchange-prepared domain

The Application Partition

Application partitions hold specific application data that the application requires. The main benefit of application partitions is replication flexibility. You can specify the domain controllers that hold a replica of an application partition, and these domain controllers can include a subset of domain controllers throughout the forest.

Currently the only application that uses the application partition is DNS, to store DNS zones in the partition as Active Directory–integrated DNS zone. Exchange Server 2010 does not use application partitions to store information.

Table 3-3 describes the application partitions commonly available in Active Directory.

TABLE 3-3 Application Partitions in Active Directory

APPLICATION PARTITION	DESCRIPTION
ForestDnsZones	Replicates to all DNS servers in forest
DomainDNSZones	Replicates to all DNS servers in domain (is created once you add the second DNS server to the domain)

Of course only DNS servers that run on Domain Controller can access the application partitions; thus all DNS zones that are stored in this partition are Active Directory–integrated.

> ***NOTE*** **Using ADSI Edit you do not see application partitions by default as well-known naming contexts. To look at them you need to directly address them using their distinguished names (DNs). You can identify the DN using a tool such as *repadmin /showrepl.***

Active Directory Replication Impact on Exchange 2010

Active Directory replication is a crucial component of Exchange 2010. As described in previous sections, the different partitions store Exchange-related configuration data. This data is automatically replicated between Active Directory sites using Active Directory replication mechanisms.

Because Exchange 2010 relies on the replication mechanisms to work correctly, you might face delays in configuration caused by replication latency. For example, if you configure an Exchange Server in the domain emea.litware.com, but your current computer is located in na.litware.com, you will see that configuration is not immediately available in the domain emea.litware.com. You need to wait until Active Directory replication takes place and replicates the changes to the domain. Normally the replication between sites happens every 15 minutes or longer depending on your Active Directory Site Link configuration.

There are two possibilities to overcome the replication delay:

- Configure your EMC or EMS so that you directly use a domain controller located in the target domain. For example, in EMS you can set the preferred domain controller using the following cmdlet:

  ```
  Set-ADServerSettings -PreferredServer <DC FQDN>
  ```

- Use Repadmin to push replication to target domain. For more information on the Repadmin tool, read the Microsoft whitepaper "Monitoring and Troubleshooting Active Directory Replication Using Repadmin" available at *http://www.microsoft.com/downloads/details.aspx?familyid=c6054092-ee1e-4b57-b175-5aabde591c5f&displaylang=en.*

Besides Active Directory replication, Active Directory sites and IP site link information are important for message routing between Exchange servers. Exchange 2010 uses the cost assignment that is part of every IP site link to determine the lowest-cost route for traffic to follow when multiple paths exist to the destination. This information is used by the Hub Transport role to decide to which Exchange Hub Transport server a message is sent to when the target Exchange Hub Transport server is not available.

More information about Active Directory sites, IP site links, and their relevance to message routing in Exchange 2010 can be found in Chapter 5, "Routing and Transport."

Active Directory Requirements

For Exchange Server 2010 Active Directory and domains must meet several requirements. Consider the following when evaluating your current Active Directory design:

- The server on which the Schema Master role runs must have at least Windows Server 2003 SP1 (32-bit or 64-bit) installed.
- You need to run Windows Server 2003 SP1 or later (32-bit or 64-bit) on global catalog servers in every Active Directory site where you plan to install Exchange Server 2010. If you still have older global catalog in your environment, it is recommended that you upgrade all your domain controllers to prevent any problems.
- Active Directory must be at least in Windows Server 2003 forest functionality mode.
- Windows Server 2008 functionality mode is supported if your Exchange organization includes Exchange 2007 and/or 2010.
- All domains that will include Exchange Server 2010 servers or recipients must be at least in Windows Server 2003 domain functional level.
- Because of the importance of the global catalog in an Exchange Server organization, you must deploy at least one global catalog in each Active Directory site that contains an Exchange 2010 server.

Single versus Multi-Forest Implementation

The following forest implementations are available:

- Single Forest
- Multi-forest

- Resource Forest
- Hybrid Forest

Figure 3-6 shows the different forest approaches and in what forest user accounts mailboxes and Exchange servers are available.

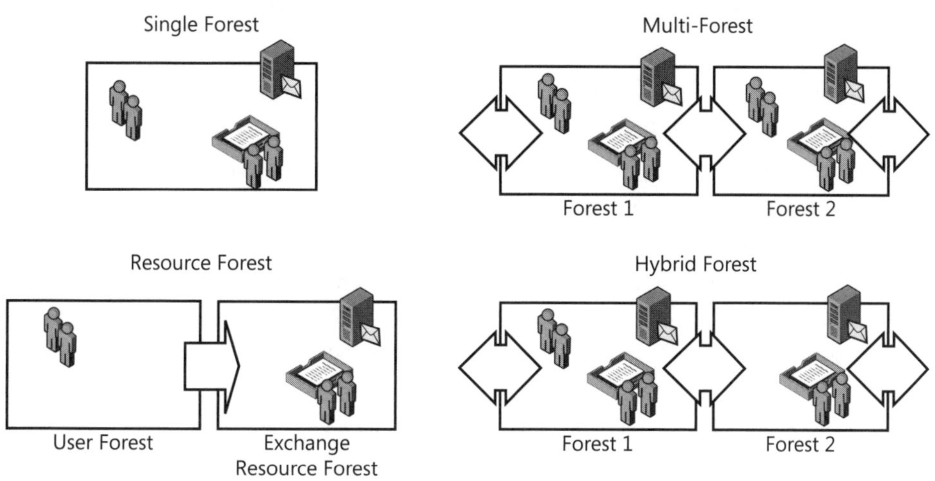

FIGURE 3-6 Exchange Forest Topologies

> **NOTE** One issue that you should keep in mind before deciding your forest design is the management effort required to administer the various types of forest. Sometimes you might make a decision regarding the kind of deployment to execute only to realize in production that it's harder to manage—and perhaps even that some tools don't work in a specific configuration. The old KISS rule (keep it stupid and simple) comes to mind here, which you should always consider if you have the chance.

Single Forest

An Active Directory forest is a set of one or more domain trees that share common configuration and schema information. A forest is a security boundary. By default, no account from outside the forest can hold security principals to access information inside the forest. A single Active Directory forest design provides the following characteristics:

- A single forest that matches the Exchange organization. (This is the most common and easiest approach.)
- No limitations to Exchange and Outlook functionality.

Multi-Forest

The multi-forest (or cross-forest) implementation consists of at least two loosely connected forests that operate independently from each other but are somewhat connected. This forest approach includes the following characteristics:

- Includes multiple Exchange organizations, often multiple SMTP addresses.
- Users are part of the different forests.
- Can include multiple service providers that administer their own forest and do not have access on another forest.
- Common when one company buys another company without integrating it into the existing Active Directory forest.
- The forests have to share a trust relationship before data can move between the forests. This is the requirement so the forests can be connected from the Exchange perspective using, for example, linked mailboxes. This approach has quite a few limitations. For example, a user cannot easily open a mailbox from another user that is located in a different forest.
- Synchronization of availability information and public folder information between forests is often very complicated.

Resource Forest

The resource forest implementation consists of one or more account forests and an Exchange forest that includes all Exchange servers, mailboxes, and distribution lists. The account forest contains the user accounts and security groups. This forest approach includes the following characteristics:

- Mailboxes are attached to disabled user accounts and associated to user accounts in the account forest.
- Administration between the account forest of the organization and the Exchange forest is separate. Most often you will create a resource forest in a hosting environment. A service provider provides the resource forest that is connected using a one-way trust to the account forest. This ensures that the service provider has no permissions in any way in the account forest and only can manage the resource forest.
- You can have better Exchange capabilities and availability with a clean resource forest that is fully controlled by the Exchange administrators.
- The concept of messaging in a cloud—such as Microsoft BPOS or the implementation of Exchange on a hosting platform—can be seen as a resource forest implementation.
- Typically reduces token bloat by moving the DL membership of a user object to a different forest.
- Because all the mailboxes are part of the same resource forest, there are no limitations to Exchange and Outlook functionality. (If this is not the situation, the implementation is called a *hybrid forest.*)

Hybrid Forest

The hybrid forest combines the concepts of a resource forest and a single forest—thus, a hybrid forest contains not only user accounts or resource mailboxes (such as user-disabled, mailbox-enabled objects) but also includes active mailboxes (mailbox-enabled user accounts where Exchange server is in the same forest). This forest approach includes the following characteristics:

- Each forest may contain a combination of enabled and disabled user accounts that are either mail enabled or mailbox enabled.
- Differs from a resource forest in that all forests have mailboxes, and you might find mail-enabled users and disabled mailbox-enabled users in the same forest.
- Contains both resource mailboxes (user-disabled mailbox-enabled objects) and active mailboxes (user-enabled mailbox-enabled objects).
- Common in a migration to or from a resource forest model or in an organization that has a resource forest for some business units but also uses the resource forest as the primary forest for other business units.
- Only the users of the same Exchange organization have no limitations to the Exchange or Outlook functionality.

NOTES FROM THE FIELD

Planning a Forest Design

Andrew Ehrensing
Principal Consultant, Microsoft Consulting Services, US Central Region

Microsoft recommends starting all designs with a single forest/single domain environment for Active Directory. On some occasions business requirements dictate a change from this model to a multi-forest model; however, this should be avoided whenever possible. Introducing multiple forests adds significant complexity and cost in both capital and operational expenses.

Single vs. Multi-Domain Implementation

After the forest design has been made, the discussion about domains follows. This discussion is only necessary if you have a multi-domain environment and your Exchange implementation will be part of a single forest design.

In such an environment, you need to decide whether you want to install all Exchange servers in a single, Exchange-dedicated domain or place Exchange in the domain where the user accounts are stored. Especially in a single forest implementation you need to consider the following domain approaches.

Single Domain

A single domain is where Exchange servers and users are located in the same domain. This approach has the following characteristics:

- Simplest implementation and thus the easiest to manage
- Centralized administration
- Used if only one domain is available

> ***NOTE*** **Always start with a Single Domain as the basic design; only move to a different domain design if forced!**

Single Exchange-Dedicated Domain

A single Exchange-dedicated domain can be found in a multi-domain forest where one domain is created just for hosting Exchange servers and managing distribution lists. This approach has the following characteristics:

- Exchange servers are maintained in their own dedicated domain. The disadvantage is that the extra domain brings the extra costs that stem from deploying and managing an additional domain.
- Exchange administration of dedicated domain can be totally independent from Active Directory administration of forest. This means that the administrators can perform all administrative tasks on the Exchange servers without requiring any administrative rights in other Active Directory domains.
- Has a special requirement for additional user domain controllers that need to be available where the Exchange servers are located.
- Common if you have your own internal service provider for Exchange.

Multi-domain

A multi-domain approach includes the Exchange servers directly in their user domains—thus, the Exchange servers are spread between the different domains. This approach has the following characteristics:

- Used if the Exchange administrations is split between different divisions or departments that own their own domains
- Used if you have a geographic domain design and thus want to add the Exchange servers to their respective regional domains

In a multi-domain environment you have to make sure that you configure the right scope in EMC and EMS. The following cmdlet configures a forest-wide scope:

```
Set-ADServerSettings -ViewEntireForest:$true
```

NOTE If you can choose between a single- or multi-domain implementation for Exchange, it is a best practice to use a single domain. This reduces complexity dramatically and will be much easier to manage.

NOTES FROM THE FIELD

A Mix of Single and Multi-Domain Implementations

A multinational electronics company with more than 70 Active Directory domains in the forest mixes a multi-domain and single Exchange-dedicated domain approach. The reason for running two different approaches was that parts of the company have a centralized Exchange administration, but some countries manage the Exchange servers on their own. However, issues in Exchange caused by replication latency and other problems supported the decision to move to a single Exchange-dedicated domain approach.

Planning Naming Conventions

Another area that needs to be considered is planning for naming conventions for your objects. In a large, complex organization (such as the scenario of Litware) it is easy to fail to understand what function a server performs at first glance; a good naming convention conveys the function of a server to an administrator without forcing the administrator to examine the server's properties.

Many organizations implement naming conventions for key components because of this requirement. Naming conventions can allow administrators and users to easily identify the purpose of an object without requiring input from others. Typically, the larger the organization, the more strict these naming conventions can become.

Naming conventions help you to easily identify key elements of an object. For example, a server's role, location, and purpose can be identified in environments that have grown beyond a tangible number.

Of course, some small companies out there have just a handful of servers, but what if you have hundreds of servers that you can no longer easily remember? In this situation, you should start thinking of naming conventions for your environment.

The most common naming convention is for the Display Name attribute of users and distribution groups. It might get complicated to identify a user when there is no strict convention, especially in companies that have mailboxes from all over the world. We've seen organizations in which some administrators created the mailboxes with the convention Firstname Lastname and others using Lastname Firstname. Of course this causes confusion and should be corrected.

Not only do you need to consider the Display Name—in Exchange 2010 it is recommended that you also define the following names:

- Server
- Database Availability Group (DAG)
- Database
- Active Directory Site
- Mailbox
- Distribution Groups
- …

Naming conventions vary according to the organization's requirements and depend on locations, geographic distribution, and other factors. There is no single best convention available.

To provide some guidance on naming conventions, the following examples were developed for this book. You can use them as basis to define your own conventions. Remember that you might need more objects to be defined than are described in this section; in general it is good to describe all names that are required, but not every name available.

Server Name

The server name can be used to identify the physical location of a server in terms of country, site, city, or datacenter. It is very common for the server name to also include service-specific information. This eases the process of identifying the role of the server by just looking at its name.

Because some city names are long, it is recommended to use an abbreviation such as an internal site code or the three-letter airport code. In this book, the server name includes the city (only cities with short names are used), the role that is running on it, and a number:

<cityname>-<2 letter service spec><2 digit number>

Table 3-4 describes the details about the service-specific abbreviations used to create the server name in this book.

TABLE 3-4 Server Name Service-Specific Abbreviations

SERVICE SPECIFICATION/ ROLE (TWO LETTERS)	DESCRIPTION
EX	Multi Exchange Role Server
MB	Mailbox Server/Public Folder
HT	Hub Transport
ET	Edge Transport

SERVICE SPECIFICATION/ ROLE (TWO LETTERS)	DESCRIPTION
CA	Client Access Server
UM	Unified Messaging
DC	Domain Controller
SV	Multi Role Server

Examples for server names include:

- Dallas-EX01 (multi-role Exchange located in Dallas)
- Munich-DC01 (DC located in Munich)
- Miami-CA01 (Client Access server located in Miami)
- Berlin-ET01 (Edge Transport located in Berlin)

Database Availability Group Name

Database availability group names can include information on physical sites included in the replication (such as Berlin and Fresno or the Active Directory site names) but for most of the implementations a simple numbering is probably sufficient. In this book, the database availability group name includes DAG name and an increasing number. The convention is as follows:

DAG<2 digit number>

DAG01 and DAG02 are both examples of database availability group names.

Database Name

In Exchange versions before 2010 Mailbox, databases always were fixed to a server name. Thus it was common practice to include the Exchange server name or server information in the database name. This practice changed in Exchange 2010—a database is no longer fixed to a server. The database is no longer associated with the server, thus the database name should include other aspects such as the DAG to which the database is associated, the main location where the database is used, or the purpose of the database (such as mailbox limits).

In this book, the database name includes the DAG it is part of, the city where it is based, and an increasing number. You can argue that we did not consider site resiliency, because having the city name as part of the database name might confuse people in the event of a cross-site database failover. However, in that scenario you can clearly identify which databases are failover databases just by looking at the name. The convention is as follows:

<DAG>-<city>-<2 digit number>

Examples of database names include:

- DAG01-Munich-01
- DAG05-Dallas-05
- DAG06-Sydney-01

Active Directory Site Name

The Active Directory site name should follow the purpose of the creation for multiple Active Directory sites—namely, to define different locations, subsidiaries, or branch offices. In most cases these are the physical boundaries of a location or a datacenter, and indicate a different connectivity between them. Thus the important factor in the name for identification is the location or datacenter name. In some cases for larger companies you might consider including the site code or street name into the site name to identify it correctly.

In this book, the Active Directory Site Name includes the word *Site*, a dash, and then the city or region the site spans. The dash needs to be included because spaces are not allowed in the site name. The convention is as follows:

Site-<city>

Examples for Active Directory site names include:

- Site-Miami
- Site-Munich
- Site-Sydney

User Names

To find the users of your system it is important to define a convention for making the user names. This can follow simple rules such as last name and first name separated by a comma or space and can include other information, such as initials when needed or departmental information after the name (such as when you have two identical names). Because many names are not unique, the general rule is to add as much information as necessary to identify the user.

In this book, the user names follow the simplest user name rule: last name followed by the first name separated by a comma. The convention is as follows:

<Lastname>, <Firstname>

Examples of user names include:

- Healy, Joe
- Richardson, Shawn

Planning Namespace

Before you set up your Exchange organization, one of the most important areas that needs to be planned is your internal (organization-facing) and external (Internet-facing) namespace. A namespace is a logical structure commonly represented by one or more domain names in DNS.

Namespace planning is most important for the Client Access Server role. However, many considerations are also needed for the Hub Transport and Edge Transport roles. This section should provide the general basis for understanding the importance for namespace planning. The topics are also discussed in Chapter 4, "Client Access in Exchange 2010"; Chapter 5, "Routing and Transport"; and Chapter 7, "Edge Transport and Messaging Security."

During migration or transitions you also might need to consider special namespace requirements. These are addressed in Chapter 14, "Transitioning from Exchange Server 2003 and Exchange Server 2007."

The official Microsoft support statement for Exchange 2010 and SLD/Disjoint/ Non-contiguous Namespaces can be found at *http://msexchangeteam.com/archive/2009/10/27/452969.aspx*.

Namespace Scenarios

When you implement your Exchange 2010 organization, you need to decide how your internal and external namespace will be defined. This is important because it affects the following areas:

- DNS configuration of your Exchange servers
- How your certificates are created and what names they include
- Client Access (Outlook Anywhere, Outlook Web App, POP3 and IMAP4, SMTP)

If you have multiple datacenters available where your Exchange 2010 servers are located, consider the following general advice for namespace planning:

- Plan your namespaces such that both datacenters can be active.
  - This still allows for incremental deployment.
  - You provide failover capabilities or can manually switch over a datacenter.
- Each datacenter needs the following namespaces, depending on your client connectivity capabilities:
  - Outlook Web App/OA/EWS/EAS namespace
  - POP3/IMAP4 namespace
  - RPC Client Access namespace
  - SMTP namespace
- Consider which datacenter will maintain the Autodiscover namespace.

To start planning your namespace, you need to consider the various locations of clients and servers and the physical connections they have to the Exchange servers. Typically the namespaces align with your DNS configuration.

You can choose from the following namespace-planning options:

- Consolidated data center
- Single namespace with proxy sites
- Single namespace with multiple sites
- Regional namespaces
- Multiple forests

Consolidated Data Center

This namespace scenario is the simplest one and includes a single namespace to access a single physical site where all the Exchange servers are hosted. The Contoso scenario described in Chapter 2 of this book is an example of a consolidated data center. This scenario has the following advantages:

- Only one or very few DNS records need to be managed.
- Only one or very few certificates are required for your Exchange organization.
- All users use the same URL to access the Exchange server.

This namespace scenario is configured by providing Internet access to the Client Access server by opening the relevant ports by a firewall or implementing an application layer firewall such as Forefront Threat Management Gateway in the perimeter network.

If you want to provide POP3/IMAP4, you need also to consider how the clients will send their messages using SMTP. To overcome this easily, you can configure the Hub Transport role on each Client Access server. Otherwise, you need to plan separately for message sending and message receiving namespaces.

Single Namespace with Proxy Sites

This model is based on the consolidated datacenter model but proxies the requests to the physical Mailbox server located at another site. One of the sites has one or more Internet-facing Client Access servers that proxy the requests.

This scenario has the following advantages:

- Only one or very few DNS records need to be managed.
- Only one or very few certificates are required for your Exchange organization
- All users use the same URL to access Exchange server.

The disadvantage of this model is that most users will access their mailboxes using proxying, thus accessing their data might be slower across latent WAN links.

To configure this namespace model, you need to configure the *ExternalURL* option of the Client Access server(s) at one site, and make sure that the *ExternalURL* settings on all the other sites are configured to *$Null*. This configuration ensures that the Client Access server does not redirect the connection to the target Client Access server, but instead proxies it. Redirect means that the Client Access server forwards the connection to the target Client Access server; proxy means that the Client Access server contacts the target Client Access server and retrieves the data for the connection.

Single Namespace with Multiple Sites

This model uses a single namespace for an organization that has multiple sites. For example, the Litware scenario would be a possible candidate for this approach because the company has multiple physical sites and wants to use a single namespace. The two possible approaches to implementing a single namespace with multiple sites are with a Client Access server proxy site or an intelligent firewall:

- The Client Access server proxy site approach includes Client Access servers based in a separate Active Directory site that is used to proxy the traffic to the site where the user's mailbox is located. To configure this namespace model, you need to configure the *ExternalURL* option to the single namespace of the Client Access servers at all sites.
- The intelligent firewall approach uses an application-layer firewall such as Forefront TMG and decides during client authentication that the traffic is forwarded to the correct target site based on configured rules. To configure this namespace model, you need to configure the *ExternalURL* option to the single namespace of the Client Access servers at all sites.

This scenario has the following advantages:

- Only one or very few DNS records need to be managed.
- Only one or very few certificates are required for your Exchange organization.
- All users use the same URL to access Exchange server.

The disadvantage of this model is that you must either have an application-layer firewall that is capable of forwarding the traffic to the correct physical sites like Microsoft Forefront TMG or a Client Access server proxy site.

Regional Namespaces

This model uses one namespace for each region or site. The users will use their regional namespace to access their messages.

This scenario has the following advantages:

- The client traffic is automatically optimized based on the region or site level. (For example, if you implement a namespace based on a city, all users of that city will use the local access.)
- Performance and end-user experience are optimized.
- Failover is provided if the regional namespace is unavailable by using a different namespace (if the Mailbox server of the site is still available).

The disadvantage of this model is that you need to manage multiple DNS records as well as multiple certificates. Additionally you have multiple Internet entry points that require a firewall.

NOTE **The regional namespaces model is recommended if your topology includes multiple sites that have their own Internet connectivity.**

Multiple Forests

The multiple forest model uses one dedicated namespace for each forest. For example if Contoso and Litware merged, Contoso users would need to access mail.contoso.com and Litware users would use mail.litware.com to access their mailboxes. Client Access server proxy redirection between the two forests does not work, so if one forest is not available, no users would be able to access their messages.

In this model, every namespace that is implemented needs its own Internet access point, DNS record, and a certificate. Within each forest, use a regional namespace model to improve customer experience.

Disjoint Namespace

The disjoint namespace model is a special scenario for planning the namespace. You face this scenario when your primary DNS suffix on domain controllers or member servers in the domain is not the same as the DNS domain name of your Active Directory domain.

For example, you have a disjoint namespace when the Exchange Server that is part of the Litware.com domain has a primary DNS suffix of Contoso.com. This computer (as the primary DNS suffix that does not match the DNS domain name) is said to be disjoint.

You might require these namespaces to be different for several reasons. For example, if DNS management in your company is split between administrators who manage Active Directory and administrators who manage networks, you may need to have a topology with a disjoint namespace.

Microsoft Exchange 2010 has three supported scenarios for deploying Exchange in a domain that has a disjoint namespace:

- **Scenario 1** The primary DNS suffix of the domain controller is not the same as the DNS domain name. Computers that are members of the domain can be either disjoint or not disjoint.
- **Scenario 2** The Exchange servers in an Active Directory domain are disjoint, even though the domain controller is not disjoint.
- **Scenario 3** The NetBIOS domain name of the domain controller is not the same as the subdomain of the DNS domain name of that domain controller.

In Exchange 2010 you may need to configure the DNS suffix search list to include multiple DNS suffixes if you have a disjoint namespace.

In a disjoint namespace environment, you must configure the following:

- All disjoint domains need to be added to the *msds-allowedDNSSuffixes* attribute of your root domain.
- The DNS suffix search list must include all DNS suffixes, including the disjoint DNS suffixes.

As mentioned, it is required to configure every disjoint domain in the *msds-allowedDNSSuffixes* attribute of your root domain. For example, if you have the disjoint namespace contoso.com that you need to add to the Litware.com forest, configure the settings on the domain level using the Windows Server 2008 Administrative Tool ADSI Edit, as shown in Figure 3-7.

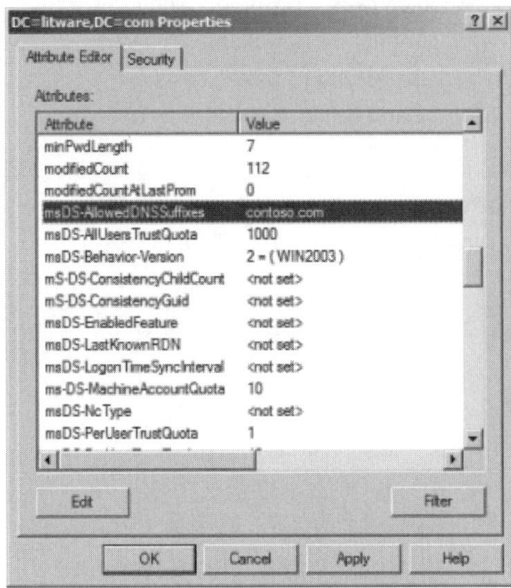

FIGURE 3-7 Configuring a disjoint namespace in the domain

Additionally, make sure that the DNS suffix search list contains all DNS namespaces that are deployed within your organization. To do this, you must configure the DNS search list for each computer in the domain that is disjoint. The list of namespaces should include not only the primary DNS suffix of the disjoint member computer and the DNS domain name, but also any additional namespaces for other servers the Exchange Servers may interoperate (such as the monitoring server).

For more information on Exchange 2010 and disjoint namespaces, see "Understanding Disjoint Namespace Scenarios" at *http://technet.microsoft.com/en-us/library/bb676377.aspx*.

NOTES FROM THE FIELD

A Disjoint Namespace Example

Carsten Allendoerfer
Head of System Services Group, Johannes Gutenberg-University Mainz, Germany

Our disjoint namespace consists of the Active Directory domain called uni-mainz.de (we have a single domain/single forest implementation) but all servers use the primary DNS suffix of zdv.uni-mainz.de. Only domain controllers use the correct suffix of the Active Directory domain.

We started to run Exchange 2010 in early beta phase and had quite a few problems caused by the disjoint namespace scenario. We still have one unsolved problem with the Active Directory Topology Discovery Service, which causes problems when the NetLogon service starts too early and no network connection is available. You can resolve this by using fixed IP addresses for the servers instead of DHCP. I assume this is a general problem in Windows Server 2008 R2 and not an Exchange 2010 problem.

Sometimes applications from Microsoft and other companies take for granted that the DNS suffixes are equal to the Active Directory Domain name. Take my advice: carefully test every application before implementing it. From what I've learned in the past 10 years running in a disjoint namespace scenario, I would never recommend it to anyone.

Single Label Domains

A single label domain (SLD) is basically a DNS domain name set equal to a NetBIOS domain name. It does not contain a suffix such as .com or .org and consists only of a single word, such as LITWARE or CONTOSO.

Before Active Directory, in Windows NT a single label domain was the basis so some companies continued to use an SLD in Active Directory. In Windows Server 2008 R2 you can no longer create SLDs—if you find an environment that still has SLDs, consider migrating to a normal namespace to prevent issues in the future.

Exchange Server 2010 supports SLDs; however, the Exchange product team does not recommend this configuration because future versions of Exchange or third-party applications might cause issues in this scenario. For that reason, you should move your organization to a normal namespace scenario.

Non-contiguous Namespaces

A non-contiguous namespace (sometimes referred as a discontiguous namespace) is a namespace where an Active Directory forest includes multiple domain trees of different names. Thus the forest is not defined hierarchically. A forest can have one or more domain trees, and these trees are defined by the DNS names. For example, contoso.com would be a domain tree in the Litware.com forest.

In Windows Server 2008 R2, you can configure multiple domain trees by using the Advanced Mode Installation in the Active Directory Domain Services Wizard (dcpromo.exe).

> ***IMPORTANT*** **If you have similar tree names (such as litware.com and litware.de), be sure to choose different NetBIOS domain names for their respective domains. If you select the same NetBIOS names for both trees, the configuration is not supported. The general rule is that each domain must still register a unique legacy NetBIOS domain name.**

If your organization has a non-contiguous namespace scenario, DNS must be configured so that every Exchange server is able to resolve all domain names in the environment. You are also required to configure *msDS-AllowedDNSSuffixes* within the Active Directory environment for all namespaces used in the forest. For more information on how to configure *msDS-AllowedDNSSuffixes* refer to the section "Disjoint Namespace" earlier in the chapter.

Planning Certificates

This section is about certificates that are generally used by Exchange 2010 to secure communication between the servers and between the client and the servers. It explains the basics about the certificates, and then dives into the details of what types of certificates are available and what you need to know to plan the names you put into your certificates accordingly.

About Digital Certificates

A digital certificate basically is an electronic representation of users, computers, or other devices or services. A digital certificate consists of a private and a public key pair.

The private key is stored only on a computer, device, or possibly a digital ID card. In many companies these keys are kept under the same security level as the user password for Windows. The public key is used to encrypt data for you and is required by everybody that wants to security communicate with you.

A digital certificate is always issued by a CA with a private and public key pair. The process is similar to applying for a passport at your local governmental office. The governmental office issues your passport, like the CA, and the passport you receive is like the digital certificate.

You use digital certificates in relation to sending and receiving e-mail in two areas:

- **Data encryption** Make sure the data you transmit cannot be decoded somewhere between the sender and the receiver.
- **Digital Signature** The receiver can verify that the data received was originated by you.

Types of Certificates

There are three types of certificates based on the authority that issues the certificate: self-signed certificates, Windows public key infrastructure (PKI)–generated certificates, and third-party certificates. Table 3-5 provides an overview of these types of certificates and their uses.

TABLE 3-5 Types of Digital Certificates

CERTIFICATE TYPE	DESCRIPTION
Self-signed certificates	When Exchange 2010 is installed, a new certificate is generated automatically if no computer certificate is available. This certificate is used by default to encrypt all communication inside and outside the Exchange organization. If you access your OWA using a Web browser, you need to confirm that the server's certificate is correct because you do not trust this certificate by default. Self-signed means that the computer itself acted as a CA and signed its own certificate.
Windows PKI–generated certificates	These certificates are issued by a Windows CA (such as Windows Server 2008 R2's Active Directory Certificate Service) and you can request them at no extra cost and install them immediately. Normally, they are not trusted publicly, so you need to make sure that the root certificate is imported at every server, client, and device that does not belong to your Active Directory. In your Active Directory forest, the information is distributed automatically.
Third-party certificates	This type of certificate is automatically trusted within the Internet and can be purchased by a third-party CA such as VeriSign. It is the easiest and least time-consuming way to implement certificates, but you need to buy them. Thus, you probably won't have an official certificate for every Exchange server in your environment.

You cannot use self-signed certificates for mutual TLS or Domain Security communication to and from the Internet in Exchange 2010—only Windows PKI–generated certificates or third-party certificates are supported there.

> ***IMPORTANT*** **If you decided to use Windows PKI–generated certificates for Internet messaging, you have to make sure that your partners' servers trust your root CA (by importing your root certificate).**

Working with Certificates in Exchange 2010

Exchange uses certificates to communicate securely between the different server roles. By default each Exchange server uses either the certificate issued by the domain or issues its own self-signed certificate and uses this one for communication. If you do not require secure communication to the Internet, a self-signed certificate works without issue. However, if you want to consider a secure Exchange 2010 implementation, some server roles require an independent certificate if they are communicating with the client. Table 3-6 provides an overview of which Exchange Server roles require which certificate for which purpose.

TABLE 3-6 Server Roles and Certificates Requirement

SERVER ROLE	PROTOCOL(S) THAT REQUIRES CERTIFICATE	TYPES OF CERTIFICATES REQUIRED
Hub Transport	SMTP over TLS	Windows PKI or third-party for external, self-signed for internal mail flow
Client Access Server	Outlook Web App (OWA) Exchange Web Services (EWS) Outlook Anywhere ActiveSync POP3 IMAP4 Autodiscover	Windows PKI or third-party
Edge Transport	SMTP over TLS	Windows PKI or third-party
Mailbox Server	—	Any certificate
Unified Messaging	SIP over TLS	Windows PKI or self-signed

SERVER ROLE	PROTOCOL(S) THAT REQUIRES CERTIFICATE	TYPES OF CERTIFICATES REQUIRED
Application Layer Firewall/Reverse Proxy[1]	SMTP over TLS Outlook Web App (OWA) Exchange Web Services (EWS) Outlook Anywhere ActiveSync POP3 IMAP4 Autodiscover	Windows PKI or third-party

[1] An application-layer firewall such as Microsoft TMG can be used to proxy traffic between the perimeter and internal network. For that reason it can proxy all Exchange protocols but does not require it.

Exchange 2010 certificates need to have a certain format to work correctly with the TLS protocol. Because the Edge Transport servers might have multiple domain names or service connection points (SCPs), you have two options:

- Use a single certificate on your server(s) with Subject Alternative Names (SAN) support, also known as Unified Communications Certificates.
- Use individual certificates.

> **NOTE** Microsoft recommends using a SAN certification because it's simpler to administer on the servers. Unfortunately, it is also more expensive than a normal certificate if purchased from a third-party CA.

Thus when considering certificates in Exchange 2010, you need to answer two key questions:

- Where do you want to place certificates? Do you want to use one certificate per server or a single certificate for all your servers? If you want to use a single certificate for all your servers, make sure you distinguish between internal and external servers. If you use an application-layer firewall in a perimeter network, consider implementing a separate certificate for it.
- What SAN names should the certificates have? If you use one certificate for all servers, you need to consider all SAN names that you want to add.

To plan for all the domains or host names that should be included in the certificate, Table 3-7 should provide you with a basic understanding of what is required.

TABLE 3-7 Creating Certificates for Exchange Roles

SERVER ROLE	CERTIFICATE NAME REQUIREMENTS	EXAMPLES (FOR LITWARE SCENARIO)
Hub or Edge Transport	■ Hub Transport server's FQDN ■ Domain name(s) used for TLS	■ Berlin-HT01.Litware.com ■ Litware.com
Client Access Server	■ Client Access server's FQDN (for internal client proxy for ECP, OCS 2007 R2) ■ Service FQDN for OWA, ActiveSync, POP3, IMAP, and so on	■ Fresno-CA01.Litware.com ■ OWA.Litware.com ■ Mail.Litware.com ■ Webmail.litware.com ■ Imap.litware.com ■ Autodiscover.litware.com
Unified Messaging	■ UM server's FQDN (for SIP over TLS)	■ Berlin-UM01.Litware.com

> ***NOTE*** **Short names or NetBIOS names are no longer required in a certificate in Exchange 2010. However, if your users are using short names in the browser to access OWA, or if you implement the certificate on legacy Exchange Servers, you should also add the short names to the certificates.**

Consider carefully the following best practices regarding creating certificates for Exchange 2010 :

- Use SAN certificates that can cover multiple host names.
- Minimize the number of certificates. If your company's security policy permits, use only one certificate for all Client Access, Hub/Edge servers, and the application-layer firewall.
- Because Office Communication Server (OCS) 2007 requires the server name in the certificate principal name (PN) and a key of <=1024 bit keys, it is recommended that you use an additional certificate if OCS is required.
- Put only the names you need in the certificate.
- Don't list computer host names on certificate host name lists, if at all possible.
- If using a certificate for each datacenter, ensure that the Certificate Principal Name is the same on all certificates. Otherwise, Outlook Anywhere will not connect in a site failover scenario.

Planning Exchange Server 2010 Placement

This section explains the planning aspects you need to consider to plan Exchange 2010 server placement at your company's locations. It starts with considering the domain controllers because they play an important role when Exchange Server 2010 is installed and then discusses what Exchange roles should be planned at which site.

Domain Controller and Global Catalog Placement

In planning your Exchange 2010 server placement, never forget to include domain controller or global catalog servers. Because Exchange 2010 requires good communications with Active Directory to access its configuration, the logical starting point is to consider domain controllers and global catalog servers that already exist and verify whether additional servers are needed. This is especially important because Exchange 2010 won't start without communicating to a global catalog server. For that reason it is important that you consider the following areas in your planning:

- At least one global catalog (which obviously is also a domain controller) must be available in the same Active Directory site where you plan to install Exchange 2010.
- For redundancy reasons, it's always good to have at least two global catalog servers available in an Active Directory site where Exchange 2010 will be installed.
- Using 64-bit domain controllers increases the directory service performance significantly, although 32-bit domain controllers are still supported.
- As in Exchange 2007, the recommended 4:1 ratio of Exchange processor cores to global catalog processor cores (32-bit) still applies for Exchange 2010. If you have 64-bit global catalogs with enough memory to house the ntds.dit, the ratio increases to 8:1. For example, if you have two Exchange servers with four processor cores per server, you should have at least one global catalog processor core for Exchange 2010 server requests. As you cannot dedicate GCs to Exchange as the servers will deal with requests from other applications, you need to make sure to deploy sufficient GC capacity to deal with Exchange and the other applications.
- If you're planning to host Exchange servers for multiple domains at a single Active Directory site you must include domain controllers from each domain you host resources for. This ensures that a domain controller of their own domain is always referred to your Outlook clients.

> ***IMPORTANT*** **Exchange Server 2010 does not support Windows Server 2008 Read-Only-Domain Controllers (RODCs) or Read-Only Global Catalogs (ROGCs) existing in the same Active Directory site. If you are using RODCs or ROGCs, you cannot install Exchange 2010 in those Active Directory sites—you need to create separate ones for Exchange.**

Using Exchange Server 2010 on Member Servers or Domain Controllers

You must also consider on which Windows 2008 server role you want to install Exchange Server 2010: member servers or domain controllers. Even though Microsoft supports the installation of Exchange Server 2010 on domain controllers, we strongly advise against it. This is because you need to be a local administrator to manage an Exchange Server 2010 server, and local administrators will automatically receive Admin permissions on all of your domain controllers.

In some circumstances, such as branch-office situations, you may not have a choice because hardware is spare or budget is limited. We've seen situations where a single piece of hardware held everything: domain controller, Exchange Server, and file and print services. However, avoid that if possible. You can use virtualization to separate domain controllers and Exchange servers easily when using virtualization such as Windows Server 2008 R2 Hyper- and still run everything on a physical computer.

> ***NOTE*** **As a protective feature, Dcpromo—the command to promote a Windows Server 2008 member server to a domain controller—cannot be run again after you have installed Exchange Server 2010 on a Windows 2008 member server. After Exchange Server 2010 is installed, changing the role from a member server to a domain controller or vice versa is not a Microsoft-supported scenario.**

Exchange Server Role Placement

To manage Exchange Server 2010 in a more natural way, server roles were implemented. These roles enable administrators to easily choose which features should be installed on an Exchange server. They provide the following advantages over the architecture used in Exchange versions before Exchange 2007:

- They reduce attack surface because only required roles are installed.
- They allow you to install the servers for their intended role only.
- They provide more possibilities for scalability and reliability.
- They lower complexity to reduce system outages.

In Exchange Server 2010 you can choose from five server roles: Mailbox server, Hub Transport server, Client Access, Unified Messaging server, and Edge Transport server. Figure 3-8 provides an overview of all Exchange Server 2010 roles, their functionality, and their connections.

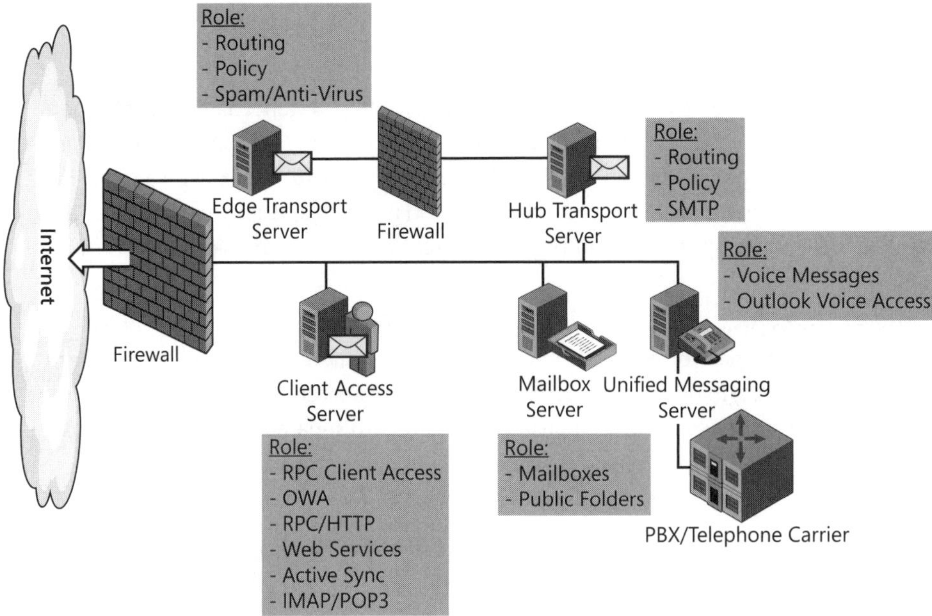

FIGURE 3-8 Exchange Server 2010 roles

As you can see in the figure, you must follow certain rules to develop a plan of which roles you place at which Active Directory sites. Table 3-8 provides an overview as well as the main planning aspects for each role. More details about the Exchange Server 2010 roles are covered in later chapters of this book.

TABLE 3-8 Exchange Server 2010 Roles and Planning Aspects

SERVER ROLE	DESCRIPTION	PLANNING ASPECT
Mailbox Server	Hosts your mailboxes as well as public folder databases.	You must plan to position Exchange servers at the Active Directory sites where most of the users are located or depending on your IT strategy in key regional datacenters. Because your users no longer directly connect to the Mailbox server in Exchange 2010 (only for public folder access), you need to have at least the Client Access and Hub Transport server roles available in the same Active Directory site.

SERVER ROLE	DESCRIPTION	PLANNING ASPECT
Client Access Server	This role hosts RPC Client Access; availability service and Autodiscover for Outlook 2007 or later; Exchange ActiveSync; client protocols such as MAPI, POP3, IMAP4, Outlook Web App (OWA), Outlook Anywhere and Exchange Web Services (EWS). All client traffic flows through the Client Access Server role in Exchange 2010, including MAPI connections from Outlook clients that are handled by the RPC Client Access layer.	Required in every Active Directory site where a Mailbox server is installed. The recommendation is three Client Access server processor cores per four Mailbox processor cores.
Hub Transport Server	Manages all internal message routing within the Exchange organization and hosts transport rules that can be applied to messages. It also accepts all SMTP types of messages even if they come from the user.	Required in every Active Directory site where a Mailbox server is installed. In this Active Directory site a global catalog must be available. The rule of thumb regarding sizing (with antivirus) is one Hub Transport processor core per five Mailbox server processor cores. For redundancy reasons you should have at least two Hub Transport servers in larger or critical Active Directory sites.
Edge Transport Server	Acts as a smart host and SMTP relay in your perimeter network and handles all Internet-facing mail flow. Provides anti-spam and antivirus functionality. Provides address rewriting and Transport rules to protect the internal network.	Depending on the size of your organization, you should plan at least two Edge Transport servers to provide redundancy in case of problems.
Unified Messaging Server	Connects Exchange with your telephone system or private branch exchange (PBX) to provide voice access to your mailbox.	Supports a maximum of 100 concurrent calls per server. The planning aspect should include the number of users and how they use Unified Messaging. A single Unified Messaging server can host approximately 3,000 users. You need at least one Hub Transport server available in the same site.

Exchange Server 2010 server roles can coexist on a single Exchange computer with a few rules to consider:

- The Mailbox role, Hub Transport role, Client Access role, and Unified Messaging role can coexist on a server.
- On a Mailbox server that is member of a DAG, you cannot use Windows Network Load Balancing (NLB).
- Edge Transport cannot be shared with any other server role.

In a smaller organization you will probably end up having a server that hosts multiple roles, mainly the Mailbox, Client Access, and Hub Transport roles. The larger the organization, the more dedicated those server roles will get.

NOTES FROM THE FIELD

Planning Exchange Server Roles and Placement

Joe Cirillo
Senior Engineer and Architect, Horizons Consulting, US/Central Region

When I prepare to install a new Exchange messaging system or integrate with an earlier version of Exchange I always take the same approach. Whether I am installing one physical server with multiple roles or installing individual roles on dedicated hardware I always begin by first installing the Client Access Server role.

Because the Client Access server is used by every mail client, you can fully prepare the Client Access server for client access before installing the Mailbox server role, thus ensuring that once the Mailbox server is online, users will be able to successfully connect to their mailboxes based on your preconfigured settings.

When I prepare the Client Access server, I like to do the following:

- **If there will be a high volume of content conversion, move the %TMP% folder to a dedicated set of drive spindles for improved performance.**
- **Replace the self-signed certificate with a public certificate, typically a SAN certificate.**
- **Create the necessary DNS records to support the services to be used.**
- **Configure Exchange services for the Autodiscover Service.**
- **Enable Outlook Anywhere.**
- **Create a Client Access Array using EMS (new in Exchange 2010).**
- **Configure the hardware load balancer.**

After I have fully configured and tested access and functionality of the Client Access server, I install the Hub Transport role. This way I can ensure that message transport is working properly. Again, having this role installed and configured before the Mailbox server role will ensure that once I provision a mailbox to a user, that user will be able to successfully send and receive e-mail messages.

When I prepare the Hub Transport server, I like to do the following:

- Confirm that message tracking is enabled.
- Change the location of the Queue Database and Queue Database Transaction Logs for improved performance.
- If necessary, modify the organizational level send and receive message size limits.
- If necessary, modify the default receive connector to accept anonymous connections.
- If necessary, modify the default receive connector's message size limit.
- If necessary, create an additional receive connector for applications that require relay access.
- Configure remote domains.
- Configure accepted domains.
- Configure e-mail address policies.
- Create send connectors.
- If necessary, modify send connector message size limits.
- Configure the hardware load balancer.

Once the Hub and Client Access servers are in place and properly configured I can safely install the Mailbox server role, comfortable in the knowledge that my users will be able to successfully connect to their mailboxes and send and receive e-mail.

When I prepare the Mailbox server, I like to do the following:

- Change the file location of the default database and logs.
- Create additional databases.
- If necessary, modify mailbox database settings (storage limits, deleted item retention, and so on).
- If necessary, create a Public Folder database.
- Configure the mailbox limits cache (see *http://technet.microsoft.com/en-us/library/bb684892(EXCHG.80).aspx*).
- Publish offline address books to the required distribution mechanisms (public folders and/or Exchange File Distribution on a Client Access server).

- Control Outlook Access to Exchange based on client version.
- Configure any settings required to enable high availability such as joining a server to a DAG.

For designs that call for a distributed messaging infrastructure where Exchange Servers will exist in multiple locations I still follow the basic guideline on installation order of Client Access, then Hub, and then Mailbox. Again, this ensures that all my services are working (even between sites) prior to provisioning a mailbox on a Mailbox server.

Planning Network Port Requirements

When the first versions of Exchange came out, security was not a major consideration. Of course, security was of concern in 1996 but the level of Internet connectivity that systems have today, together with the threat posed by being connected to the Internet, make it quite different. Obviously, this has changed in recent years. Windows Firewall is now a main component of every Windows Server 2008 operating system. Windows Firewall basically filters inbound and outbound traffic based on firewall rules. Exchange Server 2010 creates the Windows Firewall rules to open the ports required during Exchange Setup—thus you no longer need to configure these settings manually.

Some companies want to put certain server roles into a perimeter network. A perimeter network is a network zone that is deployed between the Internet and a company's intranet as defense-in-depth and is protected by one or more firewall systems.

IMPORTANT **When defining your firewall ports, always consider the concept of "less is more." The fewer ports you allow to open, the more secure your system will be.**

To provide an easy overview of the masses of ports, this section is organized according to the Exchange Server roles. The tables are sorted according the required ports so you can recognize which ports are used for which services or data paths.

For more information about firewall configuration see the Exchange Network Port Reference at *http://technet.microsoft.com/en-us/library/bb331973(printer).aspx.*

Mailbox Server

The Mailbox server role hosts the mailbox and public folder databases. Apart from public folders, the clients do not communicate directly with the Mailbox server but instead use the Client Access server for communication that then establishes the connection to the Mailbox server. For this reason it is not recommended to separate a Mailbox and Client Access server with a firewall.

Table 3-9 shows which ports are required for services or data paths to and from the Mailbox server role. It's important to understand that RPC traffic is always encrypted.

TABLE 3-9 Network Ports for Mailbox Role

DATA PATH	REQUIRED PORTS	ENCRYPTED BY DEFAULT?
Messaging application programming interface (MAPI) access, Availability Web service (Client Access to Mailbox server), Content indexing, Recipient Update Service RPC access (Exchange 2003 only), Microsoft Exchange Active Directory Topology Service access, Microsoft Exchange System Attendant service legacy access, Offline address book (OAB) accessing Active Directory, Recipient Update Service RPC access. RPC Endpoint mapper	135/TCP (RPC)	Yes
Mailbox Assistants, Admin remote access (remote registry), Microsoft Exchange System Attendant service legacy access (listen)	135/TCP (RPC)	No
Clustering or DAG to communicate between cluster nodes (status and activity)	135/TCP (RPC), 3343/UDP + randomly high TCP ports	No
DAG (Log shipping, seeding)	64327/TCP (customizable)	No
Active Directory access, DSAccess to Active Directory	389/TCP/UDP (LDAP), 3268/TCP (LDAP GC), 88/TCP/UDP (Kerberos), 53/TCP/UDP (DNS), 135/TCP (RPC Netlogon)	Yes
Microsoft Exchange System Attendant service legacy access to Active Directory, Recipient update to Active Directory	389/TCP/UDP (LDAP), 3268/TCP (LDAP GC), 88/TCP/UDP (Kerberos), 53/TCP/UDP (DNS), 135/TCP (RPC Netlogon)	Yes
Admin remote access (SMB/File)	445/TCP (SMB)	No
Outlook accessing Offline Address Book (OAB)	80/TCP, 443/TCP (SSL)	Yes (SSL)

Hub and Edge Transport Servers

Exchange Server 2010 includes two roles that perform message transport functionality: Hub Transport server and Edge Transport server. You will need to consider this section when you are planning to implement an Edge Transport server role in your organization. The Hub Transport server takes care of messages that are routed within an organization; the Edge Transport server role routes messages inside and outside of the organization. For that reason Edge Transport servers are always placed in a perimeter network, whereas Hub Transport servers are always installed behind the network perimeter and belong to the corporate network.

Table 3-10 explains which ports are required for services or data paths to and from the Hub Transport and the Edge Transport server roles.

> ***NOTE*** **Because the Edge Transport server is designed to be located in the perimeter network, it is assumed that only the communication between Hub Transport and Edge Transport needs to be protected by firewalls. Of course, Edge Transport communication to the Internet also should be protected if the Edge Transport server is located in the perimeter network.**

TABLE 3-10 Network Ports for Hub and Edge Transport Servers

DATA PATH	REQUIRED PORTS	ENCRYPTED BY DEFAULT?
Hub Transport server to Hub Transport server, Hub Transport to Edge Transport and vice versa, Edge Transport to Edge Transport, Unified Messaging server to Hub Transport server and vice versa	25/TCP (TLS)	Yes
Active Directory access from Hub Transport server	389/TCP/UDP (LDAP), 3268/TCP (LDAP GC), 88/TCP/UDP (Kerberos), 53/TCP/UDP (DNS), 135/TCP (RPC Netlogon)	Yes
Microsoft Exchange EdgeSync service (from Hub to Edge)	50636/TCP (SSL)	Yes
Active Directory Rights Management Services (AD RMS) access from Hub Transport server	443/TCP (HTTPS)	Yes
Mailbox server to Hub Transport and vice versa	135/TCP (RPC)	Yes
Clients to Hub Transport server (using SMTP)	25/TCP (SMTP) or 587/TCP (SMTP)	Yes for TLS

As the table shows, encryption is the default in many situations. Hub Transport to Hub Transport is encrypted by default using the Exchange server's certificate. If no machine certificates are available for your Exchange server, the system will use self-signed certificates for encrypting the communication. The same is true for Hub Transport to Edge Transport communication.

If clients such as Windows Messaging directly communicate with the Hub Transport server, the only encryption possible is TLS over SMTP.

Client Access Server

The Client Access Server role manages all client requests and communicates directly with the Mailbox role. Therefore it is best practice not to separate Mailbox and Client Access Server roles with a firewall but instead to keep them in the same network. Remember, Microsoft doesn't support a firewall being placed between Client Access and Mailbox servers.

Table 3-11 describes which ports are required for services or data paths to and from the Client Access Server role.

TABLE 3-11 Network Ports for Client Access Servers

DATA PATH	REQUIRED PORTS	ENCRYPTED BY DEFAULT?
Active Directory access	389/TCP/UDP (LDAP), 3268/TCP (LDAP GC), 88/TCP/UDP (Kerberos), 53/TCP/UDP (DNS), 135/TCP (RPC Netlogon)	Yes
Autodiscover service, Availability service, Outlook Web App (OWA), Outlook Anywhere, Exchange ActiveSync, Client Access server to Client Access server for Exchange ActiveSync and OWA	80/TCP or 443/TCP (SSL)	Yes
Client Access server to Client Access server for Exchange Web Services (EWS)	443/TCP (SSL)	Yes
POP3	110/TCP (TLS) or 995/TCP (SSL)	Yes (TLS/SSL)
IMAP4	143/TCP (TLS) or 993/TCP (SSL)	Yes (TLS/SSL)
Client Access server to Unified Messaging server	5060/TCP, 5061/TCP, 5062/TCP + a dynamic port	Yes
Client Access server to Exchange Server 2010 Mailbox server	135/TCP (RPC) + dynamic ports	Yes

DATA PATH	REQUIRED PORTS	ENCRYPTED BY DEFAULT?
Client Access server to a Mailbox server that is running Exchange Server 2003 or before	80/TCP, 443/TCP (SSL)	No
Client Access server to Client Access server (POP3)	995 (SSL)	Yes
Client Access server to Client Access server (IMAP4)	993 (SSL)	Yes

When a Client Access server proxies POP3 requests to another Client Access server, the communication occurs over port 995/TCP, regardless of whether the connecting client uses POP3 and requests TLS or connects on port 995/TCP using SSL. The same applies to IMAP4 connections where Client Access Server always uses port 993/TCP to proxy requests.

> ***NOTE*** **When your Exchange 2010 Client Access server is communicating with an Exchange 2003 server, it is a best practice to use Kerberos authentication (disable NTLM and Basic authentication) and configure OWA to use forms-based authentication.**

Unified Messaging Server

The Unified Messaging server role is used to play voice messages to users using a IP gateway or a IP PBX (Private Branch eXchange). This server role communicates to all other server roles and is always placed in the organization's internal network.

Table 3-12 explains which ports are required for services or data paths to and from the Unified Messaging server role.

TABLE 3-12 Network Ports for Unified Messaging Servers

DATA PATH	REQUIRED PORTS	ENCRYPTED BY DEFAULT?
Active Directory access	389/TCP/UDP (LDAP), 3268/TCP (LDAP GC), 88/TCP/UDP (Kerberos), 53/TCP/UDP (DNS), 135/TCP (RPC Netlogon)	Yes
Unified Messaging to Mailbox server	135/TCP (RPC)	Yes
Unified Messaging to Hub Transport server	25/TCP (TLS)	Yes

DATA PATH	REQUIRED PORTS	ENCRYPTED BY DEFAULT?
Unified Messaging to Client Access server	5075/TCP, 5076/TCP, 5077/TCP	Yes
Unified Messaging to Client Access server (Play on Phone)	135/TCP (RPC)	Yes
Unified Messaging to private branch exchange (PBX)	5060/TCP, 5065/TCP, 5067/TCP (unsecured) or 5061/TCP, 5066/TCP, 5068/TCP (secured) and a dynamic TCP and UDP port	No
Unified Messaging Web Service	80/TCP, 443/TCP (SSL)	Yes

International Considerations

You need to consider certain areas when implementing Exchange 2010 in a global, heterogeneous, or multi-language environment. This section considers the most important factors of a global implementation: the language, time and message format, and message text encoding factors.

Multiple Language Support for Exchange

An important factor in international implementations to consider is the language for Exchange that should be installed. By default, Exchange Server 2010 only includes the English language for Exchange, but optionally you also can install additional language bundles.

> ***NOTE*** **If you install from the Exchange 2010 DVD, most of the language packs are automatically included.**

Exchange 2010 comes with two different language bundles:

- **Language Pack for Exchange** You need this if you want to provide a localized version of the Exchange management tools (EMC and ECP) and OWA prompts for a specific language. A language pack includes the names of the default folders, user interface and layout, translated help text, and so on.
- **Unified Messaging Language Packs** You need these when you want to provide the Exchange Server 2010 Unified Messaging feature for a specific language.

Language Packs for Exchange

Depending on the Outlook Web App (OWA) languages you want to support, you need to install the respective Language Pack for Exchange. This provides localized messages for the users. It provides, for example, OWA in the local language on Client Access servers. On Mailbox servers it provides the default folder names in that language. On Hub Transport servers it provides key strings such as "Read", "Not Read", or "Undeliverable" in the local language.

The following are some general recommendations when using language packs:

- Always consider applying language packs for Exchange to all Exchange roles of that specific site. This is to prevent a mix of non-English and English strings in OWA and Outlook for users who set their language to non-English.
- You should deploy the language packs starting with your Mailbox servers.
- After installing the Exchange language packs, restart the computer to complete the installation of the language packs.
- If no Exchange language pack is deployed, English will be the only language available in Exchange and OWA, regardless of the operating system language.

You can find an overview of available language packs for Exchange 2010 at *http://technet.microsoft.com/en-us/library/dd298152.aspx*.

If you want to install the full language pack bundle for Exchange, you can download it at *http://go.microsoft.com/fwlink/?LinkId=147077*.

> ***NOTE*** **To add a language pack for Exchange after you've installed Exchange, you need to run Setup from your CD, not by going through Control Panel. Basically you add the language pack as though you were installing a new Exchange server.**

What language packs are installed on an Exchange server? On a Client Access server that's easy to answer: You can see the language packs when logging on to OWA. On the Regional tab, under Settings, select the Language drop-down menu.

On Hub Transport or Mailbox servers, this is a bit more complicated. You have to use Regedit.exe and look into the \HKLM\Software\Microsoft\ExchangeServer\v14\Language Packs key to see what languages are installed on that specific Exchange server, as shown in Figure 3-9.

To remove a language you need to remove the entire key entry for that specific language found under HKLM\Software\Microsoft\ExchangeServer\v14\Language Packs\Client.

The language codes follow the ISO 639-1 codes (as described at *http://en.wikipedia.org/wiki/List_of_ISO_639-1_codes*) except where more specific languages (such as zh-Hant) or specific cultures (pt-pt, for example) have been added. Be aware that removing languages directly from the Registry may cause issues in future versions of Exchange.

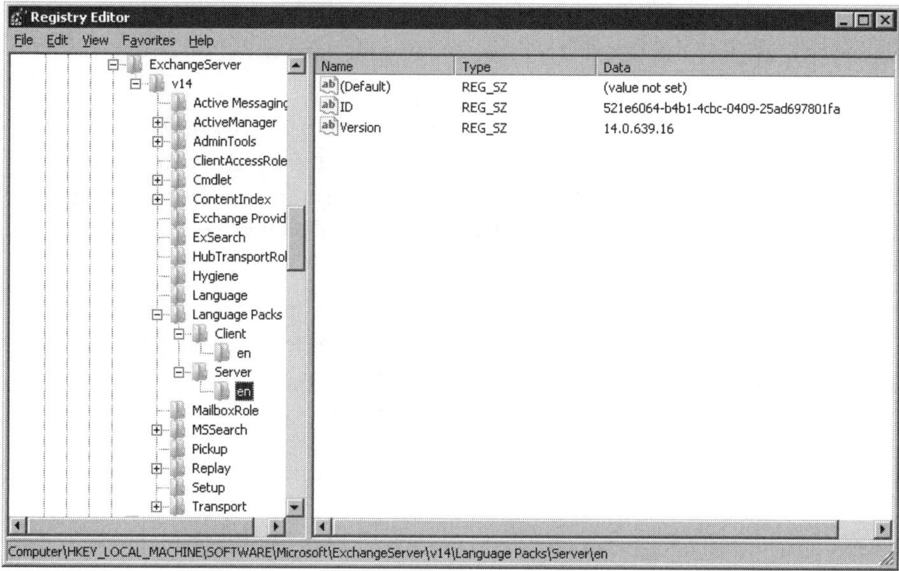

FIGURE 3-9 Identifying installed language packs in the Registry

Unified Messaging Language Packs

Unified Messaging Language Packs contain prerecorded prompts, grammar files, text to speech (TTS) data, Automatic Speech Recognition (ASR) files, and Voice Mail Preview capabilities for a specific language. They are only available for the Exchange 2010 Unified Messaging role and thus should not be installed on other server roles.

Install the same UM language packs to all Exchange UM server roles located in the same site. This will automatically provide the same language capabilities to all your users.

Because the UM language packs are continuously enhanced, you can download the latest language packs at *http://www.microsoft.com/downloads/details.aspx?FamilyID=3fdf49db-cb84-4dfe-8b8b-b30178b1a514&displaylang=en.*

Time, Time Zone, and Daylight Saving

Time zone settings on Exchange Server 2010 computers are similarly crucial to those on domain controllers in your Windows environment. If the servers run out of time synchronization, you will receive errors because Exchange assumes it is no longer working correctly. The EMS uses Kerberos when users authenticate themselves when they create a new Remote Windows PowerShell session. If Kerberos doesn't work, users won't be able to authenticate and the session cannot be created. If the time is not set correctly, EMS will fail to work. Every message is time stamped, so if message servers stamp the wrong time, this will screw up operations like message tracking.

Time is stored internally by Exchange using the Coordinated Universal Time (UTC) time zone to prevent issues from time conversions. All log files include the time in UTC format, which is sometimes confusing.

It is important to make sure you synchronize your time accordingly. Exchange Server 2010 automatically synchronizes the time within the domain if the server is a member of the domain. You therefore should configure your forest to synchronize the time. Detailed steps can be found on the Configure the Windows Time Service on the Forest Root Domain Controller Web page at *http://technet.microsoft.com/en-us/library/cc778920(WS.10).aspx.*

With Exchange servers that are not part of the domain like Edge Transport servers, you need to take care. Best practice is to configure a time server for every Edge Transport server that automatically receives the current time using the Network Time Protocol (NTP) from a server in your organization or directly from the Internet. You can use the following command to configure a NTP server:

```
net time /setsntp: <ntp server>.
```

In a multi-forest environment, make sure that the NTP servers you configured in each forest synchronize the time between them or with the same source.

The Daylight Saving Time (DST) changes every year, so you are well advised to keep your Exchange Servers during this time updated. You only need to consider this when you operate multiple Exchange Servers in different time zones, or if you're planning to do so.

> ***NOTE*** **Always enable the clock as a system icon on your taskbar; it helps prevent time issues from happening. Enabling the clock will show you the current system time whenever you log on to the server. You can immediately correct it if there is an issue.**

Message Format and Encoding

Because binary files cannot be sent directly using SMTP, they need to be encoded into a different message format. This is because SMTP messages can only consist of characters with 7 bits (or ASCII printable), meaning that you need to translate all 8-bit characters into 7-bit characters to transfer them using SMTP. This process is called *message encoding.*

Exchange Server 2010 supports the following message encoding formats:

- Uuencode (or UNIX-to-UNIX encoding) is one of the oldest encoding formats that supports encoding binary data. Three bytes of the binary file (24 bit) are divided into four of six bytes, and these six-byte values are associated with printable ASCII code. Uuencode has been widely replaced by MIME, but you still might need it if you're communicating with native UNIX SMTP servers to overcome message conversation issues.
- MIME (or Multipurpose Internet Mail Extensions) is the most common encoding format used today on the Internet. MIME nowadays is not only used by SMTP messaging,

but also by protocols such as HTTP. With MIME it is possible to exchange information about the type of messages (the content type) between the sender and the recipient of the message. MIME also defines the art of coding (Content-Transfer-Encoding).

To encode non-text elements, Exchange 2010 uses by default MIME encoding. This coding of non-ASCII characters is based on quoted-printable (QP) coding the binary data, typically using Base64-coding. As mentioned in the "Mail Client Support" section that follows, some UNIX or Linux clients cannot understand this message format and have issues with special characters that are not part of ASCII, such as German vocal or Chinese character sets. In such situations you might need to adapt the encoding format to solve the problem.

In addition to the encoding format, Exchange Server and Outlook use the Transport Neutral Encapsulation Format (TNEF) as the file format for attachments in e-mail messages. Attachments in this format often contain files called winmail.dat or win.dat. This format allows Outlook users to use some advanced features, but message programs other than Outlook cannot use it and receive an attachment called winmail.dat.

Mail Client Support

This section describes supported client and browser versions for Exchange 2010 and provides a feature overview of Microsoft Office Outlook 2003, Outlook 2007, and Outlook 2010.

Microsoft Outlook/Entourage

Several client programs supporting Exchange 2010 are available. Outlook 2010 for Windows and Entourage 2008 for Mac OS provide the most features for Exchange 2010 because they are engineered by Microsoft to work together well. Thus they include features such as MailTips that maximize the use of Exchange functionality. Because they are available in different versions, the following list provides an overview of the supported clients for Exchange Server 2010:

- Microsoft Outlook 2003 or later on Windows including the latest Service Pack
- Microsoft Entourage 2008 SP2 EWS or later on Mac OS
- Microsoft Outlook on Mac OS (2010 release)

> **NOTE** Because of the functional change in Exchange 2010 whereby Outlook no longer communicates directly to the Mailbox server, Outlook 2002 (which was part of Office XP) and earlier versions cause weird issues when connected to Exchange Server 2010. I personally tested Outlook 2002 with Exchange 2010 and some features were not working correctly; consider migrating any Outlook 2002 users before moving their mailboxes to Exchange 2010. Also, Microsoft does not support Outlook 2002 or earlier for Exchange 2010.

Each version of Outlook supports different features with Exchange Server. To receive the most server-based features, you will need to use the latest Outlook Version: Outlook 2010. Table 3-13 provides feature guidance on Exchange 2003, Exchange 2007, and Exchange 2010 and which features are available in which version of Exchange Server.

TABLE 3-13 Outlook Feature Comparison by Exchange Server Version

	SERVER INDEPENDENT	EXCHANGE 2003 (SP2)	EXCHANGE 2007 (SP1+)	EXCHANGE 2010 (RTM)
E-mail	X	X	X	X
Push e-mail	—	X	X	X
Calendar (on server)	—	X	X	X
Calendar	X	X	X	X
Free/Busy information	—	X	X	X
Free/Busy details sharing	—	—	X	X
Scheduling assistant	—	—	X	X
Contacts (on server)	—	X	X	X
Contact sharing	—	—	—	X
Calendar sharing	—	—	—	X
Calendar publishing				X
Archive access	—	—	—	X
Orgizational hierarchy	—	X	X	X
GAL access	—	X	X	X
MailTips	—	—	—	X
Conversation view	—	—	—	X
Conversation actions (ignore/move always)	—	—	—	X
UM (Voice mail)	—	—	X	X
UM preview	—	—	—	X
Protected Voice Mail	—	—	—	X
Managed folders	—	—	X	X
Tasks (on Server)	—	X	X	X
Public folders	—	X	X	X
Notes (server stored)	—	X	X	X

	SERVER INDEPENDENT	EXCHANGE 2003 (SP2)	EXCHANGE 2007 (SP1+)	EXCHANGE 2010 (RTM)
IRM protected messages	—	—	X	X
Policy management (group policy)	X			
Offline address book	—	X	X	X
AutoDiscover	—	—	X	X
OOF	—	X	X	X
External/Internal OOF	—	—	X	X
OOF Scheduling	—	—	X	X
Voting Buttons	—	X	X	X
Search folders			X	X
Search			X	X
Favorites folders			X	X
Journal (on Server)	—			
RSS Feeds (on Server)	—		X	X
Custom forms				
Custom dictionaries				
Mail rules	—	X	X	X

NOTES FROM THE FIELD

Consider Outlook RPC encryption

Ross Smith IV

Senior Program Manager, Exchange Server Product Group, Microsoft Corporation

Because Exchange Server 2010 requires Outlook traffic to be RPC encrypted, you might run into issues if you already have Outlook 2003 or Outlook 2007 in place today. By default, Outlook 2003 and Outlook 2007 do not use RPC encryption, so you will need to enable it before they're able to connect to an Exchange Server 2010. For details on how to prepare for this situation, you can find more information at *http://support.microsoft.com/kb/2006508*.

Outlook Web App

Exchange Server 2010 also supports various browsers not only in Outlook Web App Light but also with the Outlook Web App Premium edition that also provides rich features to browser users. OWA Premium includes features such as drag-and-drop, Junk-Mail filter configuration or voicemail configuration options that are not available in OWA Light. For Outlook Web App, the following browsers are supported:

- **Outlook Web App Premium on Microsoft Windows Vista or later** Internet Explorer 7 or later, Firefox 3.0.1 or later, Google Chrome 3.0.195.27 or later
- **Outlook Web App Premium on Apple Mac OS X** Safari 3.1 or later, Firefox 3.0.1 or later
- **Outlook Web App Premium on Linux** Firefox 3.0.1 or later
- **Outlook Web App Light** Almost any other browser or operating system

> ***NOTE*** Even though browsers that run on operating systems other than Windows support Outlook Web App Premium, remember that it still has some limitations. For example, if you want to use the S/MIME control provided by Exchange for digital signatures or message encryption in Outlook Web App, you need to run Internet Explorer and Windows.

A full list of browsers that support Outlook Web App can be found at *http://help.outlook.com/en-us/140/bb899685.aspx*.

IMAP and POP3 Clients

Exchange Server 2010 also provides support for IMAP and POP3 protocols. Any IMAP4/POP3 client (such Outlook Express or Thunderbird) can be used. However, you need to consider that some native IMAP or POP3 clients such as MailX have problems with the Microsoft internal content-encoding. By default Exchange 2010 converts the content of message attachments to quoted-printable (QP) format. If you client has issues reading it you might need to use a different client. Most of the Windows or Mac OS IMAP/POP3 clients do not cause issues, but for some in the area of LINUX such as MailX you need to consider this.

Additional Resources

- Windows Server 2008 R2 Components: *http://www.microsoft.com/downloads/details.aspx?displaylang=en&FamilyID=64a5cc28-f8a1-4b30-a4a2-455c65bda8d7*
- How to disable certain Internet Protocol version 6 (IPv6) components in Windows Vista, Windows 7 and Windows Server 2008: *http://support.microsoft.com/kb/929852/*
- IPv6 for Microsoft Windows FAQ: *http://go.microsoft.com/fwlink/?LinkId=147465*

- Outlook Anywhere Scalability with Outlook 2007, Outlook 2003, and Exchange 2007: *http://technet.microsoft.com/en-us/library/cc540453(EXCHG.80).aspx*
- Exchange Load Generator 2010 Beta (64 bit): *http://www.microsoft.com/downloads/details.aspx?displaylang=en&FamilyID=cf464be7-7e52-48cd-b852-ccfc915b29ef*
- Sysinternals BgInfo Tool: *http://technet.microsoft.com/en-us/sysinternals/bb897557.aspx*
- Active Directory Logical Structure and Data Storage: *http://go.microsoft.com/fwlink/?LinkId=179859*
- Monitoring and Troubleshooting Active Directory Replication Using Repadmin: *http://www.microsoft.com/downloads/details.aspx?familyid=c6054092-ee1e-4b57-b175-5aabde591c5f&displaylang=en*
- The official Microsoft support statement for Exchange 2010 and SLD/Disjoint/Non-contiguous Namespaces: *http://msexchangeteam.com/archive/2009/10/27/452969.aspx*
- DNS Requirements for Installing Active Directory: *http://technet.microsoft.com/en-us/library/cc739159(WS.10).aspx*
- Language packs for Exchange 2010: *http://technet.microsoft.com/en-us/library/dd298152.aspx*
- Language pack bundle for Exchange 2010: *http://go.microsoft.com/fwlink/?LinkId=147077*
- Language codes as defined in ISO 639-1 codes: *http://en.wikipedia.org/wiki/List_of_ISO_639-1_codes*
- Exchange Server 2010 UM Language Packs: *http://www.microsoft.com/downloads/details.aspx?FamilyID=3fdf49db-cb84-4dfe-8b8b-b30178b1a514&displaylang=en*
- Configure the Windows Time Service on the Forest Root Domain Controller: *http://technet.microsoft.com/en-us/library/cc778920(WS.10).aspx*
- Wikipedia information about Microsoft Office 2010 for Mac OS X: *http://en.wikipedia.org/wiki/Microsoft_Office_2010_for_Mac*
- Exchange 2010 Outlook Web App Supported Browsers: *http://help.outlook.com/en-us/140/bb899685.aspx*

PART II

Designing Exchange Server 2010

CHAPTER 4

Client Access in Exchange 2010

In this chapter the various aspects of designing the Client Access Server role are described, starting with an in-detail explanation of the Client Access Server role including the RPC Client Access layer and the provision of the Availability and AutoDiscover services. This chapter will provide design guidelines for designing Client Access services with Exchange Server 2010, and will provide best practices for installing the Client Access Server role.

Client Access Server Architecture

You can already guess by looking at the name of this Exchange Server role that it enables a mailbox-enabled user to gain access to his or her mailbox using any of the supported Client Access protocols: MAPI/RPC, POP3, IMAP4, HTTP, and Exchange ActiveSync.

Client Access Server Features

The Client Access Server role has grown from previous versions. Microsoft introduced the Client Access Server role in Exchange 2007 to replace the previous situation where all mailbox clients either directly connected to the mailbox server or via a proxy. The mailbox server did all of the logic and rendering of data. A major architectural change came in Exchange 2007 and most of the Client Access protocols were consolidated on the Client Access Server. This included Outlook Web Access (OWA), IMAP4, POP3, Exchange Web Services, and Exchange ActiveSync. MAPI and WebDav clients still connected to the mailbox server directly.

Now in Exchange 2010, all business logic and data rendering takes place on the Client Access Server. Figure 4-1 illustrates all of the middle-tier services provided by the Exchange 2010 Client Access Server.

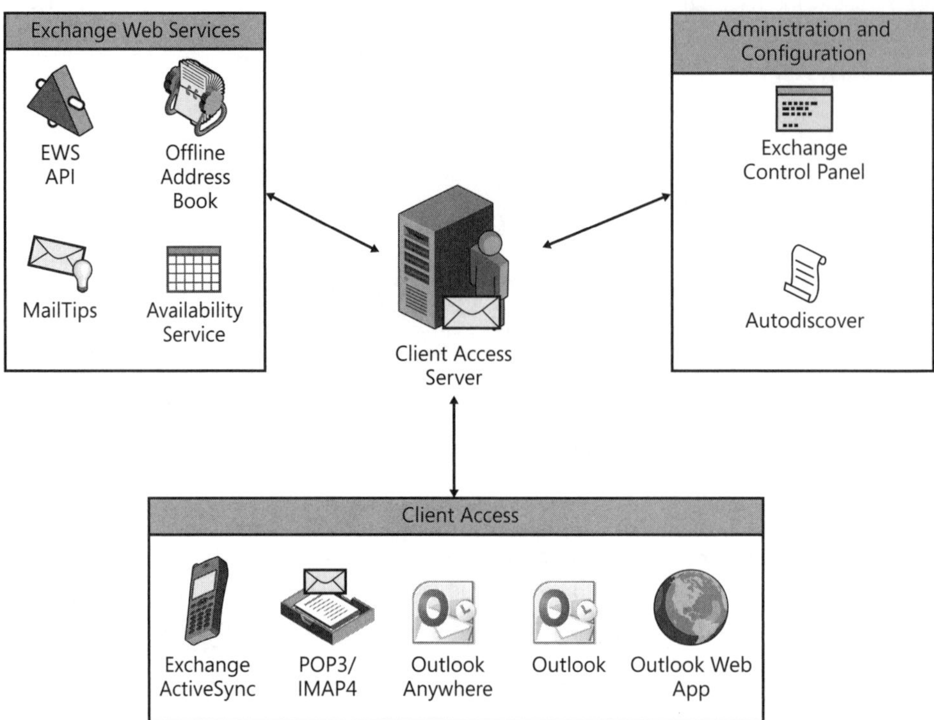

FIGURE 4-1 Client Access Server role

Along with this new architecture, the Client Access Server hosts a number of new features, as shown in Table 4-1.

TABLE 4-1 Client Access Server Features

FEATURE NAME	DESCRIPTION
Outlook Web App	Outlook Web App enables Web-based clients to access their mailboxes.
RPC Client Access	RPC Client Access enables MAPI clients to access their mailboxes (such as Microsoft Outlook).
POP3/IMAP4	POP3/IMAP4 enables clients such as Windows Live Mail to access their mailboxes.
Outlook Anywhere	Outlook Anywhere enables Microsoft Outlook 2003 or later clients to access their mailboxes using HTTP(S).
ActiveSync	ActiveSync enables mobile phones running Exchange ActiveSync to synchronize e-mail, contacts, calendar information, and tasks to the device.
Availability Service	The Availability Service provides clients with free/busy information.
Exchange Web Services (EWS)	Exchange Web Services provides an XML/SOAP interface for programmatic access to Exchange Server functionality.

FEATURE NAME	DESCRIPTION
MailTips	MailTips analyzes message properties, including the recipients, and notifies users of potential issues with the message before it is sent.
Exchange Control Panel (ECP)	The Exchange Control Panel is a Web-based management interface that allows administrators access to a set of administrative tasks. ECP also provides user self-service capabilities.
AutoDiscover	AutoDiscover enables Outlook 2007 and Outlook 2010 clients and Windows Mobile 6.1 or later clients to auto-configure user profile settings.
Address Book Service	The Address Book Service replaces DSProxy for handling directory-related requests.

Windows Services

Table 4-2 lists the Exchange services added to Windows when the Client Access Server role is installed.

TABLE 4-2 Exchange Services for the Client Access Server role

SERVICE	DESCRIPTION	BEST PRACTICE INFORMATION
Microsoft Exchange Active Directory Topology	This service reads information from all Active Directory partitions. The data is cached and then used by Exchange 2010 servers to discover the Active Directory site location of all Exchange services in the organization. It is also responsible for updating the site attribute of the Exchange server object in Active Directory.	Runs on all Exchange servers except Edge servers. Stopping this service is the quickest way to stop all Exchange services.
Microsoft Exchange Address Book	This service manages client address book connections and is dependent upon the Microsoft Exchange Active Directory Topology service.	This service is required to register the Client Access server as the Name Service Provider Interface (NSPI). This performs all directory connections for clients.
Microsoft Exchange File Distribution	This service is responsible for distributing the offline address book (OAB) files, unified messaging prompts, and group metrics files. This service is dependent on the Microsoft Exchange Active Directory Topology and Workstation services.	This service is required to distribute the OAB files from the OAB generation server to the Client Access server distribution points.

SERVICE	DESCRIPTION	BEST PRACTICE INFORMATION
Microsoft Exchange Forms-Based Authentication Service	Provides forms-based authentication to Outlook Web App and the Exchange Control Panel. This service has no dependencies.	If this service is stopped, OWA and ECP users cannot authenticate.
Microsoft Exchange IMAP4	Provides IMAP4 service to users. This service is dependent on the Microsoft Exchange Active Directory Topology service.	This service is set to Manual by default. It must be set to Automatic if IMAP4 clients are connecting to this Client Access server.
Microsoft Exchange Mailbox Replication	This service processes mailbox move requests and is dependent on the Microsoft Exchange Active Directory Topology service and the Net.Tcp port-sharing services.	This is an optional service.
Microsoft Exchange Monitoring	This service allows applications to call the Exchange diagnostic cmdlets. It has no dependencies.	This service should be started when you consider implementing monitoring tools such as System Center Operations Manager.
Microsoft Exchange POP3	Provides POP3 service to users. This service is dependent on the Microsoft Exchange Active Directory Topology service.	This service is set to Manual by default. It must be set to Automatic if POP3 clients are connecting to this Client Access server.
Microsoft Exchange Protected Service Host	Replaces services from the System Attendant functions in previous versions of Exchange.	
Microsoft Exchange Service Host	Used to do GroupMetrics calculations for MailTips and ensures ValidPorts registry keys for Outlook Anywhere.	
Microsoft Exchange RPC Client Access	This service manages client RPC connections and is dependent on the Microsoft Exchange Active Directory Topology service.	This is a required service for MAPI clients to connect to their mailbox data.

New Features

This section introduces several of the new or improved Client Access Server features.

Outlook Web App (OWA)

OWA has been renamed from Outlook Web Access in previous versions of Exchange. OWA allows users to access their mailboxes using a large number of Web browsers, including Internet Explorer 6.0+, Firefox, Safari, and Chrome. As with each new version of Exchange Server, OWA includes more enhancements and comes even closer to the full client experience. The following list highlights several of the new features:

- Conversation View
- MailTips
- Instant Messaging Integration with OCS 2007 R2
- Predefined Search Filters for quick search of folder contents
- Enhanced Right-Click
- Attach messages to messages

Another notable change is with OWA policies. Past versions of Exchange applied OWA policies against the IIS virtual directory. In Exchange 2010, the policy settings are now created at a global level, and can be applied per user. A default policy is created during role installation, but it is not applied to any mailboxes. The default policy enables all the options. OWA policies can be applied during a new user creation, or later on with the *Set-CasMailbox* cmdlet or EMC.

Service Pack 1 introduces a new look and feel to simplify the UI and provide a clean view that emphasizes content. The new interface scales well with different screen sizes and resolutions, particularly for Netbooks. Figure 4-2 shows an example of the new interface.

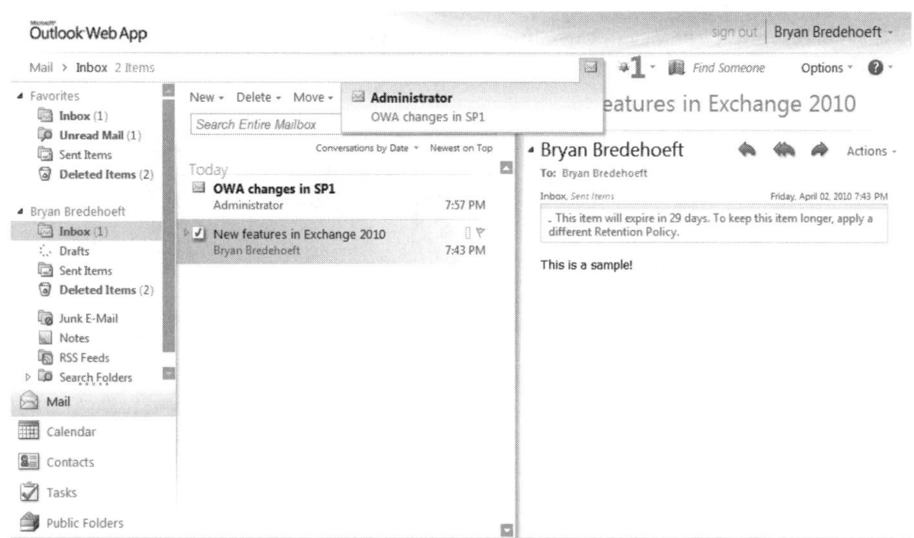

FIGURE 4-2 OWA SP1

Part of the new OWA experience is an updated options menu. The most frequently accessed options are now displayed in a drop-down menu, as shown in Figure 4-3. Additionally, users now have the ability to apply a theme to OWA.

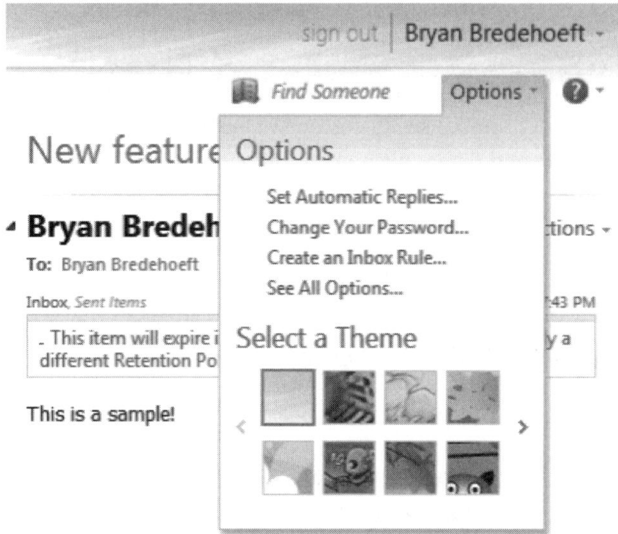

FIGURE 4-3 OWA themes

A very welcome addition in Service Pack 1 is the ability to print custom calendars in OWA. Users can view a printable calendar in Daily/Weekly/Monthly/Agenda views.

RPC Client Access

One of the major new architectural changes in Exchange 2010 is how RPC (or MAPI) clients access their mailbox and directory information. Figure 4-4 illustrates the new Exchange 2010 RPC architecture.

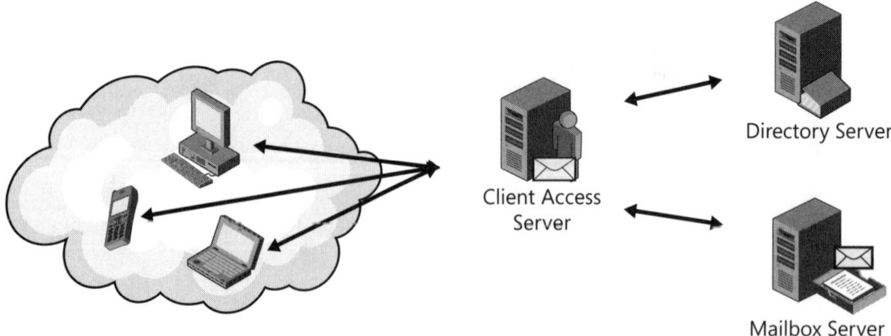

FIGURE 4-4 RPC Client Access changes

Previously, RPC clients such as Microsoft Outlook made a connection directly to the server running the Mailbox role. In Exchange 2010, the Client Access Server handles the task of processing all RPC requests in place of the Mailbox server. This is not 100-percent true because public folder connections still require direct connections to a Mailbox Server role after being authenticated with the Client Access Server, but these connections still use the Microsoft Exchange RPC Client Access Service on the Mailbox server.

These changes result in several benefits. The first advantage is that all Client Access uses a common route for mailbox access shown in Figure 4-5. This allows for consistent application of business logic and rules regardless of the client. Previously, clients either behaved differently or redundant code sat on multiple tiers. Features that take advantage of change include the Calendar Repair Assistant and the content conversion code.

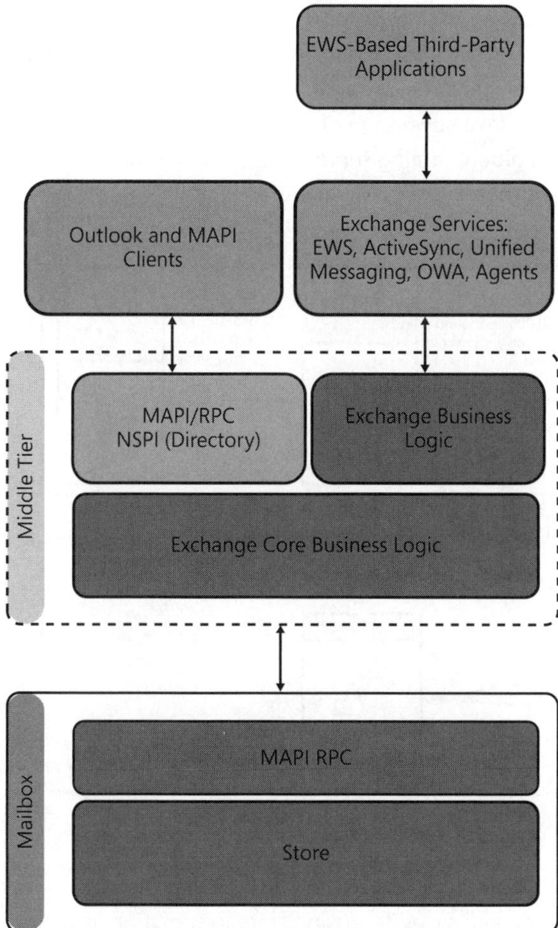

FIGURE 4-5 Middle tier

The second benefit of channeling client connections through a common path is that it makes more efficient use of network connections, and provides better scaling (more users per mailbox server). Using a 64-bit operating system allowed Exchange 2007 to scale better than previous versions. Removing the traditional bottlenecks (such as memory) allowed new bottlenecks to appear. TCP connections became a limiting factor when trying to scale mailbox servers to large numbers of users. A connection is made up from the source IP address, source port, destination IP address, and destination port. A common issue occurred between the Client Access server and the Mailbox server. On Windows 2003, the Client Access server can use only a single source port per IP address when making an outbound connection to another computer. After the source port has been used, it is not available for any other outbound connections on the server. This becomes an issue when large numbers of connections are required, such as when Outlook Anywhere is heavily used. This was addressed in Windows 2008 by allowing the source port to be used once per source IP address. By adding additional IP addresses, the Client Access server could scale past 60,000 connections. However, DSProxy—used to provide directory access to Outlook clients when connected over Outlook Anywhere—did not take advantage of this change, and was still limited to 60,000 outbound connections to global catalog servers. Figure 4-6 shows the Exchange 2007 connection architecture and where the TCP connection limitations were.

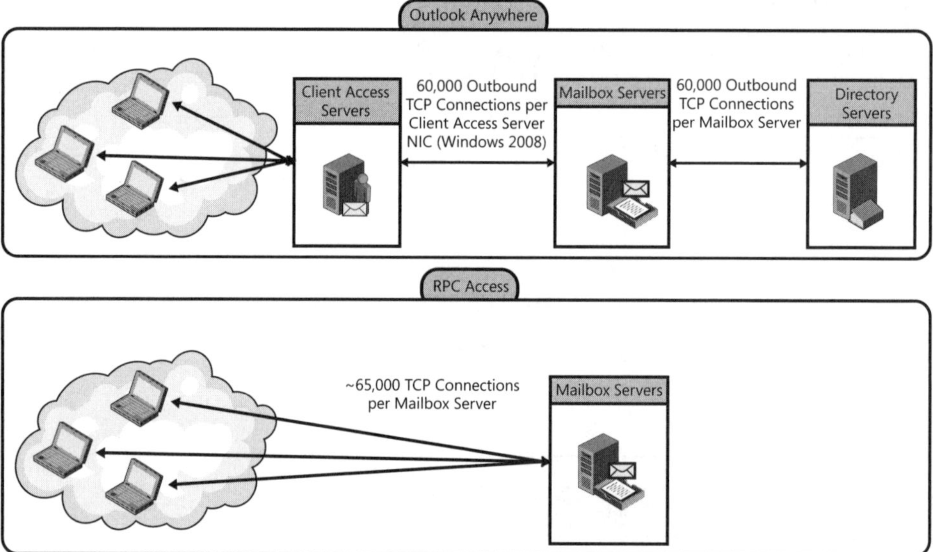

FIGURE 4-6 Exchange 2007 Client Access scale

Compare this to the Exchange 2010 situation shown in Figure 4-7. The Client Access server now disconnects the user's connection and saves its session state information. Instead of maintaining a connection for each user between the Client Access server and Mailbox server, there is a shared pool of 100 connections. If the user's connection is not active, it just stays in a disconnected state. This design allows for the Client Access server to scale better without having to add additional NICs. The number of shared connections is not configurable or exposed to administrators, and Microsoft did significant testing during product development that suggests companies will not need to change this value. Even though Figure 4-7 shows a Client Access Array, this mechanism operates in the same way with a single Client Access server.

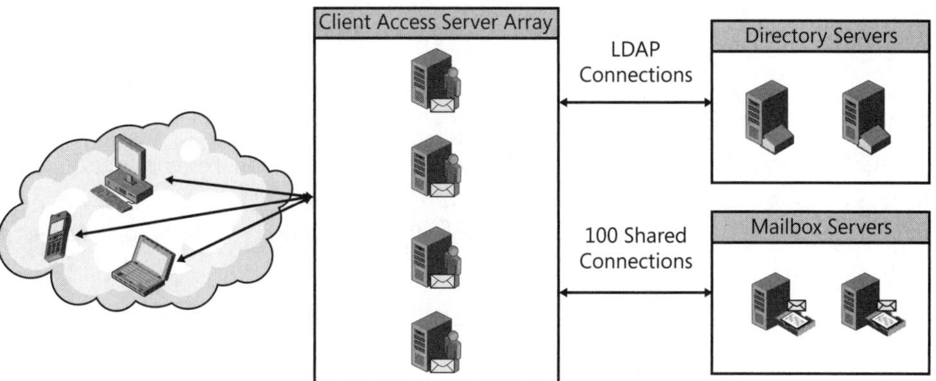

FIGURE 4-7 Exchange 2010 Client Access Scale

This architectural change also impacts directory access. The Client Access server now implements the Address Book Service to replace the DSProxy interface on servers with the Mailbox role. In Exchange 2000 through 2007, DSProxy was a true proxy and the global catalog provided the NSPI endpoint when clients connected using Outlook Anywhere. In Exchange 2010, the Client Access server is the endpoint and makes calls on behalf of the client to the global directory. Why the significant change? The DSProxy implementation caused a few issues. One concerned Outlook Anywhere and split connections, described in detail later in this chapter. At a high level, split connections could cause a user with Outlook Anywhere to end up with directory service calls being dropped.

Another common issue was that Outlook frequently connected to a domain controller that did not hold a writable copy of a group that users wanted to manage so they got errors when trying to perform group management. Several changes were implemented over the years to address multi-domain DL updates, but the only completely effective solution was to move all users and distribution lists to the same domain. For most companies, this is simply not possible, so they end up creating a complete group management portal, or using operations processes to control user requests. The Address Book Service detects modification of DL membership, delegate management, and certificate management and calls the appropriate cmdlets to make the necessary changes on a domain controller that has a writeable copy of the object. The service uses RBAC security to ensure that the user has the required permissions to make the change. Another great benefit of the Address Book Service is that future reads from the client session go to the same domain controller and the change is reflected immediately.

Previously, users hidden from the Global Address List (GAL) could not create profiles. The changes in Exchange 2010 also solve this known issue. Now, users can create a profile whether or not they are hidden from the GAL.

Finally, moving Client Access helps with faster and more seamless failovers, because the client maintains a connection with the Client Access server, the client is not aware of which mailbox server is hosting the active database. Therefore, it is possible to failover a single database instead of requiring the entire storage group, as in Exchange 2007. Microsoft's target failover time before users are reconnected to their mailboxes in Exchange 2010 is fewer than 30 seconds; CCR was about 2 minutes.

Exchange Control Panel

The Exchange Control Panel (ECP) is a completely new Web application. For end users, it provides a way to configure mail options, as shown in Figure 4-8. ECP is not only used seamlessly with OWA, but it is also used in Outlook 2010 when a user manages voicemail options.

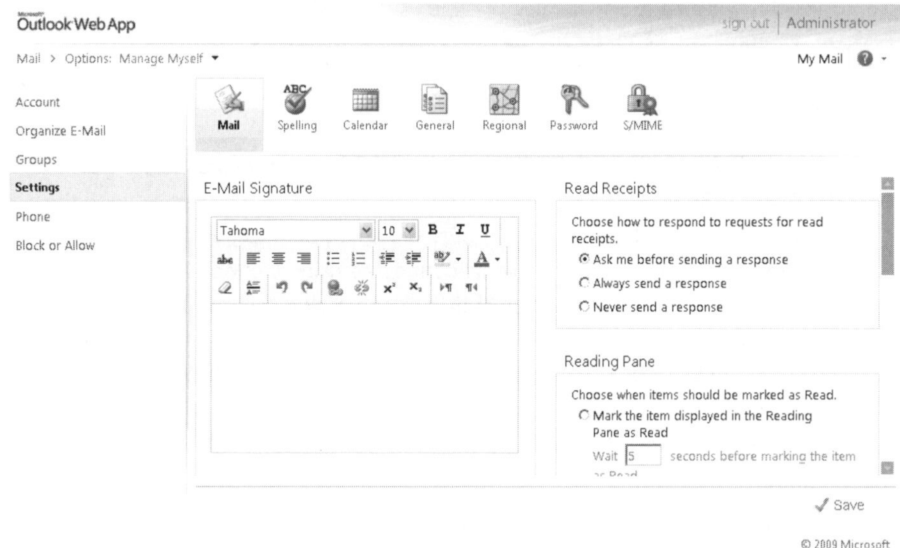

FIGURE 4-8 ECP user options

ECP is not only for end users, but is also used by administrators for organization-level management. Figures 4-9 and 4-10 show some of the functionality provided to administrators. Figure 4-9 illustrates how an administrator can create and edit mailboxes, create groups and contacts, and administer roles. Service Pack 1 adds support for Syndicated Admins. Prior to Service Pack 1, administrators must have a mailbox to access ECP. With Syndicated Admins it is now possible to log on to ECP without having a mailbox. For example, you can use the *Add-RoleGroupMemeber* cmdlet to grant an administrator account to the '*OrganizationConfiguration*' role. This admin account does not have a mailbox, but is able to open the ECP and perform administrative operations. Pre-SP1, if the account did not have a mailbox, the *Add-RoleGroupMember* cmdlet would fail. This is useful for companies that require administrators to have two accounts for security role separation and do not want administrative accounts to be mail-enabled.

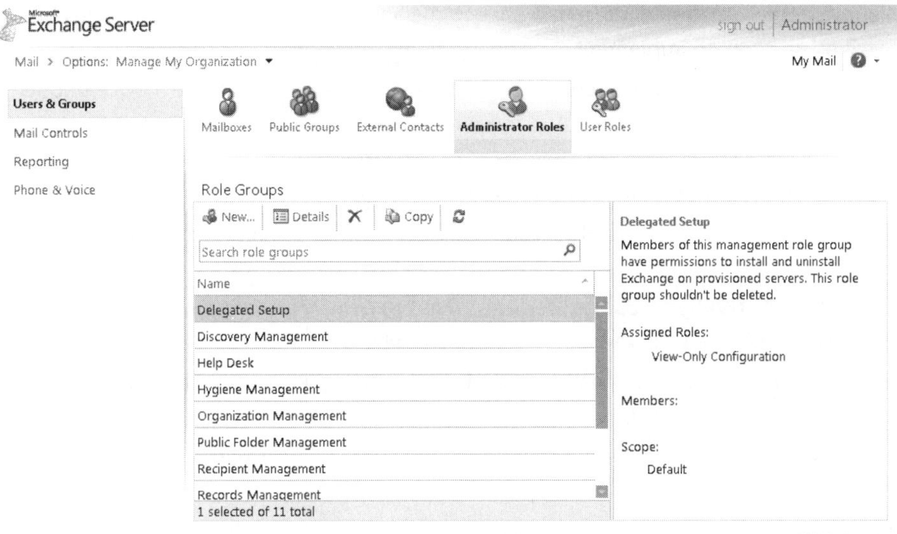

FIGURE 4-9 ECP management

Figure 4-10 shows an example of the new multi-mailbox search feature that allows users who have the Discovery Management role to perform searches based on keywords or other criteria.

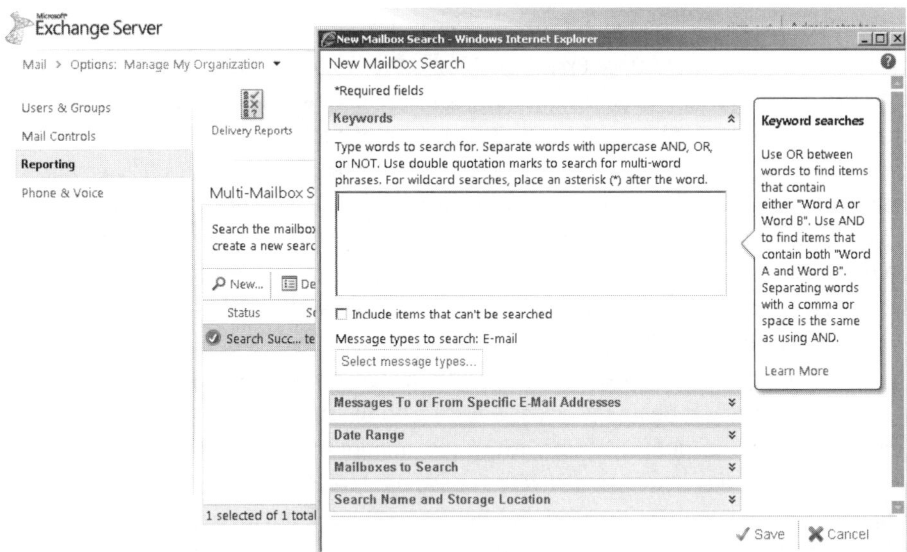

FIGURE 4-10 Exchange Control Panel Multi-Mailbox Search

Exchange ActiveSync

Exchange ActiveSync (EAS) is the Exchange feature that syncs mailbox information with mobile phones. Mobile clients can sync e-mail, contacts, calendar data, and tasks. Microsoft has licensed ActiveSync technology to other mobile phone manufacturers, such as Apple Inc.,

Nokia, Palm, Google, and Sony Ericsson. It is up to the licensee to decide which features of the ActiveSync protocol to implement.

One feature of ActiveSync is DirectPush technology. DirectPush allows the mobile phone to maintain a connection to Exchange and receive updates in real time as opposed to polling the server for new mail.

Exchange 2010 includes the ability to generate ActiveSync Reports. An administrator runs the *Export-ActiveSyncLog* cmdlet to generate a report with the following information included:

- **Exchange ActiveSync Usage Report** Used to give information related to total bytes sent and received, item counts, and item types.
- **Hits Report** Used to see the total number of sync requests per hour, and number of unique devices syncing.
- **HTTP Status Report** Used to summarize the overall performance of the Client Access server.
- **Policy Compliance Report** Reports on the number of fully compliant, partially compliant, and non-compliant devices syncing with the organization. Compliancy depends on the level of enforcement the mobile device implements.
- **User Agent List** Reports the total number of unique users sorted by the mobile phone's operating system.

Administrators now have access to a wealth of information that helps with capacity planning and service level management.

Another great advancement since Exchange 2007 is the security policies for mobile devices. In Exchange 2007, an administrator has the ability to define a security policy and enforce the policy on a per-user basis. This is problematic for users who use multiple devices because the policy affected every device. If not all of the user's devices fully enabled all of the security features, the user would have to either have all devices enabled or no devices enabled. Exchange 2007 gave administrators control at the device level, using deviceID to define ActiveSync device access rules. Exchange 2010 expands this functionality with several new capabilities. An administrator can define the default action for when a new device attempts its initial sync. The possible actions are to allow, block, or quarantine the device. If an administrator configures quarantine, the user receives a notification that the request for device syncing is being reviewed, while the administrative account configured will receive notification to approve the request. You configure this feature with the *Set-ActiveSyncOrganizationSetting* cmdlet with the *DefaultAccessLevel* and *AdminMailRecipients* parameters. You can then configure specific device policies that override the default by using the *new-ActiveSyncDeviceAccessRule* cmdlet. In Service Pack 1, administration of policies and devices was added to the ECP. Again, you must set the access level. Additionally the rule can be based on the following characteristics:

- Device model
- Device type
- Device operating system
- Device user agent

Users and administrators can view this information for existing ActiveSync partnerships using OWA to view the mobile phone details. For example, a phone partnership may show the following:

- Device Name: Touch Pro
- Device Model: HTC Touch Pro T7272
- Device Type: PocketPC
- Device OS: Windows CE 5.2.19965
- Device User agent: MSFT-PPC/5.2.19965

The administrator can use this information to build a policy specific to this device type, name, and so on. For example, if the administrator wants to always allow PocketPC device types under any circumstance, she would use the following cmdlet:

```
New-ActiveSyncDeviceAccessRule -QueryString PocketPC -Characteristic
DeviceModel -AccessLevel Allow
```

With this policy in place, all PocketPCs will be allowed to sync regardless of specific features the phone supports. Currently, these policies can only be managed through EMS cmdlets. The default ActiveSync policy allows any device to synchronize.

Internet Calendar Sharing

An interesting new feature in Service Pack 1 is for the ability to share calendars externally without federation. Similar to federated sharing, an administrator must enable and configure the feature to be available. Once enabled, users can share their calendar with anyone through OWA. By default, Internet Calendar Sharing is disabled. There are two types of URLs that can be published: restricted and public. With restricted URLs, the URL is obfuscated and must be sent to the external user directly. Public certificates, on the other hand, can be searchable on the Internet. This is shown with examples in Table 4-3.

TABLE 4-3 Internet Calendar URLs

PUBLISHING TYPE	EXAMPLE
Restricted	*http://mail.contoso.com/owa/calendar/ 8ef9b849292043c18afbc17c09fd6eb4@.contoso.com/ addb62995eae4f7ab3d06308d0eff28e/calendar.html*
Public	*http://mail.contoso.com/owa/calendar/user@.contoso.com/ published_calendar/calendar.html*

Additional security measures are in place to protect Exchange because this feature exposes data to anonymous external users. First, the feature was created with total isolation from other Exchange resources. Sharing was implemented with a dedicated virtual directory. Second, the application uses a separate application pool. Third, the http access is limited to the dedicated virtual directory. Finally, throttling is enabled to prevent excessive resource consumption. Requests are throttling both on requests per mailbox and limits on CPU utilization per Client Access Server.

Client Access Throttling Policies

At times, clients consume server resources to the point where everyone is affected. For example, some third-party search programs can send a large number of RPC requests when they perform indexing. The sheer number of RPC requests from these clients can cause performance problems on the backend. Exchange 2010 uses client-throttling policies to prevent this situation. A default client-throttling policy is configured when the Exchange organization is created. The default policy can be customized or additional policies can be created. The default policy settings are shown in Table 4-4. Do not make changes directly to the default policies—create a copy of the default and make the changes to the new policy. This will enable an administrator to quickly revert back to defaults if the need arises.

TABLE 4-4 Default Client-Throttling Policy Settings

PROPERTY	SETTING	COMMENT
EASMaxConcurrency	10	The number of concurrent connections an ActiveSync user can have running concurrently.
EWSMaxConcurrency	10	The number of concurrent connections an Exchange Web Services user can have running concurrently.
EWSFastSearchTimeoutInSeconds	60	The length of time, in seconds, searches made by EWS run before timing out.
OWAMaxConcurrency	5	The number of concurrent connections an Outlook Web App user can have running concurrently.
POPMaxConcurrency	20	The number of concurrent connections a POP3 user can have running concurrently.
PowerShellMaxConcurrency	18	For Remote Windows PowerShell users, the number of remote Windows PowerShell concurrent sessions. For Exchange Web Services, the number of concurrent cmdlet executions that a user can have at the same time.
RCAMaxConcurrency	20	The number of concurrent connections an RPC Client Access user can have running concurrently.
CPUStartPercent	75	The per-process CPU percentage at which users begin to be backed off.

NOTE It is a best practice to make sure that no throttling policy parameters are set to *$null* (no limit). This prevents users from unintentionally placing a high load on the server.

INSIDE TRACK

BlackBerry and Performance Impacts

Robin Thomas
Program Manager, Exchange Mailbox, Microsoft Corporation

Soon after Exchange 2010 was released, customers who used RIM BlackBerry Enterprise Server (BES) discovered that BlackBerry devices may experience some issues caused by the new throttling functionality. For example, users who made a change to calendar items, such as deleting an appointment, would not have that change replicated to Exchange. Also, if a BlackBerry user was sent a meeting invite, it would not show up on the device. To fix this issue, you need to disable client throttling. Although disabling throttling completely will certainly fix the problem, you are giving up a lot of protection from this new feature. A better solution is to create a new policy and assign it only to the BES service account. You can create and apply the appropriate throttling policy for the BES service account by typing these two commands into EMS.

1. New-ThrottlingPolicy BES –RCAMaxConcurrency $null -RCAPercentTimeInCAS $null –RCAPercentTimeInMailboxRPC $null –RCAPercentTimeInAD $null
2. Set-Mailbox BESAdmin –ThrottlingPolicy BES

BES is the name of the throttling policy and can be anything. BESAdmin is the BES service account.

At this point, you can run *Get-ThrottlingPolicy BES* to see the details. BES servers access Exchange using *RpcClientAccess service,* so the only values that are relevant here are RCA*.

For Exchange 2010 RTM, a second configuration change is required for BlackBerry Enterprise Servers to work correctly. In Exchange 2010 SP1 and later, this configuration is covered via the previously-mentioned throttling policy. By default, Exchange only allows 50 concurrent address book connections. The BES account makes lookups on behalf of the users, so you may exhaust this connection limit very quickly. RIM recommends changing the *MaxSessionsPerUser* value to 100,000 (this is located in the microsoft.exchange.addressbook.service.exe.config file). Unfortunately, unlike the throttling policy, you cannot configure this setting per user, so it will raise the limit for all users. You may want to start with a smaller number and increase as your number of BlackBerry devices increases.

For more information, visit RIM's Web site for configuring the BlackBerry Enterprise Server with Exchange 2010 help document: ***http://docs.blackberry.com/en/admin/deliverables/12070/Configuring_Exchange_2010_environ_962756_11.jsp.***

Service Pack 1 includes several improvements for client throttling. In RTM code, the client that has been throttled will end up with failed requests. This can result in poor user experience. Take, for example, an Entourage client that is syncing a mailbox and is constantly going over budget. Any other user requests, such as a name resolution, will also fail. In Service Pack 1, however, instead of failing requests, the request is added to an asynchronous queue that will delay processing. This sleep time is equal to a backoff time plus 1 millisecond. At the time of this writing, the backoff time had not been finalized. For batch operations, processing will pause until the caller has regained 1 millisecond of budget. Then, processing will continue starting with the item left off, and it will stream the items back to the caller as they are processed.

MailTips

MailTips is a very useful new feature that will make a lot of users happy. It is important to first understand the feature before we look at the mechanics and performance impact of turning it on.

How many times have you sent an e-mail only to receive an out-of-office notification? MailTips provides feedback while composing a message, *before* you hit send. Figure 4-11 shows an example of an e-mail with two informational messages. MailTips lets the user know that he is sending mail to a distribution list that has a large number of members. Also, Jeffrey is out of the office, so the user may want to send the message to one of Jeffrey's peers.

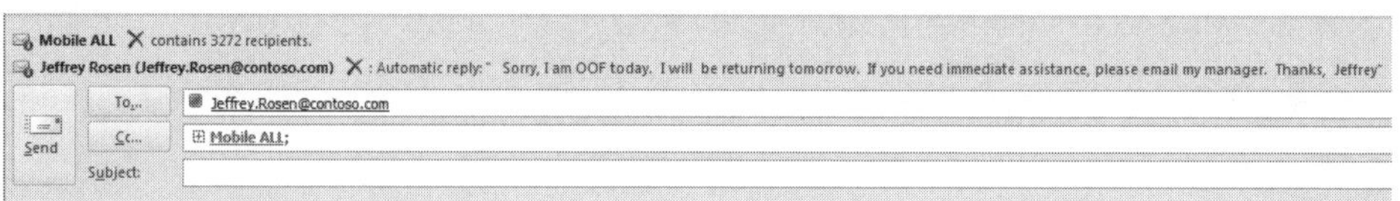

FIGURE 4-11 MailTips example

Keep in mind that MailTips is not a security measure, meaning that is does not prevent users from taking action. Rather, the MailTips feature only provides useful information to help users make better decisions before hitting Send. There are a number of prebuilt MailTips, as listed in Table 4-5.

TABLE 4-5 Exchange 2010 MailTips

MAILTIP	DESCRIPTION	DATA SOURCE	AVAILABLE OFFLINE
Invalid Internal Recipient	Informs the user that a user does not exist for an e-mail address within the organization.	Active Directory	No
Mailbox Full	A recipient has a full mailbox.	Mailbox Store	No
Automatic Replies	A recipient has an automatic reply enabled (such as out-of-office).	Mailbox Store	No

MAILTIP	DESCRIPTION	DATA SOURCE	AVAILABLE OFFLINE
Custom	A recipient has a custom MailTip enabled.	Active Directory	Yes
Restricted Recipient	A recipient has a mail delivery restriction configured.	Mailbox Store	No
External Recipients	A recipient is external or part of a distribution list.	Group Metrics	Yes
Large Audience	A distribution list contains more than 25 members (configurable).	Group Metrics	Yes
Moderated Recipient	A recipient is enabled for moderation.		Yes
Reply-All on BCC	The user replies all to a message on which he or she was bcc'd.		
Oversize Message	The message is larger than the organizational limit, maximum send size on the user's mailbox, maximum receive size on the recipient's mailbox, or maximum request length setting for OWA.		Yes

MailTips are triggered by the mail client during one of the following operations:

- Adding an attachment
- Adding a recipient
- Reply or Reply-All
- Opening a message from the Drafts folder

MailTips processing occurs in a background thread, so it will not impact the user working with their message. In other words, users do not have to wait for MailTips to finish processing before they send a message, if that is what they want to do.

Figure 4-12 provides a deeper look at the MailTips architecture. The source for MailTips data comes from Active Directory, Exchange Mailbox Server, and Group Metrics data.

The Groups Metrics process is responsible for collecting and recording information about the size of distribution lists and external recipients. This information is used for the external recipient and large audience MailTips.

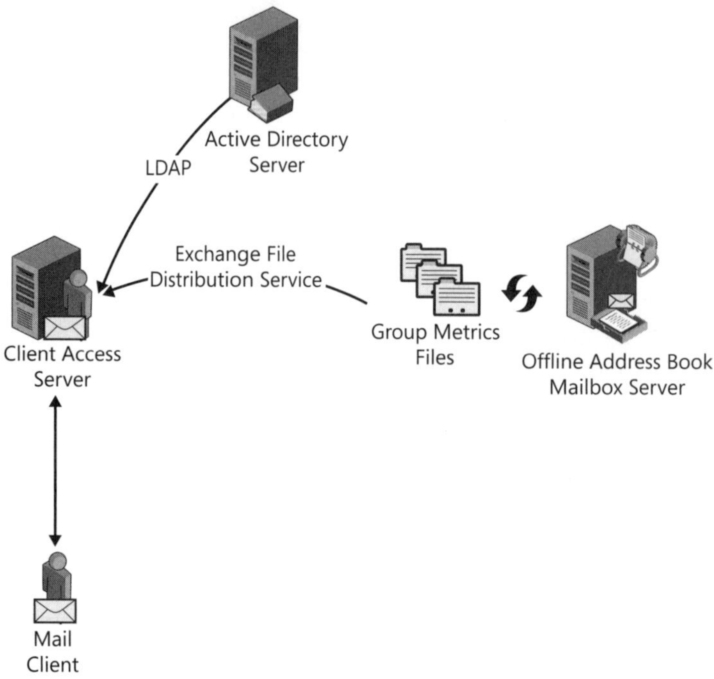

FIGURE 4-12 MailTips architecture

Groups Metrics generation happens by default on the Mailbox server that is responsible for creating the OAB and can be assigned to another Mailbox server, which is important in a large organization. On Sunday, a full generation runs for every group (both static and dynamic) within a random time two hours from midnight. Each day, the process will generate incremental results. The day for full generation is hard-coded, but the generation time can be set using the *set-mailboxserver* property named *GroupMetricsGenerationTime* (24-hour format). If you change the *GroupMetricsGenerationTime* property, the next generation occurs according to the old schedule. Subsequent generations will start at the new time. You can force regeneration by restarting the Microsoft Exchange Service Host service or rebooting the server. The process creates files by default in the <Exchange_Install_Path>\GroupMetrics. The files created are shown in Table 4-6.

TABLE 4-6 GroupMetrics Files

FILENAME	DESCRIPTION
GroupMetrics-<date>T<time>.bin	Binary file containing the membership and external members count
GroupMetrics-<servername>.xml	XML file containing information about the Group Metrics generation server
ChangedGroups.txt	Plaintext file containing the list of groups that were updated since the last time Group Metrics was run

Every eight hours, the Microsoft Exchange File Distribution Service on the Client Access server builds a list of Mailbox servers that have Group Metrics generation enabled. By default, the organizational configuration setting for Group Metrics is enabled. This means that Group Metrics will be generated on every mailbox server that generates an OAB and will also generate Group Metrics data and be included in the list. In addition, the list includes mailbox servers that are explicitly enabled for GroupMetrics generation. The property *GroupMetricsGenerationEnabled* is used to manually enable generation for a Mailbox server and is set to false by default. After the list is created, the Client Access server will pull the Group Metrics data from the best server. The best server is based on Active Directory sites and link costs. One option is to leave *GroupMetricsGenerationEnabled* set to false and let the Client Access server use the OAB topology. This is one less topology that needs to be designed and maintained. For organizations that do not use OABs or need more control, the option still exists to create your own topology.

To support offline clients, the OAB was extended to have MailTips data. Table 4-5 lists which MailTips are available offline.

The process for evaluating MailTips is shown in Figure 4-13.

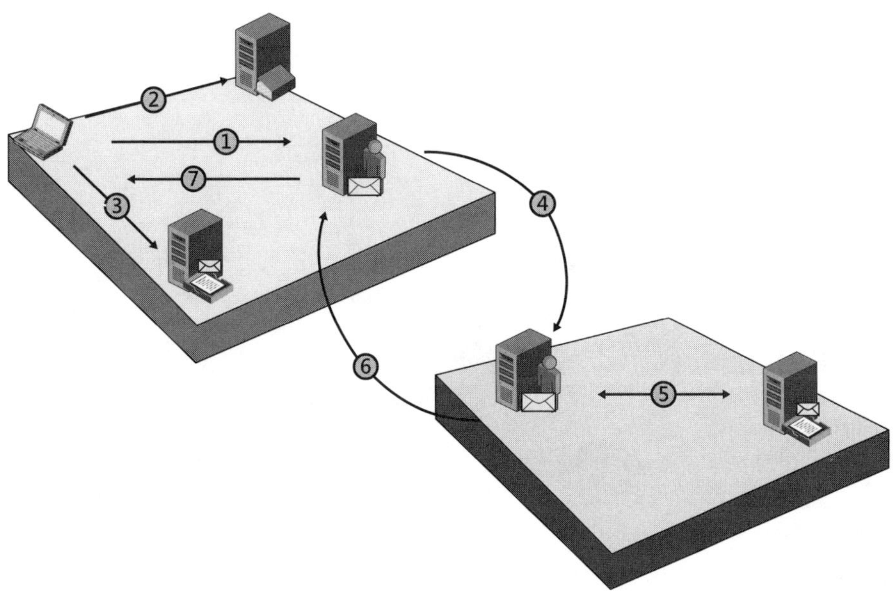

FIGURE 4-13 MailTips evaluation process

1. The mail client makes a request to the local Client Access server.
2. The Client Access server retrieves data from Active Directory and reads the Group Metrics data (locally).
3. For local recipients in the message header, the Client Access server queries the Mailbox server.
4. For each remote recipient, the Client Access server makes a request to the remote recipient's Client Access server.

5. The remote Client Access server makes RPC requests for data from the remote Mailbox server.
6. The remote Client Access server returns MailTips information about the remote recipients to the local Client Access server.
7. The Client Access server returns the MailTips information back to the client.

To limit performance impact, you should be aware of a few constraints. First, only messages with less than 200 recipients will be evaluated for MailTips. Second, individuals in a distribution group are not separately evaluated. Finally, the MailTips for Automatic Replies and Mailbox Full are reevaluated every two hours for draft messages that are left open for extended periods when being composed. This ensures a user has fresh information when they leave a message open for a long period of time.

Planning Client Access to Exchange

When planning Client Access Server architectures, you need to consider several points. Figure 4-14 shows the components—the physical architecture, the certificates and namespaces, and site resiliency requirements—that define a design.

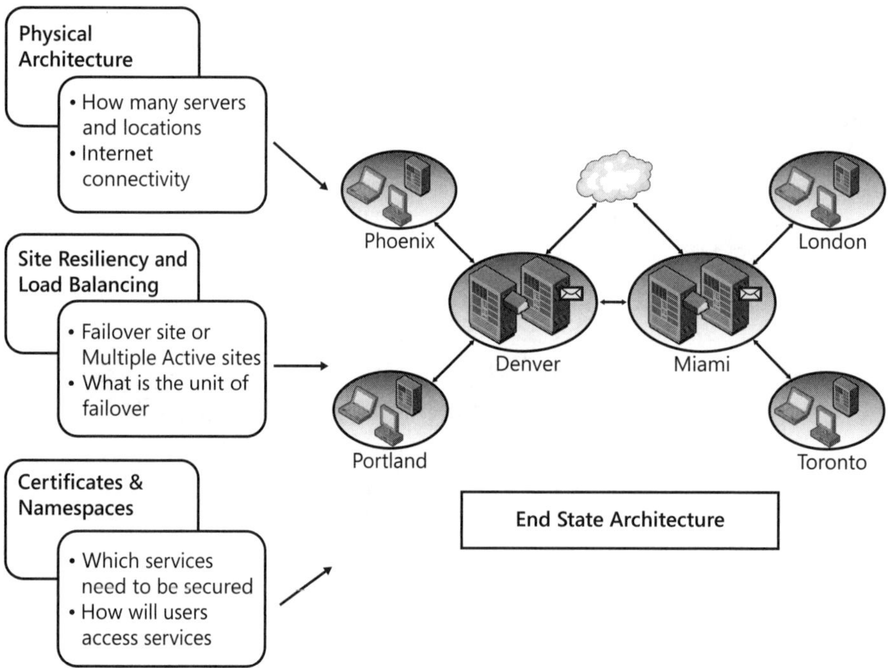

FIGURE 4-14 Client Access Server planning

What is namespace planning? As you will see, the term *namespace* can be applied to many different things. Recall that Chapter 3, "Exchange Environmental Considerations," had some discussions on namespace planning for Active Directory and Client Access. The options discussed were consolidated datacenter, single namespace with proxy site, single namespace with multiple sites, regional, and multiple forests. Namespaces can apply to other objects, such as Active Directory site design, certificate planning, or how users access their mailboxes (OWA, OA, POP3, and so on).

Namespace in general refers to any name you assign to your servers, a group of servers, a site, an Internet POP, and more. It refers to the names you configure as internal URL and external URL to allow users to find the servers that they need to connect to when they want to for download the OAB, retrieving Free and Busy information, and changing UM settings for a mailbox in your organization. It also includes properties such as the common name on a certificate and any additional subject alternative names set for those certificates as you begin to publish your Client Access services both inside and outside your network.

The Client Access Server, unlike other roles (such as Transport), *needs* to be configured with suitable certificates, load-balanced URLs, and other settings before it will work correctly for all but the simplest environments. Because each design may differ in requirements and complexity, no one design fits every situation.

You have to plan your namespace usage if any of the following are true:

- You are not able to take advantage of split DNS, which prevents you from using the same names to gain access to your servers on the inside and from the outside.
- You want to introduce load balancing and fault tolerance by having multiple Client Access servers in one site.
- You have multiple Active Directory sites and you need to make sure your clients retrieve information from the correct site.
- You have different clients accessing Exchange.

Client Access Services and Physical Architecture

Understanding Client Access planning starts with an understanding of each service and how clients access their mailbox data given different physical topologies.

AutoDiscover

AutoDiscover plays an important role in creating users' mail profiles and providing the client URLs for features such as free/busy, Unified Messaging, and the OAB. Because AutoDiscover information is refreshed when the client starts and at regular intervals (every 60 minutes), it provides a mechanism to move a mailbox around and not have to manually reconfigure every mail client. This interval can be changed with the *Set-OutlookProvider* by setting the *TTL* parameter to the number of hours for the interval. However, Windows Mobile devices can use AutoDiscover for its initial profile creation, but it does not reconfigure the client once the profile has been created.

The client finds the URL for AutoDiscover differently based on whether the client has internal access or external access.

INTERNAL AUTODISCOVER

Internal clients are clients that are domain joined and can successfully query an Active Directory server for AutoDiscover information. Figure 4-15 shows the process internal clients use for AutoDiscover.

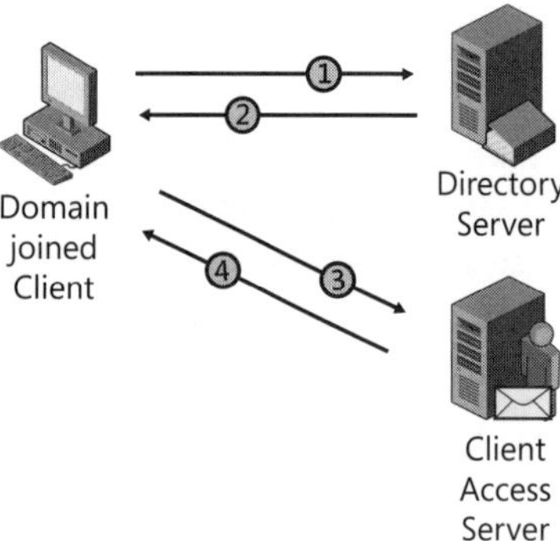

FIGURE 4-15 Internal AutoDiscover process

1. Clients search Active Directory for a service connection point object (SCP).
2. Active Directory returns a SCP that includes the location of the client's nearest AutoDiscover service.
3. The client securely (HTTPS) requests AutoDiscover information.
4. The Client Access server returns the best available service URLs for the client request.

An SCP object is created in Active Directory during the Client Access server's installation with an *AutoDiscoverServiceInternalURI* value equal to that of the FQDN of the server itself. The *AutodiscoverSiteScope* property is also configured with the Active Directory site that the host was in when the Client Access Server role was installed. This property defines the Active Directory sites that the Client Access server provides coverage for. These properties are never changed automatically, even if the host moves to a different Active Directory site. It is critical to change this property if your standard build process is to install servers and move them to a new Active Directory site when servers are placed into production. As you will see in the example in Figure 4-16, failure to correct the *AutodiscoverSiteScope* property will result in a Client Access server never being used, potentially being overburdened, or a non-optimal server being selected.

Another key concept to understand is that the client attempts to connect to the Client Access server closest to the client computer making the request, but the URLs and configuration the server returns to the client are for a Client Access server in an Active Directory site closest to the user's mailbox.

Few organizations will have large numbers of Active Directory sites, but in the event your organization does, you will meet the upper limit of the *AutoDiscoverSiteScope* property of the SCP object, which can store about 800 entries. If you try to go over this limit your *set-ClientAccessServer* cmdlet will return an ADMIN_LIMIT_EXCEEDED error. One possible workaround is if you have an Active Directory site with more than one Client Access server, you can split up the list among them. For example, assign 400 to one Client Access server and 400 to the other. This only works if you also change the *AutoDiscoverServiceInternalURI* parameter to reference a load-balanced name that includes all Client Access servers within an Active Directory site. This is discussed further when we discuss load balancing later in the chapter.

> **NOTE** **If you have a large number of sites that do not have Exchange servers, check out Brad Hugh's blog for a script that automates site assignment:** ***http://blogs.msdn.com/brad_hughes/archive/2008/05/20/autodiscover-and-client-only-sites-revisited.aspx.***

Figure 4-16 has three Active Directory sites, with Client Access servers and Mailbox servers are located in sites A and B. Outlook 2007 clients are located in all sites. By default, the *AutoDiscoverSiteScope* for the Client Access servers in site A is set to site A. The *AutoDiscoverSiteScope* for the Client Access servers in site B is set to site B. The client computers in site A will only AutoDiscover to Client Access servers in site A. The client computers in Site B will only AutoDiscover to Client Access servers in site B. Clients in Site C will AutoDiscover to Client Access servers in either site A or site B because none of the Client Access servers is specifically configured to cover site C. This could mean a client in one country could AutoDiscover to a Client Access server overseas, possibly resulting in a poor user experience. To correct this issue, set the *AutoDiscoverSiteScope* on the Client Access servers in site B to cover sites B and C. Clients in those sites will only use the Client Access servers in Site B for AutoDiscover. This is the optimal setup for this topology.

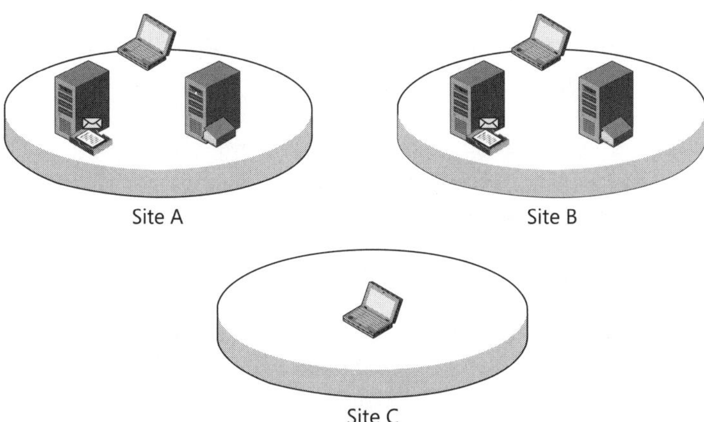

FIGURE 4-16 *AutoDiscoverSiteScope* example

Remember that the configuration information the Client Access server returns is for the Client Access server closest to the user's mailbox, regardless of the location of the client computer. All subsequent AutoDiscover requests still go to the Client Access server closest to the client computer—not the Client Access server closest to the mailbox.

To achieve this configuration you would add the AD site names by running a command such as the following:

```
Set-ClientAccessServer -Identity SiteACAS -AutoDiscoverSiteScope "Site A", "Site C"
```

Another problem will arise with the default configuration. If the site contains multiple Client Access servers, Outlook does not automatically load-balance its connections among the available hosts. Remember that Outlook receives a list of SCP records from Active Directory and will attempt to connect in the order it was received. When Active Directory generates the list, it orders the hosts by creation date of the SCP record (created during the Client Access server installation). The combination of these two operations means the one Client Access server (the oldest Client Access server) will handle all of the AutoDiscover traffic in that site. Additionally, the service URLs returned by the Client Access server are not equally load-balanced either. They are randomly chosen from all the Client Access servers within the mailbox server site.

The solution is to change the SCP record to provide a load balanced URL for AutoDiscover. To enable this, use the *set-ClientAccessServer* cmdlet with the *AutoDiscoverServiceInternalUri* property. Of course, this means you will need a load-balancing mechanism, such as Windows Network Load Balancing (NLB), round robin DNS, or a hardware load balancer.

This load-balanced name is another example of a namespace that you need to consider and plan for. In this case it is a namespace that is common for all of the Client Access server within a single Active Directory site.

INSIDE TRACK

Service Connection Points and AutoDiscover

Greg Taylor
Senior PM, Exchange Product Team, Microsoft Corporation

The way Outlook uses SCP records to find the closest AutoDiscover Service becomes even more of an exercise in namespace planning if you choose to install Exchange Server 2010 into an existing Active Directory site that already contains Exchange Server 2007 servers.

It becomes a challenge when a user's mailbox is on an Exchange 2010 mailbox server because this means a 2010 Client Access server must be used to service the user's AutoDiscover request. Exchange 2007 SP2 introduced some code to redirect any requests for 2010 users to a 2010 Client Access server, which is great, but once you understand the logic, as explained in this chapter, it raises some questions.

Remember, in any SCP lookup the client gets back a list of Client Access servers to query: either all those *in-site*, meaning the *SiteScope* attribute matches the AD site of the client computer, or all other Client Access servers *out-of-site*, meaning all the others. The client then attempts to connect the Client Access server at the top of that list, which will always be the oldest.

In a mixed 2007/2010 Active Directory site, the oldest Client Access server will almost always be a 2007 Client Access server (unless your deployment went down a very interesting or bizarre route). So the oldest 2007 Client Access server will get all the AutoDiscover requests, and will redirect those meant for 2010 Client Access server to a 2010 Client Access server.

But what if you have changed all the *AutoDiscoverServiceInternalURI* properties in the SCP objects to load-balanced names (as you should) to avoid making one Client Access server a single point of failure? Now you need *two* internal namespaces in that site, so a 2007 Client Access server can redirect to a 2010 Client Access server. If you set the value of *AutoDiscoverServiceInternalURI* on all Client Access servers in the site to be the same value, how could one Client Access server redirect to another? It can't. So, in a mixed-version site, plan for two internal (and two external) namespaces to be sure you can provide clients with redirection and URLs that point to the correct version of Exchange—that is, the one matching the mailbox version of the user.

EXTERNAL AUTODISCOVER

If the client is external or non-domain joined, there is a different process for AutoDiscover, as shown in Figure 4-17.

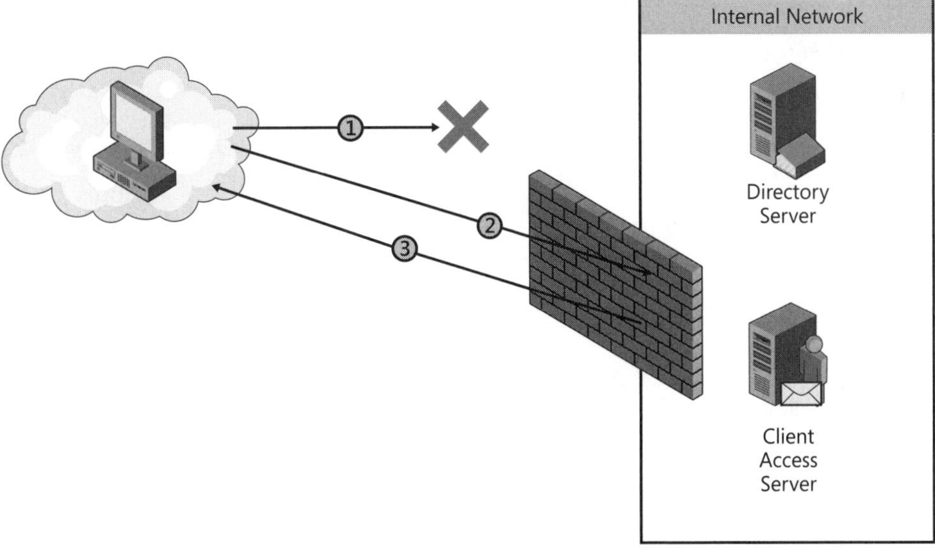

FIGURE 4-17 External AutoDiscover process

1. The client attempts to search Active Directory and fails.
2. The client attempts to connect to the AutoDiscover service using a well-known URL made with the user's primary SMTP address (just the domain parts after the @). These well-known URLs include the following:
   - *https://<smtp-address-domain>/autodiscover/autodiscover.xml*

- *https://autodiscover.<smtp-address-domain>/autodiscover/autodiscover.xml*
- A local XML file if one has been configured; if found, this overrides any other settings
- SRV record (only applies to Outlook 2007 clients with Service Pack 2 or later)

3. The Client Access server processes the request and returns the best available service URLs for the user.

DEPLOYING A STATIC AUTODISCOVER XML FILE

Another possible option for AutoDiscover is to deploy a static XML file to the client. This is particularly useful when you have two forests using the same SMTP address. This may happen during a company acquisition when the acquired company starts using the parent company's domain. Outlook 2007 or later clients may look to the wrong Exchange organization in this case. A registry entry can also force the static XML to be preferred over any other method.

To enforce the XML check first set the following registry keys:

Office 2007 – HKEY_CURRENT_USER\Software\Microsoft\Office\12.0\Outlook\Autodiscover\PreferLocalXML

Office 2010 – HKEY_CURRENT_USER\Software\Microsoft\Office\14.0\Outlook\Autodiscover\PreferLocalXML

Value: 1

Type: DWORD

To set the path to the local XML file, set the following:

Office 2007 – HKEY_CURRENT_USER\Software\Microsoft\Office\12.0\Outlook\Autodiscover\[Domain Name]

Office 2010 – HKEY_CURRENT_USER\Software\Microsoft\Office\14.0\Outlook\Autodiscover\[Domain Name]

Value: Full Path to XML file

Type: STRING

For example, litware.com, and its value is the full path to the XML file,

C:\Program Files\Microsoft\Office12\Outlook\AutoDiscover\litware.com.XML

Of course, you will need a way to deploy this XML file to all of your client computers. An example XML file, and the schema for the is explained in the Technet article found at *http://technet.microsoft.com/en-us/library/cc511507.aspx*. You can use products such as System Center Configuration Manager or Active Directory Group Policies to push it out.

SRV RECORD

A new option was introduced in an Outlook 2007 hotfix (and is included in Service Pack 1 and later). This added an additional check for a DNS SRV record. This option is extremely useful for Exchange organizations that have a large number of SMTP domains, or frequently change the SMTP domains. Let's use Litware as an example. Litware may have 100 additional SMTP domains. Some are "vanity" addresses that groups within Litware use, and the addresses have brand recognition, so retiring the addresses is not an option. For this example, we will use LitwareInc.com as one of these vanity domains. One option is to purchase a SAN certificate with each SMTP domain name and point all of the autodiscover.vanitydomain.com DNS records at the one location; however, this can become expensive and is difficult to maintain.

By using an SRV record, AutoDiscover will find the LitwareInc.com domain and the SRV record pointing at a host (mail.litware.com, for example) that is providing the AutoDiscover service and then redirect the client to the mail.litware.com address. The end user will get a message asking permission for the user to allow the redirection, as shown in Figure 4-18.

FIGURE 4-18 AutoDiscover Redirect dialog box

The user can then select the check box Don't Ask Me About This Website Again and thus will not see the prompt again. Another option is to set a registry key so that the user will never see the dialog box. The registry key is described in KB article 956528 (*http://support.microsoft.com/?kbid=956528*). You create a new string value with a delimited list of HTTPS servers to which AutoDiscover can be redirected without prompting for confirmation from the user. You can then use any distribution method to push out the registry change.

With either method, the connection to the Client Access server is secured using SSL and certificates. For a secure connection to succeed, the certificate must be valid by having a trusted root (and chain) and a name that matches the URL the client connects to, and the certificate cannot be expired. For Outlook 2007 domain-joined clients, Outlook will ignore the requirement for trusting the root certificate, allowing the out-of-box self-signed certificate to work. It is a good idea under all circumstances to replace the self-signed certificate with a valid commercial or internal PKI-generated certificate.

> ***NOTE*** **Outlook 2010 reverses this behavior and will display a warning to the user if there is a self-signed certificate—even for domain-joined clients. This again reinforces the best practice to always replace the self-signed certificate for all installations.**

You can change the order—or even exclude specific steps—of the AutoDiscover process. To change the settings add one or more of the following registry keys described in Table 4-7:

Office 2007 – HKEY_CURRENT_USER\Software\Microsoft\Office\12.0\Outlook

Office 2010 – HKEY_CURRENT_USER\Software\Microsoft\Office\14.0\Outlook

Key: AutoDiscover

Value: 0 (default; use typical AutoDiscover process) or 1 (enable XML file lookup)

Type: DWORD

TABLE 4-7 AutoDiscover Order Registry Settings

KEY	DESCRIPTION
PreferLocalXML	Forces Outlook to use the local Autodicover.xml file before any other lookups.
ExcludeHttpRedirect	Excludes lookups for a redirect from HTTP against the SMTP domain. Example: *http://Autodiscover.Contoso.com/Autodiscover/Autodiscover.xml*
ExcludeHttpsAutodiscoverDomain	Excludes lookups for Autodiscover.[SMTP domain].com/Autodiscover/Autodiscover.xml. Example: *https://Autodiscover.Contoso.com/Autodiscover/Autodiscover.xml*
ExcludeHttpsRootDomain	[SMTP Domain]/Autodiscover/Autodiscover.xml Example: *https://Contoso.com/Autodiscover/Autodiscover.xml*
ExcludeScpLookup	Excludes the Active Directory query for the Service Connection Point (SCP) object.
ExcludeSrvRecord	Excludes the DNS SRV record check.

Outlook Web App and Exchange Control Panel

Exchange Control Panel follows the same architecture as OWA. The guiding principle with OWA is to use a Client Access server closest to the user's mailbox, not the Client Access server closest to where the user is. This is because the communication between the Client Access server and the Mailbox server uses RPC communication, which needs low latency and high bandwidth. Exchange achieves this via two mechanisms: redirection and proxying. Understanding these concepts will help you later in the chapter when we look at the access scenarios.

Proxying is used to access Client Access servers that are not externally available. Figure 4-19 shows two of Fabrikam's datacenters. Because only the Denver datacenter has Internet connectivity, users with mailboxes in the Miami datacenter do not have a direct way to access their Client Access server. In this scenario, the user points the Web browser to his OWA URL, and the Denver Client Access server proxies the request using HTTPS to the Client Access server in the Miami datacenter. The Denver Client Access server uses the Miami Client Access server's certificate to encrypt the conversation. It does not use the certificate for authentication, so the Miami host can continue to use the default self-signed certificate without problems. It is also worth noting that for one Client Access server to proxy to another, the authentication used on the /OWA or /ECP Virtual Directory must be changed from the default of Forms Based Authentication to Windows Integrated Authentication.

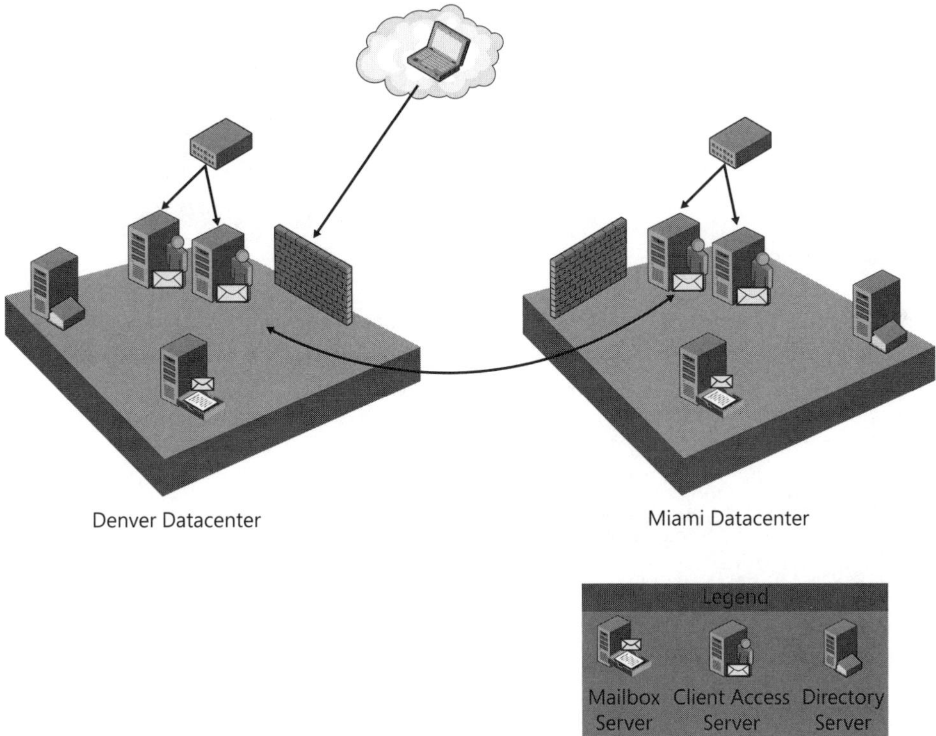

FIGURE 4-19 OWA proxying

If both datacenters have an Internet connection, as shown in Figure 4-20, the client can make a more optimal connection. For redirection to work, the external URL must be configured with an externally resolvable address.

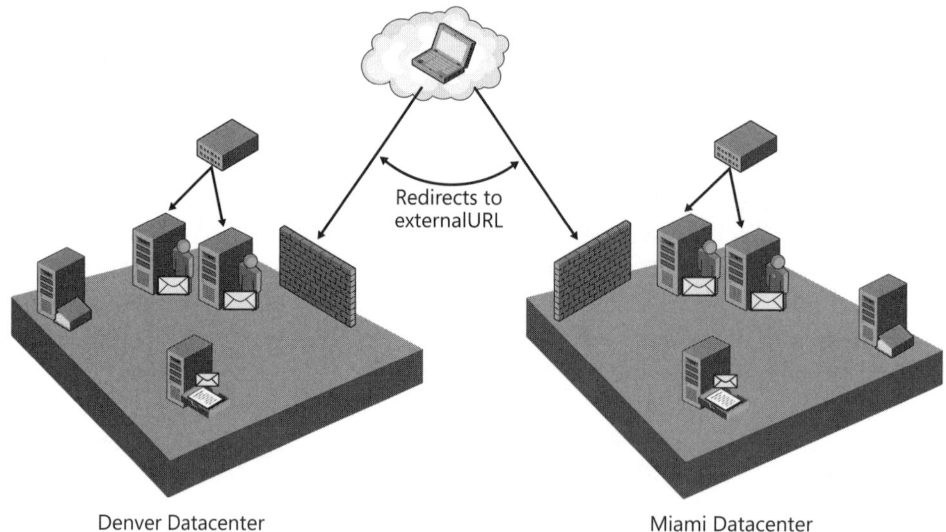

FIGURE 4-20 OWA redirection

For example, if a user whose mailbox is in the Miami datacenter opens her browser to connect to OWA for a mailbox in Denver, Exchange will redirect the client to the appropriate Client Access server with a message similar to that shown in Figure 4-21.

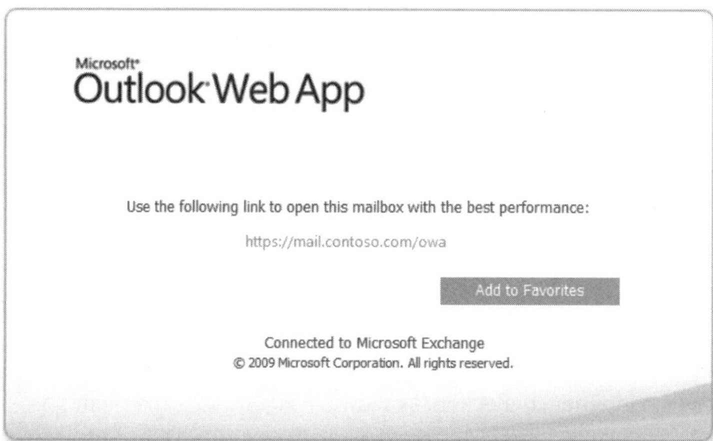

FIGURE 4-21 OWA redirect message

NOTES FROM THE FIELD

Redirecting OWA URLs in Exchange 2010

Brian Desmond
Microsoft MVP, Directory Services, Brian Desmond Consulting, North America

One of the things I've been doing for as long as I can remember is redirecting requests that don't go to *https://mail.contoso.com/owa* (or */exchange*) to the correct URL. So, if someone goes to *http://mail.contoso.com* or *https://mail.contoso.com*, he gets redirected to the correct (secure) URL. Historically I've always done this with two components:

- A custom Web site listening on Port 80 on each Client Access server
- A default.aspx file in the root of the Default Web Site redirecting to /owa

This approach no longer works with Exchange 2010 Client Access server because the PowerShell virtual directory actually operates over Port 80 (authentication is Kerberized). If you try to tinker with this, you'll start getting errors like the following from Remote Windows PowerShell:

> *... The WinRM service cannot process the request because the request needs to be sent to a different machine. Use the redirect information to send the request to a new machine. Redirect location reported: https://owa.customer.com/owa/PowerShell....*

To work around this, you need to use the HTTP Redirection feature in IIS (the default.aspx trick mentioned in the second bullet in the preceding list should work, too), and also remove the requirement for SSL at the top-level Default Web Site object. You have to be careful when you do this because when you configure settings on the Web site, IIS will push them down to any virtual directory below which does not explicitly set that setting itself. To set up the redirect, select Default Web Site in IIS Manager, and open the HTTP Redirect option under IIS. Complete it as shown in Figure 4-22.

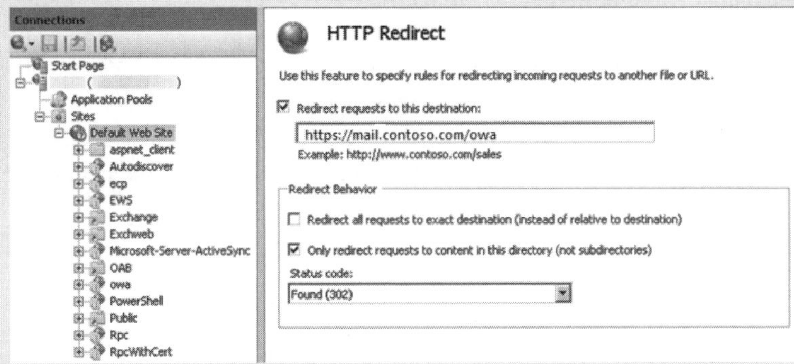

FIGURE 4-22 HTTP Redirect

WARNING It's very important that you select the check boxes as shown in the figure!

After this step is complete, you need to remove the enforced redirect from each of the virtual directories under the Default Web Site. To do this, select each virtual directory individually, and then open the HTTP Redirect property and clear the Redirect Requests To This Destination check box. You'll need to do this on the following virtual directories:

aspnet_client	AutoDiscover	ECP
EWS	Microsoft-Server-ActiveSync	OAB
Windows PowerShell	Rpc	

If at this point if you simply browse to *http://cas01.customer.com*, you'll get an HTTP 403.4 error. This is because SSL is required at the top-level Web site. To get the redirect working, you need to disable SSL for the top-level Web site while leaving it enabled for the relevant child virtual directories.

Select Default Web Site, open the SSL Settings properties, and clear the Require SSL check boxes. Like the redirection settings, this change will be inherited down the tree for any virtual directory that does not explicitly configure the setting independently. Ensure that SSL is required for the following virtual directories:

aspnet_client	AutoDiscover	ECP
EWS	Microsoft-Server-ActiveSync	OAB
Windows PowerShell	Rpc	

WARNING If you require SSL for the Windows PowerShell virtual directory, you will render Remote PowerShell inoperable!

After you've configured the redirection and SSL settings, open a command prompt and run *iisreset*. At this point you should be able to browse to *http://localhost* on the Client Access server and get redirected to *https://owa.customer.com/owa*. These steps were tested on Windows Server 2008 R2. They should be similar under Windows Server 2008, but they may not be identical.

Exchange ActiveSync (EAS)

Exchange ActiveSync enables mailbox access for compatible mobile devices. Its access methods are very similar to OWA. EAS proxying is shown in Figure 4-23.

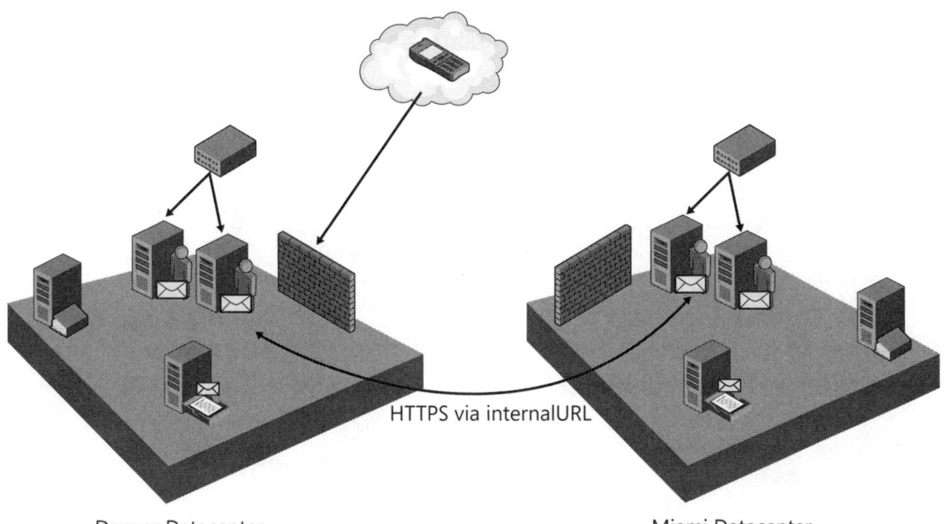

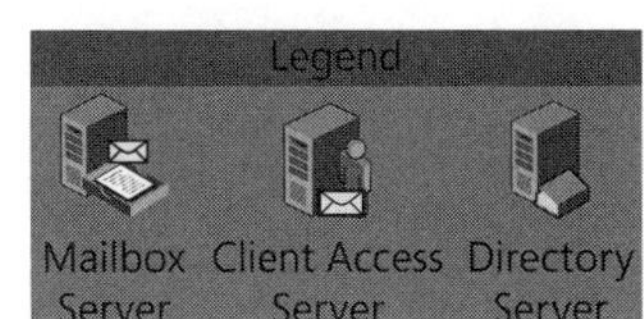

FIGURE 4-23 EAS proxying

If the client accesses the Client Access server in Denver, it will look up where the user's mailbox resides, which in this example is in Miami. It checks that the remote Client Access server has no *externalURL* property set and the /Microsoft-Server-ActiveSync Virtual Directory is configured for Windows Integrated authentication. If it passes these checks, the connection is proxied to the remote server's *internalURL* specified on the ActiveSync Virtual Directory. If the Authentication is incorrectly set or the *internalURL* is not reachable, the request fails.

EAS redirection logic is similar to that of OWA. Only Windows Mobile phones 6.1 and later have the functionality we are about to examine. Older Windows Mobile phones or phones that license ActiveSync technology may not behave the same way. As shown in Figure 4-24, when a client goes to the Client Access server in Denver, it will look up where the user's mailbox resides and determine whether the remote server's *externalURL* property is set. If it is, the Client Access server returns an HTTP error code 451, which is a client redirect containing the URL for the optimal Client Access server.

It is recommended that Exchange Active Sync be load-balanced for internal- and external-facing sites. The synchronization state is stored in the user's mailbox. If the Client Access servers are not load-balanced, the sync will be tied to a specific Client Access server. If that host becomes unavailable, synchronization will fail until the service is restored.

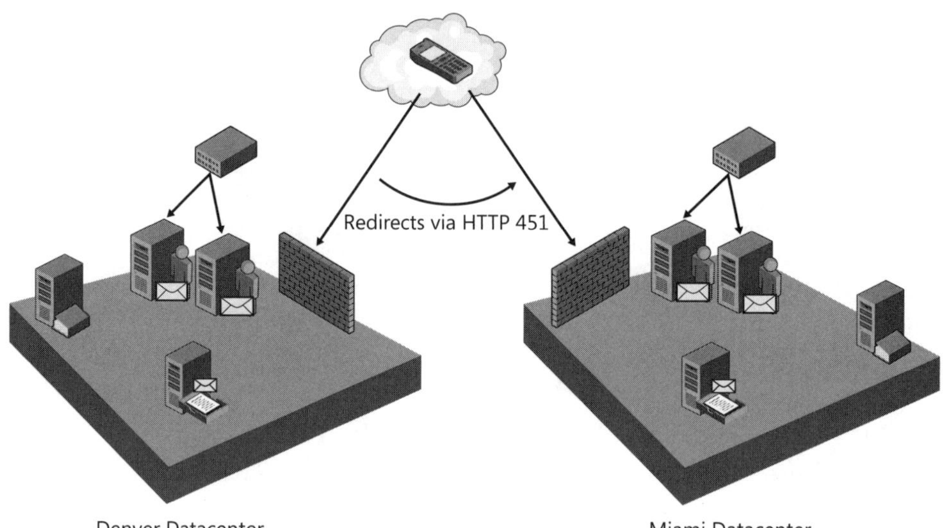

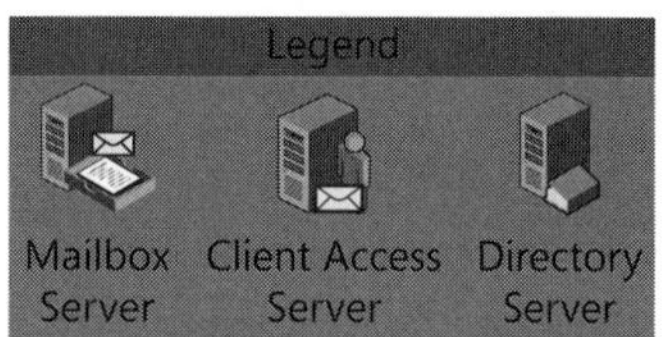

FIGURE 4-24 EAS redirection

INSIDE TRACK

ExternalURLs

Greg Taylor
Senior PM – Exchange Product Group, Microsoft Corporation

Quite often I am asked by customers if setting the *externalURL* property is required, and like all good ex-consultants, I answer, "It depends." That's because all clients work in different ways, so the question I respond with is "What client are we talking about?"

This is the ActiveSync section of the book, but let's talk about OWA first: if you don't set an *externalURL* on a VDir, does that mean you cannot connect? No, it doesn't—you can connect just fine as long as the client can resolve the name to an IP, the certificate is valid, and the right authentication is enabled. What if you have two Active Directory connected sites? If you don't set an *externalURL*, how can you redirect a client to the other site? You can't—so having *externalURL* configured for OWA is not strictly necessary unless you need redirection. Still, I would always recommending setting them, and setting them all to the same value within an Active Directory site.

Now, back to ActiveSync. This is where things get more interesting in a nerdy kind of way. When an ActiveSync client performs an AutoDiscover request, the Client Access server returns to the client the server configuration it should use. And that setting is (drum roll please) the value of *externalURL* on the Internet-facing Client Access server. What if, like OWA, you didn't set it during install, or since? No AutoDiscover. So if you want AutoDiscover to work, you need to set it on all the Client Access servers in the Internet-facing Active Directory site(s).

Exchange Web Services

Exchange Web Services (EWS) is different than the other services discussed so far because it only supports proxying. It relies on AutoDiscover to provide clients, whether Outlook or an application, with the correct URLs. Figure 4-25 depicts the proxy scenario for EWS.

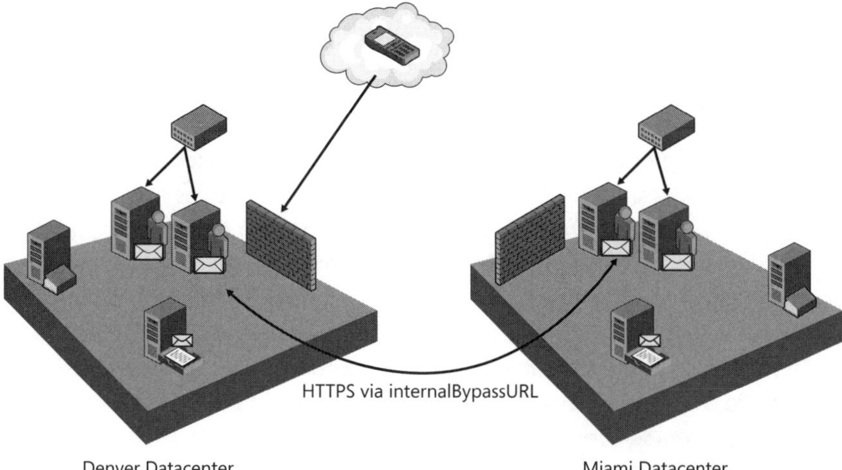

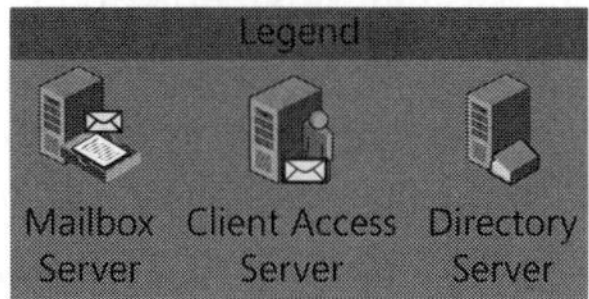

FIGURE 4-25 EWS proxy

EWS calls are generally stateless, but a number of operations require EWS to maintain state. For example, subscriptions require affinity (reconnecting to the same host) to work. However, the Availability Service is an example of an Exchange Web Services that is stateless. Even with the Exchange Web Services that are stateless, maintaining state has performance benefits.

A problem arises when Denver has to proxy to Miami. As you can see in Figure 4-25, when Denver has to proxy to Miami, Miami's Client Access servers are behind a load balancer (and the *internalURL* would appropriately be set to the array). For affinity to be maintained, the proxy process uses the *internalNLBBypassURL*. The *internalNLBBypassURL* is set by default to the FQDN of the host. This value should never be changed.

Also note that in Service Pack 1, EWS now supports certificate authentication. This addition can enforce extra security from clients and provide more control over who and what applications can access EWS.

RPC Client Access

The introduction of the RPC Client Access layer means that Outlook clients now connect to the Client Access server to access a user's mailbox. It is a requirement to have at least one Client Access server per Active Directory site where a Mailbox server has been installed.

AutoDiscover uses the *RPCClientAccessServer* setting on the mail database to configure a client to use the Client Access server in the Mailbox server's site. The *RPCClientAccessServer* property is automatically set to a randomly selected FQDN of a Client Access server in the same site as the database if an array has not already been created. If it has already been created, it will be set to that instead. Note that this setting is not updated in the event of changes, such as removing the Client Access server array or installing additional Client Access servers.

There is not a concept of proxy or redirection for RPC access in Exchange 2010 RTM. Client Access servers will make a direct connection to a Mailbox server across sites. The only way to prevent this is to change the *RPCClientAccessServer* setting on the database. In Service Pack 1, redirection logic and the ability to disable cross-site direct connections were added for RPC Client Access. Redirection is controlled by three properties (in addition to enabling redirection)—the Home Server property on the user's directory object, the preferred database site (such as the *RPCClientAccessServer* property), and the Active database site. Disabling cross-site connections forces redirection behavior and the Outlook client will reconnect to the Client Access server array in the other site.

The default setting for RPC Client Access is that encryption is required. By default, older Outlook clients such as Outlook 2003 do not enable encryption. You have two options when using such clients: either enable encryption on the client or remove the encryption requirement on the Client Access server. It is recommended that security be preserved and the Outlook clients have their settings changed. This, however, may be difficult to do in organizations that do not have automated processes in place.

To provide for load balancing of the RPC Client Access, Exchange uses the *ClientAccessArray* concept. As explained earlier, the *RPCClientAccessServer* setting controls where RPC clients go for service. To allow for load balancing, this property is set to *ClientAccessArray* instead of a single host. When an administrator creates the array, it does not create any form of load balancing itself; it really is just a logical object representing an array of servers that must be separately configured to perform load balancing. This can be done using either hardware- or software-based load balancing. Only one array is allowed per Active Directory site, and multiple DAGs can utilize the same Client Access server array.

One option frequently recommended when load balancing RPC services is to restrict the ports required. Without restrictions in place, a large range of ports need to be configured, which can overwhelm some load-balancing devices. The static port for RPC Client Access is configured in the registry using the following key. The key needs to be set on every Client Access server to the value of the port used for TCP connections,

Key: HKEY_LOCAL_MACHINE\SYSTEM\CurrentControlSet\Services\MSExchangeRPC\ParametersSystem

Value: TCP/IP Port

Type: DWORD

It is recommended that you set this value to a high port that is not used by any other application, such as 50,000.

This setting does not affect Outlook Anywhere connections because those are hard-coded to use port 6001.

Additionally, the static ports for the two RPC endpoints for the Exchange Address Book Service are set in the Microsoft.Exchange.AddressBook.Service.Exe.config file. This file is located in the bin directory of the Exchange installation path. The *RpcTcpPort* value should be set to the TCP port to be used for connections. Again, setting this to a port not used by any other application is recommended, such as 50,001.

> **NOTE** Do not change the values for *NspiHttpPort* and *RfrHttpPort*—changes may result in delays in Outlook Anywhere connecting to Exchange.

After these two changes are made, and the Microsoft Exchange RPC Client Access Service and the Microsoft Exchange Active Directory Topology Service are restarted, Outlook will still connect to the RPC Endpoint Mapper to be told which port to use for service, but instead of being provided with a dynamic port, as would be the default, Outlook uses the two statically configured ports.

INSIDE TRACK

Client Access Server Array Names

Greg Taylor

Senior PM – Exchange Product Team, Microsoft Corporation

When considering what names to put onto certificates and what FQDN's to set the various VDirs and parameters to, I am sometimes asked which FQDN the Client Access server array should be set to and whether that name should be on the certificates used.

Taking those questions in reverse order (the second question is easier to answer), Outlook connects to the array using RPC, not SSL. So no, the FQDN you use for the array does not need to be on any certificate, unless you happen to be using the same FQDN for other services—EWS, OAB, and so on.

So, what should you call your array? I think Greg is an excellent name—you should call it that. If you can't, you should name it something simple and easy to understand but which only resolves in *internal* DNS. Why? Let's say you named it *mail.fabrikam.com* and that name exists in both internal and external DNS. When you fire up Outlook at home it will try to connect to mail.fabrikam.com using RPC, and if it can resolve that name to an IP, it will keep trying and trying, until it times out and then falls back to trying to connect over HTTPS (which likely will work, but the delay is a killer if you are an e-mail addict like me). If, however, you had named it *outlook.fabrikam.com*, or better still *greg.fabrikam.com*, and neither of those exist in external DNS, Outlook immediately starts trying to connect over HTTPS.

Outlook Anywhere

Outlook Anywhere enables the full Outlook client to access Exchange using HTTPS by wrapping the RPCs that Outlook usually uses to access a Mailbox server with HTTPS to enable passage through firewalls. The advantage is that this design gives users access to their mailboxes over virtually any network, without special VPN solutions or additional firewall rules that most companies already enable for Internet access.

Enabling Outlook Anywhere requires several steps, but the important part to understand is that AutoDiscover provides the Outlook Anywhere host name and Web service *externalURL* properties to configure the client to connect to Exchange. If you have more than one Internet facing Active Directory site, it is recommended that each site have a separate external host name. The AutoDiscover service will always provide service URLs for the Client Access server closest to the user's Mailbox server. In Figure 4-26, the Miami datacenter does not have Internet connectivity. In this case, a user with a mailbox in Miami will first access the Client Access server in Denver because it is externally accessible. The Denver Client Access server will make an RPC connection to the RPC Client Access server in Miami, which in turn connects to the Miami mailbox.

Because Outlook Anywhere utilizes the HTTP protocol, its connections are *half-duplex*. This means two connections are created for a conversation, RPC_DATA_IN and RPC_DATA_OUT, as shown in Figure 4-27. Each connection is tagged with a client session ID. The RPC server on the endpoint uses this client session ID to know that data it receives via RPC_IN_DATA must be returned using the RPC_DATA_OUT with the same client session ID.

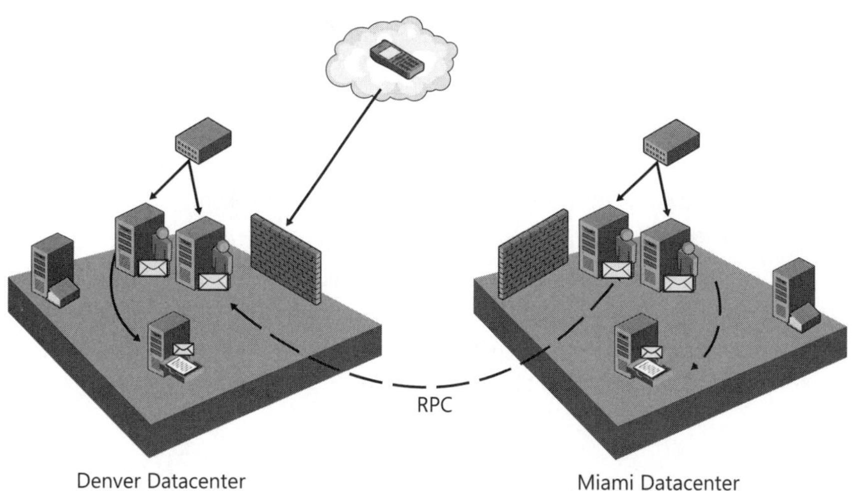

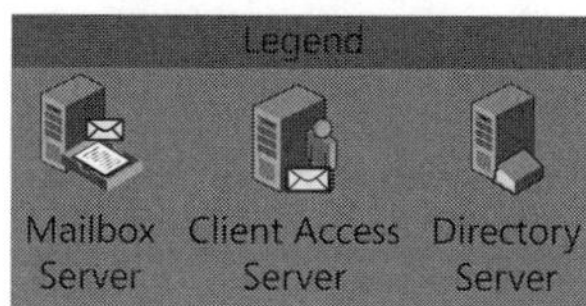

FIGURE 4-26 Outlook Anywhere

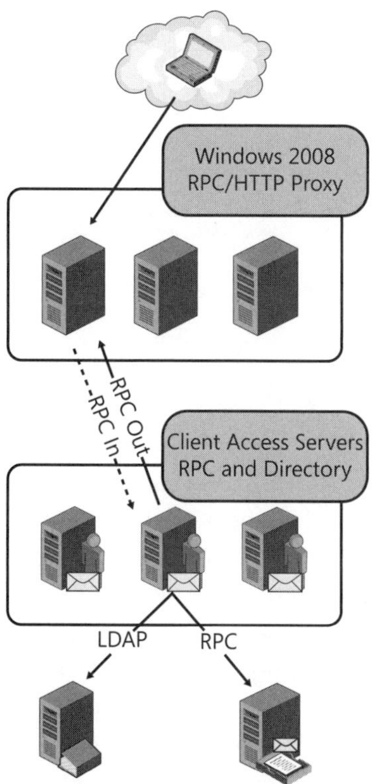

FIGURE 4-27 Outlook Anywhere data flow

This mechanism sometimes presented a problem in Exchange Server 2007 when an SSL ID-based load-balancing solution was placed between the Client Access server and clients. The load balancer does not recognize that these sets of paired connections need to be sent to the same Client Access server, so often it distributed these connections to all the Client Access servers in the load-balancing pool. This meant connections were sometimes split between different Client Access servers and so bidirectional connectivity was broken.

In Exchange Server 2010—or more precisely, in Exchange Server 2010 running on Windows Server 2008—this issue is solved by a component called the Load Balancing Service (LBS). Oddly, LBS has nothing to do with load balancing itself. What it does is detect when sessions from the same client have been split across multiple servers configured in an array and proxy connections between the hosts to ensure that split sessions no longer cause problems.

CERTIFICATES

A few settings for Outlook Anywhere impact certificate namespaces. Figure 4-28 shows the Microsoft Exchange Proxy Settings dialog box.

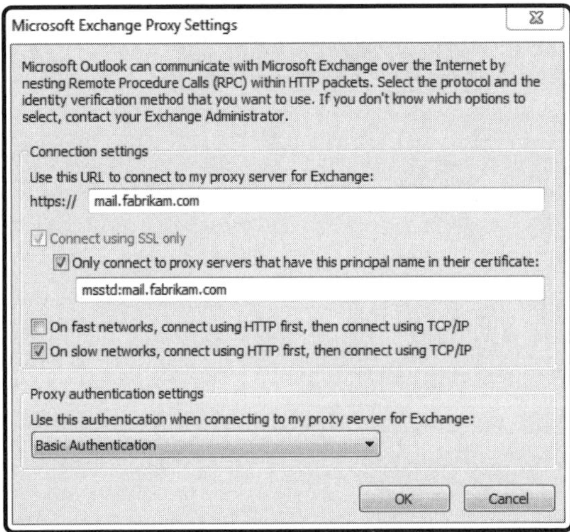

FIGURE 4-28 Outlook Anywhere Proxy Settings in Outlook

The dialog box itself has changed slightly through different Outlook client versions. It is generally accessed through the account settings for Exchange (in the profile) on the Connection tab. On the Connection tab there is a section that refers to connecting to Exchange via HTTP, and there is a button for Exchange Proxy Settings.

The first setting to understand is the URL used to connect to the proxy (Client Access server). This is the URL location Outlook will use to connect to Exchange. The second text box is for the certificate name in the Microsoft standard form (msstd). This is the subject name Outlook expects to find on the certificate presented from the Client Access server when making a connection. This name should not be a SAN because of incompatibilities in the operating system and with Outlook. (This became less of an issue after Windows Vista SP1 was released.) The default configuration on the Client Access server will set these to the same value (the Outlook Anywhere *ExternalHostname*). For now, let's focus on the mechanisms Outlook Anywhere uses. In Chapter 11 we will look at the impact these properties have on choosing a high-availability architecture for the Client Access server.

NOTES FROM THE FIELD

Client Access Server Sizing Tips

Andrew Ehrensing
Principal Consultant, Microsoft Consulting Services, US Central Region

When planning for Client Access server sizing, particularly for Outlook Anywhere, it is important to know how many connections you can expect. This also helps capacity planning when running connections through a hardware load balancer or intelligent firewall. To get an accurate client connection count, you cannot rely on the hidden Outlook connection status dialog box. You can, however, use Microsoft's TcpView utility (*http://technet.microsoft.com/en-us/sysinternals/bb897437.aspx*) or a network sniffer. Another good resource can be found in the whitepaper "Outlook Anywhere Scalability with Outlook 2007, Outlook 2003, and Exchange 2007," available at *http://technet.microsoft.com/en-us/library/cc540453(EXCHG.80).aspx*. Even though this whitepaper has not yet been updated for Exchange 2010, the information it provides good guidance for planning purposes.

POP3/IMAP4

POP3 and IMAP4 are both client protocols used to access mailbox data. Table 4-8 highlights some of the main differences between the protocols. Although both protocols are used to retrieve mail, they rely on an SMTP service to send mail.

TABLE 4-8 POP3 and IMAP4 Comparison

FEATURE	POP3	IMAP4
Mail Storage	All mail is copied and used locally. Some clients have an option to leave a copy on the server.	Mail is stored on the server, and can be used online or locally.
Syncing	POP3 supports syncing the Inbox folder only	IMAP4 supports syncing all folders
Connection	Temporary, connected only long enough to download mail. POP3 supports only a single client connection to the mailbox.	Maintains connection as long as client is running. IMAP4 supports multiple clients simultaneously connected to the mailbox.

FEATURE	POP3	IMAP4
Message State	POP3 does not record any message state information such as read/unread state.	IMAP4 can keep track of message state such as read/unread state.
Server-Side Searches	Not supported	Supported

One way to let users know their SMTP service settings is to configure the *set-ReceiveConnector* cmdlet with the *AdvertiseClientSettings* parameter. This parameter enables the help menu in Outlook Web App to display the SMTP server name, port number, and authentication settings.

POP3 and IMAP4 only support proxying, as shown in Figure 4-29. Proxy configuration is now automatic, and no additional configuration is needed to enable cross-site support.

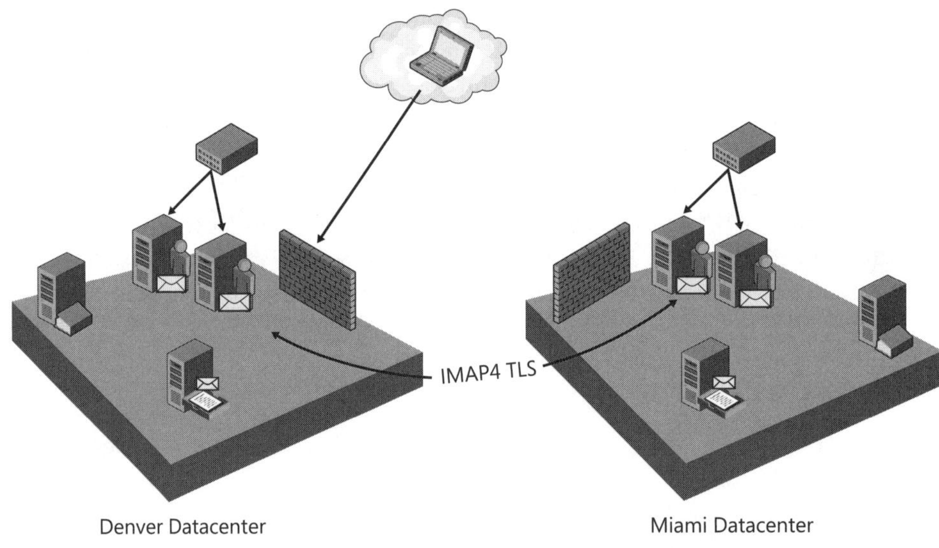

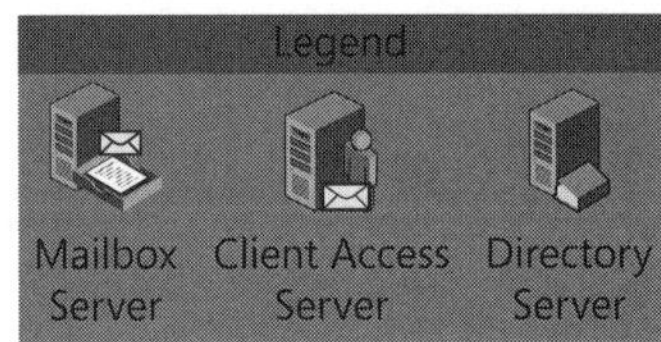

FIGURE 4-29 POP3 and IMAP4 proxy

One significant change in Exchange 2010 is in its security settings. Exchange 2010 no longer supports NTLM authentication for POP3 or IMAP4. *PlainTextAuthentication* no longer allows Secure Password Authentication (SPA) and the client must support Kerberos authentication. It is still a best practice to leave the default setting to *SecureLogin*, which requires TLS encryption and provides the best security.

> **NOTE** The Client Access server blocks POP3 and IMAP4 from the Anonymous and Guest accounts. Additionally, the administrator account cannot be used either. To access the Administrator mailbox, you must use Outlook or Outlook Web App.

A few other settings worth mentioning are used to control the number of POP3 and IMAP4 connections. They are listed in Table 4-9.

TABLE 4-9 POP3/IMAP4 Connection Settings

NAME	DEFAULT AND RANGE
MaxConnectionFromSingleIP	2,000; 1–25,000
MaxConnections	2,000; 1–25,000
MaxConnectionsPerUser	16; 1–25,000

MaxConnectionsFromSingleIP may need to be configured to a higher number if clients are coming through a firewall or load balancer that uses NAT. In this configuration, all of the connections coming into the Client Access server will appear to originate from the same IP address. Organizations with large numbers of clients utilizing POP3 or IMAP4 may need to raise the number of *MaxConnections*. This setting controls the overall number of simultaneous connections that can be made to the Client Access server. Finally, *MaxConnectionsPerUser* controls the number of connections originating from a single user. In the case where you have an application (such as third-party voicemail integration software) that makes a connection with a service account this setting may need to be raised. As with all of these settings, there is a trade-off between number of connections and server performance. You can't apply a simple formula to determine what the settings should be. It will depend on factors such as server hardware, client software, and user profiles.

Client Access Summary

As you can see, the mixture of protocols, client versions, and other factors makes Client Access server planning complex. Table 4-10 summarizes each access method and its ability to redirect and proxy Client Access Server connections.

TABLE 4-10 Redirect and Proxy Summary

ACCESS METHOD	REDIRECT SUPPORTED	PROXY SUPPORTED	COMMENT
Outlook Web App	Yes	Yes	
Exchange ActiveSync	Yes (for Windows Mobile 6.1 and above or other compatible clients)	Yes	

ACCESS METHOD	REDIRECT SUPPORTED	PROXY SUPPORTED	COMMENT
Exchange Web Services	No, except for the EWS elements of Outlook Anywhere or for any application using AutoDiscover.	Yes	
Exchange Control Panel	Yes	Yes	
Outlook Anywhere	No	No	Outlook Anywhere will access remote mailbox directly via RPC or AutoDiscover will provide the correct end points for the client to use.
POP3/IMAP4	No	Yes	

Table 4-11 summarizes each service's *internalURL* and *externalURL* configuration settings. The *externalURL* settings will depend on whether the services are in an Active Directory site with Internet connectivity.

TABLE 4-11 Summary of Load Balanced URLs

SERVICE	*INTERNALURL*	*EXTERNALURL* (INTERNAL-FACING)	*EXTERNALURL* (EXTERNAL-FACING)
OWA	Server FQDN/NLB FQDN *	NLB FQDN	$null
Exchange ActiveSync	NLB FQDN	NLB FQDN	$null
Exchange Web Services	NLB FQDN	NLB FQDN	$null
Exchange Control Panel	Server FQDN/NLB FQDN *	NLB FQDN	$null
OAB	NLB FQDN	NLB FQDN	$null

Use the Server FQDN if the site is the target of a proxy, otherwise use the NLB FQDN. The AutodiscoverServiceInteralURI (SCP record) should always be configured to the NLB FQDN.

Client Access High Availability

This section will work through the complex task of designing a highly available Client Access layer. Removing single points of failure requires that redundant Client Access servers be available. However, after you add multiple hosts, you have two problems to solve:

1. How to direct traffic between hosts
2. How to maintain session information if required

Affinity

Some Exchange applications are stateful, meaning the application needs to remember what the client was doing previously. However, if you have multiple hosts, or when you're using stateless protocols such as HTTP, this state information will be lost between client calls. In the case of multiple load-balanced hosts, affinity is a mechanism to direct calls to a host that was chosen in the initial request.

Before we go into a deeper discussion on load-balancing solutions, it is important to understand the different types of affinity and how they are used. The Client Access server uses a number of protocols that will need to be load balanced, including HTTP and RPC. Remember also that some Client Access server services require affinity and some do not. When choosing a load-balancing solution that will meet the potentially diverse requirements, remember that it may need to support a variety of affinity types.

EXISTING COOKIES

This type of affinity uses cookie information transmitted during typical client/server sessions. This type of affinity is only useful for protocols using HTTP. This would not be an option for RPC Client communication, for example, but OWA using forms-based authentication is an example of an application that does use existing, or application, cookies.

LOAD BALANCER COOKIES

Using load balancer cookies are similar to the previous affinity, except that the load balancer creates the cookie itself and does not rely on existing cookies. Again, this is only usable with protocols using HTTP. Additionally, the client must support the addition of load balancer–generated cookies. Exchange ActiveSync, Outlook Anywhere, and some Exchange Web Services do not support this capability. OWA, ECP, and Remote Windows PowerShell are very good candidates for this type of affinity.

SOURCE IP

Source IP is perhaps the most common and widely supported type of affinity. With source IP load balancing, the load balancer maps a client's IP address and destination host. All traffic from that source IP will continue to go the same destination host. Source IP load balancing has two main drawbacks.

First, affinity breaks when clients change their IP addresses. If you have an environment where this happens frequently, such as mobile clients roaming between wireless networks, this will cause issues visible to users. They may experience symptoms such as having to re-authenticate.

Second, if you have an environment where many clients share the same source IP, such as when a device performing Network Address Translation (NAT) is used, the load will not be evenly distributed.

SSL SESSION ID

SSL session ID is generated during the establishment of an SSL encrypted session. SSL session ID has a big advantage over source IP affinity in that it can uniquely identify clients sharing the same source IP address. Another advantage is that there is no requirement to decrypt the SSL traffic to load balance. This is a hard requirement for using client certificate authentication. Renegotiating the SSL session ID puts extra overhead on the server. Directing traffic to the same server saves processing time and prevents performance impacts.

SSL session ID does not work well with all clients. Some browsers, such as Microsoft Internet Explorer 8.0, create a new SSL session for each browser process. Every time a user creates a new mail, a separate window pops up, creating a new SSL session. The exception to this is when users use client certificate authentication. The same SSL session ID is used for all communication to a specific host. Outlook Anywhere and some mobile clients, such as the iPhone, open several Client Access Server sessions. Because each session gets a different SSL session ID, each session could end up on a different server. As discussed earlier, this is not a problem because the LBS component of Windows Server 2008 will correlate the RPC_IN_DATA and RPC_OUT_DATA. However, this will cause additional overhead and can have an impact on server performance.

Load-Balancing Solutions

To provide redundancy and not have a single point of failure requires multiple Client Access servers in the same Active Directory site. Given this requirement, a mechanism is needed to provide failover redundancy if a host becomes unavailable. It is also needed to effectively distribute client traffic. Three types of traffic need to be load balanced:

- Traffic from internal networks
- Traffic from external (internet) networks
- Traffic from other Client Access servers (proxy)

A goal is to use a single load-balancing solution that works for each of these types of traffic to lower complexity and cost. Because you have a number of load-balancing options, consider the following when choosing a solution:

- **Features** Does it perform SSL offloading?
- **Manageability** How easy is it to configure and maintain the solution?

- **Failover detection** Does it support advanced detection (service awareness), or simple ping (host awareness)?
- **Affinity** What options does it support to keep client connections returning to the same host?
- **Cost** How much to implement the solution?
- **Scale** How does the solution work as the number of hosts increases?

WINDOWS NETWORK LOAD BALANCING (WNLB)

Windows Network Load Balancing (WNLB) has been part of the Windows Server operating system since NT 4.0. Of course, a lot has changed since its early days. WNLB can scale to 32 hosts, but the practical limit for Exchange is 8 hosts based on Microsoft's internal deployment experience. One of WNLB's advantages is that it is relatively inexpensive to implement.

One disadvantage of WNLB is that you cannot use it combined with Windows Clustering. If you are trying to configure an all-in-one server that has the Mailbox role and Client Access Server role, and you are using DAGs, you must use a hardware-based load-balancing solution for Client Access. Another drawback is that WNLB only supports source IP affinity or no affinity. This may limit its ability to effectively load balance across all of the Client Access protocols.

HARDWARE LOAD BALANCERS

If you need to support more than eight nodes in your Active Directory site, you must consider a hardware load balancer. Having a dedicated piece of specialized hardware allows for the best performance and a considerable amount of features. Most hardware load balancers support multiple affinity types, and even allow for the ability to try fallback if one type fails. Typically, hardware load balancers support more advanced node health checks. These range from a simple ping test to measuring response times to a custom Web page. More expensive solutions also provide hardware redundancy, further eliminating any single points of failure.

Probably the biggest disadvantage of a hardware load balancer is the cost of deploying a hardware solution. For large-scale deployments, however, this is typically the solution selected.

INTELLIGENT FIREWALLS

Intelligent firewalls, such as Microsoft Threat Management Gateway (TMG) or Forefront Unified Access Gateway (UAG), are similar to the hardware load balancer solution, but provide additional security features. All of these products can create additional policies to further control the services they reverse proxy for. For example, with Active Directory groups, you can control what time during the day groups of users can access OWA. And as you will see later on in the chapter, you can unify the namespace and use groups to control routing and load-balancing decisions.

One disadvantage is that with great power comes great complexity. These solutions require more testing and more administration and operational support than the other solutions. One way to mitigate this is to buy an appliance. Appliances are prebuilt solutions that generally provide additional tools for administration and are optimally configured by the vendor.

DNS ROUND ROBIN

DNS round robin takes advantage of DNS's ability to map multiple hosts to a common name. For example, if we have three Client Access servers registered in DNS, the A record entries would look like this:

```
mail.litwareinc.com       192.168.1.2
mail.litwareinc.com       192.168.1.3
mail.litwareinc.com       192.168.1.4
```

The first request returns the IP address of 192.168.1.2. The second request returns 192.168.1.3, and the third request returns 192.168.1.4. The fourth request returns the first IP address again, and the pattern would continue.

The main advantages of DNS round robin are its low cost to implement and ease of configuration. Unfortunately, the limitations of DNS round robin limit its use to labs, or very small implementations (such as proofs of concept). One of these limitations is no support for affinity. It is up to the application to maintain affinity. For example, a Web browser navigating to *webmail.contoso.com* will actually use the IP address the DNS server returns from the name resolution query. Internet Explorer actually caches DNS entries for 30 minutes. Because of this caching, the Web browser could try to reach an unavailable server until its cache expires. And what's (possibly) worse, even if the host you are currently using stays available, after the cache expires it is likely that the next time the name is resolved a new Client Access server will be returned. This will result in a loss of all state information and the session is lost.

DNS round robin also does not have any health checks or dead node removal. In the preceding example, if 192.168.1.3 becomes unavailable, DNS round robin will happily continue to return the down host's IP address every third request.

Finally, changes to DNS can take time to propagate. If a new Client Access server is added to DNS, it will be underutilized until the record propagates fully.

LOAD-BALANCING SUMMARY

As you can see, you have a variety of solutions to choose from, depending on the business requirements and budget. Figure 4-30 offers a handy chart comparing affinity, load balancing, and other considerations for choosing a load-balancing solution.

	Type	Cost	Scale	Affinity	Benefits	Drawbacks
Hardware	Hardware NLB (F5, Cisco, Citrix)	$$$	⚖⚖⚖	All Types	+ Automatic Failover + Combines with Windows Clustering + Best Performance	– Cost
Software	Intelligent Firewall (ISA, TMG, UAG)	$$	⚖⚖	Source IP Cookie	+ SSL Bridging + Enhanced Security + AD Integration	– Complex
	Software Network Load Balancing (WNLB)	$	⚖	Source IP	+ Included in OS + Easy to Deploy	– Limited Scale – Cannot use with Windows Clustering
	DNS Round Robin	$	⚖⚖⚖	Random IP	+ Simple to Configure	– Manual Failover – Long Caching Time

FIGURE 4-30 Load-balancer summary comparison

Certificates for Client Access Services

Out of the box, Exchange 2010 provides self-signed the certificates to ensure without any configuration changes that basic security is in place. For most organizations, this is not good enough, for a few reasons. First, because the Exchange server itself signs the certificate, most internal clients and all servers outside the Exchange organization will not trust it. Second, the self-signed certificates use the host name as the subject name. Very few companies want users, for example, to access Exchange services such as OWA with a Client Access server's host name (as opposed to a friendly URL such as *webmail*). Finally, in a fault-tolerant design it may be impossible to load self-signed certificates onto a hardware load balancer.

SELECTING A CERTIFICATE AUTHORITY

Recall the discussion of certificate basics in the last chapter. If your company has an internal PKI, that is one option for replacing the self-signed certificates. However, it may be challenging to deploy the internal certificate to mobile devices or non-corporate managed assets. Another option is to buy a third-party certificate. If you are purchasing a certificate, consider the following:

- Ensure that the certificate authority (CA) root is trusted by all of the clients in your organization (operating system, browser, smartphones, and so on).
- Use a CA that is a Unified Communication Certificate Partner for Exchange and OCS. (Refer to *http://support.microsoft.com/kb/929395* for more information on UC certificates.)
- The certificate vendor sells the type of certificate you require (SAN, Wildcard).
- The certificate vendor has a flexible pricing model that allows you to add or change names at any time or load the certificate on multiple hosts without penalty.

OBTAINING THE CERTIFICATE

The next few figures show the Certificate Wizard in action. The wizard is located in the Action pane when the Server configuration node is selected in the console tree and the Client Access server is selected in the result pane.

The first step is to pick a friendly name for the certificate. This name has no effect on any URLs or configuration later on; it is simply used as an easy way to identify the certificate in the Exchange Management Console. The second step is to request a wildcard certificate. In Figure 4-31, this setting is not enabled and the certificate will use SANs instead.

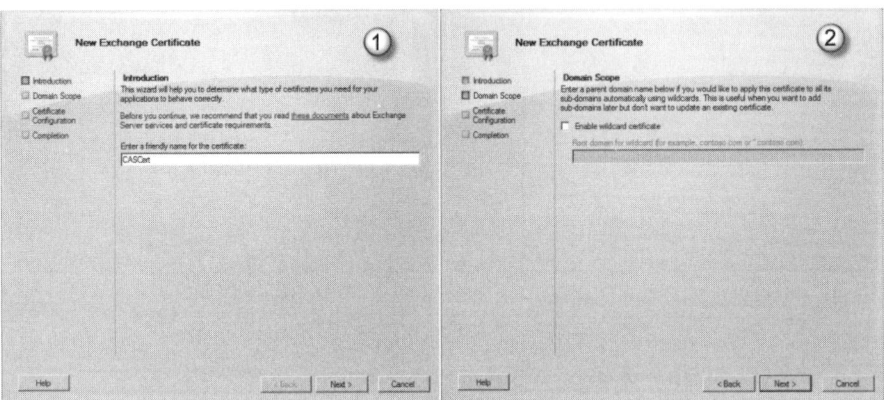

FIGURE 4-31 Certificate Wizard Steps 1 and 2

Figure 4-32 shows Steps 3 and 4. In Step 3, the administrator selects which services the Client Access server will enable and picks the URLs that users will use to access that service. For this example, OWA is enabled internally and externally at *mail.litewareinc.com.* Step 4 shows a summary of the names that will be requested for the certificate. On this step you can make modifications, such as adding the Client Access server host names if required. One name will need to be set as the certificate's common name; the selected name is shown in bold. Later in this chapter we'll discuss how this setting in particular impacts Outlook Anywhere.

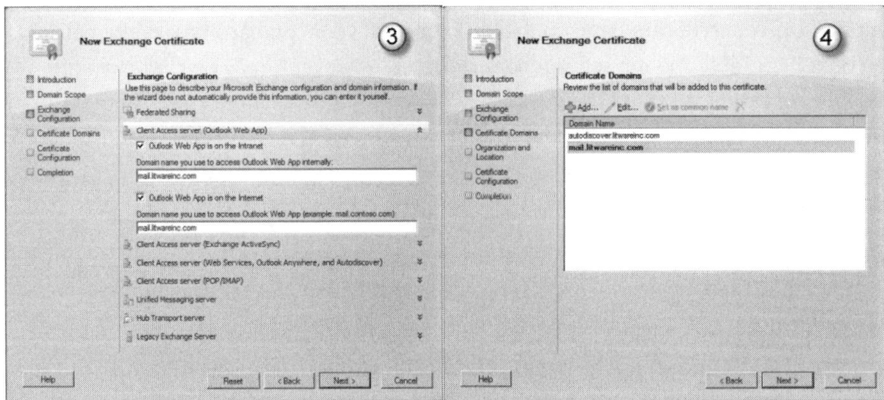

FIGURE 4-32 Certificate Wizard Steps 3 and 4

The last two steps are shown in Figure 4-33. In Step 5, the administrator inputs the metadata for the certificate request. This includes information such as state, city, and organization. Finally, Step 6 is the last review before the administrator clicks the New button to generate the certificate request.

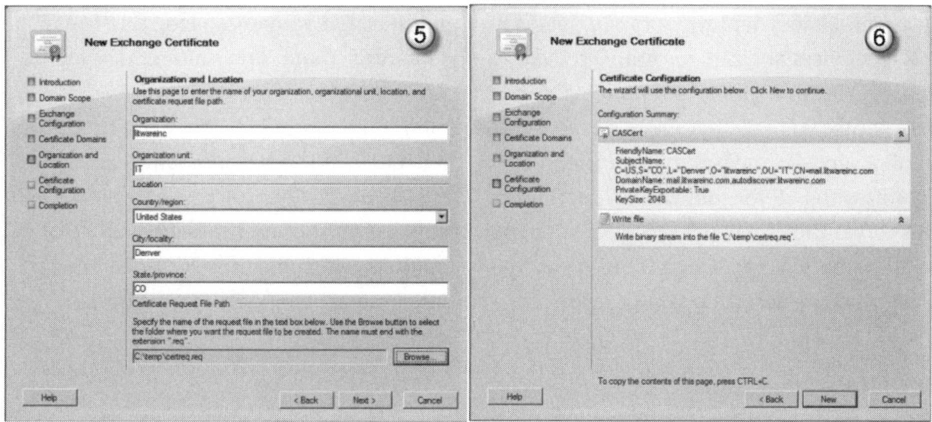

FIGURE 4-33 Certificate Wizard Steps 5 and 6

If the cmdlet is successful, the management console gives the cmdlet syntax that was used by the wizard. For this example, the cmdlet was:

```
New-ExchangeCertificate -FriendlyName 'CASCert' -GenerateRequest -PrivateKeyExportable
$true -Keysize '2048' -SubjectName 'C=US,S="CO",L="Denver",O="litwareinc",OU="IT",CN=
mail.litwareinc.com' -DomainName 'mail.litewareinc.com','autodiscover.litwareinc.com'
-Server CAS01
```

At this point the administrator can submit the output file to the certificate authority. The Certificate Wizard greatly simplifies the request process.

CERTIFICATE BEST PRACTICES

Use as few numbers of certificates as possible. You can secure each Exchange service with a unique certificate, but that will be harder to manage and possibly cost more money in the end. Namespaces are the reason you may need multiple certificates. For example, in companies using POP3 or IMAP4, the friendly URL could be *imap.company.com*, whereas POP could be *pop.company.com*. Instead of these separate names, they could both share *mail.company.com*.

Internet Information Server (IIS)

Many of the Exchange services are exposed through Internet Information Server (IIS) in Windows. By default, they share the same certificate because they are all in the default Web application pool. These services include:

- Outlook Web App
- Exchange Control Panel
- Exchange Web Services

- Exchange ActiveSync
- Outlook Anywhere
- AutoDiscover
- Offline Address Book

In general, most deployments can get away with just using two namespaces: one for all of the IIS services and one for AutoDiscover. As documented, there is no requirement for the host FQDN as a subject alternate name, with a few exceptions. First is the ECP. Earlier in this chapter you saw that Client Access servers that are the target of a proxy site should be configured with the host name instead of the NLB FQDN. This is because Outlook 2010 integrates with ECP for some of its functionality. Outlook, unlike Client Access server-to-Client Access server proxy, will not ignore mismatched certificate settings and will signal an error if the host name is not on the certificate. Another scenario in which the host FQDN is required is when users are accessing services with short names. For example, users may just type **https://mail** into their Web browsers to access OWA.

POP3/IMAP4

As mentioned earlier, these services can have separate namespaces or share a common one with the IIS services. It is recommended that you limit the number of certificates and certificate namespaces wherever possible.

Live Federation

The certificate used for Live Federation can have any name on it. During the configuration of this service you must select the certificate to be used. This certificate must be issued by a third-party certificate authority that is trusted by Windows Live.

Client Access Server to Client Access Server Proxy

In more complex multi-site scenarios, sometimes Client Access servers do not have Internet connectivity. For users to reach their mailbox stores, the Internet-facing Client Access server must proxy the requests to the internal-only host. All communication between Client Access servers is secured with SSL over HTTP. Remember that the goal is to always have the Client Access server closest to the mailbox process requests. Client Access servers use specific host names when making proxy requests. In spite of this, the FQDNs are not required because in this case, the Client Access server ignores most of the certificate information. The certificate is used strictly for encryption and not authentication. If your organization requires a higher level of security for these internal requests, set the following registry key:

Key: HKEY_LOCAL_MACHINE\SYSTEM\CurrentControlSet\Services\MSExchangeOWA\AllowInternalUntrustedCerts

Value: 0

Type: DWORD

Office Communication Server (OCS) Integration

The OCS R2 server needs to communicate securely with the Client Access server for the instant messaging integration to work. The OCS R2 server needs to be configured to allow access to the subject name listed on the certificate.

Pulling It All Together

Now that the architecture, load balancing, affinity, and features have all been explained, the next section pulls all of the information together and case studies for illustration.

Contoso Case Study

The first case study from Chapter 2, "Exchange Deployment Projects," is Contoso, shown in Figure 4-34. Because a single Client Access server is relatively straightforward design, assume for this chapter that Contoso wants to make minimal investments to increase their availability when deploying Exchange 2010. Contoso's end state will include two Client Access servers in the Seattle datacenter.

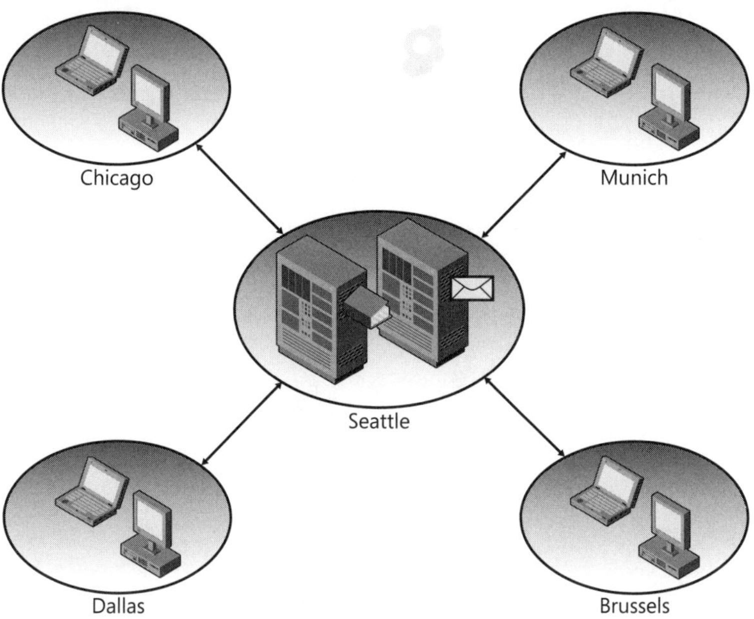

FIGURE 4-34 Contoso logical architecture

Contoso proposes using Windows Network Load Balancing (WNLB) to provide high availability for their Client Access Server role. They have to weigh the cost of servers against the cost of purchasing a hardware load balancer. A hardware load balancer would be required if Contoso chose to combine all roles on the two servers using a DAG as well. Contoso selects WNLB because they have strong Windows Server administration skills and they do not want to introduce new technology in their datacenter, as shown in Figure 4-35.

An administrator will configure WNLB with a FQDN of mail.contoso.com. The administrator then needs to create a DNS A record entry for mail.contoso.com and outlook.contoso.com, both pointing to the virtual IP address (VIP) of the WNLB array. The administrator creates an RPC Client Access array object named *outlook.contoso.com* and ensures that the each mailbox database has the *RpcClientAccessServer* property set to that value for the Outlook clients.

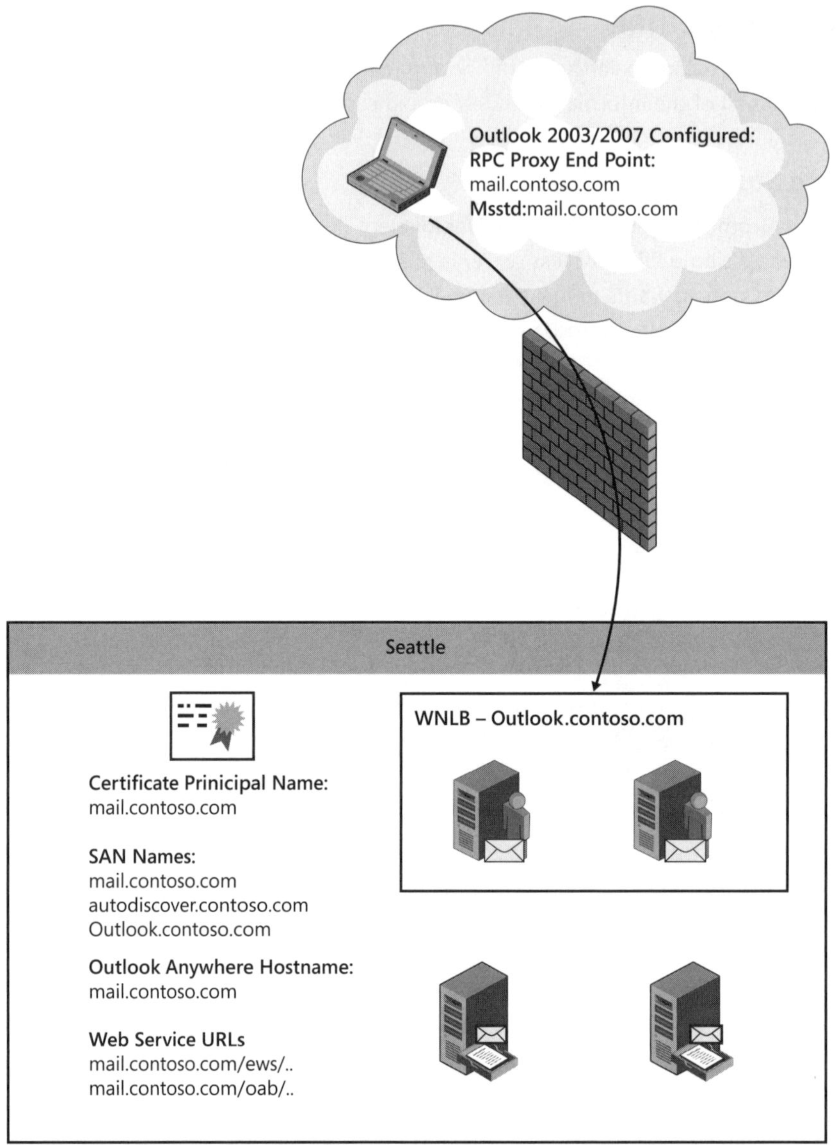

FIGURE 4-35 Proposed Contoso architecture

The service's internal and external URLs need to be updated with the load-balanced FQDN, including the *AutoDiscoverServiceInternalURI*. Because there are no proxy sites, all services should use the load-balanced FQDN. The *ExternalHostname* for Outlook Anywhere should be configured to match the certificate principal name mail.consoto.com.

Fabrikam Case Study

The next scenario is more complex. Fabrikam, from Chapter 2, is our base architecture. As shown in Figure 4-36, Fabrikam has two datacenters, one in Denver and one in Miami.

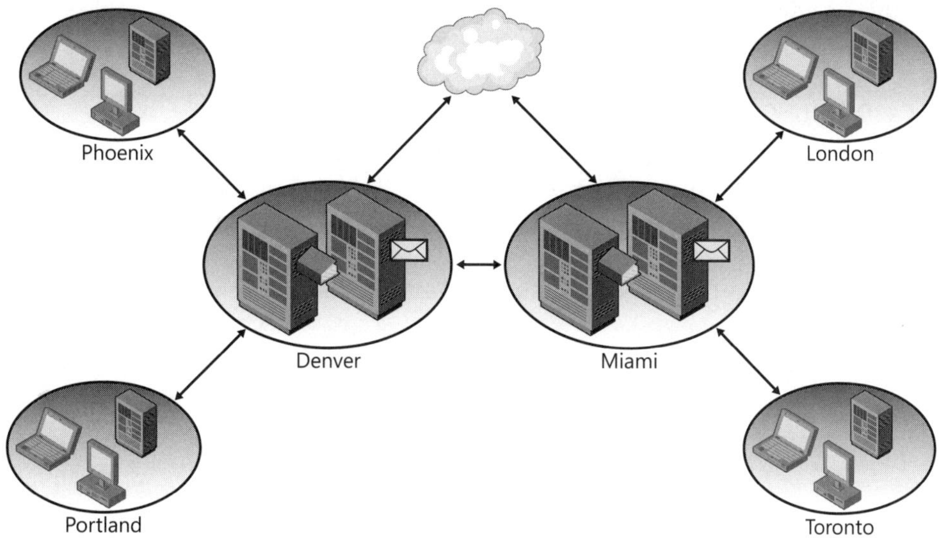

FIGURE 4-36 Fabrikam logical view

Similar to Contoso, Fabrikam has for this case study fully deployed Exchange 2010. In each datacenter, Fabrikam has deployed two load-balanced Client Access servers, and the Mailbox servers are configured in a DAG. The network between the datacenters is fast enough to host all users in both everyday operations as well as in the event of a failover.

In addition to the client version, types, and access methods, a number of factors that can impact your design, including the following:

- Are both datacenters considered active, or is one datacenter reserved for site resiliency only?
- How do external clients reach the Client Access servers (intelligent firewall, load balancer, other)?
- Is there split DNS?
- Will you need to support partial failovers?

Most often in a scenario such as Fabrikam's, the best practice is to use a separate namespace for each Active Directory site. So Fabrikam users in Denver would access OWA through *https://mail.denver.fabrikam.com/owa,* whereas users in Miami would use *https://mail.miami.fabrikam.com/owa*. What happens when users move from one datacenter to the other? They need to use a different URL, which could be very confusing. Because Fabrikam treats the two datacenters as one, they want a design that has a common namespace: *https://mail.fabrikam.com*.

Using the same physical datacenter design, you have five different ways to design high availability:

- Using wildcard certificates
- Deploying the same configuration across sites
- Using SAN Certificate and manipulating the MSSTD values provided to the client

- Using hardware load balancers
- Deploying intelligent firewalls

WILDCARD CERTIFICATES

A wildcard certificate is used to secure a namespace and all of its subdomains. For example, Fabrikam buys a wildcard certificate for *.fabrikam.com. *Mail.fabrikam.com, smtp.fabrikam.com*, and *autodiscover.fabrikam.com* are all secured by the single wildcard certificate, as shown in Figure 4-37.

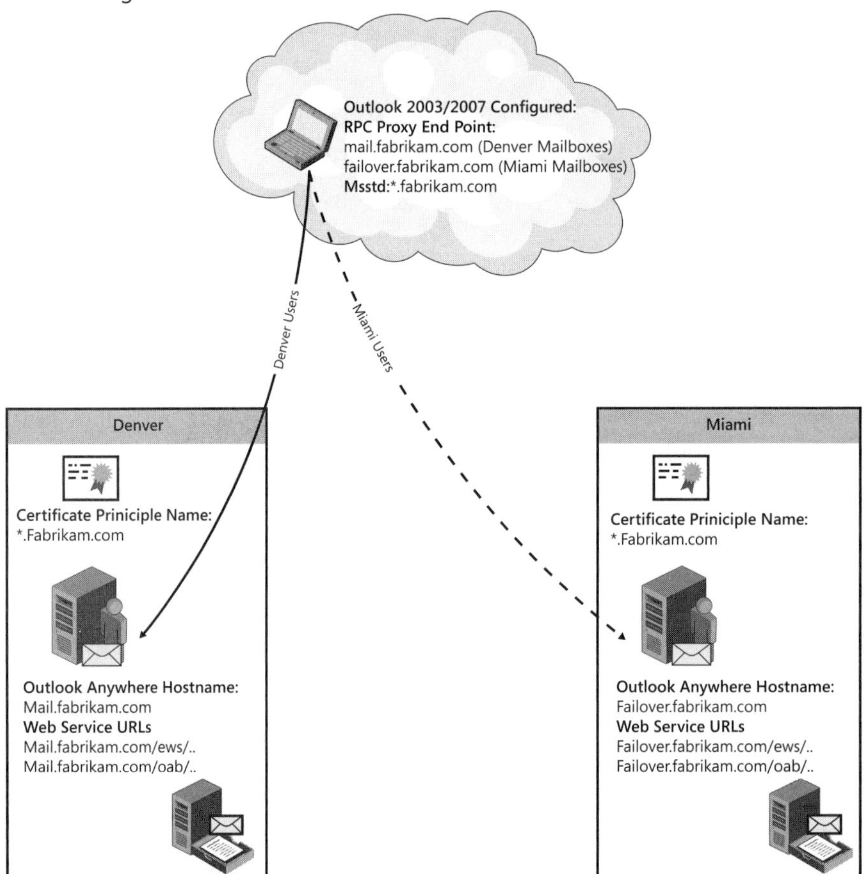

FIGURE 4-37 Fabrikam wildcard example

In this scenario the wildcard certificate allows Fabrikam to use a single namespace. The design will change slightly on Fabrikam's requirement to either try to use both datacenters actively, or treat Miami as a failover site. If Miami is only a failover site, it will be used only when all service is lost in Denver. In this case, the external DNS record for AutoDiscover needs to be updated to resolve to a Client Access server in Miami.

Users accessing OWA with *Mail.fabrikam.com* will resolve via external DNS to a Client Access server in Denver. If *externalURL* is configured on the Client Access servers in Miami, users with mailboxes in Miami will be redirected. The other option is to leave *externalURL* blank and proxy all requests, but this assumes that the correct authentication type, Windows Integrated, is enabled in each location.

Users in Miami will have their Outlook Anywhere connections set to failover.fabrikam.com, but there will be no certificate warning because we changed the global setting for *certprincipalname* to **.fabrikam.com* with the following Windows PowerShell cmdlet:

```
Set-outlookprovider EXPR -certprincipalname msstd:*.fabrikam.com
```

Note that during a move mailbox for user from Denver to Miami, the Outlook Anywhere connection may use a Client Access server in Denver and cross-site access the mailbox in Miami (and vice versa for moves in the opposite direction).

SAME CONFIGURATION IN BOTH SITES

In this design we use the same configuration in both Denver and Miami. By doing this, we can only use this design for using Miami as a failover site. As you can see from the illustration in Figure 4-38, external DNS can only resolve to one site, so an administrator must manually update the DNS entries in a failover scenario. If Fabrikam could make this one Active Directory site, it's possible to make this configuration work for single database moves.

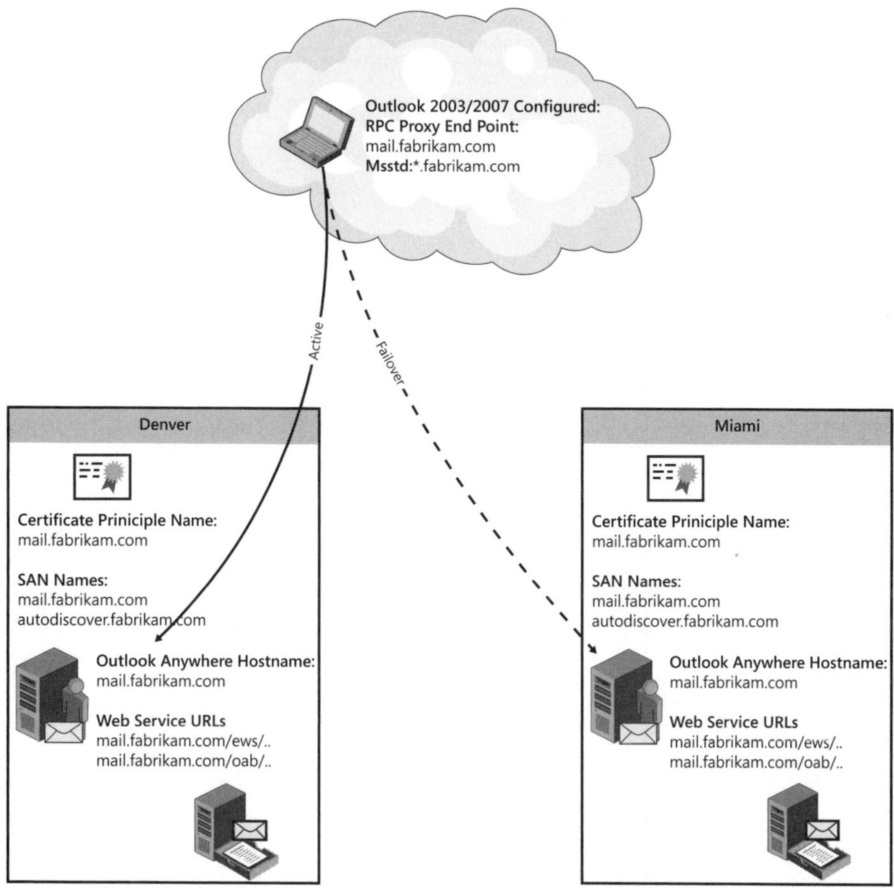

FIGURE 4-38 Fabrikam same configuration deployed in both site examples

SAN CERTIFICATE AND MSSTD

This configuration is very similar to the wildcard architecture except that it uses a certificate that supports SANs. The main reasons to use this design are the expense of using a wildcard certificate and also the maximized compatibility. Most newer clients work with wildcard certificates, but some older clients, such as Windows mobile 5.x and some Web browsers, may not work at all. The certificate must list all of the possible service points, and the subject name must be set to *mail.fabrikam.com.*

By default the MSSTD setting matches the *ExternalHostname* when enabling Outlook Anywhere. For this architecture to work, we must change the global setting for *certprincipalname* to *mail.fabrikam.com* with the following Windows PowerShell cmdlet:

```
Set-outlookprovider EXPR -certprincipalname msstd:mail.fabrikam.com
```

This way users will not get a certificate warning because the MSSTD setting matches the certificate principal name in both sites. Figure 4-39 shows this architecture.

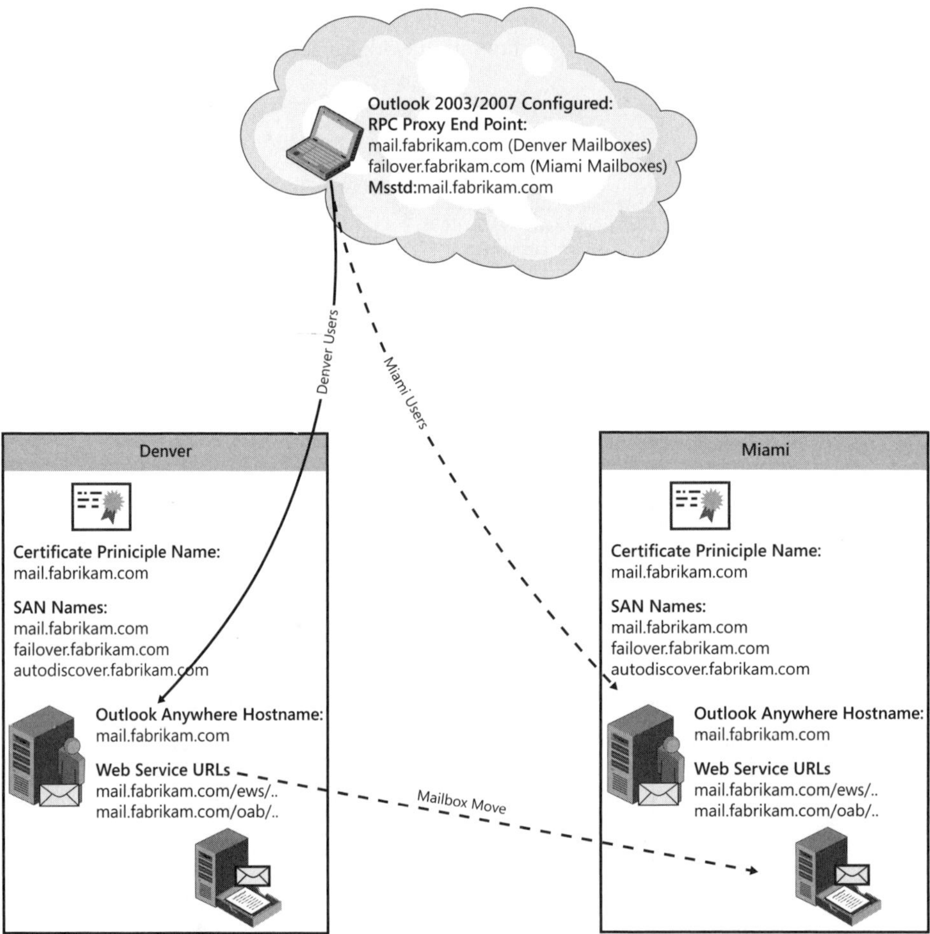

FIGURE 4-39 Fabrikam SAN certificate and MSSTD example

In the event of a failover, Outlook Anywhere 2007/2010 users will not see that they are connecting to failover.fabrikam.com because this is automatically configured with AutoDiscover. Outlook 2003 users will not have to change their profiles because the mail.fabrikam.com end point they were using still exists as a SAN on the certificate and the Certificate Principal Name has not changed. In this case, it is possible that after a mailbox move or site failure the user will have a Client Access server that accesses his mailbox across sites. A total site failure in Denver would require administrators to reconfigure AutoDiscover and mail URLs to the Client Access servers in Miami.

HARDWARE LOAD BALANCER

Another possible option is to use multiple namespaces and a hardware load balancer to route to the correct Client Access server. This concept is demonstrated in Figure 4-40.

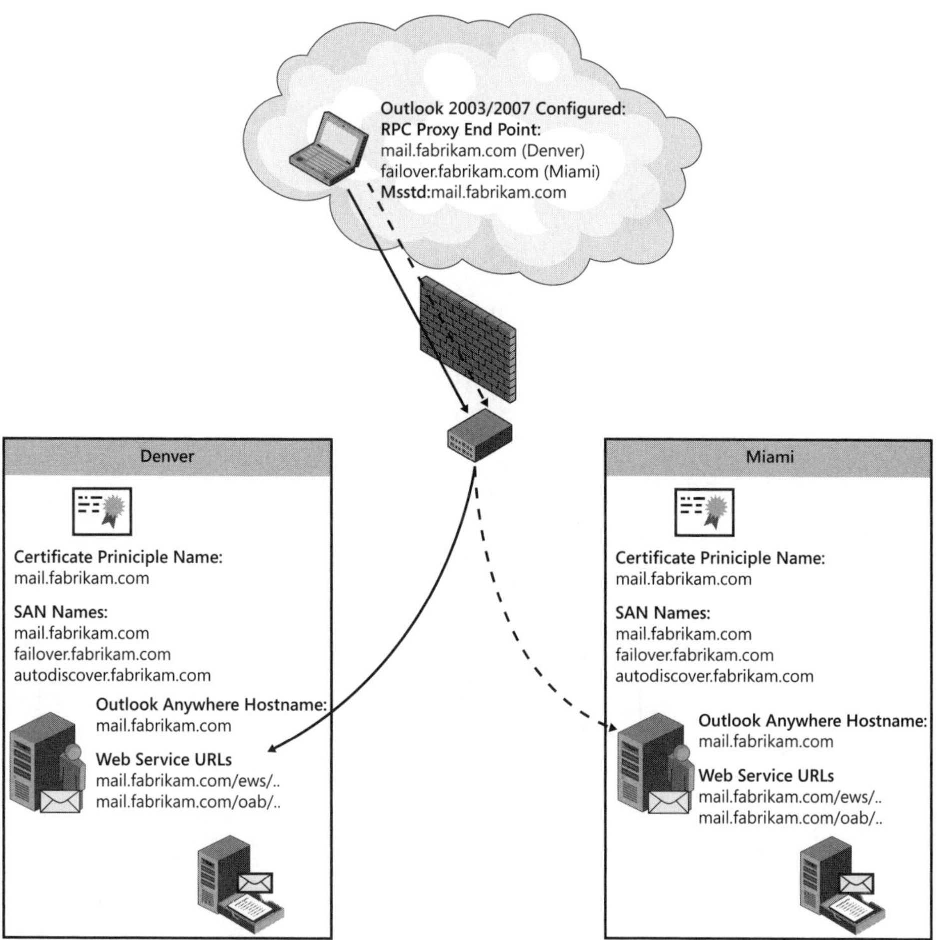

FIGURE 4-40 Fabrikam hardware load-balancer example

In practice, this is a just a slightly different configuration compared to the wildcard certificate solution. Here, the external URLs are directed to the hardware load balancer. The main advantage in this design is that the hardware load balancer handles the upfront connection, removing the extra processing required by the Client Access server in Denver in the other solution.

For smaller implementations, the extra cost of a hardware load balancer may be hard to justify. However, many newer devices are available at a lower price. To fully eliminate the hardware load balancer as a single point of failure, multiple hardware devices may be required.

INTELLIGENT FIREWALL

An intelligent firewall and a hardware load balancer are very similar; however, the intelligent firewall offers additional flexibility over most hardware load balancers. An intelligent firewall, such as Microsoft's Thread Management Gateway (TMG), can use Active Directory groups to make decisions on how to route users, as shown in Figure 4-41.

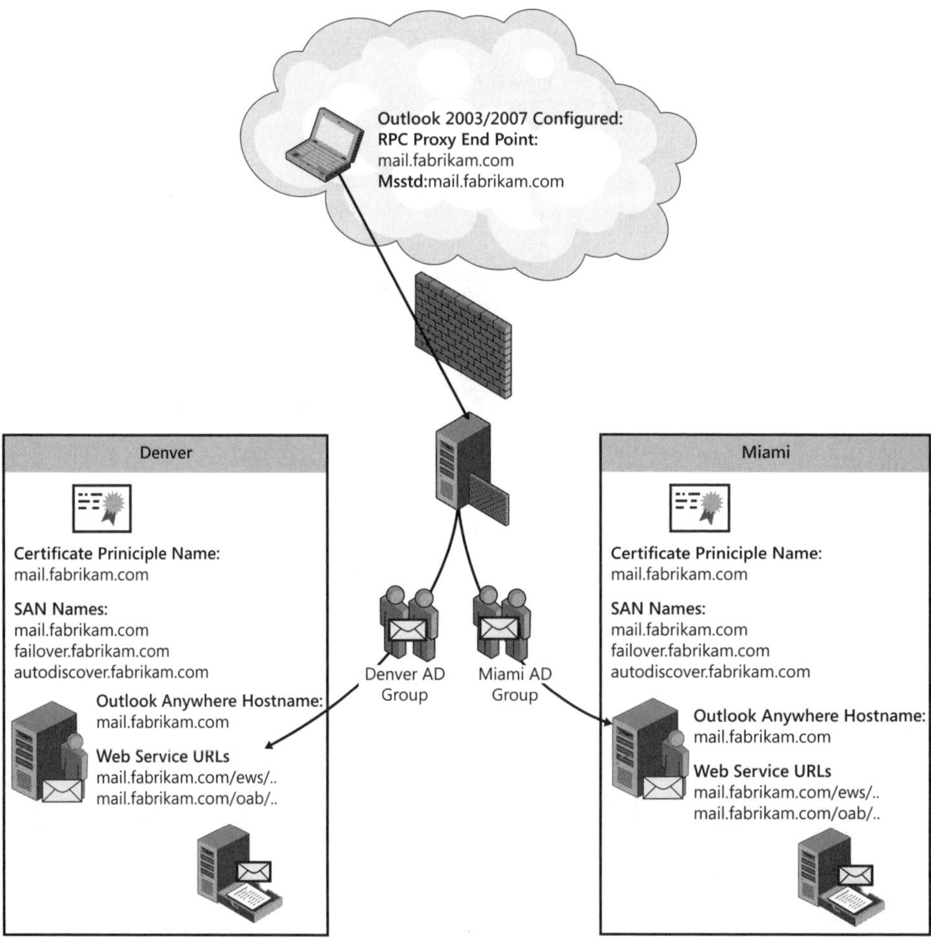

FIGURE 4-41 Intelligent firewall example

Of course, this means processes must be in place to keep group information up to date. This also places an additional dependency on Active Directory replication to keep group information current across sites.

Intelligent firewall is one of the more complex designs, but it can offer complimentary features, including link translation and URL filtering. Table 4-12 summarizes the different strategies discussed in this case study.

TABLE 4-12 Certificate Summary

METHOD	ADVANTAGES	DISADVANTAGES
Wildcard Certificate	■ Only one certificate is required. ■ Flexible if there are name changes.	■ Wildcard certificates can be expensive. ■ Some mobile and Web clients are not compatible.
Intelligent Firewall	■ Traffic is forwarded to the correct Client Access server. ■ Has additional security features.	■ High complexity. ■ Additional hardware required. ■ Requires maintaining group membership.
Hardware Load Balancer	■ HLB can listen for both external names and forward to the correct Client Access server. ■ Highest performance and scaling	■ Requires multiple certificates. ■ Requires multiple IPs. ■ Additional hardware required.
Same Configuration in Both Sites	■ Only a DNS A record change is required after site failover. ■ No additional hardware.	■ No way to run failover site as active.
SAN Certificate and MSSD	■ Minimal configuration changes required after failover. ■ Works with all clients. ■ No additional hardware.	■ Certificate Principal Name is global to all Client Access servers in forest.

FABRIKAM SOLUTION

Fabrikam picked the SAN Certificate and MSSTD as their solution. This configuration was beneficial because it did not require additional hardware purchases. Fabrikam was fortunate to have enough network infrastructure between its datacenters to support the extra traffic of supporting cross-WAN traffic.

Litware Inc. Case Study

The last case study is for the global company Litware Inc shown in Figure 4-42.

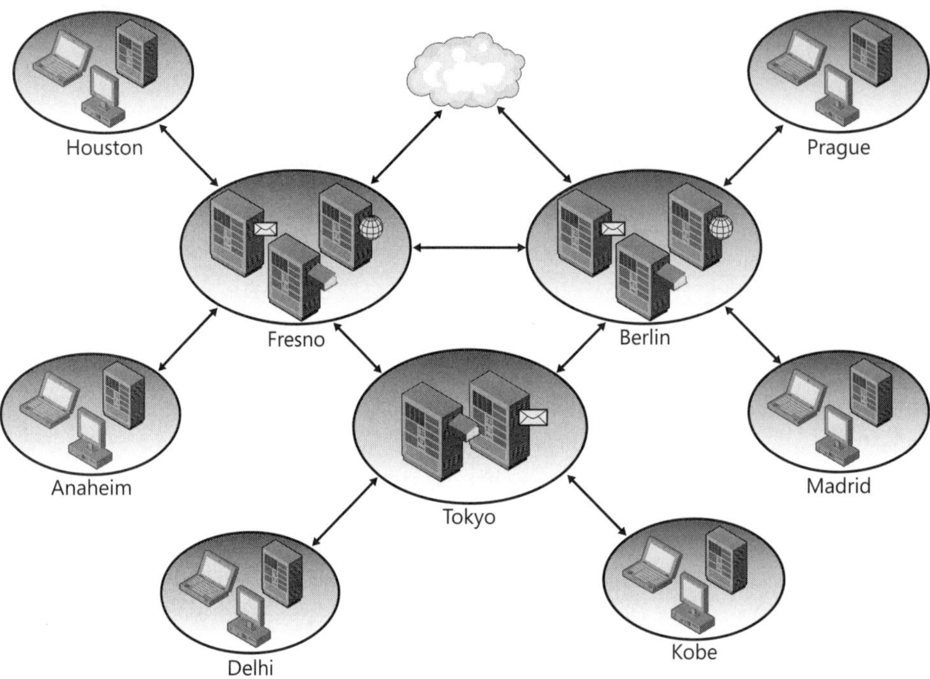

FIGURE 4-42 Litware Inc logical view

Litware Inc will implement a very similar design to Contoso, except that it will use regional namespaces to ensure that traffic does not cross its WANs. Litware Inc will deploy a high-availability solution within the regional datacenter, either with a software or hardware load balancer. Only the three hub sites—Fresno, Berlin, and Tokyo—have Exchange servers. The spoke sites, such as Kobe, Prague, and Madrid, will not have Exchange servers locally. Figure 4-43 shows how the sites will configure their certificates and URLs. Fresno, Berlin, and Tokyo will replace *Region* with the region-specific information. Tokyo, for example, will use *Tokyo.litwareinc.com* as their URL for OWA.

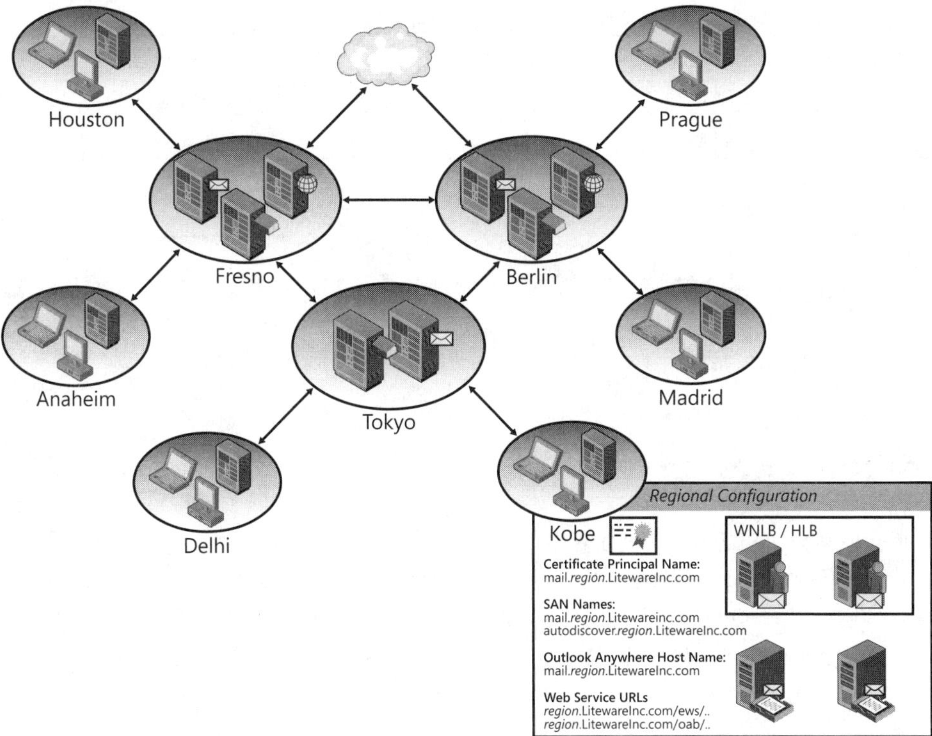

FIGURE 4-43 Proposed Litware Inc architecture

Case Study Summary

When planning namespaces for client access, a helpful process is to list each possible client along with each access type or failure scenario. We can then use the information presented earlier in the chapter to understand if our design will meet the business high-availability requirements.

As you can see in Table 4.13, be as specific as possible with the clients. Using this type of worksheet to evaluate each client, access type, and access scenario against your design will help ensure a successful deployment.

TABLE 4-13 Sample Design Worksheet

CLIENT	EXTERNAL ACCESS	COMPLETE PRIMARY SITE FAILURE	PARTIAL PRIMARY SITE FAILOVER
Outlook 2003 RPC/HTTPs			
Outlook 2007 Outlook Anywhere			

CLIENT	EXTERNAL ACCESS	COMPLETE PRIMARY SITE FAILURE	PARTIAL PRIMARY SITE FAILOVER
Outlook 2003 internal access			
Outlook 2007 internal access			
Windows Mobile 6.x			
External Outlook Web App			

Additional Resources

- Outlook Anywhere Scalability with Outlook 2007, Outlook 2003, and Exchange 2007: *http://technet.microsoft.com/en-us/library/cc540453(EXCHG.80).aspx*
- Exchange Remote Connectivity Analyzer: *https://www.testexchangeconnectivity.com*
- Configuring the Blackberry Enterprise Server with Exchange 2010: *http://docs.blackberry.com/en/admin/deliverables/12070/Configuring_Exchange_2010_environ_962756_11.jsp*
- Unified Communication Certificate Partners for Exchange and OCS: *http://support.microsoft.com/kb/929395*
- Brad Hughes's blog (script to automate Client Access server site assignment): *http://blogs.msdn.com/brad_hughes/archive/2008/05/20/autodiscover-and-client-only-sites-revisited.aspx*
- You cannot suppress the AutoDiscover redirect warning in Outlook 2007: *http://support.microsoft.com/?kbid=956528*
- TCPView for Windows: *http://technet.microsoft.com/en-us/sysinternals/bb897437.aspx*
- Automatically configure Office Outlook 2007 user accounts *http://technet.microsoft.com/en-us/library/cc511507.aspx*

CHAPTER 5

Routing and Transport

Routing messages is the most important feature of a messaging service. If your message servers don't deliver messages to other servers anymore, you are in deep trouble. And that's exactly what this chapter is about: routing and transport.

In this chapter you will learn about the Transport Server architecture, including a detailed description of Transport server services, the queue database, the message transport components, and how they work together. The architecture section focuses on Hub Transport and Edge Transport servers, which function similarly. Then you will read about transport agents and the events they can trigger. Even though many administrators don't use or even know about transport agents, it is good to understand their purpose so that you can advise your users if they have a special message-application need.

Finally, you will learn everything about message routing and the features and functions available in Exchange 2010 to manipulate and optimize message routing. In most situations message routing is fairly easy, and only needs special consideration in complex organizations.

Details on the Edge Transport server especially in the areas of anti-spam and antivirus features are covered in Chapter 7, "Edge Transport and Messaging Security."

Exchange Transport Server Architecture

The Exchange Transport Server architecture includes several areas whose interdependence and configuration options you should understand.

Components of Message Transport

The Transport Pipeline in Exchange Server 2010 consists of several components that work together to route messages. There are four mechanisms to submit a message into the transport pipeline:

- **SMTP Protocol** SMTP servers or messaging clients can submit mail using the standard SMTP protocol. The message enters the transport pipeline using an SMTP Receive connector.

- **Store Driver** Mail from Mailbox Servers is submitted via Store Driver.
- **Pickup/Replay Folders** Properly formatted messages can be dropped into the file system and the server will pick them up and process them.
- **Agent/System Generated** The system can generate messages such as Non-Delivery Reports (NDRs) or Delivery Reports, and agents can generate messages such as Journal messages.

Figure 5-1 illustrates the Transport Pipeline and all components of a message transport to route messages through a Hub Transport server. As described later in the chapter, not all of these components are available for Edge Transport servers.

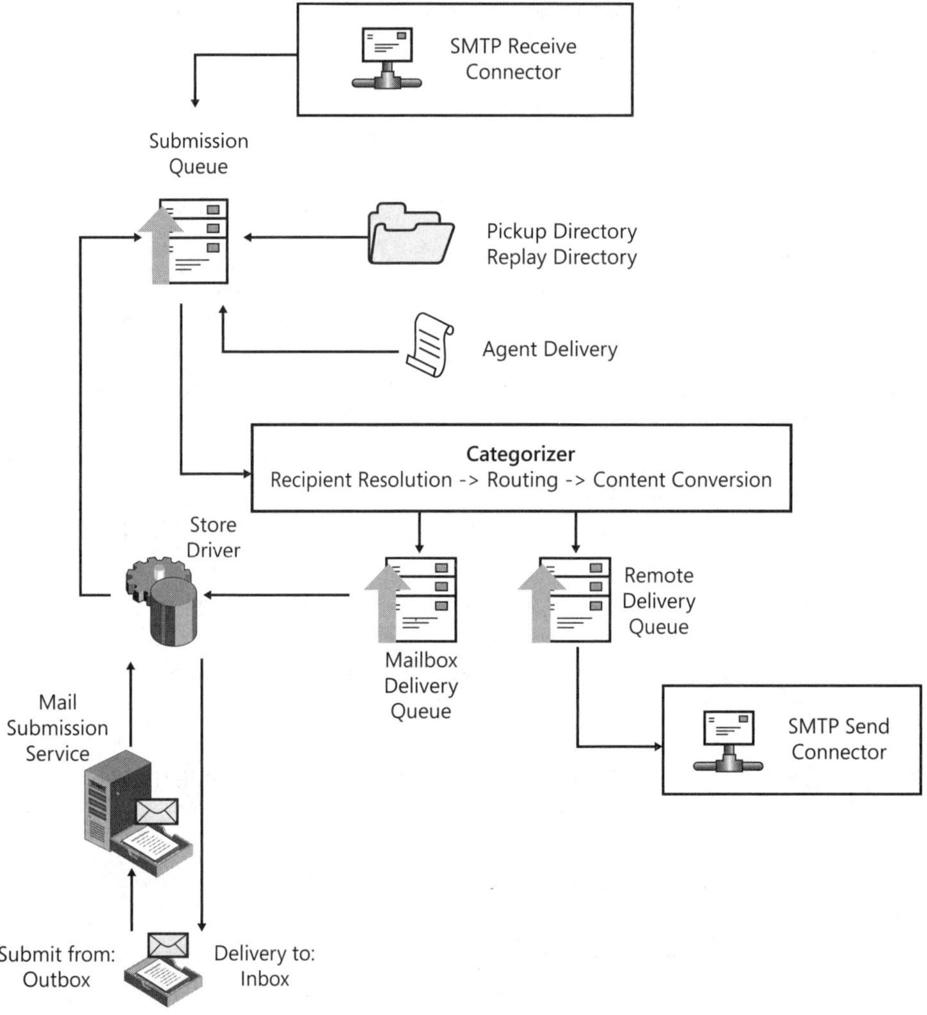

FIGURE 5-1 Message transport components

In the figure, the black arrows refer to message delivery or receiving a message; the dotted arrows illustrate how a message is submitted or sent.

Submission Queue

When the Microsoft Exchange Transport service starts, the categorizer creates one Submission queue on each Edge Transport server and Hub Transport server. The Submission queue stores all messages on disk until the categorizer processes them for further delivery. The categorizer cannot process a message unless a server promotes it to the Submission queue. While the categorizer processes a message, it remains in the Submission queue. After successful categorization, the message is removed from the submission queue.

INSIDE TRACK

Troubleshooting Submission Queue

Charlie Chung
Program Manager, Microsoft Corp, Redmond

What's useful about knowing that the submission queue is behind the categorizer is that if the submission queue is growing, you need to look at categorizer to figure out why messages are backing up. For example, most antivirus products are registered on a categorizer event. If that agent is misbehaving, the submission queue will grow.

On the Hub Transport server, message submission can occur through the store driver, through the pickup or replay directory, directly by an agent, or by the Receive connector. On the Edge Transport server, submission is generally only through the Receive connector because messages flow in from the Internet, although pickup or replay directories exist.

Delivery Queue

Delivery queues hold messages before they are delivered to their target database. Depending on where they should route the messages to, they are called *mailbox delivery queue* and *remote delivery queue.*

- Mailbox delivery queues hold messages that are being delivered to a mailbox server located in the same site by using encrypted Exchange RPC. Mailbox delivery queues, one queue for each database, exist on Hub Transport servers only.
- Remote delivery queues hold messages that are being delivered to a remote server by using SMTP. Remote delivery queues can exist on both Hub Transport servers and Edge Transport servers, and more than one remote delivery queue can exist on each server. On an Edge Transport server, these destinations are external SMTP domains or SMTP connectors. On a Hub Transport server, these destinations are SMTP connectors that are outside the Active Directory site in which the Hub Transport server is located or a remote SMTP connector.

Categorizer

The categorizer retrieves one message at a time from the Submission queue, and always picks the oldest message first. On Hub Transport servers, the categorizer completes the following three steps: recipient resolution, routing resolution, and content conversation. On Edge Transport servers the categorizer puts the message into the delivery queue and routes it to a Hub Transport server.

Store Driver

Messages sent from mailboxes enter the transport pipeline from the sender's Outbox. After the message is put in the sender's Outbox, the store driver is alerted by the Microsoft Exchange Mail Submission service, the store driver retrieves the message from the sender's Outbox, and then puts it into the Submission queue on a Hub Transport server in the same Active Directory site of the Mailbox server.

The store driver is also responsible for picking up messages that should be delivered locally (delivered in the same Active Directory site) from a delivery queue. The store driver puts the message in the recipient's inbox on the respective Mailbox server.

It is important to understand that store driver is an interface between the Hub server and the Mailbox server. That is why you see it in the beginning and the end of the Transport Pipeline—it is used to for messages submitted by the Mailbox server and to deliver messages to the target mailbox database.

Microsoft Exchange Mail Submission Service

The Microsoft Exchange Mail Submission service is a notification service running on Mailbox servers. It notifies the store driver on a Hub Transport server in the local Active Directory site when a message is available for retrieval from a sender's Outbox.

Pickup and Replay Directory

The Pickup and Replay directories serve basically the same purpose: to process properly formatted text files usually generated by applications into messages. The pickup directory is used by applications or users; the Replay directory is used to resubmit exported Exchange messages and to receive messages from foreign gateway servers. Because their purpose is almost identical, this section only focuses on the Pickup directory. Details about the Replay directory can be found at *http://technet.microsoft.com/en-us/library/bb124230.aspx*.

The Pickup directory is another way for messages to enter the message transport pipeline by being placed into the Pickup directory on a Hub Transport server or an Edge Transport server. The Pickup directory is by default located under *<Exchange_Installation_Path>*\TransportRoles\Pickup. It can be modified using the following cmdlet:

```
Set-TransportServer <Servername> -PickupDirectoryPath "C:\Pickup"
```

The Pickup directory is used to support legacy applications that are not capable of sending messages using MAPI or SMTP protocol but instead by using a simple text file (extension .eml) that is stored in the Pickup directory.

The text file has to include a certain formatting so that Exchange can compose a message out of the text file and sent it. The following requirements must be met:

- The message file must be a text file that complies with the basic SMTP message format. MIME message header fields and content are supported.
- Only one e-mail address can exist in the Sender field. Multiple e-mail addresses aren't allowed.
- At least one e-mail address must exist in the To, Cc, or Bcc fields.
- A blank line must exist between the message header and the message body.

The following is an example of a valid message that can be processed by the Pickup directory:

```
To: Joel@litware.com
From: Sigi@fabrikam.com
Subject: Pickup Directory Test

Hi!
This is a Pickup Directory Test
Sigi
```

The pickup process is quite simple: you store a message as a <*message*>.eml file in the directory, the Pickup directory is checked every five seconds (this cannot be changed), and then .eml files will be processed.

The processing of messages in the pickup directory always follows the same scheme:

1. Rename <*message*>.eml to <message>.tmp. (If the file exists, the date and time are added to the name as well.)
2. If the <*message*>.eml did not include the required formatting, the file is renamed to <*message*>.bad.
3. After the message is successfully queued for delivery, a close command is issued, and the .tmp file is deleted from the Pickup directory.

> ***NOTE*** **If the Microsoft Exchange Transport service is restarted when there are .tmp files in the Pickup or Replay directories, all .tmp files are renamed as .eml files and are reprocessed. This could lead to duplicate message transmission.**

Message Queues on Transport Servers

Every message that is sent between Transport servers is temporary stored on the Transport server in a place called a *message queue*. In this location, the message waits for the next step in processing. As explained in Table 5-1, six different message queues are available on a Transport server. You will find more details on the specific queues later in this chapter.

TABLE 5-1 Message Queues in Exchange 2010

QUEUE NAME	DESCRIPTION
Mailbox delivery queue (or MAPI delivery)	Delivers messages to mailbox databases located in the same Active Directory site. One queue is available per database. This queue only exists on Hub Transport servers.
Remote delivery queue	On Hub Transports, delivers messages to a Hub Transport server in a remote Active Directory site. On Edge Transport servers, delivers messages to remote SMTP domains.
Submission queue	Stores messages that are then processed by the categorizer for further delivery.
Shadow redundancy queue	Copies of messages that are sent to a remote Hub Transport that did not yet report successful delivery of the message are stored here.
Poison message queue	Stores isolated messages that are detected to be potentially harmful to the Exchange 2010 system.
Unreachable queue	Contains messages that can't be routed to their destinations, most likely because of Active Directory replication latency or other configuration issues.

Exchange 2010 stores all queues in the queue database, which is described in the next section. The queues itself can be managed using either the Queue Viewer or using the *Get-Queue* cmdlet, as shown in Figure 5-2.

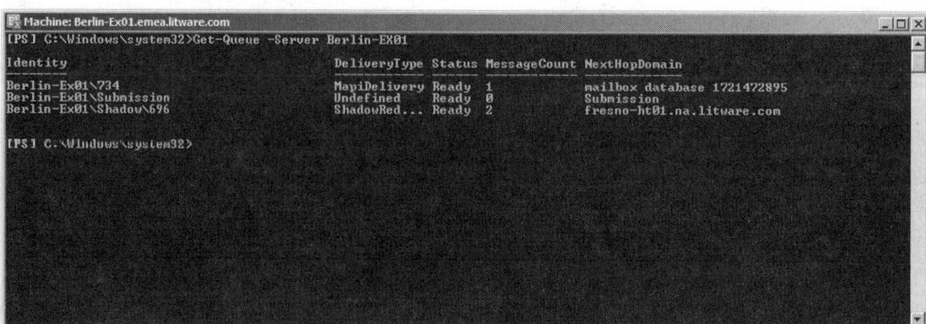

FIGURE 5-2 Viewing messages queues using the *Get-Queue* cmdlet

Queue Database

All message queues are stored in a single database called a *queue database*. The queue database is based on the Extensible Storage Engine (ESE) database technology, which is also used by the Mailbox Server. The queue database is made up of a database file and several log files to record transactions. The checkpoint file tracks which transaction log files have been committed to the database. During a service shutdown of the Microsoft Exchange Transport service, all transaction log files are always committed to the database.

The queue database uses circular logging, which means that the history of committed transactions that are stored in the transaction log files is not maintained. Any transaction log file older than the current checkpoint is immediately and automatically deleted and thus cannot be used to replay queue database recovery.

Queue Database Files

The queue database consists of several files, which are stored in the following default location: <*Exchange_Install_Path*>\TransportRoles\data\Queue. Table 5-2 provides an overview of the queue database files and their purpose.

TABLE 5-2 Queue Database Files and Purpose

FILE	DESCRIPTION
Mail.que	This file is the queue database and stores all queued messages after they are committed from the transaction log files.
Tmp.edb	This temporary database file is used to verify the queue database schema on startup.
Trn*.log	This transaction log records all changes to the queue database. Changes to the database are first written to the transaction log and are then committed to the database. Trn.log is the current active transaction log file. Trntmp.log is the next provisioned transaction log file that is created in advance. If the existing Trn.log transaction log file reaches its maximum size of 5 MB, Trn.log is renamed to Trn*XXXX*.log, where *XXXX* is a sequence number. Trntmp.log is then renamed Trn.log and becomes the current active transaction log file.
Trn.chk	The checkpoint file. It tracks the transaction log entries that have been committed to the database. This file is always in the same location as the mail.que file.
Trnres00001.jrs Trnres00002.jrs	These files are used to reserve emergency storage if the transaction log volume becomes full.

Queue Database Configuration Options

Several configuration options exist for the queue database. Unlike Mailbox or public folder databases, settings for the queue database cannot be configured in the Exchange Management Console or with EMS; instead, you need to change the settings in the EdgeTransport.exe.config file located at <*Exchange_Server_Install*>\Bin. If you change any settings, you need to restart the Microsoft Exchange Transport service for the changes to take effect.

Table 5-3 provides an overview of options available to configure the queue database.

TABLE 5-3 Overview of Parameters to Configure the Queue Database

PARAMETER	DESCRIPTION
QueueDatabasePath	Directory of the queue database files. If you change the directory, make sure that the new directory exists or use the Move-TransportDatabase.ps1 script.
QueueDatabaseLoggingPath	Directory of the queue database log files. If you change the directory, make sure that the new directory exists or use the Move-TransportDatabase.ps1 script.
QueueDatabaseBatchSize	Defines the number of database I/O operations that can be grouped together before they are executed. Default: 40.
QueueDatabaseBatchTimeout	Defines the maximum time in milliseconds that the database will wait for multiple database I/O operations to group. Default: 100.
QueueDatabaseMaxConnections	Defines the number of ESE database connections that can be open. Default: 4.
QueueDatabaseLoggingBufferSize	Specifies the memory that is used to cache the transaction records before they are written to the transaction log file. Default: 5,242,880 bytes.
QueueDatabaseLoggingFileSize	Defines the maximum size of a transaction log file before a new log file is opened. Default: 5,242,880 bytes.
QueueDatabaseMaxBackgroundCleanupTasks	Defines the maximum number of background cleanup work items that can be queued to the database engine thread pool. Default: 32.
QueueDatabaseOnlineDefragEnabled	Enables or disables scheduled online defragmentation. Default: $true.

PARAMETER	DESCRIPTION
QueueDatabaseOnlineDefragSchedule	Defines the time to start the online defragmentation. Default: 1:00:00 (1:00 A.M.).
QueueDatabaseOnlineDefragTimeToRun	Specifies the maximum time the online defragmentation task is allowed to run. If the defragmentation task is not finished in time, the queue database is left in a consistent state. Default: 3:00:00 (3 hours).

To change the folder or drive of the queue database or log files, you can use the use the Move-TransportDatabase.ps1 script available in the *<Exchange_Server_Install>*\Scripts folder. For example, if you want to move the queue database and log files to the D:\Queue folder, you use the *.\Move-TransportDatabase.ps1 –QueueDatabasePath D:\Queue –QueueDatabaseLoggingPath D:\Queue* command.

Transport Server Services

Exchange Server 2010 installs various Windows services so that Exchange can automatically run during startup and does not depend on administrative interaction. In most situations you do not need to consider their purpose because they are configured automatically during Exchange 2010 setup. However, once you face issues or a service does not start automatically during Exchange startup, it is good to know the purpose of the service and whether there are any implications when the service is not started.

Hub Transport Services

Table 5-4 shows the services that are added to the operating system when adding the Exchange Server Hub Transport role to a server.

TABLE 5-4 Exchange Services for Hub Transport Role

SERVICE	DESCRIPTION	BEST PRACTICE INFORMATION
Microsoft Exchange Active Directory Topology	This service reads information from all Active Directory partitions. The data is cached and then used by Exchange 2010 servers to discover the Active Directory site location of all Exchange services in the organization. It is also responsible for updating the site attribute of the Exchange server object in Active Directory.	Runs on all Exchange servers but Edge servers. Stopping this service is the quickest way to stop all Exchange services because all other Transport related services will also be stopped.

SERVICE	DESCRIPTION	BEST PRACTICE INFORMATION
Microsoft Exchange Anti-spam Update	This service manages the anti-spam automatic updates for Exchange. It installs the Microsoft standard set of anti-spam signature files received by Windows Update.	You can stop this service and change it to service startup manual on Hub Transport servers that do not have or need the Microsoft anti-spam feature enabled. You don't need this service if you use Microsoft Forefront Protection for Exchange 2010 because it will install its own premium update service.
Microsoft Exchange EdgeSync	This service is responsible for the EdgeSync feature to synchronize the directory information with an Edge AD LDS.	This service needs to run on any hub transport server that participates in an Edge Synchronization.
Microsoft Exchange Monitoring	This service allows applications to call the Exchange diagnostic cmdlets.	This service should be started when you consider implementing monitoring tools such as System Center Operations Manager. Otherwise you don't need to start it.
Microsoft Exchange Service Host	This service is the replacement for the System Attendant service found in previous Exchange version and is responsible, for example, for calculating MailTips.	The service should always be in a running state; otherwise, the *Test-ServiceHealth* cmdlet will recognize it and report a fail.
Microsoft Exchange Protected Service Host	Provides a host for several Microsoft Exchange services that must be protected from other services.	This service is started automatically and is used by Exchange for internal processing.
Microsoft Exchange Transport	This is the core transport service and is responsible for routing messages between servers.	This service is required for every Hub or Edge Transport server.
Microsoft Exchange Transport Log Search	Provides remote search capability for Microsoft Exchange Transport log files.	This service should be started if you want to use the Tracking Log Explorer or provide Delivery Reports to your users. The CAS servers will access it to retrieve tracking information.

Edge Transport Services

The Edge Transport services are installed to the Windows OS during Exchange setup. Table 5-5 lists Edge Transport–specific services (that differ from Hub Transport services) along with their purpose and best practice information.

TABLE 5-5 Exchange Services for Edge Transport Role

SERVICE	DESCRIPTION	BEST PRACTICE INFORMATION
Microsoft Exchange ADAM	Stores configuration data and recipient data in AD LDS database on the Edge Transport server.	All other Exchange services depend on this service, so stopping this service is the quickest way to stop all services.
Microsoft Exchange Credential Service	Monitors credential changes that occur in the Exchange organization and are replicated to AD LDS and installs these changes on the Edge Transport server.	This service is required for every Edge Transport server.

Delivery Status Notifications

Delivery status notifications (DSNs) notify the Microsoft Exchange Server 2010 administrator or e-mail sender of the status of a particular message. DSN messages are a critical part of troubleshooting e-mail connectivity issues between local Exchange recipients and issues between your Exchange organization and the remote e-mail servers on the Internet.

DSN messages occur with the following error code areas:

- **4.x.x** This indicates a temporary problem where for example a mailbox server was unavailable and typically resolve themselves.
- **5.x.x** This status code indicates a permanent problem and results in a Non-delivery Report (NDR) being sent to the originator of the message.

For messaging administrators the 5.x.x DSN status codes are the more interesting ones for troubleshooting for example. Table 5-6 provides a description of important DSN status codes.

TABLE 5-6 Overview of 5.x.x DSN Status Codes

DSN STATUS CODE	DESCRIPTION
5.1.1	Bad destination mailbox address. E-mail address or domain does not exist.
5.1.4	Destination mailbox address ambiguous. Two or more recipients in the Exchange organization have the same address.

DSN STATUS CODE	DESCRIPTION
5.2.2	Mailbox full. The recipient's mailbox has exceeded its storage quota and is no longer able to accept new messages.
5.3.4	Message too big for system. The message exceeds the size limit configured.
5.4.6	Routing loop detected. A configuration error has caused an e-mail loop.
5.5.3	Too many recipients. The total of recipients of the message exceeds the total number of recipients allowed in a single message.
5.7.1	Delivery not authorized. The sender of the message is not allowed to send messages to the recipient.
5.7.2	Unable to relay. The sending e-mail system is not allowed to send messages to an e-mail system where that e-mail system is not the final destination of the message.
5.7.3	Client was not authenticated. The sending e-mail system did not authenticate.

DSN messages and DSN codes are commonly configured either to modify the DSN message or to configure what DSN codes are copied to the Postmaster mailbox.

Modifying DSN Messages

Exchange 2010 is extremely customizable with regard to system messages and allows you to modify any DSN message using the *New-SystemMessage* cmdlet. You can define the DSN message, the language that is used, and whether the message is available internally only. For example, to configure a custom text message for the DSN code 5.1.1 use the following cmdlet:

```
New-SystemMessage -DSNCode 5.1.1 -Text "E-Mail Address does not exist" -Internal $false
-Language En
```

Customizing your DSN message is quite a timely effort. However, when your company's policy requires displaying custom system messages—for example, to provide user guidance—you can use this feature.

Creating DSN Message Copies

By default Exchange does not keep a copy of DSN messages but instead discards them automatically to preserve space. In some situations you will want to receive a DSN message to understand your messaging system. For example, when you're migrating from a different e-mail system and you just created all mailboxes with their respective original e-mail addresses, you may want to verify which e-mail addresses are not yet available in the system. Therefore, you'd want to determine which e-mail addresses are currently rejected.

If you want to keep DSN messages, you first need to configure the Exchange Recipient Reply Recipient (also known as Postmaster mailbox) using the following cmdlet:

```
Set-OrganizationConfig -MicrosoftExchangeRecipientReplyRecipient <PostmasterMailbox>
```

Then you need to specify the DSN status codes for which you want Exchange to send DSNs to the Postmaster mailbox. This is done using a cmdlet such as the following:

```
Set-TransportConfig -GenerateCopyOfDSNFor 5.1.1
```

> ***IMPORTANT*** **In an Exchange organization with EdgeSync, all these settings are configured on a Hub Transport server in your Exchange organization, not on the Edge Transport servers. If you run Edge Transport servers without EdgeSync, you need to configure the *Set-TransportConfig –ExternalPostmasterAddress <E-Mail Address>* cmdlet as well.**

Message Latency Measurement

New to Exchange 2010 is the ability to measure service levels for messages that flow through the system. Latency measurements are implemented into the core transport service and logged in Message Tracking.

Exchange 2010 comes with the ConvertTo-MessageLatency.ps1 script (found in the *<Exchange_Install_Path>*\Scripts folder) that extracts server and end-to-end latency information from the tracking log. It can be used to convert the data structure of a tracking log event to present a more friendly presentation of the component latency data. Thus you can use the script to identify messages why they've taken a long time to deliver to the users and what Hub Transport servers caused the delay. An example is found in Figure 5-3.

```
Machine: Fresno-HT01.na.litware.com
[PS] C:\Program Files\Microsoft\Exchange Server\V14\Scripts>Get-MessageTrackingLog | .\ConvertTo-MessageLatency.ps1

InternalMessageId   : 2
MessageId           : <1a3e15b3-0cc8-4040-b6ae-f486235e4c27@FRESNO-HT01.na.litware.com>
MessageLatency      : 00:00:03.9690000
MessageLatencyType  : LocalServer
ComponentServerFqdn : FRESNO-HT01.na.litware.com
ComponentCode       : TOTAL
ComponentName       : Total Server Latency
ComponentLatency    : 00:00:04

InternalMessageId   : 2
MessageId           : <1a3e15b3-0cc8-4040-b6ae-f486235e4c27@FRESNO-HT01.na.litware.com>
MessageLatency      : 00:00:03.9690000
MessageLatencyType  : LocalServer
ComponentServerFqdn : FRESNO-HT01.na.litware.com
ComponentCode       : SMSC
ComponentName       : SMTP Send Connect
ComponentLatency    : 00:00:01

InternalMessageId   : 2
MessageId           : <1a3e15b3-0cc8-4040-b6ae-f486235e4c27@FRESNO-HT01.na.litware.com>
MessageLatency      : 00:00:03.9690000
MessageLatencyType  : LocalServer
ComponentServerFqdn : FRESNO-HT01.na.litware.com
```

FIGURE 5-3 Running the ConvertTo-MessageLatency.ps1 Script

Additionally, the tracking logs are processed automatically and are summarized in log files located in the following directories found under *<Exchange_Installation_Path>*\TransportRoles\Logs on each transport server:

- ActiveUserStats (exported every eight hours)
- ServerStats (exported every hour)

The logs are in CSV format and are automatically produced to provide statistics for a single server. You can thus use Microsoft Excel to look at the log files.

If you use System Center Operations Manager (SCOM), including the Exchange Management Pack (MP), the log files are aggregated to the System Center data warehouse database. This is where the reports are generated. These reports show hourly and daily server statistics as well as active users and distribution group usage.

Shadow Redundancy

Exchange Server 2010 introduces the shadow redundancy feature, which provides redundancy for messages for the entire time they are in transit. Copies of messages that are submitted to a Hub Transport server are stored in the transport queue until the next hop reports successful delivery of the message. If the next hop doesn't report successful delivery and it fails, the message is resubmitted for delivery. Shadow Redundancy is actually made of three shadowing techniques:

- **Shadow Queue** Stores messages not yet confirmed by the next hop to be delivered.
- **Delayed Acknowledgment (Transport Wormhole)** The connections are held open until the delivery is confirmed on the next hop.
- **System Generated Reference Count** Includes a pattern to ensure that system-generated messages are also copied to the shadow queue.

The Shadow Redundancy Manager (SRM) is the core component of a Transport server that is responsible for managing shadow redundancy. The SRM is responsible for maintaining the following information for all the primary messages that a server is currently processing:

- The shadow server for each primary message being processed
- The discard status to be sent to shadow servers

The SRM is responsible for the following actions for all the shadow messages that a server has in its shadow queues:

- Maintaining the list and checking primary server availability for each shadow message
- Processing discard notifications from primary servers
- Removing shadow messages from the database once it receives all expected discard notifications
- Deciding when the shadow server should take ownership of shadow messages, thus making it the primary server

Figure 5-4 shows how shadow redundancy keeps a copy of the messages that have not yet been delivered by the Hub Transport server located in the Active Directory site Site-Fresno. As soon as the Hub Transport in Fresno is able to send the message to the next hub, the Hub Transport located on Berlin-Ex01 receives an acknowledgment and will remove the messages from the shadow redundancy queue.

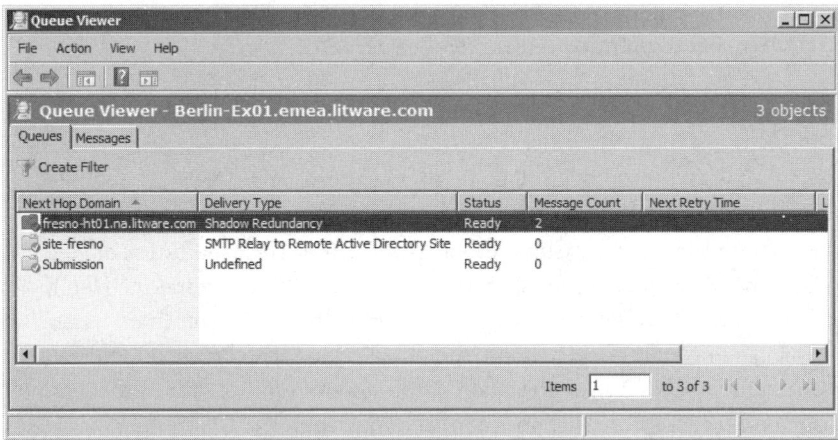

FIGURE 5-4 Shadow Redundancy Queue in Queue Viewer

Shadow redundancy is a high-availability feature; you will find more information, including configuration options, in Chapter 11, "Designing High Availability."

Message Throttling

Message throttling is a new feature of Exchange 2010 that implements limits on Hub Transport or Edge Transport servers to prevent accidental or intentional inundation of system resources. These limits are defined on areas such as the number of messages or connections that are processed by the Transport server.

Message throttling involves limits on message processing rates, SMTP connection rates, and SMTP session timeout values. These limits protect the Transport servers from being overwhelmed by accepting and delivering too many messages or connections.

Message throttling is enabled by default but you can adapt message throttling options on the Transport server, the Send connector and Receive connector. Options that you can define include the *MaxConcurrentMailboxDeliveries* parameter on Transport servers and the *MaxInboundConnection* and *MaxProtocolErrors* parameters on Receive connectors.

Exchange 2010 Service Pack 1 adds Delivery Class Throttling to the feature set. This adds the ability to classify a message based on certain characteristics and assign it a delivery class. Throttling will investigate messages when they are sent by individual users and add a cost to each message based on message size, number of recipients, and frequency. This cost factor allows assigning a delivery class to the messages.

The behavior is similar to postal mail. First-class mail gets delivered faster than regular postage mail. The higher the delivery class, the higher the message priority is in the connector queue. For example, Delivery Class Throttling will prioritize small messages with just a couple of recipients over large bulk messages with many recipients in the message queue.

For more information about message throttling, including all available message throttling options, see *http://technet.microsoft.com/en-us/library/bb232205.aspx*.

Back Pressure

Back pressure is a system-resource monitoring feature of the Microsoft Exchange Transport service available on the Hub Transport or Edge Transport server role.

Back pressure monitors important system resources, such as available hard-disk drive space and available memory. If utilization of a system resource exceeds the specified limit, the Exchange server stops accepting new connections and messages. This prevents system resources from being completely overwhelmed, and enables the Exchange server to deliver the messages queued to be sent. When utilization of the system resource returns to a normal level, the Exchange server accepts new connections and messages.

For each monitored system resource on a Hub Transport server or Edge Transport server, the following three levels of resource utilization are applied:

- **Normal** The resource is not overused. The server accepts new connections and messages.
- **Medium** The resource is slightly overused. Back pressure is applied to the server in a limited manner. Mail from senders in the authoritative domain can flow. However, the server rejects new connections and messages from other sources.
- **High** The resource is severely overused. Full back pressure is applied. All message flow stops, and the server rejects all new connections and messages.

> ***NOTE*** **Because Microsoft does not recommend modifying any back pressure settings, parameters were not included in this section, but you can access them at *http://technet.microsoft.com/en-us/library/bb201658.aspx*. You configure back pressure settings in the EdgeTransport.exe.config file located at <*Exchange_Server_Install*>\Bin.**

Understanding Transport Agents

Transport agents allow you to install custom software on a Hub or Edge Transport server role in Exchange Server 2010. Based on an action when a message flows through the transport pipeline, the software then can process messages. The backscatter agent, is an example of a transport agent.

> ***IMPORTANT*** **Transport agents have full access to all e-mail messages that they encounter. There are no restrictions on a transport agent's behavior. Transport agents that are unstable or contain security flaws may affect the stability and security of Exchange. Do not install transport agents that haven't been fully tested in a test environment!**

Default Transport Agents

Exchange Server 2010 includes several transport agents that enable it to provide additional features such as rights management service (RMS) or journaling. Table 5-7 lists default transport agents sorted by Hub Transport and Edge Transport server roles.

TABLE 5-7 Default Transport Agents

HUB TRANSPORT AGENTS	EDGE TRANSPORT AGENTS
Transport Rule agent	Connection Filtering agent
RMS Encryption agent	Address Rewriting Inbound agent
RMS Decryption agent	Edge Rule agent
Prelicensing agent	Content Filter agent
Journaling agent	Sender ID agent
Journal Report Decryption agent	Sender Filter agent
Text Messaging Routing agent from Text Messaging Delivery Agent Connector	Recipient Filter agent
	Protocol Analysis agent
	Attachment Filtering agent
	Address Rewriting Outbound agent

You can get a list of all transport agents currently configured on an Exchange Transport server by running the *Get-TransportAgent* cmdlet. For a list of Transport Agents that have been used to process messages since the last time the transport service was restarted, use the *Get-TransportPipeline* cmdlet as shown in Figure 5-5.

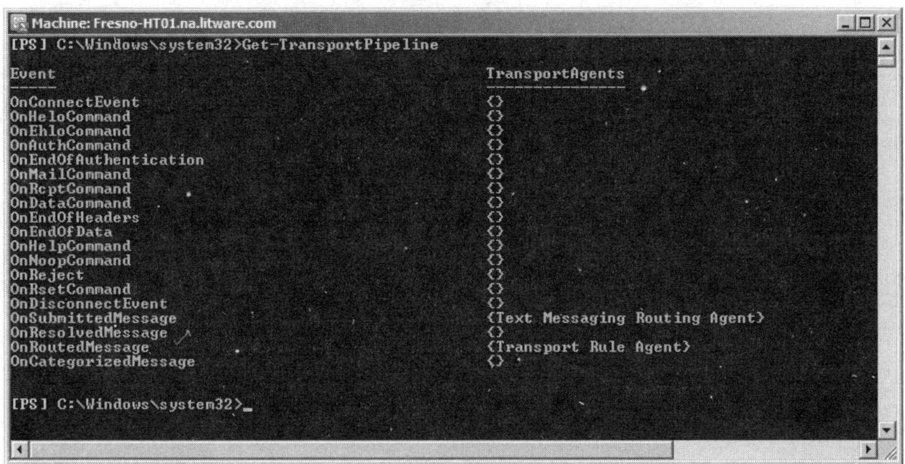

FIGURE 5-5 Default Transport Agents on a Hub Transport server

Events That Trigger Transport Agents

Exchange 2010 Transport agents use SMTP events to trigger the agent when a message moves through the transport pipeline. Three areas can trigger events: SMTP Receive events, Categorizer events, and Connection Manager events.

Even though all events available are listed in the following subsections, this chapter does not explain in detail how to develop a transport agent, but merely provides an overview of what you can do using Exchange 2010. More information about Transport Agents can be found at *http://technet.microsoft.com/en-us/library/bb125012.aspx.*

SMTP Receive Events

SMTP Receive events are triggered whenever an SMTP connection is made or an SMTP command is sent, as listed in Table 5-8. Using SMTP Receive events you can interact with the system at almost every stage of an SMTP communication.

TABLE 5-8 SMTP Receive Events Overview

EVENT	DESCRIPTION
OnConnect	This event is triggered upon initial connection from a remote SMTP host.
OnEhloCommand	This event is triggered when the EHLO SMTP verb is issued by the remote SMTP host.
OnHeloCommand	This event is triggered when the HELO SMTP verb is issued by the remote SMTP host.
OnAuthCommand	This event is triggered when the AUTH SMTP verb is issued by the remote SMTP host.
OnEndOfAuthentication	This event is triggered when the remote SMTP host has completed authentication.
OnMailCommand	This event is triggered when the MAIL FROM SMTP verb is issued by the remote SMTP host.
OnRcptToCommand	This event is triggered when the RCPT TO SMTP verb is issued by the remote SMTP host.
OnDataCommand	This event is triggered when the DATA SMTP verb is issued by the remote SMTP host.
OnEndOfHeaders	This event is triggered when the remote SMTP host as completed submitting the e-mail message headers.
OnEndOfData	This event is triggered when the remote SMTP host issues <CRLF>.<CRLF>, which indicates the end of data.

EVENT	DESCRIPTION
OnHelpCommand	This event is triggered when the HELP SMTP verb is issued by the remote SMTP host. This event can occur at any time after the *OnConnect* SMTP event and before the *OnDisconnect* SMTP event.
OnNoopCommand	This event is triggered when the NOOP SMTP verb is issued by the remote SMTP host. This event can occur at any time after the *OnConnect* SMTP event and before the *OnDisconnect* SMTP event.
OnReject	This event is triggered when the receiving SMTP host issues a temporary or permanent delivery status notification (DSN) code to the sending SMTP host. This event can occur at any time after the *OnConnect* SMTP event and before the *OnDisconnect* SMTP event.
OnRsetCommand	This event is triggered when the RSET SMTP verb is issued by the sending SMTP host. This event can occur at any time after the *OnConnect* SMTP event and before the *OnDisconnect* SMTP event.
OnDisconnect	This event is triggered upon disconnection of the SMTP conversation by either a receiving or sending SMTP host.

Categorizer Events

The Categorizer events are triggered when a message enters, is processed by, or leaves the categorizer, as listed in Table 5-9.

TABLE 5-9 Categorizer Events Overview

EVENT	DESCRIPTION
OnSubmittedMessage	This event is triggered upon submission of a message into the Submission queues on the receiving SMTP host. All messages encounter this event whether they arrived via SMTP submission, MAPI submission, or the Pickup or Replay directories.
OnResolvedMessage	This event is triggered after all the recipients have been resolved but before the next hop has been determined for each recipient. The *OnResolvedMessage* routing event enables subsequent events to override the default routing behavior by using the per-recipient *SetRoutingOverride* method.
OnRoutedMessage	This event is triggered after messages have been categorized, distribution lists have been expanded, and recipients have been resolved.
OnCategorizedMessage	This event is triggered when the Categorizer completes processing the message.

Connection Manager Events

Connection manager events are only available to delivery agents such as the Text Messaging Routing agent from Text Messaging Delivery Agent Connector. As mentioned previously in this chapter, delivery agents should succeed Foreign Connectors because they are more flexible. Table 5-10 provides an overview of the events raised by the connection manager component.

TABLE 5-10 Connection Manager Component Events Overview

EVENT	DESCRIPTION
OnOpenConnection	This event is raised when there are messages in the queue to be delivered to the foreign system. It notifies the delivery agent to initiate a connection to the foreign system.
OnDeliverMailItem	This event notifies the delivery agent to retrieve the next item from the queue.
OnCloseConnection	This event is raised when there are no more messages in the queue to be delivered to the foreign system. It notifies the delivery agent to close the connection to the foreign system.

Message Routing in Exchange 2010

Message routing might seem very easy in small organizations like the one in the Contoso scenario, but it gets more complex as the organization grows. For larger organizations, like the Litware scenario described in this book, you definitely have to understand all the possibilities and parameters available to you for planning, configuring, and optimizing message routing.

Message Routing within an Exchange Organization

In Exchange versions prior to 2007 you defined message routing inside an Exchange organization by using routing groups and routing group connectors. Exchange Server 2007 introduced changes to internal message routing that are still valid for Exchange 2010:

- The message-routing topology and routing decisions are based on the Active Directory site topology (Active Directory sites and IP site links).
- Routing is configured automatically, so you do not need to configure any routing group connectors.
- The SMTP protocol is used for all message transport.

NOTE Exchange Server 2010 automatically creates internal Send connectors on Hub Transport servers that are required for mail flow within the organization. These are implicit connectors that are not visible in the Exchange management tools, and you cannot modify them.

Table 5-11 provides an overview of internal message routing in Exchange Server 2007 and Exchange Server 2010 as it correlates to Exchange 2000 and Exchange 2003.

TABLE 5-11 Routing Comparison Between Exchange Versions

EXCHANGE SERVER 2007 AND EXCHANGE SERVER 2010	EXCHANGE SERVER 2000 AND EXCHANGE SERVER 2003
Hub Transport server	Dedicated bridgehead server
Active Directory site	Routing group
IP site link	Routing group connector
Cost of IP site link	Cost of routing group connector

This chapter only describes routing between Exchange Servers that are either 2007 or 2010. Routing between Exchange Server 2010 and Exchange 2003 is explained in Chapter 14, "Upgrading from Exchange Server 2003 and Exchange Server 2007."

Point to Point Routing in Exchange 2010

The Hub Transport server role is the only Exchange server role that can route messages within an Exchange organization. Of course, the Edge Transport role can also route messages, but only to and from the Internet.

NOTE Since Exchange Server 2007, all messages in Exchange 2010 flow through a Hub Transport server, even if the recipient is on the same Mailbox server as the sender.

Internal message routing in Exchange Server 2010 is also known as Point to Point routing and follows two basic rules:

- If the message target recipient is within the same Active Directory site, the Hub Transport server delivers the message directly to the Mailbox server where the recipient mailbox resides.
- If the message is addressed to a recipient located in a different Active Directory site, the Hub Transport server sends it directly to a Hub Transport server in the target Active

Directory site. This means that the message does not relay to each Active Directory site along the least-cost routing path as Exchange versions before 2007 did! It will choose the target Hub Transport server using round-robin load-balancing mechanisms. Only if the selected Hub Transport server becomes unavailable will it choose another Hub Transport server.

> ***NOTE*** **By default Hub Transport and Edge Transport servers communicate with each other using TLS over SMTP. This means that the communication between the servers is always encrypted, even if the message transmitted is not encrypted. TLS uses the local digital certificate available on the Exchange server. If you did not configure a certificate it uses the self-signed certificate that was created when Exchange was installed.**

Most large-scale network environments are complex, so some situations require special configurations. What happens when the target Active Directory site is offline because of network problems? What happens to firewall settings where network traffic is forced to flow through specific Active Directory sites? These issues are covered in the following paragraphs.

NOTES FROM THE FIELD

Disable TLS for Hub to Hub Transport Communication

Andy Schan
Senior Consultant, Schan Consulting Inc., Canada

By default Hub Transport to Hub Transport communication is encrypted using TLS. However, if your company uses WAN Optimizing Controller (WOC) devices, you might want to turn off TLS to optimize the WAN traffic using this device. Exchange 2010 now supports disabling TLS to support this scenario. If you have a specific WAN link you want to disable TLS for, you basically configure a Hub Site for both Active Directory sites (the Active Directory sites between the link) so that no messages are sent directly to the target site but stop before the link with the WOC device. Then you create new Receive connectors for both sites using the IP address range of the distant site and configure the Receive connectors to disable TLS.

Now all messages that want to use the WAN link are sent without using TLS encryption; thus the WOC device can optimize the traffic. You can find more details how to configure it at *http://technet.microsoft.com/en-us/library/ee633456.aspx*.

Exchange 2010 Version-Based Routing

Exchange Server 2010 also implemented a new transport server routing rule called *Version-Based Routing* or just *Versioned Routing*. This rule means that a Hub Transport can only communicate with a Mailbox server role of the same Exchange version. The idea behind version-based routing is that different and incompatible versions of the Exchange API used to get messages in and out of the store are implemented in Exchange 2007 and 2010. An Exchange 2010 server cannot talk directly to an Exchange 2007 mailbox server and vice versa. However, the Hub Transport servers of both versions can communicate together.

If you have Exchange 2007 and Exchange 2010 servers in your organization located in the same Active Directory site, the rule prevents Exchange 2007 Hub Transport servers from directly communicating with Exchange 2010 Mailbox servers and Exchange 2010 Hub Transport servers from communicating to Exchange 2007 Mailbox servers.

In the Fabrikam scenario this will be the situation during migration. During that time, all messages sent from Exchange 2007 mailboxes to Exchange 2010 mailboxes will be sent from the Exchange 2007 Mailbox server to the Exchange 2007 Hub Transport, and from there will be transferred to the Exchange 2010 Hub transport and then to the Exchange 2010 Mailbox server.

Version-based routing was implemented to overcome the requirement to have separate Active Directory sites for Exchange 2010 servers.

Least-Cost Routing Path

When multiple routing paths exist for a message, the routing path is calculated based on an algorithm to select a single path over which the message will be routed. This is called *least-cost routing path calculation* and it uses the following logic:

- Calculate the cost to the target Active Directory site by adding all IP site link costs or connector costs between the source and the target site. If an Exchange cost is configured on an IP site link, the Exchange cost is used instead of the Active Directory cost. If there are multiple paths, only the path with the lowest aggregated cost will be used.
- If there are multiple paths with the same lowest aggregated costs, the routing path with the fewest hops is selected.
- If multiple paths are still available, the site name with the lowest alphanumeric name is selected. Starting with the site name to the target Active Directory site, the algorithm will go backward along the path until it finds a site name that doesn't match.

NOTE Other factors, such as message size limits or connector scope, can influence the least-cost routing path.

The two concepts described in the following sections are based on the least-cost routing path: queue at point of failure and delayed fan-out.

QUEUE AT POINT OF FAILURE

If a Hub Transport server cannot deliver a message to a Hub Transport server in the destination site, the Hub Transport server uses the least-cost routing path to deliver the message as close as possible to the destination site. This is called *queue at point of failure*.

Technically, the least-cost routing path will be used in reverse order: from the destination Active Directory site to the source Active Directory site. All Active Directory sites are contacted along this path, and if a Hub Transport server is available, the message is queued there in a retry state. Thus the message is delivered to a Hub Transport server that seems to be the closest one to the target Hub Transport server from the IP site link cost perspective. If Hub Transport servers are not available in any site along the least-cost route, the message is queued on the local Hub Transport server.

For example, use the Litware scenario and assume all site link costs are the same and the links are configured exactly as shown in Figure 5-6.

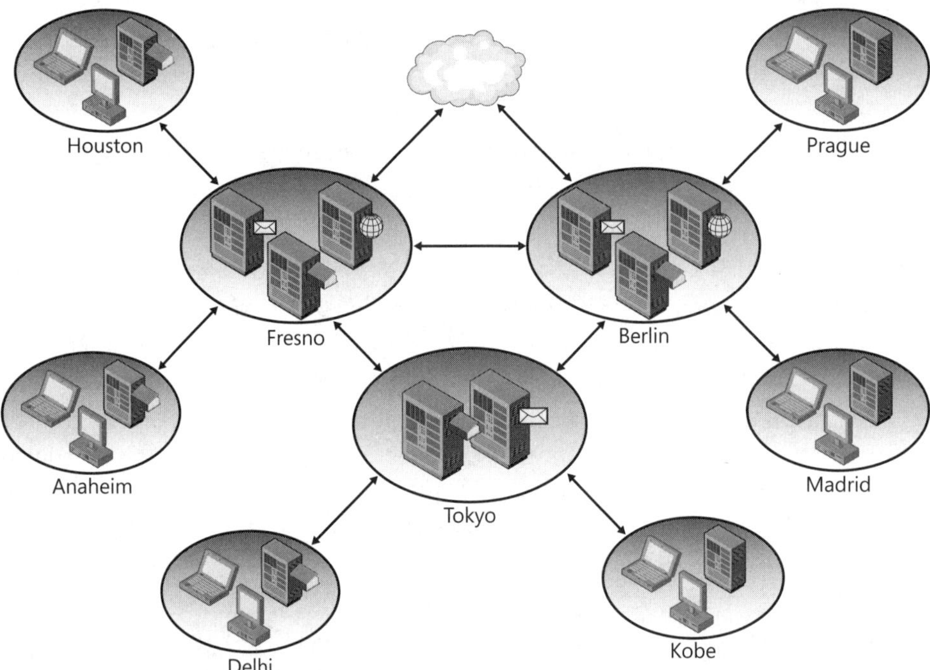

FIGURE 5-6 Litware Active Directory site scenario

Now a message is sent from Madrid to Houston. Normally the Hub Transport server of Madrid would directly connect to a Hub Transport server in Houston to submit the message. However, if no Hub Transport server in Houston is reachable, the message cannot be sent directly.

Queue at point of failure takes place and the closest site to Houston that has Hub Transport servers is selected. In this example, the message is transferred to a Hub Transport server in Fresno because Fresno is closer to Houston than Madrid.

DELAYED FAN-OUT

When sending a message that is addressed to multiple recipients, point-to-point routing normally means creating a copy of the message for every Exchange server that hosts a recipient and sending the message to the target Hub Transport servers directly. However, Exchange Server 2010 uses a technique called *delayed fan-out* to preserve bandwidth when routing messages with many recipients.

After each recipient has been resolved by the Hub Transport server, Exchange Server 2010 compares the routing path for each recipient. The splitting of messages into multiple copies does not occur until a Hub Transport server is reached, which splits up the routing path. Microsoft calls such a Hub Transport server a *fork* in the routing path.

Take a look at the Litware scenario in Figure 5-6. A message is sent from Madrid to recipients in Fresno, Houston, and Anaheim. Because of delayed fan-out, a single message is then transferred to Fresno, where the local Hub Transport delivers a local copy to the Fresno recipient, then creates two copies of the message, sending one to Houston and one to Anaheim. As you can see, especially for messages with large numbers of recipients, this feature saves a lot of bandwidth.

External Routing Connector Selection Process

Exchange 2010 also needs to decide what Send connector it will use to route messages that are destined to the organizational parameter network such as the Internet. This selection process is done by first eliminating all connectors whose message size restrictions are less than the size of the message to be routed and then determining a single connector using the following steps:

1. The connector must be enabled; if the connector is a scoped send connector, it must be in-scope for the local Hub Transport server and the address space must include the recipient's domain. (In other words, the connector must appear in the hub transport server's routing table.)
2. If more connectors remain, the most specific address space match will be used.
3. If still more than one connector matches, the following logic will be used until a unique connector is identified:
   a. *Connector cost* (All IP site link costs are aggregated.)
   b. *Proximity* (A local server is chosen over another Hub Transport server in the same Active Directory site, and a server in the local Active Directory site is chosen over a source server in a remote Active Directory site.)
   c. *Alphanumerically* (The lowest connector name will be used—for example, ConnectorA will be preferred over ConnectorB.)

> ***NOTE*** **Remember that this selection process takes place at every Hub Transport server along the routing path used by the message. If there is a scoped connector along the least-cost routing path available that includes the address space, the route may change when the message is routed through this Active Directory site.**

Routing Table

Every Hub Transport or Edge Transport server calculates the routing topology based on the Active Directory configuration. This includes Active Directory sites, Active Directory site links, Exchange servers and their relation to Active Directory sites, SMTP connectors, third-party connectors, mailbox and public folder stores, and legacy Exchange 2003 routing groups and connectors. This will make up what is called the *routing table*. A routing table is built every time one of the following events occurs:

- The Microsoft Exchange Transport service is started.
- After a periodic reload interval (six hours by default).
- After Active Directory change notifications such as changes in Active Directory site links.

> **NOTE** All Active Directory changes are collected into a batch to process them in a single operation. Each notification causes a five-second delay; thus if many changes occur at the same time, routing calculation is delayed until all changes are received and then processed as a single operation.

By default, the routing table log files can be found in <*Exchange_Installation_Path*>\TransportRoles\Logs\Routing.

Using the *Set-TransportServer* cmdlet as listed in Table 5-12, you can configure a few parameters to configure the routing table creation.

TABLE 5-12 Set-TransportServer Options for Routing Table Configuration

PARAMETER	DESCRIPTION
RoutingTableLogPath	Specify the location of the routing table log files.
RoutingTableLogMaxDirectorySize	Specify a maximum size for the directory that contains routing table log files. Default: 50 MB.
RoutingTableLogMaxAge	Specify a maximum age for the routing table log files. Default: 7 days.

In addition to these parameters, you can configure the periodic interval the routing table is automatically recalculated using the *RoutingConfigReloadInterval* parameter in the EdgeTransport.exe.config file. By default, this is set to 12 hours but because every Transport server renews its Kerberos token after 6 hours, the routing table is created more frequently. This means that other parameters interfere with changing the *RoutingConfigReloadInterval* parameter, so you should be careful when changing it.

You can view the Routing Table logs using the Routing Log Viewer available in Exchange Management Console. You can find more information how to use the Routing Log Viewer in the "Verifying Configuration Using the Routing Log Viewer" section later in this chapter.

Reviewing and Configuring Message Routing Between Active Directory Sites

Hub Transport servers route messages to other Hub Transport servers based on the Active Directory site and site link topology. Therefore, for Exchange 2010 to work correctly, it is crucial that the Active Directory topology does not cause any negative effects on message routing or Exchange servers. This section focus on how to make sure that your Active Directory site topology is suitable for Exchange 2010 and what you can do to modify the topology with Exchange-related settings.

Review Active Directory Site and Site Links Topology

Before you consider configuring Active Directory sites and Active Directory site links to optimize message routing, you need to clearly understand the current Active Directory topology of your organization. You can do this using the Active Directory Sites and Services snap-in. However, in a large environment with many Active Directory sites and site links, you may lose the overview. For that reason you can also use a tool called Microsoft Active Directory Topology Diagrammer that allows you to visualize the Active Directory topology in a Microsoft Office Visio file. The tool was tested with Visio 2003 or Visio 2007. Having a graphical representation that you can put on the wall helps you to identify areas that might need to be optimized for message routing. Figure 5-7 shows an example of a diagram created from the Litware Scenario. The tool can be downloaded at *http://www.microsoft.com/downloads/details.aspx?familyid=cb42fc06-50c7-47ed-a65c-862661742764&displaylang=en.*

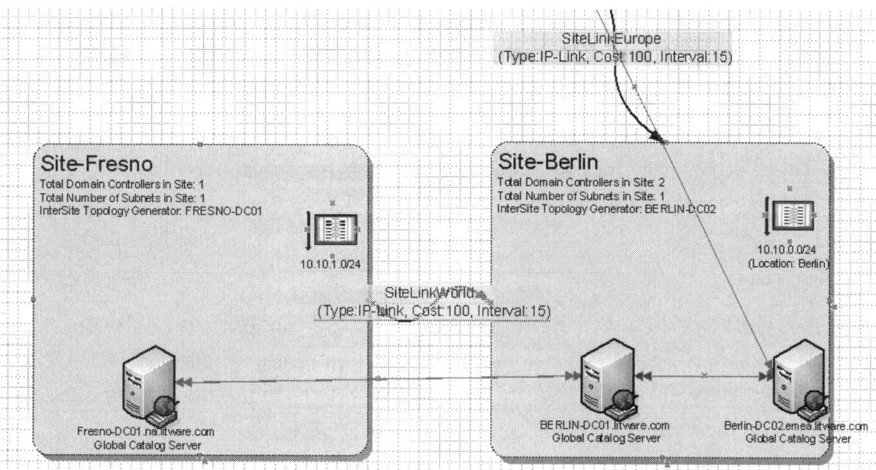

FIGURE 5-7 Sample Active Directory topology diagram from the Litware scenario

Configuring Active Directory Sites

An Active Directory site is a logical definition of a physical connected network, normally based in the same local area network (LAN) and thus sharing a very fast network connection within the Active Directory site. You define a site based on an IP subnet in the Active

Directory Sites and Services snap-in. The primary purpose for creating an Active Directory site is to define which subnets in the network are connected in a way that optimizes control of Active Directory replication traffic.

The Active Directory site is a routing boundary for Hub Transport servers to make routing decisions based the Active Directory site topology as described in the previous chapter. To meet this requirement you must make sure that every Exchange server role belongs to an Active Directory site. You should also verify that each Active Directory site is based on one or more subnets based on LAN-quality networks. Otherwise, consider splitting these Active Directory sites into multiple sites.

You can get a list of all Exchange servers and their respective Active Directory site using the following cmdlet: *Get-ExchangeServer | ft Name, Site.*

> ***NOTE*** **Many companies split the administration between the Active Directory forest and Exchange into different teams. If this describes your situation, you need to remember that you can only configure Active Directory sites and Active Directory site links if the Active Directory team has provided you with sufficient permission and you have secured the buy-in from that team to make the changes to the production Active Directory infrastructure.**

Configuring Site Links and Site Link Costs

Site links are logical paths between Active Directory sites and always include a site link cost to be able to configure specific routes for Active Directory replication traffic. The same information is used by Exchange 2010 to calculate the least-cost routing path.

> ***NOTE*** **Site links are only used for routing when direct Hub Transport server to Hub Transport server connections are not possible. The vast bulk of deliveries occur via direct connections.**

A site link does not force the actual path that is taken by network packets on the physical network but define the way Active Directory replication is done within the forest. However, every so often the cost assignment to the site link typically relates to the underlying network speed and available bandwidth.

It is important for the Exchange designer to understand the site topology as well as the site links and site link costs to make sure that Exchange routing is done as defined. To verify how Exchange uses the current topology, you can use the Routing Table Log Viewer after the first Exchange 2010 server is installed in the forest. If an Exchange server is not yet installed, use the Microsoft Active Directory Topology Diagrammer to get an Active Directory topology overview.

NOTES FROM THE FIELD

A Practical Way to Define Site Link Costs

Brian Day
Senior Systems Administrator, Messaging & Directory Services, Commonwealth of Massachusetts

Active Directory site link costs: What can they cost you? Misconfigured site link costs can cost you hours of frustration if not planned correctly from the start.

In 2005 I joined an employer whose Active Directory architecture was very complex across hundreds of physical sites, and a little bit out of control. It grew faster than anyone expected and some things got overlooked, including site link configuration. Part of my role was to help clean up the environment and optimize it where possible. At the time, WAN connections for these hundreds of sites were primarily all frame relay, ranging in speeds from 384 Kbps to multiple T-1 circuits bonded together. Site link costs were of the Wild West variety, with no uniformity. Values existed from more than 1,000 all the way down to 10 and anything in between, even though we only had 5 or 6 different speed links. In many cases circuits of the same speed didn't have the same costs. Taking a step back and looking at the situation I could see what had happened—there was no proper planning for the future and multiple schemes were actually in use regarding site link cost, depending on who had originally entered the site links.

I knew I had to find a way to future-proof ourselves and come up with a way to deal with new WAN connections in the future without having to go back and reconfigure old ones every couple of years. While researching methods other people use to determine costs I found a great article on Microsoft TechNet called "Determining the Cost" available at *http://technet.microsoft.com/en-us/library/cc782827(WS.10).aspx*. Buried on this page was a formula Microsoft suggested for site link costs: *[1024/Log*$_{10}$*(Kbps of WAN Link)]=Cost*. At first glance I looked at this and thought, What mathematics nerd had too much time on his hands? That is, until I gave it an honest try.

Suddenly I had a desire to call my old math teacher and let him know that logarithms *did* actually end up being useful in the real world! As you can see in Table 5-13, the formula provided us with costs that can grow (and shrink) as WAN speeds matured, becoming faster and faster. It also left enough space between costs so that I could configure primary/secondary site links by creating a second site link with a value of *Cost+1*. I've often seen people establish costs with no space between them, leaving no room for this type of configuration. Perhaps if you have other finicky site links that have the speed but are not always the most reliable (like a satellite connection) compared to other site links of similar throughput, you could also adjust them by bumping the cost a couple points. I have a sneaking suspicion that I will be gone from this planet by the time WAN connections exist that are fast enough to cause this formula to reach the lowest value of 1.

TABLE 5-13 Site Link Costs Defined by Bandwidth

DESCRIPTION	KBPS	SITE LINK COST
Dialup	56	586
ISDN BRI	128	486
	256	425
	384	396
	512	378
	1024	340
T1	1582	320
	2048	309
10 Mbps	10240	255
100 Mbps	102400	204
GigE6	307200	187
1000 Mbps	1024000	170

Configuring Exchange Specific Settings for Site Links

The Active Directory site topology might not be optimal for Exchange message routing in specific cases. Therefore, you can assign an Exchange-specific cost to the site link that Exchange can use for routing purposes. The Exchange-specific cost for the IP site link will not modify or affect the current Active Directory site cost that is used for replication. Of course, if you set an Exchange cost, you will override the Active Directory cost for message-routing purposes, but this won't interfere with Active Directory replication.

After reviewing your Active Directory site topology and installing your Exchange servers in the right Active Directory sites, you should carefully consider whether you need to implement Exchange-related IP site link costs, which are quite hard to manage. They only make sense in large deployments where you have many Active Directory sites with Active Directory site links that are not in the control of Exchange and are known to be changed without your notification. Don't try to configure a message routing path—remember that most of the time the Hub Transport servers communicate directly to each other anyway.

Consider the Litware Scenario where the IP Site Link SiteLinkWorld is configured with a cost of 100. The following Exchange Management Shell (EMS) cmdlet assigns an Exchange-specific cost of 20 to it:

Set-ADSiteLink -Identity "SiteLinkWorld" -ExchangeCost 20

NOTE You can also use the *Set-AdSiteLink –Identity <ADSiteLink> – MaxMessageSize <value>* cmdlet to assign a maximum message size limit for messages sent between Active Directory sites. This is especially useful if you have branch offices that have low-bandwidth network links so that you make sure only small messages can be sent over the network. All the larger messages will generate a non-delivery report (NDR).

As shown in Figure 5-8, the Active Directory site link still has the Active Directory cost of 100, but additionally has an Exchange cost of 20 assigned, and a message size limit is not configured. From now on, least-cost routing calculation will consider only the Exchange cost and ignore the Active Directory cost.

```
Machine: Fresno-HT01.na.litware.com
[PS] C:\Windows\system32>Get-AdSiteLink -id SiteLinkWorld |fl

RunspaceId          : 2b04467e-dfa3-4e61-b561-e05a87142926
Cost                : 20
ADCost              : 100
ExchangeCost        : 20
MaxMessageSize      : unlimited
Sites               : {litware.com/Configuration/Sites/Site-Fresno, litware.com/Configuration/Sites/Site-Berlin}
AdminDisplayName    :
ExchangeVersion     : 0.1 (8.0.535.0)
Name                : SiteLinkWorld
DistinguishedName   : CN=SiteLinkWorld,CN=IP,CN=Inter-Site Transports,CN=Sites,CN=Configuration,DC=litware,DC=com
Identity            : litware.com/Configuration/Sites/Inter-Site Transports/IP/SiteLinkWorld
Guid                : 20a050d2-2255-4d97-acde-e870251caf9c
ObjectCategory      : litware.com/Configuration/Schema/Site-Link
ObjectClass         : {top, siteLink}
WhenChanged         : 1/14/2010 11:17:28 AM
WhenCreated         : 12/8/2009 11:07:38 AM
WhenChangedUTC      : 1/14/2010 7:17:28 PM
WhenCreatedUTC      : 12/8/2009 7:07:38 PM
OrganizationId      :
OriginatingServer   : Fresno-DC01.na.litware.com
IsValid             : True
```

FIGURE 5-8 Active Directory site link with exchange costs assigned

NOTES FROM THE FIELD

Using Exchange Costs on IP Site Links

Ulf Hansen

Principal Systems Administrator, Central Administration Exchange, Siemens AG (Germany)

My company has a very large forest with more than 1,000 different Active Directory sites and many hundreds of IP site links. Domain administration is done independently and administrators have a huge influence on configuring their Active Directory sites because Active Directory sites are also used for services other than Exchange. Thus we started first to think about building Active Directory sites just for Exchange to be in charge of the routing costs, but finally decided against it.

Because we were not in charge of defining the Active Directory costs and we did not want to interfere or change our complex Active Directory routing in any way, we agreed to configure all Active Directory sites automatically with the maximum cost of 999. As a result, Exchange considers all Active Directory sites equal and uses the route with the fewest hops as the least-cost route.

Remember, Exchange costs will be used over Active Directory costs, and if multiple paths are available with the same costs, the path with the fewest hops is selected if a direct connection to a Hub Transport server in the target Active Directory site cannot be made.

We discovered that messages didn't take the route that we anticipated; our solution was to reduce the Exchange cost to force messages and correct the routing. However, we still see some limitations when Active Directory costs are used that cause problems in our Exchange environment. For example, Public Folder stores that have an AD cost of more than 500 from the Exchange server are not considered for Outlook 2003 Free/Busy Public Folder lookups.

Configuring Hub Sites

One way to interfere with the least-cost routing path is by defining hub sites through which all message flow must be relayed. You can think of this situation as a form of hub-and-spoke design with a messaging backbone.

You might have hub sites if a firewall prevents direct communication between certain Active Directory sites or if a company policy exists whereby all message traffic must be routed through a special Active Directory site.

NOTE A hub site is considered only when it is located on the least-cost routing path calculated by the Hub Transport server. The source Hub Transport server always calculates the lowest-cost route first, and then determines whether any of the sites on the route are hub sites. If the lowest-cost route does not include a hub site, the Hub Transport server will directly connect to a Hub Transport server in the target site.

Before you implement hub sites, it is important that you review your Active Directory topology to make sure that the least-cost routing path always includes the Active Directory sites you want to define as hub sites.

You can view all hub sites available using the *Get-AdSite* cmdlet and configure them using the Exchange Management Shell and the *Set-AdSite* cmdlet. You have to do this site by site, so keep track of the changes you make!

The following cmdlet shows an example where Site-Berlin *is configured* as a hub site:

Set-AdSite -Identity „Site-Berlin" -HubSiteEnabled $true

Configuring Expansion Servers for Distribution Groups

You also can modify the default routing topology by assigning expansion servers for distribution groups. By default, when a message is sent to a distribution group, the first Hub Transport server that receives the message expands the distribution list and calculates how to route the messages to each recipient in the list.

If you configure an expansion server for the distribution list, all messages sent to the distribution list are sent to the specified Hub Transport server, which then expands the list and distributes the messages. For example, you can use expansion servers for location-based distribution groups to ensure that the local Hub Transport server resolves them. This configuration only sends one message addressed to a location-based distribution to the location and is then expanded at the target location by the defined expansion server.

> ***IMPORTANT*** **Because you only can define a single Hub Transport server, distribution list expansion will fail if this expansion server is not available. Thus you might negatively impact your message flow. There is no way to configure more than one expansion server, so you have to decide either to use one expansion server or let the distribution list expand at all servers.**

Even though distribution group expansion was available in previous Exchange versions, it is improved in Exchange 2010 in two ways: You can now configure a memory caching limit to prevent the cache from consuming too much memory, and the processing of large distribution groups with delivery restrictions is done more efficiently.

You configure the distribution group cache by adding the parameters as found in Table 5-14 to the EdgeTransport.exe.config file located at <*Exchange_Server_Install*>\Bin.

TABLE 5-14 Parameters to Configure Distribution Group Cache

PARAMETER	DESCRIPTION
MaxResolveRecipientCacheSize	This cache is only used to avoid duplicate delivery to one-offs and distribution lists (DLs). So if you notice that delivery to some DLs (with more entries than this cache size) still result in duplicate deliveries, you can make the size larger. The Information Store would still do duplicate detection, but this feature is to prevent from trying to deliver in the first place.
MaxResolverMemberOfGroupCacheSize	This cache includes group members for the sender. So if a person sends to a DL, this cache tracks membership of that person so that if restrictions apply to any sub DL, it doesn't have to be looked up again. You would want to make this larger if you notice a lot of Active Directory queries for messages to large DLs with complex delivery restrictions.

Verifying Configuration Using the Routing Log Viewer

The Routing Log Viewer is one of the most important tools to understand how Exchange is interpreting your configuration changes in means of Active Directory sites, Active Directory site links, and so on. You use the Routing Log Viewer to open a local Routing Table log file located on your Hub or Edge Transport servers.

> **NOTE** The Routing Log Viewer only shows you the routing table of a single Hub Transport server. This means you always need to connect to the Hub Transport server that causes the message routing problem to investigate its local routing table. If you are connected to a different transport server, you might not be able to detect the issue!

After opening a routing table log file (normally you open the latest one available), the routing table is organized into four tabs: Active Directory Sites (and Routing Groups if you have Exchange 2003 servers in your organization), Servers, Send Connectors, and Address Spaces.

If you want to read more about the Routing Log Viewer and how to use it, the TechNet article "Viewing the Routing Table Log" is available at *http://technet.microsoft.com/en-us/library/bb691033(EXCHG.80).aspx.*

ACTIVE DIRECTORY SITES TAB

On this tab you can make sure that your Exchange servers belong to the correct Active Directory site, and also determine whether any Hub sites are identified incorrectly. You can also see the least cost to each of the other sites by identifying the Total Active Directory cost item, as shown in Figure 5-9. You do not see the difference between Active Directory costs and Exchange costs assigned to an Active Directory site link, but the routing table just provides you with the cost information used by the Hub Transport server.

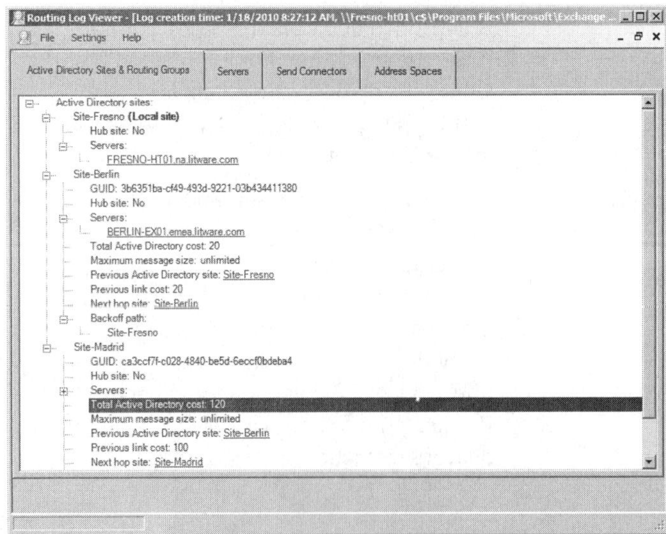

FIGURE 5-9 Viewing Active Directory sites in Routing Log Viewer

SERVERS TAB

The Servers tab provides an overview of all Exchange servers in your Exchange organization. You get an overview of the roles installed, the routing cost to reach the server, any MDB databases (mailbox databases) available on this server, and its Legacy DN.

SEND CONNECTORS TAB

This tab provides you with an overview of send connectors that are available for this specific Active Directory site, as shown in Figure 5-10. It includes the address space, information about the proximity of the connector, whether the message is delivered using a smart host or DNS, whether it is a scoped connector, and the message size restriction set on it.

> ***NOTE*** **Scoped connectors are only available in the local Active Directory site—thus the address space of a scoped connector does not show up in another Active Directory site's Send Connector tab.**

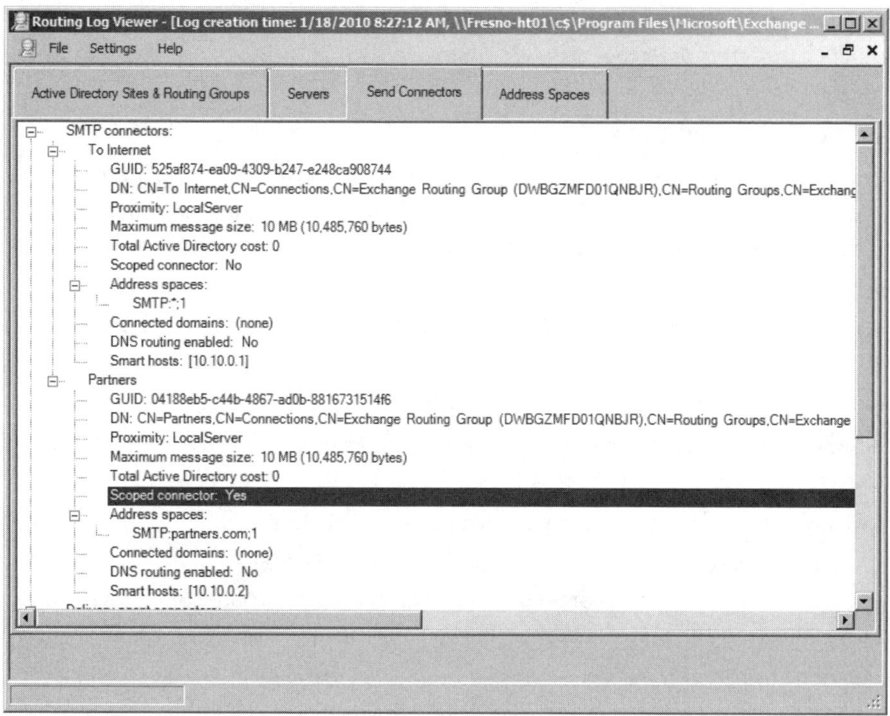

FIGURE 5-10 Viewing Send Connectors in Routing Log Viewer

ADDRESS SPACE TAB

The Address Space tab provides a hierarchical list including all address spaces available for this Hub Transport server. You can expand the list until you find the Send connector that serves the address space.

This tab is especially important in organizations that have many address spaces configured, which might also have a lot of connectors. In this situation it is maybe easier to search for a Send connector by looking through the available address spaces on this tab than to examine the connectors listed on the Send Connector tab.

Planning Message Routing to the Organization Perimeter

In Exchange Server 2010, connectors are classified in the following ways:

- Send connectors
- Receive connectors
- Foreign connectors
- Delivery Agent connectors

These types of connectors can be configured on Hub Transport and Edge Transport servers. Connectors can be configured using the Exchange Management Console, but many more details are available when using the Exchange Management Shell.

Send and Receive connectors always use SMTP as their message protocol. Foreign or Delivery Agent connectors use other message protocols, such as X.400, to transmit messages.

Configuring Send Connectors

A Send connector is a connector that transmits a message to the Exchange organization perimeter using SMTP as the communication protocol. Thus by default it sends the message using TCP port 25. You use Send connectors to configure how your messages leave the organization. Send connectors allow you to do the following:

- Set one or more source Hub Transport server(s) that the connector uses to deliver messages.
- Configure one or more dedicated address space(s) for the connector.
- Decide where to route the messages (by using a smart host or just using DNS MX record resolution).

Here's what you should consider when planning Send connectors:

- Hub Transport servers communicate automatically with each other—you do not need Send connectors for internal communication. Nor should you try to configure internal routing with send connectors because you could cause internal routing issues.
- If you don't use Edge Transport servers as Internet smart-relay hosts, you should include a Send connector with the SMTP:* address space pointing to the network connection point to the Internet or to a smart host that is able to send messages to the Internet.

- For organizational internal message re-routing meaning where you have other SMTP systems inside your company, you should add the address spaces to the Send connectors. Whether you create one connector for many partners or one connector per partner depends on whether you want to manage the connectors using DNS with MX-records or using smart hosts. Also consider the management aspect when deciding on one or more connectors.
- You can put a scope on the Send connector to prevent other Active Directory sites from using it. However, don't forget that a connector with scoped address space should not be located in the same site as the alternate least-cost route connector with non-scoped address space. Thus you also should not configure a scoped address space at Hub sites.

INSIDE TRACK

Scoping Send Connectors Correctly

Todd Luttinen
Principal Program Manager, Microsoft Corp, Redmond

If you put a scope (an assigned address space) on a Send or Foreign connector, you prevent Hub Transport servers located in other Active Directory sites from seeing it in their local routing tables. Because these transport servers will not see the connector and its associated scoped address space, they are prevented from using the scoped address space and associated connector to compute least-cost routes for external recipient delivery.

However, you need to consider that the routing calculation is done not only at the source Hub Transport, but also at every Hub Transport the message is forwarded to. It will be checked against the local routing table of each Hub Transport server to find the optimum connector based on least cost and maximum message size. If one Hub Transport along the way includes a scoped connector that is more suitable for the message to follow, it will use it.

For example, assume you're in the Site-Fresno of the Litware Exchange organization. The Site-Fresno has two Send connectors: one to the Internet with SMTP:*, and one connector with a Scope to Partners with SMTP:Partners.com. You now send a message from Site-Berlin to the Internet, which automatically uses Site-Fresno to forward the message to the Internet. The message will see the scoped Send connector and use the Partners connector to deliver the message. The best way to prevent this from happening is not to use scoped Send connectors in Hub sites or sites where all messages are sent through.

SEND CONNECTORS AND INTERNET MESSAGE DELIVERY

If you consider using Send connectors that deliver messages to the Internet, you have the following two possibilities to resolve the domains used in recipient addresses:

- Using a smart host to deliver the messages to the Internet (the most common scenario when you do not use Edge Transport servers in your organization).
- Using DNS MX records to resolve Internet addresses on your own when using an Edge Transport server.

> ***IMPORTANT*** **Microsoft does not recommend connecting a Hub Transport server directly to the Internet. Thus it is best practice to install a smart host between the Internet and your Exchange organization.**

When using DNS to resolve message addresses, Exchange queries an external DNS to find the DNS records required for message delivery. The DNS servers are queried for the following information:

- **Mail exchange (MX) records** The MX record contains one or more fully qualified domain names (FQDNs) of the server that are responsible for accepting messages for the domain and a preference value. The lowest preference value is always selected first. To optimize fault tolerance, most organizations use multiple messaging servers and multiple MX records that have different preference values. If one server fails, the other is used because of the higher preference value.
- **Address (A) records** Every server that has an MX record also has an A record assigned to it. The A record includes the IP address of the server.

INSIDE TRACK

Configuring a Failover Scenario with MX Records

Ross Smith IV
Senior Program Manager, Exchange Server Product Group, Microsoft Corporation

There are many different ways to deploy MX records for controlling inbound Internet mail flow. To frame this discussion, consider a customer who has two physical locations with an ideal configuration that ensures both locations are used in some fashion for internal and external mail routing. As a result, there are three possibilities:

- One physical location is considered primary and the other physical location is a backup.
- Both physical locations are utilized for mail flow.
- Use a single MX record.

For the first possibility, the DNS configuration can be set as follows:

```
Customer.com              MX preference = 10,
                             mail exchanger = maila.Customer.com
maila.Customer.com         A          IP1
maila.Customer.com         A          IP2
...

Customer.com              MX preference = 20,
                             mail exchanger = mailb.Customer.com
mailb.Customer.com         A          IP3
mailb.Customer.com         A          IP4
...
```

With this mechanism, both MX records are provided to the sending SMTP system, but the lowest-cost MX record is utilized first. When the TCP/IP address of the host is resolved, the DNS name server rotates the address values that it returns (via a round-robin mechanism). In this way, DNS guarantees maila.Customer.com hosts are cycled through and used equally for receiving inbound mail. Using this approach means that you take control for cycling through the mail systems: you are not at the mercy of the sender's SMTP implementation and thereby balancing mail volume efficiency across all of the Edge Transport servers. The first MX record is associated with SMTP servers in one data center, whereas the second, higher-cost MX record is associated with SMTP servers in the second data center.

This configuration can also be invoked for load-balancing data across physical locations. For example, maila.Customer.com can be associated to IP addresses in primary datacenter and IP addresses in second datacenter. The same can be done for mailb.Customer.com. The end result in this scenario is that only half of the existing Edge Transport servers are used at any given time, with an equal distribution of messages between the two data centers.

Another solution for load balancing across physical locations is to utilize two equal cost MX records:

```
Customer.com          MX preference = 10,
                         mail exchanger = maila.Customer.com
maila.Customer.com     A          IP1
maila.Customer.com     A          IP2
...

Customer.com          MX preference = 10,
                         mail exchanger = mailb.Customer.com
mailb.Customer.com     A          IP3
mailb.Customer.com     A          IP4
...
```

The difference here is that maila.Customer.com is associated to IP addresses in one datacenter, whereas mailb.Customer.com is associated to IP addresses in the other data center. Although this solution cannot guarantee an equal distribution of messages between datacenters, it can guarantee an equal distribution of messages for a particular MX record.

The third possibility is to utilize a single MX record:

```
Customer.com                  MX preference = 10,
                                 mail exchanger = maila.Customer.com
maila.Customer.com      A            IP1
maila.Customer.com      A            IP2
maila.Customer.com      A            IP3
maila.Customer.com      A            IP4
...
```

With this configuration, all Edge Transport servers in both datacenters are associated to the MX record. This configuration utilizes all SMTP servers and ensures an equal distribution of messages between all of the SMTP servers in both datacenters. If the customer's goal is to have mail flow come into either datacenter, this is the best configuration option. However, if the customer's goal is to ensure that mail flow is controlled in terms of datacenter usage, the first scenario is the best configuration option.

SEND CONNECTORS IN FABRIKAM SCENARIO

If you implement Edge Transport servers, you do not need to create additional Send connectors by default because they are all created using a default configuration. However, as in the Fabrikam scenario that uses smart host servers to send messages to the Internet, you need to create a Send connector so that your Exchange servers are able to send messages to the Internet.

For example, assume you're the Fabrikam administrator and you need to create a Send connector to your smart host including the SMTP:* address space. The connector needs to be configured on the Hub Transport server Fresno-HT01. Here's the cmdlet that would create the Send connector to the smart host:

```
New-SendConnector -Name 'To Internet' -Usage 'Internet' -AddressSpaces 'SMTP:*;1'
-IsScopedConnector $false -DNSRoutingEnabled $false -SmartHosts 'smarthost
.fabrikam.com' -SmartHostAuthMechanism 'None' -UseExternalDNSServersEnabled $false
-SourceTransportServers 'FRESNO-HT01'
```

Fabrikam might create additional Send connectors for the following reasons:

- They have a dedicated Partner WAN link that they would like to use to send messages between both companies.
- They have an internal SMTP server that shares the same address space, so they forward all messages not resolved by the Exchange organization to that SMTP server.

SEND CONNECTOR PARAMETERS

Many parameters are available to configure Send connectors. Table 5-15 provides an overview of the most important parameters, what they are used for, and when you need to consider changing them.

TABLE 5-15 *Set-SendConnector* Parameters

PARAMETER	DESCRIPTION	WHEN SHOULD IT BE CHANGED?
AddressSpaces	Address space(s) are processed by this connector.	To configure target Address Spaces (for example, "SMTP:*" to send all messages through it).
AuthenticationCredential	Defines authentication credentials (user name and password).	When your target connector requires authentication.
Comment	Defines comments for this connector.	To provide additional details regarding the purpose of the connector.
ConnectedDomains	For Exchange 2003 support, includes connected routing groups.	Cannot be changed.
ConnectionInactivityTimeOut	Times when to disconnect an idle connector.	Can be changed to reduce the amount of idle connections.
DNSRoutingEnabled	Specifies that the connector will use the local DNS Server to resolve the message.	If you don't have a smart host to relay messages, you need to use this option.
DomainSecureEnabled	Configures Domain Security using TLS on this connector.	Enable if you want to support Domain Security to partners or others.
Enabled	Enables or disables this connector.	Only if you want to disable the connector. Remember, disabling connectors causes issues with Exchange 2003.
ForceHELO	You can configure the server to respond to SMTP connections with HELO rather than EHLO.	You need to change this if your target SMTP server requires the HELO command to be sent.

PARAMETER	DESCRIPTION	WHEN SHOULD IT BE CHANGED?
Fqdn	Specifies the FQDN that will be provided after EHLO or HELO.	If the target server requires a specific response after EHLO, you can change it here.
HomeMTA	For Exchange 2003 support, includes Microsoft MTA.	Cannot be changed.
HomeMtaServerId	Transport Server on which the connector was created.	Cannot be changed.
Identity	GUID of connector.	Cannot be changed.
IgnoreSTARTTLS	Configures whether the connector uses TLS if offered.	Change it only if you want to disable TLS for this connector.
IsScopedConnector	Defines the scope of this connector.	When changed, the connector can only be used by Hub Transport servers in the same site.
IsSmtpConnector	Specifies SMTP as protocol.	Cannot be changed.
LinkedReceiveConnector	Forces all messages received by a specified Receive connector to be sent over this connector.	Useful if you want to forward all messages for inspection, such as to a third-party anti-spam service.
MaxMessageSize	Maximum message size the connector can send.	Configure a specific message size.
Name	Name of the connector.	Change the name.
Port	Port number to communicate.	If the send connector uses a port other than port 25.
ProtocolLoggingLevel	Configures the logging level for SMTP.	Enable verbose logging for troubleshooting connector issues.
RequireTLS	Configures that communication must be encrypted using TLS.	Change this only if you're sure that all target servers support TLS.

PARAMETER	DESCRIPTION	WHEN SHOULD IT BE CHANGED?
SmartHostAuthMechanism	Defines the authentication mechanism when using a smart host.	If the smart host requires specific authentication, this option needs to be configured accordingly.
SmartHosts	Defines IP address, MX records, or A record(s) of any smart host(s) used.	Configure a smart host if you want to forward all messages to the specified server(s).
SmartHostsString	Includes the *SmartHosts* parameter as a string.	Cannot be changed.
SmtpMaxMessagesPerConnection	Maximum messages this connector can send per connection.	If the target connector is configured to receive more messages, it can be changed accordingly.
SourceIPAddress	Specifies a specific IP address that will be shown to the target connector.	If your local server has multiple IP addresses and the target server requires one specific IP address, such as for authorization.
SourceRoutingGroup	Routing group the connector belongs to. Only used for backward compatibility with Exchange 2003.	Cannot be changed.
SourceTransportServers	Specifies the names of the Transport servers that can use this connector.	For redundancy, you should always add all Hub Transport servers that can use it.
UseExternalDNSServers Enabled	Uses DNS server(s) that were specified in *Set-TransportServer*.	If this connector needs to use another DNS server that is configured locally.

Configuring Receive Connectors

To receive inbound SMTP messages from external domains, you need a Receive connector in Exchange 2010. This connector acts as an inbound connection point that you can configure to accept connections based on IP address ranges and port numbers. You can configure a Receive connector on a per-server scope only. Thus, if you want to have many servers receive messages, you need to configure one connector for every server.

Receive connectors have configuration limits that you can set, such as number of active connection, maximum message size, or maximum recipients per message. You also can set the type of authentication required to send a message.

By default two Receive connectors are created on every Hub Transport server that are almost identical, but with one important difference: You configure the *Client <servername>* Receive connector to listen on port 587 rather than on port 25. As described in RFC 2476, port 587 has been proposed for use only for message submission from e-mail clients that require message relay.

> **NOTE** A Receive connector by default only accepts e-mail domains that are defined in Accepted Domains that you can list using the *Get-AcceptedDomain* cmdlet. All other domains are considered Message Relaying and need additional permissions to be processed.

What does this have to do with planning? Well, you should configure Receive connectors at every Hub Transport server serving an external inbound connection. Also, you should have dedicated Receive connectors for your applications that want to send messages so that you understand how many applications send messages to your system.

RECEIVE CONNECTORS IN FABRIKAM SCENARIO

Which Receive connectors do you need for a specific environment like the Fabrikam Scenario? As mentioned, Fabrikam has Apple Macintosh clients that use IMAP4 to receive their messages from the CAS server. However, POP3 and IMAP4 need to use SMTP to send messages. They also use a smart host to send and receive messages from the Internet.

To ease management, you create new Receive connectors (instead of using the default connectors) enforcing authentication as well as encrypted client-to-server communication using TLS. For your sample scenario the following Receive connectors should be created:

- Receive connector to receive messages from Internet smart host
- Receive connector to receive messages from IMAP4 clients using TLS

You can create an example Receive connector configuration for the IP range of 10.10.0.1 (Subnet 255.255.255.0), enforcing TLS encryption, and only allowing Exchange mailbox users and Exchange servers to use it on the local Exchange server by using the following cmdlet:

```
New-ReceiveConnector -Name "Client SMTP TLS" -Bindings "0.0.0.0:25" -AuthMechanism
"Tls, BasicAuth, BasicAuthRequireTLS, ExchangeServer" -PermissionGroups "ExchangeUsers,
ExchangeServers" -RemoteIPRanges 10.10.0.1-10.10.0.255
```

> **NOTE** The most important task after creating a Receive connector is to test its functionality. You can use Telnet *<servername>* 25 to connect to the Receive connector or use a client to check it. Remember that the Telnet Client is now a Windows Server 2008 feature that is not installed by default.

Additional reasons to create Receive connectors are as follows:

- To receive messages from an Internet smart host (if you do not use Edge Transport servers to receive messages from the Internet)
- If you need to turn off user authentication for specific clients based on IP address
- To allow relaying of messages accepted from SMTP servers
- For using a dedicated Receive connector for Domain Security on Edge Transport servers

NOTES FROM THE FIELD

Configuring Relaying in Exchange Server 2010

Christian Schindler
Senior Consultant, NTx BackOffice Consulting Group, Austria

In previous versions of Exchange Server you enabled relaying by simply activating a check box on the Properties page of an SMTP Virtual Server and adding IP Addresses to a list. In Exchange Server 2007 and 2010 this has changed a bit.

First, the SMTP Virtual Server no longer exists—the replacement is a Receive connector. Second, there's no check box to simply activate relaying—we have to use permissions in Active Directory to allow for relaying. However, we still need to specify which IP Addresses are allowed to relay.

To enable Relaying on an Exchange Server 2010 Hub Transport Server, you create a new Receive connector. Then you specify the server's IP addresses that are allowed to relay by configuring the RemoteIPRanges parameter of the Receive connector. As a final step, you need to set permissions on the Send connector to grant Anonymous the right to relay. This can be done either via ADSIEDIT or by using the following Windows PowerShell command:

```
Get-ReceiveConnector <Name of Connector> | Add-ADPermission -User "NT
AUTHORITY\ANONYMOUS LOGON" -ExtendedRights "ms-Exch-SMTP-Accept-Any-
Recipient"
```

During a migration from previous version of Exchange, you need to create relaying connectors with the same settings as on the original servers. Getting the list of allowed server IP addresses is particularly important. When you have a large list, it is crucial to automate this step to avoid human errors. This can easily be done by using the ExIpSecurity.exe Tool, which can be downloaded from the Microsoft Download Center. It allows you to export the list of allowed IP addresses to a file. The file can easily be used in a Windows PowerShell script to create the necessary Receive connectors in Exchange Server 2010.

CREATING A LINKED CONNECTOR

A linked connector is a Receive connector that is linked to a Send connector. For linked connectors, the regular routing logic that is based on the destination domain is overridden. All messages that are received by the Receive connector are forwarded to the linked Send connector.

You can see an example of a linked connector in the Fabrikam scenario: they want to outsource their anti-spam and antivirus service. They thus create a linked connector at the Internet message entry point in their Exchange organization and forward all messages to a third-party service provider for scanning. Then they receive the message back from the service provider using a dedicated Receive connector that is no longer linked.

The following list describes the requirements that you must meet to create linked connectors:

- Only one Receive connector can be linked to one Send connector.
- The Receive connector must exist before it can be linked to a Send connector.
- A linked Send connector must route messages to a smart host.

You can only link a Receive connector to an existing Send connector by using the *LinkedReceiveConnector* parameter in the *Set-SendConnector* cmdlet.

RECEIVE CONNECTOR PARAMETERS

Table 5-16 provides an overview of the most important parameters for Receive connectors. However, many more parameters can be configured on Receive connectors. You do not need to know them by heart, but should remember what options are available if you need them.

TABLE 5-16 *Set-ReceiveConnector* Parameters

PARAMETER	DESCRIPTION	WHEN SHOULD IT BE CHANGED?
AuthMechanism	Defines the advertised and accepted authentication mechanisms.	If you want to enforce TLS encryption or a specific Authentication type, you need to configure it here.
Banner	The *Banner* parameter specifies an override to the default SMTP 220 banner.	If you like to respond in a customized way to requests, this can be changed.
BinaryMimeEnabled	Specifies whether the BINARYMIME EHLO keyword is advertised and is available for use.	

PARAMETER	DESCRIPTION	WHEN SHOULD IT BE CHANGED?
Bindings	Specifies the local IP and port number the connector listens to.	If you change the bindings to a different port, make sure that all sending servers also use the same port.
ChunkingEnabled	Chunking enables large message bodies to be relayed by the remote server to the Receive connector in multiple, smaller chunks.	
DeliveryStatusNotificationEnabled	Specifies whether the delivery status notification (DSN) EHLO keyword is advertised in the EHLO response to the remote server and is available for use.	
DomainSecureEnabled	Enables or disables Domain Security (also known as mutual TLS).	Domain Security is normally only enabled on Edge Transport servers to securely communicate over the Internet.
EightBitMimeEnabled	Enables or disables 8-bit MIME.	MIME 8-bit should only be disabled if you face issues when receiving binary data, such as attachments.
EnhancedStatusCodesEnabled	Enables or disables enhanced Status Codes.	
LongAddressesEnabled	Enables the Receive connector to accept long X.400 e-mail addresses.	
OrarEnabled	Specifies whether to enable the Originator Requested Alternate Recipient (ORAR).	
SuppressXAnonymousTls	Defines whether standard TLS encryption for incoming connections is available.	If you use WOC devices to optimize WAN links, you want to change the default setting to turn off TLS.

PARAMETER	DESCRIPTION	WHEN SHOULD IT BE CHANGED?
AdvertiseClientSettings	Defines whether the SMTP server name, port number, and authentication settings are displayed in the Outlook Web App About page, which is accessed from the Help menu.	Especially in CAS arrays you should enable this to be able to identify the CAS server the client is connected to.
Enabled	Enables or disables this connector.	
ConnectionTimeout	Specifies the maximum time that a connection can remain open, even if the connection is actively transmitting data.	If you have SMTP clients that transmit large amounts of data over a slow link, consider increasing this setting.
ConnectionInactivityTimeout	Defines the maximum amount of idle time before a connection is closed.	Change this setting if you want to fine-tune message throttling options.
MessageRateLimit	Defines the maximum number of messages that can be sent by a single client IP address per minute.	Change this setting if you want to fine-tune message throttling options.
MessageRateSource	Specifies how the message submission rate is calculated (None, IPAddress, User, All).	
MaxInboundConnection	Defines the maximum number of inbound connections that this Receive connector serves at the same time.	Change this setting if you want to fine-tune message throttling options.
MaxInboundConnectionPerSource	Defines the maximum number of inbound connections that this Receive connector serves at the same time from a single IP address.	Change this setting if you want to fine-tune message throttling options.

PARAMETER	DESCRIPTION	WHEN SHOULD IT BE CHANGED?
MaxHeaderSize	Specifies in bytes the maximum size of the SMTP message header.	
MaxHopCount	Specifies the maximum number of hops that a message can take before the message is rejected by the Receive connector.	
MaxLocalHopCount	Specifies the maximum number of local hops (for example, internal Exchange servers) that a message can take before the message is rejected by the connector.	For large organizations, you might need to increase the value if you configure many Hub sites for Exchange,.
MaxLogonFailures	Number of logon failures that the Receive connector retries before closing the connection.	
MaxMessageSize	Specifies the maximum size of a message.	
MaxProtocolErrors	Specifies the maximum number of SMTP protocol errors before closing the connection.	Change this setting if you want to fine-tune message throttling options.
MaxRecipientsPerMessage	Defines how many recipients a single message can address.	
Name	Administrator-defined name of connector.	
PermissionGroups	Defines the groups or roles that can submit messages to the Receive connector: *ExchangeUsers*, *ExchangeLegacyServers*, and so on.	

PARAMETER	DESCRIPTION	WHEN SHOULD IT BE CHANGED?
PipeliningEnabled	Enables or disables Pipelining in SMTP to send requests without awaiting a response.	
ProtocolLoggingLevel	Specifies whether to enable protocol logging for the specified Receive connector.	If you have trouble with the connector, enable Verbose logging to see the full SMTP communication in the log directory.
RemoteIPRanges	Defines the remote IP addresses that can use this connector.	
RequireEHLODomain	Specifies whether the remote computer must provide a domain name in the EHLO handshake.	
RequireTLS	Configured if a session requires TLS encryption.	Set this to $true if you want to make sure the communication is encrypted.
EnableAuthGSSAPI	Specifies how to control the advertisement of the Generic Security Services application programming interface (GSSAPI) authentication method when Integrated Windows authentication is enabled on this connector.	
SizeEnabled	Specifies whether the SIZE SMTP extension is enabled.	You can change this on Edge Transport servers to advertise the maximum message size that is allowed in EHLO banner.

PARAMETER	DESCRIPTION	WHEN SHOULD IT BE CHANGED?
TarpitInterval	Specifies the period of time to delay an SMTP response to a remote server that Exchange determines may be abusing the connection. Authenticated connections are never delayed in this manner.	Change this setting if you want to fine-tune message throttling options for anonymous senders.
MaxAcknowledgementDelay	Specifies the time a Transport Server waits when sending a message to a server that doesn't support shadow redundancy before sending the acknowledgment.	

Configuring Delivery Agent Connectors

A delivery agent connector is similar to the Foreign connector in that it is used to route messages to foreign systems that don't use the SMTP protocol, such as an X.400-based messaging system that does not have an SMTP connector available. When a message is routed to a delivery agent connector, the associated agent performs content conversion and message delivery.

The advantage of using the delivery agent connector is that the agent already performs content conversation and message delivery—thus there is no need to store messages on the file system in a Drop or Pickup directory as required by the Foreign connector.

The delivery agent functions as follows:

1. It establishes a connection to the foreign system.
2. It retrieves messages from the Hub Transport's remote delivery queues.
3. It delivers the message to the foreign system and receives an acknowledgment for each successful delivery.
4. It retrieves waiting messages from the foreign system.

In comparison to the Foreign connector, where you place the message only in a drop directory and wait until it is processed, a delivery agent connector acknowledges the message delivery to the foreign system and thus allows service level agreement (SLA) analysis as you can track message latency to the foreign system. You also can use Exchange's Queue Viewer to verify message delivery, which is not the case with Foreign connectors.

> ***NOTE*** **While the Foreign connector architecture remains in Microsoft Exchange Server 2010, Microsoft recommends using delivery agents for routing messages to non-SMTP systems whenever possible.**

Exchange Server 2010 by default only comes with one Delivery Agent Connector: the Text Messaging Delivery Agent connector. This connector is used to route messages to mobile phones using the Address Space MOBILE:*, as shown in Figure 5-11.

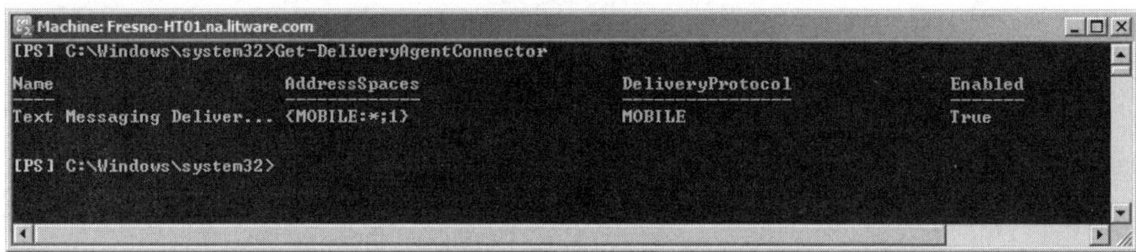

FIGURE 5-11 Default Delivery Agent connectors

Microsoft's intention is to replace connectors with other non-SMTP mail systems that were written with the old Exchange 2003 SDK (Foreign connectors) with new Delivery Agent connectors written using the Exchange 2010 SDK. Therefore, you would buy a new Delivery Agent connector for a foreign e-mail system such as Lotus Notes or Novell GroupWise from a third-party developer or you'd build your own connector if you had the time, patience, and expertise.

You use the *Set-DeliveryAgentConnector* cmdlet to configure the connector; you get information about the connector's configuration using the *Get-DeliveryAgentConnector* cmdlet.

Configuring Foreign Connectors

A Foreign connector is a connector that does not use the SMTP protocol for communication and was implemented with Exchange Server 2003 SDK. Even though it is not the recommended way to connect Exchange to a foreign system because Exchange 2010 implements Delivery Agent connectors to handle messages to foreign systems in a more sophisticated way, it still exists and can be used for existing third-party connectors.

To be able to communicate with third-party systems, the Foreign connector uses a Drop directory to send messages to the foreign gateway servers. Foreign gateway servers can send messages to Exchange Server 2010 by using the Replay directory found on every Hub Transport server in <*Exchange_Installation_Path*>\TransportRoles\Replay.

Every Foreign connector has an address space assigned to it that includes the following elements:

- **Connector Scope** Hub Transport servers that can use the connector
- **AddressSpaceType** For example, FAX or X.400
- **AddressSpace** A valid address space for the AddressSpaceType
- **AddressSpaceCost** Routing costs

Planning for Foreign connectors is a key task when doing an Exchange Server 2010 design. You should consider the following in your plan:

- Plan for fault tolerance when implementing Foreign connectors; make sure the Drop directory is available.
- Make sure the third-party connector fully supports Exchange Server 2010 before you move it over to the Exchange server, especially if you are in an environment where Exchange 2003 still exists. Alternatively, you can simply keep an Exchange 2003 server in place to host the old connector until you can either replace it with a new Delivery Agent connector or work out how to route messages to the other e-mail system with SMTP.

Planning and Configuring Your SMTP Namespace

Another important aspect is to plan and configure an SMTP namespace. The SMTP message protocol is the internal message protocol of Exchange 2010. Thus, you identify an Exchange organization by its primary SMTP namespace.

The SMTP namespace is configured in the Internet using one DNS MX record per SMTP domain that points to your Exchange organization. You need to make sure Exchange understands what to do with the SMTP namespaces that enter your Exchange organization.

Accepted Domains

The accepted domain property specifies one or more SMTP domain names for which the Exchange server receives mail. If an SMTP Receive connector on the Exchange Server 2010 Hub Transport server receives a message that is addressed to a domain that is not on the accepted domain list, it rejects the message and sends a relaying denied response.

When you create a new accepted domain, you have three options for the domain type you can create:

- **Authoritative Domain** Select this option if every e-mail addresses for this domain name exists in Active Directory (as mailbox, contact, and so on). If a message is received that has a recipient e-mail address that is not in the Active Directory, an NDR will be created for that message. The Contoso scenario, where you only use Exchange as the messaging system, is an example where you define all domains as authoritative.
- **Internal Relay Domain** This option is to configure a shared address space with one or more messaging systems. If the e-mail address does not exist in your Active Directory, Exchange will forward the message using a Send connector. You need at least one Send connector with the internal relay domain configured as address space so that the Hub Transport servers will send the message that are not found in your Exchange organization to the correct target SMTP server. For example, you would use this option during a migration in which your legacy messaging system and your new messaging system share the same e-mail addresses.
- **External Relay Domain** Select this option to relay messages to an SMTP server outside of the Exchange organization or the organization's network. An Edge Transport server is responsible for routing the messages received to the target SMTP server.

Your organization is therefore responsible for the DNS MX record of this company and forwards every message received to the target server. It requires a Send connector from the Edge Transport servers to the external relay domain's SMTP server that includes the external relay domain as address space.

> **NOTE** To configure accepted domains using the Exchange Management Shell, use the *New-AcceptedDomain* or *Set-AcceptedDomain* cmdlets. This allows you to easily create or modify many domains with a single operation.

Remote Domains

Remote domains define SMTP domains that are external to your Exchange organization. You can create remote domain entries to define the settings for message transfer between the Exchange Server 2010 organization and domains outside your AD DS forest.

When you create a remote domain entry, you control the types of messages that are sent to that domain. You can apply message-format policies and acceptable character sets for the messages that are sent from your organization's users to the remote domain as well as determine out-of-office message settings.

OUT-OF-OFFICE MESSAGE SETTINGS

The out-of-office message settings control the messages that are sent to recipients in the remote domain. The types of out-of-office messages that are available in your organization depend on both the Microsoft Office Outlook client version and the Exchange Server version on which the user's mailbox is located.

An out-of-office message is set on the Outlook client but is sent by the Exchange server. Exchange Server 2010 supports three out-of-office message classifications: external, internal, and legacy, as shown in Figure 5-12.

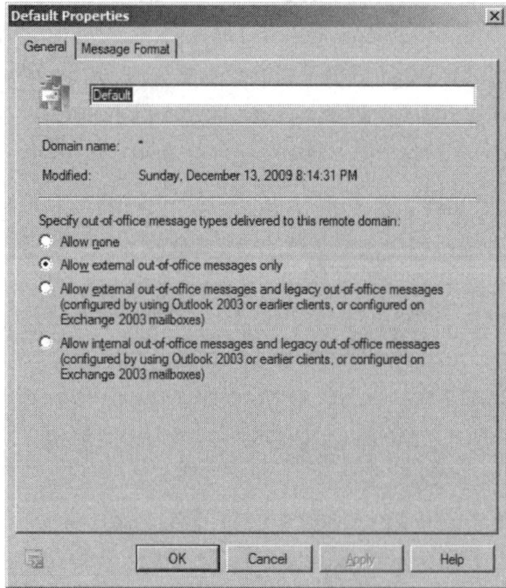

FIGURE 5-12 Out-of-office settings for remote domains

MESSAGE FORMAT OPTIONS INCLUDING ACCEPTABLE CHARACTER SETS

You can configure multiple message format options to specify message delivery and formatting policies for the messages that are sent to recipients in the remote domain. The first set of options on the Message Format tab apply restrictions to the types of messages that can be sent to the remote domain, how the sender's name displays to the recipient, and the column width for message text. These options include:

- Allow automatic replies.
- Allow automatic forward.
- Allow delivery reports.
- Allow non-delivery reports.
- Display sender's name on messages.
- Use message text line-wrap at column.

EXCHANGE RICH TEXT FORMAT SETTINGS

Use the Exchange rich-text format settings to determine whether e-mail messages from your organization to the remote domain are sent by using Exchange Rich Text Format (RTF). Remember that the Microsoft RTF format is not automatically supported by every LINUX or UNIX SMTP server; thus if the recipients of messages from your organization complain about weird attachments or missing attachments, you should try to disable RTF for that domain.

CHARACTER SETS

The Characters Sets options let you select a MIME character set and a non-MIME character set to use when you send messages to a remote domain.

TargetAddress Routing

Another way to modify message routing is to add a SMTP address to the *TargetAddress* attribute of a mail-enabled user account object or a contact object. After the attribute is added, the object is available in the Global Address List (GAL) and also can be addressed by using its primary SMTP address. Messages sent to the object will be automatically forwarded to the SMTP address defined in *TargetAddress*.

The first time I used this technology was back in the old Exchange 5.5 days, with an Exchange migration product called *Quest Exchange Migration Wizard*. This tool created one contact for every mailbox and used the *TargetAddress* attribute to forward messages to the target environment.

The *TargetAddress* attribute is defined on a per-object level; thus you can define which objects are redirected and which are not. You should consider the following if you're planning to use *TargetAddress* routing in your environment:

- You need to configure a Send connector that includes the target domain as address space.

- To share one address space, create an Internal Relay Domain for it. The internal relay domain should be the primary SMTP address of the objects. This is required to have users in both messaging systems (source and target) be able to address the contacts or mailboxes in both system by using their primary SMTP address.
- You need to create one contact or mail-enabled user account per e-mail address to be capable of forwarding it. The *TargetAddress* attribute will include a dedicated SMTP address for the target messaging system.

> **NOTE** Remember that as soon as you mailbox-enable a user account, the *TargetAddress* attribute will be removed and any message forwarding will be stopped.

Additional Resources

- Understanding the Pickup and Replay Directories: *http://technet.microsoft.com/en-us/library/bb124230.aspx*
- Microsoft Active Directory Topology Diagrammer: *http://www.microsoft.com/downloads/details.aspx?familyid=cb42fc06-50c7-47ed-a65c-862661742764&displaylang=en*
- Viewing the Routing Table Log: *http://technet.microsoft.com/en-us/library/bb691033(EXCHG.80).aspx*
- Understanding Message Throttling: *http://technet.microsoft.com/en-us/library/bb232205.aspx*
- Understanding Back Pressure: *http://technet.microsoft.com/en-us/library/bb201658.aspx*
- Understanding Transport Agents: *http://technet.microsoft.com/en-us/library/bb125012.aspx*

CHAPTER 6

Mailbox Services

The primary function of the Mailbox role in Exchange Server 2010 is to serve and store mailbox data. In this version, advances have been made to the Mailbox role to increase the sophistication of high-availability options while reducing the non-core services by moving them to other Exchange roles. Without a solid core database, the other services are irrelevant. Although rumors have circulated since the debut of Exchange 2000 Server about replacing the Exchange ESE (JET Blue) database with a Microsoft SQL Server–based database, the ESE database is still in the product, performing better and providing unique high-availability solutions that other messaging and relational databases are not able to provide. This chapter covers the basic Mailbox server architecture, and new features and functionality in the Mailbox server role, and then applies some real-world administrative guidelines for configuration and maintenance.

Introduction to Exchange Server 2010 Mailbox Services

The Exchange server product has slowly evolved to be much more than simple e-mail services; however, the heart of the product still lives on in the Mailbox role. Microsoft's original mail product, Microsoft Mail, was little more than message items stored on disk and some external applications that acted as message transport agents (MTAs) that were used to move mail around. As electronic messaging became more important to businesses, it was clear that the architecture of Microsoft Mail would not scale to meet growing business needs; it was then replaced with the Exchange Server product. Version 4.0 was the first version of Exchange Server, coming to the market in 1996 to provide improved scalability and improve the connectivity of the e-mail system to other systems.

Exchange Server 4.0 did provide a more scalable product, with a unified address book and a way to interface with a variety of e-mail systems. As Exchange Server 5.0 and Exchange Server 5.5 came to market, additional connectors were made available to embrace emerging Internet standards like SMTP. Also added in Exchange Server 5.5 was a Web-based client originally named the Exchange Web Client and then renamed Outlook Web Access (now renamed Outlook Web App in Exchange Server 2010).

With the introduction of Exchange 2000 Server, Outlook Web Access also ran not only on the same server, but the core functionality ran in the Information Store (store.exe), which was the same process that handled the database functionality. Exchange 2000 Server also introduced the streaming database file (STM) to store the content of messages that were not in native MAPI format. When these messages were accessed by a MAPI client, the data would be promoted into the ESE Exchange database; however, if the message was accessed with an IMAP or POP3 client no conversion would happen. The intent was to reduce the amount of conversions that needed to happen and thereby reduce the overall resources required on the Exchange Server. The streaming database file was discontinued starting with Exchange Server 2007.

Beginning with Exchange Server 2007, the development team began peeling out many of these functions from the database to reduce the bloat and sensitivity to any code changes. For example, in Exchange 2007 the Outlook Web Access (OWA) was completely rewritten. OWA no longer used the Information Store to render the HTML for OWA. Also, the Exchange Server 2007 introduced server roles, allowing separation of functionality onto different servers, only needing to run the required roles on specific servers. Again in Exchange 2010 additional functionality was removed from the database and moved to other roles. For example, in Exchange Server 2010, MAPI-based client connectivity has been moved from the Mailbox role to the Client Access Server role. Having fewer non-core functions running within the information store process has improved performance and stability and added in additional high-availability functionality.

Exchange Mailbox Services Architecture

A database schema is the definition of how the data is stored in the database file. As shown in Table 6-1, in all earlier versions of Exchange Server, each database has a mailbox, folder, message, and attachment table. These tables are used to store all information for all mailboxes in the database. This provides the ability to only store a message and attachment once for each of the mailboxes in the database. The previous database schema also includes a table for each folder to store the item contents of each folder.

TABLE 6-1 Exchange Server 2007 Table Structure

PER DATABASE				PER FOLDER
MAILBOX TABLE	**FOLDER TABLE**	**MESSAGE TABLE**	**ATTACHMENT TABLE**	**MESSAGE/FOLDER TABLE**
Terry	Terry: Sent Items	Terry: Message 42	Terry: Word.docx	Terry: Inbox: MH1
Ankur	Ankur: Unread	Ankur: Message 26	Ankur: Manual.pdf	Terry: Inbox: MH2
Joel	Joel: Inbox	Joel: Message 144	Joel: Pricing.xlsx	Terry: Inbox: MH3

Single instance storage no longer provides the space savings that it did when it was first introduced, because of a number of factors. The architecture used to support single instance storage also no longer provides adequate performance for SATA-based storage (this will be covered in more detail later in this chapter). The database structure in Exchange Server 2010, shown in Table 6-2, was re-architected to now only have one per database table—the mailbox table. All of the folders, message headers, and message bodies are stored in a table for each mailbox. There is also a table for each view, which stores the contents and status of each message included in each view.

TABLE 6-2 Exchange Server 2010 Table Structure

PER DATABASE	PER MAILBOX			PER VIEW
MAILBOX TABLE	FOLDER TABLE	MESSAGE HEADER TABLE	BODY TABLE	VIEW TABLES
KC	KC: Sent Items	KC: Message 42	KC: Word.docx	KC: MH1
Jeff	KC: Unread	KC: Message 26	KC: Manual.pdf	KC: MH2
Liberty	KC: Inbox	KC: Message 144	KC: Pricing.xlsx	KC: MH3

This new database structure allows data to be stored contiguously and to keep frequently accessed data located more closely together, as can be seen in Figure 6-1. When the data is contiguous, the amount of I/O that is required is reduced.

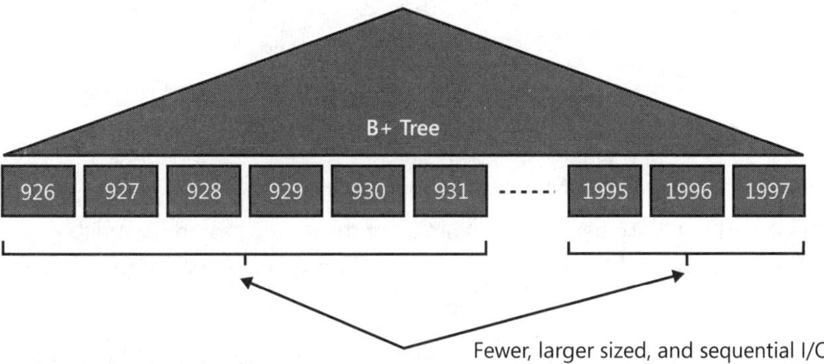

FIGURE 6-1 Contiguous database structure

Database Files

The mailbox data is stored in the Extensible Storage Engine (ESE) database, which is represented in a number of files that are stored on the Mailbox Server. Each database is represented by a single instance of the ESE instance and shares a single set of transaction log files. Whenever a transaction occurs, ESE first records the transaction in memory to the log buffers and then to a transaction log. The transaction logs contain a history of all the bit-level changes that are committed to the database. In the default database configuration, transaction logs will continue to build up until they are truncated.

Truncation, or deletion of the committed transaction logs, usually occurs when a backup of the database is completed. However, if the database is configured for circular logging, after the transaction logs are committed into the database, the transaction logs are replaced with new transaction logs. Therefore, the most current state of an Exchange service is represented by the database file plus the current log files. Checkpoint files are used to keep track of which transaction logs have been committed to the database. Checkpoint files are named E*nn*.chk and normally reside in the same directories as the transaction log files.

The basic database files for a database named Dallas-EX01-MB04 are shown in Figure 6-2.

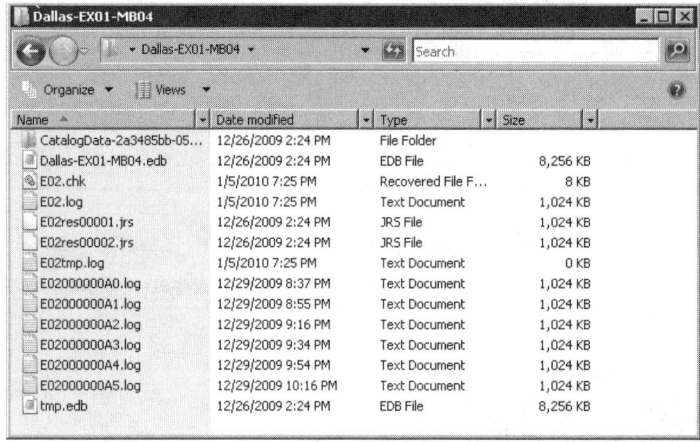

FIGURE 6-2 ESE files

- Database Name.edb (Dallas-EX01-MB04.edb)

  This file is the B-tree database file. This is where all of the data is stored for mailboxes and in the case of a public folder database where public folder data is stored.

- E*nn*.chk (E02.chk)

  The checkpoint file contains a record of the committed transaction logs and which logs are yet to be committed. The checkpoint file, as well as many of the other files, is named with the log file prefix, such as E00 for the first database on a server, E01 for the second database, and so on.

- E*nn*.log (E02.log)

  This is the current transaction log file for the first database. Data is still being written into this file. When the data in this log reaches 1,024 KB or if the server is idle for a period of time, it will be renamed to the next sequential number for the database. A new Exx.log file will then be created, and transactions will be written to it until it is full.

- E*nn*res00001.jrs and E*nn*res00002.jrs (E02res00001.jrs and E02res00002.jrs)

  These files are used to reserve emergency storage if the transaction log volume becomes full. In the event that the volume becomes full, these files are deleted to make room for the transactions being processed to be written to disk, and the databases are dismounted. By having two reserved transaction logs, Exchange can reduce the likelihood that transactions will be lost during this process. These files are always 1,024 KB in size.

- E*nn*hhhhhhhh.log (E0200000A0.log through E0200000A5.log)

  These files are older transaction log files and are named with the log prefix, such as E01, followed by an eight-character hexadecimal number. Thus the file named E0100000001.log is the first log file for the second database on the server. The transaction logs are named with the numbers 1 through 0 and the letters A through F as are used in hexadecimal numbering system. These files will always be 1,024 KB in size. These files are kept until they are truncated—which is done after a successful full backup of the database—or are overwritten after they are committed when circular logging is enabled.

- Tmp.edb

  This file is a temporary workspace for processing active transactions. This file is typically only a few megabytes in size and is deleted automatically when the database is dismounted or the Information Store process is stopped.

- E*nn*tmp.log

  This file serves as the transaction log file for the Tmp.edb workspace. This file will never be larger than 1,024 KB in size.

Single Instance Storage

During the development of Exchange Server, disk capacity compared to I/O capacity was at a premium; to solve this problem, single instance storage was included in the design. Single instance storage writes a single copy of an e-mail message or attachment once in the database and creates pointers for each mailbox in the same database that has a copy of the object, rather than duplicating the data for each copy. This allows a single 1 MB Microsoft Word document to be sent to 200 recipients on the same mailbox database but only be stored a single time, thereby only consuming only 1 MB of space in the database file rather than 200 MB of space. The potential capacity savings in some environments was significant.

A number of changes have happened over the years that have made single instance storage less and less practical. First, mailboxes have become larger. In 1996, it was not uncommon to see a maximum mailbox size of 10 or 25 MB, whereas today 1 GB and larger mailboxes are becoming commonplace. You might think that this indicates that single instance storage is now more important than ever, but this is not really the case. Prior to Exchange 2000 Server there was only an option to create a single Exchange database on the server, which made it possible to use single instance storage across all of the mailboxes on the server. However, now that mailboxes have become larger, more databases are needed on the server to reduce the individual database size, and because the logical boundary for single instance storage is at the database level, the return on single instance storage is diminished with the number of databases that are created.

The Enterprise edition of Exchange 2010 provides you with the ability to create up to 100 databases on a single server, which dilutes the potential for single instance storage savings even more. Hard drives have also become very large in the last 15 years and will continue to increase in size, and Exchange server has become increasingly more efficient at working with lower-performance disk technologies, making space even less of a premium. As a result of this and the performance improvements made in Exchange 2010, single instance storage is no longer included in the product. More information about the decision to remove single instance storage can be found at *http://msexchangeteam.com/archive/2010/02/22/454051.aspx.*

The Exchange Services

The Exchange Server Mailbox role installs a number of unique services. It is important to understand what the Mailbox role does and which services are responsible for specific functionality so that if problems arise they can be pinpointed and corrected quickly. Table 6-3 lists the services that are installed specifically to support the Mailbox functions.

TABLE 6-3 Exchange Mailbox Role Services

SERVICE NAME	DESCRIPTION	BEST PRACTICE INFORMATION
Microsoft Exchange Information Store	This required service mounts and manages mailbox and public folder databases.	This service must be started, otherwise none of the mailboxes or public folders will be available.
Microsoft Exchange Mail Submission Service	This required service submits messages that are placed in the hosted mailbox's Outbox to the Hub Transport servers. This service is needed because the Mailbox server does not have an SMTP-based delivery service.	In order to send e-mail from a mailbox this service must be running.
Microsoft Exchange Mailbox Assistants	This required service manages the background processing of mailboxes in the Exchange store, including the processing of out-of-office (OOF) messages and the managing of calendars for resource mailboxes.	To provide full functionality for mailboxes, this service should always be started.

SERVICE NAME	DESCRIPTION	BEST PRACTICE INFORMATION
Microsoft Exchange Replication Service	This service provides the continuous replication functionality for Mailbox servers in a database availability group.	This service should be running on all members in a DAG.
Microsoft Exchange Search Indexer	This service is responsible for indexing mailbox content.	This service should be enabled to maintain search indexes.
Microsoft Exchange Server Extension for Windows Server Backup	This service enables Windows Server Backup to work with Exchange Server 2010.	This service can be disabled if other backup methods are used.
Microsoft Exchange System Attendant	This is a required service that is responsible for generating e-mail addresses and offline address books, updating free/busy information for legacy clients, and maintaining permissions and group memberships for the server.	This service should never be disabled or stopped.
Microsoft Exchange Throttling	This required service limits the rate of user operations to ensure that a user cannot create a denial-of-service situation by consuming more than the allowed transactions.	This service should be started to reduce the possibility of a single user consuming an unfair amount of resources.

What Is New in Exchange Server 2010

With Exchange Server 2010, Microsoft has delivered on the following new items: larger mailbox support through improved performance, better availability options, and a reduction in the requirements for restores and reduce storage costs.

Large Mailboxes

More and more data is being stored in mailboxes for a variety of reasons. First, users now send and receive a larger quantity of e-mail messages and the messages are larger in size and contain different types of attachments than they did in years past. Second, many organizations must retain more messages in case of litigation or to meet regulatory requirements. With previous versions of Exchange it was often necessary for users to move data out of their mailboxes and into Personal Storage Folders (PSTs) because it was too costly for some organizations to provide large enough mailboxes to meet user's storage requirements. This could lead to a number of potential issues, which are described in this section.

With more room in their mailboxes, end users spend less time juggling data to decide which data should be kept to maintain a threshold under the mailbox limit. Another issue is that PST files can be lost, stolen, or to a lesser extent become corrupted, potentially losing or misplacing important or sensitive information. And having data stored in PST files reduces the likelihood and increases the complexity of a legal discovery being successful in finding the pertinent and required information and often violates regulatory compliance. Storing messages within the user's mailbox rather than in a PST also allows the end user to be able to access all of her e-mail from all available supported clients such as OWA, Outlook client, and Outlook Mobile. By architecting and optimizing Exchange Server 2010 to support larger mailboxes all the issues described above have been addressed.

Deleted Item Recovery and Dumpster 2.0

In previous releases of Exchange Server, as items were deleted they were put into the Deleted Items folder until the folder was emptied. This gives the end user the opportunity to review and recover the items before they are permanently deleted. When the Deleted Items folder is emptied, the messages are specially flagged to be included in the dumpster and essentially removed from the mailbox. If the end user needs the information after emptying the deleted items folder, the user can use the Recover Deleted Items option to retrieve the deleted data for the duration of the deleted items retention set for the mailbox. The items in the dumpster exist for the duration of the deleted item retention policy or until the items are manually deleted from the dumpster. The messages in the dumpster are not searchable; there is no way to enforce quotas on the deleted items and there is no method to block end users from manually purging the data from the dumpster.

Although the dumpster feature is invaluable in being able to recover deleted information by greatly reducing or eliminating the need for database restores and performing MAPI-based mailbox (brick-level) backups, these shortcomings limit the usefulness of the feature. In Exchange Server 2010, investments have been made to improve this feature.

> **NOTE** In versions of Outlook earlier than Microsoft Office Outlook 2007, connected to Exchange Server 5.5 and later, the Recover Deleted Items option is only shown for the Deleted Items folder. This often leads some to believe that using Shift+Delete to remove messages permanently purges the information; however, the deleted information actually still exists in the dumpster for the folder containing the original message. The Recover Deleted Items option can be enabled in Outlook by setting the DumpsterAlwaysOn registry key. More information on setting this registry key can be found at: *http://support.microsoft.com/kb/886205*.

Exchange Server 2010 introduces a new version of the dumpster, sometimes referred to as Dumpster 2.0. Unlike in the previous iteration of the dumpster where the items were flagged and hidden, Dumpster 2.0 is implemented as a non-IPM folder called Recoverable Items in each user's mailbox. Non-IPM folders do not show up as standard folders within the Outlook or Outlook Web App. This folder has three subfolders: Deletions, Versions, and Purges. Each is used to provide enhanced functionality to Dumpster 2.0.

Deletions Folder

The items that are moved to the Deletions folder are items that are soft-deleted and that would have ended up in the per-folder dumpster in previous versions of Exchange Server. To ensure that this works with Outlook 2003 and Outlook 2007, which only understands how the dumpster works in previous versions of Exchange, the RPC Client Access server will translate any calls made to the dumpster into calls into the Recoverable Items\Deletions folder. The Deletions folder data is subject to the Deleted item rendition time set on the database or on the mailbox.

Using a non-IPM folder to store deleted items allows the following:

- Deleted information can be stored per mailbox instead of per folder.
- Deleted information can be indexed and searched.
- Deleted information can be moved when the mailbox is moved to another database.

> ***NOTE*** **In Exchange Server 2010, each mailbox can also have an associated online archive mailbox, which has a separate Recoverable Items\Deletions folder to store data deleted from the online archive mailbox.**

Purges Folder

The Purges subfolder is used when Single Item Recovery is enabled on the mailbox—if Single Item Recovery isn't enabled, deleted items are moved into the Deletions folder. If items are removed manually from the Deletions folder (when Single Item Recovery is enabled) before the deleted item retention time has transpired, the messages are moved into the Purges folder for the duration of deleted item retention. The Purges folder cannot be accessed by end users and would be used by the administrator to recover deleted data; therefore, this feature solves one of the deficiencies of previous versions of Exchange where end users could manually remove deleted items allowing potentially incriminating information to be deleted, if other measures were not employed. The functionality and usefulness of this feature will be covered in more detail in Chapter 8, "Automated Message Processing, Compliance, and Archiving."

> ***NOTE*** **Regardless of whether Single Item Recovery is enabled, calendar items are maintained in the Recoverable Items folder structure for 120 days. However, a legal hold can enable longer-term data preservation to disable the expiration of the items.**

Versions Folder

The Versions subfolder is used when either Single Item Recovery or Litigation Hold is enabled. Anytime a message in the enabled mailbox is modified the original message is copied to the Versions subfolder. Each version is kept and can be searched by a user assigned the Discovery Management role. This is invaluable in finding e-mail messages that might have been modified to hide or alter the original content of the message. Messages stored in the Drafts folder are exempt from this behavior to reduce the amount of unnecessary data in the folder.

The prospect of capturing the versions of modified e-mail messages further reduces the need for restores resulting from messages being modified. The functionality and usefulness of this feature will also be covered in more detail in Chapter 8.

The Dumpster 2.0 configuration options are summarized in Table 6-4.

TABLE 6-4 Dumpster 2.0 Configuration Options

FEATURE STATE	DELETED ITEMS KEPT IN DUMPSTER 2.0	VERSIONS AND HARD-DELETED ITEMS KEPT IN DUMPSTER 2.0	USER CAN PURGE ITEMS FROM DUMPSTER	AUTOMATICALLY PURGE DUMPSTER ITEMS
Single Item Recovery disabled	Yes	No	Yes	Yes, using deleted item retention for e-mail and 120 days for calendar items
Single Item Recovery enabled	Yes	Yes	No	Yes, using deleted item retention for e-mail and 120 days for calendar items
Litigation Hold enabled	Yes	Yes	No	No

Discontinuation of Storage Groups

In earlier versions of Exchange Server, you could create multiple databases that used a single set of log files. These collections were called *storage groups* and were allowed so that databases could be kept smaller and more manageable. However, because of the limited cache memory available in 32-bit versions of Exchange Server, only four storage groups with a maximum of 20 databases could be created on a single server.

Storage groups continue to exist in Exchange Server 2007; however, having multiple databases in a single storage group is generally discouraged or prohibited in many configurations. With the ability to create up to 50 storage groups and as many databases on a single server, the best practice is to never create more than one database in each storage group, but rather create a storage group for each database.

In Exchange Server 2010, storage groups have been completely eliminated. Now each set of transaction log files only supports one mailbox or one public folder database. Not only have the storage groups been eliminated, but databases are also no longer specifically owned by any single server. All of the database objects now reside within a single database container for the entire Exchange organization. In the Exchange Server versions 2000, 2003, and 2007, a database name only had to be unique within a storage group. A database could be distinguished by the server it was created on and the storage group it was created within, as shown in Figure 6-3. Because of this many companies could have rightly used the same database names multiple times across the entire Exchange organization.

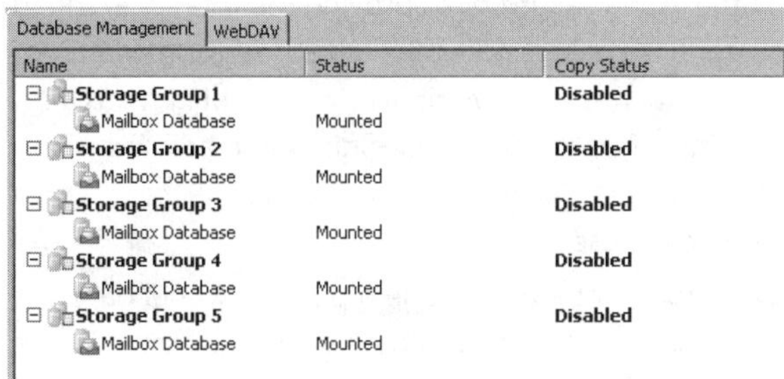

FIGURE 6-3 Distinguishing database names in Exchange 2007

In Exchange 2010 databases are no longer tied to a specific server. Therefore, each mailbox database name must be unique across the entire organization, as shown in Figure 6-4. This means that proper attention must be given to creating a naming standard that works for your organization. The best practices for creating a naming standard for an organization are discussed in further detail in Chapter 3, "Exchange Environmental Considerations."

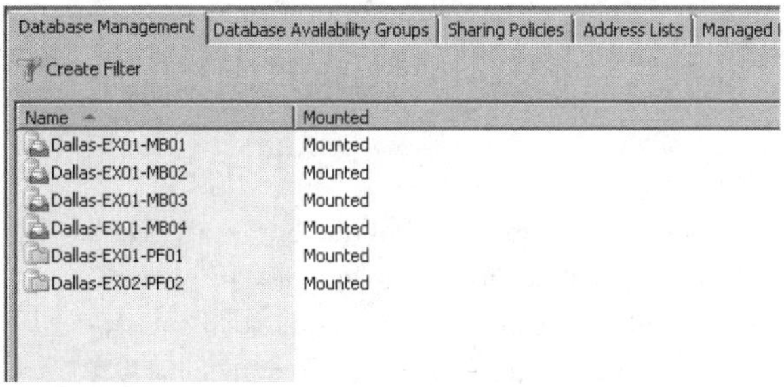

FIGURE 6-4 Distinguishing database names in Exchange 2010

Exchange Server 2003 also introduced the Recovery Storage Group feature; this feature enables an administrator to restore database backups into a special storage group for recovery. This functionality still exists within Exchange 2010; however, with the removal of storage groups it is now called a *recovery database (RDB)*. The functionality and best practices for using RDBs are covered in Chapter 12, "Backup/Restore and Disaster Recovery."

Performance Improvements

The overall theme for the storage changes in Exchange Server 2010 was to move away from doing many random, small, disk IOs to a few sequential, large, disk IOs. A number of changes were done to accomplish this, such as a larger page size, improved data contiguity, and more intelligent I/O operations.

The importance of optimizing I/O can be better understood by reviewing how disk technology functions. Random disk I/O is bound by the speed at which the disk head can move around and get data. The more the disk head has to move the longer it takes to read or write data. When data is read or written contiguously the disk head does not need to move between operations and can execute I/O at a much higher rate, primarily dependent on the speed at which the disk spins.

Although improvements have been made in this regard by improving the rotational speed and the aerial density of the disk platters, random reads and writes do not perform nearly as well as sequential reads and writes. The performance improvements for sequential reads and writes have far outpaced the performance improvements for that of random reads and writes. Thus by changing the format that the data is read and written in, more performance can be extracted from the same disk hardware already in use.

Optimizing this I/O opens up possibilities for you to use storage types that would have never even been considered, such as SATA disks, which generally have good sequential I/O performance, higher storage density, and lower cost than Fibre Channel or Serial Attached SCSI storage technologies, but have poorer random I/O performance. The size and speed of the database storage are typically the largest capital cost factors in an Exchange solution. In the end, optimizing Exchange to allow for the design of solutions using lower-cost SATA disks means lower-cost solutions with better performance.

NOTES FROM THE FIELD

Choosing a Disk Technology

Steve McIntyre
Solutions Architect, Dell Inc.

Choosing the right technology for a messaging system requires that both current and future needs are met. To do that it is important to choose the right disk technology that meets the performance and storage needs of the Exchange Server deployment. The following tables show the current state and predicted future advances in both Serial ATA (SATA) and Fibre Channel (FC) and Serial Attached SCIS (SAS) disk technology. The first table shows the past and estimated capacity and speed of 3.5-inch SATA disk drives.

	2006	2010	2013
Drive Capacity (GB)	750	2,000	8,000
Rotational Speed (RPM)	7,200	7,200	10,000

The second table shows the past and estimated capacity and speed of 3.5-inch FC and SAS disk drives.

	2006	2010	2013
Drive Capacity (GB)	300	600	2,400
Rotational Speed (RPM)	15,000	15,000	15,000

As you can see, the RPM for FC and SAS disks is not expected to improve at all in the next few years. Therefore, there will be no random I/O performance gains for Exchange Server. Also, the capacity available in SATA disks far outstrips the capacity available in FC/SAS disks, which means that optimizing Exchange to use SATA technology provides a greater "bang per buck" for companies deciding on their disk technology.

Increased Database Page Size

To accomplish these performance goals, a number of core changes were made to the database. The information inside the database is stored in B-trees, and these B-trees are segmented into pages where the data is written. The page size then sets the minimum size for any sort of I/O operation to the database. The first fundamental design change was that the page size was increased from 4 KB to 8 KB in Exchange Server 2007, which contributed to a large improvement in performance. In Exchange Server 2010 the page size has been increased all the way up to 32 KB. This increase in page size means that each I/O can now either write or read four times the amount of data than in Exchange Server 2007, which translates into needing less I/O and improved performance.

Improved Data Contiguity

To perform fewer random I/O operations the data needs to be written to the disk in a predictable, non-random fashion. When data is made contiguous and database pages are written to the database in order, the database gains a little extra whitespace. When data is compacted, the data is moved in the database to consolidate the whitespace in one area within the database file. As might be apparent here, contiguity and compaction work in direct opposition. Compaction preserves and consolidates whitespace and contiguity often leaves whitespace within the database to ensure that data is written contiguously. In the earlier versions of Exchange, the defragmentation process favored compaction over data contiguity to maintain the smallest available database file size.

In Exchange Server 2010, contiguity of data is preferred over compaction of data. In testing, the changes that were made to the database added about 20 percent of whitespace into the database. To combat this bloat, compression of message headers and text or html message bodies was added to the database, which in testing again shrank the database size around 20 percent. The results of these changes leave a much more contiguous file with better read and write performance than previous versions of Exchange Server.

As the data is written into the database, the store will look for space within the database so that the data can be written contiguously. Figure 6-5 shows how a single empty page is skipped to store a message header and message body contiguously within the database.

Data that does not need to be written contiguously will opportunistically be stored in the blank pages; the figure shows a page with event history being written to the empty page.

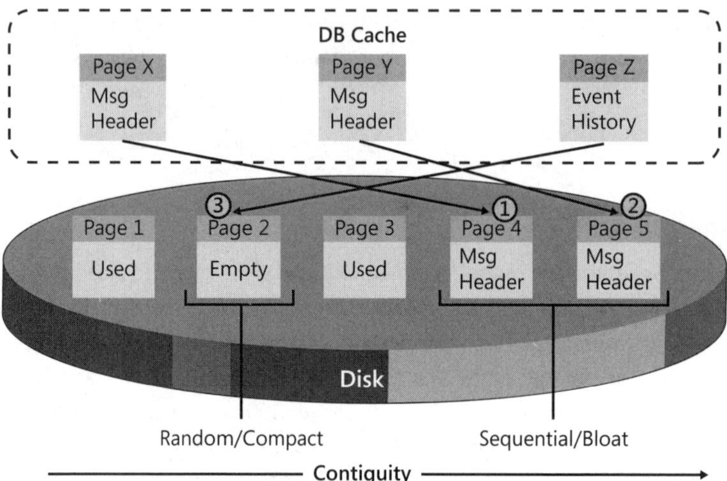

FIGURE 6-5 Contiguous page usage

Not only is contiguity built into the initial creation of the data, but processes are also in place to ensure that the data is maintained in this state, even as it is accessed and modified by the end clients.

The database defragmentation process has been improved to reduce I/O operations. Defragmentation is now performed in-place, rather than creating a new B-tree and then renaming all of the indexes and tables. This reduces the number of I/O operations that need to be completed. Data is read from and written to the hard disk from right to left—right merges require more disk head movement to complete. The defragmentation process in previous versions used right merges, meaning the data is read and then moved to the left or earlier in the file. With left merges, the data is read and then moved to the right, or the same direction as the I/O operation. Because space is allocated also from left to right, and page moves need to allocate a new page, defragmenting the database from left to right is much more efficient because it reduces the need to move the hard disk head.

With the improvements to the performance and added throttling to the defragmentation process, it is no longer required to run the process only during off hours. To be sure that contiguity is maintained, defragmentation is set by default to run continuously. As shown in Figure 6-6, the defragmentation and compactions processes will move items to maintain the optimal contiguity of the database, even after a user has disrupted the original contiguous layout.

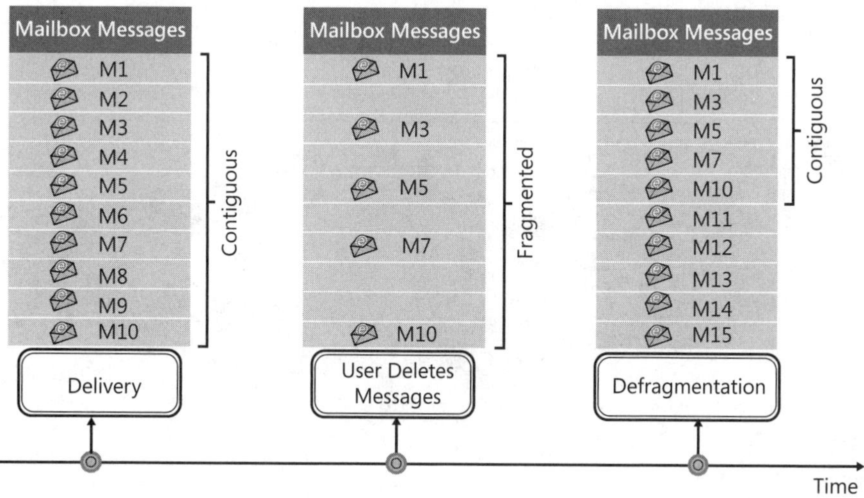

FIGURE 6-6 Maintaining contiguity over time

Intelligent I/O Operations

Not only has the schema and contiguity been improved, but there are also a number of changes to improve the way I/O is done. (As the saying goes, work smarter, not harder.) Rather than pushing the limits of the hardware, intelligence was built in the product to improve how and when I/O operations are done. These improvements include I/O gap coalescing, smarter view updates, and smoother database writes.

GAP COALESCING

With improved contiguity, coalescing—combining adjacent I/O operations—is now more viable. Exchange Server 2007 was able to coalesce adjacent I/O operations to reduce the number of I/O needed to write database changes. Exchange Server 2010 introduces the ability for gap coalescing, which is the ability to group nearby read or write operations together into a single I/O operation. This can be illustrated, as shown in Figure 6-7, when Exchange is reading a message from disk. Rather than initiating a read I/O for the page that contains the message header and then several additional read I/O operations to get each of the pages that contain the message body, Exchange will initiate a single read I/O that reads all contiguous pages from the message header through the last page that contains the message body and discard any unneeded pages. In this example the Exchange Server 2010 gap coalescing would require two fewer read I/O operations, and provide a much higher rate of I/O.

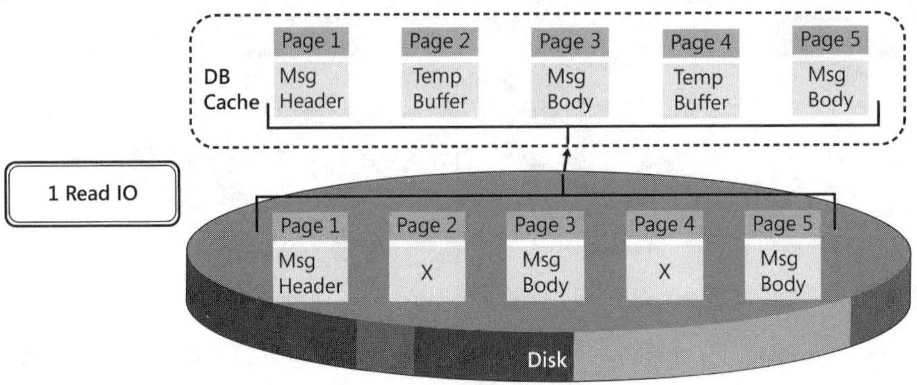

FIGURE 6-7 Coalesced read operations in Exchange Server 2010

ON-DEMAND VIEW UPDATES

In Exchange Server 2007 and earlier, anytime that an e-mail message impacted a view, the view was immediately updated. In Exchange Server 2010 the only time the view is updated is when it is being accessed. This is shown in Figure 6-8 using the Unread or Flagged items view. The top of the figure shows how, in Exchange Server 2007, any changes to the view require it to be updated immediately. At the bottom of the figure you can see that in Exchange Server 2010, the same actions occur; however, the view is only updated once, when that view is accessed by a client. This example has a five-fold reduction in the number of I/O operations that are required. This again greatly reduces the number of I/O operations that need to occur. It might seem that making the updates when a view is accessed would add latency; however, with the other database changes that have been made the overall performance is still improved.

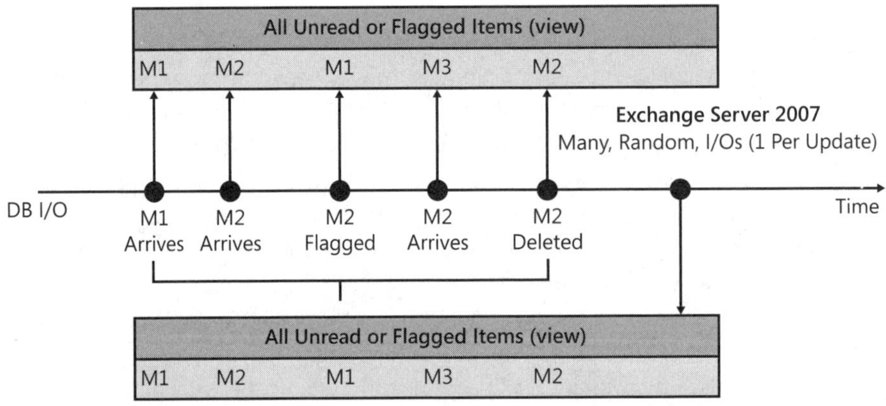

FIGURE 6-8 View updates utilizing sequential I/O

DATABASE WRITE SMOOTHING

In a typical database, anytime I/O needs to occur the database will immediately send all of the I/O requests to the storage. This causes larger bursts of work that needs to done. Most applications will allow the burst of work to be handled by adding disks or cache to the disk subsystem. However, with these bursts of work also comes disk contention, which means that the work takes additional time to complete, or adds latency. As mentioned earlier in the chapter, the faster the disk spins the faster that random I/O operation can occur. This also correlates with the number of concurrent operations that a disk can handle adequately.

Disk contention during these bursts can be likened to pouring a liquid into a funnel. When you pour the liquid into the funnel at roughly the same rate the liquid passes through the bottom of the funnel, the funnel will not overflow. If the liquid is poured too fast, it will overflow and cause a mess. The solution is to get a bigger funnel or change the rate at which the liquid is poured into the funnel. Rather than requiring a bigger funnel—more expensive hardware—Exchange Server 2010 uses database write smoothing.

Database write smoothing throttles disk writes to reduce disk contention while still maintaining the checkpoint target. This also better accommodates slower-spinning disks and multiple workloads on each disk. Database write smoothing cannot be manually configured and is always enabled, following these rules:

- When the checkpoint depth equals 1 to 1.24 times the checkpoint target, database write smoothing limits the maximum writes for each LUN to one.
- When checkpoint depth equals 1.25 times or more of checkpoint target, database write smoothing begins to increase the maximum writes for each LUN. The farther the target falls behind the checkpoint, the more aggressively it raises the maximum outstanding writes/LUN, with a total maximum of 512.

IMPROVED CACHING

Caching information in memory reduces the number of times the disks need to be accessed. Because memory is far faster than disk, the more accurate and complete the caching is, the less disk I/O is needed and the faster the information can be used. Cache warming is a process that preloads queries that were executed against a database the last time the database was started. After a server restart, failover, or switchover, the larger I/O allows ESE to increase the rate at which the cache is warmed. The information store process is now used to replay the logs on the passive copy of the database, which allows a cache to be populated with recently used information to be in memory. This is unlike Exchange Server 2007, which used a separate process to replay the logs, limiting the cache effectiveness in a switchover scenario.

Another way caching was improved was by increasing the checkpoint depth. The checkpoint depth is the amount of data waiting to be committed into the database file. The checkpoint depth has been increased to 100 MB when the database is configured in a Database Availability Group (DAG); however, the limit is still 20 MB for databases not configured in a DAG. It turns out that when a database page is written to, it often is rewritten to shortly thereafter. This makes sense, because when a user receives an e-mail message, he may read it, set it for follow-up, or move it to another folder. By waiting longer to commit the changes to the database pages, the subsequent changes are made in the database cache, and then a single I/O is performed to the disk that encompasses all of the changes.

In Exchange 2000 Server, it was common and supported to manually reduce the checkpoint depth from the default 20 MB to a lower depth in a clustered environment to improve switchover times. This is because when a switchover occurred from one clustered node to another, all of the outstanding transactions needed to be completed on the active node before the switchover or shutdown could complete. In Exchange Server 2010, this does not happen because the passive copies of the databases have a checkpoint depth of only 5 MB. With only up to 5 MB of outstanding transactions, these can be committed quickly, allowing for faster switchover operations. Also, Exchange 2010 allows all databases to failover in parallel, which improves the shutdown and the speed of committing the data before the switchover.

No matter how large the cache is, if it doesn't have valid or useful cached information it doesn't do any good. To keep the cache fresh with valid cache data, the Exchange Server 2010 cache allows lower priorities to be set to cache data that has limited usefulness. Cache data generated from database maintenance activities such as online defragmentation, database check summing, and passive copy log replay all are given lower priorities so that the data can be evicted from the cache more quickly.

With page sizes four times larger than previous versions, only a fourth of the number of pages can be cached in the same amount of memory. To combat this potential ineffectiveness, database cache compression, also known as *cache dehydration,* was introduced. This removes the whitespace and only stores the active data from each of the 32 KB database pages in memory. For example, if a database page only has 16 KB of data written to it, only the 16 KB of data is stored cached, rather than caching the entire 32-KB page. This allows additional pages to be cached and provides a more effective database cache.

Online Archive

Personal Storage Files (PSTs) are a problem for many Exchange users because they are not backed up or physically protected and can contain confidential information or have data needed for legal discovery. This information can be lost or fall into the hands of unauthorized people. Many solutions have been put on the market to help control the PST sprawl in a company. Some of these solutions will search for and then gather and index the data within the PSTs and store them in centralized repository. These solutions can scale well and have become fairly mature products. However they often require a separate access method or Outlook plug-ins to access the archived data. The online archive, although it lacks some of the more sophisticated tools that third-party products offer, does allow access to the archived data through Microsoft Office Outlook 2010 as well as through Outlook Web App (OWA) without requiring the installation of additional software on each client computer or device.

High-Availability Improvements

In recent years the market trend has been to use larger and more sophisticated SANs (storage area networks) to provide redundancy and failover solutions.

In stark contrast, the Exchange product team has been reducing the need for expensive SANs and complicated replication topologies by reducing the disk I/O requirements for the product and by building robust replication technologies directly into Exchange that are better able to understand the health of the application. The two factors that influence the high-availability options in Exchange Server 2010 are the reduction in disk I/O requirements and subsequent improved performance on inexpensive and non-RAID protected disk, and the introduction of the DAG.

NOTES FROM THE FIELD

RAID-less Storage Deployments: An Emerging Industry Trend

With the emergence of cloud computing, the trend has been toward inexpensive, highly available computing and storage. Cloud computing vendors offer large amounts of storage over the Internet for a small monthly fee. To drive down costs many of these storage vendors rely on commodity hardware and custom-written software to provide redundancy rather than expensive RAID and SAN configurations. The storage is often comprised of low and mid-tier high-capacity hard drives attached to server computers without RAID controllers or SAN connectivity. RAID and SAN configurations copy data at a bit level on the disk, usually with little understanding of the files and format of the data.

Clients then attach to the service using a common storage protocol or proprietary API, and the storages service takes care of making multiple copies of the data, either on separate disks on different servers in the same site or in multiple sites to provide redundancy. This configuration for cloud storage vendors saves money during the initial purchase because it does not require a SAN configuration, and it does not require specialized datacenter staff to manage and maintain a SAN. This also provides fewer single-points-of-failure because the data is spread out on multiple disks and multiple servers. If any single failure were to occur, the likelihood that it would affect data availability is greatly reduced.

Traditional SANs will present a logical unit number (LUN) to a host server that has a specific RAID type. All data that is stored on this LUN is striped or mirrored across all of the physical disks on the underlying group. Therefore, all files stored on this LUN share the same redundancy. Using software to provide redundancy on multiple independent storage devices provides additional flexibility because each file can be given a different protection level and copied as many times as needed for redundancy and availability.

The cloud is not the only place this trend away from hardware RAID has been seen. Microsoft Home Server, a consumer product aimed at home storage networking, also uses software to control data redundancy at a file level rather than relying on software or hardware RAID. This allows the product to aggregate storage across different hard drive sizes and technologies and provides a unified files system to store data and still provide redundancy in case of inevitable hardware failure.

It is clear this is a new trend toward file-based, RAID-less redundancy in the industry—a trend that is apparent in the design of Exchange 2010.

Exchange Server 2007 introduced a number of new options for availability that previously required special network and SAN hardware. The following availability options are available in Exchange Server 2007 SP1:

- Cluster Continuous Replication (CCR) is a two-node clustering solution that requires no shared storage and maintains two full copies of the databases to protect against server and storage failures. The data is kept in sync by replicating the transaction logs from the active to the passive node of the cluster. The passive node then applies the transaction logs to the passive copy of the database.
- Standby Copy Replication (SCR) is an availability option that does not require clustering, and can provide multiple passive database copies on multiple servers. The database copies can be set to not apply logs for up to seven days so as to provide for point-in-time recovery. Activating a passive copy requires administrative intervention. SCR was first introduced in Exchange Server 2007 SP1.
- Single Copy Cluster is similar to traditional Exchange clustering in that it does use shared storage; however, in Exchange Server 2007 the setup process, stability, and overall management process was greatly improved.
- Local Continuous Replication is a single-server, data-redundancy solution that maintains two full copies of the databases to protect against local storage failures. Activation of the passive copy requires administrative intervention.

The improvements included in Exchange Server 2010 combine many of the benefits available in Exchange Server 2007 SP1 along with a few other improvements into the DAG. The DAG is a group of up to 16 Exchange Server 2010 Mailbox servers that can each maintain up to 100 databases with a total of up to 16 copies of each database on as many different servers in the DAG.

The DAG differs from Exchange Server 2007 SP1 in the following ways:

- With CCR, there can be only two copies of the database within the cluster; within the DAG there can be up to 16 copies of each database.
- With SCR, the activation process required administrative intervention; within a DAG, failover between individual database copies can happen automatically.
- With SCC, a single copy of the database consumes less storage but provides no redundancy. There is no configuration in Exchange Server 2010 that replaces this functionality, although some third-party solutions may provide similar functionality.
- With LCR, a single-server configuration allows two copies of a database to reside on different storage connected to the same server. There is no configuration in Exchange Server 2010 that replaces this functionality.

NOTES FROM THE FIELD

Discontinuation of Single Copy Clusters

During the development of Exchange Server 2010, a small number of people hung onto the legacy high-availability and data redundancy solutions such as SCC, and requested that these functions be retained in the product. In the end, the benefits did not outweigh the negatives. SCC was usually deployed in situations where failover operations needed to be minimized or where companies already had a significant investment in SAN hardware. However, SCC was never promoted as a best practice by Microsoft. There are a number of reasons for the diminishing return of SCC:

- It does not cover for storage failures.
- It requires third-party products for multi-site failover.
- It only provides protection from hardware failures and operating system issues and reduces downtime for software updates.
- It requires shared SAN storage—often the most expensive disk.
- In the event of an information store issue, the service restarts on the same cluster node without any protection from downtime.

The fact remained that the solution still maintained the most critical single point of failure—a single copy of the database—did not meet the requirements of customers. A DAG configuration covers the single-point-of-failure problem and also protects against hardware and operating system issues. With the reduction in the required disk I/O, high-performance SAN-based disk is no longer required. Therefore, even if double the amount of disk is required to provide two copies of the database, quite often the storage costs are still significantly less for an Exchange Server 2010 DAG over a similarly configured Exchange Server 2007 SCC cluster.

Exchange Mailbox Services Configuration

Much of the configuration that is done for the Mailbox server role is done during the hardware configuration and installation of the Mailbox role. After the Mailbox role is installed, creating and configuring databases usually completes most of what needs to be done. After the deployment is completed, management of mailboxes and public folders is usually the extent to which the Mailbox server is managed. When you install Exchange, you need to consider a number of important things.

One of the biggest considerations is where Exchange should be installed and how the disks should be configured for the databases. As best practice it is always good to have the operating system and the system page file configured on separate RAID1 or RAID10 disks.

As with Exchange Server 2007, each database needs to be located on the same path on each server that will host a copy. When deploying a DAG with more than 22 different databases, managing drive letters might be a challenge. Rather than assigning each drive a new letter, they should be assigned mount points on a RAID-protected volume. Following this best practice will allow more than 24 disks to be used and provide flexibility to remount a replacement disks to that mount point quickly in case of a failure. If the disk that hosts the mount points fails, the mount points will also become unavailable. Protecting the mount point host volume with RAID will ensure that a single disk failure will not cause all of the databases to go offline.

This chapter has covered a number of the storage improvements that have been made in Exchange Server 2010. These changes affect all aspects of design and should cause experienced Exchange administrators to reconsider a lot of the accepted assumptions that have become rote. One of these is the need to ensure that the transaction logs and the database must be on separate physical disks. With the lower I/O requirements and database write smoothing, this no longer becomes a problem with disk contention. There are still reasons that it might be good to split the transaction logs and databases on separate volumes or disks. One such reason is to not allow growing transaction logs to run the disk out of space and cause the database to go offline. In a stand-alone deployment it is still important to store the transaction logs on separate disks from the database so that in the event of a disk failure, both the transaction logs and the database are not lost. In a high-availability deployment, multiple copies of the data already exist on other servers.

NOTES FROM THE FIELD

Segregating Database and Transaction Logs

Thierry Demorre
Senior Director, Infrastructure Services Line, East Operating Unit, Avanade Inc.

Placing Exchange database files and transaction logs on disk has always been a subject of discussion between Exchange design engineers and the storage engineers. Usually the former wanted to split those files across different physical disks while the latter preferred a single large aggregate and lay out all of those files together. Exchange Server 2010 provides a simple solution to this design argument thanks to two major improvements over previous Exchange versions: DAGs and a new I/O profile.

Database Availability Groups

Three or more copies of a database means more redundancy than in a typical RAID 1 or RAID 5 configuration, which is enough redundancy for your database and transaction log files. In the event of a failure of one of the instances, the remaining data is not affected. Therefore, having the database and transaction log files sharing the same physical disks should not be a concern.

Extensible Storage Engine (ESE) I/O Profile

The ESE went through a major overhaul in the way it handles disk writes. All of the previous versions of Exchange have always written small, random blocks of data. Now, ESE has been optimized for large sequential writes, which from a disk activity perspective translates to most database writes being sequential. Because transaction log writes are also sequential, mixing those two I/O profiles on the same physical disks will not affect the scaling capability.

Determining the Number of Mailboxes for Each Server

A number of factors go into deciding the number and size of mailboxes that should be placed on a single server and how to configure the number of mailboxes that should be placed in each database. The final decision will weigh several key factors, such as the size, relative importance, and, most important, the service level agreement (SLA) required for the mailboxes.

Although 10,000 mailboxes provided to university students with a maximum quota size of 25 MB at no cost may take up more space than 250 executives with a maximum quota of 10 GB, the former mailboxes are arguably far less important. Weigh this relative importance against the number of mailboxes that can be recovered within the SLA. When it comes down to it, database size is often governed by your redundancy design. Designing a solution for backup and recovery that meets these needs will be covered in more detail in Chapter 12; designing highly available solutions that may reduce the need for restores will be covered in detail in Chapter 11, "Designing High Availability." In both of these areas improvements have been made to reduce the need and improve the speed of recovery should it be required. With these changes and careful planning it usually is possible to increase the size that the databases should be allowed to grow.

NOTES FROM THE FIELD

How Many Mailboxes Should Be Created on a Server?

Thierry Demorre
Senior Director, Infrastructure Services Line, Avanade Inc.

Two of the most common questions about Exchange are "How many mailboxes can I fit on this server?" and "With this new version of Exchange, will we get twice as many mailboxes on a server than in the previous version?" Unfortunately, these questions have no definitive answers, because of a number of contributing factors to both the performance and the space requirements for an Exchange mailbox server. These are the two principle factors to take into consideration for appropriately sizing an Exchange Mailbox server.

Actually, asking how many mailboxes can be hosted on a server is not the correct question. A better way to approach the question would be to ask, "How many 1-GB mailboxes, with a medium profile usage, having a 90 KB average message size, with single item recovery configured for 20 days and calendar versioning can I host on my server with 16 cores that run at 3.4G Hz and have 32 GB of RAM and are connected to 48, 1-TB-large form factor 10,000 RPM SAS hard drives?" Although the qualification statement is wordy, it does properly identify the target usage for the mailboxes. Having this level of detail when asking this question will provide a better basis for answering the question using the right tools.

The best practice here really is two-fold: first you need to understand what you are sizing for, and second you need to validate your assumptions against the Mailbox Server Role Requirements Calculator published by the Exchange product group. To do the former you must investigate the current environment and profile the users that will be migrated or transitioned to the new environment. To do the latter you should download and learn to use the calculator. The calculator takes extensive testing done by the product group and wraps it into a fairly simple Microsoft Office Excel spreadsheet. This calculator should be the starting point at any serious Exchange design. After gauging the configuration sizing using the calculator you should use the information you have gathered to configure tools such as JetStress and Load Simulator to prove the calculations are correct.

After verifying the number of mailboxes that can be hosted on the configured servers, the last question that needs to be answered is how many is too many? As the number of mailboxes on a server grows, the number of users that would be affected in the event of a single server outage or degradation of service increases. Employing high-availability best practices can curb many of these problems; however, there is still risk in placing too many mailboxes on a single server rather than scaling out the same number of users across multiple servers.

Determining Where to Host Mailboxes

A number of best practices are defined for placing mailbox servers and mailboxes on these servers. As you define the location of each of your user populations, the network connectivity, server and storage capabilities, and skill sets available at each site, where to place the servers may become clearer.

Several configurations are used to define the configuration, as seen in the example solutions used in this book. The Litware deployment is a distributed environment with Exchange mailbox and other services pushed out to the remote sites. This has several advantages, especially if the users at the remote offices primarily communicate with each other. Because users primarily communicate with each other, the majority of the e-mail messages stay within the site and do not need to traverse the network. The side benefit of this is that in the event of network issues where the remote site loses connectivity back to one of the corporate sites, the local users can continue to send and receive e-mail. The downside of this configuration is that support for the remote servers can be challenging especially if physical access is needed to repair the hardware.

The Fabrikam deployment uses a more centralized deployment. The benefit of this type of deployment is that mailbox services are concentrated in locations that have appropriate network connectivity and support staff to handle monitoring and maintenance of the hardware and software.

The best practice for determining where to host mailboxes depends on what fits the business requirements, network requirements, and administrative requirements. The principle should always be to keep the design as simple as possible while still achieving the goals. You need to ask several key questions when determining where to host mailboxes:

- Is there adequate and redundant bandwidth available between the clients and the Exchange servers?
- If the Exchange servers will be hosted at a remote location, how will backups, hardware maintenance, and monitoring be accomplished?
- Does the remote site have adequate power, cooling, and network connectivity?

Database Maintenance

Database maintenance is divided into two parts: store mailbox maintenance and ESE database maintenance. Store maintenance includes performing cleanup within the database; ESE database maintenance includes online database scanning (database checksum), defragmentation, and compaction.

Database Cleanup

Database cleanup involves identifying newly disconnected mailboxes and evaluating the deleted item retention period on deleted messages and mailboxes and purging any items that have expired. Database cleanup is now the only task that is, by default, configured to run during the online maintenance window. Although online maintenance no longer consumes as many resources as it did previously, it is recommended to schedule the maintenance window after the backup window. This will allow backups to capture data before they are purged from the database. Configuring the online maintenance schedule is shown in Figure 6-9.

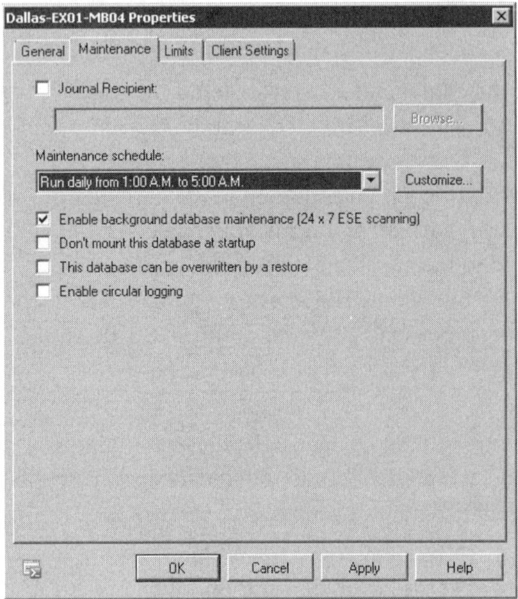

FIGURE 6-9 Configuring the database online maintenance schedule

Online Database Scanning

The integrity of data within the database is of the utmost importance—if there is a physical page corruption, it is important to know about it so that something can be done. Often this type of corruption is due to a problem with the underlying storage. In Exchange Server 2007 RTM and earlier versions, each page was scanned during backups using the streaming API. With the deprecation of the streaming backup API in Exchange Server 2007 and the removal of it in Exchange Server 2010, another facility to ensure data integrity was needed. In Exchange Server 2007 SP1 an option was introduced to run a database checksum during the scheduled online maintenance window.

In Exchange Server 2010, the default setting allows the online database scanning to run in the background continuously. Alternatively, the online database scan process can be set to run only during the schedule online maintenance window; however, because of the time it takes to complete, this is only recommended for databases smaller than 1 terabyte (TB). The best practice is to leave the default setting and allow the scanning to run continuously.

Defragmentation and Compaction

Defragmentation and compaction happen at run time and are balanced to provide data contiguity rather than to optimize space. Table 6-5 summarizes each type of online maintenance activity and how they have been improved in Exchange Server 2010.

TABLE 6-5 Comparing Online Database Maintenance Operations

DATABASE FUNCTION	EXCHANGE SERVER 2007 WITH SERVICE PACK 1	EXCHANGE SERVER 2010
Cleanup	Performed during online defragmentation, which occurs during online maintenance	ESE performs cleanup at run time when a store hard delete occurs. This happens during dumpster cleanup during the online maintenance.
Database checksum	When configured, half of OLD maintenance window reserved for sequential scan (Checksum), manual throttle. Active DB copy only.	Two options (both active and passive copies): **1.** Run DB Checksum in the background 24 × 7 (default). **2.** Run DB Checksum during online maintenance.
Maintain contiguity	N/A (compaction activities during online defragmentation prevent data contiguity).	Database is analyzed at run time and is defragmented in the background.
Space compaction	Database is compacted and whitespace is reclaimed during online defragmentation.	Database is compacted and space reclaimed at run time.

Offline Maintenance

One of the most frequently asked questions continues to be, "How often should you do an offline defragmentation of a database?" The trigger of this question in previous versions of Exchange Server was often Event ID 1221, which detailed the amount of free space available within each database after a full online database defragmentation pass was completed. Many messaging administrators would see this free space as an indicator of inefficiency and want to reduce the size of the database to improve performance and reduce the backup size. Because defragmentation and compaction are now continuous processes in Exchange Server 2010, there is no longer a point in the process when the free space within the database base is published to the event log. There is a way, however, to get this information using the Exchange Management Shell. For example, the cmdlet to find the free space in Dallas-EX01-MB04 would look like this:

```
Get-MailboxDatabase Dallas-EX01-MB01 -Status | Format-List AvailableNewMailboxSpace
```

NOTE When using the *Get-MailboxDatabase* cmdlet, the *–Status* switch must be specified to be able to view the available space, whether online maintenance is running, whether the database is mounted, or whether a backup is in process. If the *–Status* switch is not specified, the information returned by the cmdlet is retrieved from Active Directory Domain Services. When the *–Status* switch is specified, the additional information is retrieved directly from the Mailbox server.

As with previous versions of Exchange, even with a significant amount of free space available in the database, more efficient ways are available for reclaiming this space. Using database tools such as ESEUtil.exe requires that the database be taken offline and that enough space is available on disk to complete the maintenance. Although the performance of ESEUtil has improved, it still requires extended downtime for all mailboxes hosted within that database. A much more reasonable approach would be to create a new blank database and move all of the mailboxes from the bloated databases into the newly created database. For example, the command to move all mailboxes from Dallas-EX01-MB02 into Dallas-EX01-MB22 would look like this:

```
Get-Mailbox -Database Dallas-EX01-MB02 | New-MoveRequest -Local -TargetDatabase Dallas-
EX01-MB22
```

If a physical corruption is found in the database during the online database scanning (database checksum), this same process can be used to move all mailboxes to a newly created database and delete the problematic database. This eliminates the need to take the database offline to repair it, which caused extended downtime for the affected mailboxes.

Mailbox Limits

As a seasoned Exchange administrator you have most likely heard from someone that "Storage is cheap, why must you put a limit on my mailbox rather than just adding more disks?" For a number of really important reasons, adding disk alone is not the answer. The primary reason is to meet SLAs. Without established mailbox limits, an SLA violation could occur in a number of ways. For instance, if none of the 5,000 mailboxes on a mailbox server had limits imposed, any single mailbox could consume all of the disks on a server in a matter of minutes. Although this could happen as the result of a malicious act, it can also be unintentional in a case where an Outlook rule or outside service continues to send e-mail messages to a mailbox, causing it to grow larger until the underlying storage fills up. With the improved performance and faster server hardware, these sorts of actions can happen in a matter of just a few minutes.

The other way mailbox limits play into achieving an SLA and controlling the size of databases has to do with achieving expected backup and recovery times. To recover the data in a database within the agreed-upon SLA, the databases must be under a specific size. For example, if you can restore 150 GB of data from your backup solution in three hours, and you have a four-hour SLA to restore the data, you do not want to allow the database to grow larger than 150 GB; otherwise, anytime a restore is required, the SLA will be violated. The easiest way to implement and maintain control over the size of the databases is to establish limits on the mailboxes and thereby not allow them to cause the database to grow beyond the size that prevent SLAs from being met.

This really means there is no hard and fast rule on how big mailboxes should be—just that a maximum size should be set. The best practice is to set a limit that in aggregate is less than the available disk space. That way if all mailboxes on the server reach the limit, the server will still have space to continue operating. That said, this may not be completely feasible, nor is it probable that all users will use their entire quota at the same time, unless there is malicious intent. In this case it is important to weigh the risks and costs involved.

NOTES FROM THE FIELD

Appropriately Sizing Mailboxes

Thierry Demorre

Senior Director, Infrastructure Services Line, Avanade Inc.

At some point during the design phase of a new Exchange environment comes the decision of the mailbox size. This decision prompts questions like "How much should we allocate?", "Should all mailboxes have the same limits and retention policies?", and "Should users have mailbox sizes that coincide with their job function, and if so how would that be determined?" It is appropriate to answer all of these questions before doing everything else, and that requires knowing the big picture of where you are deploying Exchange. To do this you will need to interview the legal team to understand what the retention policy needs to be. For example, if the legal team wants everything older than six months purged and inaccessible, that will need to be the starting point for evaluating the mailbox size.

On the other hand, if no restrictions are to be put in place, evaluation of the Exchange Server 2010 online archive or third-party archiving solution should be done along with determining the potential impact to the configuration and performance of implementing the archiving solution. Most of these archiving companies have been singing the praises of their products, and especially how stubbing items being archived was a way to save space in your online mailbox. As a best practice, however, using any form of stubbing is a bad approach. This has always been a limiting factor in Outlook—performance can degrade when the number of items grows out of control. While Outlook 2007 SP2 and Outlook 2010 introduce technology improvements for many more items in each folder, as well as larger mailboxes, keeping the environment under control is of paramount importance to keep the performance optimal for the end user. It is important to archive smart, rather than retaining data just for the sake of retention.

The appropriate course is to evaluate this question as any other critical aspect of your design. It would be wise to interview representatives from a number of user groups and obtain their requirements. It might be that one group only cares about the last three weeks' worth of e-mail, and another group that has a completely different or conflicting requirement. It would also be good to obtain some less subjective data, perhaps by creating a trend of current mailbox sizes. Because older versions of Outlook may not perform properly with large mailboxes or will not provide access to new features available in Exchange Server 2010, it is important to identify the client software that will be used. I know of companies that will deploy Exchange Server 2010, and then continue to use Microsoft Office Outlook 2003 to connect to their new messaging system.

So, how do you answer the question, "Can I create a 1-TB mailbox?" It is true that Exchange Server 2010 will certainly allow this. However, the reciprocal question would be, "Will you use it?" If you fill that mailbox with messages with an average size of 50 KB, that is approximately 24.5 million messages!

Configuring Deleted Item Recovery Quotas

Configuring the deleted item recovery setting needs to be done after the business needs are captured and understood. However, a couple of settings should be configured to ensure that malicious users cannot cause Denial of Service attacks by placing large amounts of data into the dumpster and running the server out of space. To do this the *RecoverableItemsQuota* and *RecoverableItemsWarningQuota* settings should be set per database. However, the settings can also be done per mailbox. These settings are similar to mailbox quotas except that they apply to items in the dumpster:

- **RecoverableItemsQuota** The default limit is 30 GB; however, this can be set as needed. When the limit is reached all soft deletes will fail and an event log entry will be made the first time it occurs and once daily if the condition continues.
- **RecoverableItemsWarningQuota** The default limit is 20 GB; however, this can be set as needed. When the limit is reached, an event log alert will be made and will continue once daily afterward if the condition continues. The oldest items in the dumpster will be deleted to make room for new dumpster data.

Poison Mailbox Detection and Correction

Exchange Server introduced poison message detection, placing messages that cause issues with the transport service in a queue and allowing the transport service to continue processing other messages. Exchange Server 2010 applies this same concept to mailboxes. In some cases a single mailbox with corrupt data caused the Exchange Store to crash or even to crash repeatedly. With poison mailbox detection the Exchange information store is able to detect and then isolate the poison mailboxes.

A mailbox will be tagged as a potential threat if:

- A mailbox has had more than five threads running that have not made progress for 60 seconds; or
- A mailbox has a thread doing work that crashes.

When a mailbox meets either of these criteria, an entry in the registry is made for the database along with the number of times the problem has occurred. Storing this information in the registry allows this information to be replicated to other servers in the DAG by the Windows Cluster service. This allows this information to be preserved during a failover. This information is stored in the following locations in the registry:

- HKLM\SYSTEM\CurrentControlSet\Services\MSExchangeIS\<Server Name>\Private-{Database GUID}\QuarantinedMailboxes\{Mailbox GUID}\Crash Count
- HKLM\SYSTEM\CurrentControlSet\Services\MSExchangeIS\<Server Name>\Private-{Database GUID}\QuarantinedMailboxes\{Mailbox GUID}\\LastCrashTime

The default settings can be adjusted for how many crashes lead to quarantining a mailbox as well as how long a mailbox should stay quarantined are stored. You can adjust these settings by modifying the following registry keys:

- HKLM\SYSTEM\CurrentControlSet\Services\MSExchangeIS\<Server Name>\Private-{Database GUID}\QuarantinedMailboxes\MailboxQuarantineCrashThreshold The default setting for this key is three crashes.
- HKLM\SYSTEM\CurrentControlSet\Services\MSExchangeIS\<Server Name>\Private-{Database GUID}\QuarantinedMailboxes\MailboxQuarantineDurationInSeconds The default setting for this is 21,600 or six hours.

The Exchange information store will also keep information on when the mailbox was flagged as a poison mailbox. When a database is brought online and periodically thereafter, the information store reads the time that the mailboxes were identified as potential threats. If the mailbox was quarantined more than two hours prior, the registry key for the mailbox will be wiped out.

After a mailbox is flagged and quarantined, no access is allowed to the mailbox by any end users or any of the Exchange processes. If the mailbox hasn't caused any crashes in the last two hours and is not quarantined, the registry path for the mailbox will be cleaned up by the information store. If a mailbox has been quarantined for longer than the *MailboxQuarantine DurationInSeconds* since the last time it caused a crash, it will automatically be removed from quarantine. If the problematic mailbox has been fixed, the mailbox can also be removed from quarantine manually by deleting the registry key and then remounting the affected database.

To be sure to keep ahead of any impending issues, you should monitor these registry keys to ensure that there is not a systemic problem causing multiple mailboxes and databases to become corrupt. This will also allow administrators to track down any issues and fix them.

Client Configuration

A variety of clients are able to connect to Exchange Server 2010. Other than receiving e-mail, the client's activity is the largest driving factor on how a mailbox server performs. A number of things should be done to improve performance and protect the mailbox services.

In Office Outlook 2003, a new feature was introduced called *Cached Exchange Mode*. This was different than offline mode, available in previous versions. Offline mode provided a way for portable computers to synchronize data and then be able to work offline. Cached Exchange Mode solved the same problem offline mode did; however, it also reduced the bandwidth requirements between the client and Exchange server for clients that were connected to the server. This allows users access to the local copy of the messages stored in a OST file very quickly and synchronize the changes between the server and the client. This reduced the I/O and bandwidth (after the initial synchronization) by up to 20 percent, a great way to deploy Outlook in most situations.

> ***NOTE*** **For Outlook 2007 clients, ensure that the February 2009 cumulative update for Outlook 2007 Service Pack 1 or later has been deployed to provide the best performance.**

Cached Exchange Mode does not work well in just a couple of situations. If a mailbox is 100 MB, that data is stored locally and then synchronized as changes are made. As the mailbox size grows, more resources are needed on the client to cache and synchronize the data. On older clients that do not have enough drive space to index and manage the amount of e-mail in a mailbox, large mailboxes may perform poorly, even if the mailbox server is not performing poorly. It could be that additional resources should be planned for clients with large mailboxes that will use Cached Exchange Mode. When you deploy client computers that are running Outlook in Cached Exchange Mode, consider the following performance improvement guidelines:

- Ensure that the February 2009 cumulative update for Outlook 2007 Service Pack 1 or later has been deployed. This update included a new OST schema which reduces I/O requirements. Outlook 2010 also includes these performance improvements. For more information about the update for Outlook 2007, read the Knowledge Base article at *http://support.microsoft.com/kb/961752*.
- For mailboxes up to 5 GB, most client computers capable of running Outlook 2007 or higher should perform well.
- For mailboxes larger than 5 GB and up to 10 GB, additional hardware may be required. This will often be limited by disk I/O and the amount of memory. Using a RAID10, solid-state disks, and faster traditional hard drives for storage of the OST file will greatly improve performance.
- For mailboxes with more than 10 GB, additional hardware and memory will be needed. Archived data should be moved to an online archive and is thus exempt from being cached locally.

- For mailboxes that have more than 100,000 items in a single folder, views other than Arranged By: Date may be slower.
- Limit the amount of data that is available in the cache. By using the filter options available on each folder, the amount of data that is cached on the local computer can be limited. A typical example of this might be to only cache data that is less than a year old.

For more information on optimizing Outlook performance, see the Knowledge Base article KB640226 located at *http://support.microsoft.com/?kbid=940226*.

Up until Outlook 2010, one of the other places where Cached Exchange Mode is not supported is when Outlook is hosted on Remote Desktop Services (RDS), formerly known as Terminal Services. In RDS multiple servers will be logged on to a single server accessing Outlook, sending and receiving e-mail. The best practice in deploying RDS for high availability is to use roaming profiles and to not store the user's data on each RDS server in the farm. RDS is deployed in the datacenter so that it can be managed by the IT staff. The users that access the RDS may be located in other locations or have limited bandwidth, which is a good reason to have Outlook run in the datacenter. The RDS servers are typically located near the Exchange servers; RDS users don't usually store data on each server. Therefore, if you're using an OST to synchronize data—especially if each time the user logged in Outlook had to cache all of the mailbox data—it is understandable why using Cached Exchange Mode is not recommended nor is it supported in that configuration.

Using Cached Exchange Mode performance can be limited by the local hardware. When using Online Exchange Mode, the client requests information directly from the server. In Exchange Server 2010 using Outlook in Online Mode or Outlook Web App, the guideline is to limit the number of items in each folder to fewer than 100,000 provided there are no third-party applications installed that index e-mail content. This is a huge jump from Exchange 2007 SP2 where the guideline was a maximum of 20,000 items for Inbox and Sent folders and 5,000 for Calendar and Contacts folders.

Many Outlook add-ins and desktop search software will add additional load to the client and the mailbox server if they perform indexing or data mining. Providing end users with guidance on software that they should avoid or using permissions and policy to restrict users from installing these applications helps to reduce the likelihood that these applications can negatively impact performance.

Configuring Public Folders

Public folders have received a lot of attention for the last two releases of Exchange Server. The rumors of the removal of public folders in Exchange Server 2007 caused an uproar in the messaging community. The fact is that public folders are still supported in Exchange Server 2007 as well as Exchange 2010, and there is good reason for the feature's continued existence as it still fills a need that in some cases is not easily solved by other solutions such as Microsoft Office SharePoint Server or InfoPath. As Table 6-6 shows, in a number of scenarios public folders still provide a viable solution.

TABLE 6-6 Deciding to Deploy Public Folders

SCENARIO	USING PUBLIC FOLDERS?	NEW TO PUBLIC FOLDERS?
Calendar Sharing	No need to move	Use either
Contact Sharing	No need to move	Use either
Custom Applications	Consider SharePoint	Consider SharePoint
Discussion Forum	No need to move	Use either
Distribution Group Archive	No need to move	Use either
Document Sharing	Consider SharePoint	Deploy SharePoint
Organizational Forms	No need to move	Use InfoPath

One of the current solutions that SharePoint Server does not fill is that of a multiple-master document share, where document repositories can be replicated to multiple sites to provide access to data at remote sites.

In Exchange Server 2010 public folders support and features have not changed appreciably since Exchange Server 2007 SP1. Despite being a great solution for many client use cases, public folders still remain complex to manage in large environments and complex to recover from when problems arise without third-party tools. One of the only improvements made in Exchange Server 2010 with regard to public folders is that they can now be placed on multiple servers that are in a high-availability configuration, whereas before they were only supported on a single high-availability–configured server and its copy. This may now reduce the number of servers that are deployed because a dedicated public folder server is no longer required.

The choice to use public folders most likely means that either the application requirements are not met by another technology or the company use of public folders is so innate that the migration will take a number of years to complete. It is still important to bear in mind that public folders as they exist today will eventually cease to exist. A new large deployment of public folders should be very carefully scrutinized as to whether it is the best solution.

To understand where public folder replicas need to be placed, it is important to remember how clients find and access replicas. When a user connects with Outlook or Outlook Web App to a public folder the following occurs:

1. The default public folder database for the user's account is always the initial target for all requests. If there is a replica available in that public folder, Exchange Server directs the client to this database for the public folder contents.
2. If a replica is not in the user's default public folder database, Exchange Server redirects the client to the least-cost Active Directory site that stores the public folder database. The Active Directory site must include a computer that is running Exchange Server 2010 or Exchange Server 2007.

3. If no computer running Exchange Server 2010 or Exchange Server 2007 in the local Active Directory site has a replica of the public folder, Exchange Server redirects the client to the Active Directory site with the lowest-cost site link that does have a copy of the public folder contents.
4. If no computer running Exchange Server 2010 or Exchange Server 2007 has a copy of the public folder contents, Exchange Server redirects the client to a computer running Exchange Server 2003 that has a replica of the public folder contents, using the cost assigned to the routing group connector(s). This behavior, however, is not the default—to allow public folder referrals across the routing group connector the properties of the routing group connector must be modified.
5. If no public folder replica exists on the local Active Directory site, a remote Active Directory site, or on a computer running Exchange Server 2003, the client cannot access the contents of the requested public folder.

Figure 6-10 shows how Exchange Server uses Active Directory sites to provide clients with the closest replica of a public folder for a public folder that is not available in the user's default public folder database.

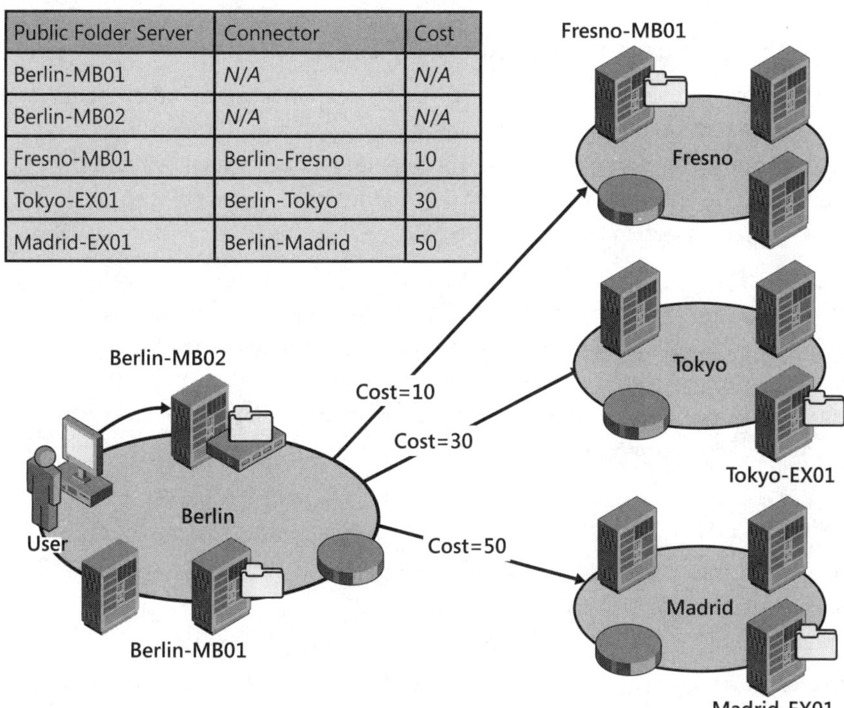

Public Folder Server	Connector	Cost
Berlin-MB01	*N/A*	*N/A*
Berlin-MB02	*N/A*	*N/A*
Fresno-MB01	Berlin-Fresno	10
Tokyo-EX01	Berlin-Tokyo	30
Madrid-EX01	Berlin-Madrid	50

FIGURE 6-10 Connecting to the closest public folder replica

Configuring public folder replicas requires that a detailed Active Directory site topology is understood as well as the methods and locations that the public folder data will be accessed from. A number of methods are chosen for creating replicas for public folders. The primary goal is to keep as few replicas for each folder while maintaining the appropriate access and redundancy.

Configuring Public Folders for Site Redundancy

As an example, let's look at how Fabrikam uses public folders. A special project team located in the Fresno office uses a set of public folders to store information about their project. Because all of the users are located locally, there is no need to create a replica of the project folders offsite. However, to ensure that data is not lost in the case of a local server failure, at least one offsite replica should be created.

> ***NOTE*** **Often, especially when users are allowed to create public folders, replicas are not created when a new folder is created. This leaves database backups a primary recovery point for data in these public folders in case of a server failure. Create and schedule an Exchange Management Shell script to periodically report on any public folders that only have one replica.**

Configuring Public Folders for Distributed Access

Another example of how public folders can be used can be seen at Litware. Rather than employing SharePoint at this time, the HR department uses a public folder to distribute documentation to all employees for review. This documentation does not change often; however, it is used by all employees on a regular basis. In this case a replica of the public folder should be created at each location so that employees have quick access to these files.

> ***NOTE*** **Creating a large number of replicas will increase the amount of data that needs to be replicated to each server. This may affect the available bandwidth between sites. Care should also be taken when adding replicas so as not to add too many at a single time, which will reduce or eliminate the bandwidth required to transfer more important messages or other critical business functions.**

Designing Public Folder Deployments

In environments where public folders are heavily used, it is a best practice to deploy dedicated public folder servers. This allows for dedicating CPU, memory, and disk resources to isolated server functions, reducing the likelihood of resource contention.

It is also beneficial to have fewer larger public folder databases, rather than having smaller public folder databases. This scales well and is more easily managed and monitored than having several smaller public folder databases. This also reduces the amount of replication traffic that must occur. As with many best practices, it still requires that adjustments be made to fit each environment. As the public folder configuration is designed, the number of databases needed to be deployed must be balanced by the cost of replication traffic and against the costs of management complexity, database backup, maintenance, and restore times.

Another factor to consider is the hierarchy of the public folders. As a general rule, because of how replication is structured it is best to have more nested folders rather than having more folders at the root of the hierarchy. When designing the hierarchy it is also important to consider the permissions that will be granted on the folders. The goal should be to simplify administration and reduce complexity as much as possible when assigning permissions. It is good to have the folders that will have the least restrictive permissions toward the top of the hierarchy, with the folders that require more restrictive permissions to the bottom. Often enterprises will create root folders for each business unit or region and allow departments and project folders to be created below the root folders. However, it is best not to have more than 250 subfolders in each folder.

Additional Resources

- Optimizing Outlook 2007 Cache Mode Performance for Very Large Mailboxes: *http://msexchangeteam.com/archive/2007/12/17/447750.aspx*
- How to Troubleshoot Performance Issues in Outlook 2007: *http://support.microsoft.com/kb/940226*
- Wikipedia: B+ Tree Structures: *http://en.wikipedia.org/wiki/B%2B_tree*
- Exchange 2010 Mailbox Server Role Requirements Calculator: *http://msexchangeteam.com/archive/2009/11/09/453117.aspx*

CHAPTER 7

Edge Transport and Messaging Security

The Edge Transport server role is designed to be placed directly in a perimeter network, exposed to the Internet. Placing a server directly in the Internet can be the cause of numerous security concerns. This chapter describes how to plan for and deploy a Microsoft Exchange Server 2010 Edge Transport server role and the security issues related to the deployment.

This chapter also describes how to configure secure Simple Mail Transfer Protocol (SMTP) messaging as well as Domain Security, a feature available in Exchange Server 2007 and later versions. The Edge Transport role provides powerful anti-spam functionalities, and some antivirus features. Because the Edge Transport role does not include a virus scanner, you can integrate additional antivirus products such as Microsoft Forefront Protection 2010 for Exchange Server.

Implementing Edge Transport Server

The Edge Transport server role in Exchange Server 2010 provides a secure SMTP gateway for all incoming and outgoing e-mail in an organization. As an SMTP gateway, the Edge Transport server's primary role is to maintain message hygiene, which includes anti-spam and antivirus filtering. You also can use the Edge Transport server to apply messaging policies to messages that are sent to the Internet.

When planning to deploy Edge Transport servers, consider the following factors:

- You cannot install the Edge Transport server role along with any other Exchange Server 2010 server role. The Edge Transport functions require a very separate level of security and must be separated from your Exchange organization. To provide increased security, you must install the Edge Transport server role on a separate computer, which can be virtual or physical.

- Edge Transport servers should be installed in the perimeter network and should be physically secure and well separated from servers in the internal network.
- The computer should not be a member of an internal Active Directory domain.

> **NOTE** You should not install the Edge Transport server role on a computer that is a member of the internal Active Directory domain, but you can install it in a perimeter Active Directory forest. Microsoft IT and other large companies have a dedicated Active Directory domain for servers in the perimeter network. This makes security updates and other maintenance/management easier than when you're dealing with non-domain-joined computers.

Considering Firewall Ports

Because the Edge Transport server role is installed in a perimeter network and thus is directly connected to the Internet, you should also plan to place a firewall between the Internet and your Edge Transport server to increase protection. This firewall should be configured to open certain ports.

This section is about what network ports you should open in the firewall that is between the Internet and the perimeter network (external) and the perimeter network and the internal corporate LAN (internal), as described in Table 7-1. You can take this as the minimum number of ports you should open, but remember that you can also configure the Edge Transport to use network ports other than those listed here.

The table includes only the Edge Transport server role. A list of firewall ports for all server roles can be found in Chapter 3, "Exchange Environmental Considerations."

TABLE 7-1 Firewall Ports Required for Edge Transport Server Role

FIREWALL DIRECTION	FIREWALL RULE	DESCRIPTION
External	Allow port 25 from all external IP addresses to the Edge Transport server.	Enables SMTP hosts on the Internet to send SMTP messages to this server.
External	Allow port 25 to all external IP addresses from the Edge Transport server.	Enables the Edge Transport server to send SMTP messages to the Internet.
External	Allow port 53 to all external IP addresses from the Edge Transport server.	Enables the server to resolve Domain Name System (DNS) names on the Internet.
Internal	Allow port 25 from the Edge Transport server to specified Hub Transport servers.	Enables the transmission of inbound SMTP messages onward to internal Hub Transport servers.

FIREWALL DIRECTION	FIREWALL RULE	DESCRIPTION
Internal	Allow port 25 from specified Hub Transport servers to the Edge Transport server.	Enables the transmission of outbound SMTP messages from internal Hub Transport to the Edge Transport server.
Internal	Allow port 50636 for secure Lightweight Directory Access Protocol (LDAP) from Hub Transport servers that participate in EdgeSync to the Edge Transport server.	Enables the Hub Transport server to replicate directory information to the Edge Transport servers using Edge Synchronization.
Internal	Allow port 3389 for Remote Desktop Protocol (RDP) from the internal network to the Edge Transport server.	Enables remote desktop administration of the Edge Transport server (recommended).

NOTES FROM THE FIELD

Edge Transport Role and Forefront TMG

Henrik Walther
Technology Architect, Timengo Consulting, Copenhagen Denmark

Microsoft Forefront Threat Management Gateway (TMG), Microsoft's application layer firewall solution, and Exchange 2010 Edge Transport role can now be installed together on the same computer. This is especially an attractive configuration for SMORGs (small and medium organizations) that are bound by a limited IT budget. Even though Microsoft ISA 2006 is supported with Exchange 2010, Microsoft recommends using Forefront TMG to prevent configuration issues. You also cannot install Edge Transport and Microsoft ISA 2006 on the same computer because ISA 2006 does not support 64-bit operating systems.

If you plan to use Microsoft ISA or Forefront TMG to separate Edge Transport and Hub Transport server roles, you need to remember either to add Exchange SMTP verb commands to the SMTP add-in filter or to disable the filter altogether. You can find the details at *http://technet.microsoft.com/en-us/library/bb851514(EXCHG.80).aspx*.

Planning and Configuring Edge Synchronization

The Edge Transport server does not use Active Directory to store its configuration information; instead, Edge Transport servers use Active Directory Lightweight Directory Services (AD LDS) to store this data. AD LDS is the successor of Active Directory Application Mode (ADAM), a service that was available in Windows Server 2003.

About AD LDS

AD LDS is a special mode of the AD DS that stores information for directory-enabled applications. AD LDS is an LDAP-compatible directory service that runs on servers running the Windows Server 2008 or Windows Server 2008 R2 operating system. AD LDS is designed to be a stand-alone directory service. It does not require the deployment of DNS, domains, or domain controllers; instead, it stores and replicates only application-related information.

Before you can install the Edge Transport server role, you must install the AD LDS server role on the same Windows Server 2008 computer that will host the Edge Transport role. This is because AD LDS stores configuration data for your Edge Transport server role. During Exchange installation, AD LDS is then configured automatically. The following types of information are stored in AD LDS:

- Schema
- Configuration
- Recipient information

The AD LDS database is stored in the <*Exchange_Install_Path*>\TransportRoles\data\Adam directory. Similar to the queue database as described in Chapter 5, "Routing and Transport," the AD LDS service also uses the Extensible Storage Engine (ESE) database engine, so the files that are used for its database are comparable to other ESE databases such as queue databases or mailbox databases.

IMPORTANT **The AD LDS stores configuration and recipient information. The Queue database also exists on every Edge Transport to store message queues.**

The AD LDS instance does not need much administration because all the information that it contains is synchronized using Edge synchronization from the Active Directory instance that holds all of the Exchange organizational configuration data and information about mail-enabled objects. Even if the database is lost, you just start EdgeSync again and the database will be newly created.

However, always consider that the database does not include all configurations and settings, so it is best practice to back up the Edge server configuration using the ExportEdgeConfig.ps1 script.

Edge Synchronization

Edge synchronization, or EdgeSync, is a process that replicates information from your internal Active Directory to the AD LDS located on the Edge Transport server.

Because Edge Transport servers are not joined to the internal Active Directory domain, they cannot directly access the configuration or recipient information that is stored in Active Directory.

You can deploy Edge Transport servers without using EdgeSync, but using EdgeSync can decrease the effort needed to administer the Edge Transport servers. Active Directory contains much of the configuration information required by the Edge Transport server. For example, if you configure accepted domains in Exchange Management Console for all Hub Transport servers centrally, these accepted domains are replicated automatically using

EdgeSync to the Edge Transport servers. Every Edge Transport server needs its own Edge Subscription to synchronize with Active Directory.

To enable any filtering or transport rules that are based on recipients, you must implement EdgeSync to replicate the recipient information to AD LDS.

EDGESYNC REPLICATION

After you enable Edge Synchronization, the EdgeSync process establishes a point of synchronization between one Hub Transport server in the Active Directory site that was selected and the Edge Transport server, and synchronizes configuration and recipient information between Active Directory and AD LDS.

Even though EdgeSync is very similar to Exchange Server 2007, in Exchange 2010 EdgeSync keeps track of synchronized information and only synchronizes the changes since the last replication cycle. Of course, this is much more efficient than EdgeSync in Exchange 2007.

> ***IMPORTANT*** **Only the internal Hub Transport servers, not the Edge Transport servers, initiate EdgeSync replication. EdgeSync replication traffic is always encrypted using Secure LDAP.**

During synchronization, EdgeSync replicates the following data:

- Accepted domains
- Send connectors
- Hub Transport servers list (for dynamic connector generation)
- Recipients (one-way hashed)
- Safe senders, safe recipients, and blocked senders (one-way hashed)
- Domain Secure List (such as the *TLSSendDomainSecureList* and *TLSReceiveDomainSecureList* properties)

> ***NOTE*** **All options that are synchronized by EdgeSync are managed in Active Directory, so you can no longer change them on the Edge Transport server. You need to change them using EMC or EMS connected to your internal Exchange organization and allow EdgeSync to transfer the configuration settings to the Edge Transport servers.**

Some configuration settings have to be made on the Edge Transport server role level because these configurations are not replicated using EdgeSync. The following list includes all areas that you need to configure for every Edge Transport server or use Edge Transport cloning to share a single configuration between all Edge Transport servers:

- All Edge Transport server settings (external or internal DNS Lookups, Log Settings, Limits, and so on)
- Exchange Product Key
- Anti-spam settings
- Receive connectors

- Transport rules
- Digital Certificates and Exchange services enabling digital certificates to secure communications

HOW DOES EDGESYNC WORK

To establish Edge Synchronization between an Edge Transport and Hub Transport server, you need to follow these steps:

1. Create an Edge subscription file on Edge Transport.
2. Import an Edge subscription file on Hub Transport.
3. Start and verify the EdgeSync Process.

Create an Edge subscription file on Edge Transport

If you want to perform EdgeSync on your Edge Transport server, you should consider the following areas before creating the Edge subscription file:

- An Edge Transport server needs a fully qualified domain name (FQDN) configured.
- You must register the FQDN with your DNS server.
- The FQDN must be resolvable and reachable from the Hub Transport servers in the site where you add the Edge subscription file.
- EdgeSync and the Connectors use the computer certificate of the Edge Transport server, so make sure you've already installed the correct certificate (for example, that supports TLS if required).

> ***IMPORTANT*** **The hub server must be able to communicate with the Edge Transport server using the FQDN as defined in the Edge Subscription file! Remember, by default the Firewall on the Edge Transport server refuses a PING response!**

You create an Edge subscription file by using the *New-EdgeSubscription* cmdlet in EMS started with Run as Administrator. The default EMS will not provide sufficient permissions to create an edge subscription. This will create an XML file, as shown in Figure 7-1.

As you can see, the sample Edge subscription file includes certain information such as the Edge servers' FQDN, the Edge server's public certificate, the default SSL port that is used for AD LDS, and the server's Exchange version. You have to use the Edge subscription file on a Hub Transport server within 1,440 minutes or the XML will expire.

> ***NOTE*** **The Edge Transport server isn't limited by version control (like Hub Transport or UM server role), meaning you can subscribe an Exchange 2010 Edge Transport server to an Exchange 2007 Hub Transport server just fine. You just won't benefit from incremental EdgeSync. You can also have an Exchange 2007 Edge Transport server in front of an Exchange 2010 Hub Transport server.**

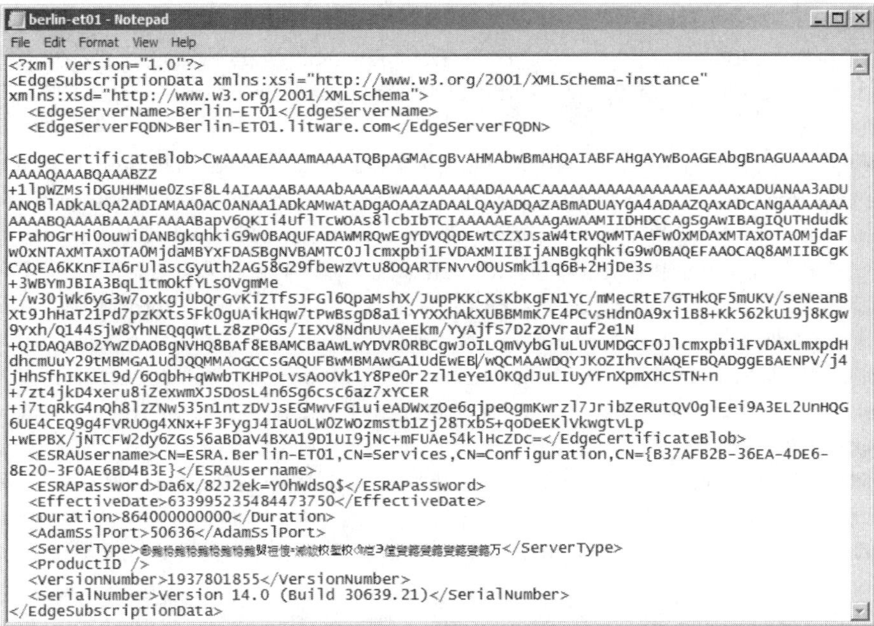

FIGURE 7-1 Sample Edge subscription file

Import Edge subscription file on Hub Transport

After you create the Edge subscription file, you need to copy it to a Hub Transport in the Active Directory site that you want to link the Edge Transport server to. On the Hub Transport server, use the *New-EdgeSubscription* cmdlet to import the Edge subscription file.

Be aware that you cannot pass the filename directly to the cmdlet—you need to pass the data string, as shown in Figure 7-2. This is because of remote Windows PowerShell. Since the script is not running locally, you can't give a local path but have to pass the file data in the cmdlet.

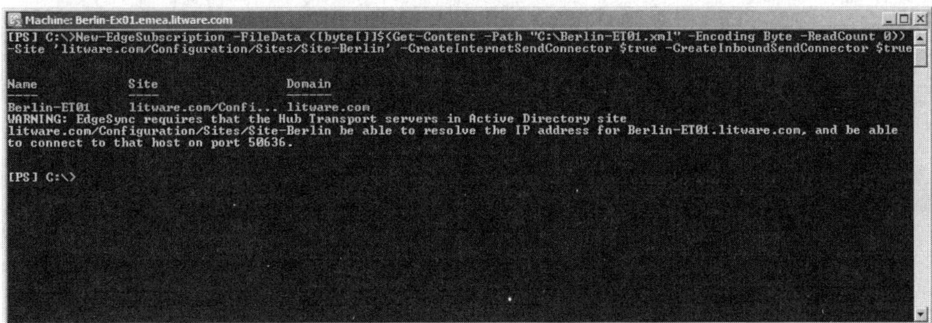

FIGURE 7-2 Importing an Edge subscription file using EMS

Start and Verify the EdgeSync Process

After the Edge subscription file is imported to the Exchange configuration, the EdgeSync replication process starts automatically. The default port for synchronization is port 50636 as defined in the Edge subscription file.

To change the default EdgeSync communication port you can use the ConfigureAdam.ps1 script located in the <*Exchange_Install_Path*>\Scripts folder. For example, if you want to change the communication port to 50222, run *.\ConfigureAdam.ps1 –Sslport:50222* with EMS.

The first Hub Transport in the Active Directory site where you created the Edge subscription that notices the subscription seizes the lease and will use the Microsoft Exchange EdgeSync service to start the synchronization with the Edge Transport server. This Hub Transport server will keep the lease until it goes offline or is otherwise unable to service the subscription which will then result in the next Hub Transport available in the Active Directory site seizes the lease.

If you like to force immediate replication, you can use the *Start-EdgeSynchronization –TargetServer <EdgeTransportName> -Server <HubTransportName>* cmdlet, which will trigger the replication and show you some information about recent changes in Active Directory.

> ***NOTE*** **You can use the Windows LDP client to look at the AD LDS database on the Edge Transport server by connecting to port 50389. Even though most entries are encrypted, you can check that replication is working.**

Alternatively you can make sure that the EdgeSync process finished successfully by running the *Test-EdgeSynchronization –FullCompareMode* cmdlet on a Hub Transport server in the connected Active Directory site that will compare Active Directory with the AD LDS on all Edge servers that are subscribed to the Active Directory site to make sure they are synchronized correctly. You will receive detailed information as output, as shown in Figure 7-3.

```
Machine: Berlin-Ex01.emea.litware.com

[PS] C:\>Test-EdgeSynchronization -FullCompareMode

RunspaceId                  : 8fcbd06b-c323-44a3-b08f-57cf235b1a26
SyncStatus                  : Normal
UtcNow                      : 1/20/2010 3:35:50 PM
Name                        : Berlin-ET01
LeaseHolder                 : CN=BERLIN-EX01,CN=Servers,CN=Exchange Administrative Group (FYDIBOHF23SPDLT),CN=Administr
                              ative Groups,CN=Litware,CN=Microsoft Exchange,CN=Services,CN=Configuration,DC=litware,DC=
                              com
LeaseType                   : Option
FailureDetail               :
LeaseExpiryUtc              : 1/20/2010 4:34:45 PM
LastSynchronizedUtc         : 1/20/2010 3:34:45 PM
TransportServerStatus       : Synchronized
TransportConfigStatus       : Synchronized
AcceptedDomainStatus        : Synchronized
RemoteDomainStatus          : Synchronized
SendConnectorStatus         : Synchronized
MessageClassificationStatus : Synchronized
RecipientStatus             : Synchronized
CredentialRecords           : Number of credentials 3
CookieRecords               : Number of cookies 4
```

FIGURE 7-3 Running the *Test-EdgeSynchronization* cmdlet

Edge Transport Configurations

This section describes Edge Transport configurations that you should consider when planning for this server role: cloned configuration, delivery status notifications, header firewall, and address rewriting.

Edge Transport Cloned Configuration

Cloned configuration is the process of configuring multiple Edge Transport servers with identical configurations. You can use the cloned configuration scripts provided as part of the Exchange installation kit with EMS to duplicate the configuration of a source server to a target server.

Edge Transport servers do not support Windows Failover Clustering. A failover cluster provides high availability by making application software and data available on several servers that are linked together in a cluster configuration. But because failover clustering is not available, to achieve high availability for messaging transport, you should implement multiple Edge Transport servers.

> **NOTE** Even though AD LDS supports directory replication, Exchange Server 2010 does not provide an option to use directory replication for configuring multiple Edge Transport servers. The only way to copy the configuration between the Edge Transport servers is to use cloned configuration. This needs to be done whenever you do any configuration changes to one of the servers.

You can use cloned configuration to ensure that all the Edge Transport servers have the same configuration. You only configure one server, and export the configuration to an XML file that is then imported to the target servers.

The XML file includes the following configuration information:

- Transport server file paths and all log files paths (such as the Message Tracking log path)
- Transport agents, including status and priority
- All Send and Receive connector–related settings (including Send connector passwords encrypted with a default encryption key)
- Accepted Domain information
- Anti-spam features and configuration settings

> **NOTE** Don't forget that any Transport Rule configured on the Edge Transport server is not exported, so you need to export the rules with the *Export-TransportRuleCollection* cmdlet and import them on the target Edge Transport servers.

Some settings are not cloned; however, they are synchronized by EdgeSync and therefore only need to be considered in a configuration where EdgeSync is not used:

- *TLSReceiveDomainSecureList*
- *TLSSendDomainSecureList*
- *InternalSMTPServers*

To configure cloned configuration, use the ExportEdgeConfig.ps1 and ImportEdgeConfig .ps1 scripts located in the <*Exchange_Install_Path*>\Scripts folder to export configuration information from one Edge Transport server to an identically configured Edge Transport server.

You can also use the tool to test configuration changes and offer rollback assistance or to assist in disaster recovery when you deploy a new Edge Transport server or replace a failed server.

To configure cloned configuration, follow these steps:

1. Use the ExportEdgeConfig.ps1 script to export the configuration information on the source Edge Transport server.
2. Validate configuration and create an answer file using the ImportEdgeConfig.ps1 script on the target Edge Transport server. The answer file will contain entries for every source server setting that is not valid for the target server.
3. Edit answer file and change all server-specific settings, such as the server name, to reflect the target server settings.
4. Import configuration using the ImportEdgeConfig.ps1 script with the -IsImport $true parameter to import the information from both the intermediate XML file and the answer file on the target Edge Transport server.

> ***NOTE*** **When importing the configuration, depending if the target Edge Transport configuration is part of Edge Synchronization or not, you may face error messages that some settings, such as Accepted Domains, cannot be imported. This situation is normal and can be ignored.**

5. Delete the configuration and answer XML files to prevent retrieval of Send Connector passwords (if used).

Understanding Header Firewall

Every Receive or Send connector adds information to the message it is transferring. This information is available in the SMTP message header and includes information such as all the servers that transferred that message and at what time. To prevent spoofing of such information, Exchange 2010 includes a feature called *Header Firewall* that (if configured) removes all additional information from inbound and outbound messages. But let's first start with an overview of the X-header fields. If you want to read more information about this topic, you can access the Exchange 2010 Help file article "Understanding Header Firewall" at *http://technet.microsoft.com/en-us/library/bb232136.aspx.*

OVERVIEW OF EXCHANGE 2010 X-HEADERS

Exchange Server 2010 adds X-header fields to every message to transfer Exchange-internal information. X-header fields are an unofficial but generally accepted way to add header fields to a message.

The purpose of X-header fields is to transfer information about the message to the other Transport servers. For example, a message is scanned by the Content Filter agent only at the first Transport server, which adds the spam confidence level (SCL) rating to the X-MS-Exchange-Organization-SCL field to the header of the message. All subsequent

Transport servers can then use this information and do not need to scan the message again. In Figure 7-4 you see a message that contains various X-header fields by looking at the Internet headers field in Microsoft Outlook.

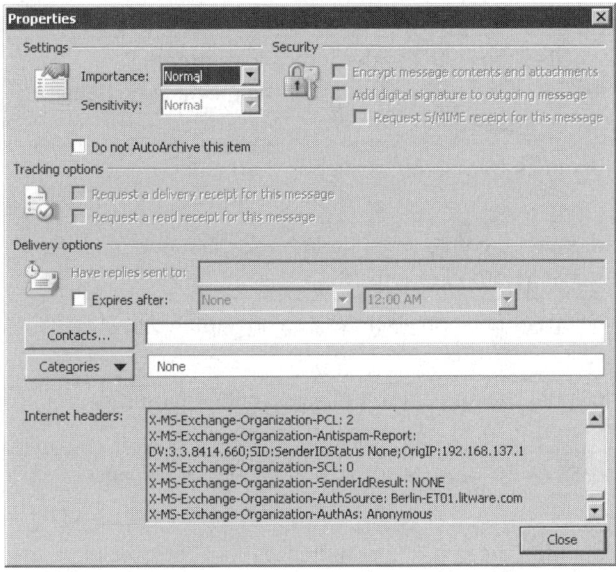

FIGURE 7-4 Viewing X-headers in Outlook

To read the message headers correctly, it is important to understand their meaning. Exchange Server 2010 includes several X-header fields and they are listed in Table 7-2.

TABLE 7-2 X-Header Fields Used by Exchange 2010

X-HEADER FIELD	DESCRIPTION
X-MS-Exchange-Forest-RulesExecuted	Lists all transport rules that processed this message.
X-MS-Exchange-Organization-Antispam-Report	Provides a summary report of the anti-spam filter results that have been applied to the message by the Content Filter agent. Detailed information can be found on TechNet "Understanding Anti-Spam Stamps" at *http://technet.microsoft.com/en-us/library/aa996878.aspx*.
X-MS-Exchange-Organization-AuthAs	Specifies the authentication source. The possible values are Anonymous, Internal, External, or Partner.
X-MS-Exchange-Organization-AuthDomain	This field is only added when Domain Secure authentication took place and includes the fully qualified domain name (FQDN) of the remote authenticated domain.

X-HEADER FIELD	DESCRIPTION
X-MS-Exchange-Organization-AuthMechanism	Specifies the authentication mechanism for the submission of the message as a two-digit hexadecimal number.
X-MS-Exchange-Organization-AuthSource	Specifies the FQDN of the server computer that evaluated the authentication of the message on behalf of the organization.
X-MS-Exchange-Organization-Journal-Report	Identifies journal reports in transport.
X-MS-Exchange-Organization-OriginalArrivalTime	Identifies the time when the message first entered the Exchange organization.
X-MS-Exchange-Organization-Original-Sender	Includes the original sender of a quarantined message.
X-MS-Exchange-Organization-OriginalSize	Includes the original size of a quarantined message.
X-MS-Exchange-Organization-Original-SCL	Includes the original SCL of a quarantined message.
X-MS-Exchange-Organization-PCL	Identifies the phishing confidence level. The possible phishing confidence level values are 1 through 8.
X-MS-Exchange-Organization-Quarantine	Indicates that the message has been quarantined in the spam quarantine mailbox and a delivery status notification (DSN) has been sent. Alternatively, it indicates that the message was quarantined and released by the administrator.
X-MS-Exchange-Organization-SCL	Includes the SCL of the message. The possible SCL values are 0 through 9. A larger value indicates a suspicious message. The special value -1 means that it is an internal message that is not processed by the Content Filter agent.
X-MS-Exchange-Organization-SenderIdResult	Includes the results of the Sender ID agent. The Sender ID agent uses the sender policy framework (SPF) to compare the message's source IP address to the domain used in the sender's e-mail address.
X-MS-Exchange-Organization-PRD	Includes the result of the Sender ID agent, especially the Purported Responsible Domain (PRD). This is the domain of the purported responsible address as determined by the Sender ID agent.

Besides X-header fields, Header Firewall also controls Routing headers. Routing headers include information about all messaging servers used to deliver the message.

CONFIGURING HEADER FIREWALL

In some situations you need to implement Header Firewall to prevent someone from creating a message that will spoof X-headers and thereby imitate an Exchange Transport server in order to have their messages accepted as legitimate by the receiving server. This is especially crucial if your organization does not include a smart host that removes these headers.

Header Firewalls are configured by assigning Active Directory permissions on the respective Send connector or Receive connector. A dedicated *ExtendedRight* attribute and Deny permission is used to control enabling or disabling a Header Firewall. The following principle applies:

- If Deny is enabled (or True), the Header Firewall is *turned on* for the specified area and headers are removed.
- If Deny is disabled (or False), the Header Firewall is *turned off* and the headers are preserved by the connector.

By default, no Send or Receive connector is configured for Header Firewall. In a situation where you use an Edge Transport server, the X-header is overwritten anyway when a message enters the organization. But for outbound messages, Routing headers might disclose too much information about your company. For example, the name of any internal Hub Transport server that processes the message is shown in the Routing header.

Several Extended Rights control Header Firewalls on Send connectors and Receive connectors. Table 7-3 provides an overview of possible Extended Rights.

TABLE 7-3 Connectors and Extended Rights for X-Header Configuration

CONNECTOR	EXTENDED RIGHT	DESCRIPTION
Receive connector	*ms-Exch-Accept-Headers-Forest*	Configures Header Firewall on "X-MS-Exchange-Forest …" headers
	ms-Exch-Accept-Headers-Organization	Configures Header Firewall on "X-MS-Exchange-Organization …" headers
	Ms-Exch-Accept-Headers-Routing	Configures Header Firewall on "Resent- …" and "Received:" headers
Send connector	*Ms-Exch-Send-Headers-Forest*	Configures Header Firewall on "X-MS-Exchange-Forest …" headers
	Ms-Exch-Send-Headers-Organization	Configures Header Firewall on "X-MS-Exchange-Organization …" headers
	Ms-Exch-Send-Headers-Routing	Configures Header Firewall on "Resent- …" and "Received:" headers

To configure Header Firewalls, you can either use EMS or directly access the Permissions tab of the connector's Advanced Security Settings using ADSIEdit, as shown in Figure 7-5. You can see Advanced Security Settings of the Send connector on the Edge Transport server that connects to the Internet. Because Deny is set for Anonymous Logon on Send Routing Headers permission, all internal message servers are removed from the routing path.

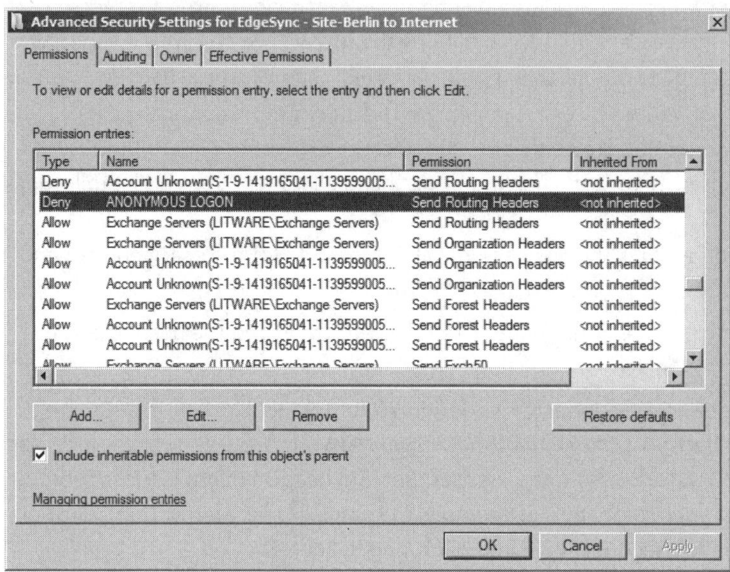

FIGURE 7-5 Configuring Header Firewall using ADSIEdit

When using ADSIEdit in Active Directory to configure permissions, remember that you can configure Edge Transport Receive connectors only directly on the Edge Transport server. Thus you can only configure Send connectors using ADSIEdit in Active Directory, for configuring Edge Transport Receive connectors you need to use EMS on the Edge Transport directly, as Receive connectors are not synchronized to Active Directory with EdgeSync.

Configuring Header Firewall using EMS is not trivial—many groups are involved and you have to configure the right group to turn Header Firewall on or off. The best approach is to look at your existing connectors to identify the groups you need to configure. The following cmdlet is an example to show you the Extended Rights of a Receive connector:

```
Get-ReceiveConnector <ReceiveConnectorName> | Get-ADPermission | ft user, deny,
ExtendedRights
```

To configure Header Firewall in your scenario you just need to change the permissions on the respective Receive or Send connector. For example, let's turn on Header Firewall for Routing headers on the Send connector to the Internet for all non-authenticated target servers. You can configure this using the following cmdlet on the Send connector that sends messages to the Internet:

```
Add-ADPermission -id "<SendConnectorName>" -User "NT Authority\Anonymous
Logon" -ExtendedRights Ms-Exch-Send-Headers-Routing -Deny
```

Remember that after you configure the permissions, you need to restart the Microsoft Exchange Transport service on all Hub Transport servers that are configured to use the Send connector so that Header Firewall will take immediate effect.

You can verify whether Header Firewall is turned on by enabling verbose logging on the Receive connector in EMC or using the *ProtocolLoggingLevel Verbose* parameter in the *Set-ReceiveConnector* cmdlet. You will now receive a detailed protocol log in the <*Exchange_Install_Path*>\TransportRoles\Logs\ProtocolLog\SMTPReceive folder. In the current log file, you will find the following entries for each SMTP session that has Header Firewall turned off:

- *AcceptRoutingHeaders*
- *AcceptForestHeaders*
- *AcceptOrganizationHeaders*

For every entry that's missing, Header Firewall is enabled!

NOTES FROM THE FIELD

Make Sure Edge and Hub Authenticate Correctly

Christian Schindler
Senior Consultant, NTx BackOffice Consulting Group, Austria

One of my customers once had an issue where inbound mail delivery from Edge Transport to Hub Transport was working correctly, but anti-spam—although correctly configured—didn't work as expected: X-AntiSpam- and Antivirus-Headers (SCL, SenderID, and so on) weren't part of the message header when the message reached Outlook.

After digging into the issue, I finally discovered that authentication methods between the Edge and Hub Transport server were modified from the default settings. I re-enabled Exchange Server authentication on the connectors, which fixed the issue.

So why is authentication between Edge and Hub Transport important in my scenario? Because Exchange only accepts X-AntiSpam- and AntiVirus-Headers through authenticated SMTP Sessions. This makes it nearly impossible for spammers or hackers to send fake X-AntiSpam or X-Antivirus Headers.

HEADER FIREWALL FOR CONTOSO SCENARIO

For most scenarios, especially if you use Edge Transport servers, you do not need to change Header Firewall settings—their default configuration is sufficient for most scenarios. However, if you do not use Edge Transport servers, you should enable Header Firewall for the Receive connector and Send connector to the Internet.

In the Contoso scenario, the Hub Transport server receives messages from a smart host from the Internet. To prevent spoofing of X-headers it is best practice to configure your Receive connector that receives the messages from the Internet to enable Header Firewall. This is done using the following cmdlet:

```
Add-ADPermission -id <ReceiveConnectorName> -User "NT Authority\Anonymous Logon"
-ExtendedRights ms-Exch-Accept-Headers-Organization -Deny
```

Figure 7-6 shows you the header configuration as performed through EMS for X-headers Organization and the command to verify that the permission was configured correctly. As seen in the figure, only the ms-Exch-Accept-Headers-Organization has a Deny permission configured; thus only this X-header has Header Firewall turned on.

```
Machine: Berlin-ET01 | Scope:
[PS] C:\>Add-ADPermission -id "Default internal receive connector Berlin-ET01" -User "NT Authority\Anonymous Logon" -ExtendedRights Ms-Exch-Accept-Headers-Organization -Deny

Identity             User                  Deny  Inherited
--------             ----                  ----  ---------
Berlin-ET01\Defau... NT AUTHORITY\ANON... True  False

[PS] C:\>Get-ReceiveConnector | Get-ADPermission | ft user, deny, extendedrights

User                                Deny                          ExtendedRights
----                                ----                          --------------
NT AUTHORITY\ANONYMOUS LOGON        True                          {ms-Exch-Accept-Headers-Organization}
NT AUTHORITY\ANONYMOUS LOGON        False                         {ms-Exch-SMTP-Accept-Authoritative-D...
NT AUTHORITY\ANONYMOUS LOGON        False                         {ms-Exch-SMTP-Submit}
NT AUTHORITY\ANONYMOUS LOGON        False                         {ms-Exch-Send-Headers-Routing}
NT AUTHORITY\ANONYMOUS LOGON        False                         {ms-Exch-SMTP-Accept-Any-Sender}
NT AUTHORITY\ANONYMOUS LOGON        False                         {ms-Exch-Accept-Headers-Routing}
MS Exchange\Partner Servers         False                         {ms-Exch-Accept-Headers-Routing}
MS Exchange\Partner Servers         False                         {ms-Exch-SMTP-Submit}
MS Exchange\Hub Transport Servers   False                         {ms-Exch-SMTP-Accept-Any-Recipient}
MS Exchange\Hub Transport Servers   False                         {ms-Exch-SMTP-Accept-Exch50}
MS Exchange\Hub Transport Servers   False                         {ms-Exch-SMTP-Accept-XShadow}
MS Exchange\Hub Transport Servers   False                         {ms-Exch-SMTP-Accept-Any-Sender}
MS Exchange\Hub Transport Servers   False                         {ms-Exch-SMTP-Accept-Authoritative-D...
```

FIGURE 7-6 Configuring Header Firewall configuration in EMS

Configure Address Rewriting

Edge Transport servers include Transport agents that allow you to modify e-mail addresses for inbound or outbound messages. This process is called *address rewriting*.

Two Transport agents provide the capability for address rewriting: Address Rewriting Inbound agent and Address Rewriting Outbound agent. They should be enabled for address rewriting to work correctly.

But why do address rewriting? You need to implement it for several reasons, including the following:

- **Group consolidation or Partners** This is when your company includes several groups that have separate e-mail addresses internally. For example, you have a group that uses the e-mail address @sales.contoso.com but your company wants to move to a single e-mail address and thus replace all messages with the originator of @sales .contoso.com with @contoso.com.
- **Mergers and acquisitions** This situation occurs when your company purchases a new company that is running in a separate messaging system. For this situation all messages get rewritten to a common e-mail address. For example, Fabrikam purchases Contoso, and because they should use the Fabrikam e-mail address, they rewrite every @contoso.com address into @fabrikam.com.

NOTE Address rewriting will replace the e-mail addresses of messages. You have to make sure that the properties of the recipient mailboxes include the replaced e-mail address in their proxy addresses; otherwise a reply will receive an NDR.

In some situations—for example, signed, encrypted, or rights-protected messages—you cannot change an e-mail address because that would, for example, make a signed message invalid. The address rewriting agent thus will not change the message in any way as it would make the message unreadable.

IMPORTANT Using address rewriting can break your federating calendaring requests because the domain name is changed. If you use address rewriting and you want to implement federated sharing, ensure that all domains involved in the address rewriting are defined in your federated organization identifier. For more information see Chapter 10, "Federated Sharing."

Address rewriting is configured using the Exchange Management Shell (EMS); you cannot configure address rewriting in the Exchange Management Console.

You configure address rewriting using the *New-AddressRewriteEnty* cmdlet. You can configure address rewriting in the following ways:

- Rewrite a single e-mail address, one domain, or a domain including all its subdomains.
- Rewrite addresses on either inbound and outbound messages or just outbound messages.

Let's go back to our scenario where Fabrikam buys Contoso. Contoso's Exchange organization is currently not your responsibility, but every message they sent to the Internet is transported over Fabrikam's Edge Transport servers. You want to make sure that every outbound Contoso.com e-mail address is replaced with Fabrikam.com. So first you have to make sure that every Contoso recipient exists in the Fabrikam Exchange organization with an e-mail address that matches both their Contoso.com and the Fabrikam.com address. Additionally there must be a Send connector to forward messages for Contoso users (addressed with their Fabrikam.com mail address) to the Contoso Exchange organization.

If that's guaranteed, you can use the following cmdlet on your Edge Transport servers to enable address rewriting:

```
New-AddressRewriteEntry -Name "Contoso to Fabrikam" -InternalAddress Contoso.com
-ExternalAddress Fabrikam.com -OutboundOnly $true
```

Planning for Anti-Spam

Planning for anti-spam to reduce the massive number of spam messages that circulate nowadays through the Internet has become one of the most important tasks of message administrators. Unfortunately, spammers and malicious senders use a variety of techniques to send unwanted messages to your organization. No single tool or process can eliminate all spam.

By default the anti-spam agents are installed only on the Edge Transport server role. However, they can also be enabled on Hub Transport servers where needed.

> ***IMPORTANT*** **Any change to the anti-spam agents is immediately activated. If, for example, you add an IP address to an IP Block List, it is immediately blocked without any service restart.**

How Exchange 2010 Does Spam Filtering

Exchange 2010 includes a variety of anti-spam features designed to work cumulatively to reduce the amount of spam messages that enter your organization. This is done by using spam-filtering agents to examine each SMTP connection and each message sent through it.

As illustrated in Figure 7-7, the sequence of spam agents that will inspect a connection or message is defined carefully.

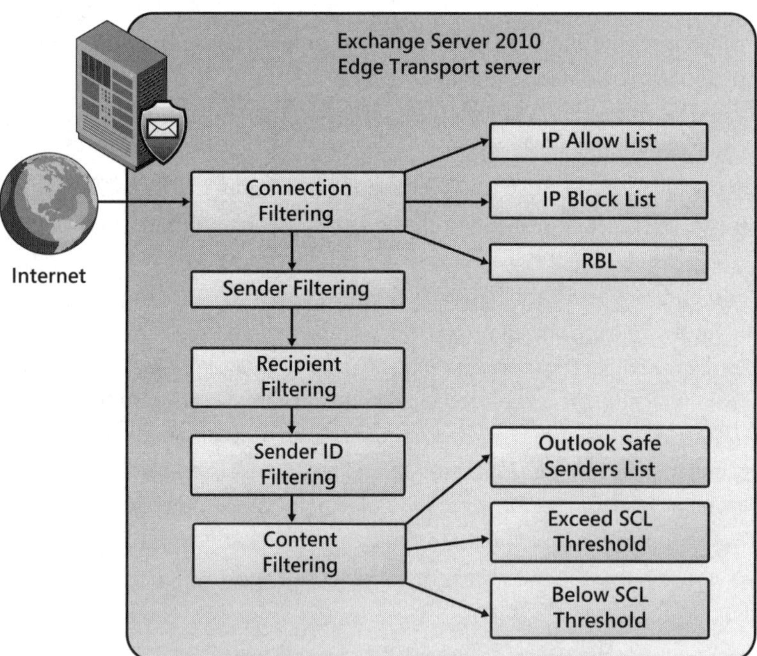

FIGURE 7-7 SPAM agent filtering sequence

When an SMTP server on the Internet connects to the Edge Transport server and initiates an SMTP session, the Edge Transport server examines each message using the following sequence:

1. When the SMTP session is initiated, the Transport server applies connection filtering using the following criteria:
   - IP Allow list and IP Allow List Provider

- IP Block list
- Real-time block list (RBL) of any IP Block List Provider

2. The Transport server compares the sender's e-mail address with the list of senders configured in sender filtering.
3. The Transport server examines the recipient against the Recipient Block list configured in recipient filtering.
4. Exchange Server 2010 applies Sender ID filtering. Depending on how the Sender ID filtering is configured, the agent might delete, reject, or accept the message that failed Sender ID validation. If the message is accepted, the server adds the Sender ID validation stamp to the message properties. Although incremental, the failed Sender ID status is included as one of the criteria when content filtering processes the message.
5. The Edge Transport server applies content filtering and performs one of the following actions:
   - Content filter compares the purported sender to the list of senders in the per-recipient Safelists aggregated from Microsoft Office Outlook users. If the sender is on the recipient's Safe Senders List, the message is assigned a spam confidence level (SCL) rating of -1, excluded from further anti-spam processing, and after antivirus scanning delivered directly to the end user's Inbox richly rendered. If the sender is not on the recipient's Safe Senders List, the message is scanned and assigned an SCL rating.
   - If the SCL rating is higher than one of the configured SCL thresholds, a content filtering agent takes the appropriate action of deleting, rejecting, or quarantining the message.
   - If the SCL rating is lower than one of the SCL thresholds, the message is assigned an appropriate SCL verdict and delivered to the Mailbox server, which decides where to deposit the message based on the recipient's mailbox settings. The message can end up either in the Junk E-mail folder or in the Inbox.

How Anti-Spam Updates Work

Spam is changing continuously, so Exchange 2010 also includes an automatic anti-spam update service that handles content filter updates. This service requires your Transport server to have either direct Internet access, Web access using a proxy, or a Windows Update Service (WUS). Anti-spam updates can be configured in two different types: manual or automatic.

Manual updates only include Content Filter updates but do not require additional licenses; automatic updates also include Content Filter and add Spam Signature and IPReputation updates. However, automatic updates require an Enterprise Client Access License (E-CAL) that needs to be purchased for every mailbox in your organization.

Manual Content Filter updates will be downloaded and installed when the update is made available by Microsoft; this is commonly done on a biweekly basis. Thus you can only describe this anti-spam protection as being very basic—more suitable for small organizations. You should consider purchasing E-CALs for automatic updates which provide multiple anti-spam updates per day if you're planning for a larger company. E-CALs also include the required licenses for Forefront Protection 2010 for Exchange Server (FPE 2010), which you can optionally deploy to add an extra level of protection for anti-spam.

You configure the anti-spam update service using the *Enable-AntispamUpdates* cmdlet and receive information on what pattern versions are installed using the *Get-AntispamUpdates* cmdlet as shown in Figure 7-8.

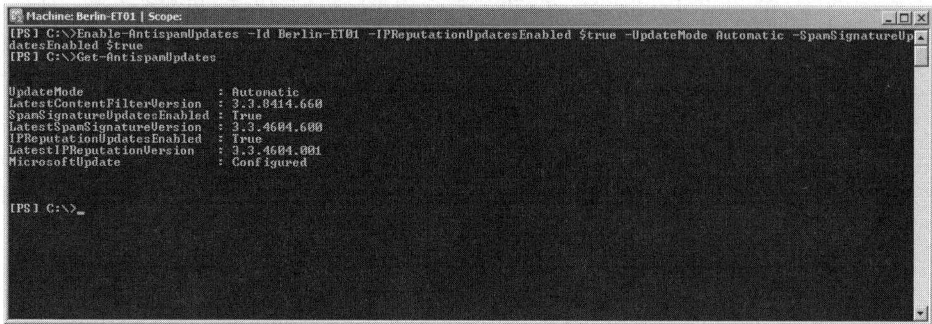

FIGURE 7-8 Configuring automatic anti-spam updates

You can see that multiple update patterns are available in the anti-spam update of Exchange 2010. Table 7-4 lists all available pattern updates.

TABLE 7-4 Anti-Spam Pattern Updates

PATTERN UPDATE	PURPOSE
Content Filter	Content Filter updates. The filter is based on Microsoft's SmartScreen technology and is used for scanning the body of the messages and assigning SCL ratings.
Spam Signature (E-CAL required)	Identifies the most recent spam campaigns.
IP Reputation (E-CAL required)	Provides sender reputation information about IP addresses that are known to send spam.

All patterns are part of a single update process—no separate processes are required.

LESSONS LEARNED

Anti-Spam with Forefront Protection 2010 for Exchange

Alexander Nikolayev
Program Manager, Forefront Server Security, Microsoft Corporation

At Microsoft, we use Forefront Protection 2010 for Exchange (FPE) for anti-spam. If you use FPE 2010, you might consider these three best practices for enabling the most effective anti-spam defense.

First, where will you reject spam? The most efficient FPE positioning is to scan the messaging stream at the entry point into Exchange organization. An early rejection of unwanted e-mail will prevent wasted resources to push unnecessary payloads through the network and save some bandwidth. Best hygiene practices call not only for physical positioning of FPE on the perimeter of the organization's network but also to enable early rejection of spam inside the FPE, which is a layered anti-spam solution. The first layer, Connection Filtering, is based on new Forefront DNSBL technology. When enabled, our testing shows that Forefront DNSBL will reject around 90 percent of spam based on the connecting IP address even before it begins to examine the content of the message. Forefront aggregates RBL feeds from multiple vendors, and the DNSBL feature is configuration-free, so it's not only very effective but also simple to use.

Second, what messages will you reject? One person's ceiling is another person's floor, right? What is considered as spam by some recipients is legitimate mail to others. To help FPE figure out for whom to reject and for whom to accept a given piece of mail, it is important to enable recipients' Outlook Safe/Block Lists aggregation. The FPE Content Filter, based on Cloudmark CMAE engine, will take these lists into consideration on a per-recipient basis to provide the desired granularity level. Using the default SCL settings on the content filter will reject the rest of spam; however, if you need to relax the filter you can lower SCL thresholds to quarantine questionable mail for triaging.

And finally, where to triage? Previously, Microsoft recommended quarantining questionable e-mail in a dedicated Exchange mailbox so that an administrator could access, review, retrieve, and resend false positives. This was not always an easy task because of the volume of quarantined messages. Forefront makes triaging easier because the messages by default are stored in Forefront quarantine. However, with the volume of quarantined messages now drastically reduced, it makes sense to review our default approach to triaging and perhaps allow these messages to be deposited into a recipient's Junk Mail folders. The amount of suspected spam is very small. For example, based on internal Microsoft data, only about 50 messages per 1 million of external mail submissions are quarantined. To determine the volume of quarantined mail, run the *Get-FseSpamReport* cmdlet and look for the number of messages with SCLs between five and eight inclusive—these are the messages that will be quarantined by default. If you see that the amount is small, maybe it's time to entrust your recipients with the responsibility of triaging suspected spam, considering that they will get only a couple of such messages per month.

In addition, do not forget to enable Backscatter filtering. Backscatter filtering will protect your organization from bogus NDRs to recipients who never sent the NDR mail in the first place. This happens when a malicious user spoofs the MAIL FROM address as someone from your organization; the receiving server might generate an NDR back to an unsuspecting victim. For the filter to work correctly you need to have the same set of keys installed on every transport server that participates in sending to or receiving mail from the Internet.

Enable Anti-Spam on Hub Transport Servers

Even though it is not enabled by default, you can also enable anti-spam on Hub Transport servers. This is especially a good idea if your Hub Transport server connects Exchange to a smart host that handles inbound Internet traffic for a company. Many companies deploy UNIX- or Linux-based servers in this role, so you can provide another, different layer of anti-spam if you enable it on the Hub Transport servers.

You enable the anti-spam features by running the Install-AntispamAgents.ps1 script available in the <*Exchange_Install_Path*>\Scripts folder. After running the script you need to restart the Microsoft Exchange Transport service to make sure the changes are applied.

> ***IMPORTANT*** **For anti-spam features to work correctly, you must have at least one IP address of an internal SMTP server set on the *InternalSMTPServers* parameter on the *Set-TransportConfig* cmdlet. If you only have one Hub Transport server in your organization, enter the IP address of that computer.**

Connection Filtering

Connection filtering inspects the IP address of the remote server that is trying to send the message to determine what action to take on an inbound message. If a specific server is found on the IP Allow list or on the list of an IP Allow list provider, the message is not scanned anymore but directly marked as not spam. Similar to the IP Allow list, an IP Block list also exists that consists of servers that are not allowed to send messages because they have been identified as spam senders. The following sections discuss IP Allow lists and IP Block lists as well as list providers.

> ***IMPORTANT*** **It might seem obvious, but if your Exchange organization receives all messages from a smart host server, the sender's IP address will always be the same. To enable Connection Filtering to work correctly, you need to add this smart host server's IP address, along with the IP addresses of all SMTP servers capable of routing e-mail, to the *InternalSmtpServers* list via the *Set-TransportConfig* cmdlet. If the Hub server where you enable anti-spam is the only SMTP server in your organization, you must add its own IP address to the list.**

IP Allow List

An IP Allow list is a static list of trusted IP addresses manually created and managed by the Exchange server administrator. IP Allow list inspection is the first in the execution chain of Connection Filtering. You can include trusted IP addresses in the IP Allow list, such as the IP addresses of SMTP servers at your partner organizations. If a connection request comes from an IP address on the IP Allow list, the server does not apply additional anti-spam filtering and accepts the message.

To configure an IP Allow list and either add a single IP address or an IP range to the list, you need to use the *Add-IPAllowListEntry* cmdlet.

IP Allow List Providers

IP Allow List Providers is a feature that allows you to take advantage of dynamic safe lists of IP addresses maintained by a third-party providers. To use these lists you need to configure an external provider that maintains a safe list of SMTP servers instead of defining it yourself. In essence, configuring IP Allow List Providers is very similar to configuring IP Block List Providers and both use the same technology to retrieve the verdict about the connecting IP address from the providers.

NOTE Most of the messaging administrators I know do not consider IP Allow List Providers for deployment and infrequently use IP Allow lists. This is due to the fact that all messages submitted from the addresses on IP Allow lists are immediately extracted from the anti-spam scanning and if a spam attack comes through one of the addresses on an IP Allow list, it won't be detected by the consecutive anti-spam layers and spam will penetrate the Exchange organization. Although the adoption of the IP Allow List Providers feature is not very significant, a carefully implemented static IP Allow list allows you to receive e-mail from trusted parties fast, without the loss of content, increasing end users' satisfaction.

IP Block List

Similar to the IP Allow list, the IP Block list feature examines connecting IP addresses against the static local list of IPs manually maintained by the Exchange administrator. In many cases administrators include on the list IP addresses of SMTP servers known to send spam or other MTAs from which they do not want to receive e-mail. If the Connection Filtering agent finds the IP address of the sending server on the local IP Block list, the server rejects the message without allowing the connecting party to initiate SMTP mail transaction.

You can configure a single IP address or IP address ranges that are blocked, and you can also define an expiration time on each entry so that you can block an IP address temporarily.

If you enable Sender Reputation filtering, it will add the IP addresses that exceed defined Sender Reputation Level (SRL) to the IP Block list for the configured amount of time.

IP Block List Providers

IP Block List Providers, or real-time block lists (RBLs), contain a list of known IP addresses of SMTP servers that are considered risky for sending spam. Because spammers use a variety of techniques to send spam and fool the receiving servers into accepting it, identifying their IP addresses and verifying them for "spamminess" is a very useful way to prevent spam from entering Exchange organizations.

If enabled, the Agent will send a DNS query to a manually configured IP Block List Provider and if the response from the provider indicates that the connecting IP is on the list, the Connection Filtering agent will reject mail transaction after the RCPT TO: command.

The rejection logic has been designed to accommodate various exceptions or cases when one or more recipients in the Exchange organization might need to receive all e-mail sent from the block-listed IP because of various business needs. (For example, spam analysts might need to investigate a newly unfolding spam attack or the Exchange administrator might set up a honey pot account to collect mail for forensics.) Whatever the reason, you can configure specific e-mail addresses as exceptions so that they will receive all messages, even if the connecting IP is on the RBL.

There are multiple real-time IP Block List Providers who maintain and service RBLs. You need to account for many factors when deciding which RBL provider to use. Some of the most important factors are the ability of the provider to service requests for removal of mistakenly or maliciously block-listed IP addresses, supportability channels, and responsiveness to customer issues. Of course, you also need to account for the cost of using the provider's services. Most RBL providers do not charge fees if the number of DNS queries is relatively low—for example it does not exceed 250,000 queries per day. However, if the number of queries exceeds this threshold, the provider won't service requests originating from high-volume IP addresses and instead will ask you to obtain their list via a zone file transfer, and the provider will charge a fee for that. Many RBL providers are available on the market, including the following:

- cbl.abuseat.org
- dnsbl.sorbs.net
- spamhaus.org
- bl.spamcop.net

> ***IMPORTANT*** **The list of common IP Block List Providers should be handled with care because the results change over time. Please watch your Agent Log carefully to prevent the blocking of messages without a reason. You should consider writing a PowerShell script that is automatically executed every day to look for problems in the Agent Log as the size of the log might increase very quickly.**

A very useful cmdlet to determine whether your IP Block List Providers are working correctly is the *Test-IPBlockListProvider* cmdlet. You can either test a single RBL or you can test an IP address using all your configured RBLs, as shown in Figure 7-9.

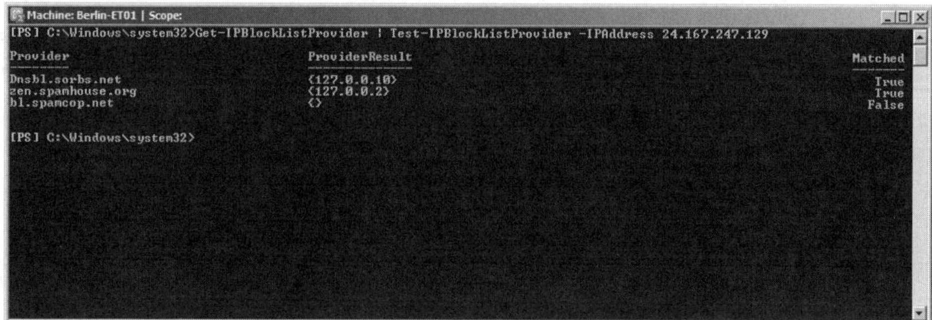

FIGURE 7-9 Testing IP Block List Providers in EMS

Please be aware that the more RBLs you configure, the longer the verification process will take. Thus it is recommended not to exceed two or three RBLs. One positive match is sufficient to block the sender.

Another advantage of using Forefront Protection 2010 for Exchange Server is that it relieves administrators of the work required to configure, maintain, and administer IP block lists. The product comes with a feature called Forefront DNSBL, which is an aggregation of multiple feeds from many RBL providers, including SpamHaus and internal Microsoft feeds such as the block list from the Forefront Online Protection for Exchange team. The aggregated feeds are combined into a single database and positioned on a Microsoft-owned DNS infrastructure. The feature is administration- and maintenance-free, meaning the Exchange administrator has nothing to configure or monitor/maintain.

Sender Filtering

The Sender filter compares the sender on the MAIL FROM: SMTP command to a list of senders or sender domains that are prohibited from sending messages to the organization. After the sender is filtered, there are two possible actions: reject the message or stamp the message and deliver it. The blocked sender information is included as one of the criteria when content filtering processes the message.

> ***NOTE*** **As a best practice you should select the Block Messages That Don't Have Sender Information option in Sender filtering properties. If a message does not contain a sender address, it is extremely likely to be spam anyway.**

Recipient Filtering

The Recipient filter compares the message recipients on the RCPT TO: SMTP command to an administrator-defined Recipient Block list. If a match is found, the message is not accepted for the recipient specified on the Recipient Block list but will be delivered to other recipients who are not on the list. If multiple recipients are listed on the message and some are not on the Recipient Block list, further processing is done on the message. The Recipient filter also compares recipients on inbound messages to the local recipient directory to determine whether the message is addressed to valid recipients. When a message is not addressed to valid recipients, such a message can be safely rejected during SMTP transaction.

> ***NOTE*** **As a best practice you should select the Block Messages Sent To Recipients That Don't Exist In The Directory option in Recipient filtering properties. This will automatically reject any message destined for e-mail addresses that do not exist in Active Directory. This will be verified to all authoritative, configured Accepted Domains. For internal relay domains this option will not be considered.**

Enabling the Block Messages Sent To Recipients That Don't Exist In The Directory option might disclose your Active Directory recipient information to malicious users executing a Directory Harvesting Attack (DHA) against your organization. To circumvent such attacks Exchange server enables you to configure tarpit intervals (*tarpits* are delays between the command coming from a remote computer and when Exchange server replies confirming or rejecting valid recipients). This is a highly effective technique that renders DHAs against Exchange organizations not feasible. The tarpit option is configurable and the default value is 5 seconds (which means Exchange server will delay response to every invalid recipient command for 5 seconds).

Sender ID Filtering

The Sender ID framework is an industry standard that allows companies to verify the IP addresses for incoming messages to ensure that they come from authorized servers. The Sender ID Framework provides highly effective protection against e-mail domain spoofing and phishing schemes. However, Sender ID is not used by many large corporations.

To take an advantage of the Sender ID Framework, domain owners must register all the IP addresses for all the SMTP servers that send e-mail from their SMTP domain with special DNS records. When using Sender ID filtering, the recipient messaging server initiates a DNS lookup to verify that the connecting IP is allowed to deliver messages on behalf of that domain. If the domain information does not contain the connecting server's IP address, the messages can be filtered out. Figure 7-10 illustrates the Sender ID filtering process.

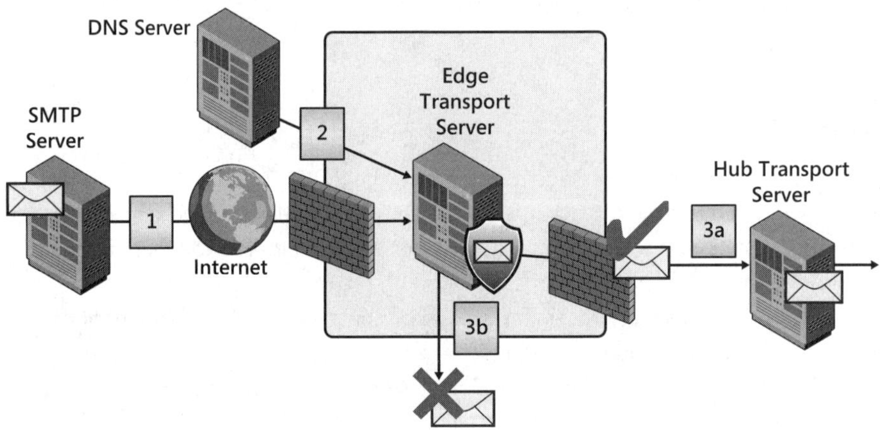

FIGURE 7-10 How Sender ID filtering works

As displayed in the figure, Sender ID filtering follows these steps:

1. The message is received by the Exchange Edge Transport server.
2. The Edge Transport server checks the IP address of the sending SMTP server and queries DNS for the Sender ID record. Sender ID records are in fact Sender Policy

Framework (SPF) compatible records and both SPF versions are supported in the Sender ID Framework.

3. Depending on the result, the following actions are taken:
   - If the Sender ID record matches the sending SMTP server, the Edge Transport server accepts the message into the Exchange organization.
   - If the Sender ID record does not match, the Edge Transport server will respond in the configured way—meaning it either rejects, deletes, or forwards the message with additional information added to its header indicating that it failed authentication.

If you're interested in additional information about the Sender Policy Framework (SPF), you can access it at *http://www.openspf.org/*.

Sender ID and Sender Policy Framework (SPF) records

To take an advantage of the Sender ID Framework and protect their own name brand and reputation, each e-mail sender must create a Sender ID or SPF record and add it to their domain's DNS records. The record is a single text (TXT) record in the DNS database that identifies each domain's e-mail servers. Sender ID records can use several formats, including the SPF record format examples as listed in Table 7-5.

TABLE 7-5 SPF Record Configuration Examples

DNS CONFIGURATION	DESCRIPTION
`Litware.com. IN TXT "v=spf1 mx -all"`	This record indicates that all servers that have an MX record for the Litware.com domain are allowed to send messages.
`Litware.com IN TXT "v=spf1 ip4:10.10.0.20 -all"`	This record indicates that only the server with the IP address 10.10.0.20 is allowed to send messages for Litware.com.
`Litware.com IN TXT "v=spf1 a -all"`	This record indicates that any host with an A record can send mail.
`Litware.com IN TXT "v=spf1 mx mx:berlin-et01 .emea.litware.com mx:berlin-et02.emea .litware.com -all"`	This record indicates that only the listed servers are allowed to send messages for Litware.com.

Additionally, you should be aware of the different configuration options you have using the *all* part of the SPF record in DNS. The options are listed in Table 7-6.

TABLE 7-6 SPF Record *all* Options

SPF RECORD	DESCRIPTION
-all	Only IPs in the text record can legitimately send mail on behalf of the domain—otherwise the e-mail is a forgery. For example, "v=spf1 mx –all" means only IPs of MX records can legitimately send on behalf of the domain; all others are forgeries. You should always consider this SPF record as the default. However, "v=spf1 –all" means no IPs are associated with sending domain and as such this domain is not involved in sending mail at all, so all mail claimed to be from the domain is a forgery. This option maps to hardfail status in Sender ID filter and the message will be deleted.
~all	E-mail is likely a forgery but this is clear. Sender ID filter, encountering such an option, will provide softfail status and the e-mail won't get deleted, but instead will get accepted into the Exchange organization.
+all	Use this option with care as it maps to the PASS status in Sender ID filter. By implementing this syntax you guarantee that your domain never sends spam.
?all	It's ambiguous if the e-mail is a spoof or good. The option is used for testing Sender ID functionality and maps to Neutral status and e-mail will be accepted into the Exchange organization.

Microsoft provides the Sender ID Framework SPF Record Wizard to verify your organization's Sender ID and SPF records in DNS. It is available at *http://www.microsoft.com/mscorp/safety/content/technologies/senderid/wizard/*. The wizard allows you to create a Sender ID record that meets your organization's exact needs.

Configuring Sender ID Filtering

Sender ID filtering is enabled by default with the option to stamp the header with Sender ID verdict and continue message processing. Other possible options are Reject and Delete.

It is very important to understand that the filter will implement Reject or Delete actions if and only if the Sender ID validation on the connecting IP failed. This means that the connecting IP cannot legitimately send mail on behalf of the domain it claims to be from, which is pretty much a spoofing attempt. In all other cases (for example, in the event of a transient DNS error, or if Sender ID records are misconfigured, do not exist, or are temporarily not available) the filter will not reject or delete message. It will stamp the verdict onto the message and pass it on to the next filtering technology.

Sender ID is not a mandatory requirement in Internet SMTP messaging; however, it is the technology that will help protect your company's name brand and prevent spoofing attacks. But the evidence is that many large companies don't use Sender ID yet. For example, at the time of this writing, neither HP nor GE nor Siemens publish Sender ID records in DNS; whereas IBM, Microsoft, and Google do.

In many cases Sender ID is your best and only defense when Zero Day attacks unfold, so it is recommended that you create and maintain Sender ID records and implement Sender ID filtering in Reject mode. Sender ID, when correctly implemented, is very safe to use and helps to improve your reputation as a responsible, legitimate sender.

To verify Sender ID, you can use the *Test-SenderID* cmdlet and enter a domain as well as the Server IP address to see the result.

Content Filtering

The Content Filter agent uses SmartScreen technology to analyze the content of every message and evaluate whether it is spam.

SmartScreen technology is the name for the underlying content filtering core technology developed by Microsoft Research and used in multiple Microsoft products under various names. In Exchange it is used under the name IMF (Intelligent Message Filter), whereas Outlook uses SmartScreen in its Junk E-mail Filter. The same core engine is used in Hotmail as well. The content filter uses the Microsoft Exchange Anti-Spam Update service to update its filters.

After the message is received, the Content Filter agent evaluates the message's content for recognizable patterns and then assigns a rating based on the probability that the message is spam. This rating is attached to the message as an SCL, which is a numerical value between -1 and 9. Table 7-7 provides an overview of the SCL ratings and the spam confidence level definition.

TABLE 7-7 SCL Ratings and Definitions

SCL RATING	SPAM CONFIDENCE LEVEL DEFINITION
–1	Messages are from a trusted source (internal, authenticated, or safelisted).
0	Messages are categorized as not spam.
1 – 4	The likelihood of being spam is extremely low to low.
5 – 9	The likelihood of being spam is high to extremely high.

The Content Filter agent scans messages only on Edge Transport servers and Hub Transport servers that have the anti-spam agents installed.

The SCL rating of the message is stored in the header of the message and can be found by identifying the *X-MS-Exchange-Organization-SCL* value, as displayed in Figure 7-11.

Content filtering is enabled by default on Edge Transport servers (or Hub Transports that have the anti-spam agents installed) and is configured to reject all messages with an SCL rating equal or greater than seven.

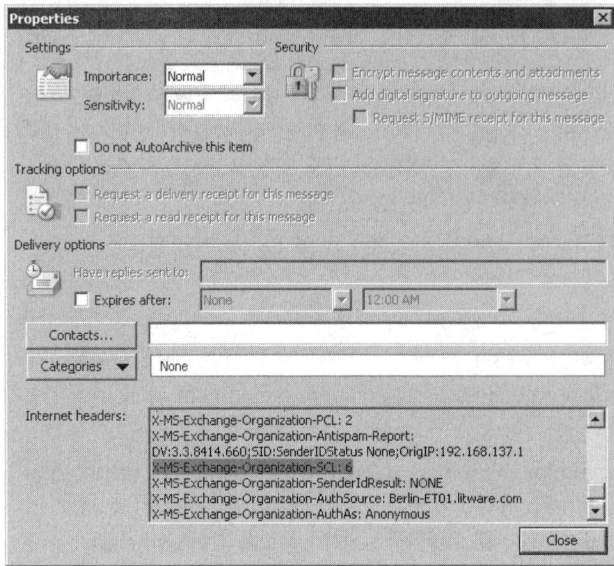

FIGURE 7-11 Viewing the SCL rating of a message in Microsoft Outlook

Configuring the Content Filter

You can modify the default content filtering settings by using the Exchange Management Console or the Exchange Management Shell:

- **Configure Custom Words** You can specify a list of keywords or phrases to prevent the blocking of any message containing those words. This feature is useful if your organization must receive e-mail that contains words that the Content Filter agent normally would block. You also can specify keywords or phrases that cause the Content Filter agent to block a message containing those words.
- **Specify Exceptions** You can configure exceptions to exclude any messages to recipients on the exceptions list from content filtering.
- **Specify Actions** You can configure the SCL thresholds and threshold actions. You can configure the Content Filter agent to delete, reject, or quarantine messages with an SCL rating equal or greater than the value you specify. You can also define the quarantine mailbox.

> **NOTE** When the Content Filter agent rejects a message, it uses the default response of "550 5.7.1 Message rejected due to content restrictions". You can customize this message using the *Set-ContentFilterConfig* cmdlet in the Exchange Management Shell.

Configure SCL Junk E-Mail Folder Threshold

Besides configuring the Content Filter to reject, quarantine, or delete messages on the incoming stream, you can also configure SCL threshold levels to move mail items automatically to the Junk folder of the mailbox. You can configure this either on a mailbox level or an organizational level.

NOTE The SCL Junk E-mail threshold configuration means that Exchange automatically moves the messages to the Junk folder. If the messaging client of your users does not allow the Junk folder to be accessed, users will never be aware of the junk mail. This is not a problem if your users are using Outlook or OWA. For POP3 clients, if you turn on the SCL thresholds, recipients won't be able to see mail sent to the Junk E-mail folder (as the POP3 protocol doesn't know the Junk E-mail folder), and IMAP4 clients should include the Junk E-mail folder in the list of subscribed folders for their client.

SCL CONFIGURATION ON A MAILBOX LEVEL

To configure specific junk mail parameters on a single mailbox, you need to use the *Set-Mailbox* cmdlet. This cmdlet includes various parameters that allow you to configure SCL thresholds and their actions. Table 7-8 provides an overview of which SCL thresholds can be configured.

TABLE 7-8 *Set-Mailbox* Cmdlet Anti-Spam Parameter Overview

SET-MAILBOX PARAMETERS	RESULT
AntispamBypassEnabled	If set to $*true*, no anti-spam agent will scan a message from or to this mailbox.
RequireSenderAuthenticationEnabled	If this is configured, any sender that addresses this mailbox must be authenticated.
SCLDeleteEnabled *SCLDeleteThreshold <SCL#>*	Defines the SCL threshold for the mailbox that deletes any messages rated equal or above the threshold.
SCLJunkEnabled *SCLJunkThreshold*	Defines the SCL threshold for the mailbox that moves any message rated equal or above the threshold to the Junk folder. When *SCLJunkEnabled* is set to $True and *SCLJunkThreshold* is a value such as 5, the setting ignores the organizational setting.
SCLQuarantineEnabled *SCLQuarantineThreshold*	Defines the SCL threshold for the mailbox that moves any message rated equal or above the threshold to the quarantine mailbox.
SCLRejectEnabled *SCLRejectThreshold*	Defines the SCL threshold for the mailbox that rejects any messages rated equal or above the threshold.

SCL CONFIGURATION ON AN ORGANIZATIONAL LEVEL

You can also define an SCL threshold level for every mailbox in your Exchange organization by using the following cmdlet:

```
Set-OrganizationConfig -SCLJunkThreshold <SCL #>
```

If the SCL rating for a specific message exceeds the SCL Junk E-mail folder threshold, the Mailbox server moves the message to the user's Junk E-mail folder. The default value is 4.

NOTES FROM THE FIELD

Create a Transport Rule to Process SCLs

Andreas Bode
Messaging Consultant, Siemens AG, Germany

One of my customers wanted to identify SPAM by adding the word SPAM: to the message subject as a prefix. Using Transport rules it is very easy to add the word SPAM: as the prefix for the SCL rating I defined. However, I recognized that the rule did not catch the SCL rating at all.

After some research I found out that the problem was caused by the priority at which the Transport agents are processed. By default, Edge Rule Agent has a priority of 3 and Content Filter Agent of 4. Practically, this means that the rule is executed before the Content Filter agent sets an SCL rating on the message.

To solve this problem I executed the following cmdlet to move the Content Filter Agent in priority before the Edge Rule Agent: *Set-TransportAgent "Content Filter Agent" –Priority 3* cmdlet. After a Transport service restart, my Transport rule marked all messages that exceeded the SCL threshold I defined accordingly.

Safe List and Block List Aggregation

In Exchange Server 2010, the Content Filter agent on the Edge Transport server uses the Microsoft Outlook Safe Senders lists, Safe Recipients lists, and trusted contacts to optimize spam filtering. Safelist aggregation is a set of anti-spam functionality that Outlook and Exchange Server 2010 share. This anti-spam functionality collects data from the anti-spam safe lists that Microsoft Outlook or OWA users configure, and makes this data available to the anti-spam agents on the Edge Transport server.

Unlike in Exchange 2007, in Exchange 2010 safelist aggregation is enabled by default. The Mailbox assistant does the safelist aggregation automatically. Another difference between Exchange 2007 and Exchange 2010 servers is Block list aggregation. In Exchange 2007 the Block list logic was triggered at the client end but in Exchange 2010 server the logic is transferred to the Sender filter and executed much earlier in the anti-spam processing. So in addition to existing Safe Sender/Recipient lists aggregation Exchange 2010 server also aggregates Block list entries, making them available to Sender filtering.

The safelist collection is stored in a hidden item in the root folder of the user's mailbox. A user can have up to 1,024 unique entries in a safelist collection. Exchange 2010 and the Junk

E-mail Options mailbox assistant then replicate the changes from the mailbox to the user's Active Directory account (namely to the *msExchSafeSenderHash*, *msExchSafeRecipientHash*, and *msExchBlockedSendersHash* attributes).

EdgeSync then synchronizes the safelist collections to the Edge Transport servers where the aggregated data is used by the Content Filtering agent.

Unlike Exchange 2007, you do not need to run *Update-Safelist* cmdlet to gather and prepare safelist data from user mailboxes anymore. However, you can use the *Update-Safelist* cmdlet to manually update the safelist in Active Directory.

You can find more details at *http://technet.microsoft.com/en-us/library/bb125168.aspx*.

Sender Reputation Filtering

The Exchange Server 2010 Sender Reputation feature makes message-filtering decisions based on information about recent e-mail messages received from specific senders. The Sender Reputation agent analyzes various properties about the sender and the e-mail message, to create a Sender Reputation Level (SRL). This SRL is a number between 0 and 9, where a value of 0 indicates less than a 1 percent chance that the sender is sending spam, and a value of 9 indicates more than a 99 percent chance of it. If a sender appears to be the spam source, the Sender Reputation agent automatically adds the IP address for the SMTP server that is sending the message to the IP Block list.

How Sender Reputation Filtering Works

When the Transport server receives the first message from a specific sender, the SMTP sender is assigned an SRL of 0. As more messages arrive from the same source, the Sender Reputation agent evaluates the messages and begins to adjust the sender's rating. The Sender Reputation agent uses the following criteria to evaluate each sender:

- **Sender open proxy test** An open proxy is a proxy server that accepts connection requests from any SMTP server, and then forwards messages as though they originated from the local host. This also is known as an *open relay server*. When the Sender Reputation agent calculates an SRL, it does so by formatting an SMTP request in an attempt to connect back to the Edge Transport server from the open proxy. If an SMTP request is received from the proxy, the Sender Reputation agent verifies that the proxy is an open proxy and updates that sender's open proxy test statistic.
- **HELO/EHLO analysis** The HELO and EHLO SMTP commands are intended to provide the receiving server with the domain name, such as Contoso.com, or the IP address of the sending SMTP server. Spammers frequently modify the HELO/EHLO statement to use an IP address that does not match the IP address from which the connection originated, or to use a domain name that is different from the actual originating domain name. If the same sender uses multiple domain names or IP addresses in the HELO or EHLO commands, there is an increased chance that the sender is a spammer.

- **Reverse DNS lookup** The Sender Reputation agent also verifies that the originating IP address from which the sender transmitted the message matches the registered domain name that the sender submits in the HELO or EHLO SMTP command. The Sender Reputation agent performs a reverse DNS query by submitting the originating IP address to DNS. If the domain names do not match, the sender is more likely to be a spammer, and the overall SRL rating for the sender is adjusted upward.
- **SCL ratings analysis on a particular sender's messages** When the Content Filter agent processes a message, it assigns an SCL rating to the message. This rating is attached to the message as an SCL. The Sender Reputation agent analyzes data about each sender's SCL ratings, and uses it to calculate SRL ratings.

The Sender Reputation agent calculates the SRL for each unique sender over a specific time. When the SRL rating exceeds the configured limit, the IP address for the sending SMTP server is added to the IP Block list for a specific amount of time.

Sender Reputation Configuration

You can configure the Sender Reputation settings on the Edge Transport server. By using the Exchange Management Console, you can configure the Sender Confidence (enable or disable Sender open proxy test), the Sender Reputation block threshold, and the timeout period for how long a sender will remain on the IP Block list. Figure 7-12 shows the default settings of Sender Reputation filtering.

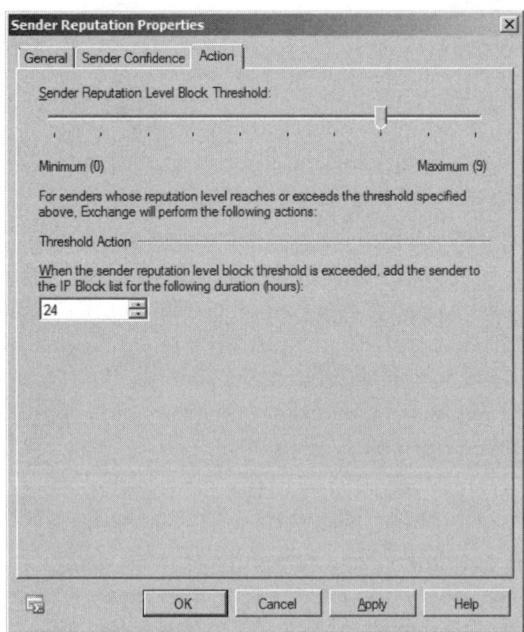

FIGURE 7-12 Sender Reputation default settings

If you want to configure advanced settings, you need to use the *Set-SenderReputation* cmdlet, which allows you to fine-tune this feature.

Attachment Filtering

Attachment filtering allows you to choose the attachment names, file extensions, or file MIME content types your users can receive. This is necessary to protect your users from malicious messages. One of the most famous viruses in messaging history, the Melissa virus, was spread using a malicious attachment. Obvious dangerous attachments such as scripts or executables are now removed after causing a complete mail disruption for large organizations years ago. You may remember the "I love you" virus that sent messages to all contacts of the local mailbox. That's just one good reason to consider attachment filtering!

Attachment filtering in Exchange 2010 can be based on the following filtering criteria:

- Filename or filename extension
- File MIME content type

You can use the *Get-AttachmentFilterEntry* cmdlet to display the currently configured attachment filters, as shown in Figure 7-13.

```
Machine: Berlin-ET01 | Scope:
[PS] C:\Windows\system32>Get-AttachmentFilterEntry

       Type Name                             Identity
       ---- ----                             --------
ContentType application/x-msdownload         ContentType:application/x-msdownload
ContentType message/partial                  ContentType:message/partial
ContentType text/scriptlet                   ContentType:text/scriptlet
ContentType application/prg                  ContentType:application/prg
ContentType application/msaccess             ContentType:application/msaccess
ContentType text/javascript                  ContentType:text/javascript
ContentType application/x-javascript         ContentType:application/x-javascript
ContentType application/javascript           ContentType:application/javascript
ContentType x-internet-signup                ContentType:x-internet-signup
ContentType application/hta                  ContentType:application/hta
   FileName *.xnk                            FileName:*.xnk
   FileName *.wsh                            FileName:*.wsh
   FileName *.wsf                            FileName:*.wsf
   FileName *.wsc                            FileName:*.wsc
   FileName *.vbs                            FileName:*.vbs
   FileName *.vbe                            FileName:*.vbe
   FileName *.vb                             FileName:*.vb
   FileName *.url                            FileName:*.url
   FileName *.shs                            FileName:*.shs
   FileName *.shb                            FileName:*.shb
   FileName *.sct                            FileName:*.sct
   FileName *.scr                            FileName:*.scr
   FileName *.scf                            FileName:*.scf
   FileName *.reg                            FileName:*.reg
   FileName *.prg                            FileName:*.prg
   FileName *.prf                            FileName:*.prf
   FileName *.pif                            FileName:*.pif
   FileName *.pcd                            FileName:*.pcd
   FileName *.ops                            FileName:*.ops
   FileName *.mst                            FileName:*.mst
   FileName *.msp                            FileName:*.msp
   FileName *.msi                            FileName:*.msi
```

FIGURE 7-13 Default attachment filter entries

When a filtering criterion is met, the following actions can be performed on the message:

- **Strip attachment but deliver message**
- **Block message and attachment** This blocks the message from entering the system but will inform the sender of the message that the message contained an unacceptable attachment.
- **Silently delete message and attachment** This will delete the message before entering the system without sending any notification to the sender or recipient.

Attachment filtering is only available on Edge Transport servers, not on Hub Transport servers, even if you installed the anti-spam agents.

NOTE The Attachment Filter agent included with Exchange 2010 detects file types even if they have been renamed. Attachment filtering also ensures that compressed files (.zip or .lzh files) don't contain blocked attachments by performing a filename extension match against the files in the compressed files.

Anti-Spam Reporting

Exchange 2010 comes with a couple of scripts to create anti-spam activity reports that are available in the <*Exchange_Install_Path*>\Scripts folder. These scripts can run on Edge and Hub Transport servers. Table 7-9 provides an overview of available scripts and their usage.

TABLE 7-9 Anti-Spam Reporting Scripts

SCRIPT	PURPOSE
Get-AntispamFilteringReport.ps1	Creates a top-ten list of sources (such as agents) that are responsible for either rejecting connections and commands or for rejecting, deleting, or quarantining a message.
Get-AntispamSCLHistogram.ps1	Retrieves all entries for the Content Filter and groups them by SCL values.
Get-AntispamTopBlockedSenderDomains.ps1	Lists the top sender domains that were blocked by anti-spam agents.
Get-AntispamTopBlockedSenderIPs.ps1	Lists the top sender IPs that were blocked by anti-spam agents.
Get-AntispamTopBlockedSenders.ps1	Lists the top sender IPs that were blocked by anti-spam agents.
Get-AntispamTopRBLProviders.ps1	Lists the top reasons for rejection by Block List Providers.
Get-AntispamTopRecipients.ps1	Lists the top recipients that were rejected by anti-spam agents.

All of these example Windows PowerShell scripts use the transport agent logs and analyze them. All anti-spam agents log information about connections and messages acted on, plus some contextual information such as the name of the RBL or the SCL of the e-mail. The transport agent log files are located at <*Exchange_Install_Path*>\TransportRoles\Logs\AgentLog.

NOTES FROM THE FIELD

Custom Agent Log Analyzer

Jon Webster
Systems Engineer, Elephant Outlook, U.S. Southeast

Exchange 2010 and Forefront Protection 2010 for Exchange Server (FPE) both store their transaction and agent logs in CSV files.

The built-in *Get-AgentLog* cmdlet first loads the entire set of CSV file(s) into Windows PowerShell objects; then they can be filtered further. I have achieved a significant performance boost using my Select-CSVString script (available at *http://poshcode.com/1649*) by filtering the lines as text first, and then converting just those results to Windows PowerShell objects.

Let's assume the following: A user on our system has opened a support ticket saying she was supposed to get an e-mail from someone at *fabrikam.com,* and it never arrived. Rather than getting the sender to locate the bounce message, we can search the agent logs and see if something from that domain was rejected within the last few days.

To look for this rejection using the built-in tool, I would use something like this:

```
Get-AgentLog |?{ ($_.p1fromaddress -match "fabrikam.com" -or
$_.p2fromaddresses -match "fabrikam.com") -and $_.action -eq
"RejectMessage"}
```

Get-AgentLog loads several gigs of agent logs, filters through potentially hundreds of thousands of results, and finishes several minutes later.

To look for the same line with *Select-CSVString,* I would use something like this:

```
Select-CSVString -pattern "fabrikam.com.*Reject"
```

Select-CSVString searches several gigs of agent logs for the above regular expression, converts just those results into Windows PowerShell objects, and return similar results in under 30 seconds. I say similar, because Exchange and Forefront can actually use multiple lines for a single message (multiple recipients) that *Select-CSVString* doesn't handle—it could, but there just hasn't been much interest.

Couple that with another script to run *Select-CSVString* against all edge servers and Hub Transport servers that run the anti-spam agents using WinRM, and you can imagine the time it saves your support staff.

Antivirus Considerations

Besides planning for anti-spam, you need also to consider protecting your Exchange organization from viruses or other dangerous software applications.

Exchange Server 2010 Antivirus Protection

E-mail is one of the most common ways to spread viruses from one organization to another. The security community even refers to email as a vector used to spread viruses. One of the primary tasks in protecting your Exchange Server organization is to ensure that all messages containing viruses are stopped at the messaging environment's perimeter.

Although Exchange Server 2010 already provides some basic antivirus features, it is important to implement a separate antivirus product based on VSAPI that supports Exchange 2010.

Exchange Server 2010 includes the following virus protection features:

- **VSAPI Support of the Virus Scanning application programming interface (VSAPI)** In Exchange Server 2010, Microsoft maintains support for the same VSAPI used in Exchange Server 2003 and Exchange Server 2007. VSAPI does not reduce any viruses unless you install a product that uses VSAPI to scan your messages and remove viruses when messages have been infected.
- **Transport agents that filter and scan messages** Exchange Server 2010 includes the concept of transport agents—such as the attachment filtering agent—to remove spam and viruses from the messaging stream. By enabling attachment filtering on the Edge Transport or Hub Transport servers, you can reduce the spread of malware attachments before they enter the organization. Additionally, third-party vendors can create transport agents that specifically scan for viruses. Because all messages must pass through a Hub Transport server, this is an efficient and effective means to scan all messages in transit.
- **Antivirus stamping** Antivirus stamping reduces how often a message is scanned as it proceeds through an organization. It does this by stamping scanned messages with the version of the antivirus software that performed the scan and the scan results. This antivirus stamp travels with the message as it is routed through the organization, and determines whether additional virus scanning must be performed on a message.

Considerations for Deploying an Antivirus Solution

Many antivirus solutions are available on the market. Exchange 2010 requires a solution that supports VSAPI, such as Symantec Mail Security for Microsoft Exchange, Trend Micro ScanMail Suite for Microsoft Exchange, or the Microsoft's Forefront Protection 2010 for Exchange Server. Just make sure VSAPI and Exchange 2010 are supported when you evaluate the best antivirus solution for your company.

Although implementing an antivirus solution in Exchange Server is straightforward, you should keep some factors in mind when choosing and configuring an antivirus solution.

Implementing Multiple Antivirus Layers

To provide enhanced security against viruses, you should implement multiple layers of antivirus protection. A virus can enter your organization from the Internet through an e-mail or from a non-protected client within your company. Thus, it is a best practice to implement several layers of antivirus protection such as a firewall, a bastion server such as an Edge Transport server, and at the client-computer level.

Maintaining Regular Antivirus Updates

Installing the antivirus product does not automatically mean that your organization is fully protected. Regular antivirus pattern updates are critical to a well-implemented antivirus solution. You should also monitor that your antivirus patterns are updated frequently.

If you have a Microsoft System Center Operations Manager 2007 R2 environment in your organization, you can make sure that pattern updates of your antivirus solution are monitored with a respective SCOM management pack if available. This will ensure that you are notified when a pattern update does not occur in a timely manner.

Using Forefront Protection 2010 for Exchange Server

Forefront Protection 2010 for Exchange Server is a separate message-hygiene software package that you can integrate with Exchange Server 2010 to provide antimalware and anti-spam protection for the Exchange environment.

Benefits of Forefront Protection

Forefront Protection 2010 for Exchange Server (FPE) was specifically developed for Exchange Server and thus provides rich antivirus and anti-spam functionality for medium to large enterprises. FPE supports Exchange 2007 SP1 and later versions.

Forefront Protection 2010 for Exchange Server extends Exchange Server 2010 with the following advanced protection features:

- Simple configuration/maintenance-free setup
- Auto-configured anti-spam agents with smart defaults
- Unified management of FPE, Exchange, and Forefront Online Protection for Exchange
- Premium multiple engine antimalware protection
- Leading anti-spam content filter engine with spam catch rate above 99 percent

An overview of the ways FPE provides benefits when implementing it together with Exchange 2010 can be found in Table 7-10.

TABLE 7-10 Forefront Protection 2010 for Exchange Server Overview

FEATURE	DESCRIPTION
Malware scan with multiple engines	You can automatically scan messages using multiple malware pattern engines, not just a single one. Single antimalware engine creates a single failure point in the entire deployment; with Forefront you can use five engines scanning the messaging stream simultaneously and thus remove this deficiency.
New Microsoft antispyware engine	Scans messages for spyware.
Intelligent Engine Management	Automatically tracks the most efficient and performing engines and forces them to execute on the messaging stream first. Enables these engines as a part of dynamically chosen subset of engines.
Full support for VSAPI	Forefront Protection 2010 for Exchange Server fully supports the Exchange VSAPI.
Forefront DNSBL service	Provides aggregated sender reputation information supplied by multiple external and internal vendors about IP addresses that are known to send spam. This is an IP Block list offered exclusively to Exchange Server.
Premium spam protection	Includes the new Cloudmark-based Content Filter engine.
Automatic content filter updates	Automatic updates for the content filter directly from the vendor's update site. Microupdates are available every 30 to 45 seconds without any manual interaction.
Backscatter protection	Forefront Protection 2010 includes new backscatter filter to prevent bogus NDRs from entering Exchange organization.
Integration with Forefront Online Protection via Hybrid Model	Allows you to implement both on-premises and online protection from a single connection point (via Forefront UI) and apply a single policy to both online and on-premises protection. This also allows for lowering TCO of messaging hygiene and malware protection.
Unified protection management	New administrative and monitoring model via Windows PowerShell support with new dashboard implementation. Consolidated support for all protection features and technologies including basic Exchange anti-spam filters.

FEATURE	DESCRIPTION
Hyper-V support	Is fully supported in a Hyper-V virtual environment.
True Type File Filtering	Enables Real File Type inspection (not just extension) and actionable scanning of nested files/within .zip attachments.
Global Exception Lists	Single access point to sender and recipient exception lists to enforce allow and block actions from a single place.
Streamlined SCL ratings	Less ambiguous SCL ratings to simplify spam categorization and decrease the false positive rate. The vast majority of mail is correctly classified as either spam or good, legitimate mail.
Sender/sender domain, File, Keywords, and Subject Line filters	Allow scanning of incoming, outgoing, and internal messaging streams.

Forefront Protection 2010 Deployment Options

When you implement Forefront Protection 2010 for Exchange Server, you must consider the various deployment options.

First, you need to determine the servers on which you plan to install Forefront Protection 2010 by considering the following criteria:

- As a baseline, you should at least deploy Forefront Protection 2010 for Exchange Server on all Edge and Hub Transport servers.
- For full protection, you should deploy Forefront Protection 2010 for Exchange Server on all Edge Transport, Hub Transport, and Mailbox servers.

NOTE **You do not need to install Forefront Protection 2010 on the Client Access Server role because Forefront is only needed on the Mailbox, Edge, or Hub Transport server roles.**

By default, FPE scans each e-mail only once and then stamps it with a special AV Stamp so that other servers do not scan that message again. However, if necessary, you can enable rescanning of messages already scanned by FPE. Best practices also call for enabling FPE on Mailbox servers, but you need to rationalize the number of engines to run. Scanning with a dynamically allocated subset of engines looks like very attractive option and it is recommended that you have at least one engine enabled for scanning Mailbox servers. Periodic rescanning of databases provides additional assurance that there are no missed or hidden threats in the accepted messages and allows for proactive protection against various threats. You should also consider enabling periodic on-demand scanning of mailboxes to remove offensive or malicious content delivered in the past.

As a best practice, you should enable at least three scan engines and select the Scan With A Dynamic-Chosen Subset of Engines option, which provides optimal protection without significantly sacrificing server performance or messaging throughput.

Forefront Protection 2010 for Exchange Server, compared to Forefront Security for Exchange 2007, improves messaging throughput from 25 to 40 messages per second with all five engines running.

Planning for Messaging Security

Secure messaging in Exchange 2010 can be separated into three levels: network-based, session (or SMTP)–based, and client-based. It is important to understand at what level you want to implement protection. For example, if you implement network- or session-based security, messages are still not encrypted in a user's mailbox. Only client-based security does this. Alternatively you can also consider implementing security at every level, which definitely never can be reached.

Implementing Network-Based Security

Network-based security basically protects the communication on the network layer using protocols such as IPsec or VPN.

IPsec provides a set of extensions to the basic IP protocol and is used to encrypt server-to-server communication. It can be used to tunnel traffic or peer-to-peer to secure all IP communications natively. Because IPsec operates on the transport layer, applications such as Exchange 2010 don't need to be aware of IPsec. You use IPsec normally to secure server-to-server or client-to-server communication. You do not need another encryption method when using IPsec.

Virtual private network (VPN) also operates on the transport layer, and very often uses IPsec as the underlying protocol. VPN is used for site-to-site or client-to-site connections. Both operate on the transport layer, which can be an advantage over application-layer protocols such as Secure MIME (S/MIME), which does not require the application on both ends to know about the protocol.

Because Exchange 2010 by default encrypts its network traffic using TLS and self-signed certificates (if you do not by default roll out server certificates), the requirements for using network-based security for Exchange 2010 are not that important anymore.

Of course, Exchange 2010 also takes advantage of whether you have already implemented network-based secure communication. You don't need to do anything to make Exchange 2010 work; however, to optimize performance, you should consider configuring your connectors accordingly when you have network-based security in place.

Let's assume IPsec is mandatory for all Exchange servers in your organization. You now only need to configure the Receive connectors of your Hub Transport servers and enable Externally Secured on the Authentication tab, as shown in Figure 7-14. Externally Secured means that the connection is considered secured by a security mechanism that is external to Exchange 2010.

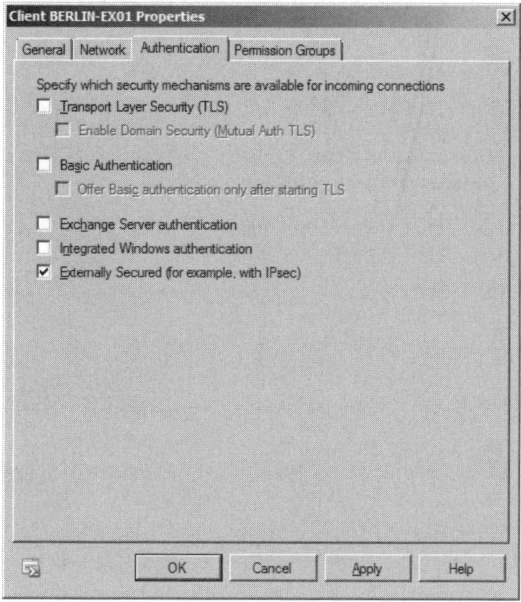

FIGURE 7-14 Configuring network-based security on a connector

Normally you don't need any other authentication method, but you're able to add only Transport Layer Security (TLS) on top of your network security. However, this will decrease the performance of message transfers because the communication gets encrypted several times. Other options, such as Exchange Server authentication, do not work with Externally Secured. Additionally, you need to configure Exchange Servers on the Permission Groups tab of the Receive connector because this group is used to permit a connection to the server.

> ***NOTE*** **Implementing network-based security is a work-intensive solution. Unless you have already implemented IPsec or other network-based protocols, you may want to consider other options for Exchange 2010.**

Planning for Session-Based Security

The TLS protocol is the default protocol used in an Exchange 2010 organization to encrypt server-to-server communication. TLS uses either an available local computer certificate or self-signed certificates that are created during Exchange 2010 setup. This means self-signed certificates provide Exchange 2010 administrators with an easy way to have OWA or other services automatically secured. Self-signed certificates are also used to automatically encrypt messages between Hub Transport and Edge Transport servers to encrypt traffic. They also are used to encrypt traffic between two Edge Transport servers located in different organizations.

If you're planning to implement Exchange 2010 Domain Security to provide secured message paths between Exchange 2010 Edge Transport servers over the Internet, you need real certificates. Self-signed certificates do need extra work when you want to implement Domain Security such as exchanging, installing, and trusting the root Certificate Authority (CA) between both companies.

Domain Security uses TLS with mutual authentication (mutual TLS) to provide session-based authentication and encryption. Standard TLS is used to provide confidentiality by encrypting but not authenticating the communication partners. This is typical of Secure Sockets Layer (SSL), which is the HTTP implementation of TLS.

Certificates and TLS

The section "Planning Certificates" in Chapter 3 already included the basics about digital certificates and Exchange Server 2010. It also mentioned the requirements for Hub and Edge Transport servers when using TLS.

Because Hub Transport servers can also use self-signed certificates for their internal communication, what you need to consider here are your Internet-facing Transport servers. On these servers it is recommended that you use an official certificate purchased from a third-party certificate authority (CA) that is well trusted.

The most important requirement on a certificate is to include the following names as SANs:

- The top-level domain for your Exchange organization that your users use in their official e-mail addresses, such as Litware.com
- All FQDNs of the Edge Transport servers

> ***IMPORTANT*** **Remember that you cannot modify the SANs of a certificate afterward; if you miss a name in the certificate request, you have to create a new one.**

Any certificate that you want to use for TLS requires the following:

- It must be a certificate that was either issued by a trusted party (by importing their root certificate) or by a third-party CA.
- It needs to be installed on the computer's certificate store.
- The certificate must be valid.
- It must be enabled on the Edge Transport server(s) for SMTP service.

On the Edge Transport server you cannot configure certificates in EMC; you have to use the Exchange Management Shell. The cmdlet to enable services for a certificate is

Enable-ExchangeCertificate. The cmdlet to verify that the certificate is enabled you can use is *Get-ExchangeCertificate |fl*, as shown in Figure 7-15.

```
Machine: Berlin-ET01 | Scope:
[PS] C:\Windows\system32>Get-ExchangeCertificate | Enable-ExchangeCertificate -Services SMTP
[PS] C:\Windows\system32>Get-ExchangeCertificate |fl

AccessRules        : {System.Security.AccessControl.CryptoKeyAccessRule, System.Security.AccessControl.CryptoKeyAccessR
                     ule, System.Security.AccessControl.CryptoKeyAccessRule, System.Security.AccessControl.CryptoKeyAcc
                     essRule}
CertificateDomains : {Berlin-ET01, Berlin-ET01.litware.com}
HasPrivateKey      : True
IsSelfSigned       : True
Issuer             : CN=Berlin-ET01
NotAfter           : 10.01.2015 11:04:27
NotBefore          : 10.01.2010 11:04:27
PublicKeySize      : 2048
RootCAType         : None
SerialNumber       : 5131DDB9D9053DA84E1AB1E2D28BB088
Services           : SMTP
Status             : Valid
Subject            : CN=Berlin-ET01
Thumbprint         : 5967ED65A5664CB220C65071CCB9ED19B05F0BE0


[PS] C:\Windows\system32>_
```

FIGURE 7-15 Enabling a certificate for SMTP service

To verify that your Edge Transport server is ready to serve mutual TLS requests, you should use the command TELNET <servername> SMTP and verify that when you enter the SMTP command **EHLO** you see STARTTLS listed. If it is not listed, check your Event Viewer's application log to find out what is wrong with your certificate.

Planning for Domain Security

Domain Security in Exchange 2010 is used as a relatively low-cost alternative to S/MIME or other message-encryption solutions. It uses mutual TLS, where each server verifies the identity of the other server by validating the certificate that is provided by the other server. It is an easy way for administrators to manage secured message paths between domains over the Internet.

TLS with mutual authentication differs from TLS in its usual implementation. Typically, when you implement TLS, the client verifies a secure connection to the intended server by validating the server's certificate, which it receives during TLS negotiation. With mutual TLS, each server verifies the connection with the other server by validating a certificate that the other server provides.

Domain Security is manually enabled for every domain by an Exchange organization administrator, so you must coordinate with the communication partner to make it work. It cannot be enabled only on one side, but must be configured in both the sending and receiving organizations.

> ***NOTE*** **Typically, Domain Security is enabled only on an Edge Transport server because the server needs to reside in the perimeter network or directly on the Internet to communicate with other domains. However, you also can enable Domain Security on a Hub Transport server if needed.**

The high-level steps to implement Domain Security are as follows:

1. Request and install a SAN certificate on the Edge Transport server(s) where you want to enable mutual TLS.
2. Test that TLS is working on both your side and the partner's side.
3. Configure outbound and inbound Domain Security.
4. Test mailflow.

> ***IMPORTANT*** **Don't forget to check your partner's domain to verify that it supports mutual TLS before configuring outbound and inbound Domain Security. If a mutual TLS connection cannot be made, all message traffic will stop.**

To configure Domain Security, you need to connect to a Hub Transport server (because it is synchronized to the Edge server using EdgeSync) and run the following commands in the EMS:

- To enforce Domain Security on an outbound connection, use the following cmdlet:

```
Set-TransportConfig -TLSSendDomainSecureList <DomainList>
```

- To enforce domain security on an inbound connection, run this cmdlet:

```
Set-TransportConfig -TLSReceiveDomainSecureList <DomainList>
```

You need to configure this on a per-domain level. The domain list is not additive—new domains are not automatically added, but replaced. You have to separate the domains using a comma. For example, you can use the following cmdlet to configure outbound domain security for the domains litware.com and fabrikam.com:

```
Set-TransportConfig -TLSSendDomainSecureList litware.com,fabrikam.com
```

> ***NOTE*** **Because you are performing this configuration on your Hub Transport servers, it takes a synchronization cycle before your Edge servers will recognize it. To speed up this process, you can use the *Start-EdgeSynchronization* cmdlet.**

Your last task is to make sure that the Send connectors and Receive connectors are enabled for Domain Security (Mutual Auth TLS). This is the default configuration, which is enabled if you do not change anything. The Send connector must be configured on the Hub Transport server; the Receive connector must be configured directly on the Edge Transport server.

When you've configured everything correctly, messages from any domain that are on the Domain Secure List should display the Domain Secured icon in Outlook 2007 or later, as seen in Figure 7-16. If the icon is not displayed, Domain Security might not work correctly and you should do the following to find the issue:

- Check the Event Viewer's application log.
- Check the Queue Viewer in the Exchange Management Console's toolbox.
- Enable Protocol logging on the Internet-facing connectors and take a look into the SMTP log conversation.

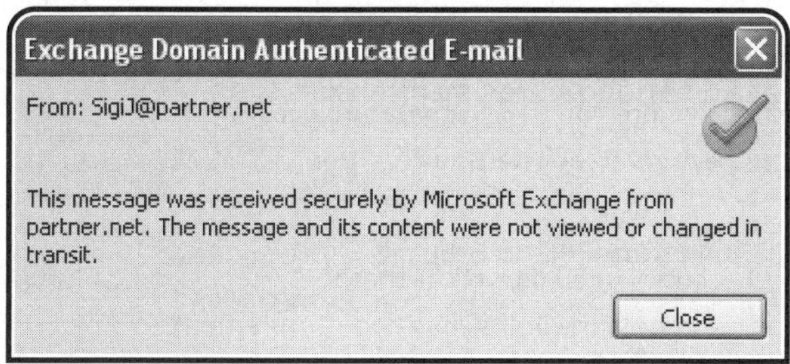

FIGURE 7-16 Domain Secured icon in Outlook 2007

Implementing Client-Based Security

When you consider client-based security, usually you must also consider Secure Multipurpose Internet Mail Extensions or S/MIME. S/MIME is a standard for public-key encryption and signatures of e-mail messages. Encryption is used to protect the content of a message so that only the intended recipients can read it. Signing a message means that the recipient can verify whether the message has been changed on the way from the sender to the recipient.

S/MIME is a client-based encryption and signing protocol that provides end-to-end security from the sending mailbox to the receiving mailbox. Unlike other encryption protocols that are session-based on the transport layer (such as TLS), the message also remains encrypted and signed within the mailbox. Even administrators cannot decrypt it if their digital certificate does not allow them to do so. Implementing S/MIME offers the following abilities:

- Use digital signatures as a way to prove to your communication partners that the content was not altered.
- Authenticate messages (especially for crucial functions such as when your boss approves your travel requests).
- Encrypt messages to prevent accidental disclosure of the content.

To support S/MIME in your Exchange organization, you must either have a public key infrastructure (PKI) available or your clients need to configure their certificates locally on each client (both their own and the public certificates from the person with whom they want to communicate securely).

If you use Windows PKI, all public certificates of your users are stored in your Active Directory. This allows your users to securely communicate with each other internally. However, if your users often communicate with external partners, you can also make the partner's certificate available in Active Directory. You do this by creating a contact and then publishing the contact's public certificate to it. You can find more information in the "Publish certificates for external contacts in Active Directory" available at *http://msexchangeteam.com/archive/2008/04/23/448761.aspx.*

> **NOTE** By default, Exchange Server 2010 fully supports S/MIME for message encryption and signatures. Unlike in previous versions where you had to configure every mailbox database, you do not need to configure any server-side setting to support S/MIME.

Because S/MIME provides end-to-end security, it is important that the e-mail application you use to read and write S/MIME messages meets the following two requirements:

- It must support S/MIME encryption and signatures.
- The digital signature must be configured in the e-mail application.

Outlook Web App running on a Windows system supports S/MIME. If you run OWA on a LINUX system, you do not have the S/MIME feature available and thus you cannot encrypt or decrypt S/MIME messages.

Additional Resources

- Understanding Header Firewall: *http://technet.microsoft.com/en-us/library/bb232136.aspx*
- Understanding Anti-Spam Stamps: *http://technet.microsoft.com/en-us/library/aa996878.aspx*
- Sender Policy Framework – Project Overview: *http://www.openspf.org/*
- Sender ID Framework SPF Record Wizard: *http://www.microsoft.com/mscorp/safety/content/technologies/senderid/wizard/*
- Understanding Safelist Aggregation: *http://technet.microsoft.com/en-us/library/bb125168.aspx*
- Publish certificates for external contacts in Active Directory: *http://msexchangeteam.com/archive/2008/04/23/448761.aspx*

CHAPTER 8

Automated Message Processing, Compliance, and Archiving

The messaging landscape has changed considerably over the last 10 years with the introduction of a great deal of government and regulatory body legislation and regulation. This has added to the already existing possibility of legal discoveries resulting from litigation or other legal action, with their attendant cost in time and resources. All of these factors have caused compliance requirements to become a major concern for messaging professionals in organizations of all sizes. Historically, Exchange did not offer features to manage messaging compliance and these requirements were met with third-party solutions, sometimes using the journaling capabilities in Exchange Server 2003 and earlier versions, or providing similar capability through their own solutions. Exchange Server 2007 introduced capabilities and features that have allowed organizations to meet some of these compliance requirements in a cost-effective manner without having to integrate third-party solutions, and Exchange Server 2010 has expanded on these capabilities to further build upon your ability to meet these needs out of the box.

Messaging Compliance Overview

The e-mail compliance capabilities introduced in Exchange Server 2007 and built on in Exchange Server 2010 are focused on regulatory compliance and legal discovery. In this context, legal discovery refers to the requirement to produce all relevant e-mail during litigation, usually as the result of a subpoena. Compliance can generally be divided into three categories:

- **Regulatory** Governmental regulations are normally the driving force behind regulatory compliance. Regulatory compliance has been a predominant concern to the financial services and healthcare sectors, but is also a matter of importance to virtually all public and private sectors. Public sector organizations typically also are expected to comply to access to information requests from citizens. Some examples of regulations affecting the private sector in the United States include Sarbanes-Oxley, SEC Rule 17A-4, Gramm-Leach-Bliley, and the Health Insurance Portability and Accountability Act (HIPAA); concerns for the public sector include the Freedom of Information Act and the Federal Information Security Management Act (FISMA). Finally, protection of privacy information is a primary concern for all organizations, whether in the public or private sectors.
- **Legal (court-ordered)** Litigation is commonly the driving force behind legal compliance.
- **Internal** Internal compliance in most cases boils down to risk mitigation for the organization. These risks can encompass concerns such as privacy breaches, financial loss, human resources concerns such as harassment/discrimination, corporate liability (criminal or civil), intellectual assets disclosure, and breach of client/attorney privilege.

Some sources estimate that as much as 90 percent of compliance costs for an organization are staff-related, and that the overall cost of compliance runs into the billions for sectors such as financials and securities. The features provided in Exchange Server 2010 can enable organizations to meet their compliance requirements with a much lower price tag in cost and effort as well as reduced complexity.

As part of their design goals to satisfy customer needs for messaging compliance within Exchange, Microsoft determined that although regulations vary widely across different jurisdictions, a complete e-mail compliance solution can primarily be defined by the following capabilities:

- **Message Retention** Defined not only as the ability to retain e-mail automatically for pre-determined time periods, but also the functionality to locate and retrieve those e-mails when necessary. If you've retained the records, but can't find them when needed, retention alone has done no good. Legal discoveries (subpoenas) in the private sector as well as access to information requests in the public sector are the primary drivers behind message retention. In Exchange Server 2010, these capabilities are provided by journaling, retention policies, retention policy tags, personal archives, and multi-mailbox search.

- **Controlled Access** Aside from retaining records as required, another capability required by a compliance solution is the ability to protect privacy information and prevent unauthorized access to data, both in transit and at rest. Exchange Server 2010 provides this capability through integration with Active Directory Rights Management Services (AD RMS), transport rules, and Transport Layer Security (TLS) for SMTP.
- **Information and Process Integrity** This capability encompasses message classification and processing messages based on their classification. It may also include *ethical walls* to block communication between specified departments or individuals of the organization to help preclude conflicts of interest. An example of an ethical wall is a financial institution that provides both brokerage and market research services; these groups are typically mandated by regulations to not communicate with each other in any way. Message classifications are an integrated component in Exchange Server 2010, whereas ethical walls can be implemented using transport rules in Exchange Server 2010. Both message classifications and transport rules were introduced in Exchange Server 2007.

INSIDE TRACK

Successfully Implementing Messaging Compliance Technologies

Ed Banti
Program Manager, Microsoft Corporation, Redmond, WA

Any technology implementation intended to impose certain behavior on end users or for policy enforcement (and the technologies discussed in this chapter certainly fall into these categories) can encounter challenges along the way that prevent the implementation from being a success. Primary among these challenges is the lack of a clearly defined and enforced corporate e-mail policy; this policy is the cornerstone of a successful compliance implementation. A large portion of messaging compliance is fundamentally policy enforcement, so without a defined policy in place you're like a dog chasing its tail; you may be getting good exercise, but you're not accomplishing anything.

A corporate e-mail policy is not a technical document—it's a business policy created by your compliance or risk officers that includes compliance measures based on the relevant regulations and/or laws for your industry. Areas of risk and potential liability should also be defined in the policy.

Exchange Server 2010 messaging compliance-related technologies such as retention policies, Information Rights Management (IRM) integration, and to a lesser extent message classification may be seen by end users as intrusions or obstacles to doing their job, and these perceptions can result in the project failing through no fault of the technology. Resistance such as this is the result of several factors in the majority of cases:

- An unclear or non-existent e-mail policy
- Insufficient (or non-existent) communication to end users regarding the purpose of the new features
- Lack of upper management sponsorship for the compliance initiative
- Forcing a taxonomy or classification system on your end users that is so rigid that it impedes their daily work
- Policies that are so disruptive to daily work that users find ways to get around them
- All of the above

As with any technology implementation, if you design and present your messaging compliance deployment as something that meets the needs of the organization, rather than an obstacle to be overcome, the project is much more likely to be a success.

Designing and Implementing Messaging Records Management

The messaging records management (MRM) technology in Exchange Server 2010 provides the message retention capability discussed in the "Messaging Compliance Overview" section of this chapter. This allows your organization as well as your individual users to retain or remove messages as required for company policy compliance, government regulations, or legal needs, as well to remove e-mail that doesn't need to be retained, such as personal e-mail or newsletter subscriptions. Removing messages that don't need to be retained can assist in controlling mailbox growth and the resources required to support that growth. When the age limit for retention is reached, an e-mail can be deleted or archived, an event can be logged, or the message can be flagged for user attention. When combined with message classification, AD RMS integration, and transport rules, MRM can provide a comprehensive e-mail compliance solution.

The MRM implementation in Exchange Server 2010 is composed of retention tags and retention policies; retention policies are collections of retention tags, which are then applied to mailboxes. We will cover retention policies in more detail in the "Retention Policies" section of this chapter.

Managed folders and managed folder mailbox policies, the Exchange Server 2007 implementation of messaging records management, are also supported in Exchange Server 2007. Managed folders can be migrated to retention policies; this will be covered in detail in the "Migrating from Managed Folders to Retention Policies" section of this chapter.

Managed folders and retention policies represent two different approaches to messaging records management. Managed folders can be used to apply retention settings to default mailbox folders (for example, Inbox, Sent Items, and Calendar) and custom managed folders created by the administrator; similar functionality can be implemented using retention policies and retention policy tags. However, retention policy tags provide the added flexibility of users being able to apply retention settings to individual mail items or folders they have created in their mailboxes; with managed folders, a user is required to move an item to a managed folder with the appropriate retention settings applied to it. By applying personal folder retention policy tags to messaging items or folders, a user can retain her folder structure and file her messaging data to her liking, and still apply the necessary retention policies to the data. The various types of retention policy tags and their usage will be discussed in more detail in the "Retention Policies" section of this chapter.

IMPORTANT Outlook 2007 or earlier clients don't include all of the required client features and thus are not supported when a retention policy is assigned to the mailbox to deliver the client experience. Outlook 2007 or earlier clients can be used if the applicable retention policies do not include personal tags.

In addition, journaling is not presently available with retention tags, so if you require journaling you will need to deploy new managed folders or retain your existing ones.

With either technology (managed folders or retention policies), your users are taking part in the MRM process by categorizing their messages according to their content and associated retention requirements. Conceptually, this categorization thought process is similar to that for message classification. (Message classification will be discussed in further detail in the "Designing and Implementing Transport Rules" section of this chapter.)

NOTE MRM requires an Exchange Server 2010 Enterprise Client Access License (CAL) for every mailbox configured for MRM.

Retention Tags and Retention Policies

In Exchange Server 2010, retention tags and retention policies replace or supplement the managed folder mailbox policies introduced in Exchange Server 2007. Exchange Server 2010's messaging records management strategy of retention tags and retention policies is illustrated in Figure 8-1.

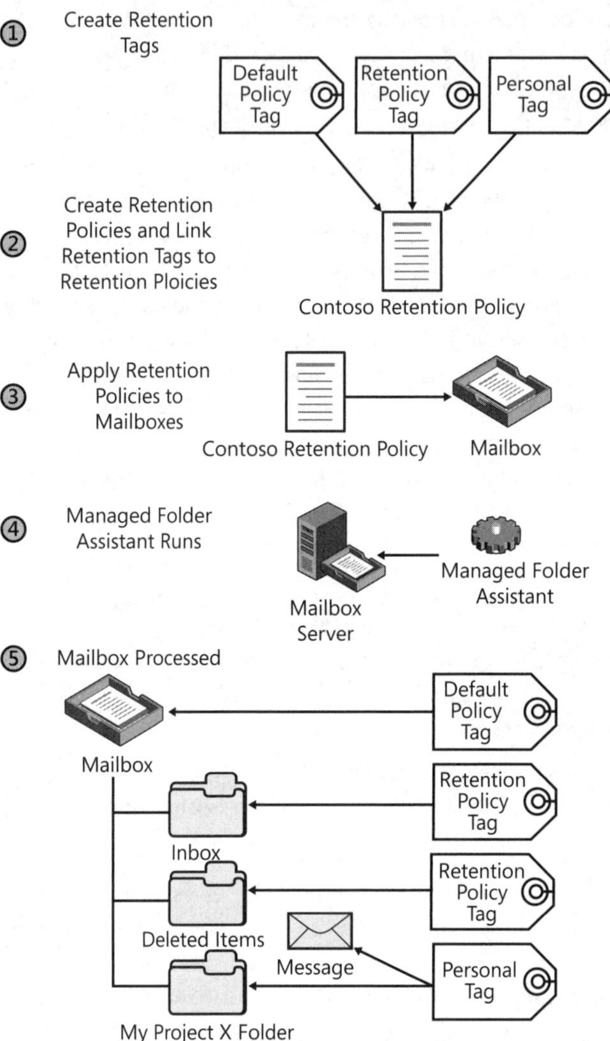

FIGURE 8-1 Retention tags and retention policies in Exchange Server 2010

Retention Tags

Retention tags are definitions of retention settings that are applied to folders and/or individual items within folders such as messages or other item types. These settings specify the retention period for the item type, and what action is taken when the specified age is reached; the age is calculated in days from the delivery date, or from the creation date if the item wasn't delivered but created within the mailbox. Retention tags differ from managed folders in that users don't have to file items in managed folders to satisfy retention requirements; they can tag items and folders within their own folder structure.

The following actions can be specified when a message reaches its retention age:

- **Mark As Past Retention Limit** Marks a message as past the limit, but does not take any further action.
- **Move To Deleted Items** Moves the item to the Deleted Items folder.
- **Delete And Allow Recovery** Item is deleted, but can be retrieved from Deleted Items Recovery within the deleted items retention period set on the mailbox database.
- **Permanently Delete** The item is not recoverable from Deleted Items Recovery, unless litigation hold is enabled for the mailbox.
- **Move To Archive** The item is moved to the user's configured archive mailbox.

Localized language settings can also be specified for your retention tag using the *New-RetentionPolicyTag* or *Set-RetentionPolicyTag* cmdlets. Localized names are specified in the form of the *"ISO Language Code":"Tag Name"* with the *LocalizedRetentionPolicyTagName*; for example, *-LocalizedRetentionPolicyTagName* EN-US:"Business Critical". You can also specify localized comments with the *LocalizedComment* parameter (for example, *-LocalizedComment* EN-US:"This is a localized comment in U.S. English"). Localized text (*LocalizedRetentionPolicyTagName* and *LocalizedComment*) is visible within Outlook 2010.

You can create three types of retention tags: retention policy tags, default policy tags, and personal tags.

RETENTION POLICY TAGS

Retention policy tags (RPTs) apply retention settings to default folders within the mailbox, such as Deleted Items, Sent Items, and Contacts. You cannot apply an RPT to individual items, although you can apply a different tag to items within a folder with an RPT applied to it. In addition, users can't apply a different tag to a default folder.

You can create RPTs for the following default folders:

- Calendar
- Deleted Items
- Drafts
- Inbox
- Junk E-Mail
- Journal
- Notes
- Outbox
- Sent Items
- Tasks
- RSS Feeds
- Sync Issues
- Conversation History

DEFAULT POLICY TAGS

In addition to the preceding list, a default policy tag (DPT) can be created; when a DPT is added to a retention policy and that retention policy is assigned to a mailbox, the tag settings apply to all folders and items within the mailbox that do not have other tags assigned or through inheritance on the folder.

> ***NOTE*** **A retention policy can only contain a single DPT.**

PERSONAL TAGS

Finally, you can create personal tags. When you create a personal tag and add it to a retention policy, a user whose mailbox the policy has been assigned to can tag individual items or non-default folders within his mailbox with that personal tag. The result is that the settings defined within the personal tag are applied to the item or folder; if applied to an item, the personal tag overrides other tags that may be assigned to the folder, or any default policy tag applied to the mailbox. If applied to a non-default folder, the tag replaces any tag previously assigned to that folder.

> ***NOTE*** **Personal tags cannot be applied to default folders.**

CREATING RETENTION TAGS

In Exchange Server 2010 SP1, retention tags and retention policies can be created through the Exchange Management Console (EMC). The New Retention Policy Tag Wizard is shown in Figure 8-2. A default policy tag is created by selecting All Other Folders In The Mailbox as the tag type in the wizard, whereas a personal tag is created by selecting Personal Folder. Selecting any other tag type creates a retention policy tag.

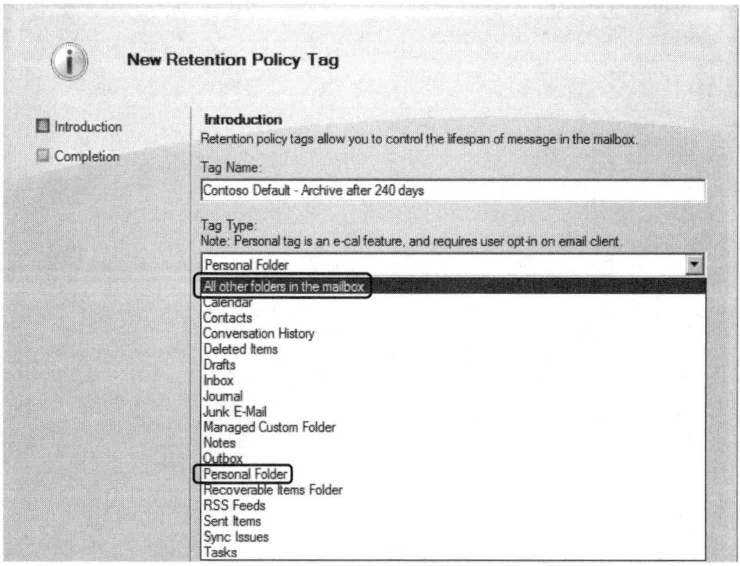

FIGURE 8-2 The Exchange Server 2010 New Retention Policy Tag Wizard

Retention tags can also be created via the Exchange Management Shell (EMS); it is worth noting that localized tag names and message class settings can only be configured through the EMS.

> **NOTE** A mantra to keep in mind for retention tags—especially personal tags, which are visible to the end users as choices they can make—is *keep it simple*. If an excessive number of retention tag choices are presented in the Outlook 2010 or OWA interface, the user will be more likely to give up on her attempts to use them. The best approach is to design the absolute minimum number of retention tags and retention policies required to meet the needs of your corporate e-mail policy for the organization as a whole, keeping policies broad enough to be used across as many mailboxes as possible. You can then use these policies and tags as a baseline to design and deploy other retention policies for specific sections or departments as required, while re-using retention tags where possible. This not only keeps the Outlook or OWA interface uncluttered, but also greatly reduces your management overhead. Although the technology will support creating hundreds of retention tags in hundreds of retention policies, you will seldom have a good reason to do so.

Retention Policies

Retention policies are collections of retention tags that you apply to mailboxes to implement retention settings for items and folders in those mailboxes. Retention tags cannot be applied to a mailbox directly; they must be included in a retention policy, and that policy is then assigned to a mailbox or mailboxes. A mailbox cannot be assigned more than one retention policy, although retention tags can be added to or removed from a retention policy at any time.

A retention policy can be composed of:

- One or more retention policy tags for default folders, although you can't link more than one RPT of a particular type (such as Inbox) to a particular retention policy.
- One default policy tag.
- Any number of personal tags, although it is recommended to have no more than 10 to keep it simple for users.

MANAGED FOLDER ASSISTANT

Once retention policies have been applied to mailboxes, those mailboxes are then processed by the Managed Folder Assistant, which runs on mailbox servers and provisions retention tags in mailboxes on a scheduled process (by default, from 01:00 to 09:00 (1 AM to 9 AM)). If you have implemented database availability groups (DAGs) and you wish to modify the Managed Folder Assistant schedule, be certain to modify it on all mailbox servers in the DAG to ensure consistent behavior in the event of a database being activated on a different server.

Additionally, if you wish to have the Managed Folder Assistant process a mailbox immediately, you can run the *Start-ManagedFolderAssistant* cmdlet. With no parameters, this causes the Managed Folder Assistant to process all mailboxes on the local server. You can target specific mailbox servers with the *Identity* parameter, or specify particular mailboxes with the *Mailbox* parameter. The following example retrieves all mailboxes that resolve from the ambiguous name resolution (ANR) search on the string "Dav"; for example, David Jones, Dave Barnett, Velimir Davidovski:

```
Get-Mailbox -Anr Dav | Start-ManagedFolderAssistant
```

REMOVING OR DELETING A RETENTION TAG FROM A RETENTION POLICY

Removing a retention tag from a retention policy does not remove the settings defined in that tag from items in the mailboxes the retention policy has been applied to. The Managed Folder Assistant continues to process items stamped with that tag, and the retention parameters specified in the tag continue to be applied to those items. However, removing the retention tag does make the tag unavailable to the user; the removed tag can no longer be applied to items in the mailbox.

To remove the retention tag's settings from mailbox items that have been stamped with it, the retention tag must be deleted. Retention tags can be deleted from the Exchange Server 2010 SP1 EMC, or with the *Remove-RetentionPolicyTag* cmdlet in the EMS.

> ***IMPORTANT*** **Deleting a retention tag causes the Managed Folder Assistant to process all items that have the removed tag applied and restamp them the next time the Managed Folder Assistant runs. This may consume significant resources on your mailbox servers depending on the number of mailboxes and mailbox items affected.**

You can also disable retention tags in lieu of deleting them; this causes the Managed Folder Assistant to ignore all items stamped with that tag rather than restamping them. However, these items are still considered tagged, so any default policy tag applied to the mailbox will not affect them; in effect, you have suspended retention for any items marked with that retention tag. A retention tag is disabled by selecting Disable This Tag in the Properties dialog box for the tag in EMC, or by setting the *RetentionEnabled* property to *$False* using the *Set-RetentionPolicyTag* cmdlet in the EMS.

CREATING A RETENTION POLICY

You can create a retention policy using the *New-RetentionPolicy* cmdlet or through the Exchange Server 2010 SP1 EMC. Creation consists of specifying a name for the policy and optionally adding retention tags to the policy and assigning the policy to mailboxes. The name of the retention policy must be unique in the organization, and there should be existing retention tags to link to the policy as it is created. Although it is possible to create a retention policy with no retention tags linked to it, it is not recommended because an empty policy applied to a mailbox may cause items in that mailbox to never expire.

Retention policies are created in the Exchange Server 2010 SP1 EMC by navigating to the Mailbox node under Organization Configuration and then selecting New Retention Policy from the Actions pane to start the New Retention Policy Wizard. The New Retention Policy Wizard is shown in Figure 8-3.

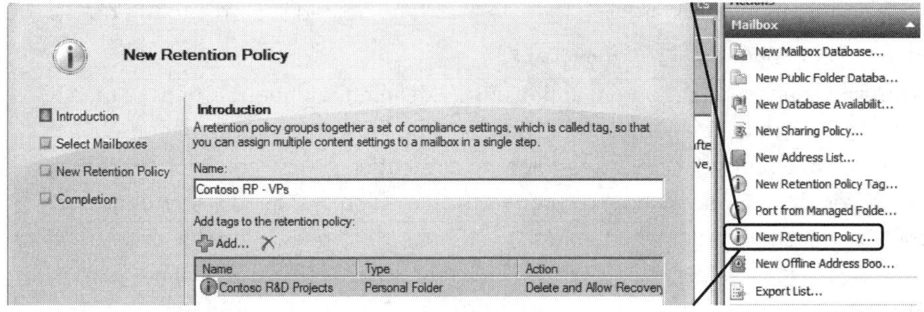

FIGURE 8-3 The New Retention Policy Wizard

The same retention policy example shown in Figure 8-3 can also be created in the EMS using the *New-RetentionPolicy* cmdlet:

```
New-RetentionPolicy "Contoso RP - VPs" -RetentionPolicyTagLinks "Contoso R&D Projects"
```

APPLYING A RETENTION POLICY TO MAILBOXES

After a policy is created and retention tags have been linked to it, you can apply that policy to mailboxes; no single mailbox can have more than one policy applied to it at the same time. Retention policies are applied using the *Set-Mailbox* cmdlet with the *RetentionPolicy* parameter. They can also be applied through the properties of the retention policy or the Messaging Records Management properties of a mailbox in the Exchange Server 2010 SP1 EMC. The Messaging Records Management properties dialog box of a mailbox is shown in Figure 8-4.

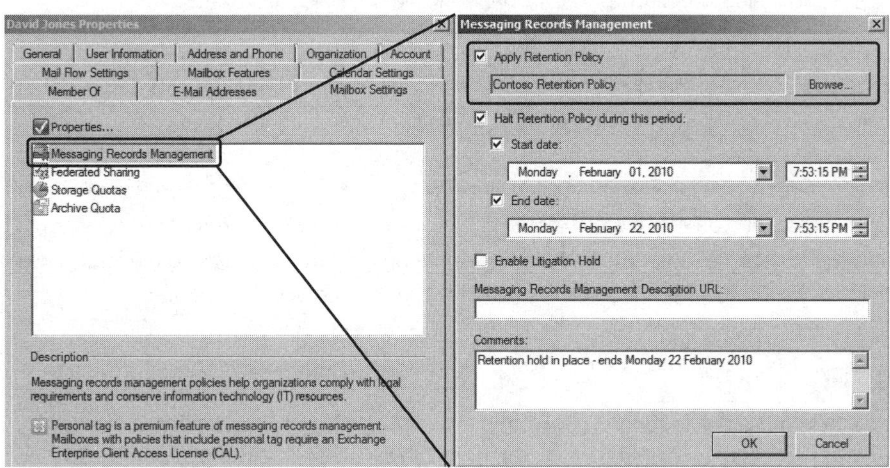

FIGURE 8-4 Applying a retention policy to a mailbox

Migrating from Managed Folders to Retention Policies

Migrating from managed folders to retention tags and retention policies is essentially a three-step process:

1. Create retention tags based on the existing managed folders and their managed content settings.

2. Create a retention policy and link the retention tags created in Step 1 to this policy.
3. Apply the retention policy to mailboxes.

Rather than creating a retention tag and manually defining retention settings to match the managed folder and managed content settings to be replaced, you can migrate the functionality of a particular managed folder to a retention policy tag as the tag is created. A retention policy tag can be created from an existing managed folder using the *New-RetentionPolicyTag* cmdlet with the *ManagedFolderToUpgrade* parameter, or by using the Port From Managed Folder To Tag Wizard in Exchange Server 2010 SP1. This wizard is shown in Figure 8-5.

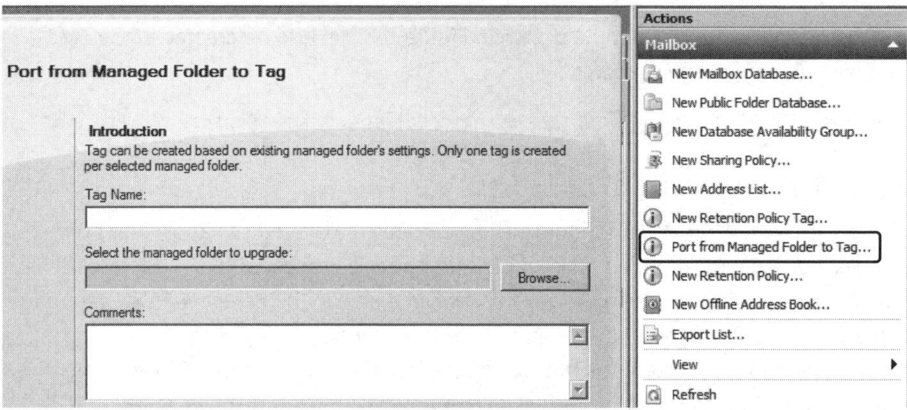

FIGURE 8-5 The Exchange Server 2010 SP1 Port From Managed Folder To Tag Wizard

> ***NOTE*** **If you create a retention tag by porting an existing managed folder with EMC or EMS, the tag created is automatically applied to the corresponding managed folder.**

Creating retention policies was covered in detail in the "Creating a Retention Policy" section of this chapter; you can create retention policies using the *New-RetentionPolicy* cmdlet or by using the Exchange Server 2010 SP1 EMC. Applying a retention policy to mailboxes was covered in the "Applying a Retention Policy to Mailboxes" section of this chapter.

Retention Hold

A mailbox can be placed on retention hold when the user is absent for an extended period of time with no access to e-mail; this retention hold can be indefinite, or have scheduled start and stop dates and times. This temporarily suspends retention policy processing for that mailbox, so that messages are not deleted or moved to the user's personal archive before he has an opportunity to review them on his return. A retention comment can also be configured; this comment can inform the user about the retention hold, including when the hold is scheduled to start and end. Retention comments are displayed in supported Outlook clients (Outlook 2010 and later), and can be localized so that the user sees the comment in his preferred language. Retention comments are also used for litigation hold, as discussed in the "Litigation Hold" section of this chapter, and are displayed in the Outlook 2010 Backstage view as shown in Figure 8-13.

A retention hold can be configured on a mailbox via the Exchange Control Panel or the EMC. In the EMC, they are configured by accessing the Properties dialog box for the mailbox and then accessing the Messaging Records Management properties from the Mailbox Settings tab as shown in Figure 8-6.

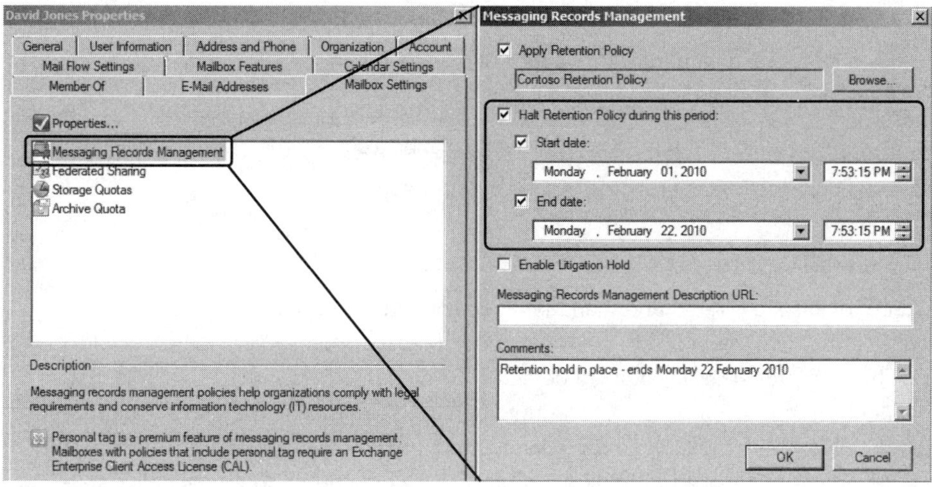

FIGURE 8-6 Configuring a retention hold via the EMC

Managed Folders

Although they are de-emphasized in Exchange Server 2010, Managed Folders are another technology that provides MRM; it is recommended that you migrate any existing Managed Folders to retention policies, and that you deploy retention policies for new MRM implementations.

Managed Folders are composed of the following components:

- Managed folders (default and custom)
- Managed content settings
- Managed folder mailbox policies
- Managed Folder Assistant

Managed Folders Requirements

A mailbox must reside on an Exchange Server 2010 or Exchange Server 2007 computer to be able to apply a managed folder mailbox policy to it. Mailboxes with a managed folder mailbox policy applied to them can be accessed via Outlook 2010, Outlook 2007, Outlook 2003 SP2, Exchange Server 2010 Outlook Web App, and Exchange Server 2007 Outlook Web Access; versions of Outlook older than Outlook 2003 SP2 are not supported. Outlook 2003 SP2 clients will not have access to all the features that are available to Outlook 2007 or higher clients, although they can access the mailbox. For example, they do not see any managed folder comments that have been configured by the administrator.

Deploying Managed Folders

With a defined corporate e-mail policy to use as a framework, your managed folders can be planned and deployed. The following steps are involved in deploying managed folders:

1. Create managed folders.
2. Create managed content settings for the managed folders.
3. Define managed folder mailbox policies.
4. Apply managed folder mailbox policies to mailboxes.
5. Configure the Managed Folder Assistant (optional).

CREATING MANAGED FOLDERS

Managed folders are created and then managed content settings are applied to them, as required to satisfy your corporate e-mail policy. Managed folders are Active Directory objects holding properties for defined default and custom folders within a mailbox that the content settings are applied to. Custom folders are presented in the user's mailbox in a discrete folder hierarchy under a top-level folder named Managed Folders. An example of a requirement that managed folders can satisfy is if your corporate e-mail policy states that messages pertaining to client projects are retained for three years, whereas messages containing privacy data as defined by legislation are retained for 30 days. To satisfy this type of requirement, you can create two managed custom folders with defined retention periods of 3 years and 30 days respectively. Users then file the appropriate messages in each custom folder, and the Managed Folder Assistant applies the defined retention settings to the messages in those folders.

Default folders are folders created in a user's mailbox by default with or without MRM implemented. These folders include the Inbox, Sent Items, and Deleted Items folders. Within managed folders, a managed default folder named One-Year Retention of (for example) type Inbox can be created and managed content settings applied to it. When this managed folder is included in a policy and assigned to a user, the user's Inbox folder is subjected to the retention settings defined for that managed default folder.

> ***NOTE*** **Managed default folders are always displayed in the user's mailbox with the standard default name. For instance, in the example outlined earlier, because the folder is of the Inbox type, users with the One-Year Retention folder assigned to them would see the folder in their mailbox as Inbox; the One-Year Retention name assigned to the folder when it was created is not visible to them.**
>
> **In addition, you can assign only one managed default folder of any particular type, such as Inbox, to a managed folder mailbox policy, and only one managed folder mailbox policy can be assigned per mailbox.**

Managed custom folders are created solely for MRM purposes, and appear in a mailbox's folder list separately from default folders, under a special default folder named Managed Folder. Created and assigned to users or groups of users through the use of a managed folder mailbox policy, these folders display in Outlook 2007 or higher with a special folder icon, as shown in Figure 8-7. The managed folders are displayed similarly in Exchange Server 2010 Outlook Web App.

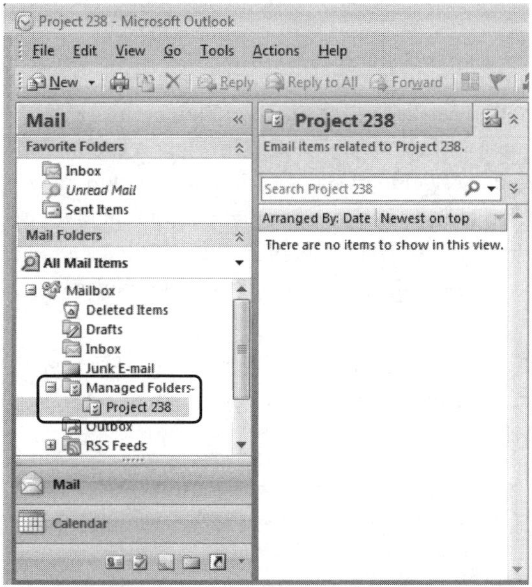

FIGURE 8-7 A managed custom folder in Outlook 2007

To create a managed custom folder named Contains Privacy Information using the EMS, use the following:

```
New-ManagedFolder -Name 'Privacy Act' -FolderName 'Contains Privacy Information'
-StorageQuota 'unlimited' -Comment 'Email content containing privacy information; to be
retained for 90 days'
```

MANAGED CONTENT SETTINGS

After creating managed default and custom folders, the next step in your managed folder implementation is defining managed content settings for those folders. These settings manage the life cycle of items in users' managed folders by controlling retention periods and applying actions to content when the retention period has been reached. Relevant content can also be journaled to a storage location outside the mailbox; journaling is discussed in the "Designing and Implementing Message Journaling" section of this chapter.

You can define when the retention period starts in one of two ways:

- When delivered for messages or the end date for calendar and recurring tasks
- When an item is moved to the folder

In addition, the following actions can be defined to occur at the end of the retention period:

- Move to the Deleted Items folder
- Move to a managed custom folder
- Delete and allow recovery
- Permanently delete
- Mark as past retention limit

Managed content settings can also be configured to journal content placed in the managed folder to another location; this location can be any destination that has an SMTP e-mail address, including a mail contact or another Exchange mailbox. Text labels can be assigned to messages as well to facilitate the preservation of classification information; they can also enable automated sorting of journaled messages by the recipient. A journaled item is attached as an unaltered copy to a new e-mail message: certain properties of the journaled item are assigned as properties of the e-mail message they're attached to. This enables automatic sorting and review of the content.

The following EMS example creates managed content settings for the Contains Privacy Information folder, using Retain For 90 Days as the name for the managed content settings and configuring the retention period for 90 days:

```
New-ManagedContentSettings -Name 'Retain for 90 days' -FolderName 'Contains
Privacy Information' -RetentionAction 'MoveToDeletedItems' -AddressForJournaling
$null -AgeLimitForRetention '90.00:00:00' -JournalingEnabled $false
-MessageFormatForJournaling 'UseTnef' -RetentionEnabled $true -LabelForJournaling ''
-MessageClass '*' -MoveToDestinationFolder $null -TriggerForRetention 'WhenMoved'
```

MANAGED FOLDER MAILBOX POLICIES

After managed folders have been created, and managed content settings have been defined for those folders, you can create managed folder mailbox policies and assign managed folders to them.

Managed folder mailbox policies are logical groupings of managed folders that are used for deployment and management purposes. These policies are applied to users' mailboxes; this, in a single operation, deploys all the managed folders contained in the policy to those mailboxes. You can create as many managed folder mailbox policies as required, and each policy can contain as many managed folders as necessary. Keep in mind, though, that any one mailbox can be assigned only one managed folder mailbox policy.

The following example creates a managed folder mailbox policy consisting of the Contains Privacy Information managed custom folder:

```
New-ManagedFolderMailboxPolicy -Name 'Privacy Information Compliance Policy'
-ManagedFolderLinks 'Contains Privacy Information'
```

APPLYING MANAGED FOLDER MAILBOX POLICIES TO USERS

After you have created managed folder mailbox policies and assigned managed folders to them, these policies can be assigned to users. Policies can be applied to users via the EMS, where you can script a solution that incorporates powerful selection and filtering criteria to configure users in bulk and target specified groupings of users.

The following example retrieves all users whose title equals Human Resources Analyst, then applies the Privacy Information Compliance Policy managed folder mailbox policy to their mailboxes:

```
Get-User | Where-Object {$_.RecipientType -eq "UserMailbox" -and $_.Title -eq "Human
Resources Analyst"} | Set-Mailbox -ManagedFolderMailboxPolicy "Privacy Information
Compliance Policy"
```

As with retention policies, after you have assigned managed folder mailbox policies to mailboxes, those mailboxes are then processed by the Managed Folder Assistant. The Managed Folder Assistant is discussed in detail in the "Retention Policies" section of this chapter.

Designing and Implementing Transport Rules

In Exchange Server 2010, transport rules provide the ability to apply e-mail and compliance policies to messages as they flow through your organization, providing the controlled access and information and process integrity capabilities discussed in the "Messaging Compliance Overview" section of this chapter. Transport rules are configured and managed on an organizational level as a component of the Hub Transport configuration.

Transport rules are composed of the following components:

- **Conditions** Conditions consist of one or more predicates that define which portions of a message to examine, and what criteria to use for identifying messages that the rule is applied to. For example, the To: field could contain David Jones, or the subject or body of the message could contain the phrase "Top Secret". Most predicates require a comparison operator (equals, does not equal, contains) and a value to look for. Think of the conditions as the *if* portion of an *if-then* statement. Exchange Server 2010 includes new predicates that were not available in Exchange Server 2007, such as messages sent to partners, if the sender and recipient's specified Active Directory attribute matches a defined value, or if a message is not marked with a message classification. If no conditions are defined, the rule will apply to *all* messages unless exceptions are defined.
- **Exceptions** Exceptions are composed of the same components as conditions except that they identify messages that transport rules should *not* be applied to. Exceptions override conditions; a message identified by an exception will not have the rule applied to it, even if it meets all of the conditions. Exceptions are optional; they are included only if necessary.

- **Actions** Actions specify what to do with messages that meet the defined conditions and do not match any exceptions in the rule. A large number of actions are available for transport rules. Exchange Server 2010 includes new actions in addition to those offered in Exchange Server 2007; for example, adding the sender's manager as a specific recipient type, forwarding the message to a specified address or manager for moderation, or applying rights management protection with an AD RMS template. AD RMS integration will be covered in more detail in the "Designing and Implementing AD RMS Integration" section of this chapter. Actions are mandatory; you cannot create a rule without defining at least one action, although you can define multiple actions in the same rule.

Rules Agents

Rules agents are responsible for applying transport rules on Hub Transport and Edge Transport servers. The Transport Rules agent applies rules on the Hub Transport, whereas the Edge Rules agent performs this task on the Edge Transport server. Although these two agents are comparable in function, they are each unique in the predicates and actions available to them, the priority of the rule agent relative to other transport agents, and what transport event the agent fires on.

Transport Rules Agent

The Transport Rules agent runs on the Hub Transport server, and fires on the *OnRoutedMessage* transport event. Hub Transport rules are created and managed at the Exchange organization level, stored in Active Directory, and processed on all Hub Transport servers in the organization. This provides Exchange Server 2010 with the ability to consistently apply a uniform set of rules across the entire organization, but because the rules are stored in Active Directory, the availability of the rules across the organization is dependent on Active Directory replication.

Edge Rules Agent

Transport rules are processed on the Edge Transport server by the Edge Rules agent, which fires on the *EndOfData* transport event. The primary purpose of the Edge Transport role is to act as an e-mail gateway between your internal Exchange organization and the Internet, so it is an ideal place to apply antivirus and anti-spam checks and policy restrictions to inbound messages, so that unwanted messages can be filtered out without consuming resources on your internal Exchange servers.

> ***NOTE*** **Edge Transport rules can also be used to process outbound Internet e-mail for policy and compliance purposes. However, you cannot apply disclaimers to outbound Internet e-mail with Edge Transport rules; this must be done with Hub Transport rules.**

Rules created on Edge Transport servers are stored in the Active Directory Lightweight Directory Services (AD LDS) database, formerly known as Active Directory Application Mode (ADAM), on each Edge Transport server. Rules configured on one Edge Transport server are not replicated to other Edge Transport servers, regardless of whether EdgeSync is configured. This means that if you want the same rules applied on multiple Edge Transport servers, they must be configured on each Edge Transport server, although you can use the *Export-TransportRuleCollection* and *Import-TransportRuleCollection* cmdlets to automate the process. This requirement does provide you with the flexibility to configure unique rules on each Edge Transport server, however, which can be desirable in many cases—for example, to configure unique rules based on the Edge Transport server's address or type of e-mail traffic that it handles.

Creating Transport Rules

Transport rules can be created via the EMC, the ECP, or by using the *New-TransportRule* cmdlet in the EMS. One significant difference in Exchange Server 2010 is that, unlike with Exchange Server 2007, you no longer need to instantiate predicates and actions with the *Get-TransportRulePredicate* and *Get-TransportRuleAction* cmdlets for use in the *New-TransportRule* cmdlet. The *Get-TransportRulePredicate* and *Get-TransportRuleAction* cmdlets now only list the predicates and actions available for use on the Hub Transport or Edge Transport servers that you run the cmdlet on. In Exchange Server 2010, all the predicates and actions are available as parameters for the *New-TransportRule* and *Set-TransportRule* cmdlets, providing the means for you to create or modify a transport rule with a single command.

The predicates available on Exchange Server 2010 Hub Transport servers are outlined in Table 8-1; the variables that can be configured for each predicate are indicated in italics. These predicates are listed by their display names as they appear in the New Transport Rule or Edit Transport Rule wizards in the Exchange Server 2010 EMC.

TABLE 8-1 Hub Transport Rule Predicates

From *people*	When any of the recipients in the To field is a member of *distribution list*	With a spam confidence level (SCL) rating that is greater than or equal to *limit*
From a member of *distribution list*	When any of the recipients in the Cc field is *people*	When the size of any attachment is greater than or equal to *limit*
From users that are *inside* or *outside* the organization	When any of the recipients in the Cc field is member of *distribution list*	Marked with *importance*
Sent to *people*	When any of the recipients in the To or Cc fields is *people*	If the message is *Message Type*

Sent to a member of *distribution list*	When any of the recipients in the To or Cc fields is a member of *distribution list*	When the sender's properties contain *specific words*
Sent to users that are *inside* or *outside* the organization, or *partners*	Marked with *classification*	When the sender's properties match *text patterns*
Between members of *distribution list* and *distribution list*	When the Subject field contains *specific words*	Not marked with a message classification
When the manager of any *sender* is *people*	When the Subject field or message body contains *specific words*	When an attachment's content contains *words*
When the sender is the *manager* of a recipient	When the message header contains *specific words*	When an attachment's content matches *text patterns*
If the sender and recipient's Active Directory Attributes are *attribute value*	When the From address contains *specific words*	When an attachment is unsupported
When a recipient's address contains *specific words*	When the Subject field contains *text patterns*	
When a recipient's address contains *text patterns*	When the Subject field or the message body contains *text patterns*	
When a recipient's properties contains *specific words*	When the message header matches *text patterns*	
When a recipient's properties contains *text patterns*	When the From address matches *text patterns*	
When any of the recipients in the To field is *people*	When any attachment file name matches *text patterns*	

The predicates listed in Table 8-1 also have equivalent exceptions that can be configured in the New Transport Rule and Edit Transport Rule wizards, as well as with the *New-TransportRule* and *Set-TransportRule* cmdlets. Exceptions are expressed as the predicate preceded with *ExceptIf*. For example, the exception parameter for the *FromMemberOf* predicate is called *ExceptIfFromMemberOf*. Because the same predicate object contains the logic for use in a transport rule condition and exception, exceptions aren't shown separately when you use the *Get-TransportRulePredicate* cmdlet to list predicates.

The predicates available on Exchange Server 2010 Edge Transport servers are listed in Table 8-2. The available predicates for Edge Transport rules are for the most part a subset of the Hub Transport rule predicates, along with a couple of predicates that are unique to the Edge Transport.

TABLE 8-2 Edge Transport Rule Predicates

PREDICATE	AVAILABLE ON HUB TRANSPORT?
When the Subject field contains *specific words*	Yes
When the Subject field or message body contains *specific words*	Yes
When the message header contains *specific words*	Yes
When the From address contains *specific words*	Yes
When any recipient address contains *specific words*	No
When the Subject field matches *text patterns*	Yes
When the Subject field or the message body matches *text patterns*	Yes
When the message header matches *text patterns*	Yes
When the From address matches *text patterns*	Yes
When any recipient address matches *text patterns*	No
With an SCL rating that is greater than or equal to *limit*	Yes
When the size of any attachment is greater than or equal to *limit*	Yes
From users that are *inside* or *outsid*e the organization	Yes

NOTE As discussed in Chapter 14, "Upgrading from Exchange Server 2003 and Exchange Server 2007," Exchange Server 2010 supports many new transport rule predicates and actions, and has changes to some predicates and actions from Exchange Server 2007. Because Exchange Server 2007 Hub Transport servers can't process these new and changed predicates and actions, transport rules are stored in a different format and location in Active Directory. Thus, any Exchange Server 2010–specific transport rules are only processed when the message traverses an Exchange Server 2010 Hub Transport server.

In a coexistence environment with Exchange Server 2007 and Exchange Server 2010, any changes to transport rules in Exchange Server 2007 or Exchange Server 2010 must be applied to the other version as well. The methods and cmdlets to do this are discussed in detail in Chapter 14.

Transport Rule Examples

In this section, we'll discuss a few examples of transport rules used to meet compliance requirements.

DISCLAIMERS

Disclaimers are typically used to provide warnings about unknown or unverified e-mail senders or legal information, or for other reasons as determined by an organization. In Exchange Server 2010, you now have the ability to use HTML for disclaimers to e-mail messages that are processed on Hub Transport servers; this is in addition to the ability to apply plain-text disclaimers, which was introduced in Exchange Server 2007. HTML tags can also include images by using IMG tags; note, however, that these images are not embedded in the message and so should be located on a Web server that is accessible to the e-mail's recipients. In addition, you should remember that Exchange Server 2007 Outlook Web Access, Outlook Web App, and Outlook 2007 and later block external Web content (including images) by default, so it is recommended to test your disclaimers to verify that the recipient's experience is what you are expecting.

With Exchange Server 2010, Active Directory attributes can also be added to disclaimers (*DisplayName*, *FirstName*, *LastName*, *Department*, and *Company*). The attribute names are replaced by the values from the sender's Active Directory user account when the disclaimer rule is triggered. The attribute is enclosed in two percent signs (%%) to use it in the disclaimer; for example, to use the *DisplayName* attribute you include **%%DisplayName%%**.

Disclaimers can be appended or prepended to messages. When a disclaimer is appended (the default), it is inserted at the bottom of the message thread; Exchange Server 2010 doesn't check whether disclaimers have been added previously. A prepended disclaimer is inserted before the text of the newest message in the thread.

Disclaimers are configured as actions in Hub Transport rules; as mentioned in the "Edge Rules Agent" section of this chapter, disclaimers cannot be configured using Edge Transport rules.

The following EMS example creates a transport rule that applies a disclaimer using HTML formatting to all messages sent to recipients outside of the organization:

```
New-TransportRule -Name ExternalDisclaimer -Enabled $true -SentToScope
'NotInOrganization' -ApplyHtmlDisclaimerLocation 'Append' -ApplyHtmlDisclaimerText
"<h3>Disclaimer Title</h3><p>This is the disclaimer text.</p>"
-ApplyHtmlDisclaimerFallbackAction Wrap
```

ETHICAL WALLS

As discussed in the "Messaging Compliance Overview" section of this chapter, ethical walls are used to block communication between specified departments or sections of your organization. Although an ethical wall can encompass numerous methods of communication, including telephone, instant messaging, and postal mail, in the context of e-mail an ethical wall is implemented using transport rules in Exchange Server 2010. In a typical configuration, when a message is sent that matches the conditions defined in the transport rule, Exchange Server 2010 rejects the message and returns a non-delivery report (NDR) to the sender informing them that the message was rejected due to policy restrictions. This NDR can be modified by customizing the delivery status notification (DSN) code used to provide the sender with specific instructions or hypertext links to inform the sender of the policies or regulations that prevented delivery.

> ***IMPORTANT*** **The primary purpose of an ethical wall is to prevent communication, so when implementing the transport rule for the ethical wall it is crucial to properly define the scope (conditions and exceptions) of the rule. An improperly defined scope can potentially block all messages sent to or from all recipients or senders in your organization.**

The following example shows how to create a transport rule that implements an ethical wall using the EMC. This example specifies a new, custom DSN code in the *RejectMessageEnhancedStatusCode* property:

```
New-TransportRule "Sample Ethical Wall" -Enabled $true -BetweenMemberOf1 BrokerageGroup@
contoso.com -BetweenMemberOf2 SalesGroup@contoso.com -ExceptIfFromMemberOf
ExecutivesGroup@contoso.com -RejectMessageReasonText "Sample Rejection Message"
-RejectionMessageEnhancedStatusCode '5.7.228'
```

This example then creates the custom DSN code and its specified text that is returned to the sender with the DSN code:

```
New-SystemMessage -DsnCode 5.7.228 -Internal $true -Language En -Text "A message was
sent that violates company policy #123. For more information, please contact the
Compliance department."
```

Designing and Implementing Message Journaling

Archiving refers to reducing the amount of data in a user's primary mailbox by moving it to different storage (another mailbox, in the case of Exchange Server 2010 archiving); *journaling* is the ability to record all e-mail communications in an organization for archival purposes to meet with compliance and regulatory requirements. We'll discuss archiving in detail in the "Designing and Implementing Archiving" section of this chapter.

Although a specific regulation may not specifically require journaling, journaling may achieve compliance under certain regulations. One example is corporate officers in a financial sector that may be held liable for the claims made to their customers by their employees. To verify that the claims are accurate, a system can be set up where a portion of employee-to-client communications is regularly reviewed by managers on a quarterly basis to verify compliance and approve employees' conduct. When every manager has formally reported approval to the corporate officer, the corporate officer can, on behalf of the company, report compliance to the regulating body. E-mail messages are likely one type of the employee-to-client communications reviewed by managers; in this case, all e-mail messages sent by client-facing employees can be collected by journaling. Other client communications that may also be subject to regulation, and thus monitored, include faxes and telephone conversations; journaling all classes of data in an enterprise is an ability that is a valuable functionality of the IT architecture.

Journaling can be a requirement in particular regions or industries because of governmental regulations such as the European Union Data Protection Directive (EUDPD), Sarbanes-Oxley Act of 2002 (SOX), and the Securities and Exchange Commission Rule 17a-4 (SEC Rule 17a-4). Because these are regulatory or business issues, journaling requirements for your Exchange Server 2010 environment are best determined through consultation with your organization's compliance and security staff.

Journaling is implemented in Exchange Server 2010 via the Journaling agent and journal rules, and the output from the Journaling agent is journal reports—one report for each message that is journaled; this output is stored in designated journaling mailboxes (one mailbox per journal rule). We will discuss each of these concepts in detail in the following sections of this chapter.

> ***IMPORTANT*** **Journaling mailboxes can contain sensitive data, so access to these mailboxes should be tightly controlled and monitored.**

Journaling Agent

The Journaling agent is a transport agent focused on compliance; it processes messages on Hub Transport servers. The Journaling agent fires on the *OnSubmittedMessage* and *OnRoutedMessage* transport events. The Exchange Server 2010 Journaling agent is a built-in agent; agents of this type are not included in the output of the *Get-TransportAgent* cmdlet.

The Journaling agent in Exchange Server 2010 provides two types of journaling:

- **Standard journaling** Standard journaling is configured on a per-mailbox database basis and allows the journaling of all messages sent to and from mailboxes located on the targeted mailbox database. You must configure journaling on all mailbox databases in the organization to journal all messages in the organization.
- **Premium journaling** More granular journaling is accomplished by using premium journaling with journal rules. You can configure journal rules to match your organization's needs by journaling individual recipients or members of distribution groups instead of journaling all mailboxes residing on a mailbox database. An Exchange Enterprise client access license (CAL) is required to use premium journaling.

Both types of journaling store their configuration information in Active Directory where it is read by the Journaling agent and applied to the appropriate database in the case of standard journaling, or recipient in the case of premium journaling. The journaling rules used with premium journaling are also stored in Active Directory and accessed by the Journaling agent from there.

Standard journaling is implemented on a mailbox database using the *Set-MailboxDatabase* cmdlet and specifying the journaling mailbox with the *JournalRecipient* parameter; the journaling mailbox is the mailbox used to store the journal reports generated by the Journaling agent. Standard journaling can also be configured with the EMC on the properties of the mailbox database, as shown in Figure 8-8.

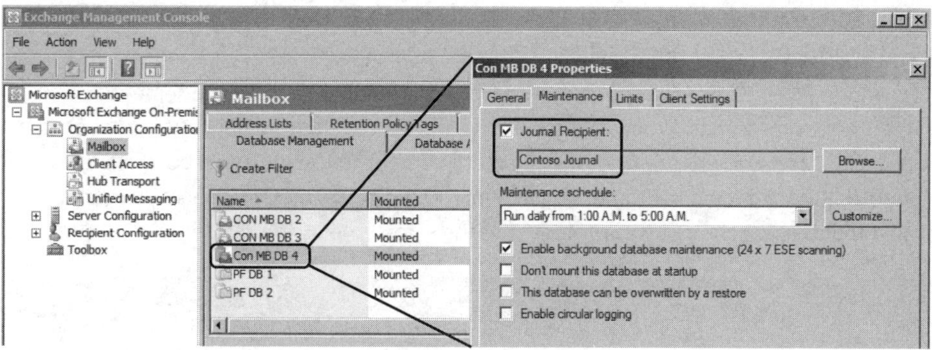

FIGURE 8-8 Implementing standard journaling on a mailbox database

Premium journaling is implemented with journal rules on an organizational level as a component of the Hub Transport configuration, similar to transport rules. You can start the New Journal Rule Wizard from the Actions pane of the Hub Transport organization configuration, as shown in Figure 8-9. Exchange Server 2010 SP1 also introduced the ability to create journal rules from the ECP.

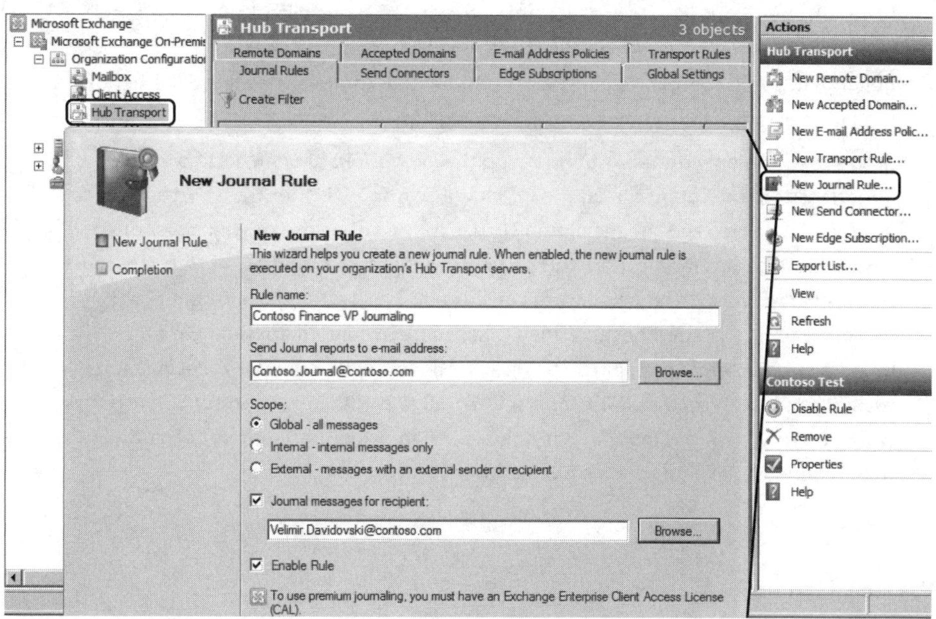

FIGURE 8-9 Creating a journal rule

Journal Reports

The output generated by both standard and premium journaling is a journal report; this is the message generated by the Journaling agent when submitting a message to the journaling mailbox. The original message matching the journal rule is attached unaltered to the journal report. Information from the original message such as the sender e-mail address, message subject, message-ID, and recipient e-mail addresses is included in the body of the journal report. This is the only journaling technique supported in Exchange Server 2007 and Exchange Server 2010, and is referred to as *envelope journaling*.

Exchange Server 2010 also supports journaling Information Rights Management (IRM)–protected messages. When IRM support is configured, Journal Report Decryption can include a clear-text copy of the message as an attachment to the journal report, along with the original IRM-protected message. Any IRM-protected attachments are also decrypted, provided that the attachment was protected at the same time as the message.

NOTES FROM THE FIELD

Journaling and Distribution Lists

Thierry Demorre
Senior Director, Avanade, USA

Exchange Server 2010 Hub Transport servers have a default value for the distribution list chipping size (how many recipients are processed when expanding the DL to start sending messages as soon as possible) of 1,000. So if a DL has 1,001 members, Exchange will send two messages, one with 1,000 recipients and one with 1 recipient, which will translate into two journal reports being generated. Some companies consider this to be non-compliant because neither of the two messages accurately captures the envelope recipients.

In this case, the only option is to bump up the *ExpansionSizeLimit* setting in the edgetransport.exe.config file on the Exchange Server 2010 Hub Transport servers to a value that will exceed the maximum DL size in the enterprise or whichever one the legal department is monitoring; this setting should be changed on all Hub Transport servers in the environment to ensure consistency. This setting has no significant performance implication because the DL has to be expanded anyway; the only difference between expanding a 50,000-member DL with *ExpansionSizeLimit* set to 1,000 and with *ExpansionSizeLimit* set to 50,000 is that in the former 50 messages would be sent, whereas in the latter only 1 message would be sent but after the time required to expand the 50,000 members.

Journal Rules

The journal rules used by premium journaling are composed of three components:

- **Journal Rule Scope** The scope determines which messages are to be journaled:
  - **Internal** A journal rule with an internal scope targets messages sent and received by recipients inside the organization.
  - **External** Setting an external scope targets the journal rule on messages sent to or received from recipients outside the organization.
  - **Global** A global scope targets all messages that pass through the Hub Transport server, whether external or internal.

- **Journal Recipients** The journal recipient specifies the SMTP address of the recipient to be journaled; specifying a journal recipient causes all messages both sent to or from that recipient to be journaled.
- **Journaling Mailbox** The journaling mailbox is used to store the journal reports generated by standard or premium journaling.

> **NOTE** You can also opt to journal or to not journal messages containing voicemail messages and missed call notification messages generated by Unified Messaging. However, messages containing faxes that have been generated by a Unified Messaging server are always journaled; this is true even if you have specified to not journal voicemail and missed call notifications.

Designing and Implementing Personal Archives

Exchange Server 2010 introduces an integrated archive solution named personal archives; this solution provides an alternative to personal store (.pst) files, providing you with the means to phase out these files by importing them to the personal archive associated with the user's mailbox. Eliminating .pst files rids you of the many headaches associated with them:

- Access from file shares is not supported.
- They can be challenging to deal with during a legal or regulatory discovery request. (Searching .pst files scattered across file servers, laptops, desktops, and removable storage can be difficult if not impossible.)

A personal archive is a mailbox that can be used for alternative storage, and is optionally created when the user's primary mailbox is created, or it can be enabled on an existing mailbox. The personal archive is accessible by the user in Outlook 2010, Exchange Server 2010 OWA, or Outlook 2007 (with the appropriate updates). In addition, the personal archive is not accessible to offline clients, such as Outlook in cached mode; this may be seen as a limitation to some users who have grown accustomed to having their .pst files available on their local computer. Enabling a personal archive for an existing mailbox is shown in Figure 8-10.

> **NOTE** Exchange Server 2010 personal archives functionality requires an Enterprise CAL for each mailbox configured with a personal archive.

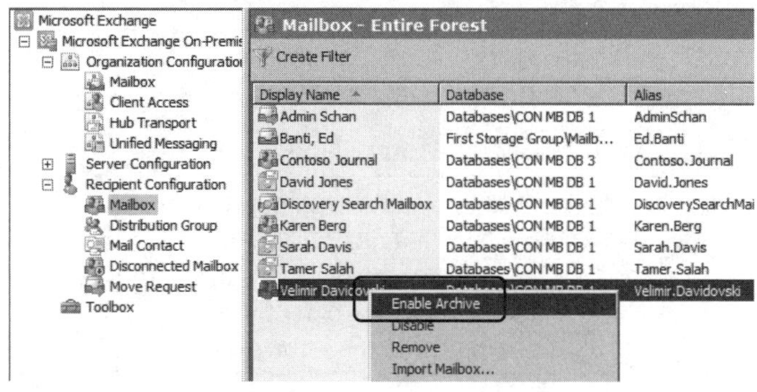

FIGURE 8-10 Enabling personal archive for an existing mailbox

> ***IMPORTANT*** **In the initial Exchange Server 2010 release, the personal archive was restricted to the same database the user's primary mailbox resided on; however, in Exchange Server 2010 SP1 the archive mailbox can be placed on any database in the organization, or in Exchange Online.**

When a new mailbox is created with the New Mailbox Wizard in the EMC, a personal archive can be created on the Archive Settings page of the wizard as shown in Figure 8-11.

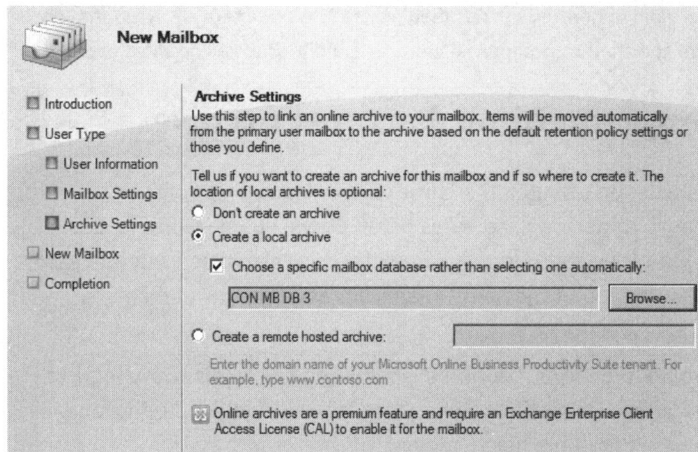

FIGURE 8-11 The Archive Settings page of the New Mailbox Wizard

> ***NOTE*** **When an archive mailbox is created, content is moved automatically from the user's primary mailbox to his archive based on the default archive policy if no retention policy is assigned to the mailbox. If a retention policy is assigned to the mailbox, that policy supersedes the default archive policy and items are moved to the archive based on the assigned retention policy. Refer to the "Retention Tags and Retention Policies" section of this chapter for details on configuring retention tags and policies.**

The default archive policy is a retention policy composed of the retention tags outlined in Table 8-3.

TABLE 8-3 Contents of the Default Archive Policy in Exchange Server 2010

RETENTION TAG NAME	TAG TYPE	DESCRIPTION
Default two-year move to archive	Default	This tag applies to all items in the mailbox that don't have a retention tag applied directly or are inherited from the folder; items older than two years are moved to the archive.

RETENTION TAG NAME	TAG TYPE	DESCRIPTION
Personal one-year move to archive	Personal	Items or folders assigned this tag are automatically moved to the archive mailbox after one year.
Personal five-year move to archive	Personal	Items or folders assigned this tag are automatically moved to the archive mailbox after five years.
Personal never move to archive	Personal	Items or folders assigned this tag are never archived automatically.

NOTE The storage quotas for personal archives are set separately from the quotas on the user's primary mailbox, and are configured for unlimited storage by default; if unlimited quotas are not suitable for your environment, the archive warning quota can be set in the Archive Quota dialog box on the Mailbox Settings tab of the user's mailbox properties in the EMC. You can modify the archive warning quota as well as the archive quota with the *Set-Mailbox* cmdlet using the *ArchiveQuota* and *ArchiveWarningQuota* switches. The archive quota sets at what point the user will no longer be able to move items to the personal archive.

The retention tags linked to the default archive policy are system tags created by Exchange Server 2010 setup, and by default are not returned in the output of the *Get-RetentionPolicyTag* cmdlet unless you specify the *IncludeSystemTags* parameter.

Multi-Mailbox Search

Multi-Mailbox Search (also known as a discovery search) in Exchange Server 2010 provides your organization with the ability to respond to legal discoveries or other internal investigations as required by facilitating discovery search across multiple mailboxes. The ability to use Multi-Mailbox Search is delegated through Role-Based Access Control (RBAC) using the management role group Discovery Management; RBAC is discussed in detail in Chapter 16, "Managing Exchange." Non-technical users who have been delegated to perform discovery searches can perform these searches through the ECP, without requiring Exchange administrative access or other elevated privileges.

Multi-Mailbox Search uses the Exchange Search content indexes, and queries are constructed using the Advance Query Syntax (AQS), which is also used by Windows Search and Instant Search in Microsoft Outlook 2007 and later, so that users delegated the Discovery Management role can create queries using syntax they're already familiar with.

A target mailbox must be specified when performing a discovery search; mailboxes of the type discovery are the only targets that can be selected when you perform a discovery search using the ECP. Exchange Server 2010 creates one discovery mailbox with the display name Discovery Search Mailbox, but others can be created as necessary. Discovery mailboxes can only be created in the EMS with the *New-Mailbox* cmdlet using the *Discovery* switch, and by default a newly created discovery mail has no mailbox access permissions assigned. In addition, by default discovery mailboxes are visible in address lists, but users can't send e-mail to them; delivery is prohibited with delivery restrictions.

Multi-Mailbox Search also relies on a system mailbox named SystemMailbox{e0dc1c29-89c3-4034-b678-e6c29d823ed9}. This mailbox (like other system mailboxes) is not visible in the EMC, nor does it appear in any address lists; the purpose of this mailbox is to host metadata for the Multi-Mailbox Search functionality.

Litigation Hold

The litigation hold functionality in Exchange Server 2010 provides the means for your organization to respond to impending litigation or internal investigations. When expectations such as these arise, all records, including e-mail, relating to the litigation or internal investigation are expected to be retained. Whereas one means of addressing this may be to configure journaling, journaling can present additional challenges to IT personnel such as database growth and performance implications (each message is sent twice). These challenges can be especially significant for impending events such as litigation because the full scope of the resultant discovery are likely not fully defined yet, which means that you may have to configure a much larger group of mailboxes for journaling than will ultimately be required for the actual discovery to ensure that you are compliant to avoid severe penalties.

Litigation hold addresses these issues by preventing items in the Recoverable Items folder from being purged permanently while the litigation hold is in place. The Recoverable Items folder replaces the dumpster in previous versions of Exchange and is covered in detail in Chapter 12, "Backup/Restore and Disaster Recovery."

In brief, though, when a user *hard deletes* an item (by pressing Shift+Delete simultaneously) or empties her Deleted Items folder, the items are placed in the Deletions subfolder of Recoverable Items; the contents of the Deletions subfolder are what is visible through the Recover Deleted Items tool in Outlook or OWA; this is the only folder within Recoverable Items whose contents are accessible by the user. When an item is deleted using the Recover Deleted Items tool in Outlook or OWA, it's moved to the Purges subfolder of Recoverable Items, and is purged from this folder the next time the Managed Folder Assistant runs; the Managed Folder Assistant is discussed in detail in the "Retention Policies" section of this chapter. When a mailbox is placed on litigation hold, items are no longer purged from the Purges subfolder. If a mailbox has been configured with a personal archive, when litigation hold is enabled the deleted content in the archive mailbox goes into the Recoverable Items folder of the archive mailbox.

A final subfolder of Recoverable Items is the Versions folder; again, this folder and its contents are not visible to the user. The Versions folder is used for litigation holds; when a mailbox is placed on litigation hold, any changes to certain properties on any items within the mailbox causes a copy of the original item to be stored in the Versions folder in a process called *copy on write*. The properties that initiate a copy on write are outlined in Table 8-4.

> ***NOTE*** **The behavior of retaining items in the Purges folder, and retaining copies of modified items, can also be attained by enabling Single Item Recovery on a mailbox. When Single Item Recovery is enabled, items are retained in the Purges folder for the duration of the deleted items retention period configured on the mailbox (or on the mailbox database, if it has not been set on the mailbox directly). When a litigation hold is configured on the mailbox, items are retained in the Purges folder for the duration of the litigation hold, regardless of the deleted items retention period set on the mailbox or database.**

TABLE 8-4 Properties That Initiate a Copy on Write

ITEM TYPE	PROPERTIES THAT INITIATE COPY ON WRITE
Messages (IPM.Note*) Posts (IPM.Post*)	■ Subject ■ Body ■ Attachments ■ Senders/Recipients ■ Sent/Received Dates
Items other than messages and posts	Any change to a visible property, except the following: ■ Item location (when an item is moved between folders) ■ Item status change (read or unread) ■ Changes to retention tag applied to an item
Items in the default folder Drafts	None (items in the Drafts folder are exempt from copy on write)

> ***IMPORTANT*** **All items in the Recoverable Items folder, including items in the Purges and Versions folders, are indexed by Exchange Search, and are discoverable using Multi-Mailbox Search, even though the Purges and Versions folders and their contents are not visible to the user.**

Placing a Mailbox on Litigation Hold

A mailbox can be placed on legal or litigation hold by users who have been assigned the Legal Hold Management role or been added to the Discovery Management RBAC role group; this is accomplished through the ECP or EMC in Exchange Server 2010 SP1 or via the EMS using the *Set-Mailbox* cmdlet with the *LitigationHoldEnabled* parameter set to *$true*; to remove a legal hold, set the *LitigationHoldEnabled* parameter to *$false*. In Exchange Server 2010 RTM, legal holds can only be configured via the EMS using the *Set-Mailbox* cmdlet.

In addition, if your organization requires that users are informed when a legal hold is enabled, the Retention Comment property can be set as well; when configured, this property provides a notification for both retention and legal holds. We covered retention holds in the "Designing and Implementing Messaging Records Management" section of this chapter.

The following example enables a legal hold on a mailbox and configures a Retention Comment to notify the user of the legal hold:

```
Set-Mailbox tamer.salah -LitigationHoldEnabled $true -RetentionComment "This mailbox
has been placed on legal hold; you will be unable to permanently delete any items until
further notice."
```

> **NOTE** It may take up to one hour for the legal hold to take effect.

Figure 8-12 shows the same litigation hold being configured via the ECP.

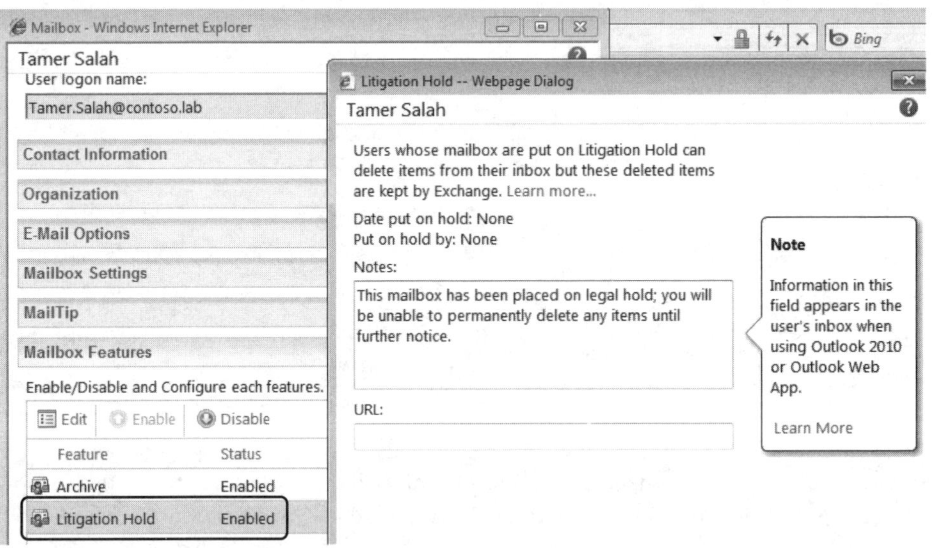

FIGURE 8-12 Configuring a litigation hold via the ECP

The Retention Comment configured with the preceding example is displayed in Outlook 2010, in the Backstage view, as shown in Figure 8-13. The Retention comment is not visible in Exchange Server 2010 Outlook Web App.

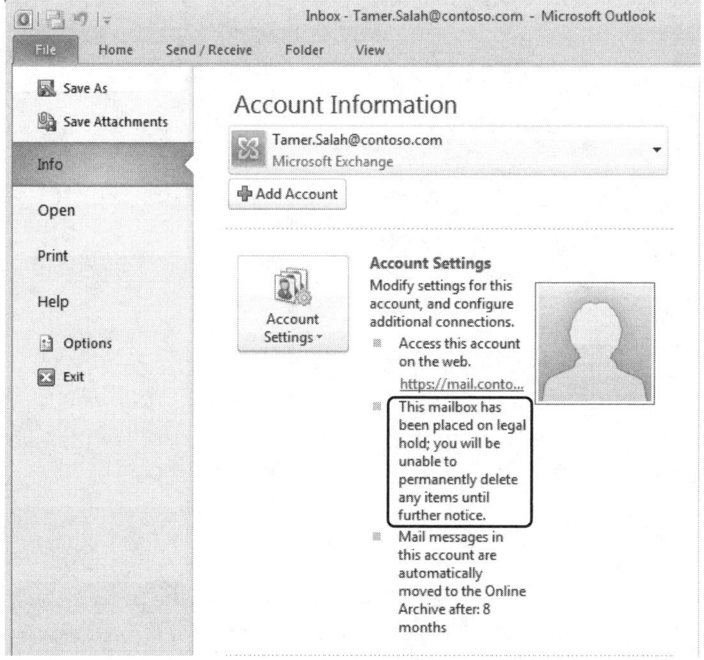

FIGURE 8-13 Retention comment for a litigation hold as seen in Outlook 2010

Performing a Multi-Mailbox Search

A Multi-Mailbox Search can be initiated through the ECP, or by using the EMS, assuming you have been added to the Discovery Management RBAC role group. If you are performing a search across all mailboxes in your organization that may return a large number of items, Exchange Server 2010 SP1 provides the option to estimate the search result size. This option is selected initially by default, as shown in Figure 8-14; it is recommended that you keep this selection, as this will provide you with an estimate of the size of the search results, thus allowing you to determine beforehand that the disk volumes holding the mailbox database and transaction logs have sufficient free space to hold the expected search results.

In addition, for searches that will return a large number of items Exchange Server 2010 SP1 also provides the Copy Only One Instance Of The Message option as shown in Figure 8-13. This will reduce the size of the results by removing any duplicate messages from the search results.

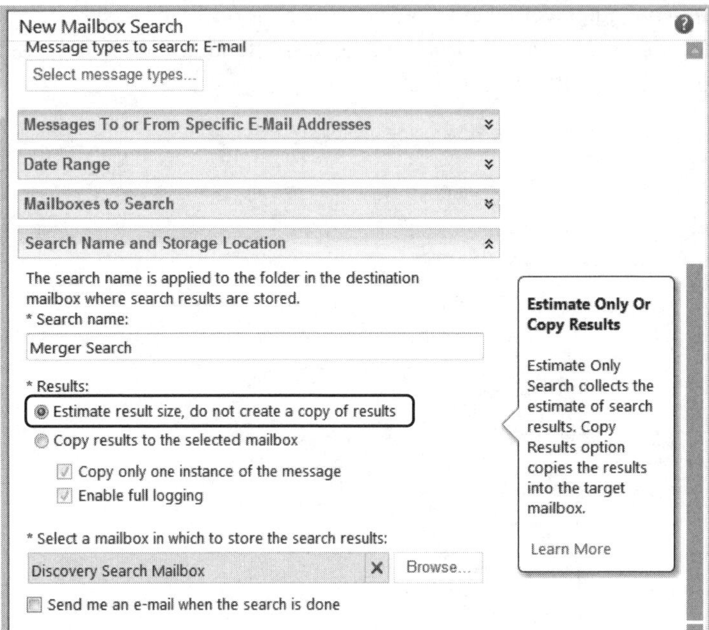

FIGURE 8-14 Creating a New Multi-Mailbox Search in the ECP

The following example creates a search using the EMS; this search covers the period 1 January 2010 to 31 December 2010, looks for e-mail items only, searches for e-mail that contains the phrases "last quarter" or "Project Contoso" or the word *merger*, and returns unsearchable items as well:

```
New-MailboxSearch -Name "Merger Search" -StartDate "1/1/2010" -EndDate "12/31/2010"
-TargetMailbox "Discovery Search Mailbox" -SearchQuery '"last quarter" OR merger OR
"Project Contoso"' -MessageTypes Email -IncludeUnsearchableItems -LogLevel Full
```

A search object is created in the Exchange Server 2010 system mailbox when you perform a search; manipulating this object allows you to start, stop, modify, and remove the search.

The following parameters are applied when performing a discovery search:

- **Keywords** Keywords and phrases can be specified to focus the search.
- **Messages To Or From Specific E-Mail Addresses** You can limit your search by specifying the senders or recipients of messages to search for. Senders or recipients can be specified by e-mail address, display name, or domain (such as @contoso.com).
- **Date Range** Searches aren't limited by date range by default, but you can specify start and end dates to narrow the search. If you define a start date but no end date, the latest results will be returned each time the search is restarted.
- **Mailboxes To Search** You can scope the search to include all mailboxes in the organization, or limit the search by specifying mailboxes to include. Distribution

groups can also be specified; this will include mailboxes that are members of the distribution group.

- **Personal Archive** Multi-Mailbox Search includes personal archives by default. If you want to exclude personal archives, you must create or modify the search using the EMS; this option is not available via the ECP.
- **Message Types** Your search can be configured to include all message types or it can be limited to selected types. You can select to search the following message types:
  - E-mail
  - Meetings
  - Tasks
  - Notes
  - Documents
  - Journal
  - Contacts
  - Instant messaging conversations
- **Attachments** Attachment types supported by Exchange Search are included in the search. Additional file types can be supported by installing search filters (also known as iFilters) for that file type on the Mailbox servers.
- **Include Items That Can't Be Searched** You can specify items that can't be indexed by Exchange Search in the search results. Reasons for unsearchable items can include file types for which no search filters are installed, filter errors, and encrypted messages such as those encrypted by S/MIME.
- **Safe List** Exchange Server 2010 setup creates a safe list of file types that contain content that can't be indexed by Exchange Search; mailbox items containing these items are not returned in the list of failed items. These file types include image files such as bitmaps and multimedia files such as .mp3 and .mpg files.
- **IRM-Protected Messages** Messages protected using AD RMS can be indexed and returned in search results if Exchange Server 2010 has been configured for AD RMS integration. AD RMS is discussed in details in the "Designing and Implementing AD RMS Integration" section of this chapter.

IMPORTANT If Exchange Search fails to index an IRM-protected message, that item is not returned in the failed items list. You can compensate for this by creating a second discovery search to return messages with .rpmsg attachments by using the query string attachment:rpmsg.

Search results are copied to the discovery mailbox specified when the search was created, in a folder with the same name as the search. Underneath this folder, subfolders are created for each searched mailbox, provided the Copy Only One Instance Of The Message option has not been selected for the search. These folders are named using the mailbox's display name and the date and time the search was created. In each mailbox folder, messages are copied to a folder that has the same name as their location in the user's mailbox. The following example of this folder structure shows a search named Merger Search that returned results in the Inbox of the primary mailbox of a user named Tamer Salah:

```
Merger Search > Tamer Salah -25/2/2010 9:57:10 PM > Primary Mailbox > Inbox
```

The search results as they appear in Outlook 2010 are shown in Figure 8-15. If the Copy Only One Instance Of The Message option was selected for the search, then all results are copied to a single folder; in this example, a single folder named Results and the date and time the search was created would be created underneath the Merger Search folder.

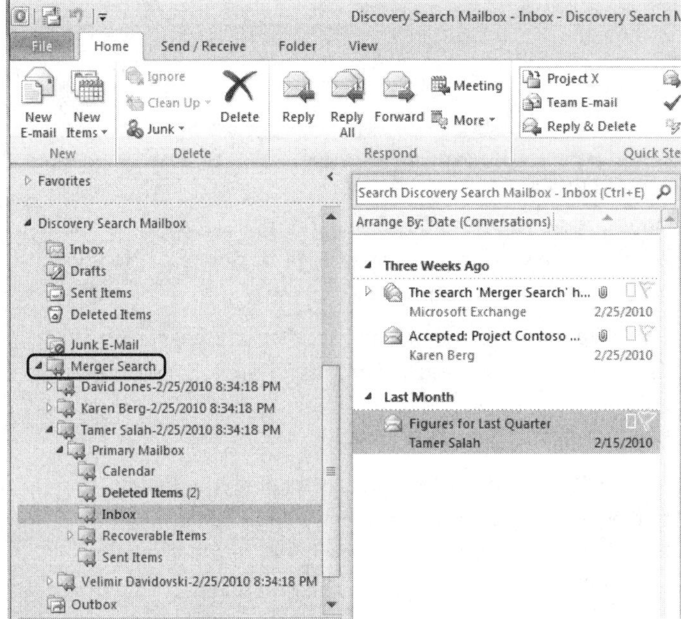

FIGURE 8-15 Search results in the discovery mailbox

Finally, if a discovery mailbox other than the default Discovery Search Mailbox is specified for the search, mailbox access permissions must be configured separately for authorized users to access the mailbox. These users can access the mailbox with either OWA or Outlook. Access to the default Discovery Search Mailbox is granted through adding the authorized user to the Discovery Management RBAC role group.

Designing and Implementing AD RMS Integration

In this section, we will discuss the integration of AD RMS with Exchange Server 2010, starting with an overview of the AD RMS technology in Windows Server 2008 and Windows Server 2008 R2.

AD RMS Overview

AD RMS is information-protection or information rights management (IRM) technology that provides organizations with the means to better safeguard sensitive information. It does this by enforcing policy through applying persistent protection to the e-mail or document, allowing the publishers of confidential e-mail messages and documents to control who can view their content. This is done using public key technology using XrML (Extensible Rights Markup Language)–based certificates.

> ***NOTE*** **AD RMS is not a replacement for your X.509 PKI implementation, even though AD RMS is based on public/private key technology; the two are complementary, and provide different solutions for different problems. In the same vein, deploying RMS does not require you to implement a PKI certificate authority (CA).**

Persistent content protection is the fundamental distinguishing feature of AD RMS that differentiates it from other encryption technologies such as S/MIME or PGP. A user who has opened an S/MIME encrypted e-mail message using his keys has complete control over the message while he has it opened; he can forward it, cut/copy/paste the contents, print the message, and so on. The persistent content protection provided by AD RMS means that as well as when the material is unopened, the rights the user has over the content are also explicitly defined and enforced while the user has the e-mail or document open. Those rights also persist with the message whether it is in an Exchange Server 2010 mailbox, in a PST file, or wherever else it may exist. The most important concept is that rights are enforced while the message is opened, meaning that the recipient cannot forward, print, cut, copy, or paste the message unless the explicit rights to perform these actions have been granted.

Users present valid Active Directory credentials to the AD RMS server and are then granted a Rights Account Certificate (RAC—their RMS credentials). The AD RMS client on the user's computer also generates a certificate for the client computer, and the user's RAC is encrypted with this machine certificate. If the user moves to a different client computer, another instance of her RAC is obtained from the RMS server, encrypted for the new client computer.

In addition to the RAC, a user is also issued a Client Licensor Certificate (CLC). The CLC enables the user to encrypt (protect) content without contacting the AD RMS server, to facilitate working offline; offline publishing is the default behavior for the RMS client.

When an RMS-protected e-mail is received by a user, that user is provided a use license issued by the RMS server which grants them rights for that e-mail. Use licenses are encrypted with the user's RAC and bound to a specific client computer with that client computer's machine certificate, similar to the user's RAC. RMS-protected content can be encrypted to a single user or to distribution groups.

The various certificates issued to users can be viewed in the user's profile, including RACs, CLCs, use licenses, and the machine certificate. Note that if the user only accesses RMS-protected e-mail via Outlook Web App, these certificates won't be stored in his local user profile and instead will be stored on the Exchange Server 2010 Client Access server. In Windows 7, these certificates are located at %userprofile%\AppData\Local\Microsoft\DRM.

The components of an AD RMS implementation are outlined in the following list; all of these components are required except for AD RMS templates. Templates are not required for the base functionality, but may be required to use some of the features of AD RMS integration with Exchange Server 2010.

- **Active Directory** AD RMS uses Active Directory to authenticate and authorize users as well as to look up group memberships for content protected to groups. This is done by referencing the user or group's SMTP addresses, including proxy addresses. To reduce the number of Active Directory lookups performed by AD RMS, group memberships are cached in SQL.
- **AD RMS cluster** An AD RMS cluster is composed of one or more AD RMS servers. The AD RMS server is a Windows Server 2008 SP2 or Windows Server 2008 R2 computer on which the AD RMS role has been installed. This role has a Web service that handles the XrML-based licensing of rights-protected information, enrollment of servers and users, certification of trusted entities such as users and computers, and administration functions. The AD RMS server role requires the Microsoft Message Queuing service, IIS, and ASP.NET; these required services are installed automatically when the AD RMS role is installed.
- **Database server** AD RMS uses a SQL Server database—either SQL Server 2000 SP4 and higher, SQL Server 2005 SP3 and higher, or SQL Server 2008 SP1 and higher. A single-server AD RMS cluster can use the Windows Internal Database feature of Windows Server 2008 or Windows Server 2008 R2 for testing purposes, but is not recommended for use in a production deployment.
- **AD RMS client** The AD RMS client software is an integrated component of Windows Vista, Windows 7, Windows Server 2008, and Windows Server 2008 R2. For Windows XP SP2, Windows Server 2003, and Windows Server 2003 R2, the SAD RMS client is a separate download and install.
- **RMS-aware applications** Applications must be AD RMS–aware to be able to use its capabilities.

  An application being AD RMS–aware means that:

  - It relies on the AD RMS client for encryption/decryption.
  - It enforces the rights defined in the publishing license for the document or e-mail.
  - It can directly or indirectly call the RMS Web services.
  - It is certified by Microsoft via an application manifest signing process.

  From a client computer perspective, Office 2003 Professional and higher or Office 2007 Professional Plus and higher are supported out of the box for protecting content. Office 2003 Standard and Office 2007 Professional can access RMS-protected content only; they cannot access RMS-protect content. Outlook e-mail messages and Microsoft Word, Microsoft PowerPoint, and Microsoft Excel files can all be RMS-protected, as can XML Paper Specification (XPS)–based documents. RMS functionality can be extended with third-party products into other applications and file formats, such as PDF, CAD/CAM file formats, and BlackBerry Enterprise Server. Exchange Server 2010 is also AD RMS–aware; in many ways, from the perspective of the AD RMS cluster, Exchange Server 2010 is simply another client.

- **AD RMS templates** AD RMS templates provide a predefined set of user/group and rights combinations that facilitate the consistent application of RMS protection to content. These templates are defined on the AD RMS server and stored in the SQL database used by AD RMS. The AD RMS templates are also exported in XML files to a location configured on the AD RMS cluster for use by AD RMS clients. These XML files are used by clients to view and select the AD RMS template to apply to the content. To be usable for end users, the AD RMS template XML files must be made available to them.

> ***NOTE*** **AD RMS templates are best used sparingly to keep the AD RMS deployment manageable and so that the list of options presented to end users is as short as possible. As an example, an organization of more than 250,000 users uses AD RMS with fewer than five templates for the entire organization.**

AD RMS Templates

Although AD RMS templates (also known as distributed rights policy templates) are optional for end users who are applying IRM permissions to documents or e-mail messages manually, they are required for Exchange Server 2010 to apply IRM protection via either transport rules or Outlook Protection rules.

Exchange Server 2010 uses AD RMS templates when applying IRM to e-mail messages. If no templates have been defined by the AD RMS administrator, the built-in Do Not Forward functionality can be used. Do Not Forward is a client-side template that grants edit, view, reply, and reply all permissions to recipients of an e-mail message. This client-side template is a built-in function of the AD RMS client, and is available to Outlook and Exchange Server 2010 as a selectable template for Exchange Server 2010 transport rules and Outlook Protection rules, independent of whether AD RMS distributed rights policy templates have been created.

The components of an AD RMS template are as follows:

- **Template Identification** The template identification defines the language or languages of the template, the template name (displayed in the Permissions menu in Outlook or Outlook Web App), and a template description (displayed to the recipient of the IRM-protected e-mail). The template name and description are configured separately for each language supported in the template.

- **User Rights** The user rights define what users or groups are granted permissions by this template and what permissions those users or groups receive. You can have multiple users or groups specified, with each entry receiving different permissions. For example, All Employees could be granted Full Control, whereas Sub-Contractors may be granted only View permissions.
- **Expiration Policy** The expiration policy dictates how long content is accessible by recipients. For example, the policy can be defined to not allow access after 31 December 2010, or to not allow access after 30 days. By default, the author of the content always has access, even after the content has expired.
- **Extended Policy** The extended policy dictates whether users can view content using a Web browser add-on, or whether clients need to obtain a new use license (contact the AD RMS cluster) every time content is consumed. Caution should be used when configuring a template to require a new use license every time content is consumed; this will increase network traffic and make the content unavailable to offline users. By default, use licenses are cached with the IRM-protected content, so the client only needs to contact the AD RMS cluster the first time content is consumed. Note that requiring a new use license every time content is consumed means that Exchange Server 2010 will be unable to pre-fetch use licenses for e-mail protected with that template.
- **Revocation Policy** Using revocation policies provides you the ability to revoke content protected using this template. This option is not typically used because it requires additional administrative overhead and requires that the published revocation list be always available to all clients when they attempt to obtain a use license for content protected with this template. If the revocation list is unavailable, clients will be unable to access content protected with this template, although users (content owners) by default always have access to content they have created.

CREATING DISTRIBUTED RIGHTS POLICY TEMPLATES IN AD RMS

For AD RMS clients—including Exchange Server 2010—to use AD RMS templates, the XML files associated with those templates must be made available to the clients. This is accomplished with the following steps:

1. Log on to a server in the AD RMS cluster with an Active Directory account that is a member of the local AD RMS Enterprise Administrators group on the server.
2. Start the Active Directory Rights Management Services management console from Administrative Tools.
3. In the Active Directory Rights Management Services management console, expand the AD RMS cluster in the left-hand pane and select Rights Policy Templates. In the Results pane, click the Change Distributed Rights Policy Templates File Location link and then select the Enable Export check box as shown in Figure 8-16. Enter the UNC path for the file share to export the template files to and then click OK.

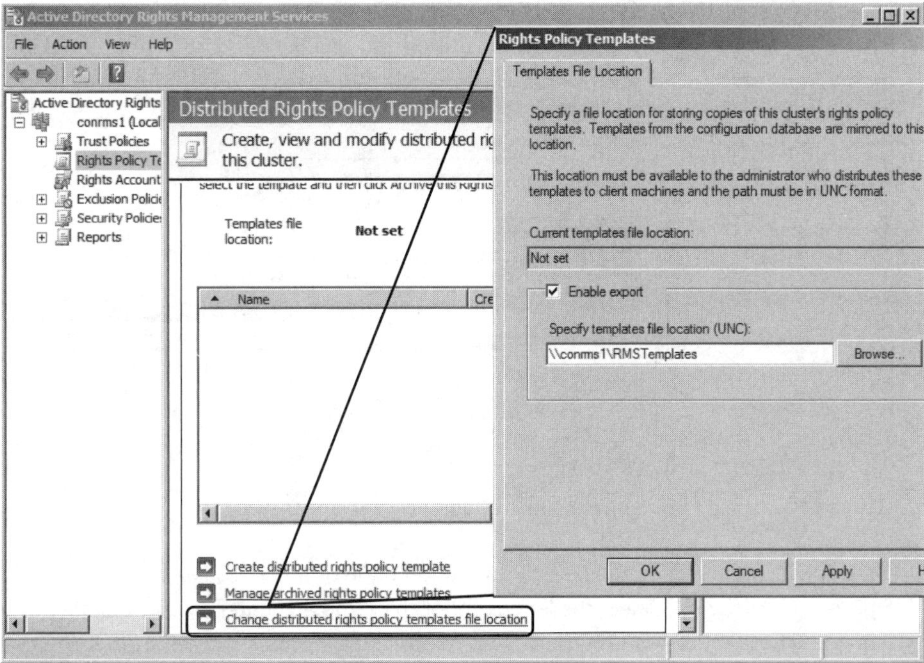

FIGURE 8-16 Configuring the templates file location for AD RMS

> ***NOTE*** **The file location specified should already exist, and the RMS service account needs to have write permission to the file share. In addition, clients accessing the template files from this location need to have at least read permission to the file share.**

When the distribution point for the template XML files has been configured, you create distributed rights policy templates using the Create Distributed Rights Policy Template Wizard in the AD RMS management console as shown in the following steps:

1. Log on to a server in the AD RMS cluster with an Active Directory account that is a member of the local AD RMS Enterprise Administrators group on the server.
2. Start the Active Directory Rights Management Services management console from Administrative Tools.
3. In the Active Directory Rights Management Services management console, expand the AD RMS cluster in the left-hand pane and select Rights Policy Templates. In the Actions pane, click Create Distributed Rights Policy Template as shown in Figure 8-17 to start the Template Creation Wizard.

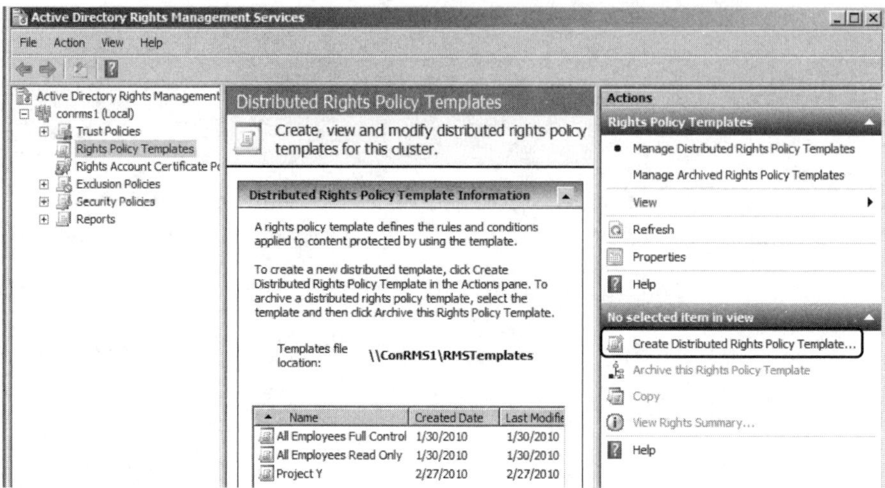

FIGURE 8-17 Starting the Create Distributed Rights Policy Template Wizard

4. On the Add Template Identification Information page of the wizard, shown in Figure 8-18, click Add. Select the language for the template, enter an appropriate name and description, and then click Add to apply the settings and return to the wizard. Click Next.

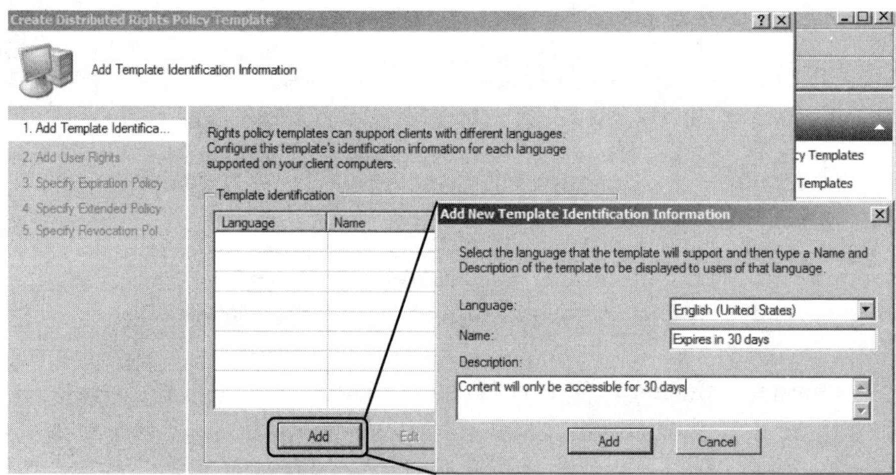

FIGURE 8-18 Setting a language and name for a template

5. On the Add User Rights page of the wizard, click Add to add the appropriate user or group to the template. Back on the Add User Rights page, highlight the added entry and select the appropriate rights for the user or group as shown in Figure 8-19. Click Next.

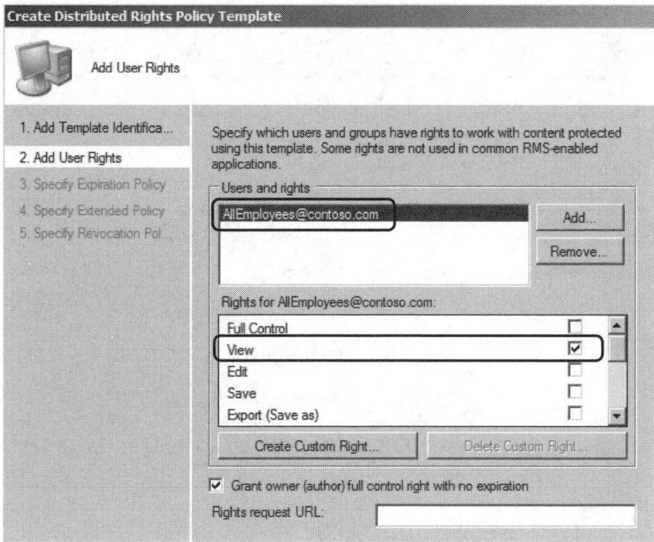

FIGURE 8-19 Adding user rights to an AD RMS template

6. On the Specify Expiration Policy page, configure the content expiration settings as appropriate and click Next.
7. On the Specify Extended Policy page of the wizard, click Next.
8. Click Finish on the Specify Revocation Policy page to complete the wizard and create the template.

AD RMS and Outlook

Some editions of Microsoft Office can create and consume (open) IRM-protected content, whereas other editions can only consume content (read-only). Table 8-5 outlines the IRM capabilities of the various Microsoft Office editions.

TABLE 8-5 Office Editions and IRM Content Protection and Consumption

CREATE AND CONSUME IRM-PROTECTED CONTENT	CONSUME IRM-PROTECTED CONTENT (READ-ONLY)
Office 2003: ■ Enterprise ■ Professional	Office 2003: ■ Standard ■ Basic ■ Small Business ■ Student and Teacher ■ Word Viewer 2003 ■ Excel Viewer 2003 ■ PowerPoint Viewer 2003

<table>
<thead>
<tr><th>CREATE AND CONSUME IRM-PROTECTED CONTENT</th><th>CONSUME IRM-PROTECTED CONTENT (READ-ONLY)</th></tr>
</thead>
<tbody>
<tr><td>Office 2007:
■ Ultimate
■ Enterprise
■ Professional Plus</td><td>Office 2007:
■ Professional
■ Small Business
■ Home and Student
■ Standard
■ Word Viewer 2007
■ Excel Viewer 2007
■ PowerPoint Viewer 2007</td></tr>
<tr><td>Office Mobile (version 6.0 and higher):
■ Outlook</td><td>Office Mobile (version 6.0 and higher):
■ Word
■ Excel
■ PowerPoint</td></tr>
<tr><td>Office 2010:
■ Professional Plus
■ Professional
■ Professional Academic</td><td>Office 2010:
■ Standard
■ Home and Business
■ Home and Student
■ Office Starter</td></tr>
</tbody>
</table>

AD RMS and Exchange Server 2010

Assuming that an AD RMS infrastructure has been established on the network, AD RMS can be integrated with Exchange Server 2010 for automatic application of IRM through transport rules and Outlook protection rules with Outlook 2010 defined by the Exchange administrator, and for manual application with Exchange Server 2010 Outlook Web App and Outlook 2003 or higher. Applying IRM to messages with Outlook uses the IRM functionality built in to Outlook, and is independent of the AD RMS integration with Exchange Server 2010. In Exchange Server 2010, if AD RMS is implemented, voicemail messages marked as Private also have IRM protection applied to them.

In Exchange Server 2007 and Exchange Server 2003 OWA, IRM functionality was limited to reading messages only; you could not create new IRM-protected messages or reply to existing ones. In addition, this functionality was limited to Internet Explorer on Windows, and the AD RMS client had to be installed on the computer if the operating system was not Windows Vista, Windows 7, or Windows Server 2008 and higher. An IRM-protected message as viewed in Exchange Server 2007 OWA is shown in Figure 8-20.

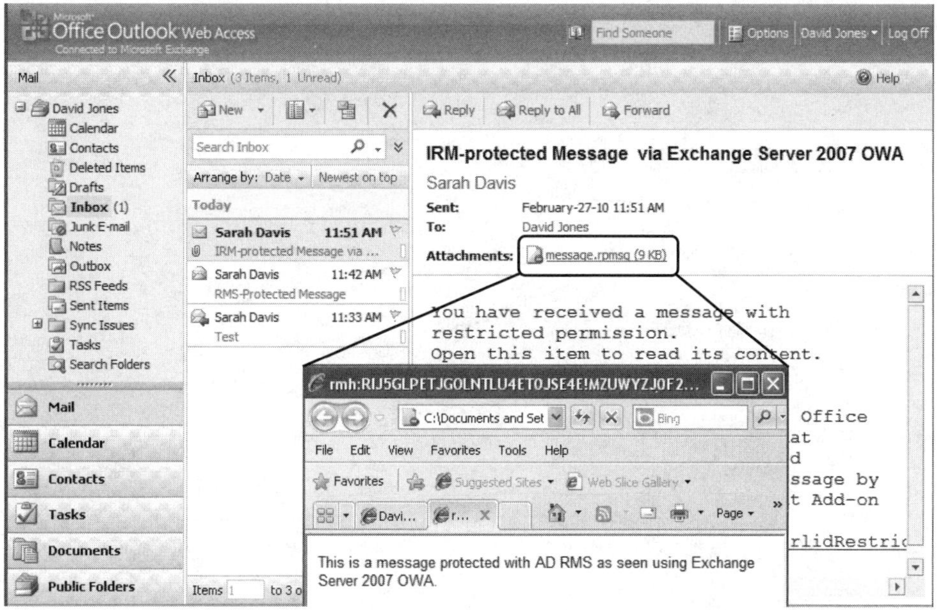

FIGURE 8-20 An IRM-protected message in Exchange Server 2007 OWA

Protecting Messages with AD RMS

For an e-mail message to be protected using Outlook 2003, Outlook 2007, or Outlook 2010, the client computer requires the AD RMS client to be installed; if the client operating system is Windows Vista, Windows 7, Windows Server 2008, or Windows Server 2008 R2, the RMS client is integrated with the operating system. The RMS client is a separate download and installation if the client operating system is Windows XP, Windows Server 2003, or Windows Server 2003 R2.

In addition, Exchange Server 2010 provides the capability for the end user to apply IRM protection to new messages manually and reply to IRM-protected messages via Outlook Web App, using Internet Explorer 7 and higher, Firefox 3 and higher, or Safari 3 and higher, running on any client operating system. Figure 8-21 shows an IRM-protected message in Exchange Server 2010 Outlook Web App; note that the message displays correctly in the Preview pane, and that the Reply and Reply All functionality is available.

Exchange Server 2010 also provides you with the ability to apply IRM protection automatically through transport rules on Exchange Server 2010 Hub Transport servers and Outlook Protection Rules. Transport rules are covered in detail in the "Designing and Implementing Transport Rules" section of this chapter.

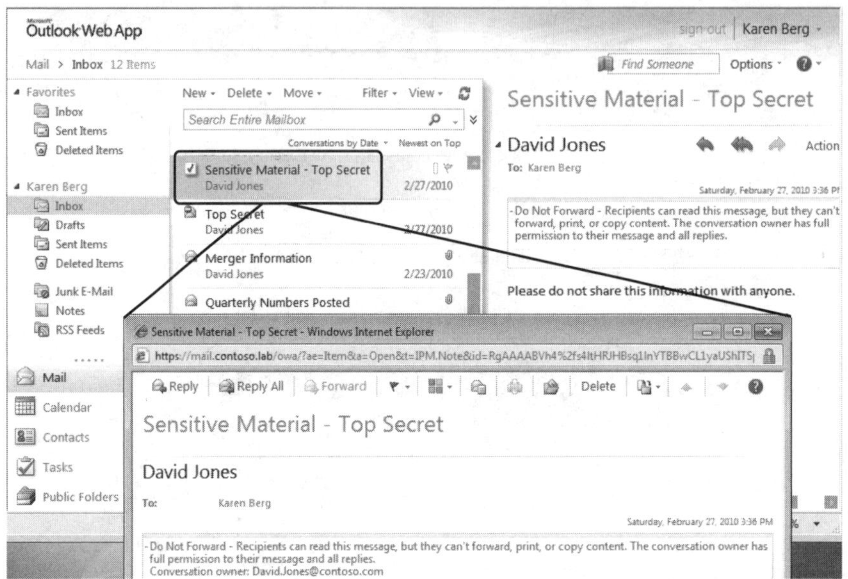

FIGURE 8-21 An IRM-protected message in Exchange Server 2010

OUTLOOK PROTECTION RULES

Although users can apply IRM protection to messages manually before they send them, they may occasionally neglect to do so for messages that should be protected. Outlook protection rules in Exchange Server 2010 can help in protecting your organization from information leakage by applying IRM protection to messages automatically when they are sent from Outlook 2010. When IRM protection is applied to a message, any attachments in supported file formats have IRM protection applied to them as well. Because Outlook protection rules are applied within Outlook, the client must be running Outlook 2010 because this is the only version of Outlook that can use Outlook protection rules.

Outlook protection rules are similar in functionality to transport rules that apply IRM protection, but with the following differences:

- With Outlook protection rules, IRM is applied in Outlook 2010, before the message leaves the user's computer. Transport rules on Hub Transport servers apply IRM when the message enters the transport pipeline.
- The IRM protection applied with Outlook protection rules is also applied to the copy of the message in the user's Sent Items folder.
- Users are aware if IRM protection is applied to a message with an Outlook protection rule; when a message is protected by a transport rule, the sender has no indication of this.
- If the Outlook protection rule allows it, users can choose to override the protection applied by the rule. If the rule is overridden by the user, an x-header named *X-MS-Outlook-Client-Rule-Overridden* is inserted in the message by Outlook 2010. By default, users can override the Outlook protection rule unless *UserCanOverride* is set to false.

NOTE Outlook protection rules can be used to automatically protect content in scenarios where you do not want to enable your Exchange servers for IRM integration; for example, when the Exchange infrastructure is hosted/managed by a third party. However, you need to be aware of the following information if Exchange does not have RMS super-user permissions:

- The Exchange server will not be able to perform content filtering or anti-virus filtering on protected content.
- Exchange Server 2010 will be unable to apply certain transport rule predicates or actions—such as when the Subject field or message body contains predicates—or being able to append disclaimers to messages.
- Protected content will not be available through OWA, will not be journaled in clear text, and will not be indexed or discoverable.

Outlook protection rules must be created using the *New-OutlookProtectionRule* cmdlet in the EMS; the following example creates a new Outlook protection rule that applies the Do Not Forward RMS template to messages sent to the Engineering distribution group:

```
New-OutlookProtectionRule -Name "Project X" -SentTo "Engineering@contoso.com"
-ApplyRightsProtectionTemplate "Do Not Forward"
```

The following predicates can be used in Outlook protection rules:

- **FromDepartment** This predicate compares the sender's department attribute in Active Directory to the department specified in the rule, and IRM protects the message if there's a match. This will cause all messages sent by (for example) the Research department with Outlook 2010 to be IRM protected.
- **SentTo** The *SentTo* predicate causes all messages sent to the specified recipient to be IRM protected. For example, you can specify that all messages sent to the Finance distribution group have IRM protection applied to them.
- **SentToScope** This predicate allows you to specify that messages sent inside or outside the organization be IRM protected. This can be combined with the *FromDepartment* predicate; for example, you can create an Outlook protection rule that directs that all messages sent by the Research department to internal recipients have IRM protection applied.

When Outlook protection rules are created, they are automatically distributed to Outlook 2010 clients with Autodiscover and the Exchange Web Services on Exchange Server 2010.

If you want to block any e-mail clients that do not use Outlook Protection Rules, you can implement blocking of all versions of Outlook except Outlook 2010 by using the *Set-CASMailbox* cmdlet with the *MAPIBlockOutlookVersions* parameter.

Consuming IRM-Protected Messages

IRM-protected messages can be accessed with Outlook 2003, Outlook 2007, or Exchange Server 2010 Outlook Web App, assuming that the recipient has been granted appropriate RMS rights to the message. To enable IRM for Outlook Web App, the Federated Delivery

Mailbox must be granted AD RMS Super Users privileges by adding it to the Super Users group defined for the AD RMS cluster; the Federated Delivery Mailbox is a system mailbox created by Exchange Server 2010 Setup. The configuration of AD RMS for Exchange Server 2010 integration, including Super Users, is covered in detail in the "Configuring AD RMS for Exchange Server 2010" section of this chapter.

Exchange Server 2010 SP1 Outlook Web App also provides the ability to access attachments that are IRM protected using Web Ready Document Viewing.

> ***IMPORTANT*** **Although Outlook Web App provides the ability to read and reply to IRM protected messages, unlike Outlook and other Office applications it can't prevent users from performing screen captures by using Print Screen.**

IRM for Outlook Web App and Exchange ActiveSync (EAS) is enabled by default, and is available after AD RMS is configured and the Federated Delivery Mailbox is granted AD RMS Super Users privileges. To disable IRM for OWA and EAS, you can use the *Set-IRMConfiguration* cmdlet with the *ClientAccessServerEnabled* parameter:

```
Set-IRMConfiguration - ClientAccessServerEnabled $false
```

Conversely, to enable IRM for OWA and EAS, set the *ClientAccessServerEnabled* parameter to true.

The *Set-IRMConfiguration* cmdlet is used to disable or enable IRM for Outlook Web App for the entire organization. If you want to enable or disable IRM for certain Outlook Web App users, you can accomplish this with Outlook Web App mailbox policies. IRM is enabled or disabled using the *Set-OwaMailboxPolicy* cmdlet with the *IRMEnabled* parameter.

Transport and Journal Report Decryption

Exchange Server 2010 can also be configured to decrypt IRM-protected content, to allow for content scanning, applying disclaimers, facilitating discovery searches, and allowing the journaling of decrypted copies of messages.

TRANSPORT DECRYPTION

Transport decryption provides the ability for you to enforce messaging policies access on IRM-protected messaging content by allowing access to the content by agents in the transport pipeline. When enabled, IRM-protected messages are decrypted by the Decryption agent; only messages protected with the AD RMS clusters in your organization can be decrypted. The Decryption agent is a built-in transport agent; built-in agents are not returned in the output of the *Get-TransportAgent* cmdlet.

Messages that have been IRM protected using transport rules do not need to be decrypted by the Decryption agent; the transport rules apply protection when fired by the *OnRoutedMessage* event, whereas the decryption agent fires on the *OnEndOfData* and *OnSubmit* transport events.

IMPORTANT After the Decryption agent decrypts the message, it is available to custom or third-party agents that are installed on the Hub Transport server so that these agents can perform their actions on the message. Although the message is always encrypted again before leaving the Hub Transport server, you need to test the behavior of these custom or third-party agents before deploying them in a production environment.

For example, if the actions of a custom or third-party agent cause a new message to be created and the original message to be attached to it, only the new message is re-encrypted; the original attached message is left unencrypted. This means that the final recipients of the new message have access to the original message in an unprotected state, and can take any action they wish with it, such as cutting, copying, printing, or forwarding it.

If an error occurs while decrypting a message, or re-encrypting it before the message is passed on, the Hub Transport server attempts the action twice more. If the third attempt fails, the Hub Transport considers this a permanent error and takes the following action:

- If the permanent error occurred during decryption and if transport decryption is set to *Mandatory*, an NDR is sent that includes the encrypted message. If transport decryption is set to *Optional*, no action is taken and the message is delivered even if decryption fails.
- An NDR is always returned if the permanent error occurs during re-encryption; this NDR never includes the decrypted message.

To configure transport decryption, the Federated Delivery Mailbox must be granted Super Users privileges for your AD RMS cluster; this is covered in detail in the "Configuring AD RMS for Exchange Server 2010" section of this chapter. When Super Users privileges have been configured, enable transport decryption using the *Set-IRMConfiguration* cmdlet. The following example enables transport decryption and rejects messages that can't be decrypted, returning an NDR to the sender:

```
Set-IRMConfiguration -TransportDecryptionSetting Mandatory
```

The acceptable values for *TransportDecryptionSetting* are *Mandatory*, *Optional*, or *Disabled*.

JOURNAL REPORT DECRYPTION

If your organization uses premium journaling, any messages protected with IRM may need to be journaled unencrypted to enable successful discovery of that content in the event of a legal or regulatory discovery request. When enabled, journal report decryption saves a clear-text copy of the IRM-protected message in the journal report along with the original IRM-protected message.

NOTE Journal report decryption only supports premium journaling, and thus requires an Exchange Enterprise client access license (CAL).

The decryption of the IRM-protected message is performed by the Journal Report Decryption agent, a built-in transport agent. This agent fires on the *OnCategorizedMessage* event while transport rules protect messages with IRM on the *OnRoutedMessage* event, before the Journal Report Decryption agent sees them. Thus, messages protected by transport rules are decrypted again by the Journal Report Decryption agent. Similar to transport decryption, the Journal Report Decryption agent only decrypts messages IRM protected by the AD RMS cluster in your organization.

Generally, only sensitive information is protected with IRM, so when you enable journal report decryption the journaling mailbox may contain sensitive information that is not encrypted. Best practice thus dictates that access to the journaling mailbox be monitored closely and access allowed only to authorized individuals.

As with transport decryption, the Federated Delivery Mailbox must be granted Super Users privileges for your AD RMS cluster before journal report decryption can be enabled; this is covered in detail in the "Configuring AD RMS for Exchange Server 2010" section of this chapter. After Super Users privileges have been configured, journal report decryption is enabled using the *Set-IRMConfiguration* cmdlet:

```
Set-IRMConfiguration -JournalReportEncryptionEnabled $true
```

Applying IRM with Transport Rules

Once IRM integration with Exchange Server 2010 has been implemented, the action Rights Protect Message With RMS Template can be selected for a transport rule, as shown in Figure 8-22. The RMS template selected can be any distributed rights policy template configured on the AD RMS cluster or the Do Not Forward client-side template. IRM protection can be selected as an action for a rule on a Hub Transport server only.

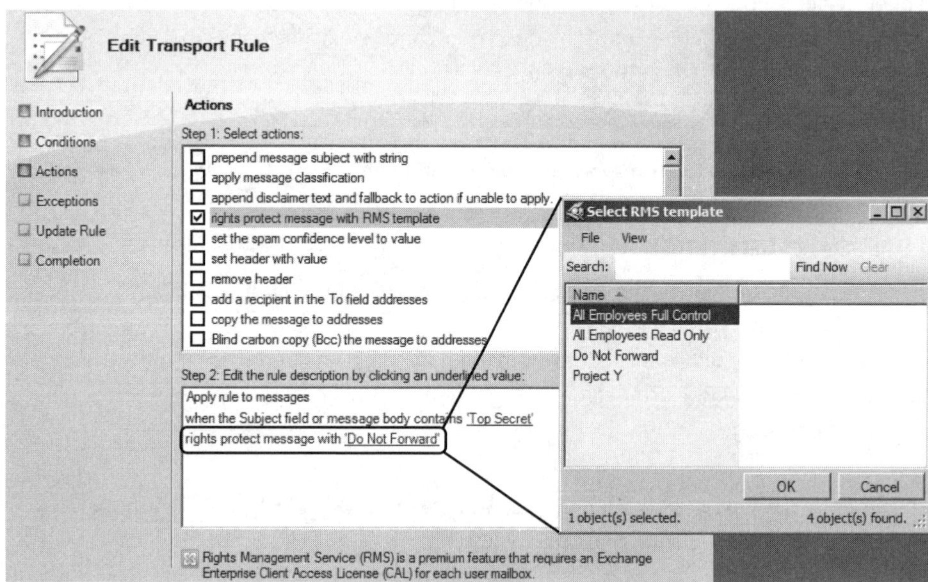

FIGURE 8-22 Applying IRM protection via a transport rule

Configuring AD RMS for Exchange Server 2010

Before you can use the IRM functionality in Exchange Server 2010, you must configure your AD RMS infrastructure. Your AD RMS cluster must be Windows Server 2008 R2 or Windows Server 2008 SP2 with hotfix 973247, and the AD RMS Service Connection Point (SCP) must be registered in Active Directory. In addition, the AD RMS server certification pipeline must be enabled and access granted to the Active Directory Exchange Servers group; this must be configured on each server in your AD RMS cluster.

Finally, to enable IRM in Outlook Web App, IRM for Exchange Search, transport decryption, or journal report decryption, the Federated Delivery Mailbox must be granted Super Users privileges in the AD RMS cluster. The Federated Delivery Mailbox is a hidden system mailbox that is created by Exchange 2010 Setup; the Active Directory account associated by this mailbox is disabled by default.

REGISTERING THE AD RMS SERVICE CONNECTION POINT

You register the SCP for AD RMS by following these steps:

1. Log on to a server in the AD RMS cluster with an Active Directory account that is a member of the local AD RMS Enterprise Administrators group on the server and a member of the Enterprise Administrators group in Active Directory.
2. Start the Active Directory Rights Management Services management console from Administrative Tools.
3. In the Active Directory Rights Management Services management console, right-click the AD RMS cluster in the left-hand pane and select Properties. Click the SCP tab in the properties dialog box, as shown in Figure 8-23, and then select the Change SCP check box. Click OK to register the SCP and click Yes in the confirmation dialog box to apply the changes and exit the Properties dialog box.

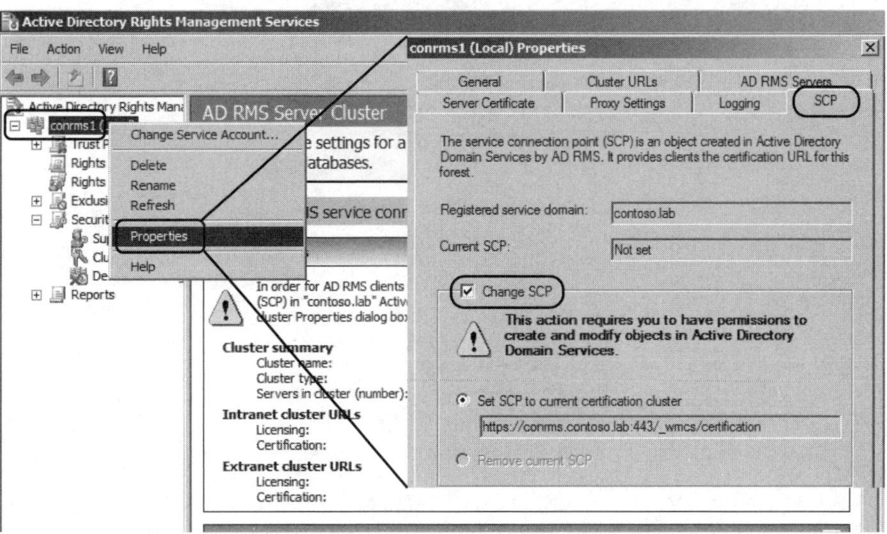

FIGURE 8-23 Registering the AD RMS SCP

CONFIGURING THE AD RMS SERVER CERTIFICATION PIPELINE

Configure the server certification pipeline in AD RMS for Exchange Server 2010 integration by following these steps:

1. Log on to a server in the AD RMS cluster with an Active Directory account with local administrative privileges.
2. Click Start, and then click Computer to open Windows Explorer. Navigate to C:\Inetpub\wwwroot_wmcs\Certification, right-click ServerCertification.asmx, and select Properties to open the Properties dialog box.
3. In the ServerCertification.asmx Properties dialog box, click the Security tab and then click Advanced. Click Continue on the Permissions tab of the Advanced Security Settings For ServerCertification.asmx dialog box.
4. In the Advanced Security Settings For ServerCertification.asmx dialog box, select the Include Inheritable Permissions From This Object's Parent check box, as shown in Figure 8-24, and then click OK twice to apply the change and return to the ServerCertification.asmx Properties dialog box.

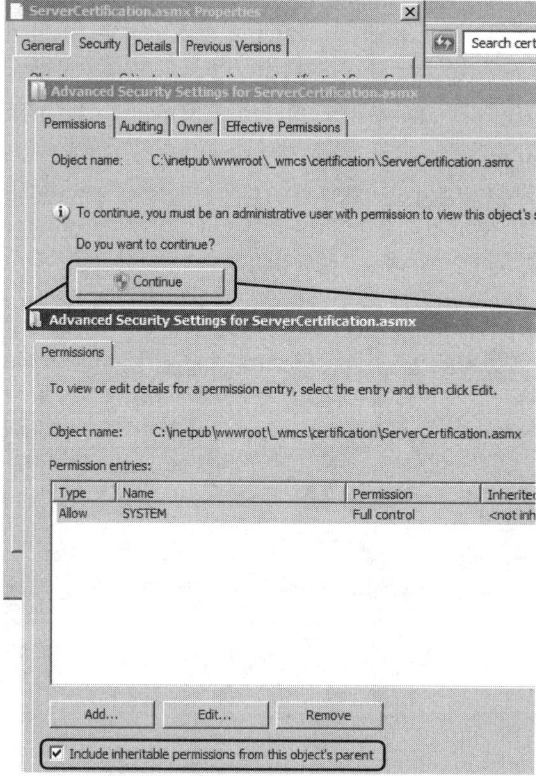

FIGURE 8-24 Setting inheritable permissions on ServerCertification.asmx

5. Back on the Security tab of the ServerCertification.asmx Properties dialog box, select Continue to open the Permissions for ServerCertification.asmx dialog box as shown in Figure 8-25.

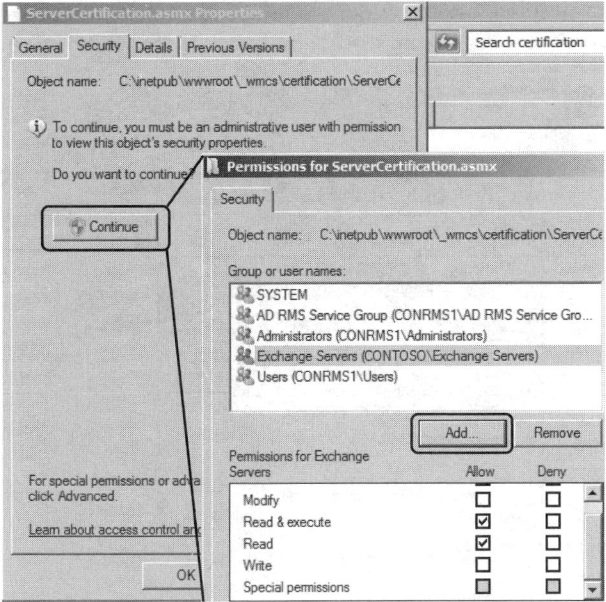

FIGURE 8-25 Granting the Exchange Servers Group Access to ServerCertification.asmx

6. In the Permissions for ServerCertification.asmx dialog box, click Add and then add the Exchange Server group from Active Directory, granting this group Read and Read & Execute permissions to the file. Apply the changes, and then close all dialog boxes to return to Windows Explorer.
7. Repeat Steps 1 through 6 on all other servers in the AD RMS cluster.

CONFIGURING AD RMS SUPER USERS

To use the IRM in Outlook Web App, IRM for Exchange Search, transport decryption, or journal report decryption functionality in Exchange Server 2010, the Super Users feature in AD RMS must be enabled and assigned to a group containing the Federated Delivery Mailbox. There is only one Federated Delivery Mailbox per organization, and it is created by the */PrepareAD* process. If this mailbox is deleted or disabled, IRM functionality will not work; the associated Active Directory account for the Federated Delivery Mailbox is disabled by default. You can re-create the Federated Delivery Mailbox if necessary by running */PrepareAD* again.

Enable and configure the AD RMS Super Users feature by following these steps:

1. If a Super Users group is not already created, create a distribution group named **ADRMSSuperUsers** and add the FederatedEmail.4c1f4d8b-8179-4148-93bf-00a95fa1e042 user to this group.
2. Log on to a server in the AD RMS cluster with an Active Directory account that is a member of the AD RMS Enterprise Administrators local group.
3. Start the Active Directory Rights Management Services management console from Administrative Tools and expand the cluster in the left-hand pane.

4. In the console tree in the left-hand pane, expand Security Policies and then select Super Users. Click Enable Super Users from the Actions pane, as shown in Figure 8-26.

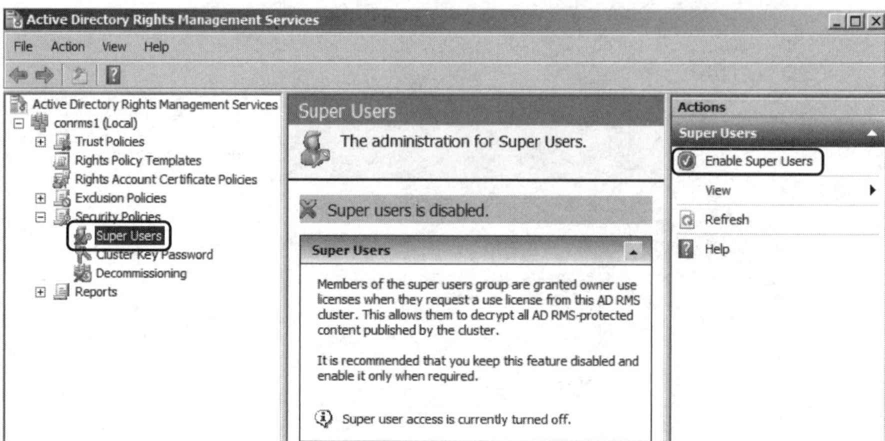

FIGURE 8-26 Enabling Super Users in AD RMS

5. Back in the Results pane, click Change Super User Group as shown in Figure 8-27. In the Super Users dialog box, type in the e-mail address of the Super Users group created in Step 1, or click Browse to select the group from Active Directory. Click OK to apply the group.

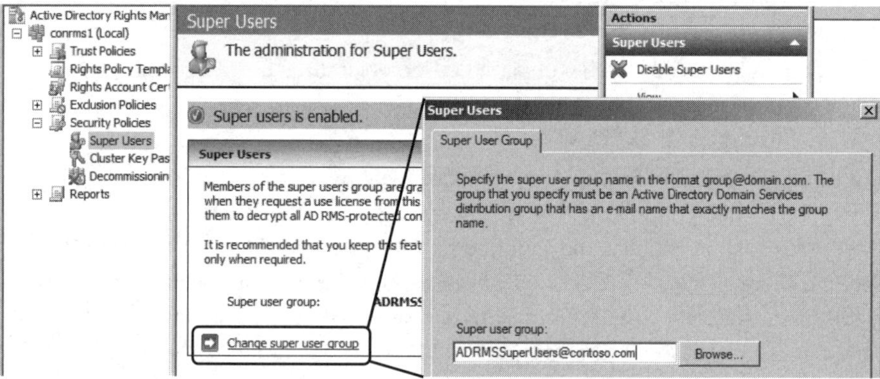

FIGURE 8-27 Setting the AD RMS Super Users group

NOTE **If Super Users is already enabled for a group, and the Federated Delivery Mailbox is later added to that group, it may take between 12 and 24 hours for the change to take effect because AD RMS caches group memberships in SQL and only updates them from Active Directory when this cache has expired.**

Designing and Implementing Message Classifications

The typical organization has invested heavily in solutions protecting against threats from inbound e-mail such as malware (viruses, worms, Trojans, and phishing, for example) and spam. However, the compliance and intellectual property risks of internal and outgoing e-mail have not generally been given much consideration. The retention policy and managed folder technologies that provide messaging records management in Exchange Server 2010 can aid in dealing with these issues for e-mail residing in mailboxes (at rest), but they depend to a large extent on decisions made on the content of messages by end users and, in some cases, administrators. These decisions typically focus on the designation of messages based on their content, principally in the context of their intended use, audience, retention, and so on.

E-mail classification adds visual labels and metadata to e-mail messages to describe the intended use of or audience for a message to enable processes to make decisions based on those designations. The message sender typically applies the message classifications, as a decision made on the content of the message before it is sent. These classifications typically indicate the sensitivity, intended distribution, retention periods, or other designations, usually as required by the organization. If deployed with some pre-planning, message classifications can offer a crucial piece of an effective strategy for managing and controlling e-mail by ensuring regulatory compliance and maintaining policy.

Unclassified, Confidential, and Secret are some examples of message classifications used by organizations, whereas others may employ designations such as Non-Business, Partner Confidential, Mergers and Acquisitions, Privacy Act, and so on.

As with retention tags, AD RMS templates, and managed folders, the number of message classifications should be kept to a minimum. This aids in keeping the interface uncluttered for end users, which will in turn encourage them to actually use this new technology.

In Outlook 2007, Outlook 2010, and Outlook Web App in Exchange Server 2010, the message classification applied can display visual labels for the sender and the recipients of the e-mail in the form of a user-friendly description of the classification.

> ***IMPORTANT*** **Message classifications in Exchange Server 2010 are informational only; they are not integrated with any transport rules or messaging records management functionality. However, they can be used as a predicate in transport rules, and transport rules can be configured to apply a message classification as an action.**
>
> **In addition, Exchange Server 2010 message classifications set on a message are only visible to the recipient when viewed in Outlook Web App, or with Outlook 2007 or Outlook 2010; Outlook 2007 and Outlook 2010 require additional configuration to apply and view Exchange Server 2010 message classifications.**

When a user composes a message in Outlook Web App and Outlook 2007 and higher, the message classifications configured in Exchange Server 2010 are listed in the Permissions dialog box, along with AD RMS templates, as shown in Figure 8-28. In this example, Privacy Act is a message classification, whereas the rest of the entries in the list are AD RMS templates.

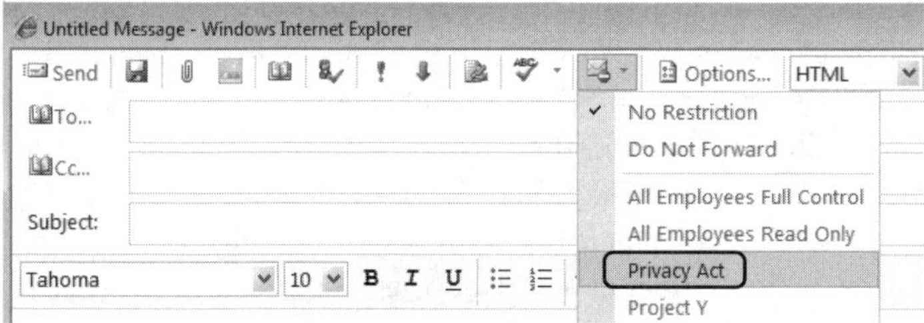

FIGURE 8-28 Selecting a message classification in Outlook Web App

Message classifications are created using the EMS and the *New-MessageClassification* cmdlet. It is worth noting that the message classification selection seen in Figure 8-28 is just the display name of the classification. You specify the classification's display name with the *DisplayName* parameter; this defines the label seen from the selection menu by the sender. The *SenderDescription* parameter defines the description that is shown to the sender in the composed message, as shown in Figure 8-29.

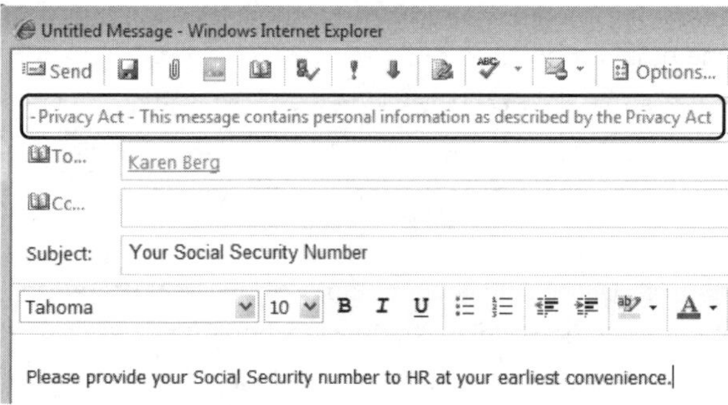

FIGURE 8-29 Message classification sender description in a composed message

You can configure separately the text displayed to recipients of a classified message with the *RecipientDescription* parameter; the recipient description for the message composed in Figure 8-29 as seen in Outlook Web App is shown in Figure 8-30. If the recipient description is not configured, the text configured for the sender description is displayed.

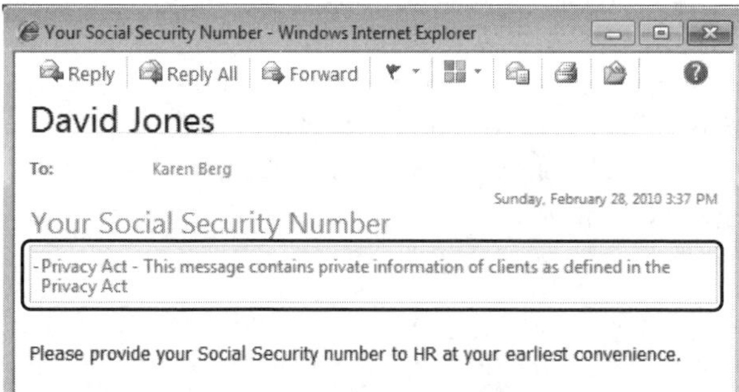

FIGURE 8-30 Message classification as seen by an Outlook Web App recipient

INSIDE TRACK

Simplifying the End-User Experience with Message Classifications

Ed Banti
Program Manager, Microsoft Corporation, Redmond, WA

All too often organizations will attempt to place rigid or complex policies on their end users in the name of governance, compliance, security, privacy, or a whole collection of laws and regulations. For example, I've heard of organizations that prompt their employees to classify every single e-mail and that process involves understanding the definition of hundreds of classification tags and picking the right one. I've also heard of organizations that give their employees complex instructions on when to IRM-protect documents or when it's appropriate to S/MIME encrypt versus sign an e-mail. While the intent is to keep the organization and employees out of trouble, this approach results in employee frustration and ultimately leads to the "click the default" and ignore mentality, which is contrary to the original goal and intent of the policy.

Instead of pushing complex rules to employees, organizations need to consider ways to reduce confusion and streamline the process. An easy way to do this out of the box in Exchange 2010 is via message classifications and transport rules. Message classifications are informational policies that can be tagged (either manually or automatically) to e-mail messages that can display a user-friendly description in Outlook or OWA. These message classifications can then trigger transport rules in the background. Take a look at the following example.

Contoso is a healthcare provider with patient information that needs to be kept confidential. Today they instruct their employees to include a disclaimer on all e-mails that contain patient data and they also require that these e-mails be encrypted. Half the time, employees forget to do this or they only include the disclaimer but don't encrypt the mail. To simplify, Contoso creates a set of message classifications: Patient Data, Financial Data, and Public. When an employee marks and sends a message as Patient Data, a transport rule is triggered that automatically adds the proper disclaimer to the message and protects the message using AD RMS such that the content cannot be viewable outside of Contoso. For Financial Data e-mail, a transport rule applies a different disclaimer and forces the message to be moderated before the message can leave Contoso. This ensures that no financial data is sent outside the company without approval.

As this example shows, you have access to simple and straightforward ways to use message classifications to abstract complex policies and actions from employees while encouraging them to properly handle and classify sensitive information.

Dependencies of Message Classification

Active Directory and the messaging client used are the main dependencies of message classification in Exchange Server 2010; we'll go over each of these in turn in the following sections.

Active Directory Configuration Container

As with all Exchange Server 2010 configurations, message classifications are stored in Active Directory; in particular, in the Configuration container in the path Configuration/Services/Microsoft Exchange/<*Organization*>/Transport Settings/Message Classifications/<*Locale*>. The classifications can be verified using ADSI Edit (ADSIEdit.msc), as shown in Figure 8-31.

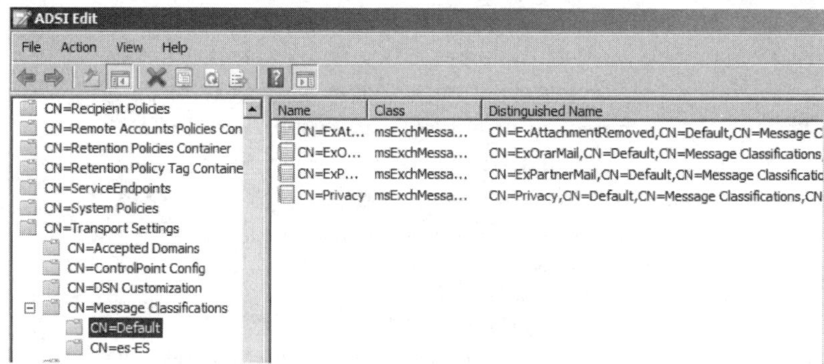

FIGURE 8-31 Message classifications in Active Directory

As inferred from what you saw in Figure 8-25, message classifications are locale-specific (language-specific). This means that you can present several versions of the same classification, so that different users see a version in their own language as determined by their client locale settings. Creating localized message classifications is covered later in the "Creating Localized Message Classifications" section of this chapter.

Messaging Client

The other primary dependency for Exchange Server 2010 message classifications is the messaging client. As stated earlier, classifications are set by the message sender on outgoing messages in Outlook 2007, Outlook 2010, and Exchange Server 2010 Outlook Web App and are viewable by recipients only in those same clients.

Creating Message Classifications in Exchange Server 2010

You can create the message classification shown earlier in Figure 8-24 using the following cmdlet:

```
New-MessageClassification -Name Privacy -DisplayName "Privacy Act" -SenderDescription
"This message contains personal information as described by the Privacy Act"
-RecipientDescription "This message contains private information of clients as defined
in the Privacy Act"
```

The common parameters used when creating new or configuring existing classifications are listed in Table 8-6.

TABLE 8-6 Message Classification Common Parameters

CLASSIFICATION PARAMETER	PARAMETER DESCRIPTION
DisplayName	This parameter specifies the display name for the message classification. This display name is shown in Outlook 2007, Outlook 2010, and Outlook Web App; it is used to select the appropriate message classification before a message is sent. The *DisplayName* parameter must be 64 characters or fewer.
SenderDescription	Provides an explanation to the sender what the message classification is intended to achieve. This is used by Outlook and Outlook Web App users to assist in selecting the appropriate message classification before sending a message. The *SenderDescription* parameter must be 1,024 characters or fewer.
RecipientDescription	Displays text to the recipient explaining what the message classification is intended to achieve. This is seen by Outlook and Outlook Web App users when a message with this classification is received. The *RecipientDescription* parameter must be 1,024 characters or fewer. If this parameter is not configured, the text set for *SenderDescription* is used.
Locale	This parameter allows you to localize the message classification for different languages when a culture code is specified. You also must also specify the *Identity* parameter of the existing message classification when you create a new locale-specific version. Values for the *Locale* parameter are the string names listed in the Culture Name column in the Microsoft .NET Class Library class reference that is available at *http://go.microsoft.com/fwlink/?LinkId=67222*.
RetainClassificationEnabled	Specifies whether the message classification should persist with the message if the message is forwarded or replied to; the default value for this parameter is true.

Creating Localized Message Classifications

Localized versions of an existing message classification can also be created for accommodating multilingual organizations. Exchange Server 2010 determines the language of the recipient by examining the recipient's mailbox when a message is classified and sent.

If a message classification in the corresponding language is found in Active Directory, the message has that classification attached to it by Exchange Server 2010. If there is no exact language match, Exchange examines the recipient mailbox's locale property to determine the locale of the recipient. In the event of no match for the specific locale of the recipient, Exchange Server 2010 looks for a version that is culture-neutral, such as es for es-MX, (Spanish-Mexico) or fr for fr-CA (French-Canada). Finally, the default message classification is used if no language-specific or culture-neutral match is found, regardless of its locale.

Localized message classifications are created with the *New-MessageClassification* cmdlet, using the *Identity* parameter to identify the existing classification and the *Locale* parameter to indicate the locale of the new classification. For example, to create a Spanish version of a message classification named Privacy, you would use the following cmdlet:

```
New-MessageClassification Privacy -Locale es-ES -DisplayName "España Example"
-SenderDescription "Este es el texto de la descripción"
```

Configuring Message Classifications for Outlook 2007 and Outlook 2010

After your message classifications have been created and configured, a few more steps are required to allow Outlook 2007 and Outlook 2010 users to be able to set message classifications. You must export the classifications from Active Directory to an XML file, and make this file accessible to the Outlook 2007 and Outlook 2010 clients. This is accomplished with the Exchange Server 2010 EMS script named Export-OutlookClassification.ps1; this script is located in the <install_drive>:\Program Files\Microsoft\Exchange Server\Scripts directory on the server running Exchange Server 2010.

After the classification XML file is exported, Outlook 2007 and 2010 clients not only require access to the file, but also require message classification to be enabled. This is done through the registry by creating the three values shown in the following example:

```
[HKEY_CURRENT_USER\Software\Microsoft\Office\12.0\Common\Policy]
"AdminClassificationPath"="c:\\Classifications.xml"
"EnableClassifications"=dword:00000001
"TrustClassifications"=dword:00000001
```

You must change the above registry key to [HKEY_CURRENT_USER\Software\Microsoft\Office\14.0\Common\Policy] for Outlook 2010 clients. This Policy key is not present by default in Outlook 2007 or Outlook 2010, so it must be created. Table 8-7 outlines the registry values configured as well as the purpose of each.

TABLE 8-7 Registry Values for Outlook 2007 and Outlook 2010 Message Classifications

REGISTRY VALUE	DESCRIPTION
AdminClassificationPath	This string value defines the location where the classification XML file is stored. This can be any location accessible to the Outlook 2007 client, including a network share.

REGISTRY VALUE	DESCRIPTION
EnableClassifications	To enable message classification functionality for the specified user, set this *DWORD* value to 00000001. Message classification functionality is disabled by setting this value to 00000000.
TrustClassifications	*TrustClassifications* should only be enabled for Exchange Server 2010 users, and is enabled by setting this *DWORD* value to 00000001. Message classifications between users on Exchange Server 2003 are also supported by Outlook; because Exchange Server 2003 doesn't support or recognize message classifications, the content and validity of the message classifications is not guaranteed. In this case, disabling *TrustClassifications* prepends the text "The sender claims:" to the message classification. This prevents the recipients from assuming incorrectly that their organization has processed the classification. Disable *TrustClassifications* by setting this *DWORD* value to 00000000.

NOTE The message classification XML file exported from Active Directory must be distributed to Outlook 2007 and 2010 clients, and this presents some challenges about where to store the XML file so that it is accessible to these clients.

Storing the XML file in a local path on the client computer ensures that message classifications are available to the user when they are offline in cached mode; however, this means that the file needs to be distributed to and updated on all of the client computers—especially if classifications are modified or added/removed.

You can store the XML file on a network share so that it is maintained in only one location, but this presents challenges for those users working offline in cached mode—they will be unable to use the message classifications while working offline.

One solution to this challenge is to store the file on a network share and force that network share to be available offline for all connected users (using Windows offline files). This ensures that message classifications are available to end users at all times, while leaving only one file location to maintain. When offline users connect to the corporate network again, any changes made to the XML file will be updated in their offline files cache.

Assigning Message Classifications with Transport Rules

As we've seen, with Exchange Server 2010 and supported messaging clients you can provide end users with the ability to assign message classifications to messages before they are sent. In addition to this, you can automatically assign classifications to messages using transport rules run by the Hub Transport role based on criteria you specify. As with any transport rules, conditions are defined for the rule and then an action is set for the rule to take when the conditions are met; in this case, applying a message classification. As a case in point, you could configure a transport rule to check for messages that contain a text pattern matching a Social Security number, then apply a message classification named Privacy Act to ensure compliance with regulatory and company policies.

Besides assigning classifications with transport rules, transport rules can also be created that act on messages that have already been classified. One example is to prevent any messages classified Company Internal from leaving the organization; another example would be to apply IRM protection to messages classified Client-Attorney Privilege. What this all means is that even though message classifications are only visible in Outlook 2007, Outlook 2010, and Outlook Web App, your organization may still find them of value.

Additional Resources

- Configure a Disclaimer: Exchange 2010 Help: *http://technet.microsoft.com/en-us/library/dd876914.aspx*
- Titus Labs security and classification solutions videos, whitepapers, case studies, datasheets, and other resources: *http://titus-labs.com/resources/index.php?resourceid=38&tabno=4*
- Exchange Server 2010 Compliance Capabilities: *http://www.simple-talk.com/sysadmin/exchange/exchange-server-2010-compliance-capabilities/*
- Hold Me Now! How to Quickly Put a Retention Hold on 1,400 Employees Using Microsoft Exchange 2007: *http://blogs.technet.com/b/ediscovery/archive/2008/07/14/hold-me-now-how-to-quickly-put-a-retention-hold-on-1-400-employees-using-microsoft-exchange-2007.aspx*
- Exchange 2007 Assists Regulatory Compliance: *http://www.directionsonmicrosoft.com/sample/DOMIS/update/2007/02feb/0207e2arc.htm*
- Single Item Recovery in Exchange Server 2010: *http://msexchangeteam.com/archive/2009/09/25/452632.aspx*
- Part 1: How to Add a Disclaimer to Exchange Server 2007 E-mail: *http://searchexchange.techtarget.com/generic/0,295582,sid43_gci1256759_mem1,00.html*
- Messaging Policy and Compliance: *http://technet.microsoft.com/en-us/library/aa998599.aspx*
- Apply Exchange Server 2010 Message Retention Tags for E-mail Archiving: *http://searchexchange.techtarget.com/generic/0,295582,sid43_gci1379660,00.html*
- E-mail Retention Policies in Exchange 2010: *http://www.windowsitpro.com/article/email/email-retention-policies-in-exchange-2010.aspx*
- Understanding Information Rights Management: *http://technet.microsoft.com/en-us/library/dd638140.aspx*
- Planning for Compliance: *http://technet.microsoft.com/en-us/library/bb201740.aspx*

CHAPTER 9

Unified Messaging

Exchange Server 2010 Unified Messaging bridges the gap between voice and messaging, thus allowing your users to access their Exchange mailboxes using a regular phone. Introduced with Exchange 2007, Exchange 2010 Unified Messaging now provides an even more sophisticated implementation that needs to be carefully planned to be implemented well.

This chapter is about designing, planning, and deploying the Unified Messaging (UM) server role for your organization, including the telephony basics you need to understand to configure the UM server role.

Additionally, the UM role is capable of being tightly integrated into an Office Communication Server 2007 (OCS) or later implementation to provide not only voice mail and Outlook Voice Access but also to provide an automated switchboard that can be fully customized for your company's needs.

This chapter is only important if you are planning on using the UM role, which requires you to connect your telephony system to Exchange. If you do not plan to use it, you can skip this chapter.

Introduction to Unified Messaging

Exchange 2010 Unified Messaging combines voice and e-mail messaging in the Exchange Server store and integrates telephony systems with Exchange. Many companies manage voice mail separately from e-mail. Usually, voice messages and e-mail exist as separate inboxes on separate servers, and users access them using different tools. Frequently, each communication tool requires a separate address list, which can make it difficult to keep all address lists synchronized. Unified Messaging brings these tools together and offers an integrated store and user experience for both voice mail and e-mail.

Exchange 2010 Unified Messaging provides the following core features:

- **Voice mail** Also known as call answering, it enables the system to answer the telephone and record a message when the user is unavailable.
- **Outlook Voice Access** OVA provides users with access to their Exchange mailbox from a phone. It enables you to use any telephone to retrieve e-mail, voice mail, calendar, personal contacts, and to access the company directory. You can also create messages to both internal and external recipients. With Exchange 2010 SP1 you can also change the sorting of the messages—for example, you can play the oldest voice mail first.

> ***NOTE*** An excellent Quick Start Guide for Outlook Voice Access 2010 is available at *http://go.microsoft.com/fwlink/?LinkId=137165.*

- **Play on Phone** This feature lets a Unified Messaging–enabled user listen to a voice message using a telephone instead of playing it over computer speakers or headphones.
- **Voicemail Preview** The Unified Messaging role uses Automatic Speech Recognition (ASR) on newly created voice messages. When users receive voice mail, they receive messages that contain the voice recordings along with a text transcription that Unified Messaging creates from recordings. UM also learns from the individual and will improve over time by using a grammar-generation algorithm for the most used words per mailbox. This algorithm is performed by the mailbox assistant once a month. Voicemail Preview is not available in all languages. Exchange 2010 SP1 increases the accuracy of voice mail preview and also includes the ability to set the UM policy to automatically send voice mail messages to Microsoft for analysis so that Voicemail Preview can be improved, especially in languages other than English. SP1 also adds additional languages such as European Spanish.
- **Protected voice mail** Unified Messaging provides this functionality so that callers can send private mail, which Microsoft Rights Management Services (RMS) protects.

However, Unified Messaging restricts users to only forwarding, copying, and extracting the voice file from mail by applying the Do Not Forward template.

- **Auto Attendant** Allows callers to look up a person and identify his or her extension number from the organization's global address list. With auto attendant you can also create custom menus for callers, define different greetings based on the business hours, describe to callers how to find the people they are calling, and connect callers to the operator.
- **Call Answering Rules** The user can configure a custom experience for incoming callers by creating and customizing call-answering rules based upon different factors such as time of day, free/busy status, Caller ID, and so on.
- **Message Waiting Indicator (MWI)** Exchange Server notifies users of the presence and number of new or unread voice mail messages on their phones.
- **Missed Call and Voice Mail Notifications via SMS** Users can receive notifications about missed calls and new voice messages on their cell phones in a text message via the Short Messaging Service (SMS).
- **Calling Name Display** Exchange 2010 SP1 enhances the support for displaying caller names if your PBXs or IP gateways pass the information in their SIP INVITE. You can identify that the name was passed from the PBX when you see the name in quotes, such as *Voice mail from "Joel Stidley"*.

INSIDE TRACK

Behind the Scenes of Unified Messaging

Ankur Kothari
Senior Technical Product Manager, Exchange Server, Microsoft Corporation

Creating a voice mail product in today's world involves looking at how people work today, which invariably differs from how voice mail solved a need in 1975. Today, people rely on many communication technologies to achieve their business needs—the telephone being only one of them.

What we learned from customers and our research was that users are overwhelmed with information—*information overload* is a term we heard many times. Helping solve this challenge is something that we hope Exchange Unified Messaging will do, by placing voice mail in your e-mail Inbox and making it accessible in a number of languages. We've done some great things in making a voice mail message very similar to the e-mail experience by introducing speech-to-text technology, which will create a text-based Voicemail Preview of a message—one of many new features that will help users to be more productive in the now.

The Basics of Telephony

Because Unified Messaging must be integrated into your company's telephony solution, it's important to understand the most crucial terms and definitions to be able to follow the discussions in this chapter.

> **NOTE** If your company is already connected to Office Communications Server 2007 or later with your telephone system, you don't need to consider the details in the following sections; Exchange 2010 will use OCS as the gateway.

Types of Telephone Systems

Three general types of business telephone systems can be integrated with Unified Messaging:

- **Centrex Phone System** Phone companies lease a Centrex phone system (also known as Central Office Telephone Exchange) to businesses. The Centrex phone system uses the phone company's central office (CO) exchange to route internal calls to an extension. A new Centrex version called *IP Centrex* is available. With IP Centrex, the organization does not rent phone lines from the telephone company's CO. Instead, the CO sends the phone calls through a VoIP gateway, which routes them over a VoIP gateway or through the Internet. At the organization's office, another VoIP gateway translates the call to a traditional circuit-switched call.
- **Key Telephone System** This phone system is similar to the Centrex system in that the organization leases several phone lines from the telephone company. However, with the Key Telephone System, each phone line connects to multiple telephones in the organization. When someone calls the company, all phones ring that are associated with that line. Businesses with Key Telephone Systems often arrange for someone to answer incoming calls, and then announce the call to the correct recipient.

> **NOTE** Some key telephone systems can work with UM if an IP gateway is added. However, some less sophisticated systems may not work even if a supported IP gateway is used. Make sure you contact your vendor before you try to use your key telephone system with Exchange 2010.

- **Private Branch Exchange System** A Private Branch Exchange (PBX) system is different from the other telephone systems in that it typically has only a single connection to the phone company and all call switching happens at the organization. The connection to the phone company usually occurs through a T1 or E1 line, both of which provide multiple channels to enable multiple calls over the same line, also called *trunk lines*. The PBX routes internal phone calls and those between external and internal users. In a PBX system, each user has a telephone extension. When an internal user places a call to another internal user, she uses only the extension number, and the PBX routes the call to the appropriate extension.

Types of PBX

PBX systems are the most common telephone system type that medium- and large-size organizations use. Several types of PBX systems are available:

- **Analog PBX** Analog PBX systems send voice and signaling information, such as the touch tones of dialed phone numbers, as actual analog sound. Analog PBX systems never digitize the sound. To direct the call, the PBX and the phone company's CO listens for the signaling information.
- **Digital PBX** Digital PBXs encode analog sound into a digital format. They typically encode the voice using a standard industry audio codec, G.711. After digital PBXs encode the sound, they send the digitized voice on a channel using circuit switching. The process of circuit switching establishes an end-to-end open connection, and leaves the channel open for the call's duration and for the call's users only. Some PBX manufacturers have proprietary signaling methods for call setup, such as Avaya Definity G3si PBX.
- **IP PBX** IP PBXs include a Network Interface Card (NIC) to provide voice over regular network. The phone converts voice into digitized packets, which it then transfers over the network. The network sends the voice packets via packet switching, a technique that enables a single network channel to handle multiple calls. The IP PBX also acts as a gateway between the internal packet-switched network and the external circuit-switched networks that phone company's use. In this situation, external phone calls arrive at the IP PBX on the normal public phone lines, and the IP PBX converts the phone call to packets sent on the internal IP-based network. An example of this is Cisco Call Manager.
- **Hybrid PBX** Hybrid PBXs provide both digital and IP PBX capabilities. This hybrid approach enables a customer to run a mixture of digital and IP-based phones. Most modern PBXs are in this hybrid category, such as SEN HiPath 4000.

VoIP Gateway Introduction

A VoIP gateway is a third-party hardware device or product that converts traditional phone-system or circuit-switching protocols into data-networking or packet-switched protocols. The VoIP gateway connects a telephone network with a data network.

Unified Messaging servers can connect only to packet-switched data networks. This means that organizations with a traditional PBX must deploy a VoIP gateway to communicate between the PBX and the Unified Messaging server.

Table 9-1 lists the types of telephony systems and explains when a VoIP gateway is required.

TABLE 9-1 VoIP Gateway Requirements for Telephone Systems

TYPES OF TELEPHONE SYSTEM	VOIP GATEWAY REQUIREMENT
Traditional Centrex	Required
IP Centrex	May not be required if supported

TYPES OF TELEPHONE SYSTEM	VOIP GATEWAY REQUIREMENT
Key Telephone System	Required, some phone systems are not supported
Analog or Digital PBX	Required
IP or Hybrid PBX	May not be required is supported

A list of supported PBXs and IP gateways for Exchange 2010 Unified Messaging can be found on Microsoft TechNet in Telephony Advisor for Exchange 2010 at *http://technet.microsoft.com/en-us/library/ee364753.aspx*.

Unified Messaging Protocols

There are a number of voice-related, IP-based protocols. A Unified Messaging environment with Exchange Server 2010 uses the following:

- **Session Initiation Protocol (SIP)** SIP is a real-time signaling protocol that creates, manipulates, and disconnects interactive communication sessions on an IP network. The UM role uses SIP mapped over Transmission Control Protocol (TCP) and supports TLS for secured SIP environments. SIP clients, such as IP/VoIP gateways and IP/PBXs, can use TCP port 5060 or port 5061 (for Secure SIP) to connect to UM server roles. You can find more information about the SIP protocol at *http://tools.ietf.org/html/rfc3261*.
- **Real-time Transport Protocol (RTP)** RTP is for voice transport between the IP gateway and the Unified Messaging server. RTP provides high-quality, real-time, streaming voice delivery. One of the issues with sending voice messages over an IP network is that voice requires real-time transport with specific quality requirements to ensure that the voice sounds normal. If the protocol uses large packets, listeners must wait for the entire packet to arrive before they can respond. Any delay in packet delivery can produce undesirable periods of midstream silence. Packet loss can cause voice garbling. You can get more information about the RTP protocol at *http://tools.ietf.org/html/rfc3550*.

Exchange Unified Messaging Architecture

The Unified Messaging server role includes connections to different components, such as the Client Access or Mailbox server roles, and also to IP PBX or IP gateways, as shown in Figure 9-1.

Generally, the UM server role communicates to an IP PBX or to a PBX using an IP gateway with the Voice over IP protocols (VoIP), Session Initiation Protocol (SIP), and Real-time Transport Protocol (RTP).

The UM server role uses MAPI protocol to communicate with Client Access and Mailbox server roles, and SMTP protocol to send voice mail messages to the destination mailbox via

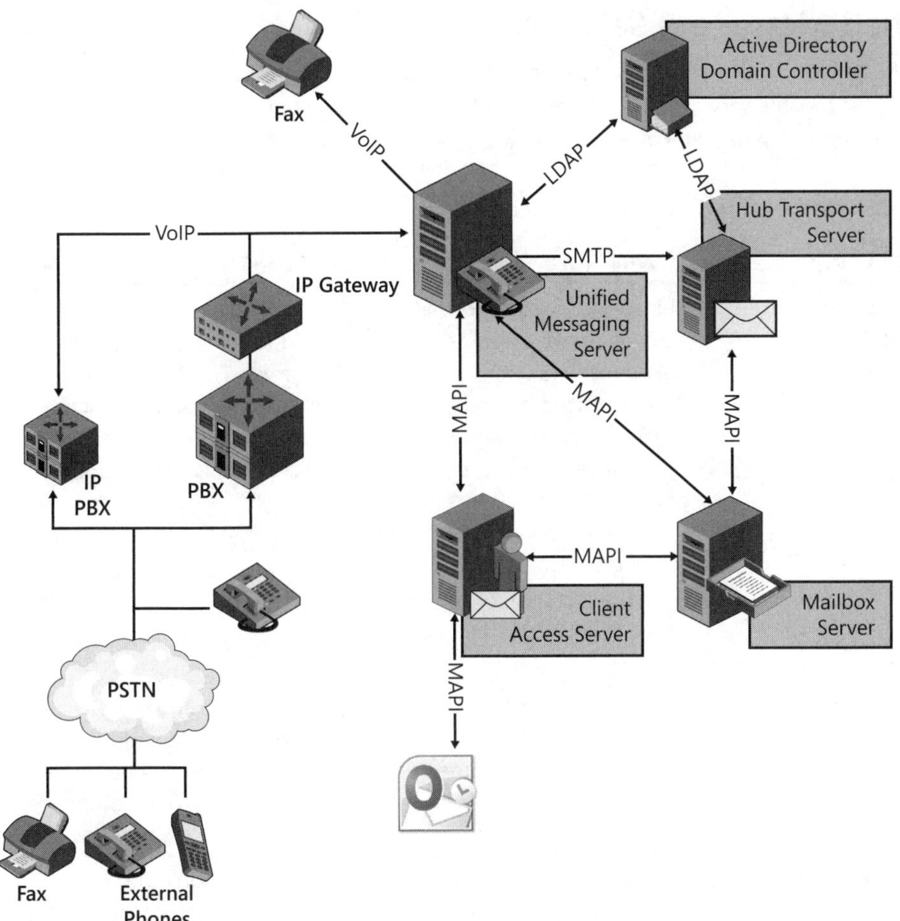

FIGURE 9-1 Unified Messaging architecture

the Hub Transport server. For Outlook Voice Access the UM server role accesses the mailbox using MAPI protocol to have full access to all items in the mailbox such as messages or contacts.

The Unified Messaging role no longer supports an inbound fax like Exchange 2007 UM. However, UM retains fax configuration properties, and continues to be sensitive to fax tones on calls that it answers and forwards these calls to a partner fax solution. The received fax messages look essentially the same as those created by Exchange 2007 UM, and will appear as a fax when the user is UM-enabled.

The communication to the other Exchange roles—namely the Hub Transport, the Mailbox, and Client Access Server roles—uses MAPI connections to perform tasks such as opening a mailbox for OVA or sending a voice mail message when the call has ended.

Unified Messaging Services

The UM server role relies on several services that are required for UM to work correctly. Table 9-2 shows the services that are added to the operating system when adding the Exchange Server Unified Messaging role to a server.

TABLE 9-2 Exchange Services for Unified Messaging Role

SERVICE	DESCRIPTION	BEST PRACTICE INFORMATION
Microsoft Exchange Active Directory Topology	This service reads information from all Active Directory partitions. The data is cached and then used by Exchange 2010 servers to discover the Active Directory site location of all Exchange services in the organization. It is also responsible for updating the site attribute of the Exchange server object in Active Directory.	Runs on all Exchange servers but Edge servers. Stopping this service is the quickest way to stop all Exchange services because all other UM-related services will also be stopped.
Microsoft Exchange File Distribution	This service is responsible for distributing files such as the UM prompts to other Exchange servers.	This service is required; otherwise, the Unified Messaging prompts are not distributed to the other Exchange UM servers.
Microsoft Exchange Monitoring	Allows applications to call the Exchange diagnostic cmdlets.	This service should be started when you consider implementing monitoring tools such as System Center Operations Manager. Otherwise, you don't need to start it.
Microsoft Exchange Service Host	This service provides a host for several Exchange services.	The service should always be in a running state; otherwise, the *Test-ServiceHealth* cmdlet will recognize it and report a fail.
Microsoft Exchange Speech Engine Service (Only Exchange 2010 RTM)	Provides speech processing services for UM.	In SP1 this service was replaced by Unified Communications Managed API 2.0 Core SDK (UCMA).

SERVICE	DESCRIPTION	BEST PRACTICE INFORMATION
Microsoft Exchange Unified Messaging	Enables Microsoft Exchange Unified Messaging features. This allows voice messages to be stored in Microsoft Exchange and gives users telephone access to e-mail, voice mail, calendar, contacts, or an auto attendant.	When you stop this service, the Unified Messaging server won't be able to accept and process incoming calls. Before stopping the service, you should consider currently active calls using the *Get-UMActiveCalls* cmdlet.

NOTE Exchange 2010 SP1 no longer relies on the Microsoft Exchange Speech Engine Service. It uses the Unified Communications Managed API (UCMA), which improves the performance of the speech engine and provides Quality of Experience metrics.

Unified Messaging Folder Structure

Similar to the other Exchange roles, the UM server role also creates a folder structure in the Exchange Installation folder. The folder structure is available in <Exchange_Install_Path>\UnifiedMessaging and is described in Table 9-3.

TABLE 9-3 Unified Messaging Folder Structure

FOLDER	DESCRIPTION
Badvoice mail	Includes voice mails that have been identified as bad or corrupt.
Grammars	Includes grammar files for all languages installed on the UM server role.
Log	Only used for special logging purposes by Microsoft CSS.
Prompts	Includes the voice prompts for all languages installed on the UM server role.
Voicemail	Used to store voice mails before they're transferred to a Hub Transport server role. If you see files in this folder, there is a problem sending them to the Hub Transport.

Planning for Unified Messaging

Planning for the UM role requires you to consider the following UM-related areas beyond server placement and configuration:

- **UM Server** The server that handles voice access. UM servers can handle calls for multiple dial plans and thus can be associated with multiple UM Servers.
- **UM Dial Plan** Represents a set of telephony-enabled endpoints (extensions), sharing a common numbering or naming plan, defined by the telephone network (such as PBX).

- **UM Hunt Group** A hunt group associates an IP gateway with a dial plan, and may have a pilot number to distinguish gateway associations with different dial plans.
- **UM Mailbox** Represents the UM-enabled user. The mailbox has an extension assigned to it in an associated dial plan. Users can have secondary extensions, and these can be in different dial plans.
- **UM Mailbox Policy** Associates the UM users with their dial plans and defines additional policies such as PIN Policies for a user.
- **UM IP Gateway** An IP gateway represents any SIP/RTP-capable peer server with which UM is allowed to communicate. This includes VoIP gateways, IP PBXs, and Office Communications Server.
- **UM Auto Attendant** An auto attendant allows administrators to provide callers with DTMF- and speech-enabled access to users, operators, and phone numbers.

Unified Messaging Servers

If you want to plan your Exchange 2010 Unified Messaging implementation, you need to consider two important factors: How many UM servers do you need, and where do you physically place your UM server roles? You can find additional information about UM server role hardware planning in Chapter 13, "Hardware Planning for Exchange Server 2010."

Planning Amount and Hardware for UM Servers

Planning for how many Unified Messaging servers you need for your environment is logically the first question that needs to be answered before considering their configuration.

Planning the amount of UM servers depends mainly on the number of concurrent calls to the server as well as how many Voicemail Previews a CPU has to produce. These assumptions are based on an average voice mail of 50k and an average voice mail length of 30 seconds.

You can follow these guidelines for UM server planning:

- From the processor power, assume that one voice mail per core per minute can be produced. The UM role supports up to 12 cores, but because this is based on a reasonable price and performance ratio, it might rise in the future.
- Each language installed and supported on an UM server adds memory and CPU overhead because it has to rebuild the language library of words every 24 hours.
- Call answering rules do not have a measurable impact on processor power.
- Every UM server can support as many as 200 concurrent calls maximum; the default configuration is 100 concurrent calls.
- If you don't know your average concurrent callers, you can calculate that roughly 1 percent of your users produce concurrent calls at peak times. This means that if you have 5,000 UM-enabled users accessing a single UM server, they produce 50 concurrent calls during peak hours.

- You should plan to have at least two UM server roles available in your organization to provide failover capabilities.
- 8 GB memory is the recommended memory configuration for a dedicated UM server. More memory will not provide much benefit, even though UM will utilize it.

At Microsoft, three dedicated, centralized Exchange 2010 UM servers are currently available that host more than 90,000 mailboxes. You can find additional hardware planning recommendations in Chapter 13.

INSIDE TRACK

Voicemail Preview and CPU Scalability

Ankur Kothari
Senior Technical Product Manager, Exchange Server, Microsoft Corporation

Scalability of the messaging role is primarily bottlenecked at the CPU. The process of taking an audio stream and determining a best-fit language model for the words spoken is primarily a processor task. We estimate that a single CPU core can handle one voice mail message per minute. An average voice mail message is roughly 25 to 30 seconds, although this can vary by industry or geography. Planning for CPU usage on this role is crucial to providing a consistent end-user experience.

UM Server Placement

If you have a small, single-site implementation of Exchange, you do not give much thought to where you physically place the UM server role. However, if you have a global implementation with several large branch offices located in different countries, you must ask yourself whether you want to place a UM server role close to the branch office's PBX or if you want to place the UM server role in the location where the mailboxes are hosted. The subsequent discussion uses the term *PBX*, meaning that the PBX can be connected to the UM role or already includes an IP PBX.

Let's use the Litware scenario and assume that you have mailboxes from your branch offices in Brussels and Amsterdam hosted on the Mailbox server in Berlin. You also have local PBXs available in Brussels and Amsterdam. Obviously you can place the UM server close to the PBX or close to the Mailbox server role. The following considerations will help you to make a valid decision for this situation:

- Placing the UM server close to the PBX but far from the Mailbox server improves the voice quality because the PBX to UM role is very close. The UM role might need a short delay to open a mailbox and read the items, but the voice quality when the message is played or sent is excellent. Having centralized UM servers and sending VoIP traffic over an unreliable or high-latency WAN should be considered carefully. A delay in opening messages could be acceptable for your users, but a delay in the voice traffic or bad voice quality is not. On the other hand, having the UM server close to the PBX but far from the Mailbox server also means that retrieving and playing personal greetings may not work well. Because the event of "leaving a voice mail" is more of a one-way conversation from the caller to the UM server, best practice is having the UM server near the Mailbox server.

- Placing the UM server close to the Mailbox role, but distant from the PBX might cause voice issues if you do not have a Quality of Service (QoS) network that prioritizes VoIP traffic over your WAN:
  - If you can guarantee or have sufficient network bandwidth available, it is best practice to place the server close to the Mailbox server role.
  - If you cannot guarantee network quality between the PBX and UM server role, your users might not be able to understand voice messages because of network latency or outages, which might cause user confusion.
- Security is another aspect worth considering. Most of the time voice mails are private, and it is sometimes difficult or even unsupported on a lot of PBXs to have the RTP protocol stream secured. This might be an easy target for eavesdropping.
- You can also consider adding a multi-role server to the site where the PBX is located, including the Mailbox, Client Access, Hub Transport, and UM roles to make sure all traffic is local and users get the best voice quality possible. However, carefully consider other implications, such as Domain Controller requirements, that you need to satisfy before installing a multi-role Exchange server onsite.

NOTE **The Microsoft recommended best practice is to place the UM server close to the Mailbox, Hub Transport, and Client Access servers. An IP PBX/IP gateway roundtrip needs to be less than 300 ms, which is higher latency than the RPC traffic between Exchange servers can tolerate and still perform well.**

UM Dial Plans

The UM dial plan is the basic Unified Messaging administrative unit and used for telephony extension-numbering. The UM dial plan, plus the extension number, provides the unique identifier for each UM-enabled user. The UM dial plan also controls the numbering scheme and the outbound dialing plan.

The UM dial plan is an Active Directory container object that is a logical representation of a Telephony dial plan that you configure on a PBX. The UM dial plan establishes a link from an Exchange Server 2010 recipient's telephone extension number in Active Directory to a UM-enabled mailbox.

Before you can use Unified Messaging, your Exchange environment requires at least one UM dial plan to be created, assigned to a UM server, and associated with a UM IP gateway.

When you configure UM dial plan settings, you have to define at least the extension length. Additionally, you can configure other UM dial plan settings:

- Access numbers for subscribers (OVA phone number) or your UM-enabled users dial to access their mailbox via a phone.
- Default greetings that is used when subscribers call into the UM server.
- Dial codes for dialing external phone numbers and international numbers.
- Features such as whether subscribers can transfer callers to other users and whom callers can contact.
- Time limits for calls, messages, and idle timeouts.
- Default language for OVA and voice prompts.
- The audio codec format for voice messages, such as MP3.

> ***IMPORTANT*** **If you want to upgrade your existing Exchange 2007 UM environment that is connected to OCS, you need to create new UM dial plans for Exchange 2010 UM to make OCS UM-version aware. Until SP1, changing a user's dial plan means de-provisioning and re-provisioning a user from the UM system. SP1 changes that by enabling the Move Request to update the UM dial plan automatically.**

Exchange 2010 SP1 will include secondary UM dial plan support, which means that you can assign two UM dial plans to your users, especially those who use two phones connected to different gateways. For more information about this feature see the "Enabling Mailboxes for Unified Messaging" section in this chapter.

UM IP Gateways

A UM IP gateway is a logical representation of a physical IP gateway hardware device that translates between the circuit-switched telephone network and an IP or packet-switched network. This represents either a VoIP gateway or an IP PBX.

The UM IP gateway contains one or more UM hunt groups and other UM IP gateway-configuration settings, including the actual IP gateway. The combination of the IP gateway object and a UM hunt group establishes a logical link between an IP gateway hardware device and a UM dial plan.

> ***NOTE*** **Before an IP gateway can process calls, a UM IP gateway must be associated with at least one UM dial plan.**

You can create a UM IP gateway using the Exchange Management Shell (EMS) or Exchange Management Console (EMC). When you create a new UM IP gateway, you enable

UM servers to connect to the VoIP gateway or IP PBX. However, you can enable or disable the UM IP gateway. You can disable a UM IP gateway in two different modes:

- **Disable After Completing Calls** Forces UM servers associated with this UM IP gateway to stop handling any new calls.
- **Disable Immediately** Forces all associated UM servers to drop existing calls for this UM IP gateway.

UM Hunt Groups

A UM hunt group is a logical representation of an existing PBX or IP PBX hunt group. When the hunt group's pilot number receives a call, the PBX or IP PBX looks for the next available extension number to deliver the call. When the call's recipient does not answer an incoming call, or the line is busy because the recipient is on another call, the PBX or IP PBX routes the call to the UM server.

UM hunt groups act as a link between UM IP gateways and UM dial plans. Therefore, you must associate a UM hunt group with at least one UM IP gateway and one UM dial plan. UM hunt groups locate the PBX hunt group from which the incoming call was received. A pilot number that is specified for a hunt group in the PBX also must be specified within the UM hunt group. The pilot number enables the UM server to associate the call with the correct UM dial plan so that it can route the call correctly.

When you create a new UM hunt group, you enable UM servers in the specific UM dial plan to communicate with the UM IP gateway. You need to specify the UM dial plan and the pilot identifier or pilot number that you want it to use with the new UM hunt group.

> ***NOTE*** **You can create UM hunt groups only if you have already created a UM IP gateway.**

UM Mailbox Policies

You configure UM mailbox policies to standardize UM configuration settings, policies, or security settings for UM-enabled users. When creating a UM dial plan, a respective UM mailbox policy is created automatically, including default settings. Using UM mailbox policies, you can configure the following settings:

- Dial plan (required)
- Maximum greeting length
- Number of unsuccessful login attempts before password is reset
- Minimum number of digits that a PIN requires
- Number of days until user must create a new PIN
- Number of previous passwords that are not allowed
- Restrictions on in-country/region or international calling
- Protected voice mail settings
- Configuring inbound faxing to a fax partner solution

IMPORTANT **Each UM-enabled mailbox must link to one UM mailbox policy.**

UM Auto Attendants

Using a UM auto attendant, you can create a voice-menu system that enables your callers to navigate through voice menus to locate or transfer calls to your UM-enabled users or departments. You can create and use your own voice prompts so that you're able to fully customize the UM auto attendant to your own needs.

The UM auto attendant uses a series of WAV files that callers hear instead of a human operator. The callers can navigate the menu system, place calls, or locate users using DTMF or voice inputs.

NOTE **You can join auto attendants together to form multi-level menus.**

The UM auto attendant allows you to provide the following:

- Corporate or informational greetings, such as business hours or directions to a location
- Custom corporate menus that you can customize to have more than one level
- A directory search function that enables callers to search the organization's name directory
- The ability for callers to connect to the telephone of—or leave a message for—UM-enabled mailboxes

You are not limited in the number of UM auto attendants you can create, and each auto attendant can support an unlimited number of extensions. However, you should design menu systems for auto attendants carefully to ensure that the user has a positive experience. If you design them incorrectly, users can become very frustrated if the time it takes to connect correctly is lengthy or navigating the system is difficult. You should especially consider creating additional UM auto attendants if you are operating in a multi-language environment so that you can provide a dial-in number for each language.

When you create a UM auto attendant, you must provide the associated UM dial plan and extension number(s) to access the UM auto attendant. After creating the UM auto attendant, you can configure alternative greetings by specifying the WAV files to use. You also can configure different settings for work and non-work hours and features such as call transferring. You can create auto attendants in the EMC or by using the *New-UMAutoAttendant* cmdlet in the EMS.

Call Answering Rules

Call Answering Rules or Personal Auto Attendants allow your users to create and customize rules to enhance the experience that callers have when their calls are answered. For example, the call answering rules can include features such as special greetings by contact or time of the day. Using call answering rules, the caller can for example decide to:

- Leave a voice message for the UM-enabled user.
- Transfer to an alternate contact of the UM-enabled user.
- Transfer to an alternate contact's voice mail.

- Transfer to other phone numbers that the UM-enabled user configures.
- Use the Find-Me feature or locate the UM-enabled user via a supervised transfer.

Your UM-enabled users can configure up to eight call answering rules in OWA Options or ECP, as shown in Figure 9-2.

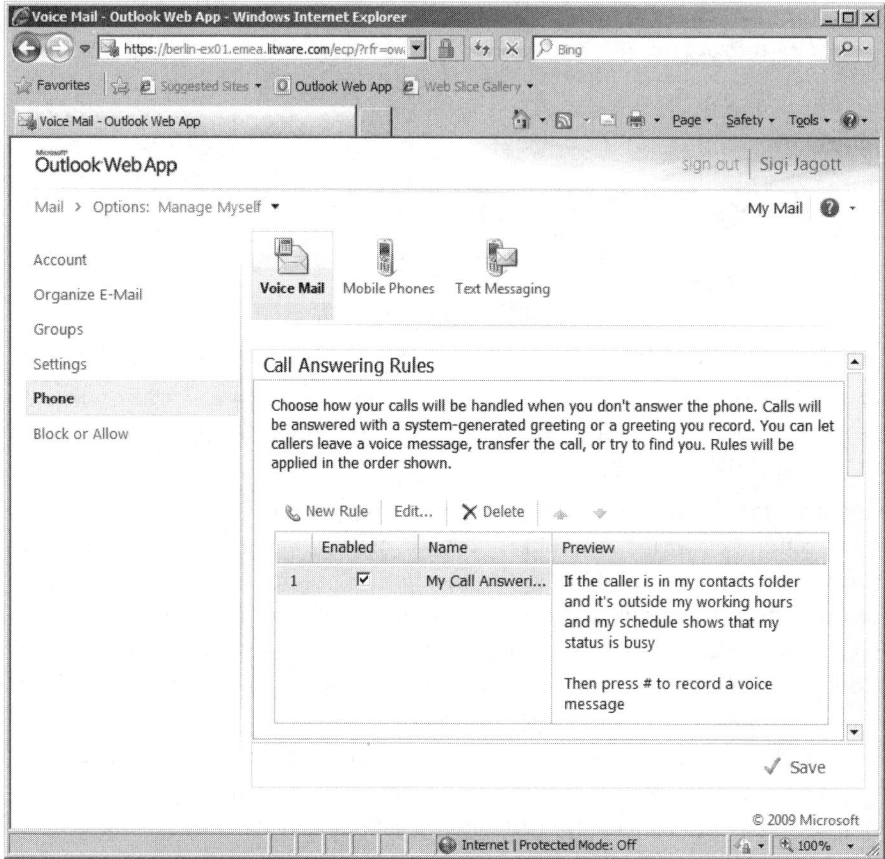

FIGURE 9-2 Configuring Call Answering rules

Call answering rules consist of conditions, a greeting and menu, and actions. You can configure call answering rules in Outlook Web App Options.

Condition

The following conditions for call answering rules are available:

- If the caller is: calling from a phone number, this specific contact, or in my contacts folder.
- If it is during this period: working hours or nonworking hours to a specific time defined.

- If the user's schedule shows a status of: free, tentative, busy, or away.
- If you turn on automatic replies, such as when you turn on an automatic Out of Office message.

Greeting and Menu

Greeting and Menu is the area where the caller can take specific actions that users predefine. For example, after hearing a greeting that you previously recorded, you can provide a prompt so that the caller can dial you at home.

> ***NOTE*** **When the users create their greetings, they have to take care of the entire caller menu—the auto attendant will no longer prompt the caller.**

Actions

Actions define the tasks that occur when callers choose specific menu selections. You can select the following actions:

- **Find Me At The Following Numbers** Defines a recording text, the number key to press to transfer, and enables you to call two phone numbers for a specific time.
- **Transfer The Call To** Defines a recording text, the number key to press to transfer, and either a phone number or a contact—or indicates that the call should transfer directly to voice mail.
- **Leave A Voice Message** Directly transfers the caller to voice mail.

Deploying Unified Messaging

Before you can use UM and OVA, you need to configure your UM server role.

Adding the UM Server Role

Before you can use UM, you need to install an Exchange server that includes the UM server role. You can add the UM role to every server role except for the Edge Transport server role.

Depending on the size of your environment, you can decide whether you want to deploy the UM role on a server that already hosts a role, or use a dedicated server to host the UM server role. You can find more details how to deploy the UM server role in Chapter 15, "Preparing for and Deploying Exchange Server 2010."

Configuring UM Dial Plans

You need to create a UM dial plan to configure the number of extensions the UM server will be accept. Each UM dial plan requires a specifically set URI type as well as VoIP security. Table 9-4 lists the available URI types and when each one is used.

TABLE 9-4 URI Types Available in UM Dial Plans

URI TYPE	DESCRIPTION
Telephone Extension	Used if this UM dial plan is directly connected to an IP gateway that cannot support SIP.
SIP URI	IP gateway uses SIP for signaling or if you are connecting to OCS 2007 R2.
E.164	Your IP gateway delivers the URI in E.164 format.

Additionally, every UM dial plan can be configured for different VoIP security levels. This basically dictates whether Mutual TLS and/or SRTP are required or disabled. An overview of the available VoIP security levels is provided in Table 9-5.

TABLE 9-5 VoIP Security Levels Available in UM Dial Plans

VOIP SECURITY	TLS	SECURE RTP	DESCRIPTION
Unsecured	No	No	UM server uses an unencrypted communication over TCP port 5060.
Secured	Yes	Yes	UM server uses TLS to encrypt communication over TCP port 5061. If you use this option with OCS 2007, Office Communicator client encryption level must be set to either Required or Optional.
SIPSecured	Yes	No	Uses SIP encrypted communication over TCP port 5061. If you use this option with OCS 2007, Office Communicator client encryption level must be set to either Rejected or Optional.

To create a UM dial plan, make sure you know the following information:

- UM dial plan name
- The number of digits needed for the extension number
- URI type
- VoIP security

NOTE If you are creating a UM dial plan for OCS, remember that you cannot use any spaces or special characters—you can only use those that are supported by OCS 2007 Location Profiles.

To create a UM dial plan, you can use the EMC as shown in Figure 9-3, or you can use the *New-UMDialPlan* cmdlet.

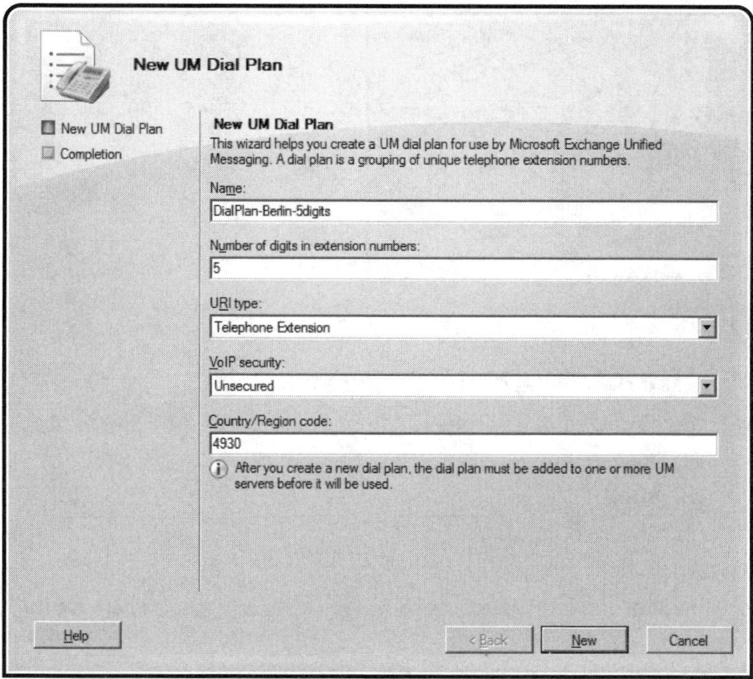

FIGURE 9-3 Creating a new UM dial plan

Configuring UM IP Gateways

You are required to create an IP gateway when you don't use OCS 2007 R2 in your environment and want to connect directly Exchange 2010 UM to your IP PBX or IP gateway. If you use OCS 2007 R2, the task of creating an IP gateway per OCS Pool will be done by the *ExchUCUtil.ps1* script.

To create an UM IP gateway, you need the following information:

- The name of the UM IP gateway
- The IP address or FQDN of the IP gateway or IP PBX that you want to connect to
- The UM dial plan the UM IP gateway will serve

To create a UM IP gateway, you can use the *New-IPGateway* cmdlet in the EMS or use the EMC as shown in Figure 9-4.

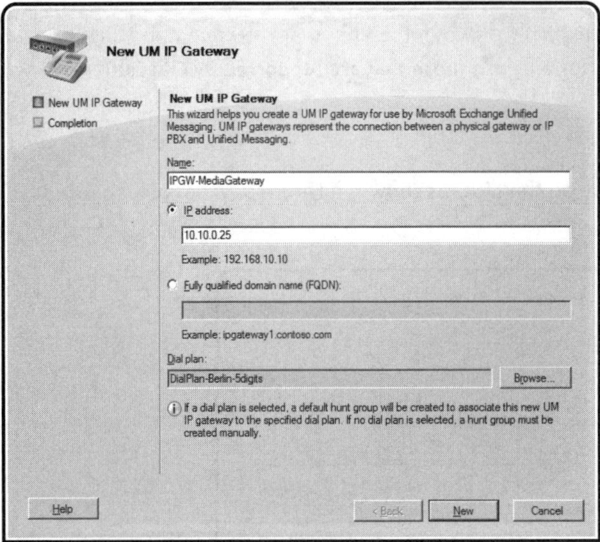

FIGURE 9-4 Creating a new UM IP gateway

Configuring UM Hunt Groups

For every UM IP gateway you also need at least one UM hunt group. To create a UM hunt group you need the following information:

- Name of the UM hunt group
- The pilot identifier for this UM hunt group
- The UM dial plan the UM hunt group is part of

You can create the UM hunt group in the EMC, as shown in Figure 9-5, or you can use the *New-UMHuntGroup* cmdlet.

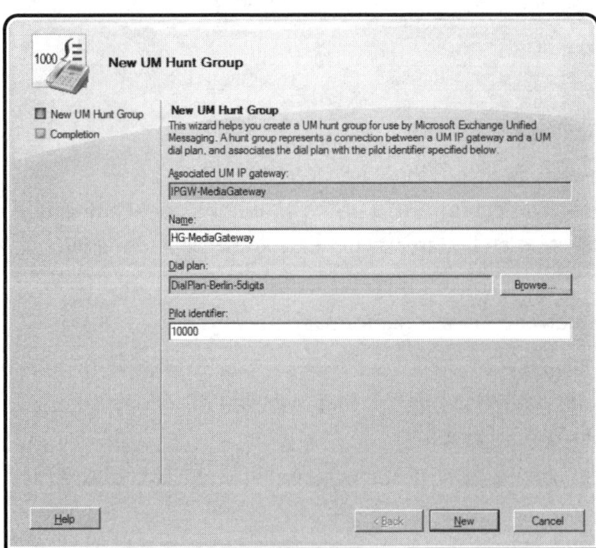

FIGURE 9-5 Creating a new UM hunt group

Configuring UM Mailbox Policies

UM mailbox policies are required when you enable users for UM. They're useful for applying and standardizing UM configuration settings for UM-enabled users. You create UM mailbox policies to apply a common set of policies or security settings to UM-enabled mailboxes and UM servers. UM mailbox policies are used to configure the following settings:

- General policies, such as allowing Voicemail Preview or configuring inbound faxes
- Message text for system messages sent by the UM server
- PIN policies
- Dialing restrictions
- Protected voice mail

You configure UM mailbox policies by using the EMC as shown in Figure 9-6, or you can use the *New-UMMailboxPolicy* cmdlet.

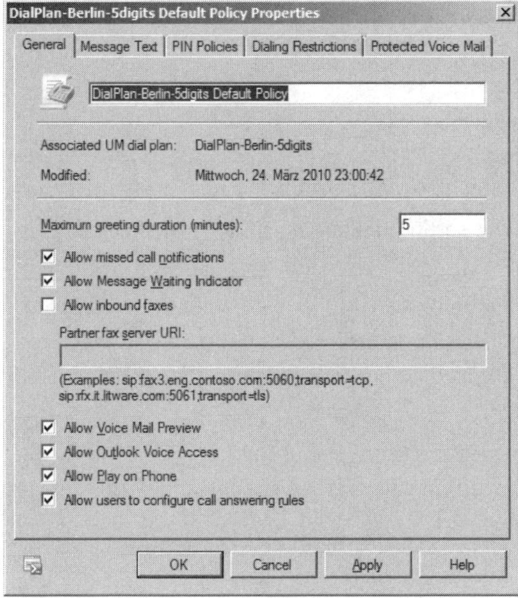

FIGURE 9-6 Configuring UM mailbox policies

Configuring UM Settings

After you've configured the UM dial plan in Organization Configuration, you need to assign the dial plan to the UM server role to enable it. In EMC you can perform this task in Server Configuration-> Unified Messaging in the UM server's properties, as shown in Figure 9-7.

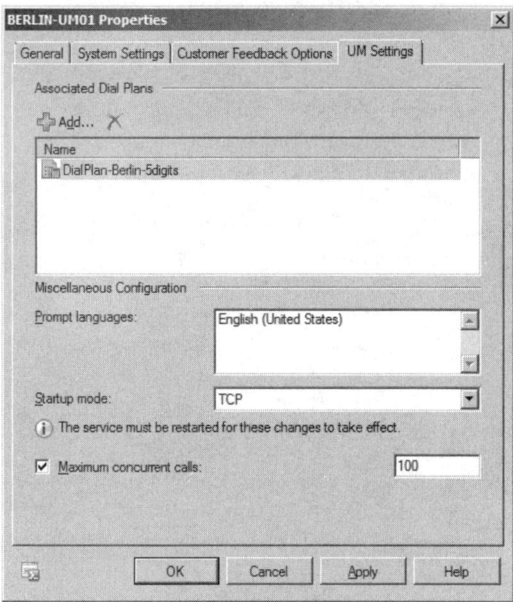

FIGURE 9-7 Configuring UM Settings in Server Configuration

On the UM server level, you can configure the following settings:

- **Associated Dial Plans Assigned** This setting defines which dial plans the UM server is serving.
- **Startup Mode** Defines the startup mode of the UM server—namely TCP, TLS, or Dual. If your UM server does not have a certificate installed, you should not switch to TLS or dual startup mode. Select TLS-enabled mandatory encrypted communication using SIP over TLS.
- **Maximum Concurrent Calls** To prevent server overconsumption, you can configure the maximum amount of concurrent calls this server can handle. The default is 100 calls; the maximum is 200 calls.

Configuring Incoming Faxes

Exchange 2010 UM no longer supports inbound fax transcripts as it was available in the core product with Exchange 2007, but the UM server role retains fax configuration properties and forwards fax calls to a partner fax solution. This happens in the following way:

- If a fax tone is detected, UM looks at the *FaxServerURI* configuration property on the UM mailbox policy objects to determine if a partner fax solution is installed (and if so, where).
- If a value is found for the property, UM will attempt to hand off the call in progress to the partner fax solution. The partner fax solution will establish a fax media session with the sender, create a fax message, and send it to the UM-enabled user's mailbox.

Messages created by partner fax solutions will look essentially the same as those created by Exchange 2007 UM, and will appear as a fax when the user is UM-enabled.

To have faxes forwarded to your partner fax solution correctly, you need to make sure that the partner fax server is configured and you need to configure UM to make your fax partner solution available to UM. When you configure the Exchange UM, make sure the following areas are configured correctly:

- Verify that UM dial plan is configured to allow users to receive faxes. You can do this using the *Set-UMDialPlan <UMDialPlan> -FaxEnabled $true* cmdlet.
- Configure the UM mailbox policy to forward faxes to the fax partner's server. You can do this using the *Set-UMMailboxPolicy <UMMailboxPolicy> -AllowFax $true -FaxServerURI "sip:<faxserverFQDN>:5060;transport=tcp"* cmdlet.
- Make sure your UM-enabled mailbox can receive faxes.
- To enable fax messages to be sent to a UM server from the partner fax server, you also need to create a Send connector that is configured with the respective authentication that the partner fax solution supports.

To find a suitable fax partner solution that meets your requirements, you can get an overview of available fax solutions by reading the Fax Advisor for Exchange 2010 available at *http://technet.microsoft.com/en-us/library/ee364747.aspx.*

International Considerations of Unified Messaging

In an international environment it is especially important to consider the foreign language aspect of UM. In governmental agencies in particular it is common to speak and work not in a common language, but in the local language, such as German.

If you add the UM server role, only one default language is added—English. Thus, you need to define the additional languages required for your users.

INSIDE TRACK

Languages for Voicemail Preview

Ankur Kothari
Senior Technical Product Manager, Exchange Server, Microsoft Corporation

A question I often receive is, "Why did you decide to ship *X* language and not *Y* for Voicemail Preview?"

Our speech model for voice mail is highly tuned to each culture and language. Dialects, vocal tones, grammar, background noise, and mumbling all challenge any voice recognition technology. A language model can even have subtle challenges, such as the method in which a phone number is recited in England is very different than in the United States.

To address these challenges, we created a unique language model for each potential language that we planned to ship. After getting each language model to an acceptable level, we ran the results through a user panel to determine whether users found the results usable or not. Different cultures, as you know, may interpret results uniquely, and we wanted to determine whether our model met the bar. In the end, we decided to ship seven languages/cultures for Voicemail Preview that exceeds both our testing and the user experience. The four new languages in Exchange 2010 SP1 are Canadian English, Polish, Portuguese (Portugal), and Spanish (Spain).

Foreign Language Support

Unified Messaging provides language packs to satisfy international UM requirements. In multiple-language environments, you should install the applicable UM language packs because some UM users prefer their voice prompts in a different language or because they receive e-mail messages in multiple languages that they need to access using OVA. If you do not install the UM language pack for a particular language, e-mail messages in that language will be illogical and incoherent when relayed to the user. OVA uses the following language selection behavior in the release version of Exchange 2010:

1. Try to find an exact match from the OWA language setting.
2. If no match is found, look for a language with the same parent language name. If multiple languages with the same parent language name are installed, the language that is last installed on the UM server wins.
3. If still no match, pick the latest language installed on the UM server.

Exchange 2010 SP1 changes the language selection behavior as follows:

1. Try to find an exact match from the OWA language setting.
2. If no exact match is found, fall back to a matching fallback language (en = en-US, fr = fr-FR, es = es-ES, pt = pt-BR, and so on).
3. If no fallback language is installed, use the default language of the UM dial plan.

Several key components rely on UM language packs to enable users and callers to interact effectively with Exchange Server 2010 UM in multiple languages. Each language pack includes:

- A Text-to-Speech (TTS) engine to read and convert messages when OVA users access their inboxes.
- The prerecorded prompts used to configure UM dial plans and auto attendants.
- ASR support for speech-enabled UM dial plans and auto attendants.

To install a language pack, use *Setup.com /AddUMLanguagePack* found in the Exchsrvr\Bin directory of the Exchange Server installation. Once you install your language packs, you can change the default language configured for each dial plan.

NOTE Users automatically use the default language if their configured language setting in Outlook Web App is not available as a language pack. For example, if you install only the English and German language packs, and the English language pack is the default on the dial plan, a user with the French language configuration in Outlook Web App will hear English prompts.

In Exchange Server 2007, each language pack included the TTS engine but only supported ASR for U.S. English. In Exchange Server 2010, all available language packs contain ASR support. However, not all language packs support Voicemail Preview.

NOTE You can access and download all available UM language packs at *http://technet.microsoft.com/en-us/library/dd638119.aspx.*

Operating UM in a Multi-language Environment

Providing UM to your users in a multi-language environment requires additional considerations so that your users receive voice prompts for their local language. Consider the following when planning a multi-language implementation:

- Create one UM dial plan for every language you support. For example, if you set up a UM server for Germany, you should configure a UM dial plan with its own subscriber number that has German configured as default language in Language Settings.
- You can only define a single text message in a UM mailbox policy. If you are in a multi-language environment, you should consider either adding a text message for all languages or using a common language only.
- Minimize the number of languages to only the needed ones. Every language installed requires time for grammar generation and language specific work. If you do install all 26 languages, this might never be finished.

NOTE You should consider a Subscriber Access number for every primary language that you want to support so that your local users can access their mailboxes in their local language.

NOTES FROM THE FIELD

Changing Language for Voice Mail

Korneel Bullens
Team Coordinator Unified Communications, Wortell, Netherlands

One of the questions I hear from my customers is "Why do I get my OVA greeting in English while my colleague has a Dutch or English intro?" This is a simple challenge. When your mailbox is created and you log on to Outlook or OWA, you encounter a language selection process. The language you pick is the language used on your voice mail. You can change this by opening Outlook Web App and changing your regional settings back to your desired language.

Managing Unified Messaging

To manage the UM server role, you need to make sure you understand the tools available and how to troubleshoot UM.

Enabling Mailboxes for Unified Messaging

For most people, enabling a mailbox for UM might seem straightforward, but it is not done in the properties of the mailbox on the Mailbox Features tab, but using Enable Unified Messaging in the Actions pane in the EMC as seen in Figure 9-8, or by using the *Set-Mailbox* cmdlet.

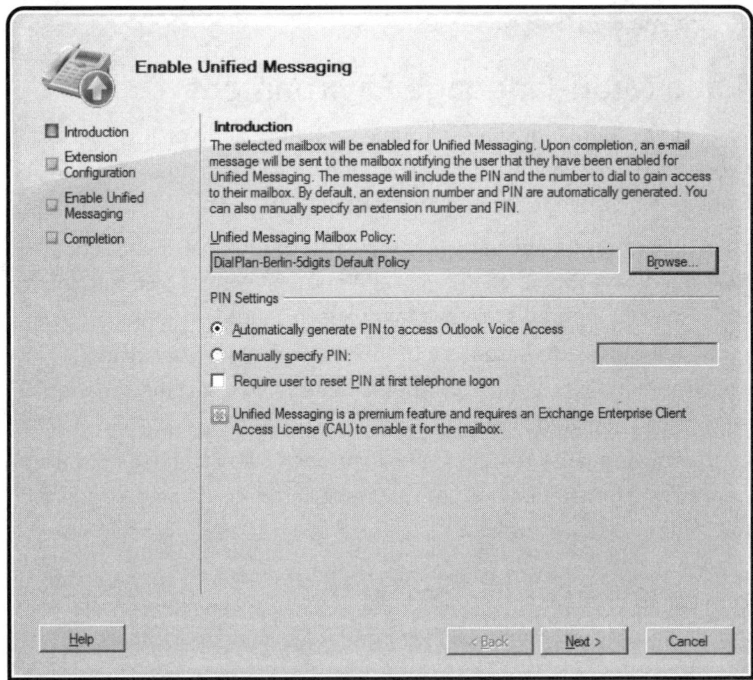

FIGURE 9-8 Enabling Unified Messaging for a mailbox

When you enable a user account for UM, you must specify a UM mailbox policy and an extension, and you must assign a PIN or configure the system to generate the user's initial PIN. After enabling a user for UM, Exchange Server sends the user an e-mail message indicating that the account is enabled. The message also contains the PIN. The user must use touch tones to input a PIN when accessing the UM-enabled mailbox. Speech recognition is not enabled for PIN input.

Since Exchange 2010 SP1 you can also add a mailbox to a secondary UM dial plan. This is especially helpful if your user has multiple phones that are not part of the same UM dial plan. For example, one of your users might be part of an OCS dial plan as well as an UM dial plan that has a direct connection to an IP gateway using the URI type Telephony Extension.

You configure a secondary UM dial plan using the *Set-Mailbox <Mailbox> -SecondaryAddress <extension> -SecondaryDialPlan <UMDialPlan>* cmdlet.

UM Reporting

For UM reports you required System Center Operations Manager 2007 and the Exchange 2010 Management Pack to be installed in Exchange 2010 RTM.

Exchange 2010 SP1 includes reports that allow you to verify UM quality metrics and see details about the UM IP gateway's specific voice mail calls performed. The call data records for UM reporting are automatically stored after the call to the discovery metadata mailbox found with the fixed name SystemMailbox{e0dc1c29-89c3-4034-b678-e6c29d823ed9} for 90 days. This is enabled by default and cannot be changed. If you want to keep the records for a longer period, you need to export them.

> ***NOTE*** **If you're using OCS QmS (Quality of Experience Monitoring Server), the data is automatically also available to OCS.**

The UM reports are available in the EMC Toolbox, ECP, or EMS. The following UM tools are available:

- **Call Statistics** Shows the calls made, the quality of the call, and so on. You also can export a report and use another program such as Microsoft Excel to analyze it. Alternatively, you also can use the *Get-UMCallSummaryReport* cmdlet in the EMS to receive an aggregated view on calls received and made through your UM environment.
- **User Call Logs** When users complain about the quality of voice mails, the administrator can verify the UM logs to identify the reason for the issue. For example, you will see a summary of the voice mails the user received and the respective IP gateway of the voice mail, as shown in Figure 9-9.

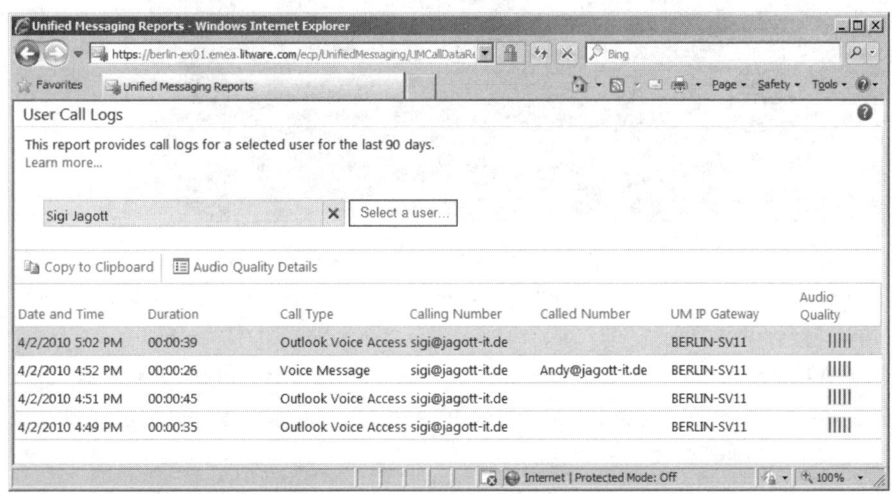

FIGURE 9-9 Viewing User Call Logs

Testing Unified Messaging Functionality

Testing the UM functionality is a bit trickier than testing other features such as message routing because it involves multiple components in the testing process such as voice, mailbox access, and so on. Only when testing this functionality end-to-end can you make sure it is working as expected. Several tools are available for testing your UM functionality.

UM Troubleshooting Tool

The UM Troubleshooting Tool is available with Exchange 2010 SP1 as a separate download to proactively test the voice mail functionality and identify any issues. The Troubleshooting Tool is able to simulate a call from OCS or IP gateway to your UM server and verifies that the UM communication is working as expected. It verifies that a call can be established, verifies that the audio flow from the UM server works, and prepares quality metrics for recorded audio.

You can install the UM Troubleshooting Tool on a workstation or server. The recommendation is to use an administrative workstation. It is available in x86 and x64 versions and requires the following prerequisites to be installed:

- Windows PowerShell v2
- .Net Framework 3.5 SP1
- Unified Communications Managed API (UCMA) v3.5

The UM Troubleshooting Tool provides you with a shell similar to the EMS and allows you to test UM connectivity with the *Test-ExchangeUMCallFlow* cmdlet, as shown in Figure 9-10.

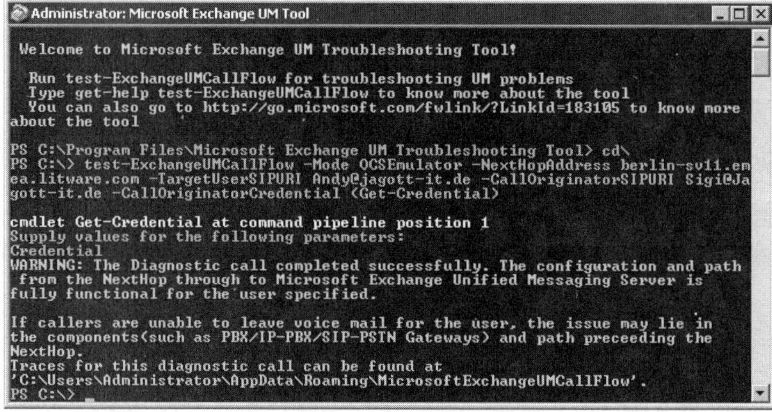

FIGURE 9-10 Microsoft Exchange UM Troubleshooting Tool

If you want to use the UM Troubleshooting Tool to test your UM server, you need to create the following:

- A UM dial plan with *Telephone Extension* as the URI type and *Unsecured* as VoIP security
- A UM IP gateway that points to the IP address of the workstation you installed the UM Troubleshooting Tool on
- A UM-enabled mailbox with an extension

After you create the prerequisites, run the *Test-ExchangeUMCallFlow –Mode GatewayEmulator –VoIPSecurity Unsecured –NextHopAddress <UMServer> -Diversion <Extension>* cmdlet to verify that the UM server is working correctly.

> ***NOTE*** You can use this tool to run against Exchange 2010 UM SP1 servers only!

Exchange UM Test Phone

The Microsoft Exchange UM Test Phone is a software phone that you can use to connect to your UM server and simulate specific IP gateway settings. It is based on the Exchange Speech Engine and can be used to troubleshoot connectivity.

The UM Test Phone (ExchangeUMTestPhone.exe) is no longer available on the Exchange 2010 DVD, but you can get it from an Exchange 2007 DVD and use it against your Exchange 2010 UM server.

> ***IMPORTANT*** **UM uses the Unified Communications Managed API 2.0 Core SDK (UCMA) in Exchange 2010 SP1; the Exchange UM Test Phone cannot connect anymore to run against SP1. You can only use it with Exchange 2010 RTM.**

You can install the Exchange UM Test Phone on a workstation or server that includes a microphone and speakers so you can verify that the speech is accurate and correct. Like the Exchange 2007 installation files, it is available in x86 and x64 versions. The UM Test Phone is shown in Figure 9-11.

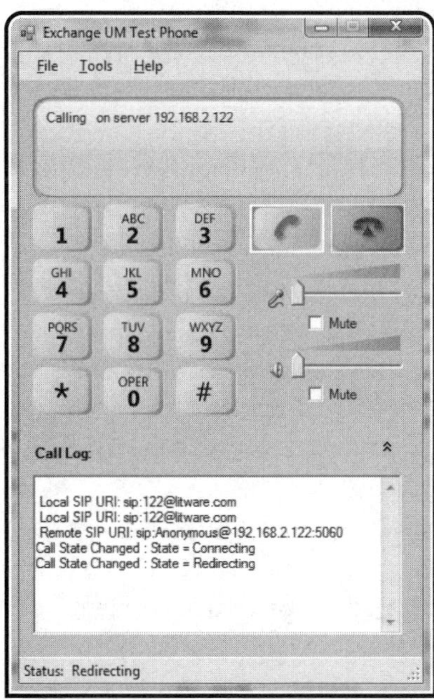

FIGURE 9-11 Using the UM Test Phone

Detailed information about how to test your UM server with the UM Test Phone can be found at *http://technet.microsoft.com/en-us/library/aa997146(EXCHG.80).aspx.*

Office Communication Server 2007 R2 Integration

Exchange Server 2010 UM provides OCS 2007 R2 with the voice mail feature, and OCS 2007 R2 can make presence information and instant messaging features available to your OWA users. You can also configure an automatic switchboard for your OCS 2007 R2 voice-enabled users using an UM auto attendant.

UM can also utilize an existing IP PBX that is configured with OCS 2007 R2—you do not need additional hardware to connect UM to your PBX if OCS 2007 R2 is installed already. Thus any PBX configuration can be managed from the OCS 2007 R2 side, and does not need to be configured again in Exchange 2010.

OCS 2007 R2 also provides other features that integrate into UM:

- **Instant messaging** The OCS 2007 R2 client provides instant messaging (IM) functionality that the OCS hosts. The solution provides IM features, such as group IM, and extends the internal IM infrastructure to external IM providers. You can implement IM directly into OWA.
- **Presence information** OCS 2007 R2 tracks presence information for all OCS users and provides this information to the OCS 2007 R2 client and other applications, such as Outlook 2007. You can implement presence information directly into OWA.
- **Web conferencing** OCS 2007 R2 can host on-premise conferences, which you can schedule or reschedule, and they can include IM, audio, video, application sharing, slide presentations, and other forms of data collaboration.
- **Audio conferencing** Users can join OCS 2007-based audio conferences using any desk or mobile phone. When connecting to an audio conference using a Web browser, users can provide a telephone number that the audio-conferencing services calls.
- **VoIP telephony** Enterprise Voice enables OCS 2007 R2 users to place calls from their computers by clicking an Outlook or Communicator contact. Users receive calls simultaneously on all their registered user endpoints, which may be a VoIP phone, a mobile phone, or an OCS 2007 R2 client. The OCS 2007 R2 Attendant is an integrated call-management client application that enables a user, such as a receptionist, to manage many conversations simultaneously.
- **Response Group service** This service enables administrators to create and configure one or more small response groups for routing and queuing incoming phone calls to one or more designated agents. Typical scenarios include an internal help desk or customer-service desks.

NOTES FROM THE FIELD

OCS 2007 R2 Integration: Extension Numbers

Korneel Bullens
Team Coordinator Unified Communications, Wortell, Netherlands

One of the things I am always asked about is when deploying OCS Enterprise Voice as PBX replacement; the users still require an extension number. When you configure the UM dial plan for OCS connectivity, you select SIP dial plan as the URI type and you still need to configure the number of digits in extension numbers for the UM dial plan. Many of the administrators I talk to would not expect to be asked for an extension number in an OCS- and UM-only scenario.

When you think about it, it's quite logical. You need a unique identifier when someone calls his voice mail from outside the company, and needs to select his own voice mail box. This is when the extension number comes into the game. You are free to assign your own extension numbers, just make sure when you create the UM dial plan, the amount of digits suits your needs. If you deploy 120 users for UM, use only three digits. Fewer digits mean fewer numbers to remember for your users.

Integrating OCS 2007 R2 in Exchange 2010 Architecture

Exchange 2010 UM completes the offering of OCS 2007 R2 with a voice mail solution based on messaging. This requires a tight integration between OCS 2007 R2 and Exchange 2010 UM. Together with the integration of IM in OWA, OCS 2007 R2 can be described as being fully connected to Exchange Server 2010, as shown in Figure 9-12.

The UM role communicates to the OCS Mediation server using the OCS Pool Name and thus contacts the OCS Front-End server. All signaling communication (SIP) and the voice stream (RTP) pass the OCS Front-End server.

When Office Communicator clients access their voice mail mailbox, they also do not directly contact the Exchange UM server role. Their communication is also handled by the OCS Front-End server.

NOTE **For more details about the communication between OCS 2007 R2 and UM, you can access the Office Communications Server 2007 R2 Workload Architecture Poster at** ***http://www.microsoft.com/downloads/details.aspx?displaylang=en&FamilyID=af2c17cb-207c-4c52-8811-0aca6dfadc94.***

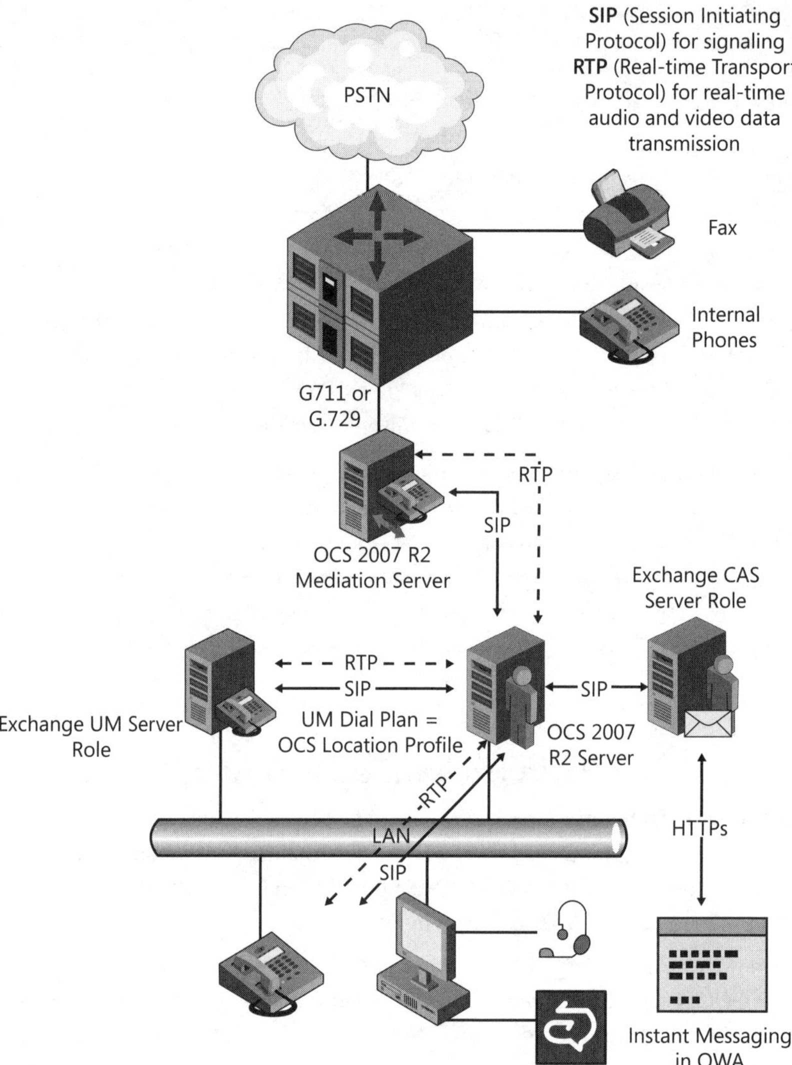

FIGURE 9-12 OCS 2007 R2 integration in Exchange 2010 architecture

Deploying UM and OCS 2007 R2 Integration

If you want to implement OCS 2007 R2 or later into your Exchange 2010 UM, your environment should consider the following requirements:

- One or more OCS 2007 R2 Front-End servers.
- At least one OCS 2007 R2 Mediation server connected to your PBX or phone system.
- UM server roles require a digital certificate that is enabled for UM service on that server.

- One or two phone numbers per OCS Location Profile—at least one for Subscriber Access and optionally one for an UM auto attendant. Particularly if you want to connect multiple office locations, you should consider at least a subscriber access number that is in the local phone range, but you can use a single UM auto attendant for the company.

Follow these steps to install OCS 2007 R2 integration for UM:

1. Create a UM dial plan for each of your available OCS Location Profiles:
   a. The dial plan name should, for example, include information about Exchange UM and only include characters supported by an OCS 2007 R2 Location Profile (such as no spaces).
   b. URI Type = SipName
   c. VoIP security = Secured or SIPSecured (OCS 2007 does not support unsecured VoIP security!)

> **NOTE** Make sure that your Office Communicator client encryption level reflects the VoIP security setting. If you configure VoIP Security as SIP Secured, you need to set it either to Rejected or Optional. If you use Secured as VoIP Security level, it must be either Required or Optional.

2. Configure your UM dial plan(s) with the correct OCS Location Profile Subscriber Access phone number.
3. Associate the UM server with the UM dial plans and make sure Startup Mode is Dual. If Startup Mode is changed, you need to restart the Microsoft Exchange UM service.
4. Run the *ExchUCUtil.ps1* script found in the *<Exchange_Install_path>*\Scripts folder. The script will perform the following tasks:
   a. Create one UM IP gateway for each OCS 2007 Enterprise Pool
   b. Create a UM hunt group for each UM IP gateway with their respective Pilot Identifiers
   c. Grant OCS 2007 servers permission to read Exchange UM objects in Active Directory
5. Use the *Set-UMIPGateway* cmdlet to configure the *Port* parameter of every created IP gateway to port 5061. You also use this cmdlet to disable outbound calling for all but one UM IP gateway. This is usually the gateway that is likely to handle the most traffic.
6. Run the *Get-UMDialPlan –Id <DialPlanName> |fl PhoneContext* cmdlet in EMS and remember the *PhoneContext* property—you'll need to create an OCS Location Profile with that exact name.
7. Create and configure required UM auto attendant(s). Assign them the correct UM dial plan and the access phone number from the OCS Location Profile.

8. On your OCS 2007 R2 Front-End server, create an OCS Location Profile in OCS 2007 R2 for the UM dial plan you created that matches the *PhoneContext* name.
9. Run the OcsUMUtil.exe tool found in the C:\Progam Files\Common Files\Microsoft Office Communication Server 2007 R2 folder. The tool will verify that OCS Location Profile and UM dial plan names match and allow you to create contacts for your Subscriber Access as well as auto-attendant access numbers.

NOTES FROM THE FIELD

Unified Messaging Transitioning and Extension Dialing

Gary A. Cooper
Senior Systems Architect, Horizons Consulting, Inc., United States

Within our organization, we had been utilizing Exchange Server 2007 UM in conjunction with Office Communication Server 2007 R2. This solution worked well, but we required the new features in Exchange Server 2010 UM—specifically RMS-protected Voicemail and Voicemail Preview. When we originally configured Exchange Server 2007 UM, we did not have enough Direct Inward Dial (DID) numbers for each mailbox that was UM-enabled, so we instead configured Exchange Server 2007 UM to use the auto attendant to answer all inbound calls and then to prompt the caller to select the appropriate person to contact. This worked well until we introduced Exchange Server 2010 and DID numbers.

To implement Exchange Server 2010, we had to create a new dial plan for OCS to route properly to the new UM server. This now forced each user to have two new EUM address entries after we moved their mailboxes to Exchange Server 2010 and migrated their UM to Exchange Server 2010 UM (by removing their old UM settings and re-provisioning them).

EUM: FirstName.LastName@Contoso.com;phone-context=<NewDialPlanName>

eum:<extension>;phone-context=<Exchange2010DialPlanName>

In testing, what we found was that if a call came into OCS for a mailbox we had already moved to Exchange 2010 UM, the main number would be answered by the auto attendant in Exchange Server 2007 UM; then, when the older UM server tried to route the caller to the Exchange 2010 UM server, it would error and tell the caller "The call has failed, please press '0' (zero) for the operator or dial someone by name or extension to reach them directly." If the caller tried to dial by name or extension number to mailboxes still on Exchange Server 2007 UM, it worked without issue. Behind the scenes, Exchange UM couldn't find the migrated mailbox and would route the call back to OCS 2007 R2, which would route it back to Exchange UM, and so on, and eventually the call failed and the caller was dropped.

In working with Product Support Services, we determined that Exchange 2007 was still looking for the proxy address for its dial plan in the following format:

eum:<extension>;phone-context=<Exchange2007DialPlanName>

We determined that when the caller entered the extension (such as - 204), Exchange Server 2007 UM would search for the user in the current dial plan (the dial plan associated with the auto attendant that answered the call)—in this case the Exchange 2007 Sip_Name dial plan. It did this search by constructing the EUM address (*204; phone-context=<Exchange 2007 Dial plan Name>.< Exchange 2007 Dial plan GUID>*) and then searching all Active Directory users to check whether any user had this stamped in their proxy addresses. However, the migrated mailbox that has been moved to Exchange 2010 UM-has been provisioned on the new Exchange 2010 Sip_Name dial plan, so it no longer has the Exchange 2007 proxy address, and so the user object is not located.

The solution we ended up implementing was to add the legacy EUM proxy address back to the mailbox object, thus enabling extension dialing from both Exchange 2007 and Exchange 2010 UM services.

Deploying Instant Messaging for OWA

A new feature in Exchange 2010 is the integration of Instant Messaging (IM) into Outlook Web App, so your OWA users can see who is online and directly chat with the users without the requirement of installing Office Communicator on their client computer.

NOTE IM integration for OWA does not require a UM server role to be installed in your environment; it just requires OCS 2007 R2 to be available. For that reason the feature also does not require an Exchange E-CAL like UM does.

To deploy this functionality, you need to install the OCS 2007 R2 Web Service Provider on all Client Access servers, enable IM on the Client Access server, and configure the OCS 2007 R2 Server to be able to access the Client Access server.

For IM integration you need the following:

- The Firewall configuration between the OCS 2007 R2 and Client Access server needs to allow the following TCP ports: 5061 (SIP), 5075, 5076, and 5077.
- The Client Access server requires a digital certificate that includes the FQDN or Client Access server array name as Subject Name and is from the same CA as the certificate of the OCS server. Certificates from different CAs—even if the CAs are trusted—might cause problems.

You must perform the following steps on every Client Access Server role where users access OWA and want to use IM:

1. Download the Microsoft Office Communications Server 2007 R2 Web Service Provider at *http://go.microsoft.com/fwlink/?LinkID=135129* and run CWAOWASSPMain.msi to extract the package:
   a. Run vcredist_x64.exe to install Microsoft Visual C++ 2008 Redistributable.
   b. Run Ucmaredist.msi to install the OCS 2007 R2 Unified Communication Managed API 2.0 Core Redistributable.
   c. Run CWAOWASSP.msi to install the OCS 2007 R2 Web Service Provider.
2. Download and install the API 2.0 Core update for Windows Server 2008 R2 with the file name UcmaRedist.msp at *http://www.microsoft.com/downloads/details.aspx?FamilyID=b3b02475-150c-41fa-844a-c10a517040f4*.
3. Identify the Client Access server's certificate subject name and thumbprint using the *Get-ExchangeCertificate |fl* cmdlet.
4. Configure the OWA Virtual Directory of the Client Access server to enable IM by running the *Get-OwaVirtualDirectory –Server <CAS-server> | Set-OWAVirtualDirectory –InstantMessagingServerName <OCS-server> - InstantMessagingCertificateThumbprint <thumbprint> -InstantMessagingEnabled $true –InstantMessagingType OCS* cmdlet, as shown in Figure 9-13.

```
Machine: Berlin-Ex01.emea.litware.com
[PS] C:\Windows\system32>Get-ExchangeCertificate |fl

AccessRules        : {System.Security.AccessControl.CryptoKeyAccessRule, System.Security.AccessControl.CryptoKeyAccessR
                     ule, System.Security.AccessControl.CryptoKeyAccessRule}
CertificateDomains : {BERLIN-EX01.emea.litware.com}
HasPrivateKey      : True
IsSelfSigned       : False
Issuer             : CN=LITWARE-CA, DC=emea, DC=litware, DC=com
NotAfter           : 3/22/2011 1:39:13 AM
NotBefore          : 3/22/2010 1:39:13 AM
PublicKeySize      : 2048
RootCAType         : Enterprise
SerialNumber       : 125338E4000000000019
Services           : IMAP, POP, IIS, SMTP
Status             : Valid
Subject            : CN=BERLIN-EX01.emea.litware.com             <- Required for OCS Configuration (Authorized Host)
Thumbprint         : B2F8BB4C70198C9C38BD5E61D609D71C8B8E021F    <- Required for Exchange CAS Configuration (see below)

[PS] C:\Windows\system32>Get-OwaVirtualDirectory -Server berlin-ex01 | Set-OwaVirtualDirectory -InstantMessagingServerNa
me berlin-svl1.emea.litware.com -InstantMessagingCertificateThumbprint B2F8BB4C70198C9C38BD5E61D609D71C8B8E021F -Instant
MessagingEnabled $true -InstantMessagingType OCS
[PS] C:\Windows\system32>_
```

FIGURE 9-13 Enabling IM on Client Access server

> ***NOTE*** **In Exchange 2010 RTM this task required modifying web.config file located in the <*Exchange_Install*>\ClientAccess\Owa folder. If you have not installed Exchange 2010 SP1 yet, please follow the instructions to configure the web.config file at *http://technet.microsoft.com/en-us/library/ee633458.aspx*.**

5. Restart World Wide Web Publishing Service to apply the changes. Remember, restarting the service will disconnect all active users.

After you have configured the Client Access Server role, you need to perform the following steps on your OCS 2007 R2 Server:

1. In the Office Server 2007 R2 Management Console, on your OCS 2007 R2 pool, open Front-End properties.
2. On the Host Authorization tab, click Add Authorized Host and configure the Client Access Server or the Client Access Server namespace. In Settings, select Throttle As Server and Treat As Authenticated, as shown in Figure 9-14.

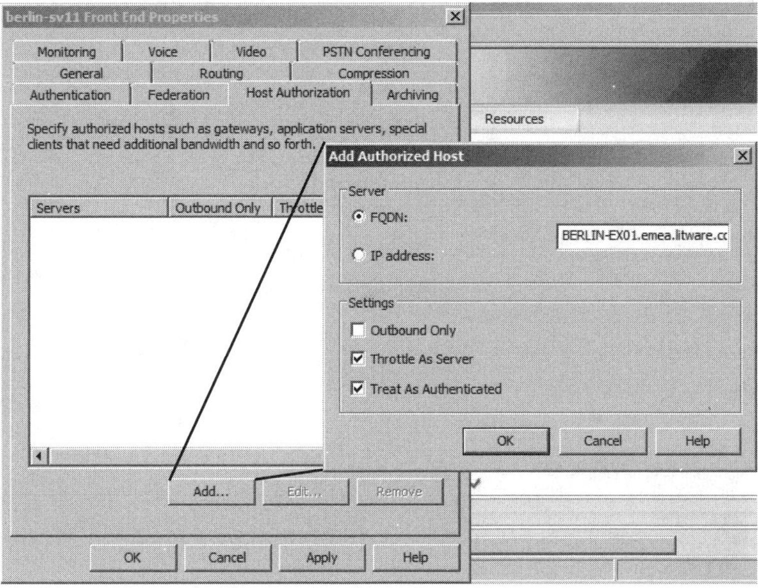

FIGURE 9-14 Adding an authorized host in OCS 2007 R2

> ***NOTE*** **The Server name must be exactly the same as the Subject name of the certificate you have configured on your Client Access server(s).**

3. For the settings to take effect immediately, you need to restart Office Communication Server Front-End service. Be aware that this will disconnect any active users.

After you've configured your OCS 2007 R2 and Client Access Server role, your users should see their presence information and should be able to chat with their contacts using OWA as shown in Figure 9-15.

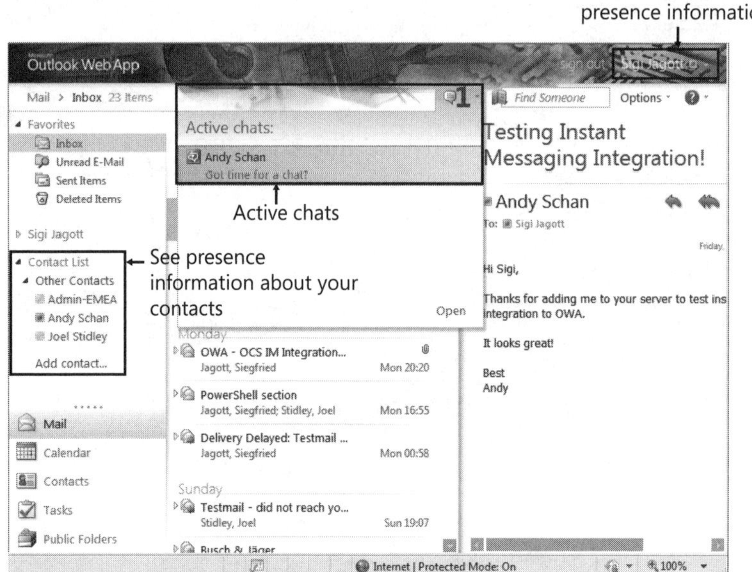

FIGURE 9-15 Instant Messaging integration in OWA

Additional Resources

- Quick Start Guide for Outlook Voice Access 2010: *http://go.microsoft.com/fwlink/?LinkId=137165*
- Telephony Advisor for Exchange 2010: *http://technet.microsoft.com/en-us/library/ee364753.aspx*
- RFC 3261 - SIP: Session Initiation Protocol: *http://tools.ietf.org/html/rfc3261*
- RFC 3550 - RTP: A Transport Protocol for Real-Time Applications: *http://tools.ietf.org/html/rfc3550*
- Fax Advisor for Exchange 2010: *http://technet.microsoft.com/en-us/library/ee364747.aspx*
- Client Language Support for Unified Messaging: *http://technet.microsoft.com/en-us/library/dd638119.aspx*
- Testing a Unified Messaging Server with the Unified Messaging Test Phone: *http://technet.microsoft.com/en-us/library/aa997146(EXCHG.80).aspx*
- Office Communications Server 2007 R2 Workload Architecture Poster: *http://www.microsoft.com/downloads/details.aspx?displaylang=en&FamilyID=af2c17cb-207c-4c52-8811-0aca6dfadc94*
- Managing Outlook Web App and Office Communications Server 2007 Integration: *http://technet.microsoft.com/en-us/library/ee633458.aspx*

CHAPTER 10

Federated Delegation

The days when a user worked exclusively with internal recipients are long behind us. Today information workers collaborate with a multitude of external recipients including customers, vendors, and partners. As part of this collaboration, users frequently need to share their availability (free/busy) information, calendar details, and even their contacts with external recipients. In addition, this ability is commonly required in cross-premises scenarios where a portion of the organization is hosted externally with the rest hosted in-house.

To provide a solution for sharing information externally in a secure fashion, an underlying trust framework is provided by federation in Exchange Server 2010. Federated delegation (formerly known as federated sharing) then uses the federation framework to allow for the secure sharing of availability, calendar details, and contacts with external recipients.

In this chapter, we will discuss the technology and best practices surrounding federated delegation, beginning with an introduction and overview of the technologies and concepts, followed by a discussion on managing federation and delegation in your environment. Then we'll go over various federation scenarios, and finally wrap things up with troubleshooting federation and federated delegation.

Introduction to Federated Delegation in Exchange Server 2010

Before jumping into managing federated delegation and a discussion of the various scenarios, let's start out with an overview of federation, its challenges, and its implementation in Exchange Server 2010.

Overview of Federation and Federated Delegation

Federated delegation in Exchange Server 2010—and the underlying federation infrastructure with the Microsoft Federation Gateway—is an innovative means of securely sharing information with external recipients with minimal management overhead compared with traditional federation technologies. A common request is for end users to determine the availability of users in other organizations when planning meetings, short of calling them on the phone and asking them what times work for them.

Federation Overview

For Star Trek fans, federation may have a different meaning, but for the purposes of this discussion federation is used in the context of federated identity. *Federated identity* means a user's authentication and authorization process across multiple IT systems (or Exchange organizations, in our case). It can also refer to the assembling of a user's identity from disparate identity management systems, but for the purposes of this discussion we are concerned with authentication and authorization.

Federation is a claims-based means of providing secure Web-based authentication and authorization across organizations and platforms without needing to replicate or reproduce the user's identity or attributes (referred to as "claims," such as e-mail address, UPN, display name, and so on) in another directory or other information silo. This means that a user can perform single sign-on (SSO) across organizational boundaries without the need for directory or GAL synchronization, or learning another set of credentials, or needing to have the other organization store and manage replicated credentials or directory objects. A user's identity, e-mail address, and other requested attributes are asserted as claims in tokens, which are presented to an application to verify the user and the user's attributes. Microsoft's federation implementation, Active Directory Federation Services (AD FS), was first introduced in Windows Server 2003 R2 and is based on the industry standard WS-Federation specification, which is part of the WS-* Web Services Architecture.

In a typical deployment, federation was enabled between organizations through each organization standing up a federation infrastructure and then establishing a secure federation trust between them. These federation trusts are conceptually similar to Active Directory forest trusts in that a trust was established between the organizations to allow one organization to trust authentication tokens issued by the other organization. In reality, a federation trust is Web-based and is enabled through the sharing of public keys between the organizations, unlike Active Directory trusts. In addition, because it is Web-based, a federation trust requires only port 443 communication between the components.

Because these federation trusts are at the organizational level, every organization must create a trust with every other organization. This means that to establish trusts with multiple organizations, (n*(n–1)) trusts are required, where n represents the number of organizations involved. This is illustrated in a configuration involving four organizations in Figure 10-1.

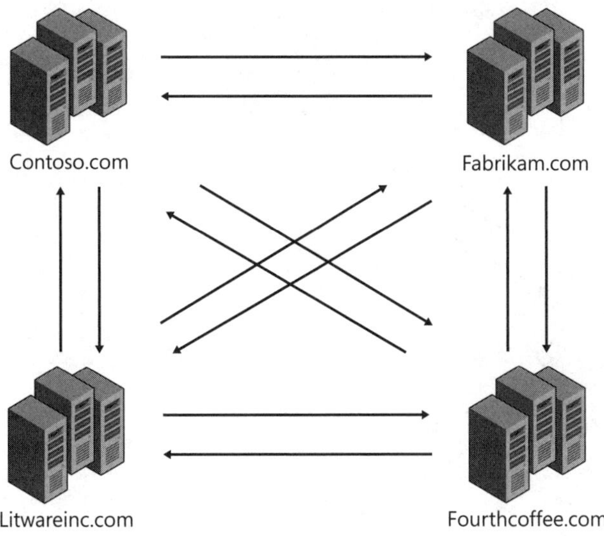

FIGURE 10-1 Multiple federation trusts in a standard federation deployment

As you can see, the standard federation deployment shown in Figure 10-1 means that the configuration and management of a large number of trusts can quickly become unwieldy as more organizations are involved, requiring you to share your public keys with each organization you have a trust with, and maintain their public keys in your organization.

Role of the Microsoft Federation Gateway

To simplify this management challenge, Exchange Server 2010 uses the Microsoft Federation Gateway (MFG) as a trust broker. The Microsoft Federation Gateway is an identity backbone that runs in the cloud, acting as a hub for federation activity between (in this case) Exchange Server 2010 organizations. This means that you only need to create one federation trust with the Microsoft Federation Gateway rather than with each organization you want to establish a relationship with. The MFG will be discussed in more detail in the next section of this chapter, but an example of the federation trusts with the MFG are shown in Figure 10-2 for the same four organizations depicted in Figure 10-1. To establish a trust with the Microsoft Federation Gateway service, your organization must obtain an X.509 certificate from a third-party certificate authority (CA) as well as verify their ownership of the domain they are federating by publishing an application identifier (appID) in a TXT resource record in the DNS zone for that domain. The certificate and DNS requirements for the federation trust are discussed in more detail in the "Federation Trust" section of this chapter.

> ***NOTE*** **It is important to point out that the Microsoft Federation Gateway acts as a broker service (intermediary) only; no credentials or passwords are stored there and no Windows Live accounts are necessary for its use. Its only function is to facilitate the federation trust to enable organizations to share information securely without needing to establish individual trusts between each other.**

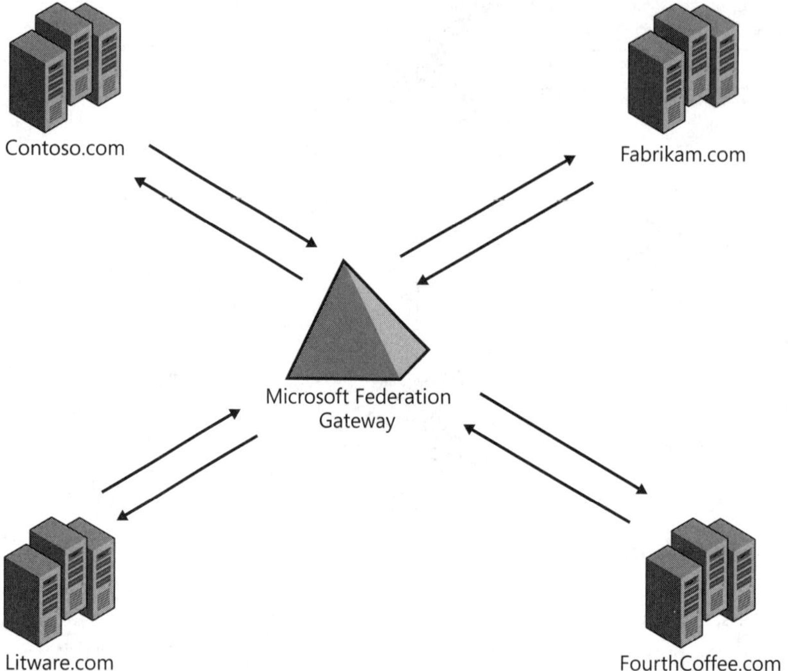

FIGURE 10-2 Microsoft Federation Gateway as trust broker

After you have created a single federation trust with the MFG for your organization, you simply configure an organization relationship with another organization to enable you to start sharing information securely; you don't need to exchange any certificates or metadata with the other organization. We will discuss federation trusts and organization relationships in more detail in the "Fundamentals and Components of Federated Delegation" section of this chapter.

Fundamentals and Components of Federated Delegation

The primary components of federation delegation are the federation trust, organization relationships, and sharing policies.

Federation Trust

The following prerequisites are necessary for creating and managing the federation trust:

- The domain used for establishing a federation trust must be resolvable from the Internet. This means that the domain must be resolvable via DNS from the Internet and that the domain is registered with a domain registrar. Best practice is to use your primary SMTP domain (for example, contoso.com) rather than your internal Active

Directory namespace, which may not be resolvable from the Internet (for example, contosocorp.local).

- For cross-premises scenarios, where an organization hosts some mailboxes on site and hosts others in the Exchange Online service, it is recommended to use a sub-domain of exchangedelegation.<*your primary SMTP domain*> to avoid namespace conflicts with the Exchange Online tenant namespace. Your primary SMTP domain should then be added as an additional URI to your federated organization identifier using the *Add-FederatedDomain* cmdlet.

- You require a valid X.509 SSL certificate issued by a Certification Authority (CA) trusted by Windows Live to be able to configure a trust with the MFG. The CAs trusted by Windows Live (and, by extension, the MFG) are listed in the "Certificate Requirements for Federation Trust" section of this chapter, along with more details on the subject name requirements.
- After the federation trust is created, you must provide proof of ownership for the domain specified by creating a TXT resource record in your external DNS. This TXT record contains the application identifier (AppID) provided in the output when the federation trust is created with either the New Federation Trust Wizard or the *New-FederationTrust* cmdlet.

Certificate Requirements for Federation Trust

The certificate used for the federation trust must meet the following requirements:

- The certificate must be issued by a certification authority trusted by the MFG. You can obtain the most current list of trusted root Certification Authorities at *http://technet.microsoft.com/en-us/library/ee332350.aspx*, but the following CAs are presently trusted:
  - Comodo
  - Digicert Global Root CA
  - Digicert High Assurance EV Root CA
  - Entrust.net CA (2048)
  - Entrust Secure Server CA
  - Go Daddy Secure Certification Authority
- The certificate must have a subject key identifier field. The X.509 certificates issued by the majority of commercial CAs have this field already.
- Certificates using Cryptography Next Generation (CNG) cryptographic service providers (CSPs) aren't supported for federation; the certificate must use a CryptoAPI CSP. A CryptoAPI provider is used when you create your certificate request using the Exchange Server 2010 New Certificate Wizard.
- The certificate must use the RSA signature algorithm.

- The private key for the certificate must be exportable. This is configured automatically when you create the certificate request using the New Certificate Wizard in the EMC or the *New-ExchangeCertificate* cmdlet.
- The certificate must be current and valid; an expired or revoked certificate cannot be used.
- The certificate must include the enhanced key usage (EKU) type Client Authentication (1.3.6.1.5.5.7.3.2); this usage type is used for proving your identity to a remote computer. The Client Authentication usage type is included by default when you use the New Exchange Certificate Wizard in the EMC or the *New-ExchangeCertificate* cmdlet to generate the certificate request.

NOTE **The certificate used for the federation trust does not have any subject name or subject alternative name requirements; the subject name can be the server's host name or the domain name—or any other name can be specified. When the trust is established, Exchange Server 2010 distributes the certificate to all other Exchange Server 2010 Client Access and Hub Transport servers in the organization automatically, as discussed in the Certificate Distribution section of this chapter.**

Creating the Federation Trust

You create the federation trust by exchanging the X.509 certificate for your organization with the MFG, and retrieving the X.509 certificate and federation metadata from the MFG. These tasks are performed for you when you create the federation trust with the Exchange Server 2010 Exchange Management Console (EMC) or Exchange Management Shell (EMS).

In the EMC, you create the federation trust by selecting the Organization Configuration node and then clicking New Federation Trust on the Actions pane as shown in Figure 10-3.

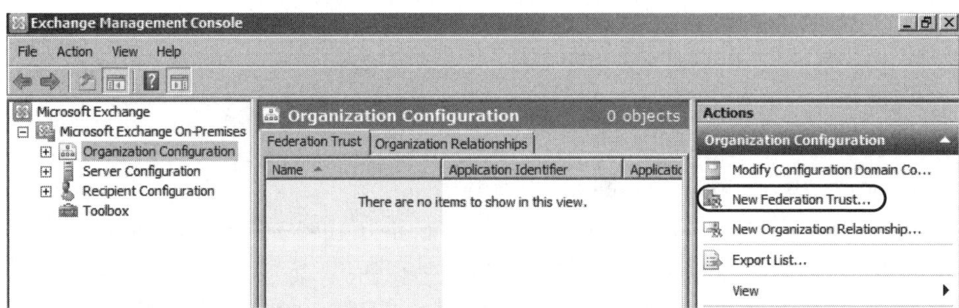

FIGURE 10-3 Creating a federation trust in the EMC

In the resultant New Federation Trust Wizard (shown in Figure 10-4), you select the certificate used for the trust and create the trust by clicking New.

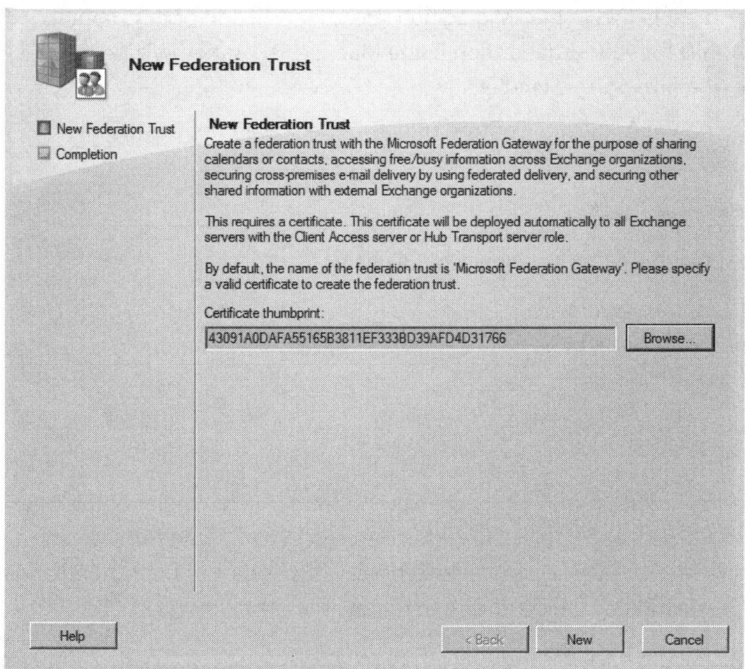

FIGURE 10-4 The New Federation Trust Wizard

> ***NOTE*** **Creating a federation trust is a one-time configuration; you can only have one federation trust per Exchange Server 2010 organization. After the trust is created, the New Federation Trust option is no longer available in the EMC.**

You can also create the federation trust using the *New-FederationTrust* cmdlet in the EMS. The parameters required for the cmdlet are *-Name* and *–Thumbprint*. *-Thumbprint* is the thumbprint of the certificate being used for the federation trust; to get a list of the certificates available and their thumbprints, use the following cmdlet:

```
Get-ExchangeCertificate | where {$_.IsSelfSigned -eq $false} | fl
```

After you obtain the thumbprint, the federation trust is created with the *New-FederationTrust* cmdlet. An example of this cmdlet for Contoso with a certificate with a thumbprint of AC00F35CBA8359953F4126E0984B5CCAFA2F4F17 is as follows:

```
New-FederationTrust -Name "Contoso-MFG Trust" -Thumbprint
AC00F35CBA8359953F4126E0984B5CCAFA2F4F17
```

After the federation trust has been successfully created, an AppID is provided in the output of the New Federation Trust Wizard (or the output of the *New-FederationTrust* cmdlet, if you created your federation trust using the EMS). This AppID is used in configuring your accepted domains for federation, as explained in the "Managing Federation" section of this chapter. You can also view the AppID for your organization in the Manage Federation Wizard in the EMC or by using the *Get-FederationTrust* cmdlet.

An example of obtaining the AppID for Contoso using the *Get-FederationTrust* cmdlet is as follows:

```
Get-FederationTrust | fl name, appl*
```

The output of this cmdlet should be similar to the following:

```
Name                  : Contoso-MFG Trust
ApplicationIdentifier : 000000004001A66A
ApplicationUri        : contoso.com
```

CERTIFICATE DISTRIBUTION

When you create the federation trust with either the *New-FederationTrust* cmdlet or the New Federation Trust Wizard, the task also copies the certificate used to all CA and Hub servers in the same Active Directory site. The Cert Distribution Service, which is part of the MS Exchange Service Host service, then distributes the certificate to remote sites as follows:

The Cert Distribution Service on CA and Hub servers in remote Active Directory sites monitors Active Directory for changes on the certificates and tries to retrieve the new certificate immediately on any change. The service detects new certificates through reading the certificate thumbprint stored in Active Directory.

- The Cert Distribution Service will first attempt to retrieve the new certificate from a CA or Hub server within the same Active Directory site.
- If the certificate is not available within the same site, the service will attempt to retrieve the new certificate from CA or Hub servers in adjacent sites, such as any that are one hop away. It will try the sites in the order of least Active Directory cost.
- If retrieving the new certificate from an adjacent site fails, an error is logged and the service attempts to retrieve the certificate again in one hour.

Managing Federation

After you have created your federation trust, you must perform some management and configuration steps.

CONFIGURING DNS FOR PROOF OF OWNERSHIP

After you have created your federation trust, you must provide proof of ownership for the domain specified during the creation of the trust, as well as any other accepted domains you will be using with federation; we will discuss configuring additional accepted domains for federation in the "Configuring Domains for Federation" section of this chapter. Providing proof of ownership is accomplished by creating a TXT resource record in your external DNS containing the AppID provided when the federation trust was created. This TXT record is created in the DNS zone for each accepted domain using federation. The following is an example of this text record for Fabrikam:

```
fabrikam.com IN TXT AppID=000000004001A66A
```

CONFIGURING DOMAINS FOR FEDERATION

You specify which authoritative accepted domains in your Exchange organization are configured for federation through the use of the federated organization identifier; domains are added to the federated organization identifier, then proof of ownership is established through creating a TXT record for that domain as outlined in the "Configuring DNS for Proof of Ownership" section of this chapter. A user must be configured with an e-mail address defined in the organization identifier for the MFG to recognize that user and allow that user to use any of the federated delegation features.

The first domain used for federation is set using the *Set-FederatedOrganizationIdentifier* cmdlet with the *–AccountNamespace* parameter; this is the only federated domain that is configured in the MFG. The URIs (Uniform Resource Identifiers) for additional domains are configured in the federated organization identifier through the use of the Manage Federation Wizard in the EMC or by using the EMS. The following cmdlet adds the domain fabrikam.co.uk as a federated domain:

```
Add-FederatedDomain fabrikam.co.uk
```

> **NOTE** It is not necessary to configure additional URIs if all users have a primary or secondary SMTP address for the domain defined in the *-AccountNamespace* parameter of your federated organization identifier. Whether the domain is their primary SMTP address is unimportant.

Adding an accepted domain using the Manage Federation Wizard in the EMC is shown in Figure 10-5.

To determine which domains in your organization are federated, you can use the cmdlet *Get-FederatedOrganizationIdentifier*; this cmdlet outputs all of the federated domains defined in the federated organization identifier. You can also view the federated domains by using the Manage Federation Wizard in the EMC.

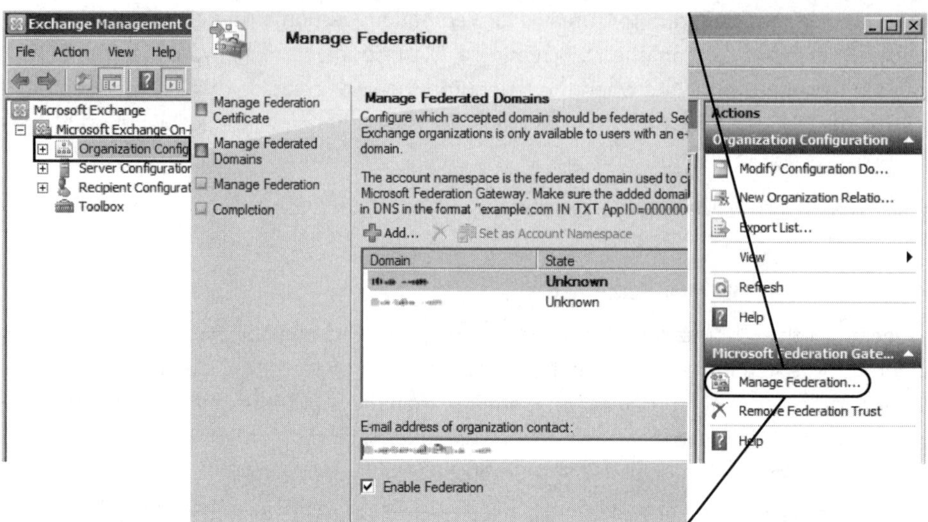

FIGURE 10-5 Adding accepted domains for federation using the Manage Federation Wizard

MANAGING CERTIFICATES FOR FEDERATION

The X.509 certificate used for the federation trust is specified during the creation of the trust and automatically distributed to all Client Access and Hub Transport servers in your organization, as outlined in the Certificate Distribution section of this chapter. If you need to replace the federation trust certificate, you accomplish this by installing the new certificate on an Exchange Server 2010 Client Access or Hub Transport server (or some other computer with the Exchange Server 2010 management tools installed) and then configuring the federation trust from that computer to designate it as the Next Certificate. Exchange Server 2010 then automatically distributes the certificate to all Exchange Server 2010 Client Access and Hub Transport servers; when this distribution has completed, the federation trust is switched to the new certificate by defining it as the Current Certificate.

You can manage the certificates used for federation with the *Set-FederationTrust* cmdlet; the *–Thumbprint* parameter configures the specified certificate as the next certificate, as shown in this example:

```
Set-FederationTrust -Identity MyFederationTrust -Thumbprint
AC00F35CBA8359953F4126E0984B5CCAFA2F4F17
```

After the next certificate has been designated, it is automatically distributed to all Exchange Server 2010 Client Access and Hub Transport servers. You can use the *Test-FederationTrustCertificate* cmdlet or the Manage Federation Wizard to check the distribution status of the certificate. The distribution process is described in detail in the "Certificate Distribution" section of this chapter.

After the distribution of the next certificate has been verified, you can set it as the current certificate, as shown here:

```
Set-FederationTrust –PublishFederationCertificate
```

Alternatively, you can manage the federation certificates using the Manage Federation Wizard as shown in Figure 10-6.

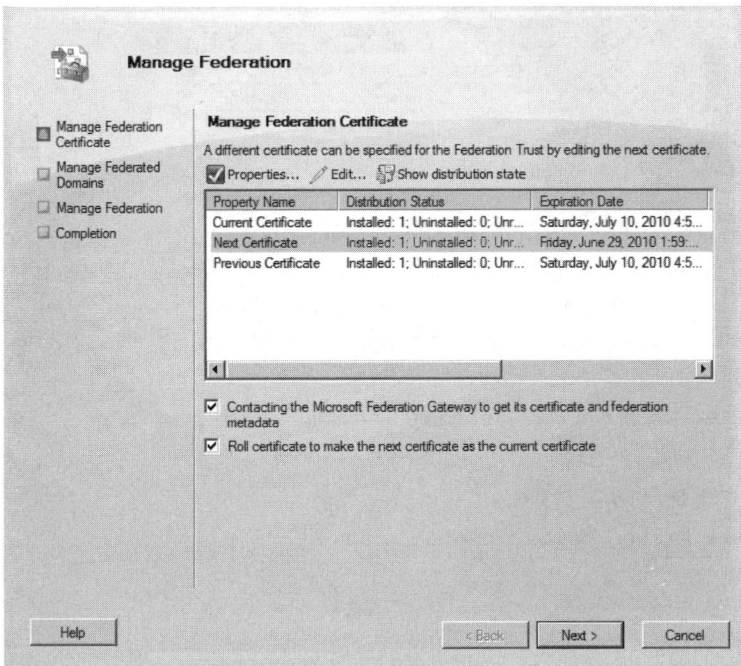

FIGURE 10-6 The Manage Federation Wizard

Organization Relationships

After you have created and configured a federation trust, you can establish organization relationships with other organizations (assuming that they have established a federation trust of their own).

Organization relationships provide the means to share availability (free/busy) information between organizations. When you create an organization relationship with an external organization, users in that external organization can access availability information for your users. For your users to access availability information from the external organization, however, an organization relationship must be configured on their side as well.

You can configure an organization relationship using either the EMC or the EMS. Having a federation trust in place is a prerequisite to successfully creating an organization relationship. In the EMC, you start the New Organization Relationship Wizard by selecting Organization Configuration on the navigation pane and then clicking New Organization Relationship on the actions pane, as shown in Figure 10-7.

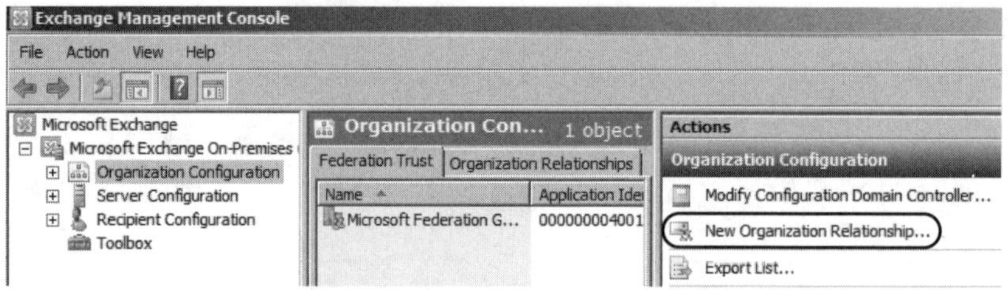

FIGURE 10-7 Starting the New Organization Relationship Wizard

To create an organization relationship to share availability information, on the Introduction page of the wizard you define a name for the relationship, define the free/busy data access level, and specify a security distribution group containing the internal members whose free busy data will be accessible via the relationship, as shown in Figure 10-8. The free/busy data access level can be set to three levels:

- No Free/Busy Access (used when organization relationship is established for federated delivery only)
- Free/Busy Access With Time Only
- Free/Busy Access With Time, Plus Subject And Location

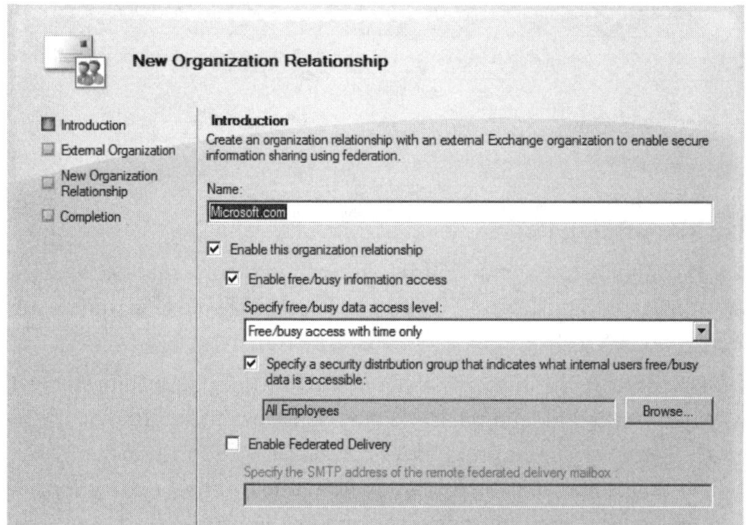

FIGURE 10-8 Introduction page of the New Organization Relationship Wizard

> ***NOTE*** Details, attachments, and attendees are not made accessible via the organization relationship; to view that level of information, the user must create a Sharing Invitation to the user in the other organization. The level of detail that can be shared via a sharing invitation is determined by the Sharing Policy assigned to the user; Sharing Policies and sharing invitations are discussed in more detail in the "Sharing Policies" and "Calendar and Contacts Sharing" sections of this chapter.

On the External Organization page of the wizard, you can specify a federated domain of the external organization and have the configuration information automatically discovered via the MFG as shown in Figure 10-9. Alternately, you can manually enter the configuration information in the bottom half of the screen.

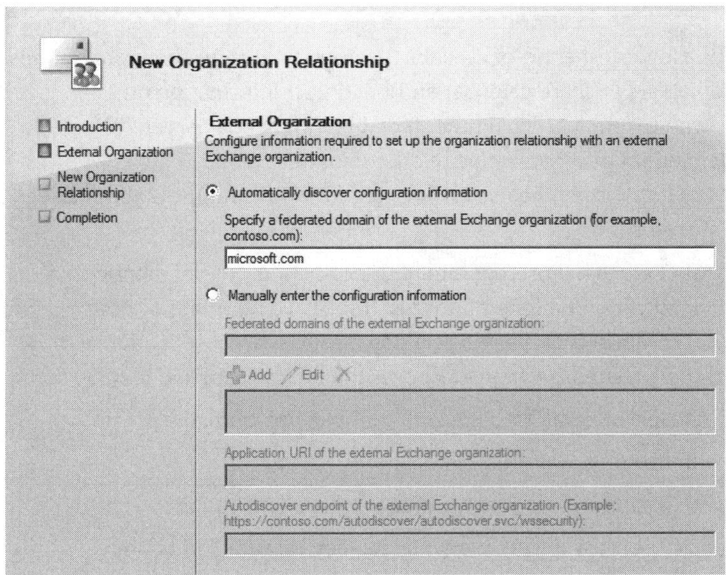

FIGURE 10-9 External Organization page of the New Organization Relationship Wizard

Via the EMS, you can create an organization relationship by automatically discovering the configuration as shown in the following example:

```
Get-FederationInformation -DomainName Contoso.com | New-OrganizationRelationship -Name
"Contoso" -FreeBusyAccessEnabled $true -FreeBusyAccessLevel LimitedDetails
```

An important point to note is that for *Get-FederationInformation* to work, DNS records must be correctly configured so that Autodiscover is resolvable to an external-facing CA server. For example, for the preceding cmdlet a CNAME record must be in place to resolve autodiscover.contoso.com to an Exchange Server 2010 Client Access server that is accessible from the Internet.

Alternatively, the following example shows how you can configure an organization relationship with Contoso by specifying the configuration information manually if Autodiscover is unsuccessful:

```
New-OrganizationRelationship -Name "Contoso" -Domainnames "contoso.com","northamerica
.contoso.com"," europe.contoso" -FreeBusyAccessEnabled $true -FreeBusyAccessLevel
LimitedDetails -TargetAutodiscoverEpr "https://mail.contoso.com/autodiscover/
autodiscover.svc/wssecurity" -TargetApplicationUri "mail.contoso.com"
```

In most cases, it is recommended to resolve any Autodiscover issues, if possible, and then create the organization relationship by retrieving the configuration information from the Microsoft Federation Gateway automatically.

Sharing Policies

Organization relationships allow for sharing of availability information between organizations. Sharing polices enable your users to share calendar and/or contact information on a person-to-person basis with external users in other federated Exchange Server 2010 organizations. This is independent of organization relationships, and requires the participation and consent of both users (the user in your organization and the external user the information is being shared with).

Having a federation trust in place is a prerequisite to using sharing policies; although sharing policies can be defined without a federation trust, they have no effect without the trust. A sharing policy is comprised of the external domains to share information with, the level of detail allowed to be shared, and the mailboxes the policy is applied to.

You can identify various levels of detail to share with the specified domains:

- Calendar sharing with free/busy information only
- Calendar sharing with free/busy information, plus subject and location
- Calendar sharing with free/busy information plus subject, location, and body
- Contacts sharing
- Calendar sharing with free/busy information only, Contacts sharing
- Calendar sharing with free/busy information, plus subject and location; Contacts sharing
- Calendar sharing with free/busy information plus subject, location, and body; Contacts sharing

Figure 10-10 shows a policy being created for Contoso users to share complete Calendar information as well as Contacts with fabrikam.com users.

After you define the sharing policy, you assign it to the appropriate users. If a user is not assigned a specific sharing policy, the default sharing policy applies to that user. One sharing policy must always be designated as the default policy.

Users can create a sharing invitation in Outlook 2010 or OWA and define the level of detail to share with the external user up to the level allowed by the sharing policy assigned to them. For example, if the sharing policy assigned allows "Calendar sharing with free/busy information, plus subject and location" with fabrikam.com, the user can either share only her availability, or share limited details with users from fabrikam.com; she will not be able to share the body of calendar entries or Contacts with fabrikam.com users.

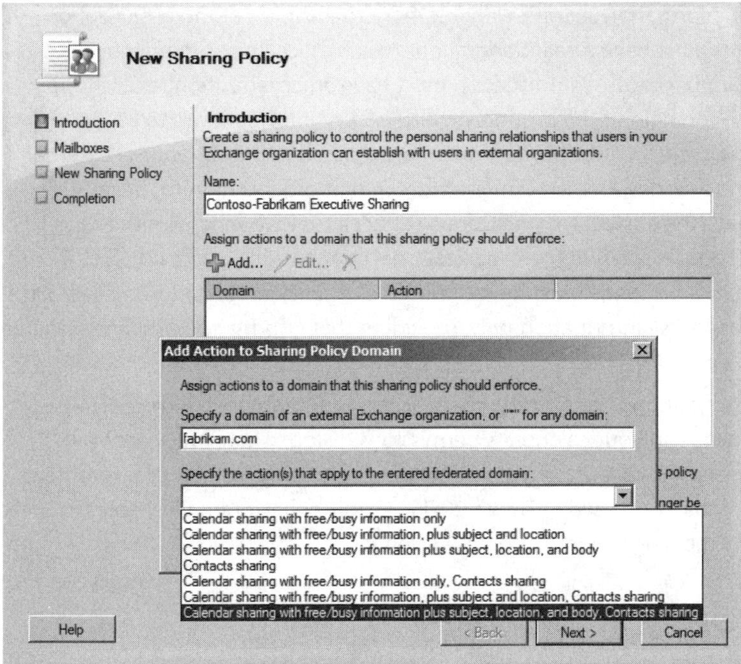

FIGURE 10-10 The New Sharing Policy Wizard

Only one sharing policy can be assigned to any one user, although a sharing policy can include numerous domain and action pairings. In addition, a sharing policy can include the * domain definition, which means that the action defined applies to *all* domains, unless a more specific domain and action pairing is defined in the same policy.

> ***NOTE*** **To disallow any person-to-person sharing for particular users, simply disable the sharing policy assigned to those users. Disabling the default sharing policy disallows person-to-person for all users except those assigned other policies that are still enabled.**

Interaction of Permissions, Organization Relationships, and Sharing Policies

Because federated delegation is a new topic for most Exchange Server 2010 administrators, let's examine the relationship between Calendar permissions (the Access Control List, or ACL, on the user's default Calendar), sharing policies, and organization relationships.

An important point to keep in mind is that any organization relationships in place honor the permissions defined for the default entry in your calendar's permissions dialog. That is, if the default entry is changed from the standard Free/Busy time setting to None, neither external nor internal users will see your free/busy information.

To enable free/busy information sharing with another organization at the organization level, both organizations must have a valid federation trust in place. In addition, the organization that is sharing free/busy information must have an organization relationship configured for the SMTP domain of the organization free/busy information is to be shared with. In a case where recipients for your organization are defined in the GAL of the external organization, you need to work with the administrators of that organization to make sure that those recipients have the correct target address set because Exchange uses the target address of an external recipient to find the organizational relationship. To provide for two-way sharing, both organizations must have applicable organization relationships in place. This offers sharing of free/busy information only, providing that information which is available via the availability service.

In contrast to an organization relationship, where access is determined by the permissions defined for the default entry in your calendar's permissions dialog, when you share your calendar with an external user via a sharing invitation, a unique entry for that user is added to the ACL for your Calendar, as shown in Figure 10-11. As this behavior implies, access is still ultimately controlled by the permissions set on the calendar.

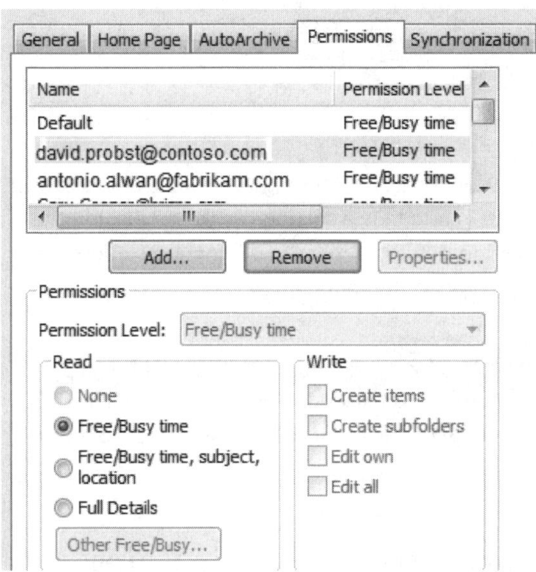

FIGURE 10-11 Calendar Permissions dialog box

However, the primary difference between organization relationships and sharing policies is that whereas organization policies provide access to the Availability service between organizations, sharing policies provide the ability for end users to share their Calendars and/or Contacts in a person-person relationship. The level of detail they can share is determined by the sharing policy applied to their mailboxes. When sharing of a Calendar or Contacts folder has been set up, that folder is synchronized to a folder in the mailbox of the person you shared the Calendar or Contacts with.

Federation Scenarios

Let's see how the basic principles of federation and federated delegation and the various components and fundamentals of federated delegation in Exchange Server 2010 all fit together. We'll do this by covering the various federation scenarios in an Exchange Server 2010 environment, and the advantages and drawbacks to each of them.

The common component in all of these scenarios is the creation of a federation trust, as discussed in the "Federation Trust" section of this chapter; for the purposes of this discussion, we will assume that the trust is in place and configured for all accepted domains in the organization.

Free/Busy Access

Although federated delegation provides a lot of new functionality with many advantages, the "killer app" is probably providing seamless, basic free/busy information—much like your users are accustomed to seeing when scheduling meetings with other internal users. This is configured at the organization level on a per-external organization basis, with one organization relationship in place with each external organization you want to share free/busy information with. This provides the other organization access to your Availability service at the level of detail specified. You can also restrict which internal users' free/busy data is accessible by specifying a security distribution group; only members of that group will have their free/busy data accessible via the organization relationship. Organization relationships are discussed in detail in the "Organization Relationship" section of this chapter.

The organization-level prerequisites to enabling two-way free/busy access between organizations are:

- Both organizations must be running Exchange Server 2010 Client Access servers.
- Both organizations must have federation trusts created and configured for the SMTP domains of the users who will be accessing free/busy between the organizations. The creation and management of federation trusts is discussed in detail in the "Federated Trust" section of this chapter.
- Both parties must have created and configured an organization relationship with the other organization as discussed in the "Organization Relationship" section of this chapter.

NOTE **Although Exchange Server 2010 Client Access servers are a prerequisite, users' mailboxes do not have to be on Exchange Server 2010 Mailbox servers. Mailboxes on Exchange Server 2007 SP2 can use federated delegation by configuring Exchange Server 2007 SP2 Client Access servers to proxy availability requests to Exchange Server 2010 Client Access with the *Add-AvailabilityAddressSpace* cmdlet. For example, to proxy the contoso.com address space, the cmdlet would be:**

```
Add-AvailabilityAddressSpace -ForestName contoso.com _-AccessMethod
InternalProxy
```

When the prerequisites and client requirements are in place, your users can access free/busy information for users in the other organization by entering the user's SMTP address in the Scheduling Assistant within a new or existing Outlook Web App or Outlook 2010 meeting request, as shown in Figure 10-12. Outlook versions prior to Outlook 2007 cannot be used because the free/busy lookup across organizations uses the availability service, and no free/busy information is posted to public folders.

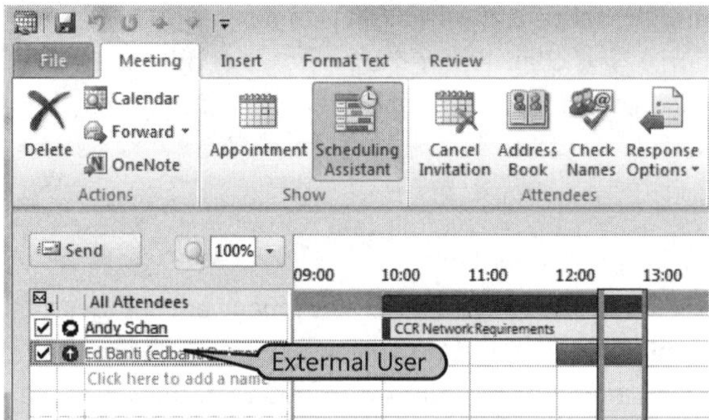

FIGURE 10-12 Accessing free/busy from a user in an external organization

INSIDE TRACK

Cross-Org Free/Busy Access with Outlook 2007 Clients

Matthias Leibmann
Program Manager, Microsoft Corporation, Redmond, WA

The only prerequisites for Outlook Web App and Outlook 2010 clients to access free/busy information across Exchange Server 2010 organizations is for both organizations to have federation trusts established and to have organization relationships in place with each other. Users of Outlook 2007, however, can't specify recipients in external organizations by SMTP address to display availability information; they are restricted to selecting recipients from the GAL. This means that GAL synchronization must be in place between the organizations for Outlook 2007 users to be able to perform free/busy lookups for users in federated domains.

Establishing GAL synchronization between organizations is a complex undertaking on both a business and technical level, so we recommend that organizations deploy Office 2010 to allow for cross-organization free/busy access, or consider utilizing Outlook Web App for this functionality.

Calendar and Contacts Sharing

Unlike free/busy access as discussed in the "Free/Busy Access" and "Organization Relationships" sections of this chapter, the sharing of Calendars and/or Contacts with users in external Exchange Server 2010 organizations is accomplished on a per-user basis, between a user in your organization and someone in an external Exchange Server 2010 organization. Calendar and Contacts sharing requires both organizations to have a federation trust in place as well as a valid sharing policy assigned to your user who is attempting to share his Calendar or Contacts, but no organization relationships are required. Similar to free/busy access, however, Calendar sharing provides your users access to the free/busy information of an external user, and potentially all other information in their calendars as well.

When these criteria are met, a user can create a sharing invitation using Outlook Web App or Outlook 2010; an example of a sharing invitation is shown in Figure 10-13. The level of information the user is allowed to share is dictated by the sharing policy assigned to her mailbox.

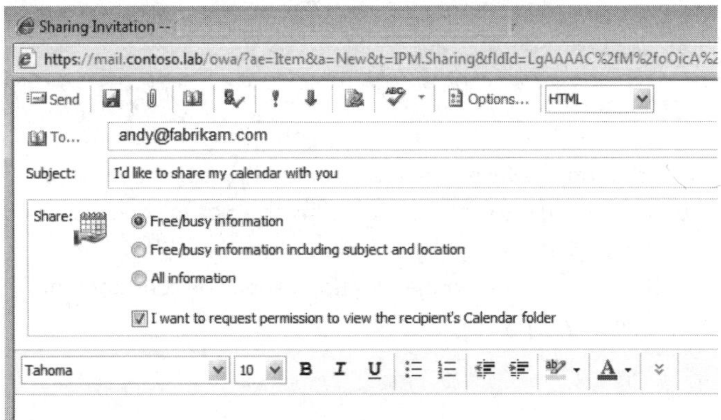

FIGURE 10-13 Creating a Calendar sharing invitation

Another difference from accessing free/busy (availability) information via an organization relationship is that Calendar sharing establishes and maintains a subscription at the server level to the requested calendar, synchronizing it into a separate subscription folder for the calendar in the requestor's mailbox. Thus, once you have established calendar sharing, the shared calendar can be viewed from any client that can view the mailbox's folders; this differs from accessing free/busy information via an organization relationship, which requires either Outlook Web App or Outlook 2010 and provides free/busy information by querying the Availability service.

Your users' Contacts folder can also be shared in a similar manner to Calendars, assuming that the sharing policy applied to the user permits Contacts sharing. To send the sharing invitation for Contacts requires Outlook 2010; you cannot share Contacts using Outlook

Web App. Like shared Calendars, after Contacts are synchronized to the mailbox, they can be viewed in any client that can view the mailbox's folders. A Contacts sharing invitation is shown in Figure 10-14.

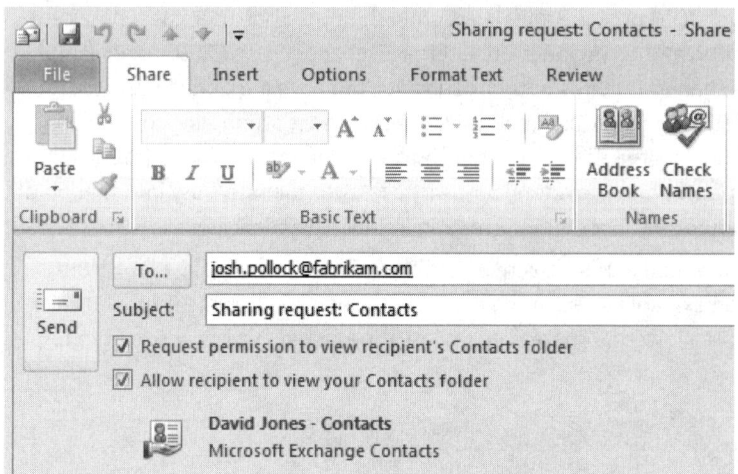

FIGURE 10-14 Creating a Contacts sharing invitation

For both Contacts and Calendar sharing, however, the level of detail you are allowed to share is dictated by the sharing policy assigned to your mailbox. An attempt to send a sharing invitation at a greater level of detail than that allowed by the sharing policy will result in an error message as shown in Figure 10-15, and the sharing invitation cannot be sent until the level of detail is reduced to that allowed by the sharing policy.

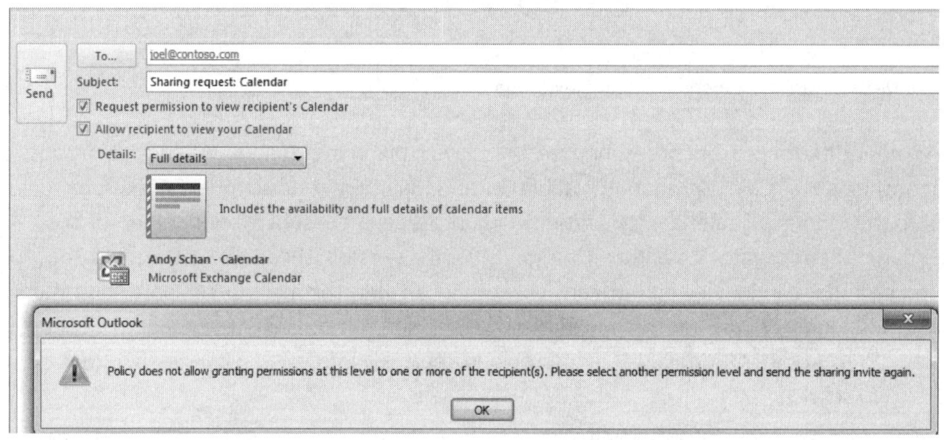

FIGURE 10-15 Level of Calendar sharing detail allowed limited by sharing policy

Federating with Online Services

Federation and federated delegation are also used in a cross-premises scenario where an organization hosts some mailboxes on-site and hosts others in the Exchange Online service. Federated delegation via the MFG provides for free/busy sharing, full calendar sharing, and mailbox moves between on-site Exchange servers and Exchange online. Single Sign-On (SSO) capability for mailboxes hosted in Exchange Online with your on-site Active Directory credentials is provided via the MFG by deploying AD FS version 2.0 on-site, in addition to the Microsoft Federation Gateway federation trust configured in Exchange Server 2010. The relationship between the various components of federation and Exchange Online is depicted in Figure 10-16.

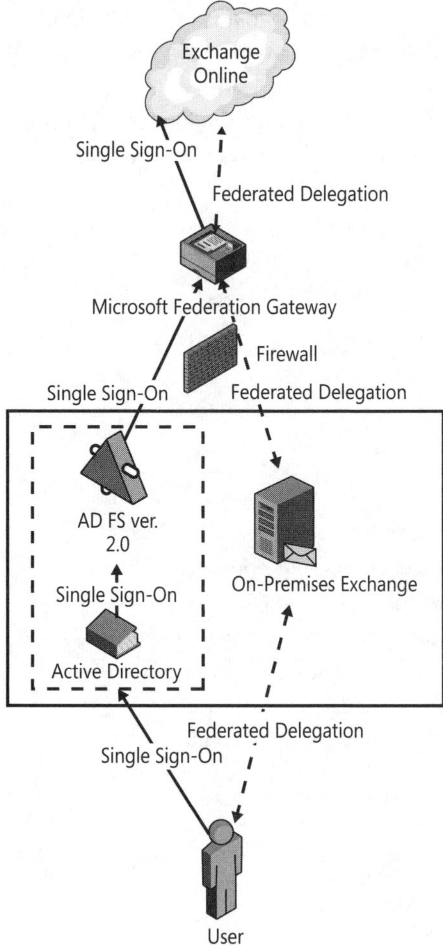

FIGURE 10-16 Federation and Exchange Online

Another point to keep in mind is that the configuration of DNS for proof of ownership for federation is separate from that required when you create an accepted domain for your Exchange Online tenant organization. Even if you have proven ownership for that domain when configuring it as an accepted domain for Exchange Online, your DNS must still be updated with a TXT record for that domain for the purposes of federation.

Configuring an organization relationship with your Exchange Online tenant organization is similar to configuring one with any other external organization; organization relationships were discussed in detail in the "Organization Relationship" section of this chapter. When you create the organization relationship with the *New-OrganizationRelationship* cmdlet, the Exchange Online tenant domain that you specify must be configured in the federation organization identifier for the Exchange Online tenant organization; the federation organization identifier was discussed in detail in the "Configuring Domains for Federation" section of this chapter. You must also configure an organization relationship in the Exchange Online tenant organization for your on-premise organization before federated delegation can be used between your on-premises organization and the Exchange Online tenant; this is the same requirement as for establishing federated delegation between your organization and any other external Exchange organization.

INSIDE TRACK

Federation Trust and the Federated Organization Identifier for Cross-Premises Scenarios

Matthias Leibmann
Program Manager, Microsoft, Redmond, WA

For federation with Exchange Online in cross-premises scenarios, we recommend that you utilize a sub-domain of "exchangedelegation.<*your primary SMTP domain*>" using the *Set-FederatedOrganizationIdentifier* cmdlet with the *AccountNamespace* parameter to avoid namespace conflicts with the Exchange Online tenant namespace. Then add <*your primary SMTP domain*> as an additional URI to the federated organization identifier using the *Add-FederatedDomain* cmdlet. You would set your account namespace as shown in this example:

```
Set-FederatedOrganizationIdentifier -AccountNamespace exchangedelegation.
fabrikam.com -DelegationFederationTrust "name_of_trust"
```

Then you configure your primary SMTP domain, as shown in this example:

```
Add-FederatedDomain -DomainName fabrikam.com
```

Keep in mind that both your primary SMTP domain and the sub-domain configured with the *AccountNamespace* parameter require a TXT record for proof of ownership.

As with configuring any other organization relationship, you can retrieve the necessary information from the tenant organization via AutoDiscover and use it to create the relationship with the Exchange Online tenant organization by piping the output of the *Get-FederationInformation* cmdlet to the *New-OrganizationRelationship* cmdlet as the following example shows:

```
Get-FederationInformation -DomainName <tenant domain> | New-OrganizationRelationship
-Name "Tenant Domain"
```

If the preceding command fails, Autodiscover may not be configured for the Exchange Online tenant organization. In that case, you can try configuring the organization relationship using the *New-OrganizationRelationship* cmdlet with the *–TargetAutodiscoverEpr* parameter. If this is not successful, and the causes for AutoDiscover not working are not possible to fix, as a last resort you may have to specify the *–TargetSharingEpr* and *–TargetApplicationUri* parameters manually to successfully create the organization relationship.

Creating the organization relationship in the Exchange Online tenant organization for your on-premises organization is similar to the above; again, the easiest approach is to obtain the information for the relationship with the *Get-FederationInformation* cmdlet and pipe it to the *New OrganizationRelationship* cmdlet as the following example shows:

```
Get-FederationInformation -DomainName <on-premises domain> | New
OrganizationRelationship -Name "OnPremisesDomain"
```

Troubleshooting Federated Delegation

We'll begin our discussion of the tools and best practices around troubleshooting federation and federated delegation in Exchange Server 2010 by looking at the federation trust, then move on to organization relationships and Calendar and Contacts sharing, and finish up by examining RMS federation.

LESSONS LEARNED

Federated Delegation and Pre-Authentication with Microsoft ISA Server and Forefront Threat Management Gateway (TMG)

Devin L. Ganger
Solutions Architect, Trace3, USA

In Exchange Server 2007, sharing calendar data with other Exchange Server 2007 organizations was on a per-foreign organization basis, and the controls around it were not very granular. This meant that your Client Access servers had to talk to their CA servers and you needed to either establish a forest trust and grant permissions to the other forest's CA servers (to get detailed per-user free/busy

information), or set up a separate user in your forest for the foreign forests to use and provide that user with these credentials (to get default per-org free/busy data). Aside from the large amount of effort and troubleshooting involved, this process used user accounts for authentication, so it worked well with ISA Server's or TMG's Web listener. During the initial Exchange 2010 deployment at a previous employer, we published Exchange 2010 with ISA 2006 SP1 configured to pre-authenticate users with FBA (Forms-Based Authentication) using a single Web listener.

However, here's the problem: with federated delegation in Exchange Server 2010, you're using SAML tokens—*not user accounts*—to authenticate against IIS for EWS calls. ISA Server doesn't know how to validate SAML tokens, so the incoming requests can't be authenticated and passed on to the Exchange Server 2010 CA server. The end result is that we couldn't get a proper sharing relationship set up and you can't federate calendar data.

When we knew what the problem was, fixing it involved modifying the OWA and ECP virtual directories on all of our Exchange Server 2010 CA servers to perform FBA, then modifying the Web listener on our ISA Server to disable pre-authentication. Finally, we needed to modify the authentication settings for each of the ISA publishing rules for ActiveSync, Outlook Anywhere, and OWA to set them to No Delegation, But Client May Authenticate Directly, and to revise the Users settings from All Authenticated Users to All Users. Revising the Users settings is important; without this, ISA won't pass any connections on to the CA servers. You may also need to verify that the authentication settings of your other Exchange virtual directories are valid; many organizations will allow basic authentication between ISA and their CAS servers, but require NTLM or Windows Integrated from external clients to ISA.

If you're using multiple Web listeners to publish Exchange 2010, then your steps may be different. The federated delegation feature requires direct access to the EWS vdir on your CAS servers, and EWS is typically published on ISA and TMG as part of the Outlook Anywhere rules. If you publish those using a separate Web listener—which will require a separate IP address, FQDN, and SSL certificate—you can simply disable pre-authentication for that Web listener, but still allow it on your OWA, ECP, and EAS directories.

Calendar sharing and ISA Server/TMG FBA pre-authentication are both wonderful features, but at this point they are not compatible.

Troubleshooting the Federation Trust

The foundation behind all aspects of federated delegation is the federation trust with the Microsoft Federation Gateway, so we'll start by looking at that.

The EMS cmdlet named *Test-FederationTrust* verifies several aspects of your federation with the Microsoft Federation Gateway. This cmdlet must be run from either an Exchange Server 2010 Hub Transport or Client Access server, and it does the following:

- It establishes a connection to the Microsoft Federation Gateway; this test verifies the communication between the Microsoft Federation Gateway and Exchange Server 2010 is functional.
- The local certificates designated for federation are verified for validity to ensure that they can be used with the Microsoft Federation Gateway. If the certificates are deemed to be not valid, you can obtain details on the certificates by using the *Get-FederationTrust* cmdlet, discussed later in this section.
- The cmdlet requests a security token from the Microsoft Federation Gateway to verify that tokens can be properly retrieved and used.

IMPORTANT **The *Test-FederationTrust* cmdlet uses a mailbox in the organization for testing, and requests a security token for that mailbox. You can use a mailbox specified with the *-UserIdentity* parameter; if no mailbox is specified the default test mailbox is used. If no mailbox is specified and the default test mailbox is not present, the *Test-FederationTrust* cmdlet fails. The default test mailbox must be created beforehand with the New-TestConnectivityUser.ps1 script found in the Scripts folder of the Exchange installation.**

Another useful cmdlet is *Test-FederationTrustCertificate*. This cmdlet verifies the distribution of the certificates used for federation on all Hub Transport and Client Access servers, and should be run prior to setting the Next certificate as the Current certificate with the *Set-FederationTrust* cmdlet or the Manage Federation Wizard in the EMC. No parameters need to be specified with the *Test-FederationTrustCertificate* cmdlet. You can also verify the distribution of the federation certificates to all CA and Hub Transport servers on the Manage Federation Certificate page of the Manage Federation Wizard by clicking Show Distribution State, as shown in Figure 10-17.

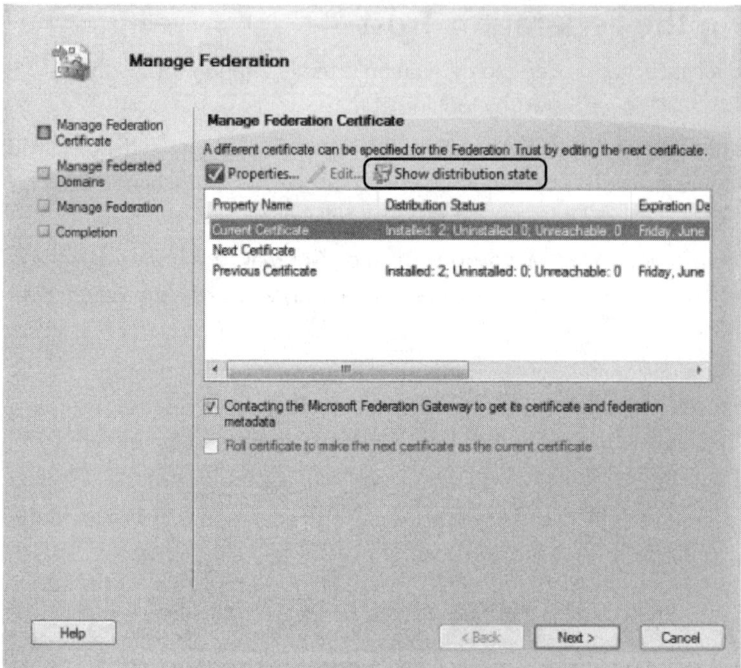

FIGURE 10-17 Verifying federation certificate distribution through the EMC

You can also use numerous *Get-* cmdlets to retrieve information useful for troubleshooting various aspects of your federation configuration:

- The *Get-FederatedOrganizationIdentifier* cmdlet retrieves the federated organization identifier for your organization as well as related details such as federated domains (accepted domains), organization contact, and status. If the *Get-FederatedOrganizationIdentifier* cmdlet is run with the *-IncludeExtendedDomainInfo* parameter, the MFG is queried for the status of each accepted domain that has been federated. The status of these domains is returned in the *Domains* property of the cmdlet's output. This cmdlet is useful in troubleshooting issues with different accepted domains in your environment.
- The *Get-FederationTrust* cmdlet is used to retrieve information on your federation trust with the Microsoft Federation Gateway. When run as *Get-FederationTrust | fl*, the following information is returned:
  - The AppID and application URI for the trust. You can use this to verify that the TXT resource record created in your external DNS when the trust was established is correct. The AppID and the associated DNS record are discussed in detail in the "Managing Federation" section of this chapter.

- The current, next, and previous certificates configured for the federation trust, including their subject, issuer, and issue and expiry dates. Certificates for federation are discussed in more detail in the "Managing Federation" section of this chapter.
- The token issuer current and previous certificates from the MFG.
- The distinguished name of the federation trust object in Active Directory.
- *WhenChanged* and *WhenCreated* date/time parameters for the federation trust.

As discussed in the "Managing Federation" section of this chapter, you can use the *Set-FederationTrust* cmdlet to manage your organization's certificates used for federation. You can also use *Set-FederationTrust* to refresh the metadata from the Microsoft Federation Gateway when you run it with the *–RefreshMetadata* parameter as part of your troubleshooting process.

LESSONS LEARNED

Troubleshooting Certificate Rolling Using Exchange Server 2010 Federation

Gary A. Cooper
Senior Systems Architect, Horizons Consulting, Inc., USA

At some point after you have deployed your federation trust, one of two certificate issues will present themselves. Either the Microsoft Federation Gateway Certificate will expire or your federation certificate will expire. If the first event occurs, the people responsible for the Microsoft Federation Gateway will manage certificate updates for the MFG. However, your CAS servers may not always update their version of the metadata that they obtain from the MFG. Typically, you will see Event ID 2009 from Source: MSExchange Certificate Deployment with a description indicating that the certificate will be expiring in less than 15 days.

To remove this warning, you can try the following cmdlet in the EMS:

```
Set-FederationTrust MyFederationTrust -RefreshMetadata'.
```

On the other hand, if it is your certificate that is about to expire, or if it has expired and you now have the updated certificate, you will need to update it within the Federation framework by telling the Microsoft Federation Gateway to begin using your new certificate. This is done with the following commands. The first command tells your CAS/Hub servers to register your new certificate as the next one to use with the MFG:

```
Set-FederationTrust -Identity <your Trust Name here> -Thumbprint <Your
new Certificate Thumbprint here>
```

The next command tells your CAS/Hub and the MFG to roll to the next certificate and to stop using the older original certificate. Before you issue this command, it is vital that this is the correct certificate and that the new certificate has replicated to ALL CAS/Hub servers in your organization. This is a one-way command and is not easily undone:

```
Set-FederationTrust <your Trust Name here> -PublishFederationCertificate
```

To verify the certificate that is currently in use, run *Get-FederationTrust |fl *cert** and look for the *OrgCertificate*, *OrgNextCertificate*, and *OrgPrevCertificate* values, which will show you the currently used, next in line to be used, and previously used certificates respectively. Pay particularly close attention to the Thumbprint and time stamps (shown as Not Before and Not After). Many times I have seen expired certificates being used or ones that haven't yet started. This is not only true for your certificates but also for those that your CAS/Hub servers are using from the MFG.

Finally, many organizations have had difficulty with managing the federated trust relationship simply because the CAS/Hub server they were working with it on did not have direct Internet access. To manage the certificate and trust relationship with MFG, the CAS/Hub server must have access to the Internet over TCP ports 80 and 443.

Troubleshooting Organization Relationships

The *Get-FederationInformation* cmdlet is arguably the most important tool in troubleshooting existing organization relationships as well as establishing new ones. This cmdlet returns information on a specified domain by querying the MFG, including federated domain names, target URLs, and the accessibility of those URLs. This output can be used for troubleshooting as well as for establishing new organization relationships by piping the output to the *New-OrganizationRelationship* cmdlet. The *Get-FederationInformation* cmdlet is also invoked in the New Organization Relationship Wizard when you select the Automatically Discover Configuration Information option on the External Organization page of the wizard, as shown in Figure 10-18.

The information retrieved by this cmdlet can tell you if there are issues with the specified domain; if no information is returned, check with the administrators of the external organization to verify that they have a federated trust in place and if they have published Autodiscover to the Internet. You may need to specify the external organization's information manually to establish the organization relationship, or they may not have established a federation trust yet—or they may have issues with the certificates for their existing federation trust.

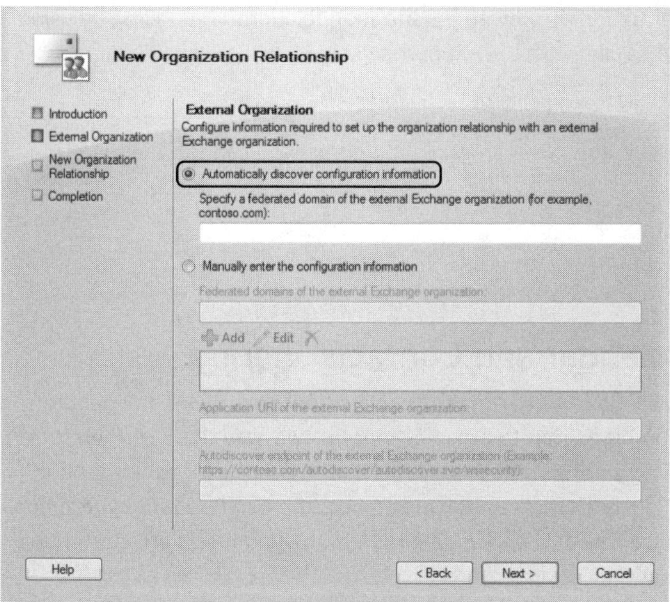

FIGURE 10-18 Retrieving federation information for a domain with the New Organization Relationship Wizard

The *Get-OrganizationRelationship* cmdlet is used to retrieve details on organization relationships, including free/busy access level, the internal security distribution group whose free/busy is accessible through this organization relationship, the application URI and Autodiscover endpoint of the external organization, and the create and last modified dates of the organization relationship. A subset of this information is also available through the properties of the organization relationship in the EMC, as shown in Figure 10-19.

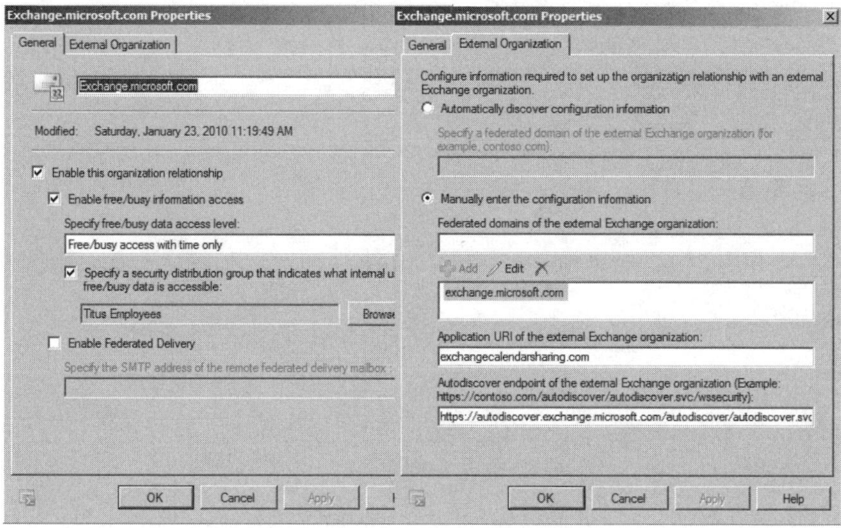

FIGURE 10-19 Properties of an organization relationship in EMC

You can also get more information on why an organization relationship is failing by using the *Get-FederationInformation* cmdlet with the *-verbose* switch:

```
Get-FedInfo -DomainName fabrikam.com -Verbose
```

To get extended information in the event an exception occurs you can run the following script:

```
$result= Get-FedInfo -DomainName fabrikam.com
$result | fl - Force
```

Troubleshooting Calendar and Contacts Sharing

Although Calendar and Contacts do not use organization relationships, they do depend on having valid federation trusts in place in both organizations for two-way sharing. Therefore, you will find the troubleshooting cmdlets and procedures outlined in the "Troubleshooting the Federation Trust" section of this chapter useful. In addition, the *Get-FederationInformation* cmdlet will help you determine whether the external organization your users are attempting to share with has a valid federation trust in place.

Another aspect to consider for troubleshooting Calendar and Contacts sharing is the permissions set on the user's Calendar or Contacts folder. Calendar and Contacts sharing is a one-to-one relationship between two users in different organizations, so the user's Calendar or Contacts folder should have a permissions entry for the external user the folder is being shared with, as shown in Figure 10-20.

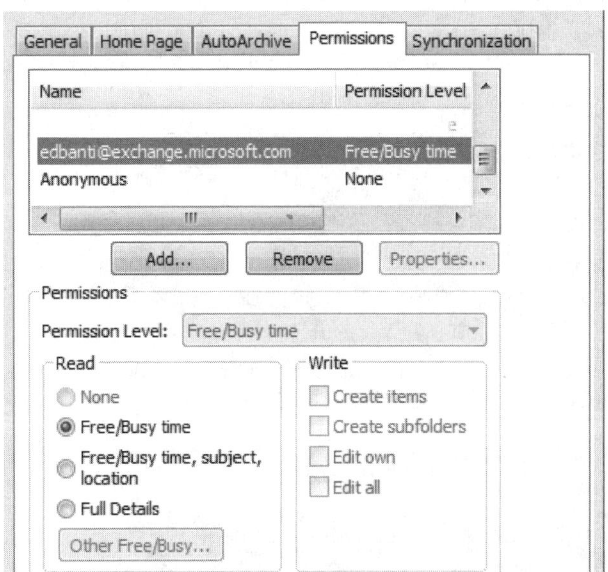

FIGURE 10-20 Permissions entry on a Calendar for an external user

Finally, if you use Outlook 2010 for free/busy access or Calendar and Contacts sharing, you can enable client logging within Outlook. This is done by clicking File, then Options, then Advanced, and then Enable Troubleshooting Logging (Requires Restarting Outlook) as shown in Figure 10-21.

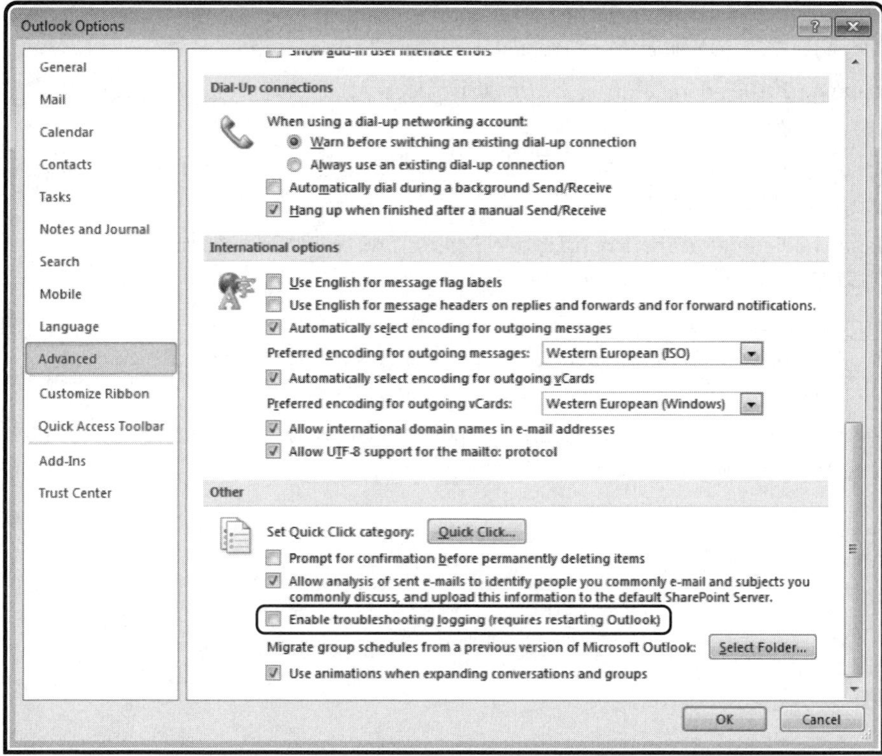

FIGURE 10-21 Enabling Client Logging in Outlook 2010

Outlook 2010 then writes logs into the logging directories. For free/busy logs, they are located at *%temp%\olkas*; look for files named **.fb.log*. For Calendar and Contacts sharing logs, they are located at %temp%\outlook logging; look for files named **-rs.log*, **-es.log*, and **-ps.log*. Depending on the issue or failure encountered, the **-ps.log* file may or may not be created.

Additional Resources

- Federated Identity Management: *http://www.networkcomputing.com/servers-storage/federated-identity-management.php*
- Microsoft Identity Lab: *http://www.federatedidentity.net/*
- Identity Federation with ADFS: Part 1: *http://ewright.spaces.live.com/blog/cns!C0C3DF24CE16DC2F!165.entry?wa=wsignin1.0&sa=378763958*

- Federated identity: *http://en.wikipedia.org/wiki/Federated_identity*
- Understanding Federation: Exchange 2010 Help: *http://technet.microsoft.com/en-us/library/dd335047.aspx*
- Microsoft Federation Gateway: *http://msdn.microsoft.com/en-us/library/cc287610.aspx*
- Exchange 2010 Federation Part I: *http://blogs.technet.com/ucedsg/archive/2009/10/28/exchange-2010-federation-part-i.aspx*
- Exchange 2010 Federation Part II: *http://blogs.technet.com/ucedsg/archive/2009/10/28/exchange-2010-federation-part-ii.aspx*
- Exchange 2010 Federation Part III: *http://blogs.technet.com/ucedsg/archive/2009/10/28/exchange-2010-federation-part-iii.aspx*
- Managing Federated Sharing: *http://technet.microsoft.com/en-us/library/dd351033.aspx*
- TechNet Webcast: Federation in Exchange 2010 (Level 300): *http://msevents.microsoft.com/CUI/WebCastEventDetails.aspx?culture=en-US&EventID=1032416725&CountryCode=US*
- Devin on Earth » Some Thoughts on FBA (part 2): *http://www.thecabal.org/2009/08/some-thoughts-on-fba-part-2/*

CHAPTER 11

Designing High Availability

High availability has become a requirement for deploying most enterprise messaging environments; however, not everyone takes the time to understand everything that it involves. Many administrators have been conditioned to think that high availability means the same thing as failover clustering, or that high availability is a feature than can be enabled. Although failover clustering and network load balancing are high-availability platforms, they do not provide high availability by themselves. It is important to understand that clustering is only one piece of high availability.

Rather than being a product feature, high availability is an achievement that requires strong management, testing, and change control processes. An organization cannot achieve high availability just by implementing a product feature. The most important requirement in achieving high availability is implementing a high-availability philosophy within the organization where administrators think, evaluate, collaborate, and then perform actions that are in harmony with that goal.

Achieving High Availability

A number of barriers stand in the way of achieving high availability. For example, a poor implementation of Exchange might be one where Exchange is installed on improperly sized servers and installed without following best practices. In this case it is possible to deploy an Exchange messaging environment over a short time period. This is easy to do quickly, but a lot of important details can be missed and availability will no doubt suffer.

By contrast, in a high-availability environment the messaging system deployment is well designed. The deployment plan will be based on the information presented in Chapter 2, "Exchange Deployment Projects." During the deployment project, organizational messaging requirements are researched. The current messaging environment is examined for inadequacies and solutions are identified. Research into how best to deploy Exchange may go on for an extended period while consultants are brought in to help build a design. Vendors are also brought in to discuss how their products will work and how they can contribute to running a highly available system. Hardware is sized and tested to meet both business and technical requirements, such as service-level agreements (SLAs), recovery point objectives, and cost considerations. Hardware will be considered that has the defined level of fault-tolerant components such as redundant memory, drives, network connections, cooling fans, power supplies, and so on.

A high-availability environment will also incorporate a significant amount of design, planning, and testing. A high-availability environment will often, but not always, include additional features, such as failover clustering and load balancing, which are designed to decrease downtime by enabling rolling upgrades and allowing for a preplanned response to failures. The messaging client software and its potential configurations can also improve availability. For example, Outlook 2003 and later offers the Exchange Cached Mode configuration that allows users to create new messages, respond to existing mail in their Inboxes, and manage their calendars (among many other tasks) even if the connection is lost to the Exchange server. Cached Exchange Mode allows users to continue working locally even though the Exchange server might be down for a short time. When the connection to the Exchange server is restored, any changes made will be synchronized. In the end, all critical business systems must be analyzed to understand the cost incurred when they are unavailable. If downtime has a significant cost, the organization should take steps to minimize downtime. This is particularly true if the cost of downtime is greater than the cost of deploying a suitable highly available solution.

The opposite of availability is downtime, both planned and unplanned. Planned downtime is the result of scheduled events, such as maintenance. Unplanned downtime is the result of unscheduled events. Events that cause unplanned downtime can be minor, such as a faulty hardware driver or a processor failure, or major, such as an earthquake, fire, or flood.

Measuring Availability

Availability is usually expressed as the percentage of time that a service is available. As an example, a requirement for 99.9 percent availability over a one-year period of 24-hour days, 7 days a week allows for only 8.75 hours of downtime, as shown in Table 11-1. In complex environments, organizations specify availability targets for each service. When dealing with an Exchange messaging environment, availability goals may be tied to specific features such as Microsoft Outlook Web App, Simple Mail Transfer Protocol (SMTP) message delivery, and Outlook MAPI connectivity. These availability targets are then turned into SLAs that hold the group operating the messaging system accountable for meeting those targets. In some cases, if those targets are not met, the salaries and bonuses of the employees and managers in the responsible group can be affected. In some instances both planned and unplanned downtime affect the overall availability target; in other environments planned downtime is exempt from the availability target. Because successfully achieving high availability includes update management to mitigate potential downtime, some planned downtime is required.

TABLE 11-1 Permitted Downtime for Specific Availability Targets

AVAILABILITY TARGET	PERMITTED DOWNTIME ANNUALLY
99 percent	87 hours, 36 minutes
99.9 percent	8 hours, 46 minutes
99.99 percent	52 minutes, 34 seconds
99.999 percent	5 minutes, 15 seconds

This bit of background should not detract from the great features provided to help achieve high availability in Exchange 2010; rather, the purpose is to provide a frame of reference as the Exchange-specific high-availability features are discussed.

Exchange 2010 High-Availability Features

Exchange 2010 builds on the solid foundation set by Exchange 2007 with regard to high availability. Exchange 2007 introduced a number of new options for availability, including cluster continuous replication (CCR), standby continuous replication (SCR), single copy cluster (SCC), and local continuous replication (LCR). Exchange 2010 introduces the Database Availability Group (DAG), which combines the best functionality available in Exchange 2007. A DAG is a group of up to 16 Exchange 2010 Mailbox servers that can each maintain up to 100 databases. A database may have up to 16 copies of each database using continuous replication.

The DAG differs from Exchange Server 2007 SP1 in the following ways:

- With CCR, there can be only two highly available copies of the database within the cluster; within the DAG there can be up to 16 copies of each database.
- With SCR, the activation process required administrative intervention; within a DAG, failover between individual database copies can happen automatically.
- With SCC, a single shared copy of the database consumes less storage but provides no redundancy. Exchange Server 2010 has no configuration that replaces this functionality, although some third-party solutions may be able to provide similar functionality by using the Third Party Replication API.
- With LCR, a single-server configuration allows two copies of a database to reside on different storage connected to the same server. No configuration in Exchange Server 2010 replaces this functionality.

Exchange 2010 provides database-level failover within the DAG. A single database failure no longer affects all mailbox databases on a server. Database failover time has also been improved since Exchange 2007. The DAG also makes it easier to implement site failover because now the DAG handles both in-site and inter-site replication.

Exchange 2010 also has improved non-mailbox high availability. Transport servers now have a feature called *shadow redundancy*, which provides redundancy for in-transit messages.

Another improvement is online mailbox moves. In previous versions of Exchange, mailboxes are moved offline which requires users to disconnect their clients in order to complete the move. Since this process impacts the users, these mailbox moves are usually scheduled during maintenance windows. Only being able to move mailboxes at night and on the weekends during a migration project does not provide enough time to complete the migration. The online mailbox move feature allows mailboxes to be moved between databases asynchronously without taking the user offline. The users will be able to maintain their connection and work while their e-mail is being moved in the background. This reduces end-user downtime and allows mailbox migrations to be performed during business hours. Online mailbox moves help improve availability for end users. More information about Exchange 2010 high-availability planning can be found in the Planning for High Availability and Site Resilience topic at *http://technet.microsoft.com/en-us/library/dd638104.aspx*.

Availability Planning for Mailbox Servers

In addition to normal IT best practices and redundant hardware, the DAG is the primary high-availability option for Exchange 2010 Mailbox servers. A DAG is a collection of servers that provides continuous replication and availability for mailbox databases, as shown in Figure 11-1.

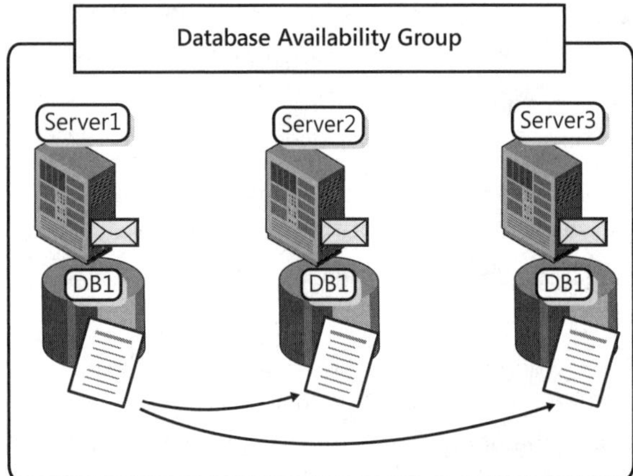

FIGURE 11-1 A Database Availability Group

Continuous replication creates a passive database copy on another Mailbox server in the DAG, and then uses asynchronous log shipping to maintain the copies.

The continuous replication process follows these steps:

1. The active transaction log is written and then closed.
2. The Microsoft Exchange Replication service replicates the closed log to servers hosting the passive database copies.

3. Because each copy of the database is identical, the Log Inspector will examine the transaction logs for the following:

   Verifies the physical integrity of the transaction log

   Verifies that the header generation is not higher than the highest generation for the current database copy

   Verifies the log header matches the generation of the file name

   Verifies the log file signature in the header matches the log file

   The transaction log is then placed in the defined transaction log directory.

4. The Information Store then validates the transaction log and then applies the logs to the database copy. The databases remain in sync.

A DAG also has the following characteristics:

- Requires the Windows failover clustering feature and uses an Enterprise version of Windows server (Windows Server 2008 or Windows Server 2008 R2), although the installation and configuration tasks occur with the Exchange Server management tools. Exchange Server does not use Windows failover clustering to handle database failover. Instead, it uses Active Manager to manage the failover process.
- Members must have the same operating system.
- You can add up to 16 servers to a single DAG and create up to 16 copies of a database. Up to 100 databases can be mounted as either a passive or active copy of the database on each server in the DAG.
- Uses an evolution of the continuous replication technology that is available in Exchange 2007.
- A DAG can be created after you install the Mailbox server. If a Mailbox server is hosting active mailbox databases, it can be added to a DAG later, it if meets the requirements.
- Allows you to move a single database between servers in the DAG without affecting other databases. Failover occurs per mailbox database, not for an entire server.
- Allows up to 16 copies of a single database on separate servers. A server can only host one copy of each database.
- Requires the database and transaction log copies for each database to be stored in the same path on all servers. For example, if you store Mailbox Database 1 in *D:\DB\Mailbox Database 1* on Dallas-MB01A, you must also store it in *D:\DB\Mailbox Database 1* on all other servers that host copies of Mailbox Database 1.
- Defines the boundary for replication, failovers, and switchovers—only servers in the DAG can host database copies. You cannot replicate database copies to Mailbox servers that are not in the same DAG.
- Does not require that all databases have the same number of copies. In a 16-node DAG, one database can have 16 copies, whereas other databases are neither redundant nor have varying number of copies.

In Exchange 2010 transaction log shipping occurs over TCP sockets as opposed to the file share (Server Message Block) used in Exchange 2007. You can view the current TCP port used for replication by running *Get-DatabaseAvailabilityGroup -Status | Format-List*. The default TCP port used for replication is 64327. This can be set using the *Set-DatabaseAvailabilityGroup -ReplicationPort* cmdlet. For this change to take effect, you need to create the Windows Firewall exceptions for the new TCP port and then restart the Microsoft Exchange Replication service on each node in the DAG. In the initial release of Exchange 2010, when you created a DAG using the EMC, the DAG was automatically configured to obtain an IP address from DHCP. To complete the configuration and assign a static IP address, you had to use the EMS. In SP1, the DAG can be configured with an IP address from within the EMC.

The target member notifies the member running the active copy of which transaction logs it expects to receive. The source member then responds by sending the required transaction log files. After the transaction logs are received from the source server, the files are placed in the target server's Inspector directory for processing. The logs are then inspected and verified for integrity and the header is inspected. After passing inspection, a transaction log is placed in the log directory on the target Mailbox server. If the transaction log does not pass inspection the target server will request it from the source up to three times before setting the mailbox database copy to Failed. When a database copy status is Failed, it will periodically attempt to copy the missing log files in order to return the database to a state of Healthy. The target Exchange server then plays the logs against the local copy of the database.

Before this transaction log shipping process can start, the database copy must first be seeded. Seeding is the process of creating a consistent database copy on a DAG member to act as a baseline that will be updated through continuous replication of the transaction log files. This can be accomplished using the following methods:

- **Automatic seeding** Automatic seeding occurs during the creation of a new database.
- **Manually copying the offline database** This method involves dismounting the database and copying the database file to the target server. If you do this, service will be interrupted while the database is dismounted.
- **Using the *Update-MailboxDatabaseCopy* cmdlet** You can use the *Update-MailboxDatabaseCopy* cmdlet in the EMS to seed a database copy.
- **Using the Update Database Copy Wizard** You can use the Update Database Copy Wizard within the EMC to seed a database copy.

Database failover occurs when the active database fails, and another copy of the database is activated on another server in the DAG. This can occur because of a number of failure types including: network, storage, and server hardware. If a entire DAG member fails, each of the active highly available databases will attempt to fail over to another configured DAG member. A switchover occurs when an administrator initiates moving an active database from one server to another.

NOTES FROM THE FIELD

Exchange High-Availability Improvements

Colin Lee

Technology Specialist, Unified Communications, Microsoft Corporation, Australia

In my opinion, Exchange 2007 is an evolutionary step in providing a complete high-availability solution with continuous replication. This provides capability for high availability, with CCR, and disaster recovery (DR), with SCR. Many customers I have worked with implemented this solution for high availability and DR with great success and were able to improve their SLA, or internal operational level agreement. As with all new technology there are areas for improvement and Microsoft continues to evolve continuous replication with Database Availability Group (DAG) in Exchange 2010. The introduction of DAGs in Exchange 2010 adds improvements that my customers requested as they were looking to improve SLAs even further. These requests are often around the active-passive nature of CCR and the ability to seamlessly failover if the disk (or raid group) the database resides on fails.

> ***NOTE*** In a CCR implementation with multiple storage groups an outage of a disk did not trigger a failover between the nodes and required some manual intervention to initiate a recovery, whether that be a restore from back for a DB or triggering a node failover.

Exchange 2010 solves this issue with the capability that makes the database the unit of failover. It also helps address the perception that a passive node was sitting around idle. This is because up to 16 members can be put in a DAG, and all members can host active mailboxes. This is a powerful perception where upper management have a tendency to view "idle" servers as inefficiencies a company can do without. The following comments are from a customer that has migrated from Exchange 2007 with a CCR and SCR implementation to Exchange 2010 with a DAG that spans multiple datacenters.

"Moving to Exchange 2010 has allowed us to provide a more highly available solution to our hotels department whilst at the same time giving us (IT) increased simplicity in managing the infrastructure. We have extremely high confidence in our DAG with its ability for single database failovers as opposed to our old CCR and SCR setup. Implementing our DAG together with Datacentre Activation Coordination mode has also given us the confidence to increase our Disaster Recovery scope from a single storage group of critical mailboxes to the entire group, yet at the same time maintaining an uncomplicated recovery process."

Active Manager

Windows failover clustering is not used to replicate or manage the active database copies in a DAG; however it is used to store information for several pieces of volatile information about the DAG such as the state of active database copies. Exchange Server uses a Windows failover cluster, but there are no cluster groups for Exchange Server, and the cluster has no storage resources. In the Failover Cluster Management Console, you will see an empty cluster, as shown in Figure 11-2. Exchange 2010 does use the cluster API library functions for cluster network (heartbeating), node management, and cluster registry functions. Although Active Manager stores database information in the cluster database, it isn't accessed directly by any other components.

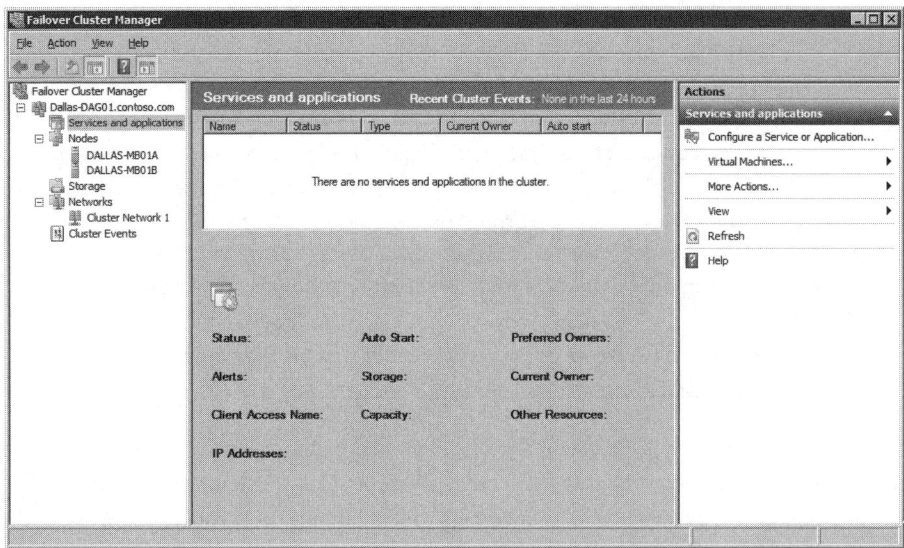

FIGURE 11-2 Windows Failover Cluster Management objects for a DAG

To manage mailbox database replication and activation Exchange 2010 includes a new component called *Active Manager,* which runs as a function of the Microsoft Exchange Replication service (MSExchangeRepl.exe). Active Manager replaces the resource model and failover management features integrated into Windows failover clustering that previous Exchange Server versions used. To simplify the architecture Active Manager runs on all Mailbox servers, even if the server is not part of a DAG.

Active Manager runs on all of the DAG members and runs as either the primary active manager (PAM) or a standby active manager (SAM). The PAM is the Active Manager in a DAG that controls which copies will be active and which will be passive. It is responsible for processing topology change notifications and reacting to server failures. The DAG member acting as the PAM is always the member that currently owns the default cluster group, as shown in Figure 11-3. In order to identify the PAM it is recommended to use *Get-DatabaseAvailabilityGroup <DAG Name> -Status | Format-List Name, PrimaryActiveManager* rather than using the Windows Failover Clustering tools. If the server that owns the default cluster group fails, the PAM function automatically moves to the server that takes ownership of the default cluster group.

```
Administrator: Windows PowerShell
PS C:\Users\administrator.CONTOSO> Import-Module FailoverClusters
PS C:\Users\administrator.CONTOSO> Get-ClusterGroup | Format-Table -Auto

Name              OwnerNode     State
----              ---------     -----
Cluster Group     dallas-mb01a  Online
Available Storage dallas-mb01a  Offline

PS C:\Users\administrator.CONTOSO> _
```

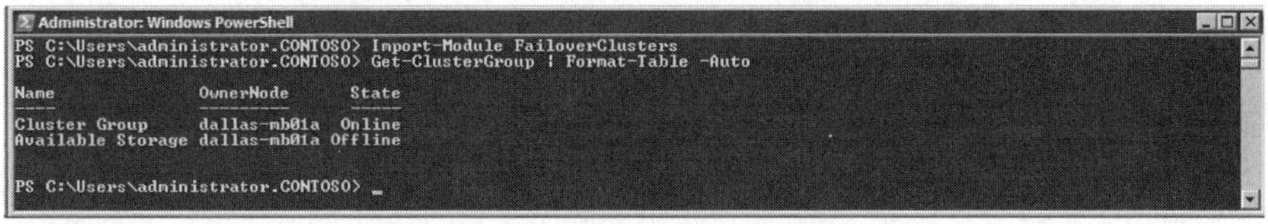

FIGURE 11-3 Identifying the DAG member that has the PAM function

If you are going to perform maintenance on the server that hosts the default cluster group, you must first manually move the PAM function to another server in the DAG, as shown in Figure 11-4, on a Windows Server 2008 R2 server. To do the same on Windows Server 2008 you run from a command prompt *cluster.exe group "Cluster Group" /MOVETO:Dallas-MB01B*.

```
Administrator: Windows PowerShell

PS C:\Users\administrator.CONTOSO> Move-ClusterGroup "Cluster Group" -Node DALLAS-MB01B
Name                          OwnerNode                                        State
----                          ---------                                        -----
Cluster Group                 dallas-mb01b                                     Online

PS C:\Users\administrator.CONTOSO> _
```

FIGURE 11-4 Moving the PAM function

Far from having a passive role, the SAM function provides information about which server hosts the active copy of a mailbox database. The SAM detects local database and Information Store failures and reacts to them by requesting the PAM to initiate a failover when a copy is available. A SAM does not determine a failover target, nor does it update a database's location state for the PAM. Each SAM accesses the state of the active database copy in order to answer any request for where the active copy is from other Exchange components like the Hub Transport of Client Access servers. The PAM also performs the functions of the SAM role on the local system.

SP1 includes *StartDagServerMaintenance.ps1,* a script that you use to take a computer out of service. The script moves active databases off of the server and blocks databases from activating on that server. It will also ensure that all critical DAG support functionality is moved to another server, and blocked from moving back. The *StopDagServerMaintenance.ps1* script is then used to complete the operation and remove the blocks and allow databases to be activated on that node.

Adding Database Copies

Creating a database availability group is just the first step in making a database highly available. A database that exists on one of the DAG members must be set up with additional copies on other DAG members. Some databases may require more copies than others.

When creating a database copy, you can specify the following details:

- The name of the database you are copying.
- The name of the Mailbox server that will host the database copy.
- The amount of time (in minutes) to delay log replay. This sets how long to wait before the transaction logs are committed to the database copy. Setting the value for replay lag time to 0 disables the log replay delay.
- The amount of time (in minutes) for log truncation delay. This controls how long to wait before truncating committed transaction logs. Setting the value for truncation lag time to 0 disables the log truncation delay.
- An activation preference number. This represents the activation preference order of a database copy when multiple databases have the same copy queue length after a failure or outage of the active copy,
- The seed copy server. This server will be used to copy the seed database and content indexing information to the new copy. Although this is specified when creating a new database copy, replication always occurs from the active database to each of the copies.

Creating databases copies should be done according to a high-availability plan. A high-availability plan should be created that identifies the level of redundancy required for your environment. If JBOD (Just a Bunch of Disks) will be used to store database files, additional copies of the database should exist on other servers to sustain a disk failure.

You can add database copies using the *Add-MailboxDatabaseCopy* cmdlet or you can use the Add Mailbox Database Copy Wizard in the EMC.

Lagged Database Copies

One of the options available when configuring mailbox database copies is to configure a lag time of up to 14 days. This lag time is the time that the transaction logs will be held before being committed to the database copy. By delaying committing the logs to a database copy, you have the capability to recover the copy to a point in time using the copy rather than having to pull data from tape-based backup media.

Lagged database copies are deployed to protect from logical corruption. Database logical corruption and store logical corruption are the two types of logical corruption that can occur in the Exchange database.

If you use multiple database copies and Single Item Recovery, only the extremely rare catastrophic store logical corruption case remains unaddressed. In the following scenarios lagged database copies can be used to recover data:

- Recovering a deleted item from within 14 days outside the retention period
- Recovering to a point in time because of virus outbreak

You should deploy lagged copies to mitigate a specific risk and lagged copies are usually not needed if you are also deploying a third-party backup solution. Lagged copies should not be treated as another high-availability database copy and should not be activated for the following reasons:

- You lose your point-in-time recoverability.
- You lose your backup copy.
- Page patching is not processed on lagged copies.
- Lagged copies take a long time to bring online as transaction logs are applied.

Lagged copies have storage implications as enough space must be available to store the transaction logs for lag period. However, rather than just meeting those requirements, it is best practice to have at least enough room for three additional days of transaction logs, to provide for potential truncation failures or periods of excessive log file generation. More information on planning for and recovering Exchange 2010 is covered in Chapter 12, "Backup, Restore, and Disaster Recovery."

Continuous Replication

Block Mode Introduced in Exchange 2010 Service Pack 1 (SP1), continuous replication–block mode reduces the exposure of data loss on failover by replicating all logs writes to the passive database copies in parallel to writing them locally. In other words, block mode replicates the transactions to the database copies as they are being written to the active local transaction log files. Enabling and disabling block mode is done automatically by the log copy process by database. Block mode will automatically become active when continuous replication file mode is up-to-date with the database copies. The replication transport is the same when granular replication is enabled or disabled.

The benefit of block mode is that it can dramatically reduce the latency between the active copy and the passive copy while also reducing the possibility of data loss during a failover and the time it takes to perform a switchover.

DAG Networks

A DAG network is a set of subnets that can be configured for replication or MAPI communication. Exchange supports the use of a single network adapter and path for DAG members. However, to provide network redundancy as well as the ability to separate replication and MAPI communication, multiple network adapters and networks (subnets) are recommended. After the network hardware is in place and configured and windows failover clustering has detected the changes, these additional physical networks can be configured by setting up additional DAG networks within Exchange.

Consider the following criteria when designing the network for a DAG deployment:

- Each DAG can have only one MAPI network. This network must provide connectivity to other Exchange servers, Active Directory, and DNS.
- Each DAG member must have at least one network adapter that is able to communicate with all other DAG members.
- Each DAG member's MAPI network must be able to communicate with each of the DAG node's MAPI network interfaces.
- Each DAG member must have the same number of networks.

- Each DAG can have zero or more replication networks.
- Regardless of location, each DAG member cannot have round-trip return network latency greater than 250 milliseconds (ms).
- DAG networks support Internet Protocol Version 4 (IPv4) and IPv6. IPv6 is supported only when IPv4 is also used; a pure IPv6 environment isn't supported.
- APIPA addresses (including manually assigned addresses from the APIPA address range) aren't supported for use by DAGs.
- Each DAG member's replication network must be able to communicate with every other DAG member's replication network.
- There should be no direct routing to allow heartbeat traffic from the replication network on one DAG member to the MAPI network on another DAG node, or vice versa.
- Each DAG requires a minimum of one IP address on the MAPI network. Additional IP addresses are required when the MAPI network is extended across multiple subnets. The DAG requires an IP address on each subnet it will be active on.
- When Internet SCSI (iSCSI) is used for storage, these networks should not be used for replication. This keeps replication communication from interfering with storage operations. It is a best practice to manually disable the iSCSI network from being used by the DAG and by the cluster. For more information see "Managing Database Availability Groups" under the DAG Networks and iSCSI Networks subheading at *http://technet.microsoft.com/en-us/library/dd298065.aspx.*

A DAG network can be configured in a couple different ways. The previous list suggested having at least two networks defined: one network dedicated for MAPI communication and one network dedicated for replication, as shown in Figure 11-5. If all of the replication networks go offline or fail the MAPI network will be used for replication.

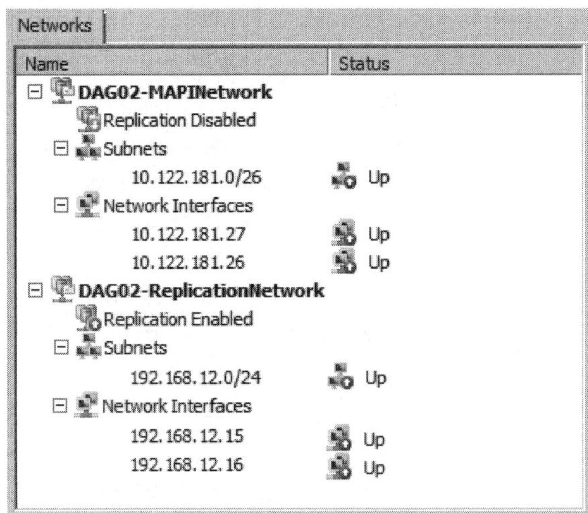

FIGURE 11-5 DAG network configuration

Database Failover Process

When a highly available mailbox database failure occurs the PAM will attempt to perform a failover of the database. Before attempting to select a suitable copy to activate the attempt copy last logs (ACLL) process occurs. ACLL makes remote procedure calls (RPCs) to each DAG node that hosts a copy of the mailbox database that is being activated. This call requests to see whether the servers are available and healthy and determines the *LogInspectorGeneration* value for the database copy. The last active mailbox database copy is used to copy any missing log files to the copy selected by Active Manager for activation. If the ACLL process fails to retrieve all of the missing log files, the configured *AutoDatabaseMountDial* value is consulted. The *AutoDatabaseMountDial* value has the following three potential values:

- **BestAvailability** This value allows the database to be automatically mounted if the copy queue length is less than or equal to 12. The copy queue length is the number of logs that the passive copies recognize and have not been replicated. When the copy queue length is less than or equal to 12, Exchange Server attempts to replicate the remaining logs to the passive copies and mount the database. This is the default value.
- **GoodAvailability** This value allows the database be automatically mounted immediately after a failover if the copy queue length is less than or equal to six. When the copy queue length is less than or equal to six, Exchange Server attempts to replicate the remaining logs to the passive copy and mount the database.
- **Lossless** This value does not allow a database to mount automatically until all logs generated on the active copy have been copied to the passive copy.

If the number of lost logs is within the configured *AutoDatabaseMountDial* value, Exchange Server mounts the database. If the number of lost logs falls outside the configured *AutoDatabaseMountDial* value, Exchange Server does not mount the database until either missing log files are recovered or an administrator manually mounts the database and accepts that the loss of data is larger than the *AutoDatabaseMountDial* setting. You use the *Set-MailboxServer* cmdlet to configure the *AutoDatabaseMountDial* setting for each DAG node.

It may seem counterintuitive to list the Best Availability as allowing for 12 missing transaction logs, and Good Availability as only allowing 6. In this case, availability is referring to the database being mounted and available, not to the possibility of lost data. In most enterprise environments, data loss is less acceptable than the loss of service. You must decide whether to keep the database available by allowing it to mount despite potential data loss or to leave it unavailable and wait for manual recovery of missing log files.

Mailbox Database Activation

When an active database failure occurs, Active Manager uses a set of selection criteria to determine which copy should be activated. It would make sense that Active Manager attempts to locate the best database copy to perform the quickest failover that is least likely to lose data. Active Manager uses a complex sorting system to determine which copy to make active.

When a failover occurs, Active Manager uses several sets of selection criteria to determine which database copy to activate. During the process for selecting the best copy to activate, Active Manager will:

1. Enumerate all the available copies.
2. Remove any copies on unreachable servers.
3. Sort available copies by how up to date they are.
4. Use the activation preference if a tiebreaker is necessary.

For more information on selection process see "Understanding Active Manager" at *http://technet.microsoft.com/en-us/library/dd776123.aspx.*

Exchange 2010 SP1 provides the *RedistributeActiveDatabases.ps1* script that provides thee ways to balance active database copies. The first option, switch parameter *-BalanceDbsByActivationPreference*, just activates the copy that has the lowest *ActivationPreference* value without taking into account Active Directory site balance. The second option, switch parameter *–BalanceDbsIgnoringActivationPreference,* attempts to balance active copies across the DAG, as shown in Figure 11-6. The third option, *-BalanceDbsBySiteAndActivationPreference,* attempts to keep active databases balanced between Active Directory sites. The version of the script included in SP1 won't move databases to less preferred copies to achieve site balance, but it will log a warning. The script will attempt to minimize an active copy imbalance during the redistribution process; this will help prevent a single node from being overwhelmed with active copies during this process.

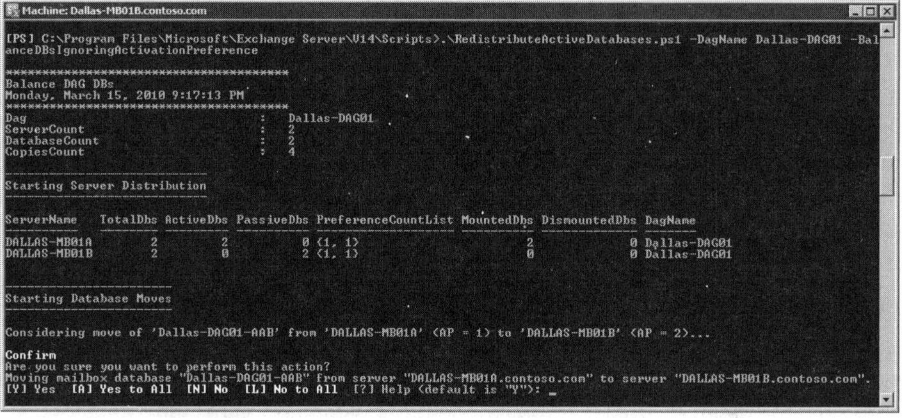

FIGURE 11-6 Running *RedistributeActivateDatabases.ps1*

Controlling Database Activation

In large environments you may want to limit which servers can host an active database in the event of a failure so that a database is not brought online in a secondary datacenter if you are performing maintenance on a server or the database is a lagged copy. A database activation policy can be set on the Mailbox server, or only the database copy can be configured to not activate. When setting this on the Mailbox server using *Set-MailboxServer ServerName –DatabaseCopyAutoActivationPolicy,* the following three policies are available:

- **Blocked** No database can be automatically activated.
- **IntrasiteOnly** This prevents database failovers from copies that are not in the same Active Directory site.
- **Unrestricted** This allows any server in the DAG to be for database activation. This is the default configuration.

These policies only affect how Active Manager calculates where to activate database copies. An administrator can manually mount the database on a server that has the activation policy set to Blocked. The server auto activation policy is usually used during periods of maintenance when you do not want a database copy to be automatically activated on a specific server.

The second way to control database activation is to suspend database activation on a specific copy of the database. This can be done by running *Suspend-MailboxDatabaseCopy <Database Name>\<Server Name> -ActivationOnly,* as shown in Figure 11-7. Suspending activation for a specific database copy should be done on copies that you do not want to be activated automatically, such as lagged database copies.

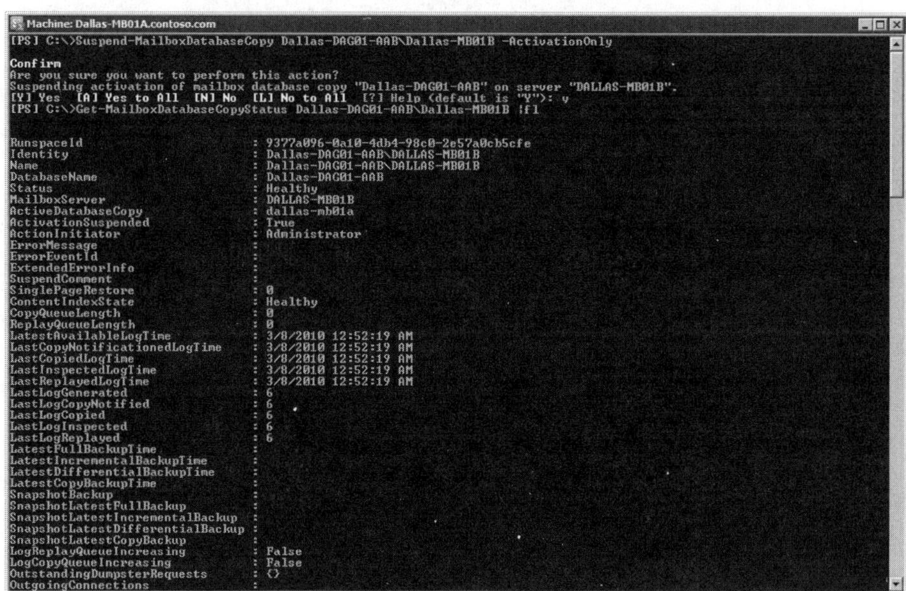

FIGURE 11-7 Suspending activation on a database copy

Unlike setting an activation policy on the Mailbox server, suspending activation on a database copy cannot be mounted directly by an administrator, as shown in Figure 11-8. However, this block can be reset in two ways: when the database copy is reseeded or if replication is suspended and then resumed.

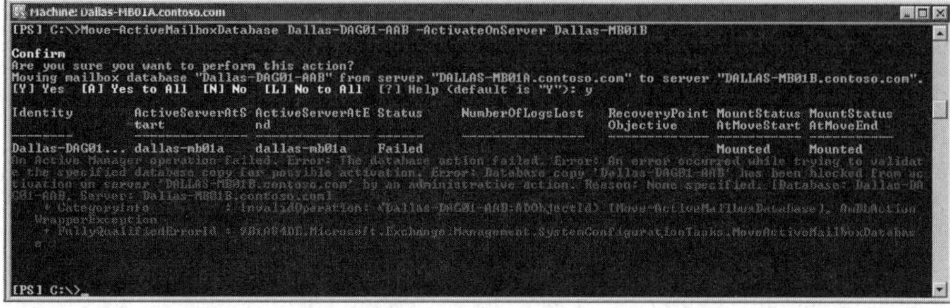

FIGURE 11-8 Attempting to activate a database copy when activation is blocked

Transport Dumpster

In case failure occurs and some transaction logs are not replicated to the passive copy, the transport dumpster is used to redeliver any recently delivered e-mail. If a database failure occurs, a request is made to the Hub Transport servers to redeliver any lost e-mail messages.

The transport dumpster only retains e-mail that has already been delivered. The local submission queue withholds any pending outgoing e-mail. After the transaction logs containing the e-mail message are replicated to and inspected by each DAG member with a copy of the database, the Hub Transport server purges the message from the dumpster.

The transport dumpster is enabled by default. Transport dumpster can be configured by using the *Get-TransportConfig* cmdlet using the following two properties:

- **MaxDumpsterSizePerDatabase** This setting defines the maximum size of the transport dumpster queue per database and is set globally for the entire Exchange organization. The recommended size is 1.5 times the maximum message size that can be sent. For example, if the maximum size for messages is 20 MB, this parameter should be set to 30 MB.
- **MaxDumpsterTime** This is the time for which the transport dumpster retains a message if the message is not purged for exceeding the maximum dumpster size. The default is set to seven days.

Managing Database Copies

You can use a number of cmdlets to manage database copies. Understanding the function of each is essential to being able to manage database copies. The following cmdlets are available:

- **Add-MailboxDatabaseCopy** This cmdlet is used to create a passive copy of an existing mailbox database on another DAG member.
- **Remove-MailboxDatabaseCopy** This cmdlet is used to delete a passive copy of an existing mailbox database.
- **Update-MailboxDatabaseCopy** This cmdlet updates or seeds a passive database copy. This is useful in situations in which seeding was not performed when the copy was created, or an error has caused the passive copy to be diverged from the active copy.

- **Suspend-MailboxDatabasaeCopy** This cmdlet suspends continuous replication to the specified database copy.
- **Resume-MailboxDatabaseCopy** This cmdlet resumes continuous replication to the specified database copy that was previously suspended.
- **Set-MailboxDatabaseCopy** This cmdlet is used to configure the activation preference, replay lag time, and truncation lag time.
- **Get-MailboxDatabaseCopy** This cmdlet is used to retrieve information about the mailbox copy, such as the activation preference, replay lag time, and truncation lag time.
- **Get-MailboxDatabaseCopyStatus** This cmdlet is used to retrieve information about the health of the mailbox database copy.

Obtaining detailed information about the status of the database copies is important. One way to do this is with the *Get-MailboxDatabaseCopyStatus* cmdlet. Figure 11-9 shows the output of *Get-MailboxDatabase* | *Get-MailboxDatabaseCopyStatus* | *Format-List*. The two properties that are of immediate interest are the Context Index State and the Status, which ideally are Healthy. Also, be sure to note the *CopyQueueLength* because this is the number of transaction log files that have not been successfully copied to the passive copies. By adding the –*ConnectionStatus* parameter, additional details about the replication networks is shown, such as listing the networks being used for log replication and seeding.

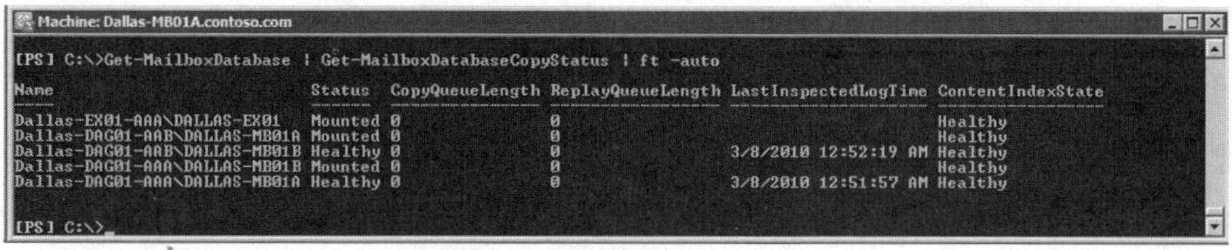

```
Machine: Dallas-MB01A.contoso.com

[PS] C:\>Get-MailboxDatabase | Get-MailboxDatabaseCopyStatus | ft -auto

Name                           Status  CopyQueueLength ReplayQueueLength LastInspectedLogTime ContentIndexState
----                           ------  --------------- ----------------- -------------------- -----------------
Dallas-EX01-AAA\DALLAS-EX01    Mounted 0               0                                      Healthy
Dallas-DAG01-AAB\DALLAS-MB01A Mounted 0               0                                      Healthy
Dallas-DAG01-AAB\DALLAS-MB01B Healthy 0               0                 3/8/2010 12:52:19 AM Healthy
Dallas-DAG01-AAA\DALLAS-MB01B Mounted 0               0                                      Healthy
Dallas-DAG01-AAA\DALLAS-MB01A Healthy 0               0                 3/8/2010 12:51:57 AM Healthy

[PS] C:\>
```

FIGURE 11-9 Running *Get-MailboxDatabaseCopyStatus*

Other potential states for database copies exist in addition to Healthy. Table 11-2 summarizes all of the possible copy status states that you may encounter.

TABLE 11-2 Database Copy Status

COPY STATUS	DESCRIPTION
ActivationSuspended	The database copy has been manually blocked from activation.
DisconnectedAndHealthy	The database copy has become disconnected from the active database copy. When it was disconnected it was in the Healthy state. This status may be reported during DAG network failures between the source copy and the target database copy.

COPY STATUS	DESCRIPTION
DisconnectedAndResynchronizing	The database copy is disconnected from the active database copy. When it was disconnected it was in the Resynchronizing state. This status may be reported during DAG network failures between the source copy and the target database copy.
Dismounted	The active copy is offline and not accepting client connections.
Dismounting	The active copy is going offline and terminating client connections.
Failed	The database copy is in a Failed state and it isn't able to copy or replay log files. In this state, the system will periodically check whether the problem that caused the copy status to change to Failed has been resolved and attempt to automatically resume.
FailedAndSuspended	The Failed and Suspended states have been set simultaneously by the system because a failure was detected, and resolution of the failure explicitly requires administrator intervention.
Healthy	The database copy is successfully copying and replaying log files.
Initializing	The system is verifying that the database and log stream are in a consistent state. This state occurs when a database copy is created; when the Microsoft Exchange Replication service is starting; and during transitions from *Suspended, ServiceDown, Failed, Seeding,* or *SinglePageRestore* to another state.
Mounted	The active copy is online and accepting client connections.
Mounting	The active copy is coming online and not yet accepting client connections.
Resynchronizing	The database copy and its log files are being compared with the active database copy to check for divergence.
Seeding	The database copy is being seeded, the content index for the mailbox database copy is being seeded, or both are being seeded. After seeding is successful, the copy status changes to Initializing.

COPY STATUS	DESCRIPTION
SeedingSource	The database copy is being used as a source for a database copy seeding operation.
ServiceDown	The Microsoft Exchange Replication service is not running on the server that hosts the mailbox database copy.
SinglePageRestore	This state indicates that a single page restore operation is occurring on the database copy.
Suspended	The database copy is in a Suspended state as a result of an administrator manually suspending the database copy by running the *Suspend-MailboxDatabaseCopy* cmdlet.

In some instances, such as during maintenance, you many need to suspend and resume continuous replication activity for a database copy. The transaction logs do not truncate the active mailbox database copy when one or more passive copies are suspended. During an extended maintenance period this may result in a large number of transaction logs accumulating in your transaction log directory. In these cases, you may opt to remove the affected passive database copy instead of suspending it. When the maintenance is complete, you can re-add the passive database copy.

Designing and Configuring DAGs

When deploying a CCR environment in Exchange 2007, the sizing was straightforward—the databases were running on one node or the other. In Exchange 2010, which offers you the ability to have 16 members with up to 1,600 databases, sizing and designing the layout is far more complex. The obvious rule is that the more servers you have in a DAG the more options you have for laying out your database copies efficiently and resiliently. Consider the implications of a three-copy, six-server DAG versus two DAGs with three servers and three copies of each database. More servers in a single DAG give you more flexibility in creating copies and to balancing load. To illustrate, if a single server fails with three active databases in a three-member DAG, the two remaining servers need to service the load from the first server, as shown in Figure 11-10.

As compared to two 3-member DAGs, a 6-member DAG can more effectively spread the results of failure across multiple servers as well as to sustain more member failures.

Normal Operation

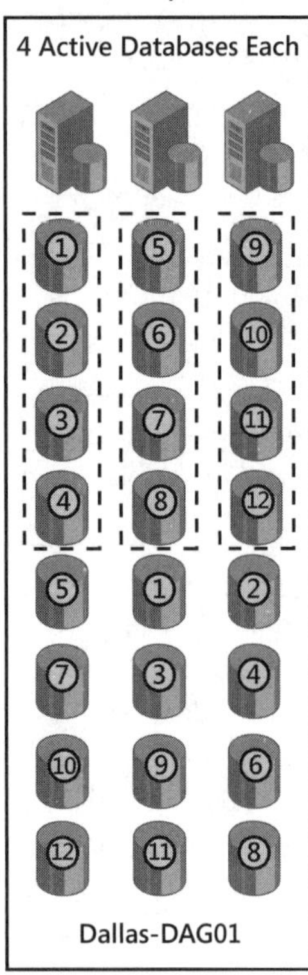

Single-Member Failure

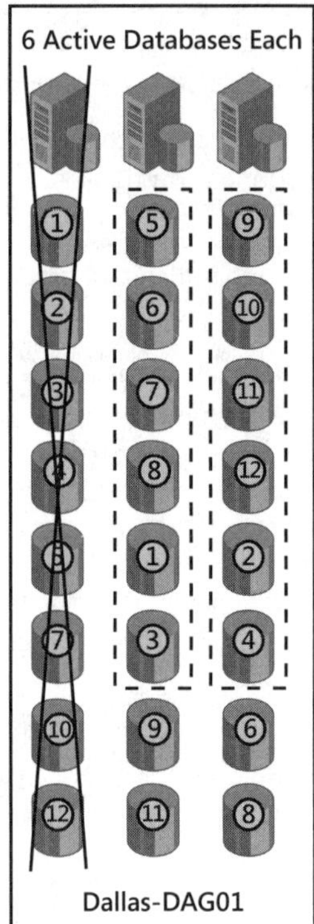

Active Databases

FIGURE 11-10 Three-node DAG failover

In Figure 11-10 the DAG was designed to sustain a single-node failure; if more than one member was down at least two databases would be offline. Simply adding a member to a DAG does not automatically enable it to sustain multiple failures, as Figure 11-11 shows. Here, servers are configured to mirror each other in a four-member DAG. If either A and B or C and D fail, a large number of databases will be unavailable. This configuration provides no better member redundancy than having two 2-member DAGs.

You should design the databases copies with the worst-case failure needed to meet your agreed-upon SLAs. The following two rules apply for redundancy:

1. One-member failure requires two or more high-availability copies, two or more servers, and a witness server.
2. Two-member failure requires three or more high-availability copies, four or more servers, and a witness server.

Rather than mirroring database copies on two servers it is better to stripe copies across the members or create copies randomly across the DAG to reduce the likelihood of a low number of failures causing outages for databases.

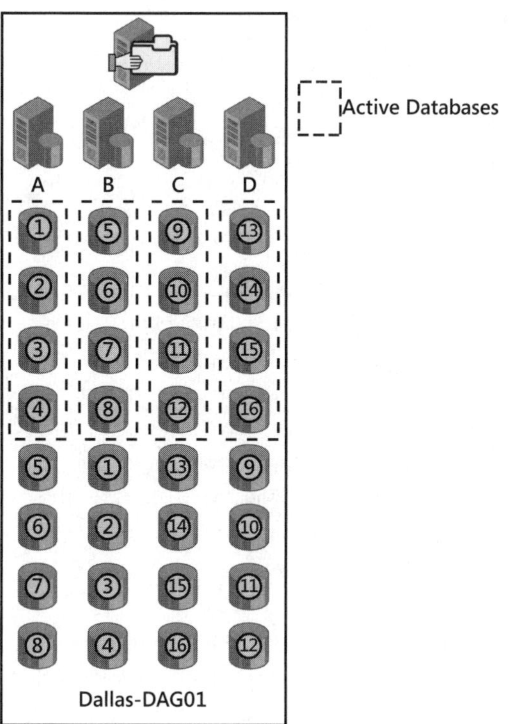

FIGURE 11-11 A four-node mirrored configuration

When determining the copy design plan for the worst case, ensure that the members can handle all of the hosted database copies becoming active. If you plan on oversubscribing the members, you can set a maximum number of simultaneous active databases on each member to ensure that more copies than the server can handle do not come online by using the *Set-MailboxServer* cmdlet with the *-MaximumActiveDatabase* parameter. When the Mailbox server has reached the maximum, no additional database mounts will be successful. If the Active Manager attempts to mount a database on the server the mount will fail and Active Manager will attempt to mount the database copy on another member if one is available. Also, as usage profiles change over time it is important to periodically evaluate the appropriate level of oversubscription and whether the number of active database copies should be modified to accommodate for hardware and usage changes.

Over the course of time, when maintenance is performed active mailbox databases may end up active on servers that they were not intended for. As part of routine maintenance activities remember to activate the database copies across the DAG. You may also use *RedistributeActiveDatabases.ps1,* which is included in SP1, to automatically load-balance active database copies across DAG members.

Deciding the number and location of database copies also involves the storage infrastructure and the operational maturity of your IT department. Assuming the operational challenges can be overcome, you should consider a few best practices when choosing whether to use RAID (Redundant Array of Independent Disks) or JBOD as summarized in Table 11-3.

TABLE 11-3 Choosing Between RAID and JBOD in a Single-Site Deployment

NUMBER OF COPIES	STORAGE OPTIONS
Two high availability	RAID
Three or more high availability	RAID or JBOD
One active and one lagged copy	RAID

When a large number of databases are hosted on each server in a DAG, disk management can become complicated, especially when you are using JBOD storage. Only 23 drive letters are available to mount additional disk drives—A and B are reserved and most likely the operating system is installed on C. When planning a DAG that will require a number of volumes, it is a best practice to use volume mount points rather than drive letters. Volume mount points allow volumes to be mounted as directories rather than drive letters. For example, you may want to mount a 1-TB volume in D:\Databases\Dallas-MB01 to store the Dallas-MB01 database files. You could then mount another 1-TB volume in C:\Databases\Dallas-MB-02 for storing the Dallas-MB02 database files. This way you are no longer constrained by the number of drive letters available.

Using mount points introduces a problem: if the drive that contains the mount points fails, you lose connectivity to all of the other drives. The best practice is to protect the volume that contains the mount points using RAID to reduce the likelihood of a single disk failure taking the entire server offline.

NOTES FROM THE FIELD

JBOD Impact on Operations and Risk Discussion

Arno Zwegers
Infrastructure Architect, Avanade Netherlands

Since the early days of Exchange, administrators have had servers that include storage-level redundancy. Usually this is a hardware-based RAID system where the data is stored across multiple disks. Although failure of one disk may affect performance, it does not affect the availability of the mailboxes. Now, with the ability to store the data on multiple servers, you can use JBOD as the storage technology on the DAG members themselves. The availability of the data is no longer handled by the underlying storage infrastructure, but by Exchange. However, the availability of the operating system and applications must be ensured with a RAID storage solution. This is important; otherwise, the failure of one disk may mean that the server must be rebuilt. A server rebuild takes time, and that means an increased risk of data loss for all mailbox database copies on the failed server because there is now one less copy of all those mailbox databases.

JBOD changes the way administrators will have to operate the servers. Monitoring and signaling of problems becomes even more important to handle quickly and efficiently. This also changes the process required to complete a failed disk replacement.

When a disk fails on an Exchange server with RAID protecting the operating system and databases and the administrator is notified, he or she will have to replace the failed disk. Depending on the RAID system used, replacing the disk will have to happen quickly if no online spare is available, or it can wait if an online spare is available. Rebuilding a RAID set will consume system resources and may impact performance. Many administrators prefer to rebuild the RAID set during a maintenance window; however, with an online spare this process starts immediately.

In this situation the administrator will perform two actions: replace the failed disk with a new one and monitor the status of the rebuilding process, noting when the rebuild is completed. During this process the availability of Exchange itself has not changed—it is unaware of what happened on the storage level.

Now consider an Exchange 2010 server with RAID protecting the operating system and Exchange databases stored on JBOD, where each disk is a separate volume within Windows. (This is important because people may interpret JBOD only as "without RAID" and then create a single Windows volume across all the disks, which increases risk significantly when using JBOD.) The monitoring mechanism for failed disks also needs to be updated, because it will need to understand and report on the database copy status when one or more copies are unavailable or no longer exist.

When a disk fails and the administrator responds, he or she will have to perform more actions than when using a RAID system. First, the failed disk is replaced and formatted, and then the Exchange databases copy needs to be restarted. Finally, the administrator must monitor the status of the database replication.

The administrator will have to consider how to re-create the database copies on the replaced disk. If the failed disk contained 1 TB of data, this amount of data will have to be copied to the replaced disk. This can be done by creating a new copy of the databases and transferring 1 TB of data over the network or by placing a copy of the database files onto the drive by means of USB-based storage or by restoring from a backup. This consideration is important because even on a 1-GB network connection, the copy may take more than two and a half hours to complete, and when copied across a 100-MB WAN connection this may take more than 24 hours.

JBOD reduces hardware costs, but it increases risk, even in the scenario where the DAG has three or more copies of the data. The time during copy re-creation increases risk, because during that time fewer are copies available; however, it can be argued that this risk is similar to the risk while this is a failed disk in the RAID set.

The fundamental change is where the data redundancy is handled. Administrators are used to RAID, which has been used for a long time. The additional activities that have to be performed within Exchange to provide redundancy are new. Without additional integration, many monitoring systems will not be able to effectively understand this new redundancy model. Confusion regarding how to handle failures increases the likelihood that an administrator may not identify the problem or respond quickly enough to the failure.

During the design process the risk of the operational excellence and the time it takes to reseed are important factors to consider in determining whether JBOD is a viable solution for you.

Availability Planning for Client Access Servers

Unlike the Mailbox server role and to some extent the Transport server roles, the Client Access Server role does not have any inherent high-availability functionality built in. That does not mean that it was designed without high availability in mind—it just requires other modalities to provide high availability. A separate product or feature is required to provide this functionality. The following sections cover choosing and configuring the best solution depending on deployment requirements.

Client Access Load Balancing and Failover Solutions

To provide Client Access high availability requires multiple Client Access servers to be deployed in the same Active Directory site. As mentioned, there is no integrated mechanism to provide load balancing and failover capabilities if a host becomes unavailable or overloaded. However, a variety of products are available that fill this need. Because the Client Access servers provide so many services with a number of different connections types—from OWA to MAPI to Web Services—three types of Client Access server traffic actually need to be load balanced:

- Traffic from internal networks
- Traffic from external (Internet) networks
- Traffic from other Client Access Servers (proxy)

Affinity

Some Exchange communications are *stateful*, meaning the application requires that the communication context be maintained with the same host until the session is completed. This is common in conversations that we have daily. If a co-worker asks what the deadline is for your project and then you walk into another co-worker's office and say "Wednesday," she will likely have no idea that you were answering John's question. This is similar to how a stateful program works: It expects to continue communication with the same context until the conversation is completed. Other protocols are stateless, such as HTTP, where state information is lost between client requests. In the case of multiple, load-balanced hosts, affinity is a mechanism to direct subsequent calls to the host that answered the initial request.

It is important to understand the different types of affinity and how they are used. The Client Access server uses a number of protocols that will need to be load balanced, including HTTP and RPC. Remember some Client Access server protocols require affinity and some do not.

EXISTING COOKIES

Existing cookie affinity uses cookie information transmitted during typical client/server sessions. This type of affinity is only useful for protocols using HTTP and thus not an option for any RPC communication. OWA using forms-based authentication is an example of an application that does use existing or application cookies.

LOAD BALANCER COOKIES

Using load balancer cookies is similar to using existing cookies except that the load balancer creates the cookie and does not rely on any existing cookies. As with existing cookies, this is only usable with HTTP. Additionally, the client must support the addition of the load balancer–generated cookie. Exchange ActiveSync, Outlook Anywhere, and some Exchange Web Services do not support this capability. However, Outlook Web App, Exchange Control Panel, and Remote Windows PowerShell are good candidates for this type of affinity.

SOURCE IP

Source IP is perhaps the most common and widely supported type of affinity. With Source IP affinity, the load balancer records a client's IP address and the initial destination host. All subsequent traffic from that source IP will continue to go to the same destination host for a period of time. However, source IP load balancing has two main drawbacks.

First, affinity breaks when clients change their IP addresses. If you have an environment where this happens frequently, such as mobile clients roaming between wireless networks, this will cause issues. Users may experience symptoms such as having to re-authenticate.

Second, if you have an environment where many clients share the same source IP, such as when a device performing Network Address Translation (NAT) is used, the load will not be evenly distributed because all clients behind the NAT will be routed to the same destination IP address.

SSL SESSION ID

SSL session ID is generated when establishing an SSL encrypted session. The SSL session ID has a big advantage over source IP affinity: It can uniquely identify clients sharing the same source IP address. Another advantage is that there is no requirement to decrypt the SSL traffic. This is a hard requirement for using client CA because renegotiating the SSL session ID puts additional overhead on the server. Directing traffic to the same server saves processing time and prevents performance impacts.

SSL session ID does not work well with all clients. Some browsers and mobile devices, such as Microsoft Internet Explorer 8.0, create a new SSL session for each browser process. Therefore, every time a user creates a new e-mail message, a separate window opens, which creates a new SSL session. The exception to this is when users use client CA. The same SSL session ID is used for all communication to a specific host.

Outlook Anywhere and some mobile clients also open several Client Access Server sessions. Each session receives a different SSL session ID, so each session could end up being connected to a different server. As discussed earlier, this is not a problem because Windows Server 2008 network load balancing can correlate the RPC_IN_DATA and RPC_OUT_DATA; however, it does cause additional overhead and can negatively impact server performance.

Selecting a Load Balancer Type

To lower cost and complexity, you should select a single load-balancing solution that works for each type of traffic. A large number of load-balancing options are available on the market; it is important to make an informed choice. Consider the following criteria during the decision-making process:

- **Features** Does the load balancer have features such as SSL offloading that you will use now and in the future?
- **Manageability** How easy is the solution to configure and maintain?
- **Failover detection** Does the solution support advanced detection (service awareness) or simple ping (host awareness)?
- **Affinity** What options does the solution support to keep client connections returning to the same host?
- **Cost** How much will it cost to implement the solution?
- **Scale** How does the solution work as the number of hosts increases?

Load balancers can be categorized into four distinct categories: Software Load Balancers, Hardware Load Balancers, Intelligent Firewalls, and Round Robin DNS. The following sections discuss each of these categories.

SOFTWARE LOAD BALANCING

Windows Network Load Balancing (NLB) has been part of the Windows Server operating system since Windows NT 4.0. Of course, a lot has changed since its early days. NLB can scale to 32 hosts on Windows Server 2008 R2, but the practical limit for Exchange is 8 hosts based on documentation provided about Microsoft's internal deployment experience. One advantage of NLB is that it is relatively inexpensive to implement.

One disadvantage of NLB is that you cannot use it combined with Windows Clustering. If you are trying to configure an all-in-one server that has the Mailbox role and Client Access

Server role, and you are using DAGs, you must use a non-Windows network load-balancing solution for client access. Another drawback is that NLB only supports source IP affinity or no affinity. This may limit its ability to effectively load balance across all of the Client Access protocols. NLB also has no built-in intelligence to test server health or functionality before sending traffic to a host. If the IIS service has stopped on one Client Access server, NLB will continue to send traffic to that node, unless it is reconfigured to stop. This can be partially overcome when NLB is deployed along with Microsoft System Center Operations Manager 2007 R2 and the NLB Management Pack, which may be an option for people that already use Operations Manager.

Other software-based load balancers are installed on a separate server or other hardware. These solutions are often more similar to hardware load balancers or application firewalls than the functionality of NLB.

HARDWARE LOAD BALANCERS

If you need to support more than eight nodes in your Active Directory site, you must consider a hardware load balancer. Having a dedicated piece of specialized hardware allows for the best performance and a considerable number of features. Most hardware load balancers support multiple affinity types, and even allow for the ability to fall back if one type fails. Typically, hardware load balancers support more advanced node health checks. These range from simple ping tests to measuring response times to custom Web pages. More expensive solutions also provide hardware redundancy, further eliminating any single points of failure.

Probably the biggest disadvantage is the cost of deploying a hardware solution. However, for large-scale deployments, this is typically the solution selected.

APPLICATION FIREWALLS

Application (Intelligent) firewalls, such as Microsoft Threat Management Gateway (TMG) or Forefront Unified Access Gateway (UAG), are similar to the hardware load balancer solution, but can also provide additional security features. For example, with Active Directory Domain Services (AD DS) security groups, you can control what time of the day groups of users can access OWA.

One disadvantage is that with this great power comes great complexity. These solutions require more testing and more administration and operational support compared to the other solutions. Another disadvantage is that these do not perform RPC load balancing; in order to do this another solution is also required.

DNS ROUND ROBIN

DNS round robin uses DNS's ability to map multiple hosts to a common name. For example, if you have three Client Access servers the DNS A record entries would look like this:

```
mail.litwareinc.com      192.168.1.2
mail.litwareinc.com      192.168.1.3
mail.litwareinc.com      192.168.1.4
```

The first client to request *mail.litwareinc.com* would have the IP address of 192.168.1.2 returned. The second request would have 192.168.1.3 returned, and the third request would have 192.168.1.4 returned. The fourth request would have the first IP address returned again, and the pattern would continue. The main advantage of this is that it has very little or no cost to implement and it's very easy to configure.

Unfortunately, the limitations of DNS round robin limit its use to lab environments and very small implementations. These limitations include no support for affinity, which requires the application to maintain affinity. For example, a Web browser navigating to *webmail.contoso.com* will actually use the IP address the DNS server returns from the name resolution query. Internet Explorer will have this DNS entry cached for about 30 minutes. If the server became unavailable during that cache period, the Web browser could not be automatically redirected to the new server. Because of this caching, the Web browser will attempt to reach an unavailable server until its cache expires. DNS round robin also does not have any health checks or dead node removal. In the preceding example, if 192.168.1.3 becomes unavailable, DNS will continue to return the down host's IP address every third request unless it is manually reconfigured. Another problem is that if multiple clients share the same local DNS server as in a LAN environment, all of those clients will use the same IP address that is cached by the local DNS server; if most of the clients are from the same location, the load will be very balanced across the servers. Finally, changes to DNS can take time to propagate. If a new Client Access server is added to DNS, it will be underutilized until the record propagates fully.

GLOBAL SERVER LOAD BALANCING

Global server load balancing (GSLB), or wide-area load balancing, is a more sophisticated version of DNS round robin available from some hardware load balancer vendors. This solution is typically deployed as a hardware device or even as a feature of a hardware load balancer. This type of load balancing uses DNS to load-balance client connectivity between sites based on a number of factors such as location of the client, response time of the servers, availability of the servers, custom weights, and more. GSLB is typically used in multiple site configurations to provide load balancing between sites. To provide full site redundancy the GSLB device should be located outside of either of the load-balanced sites or deployed in multiple sites. One way to use the GSLB is to load-balance Autodiscover to ensure that it is available even during a single site outage. In Figure 11-12, Autodiscover.constoso.com is set up for GSLB—all traffic will be sent to the IP address for the Denver Autodiscover service. In the event of a failure of Denver, the GSLB device can send all traffic for Autodiscover.contoso.com to the second site.

The GSLB device will accept DNS requests from the client and then return the appropriate IP address based on the rules defined. The TTL for the returned IP address is set low to ensure that changes are received by the client as quickly as possible. As with DNS round robin, because GSLB relies on DNS client resolution, its functionality is limited when the client DNS resolution is uncontrolled.

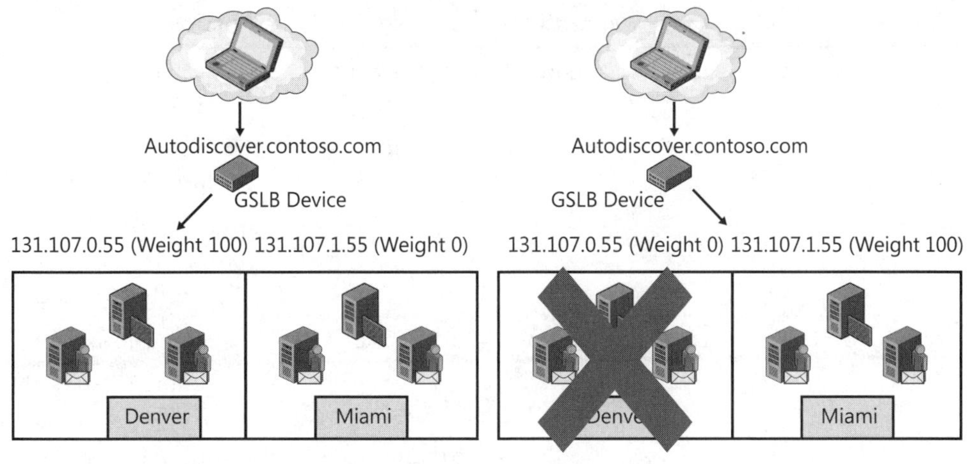

FIGURE 11-12 Using GSLB for the Autodiscover server

LOAD BALANCING SUMMARY

As you can see, you have a variety of solutions to choose from, depending on business requirements and budget. Table 11-4 combines affinity, load balancing, and other considerations when choosing a solution for load balancing.

TABLE 11-4 Load Balancer Comparison

TYPE	COST	SCALE	AFFINITY	BENEFITS	DRAWBACKS
Hardware Load Balancing	High	High	All Types	■ Automatic Failover ■ Can be used with Windows Failover Clusters ■ Service Health Checking	■ Cost ■ Complex
Application (Intelligent) Firewall	Medium	Medium	Source IP Cookie	■ SSL Bridging ■ Enhanced Security ■ AD Authentication ■ Service Health Checking	■ Complex

TYPE	COST	SCALE	AFFINITY	BENEFITS	DRAWBACKS
Software Load Balancing	Low	Low	Source IP	■ Inexpensive ■ Easy to configure	■ Limited Scale ■ Cannot be used with Windows Failover Clusters ■ No Service Health Checking
DNS Round Robin	Low	Low	Random	■ Easy to configure	■ Manual failover ■ Unpredictable traffic ■ Long failover time

Table 11-5 summarizes the configuration needed to support all of the Client Access Server protocols. If the load balancer is used to terminate the SSL certificates, the traffic between the load balancer and the Client Access server will be unencrypted; thus, the unencrypted port is used. Each of the services can be provided with separate load-balanced IP addresses to apply different load-balancing policies to each. For more information about configuring certificates and the internal and external URLs for your Client Access servers see Chapter 4, "Client Access in Exchange 2010."

TABLE 11-5 Load-Balancing Client Access Services

CLIENT ACCESS SERVICE	PROTOCOL	TCP PORT(S)	NOTES
Exchange ActiveSync	HTTP	80/443	Persistence: Source IP
IMAP4	IMAP4	143/993	
Outlook Anywhere	HTTP	80/443	Persistence: Source IP
Outlook Web App	HTTP	80/443	Persistence: Cookie or Source IP
POP3	POP3	110/994	
RPC Client Access	RPC	RPC Ports	Persistence: Source IP

By default the Outlook client will make a connection to the RPC Endpoint Mapping Service on TCP/IP port 135 on the server to negotiate a dynamic RPC port above TCP 1024 for usage. If no firewalls or load balancers are between the clients and servers this is usually not an issue. You can reduce the number ports that need to be load balanced by modifying the Client Access servers to scope down the ports that are required. You must make three modifications:

1. Modify the registry to statically set the MAPI TCP/IP port on all of the Client Access servers.
    1. Open the Registry editor and then select *HKEY_LOCAL_MACHINE\SYSTEM\CurrentControlSet\Services\MSExchangeRpc\ParametersSystem.*
    2. Add a DWORD named TCP/IP Port.
    3. Set the value of TCP/IP port to selected port number.
    4. Close the Registry editor.
2. Modify *X:\Program Files\Microsoft\Exchange Server\V14\Bin Microsoft.Exchange.Addressbook.Service.exe.config* file to statically assign the Address Book (NSPI) and Referral Service (RFR) TCP/IP port on all of the Client Access servers.
    1. Open *X:\Program Files\Microsoft\Exchange Server\V14\Bin Microsoft.Exchange.Addressbook.Service.exe.config* in Notepad or another text editor.
    2. In the *<appSettings>* section locate the line that has *<add key="RpcTcpPort" value="0" />* and then change the 0 to the selected TCP/IP port.
    3. Save the file and close Notepad.
    4. Restart the Client Access server.
3. Modify the registry to statically set the MAPI TCP/IP port on all of the Mailbox servers hosting public folders.
    1. Open the Registry editor and then select *HKEY_LOCAL_MACHINE\SYSTEM\CurrentControlSet\Services\MSExchangeRPC\ParametersSystem.*
    2. Add a DWORD named TCP/IP Port.
    3. Set the value of TCP/IP port to selected port.
    4. Close the Registry editor.
    5. Restart the Mailbox server.

After the load balancer is configured, certificates need to be applied and the internal and external URLs need to be set on each of the Client Access servers.

Creating a Client Access Server Array

Using a load-balancing product will allow you to load-balance connectivity across the Client Access servers for all communication types. To represent the RPC Client Access load-balanced cluster in a single Active Directory site a Client Access array is created. Then the name and IP address for the network load-balanced cluster must be added into the local Domain Name System (DNS). For example, you could add an A record for Dallas-Caa01.contoso.com that points to 10.1.1.25. After adding the DNS record, you can create the Client Access array and assign it to an Active Directory site using the *New-ClientAccessArray* cmdlet. If mailbox databases are already created in the Active Directory site, you must assign the Client Access array to each of the mailbox databases in the site using the *Set-MailboxDatabase* cmdlet with the *RpcClientAccessServer* parameter. To avoid this extra step, you should create the Client Access server array prior to installing any Mailbox servers into the Active Directory site.

A Client Access array exists in a single Active Directory site. Therefore, you need to create a Client Access array in each Active Directory site that will have load-balanced Client Access servers. Also, the Client Access array cannot match the DNS name for the external Outlook Anywhere host name or Outlook will attempt to the Client Access array via RPC before falling back to HTTPS. Because the Client Access server array name is used only for RPC access, any certificates obtained to support Client Access connectivity (OWA, Outlook Anywhere, and so on) don't need to have the Client Access array name included—RPC communications do not use certificates. For a full discussion of configuring certificates and the internal and external URLs for your Client Access servers, see Chapter 4, "Client Access in Exchange 2010."

When you put together a Client Access server array with a DAG, a redundant configuration is born. Figure 11-13 shows how an Outlook client will maintain connectivity when a mailbox database failover occurs. The client computer maintains connectivity to the same node in the Client Access server array based on the configuration of the load balancer and that Client Access server will connect to the second Mailbox server to maintain connectivity to the mailbox.

The other scenario where the Client Access server handles a failure is illustrated in Figure 11-14. When the Client Access server fails, the load balancer will reconnect the client computer to another Client Access server in the Client Access server array. The new Client Access Server will then connect to the Mailbox server with the active copy of the database so that the client computer will continue to be connected to the user's mailbox.

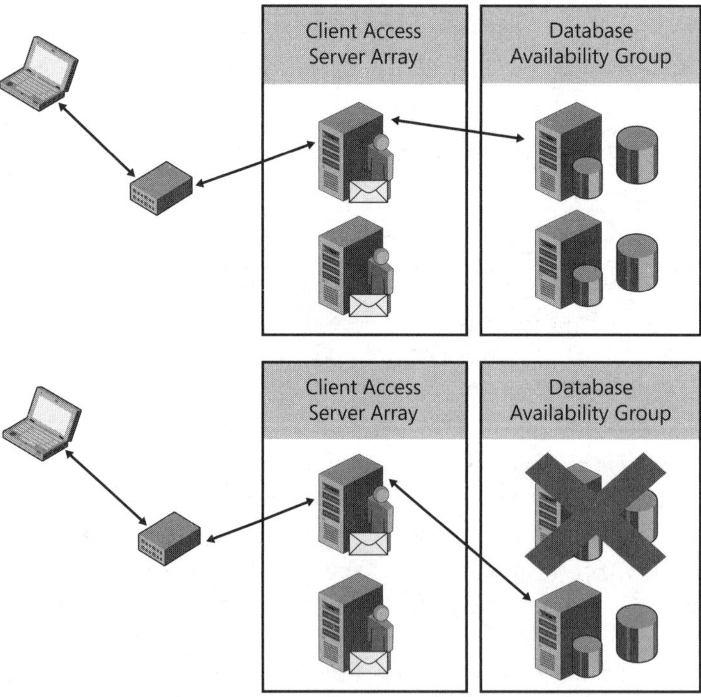

FIGURE 11-13 Client connectivity to the Client Access server during a mailbox copy failover

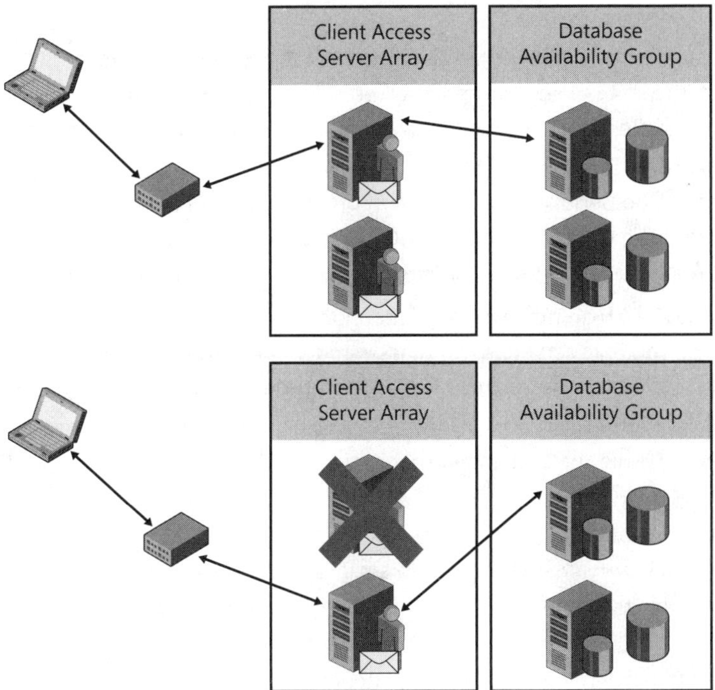

FIGURE 11-14 Client connectivity to the Client Access Server during a Client Access server failover

Availability Planning for Transport Servers

Within the Exchange organization, it is important to deploy multiple transport servers to provide message path redundancy. Deploying multiple Hub Transports in each Active Directory site automatically provides redundancy and load balancing for message delivery. Deploying multiple Edge Transport servers will also provide incoming and outgoing SMTP redundancy.

Shadow Redundancy

Exchange Server 2010 includes the shadow redundancy feature, which provides redundancy for messages for the entire time they are in transit. This is in addition to the transport dumpster. With one form of shadow redundancy, the message deletion from the transport queue is delayed until the transport server verifies that all of the next hops for that message have completed delivery. If any of the next hops fail before reporting successful delivery, the transport server resubmits the message for delivery to that next hop. If the next hop server does not support shadow redundancy, the message will be sent to the next hop and a shadow copy of the message will not be retained.

Shadow redundancy provides the following benefits:

- It eliminates the reliance on the state of the transport server queues. If redundant message paths exist, the state of any transport server isn't relevant. If a transport server fails, you can simply remove it from production without worrying about emptying its queues or losing messages currently in transit.
- If maintenance needs to be performed on the transport server the server can be brought offline without the risk of losing messages in transit.
- It reduces the need for hardware redundancy for transport servers for messages in transit.
- It consumes less bandwidth than other forms of redundancy that create duplicate copies of messages on multiple servers. With shadow redundancy the only added network traffic is the discard status being communicated between transport servers.
- It provides resilience and simplifies recovery from a transport server failure because messages still in transit within the Exchange organization are protected by the previous Exchange 2010 transport server.

IMPORTANT **Shadow redundancy does not protect messages in the transport dumpster, which is essential in being able to recover messages in the case of a DAG member failure.**

One form of shadow redundancy is implemented by extending the SMTP protocol. These service extensions allow SMTP hosts to negotiate shadow redundancy support and communicate the discard status for shadowed messages.

The protocol implementation of shadow redundancy works between Exchange 2010 transport servers. In the following scenario, a message is sent from an Exchange 2010 mailbox out to the Internet from a Hub Transport through an Edge Transport server, as shown in Figure 11-15. In this case the message flow follows these stages:

1. Hub delivers the message to Edge1:
   a. Hub opens an SMTP session with Edge1.
   b. Edge1 advertises shadow redundancy support.
   c. Hub notifies Edge1 to track discard status.
   d. Hub submits the message to Edge1.
   e. Edge1 acknowledges receipt of the message and registers Hub1 to receive discard information for the message.
   f. Hub moves the message to the shadow queue for Edge1 and marks Edge1 as the primary server. Hub becomes the shadow server.
2. Edge1 delivers the message to the next hop:
   a. Edge1 submits message to a third-party e-mail server.
   b. The third-party e-mail server acknowledges the message's receipt.
   c. Edge updates the discard status for the message as delivery complete.

3. If the message is delivered successfully, when Hub queries Edge1 for discard status:
   a. At end of each SMTP session with Edge1, Hub queries Edge1 for the discard status on messages previously sent. If Hub has not sent any other messages to Edge1, it will open an SMTP session with Edge1 to query for the discard status after five minutes and will fail over three failures or 15 minutes. This time can be configured using *Set-TransportConfig* with the *ShadowHeartbeatTimeoutInterval* parameter. The number of retries can be configured by running *Set-TransportConfig -ShadowHeartbeatRetryCount*.
   b. Edge1 checks the local discard status and sends back the list of messages registered to Hub1 that have been delivered and then removes the discard information.
   c. Hub deletes the delivered messages from its shadow queue.
4. If the message delivery fails, then Hub queries Edge1 for discard status and resubmits the message:
   a. If Hub cannot contact Edge1, Hub resumes the primary role and resubmits the messages in the shadow queue to another available transport server, Edge2.
   b. The resubmitted messages are delivered to Edge2, and the workflow starts from step 1.

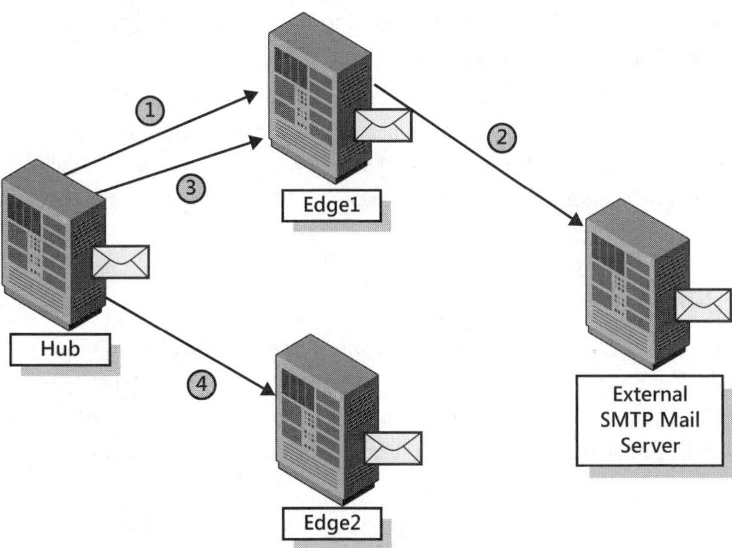

FIGURE 11-15 Transport shadow redundancy

The Shadow Redundancy Manager (SRM) is the core component of a Transport server responsible for managing shadow redundancy. The SRM is responsible for maintaining the shadow server for all of its primary messages. The SRM is also responsible for maintaining the following information for all the shadow messages in its shadow queues:

- Determining when the shadow server should take ownership of shadow messages, thus making it the primary server
- Maintaining the list and checking primary server availability for each shadow message

- Processing discard notifications from primary servers
- Removing the shadow messages from the database once after receiving the discard notification
- Sending the discard status to the shadow servers

Shadow redundancy does not require any sort of configuration. When multiple transport servers are deployed they will automatically negotiate the use of shadow redundancy. When multiple Hub Transport servers are deployed in each Active Directory site each e-mail message will exist in two places while in transit. Because each message exists in two locations you may consider deploying Hub Transport servers without RAID-protected disks because the in transit e-mail messages will exist on another server and not need to be recovered. It is not always advantageous to deploy transport servers without redundant storage for the message queue as shadow redundancy does not protect e-mail messages in the transport dumpster. In configurations with a multi-site DAG as well as others that consistently maintains a number of e-mail messages in the transport dumpster because of transaction log replication latency you should store the message queue on redundant storage to reduce the probability of losing transport dumpsters data. You can determine the number of items in the transport dumpster by viewing the *Dumpster Item Count* counter on the *MSExchangeTransport Dumpster* performance object using Performance Monitor or by trending this counter using a solution like Microsoft System Center Operations Manager.

To reduce the likelihood of a server failure causing a loss of e-mail, the Mailbox Submission service on a DAG member first attempts to load-balance submission requests across other Hub Transport servers in the same Active Directory site. If the Hub Transport role is installed on the DAG member and it cannot submit messages to any other Hub Transport server in the site, it will fall back to the local Hub Transport server.

Inbound E-mail Redundancy

Another form of shadow redundancy called *delayed acknowledgement* is used in scenarios when a transport server receives a message from a mail server that doesn't support shadow redundancy. Rather than immediately confirming receipt of the message from the submitting service, it delays sending an acknowledgement until it has confirmed that the message has been successfully delivered.

For inbound e-mail delivery with Edge or Hub Transport servers, the typical way to provide redundancy is to use an MX record for each of the e-mail servers accessible for e-mail delivery. MX records are weighted records in DNS that point to the e-mail servers responsible for receiving mail for a domain. The MX records with a lower weighting will be attempted before higher-weighted records. Records that have the same weight will be load balanced. Using MX records to provide this redundancy is part of the way SMTP was designed, so this configuration is often sufficient. In some instances where large numbers of SMTP servers are deployed, you may choose to use network load balancing to have more control over the inbound SMTP traffic, but load balancing should never be used inside the Exchange organization or against the Default Receive Connector on each Hub Transport server. Load balancing and redundancy are built in to the transport service.

NOTE More information about MX records and how they are used can be found in RFC 2821.

Planning Cross-site Failovers

The high-availability improvements in Exchange 2010 make it even easier to deploy cross-site failover solutions without a need for third-party network and storage solutions. The secondary site can be used to handle primary site outages resulting from maintenance or other, more serious failures. Even with the improvements in Exchange 2010, careful planning must be done to successfully deploy and maintain a multi-site deployment.

Cross-site DAG Considerations

The primary building block of a cross-site solution is the cross-site DAG. Extending a DAG between sites does have a couple requirements, including the following:

- Fewer than 250 milliseconds of latency between all DAG members. To ensure consistent DAG operations there should be minimal latency.
- At least one domain controller in each site. Exchange requires a domain controller in each site it is deployed; for redundancy at least two should be deployed.
- At least one Client Access server in each site. To provide client connectivity to both sites at least one Client Access server must be deployed; for redundancy at least two should be deployed.
- At least one Hub Transport server in each site. To provide e-mail transport to both sites at least one Hub Transport must be deployed; for redundancy at least two should be deployed.
- Consider the impact on supporting services to a failover. The appropriate number and configure of Client Access servers, Hub Transport, Edge Transport, Unified Messaging server roles, and domain controllers must be located at each site to support the maximum number of active mailboxes.
- In the case of a complete datacenter failure:
  - Quorum must be reestablished. To mount databases, a quorum must be established within the cluster. If a majority of the members, including the file share witness, are unavailable the DAG must be manually reconfigured to reestablish quorum.
  - Manual switchover process. To bring up the second site, the administrator must manually initiate the switchover. A complete datacenter switchover is not something to consider lightly from a business process standpoint. Requiring manual intervention was put in place to ensure that an administrator has to make the decision to initiate a full datacenter switchover.

Cross-site Considerations for Client Access and Transport

When you deploy non-Mailbox servers to support a cross-site failover, you might come across several issues, including Domain Name System (DNS) entries for Outlook Web App, Outlook Anywhere, and Autodiscover. Inbound e-mail (MX) must be redirected to reflect the secondary site's IP addresses. These record changes should be automated to provide the quickest return to service. Until the clients that connect to these services have the new addresses they will fail. These changes can be improved by deploying DNS servers in multiple locations or by using third-party global-server load balancing. If you are using a hosted anti-spam or archiving service these services must be redirected to the new site.

Proper namespace planning is needed for the failover process to run smoothly. To do this you must consider each datacenter as being active and choose a unique set of names for each Exchange service. This includes OWA, Post Office Protocol version 3 (POP3), Internet Message Access Protocol version 4 (IMAP4), Exchange Web Services, and Outlook Anywhere; however, it cannot include Autodiscover. Having this number of names requires that you configure certificates to reflect the names that each site uses. To do this, ensure that the certificates contain all required host names for services in both datacenters or use a wildcard certificate. If you choose to use separate certificates for each datacenter, you must ensure that each certificate has the same certificate principal name. To reduce the impact on Outlook connections, you must run *Set-OutlookProvider EXPR -CertPrincipalName msstd:<certificate principal name>*. For more information on namespace planning see Chapter 4, "Client Access in Exchange 2010."

NOTES FROM THE FIELD

Client Access Namespace and the Impact to High Availability and Site Resiliency

Gary A. Cooper
Senior Systems Architect, Horizons Consulting, Inc., United States

In previous versions of Exchange Server, when thinking of high availability and site resiliency, we often thought only of how to protect the mailbox database and how to make it available in another datacenter in the event that something happened to your primary copy. Although database availability and the DAG are still important factors in Exchange Server 2010, it is now equally important to consider the Client Access Server role and the overall namespace design and its impact on your high availability and site resiliency plan.

To account for the impact the namespace design has on availability, it is helpful to think about the different switchover/failover (*over) scenarios and the impact those *over scenarios have on all of the client connectivity types that your organization needs to support. When the namespace design has been drawn out, I recommend deploying the design in a lab environment so that the *over scenarios can be played out and the client types supported by the organization can be fully tested to gain the impact on users. It is important to note whether the client will continue to run without interruption or will experience a brief disconnect and then automatically reconnect. Possibly, the client will reconnect, but only after a timeout value has been exceeded (for example: DNS resolver cache expiring). During the testing phase, you can also work out any intervention steps you must take to ensure a smoother transition during a failure.

After you have fully tested the client impact, it is important to document the results both for your design documentation and so that you can articulate the results to both your senior management and to the user community at large. In this way, you can set everyone's expectations properly and avoid confusion in the event that the unthinkable disaster happens.

To visualize the different scenarios, it is often helpful to build a chart that allows you to track the success or failure of each client connection type given specific *over scenarios.

	HIGH AVAILABILITY (SINGLE-SITE AND SINGLE-NAMESPACE)		SITE RESILIENCY (TWO-SITE AND TWO-NAMESPACE)	
CLIENT TYPE	**SWITCHOVER**	**FAILOVER**	**SWITCHOVER**	**FAILOVER**
OWA	No user impact (Success)	No user impact (Success)	No user impact (Success)	No user impact (Success)
Exchange ActiveSync 5/6	No user impact (Success)	No user impact (Success)	Client failure and profile must be manually updated (Failure)	No user impact (Success)
Exchange ActiveSync 6.1+	No user impact (Success)	No user impact (Success)	No user impact (Success)	No user impact (Success)
Outlook 2007/2010 (Outlook Anywhere)	Short client disconnect and reconnect (Success)	Short client disconnect and reconnect (Success)	No user impact (Success)	No user impact (If EXPR matches certificate CN) (Success)
Outlook 2007/2010 (Internal RPC)	Short client disconnect and reconnect (Success)	Short client disconnect and reconnect (Success)	No user impact (Success)	No user impact (If EXPR matches certificate CN) (Success)
POP3/IMAP4	No user impact (Success)	No user impact (Success)	Client failure and profile must be manually updated (Failure)	No user impact (Success)

Cross-site Switchover

Deploying a DAG across two sites can allow database copies to exist in two locations and provide site resiliency. This allows a single mailbox database to fail over and switch over to the secondary site. The client software will react to the changes in one of two possible ways when the active mailbox database is moved from one site to another. Understanding these reactions is important to ensuring that you perform the correct type of failover for your needs:

- The Client Access server will directly connect to the Mailbox server.
- The client will be redirected to connect to the second site, as shown in Figure 11-16.

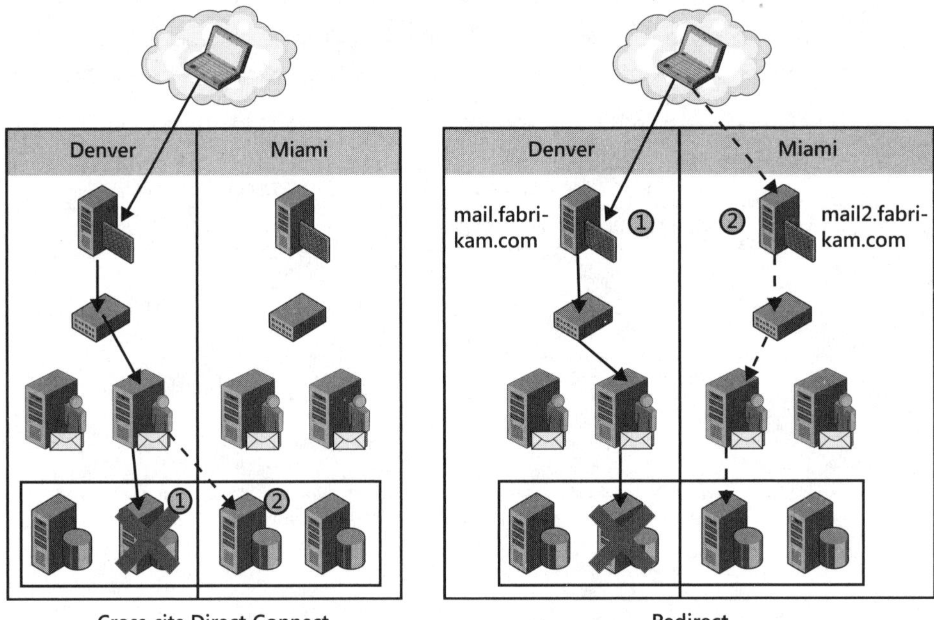

FIGURE 11-16 Comparing cross-site connections and redirect

Exchange 2010 SP1 includes functionality to control the connection behavior of Outlook when a cross-site database failover or switchover occurs. By default, Outlook will connect across from the primary Client Access server to the activated Mailbox server for temporary cross-site situations. Alternatively, the administrator can prevent all cross-site connections. Temporary and permanent cross-site moves are differentiated by the administrator explicitly resetting the database copy activation preference.

In the initial release of Exchange 2010, the default behavior is to perform a direct connect from the Client Access server array in the first datacenter to the mailbox hosting the active copy in the second datacenter. Redirection will only occur when the *RPCClientAccessServer* property is changed on the mailbox database. In SP1, you can choose to enable or disable cross-site direct connect and define an activation preference for a database.

The new SP1 behavior is based on the following three properties:

- Home server property in Outlook
- Preferred database site (*RPCClientAccessServer*)
- Active database site

Cross-site direct connect happens in the following scenarios:

- If the Outlook profile home server value, preferred database site, and mounted database site are the same, Outlook will connect (or stay connected) to the Client Access server array and that will connect to the Mailbox server cross-site.
- If the Outlook profile array site is the same as the preferred database site, and the mounted database site is different and cross-site connections are allowed, Outlook will connect (or stay connected) to the Client Access server array and will connect to the Mailbox server cross-site.
- If the Outlook profile home server property value is the same as the mounted database site, and different than the preferred database site, Outlook will connect (or stay connected) directly through the to the Client Access server array to the Mailbox server cross-site. This happens when you change the activation preference.

Redirection happens in the following scenarios:

- If the Outlook profile home server property value is different, and the preferred and mounted database sites are the same, the RPC Client Access service must redirect Outlook to the preferred and mounted database site and update the Outlook profile.
- If the Outlook profile home server property value is the same as the preferred database site, and the mounted database site is different, the Client Access server will redirect Outlook to the mounted database site if cross-site connections are not allowed.

Using cross-site direct connect is often suitable when a single mailbox server is undergoing maintenance or there are other temporary issues that will be resolved in a short period of time. Redirection may be needed when multiple systems or the entire datacenter will undergo maintenance. Performing a redirection switchover will force the clients to reconnect to the secondary site and allow maintenance to be completed. If redirection is used to switch over, it will also be done to perform the switchback to allow the clients to reconnect to the primary site. To enable cross-site direct connect, run *Set-DatabaseAvailabilityGroup <DAG Name> -AllowCrossSiteRpcClientAccess: $true* from the EMS. Conversely, to disable cross-site direct connect, run *Set-DatabaseAvailabilityGroup <DAG Name> -AllowCrossSiteRpcClientAccess: $false* from the EMS. To determine whether cross-site direct connect is enabled, run *Get-DatabaseAvailabilityGroup <DAG Name> | Format-List* as shown in Figure 11-17.

```
Machine: Dallas-MB01B.contoso.com
[PS] C:\Windows\system32>Get-DatabaseAvailabilityGroup Dallas-DAG01 -status | fl

RunspaceId                              : da130288-e3f3-4911-b391-05c33f626e88
Name                                    : Dallas-DAG01
Servers                                 : {DALLAS-MB01B, DALLAS-MB01A}
WitnessServer                           : dallas-ex01.contoso.com
WitnessDirectory                        : C:\FSW\Dallas-DAG01
AlternateWitnessServer                  :
AlternateWitnessDirectory               :
NetworkCompression                      : Enabled
NetworkEncryption                       : Enabled
DatacenterActivationMode                : DagOnly
StoppedMailboxServers                   : {}
StartedMailboxServers                   : {Dallas-MB01B.contoso.com, Dallas-MB01A.contoso.com}
DatabaseAvailabilityGroupIpv4Addresses  : {10.112.33.95}
DatabaseAvailabilityGroupIpAddresses    : {10.112.33.95}
AllowCrossSiteRpcClientAccess           : False
OperationalServers                      : {DALLAS-MB01A, DALLAS-MB01B}
PrimaryActiveManager                    : DALLAS-MB01B
ThirdPartyReplication                   : Disabled
ReplicationPort                         : 64327
NetworkNames                            : {Dallas-DAG01_MAPINetwork, Dallas-DAG01_ReplicationNetwork}
WitnessShareInUse                       : Primary
AdminDisplayName                        :
ExchangeVersion                         : 0.10 (14.0.100.0)
DistinguishedName                       : CN=Dallas-DAG01,CN=Database Availability Groups,CN=Exchange Administrative Gro
                                          up (FYDIBOHF23SPDLT),CN=Administrative Groups,CN=Contoso,CN=Microsoft Exchange
                                          ,CN=Services,CN=Configuration,DC=contoso,DC=com
Identity                                : Dallas-DAG01
Guid                                    : f6547e8f-c588-4e51-a6e3-e0163aa912ca
ObjectCategory                          : contoso.com/Configuration/Schema/ms-Exch-MDB-Availability-Group
ObjectClass                             : {top, msExchMDBAvailabilityGroup}
WhenChanged                             : 3/20/2010 4:24:14 PM
WhenCreated                             : 3/6/2010 9:35:41 PM
WhenChangedUTC                          : 3/20/2010 8:24:14 PM
WhenCreatedUTC                          : 3/7/2010 2:35:41 AM
OrganizationId                          :
OriginatingServer                       : Dallas-DC01.contoso.com
IsValid                                 : True
```

FIGURE 11-17 Retrieving the cross-site direct connect setting

Handling Datacenter Failures

To prepare for activating a secondary site in the case of a primary site failure, you must enable datacenter activation coordination (DAC) mode on the DAG by running *Set-DatabaseAvailabilityGroup <DAG Name> -DatacenterActivationMode:DagOnly.* Also in preparation you should also set the alternate witness server and alternate witness directory for a server available in the second site. This allows an administrator to activate the site even if a majority DAG members remain unavailable in the failed site, and it prevents split-brain scenarios. The Active Directory site defines the datacenter boundaries; therefore, to enable DAC mode, the DAG must span at least two sites. A datacenter failure is a catastrophic event because such a failure requires an administrator to make the decision to perform a full datacenter switchover, because the process is not automatic. The datacenter switchover process includes the following steps:

1. Evaluate the situation and then decide to perform a datacenter switchover.
2. Configure the DAG to remove the primary site's servers from the Windows Failover Cluster, but retain them in the DAG. This is done by running *Stop-DatabaseAvailabilityGroup <DAG Name> –ActiveDirectorySite <Primary Site Name> -ConfigurationOnly* in the primary site, if possible.
3. Configure the DAG to use an alternate witness server and restore the functionality in the secondary site. To do this, first stop the cluster service on each of the secondary site's DAG's servers, and then run *Restore-DatabaseAvailabilityGroup <DAG Name> -ActiveDirectorySite <Secondary Site Name>.*

4. Start the cluster service on each of the servers in the DAG in the secondary site. The remaining Active Managers will then coordinate mounting databases in the secondary site.
5. Adjust DNS records, if necessary, for Simple Mail Transfer Protocol (SMTP), OWA, Autodiscover, and Outlook Anywhere. These adjustments can be done manually or automatically using a third-party global-server load balancer.

After the primary site is recovered you may choose to perform a switchover to the primary site. This process includes the following steps:

1. Evaluate the situation and decide to perform a datacenter failback. Verify that the primary datacenter is capable of hosting Exchange services.
2. Reconfigure the DAG to add the DAG members in the primary datacenter back into the failover cluster by running *Start-DatabaseAvailabilityGroup <DAG Name> –ActiveDirectorySite <Primary Site Name>*.
3. Configure the DAG to use the primary site's witness server by running *Set-DatabaseAvailabilityGroup <DAG Name> –WitnessServer <Primary Site Witness Server>*.
4. Manually reseed or allow replication to update the primary datacenter's database copies, depending on the state of the primary site copy.
5. Schedule downtime for the mailbox databases and then dismount them.
6. Move databases back to the primary datacenter by running *Move-ActiveMailboxDatabase <Database> –ActivateOnServer <Server in Primary Site>*, and then mount the databases in the primary datacenter.
7. Adjust DNS records, if necessary, for Simple Mail Transfer Protocol (SMTP), OWA, Autodiscover, and Outlook Anywhere. These adjustments can be done manually or automatically using a third-party global-server load balancer.

In Exchange Server 2010 DAC mode tasks are available to restore service in a standby datacenter while a minority of the DAG members are available. Prior to SP1, DAC mode was limited to at least three members in the DAG. In that three-node DAG, two members needed to be in the primary datacenter (Active Directory site). In SP1, DAC mode has been improved to support a two-member DAG with a member in each datacenter. As with all DAGs with an even number of members, this implementation requires a witness server to provide the additional vote to obtain quorum.

Cross-site Best Practices

You can use the best practices described in this section to ensure a successful, highly available, multiple-site configuration. First, you can reduce failover times by lowering the Time to Live (TTL) on DNS records for the Client Access server array, Client Access server URLs, and SMTP records. A low TTL reduces the time it takes DNS clients to discover the DNS entries that point to the secondary site. If any client computers that use DNS services are outside of your control, such as a regional ISP, be sure to verify that these services will honor any TTLs set—this will impact service availability for these users. By default a DAG is configured to only compress and encrypt transaction log shipping across different subnets. To take advantage of network compression between sites, you must manually enable intersubnet compressing and encryption.

Never wait until a failure occurs to ensure that everything works as designed. You should continually monitor and verify that all messaging-system components are functioning properly. This is done by monitoring all aspects of the Exchange Server environment to ensure that it is functioning normally, and that mailbox data is successfully replicating to the secondary site in a timely manner. You should also schedule periodic switchover tests to provide an additional level of preparation and to validate the configuration and operation of the cross-site switchover process. Switchover tests are usually coordinated events where the primary servers are shut down cleanly to reduce the possibility of data loss. When performing these drills be sure to verify that you are not missing steps that would be required in a real switchover scenario where the primary datacenter becomes unavailable.

You should also follow a change management process to ensure that each Mailbox server in the DAG, each Client Access server, and each Hub Transport server are configured identically with the same updates applied. Doing so reduces the possibility of incompatibilities and unexpected behavior if a *over occurs.

Provide adequate bandwidth for replication traffic. Replication is always from source to target; therefore, multiple copies in the remote site means more bandwidth is required. To reduce the amount of bandwidth needed you should be sure that compression is enabled on the log shipping traffic for the DAG. The Exchange 2010 Mailbox calculator can be used to help estimate the bandwidth required.

Finally, you should have each DAG node connected to multiple networks. These multiple networks provide communication redundancy between DAG nodes and segregate MAPI and replication communications. To reduce network congestion and potential communications problems, you should not allow the DAG networks to route between each other. For example, you would not allow the replication network to communicate with the MAPI network or vice versa. This communication should be blocked by the network equipment, with a router or a firewall.

Multi-Site Storage Architecture

You must consider a number of factors when determining the hardware needed to support your highly available Exchange deployment, as discussed in detail in Chapter 13, "Hardware Planning for Exchange Server 2010." Having multiple database copies requires storing data on multiple disks; this reduces the requirement for having RAID-protected storage because the data is redundantly stored. Deployment decisions for RAID or JBOD should be based on cost, performance, IT operational maturity, and required resilience. To provide for storage failures, redundancy is either provided by having additional database copies or by using RAID on the storage. Table 11-6 summarizes instances when RAID or JBOD should be considered.

TABLE 11-6 Choosing Between RAID and JBOD

	2 HIGH-AVAILABILITY COPIES	3 + HIGH-AVAILABILITY COPIES	2 + HIGH-AVAILABILITY COPIES / DATACENTER	1 LAGGED COPY	2 + HIGH-AVAILABILITY COPIES AND 1 + LAGGED COPIES / DATACENTER
Primary Datacenter	RAID	RAID or JBOD	RAID or JBOD	RAID	RAID or JBOD
Secondary Datacenter	RAID	RAID or JBOD	RAID or JBOD	RAID	RAID or JBOD

Risk Mitigation

Achieving high availability requires that risks are identified and addressed. Many organizations employ risk management practices to capture and address potential disruptions to business processes. These practices usually consist of the following phases:

- **Identification** This phase includes the documentation of areas of risk within the business. These range from loss of a large customer and the associated revenue all the way to a disaster that destroys a company datacenter.
- **Assessment** This phase includes the analysis of the identified risks to determine the probability and the impact of each.
- **Mitigation** This phase includes creating a plan for mitigating each potential risk. The mitigation plans for each risk fall into the following three categories:
  - **Acceptance** This is done when a risk is accepted, usually because the probability of occurrence is so low it doesn't require mitigation or the cost outweighs the consequences of the risk. A risk that might fall into this category is the probability of datacenters that are 20 miles apart being affected by the same tornado. Although this is possible, the likelihood is so small that is acceptable.
  - **Transference** This is done when the risk is mitigated by obtaining insurance or by outsourcing the risk to others to manage. A risk that might fall into this category is outsourcing inbound anti-spam and antivirus services to Microsoft Exchange Hosted Services to handle inbound e-mail.
  - **Reduction** This is done when the risk can be managed to a point where it is less probable or can be recovered from quickly. A risk that might fall into this category is deploying a cross-site DAG in two datacenters to reduce the likelihood that a single site failure can cause a messaging system outage.
- **Implementation** This phase includes putting the risk mitigation into practice.
- **Review** This phase evaluates the risk mitigation plan to verify that it has addressed the identified risks and to evaluate whether any new risks have been introduced.

Not only should risk management be practiced at the business level, but it must also be performed for IT solutions, such as the Exchange messaging environment. As you perform risk identification for your messaging environment you may list disk failure, server motherboard failure, loss of Internet connectivity, security breaches, site failures, and employee mistakes as risks. The assessment and mitigation process may create a list similar to the one in Table 11-7.

TABLE 11-7 Exchange Risk Mitigation

RISK	MITIGATION
Mailbox Server Disk Failure	Reduction: Use a RAID configuration or rely on DAG replication.
Server Motherboard Failure	Reduction: Use a DAG for Mailbox servers and deploy multiple Transport and Client Access servers.
DNS Server Failure	Reduction: Deploy multiple DNS servers and configure servers to use them.
Domain Controller Failure	Reduction: Deploy multiple domain controllers in each site.
Network Device Failure	Reduction: Deploy redundant network devices.
Loss of Internet connectivity	Reduction: Add additional Internet providers. Transference: Host servers in a colocation facility.
Security Breaches	Reduction: Good update management; implement intrusion detection and prevention systems. Transference: Outsource security to an experienced third-party provider.
Site Failures	Reduction: Deploy a failover site.
Employee Mistakes	Reduction: Provide training for employees and automate many common tasks.

One of the best ways to mitigate risk is to periodically test any disaster avoidance or recovery practices that have been put into place. This allows these measures to be tested and refined in a controlled environment, and in the end reduces risk. Often small details can be overlooked in a plan that cause delays in the recovery. For some organizations the primary datacenter is colocated in the same facility as the office space. In a situation where the primary facility is no longer viable and the IT systems are operational in the secondary datacenter, the users will still need another location to work. The processes and procedures for accessing the new location and notifying customers must also be worked out.

These fire drills also provide the opportunity to teach the employees the importance the business places on recovery and reinforces the mind-set to work toward that goal during all of their day-to-day responsibilities.

Pulling It All Together

The following sections review how each of this book's case studies implement their high-availability Exchange 2010 environment.

Contoso Case Study

The first case study is from Chapter 2, as shown in Figure 11-18.

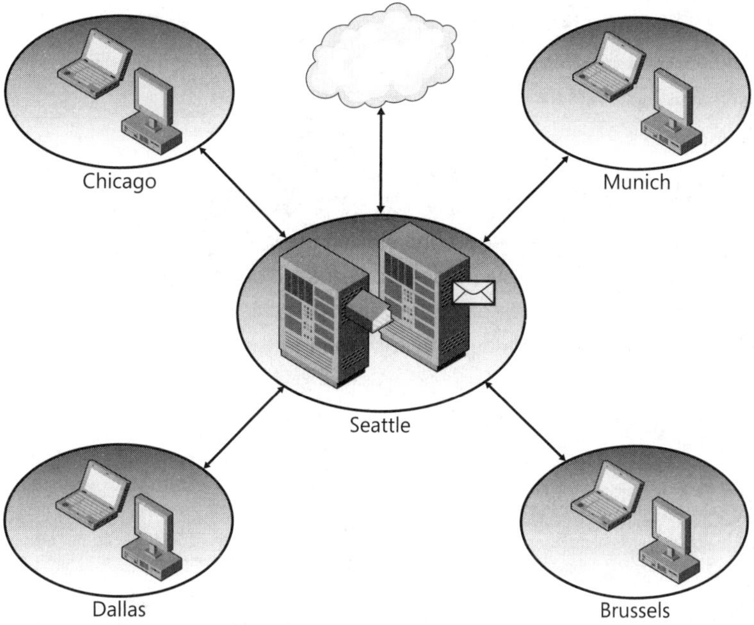

FIGURE 11-18 Contoso logical architecture

In light of high-availability requirements, Contoso proposes deploying a two-server high-availability solution. This two-server solution has both servers running Client Access, Hub Transport, and Mailbox server roles and is configured in a DAG. A file server in the site is the witness server. Although Contoso needs to purchase a third-party load-balancing solution because NLB is not supported on the same servers running Windows Failover Clustering, the money saved by purchasing half the number of servers more than makes up for the cost of the hardware load balancer, as shown in Figure 11-19.

The administrator creates an RPC Client Access array object named outlook.contoso.com and ensures that the each mailbox database has the *RpcClientAccessServer* property set to that value for the Outlook clients. The internal and external URLs also need to be updated with the load-balanced FQDN, including the *AutoDiscoverServiceInternalURI*. Because there are no proxy sites, all services should use the load-balanced FQDN. The *ExternalHostname* for Outlook Anywhere should be configured to match the certificate principle name, mail.consoto.com. An administrator will configure the load balancer with two virtual IP addresses (VIPs) that load balances both servers. The administrator will then create a DNS A record entry for mail.contoso.com and outlook.contoso.com, both pointing to separate VIPs on the load balancer.

The Contoso IT staff members have decided to deploy RAID-protected storage for each server to ensure adequate data resiliency in the event of a disk failure.

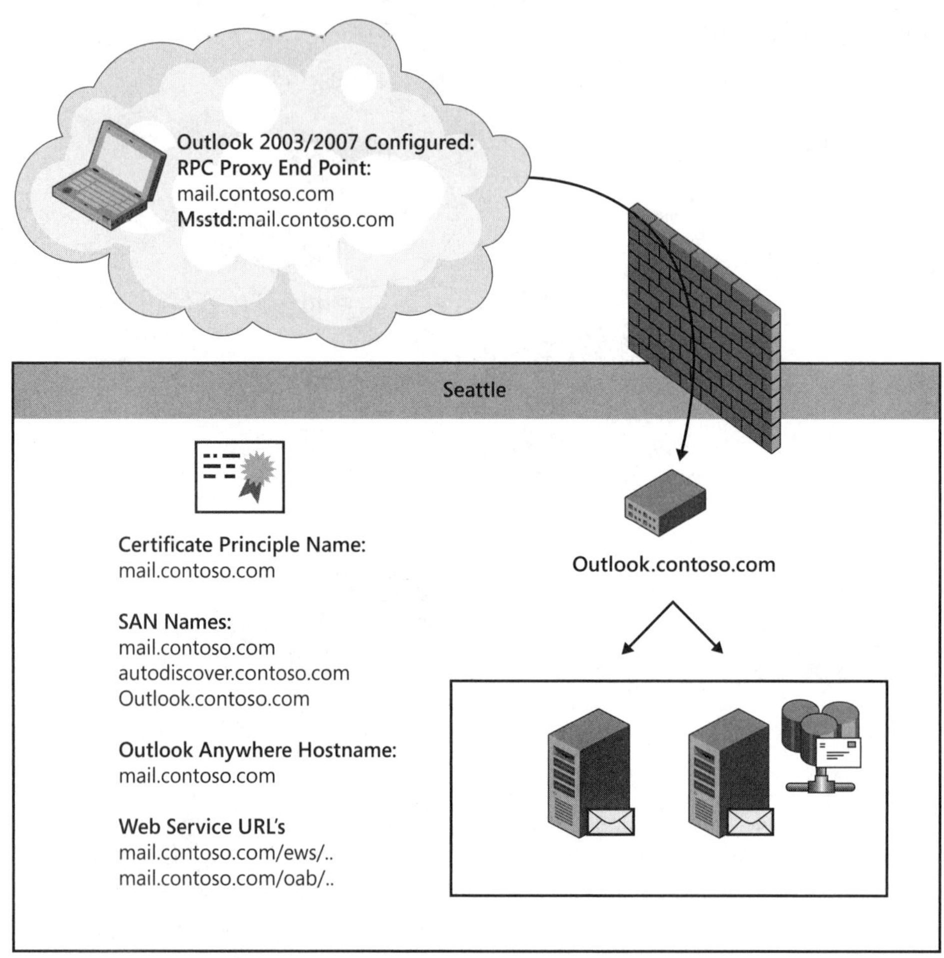

FIGURE 11-19 Proposed Contoso architecture

Fabrikam Case Study

The second, more complex case study from Chapter 2 is Fabrikam. As shown in Figure 11-20, Fabrikam has two main datacenters that will host Exchange services for all of their other sites. The Mailbox servers on the Denver site will host mailboxes for users in Phoenix, Portland, and Denver. The Mailbox servers on the Miami site will host mailboxes for user located in London, Toronto, and Miami.

In the Denver and Miami datacenters Fabrikam has deployed two hardware load-balanced Client Access servers, and the Mailbox servers are configured in a DAG. The network between the datacenters is adequate to host all client traffic both for everyday operations and in the event of a failover.

One of the key requirements for the Exchange 2010 deployment was providing a site-resilient solution. Therefore, Fabrikam has decided to migrate from their two Exchange 2007 Single Copy Clusters to a single DAG that spans both sites as shown in Figure 11-21.

In case of a Denver site failover, DAC mode is enabled and an alternate witness server is configured for a server on the Miami site.

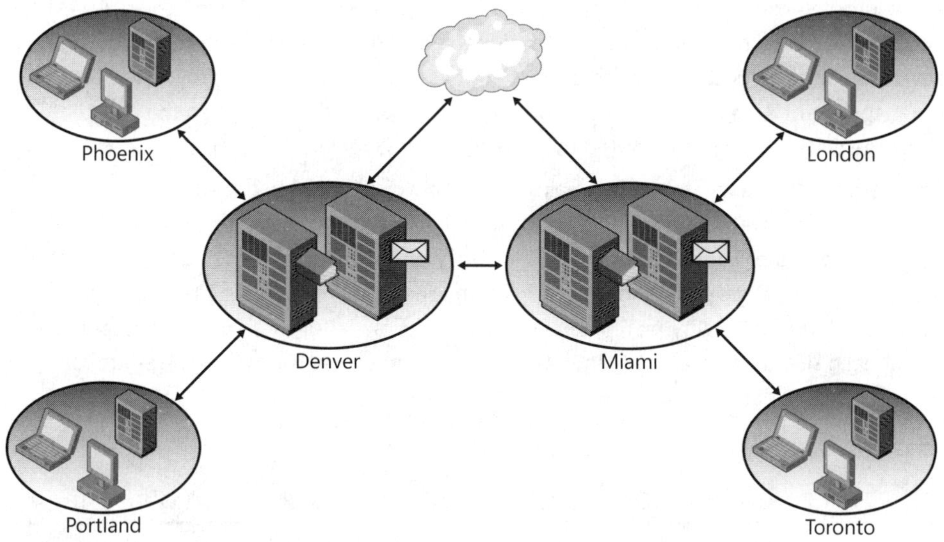

FIGURE 11-20 Fabrikam logical view

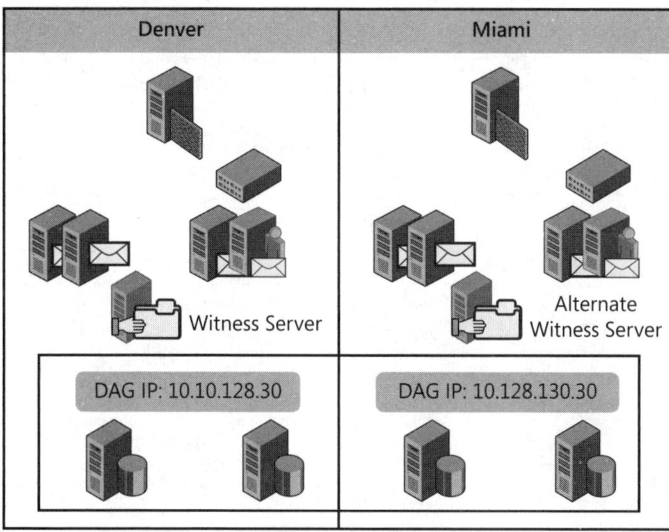

FIGURE 11-21 The Fabrikam high-availability deployment configuration

The Fabrikam Exchange 2007 deployment team followed best practice and chose to use a separate namespace for each Active Directory site. Fabrikam users in Denver access OWA using *https://mail.denver.fabrikam.com/owa,* whereas users in Miami use *https://mail.miami.fabrikam.com/owa.* To reduce confusion and support requests, Fabrikam has decided to consolidate the namespace and only instruct users to use *https://mail.fabrikam.com* for OWA, EWS, and IMAP communication. They have chosen to use GSLB to load-balance mail.fabrikam.com and autodiscover.fabrikam.com and configure the GSLB to send client computer connections to the site that is geographically closest. For example, a user connecting over the Internet from Atlanta will be directed to the IP address for the Miami Client Access servers; a user connecting from Fresno will be directed to the Denver Client Access servers. In the event that a client is connected to a site that does not host the active copy of the user's mailbox, the Client Access server will be able to use the connectivity between the datacenters because the DAG has been configured to allow cross-site direct connect.

Fabrikam has approximately 7,000 mailboxes evenly distributed between the two sites. Twenty-four databases will be created, and each will handle almost 300 mailboxes, all with a 1-GB storage quota. The database high-availability plan defines that each database will have two copies on the primary site and one copy on the secondary site. Table 11-8 summarizes the database high-availability plan. The plan does not provide for three mailbox database copies at each site; therefore, the team has chosen to deploy RAID-protected storage for all of their mailbox database storage.

TABLE 11-8 Fabrikam's Mailbox Database Copy High-Availability Plan

	DENVER-MB01A	DENVER-MB01B	MIAMI-MB01A	MIAMI-MB01B
DAG01-DB1	**Active**	Copy 1	Copy 2	No Copy
DAG01-DB2	Copy 1	**Active**	No Copy	Copy 2
DAG01-DB3	No Copy	Copy 2	**Active**	Copy 1
DAG01-DB4	Copy 2	No Copy	Copy 1	**Active**
DAG01-DB5	**Active**	Copy 1	Copy 2	No Copy
DAG01-DB6	Copy 1	**Active**	No Copy	Copy 2
DAG01-DB7	No Copy	Copy 2	**Active**	Copy 1
DAG01-DB8	Copy 2	No Copy	Copy 1	**Active**
DAG01-DB9	**Active**	Copy 1	Copy 2	No Copy
DAG01-DB10	Copy 1	**Active**	No Copy	Copy 2
DAG01-DB11	No Copy	Copy 2	**Active**	Copy 1
DAG01-DB12	Copy 2	No Copy	Copy 1	**Active**
DAG01-DB13	**Active**	Copy 1	Copy 2	No Copy
DAG01-DB14	Copy 1	**Active**	No Copy	Copy 2
DAG01-DB15	No Copy	Copy 2	**Active**	Copy 1
DAG01-DB16	Copy 2	No Copy	Copy 1	**Active**
DAG01-DB17	**Active**	Copy 1	Copy 2	No Copy
DAG01-DB18	Copy 1	**Active**	No Copy	Copy 2
DAG01-DB19	No Copy	Copy 2	**Active**	Copy 1
DAG01-DB20	Copy 2	No Copy	Copy 1	**Active**

	DENVER-MB01A	DENVER-MB01B	MIAMI-MB01A	MIAMI-MB01B
DAG01-DB21	**Active**	Copy 1	Copy 2	No Copy
DAG01-DB22	Copy 1	**Active**	No Copy	Copy 2
DAG01-DB23	No Copy	Copy 2	**Active**	Copy 1
DAG01-DB24	Copy 2	No Copy	Copy 1	**Active**

Fabrikam uses a hosted service for all inbound e-mail traffic. The hosted service provides redundancy and an SLA that meets the business and technical requirements for Fabrikam's Exchange 2010 deployment project. To provide redundancy for inter- and intra-site message transport, two Hub Transport servers will be deployed to each site.

Litware Case Study

The last case study is for the global company Litware, Inc., as shown in Figure 11-22.

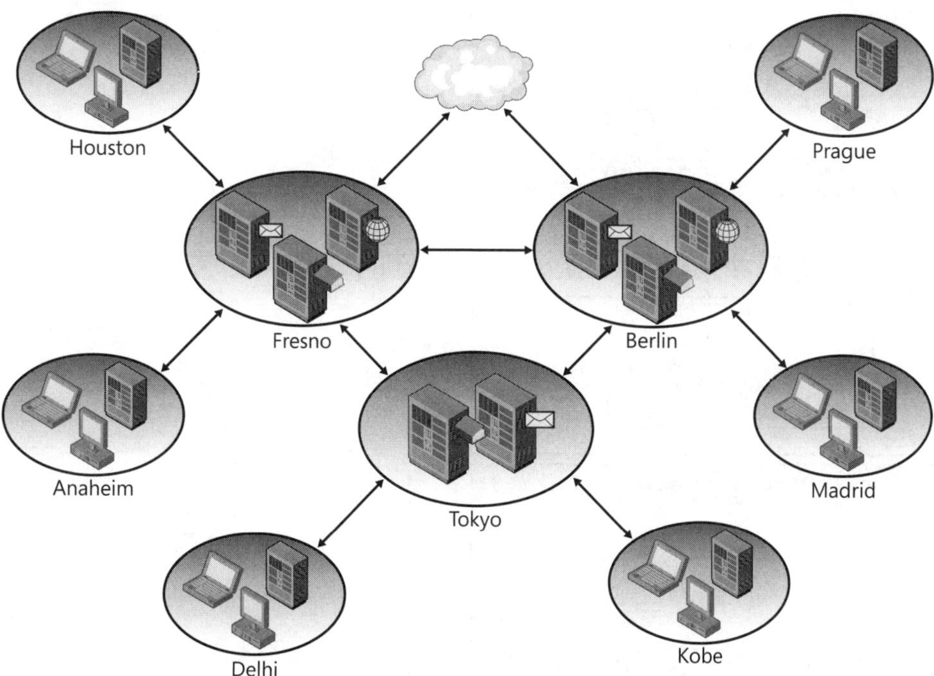

FIGURE 11-22 Litware, Inc., logical view

To reduce network costs, Litware uses regional namespaces to ensure that client traffic does not traverse the company WAN. Litware will deploy a high-availability solution within the regional datacenter, either with a software or hardware load balancer. Only the three hub sites—Fresno, Berlin, and Tokyo—have Exchange servers. The spoke sites, such as Kobe, Prague, and Madrid, will not have Exchange servers locally. Fresno, Berlin, and Tokyo will replace *Region* with the region-specific information. Tokyo, for example, will use *Tokyo.litwareinc.com* as their URL for OWA.

To provide e-mail message ingress and egress traffic to the Internet, the Edge Transport servers in Fresno and Berlin will all have a single MX record published using GSLB. When a request for the MX record for fabrikam.com is processed by GSLB, it will return the IP address for the MX record for the Edge Transport server closest to the sender. For example, if a SMTP server in Leipzig is sending an e-mail to Jeff@Fabrikam.com, GSLB will return the IP address for one of the Edge Transport servers in Berlin.

The Exchange deployment team at Litware decided to deploy their DAG using JBOD and without backups, which requires a 12-node DAG to be deployed in Fresno, Berlin, and Tokyo. To support the DAG in each location, nine Client Access servers are needed. This number was determined by using the CPU core ratio of four Mailbox server CPU cores for every three Client Access server CPU cores, will be deployed. Also, using the CPU core ratio of five Mailbox server CPU cores for every one CPU core on a Hub Transport server that is also running antivirus, five Hub Transport servers will be deployed at each location, as shown in Figure 11-23.

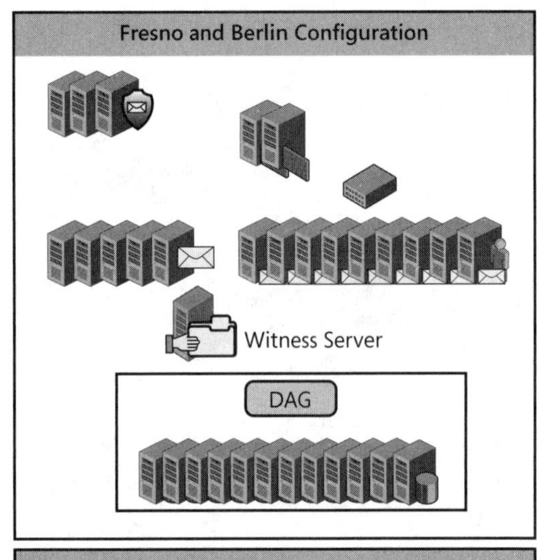

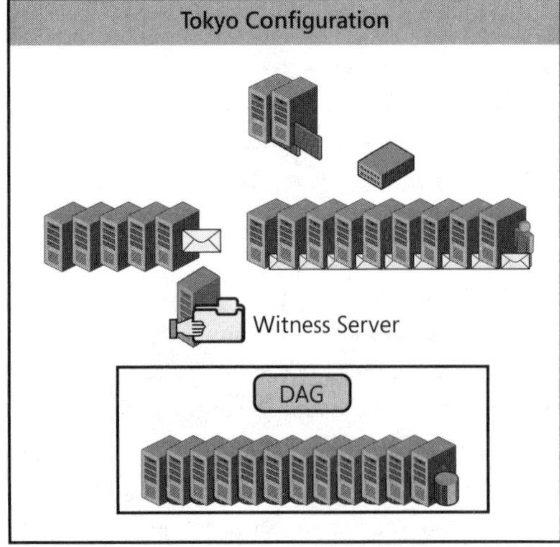

FIGURE 11-23 Litware high-availability deployment configuration

To meet Litware's business and technical requirements, each mailbox database will have three current copies and one database copy lagged for 14 days. This configuration provides enough data redundancy to eliminate having to RAID database storage and provides a lagged copy in case a point-in-time copy is required. Because of the large number of mailbox copies required, the copies will be distributed randomly across the DAG nodes and each month the Exchange administers will run an automated report to examine server load and copy distribution to determine whether adjustments need to be made to the copy distribution.

Additional Resources

- Simple Mail Transfer Protocol: *http://www.ietf.org/rfc/rfc2821.txt*
- Exchange 2010 Help: Planning for High Availability and Site Resilience: *http://technet.microsoft.com/en-us/library/dd638104.aspx*
- Exchange 2010 Help: Understanding Active Manager: *http://technet.microsoft.com/en-us/library/dd776123.aspx*

CHAPTER 12

Backup, Restore, and Disaster Recovery

Microsoft Exchange Server 2010 contains new features that you should consider implementing before using the traditional point-in-time backup approach that most organizations use nowadays. The new high-availability features of Exchange Server 2010 should also be part of your plan for backup, restore, and disaster recovery. Features such as DAGs combined with Single Item Recovery and Archiving even allow you to retire your traditional backup-to-tape solution for your messaging environment.

Changes to Backup and Restore in Exchange Server 2010

Exchange Server 2010 changes the way you back up your Exchange mailbox databases, removing the ESE streaming backup application programming interface (API) and adding a Volume Shadow Copy Service (VSS)–based plug-in for Windows Server Backup. Now the only supported online backup method is using the VSS plug-in for Windows Server Backup or an Exchange-aware VSS backup solution.

Together with the functionality that allows you to create copies of your databases on multiple Exchange servers, Exchange high-availability features closely link with disaster recovery.

Integrating High Availability and Disaster Recovery

You can integrate your high-availability deployment with disaster recovery, especially if you consider the Exchange Server 2010 high-availability features sufficient to satisfy your backup requirements.

The Link Between High Availability and Disaster Recovery

Using the high-availability features built into Exchange 2010 such as database availability groups (DAGs) allows you to minimize downtime and data loss in the event of a disaster but can also reduce the total cost of ownership of the messaging system. By combining these features with other built-in features, such as Single Item Recovery and Legal Hold, you are able to reduce or eliminate your dependency on traditional point-in-time backups and reduce the associated costs. You can spread database copies across multiple sites, which allows you to address datacenter failures and maintain offsite copies of a database.

High-Availability Provides Options Beyond Traditional Backup and Restore

Using DAGs to configure a lagged, or point-in-time, copy of a database allows you to delay committing changes to the database for up to 14 days. Thus, you continuously maintain a database at the states it went through during the previous day or week. Therefore, if you have an issue with your current database, such as a rogue administrator or a script changing many items at once, you can revert to a lagged database copy and commit the transaction logs to a specific time that you decide.

Using lagged database copies, together with maintaining multiple database copies across more sites, means that organizations can consider reducing the amount of nightly backups. This is particularly true for medium-sized and large organizations because they generally have a more complex backup and restore infrastructure in place than small companies.

Evaluate the cost of your current backup infrastructure, including hardware, installation, and license costs, as well as the management cost associated with recovering data and maintaining the backups. Depending on your organization's backup requirements, a DAG environment together with Exchange 2010 features such as Single Item Recovery may provide lower total cost of ownership (TCO) than a traditional backup environment. If you can reduce the backup-to-tape dramatically this also would save you storage costs for the tapes for example.

Large Mailbox Considerations

Mailboxes that are more than 10 GB in size require a more flexible backup and restore method because the amount of data they contain is dramatically more than those with which Exchange Server administrators typically deal. The main concern here is always about how long it takes to recover a database. Even though the Exchange Server 2010 database structure handles large mailboxes better than previous versions, you should be aware of the additional data requirements for backup.

The amount of time it takes to restore a backup during disaster recovery skyrockets when you have large mailboxes. When you're planning to implement large mailboxes, consider using multiple database copies and using the Single Item Recovery feature for Exchange Server 2010 to recover data. These features provide you with options to move away from traditional backups.

Backup and Restore Requirements in a Highly Available Deployment

Even though it may appear that highly available deployments no longer require traditional backups, they may still be needed in your environment. You may want to use existing backup strategies that provide offsite data storage at secure locations, even if Exchange 2010 can provide additional offsite database copies. Sometimes backups also serve an archival purpose, and typically organizations use tape to preserve point-in-time data for extended periods, as mandated by compliance requirements.

Additionally, remember that integrating high-availability features as an alternative to backups only works for the mailbox database, not for other Exchange Server resources, such as the Hub Transport configuration. You still may need to consider using traditional backup for your Hub Transport servers.

Removal of ESE Streaming APIs for Backup and Restore

Previously, Exchange Server used Extensible Storage Engine (ESE) streaming backup APIs as well as the Volume Shadow-Copy Service (VSS) for Exchange-aware backup and restore. Now, Exchange Server 2010 supports only VSS-based backups. To back up and restore Exchange Server 2010, you must use an Exchange Server–aware application that supports the VSS writer, such as Windows Server Backup or Microsoft System Center Data Protection Manager or a third-party, Exchange-aware, VSS-based application.

Storage Group Removal

One significant change in Exchange Server 2010 is the removal of storage groups. In Exchange Server 2010, each database is associated with a single log stream as represented by a series of 1-MB log files. Each Mailbox server with an Enterprise Server license can host up to 100 active or mounted database copies, and with a Standard Server license can host up to five active database copies. Passive database copies and recovery databases are not included in this per-server limit as you are able to create up to 257 databases per server.

Database Not Tied to a Specific Mailbox Server

Another significant change for Exchange Server 2010 is that databases are not tied to a specific Mailbox server. Database mobility expands the system's use of continuous replication by replicating a database to multiple servers. This provides better database protection and increases availability. If failures occur, the other servers with database copies can mount the database.

Using DAGs to Eliminate Traditional Point-in-Time Backups

Because you can have multiple database copies hosted on multiple servers in a DAG, you can also consider eliminating traditional point-in-time backups from your organization and turning on circular logging on your databases. This removes the transaction logs that are no longer required for any copies of the database, so they do not accumulate. Normally, transaction log files are removed when you do a full Exchange Server backup. Circular logging accomplishes the same task without doing a full backup.

Backup and Disaster Recovery Planning

As the messaging system is fundamental to the success of a business, more and more companies implement and plan their backup and disaster recovery procedures very carefully to prevent the event of message outages.

Why Backup Is Done

A backup is required to preserve the company's investment of a reliable and dependable messaging service. This is especially important when a server malfunctions and users are not able to send or receive messages. For this reason, backing up your environment to restore it quickly is a very important task in every Exchange administrator's area of responsibility.

The reasons to perform a backup include:

- **Disaster recovery** Allows you to restore configuration and user data as quickly as possible after a server failure.
- **Point-in-time database recovery** Allows you to recover a previous version of the database if the current database is not working correctly because of a logical or physical corruption, a virus attack, or a malicious administrator that destroyed or modified the data in the databases.
- **Recovery of accidentally deleted items** For when users delete items that later needed to be recovered.
- **Long-term data storage** Provides long-term storage of message data for compliance reasons or because it is company policy. Generally this involves archiving the mailboxes or storing a backup of the databases in a locked-down location only accessible to a person you completely trust.

NOTES FROM THE FIELD

Backup Pains

Colin Lee
Technology Specialist, Unified Communications, Microsoft Corporation, Australia

Over the years I've worked with many customers that had Exchange implementation ranging from small (50 mailboxes) to the very large (60,000 mailboxes). One of the more interesting customers I dealt with ran Exchange 2003 with a large number of mailboxes. Ten thousand plus mailboxes in Australia is considered large. Typical of some large customers, this customer had issues with storage capacity and backup.

This customer had a requirement to recover single e-mail items going back a number of years. To meet this requirement the customer decided to use the company's investment in an expensive tape library. The backup schedule entailed a full nightly backup to comply with the recovery requirement, which was streamed directly to the tape library with a Fiber-channel connection. What made this customer interesting is that the full nightly backup took up to 10 hours to complete on a good day. On a bad day it would take up to 23 hours (thus completing not long before the next backup schedule). This was due to the large amount of Exchange data and the fact the tape library was not dedicated to Exchange. On a really bad day the store would dismount as a result of exceeding 1,008 uncommitted transactions (see Microsoft Knowledge Base article 905801) because of lengthy backup time. The customer was initially running an Exchange 2003 cluster on a Windows 2000 operating system and thus wasn't able to take advantage of VSS backups.

The customer is now moving forward with Exchange 2010 to take advantage of the flexible storage options as well as the other enhancements that make backup easier, less painful, and less frequent. As part of the move to the new messaging platform the customer will evaluate backup solutions that will provide VSS capabilities that can take a backup from the passive DB to reduce backup time and avoid impacting production users. The customer is also looking to use a 30-plus-day Single Item Recovery period and schedule backups on a weekly or fortnightly basis.

Developing Service Levels for Backup and Restore

Before you can think of what types of backup you implement for your messaging solution and how restore will take place, you should plan some time to develop service levels for backing up and restoring your messaging environment.

Very common service levels are summarized into three industry-standard acronyms: SLA (Service Level Agreement), RPO (recovery-point objective), and RTO (recovery-time objective) as described in Table 12-1.

TABLE 12-1 Common Service-Level Definitions

SERVICE LEVEL	DESCRIPTION
Service Level Agreement (SLA)	Determines how long the mail service can be down before service has to be restored
Recovery-Point Objective (RPO)	Determines how much data can be lost; measured in minutes
Recovery-Time Objective (RTO)	Determines the maximum time allowed for recovering each service; measured in minutes

To develop your own service levels, you should consider the following questions for your own organization:

- What level of service is required after the message service fails?
- How long can it take before service is restored?
- In case of an outage, do users need their mailbox data or just messaging services?
- How rapidly is mailbox data required?
- How many and what users must be supported during an outage?
- What services are essential to restore, and in what order?
- What is the maximum amount of data that can be lost?
- What budget has to be allocated for backup and recovery?

The overall design of your backup, disaster recovery, and high-availability strategy will depend on these SLAs to cover various failure scenarios. This will not only include considering backup, but also other areas such as high-availability and disaster prevention strategies.

> ***NOTE*** **Service levels also have an impact on your database design because they dictate the size of the databases so that you're able to recover with the time you have available. For example, if your SLA is 1 hour, you need to consider the time you need to identify the problem and decide for a recovery, and then add the time needed for the recovery of the database itself. You can imagine that with an SLA of 1 hour a database recovery shouldn't take longer than 30 minutes maximum and thus enforces very sophisticated backup technology or small databases.**

Disaster Prevention Strategies

As you prepare to implement disaster recovery solutions in Exchange Server 2010, you first must identify the potential risks to the Exchange Server environment, and then identify the options for mitigating those risks, as detailed in Table 12-2.

TABLE 12-2 Potential Data-Loss Risks and Mitigation Options for Exchange 2010

POTENTIAL DATA-LOSS RISK	OPTIONS AVAILABLE
Loss of a single message	Configure Single Item Recovery settings. Recover messages from backup by using the recovery database.
Loss of a single mailbox	Configure mailbox retention settings to ensure that you can recover most deleted mailboxes before they are deleted permanently. Recover mailbox using the recovery database.
Loss of a database or server	Create a database copy on another server. Back up the Exchange Server data and recover lost mailbox databases from backup. Install Exchange Server 2010 with the */m:RecoverServer* switch.
Loss or logical corruption of a mailbox database	Create a lagged database copy in a DAG environment. Back up the Exchange Server data and recover lost mailbox databases from backup.
Loss of a public folder database	Implement public folder replicas to other Exchange servers.

Single Item Recovery

Exchange 2010 introduces a new concept called *Single Item Recovery*. Single Item Recovery, or Dumpster 2.0, the successor to Dumpster 1.0 in Exchange 2007 or earlier, provides some significant advantages over Dumpster 1.0:

- It ensures that all deleted or modified items are preserved; the user can no longer hard-delete any item from their mailbox.
- It ensures that deleted or modified items can be recovered easily.
- It stores all deleted or modified items in a hidden recoverable items folder in the mailbox that can be indexed and is searchable using discovery cmdlets.
- Because the recoverable items folder is part of the user's mailbox, all items in that folder are moved when the mailbox is moved to a different database or server.
- By default the recoverable items folder is given a quota to help prevent uncontrolled mailbox growth.

One benefit of Single Item Recovery over regular deleted items (known from Exchange 2007 or earlier) or brick-level backups is that the user can no longer manipulate or delete any items and you do not need extra backup media to store data for the brick-level backup.

As mentioned earlier, the recoverable items folder is located within the non-interpersonal messaging (non-IPM) subtree of the user's mailbox and thus is not accessible to the end user, but it is accessible to administrators assigned to the Discovery Management role. The folder includes three subfolders called Deletions, Versions, and Purges as described in Table 12-3.

TABLE 12-3 Recoverable Items Subfolders

RECOVERABLE ITEMS SUB-FOLDER	PURPOSE
Deletions	Similar to the previous Exchange version, this folder includes all the items that have been deleted or removed from the Deleted Items folder but can be recovered in Outlook or OWA using the Recover Deleted Items option.
Versions	The Versions folder includes an item that was changed and then saved back to the mailbox in its original state. It includes all types of items, but does not include flag changes such as a category change and items in the Drafts folder. This folder is only used when Singe Item Recovery or Litigation Hold (or legal hold) is enabled on the mailbox.
Purges	The Purges folder includes all items that have been manually removed from the Deletions folder to preserve them until the deleted item retention period is reached (only if Litigation Hold is not enabled). This folder is only used when Singe Item Recovery or Litigation Hold is enabled on the mailbox.

Figure 12-1 illustrates how the different folders in the Recoverable Items folder interact with each other and when they are used to store items.

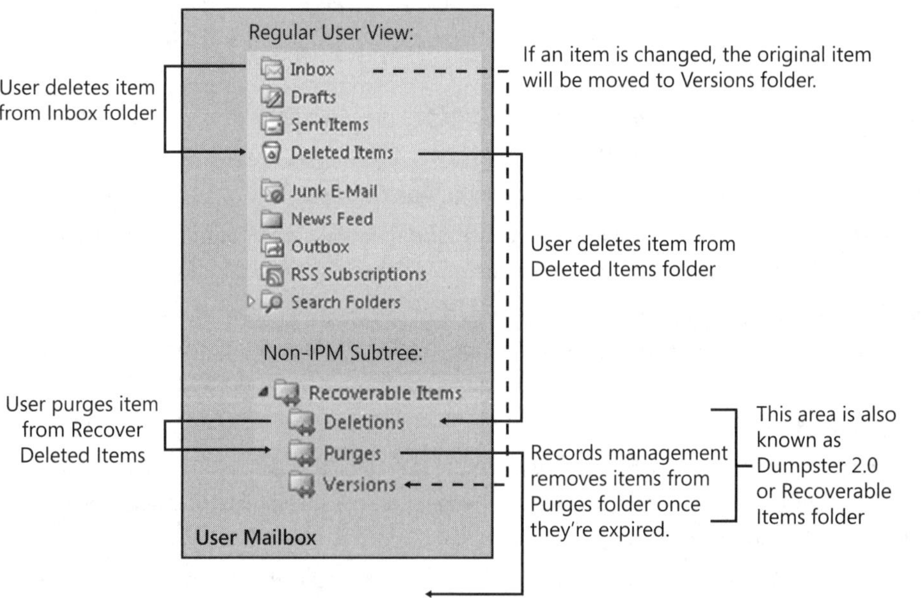

FIGURE 12-1 Single Item Recovery architecture

> ***IMPORTANT*** **In Exchange 2010, mailbox items are no longer deleted by the user, but instead will be removed by Records Management when the deletion timestamp of the item has been exceeded.**

CONFIGURING SINGLE ITEM RECOVERY

Single Item Recovery is not enabled by default, so you need to manually enable it using Exchange Management Shell (EMS). You configure deleted items recovery on a mailbox level using the following cmdlet: *Set-Mailbox <identity> -SingleItemRecoveryEnabled $true*. Alternatively you also can enable all mailboxes for Single Item Recovery using the *Get-Mailbox | where {$_.SingleItemRecoveryEnabled –eq $false} | Set-Mailbox -SingleItemRecoveryEnabled $true* cmdlet.

The default settings for Single Item Recovery are configured on the database level and include 14 days for deleted item retention and 30 GB as quota limit for recoverable items, as shown in Figure 12-2. However, you can also configure these settings on the mailbox level by overriding them for specific mailboxes.

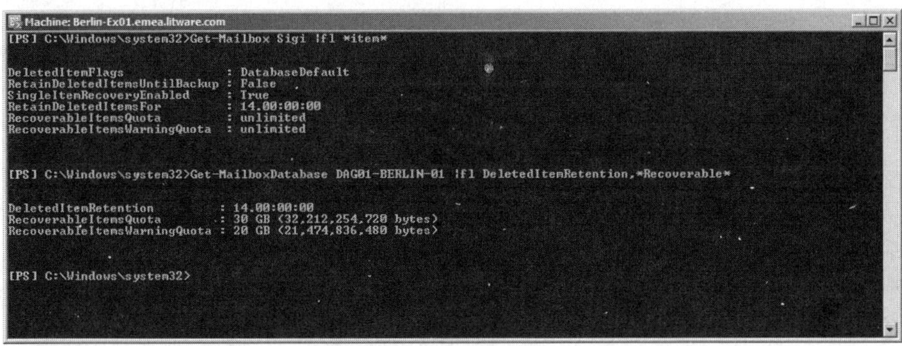

FIGURE 12-2 Configuring deleted items recovery options

RECOVERING ITEMS FROM SINGLE ITEM RECOVERY

To recover items from Single Item Recovery, you need to configure a mailbox search and then use the Discovery Search mailbox to recover the items to the correct mailbox. This action requires the following additional permissions:

- Full Access permissions on the Discovery Search mailbox for opening the mailbox and looking for the search results.
- Full Access permissions on the user mailbox for opening the target mailbox to recover the items.
- Either Mailbox Search permission or member of the Discovery Management role for defining a search in ECP. To assign this permission, you can run the following cmdlet: *New-ManagementRoleAssignment –Role "Mailbox Search" –User <account>*.

After you've assigned the permission required to the account, you need to define a mailbox search in ECP as shown in Figure 12-3.

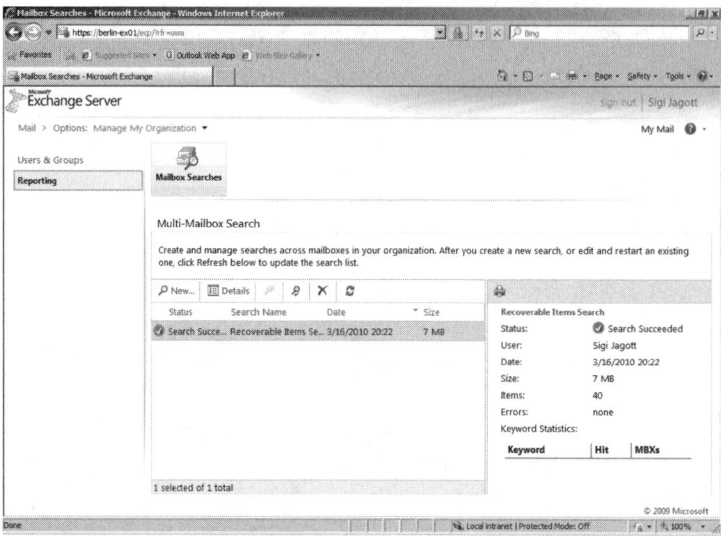

FIGURE 12-3 Creating a mailbox search for Single Item Recovery

NOTE By default the search only considers e-mail items, not other items such as contacts or appointments. If you want to restore all items, you need to select Search All Message Types Including Ones That May Not Be Listed Below in the Select Message Types dialog box.

When the Mailbox Search finishes collecting the information, you can either use the *Export-Mailbox* cmdlet, which has a disadvantage in that you need to know exact folder names, or you can use the easier approach of configuring an Outlook profile that includes the Discovery Search Mailbox and target user mailbox so that you can copy the deleted items from the Recoverable Items folder to the original folder, as shown in Figure 12-4.

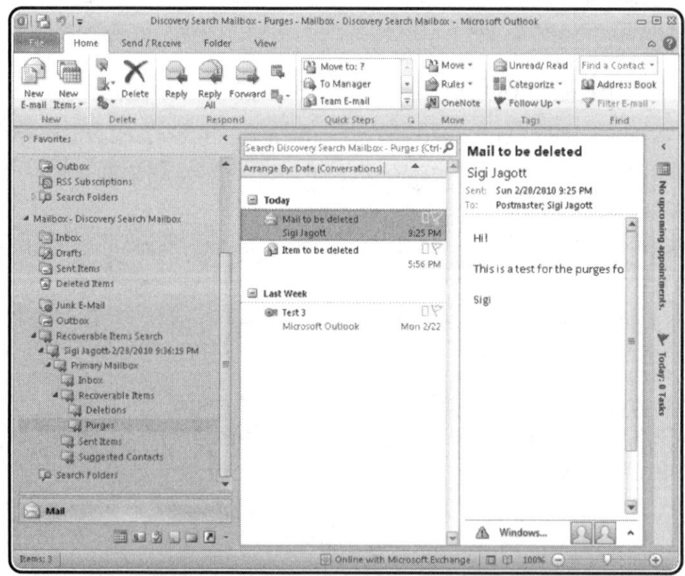

FIGURE 12-4 Using Outlook 2010 to recover items from Discovery Search Mailbox

PLANNING SINGLE ITEM RECOVERY CAPACITY

After learning about the Single Item Recovery feature, the logical follow-up question is "Do I still need backups for Single Item Recovery?" As always the answer depends on both your current backup requirements and on capacity planning.

Before performing the calculation, you should ask yourself the following questions:

- What's my current deleted item recovery time in days?
- How often do I require recovering items from backup and from what time span?
- What's my current client load pattern (see Chapter 2, "Exchange Environmental Considerations," for more information)?

Let's consider that a customer currently maintains a deleted item recovery time of 7 days and maintains backups for 60 days where users require Single Item Recovery. Let's assume the following client load pattern:

- Average message size: 50kb
- Messages sent/received per day: 100
- Items edited: 10 percent

Now let's do the math and calculate the space requirement for the recoverable items folder of a mailbox:

- Assumption: 5 working days * 100 mails = 500 mails per week
- Space requirements for Purges folder:
  - 8 weeks * 500 mails per week * 50kb per mail = 195 MB
- Space requirements for Versions folder:
  - 10 percent of 195 MB = 19.5 MB

This indicates a mailbox size increase of 215 MB per mailbox, and you don't even need a Single Item Recovery tool or backup of your mailbox databases because Single Item Recovery will be performed within Exchange.

> ***NOTE*** **After implementing Single Item Recovery you should monitor the size of the Recoverable Items folder of your mailboxes from time to time. This can be achieved using the *Get-MailboxStatistics –id <account> | fl *size** cmdlet.**

Another consideration if you implement Single Item Recovery together with high availability of databases is that you can also dramatically reduce the backup frequency.

Ultimately, if the storage subsystem is planned and designed appropriately and mailbox resiliency features of Exchange 2010 are used, traditional point-in-time backups are degraded to only a disaster recovery mechanism—if they are even needed at all.

NOTES FROM THE FIELD

The Missing Folder Information of Single Item Recovery

Jon Webster

Systems Engineer, Elephant Outlook, US Southeast

The single largest issue preventing us from embracing running without traditional point-in-time backups is that folder information is not preserved in the Recoverable Items folder. Items are only placed in their respective Deletions, Versions, or Purges folders. If someone "accidentally" deletes 17,000 items across 20 folders, recovering only the items means spending a long time rebuilding the folders.

My main concern is that people tend to archive large folders worth of items, lose the archive, and then expect us to go back 30 days to recover their deleted folder. Single Item Recovery can get the items, but figuring out which ones out of 400,000 deleted in that time period without folder information is a challenge to say the least.

We also have folks that do mass deletes when they receive a warning about their mailbox size or when they can't send mail. These we can recover within the 14-day window with a lagged copy, but it would be a lot easier if we had folder info. Let's hope Microsoft will implement this in following Exchange 2010 Service Pack or Roll-up pack. Unfortunately it's not yet implemented in SP1.

Mailbox Retention

Every Exchange mailbox consists of a user account in Active Directory and the mailbox stored in the Exchange database. If the mailbox is deleted, or a mailbox-enabled user account is deleted, that mailbox is not yet deleted from the database but is marked for deletion. The mailbox will stay as a disconnected mailbox on the database until the deleted mailbox retention setting is reached, by default 30 days. Only then is the mailbox purged from the database and thus physically removed. The main benefit is that mailbox retention allows you to recover deleted mailboxes up to the retention setting without having to restore the entire mailbox database. To reconnect the mailbox you just select the disconnected mailbox and connect it to a user account in EMC, as shown in Figure 12-5.

Even with good processes, mailboxes can be deleted accidentally or prematurely. In some instances employees are hired back shortly after they leave; in other incidents mailboxes are deleted with information required by other employees or legal departments. The mailbox retention period should take into account these scenarios and can be set differently depending on the type of user or the circumstances around the employee's departure. Defining the retention should be discussed and approved by each department and any legal counsel so as to reduce the amount of mailboxes that need to be recovered from backup.

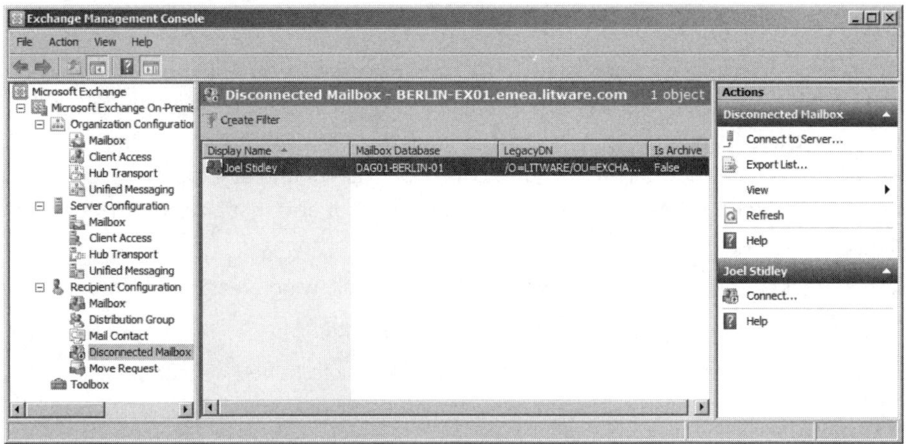

FIGURE 12-5 Using EMC to reconnect disconnected mailboxes

Mailbox retention is configured on the database level. If you want to change the configuration, you can use the *Set-MailboxDatabase <database name> -MailboxRetention 30.00:00:00* cmdlet or you can use the EMC to configure the deletion time in database properties, as shown in Figure 12-6.

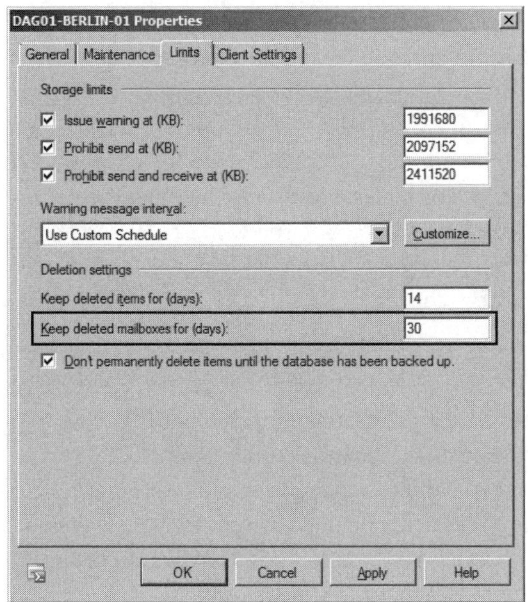

FIGURE 12-6 Configuring mailbox deletion settings in EMC

If you want to make sure that deleted mailboxes are not available as disconnected mailboxes, you can use the *Remove-Mailbox –Permanent $true* cmdlet.

Testing Your Disaster Recovery Plan

The best backup and recovery plan is useless if your administrators do not know exactly what to do during a disaster. Therefore, it is a best practice to test a disaster recovery thoroughly at least once a year with the people involved in normal day-to-day operations of your systems. This test ensures not only that your recovery plan is working as expected and that your team is well trained in how to recover from a disaster, but also that any system changes are immediately implemented into the plan.

To test your disaster recovery plan, consider testing the following areas:

- Rebuild the systems from scratch after a total datacenter loss.
- Provide alternative solutions such as dial tone recovery to bring back the service operation as quickly as possible after server failures.
- Make sure the installation sources are available and updated (for example, latest service packs must be available).
- Test recovery in accordance with your company's SLAs to make sure they are met.

Performing Backup and Recovery for Non-Mailbox Server Roles

Every Exchange role depends on different services or databases, so they have special requirements for backup and recovery. Almost all of the configuration settings for Mailbox, Hub Transport, and Unified Messaging server roles are stored in Active Directory. As with previous versions of Exchange, Exchange 2010 includes the *Setup /m:RecoverServer* parameter for recovering lost servers. It is used to rebuild and re-create a lost server by using the settings and configuration information stored in Active Directory. This works on all server roles except Client Access Server role, which loses all customizations and Edge Transport role that cannot be used with the */m:RecoverServer* switch.

Of course, you can restore only if an Active Directory domain controller is available. You must ensure that your disaster-recovery planning includes backing up and restoring Active Directory.

The Exchange Server environment includes additional information, such as the Offline Address Book, availability data that a local folder stores, and other configuration data. This information is rebuilt automatically when you rebuild the Exchange Server environment. However, if you configured custom settings such as custom audio prompts for your Unified Messaging server, you also need to consider backing up these settings. It is thus important to understand each Exchange roles' requirement to do a successful backup.

Client Access Server Backup and Recovery

The Client Access Server role stores the majority of its configuration settings in Active Directory but also has some configuration such as POP3 and IMAP4 or configurations of the EWS service stored in the file system found in the <*Exchange_Installation_Path*>\ClientAccess folder. Table 12-4 provides an overview of specific configuration files and how you should back them up.

TABLE 12-4 Client Access Server Data Backup Requirements

SERVER DATA	HOW TO BACK UP
Server Configuration	Full backup of all files on the local drives including the registry
Certificates	Full backup or export of certificates and private keys
RPC Client Access Service	File-system backup of <*Exchange_Installation_Path*>\ClientAccess\RPCProxy
Outlook Web App (OWA)	File-system backup of <*Exchange_Installation_Path*>\ClientAccess\OWA
Exchange Control Panel (ECP)	File-system backup of <*Exchange_Installation_Path*>\ClientAccess\ECP
Availability Service	File-system backup of <*Exchange_Installation_Path*>\ClientAccess\exchweb\ews
Autodiscover Service	System-state or IIS metabase backup
ActiveSync	File-system backup of <*Exchange_Installation_Path*>\ClientAccess\Sync and IIS metabase backup
POP3 and IMAP4	File-system backup of <*Exchange_Installation_Path*>\ClientAccess\PopImap

To recover a Client Access Server, you can either recover a full backup or you can run *Setup /m:RecoverServer* to get the basic configuration information from the Active Directory and then restore or configure specific service settings and certificates.

> ***IMPORTANT*** **Client Access Server role customize settings are not recovered when you use the *Setup /m:RecoverServer* command to reinstall the server. As a best practice for this situation, Microsoft recommends installing a new Client Access Server with default settings, and then use a PowerShell script for any customizations you did on the Client Access Server for recovery.**

Hub Transport Server Backup and Recovery

Hub Transport servers store most of their configuration information in Active Directory and provide protection for messages in transit with their shadow redundancy feature anyway. Thus the Hub Transport servers are not critical from the backup and restore perspective because you will only lose limited data.

The main data that is stored directly on a Hub Transport server that should be considered in a backup is the message tracking logs and (if used) the custom ESE database configuration file. However, in a good backup and restore concept every server should be considered with the same importance. Table 12-5 provides an overview of what areas you should consider for Hub Transport backup.

TABLE 12-5 Hub Transport Server Data Backup Requirements

SERVER DATA	HOW TO BACK UP
Server Configuration	Full backup of all files on the local drives including the registry
Certificates	Full backup or export of certificates and private keys
ESE database configuration	Backup of EdgeTransport.exe.config file located in <*Exchange_Installation_Path*>\Bin
Message tracking logs	File-system backup of <*Exchange_Installation_Path*>\TransportRoles\Logs

> **NOTE** It is recommended that you do a full server backup including at least a file-system backup of the <*Exchange_Installation_Path*>\ folder to successfully back up a Hub Transport server.

To recover a Hub Transport server, follow these steps:

1. Set up a server with the same name as the server that is recovered.
2. Run *Setup /m:RecoverServer* to install the Exchange role and fetch the configuration information from Active Directory.
3. Restore custom ESE configuration file and message tracking logs if required.

Unified Messaging Server Backup and Recovery

The Unified Messaging server role also does not store any user-related information on the server but includes only configuration information such as custom auto-attendant files, grammar configuration, and Outlook Voice Access files. Table 12-6 provides an overview of what areas you should consider for Unified Messaging backup.

TABLE 12-6 Unified Messaging Server Data Backup Requirements

SERVER DATA	HOW TO BACK UP
Server Configuration	Full backup of all files on the local drives including the registry
Certificates	Full backup or export of certificates and private keys (can be ignored because an UM server does not use any public certificates)
Custom audio prompts	File-system backup of <*Exchange_Installation_Path*>\UnifiedMessaging\Prompts
GAL grammar	File-system backup of <*Exchange_Installation_Path*>\UnifiedMessaging\Grammars

NOTE To perform a backup that you can recover as quickly as possible, it is recommended that you do a full backup including at least a file-system backup of the <*Exchange_Installation_Path*>\UnifiedMessaging folder to successfully back up a Unified Messaging server.

To recover a Unified Messaging server, follow these steps:

1. Set up a server with the same name as the server that is recovered.
2. Run *Setup /m:RecoverServer* to install the Exchange role and fetch the configuration information from Active Directory.
3. Restore custom prompts and audio files if required.
4. Restore GAL grammar configuration files if required.

Edge Transport Server Backup and Recovery

Edge Transport servers that participate in an Edge Synchronization store most of their configuration data in the Exchange organization's Active Directory. This configuration data is synchronized via EdgeSync to the Edge Transport server's local AD LDS database. Only a few configuration settings that are not part of the EdgeSync process, such as local transport agents, need to be considered separately.

Similar to the Hub Transport server, the shadow redundancy feature includes automatic failover functionality for message sending and receiving. Thus the Hub Transport servers are not critical from the backup and restore perspective because you will only lose limited data. Table 12-7 provides an overview of what areas you should consider for Edge Transport backup.

TABLE 12-7 Edge Transport Server Data Backup Requirements

SERVER DATA	HOW TO BACK UP
Server Configuration	Full backup of all files on the local drives including the registry
Certificates	Full backup or export of certificates and private keys
Edge specific configuration/ Content-filtering database	Use the ExportEdgeConfig.ps1 script
Edge transport rules	Use the *Export-TransportRuleCollection* cmdlet
Message tracking logs	File-system backup of <*Exchange_Installation_Path*>\ TransportRoles\Logs

NOTE As a best practice, it is recommended that you run the ExportEdgeConfig.ps1 script to export the configuration to a local disk and then do backup of all files on the local drives including the registry to successfully back up an Edge Transport server.

To recover an Edge Transport server, follow these steps:

1. Set up a server with the same name as the server that is recovered and install the Exchange Edge Transport role on it.
2. Validate and import configuration using the ImportEdgeConfig.ps1 script.
3. Import transport rules using the *Import-TransportRuleCollection* cmdlet.
4. Run the EdgeSync process if the Edge Transport server was part of an Edge Synchronization before.
5. Restore any message tracking log files if required.

Performing Backup and Recovery for Mailbox Server Roles

The Mailbox Server role hosts the most important data of your messaging environment: the mailboxes. Special considerations are required when planning for backup and recovery of mailbox servers. This section provides an overview of what options you have available so that you can plan the most suitable backup solution for your organization.

LESSONS LEARNED

Backup and Restore Options Depend on Organization Size

Colin Lee
Technology Specialist, Unified Communications, Microsoft Corporation, Australia

I've worked with a wide range of customers, and backup and restore is a topic that generates a lot of attention when it comes to Exchange 2010. The following scenarios are among the most common that come up for discussion.

- **Small Environments (50 mailboxes)** A single server environment can use the out-of-the-box backup option from Windows Server 2008 for Exchange 2010. Use Single Item Recovery to provide the capability to restore single or multiple messages for 30 days or a period that makes sense for the company. Windows Server Backup can be used to recover from an infrastructure outage.
- **Medium Environment (500 mailboxes)** This size organization benefits from the high-availability options of Exchange 2010 but is constrained by only a single server room or datacenter. For a major disaster or recovery beyond the Single Item Recovery period, the traditional tape restore is used. Backup would use VSS to snap from a passive copy of the DB to disk and then stream to tape. Alternate tape backup copies are then shipped offsite in case of major outages.

- **Large Environment (5,000 mailboxes)** This is the typical experience for an enterprise company, where multiple datacenters are available and a DAG may span multiple locations. Backup occurs regularly every week or fortnight rather than the traditional nightly or weekly with daily incremental. Single Item Recovery is used to recover single or multiple items without resorting to backup. The backup would use VSS to snap from a passive copy of the DB and then stream to tape if necessary, all from the secondary datacenter. Note that the concept of having no tape backup for Exchange is very difficult to accept for an organization that has been dependent on it for the last 10 years or so. However, the idea of reducing the amount of backup necessary is readily embraced.
- **Extra Large Environment (50,000 mailboxes)** From an infrastructure perspective this is very similar to your typical large-enterprise organization. However, in this instance the data recovery policy of the organization is no more than three months (the legal viewpoint). The organization has no need for tape backup and implements a single instance recovery period of 90 days, with three-plus copies of the DB and a lag copy across multiple datacenters (very similar to the Microsoft strategy). With the three-month data recovery policy, all data is available online without resorting to backup. Longer-term data retention can be taken care of by exception and/or by looking at other enhancements in Exchange 2010, such as the archive mailbox.

Volume ShadowCopy Service

Exchange Server 2010 only supports using Volume ShadowCopy Service (VSS) for backup and restore. Exchange 2007 or before also supported using Extensible Storage Engine (ESE) streaming backup APIs, but this option is no longer available in Exchange 2010. Therefore, the only way to create a backup of an Exchange database when it's online is by using the VSS interface.

VSS Backup Overview

VSS provides the backup infrastructure for Windows Server 2008 as well as a mechanism for creating consistent point-in-time data copies, which are known as shadow copies. The backup solution thus creates a shadow copy of the disk as the backup process begins. Then, Exchange Server creates the backup with the shadow copy rather than the working disk, so that backup does not interrupt normal operations. This method offers the following advantages:

- It produces a backup of a volume that reflects that volume's state when the backup begins, even if the data changes while the backup is in progress. All the data in the backup is internally consistent, and it reflects the volume's state at a single point in time.
- It notifies applications and services that a backup is about to occur. The services and applications, such as Exchange Server, therefore can prepare for the backup by cleaning up on-disk structures and flushing caches.

VSS produces consistent shadow copies by coordinating with business applications, file-system services, backup applications, fast-recovery solutions, and storage hardware. An architectural overview is shown in Figure 12-7.

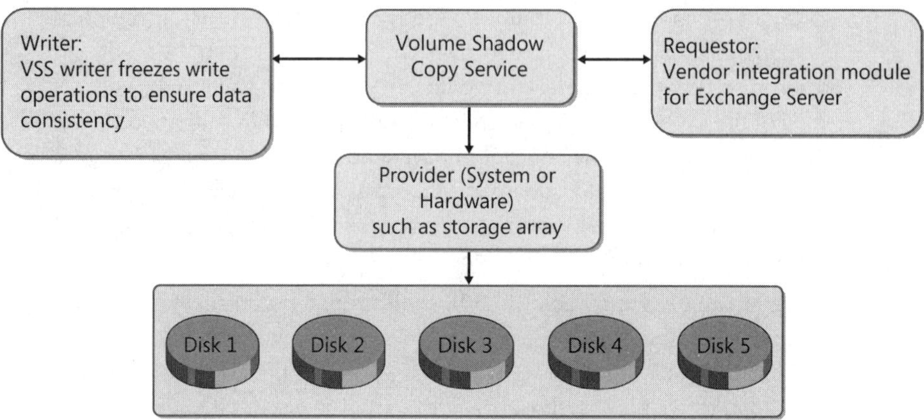

FIGURE 12-7 VSS architecture

The VSS architecture consists of several components: namely Writer, Requestor, and Provider, as described in Table 12-8.

TABLE 12-8 VSS Components

VSS COMPONENT	DESCRIPTION
Writer	The VSS writer that is included with Exchange Server 2010 and that coordinates Exchange Server 2010's input/output (I/O) with VSS. Exchange 2010 comes with two VSS writers, one in the Exchange Store to backup active database copies and one in the Microsoft Exchange Replication service that can be used to back up passive mailbox database copies
Requestor	Backup or restore application, such as Windows Server Backup
Provider	Low-level system, software, or hardware interfaces, such as storage area networks (SANs)

The VSS components interact with each other to create a consistent backup of the disk. The following steps are completed for a VSS backup:

1. The requestor starts the backup by initiating the writer.
2. When the writer finishes its tasks, it notifies the requestor that the data is ready to do a backup.
3. The requestor then contacts the provider to notify the hardware to complete the backup.
4. After the backup is completed, the requestor notifies the writer so that the writer can allow database activity to resume.

VSS providers are available in two flavors: Hardware or Software VSS solutions. Hardware VSS solutions are available with SANs; software VSS solutions can be used against SANs or direct attached storage architectures. However, be aware that hardware VSS solutions mostly require a specific LUN architecture so that you have database and log files separated on two LUNs. For more information about VSS, see *http://technet.microsoft.com/en-us/library/cc785914(WS.10).aspx.*

Exchange Server Support for VSS Backup

To back up and restore Exchange 2010, you must use an Exchange-aware application that supports VSS backups for Exchange 2010, such as Windows Server Backup. Alternatively you can use a third-party backup solution that comes with its own VSS plug-in for Exchange Server 2010, such as Microsoft Data Protection Manager 2010, or a third-party, Exchange-aware, VSS-based application.

The VSS plug-in for Windows Server Backup that ships with Exchange 2010 has the following limitations:

- VSS support is at the volume level only, not the database level.
- VSS support is for full backups and copy backups, not for incremental or differential backups.
- Without using the registry key mentioned later in this section, VSS can only be used to back up volumes containing active mailbox database copies or non-replicated databases.

Using Windows Server Backup

Exchange Server 2010 now includes full Exchange VSS backup support for Windows Server 2008 and Windows Server 2008 R2. When you install the Mailbox server role on a server running Windows Server 2008, it also updates Windows Server Backup to support Exchange Server 2010. Windows Server Backup enables you to perform VSS-based backups of Exchange Server data without extra charge.

For many smaller organizations, Windows Server Backup provides a sufficient solution. However, larger organizations may require a more robust backup strategy because Windows Server Backup includes the following limitations:

- Backups are only performed at volume level; you cannot back up a single database only.
- There is no Exchange-only backup feature. You need to back up at least a complete volume to create an Exchange-aware backup.
- You can only perform full or copy backup, not incremental or differential backups.
- Windows Server Backup has no remote server backup functionality—it must run on the Exchange server that needs to be backed up.
- Windows Server Backup is only available for Windows Server 2008 or Windows Server 2008 R2.
- Windows Server Backup PowerShell cmdlets are not compatible with the Exchange Server 2010 VSS plug-in.

For more information about Windows Server Backup, see the Microsoft TechNet article "Using Windows Server Backup to Back Up and Restore Exchange Data" at *http://technet.microsoft.com/en-us/library/dd876851(EXCHG.140).aspx.*

Backing Up Your Exchange Server with Windows Server Backup

Windows Server Backup (WSB) is the right tool for backing up Exchange databases and servers if you have just a couple of Exchange servers installed in your environment and you do not require direct connection to a storage system such as a tape library. If the backup software that supports your storage system does not include Exchange 2010 plug-in, you can use Windows Server Backup to create a backup on a file share and then use your available backup software to store the data to your storage system.

Using WSB, you can create a scheduled backup set, meaning that you decide how often the backup is done, or you can create one backup. The next option you can configure is how WSB handles Exchange log file truncation. You can choose a VSS full backup, which removes the Exchange log files after the backup, or you can choose a VSS copy backup, which preserves the log files as shown in Figure 12-8.

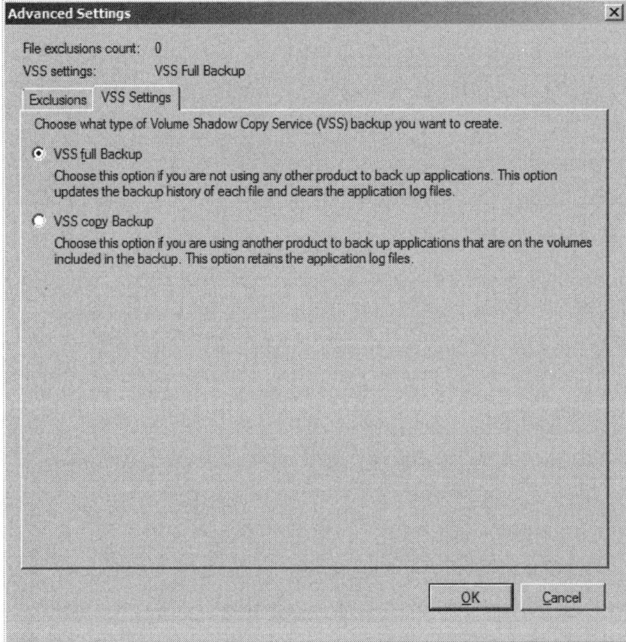

FIGURE 12-8 Exchange log file truncation options

Keep the following general considerations and best practices in mind when using WSB for creating Exchange backups:

- You need to select the backup on the volume level; you cannot back up just the Exchange folder because this will not create a valid Exchange VSS backup.
- If your database files and the log files are on different volumes, you need to back up all volumes in the same backup job to create a valid Exchange VSS backup of your database.

- Out of the box, WSB does not support backing up a volume that includes active and passive mailbox database copies. If you attempt this, the Backup Status will appear as Complete With Warnings and you won't have Applications recovery type available when recovering. The recommended workaround is to make sure that your passive database copies are either stored on one Exchange server that you do not back up or use a separate volume for them. However, a tweak is available that allows WSB to back up volumes containing both active and passive database copies. This tweak forces WSB to use the Store Writer instead of the Replica Writer for backup; thus passive databases will be ignored. To implement the tweak, you need to perform the following two tasks on the servers where you have both active and passive databases:
  - Apply the following registry key: HKEY_LOCAL_MACHINE\SOFTWARE\Microsoft\ExchangeServer\v14\Replay\Parameters\EnableVSSWriter set to 0 (DWORD type), as shown in Figure 12-9.
  - Restart the Microsoft Exchange Replication service.

> ***IMPORTANT*** **If you later change to a backup solution that does support the Replication service VSS writer, such as Microsoft Data Protection Manage (DPM), you will need to remove the registry value and restart the Microsoft Exchange Replication service!**

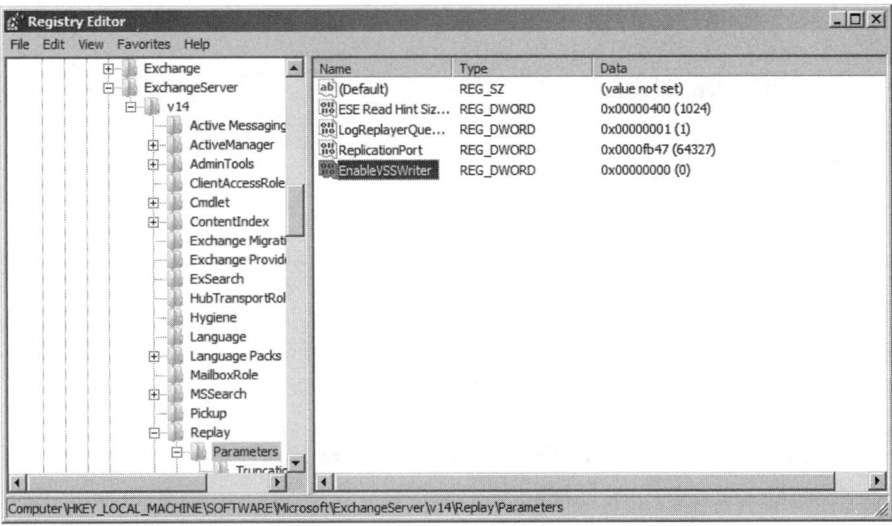

FIGURE 12-9 Tweaking Windows Server Backup to ignore passive database copies

- Consider implementing Exchange-only volumes such as disk D: for all mailbox databases and their log files so that you can perform an Exchange-only backup.
- A backup cannot be stored on the same volume that you want to back up; you must always use a volume selected for backup or a remote shared folder as a backup target.
- You can only use mount points on Windows Server 2008 R2 computers. If you have Exchange 2010 installed on Windows Server 2008 SP2, mount points are currently not supported.

Selecting the correct volumes for backup is key to successfully backing up Exchange; Figure 12-10 provides basic guidance to what items you should select when backing up Exchange.

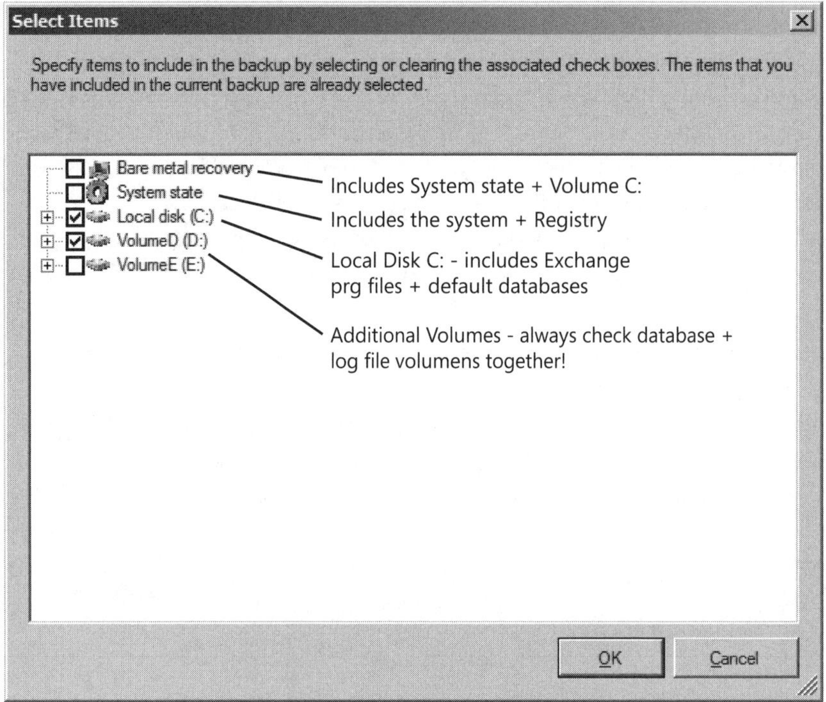

FIGURE 12-10 Windows Server Backup Select Items to back up

> ***IMPORTANT*** **Don't forget to always check the Application log in Event Viewer to verify that the Exchange backup was successful. For every Exchange database you should see Event ID 9780 for a non-replicated database or Event ID 9827 for a replicated database copy, and Event ID 224 for a successful log truncation.**

Restoring Backups with Windows Server Backup

To restore a backup that was created with WSB, you can select a backup set available either on a local drive or on a remote shared folder. After you selected the desired backup set to recover, you need to select recovery type. For Exchange backups you must have the Applications option selected, as shown in Figure 12-11.

> ***NOTE*** **If the Applications option is dimmed, the selected backup set is not a correct Exchange-aware VSS backup and thus can only be considered a file-level VSS backup. The most common reason for this is that you forgot to back up the volume containing the Exchange log files or you did not back up on a volume level but on a folder level.**

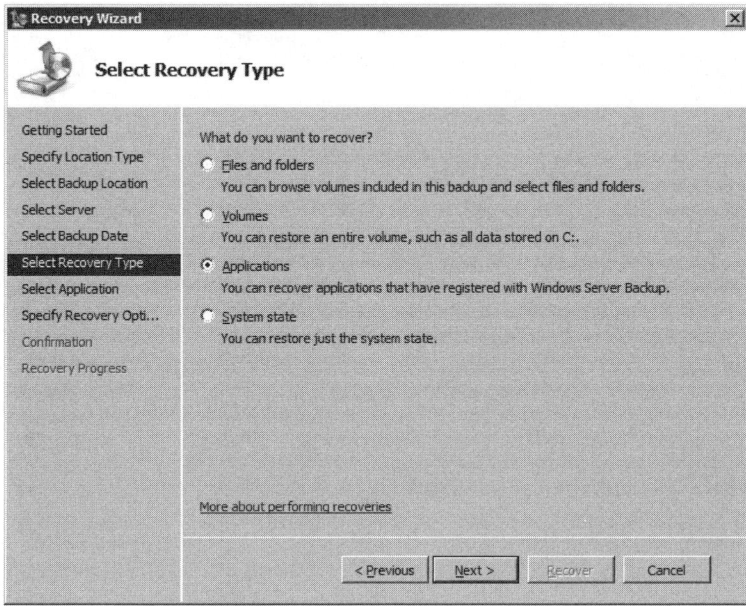

FIGURE 12-11 Selecting the recovery type in WSB

After selecting the Applications option, you will see the available applications that are part of the backup set. You also can view details on what databases are available as part of the backup set, as shown in Figure 12-12.

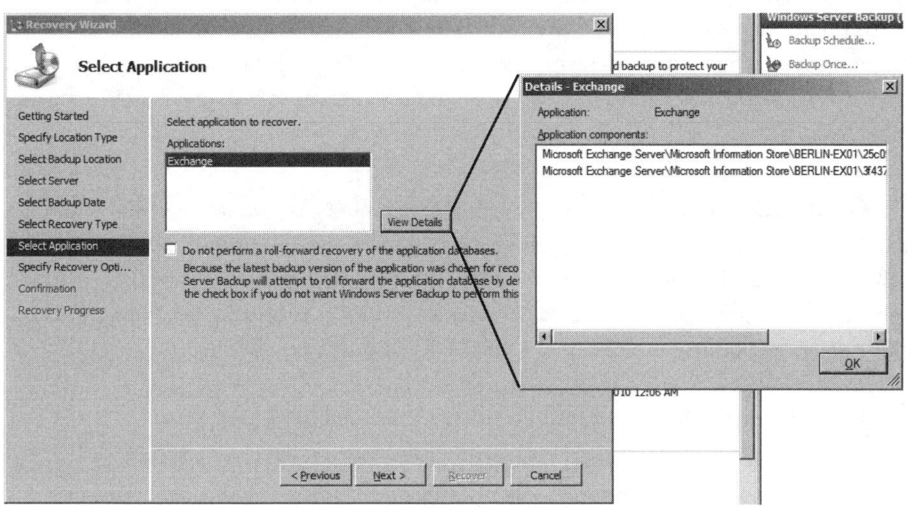

FIGURE 12-12 Viewing Exchange application backup details in WSB

You can either recover to the original location or you can restore to another location, such as a local folder or network drive as shown in Figure 12-13.

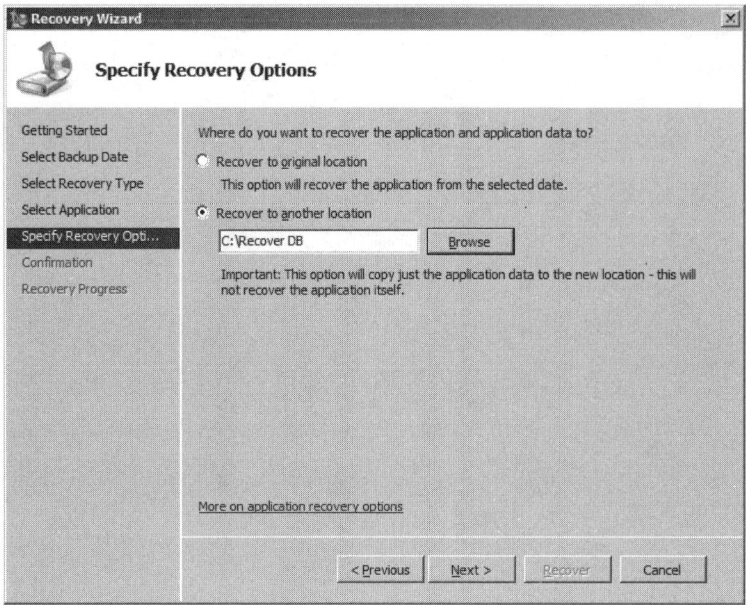

FIGURE 12-13 Specifying the recovery location

USING WINDOWS SERVER BACKUP TO RECOVER TO THE ORIGINAL LOCATION

Recovering a backup set to the original location is quick and easy. If you selected the Applications option, you will recover all Exchange databases of that respective backup set to their original location. WSB will take care of dismounting the involved databases and mounting them again after the restore is completed. If the original location of the databases was changed, you cannot recover the databases anymore but have to use recover to another location.

> ***IMPORTANT*** **Restoring a backup set to the original location is a volume-level operation and thus does not require additional Exchange configurations such as selecting This Database Can Be Overwritten By A Restore on the Maintenance tab in the Database properties of EMC. However, you should consider a restore to the original location carefully because you might overwrite a database by mistake without even realizing it!**

USING WINDOWS SERVER BACKUP TO RECOVER TO ANOTHER LOCATION

Alternatively, you can recover a backup set to another location such as a local drive or a network drive. Using the Applications Recovery Type in the Recovery Wizard, restore all Exchange databases to another local location, such as C:\Recovery, as the target folder. When the recovery is finished, the target folder will include the full folder structure including the database as well as log files for the databases.

Once the database is recovered, run the *Eseutil /mh <database.edb>* command to make sure that the database is in a clean shutdown state. If the state shows Dirty Shutdown, as shown in Figure 12-14, you need to additionally run the *Eseutil /r e00 /i /d* command to bring it to a clean state.

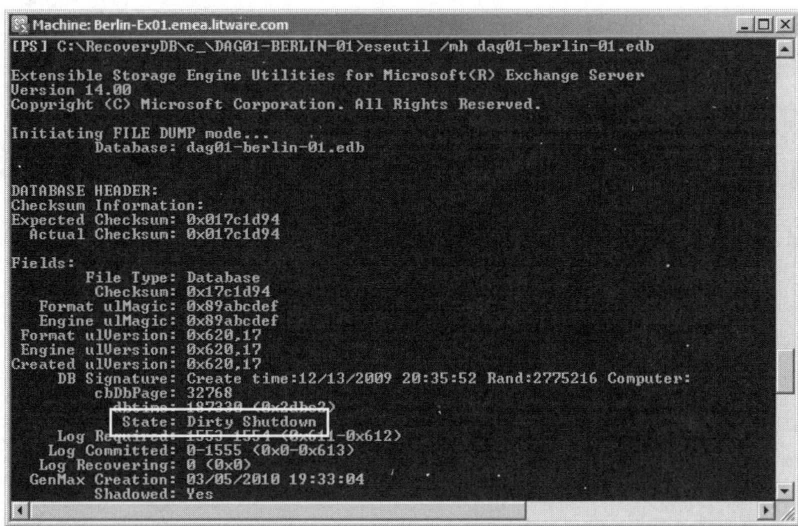

FIGURE 12-14 Verifying the state of a recovered database

Even though you can only recover all databases of a backup set using Windows Server Backup, with a few tweaks you can achieve the following:

- **Recover a single database** You need to dismount the respective database, then move all database and log files from the restored database folder to the database and log folder, and then mount the database again. Make sure the target folder is free of the existing database, log, and catalog files.
- **Recover a database as a recovery database** Move the recovered database and log files to a directory that is easy to reach, such as C:\RecoveryDB, and then create a new recovery database using the *New-MailboxDatabase -Recovery -Name RecoveryDB -Server <server name> -EDBFilePath "C:\RecoveryDB\<database name>.edb" -LogFolderPath "C:\RecoveryDB"* cmdlet. Don't forget to use the original database name of the recovered database and mount it using the *Mount-Database RecoveryDB* cmdlet. An example is shown in Figure 12-15.

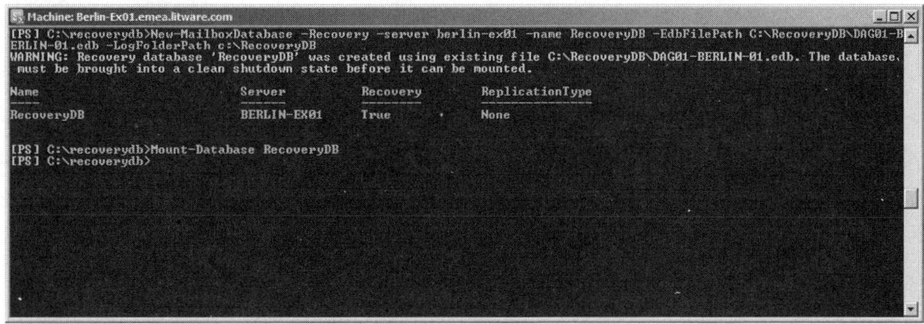

FIGURE 12-15 Creating and mounting a recovery database

IMPORTANT You can only recover mailbox databases to a recovery database. Public folder databases cannot use a recovery database!

Using Advanced Backup Solutions

If your company requires more functionality than available in WSB, you need to consider using an advanced backup solution such as Microsoft Data Protection Manager 2010 or other Exchange-aware, VSS-based backup applications from third-party vendors.

Such backup solutions provide you with the following advanced features:

- You can back up volumes containing active and passive mailbox database copies at the same time.
- You can back up and restore a single database or single database copies.
- You can restore a database into a recovery database or an alternate location.
- If the backup solution is from a hardware vendor, it includes advanced features to utilize the backup hardware.

NOTE Passive database copies are backed up using a VSS writer in the Microsoft Exchange Replication service. The Microsoft Exchange Replication service VSS writer doesn't support restores; thus you can't perform a restore directly to a passive database copy. However, you can perform a VSS restore to an alternate location, suspend replication to the passive copy, and then manually copy the database and log files from the alternate location to the location of the passive database copy.

Considerations for Selecting an Exchange Server Backup Solution

When selecting a backup solution for Exchange Server 2010, you must consider your system's characteristics and those of the software and hardware. System characteristics to consider include:

- The amount of data you are backing up.
- The time window in which the backup can occur.
- The type of backup you are performing.
- Recovery time requirements.
- Archiving requirements.
- Budgetary considerations for the backup solution.

When you understand your system characteristics, you should consider how to select the backup software required. To help you with this, Table 12-9 describes some basic criteria for selecting the software that best meets your needs.

TABLE 12-9 Backup Software Selection Criteria

SELECTION CRITERIA	DESCRIPTION
Backup architecture	Your backup software should provide support for any operating systems that you have. Additionally, the backup software should be able to back up Exchange Server to your desired media, either on the local computer or over the network.
Scheduling	Your backup software should support the ability to schedule backups that you require for your organization. Most backup software allows you to schedule jobs at any time you require. However, this is easier to configure in some software packages.
Brick-level backup support	If desired, ensure that your software supports brick-level backups. Alternatively, consider implementing Single Item Recovery.
VSS writer for Exchange 2010 API support	Your backup software must support the Exchange Server Backup VSS API to perform online backups successfully.
Tape management	Different backup software has varying degrees of flexibility for tape management. This includes automated naming of blank tapes and preventing existing tapes from being overwritten accidentally. Also, as tape media is used it becomes less reliable. It is important to manage the number of times the media is used and replace it with new media.
Vendor support	Vendor support is essential if you experience any problems during disaster recovery. Ensure that vendor support is available for your backup software.
Disaster-recovery support	Some backup software has a disaster-recovery option that provides complete disaster recovery for a failed server, including Exchange Server.
Hardware support	Your backup software must support the technologies that your company uses, including clustering or SANs. The two most common types of backup hardware are tape and disk. Many organizations use disk-based backup as the first tier, and then utilize tape as a second tier. This allows you to perform primary backups quickly to disk. Typically, any data that you need to archive offsite is backed up to tape from the disk backup.

Data Protection Manager 2010 Overview

Microsoft System Center Data Protection Manager (DPM) 2010 is a backup and recovery solution that provides all advanced features for Exchange 2010. It can back up basic file and print servers and application servers.

DPM 2010 fully complements Exchange 2010 DAGs and provides protection against total data loss resulting from logical corruptions; it helps you preserve data for point-in-time restores beyond the 14 days that a Exchange 2010 lagged copy will allow. It provides a cost-effective means of storing data for long haul on tape to meet regulatory requirements. DPM 2010 supports and enhances DAG Continuity of Service SLAs by reducing RTO and RPO times and supports item-level recovery using Exchange Recovery Database.

DPM 2010 performs disk-based backups first, and then allows you to archive to tape. The first backup to disk is a complete copy of the server. The second snapshot captures only changes and writes them to disk. Multiple backup versions exist on the disk, but the tool only uses disk space equivalent to the first backup plus changes. This is similar to VSS in that it allows you to restore multiple versions of shared files on a file server.

VSS backups snapshot the entire logical disk, not individual files. However, you can restore specific information—such as files or an Exchange Server database—rather than an entire logical disk.

You can find more information about DPM 2010 and Exchange 2010 at *http://blogs.technet.com/b/dpm/archive/2010/01/08/dpm-2010-protecting-exchange-2010-dag-in-a-single-site.aspx*

NOTES FROM THE FIELD

DPM 2010 vs. Lagged Copies

Todd Hawkins

Senior Consultant, Dell Global Infrastructure Consulting Services, US South Central Region

You can achieve the same point-in-time (PIT) recovery goal of a lagged copy with Microsoft Data Protection Manager (DPM) 2010. DPM can take PIT snapshots of your databases at up to 15-minute increments.

When restoring to a PIT with lagged copies, you need to plan what logs are needed to get to the desired recovery point, suspend replication, delete the .chk file, and use Eseutil to replay logs. You may also need to write scripts to automate some of the process. With DPM, on the other hand, you choose the date and time you want to recover from very easily in the GUI. This leads to a faster RPO and less difficulty in disaster-recovery scenarios.

In addition to being easy to use, DPM offers you more flexibility. For example, with DPM, you can move these backups to tape for offsite storage or for compliance reasons. In addition, you aren't limited to 14 days of PIT recovery—you are limited by the amount of storage you have available. DPM is not just an Exchange backup solution—you can use it to provide backup and recovery for file servers, Microsoft SQL, Windows SharePoint, and more.

Third-Party, Exchange-Aware Backup Solutions

Of course, more than just DPM 2010 is available to back up Exchange Server 2010. Many other third-party backup solutions are available that are Exchange-aware, such as Symantec Backup Exec 2010 and Commvault.

The list of Exchange-aware backup solutions is ever increasing. You can find a frequently updated Exchange 2010 Backup Product Support Matrix at *http://chrislehr.com/2010/02/exchange-2010-backup-product-support.htm.*

However, if you're already using a third-party backup solution, you should check with your vendor to make sure their solution supports Exchange Server 2010, including DAGs.

Dial Tone Recovery

Dial tone recovery is the process of implementing user access to e-mail services without first restoring data to user mailboxes. Dial tone recovery enables users to send and receive e-mail as soon as possible after a database or server loss. Users can send and receive e-mail messages, but they do not have access to the historical mailbox data.

Because your users can work with the dial tone database, you can recover the original database or server and restore the historical mailbox data without pressure. After you bring the recovered database back online, you can merge the dial tone database and the recovered database into a single up-to-date mailbox database.

When to Use Dial Tone Recovery

Use the dial tone recovery method when it is critical for users to regain messaging functionality as quickly as possible after a mailbox server or database fails, and when you cannot restore historical data from a backup quickly enough.

The loss may result from hardware failure or database corruption. If the server fails, you will need significant time to rebuild the server and restore the databases. If you have a large database that fails, restoring the database from backup may take several hours.

If the original mailbox server remains functional, or if you have an alternative mailbox server available, you can restore messaging functionality within minutes using dial tone recovery. This enables continued e-mail use while you recover the failed server or database.

Implementing a Dial Tone Database

Implementing a dial tone database should be carefully considered because it requires additional work to recover to the original situation. Consider the different dial tone recovery scenarios available such as using a different dial tone recovery server. However, all scenarios follow the same general steps:

1. Create the dial tone database. For messaging client computers to regain functionality as quickly as possible, create a new database for the client computers. Two methods are used for creating the dial tone database:

   a. Create the dial tone database on the same server as the failed database. Use this method if the drive that contained the database failed or if the database is corrupt.
   b. Create the dial tone database on a different server than the failed database. Use this method to utilize a different server as a recovery server or if the original server fails.
2. If necessary, configure the mailboxes that were on the failed database to use the new dial tone database. You must configure the mailboxes to use the new database if you create the dial tone database on a different server. To re-home all users from the old database to another, use the *Get-Mailbox -Database <OldDatabase> | Set-Mailbox -Database <dial tone database>* cmdlet.
3. Configure user profiles. If the server failed, you might need to reconfigure any user that is directly accessing the server (because you have multiple Exchange server roles hosted on a single server). Outlook profiles will be automatically updated.

> **NOTE** At this point users can connect to their mailboxes and are able to send and receive messages. However, they will find an empty mailbox not including their historical data. If your client computers are using Outlook 2003 or later and run in cached mode, users receive a prompt to connect or work offline when they connect to the dial tone database. If users choose to connect to the server, they will see an empty mailbox (local cached copy is replaced with the empty mailbox). If they choose to work offline, they will see all of the historical data stored in the offline folders (.ost) file but will not be able to send or receive new messages.

4. Restore the failed databases from backup. After the dial tone database is operational and your users can continue to send and receive messages, you can work on restoring the failed database. In a dial tone recovery scenario you should restore the failed databases into a recovery database to the same or another server.
5. Merge the data in the two databases. Because you have restored messaging functionality by implementing the dial tone database, users will be sending and receiving e-mail while you are restoring the original databases. When the recovery is complete, users should be able to access both the original and the dial tone data. This means that you must merge the contents of the dial tone database with those of the original database. To do this, you will use the recovery database as mentioned in the next section.

Using the Recovery Database

The recovery database is a database that does not affect any other databases or mailboxes running on that server. It runs separately and is limited to one mounted recovery database per Exchange server.

Users cannot access the recovery database directly. Only administrators can access it to recover single items, folders, mailboxes, or complete databases. The recovery database replaces the recovery storage group from Exchange Server 2007. You need to use the EMS to create a recovery database.

After you restore a database to the recovery database, you can copy messages to a folder or merge them into user mailboxes. The recovery database has the following requirements and characteristics:

- The server must have enough free disk space to restore the database. Effectively, there must be enough total storage space on the server to store two database copies simultaneously—the original database and the recovered version.
- The recovery database does not support public folder databases.

To create and mount a recovery storage group, the following steps are necessary:

1. Use the *New-MailboxDatabase –Recovery* cmdlet to create a new recovery database.
2. Restore the database that you want to recover to the recovery database. (For more information see the "Using Windows Server Backup to Recover to Another Location" section in this chapter.)
3. Mount the recovery database using the *Mount-Database <database>* cmdlet.

When your recovery database is mounted, you can take a look at what mailboxes are in the database by using the *Get-MailboxStatistics –Database <recovery database>* cmdlet or, if you also want to display the GUID for each mailbox, use the *Get-MailboxStatistics –Database <recovery database> |ft DisplayName. MailboxGuid, ItemCount* cmdlet as shown in Figure 12-16.

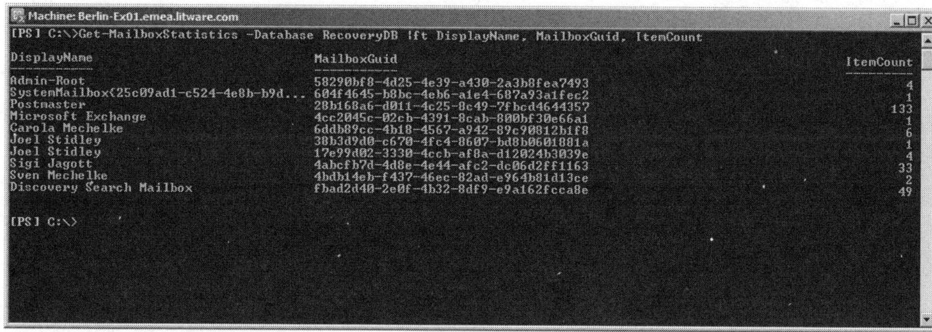

FIGURE 12-16 Listing mailboxes of a recovery database

If you want to recover the complete mailbox from the recovery database to its original location, use the *Restore-Mailbox –Identity <mailbox> -RecoveryDatabase <RecoveryDB Name>* cmdlet. This is common when you use dial tone recovery because dial tone recovery preserves all mailbox GUIDs.

NOTE Recovery to the original folder location is currently only possible if the user's mailbox GUID in Active Directory matches the one in the recovery database. If the mailbox GUID is different because the mailbox was re-created, you need to use the mailbox GUID instead of the name and define a target folder to store the recovered folders.

To restore to an alternative mailbox (or to a different mailbox GUID) or target folder, you need to use the *Restore-Mailbox -RecoveryMailbox <Name or MailboxGuid> -Identity <mailbox> -RecoveryDatabase <recoverydb name> -TargetFolder <DestinationFolder>* cmdlet to perform this task. Remember, this requires you to define a destination folder where all the items and folders will be restored.

Recover an Exchange Server

When recovering a failed Exchange Server, you have several options. The option you choose determines the process that you use to restore the server. When you need to replace a failed server, you have the following options:

- **Restore the server** You can restore the server from a full computer backup set and then restore your Exchange Server information. When you restore a server, you are reproducing the server configuration, including the server security identifier. This option is feasible only if you have a full server backup, including the System State backup, and you have replacement hardware that is the same or very similar to the failed server.
- **Rebuild the server** This option involves performing a new installation of Windows Server and an Exchange Server 2010 installation in Recover Server mode, which gathers the previous settings from Active Directory and then restores your Exchange Server databases.
- **Use a standby server** You can use a standby recovery server as part of the Mailbox server recovery strategy. This option involves keeping recovery servers available with the operating system and other software installed. Having available standby recovery servers reduces the time you need to rebuild a damaged server.

So what is better, restoring the server or rebuilding the server? The answer depends on what kind of backups your organization is taking. If you are doing backups for bare metal recovery that include system state and all server data, restoring the server from a backup is probably the best idea provided that the hardware you are restoring to is comparable to the server that was backed up.

If you are only backing up specific volumes and no system state, the best option is rebuilding the server using the */m:RecoverServer* switch to build the server using the information in Active Directory and then restoring the databases.

Running Exchange Server Setup with the */m:RecoverServer* switch causes Setup to read configuration information from Active Directory for the server with the same name as that from which you are running Setup. After you gather the server's configuration information from Active Directory, the original Exchange Server files and services then are installed on the server, and the Exchange Server roles and settings that Active Directory stored are applied to the server.

> ***IMPORTANT*** **When you run Exchange Server Setup in Recover Server mode, it must be able to connect to Active Directory and read the Exchange Server configuration information that links to the name of the computer that is running Exchange Server. This means that the computer account still must exist in Active Directory. If you delete the computer account, you will not be able to restore the Exchange Server.**

Follow these steps to restore a member server running Exchange Server 2010:

1. If the failed Exchange server was part of a DAG, you need to do the following:
   a. Verify whether there was a database copy on that server that had ReplayLagTime or TruncationLagTime configured. You can do this using the *Get-MailboxDatabase – Server <server> | fl Name,*lag** cmdlet. If the server had a lag configuration, you should write down these settings so that you can configure the same lag configuration settings later.
   b. Remove all database copies from that server (obviously from Active Directory because the copies are no longer on the server). This can be done using the *Remove-MailboxDatabaseCopy <database name>1\<server>* cmdlet.
   c. Remove the server from the DAG configuration by using the *Remove-DatabaseAvailabilityGroupServer -Identity <DAG> -MailboxServer <server>* cmdlet.
2. Install Windows Server 2008 or later on the computer that you are rebuilding. Use the same computer name and drive volume letters as the failed server. Install any Windows Server 2008 service packs and software updates that the damaged server was running.
3. Reset the Active Directory computer account for the failed server. After resetting the account, join the computer to the domain.
4. Install Exchange Server on the computer by running Exchange Server 2010 Setup in Recover Server mode by running *Setup /m:RecoverServer.*
5. Recover all drives that contained Exchange databases or log files when restoring a Mailbox role server or recover all other role-specific information for other Exchange roles.
6. If the failed Exchange server was part of a DAG, you need to add it again to the DAG, configure all previously available database copies, and configure any *ReplayLagTime* or *TruncationLagTime* settings.

> **NOTE** The Recover Server mode installation can recover only server configuration data that Active Directory stores. This means that the rebuild may not preserve every custom setting or restore data, such as custom scripts, that may have existed on the failed server. Also it won't restore custom Client Access Server role settings. Therefore, you should be prepared to re-create any Exchange Server configuration settings or files that you cannot recover from Active Directory.

Backup and Recovery of Public Folders

The area of Public Folders is one of the most controversial topics of Exchange Server. In Exchange 2007 Microsoft first de-emphasized Public Folders, but because of customer feedback they added a public folder management interface with Exchange 2007 SP1. In Exchange 2010 Public Folders should also be considered in your backup and recovery strategy.

Although public folders can be on members of a DAG, you cannot use continuous replication to make database copies, nor do the Single Item Recovery or Hold policy features apply. You also cannot use a recovery database to recover a Public Folder database. Thus you cannot protect public folders in the same way you can protect mailbox items so you need to especially consider public folders and backup.

If your company is using Public Folders, you should consider the following recommendations to make sure you can recover public folders:

- Replicate Public Folders to at least another Exchange server.
- You can configure deleted item retention settings on a public folder database or public folder level. By default it stores all deletions for 14 days, as shown in Figure 12-17.

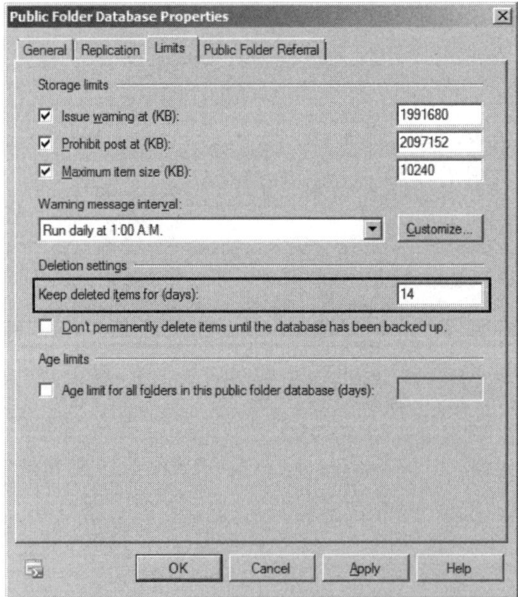

FIGURE 12-17 Public folder database deletion settings

- Use the Recover Deleted Items option to recover items and folders that have been deleted (only available in Outlook—not in OWA)

If these features do not provide sufficient protection to your public folders, or you have other requirements such as governmental regulatory or company policy that dictate you to backup public folders to a long-term storage system, you should consider an additional backup solution that provides you with the features required.

Operating Without Traditional Point-in-Time Backups

An Exchange infrastructure that uses Exchange Native Data Protection is an infrastructure in which you don't need to perform traditional point-in-time backups.

The intention to move toward an infrastructure without traditional point-in-time backups is mainly cost-driven—you can save the money for expensive backup solutions and storage facilities for tapes or disks. To deploy an infrastructure without traditional point-in-time backups, you need to consider the following:

- Create multiple database copies using DAGs to protect your database by having it copied to different Exchange servers—maybe even to different datacenters—to reduce the risk of losing a database because of a malfunction such as a disk crash.

> ***NOTE*** **As a best practice, you should create at least three database copies if you store these copies on just a bunch of disks (JBOD); at least two database copies are required if you are using additional data protection on your disks such as RAID. Lagged database copies should be considered additionally.**

- Provide deleted item recovery by implementing Single Item Recovery and hold policy so that you can recover changed or deleted items on user request. Traditionally, recovering items required a brick-level backup or a full database to be restored that you don't need anymore.
- To protect your databases from logical corruption, implement a lagged database that replays log files after a delay of up to 14 days.

If you consider implementing all these areas, you're on the best way to implementing a backup-less infrastructure. However, you should not forget about Public Folders, which are not covered in this concept. Public Folder databases can be replicated to multiple servers; thus you maintain multiple copies of them in your environment. But what happens if somebody deletes a Public Folder item or folder by mistake? As mentioned in the previous section, you can use deleted item retention to recover deleted items or folders. The big question here is whether that solution is sufficient for your organization. If your answer to that question is no, you might still need a third-party backup solution for your public folders.

Implementing DAGs and a discussion of how many database copies you should create is covered in Chapter 11, "Designing High Availability," and Single Item Recovery was discussed earlier in this chapter. This section explains using lagged databases.

NOTES FROM THE FIELD

An Exchange 2010 Implementation Without Traditional Point-in-Time Backups

Sascha Schmatz
Global Service Manager Messaging, Quimonda AG, Germany

We implemented a fully backup-less solution with Exchange 2010. My company has 12,000 employees spread over 12 locations (North America, Europe, and Asia). All Exchange 2010 servers are centralized at a single site located in Germany. To prevent problems from going backup-less, we defined the following corporate policies for the messaging service:

- A user can recover deleted messages for 14 days; older deleted messages are no longer available. VIPs get 30 days, but this is only available for fewer than 100 users.
- Public Folders are only used for Free/Busy Information and nothing else.

To realize a backup-less messaging system, we implemented DAGs with two database copies and one lagged database copy (lag time: 14 days) on a RAID. The database copies are stored on different storage systems in the same location—thus we make sure that a disk failure does not affect all copies at the same time. Because we do not run any backup, we enabled circular logging for all databases. We're also using a lagged database to protect us from logical database corruption. For that reason we can very easily give up doing backups.

For the single item restore, we configured Single Item Recovery to 14 days and enabled it for every mailbox. This increased user satisfaction; users previously had only four days of deleted items to recover. Using DAGs and Single Item Recovery enabled us to move away from backup to disk solution/snapshots that we had to maintain for Exchange 2007. As you can guess, going backup-less saved us a lot of money without interfering with our data-protection policies.

Using Lagged Database Copies

A lagged database copy is a database that uses a delayed replay lag time to commit the log files to the database. This allows you to go back to a point in time (maximum 14 days). Because 14 days is the fixed upper window for a lagged copy, this might not be the right solution for you to fit all scenarios, especially those scenarios where you need to restore items older than 14 days. By delaying the replay of logs in to a database, you have the capability to recover it to a point in the past.

Lagged database copies can protect you from the extremely rare logical corruption type cases as described in the following scenarios:

- **Database Logical Corruption** This is the case when the database pages checksum matches, but the data on the pages is logically wrong. It can occur when ESE attempts to write a database page and the operating system storage stack returns success even though the data either never makes it to disk or gets written to the wrong place. This behavior is called *lost flush*. To prevent lost flushes, ESE includes a lost flush detection mechanism in the database with a single database page restore feature.
- **Store Logical Corruption** This means data is added, deleted, or modified in a way that is not accepted by the user, so the user views it as a corruption. Typically this is caused by third-party application that issues a series of valid MAPI operations against the store. An example is a corrupt archiving solution that changes all message items of the users. Single Item Recovery or retention hold provides some protection against this case because all changed items are kept and thus can be restored. However, especially when large amounts of data are changed, it might be easier to recover the database to a point back in time before the corruption occurred.
- **Rogue Admin Protection** This is the case where the organization seeks protection against malicious or rogue administrators, particularly against administrators that by intention add, change, or remove data from the system in a way that is seen as undesirable by the users. To protect against this, the lag database copies can be placed on a server that is under separate administrative control.

If you use multiple database copies and Single Item Recovery, only the extremely rare catastrophic store logical corruption case is interesting. Depending upon which third-party applications you use and your history with store logical corruption, lagged database copies may or may not be that interesting for you.

In the following scenarios lagged database copies can be used to recover data:

- Recovering a log file that was deleted on the source
- Rolling back to a point in time because of a virus outbreak
- Recovering a deleted item that is outside the retention time

Planning Lagged Database Copies

When planning for lagged database copies, you should carefully consider the implications this brings to your storage planning. Every lagged database needs sufficient disk space for holding the database as well as the log files for the configured time.

For example, at Microsoft, 14 days of logs for one database result in about 60,000 log files or 60 GB of data. The log storage design for the lagged database copy needs to accommodate this. In addition to the space requirements, consider the following criteria when deciding the replay lag time:

- How long does it take you to identify a logical database corruption? This should include non-working days such as weekends. So if you configure a replay lag time of two days, you might not be able to identify the problem when it happens on a weekend and you're back on Monday.

- Consider the maximum time where a replay lag time makes sense. Fourteen days is the maximum time possible, but do you really need the full 14 days? In most cases, 7 days should be sufficient to identify a corruption and be able to recover using the lagged database copy.
- Don't underestimate the space requirements needed the longer the replay lag time is defined. In the previous Microsoft example you needed to reserve 60 GB for 14 days; thus 7 days would save you 30 GB per database of storage that you need to have available.
- The duration of replaying the log files is also worth considering. You should plan a test to replay all log files; this might take a considerable amount of time. Replaying 14 days of logs might require several hours before the database is up to date.

Besides the replay lag time considerations and the storage design, you should plan the following considerations carefully:

- How many lagged database copies do you need? Normally one lagged copy should be sufficient, but maybe you want more copies because of your disaster-recovery requirements. If lagged database copies are a critical piece of your disaster-recovery strategy, you will probably want to put them on a RAID system or have multiple copies of them.
- Where should you store the lagged database copies—at a server at the same site or offsite? This decision has a direct impact on the time you need to recover the lagged database copy because you need to consider available bandwidth when storing them offsite.
- On what Exchange server should you place the lagged database copies? You have the option to place them on the same server where your active database copies are stored, or you can use a single server just for all lagged database copies, such as a dedicated public folder server.
- Lagged database copies always should be activation-disabled and have the highest activation preference number available. This is required to prevent automatic activation by mistake or resulting from a system failure.

You should make the best decision for your own situation. Don't start with the maximum of 14 days for replay lag time, but make a decision that suits your needs considering both disaster recovery and budgetary (or storage design) aspects.

NOTE **Lagged database copies are not updateable with the single page restore feature. If a lagged database copy hits a page corruption, you will have to reseed to repair it (and subsequently lose the lagged aspect to the copy). It is therefore best practice to either deploy the lagged database copy on RAID or create multiple lagged database copies when using JBOD.**

Deploying Lagged Database Copies

You configure a lagged database copy using the EMS by following these steps:

1. Create a database copy to the target server where you want to store the lagged database copy.
2. Configure the *ReplayLagTime* of the database. The following cmdlet configures a lag time of 7 days to the database DAG01-BERLIN-01 located on Berlin-MB01: *Set-MailboxDatabaseCopy –id DAG01-BERLIN-01\Berlin-MB01 –ReplayLagTime 7.0:0:0.*
3. Block auto activation of this database to make sure it is not activated by mistake. You use the following cmdlet to perform this task: *Suspend-MailboxDatabaseCopy <database\server> -ActivationOnly -Confirm:$false.*
4. If you use a dedicated Exchange server that hosts all lagged database copies, you can block automatic activation of databases also on the server level by using the following cmdlet: *Set-MailboxServer <mailbox server> –DatabaseCopyAutoActivationPolicy Blocked.*

When the lagged database copy is configured, you will see that the replay queue length of the lagged database will increase, as shown in Figure 12-18.

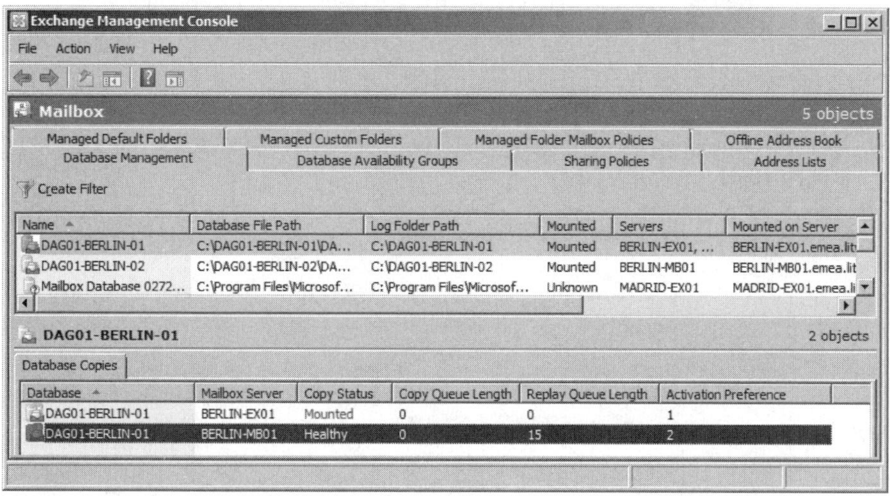

FIGURE 12-18 Viewing a lagged database copy in EMC

> ***NOTE*** **To verify that all logged database copies are not automatically activated, use the *Get-MailboxDatabaseCopyStatus –Server <name> | ft Name, Act** cmdlet and make sure that the *ActivationSuspended* property is set to true.**

Using a Lagged Database Copy to Recover Data

Using a lagged database copy to get to a specific point in time is rather difficult because you have to know the exact time frame in which something occurred. In addition, no tools are available to tell you which log file contains exactly what database change. Thus you have to estimate which log files need to be replayed so that you get the database to the point in time that you require. You must simply guess when you grab the database and logs files and then replay the logs manually before you can recover data from a recovery database.

Recovering a lagged database to a specific point in time is a manual process, so follow these steps to receive the data you're looking for:

1. Suspend replication to the lagged database copy by using the *Suspend-MailboxDatabaseCopy <database>\<server>* cmdlet.

> **NOTE** You should now decide whether you want to back up or copy the database and log files to a different location so that you have them available if you don't get to the right point in time. You alternatively can create a VSS snapshot using the *VSSAdmin CREATE SHADOW /For=<Volume that includes database>* command.

2. Use Explorer to delete or move all log files that are newer from the log file's time stamp than the time you decided to go back. For example, if you have 14 days of log files available, and you want to replay the log files to get back 10 days, you only need to commit those log files to the 14-days-old database, that are 10 days and older. In order to achieve this, you need to delete or move all log files that have a time stamp newer than 10 days, like day 9 or newer.
3. Delete the .chk file for the database and note its filename. It should normally be something like E00.chk.
4. Run the *Eseutil.exe /r E00 /a* command but replace *E00* with the filename of the .chk file. Depending on the number of log files that need to replayed, this might take several hours. A rule of thumb is that on normal 7.2K JBOD 3.5-inch disks, you can assume that you'll replay approximately 7.2 GB of transactional log files per hour. The exact value, of course, depends on your local factors such as storage performance or CPU.

> **NOTE** If you want to measure how long replaying the log files to the database takes, you can use the tool JetStress 2010, which includes a Recovery Performance measure option for this exact situation. You can download Microsoft Exchange Server Jetstress 2010 (64 bit) at *http://go.microsoft.com/fwlink/?LinkId=178616.*

5. When Eseutil is finished, the database is in clean shutdown state. You can now decide how to continue:
   a. You can create a recovery database using this database, mount it, and recover the data as described in "Using the Recovery Database" section in this chapter.
   b. You can replace the corrupt database files with the lagged database files and mount the database.

As you can see, several steps are involved here and the process is time-consuming because of the large number of logs that must be replayed. The process is not difficult, but is not something you want to be doing on a daily/weekly basis because of the operational time required. Lagged copies were not designed for the deleted item recovery case—they were designed for the once-in-a-great-while scenario where multiple database copies within a DAG combined with retention hold is not enough protection in a backup-less environment.

> **NOTE** As already mentioned, no tools are currently available from Microsoft that allow you to automate the process of recovering a lagged database copy to a specific point in time. However, third-party vendors may soon provide solutions for this situation. Check the Internet regularly for updates.

Backups and Log File Truncation

Log file truncation, or deleting the transactional log files that are no longer required for a successful database restore, takes place once you do a successful backup. But if you do not perform a backup in situations where you decided to no longer use traditional point-in-time backups, how will you make sure the log files are removed so they don't pile up? Simple: they are never removed.

For this reason you need to configure log file truncation by enabling circular logging. You can enable circular logging on a database either in EMC or in EMS using the *Set-MailboxDatabase –Identity <DatabaseName> -CircularLoggingEnabled $True* cmdlet.

Once you enable circular logging when multiple database copies are in place, you get a new type of circular logging called *continuous replication circular logging (CRCL)* which behaves differently from traditional circular logging known from Exchange 2007 and before.

CRCL is performed by the Microsoft Exchange Replication Service, not the Microsoft Exchange Information Store service. Also, CRCL requires considering log files that are required for log shipping and replay before removing them. This situation needs special logic to ensure that all database copies process the log file before it is removed, which differs from the traditional circular logging logic where the log file was deleted when it was committed to the database.

When CRCL is enabled, log file truncation for database copies that are not lagged occurs in the following way:

- The log file is checked to determine whether it is below the checkpoint.
- The log file is inspected that all other non-lagged database copies replayed the log file into their database.
- The log file has been inspected by all database copies (including any lagged database copies).

Log file truncation happens for lagged database copies in the following way:

- The log file is checked to determine whether it is below the checkpoint.

- The log file is older than *ReplayLagTime* and *TruncationLagTime*.
- The log file is already deleted on an active database copy and all copies agree on the deletion.

Reasons for Traditional Point-in-Time Backups

Even though Exchange Server 2010 supports backup-less scenarios, in some cases your organization may want to maintain its traditional backup methods. Keep in mind the following argumentations when discussing the pros and cons of a backup-less infrastructure:

- **No Available DAGs** Organizations that do not use DAGs need to consider traditional ways to back up their databases. A reason for not implementing DAGs is often that they are too expensive to deploy—DAGs require a Windows Server Enterprise Edition license.
- **Single Exchange Server Implementation** Single Exchange Server implementations are not conducive to DAG usage because they require adding more server hardware. Traditional backups to disks or tapes are the option to follow here.
- **Utilizing an Existing Backup Environment** Your company's backup strategy might force you to follow other applications if you have an existing backup environment in which all other applications will back up their data, so that even when you maintain multiple copies of your database, you are required to have a copy of it in your backup environment.
- **Compliance Requirements** You typically use tape backups if you have an archival reason to preserve data for an extended time, as governed by compliance requirements. You also need to ensure that you can access the data in the future, especially if the storage is long term—sometimes up to 10 years.

Additional Resources

- How Volume Shadow Copy Service Works: *http://technet.microsoft.com/en-us/library/cc785914(WS.10).aspx*
- Using Windows Server Backup to Back Up and Restore Exchange Data: *http://technet.microsoft.com/en-us/library/dd876851(EXCHG.140).aspx*
- DPM 2010 Protecting Exchange 2010 DAG in a Single Site: *http://blogs.technet.com/b/dpm/archive/2010/01/08/dpm-2010-protecting-exchange-2010-dag-in-a-single-site.aspx*
- Exchange 2010 Backup Product Support Matrix: *http://chrislehr.com/2010/02/exchange-2010-backup-product-support.htm*
- Microsoft Exchange Server Jetstress 2010 Beta (64 bit): *http://go.microsoft.com/fwlink/?LinkId=178616*

CHAPTER 13

Hardware Planning for Exchange Server 2010

Even with the latest software deployed and all of the new features enabled for the users, it is all useless if the underlying hardware cannot effectively run the software. Your tendency might be to buy more hardware than you need; however, most businesses don't have money in their budget to afford overspending. This is especially true in a business environment where many companies are looking to take advantage of cloud resources to reduce costs and improve operational flexibility.

Planning the hardware to use for an Exchange deployment can be overwhelming. Do not fret—you can use numerous tools, guides, and other resources to make the best possible estimate for the hardware requirement.

The first step toward defining the hardware to use is that an intimate understanding of what type of solution will deployed. Will you deploy a highly available solution? Will you deploy a solution that achieves redundancy by scaling out rather than requiring redundancy at the server-component level?

Sizing and Planning Exchange Hardware

To size a messaging environment, you need a few key pieces of information. Unfortunately finding this information can be complicated without the right tools. The number, size, and usage profile of the mailboxes is critical to properly sizing Exchange server hardware—these inputs directly impact the required resources. The Exchange Profile Analyzer tool helps you gather this information if you already have a version of Exchange deployed and have the ability to run the tool against that environment.

If you have a non-Exchange messaging system currently in place you may be able to gather information about the average e-mail message sizes and the number of messages sent and received, which can help roughly gauge equivalent Exchange usage. A word of caution, however: After a migration to Exchange—as users become more comfortable using the features of Exchange and various clients—usage patterns will change in most cases. This change in behavior often is due to the difference in features the users are able to use. For example, in the previous messaging system the user may not have had the rich calendaring features that Exchange provides; therefore, as users begin to gain experience with the calendaring features, they may use it frequently. This change in behavior will cause usage patterns and performance requirements to change over time.

Exchange 2010 has reduced storage I/O requirements, leading to a reduced overall system total cost of ownership (TCO). For more information about the storage changes in Exchange 2010, see Chapter 6, "Mailbox Services." However, the improvement in I/O is offset by some new features in Exchange 2010 that may require additional hardware resources. By planning correctly, any potential increase in server count can be minimized. Virtualization is a great way to take advantage of underutilized hardware; however, you must take care to make it work optimally. This chapter will cover all of these topics and more.

Exchange Scalability

Exchange 2010 is a componentized messaging system, meaning each server role can be separated onto different servers. In this book you have read about the different roles available and how these roles can be installed on separate servers or together on a single server. Consolidating and separating server roles both have benefits and drawbacks. Before deciding how to size your messaging system, you need to have a good understanding of what configuration you are sizing. If you have not done so already, be sure to review the chapters of this book that discuss each server role, as well as Chapter 11, "Designing High Availability," if you are going to deploy a highly available messaging system.

The Sizing Process

A lot of variables go into making an educated sizing decision. Thankfully, a number of tools have been provided to help you objectively fill in the variables to provide a more accurate sizing guidance.

A hardware sizing project has a progression, as shown in Table 13-1. First, tools are used for profiling usage in an existing environment. Then sizing estimates are created with sizing tools, and then the estimates are validated with validation tools.

TABLE 13-1 Sizing Tools

PROFILING TOOLS	CONFIGURATION SIZING TOOLS	CONFIGURATION VALIDATION TOOLS
■ Exchange Profile Analyzer (EPA) - Download from *www.microsoft.com/exchange* ■ Performance Monitor - Built in to Windows (other performance monitoring solution)	■ Exchange 2010 Mailbox Server Role Requirements Calculator - Download from *www.microsoft.com/exchange* ■ Vendor-specific sizing tools	■ Exchange Load Generator - Download from *www.microsoft.com/exchange* ■ Exchange Jetstress - Download from *www.microsoft.com/exchange*

Figure 13-1 summarizes the process of creating a user profile, creating a configuration, and then validating the configuration with load-generation tools.

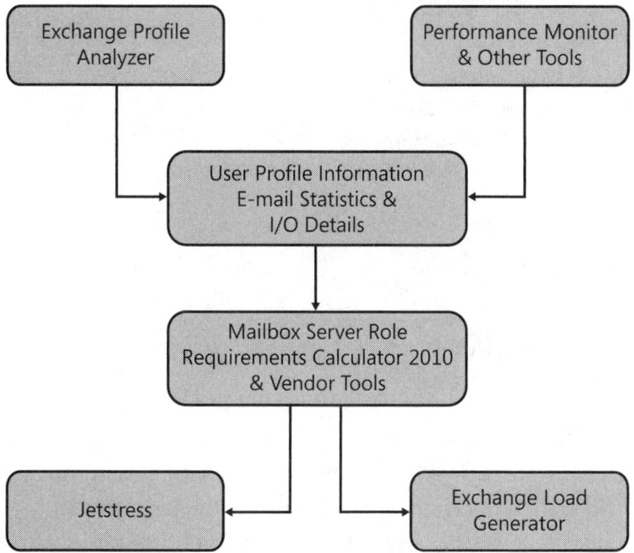

FIGURE 13-1 Exchange sizing project process

Profiling

Profiling is the first step in planning hardware for a new Exchange deployment, and can be done in two primary ways if a version of Exchange is already deployed. One is to use a tool like the Exchange Profile Analyzer and the other is to gather performance data using Performance Monitor (Perfmon.exe) or a more sophisticated tool such as Microsoft System Center Operations Manager 2007 R2. In instances where Exchange is not already deployed, tools specific to the foreign messaging solution are used to gather information about the average message sizes and quantities sent and received to provide information about the user profile.

Using Exchange Profile Analyzer

The Exchange Profile Analyzer (EPA) is a tool used to analyze a production Exchange server and generate a statistical profile of user activity. It gathers the following statistics:

- Number of e-mail messages sent/day
- Number of e-mail messages received/day
- Number of inbox rules
- Number of items
- Sizes of items

EPA version 8.03 is available in both 32- and 64-bit versions and works against Exchange 2007 and Exchange 2003 with SP2. If you have Exchange 2007 installed on Windows Server 2008, you will need to manually install and enable the WebDAV components for IIS 7.0 because Windows Server 2008 does not include these components. EPA has the following requirements for the client computer:

- The Microsoft .NET Framework Version 2.0 Redistributable Package (x86) and later versions (*http://go.microsoft.com/fwlink/?linkid=66763*).
- One of the following operating systems:
  - Windows Server 2003 with Service Pack 3 or higher (any edition)
  - Windows Server 2008 or higher (any edition)
  - Windows Server 2008 R2 (any edition)
  - Windows XP Service Pack 3, Windows Vista SP1 or higher, and Windows 7
- An account with Exchange View-Only Administrator permissions and Full Mailbox access for each sampled mailbox

The account used to run EPA must have Exchange View-Only Administrator permissions and must not be a member of the Domain Administrators or Enterprise Administrators groups—accounts in these groups inherit a Deny access control entry on user mailboxes. To grant a user these permissions on an Exchange 2007 server from Exchange Management Shell (EMS) run the following cmdlet:

```
Add-ExchangeAdministrator <UserName> -Role ViewOnlyAdmin
Get-ExchangeServer <ServerName> | Add-ADPermission -user <UserName> -AccessRights
extendedright -ExtendedRights send-as, receive-as
```

Running the EPA is resource-intensive and may affect server performance, so it is recommended that you only run it during a maintenance window and that server performance be closely monitored.

Because the process of profiling a mailbox is time consuming, profiling all of the mailboxes in an Exchange organization is usually not feasible. Therefore, a statistically sound number of mailboxes should be selected and profiled to represent an average user's activity. User usage profiles will vary by department and job role; thus a percentage of each type of user should be profiled to provide an accurate and complete data sample. For example, to gather an accurate accounting of a user in the Engineering Department of more than 1,000 people, you would not simply profile one mailbox. The number of mailboxes that you need to profile to gather this statistically sound information will vary. As a rule of thumb, the EPA sampling size should be at least 10 percent of the total number of mailboxes that will be represented.

The EPA tool consists of the following:

- **Config.xml** The configuration file used to control EPA
- **EPACmd.exe** The command-line version of EPA

- **EPAOWACmd.exe** The command-line tool used to analyze IIS logs and generate a report on OWA usage
- **EPASummarizer.exe** The command-line tool used to generate an aggregated summary report from multiple EPA collection reports
- **EPAWin.exe** The graphical user interface version of EPA
- **ExProfAn.doc** The user documentation for the tool

The EPA collects data from a single mailbox at a time. To collect data from multiple mailbox databases, you must either run multiple instances of the tool by creating multiple configuration files or by increasing the value of the *ServerThread* and *MailboxThreadPerServer* attributes in the configuration file.

Running EPAWin.exe starts up in the Scanning Wizard. You can connect to Active Directory or you can open a previously saved configuration file. Next, you choose the time range and mailbox databases for the scan and start the collection. At the end of the collection process, you can review the report, as shown in Figure 13-2.

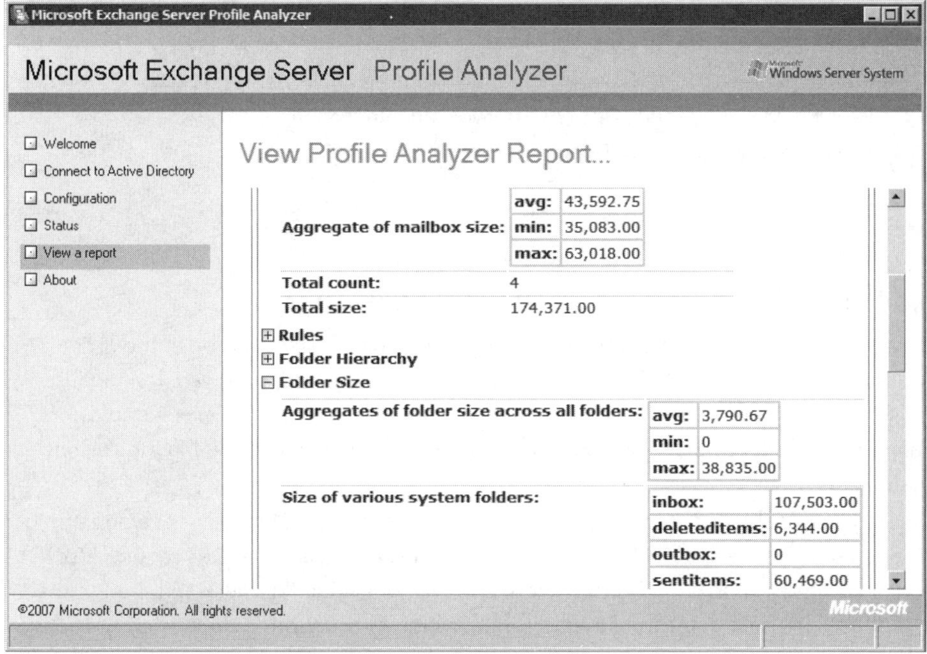

FIGURE 13-2 EPA Report

The EPA Report includes information about the user's profile. This includes information about the number of messages sent and received each day, the number and size of mailbox folders, and the number of inbox rules. This information is used later when sizing the server hardware.

NOTES FROM THE FIELD

Profiling Foreign Mail Systems

Jeffrey Rosen
UC Solution Architect, Microsoft Corporation, USA

Planning from earlier versions of Exchange can be somewhat easier because of the tools available to profile users. What do you do if you are coming from a foreign mail system? As an architect, I know one of the more important inputs to the Mailbox Role Calculator is the users' sent and received items count. Many calculations are based on these numbers, so how can you arrive at a reasonable number? First, some third-party reporting tools may provide functionality similar to that of the EPA. Another option is to migrate a set of users' data to Exchange deployed in a lab environment, and then use the EPA against the test system. This provides an interface to allow EPA to report on the user's data as if it were being used on an Exchange server. Another option is to spot-check a number of representative users. With either of these two approaches you must be careful about which users are used to get your data. In my experience, IT (especially messaging administrators) often tend to overestimate the number of average messages sent and received. For this reason, make sure you get good representation from groups outside of IT.

Using Performance Monitor (Perfmon) and other tools

After gathering information about the type and number of messages stored in the users' mailboxes, it is also important to understand how the current server hardware is handling the user activity. This may seem a little counterintuitive—most likely you will be deploying Exchange to newer hardware, which would seemingly not require determining the current hardware capabilities.

The single most significant bit of information that you should collect is the average number of I/O operations per second (IOPS) required by each mailbox user. The IOPS required for each mailbox will be used later to help determine the storage configuration required to meet the needs of your users. You can gather this information by monitoring the Logical Disk\Disk Transfers/sec counter for each of the logical disks and then dividing the peak value by the total number of mailboxes. This will give you a baseline peak IOPS for each mailbox.

Rather than just monitoring this information for a few hours, you should gather a baseline over a full business cycle. In many business environments additional load is placed on the system at certain times during the month, such as an end-of-the-month accounting process or the weekly human resources payroll process. Each business will have different peak periods, so it is important to gather a baseline that covers at least one of these full cycles. Ideally you can collect information from several of these cycles to generate an average across each cycle. The more accurate your information is, the better informed your decisions will be.

After gathering user profile information with EPA and Performance Monitor, you will have a comprehensive definition of what a user does and how the current hardware handles these activities. You can use this information with the sizing tools to better customize the solution to meet the technical requirements of your users.

Sizing Tools

The primary tool for sizing an Exchange 2010 environment is the Exchange 2010 Mailbox Server Role Requirements Calculator. Alternatively, many hardware vendors also provide sizing guidance based on their hardware. Using both tools to develop a hardware configuration can help provide needed guidance. Because vendor tools are specific to each vendor, you will need to explore the features and functionality individually.

Mailbox Server Role Requirements Calculator 2010

The Exchange 2010 Mailbox Server Role Requirements Calculator is an Excel spreadsheet created and supported by the Exchange product group. The goal of the calculator is to give you guidance on the I/O and capacity requirements and a storage design. This complex spreadsheet follows the latest Exchange product group recommendations on storage, memory, and mailbox sizing. This tool is constantly improved and updated, so be sure to check for the latest version before using it to create a new configuration. You can download the calculator from the Exchange product team blog at *http://msexchangeteam.com/archive/2009/11/09/453117.aspx*.

Before you use the calculator, you must understand what it does. If you do not use it properly, you may end up with the wrong results.

The information in the calculator is separated into seven worksheets to improve readability and simplify use:

- Input
- Role Requirements
- LUN Requirements
- Backup Requirements
- Log Replication Requirements
- Storage Design
- Version Changes

The next few sections cover each of these worksheets and how they are used to generate an Exchange configuration.

INPUT

The Input worksheet is where you enter all of the information to define your design. It is broken down into six areas or steps: Environment Configuration, Mailbox Configuration, Backup Configuration, Storage Configuration, Processor Configuration, and Log Replication Configuration.

Step 1: Environment Configuration

Step 1 is broken into six subsections that are used to define your environment. The first subsection in Step 1 is the Exchange Environment configuration, shown in Figure 13-3.

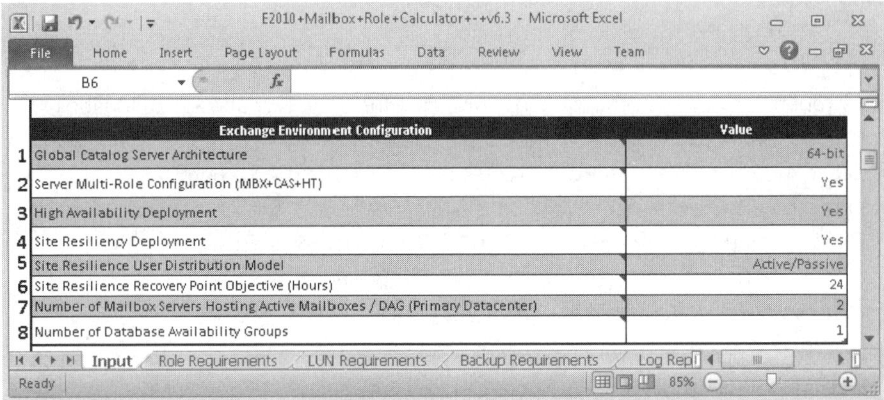

FIGURE 13-3 Mailbox server requirements calculator Environment Configuration

This section has fields for the following information:

1. Do the global catalog servers run a 32-bit or 64-bit version of Windows Server? This information is important because it affects the core ratio planning. For more information, please see the "Sizing Guidelines" section of this chapter.
2. Do these servers have multiple server roles installed? Installing other server roles affects the memory and process configuration and the type of load-balancing options available.
3. Will you be deploying a high-availability solution using a DAG? This information will provide additional choices regarding mailbox copies, storage redundancy, and backups. For more information about high availability see Chapter 15, "Preparing for and Deploying Exchange 2010."
4. If you are deploying a high-availability solution, will it be site-resilient? A site-resilient DAG is stretched across two or more datacenters; however, the calculator only allows for sizing a single active datacenter.
5. If you are deploying a site-resilient, high-availability solution you will be prompted to choose a user distribution mode. The only option available in the initial Exchange 2010 of the tool is Active/Passive. This denotes that mailboxes will be either all active in one datacenter or the other. To configure two active sites, use the tool to create two Active/Passive configurations with the number of mailboxes that will be located in each datacenter.
6. If you are deploying a site-resilient solution, how many hours of transaction logs can you afford to lose and meet your recovery point objective (RPO)? The lower the RPO,

the higher the bandwidth between datacenters needs to be to ensure that transaction logs are being transferred quickly enough.

7. How many Mailbox servers do you plan to deploy within the primary datacenter? If you specify more than one, the calculator will evenly distribute the user mailboxes across all of the Mailbox servers. As for the secondary datacenter, the calculator will determine the number of Mailbox servers you need to deploy based on requirements.
8. How many DAGs do you plan to deploy? If you specify more than one DAG, the calculator will distribute the user mailboxes to all DAGs.

The next subsection is the Mailbox Database Copy Configuration, which provides fields to define how you plan to configure high-availability and secondary site–lagged mailbox database copies.

1. Define the number of high-availability mailbox database copies you plan to deploy. Enter the number of highly available database copies you plan to have within the environment. This value excludes lagged database copies, but does account for both the active and any passive database copies, but includes both the active copy and all passive copies you plan to deploy. For optimal sizing, choose a multiple of the total number of mailbox servers you have selected.
2. Define how many lagged database copies you plan to deploy. Remember that lagged database copies should not be considered database copies. The technical limitation of the number of lagged copies is based on the number of servers in the DAG. The calculator limits you to a maximum of two lagged copies.
3. Define how many mailbox database copies you plan to deploy at the secondary datacenter.
4. Define how many lagged database copies you plan to deploy at the secondary datacenter within a DAG. If you are deploying a site-resilient solution, you can choose to have a portion or all of your lagged database copies deployed in the secondary datacenter. Additional information about lagged database copies can be found in Chapter 11 and in Chapter 12, "Backup, Restore, and Disaster Recovery."

The Database Configuration subsection is used to define your parameters for the number and size of the databases. Microsoft documentation recommends that the database on a non-high-availability Mailbox server should not exceed 200 GB in size. However, for high-availability solutions, Microsoft documentation recommends that databases should not exceed 2 TB in size. You can override these settings in this section, which may be helpful you need to reduce these limits to fit into backup or storage constraints. In this section you can also either allow the calculator to determine the optimal number of databases, or specify your own number.

The Exchange Data Configuration subsection of Step 1 is used to provide information needed to size storage for both the database and transaction log LUNs and is shown in Figure 13-4.

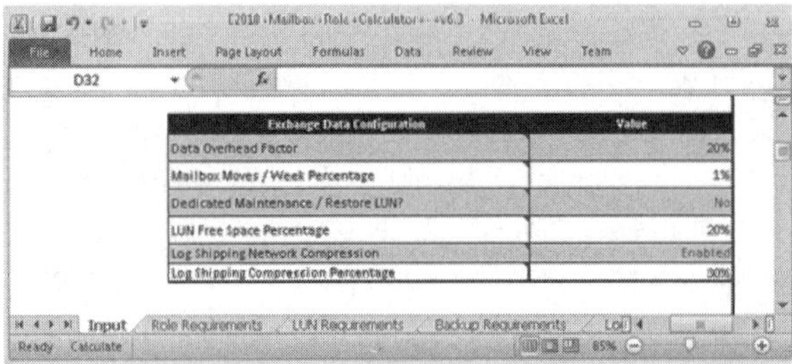

FIGURE 13-4 Mailbox Server Requirements Calculator Exchange Data Configuration

1. Define the data overhead factor. This should be set anywhere from 20 to 30 percent to account for non-mailbox data storage within the database.
2. How many mailboxes that will be moved each week? Mailbox moves generate a large number of transaction logs. The size of these transaction logs needs to be calculated in the size of the transaction log LUN.
3. Will you deploy a LUN dedicated for restore operations on each server? An additional LUN will be added into the configuration for you to use to perform mailbox maintenance and restore operations.
4. Define the percentage of free disk space that needs to be maintained on data LUNs. Many organizations like to maintain at least 20 percent free space available on each disk to maintain performance standards and reduce the likelihood of running out of storage space.
5. Will you enable log-shipping compression? The default DAG configuration will compress and encrypt the log shipping communication across IP subnets. This setting may add additional CPU load to each Mailbox server; however, it can reduce the bandwidth needed for transaction log shipping.
6. If you plan to enable log shipping compression, what compression rate do you expect to achieve? The compression rate varies by environment and by activity within the environment. Microsoft documentation recommends starting with a value of 30 percent. After you deploy Exchange 2010 in your environment you can analyze your compression rate by comparing throughput rates with it enabled and with it disabled.

The Exchange I/O Configuration subsection of Step 1 has two settings. One is to set the I/O Overhead Factor. This factor is to allow deviations from a baseline by a specified percentage. This helps allow for abnormally busy I/O times. The Microsoft documentation recommends using a 20 percent factor.

The other setting in this section allows you to add the information that you gathered using Performance Monitor when you established your user profile. If you calculate that additional I/O capacity is required to support a third-party product, you can add that overhead here.

Step 2: Mailbox Configuration

Step 2 is broken into three subsections in which you define up to three tiers or service levels of mailboxes. Some businesses will offer several tiers of mailbox service. A tier is defined by the characteristics of the mailbox service, such as the mailbox size, retention settings, and user usage profile. For example, a university may offer students 250-MB mailboxes with 7 days of deleted item retention and staff members 1-GB mailboxes with 21 days of deleted item retention. If you plan to offer something similar to your Exchange users, define the mailbox service tiers and the number of mailboxes that will be created in each tier, as shown in Figure 13-5. However, if you plan to offer a single level of service across all mailboxes, define that tier of service as Tier 1.

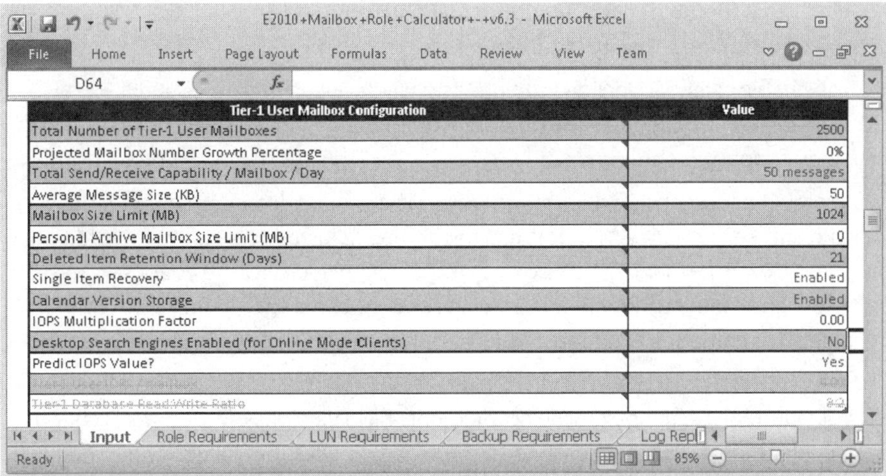

Tier-1 User Mailbox Configuration	Value
Total Number of Tier-1 User Mailboxes	2500
Projected Mailbox Number Growth Percentage	0%
Total Send/Receive Capability / Mailbox / Day	50 messages
Average Message Size (KB)	50
Mailbox Size Limit (MB)	1024
Personal Archive Mailbox Size Limit (MB)	0
Deleted Item Retention Window (Days)	21
Single Item Recovery	Enabled
Calendar Version Storage	Enabled
IOPS Multiplication Factor	0.00
Desktop Search Engines Enabled (for Online Mode Clients)	No
Predict IOPS Value?	Yes

FIGURE 13-5 Mailbox Server Requirements Calculator Tier-1 Mailbox Configuration

The following information can be specified in this section:

1. Define how many mailboxes of this tier will be deployed.
2. Define the projected percentage of mailboxes that the solution should be able to handle. For example, if the solution will grow by 25 percent and the initial deployment is 1,000 mailboxes, plan on growing to 1,250 mailboxes.
3. Define the average amount and size of e-mail messages sent and received by the average user that will be assigned this tier. The user profile information collected using EPA fits into these fields. Having this set accurately will ensure that server memory, storage, and processor scalability requirements are met.
4. Define the prohibit send and receive mailbox size limit. To control capacity requirements and ensure that a single user does not consume all of the storage, you should set a hard mailbox size limit for user mailboxes. This setting provides guidance for how much storage will be required to support this tier of user mailboxes. If these limits are not set, accurately sizing storage becomes difficult because nothing will stop users from continuing to consume more storage.
5. If you are deploying a personal archive, define the personal archive quota limit. As with the mailbox send and receive limit, to control capacity requirements you should set a hard personal archive mailbox size limit for the same reason limits should be set on the mailbox. The default quota for a personal archive is 50 GB. If you expect the archive

to be heavily used, be sure to include the sizing information in this field to include enough storage in your design.

6. Define the deleted item retention period. The default retention period is 14 days; however, this should be adjusted to match your deleted item recovery policy along with Single Item Recovery to eliminate performing restores.
7. Will you deploy Single Item Recovery? Single Item Recovery preserves deleted and modified items for the deleted item retention period. When enabled, this feature increases the storage capacity requirements.
8. Will you enable calendar version logging? This will save changes to calendar items for 120 days and can be used to repair the calendar. When enabled, this feature increases the storage capacity requirements.
9. Define an I/O per second multiplication factor. The user profile information gathered with EPA and Performance Monitor may need to be adjusted to account for additional impact on I/O performance because of third-party tools or because your users have multiple clients running simultaneously (such as a mobile device, a portable computer, and a desktop computer) and thus require additional I/O over an baseline estimated by the calculator.
10. Will your Outlook Exchange Online Mode clients have versions of Windows Desktop Search older than 4.0 or third-party desktop search engines deployed? These indexing tools cause additional I/O storage on the Mailbox server. Ideally, alternatives to these tools should be found to minimize the impact on the server; however, if you must maintain support for them, this option will account for additional I/O capacity. This option may suggest adding additional disks or faster storage to account for this overhead.
11. Will you use the calculator to predict I/O or will you define your own I/O profile based on user profile information you have gathered? The calculator predicts I/O for each mailbox based on the number of messages per mailbox and the user memory profile. If you choose to override the prediction, you can specify your I/O per second per mailbox value as well as the database read/write ratio.

Step 3: Backup Configuration

Step 3 has just one subsection and is used to define the backup methodology and failure tolerance settings and whether you will separate the transaction logs and database files on different volumes. The following information can be provided to define the backup solution:

1. Define the backup methodology that will be used from the following options: hardware-based VSS, software-based VSS, and the native Exchange data protection features. In some cases, if you are deploying adequate mailbox resiliency and Single Item Recovery, and you have no long-term retention needs, you may be able to eliminate traditional backup. Alternatively, if you still require a traditional backup for legal and compliance reasons you will need to deploy a VSS-based solution.

Hardware-based VSS solutions are available with many storage area network (SAN) solutions. However, software-based VSS solutions can be used in either a SAN or direct attached storage solution. The backup methodology affects the LUN design because hardware-based VSS solutions require a LUN architecture of two LUNs for each database—one for the transaction logs and one for the database files.

2. Define the backup frequency. Choose Daily Full, Weekly Full With Daily Differential, Weekly Full With Daily Incremental, or Bi-Monthly Full With Daily Incremental. The backup frequency affects the LUN design and the disk space requirements. To support a schedule of daily differentials, storage capacity is needed for at least seven days of transaction logs.
3. Will you segregate the transaction logs from the database files on different volumes on separate physical disks? In non-high-availability deployments, best practice is to deploy isolated database and transaction logs for recoverability purposes. For high-availability solutions, isolation is not required because the database copies are stored on separate servers and not susceptible to data corruption or loss in the case of a single failure.
4. Define the number of allowed failed backups or log truncations that can be tolerated and still provide storage for transaction log files. For example, if you perform a weekly full backup and daily differential backups, transaction log truncation occurs only once a week during the full backup. If the weekly full backup fails, an entire week will lapse before another full backup is attempted, unless you are able to reschedule the full backup. Setting this value to 1 will size the transaction LUNs to have enough capacity for transaction logs until the following week's full backup. When using Exchange native data protection features (a backup-less deployment), best practice is to specify a value of 3 to ensure enough capacity for up to three days' worth of transaction log generation.
5. Define the number of days to tolerate a network outage. The Network Failure Tolerance value ensures that you have enough storage capacity on the log LUNs to tolerate a network outage for the specified number of days. A network outage will impede replication and will keep log truncation from occurring on the source copy. In multi-site DAG deployments a network outage can cause transaction logs to accumulate. If the source log capacity is exhausted and a manual log truncation is required during the outage, the remote copies must be reseeded when the network is restored.

Step 4: Storage Configuration

Step 4 is separated into two subsections: Storage Options and Disk Configurations, and is provided for you to define your storage parameters. To consider using JBOD storage, select that value in the Storage Options subsection. Then, define the disk capacities and types you plan to deploy for databases, transaction logs, and the restore LUNs. Be sure to select the appropriate capacity and disk type. These values are used to determine the appropriate number of disks needed to support both the storage and I/O capacity of your solution.

Step 5: Processor Configuration (Optional)

Step 5 is an optional step that can be used to define the number of processor cores and megacycles you will deploy in each Mailbox server. Defining the number of processor cores for the primary, secondary, and dedicated lagged mailbox copy Mailbox servers is straightforward. However, defining the megacycles/core is a little more involved.

> ***NOTE*** **For a processor other than the Intel Xeon x5470, you must do a megacycle adjustment and specify the adjusted value into the calculator by using these steps:**
>
> 1. **Open an Internet browser and go to** ***http://www.spec.org/cgi-bin/osgresults?conf=rint2006.***
> 2. **Select Processor from the drop-down menu; then type the name of the process you would like to compare, such as x5570; and then click Execute Simple Fetch.**
> 3. **Find the server and processor in the search results and record the value for the Result column. For example, let's say you are deploying a server with two Intel Xeon x5570 2.93 GHz processors with a total of eight cores. The SPECint2006 rate results value is 256.**
> 4. **The baseline server used in the Mailbox Role Calculator has a SPECint2006 rate Results value of 150 and eight cores, or a Results value of 18.75/core.**
> 5. **To estimate the megacycles/core value of the new server use the following formula:**
>
>   *Megacycles/core = ((New Server SPECint2006 Results/New Server Total Cores) * (New Server Processor Gigahertz * 1000)) / (18.75)*
>
>   *5000.53 Megacycles/Core = ((256/8) * (2.93 * 1000)) / 18.75*

Step 6: Log Replication Configuration (Optional)

Step 6 is separated into two subsections: Log Replication Configuration and Network Configuration. The Log Replication Configuration subsection is used to set how many transaction logs are generated for each hour in the day. In this section you must specify the percentage of transaction logs that are generated for each hour in the day by measuring an existing Exchange 2003 or Exchange 2007 server in your environment. To collect this information you can use the Collectlogs.vbs script available on the Exchange Team Blog at *http://msexchangeteam.com/files/12/attachments/entry445789.aspx.*

The second subsection of Step 6 is the Network Configuration. If you have chosen to deploy a site-resilient high-availability solution, this section is used to define the bandwidth and latency of the network between the two datacenters.

ROLE REQUIREMENTS WORKSHEET

The worksheet shown in Figure 13-6 provides the solution's I/O, capacity, memory, and CPU requirements.

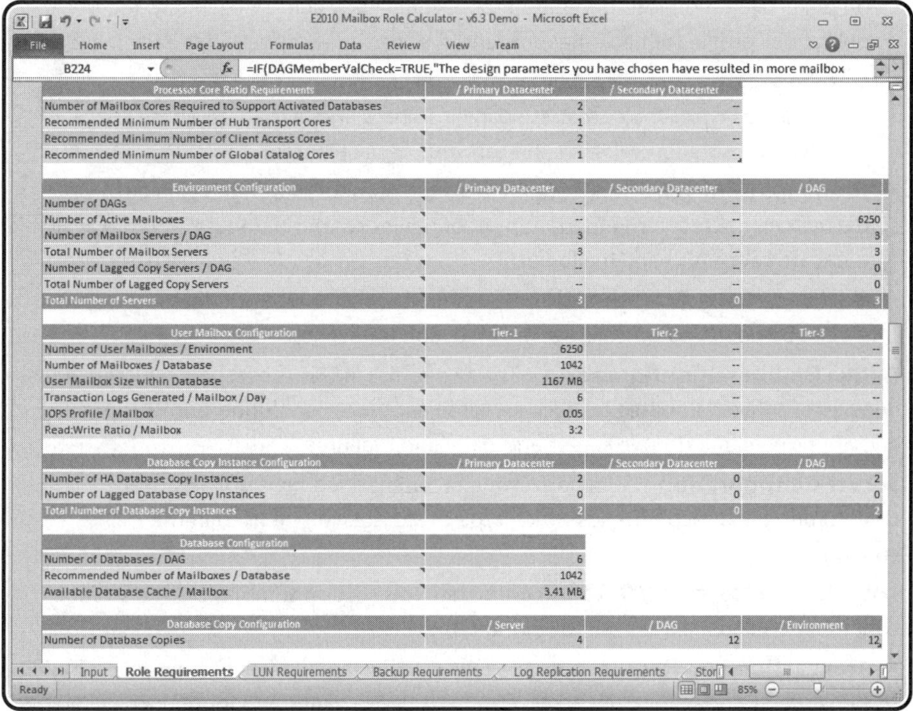

E2010 Mailbox Role Calculator - v6.3 Demo - Microsoft Excel
File Home Insert Page Layout Formulas Data Review View Team
B224
=IF(DAGMemberValCheck=TRUE,"The design parameters you have chosen have resulted in more mailbox
Processor Core Ratio Requirements / Primary Datacenter / Secondary Datacenter
Number of Mailbox Cores Required to Support Activated Databases 2 --
Recommended Minimum Number of Hub Transport Cores 1 --
Recommended Minimum Number of Client Access Cores 2 --
Recommended Minimum Number of Global Catalog Cores 1 --
Environment Configuration / Primary Datacenter / Secondary Datacenter / DAG
Number of DAGs -- -- --
Number of Active Mailboxes -- -- 6250
Number of Mailbox Servers / DAG 3 -- 3
Total Number of Mailbox Servers 3 -- 3
Number of Lagged Copy Servers / DAG -- -- 0
Total Number of Lagged Copy Servers -- -- 0
Total Number of Servers 3 0 3
User Mailbox Configuration Tier-1 Tier-2 Tier-3
Number of User Mailboxes / Environment 6250 -- --
Number of Mailboxes / Database 1042 -- --
User Mailbox Size within Database 1167 MB -- --
Transaction Logs Generated / Mailbox / Day 6 -- --
IOPS Profile / Mailbox 0.05 -- --
Read:Write Ratio / Mailbox 3:2 -- --
Database Copy Instance Configuration / Primary Datacenter / Secondary Datacenter / DAG
Number of HA Database Copy Instances 2 0 2
Number of Lagged Database Copy Instances 0 0 0
Total Number of Database Copy Instances 2 0 2
Database Configuration
Number of Databases / DAG 6
Recommended Number of Mailboxes / Database 1042
Available Database Cache / Mailbox 3.41 MB
Database Copy Configuration / Server / DAG / Environment
Number of Database Copies 4 12 12
Input Role Requirements LUN Requirements Backup Requirements Log Replication Requirements
Ready 85%

FIGURE 13-6 Viewing the Mailbox Server Requirements Calculator Role Requirements worksheet

Use this worksheet to review the solution before using the other worksheets to verify that you have entered the proper information on the Input worksheet. No changes should be made on this worksheet so as not to break any of the calculations. The Calculations Pane on the Requirements worksheet is hidden by default and lists the calculations based on the information specified on the Inputs worksheet. The Results pane on the Requirements worksheet recommends the Mailbox server architecture and is broken down into four main sections, each with a number of subsections:

- **Environment Configuration** Summarizes the information about the Exchange messaging environment. This subsection is broken into six tables:
  - **Processor Core Ratio Requirements** Identifies the required number of processor cores required to support the activated databases for the Mailbox, Hub Transport, and Client Access Server roles per datacenter. This table is only populated if you populate the processor core megacycle information on the Input tab.
  - **Environment Configuration** Identifies how many mailbox servers and lagged copy servers you will deploy in each datacenter.
  - **User Mailbox Configuration** Summarizes the information gathered and computed to design the storage I/O requirements, such as the number of mailboxes in the environment, the number of mailboxes in each database, user mailbox size

on disk, transaction logs generated for each mailbox activity each day, the I/O operations profile for each mailbox, and the read-to-write ratio for each mailbox.

    - **Database Copy Instance Configuration** Summarizes the number of high-availability mailbox database copy instances and lagged database copy instances the solution will have in each DAG or datacenter.
    - **Database Configuration** Summarizes the number of databases in each DAG or datacenter, the recommended number of mailboxes per database, and the available database cache for each mailbox.
    - **Database Copy Configuration** Summarizes the number of database copies that should be deployed on each server, DAG, and datacenter.
- **Active Database Configuration** The two tables in this subsection summarize the number of active databases on each server in each location during normal operation and after single and double server and datacenter failures.
- **Server Configuration** Summarizes the recommended memory and CPU configuration and recommends which type of storage can be used in the configuration.
- **Log, Disk Space, and I/O Requirements** This section summarizes the storage configuration and includes the following tables:
    - **Transaction Log Requirements** Summarizes the number of transaction log files generated per day for each active database, server, DAG, and in total. The average number of transaction log files generated per day as a result of mailbox move operations are also summarized. Finally, the average transaction log files generated per day is the total number of transaction log files generated per day for active database, server, DAG, and in total.
    - **Disk Space Requirements** Summarizes the disk space requirements for the databases and transaction log files. The database, transaction log file, and restore LUN space required is also defined for the solution.
    - **Host I/O Performance Requirements** Summarizes the total required I/O per second needed to sustain during peak load for the database and transaction logs. The percentage of I/O operations that will be read operations is also listed here.
- **Special Notes** Provides additional information about the design, such as when you should use GPT disks, how to configure a mailbox server to control the maximum number of active mailbox databases, and whether the design has more Mailbox servers than are supported in a DAG.

LUN REQUIREMENTS WORKSHEET

The LUN Requirements worksheet provides additional detail on how the LUNs should be sized. No changes should be made on this worksheet so as not to break any of the calculations. The Calculations pane is hidden by default and lists the calculations based on the information specified on the Inputs worksheet. This worksheet has only one subsection, the LUN Requirements Results Pane. This pane is broken into the five tables shown in Figure 13-7.

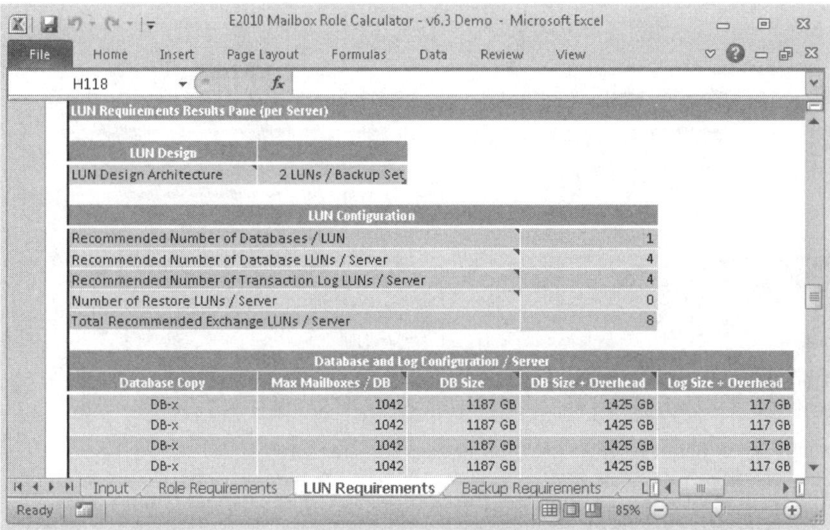

FIGURE 13-7 Mailbox Server Requirements Calculator LUN Requirements

- **LUN Design** Highlights the LUN architecture chosen for this solution. The architecture is derived from the backup type, backup frequency, and high-availability architecture chosen in the Storage Requirements section. Three types of LUN architecture can be used within Exchange 2010: one LUN per database, two LUNs per database, and two LUNs per backup set.
- **LUN Configuration** Summarizes the number of databases that should be placed on a single LUN and the number and purpose of LUNs on each server.
- **Database and Log Configuration/Server** Summarizes the number of database copies on each server, the number of mailboxes per database, the size of each database, and the size required for transaction log files for each database.
- **DB and Log LUN Design/Server** Summarizes the LUN configuration based on LUN design architecture's recommended number of databases per LUN. The LUN size specified in this list includes an additional capacity for content indexing, the configured free space percentage, and whether a restore LUN is used.

BACKUP REQUIREMENTS

The Backup Requirements worksheet provides additional detail on how backups should be configured. No changes should be made on this worksheet so as not to break any of the calculations. The Calculations Pane is hidden by default and lists the calculations based on the information specified on the Inputs worksheet. Only one subsection outlines the appropriate backup design. The two tables in this subsection are shown in Figure 13-8.

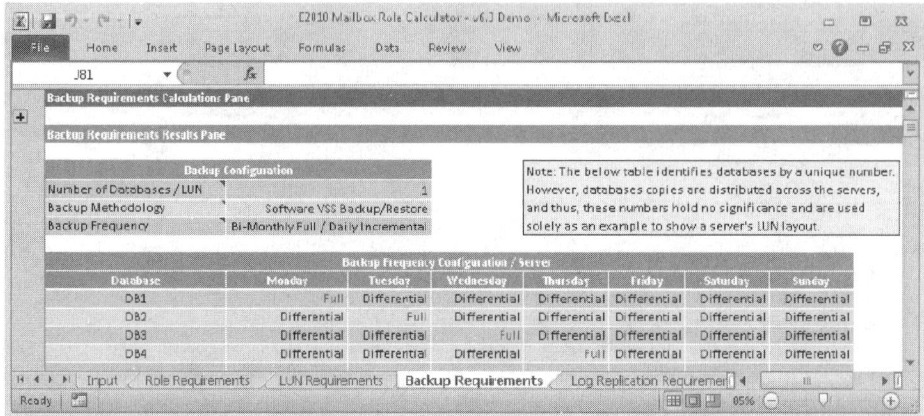

FIGURE 13-8 Mailbox Server Requirements Calculator Backup Requirements

- **Backup Configuration** Summarizes the number of databases that will be placed on a single LUN, the type of backup methodology, and the frequency the backup jobs occur.
- **Backup Frequency Configuration** Summarizes a backup schedule for each server based on the daily full backup or weekly or bi-monthly full backup frequency chosen on the Input worksheet.

LOG REPLICATION REQUIREMENTS

The Log Replication Requirements worksheet provides additional detail about what is required to support transaction log replication. No changes should be made on this worksheet so as not to break any of the calculations. The Calculations Pane is hidden by default and lists the calculations based on the information specified on the Inputs worksheet. This worksheet calculates the throughput required to replicate the transaction logs to each target database copy in the secondary data center. This worksheet has five tables:

- **Peak Log and Content Index Replication Throughput Requirements** Summarizes the peak network throughput required for transaction log replication and content indexing for each database, between datacenters for each DAG, and for the entire environment. This information only takes into account the network traffic generated by the database replication operations and does not take into account database seeding operations, Domain Controller replication, cluster heartbeat and replication, Client Access traffic, or any other application.
- **RPO Log and Content Index Replication Throughput Requirements** Summarizes the network throughput required to meet the RPO for transaction log replication and content indexing for each database, between datacenters for each DAG, and for the entire environment. This information only takes into account the network traffic generated by database seeding operations and database replication operations and does not take into account Domain Controller replication, cluster heartbeat and replication, Client Access traffic, or any other application.

- **Chosen Network Link Suitability** Summarizes the network link configuration that you chose on the Input worksheet and whether it has sufficient capacity to sustain the peak replication or the RPO replication network throughput requirements. If the chosen network link will not sustain the log replication traffic, either the network will need to be changed or the solution should be reconfigured appropriately.
- **Recommended Network Link** Identifies a suitable network link if the network link chosen on the Input worksheet does not meet the peak transaction log replication and RPO throughput requirements.

STORAGE DESIGN

The Storage Design worksheet, shown in Figure 13-9, takes the data from the Input and Storage Requirements worksheets and provides additional information to better determine the number of physical disks needed to support the databases, transaction log files, and restore LUNs. This worksheet is broken into five subsections.

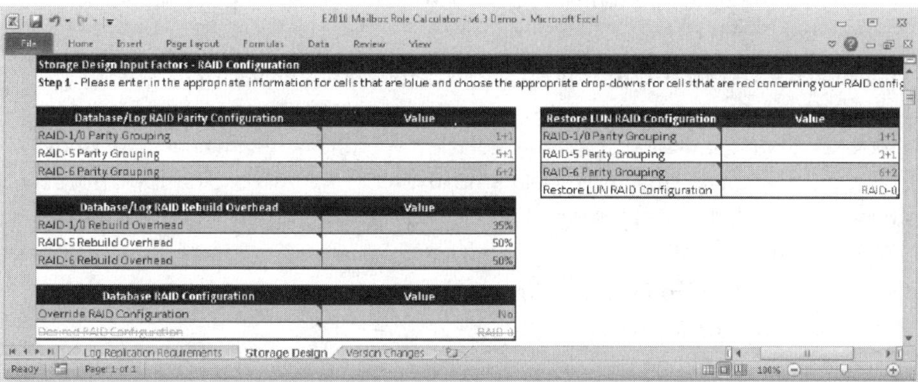

FIGURE 13-9 Mailbox Server Requirements Calculator Backup Requirements Storage Design

Not only is choosing the RAID type important for developing an accurate storage design, but the parity group also plays a factor in the amount of space available, number of effective I/O per second, and the redundancy available. As shown in Figure 13-9, four tables provide inputs to tailor the configuration to accurately reflect the deployed solution:

- **RAID Parity Configuration** Select the RAID parity group for the selected storage solution. A RAID set defines how data and data parity are written to the disks. In a RAID-1/0 data is mirrored between disks. The Mailbox Server Requirement Calculator allows a one-to-one, two-to-two, or four-to-four pairing. With RAID-5 a stripe of data is written to a set of disks and then parity is calculated on a separate disk. In a RAID-5 configuration the calculator allows a ratio of 2:1, where data is striped across two disks and parity is written to the third disk. The calculator allows selection up to 20:1 where data is striped across 20 disks and then parity is calculated and stored on the 21st disk. The higher the ratio, the fewer parity disks are used and the more usable space is available; however, each parity set can only sustain a single disk failure. With RAID-6 a stripe of data is written to a set of disks and then parity is written to two separate disks. The only option in the calculator is for six disks of data and two parity disks.

- **Database/Log RAID Rebuild Overhead** When a disk fails and is replaced in a RAID set the data on the missing data needs to be written to the replaced disk. During this rebuilding process the performance and redundancy of the RAID set is affected because additional I/O and calculations will need to be used to write this rebuilt data. This can affect performance. Because disks will eventually fail, a rebuild is inevitable; therefore, any penalties incurred during rebuild should be planned for in the design. In general, RAID-1/0 implementations have a 25 percent reduction in available performance during a rebuild and most RAID-5 and RAID-6 implementations have a 50 percent performance penalty during a rebuild. It is best to check with your storage vendor and then verify with production testing. Using Jetstress to generate I/O operations and manually failing a disk in the RAID set will allow you to capture information about this performance penalty so that you can properly input that information in this table.
- **Database RAID Configuration** The calculator will automatically recommend either RAID-1/0 or RAID-5 by evaluating capacity and I/O requirements while using the fewest number of disks. This table will allow you to override the database storage recommendation and manually select RAID-0, RAID-1/0, RAID-5, or RAID-6. However, because of performance problems, the calculator will still prevent the use of RAID-5 or RAID-6 with 5.2K, 5.4K, 5.9K, and 7.2K disk types.
- **Restore LUN Configuration** You can select the type of parity and RAID configuration you will be deploying for the Restore LUNs.

RAID Storage Architecture

The RAID Storage Architecture subsection summarizes the servers (primary datacenter servers, secondary datacenter servers, or lagged copy servers) that should be deployed on RAID storage. The RAID Storage Architecture Server table also summarizes the optimal RAID configuration and number of disks for each LUN for each mailbox server, ensuring that performance and capacity requirements are met within the design.

JBOD Storage Architecture

The JBOD Storage Architecture subsection summarizes which servers (primary datacenter servers, secondary datacenter servers, or lagged copy servers) could be deployed on JBOD storage. The JBOD Storage Architecture Server table also recommends the optimal JBOD configuration and number of disks for each LUN for each mailbox server, ensuring that performance and capacity requirements are met within the design.

Total Disks Required

The Total Disks Required subsection provides a shopping list by adding up the number of disks required for a RAID or JBOD configuration for each server, DAG, and environment.

The calculator determines the storage architecture that will use the least number of disks to the support the design. The calculator will also ensure that you have enough data redundancy to meet best practices. For example, the calculator will not recommend a JBOD deployment if you have fewer than three mailbox database copies. You can override the recommendation in this subsection and manually configure the calculator to use JBOD or RAID.

Like any software tool, the calculator does have limitations. Although countless hours have been put into making the calculations accurate and guidance sound, the output is only as good as the input data and the engineer who interpreted and implemented the guidance. After reviewing the suggested configuration, be sure to perform a detailed audit of its suggestions and make adjustments to ensure that the design fits within your business process, the abilities of your support staff, and the financial constraints of your business.

Preproduction Verification

After estimating the number of servers and the storage configuration, and all of the configuration is done, you have made a number of assumptions. To verify that the correct assumptions have been made, you should quantitatively test the hardware. Two tools are provided by Microsoft for you to use to generate a simulated transaction load against the server. Jetstress 2010 is used to simulate the storage I/O generated by an active Exchange Mailbox server. Exchange Load Generator, the second tool, is used to simulate client connections via Outlook, OWA, IMAP4, POP3, and even SMTP against a deployed Exchange server or servers.

Jetstress 2010

As previously mentioned, Jetstress is used to simulate the disk I/O generated for a database on a production Exchange server. It analyzes the server storage I/O performance for Exchange database performance, backup performance, and soft recovery performance. It should be used to validate storage performance and reliability. It cannot validate the client experience or software functionality. The tool specifically simulates the way the Exchange database uses the storage without having to install Exchange and its dependent services. Both a command line (JetstressCmd.exe) and a graphical (JetstressWin.exe) are available.

Each version of Exchange Server has a different storage I/O profile, so it is important to use the latest version of Jetstress and the resource file that matches the version of Exchange you will deploy. The Exchange 2010 version of the tool has the following new features:

- Exchange 2010 Mailbox server I/O requirements have been updated to simulate the improved I/O profile, high-availability transaction log replications, and background database maintenance.
- Multi-case database duplication reduces database copy preparation time.
- Databases and transaction logs can now be placed on the same volume.

Best practice for Jetstress is to use it before deploying Exchange so that performance of the storage design can be validated. Because the purpose of Jetstress is to put stress on the storage, you should not run Jetstress on a production Exchange Server so as to not impact performance.

To install Jetstress, download the latest copy from the Exchange 2010 TechNet site and run the installer. After installing Jetstress you will need to copy the following files into the folder where you installed Jetstress:

- X:\Setup\ServerRoles\Common\ESE.DLL
- X:\<Language>\Setup\Serverroles\Common\Perf\Amd64\<Language>\ESEPERF.DLL
- X:\<Language>\Setup\Serverroles\Common\Perf\Amd64\<Language>\ESEPERF.INI
- X:\Setup\Serverroles\Common\Perf\Amd64\ESEPERF.HXX

If you do not copy these files before running Jetstress you will receive an error similar to the one shown in Figure 13-10.

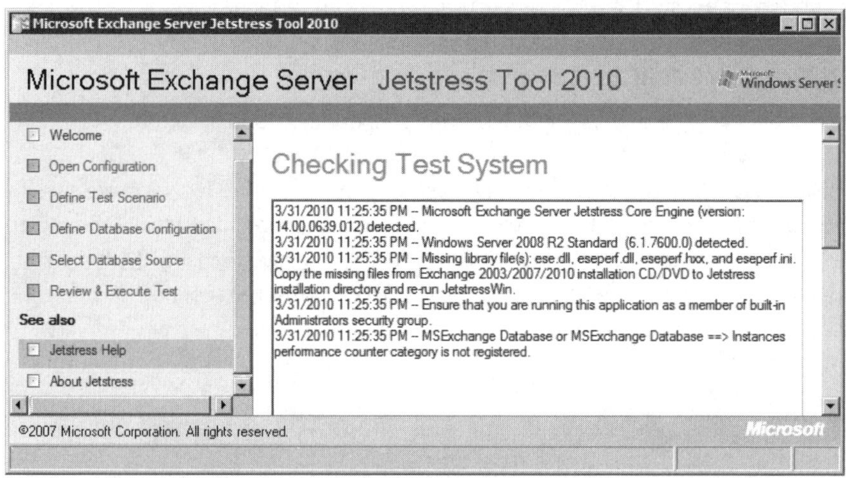

FIGURE 13-10 Starting Jetstress without the required files

If you have already installed Exchange Server, you should still copy the ESE database modules to the Jetstress installation directory; Jetstress requires these files to exist in the installation folder. If you are testing with a different version of Exchange Database Engine than the one installed with Exchange Server, you may have to uninstall the existing Exchange Database Engine counters before you run Jetstress. You can do this by running *unlodctr ESE* at a command prompt with Administrator permissions and then restarting Jetstress.

> ***IMPORTANT*** **Start Jetstress as an administrator if UAC is enabled on the server. This will ensure that Jetstress has the appropriate permission to load performance counters and create databases.**

Running Jetstress starts by defining the test scenario. You can either test disk subsystem throughput or test a specific usage profile. Use the test disk subsystem throughput to determine how the configured storage will perform database transactions, backups, and soft recovery. This is good for testing the storage system limits and when performing a storage reliability test. The mailbox profile test is used to verify a storage configuration by inputting information about the number of mailboxes, the estimated IOPS/mailbox, and the average mailbox size, as shown in Figure 13-11. Automatic tuning will attempt to adjust the number of process threads to be able to generate the required I/O; however, in some cases automatic tuning does not provide enough threads, so you can manually assign the number of threads. Adding threads can improve the amount of I/O throughput; however, having too many threads may increase I/O latency.

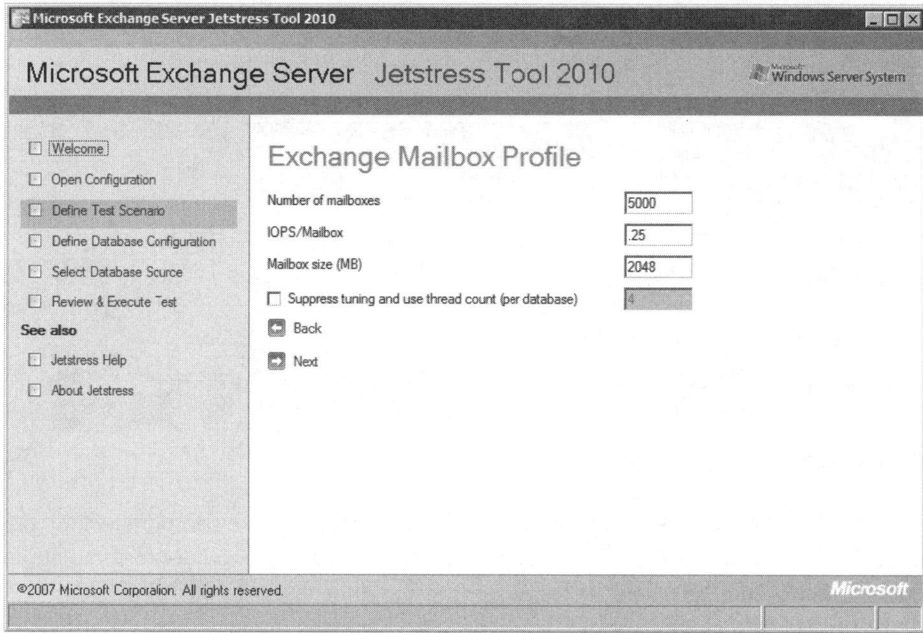

FIGURE 13-11 Setting Mailbox Profile information

After selecting the I/O profile information, you must choose one the following test types:

- **Performance** This option will simulate normal Exchange database operations.
- **Database Backup** This option will measure the performance of a backup operation.
- **Soft Recovery** This option will measure the rate at which transaction logs can be replayed.

At this point in the configuration, you must also choose to enable a multi-host test and whether to simulate background database maintenance. If you are testing storage for a DAG server and plan to leave background database scanning enabled, both of these options should be enabled.

The next step is to choose a test duration of between 2 and 24 hours. To ensure that the storage system has had ample opportunity to normalize disk cache and to ensure storage stability, a full validation should run for at least eight hours.

The next step in configuring Jetstress is setting up the disk configuration, as shown in Figure 13-12. You must define the number of databases to create, how many copies to create, and the disks each database and transaction log should be stored on. With Jetstress 2010, you can store the transaction logs and databases on the same disks; however, you cannot store more than one database or set of transaction logs on the same disk.

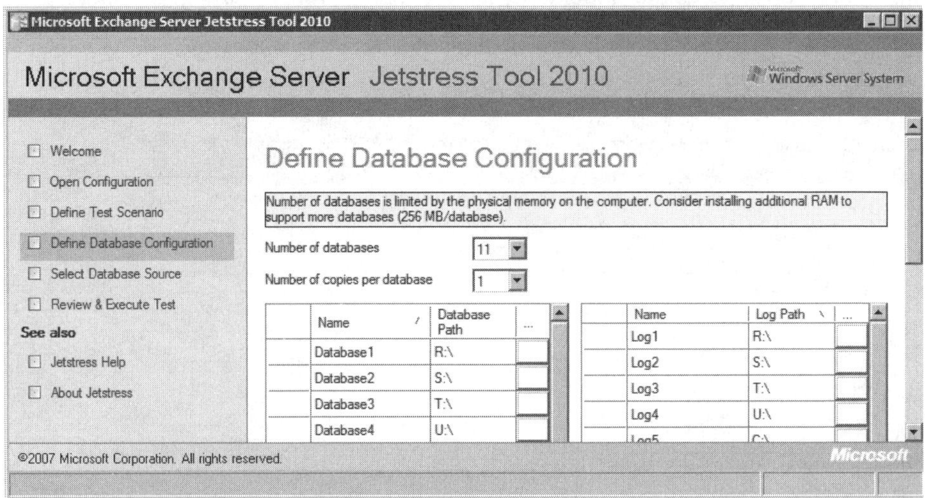

FIGURE 13-12 Defining the database configuration

The test preparation will create and attach the database files with the appropriate configuration for your test criteria. The test preparation can take a few minutes to complete. After preparation is complete, you can execute the test and then wait for the results. At the end of the test, a test summary is shown, an XML-based file is generated with the results, an HTML file is generated as a report, and the Windows Application and System log are saved for review, as shown in Figure 13-13.

The HTML report contains valuable information about whether the test was successful and about the performance metrics attributed to the storage tests. Review the report with a storage subject matter expert (SME) to ensure that performance does not exceed acceptable thresholds. The storage SME may be able to suggest configuration changes as well as thresholds specific to the type of storage. For example, the storage read and write average latencies should all be below 25 ms; otherwise, this indicates that the storage is not able to keep up with the I/O requirements. If the test shows that this threshold was exceeded, changes to the configuration or user profile may be required. For more information about performance counters and how to monitor Exchange see Chapter 17, "Operating and Troubleshooting Exchange 2010."

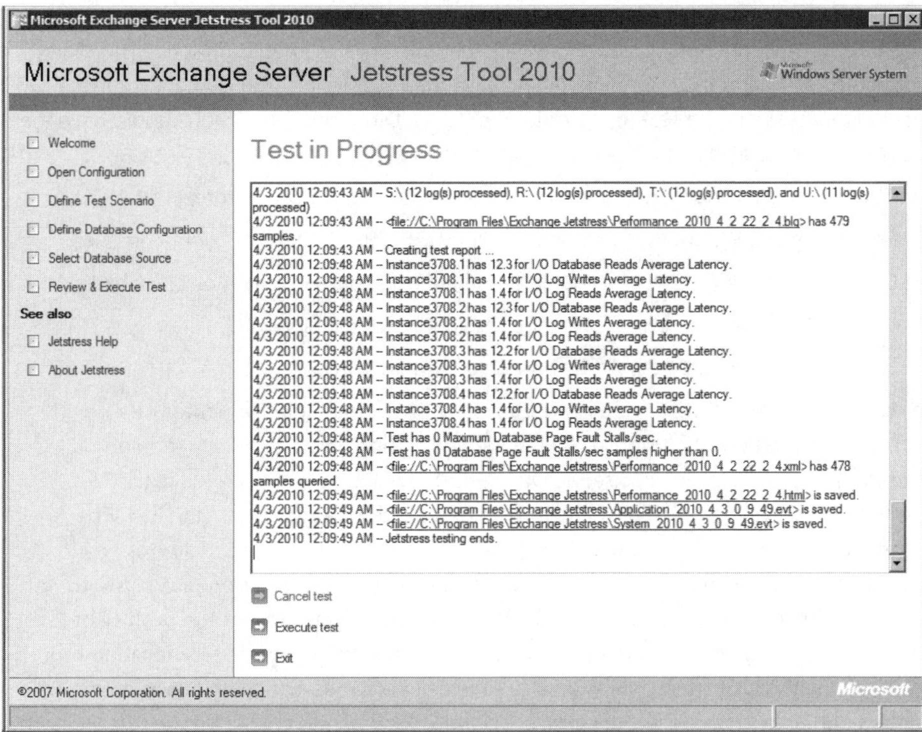

FIGURE 13-13 Jetstress test results

Exchange Load Generator 2010

Exchange Load Generator is the only supported load generator for Exchange. It replaces Loadsim and Exchange Server Stress and Performance (ESP). Exchange Load Generator has a UI and a command-line interface as well as task-based and scripted simulation modes. The existing modules can test a variety of clients and protocols, including:

- Outlook 2003/2007 (online and cached)
- Post Office Protocol (POP3)
- Internet Message Access Protocol (IMAP4)
- Simple Mail Transfer Protocol (SMTP)
- OWA
- ActiveSync

Unlike Jetstress, Exchange Load Generator requires a fully functional Exchange 2010 server environment as well as a client computer to generate the load for the Exchange servers. Load Generator should not be run in a production environment because it requires mailboxes to be created for the test, and because it generates significant client load on the Exchange servers and domain controllers that may cause noticeable performance degradation. If Exchange is already deployed in the environment, you can configure Load Generator to only generate load against non-production servers. However, test objects are created in Active Directory to support the tests and may significantly increase the load against the domain controllers in the site. If you must run the test in a production Active Directory forest, you should have the Exchange servers located in a different Active Directory site.

The Exchange 2010 Load Generation tools have a number of new features:

- Requires Vista, Windows 7, or Windows 2008 OS (SP2/R2) for the client computer.
- Does not require the Exchange Management Tools to be installed on the client.
- Does not require message files—they are created dynamically.
- Load is now generated for Active Directory connections.

To create a new test profile, install and then start Exchange Load Generator as an Administrator on the client computer. The initial test settings include information about the test duration, the domain name, a service account that will be used to create mailboxes, the password that will be used for the test mailboxes, and the logging level that will be captured. The next step allows you to select the location and number of mailboxes, contacts, and distribution lists to create as well as the type of client software to simulate, as shown in Figure 13-14. The user test groups that you define here should represent the profiles of the user that will be using Exchange in a production in environment. If you are simulating more than 1,500 simultaneous users, you will need to install Exchange Load Generator on multiple computers and then enable remote control. This will allow you to configure the master load generator to distribute the workload to multiple servers, which allows you to coordinate a larger number of users.

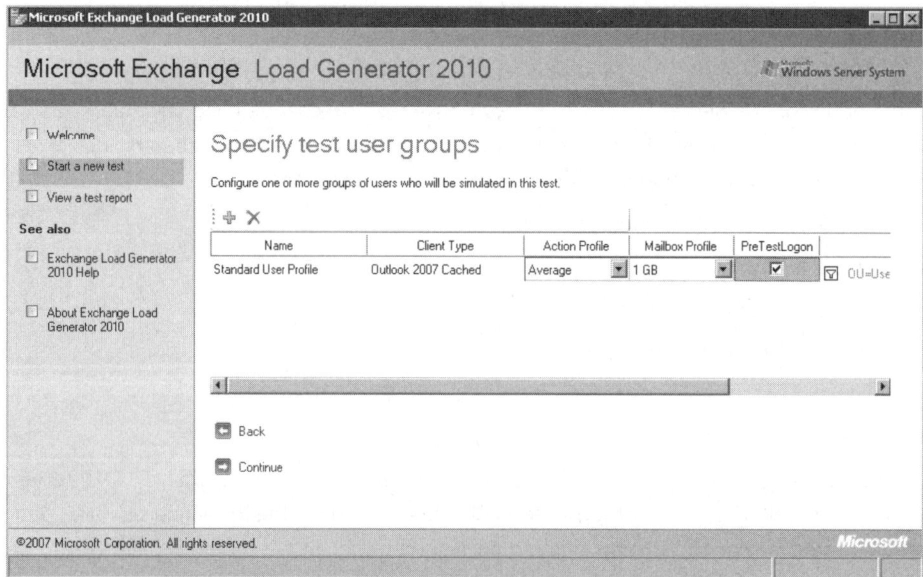

FIGURE 13-14 Specifying test settings

After the test parameters have been set you must initialize the test environment. The initialization process will create the mailboxes, distribution lists, contacts, and other objects needed to complete the tests.

Exchange Load Generator does not have a method for collecting information about the performance of the Exchange environment. It does, however, add a number of performance counters to the client computer to monitor the progress of the tests. All other performance monitoring should be done using Performance Monitor or another monitoring tool to determine how well the server is performing under load and whether performance is acceptable.

After initialization has completed, be sure to start any monitoring tools needed and then run the simulation you have defined. At the end of the simulation you will be provided with a summary report to review and verify that the test ran correctly. Be sure to verify that the tests ran correctly and review the performance data collected with a server hardware and performance SME to pinpoint any bottlenecks or other issues.

Scale Up or Scale Out

You have two fundamental choices when it comes to scaling a server infrastructure: scale up or scale out? Scaling up is the path of creating more robust single solutions with more resources. In its simplest form this includes adding memory or disk into a server. As a solution is scaled up, it becomes more costly and a single failure can impact more mailboxes and more transactions. As you add more mailboxes, you must also add more processing, memory, and storage to support these mailboxes. To fulfill these requirements as you scale up the density and speed of processors, memory and storage also need to increase.

Scaling out is the process of adding servers with the needed hardware to provide additional resources. Simply put, this might entail adding a second Mailbox sever to host additional mailboxes. Scaling out is usually done with lower-cost hardware and allows failure risk to be spread across more servers.

For example, take Litware's Fresno datacenter, where they are considering deploying 25,000 mailboxes on 10 Mailbox servers. Each Mailbox server would host 2,500 active mailboxes. If Litware chooses to scale up the Mailboxes servers and only deploy 5, each server would host 5,000 active mailboxes. Scaling up each server would require twice as many resources available and adds to the hardware cost. If a failure of the server occurs, twice as many mailboxes will be affected. The Exchange Mailbox Role Calculator estimates this scale-up deployment requires roughly 15,000 megacycles and 48 GB of RAM for each server. It also estimates the scale-out server configuration requires only 8,500 megacycles and 32 GB of RAM. Using list prices, the scale-up server configuration with more processors and memory costs almost 40 percent more than the scale-out configuration. If you take into account the software cost associated with scaling out, the price difference begins to even out. The more servers deployed, the more software licensing needed to support them; even so, the total capital cost of this example is still lower for the scale-out configuration.

If you would rather scale up servers in your environment, best practice is not to scale up a single Mailbox server to host 100,000 mailboxes; instead, you should host a reasonable number of mailboxes on the server and then add additional Exchange roles, such as Hub Transport and Client Access Server roles. Be sure to verify the sizing suggestions for multiple role server deployments later in this chapter. Another way many choose to scale up is to use virtualization to make full use of the underlying hardware. This solution, which is also covered in greater detail later in this chapter, should be approached with caution to ensure that the right decisions are made. In the case of a scale-up or a scale-out solution, it is important to validate the configuration in a test lab using tools such as Exchange Load Generator and Jetstress.

Sizing Guidelines

As you have read through this chapter you have probably noticed the emphasis on performing testing and sizing exercises in your own environment. Not every individual configuration has a concise and clear answer. As the number of processor cores increase, memory densities rise, and storage costs change, so do the specifics of a configuration. But don't worry, plenty of guidelines will do just that—guide you to a configuration that meets your needs.

The basic supported hardware requirements for installing Exchange server are:

- An x64-based processor
- Minimum of 4 GB of RAM
- Page file equal to the physical memory plus 10 MB
- Minimum of 1.2 GB of NTFS formatted disk space:
  - Additional 500 MB for each Unified Messaging language pack
  - Additional 200 MB of disk space free on the system disk
  - Additional 500 MB of free space to store the Transport queue database
- Minimum of 800 × 600 pixel screen to manage and install Exchange
- System Partition and partitions that store the Exchange binary files, the transaction logs files, the database files all formatted with NTFS

Processor Type

Exchange 2010 will only run on Windows Server 2008 x64 or Windows Server 2008 R2, which requires an x64-compatible processor. Intel processors support x64 with the Intel Extended Memory 64 Technology and AMD processors support x64 with AMD64. The x64 versions of Windows Server do not run on Intel Itanium-based processors and therefore Exchange 2010 is not supported on Itanium-based processors.

Processor Scalability

In recent years the number of gigahertz has not changed considerably; however, the number of processors cores on a chip has gone from 1 to 12 with even more on the horizon. These cores on the same chip often are on the same silicon wafer and share cache between them, making them far more efficient and faster than if the cores were in separate sockets on the motherboard. Although not instantaneous, core-to-core communication on a single processor is faster than when processors have to communicate between sockets. Another reason that more sockets does not necessary mean more performance for Exchange is that in multi-processor configurations with a Non-Uniform Memory Access (NUMA) architecture each socket has a bank of locally accessible memory and an integrated memory controller. To access memory attached to another processor's memory controller, the two processors must communicate, which adds latency to the request. Local memory is faster than memory attached to another processor, which can greatly improve application performance. To take advantage of the NUMA architecture an application must be NUMA-aware and must understand how to keep processes and its associated memory localized within a NUMA node, the local processor, and local memory. Exchange 2010 is not NUMA-aware; therefore, it does not optimize processes within a NUMA node for added performance. Adding NUMA nodes (usually by adding processor sockets) can actually reduce performance because the more NUMA nodes, the more likely remote memory will need to be accessed by Exchange. This also provides an additional reason to scale out rather than scale up.

With Intel Hyper-Threading Technology the processor provides the ability to schedule more parallel computations by presenting two virtual CPUs for every physical processor core to the operating system. Because there is only one physical processor, portions of the core must be shared when executing processes. Hyper-Threading, much like NUMA, is best exploited when an application is written specifically to take advantage of the technology. Also consider that if you have an 8-core, 3.0-GHz processor with Hyper-Threading enabled you may assume that you have a potential of 48 GHz (3 GHz × 8 Cores × 8 Hyper-Threaded cores) to execute processes. However, the physical core and the Hyper-Threaded core cannot execute a process at the same time, so this 48-GHz maximum can never be fully reached. And as discussed earlier, when trending performance—especially when working with percentages—it may be misleading that the server is reporting 25 percent CPU utilization with Hyper-Threading enabled, because a portion of that 25 percent is Hyper-Threaded resources. How effectively Hyper-Threading can execute the scheduled workload depends on the actual usage percentage of the CPU. As the processor becomes busier, Hyper-Threading becomes less effective—each virtual processor will be requesting resources, offering twice as many parallel requests for the same resources than without Hyper-Threading enabled. Exchange is designed to scale out efficiently, but you may experience diminishing returns when additional processors are added to the server. That is not to imply that Hyper-Threading is not a worthwhile option. Many workloads optimized for it—including virtualization—may benefit from Hyper-Threading. If you choose to enable Hyper-Threading in your environment, perform testing using Exchange Load Generator to determine the effects of enabling Hyper-Threading on performance and on how performance monitoring changes.

Processor Guidelines

Given all of these choices, you may have trouble determining where to start. Table 13-2 summarizes best practices for choosing the number of processors and processor cores. As shown in the table, you can exceed the recommended maximums and still have a supported configuration; however, you should expect diminishing returns in performance for the additional cost.

TABLE 13-2 Exchange Server Role Processor Recommendations

SERVER ROLE	MINIMUM NUMBER OF PROCESSOR CORES	MAXIMUM RECOMMENDED PROCESSOR SOCKETS	MAXIMUM RECOMMENDED CORES
Client Access	2	2	24
Edge Transport	1	2	24
Hub Transport	1	2	24
Mailbox	2	2	24
Unified Messaging	2	2	12
Client Access & Hub Transport	2	2	24
Client Access, Hub Transport & Mailbox	2	4	48

Processor Ratio Guidelines

Often a configuration will start with sizing out the number and configuration of the Mailbox servers. This makes sense because much of the cost associated with an Exchange deployment will be based on the amount and type of storage needed to support the Mailbox servers. To approximately gauge the number of other servers you will need, you can use a couple of ratios. These ratios work because of how closely the roles work together. To connect to a mailbox via MAPI or any other protocol, the client must connect to a Client Access Server. To be able to send or receive any e-mail messages, the Hub Transport server must be used. Any mail routing or address lookup activity requires communication with a domain controller. Table 13-3 summarizes the general guidance for processor cores of similar speed needed on server roles in the same Active Directory site. You can read more about selecting processors for your Exchange servers at *http://technet.microsoft.com/en-us/library/dd346699.aspx.*

TABLE 13-3 Processor Core Ratios

ROLES	PROCESSOR CORE RATIO
Client Access Server : Mailbox server	3:4
Hub Transport server : Mailbox server	1:5 (with Exchange-based antivirus installed) 1:7 (no Exchange-based antivirus installed)
Global Catalog server : Mailbox server	1:4 (with 32-bit GCs) 1:8 (with 64-bit GCs)

Memory

Another factor in properly sizing an Exchange server is the performance and amount of memory installed. Exchange 2010 is a 64-bit program, so it can use more than 3 GB of memory as a working set and to cache data. Not having enough memory will cause the page file to be heavily used, resulting in higher load on both the processor and the storage I/O; having too much memory is a costly mistake.

When determining the type of server and the amount of memory to purchase it is important to understand the memory architecture options available. As mentioned in the previous section, Exchange is not NUMA-aware, meaning it cannot take advantage of the benefits provided by a NUMA-based configuration.

Nonetheless, the speed, density, and configuration of memory on an Exchange server is extremely important. When choosing memory be sure to pick a server platform that has enough memory slots to handle the upper end of the amount of memory you will need during the server's life cycle. For example, if you decide that you need 8 GB of RAM today and will need to grow to 32 GB within 2 years, be sure that the server will be able meet your needs. In many cases the more memory DIMMS in the same memory channel the slower the memory must run. In most modern server platforms the following best practices should be followed:

- Purchase memory to match the CPU memory speed.
- Evenly distribute memory across memory channels.
- Always use memory with ECC to protect against memory errors.
- Read and follow the server manufacturer guidelines closely on selecting and installing memory.

Each of the Exchange server roles has specific memory requirements that also must be met to provide optimal performance. Table 13-4 summarizes the recommended memory configuration for each of the roles.

TABLE 13-4 Exchange Server Memory Recommendations

SERVER ROLE	MINIMUM SUPPORTED (GB)	RECOMMENDED (GB)
Client Access	4	2 GB per core (at least 8 GB)
Edge Transport	4	1 GB per core
Hub Transport	4	1 GB per core
Mailbox	4	4 GB plus mailbox database cache
Unified Messaging	4	2 GB per core
Client Access & Hub Transport	4	2 GB per core (at least 8 GB)
Client Access, Hub Transport & Mailbox	10	6 GB plus 1 GB per core plus mailbox database cache

More information about sizing the mailbox database cache can be found in the "Mailbox Role" section later in this chapter.

To have a supported Exchange deployment the server must be configured with a page file of the size of the amount of memory in the server plus 10 MB. Although this may seem to be an odd recommendation, there is good reason for it. Although it might seem to indicate that a crash dump file can be created to troubleshoot server errors, this is not the case because the recommendation is to store the page file on a RAID-protected disk dedicated for the page file, separate from the system drive. When the page file is not stored on the system disk it cannot be used to generate the crash dump file. On the other hand, this recommendation does segregate storage I/O to the page file from the I/O generated by the operating system and thus minimizes I/O contention and improves performance. Although the guideline states that the page file should be 10 MB more than the memory, you may need to adjust the size. To be sure your page file is sized correctly, monitor the following performance counters:

- **Memory\Available Bytes** This number should never be less than 4 MB.
- **Memory\Pages Input/Sec** This number should be fewer than 10 pages.
- **Memory\Pages/sec** This number will vary greatly depending on server load. You should establish a baseline specific to your environment; however, this should generally be below 1,000.
- **Paging File\%Usage** This number should be less than 70 percent.
- **Paging File\%Usage Peak** This number should be less than 70 percent.

Network Configuration

Each Exchange server should be configured with at least two 1 Gbps Network adapters that are teamed for redundancy. If iSCSI storage is used, a separate adapter should be dedicated for iSCSI communication. Mailbox servers in a DAG should have at least one additional adapter connected to a separate network to support cluster communication and replication. More information about configuring a highly available DAG can be found in Chapter 11.

The previous information set the guidelines for all of the Exchange server roles. The next sections cover each component in an Exchange deployment in more detail.

Domain Controllers

Domain controllers provide a critical component in an Exchange environment. Not having appropriately sized or too few domain controllers can wreak havoc on Exchange performance, causing e-mail message delivery delays, global address list lookups, and other issues.

For each Active Directory site with Exchange 2010 deployed, follow these guidelines:

- Have at least one global catalog server running at least Windows Server 2003 SP2. Two global catalog servers should be deployed to provide redundancy.
- The domain controllers should have at least 400 MB of storage for every 1,000 user accounts in the domain to store the database.

- Have at least 500 MB of additional space for SYSVOL and 500 MB of free space to store Active Directory transaction log files.
- Active Directory files should be protected with RAID redundancy to minimize the risk associated with a disk failure.

The key to memory sizing for domain controllers is to provide enough memory to be able to cache the entire Active Directory database in memory. If the Active Directory database is 2.75 GB or more, a 64-bit version of Windows Server should be used on the domain controller to provide enough memory for cache. Just as with the Exchange Mailbox server, when enough memory is provided the storage I/O is minimized and performance is optimized. If the domain controllers will also be hosting DNS, additional resources will be required to support these roles.

In many cases it is desirable to create a dedicated Active Directory site for the Exchange servers and the associated domain controllers. This effectively separates user login activities from Exchange domain activities. If this is not possible, the domain controllers will be authenticating logins for client computers, which can impact the performance of Exchange activities, especially during peak hours.

In general, in an Active Directory site dedicated to Exchange, you should plan to have one processor core on a 32-bit global catalog server for every four similar in speed processor cores on the Mailbox server in the site. When using 64-bit global catalog servers, plan to have one processor core for every eight Mailbox server processor cores. In an Active Directory site with six Mailbox servers, each with two 8-core processors, you should consider starting with three 32-bit global catalog servers, each with two 4-core processors or three 64-bit global catalog servers, each with one 4-core processor.

Hub and Edge Transport Roles

Servers with more processor cores can be efficiently used when the Hub Transport server is configured to use antivirus and anti-spam. Processor utilization is based on several factors, such as message rate, average message size, number of enabled transport agents, antivirus configuration, and third-party applications.

The Hub Transport has an increased workload in Exchange 2010 with the addition of shadow redundancy, changes to the queue database format, and compliance and retention features.

Because the Hub Transport stores the message queues in an ESE database, you should follow the memory guidelines earlier in this section to have ample database cache to minimize the disk I/O required. Another way to minimize I/O requirements is to store the queue database on a RAID-protected volume separate from the operating system. If you store the mail queue and the transaction logs on a disk attached to a RAID controller with battery-backed write cache enabled, the write cache allows transaction log writes to occur in cache rather than having to wait for the disk to acknowledge the writes. Caching these sequential transaction log writes reduces the number of IOPS the disks need to be able to sustain. The write cache needs to be battery-backed so that in case of a power failure, any data still in cache can be saved and written to disk when the power is restored.

In Exchange 2010, shadow redundancy protects e-mail in transit so that in the event of a Transport server failure, the previous server can resubmit any messages lost. In larger environments that have a number of Hub Transport servers in the same site, you may equip the Hub Transport servers with JBOD storage rather than using RAID. Deploying a Hub Transport server without RAID should only be done when every path to and from the site has multiple servers available. When considering this type of configuration, be sure to evaluate potential failure scenarios both inside and outside the Active Directory site to be sure you have no risk of data loss. Because many inbound e-mail transport agents on the Internet do not currently support shadow redundancy, it is not recommended that you deploy inbound Edge Transport servers on JBOD.

The amount of storage required for the transport queues on a Hub Transport server varies greatly in the number of messages sent or received each day, the number of days that transaction logs are kept, and whether protocol logging is enabled. To calculate how much storage each Hub Transport server needs, you need to determine the maximum number of messages you will queue in the site. When Hub Transport servers are not used to send or receive e-mail directly to the Internet, message queuing should be minimal in a functional environment. Sizing the storage for the queue database needs to take into account failure situations, so that when a failure elsewhere occurs the transport server can remain operational.

To calculate the maximum size of the queue database, take the average size of e-mail messages, multiply by the maximum number of queued messages you expect to handle, and then add about 20 percent to account for variance and database overhead. The maximum number of messages you will queue should be based on the length of time you plan to sustain delivery failures. If you want to sustain 24 hours of delivery failure, multiply the average message size by the number of messages sent and received.

As an example, Litware has an Active Directory site where 100,000 messages traverse the site daily, with an average message size of 100 KB. In this case, the queue database would need 12 GB (100,000 messages × 100 KB × 1.20 overhead) of space to store the database to sustain failure for up to one day. You also need to take into account space for the transport dumpster, which can be up to 18 MB for every mailbox database in the Active Directory site. If you have 100 active mailbox databases in a site, the transport dumpster could grow as high as 1.8 GB on each Hub Transport server. The maximum number of messages that can be queued on a Hub Transport server is 500,000. Therefore, if you need to be able to queue more than 500,000 messages in a single Active Directory site, you need to add more Hub Transport servers.

Finally, when sizing storage for a Hub Transport server, you need to account for storing message tracking and protocol logs. If you have an Exchange deployment today, use the average sizes from the current deployment. If you do not have a previous deployment, assume roughly .5 KB for each message sent or received for the message tracking logs. In the preceding example this would be 500 MB of message tracking logs generated each day. By default, message tracking logs are kept for seven days, meaning that in our example up to 3.5 GB of message tracking logs could be stored on the Hub Transport server. Protocol, Agent, and Connectivity logs store information about SMTP communication and also vary depending on the size, number, and type of messages delivered. In this example we estimated 2 GB of logs each day, and we need to maintain those logs for up to seven days for a total of 14 GB of disk space. To summarize, Litware requires:

- 12 GB for the queue data
- 500 MB of required free disk place
- 1.8 GB for the maximum transport dumpster
- 3.5 GB of message tracking logs
- 14 GB for protocol and connectivity logs

This 31.8 GB of storage is in addition to storage needed for the operating system and Exchange installation files.

Sizing Edge Transport server storage is similar to sizing storage for the Hub Transport server. However, the Edge Transport server is the ingress and egress for Internet-based e-mail, so additional time should be allowed for Internet service failures, additional space for quarantined messages, and additional storage for the Active Directory Lightweight Directory Services (AD LDS) database that stores the Edge Transport configuration. Edge Transport servers are also usually configured with antivirus and anti-spam scanning, which can add considerable processor load to the server. However, Edge Transport servers do not have a transport dumpster; therefore, sizing does not need to account for it. Use the following best practices for planning the hardware for Transport servers:

- Use 4 to 16 processor cores, up to two sockets.
- Use 4 to 8 GB of RAM or 1 GB per core.
- Use battery-backed write cache disk controller to minimize transaction log I/O requirements.
- Before deploying on JBOD, carefully evaluate I/O requirements and any potential failure points.
- Calculate the maximum length of time a failure needs to be sustained and size the mailbox and transport dumpster accordingly.
- For Hub Transport servers, use one processor core for every five Mailbox server processor cores if Exchange-based antivirus is installed; use seven if no Exchange-based antivirus is installed.

Client Access Server Role

In Exchange 2010, the Client Access Server role plays a much larger part in the architecture, now that most of the client-specific functions are handled by this server role. For example, Outlook communicates with Client Access Server to be able to connect to a mailbox. Processor-intensive activities such as rendering OWA and converting MAPI messages for non-MAPI clients are also handled by the Client Access Server role. This new functionality means that the Client Access servers require more resources than they did in Exchange 2007.

The minimum amount of memory for a Client Access server is 4 GB; however, 2 GB for each processor core installed in the server with a minimum of 8 GB is recommended. Although two processor cores are the minimum required, at least four processors cores are recommended for smaller deployments; however, since non-MAPI clients require more processor cycles, additional processor cores may be required.

The increased processor requirement for the Client Access Server role reduces the ratio of processor cores needed compared to Mailbox server processor cores in the same site. The new ratio is three Client Access processor cores for every four similar speed processors cores in the Mailbox servers in the same Active Directory site.

Use the following best practices when planning the hardware for Client Access servers:

- Use 4 to 16 processor cores, up to two sockets.
- Use 8 to 16 GB of RAM or 2 GB per core.
- Use three processor cores for every four Mailbox server processor cores.

Mailbox Role

The recommended configuration for the Mailbox server role is based predominantly on mailbox count and the user profile. Two processors, each with four, six, eight, and now even twelve processor cores can provide a good balance between price and performance. As discussed at the beginning of this chapter, sizing Mailbox servers requires an understanding of the average user profile. This profile includes the number, type, and size of messages sent and received and the average storage I/O each mailbox needs.

Memory Requirements

Basic memory configurations for each server role were discussed earlier in this chapter. One of the variables that makes sizing memory on the Mailbox server more complicated is the mailbox database cache. The mailbox database cache is the memory used to cache database I/O operations. Having ample mailbox database cache will minimize the required storage I/O. To estimate the mailbox database cache requirements, multiply the number of mailbox copies and the average I/O calculated for each mailbox and then multiply by 50 MB/IOP to obtain the amount of optimal database cache for the calculated user profile. For example: 2750 Mailboxes * 0.120 IOPS/Mailbox * 50 MB/IOPS = 16,500 MB.

> ***NOTE*** **Fifty MB/IOP is calculated from performance guidelines published by Microsoft. For more information about the Exchange mailbox database cache and other ways to estimate the optimal mailbox database cache visit** ***http://technet.microsoft.com/en-us/library/ee832793.aspx.***

After determining the amount of mailbox database cache, you must determine the amount of physical memory required. To determine the amount of physical memory required to satisfy the mailbox database cache required use the information in Table 13-5.

TABLE 13-5 Exchange Mailbox Database Cache

PHYSICAL MEMORY (GB)	MAILBOX ROLE ONLY: MAILBOX DATABASE CACHE (GB)	MULTIPLE ROLE: MAILBOX DATABASE CACHE (GB)
4	1	Not Supported
8	3.6	2
16	10.4	8
24	17.6	14
32	24.4	20
48	39.2	32
64	53.6	44
96	82.4	68
128	111.2	92

To provide 16,500 MB of cache for the preceding example, according to the table the physical server should have 24 GB of memory to provide 17.6 GB of mailbox database cache.

For more information about sizing memory for Exchange 2010 visit *http://technet.microsoft.com/en-us/library/dd346700.aspx*.

Storage Requirements

Although many of these concepts are wrapped in the Mailbox Server Role Requirements Calculator, it is also important to understand how it calculates the requirements. One of the decisions that you need to make is whether you want to use a SAN, or direct attached storage (DAS). If you choose to use DAS, you also have the option of configuring storage as JBOD or with RAID protection. This decision should be made based on the level of redundancy in the Exchange configuration, operational maturity, and storage performance. For example if you already have a SAN in place and you plan to deploy a DAG, storing all database copies in the DAG on the SAN still has the SAN as a single point of failure. In some environments this may be an acceptable risk because of the redundancy for the SAN. On the other hand, a greater level of redundancy may be achieved at a lower cost by using a DAS solution with local RAID. If you have decided to use a DAS configuration and you have planned for at least three copies of each database, do you also need to have a RAID-configured storage system? For a more thorough discussion of risk management and storage options, please see Chapter 11.

Mailbox data stored on disk that is not equal to the amount of data that Outlook reports is stored inside a user's mailbox because there is some additional overhead. To estimate the maximum size a mailbox would consume on disk, add the mailbox limit and whitespace and the dumpster size. Whitespace is the transient data in the mailbox that may take up space temporarily on disk but is shortly deleted. Whitespace can be estimated to be roughly the size of messages sent and received each day. A user profile that sends and receives 100 messages a day with an average size of 100 KB each would have an estimated whitespace of about 10 MB.

Calculating the size of the dumpster depends on the features enabled. Deleted item retention is figured simply by multiplying the average size of messages sent and received each day by the length of the retention period. If you enable Single Item Recovery, an additional 1.2 percent of the mailbox size needs to be added to the size on disk. If you leave calendar version logging enabled you must also add an additional 5.8 percent of the mailbox size.

For a mailbox with a 1,024 MB limit that has roughly 10 MB of changes each day, a 21-day retention window, and Single Item Recovery, the size would be roughly 210 MB. Add to that 12.3 MB (1,024 MB mailbox limit × 1.2 percent) for Single Item Recovery and 59.4 MB (1,024 MB mailbox limit × 5.8 percent) for calendar version logging to estimate the dumpster to be 281.7 MB. The maximum size for the 1,024 MB mailbox in this scenario would be roughly 1,317 MB (1,024 MB mailbox limit + 10 MB whitespace + 281.7 MB dumpster) on disk.

DATABASE SIZE

Deciding how large to make mailbox databases should be based on service level agreements (SLAs), whether the database will be in a DAG, and the type of storage you will be using. The primary factor for determining the maximum database size should be the service level agreement that needs to be met. In the case of a database failure you need to be able to restore mailbox data. If the damaged database has multiple copies within the DAG, recovery is instantaneous; however, you will need time to reseed the failed database copy. If the database is not highly available, recovery may need to be done from a backup copy. If the SLA requires an outage not last more than four hours, you must be able to restore the database from backup within the SLA. If you can restore 100 GB each hour from backup the database should be 400 GB smaller to be able to meet the SLA. However in a DAG with at least two copies of each database, it is still not recommended to have databases larger than 2 TB. Finally, if you are planning to use a JBOD configuration, you want to make sure that the database is small enough to leave room for transaction logs, content indexing, and other growth. If you were to use a 1.5-TB SATA drive for storing a mailbox database copy, you would want to size the database to leave room for transaction logs and content indexes.

When the maximum database size is chosen, the number of mailboxes in each database can be determined. For Litware's deployment the maximum database size has been set to be 500 GB; each database can have 379 (500 GB maximum database size / 1,317 MB mailbox size = 379 Mailboxes) of the 1,024 MB mailboxes mentioned earlier.

TRANSACTION LOGS

Transaction log files capture all changes that are made to each database. The number of transaction logs generated each depends on the number and size of changes made to the database. In cases where a backup-less configuration is deployed, circular logging should be enabled so that transaction log files are truncated after the data has been committed to each database in the DAG. For more information on backup-less environments and database recovery see Chapter 12. In cases where circular logging is not enabled, transaction logs accumulate until they are truncated with either a full or an incremental backup. In these cases, you must estimate the number of transaction logs that will be generated between successful backups so that enough storage can be provisioned. Table 13-6 shows an estimate of the number of transaction log files that will be generated depending on the average message size and the number of messages sent and received each day.

TABLE 13-6 Estimated Number of Transaction Log Files Generated per Day for Specific User Profiles

NUMBER OF MESSAGES SENT AND RECEIVED PER DAY	NUMBER OF LOG TRANSACTION LOGS (75 KB AVERAGE MESSAGE SIZE)	NUMBER OF LOG TRANSACTION LOGS (100 KB AVERAGE MESSAGE SIZE)	NUMBER OF LOG TRANSACTION LOGS (150 KB AVERAGE MESSAGE SIZE)	NUMBER OF LOG TRANSACTION LOGS (300 KB AVERAGE MESSAGE SIZE)
50	10	13	19	38
100	20	26	38	76
150	30	40	57	114
200	40	53	76	152
250	50	66	95	190
300	60	79	114	228
350	70	92	133	266
400	80	105	152	304
450	90	119	171	342
500	100	132	190	380

In some cases hardware problems or maintenance activities will cause backup jobs to not run or complete within the backup window. When this occurs transaction logs may not be truncated and will continue to accumulate. As a best practice, enough space should be available to sustain at least two failed backup attempts. Finally, as best practice, to provide for a margin of error or unexpected growth be sure to size an additional 20 percent of additional space.

For Litware's deployment with databases with 379 mailboxes that send and receive an average of 100 messages each day with an average size of 100 KB, each mailbox will generate around 26 transaction logs. Each transaction log is 1 MB, meaning that each database will need roughly 10 GB of storage to store one day's worth of transaction logs to support normal mailbox usage (9.9 GB = 379 mailboxes × 26 transaction log files × 1 MB). A full backup is run every other day; to sustain two backup failures enough space is needed for three days' worth of transaction logs or 30 GB. Additional space for transaction logs will need to be added to support mailbox moves. When a mailbox is moved between databases transaction log files are generated for all data that will be inserted into the new database. If you plan to move 5 of the 1,024 MB mailboxes each day you will need to have an additional 25 GB of transaction log storage for the three days' capacity needed. To summarize, the example database generates 10 GB of transaction logs each day for normal mailbox use and 5 GB of transaction logs for mailbox moves. Three days of transaction log storage is 54 GB (3 days × (10 GB transaction logs for normal mailbox usage + 5 GB transaction logs for mailbox moves) + 20 percent for growth).

DISK LAYOUT

You have a number of ways to design the storage for the transaction logs and database files. The strategy you use should be based on performance and backup requirements. The basic disk layout options are as follows:

- **1 LUN/Database** Both the database and its transaction log files are placed on the same LUN. This architecture should only be used for databases in a DAG with two or more database copies that doesn't use a hardware-based VSS solution. This is beneficial because it simplifies storage administration because you have fewer LUNs to manage. This option separates databases to ensure that one database cannot affect the performance of another database.
- **2 LUNs/Database** The database is stored on one LUN and the transaction log files are stored on a separate LUN. Use this option when the recovery time objective (RTO) is very small, or when VSS clones are used. In all but the smallest deployment this option will use more than the available number of drive letters; volume mount points must be used. This allows hardware-based VSS at a database level, providing single database backup and restore. This option separates databases to ensure that one database cannot affect the performance of another database. In a large deployment the number of LUNs required may exceed storage array maximums and may be complicated to administer.
- **2 LUNs/Backup Set** Placing all of the databases to be backed up on the same transaction log files and database LUN can reduce the number of LUNs needed. If a single LUN corruption occurs more databases are affected.
- **1 LUN/Multiple Databases** Placing multiple databases on one LUN can maximize space usage and reduce the number of LUNs needed. A single LUN problem will affect more databases. This configuration can also make it difficult to pinpoint I/O problems to a specific database when multiple databases are stored on the same LUN.

NOTES FROM THE FIELD

Mailbox Server Storage I/O Configuration

Arno Zwegers
Architect Infrastructure, Avanade Netherlands

Disk I/O operations are either read or write operations. The ratio and the amount of I/O is dependent on the application, its operation, and usage. Disk writes are more expensive than disk reads on a RAID storage subsystem. A write operation is more expensive because on a RAID disk subsystem—because of the redundancy it provides or as a trade-off for improved read performance—the data is written onto multiple disks. This means that multiple write operations are needed to complete a single write instruction.

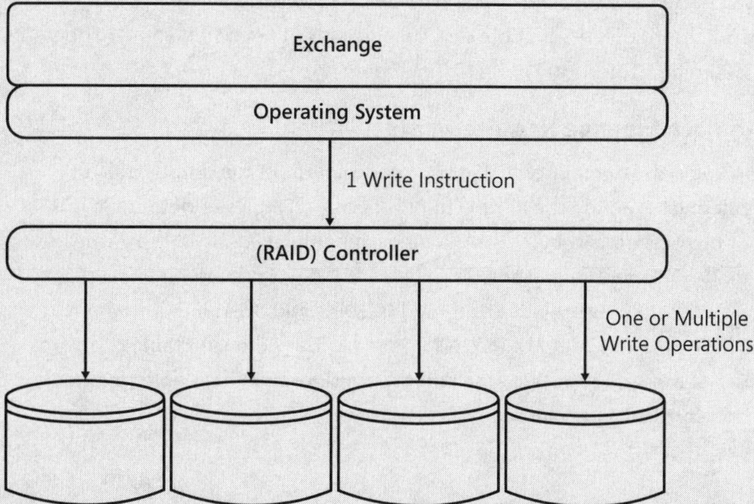

A RAID10 (0+1) set has a penalty on write of two, meaning that for every one I/O instruction two I/O operations are required to write the data to the physical disks. A RAID-5 set has a penalty on write of four (when using a 3+1 parity set) and a RAID-6 set has a penalty on write of five.

The starting points for the calculation are the I/O profile of the users, the read-to-write ratio, and the I/O and size capacity of the available disks.

IOPS Calculations

You can estimate the IOPS required for each user by using the user profile information you have gathered. If you are using Exchange 2003 and the IOPS required for each user is 2, you can conservatively estimate that each mailbox will require around 0.2 IOPS. If you are migrating from Exchange 2007 and you have identified the average IOPS required for mailboxes as .5, you can conservatively estimate .16 IOPS for Exchange 2010. If you do not have access to user profile information from a previous version of Exchange, you can use the guidance provided by Microsoft based on user profiles and the amount of messages sent/received.

The read-to-write ratio for Exchange 2010 is approximately 1:1, meaning that 50 percent of all I/O to the database is read and 50 percent is write operations. For a server with 5,000 mailboxes, each with a .2 IOPS profile, Exchange will generate about 1,000 IOPS (5,000 mailboxes × 0.2 IOPS). Out of the 1,000 IOPS generated, about 500 IOPS will be read operations and 500 will be write operations. With JBOD there is no penalty on write, so the actual IOs that the disk subsystem will need to be able to handle is the same as the amount of IOPS that the application will generate. For RAID0+1 the 500 read I/OPS are equal to 500 IOPS; however, the 500 write IOPS is 1,500 IOPS (500 read IOPS + (500 write IOPS *2 penalty)). For RAID-5 the amount of IOPS that the disk subsystem will need to be able to generate is 2,500 (500 read IOPS + (500 write IOPS * 4 penalty).

Meeting Performance Requirements

When you know the number of IOPS the storage solutions need to be able to sustain, you must examine the underlying disk characteristics to determine the number of physical disks required. SATA disks spinning at 7,200 RPM provide an average of 70 IOPS per disk; a Serial Attached SATA (SAS) or Fibre Channel (FC) disk spinning at 10,000 RPMs provides roughly 130 IOPS; and a SAS/FC disk spinning at 15,000 RPM provides roughly 180 IOPS per disk. The following table compares the number of disks of a specific type and the configuration needed to provide a specific performance benchmark.

	AVAILABLE HOST IOPS	SATA (70 IOPS/DISK)	SAS/FC 10,000 RPM (130 IOPS/DISK)	SAS/FC 15,000 RPM (180 IOPS/DISK)
JBOD	1000	15 disks	8 disks	6 disks
RAID-0+1	1500	22 disks	12 disks	10 disks
RAID-5	2500	37 disks	20 disks	15 disks

Meeting Capacity Requirements

After ensuring that the minimum performance requirements are met, you can now determine the number, type, and configuration of disks needed to meet capacity requirements. The following example compares the data needed for 5,000 mailboxes with 1-GB limits. For simplicity, the table does not account for disk free space, deleted item retention, or content indexing.

CONFIGURATION	1-TB SATA	450-GB SAS/FC 10K	320-GB SAS/FC 15K
JBOD	5 disks	12 disks	16 disks
RAID-0+1	10 disks	24 disks	32 disks
RAID-5	6 disks	13 disks	17 disks

In the previous example, there are 5,000 mailboxes, each with 1-GB mailbox limits, all stored on SATA-based disks. The performance requires a total of 15 disks configured as JBOD. Just to satisfy capacity requirements, using three disks would have been enough. However, both performance and capacity requirements must be met—which means that 15 SATA disks would meet the minimum requirements. As you can see, you must balance storage capacity with performance when determining the number, type, and configuration of storage to be used for the Mailbox server deployment.

Use the following best practices for planning the hardware for Mailbox servers:

- Use 4 to 16 total processor cores.
- More than two sockets don't usually scale as well as adding a second two-socket server.
- 4 GB RAM plus 3–30 MB per mailbox is recommended, depending on the profile.
- Use the Exchange 2010 Mailbox Server Role Requirements Calculator to determine storage configuration.
- Use Jetstress to validate storage hardware performance.

Mailbox Server High-Availability Sizing

To have a highly available Mailbox server, the configuration needs to be created taking into account server failures so that the remaining servers can remain operational despite failures on other DAG nodes. So far in this chapter we have developed sizing guidelines without specifically mentioning how multiple copies of the same database running on different nodes in the DAG affect sizing. The processors on each server in the DAG must service both active mailboxes and passive mailbox databases. A passive database copy uses CPU resources to validate and replay replicated transaction logs and to maintain the content index associated with the database copy. In general, each passive database copy requires up to 15 percent of the CPU utilization required to host the active mailbox database copy. The CPU requirements of the server hosting the active mailbox database copy increases by 10 percent for each additional database copy because of the extra work required to replicate transaction logs to the passive mailbox copies. Use the following best practices when sizing Mailbox servers for high availability:

- Plan for the possibility of double failures.
- Do not overcommit resources—spread databases across nodes in a matrix.
- Use multiple 1-GB networks or a 10-GB network to segregate MAPI and replication communication.
- Improve LAN reseed/log replication queue drain performance.

Unified Messaging Role

Multiple cores are used on the Unified Messaging server for several architectural functions such as .wav to Microsoft Windows Media Audio (WMA) conversions for voice mail messages. Servers with 2X processor cores can be used for Unified Messaging servers in organizations that don't have enough mailboxes or insufficient Unified Messaging server activity to warrant using 4X processor core servers. Use the following best practices for planning the hardware for Unified Messaging servers:

- Use two processor sockets with four, six, or eight cores, each with voice mail preview or use one processor socket with four, six, or eight cores when not using voice mail preview.
- Use 4 to 8 GB of RAM—more than 8 GB is not shown to improve scale.
- Do not combine with other roles because audio quality can be affected.
- Place Unified Messaging servers close to UM-enabled user Mailbox servers to ensure minimal latency.

Multiple Role Server

In smaller environments and in branch offices it may make sense to combine the Mailbox role with other server roles. As a general guideline, a multiple-role server should be sized to use half of the available processor cores for the Mailbox role and the other half for the Client Access and Hub Transport roles. Two processor sockets is the maximum recommend configuration. Although this configuration can use more than two processor sockets, this is not recommended because better performance and lower cost can usually be had using two smaller two-socket servers. Use the following best practices for planning the hardware for multiple role servers:

- Don't co-locate the Unified Messaging role on a server with any of the other roles installed.
- Only install the Mailbox, Client Access Server, and the Hub Transport roles.
- Use 8 to 24 cores.
- A minimum of 8 GB RAM plus 3–30MB/mailbox is recommended. Be sure to follow the mailbox database cache sizing guidance.

Designing Virtualization for Exchange 2010 Servers

Undoubtedly, one of the hottest computing trends for the last few years has been virtualization. Virtualization is showing up on desktop computers, servers, network devices, and even in the cloud. Virtualization can make better use of server hardware and can provide additional availability to many applications. Despite virtualization pervasiveness, a virtualization strategy should be adopted and each application and deployment should be carefully evaluated before you decide to deploy on virtual hardware.

There are a myriad of reasons to virtualize an Exchange deployment. These include fast operating system deployment, flexible and quick hardware configuration, and dramatically quicker system boot time because you don't have to initialize any physical hardware. Other virtualization benefits, such as better use of hardware and being able to run legacy applications on newer hardware, are not of particular benefit to an Exchange 2010 deployment if your underlying hardware is sized correctly.

Virtualization Support

If you are deploying Exchange 2010, chances are you will want to have a configuration that will be supported by the Microsoft support. There are boundaries of what virtualization configurations are supported. For the most current information about the support policies for Exchange server deployed on hardware virtualization, visit *http://technet.microsoft.com/en-us/library/cc794548.aspx*.

The basic support guidelines are as follows:

- Must run on a supported hardware virtualization platform such as Microsoft Hyper-V or others that have been validated by the Windows Server Virtualization Validation Program.
- Dynamically expanded virtual disks are not supported.
- Differencing disks or those that operate similarly are not supported.
- DAGs cannot be made highly available by the hypervisor or moved with hypervisor features such as Hyper-V Live Migration and VMware vMotion.
- Do not run more than two virtual CPUs for every physical processor cores on the host.
- The Unified Messaging role cannot be virtualized because it is extremely sensitive to response time.

It is important to take into account the overhead that the hypervisor has. The hypervisor has to coordinate and manage each running VM. If you're using Hyper-V, running Windows Server 2008 R2 Server Core helps reduce some of this overhead. The CPU overhead varies wildly—anywhere from 5 to 20 percent based on processes architecture, hypervisor configuration, and workloads. For sizing purposes, it is usually safe to assume roughly a 12 percent processor overhead. Virtual machines should be configured so as to not exceed the performance available on the server with the hypervisor overhead taken into account.

NOTES FROM THE FIELD

Virtualization—It's Complicated!

Erik Gustafson
Solutions Architect, Terremark Worldwide

Many businesses look to add virtualization into their environment to provide operational and financial efficiencies. This is a lofty yet reachable goal that requires discipline and forethought. There is a lot of complexity to provide a virtualization platform that performs and scales well and still provide the flexibility that many have come to expect in a virtualized environment. Adding a layer on top of physical hardware adds complexity and cost to the solution. That complexity shows up in all aspects of the solution: installation, configuration, monitoring, troubleshooting, life cycle management, and capacity management.

As with any business-changing decision, follow a controlled virtualization rollout. Be sure to test core application functionality and make sure that your staff is properly trained to troubleshoot and return to service the environment.

If your company has fundamental operational issues, with training, infrastructure instability, and poor change control, virtualization will most likely exacerbate these problems.

If your IT processes are advanced enough to handle a complex virtualization deployment, many benefits can be reaped with virtualization, especially for Transport servers and Client Access servers, which tend to virtualize well in most (but not all) environments.

When undertaking a virtualization project or just deciding whether to virtualize Exchange, take into account the complexity and overall cost of the decision and weigh that against the benefits.

Points to Consider

Performance counters in the guest operating systems can be misleading, especially when dealing with percentage-based counters. For example, the CPU cycles in the guest are relative to the CPU cycles provided to the guest from the virtualization layer. This can skew results, especially on busy hosts. In most cases, CPU utilization will appear to be higher within the guest than it would with the same workload on a physical server; thus monitoring thresholds will need to be adjusted to properly monitor virtual resources. As changes are made to the hypervisor and host hardware, these thresholds may change again. Be sure to do a comparison on how virtualization will affect production monitoring. Comprehensive comparison of physical resources and application consumption is difficult to achieve.

TRADE-OFFS

Exchange Virtualization—Choosing a Strategy

Jeff Mealiffe
Exchange Program Manager, Microsoft Corporation

For software developers, virtualization is one of the most useful (and really cool) technologies in terms of developer productivity. I take for granted the ability to revert to a point-in-time copy while testing a software change or take a snapshot of a production system and then test it in isolated test lab to reproduce a problem. As an Exchange administrator on my home Exchange 2010 deployment, I love that I can use only the hardware resources necessary to get the job done and share the rest of the resources on my physical servers to do other extremely important things, such as provide access to my music and movie library throughout the house. I see the value of virtualization every month on my electricity bill. What's less clear to me is the value of virtualization in a large-scale Exchange deployment. As a development lead in the Exchange product group at Microsoft, I spend quite a bit of time talking to customers and partners about Exchange virtualization, and I've been heavily involved in setting our support policies in this area for Exchange 2010.

Virtualization in the datacenter happens for a number of reasons, but I think most boil down to controlling costs. I'm all for saving money—and I do think that some Exchange deployments can benefit from some of the consolidation that comes from virtualization to save cost. I also think that it's very, very important to carefully evaluate a particular situation to see whether virtualization really does make sense. By that, I mean think about the "total" in "total cost of ownership."

With Exchange 2010 DAGs, you might be tempted to look at all of those mailbox servers that are running at some fraction of their potential capacity and think that they would be great candidates for virtualization (wow, underutilized hardware!). Just as in a physical deployment, you have to worry about what happens during failure scenarios. A server utilizing 30 percent of the CPU may suddenly need 60 percent or 90 percent of the CPU to service the workload after a failover. Given this, virtualization doesn't really help with Exchange Mailbox server consolidation. Also, running multiple mailbox servers on a single physical host complicates DAG design because you now need to consider the potential for a host server failure affecting multiple virtual machines. You don't want all of your database copies for a particular database on the same physical host, and ideally you want all copies on separate physical computers. All of this talk about DAG design difficulty might make you think that an active-passive deployment with hypervisor-based clustering might be the solution. With hosting clustering you need to have shared storage, which comes at a cost. Also, the entire virtual Exchange server fails over rather than individual databases failover, causing user-noticeable downtime. Even worse, Exchange does not communicate with all of the components at the hypervisor level, and does not understand what has failed. It's hard to argue that this would be an optimal high-availability solution.

What about the Hub Transport and Client Access Server roles? In these cases, I think virtualization becomes a lot more interesting—particularly when you consider that you now have the potential to dynamically scale your capacity up and down as necessary to handle peak loads and to scale back capacity when you anticipate workload lulls (perhaps on the weekend in a corporate messaging deployment). Virtualization provides the ability to move a large number of virtual Client Access Servers and Hub Transport servers to a smaller set of physical computers when demand is low. In these cases, excess hardware can be powered off or put in some sort of sleep mode. This process could even be automated for anticipated low-volume time periods. This could add up to very significant power and cooling savings.

From the perspective of Exchange, a virtual machine is simply hardware and an operating system. It's a platform. Nothing in the Exchange product behaves any differently when running on a virtual machine. I like to think of this as a very powerful hardware platform that provides an amazing amount of deployment flexibility. With that flexibility comes the ability to design a rock-solid deployment or a deployment that won't stand up to the challenges of a production workload, so having a complete understanding of the potential pitfalls with virtualization is key. We've tried to come up with a set of virtualization support policies that will provide enough freedom to take advantage of the flexibility offered by virtualization while at the same time protect our users from the worst potential outcomes. Our best practices, on the other hand, provide our opinions on the best way to deploy Exchange.

Additional Resources

- Understanding Processor Configurations and Exchange Performance: *http://technet.microsoft.com/en-us/library/dd346699.aspx*
- Understanding Memory Configurations and Exchange Performance: *http://technet.microsoft.com/en-us/library/dd346700.aspx*
- Understanding Storage Configurations: *http://technet.microsoft.com/en-us/library/ee832792.aspx*

PART III

Upgrading to Exchange Server 2010

CHAPTER 14

Upgrading from Exchange Server 2003 and Exchange Server 2007

The mythical "greenfield" Exchange Server 2010 deployment (deploying Exchange into an environment where no messaging services existed before) is, like the unicorn and the Yeti, something rumored but seldom actually seen firsthand. You are much more likely to be dealing with a migration from another messaging system or an upgrade from an earlier version of Exchange. Because an upgrade is the more common scenario, this chapter focuses on upgrading from Exchange Server 2003 or Exchange Server 2007 to Exchange Server 2010.

Whether you are upgrading from Exchange Server 2003 or Exchange Server 2007, you need to take some common components to your strategy into account. And, as with any implementation or upgrade project, you need to ensure that your project fulfills the business and technical requirements of your organization and that it doesn't disrupt any existing functionality that users have come to depend on. To paraphrase the Hippocratic Oath, "first, do no harm."

Designing Upgrade and Coexistence Strategies

Whether you are upgrading from Exchange Server 2003 or Exchange Server 2007, the upgrade process, in a nutshell, is similar:

1. Upgrade your existing servers (Exchange Server 2003 or Exchange Server 2007) to SP2. All Exchange Server 2003 computers must be at Exchange Server 2003 SP2. If your environment is already at Exchange Server 2007, it is recommended that you upgrade all Exchange Server 2007 computers to Exchange Server 2007 SP2. At a minimum, all your Exchange Server 2007 Client Access (CA) and Unified Messaging (UM) servers in the organization must be upgraded to SP2 before introducing the first Exchange Server 2010 computer. In addition, all the Exchange Server 2007 computers in an Active Directory site must be at Exchange Server 2007 SP2 before introducing the first server running Exchange Server 2010 to that site.
2. Deploy your Exchange Server 2010 computers beginning with your Internet-facing sites. If you are not installing all of the roles on the first server, deploy them in this order: starting with CA, then Hub, then Edge, then Unified Messaging, and finishing with Mailbox servers. This is discussed in more detail in the "Deploying Exchange Server 2010 Computers" section of this chapter.
3. Create a legacy namespace and PKI certificates for your Internet-facing Exchange Server 2003 front end or Exchange Server 2007 Client Access environment, as discussed later in this chapter in the "Upgrading Outlook and Remote Access Functionality" and "Upgrading Client Access Services" sections.
4. Switch over Client Access services to Exchange Server 2010 and activate the legacy namespace, as discussed in the "Upgrading Outlook and Remote Access Functionality" and "Upgrading Client Access Services" sections.
5. Upgrade messaging connectivity as discussed in the "Upgrading Message Connectivity" section.
6. Move mailboxes and public folders to Exchange Server 2010, as discussed in detail in the "Planning and Implementing Mailbox Moves and Coexistence" and "Planning Public Folder Access and Migration" sections.
7. Decommission the legacy Exchange servers. This is covered in more detail in the "Removing Legacy Exchange Servers" section.

Figure 14-1 illustrates the upgrade process.

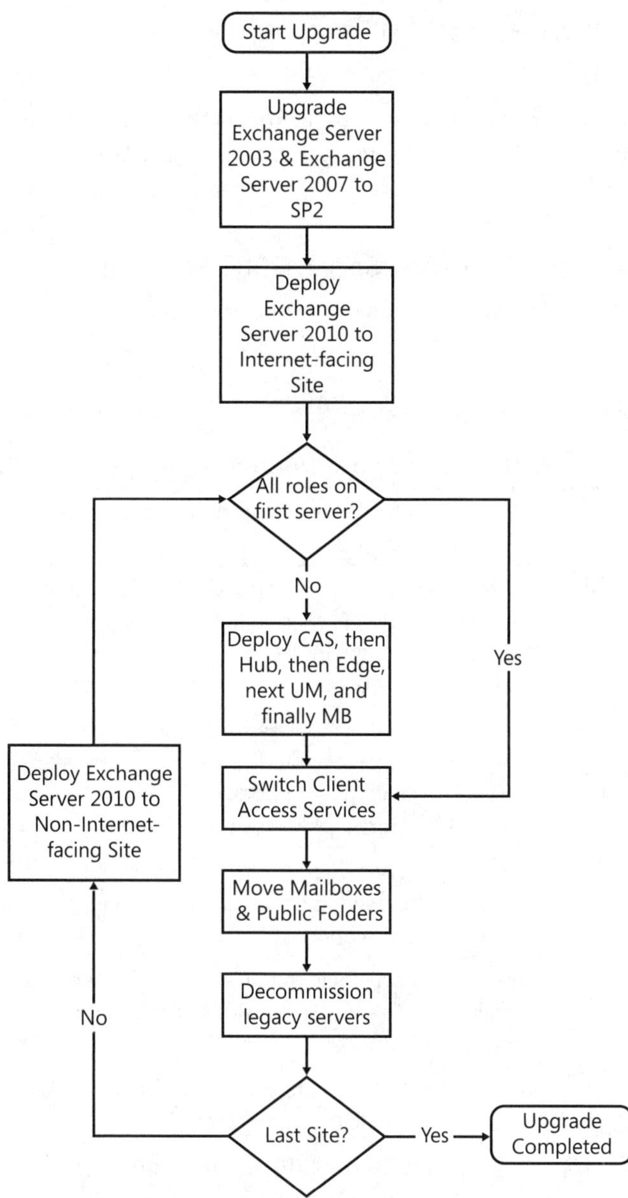

FIGURE 14-1 Upgrading to Exchange Server 2010 in a nutshell

Discontinued and De-emphasized Functionality in Exchange Server 2010

Another area that you need to look at when planning your upgrade from Exchange Server 2003 or Exchange Server 2007 to Exchange Server 2010 is that some features and functionalities have been discontinued in Exchange Server 2010, whereas others have been de-emphasized.

Discontinued and De-emphasized Exchange Server 2003 Features

Table 14-1 outlines the Exchange Server 2003 architecture features that have been discontinued in Exchange Server 2010.

TABLE 14-1 Discontinued Exchange Server 2003 Architecture Features

EXCHANGE SERVER 2003 FEATURE	COMMENTS AND MITIGATION STRATEGY
Routing groups	Active Directory site-based routing is used in Exchange Server 2010.
Administrative groups	A Role-Based Access Control (RBAC) delegation model is used in Exchange Server 2010; this is discussed in detail in the "Exchange Server 2003 Administrative Groups" section of this chapter.
Intelligent Message Filter	Exchange Server 2010 uses anti-spam agents in the Hub Transport and Edge Transport server roles. This is discussed in detail in Chapter 7, "Edge Transport and Messaging Security."
Link state routing	Exchange Server 2010 uses least cost routing, which is discussed in the "Link State vs. Least Cost Routing" section of this chapter.
Routing objects	If this functionality is required, you will need to retain an Exchange Server 2003 computer in your organization.
Network-attached storage	Internet SCSI (iSCSI) Storage Area Network (SAN) is supported in Exchange Server 2010.
Exchange Installable File System (ExIFS)	In Exchange Server 2010, this functionality is replaced by Exchange Web Services (EWS) and MAPI.
Event service	If this functionality is required, you will need to retain an Exchange Server 2003 computer in your organization.
Recovery storage group	Exchange Server 2010 uses the recovery database, which is discussed in Chapter 12, "Backup, Restore, and Disaster Recovery."

In addition, the Exchange Server 2003 connector features listed in Table 14-2 are discontinued in Exchange Server 2010.

TABLE 14-2 Discontinued Exchange Server 2003 Connector Features

EXCHANGE SERVER 2003 FEATURE	COMMENTS AND MITIGATION STRATEGY
Microsoft Exchange Connector for Novell GroupWise and migration tools	If this functionality is required, you will need to retain an Exchange Server 2003 computer in your organization.
Microsoft Exchange Connector for Lotus Notes	If this functionality is required, you will need to retain an Exchange Server 2003 computer in your organization. Alternatively, you can use the appropriate tools for coexisting and migrating from Lotus Notes, which are available at *http://go.microsoft.com/fwlink/?LinkId=58466*.

The Exchange Server 2003 protocol features that have been discontinued are outlined in Table 14-3.

TABLE 14-3 Discontinued Exchange Server 2003 Protocol Features

EXCHANGE SERVER 2003 FEATURE	COMMENTS AND MITIGATION STRATEGY
Network News Transfer Protocol (NNTP)	If this functionality is required, you will need to retain an Exchange Server 2003 computer in your organization.
X.400 message transfer agent (MTA)	If this functionality is required, you will need to retain an Exchange Server 2003 computer in your organization.
SMTP virtual server instances	This functionality is replaced with Exchange Server 2010 SMTP connectors, which are discussed in detail in Chapter 5, "Routing and Transport."

In addition to the features outlined in Table 14-3, Outlook Mobile Access has been removed in Exchange Server 2010.

Discontinued Exchange Server 2003 public folder features are outlined in Table 14-4. Public folder migration is discussed in detail in the "Planning Public Folder Access and Migration" section of this chapter.

TABLE 14-4 Discontinued Exchange Server 2003 Public Folder Features

EXCHANGE SERVER 2003 FEATURE	COMMENTS AND MITIGATION STRATEGY
Non-MAPI top-level hierarchies in a public folder store	If this functionality is required, you will need to retain an Exchange Server 2003 computer in your organization.
Public folder access with NNTP	If this functionality is required, you will need to retain an Exchange Server 2003 computer in your organization.
Public folder access with IMAP4	If this functionality is required, you will need to retain an Exchange Server 2003 computer in your organization.

In addition, using Integrated Windows authentication (NTLM) for POP3 and IMAP4 users is not supported in Exchange Server 2010; the recommended alternatives are Kerberos, or plain text authentication with SSL. If Integrated Windows authentication is required, you will need to retain an Exchange Server 2003 computer in your organization.

The tools and management features from Exchange Server 2003 that have been discontinued are listed in Table 14-5.

TABLE 14-5 Discontinued Exchange Server 2003 Tools and Management Features

EXCHANGE SERVER 2003 FEATURE	COMMENTS AND MITIGATION STRATEGY
Active Directory Users and Computers (ADUC) snap-in extension for Exchange	In Exchange Server 2010, recipient management is included in the EMC and EMS.
Exchange Server Mailbox Merge wizard (ExMerge.exe)	This functionality is replaced with the *Export-Mailbox* cmdlet in Exchange Server 2010 RTM, and the *New-MailboxExportRequest* cmdlet in Exchange Server 2010 SP1.
Recipient Update Service	Recipients are deployed fully provisioned in Exchange Server 2010, although the *Update-AddressList* and *Update-EmailAddressPolicy* cmdlets do perform some of the functions that the RUS used to perform. Migrating the RUS is discussed in the "Recipient Update Service Migration" section of this chapter.
Monitoring and status node in the Exchange Server 2003 Exchange System Manager	Exchange Server 2010 provides some test cmdlets, or a monitoring solution such as Microsoft System Center Operations Manager can be deployed. This is discussed in more detail in Chapter 17, "Operating and Troubleshooting Exchange Server 2010."

EXCHANGE SERVER 2003 FEATURE	COMMENTS AND MITIGATION STRATEGY
Message Tracking Center node and tracking mechanism in the Exchange Server 2003 Exchange System Manager	Exchange Server 2010 provides the Tracking Log Explorer and Message Tracking tools; message tracking is discussed in detail in Chapter 17.
Mailbox Recovery Center	This is replaced in Exchange Server 2010 with the *Restore-Mailbox* cmdlet.
Mailbox Management Service	Exchange Server 2010 provides messaging records management (MRM), which is discussed in detail in Chapter 8, "Automated Message Processing, Compliance, and Archiving."
Clean Mailbox tool	This functionality is replaced with the *Export-Mailbox* cmdlet in Exchange Server 2010 RTM and the *New-MailboxExportRequest* cmdlet in Exchange Server 2010 SP1 as well as the *Move Request* cmdlet set.
Migration wizard	Exchange Server 2010 replaces this functionality with the *Move Request* cmdlet set in the EMS and the Move Request Wizards in the EMC.
Exchange Profile Redirector tool (ExProfRe)	This functionality is replaced with the AutoDiscover service in Exchange Server 2010. AutoDiscover is discussed in detail in Chapter 4, "Client Access in Exchange 2010."

Finally, the following features have been de-emphasized in Exchange Server 2010; they still work with Exchange Server 2010, but they will likely be removed in some future release. These functionalities are now provided by Exchange Web Services (EWS), so any applications or services that rely on these services will need to be upgraded to use EWS:

- CDO 1.2.1
- MAPI32
- CDOEX (CDO 3.0)
- Exchange WebDAV extensions
- ExOLEDB
- Store events

Discontinued Exchange Server 2007 Features

This section outlines the Exchange Server 2007 features that are not supported in Exchange Server 2010.

In Exchange Server 2010, Exchange WebDAV has been discontinued; this functionality is replaced with Exchange Web Services; alternatively, you can maintain an Exchange Server 2007 Mailbox server for mailboxes that are managed with applications that use WebDAV.

The Exchange Server 2007 architecture features that have been discontinued in Exchange Server 2010 are outlined in Table 14-6.

TABLE 14-6 Discontinued Exchange Server 2007 Architecture Features

EXCHANGE SERVER 2007 FEATURE	COMMENTS AND MITIGATION STRATEGY
DSProxy	Exchange Server 2010 replaces the DSProxy with the Address Book service, which is discussed in Chapter 4.
Storage groups	Exchange Server 2010 uses database copy functionality. Database mobility and database copies are discussed in detail in Chapter 6, "Mailbox Services."
Extensible Storage Engine (ESE) streaming backup APIs	Exchange Server 2010 uses Volume Shadow Copy Service (VSS)–based backups, which are discussed in Chapter 12.

Exchange Server 2010 also replaces the mailbox high-availability features of Exchange Server 2007 database availability groups (DAGs) and mailbox database copies, which are discussed in detail in Chapter 6.

The Exchange Server 2007 mailbox features that have been removed are:

- Cluster continuous replication (CCR)
- Local continuous replication (LCR)
- Standby continuous replication (SCR)
- Single copy cluster (SCC)

And as explained in the "Discontinued and De-emphasized Exchange Server 2003 Features" section of this chapter, using Integrated Windows authentication (NTLM) for POP3 and IMAP4 users is not supported in Exchange Server 2010; the recommended alternatives are Kerberos, or plain text authentication with SSL. If Integrated Windows authentication is required, you will need to retain an Exchange Server 2007 server in your organization.

The Exchange Server 2007 Outlook Web Access (OWA) features outlined in Table 14-7 are discontinued in Exchange Server 2010.

TABLE 14-7 Discontinued Exchange Server 2007 OWA Features

EXCHANGE SERVER 2003 FEATURE	COMMENTS AND MITIGATION STRATEGY
SharePoint document libraries and Windows file share access	Access to SharePoint document libraries and Windows file share via OWA is discontinued in Exchange Server 2010.
Web Parts	Web Parts were not available in Exchange Server 2010 RTM, but are available again in SP1.
Reading pane at the bottom of the page	It is not possible to display the reading pane at the bottom of the Exchange Server 2010 OWA window.

Finally, the Exchange Server 2007 *Move-Mailbox* cmdlet has been replaced in Exchange Server 2010 with the *Move Request* cmdlet sets and wizards. *Move Requests* are discussed in the "Moving Mailboxes from Exchange Server 2003 to Exchange Server 2010" section of this chapter.

Useful Tools for an Upgrade

A number of useful tools are available for planning, deploying, and troubleshooting your upgrade to Exchange Server 2010, four of which are covered here:

- Exchange Server Deployment Assistant
- Exchange Best Practices Analyzer
- Exchange Pre-Deployment Analyzer
- Exchange Server Remote Connectivity Analyzer

Exchange Server Deployment Assistant

A valuable, free online resource for planning your upgrade to Exchange Server 2010 is the Exchange Server Deployment Assistant, available at *http://technet.microsoft.com/en-ca/exdeploy2010/default.aspx#Home*. For on-premises upgrades, this checklist-driven tool creates instructions that are customized for your environment. You answer a small set of questions, which generate a set of instructions designed to get you up and running on Exchange Server 2010. The Deployment Assistant condenses the 2000-plus topics in the Exchange Server 2010 library down to enough customized content to get you started on your upgrade. Figure 14-2 shows a page of the Deployment Assistant for Exchange Server 2003 after the initial set of questions are answered and instructions were generated.

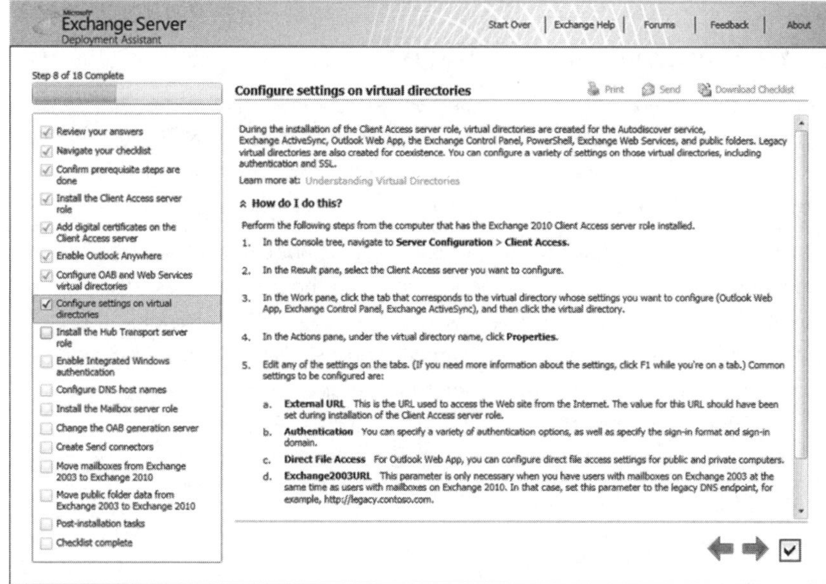

FIGURE 14-2 The Exchange Server Deployment Assistant

Exchange Best Practices Analyzer

The Exchange Best Practices Analyzer (ExBPA) is another useful tool included in the management tools in the Exchange Server 2010 Exchange Management Console. You should run the ExBPA after making any changes to your Exchange organization, especially during your upgrade to Exchange Server 2010.

The scan options available in the ExBPA are shown in Figure 14-3.

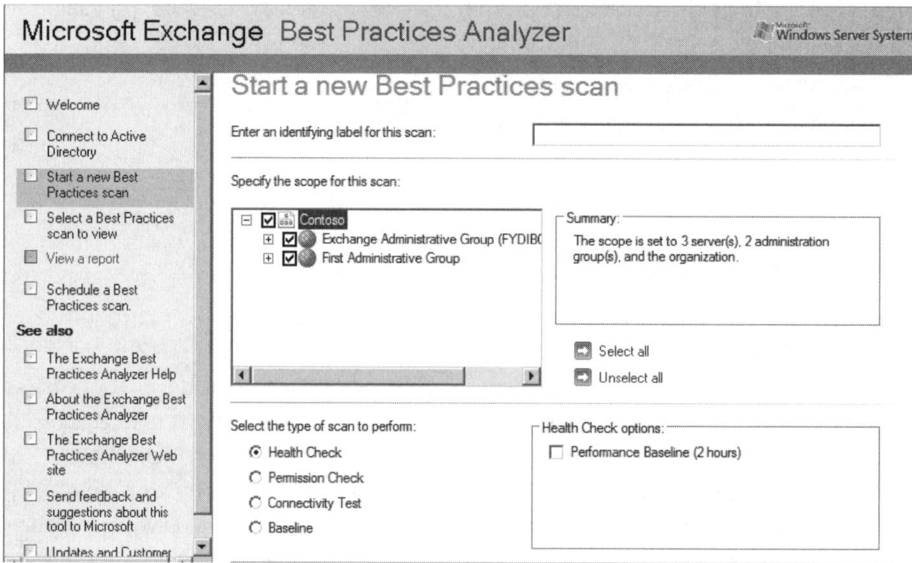

FIGURE 14-3 The Exchange Best Practices Analyzer

Exchange Pre-Deployment Analyzer

A new downloadable tool released for Exchange Server 2010 is the Exchange Pre-Deployment Analyzer (ExPDA). This tool provides an Exchange 2010 Readiness Check; previously, the Exchange Server 2007 Readiness Check was provided as part of the downloadable version of the ExBPA. The Start A New Scan screen of the ExPDA is shown in Figure 14-4.

When the scan is run, a detailed analysis of your existing Exchange organization is performed, and a comprehensive report is generated detailing the preparedness of your organization for the introduction of Exchange Server 2010 as well as providing the appropriate corrective measures to take. In the example report shown in Figure 14-5, you can see that an Exchange Server 2003 server in the organization does not have link-state suppression enabled. Suppressing link state updates will be discussed in detail in the "Preparing the Environment" section of this chapter.

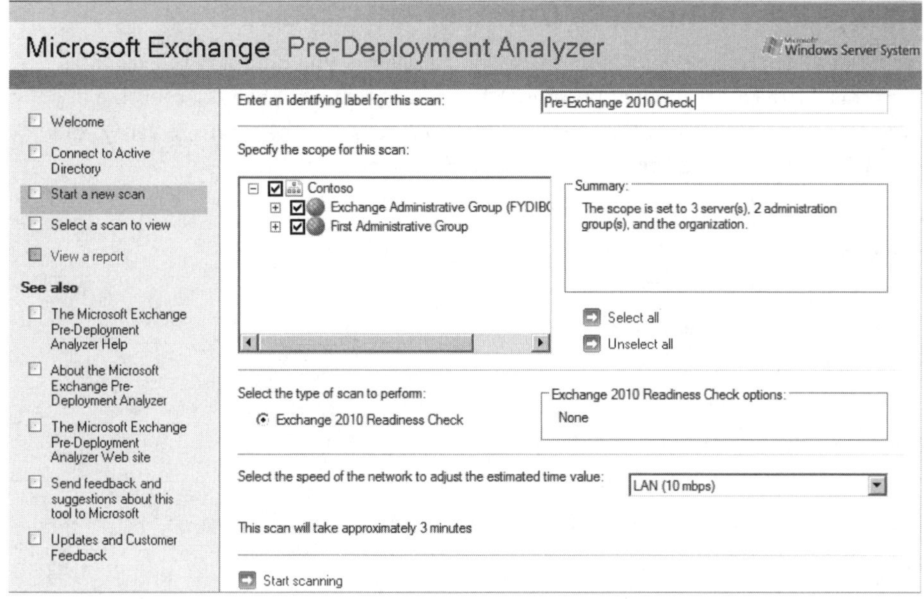

FIGURE 14-4 Starting a new scan with the Exchange Pre-Deployment Analyzer

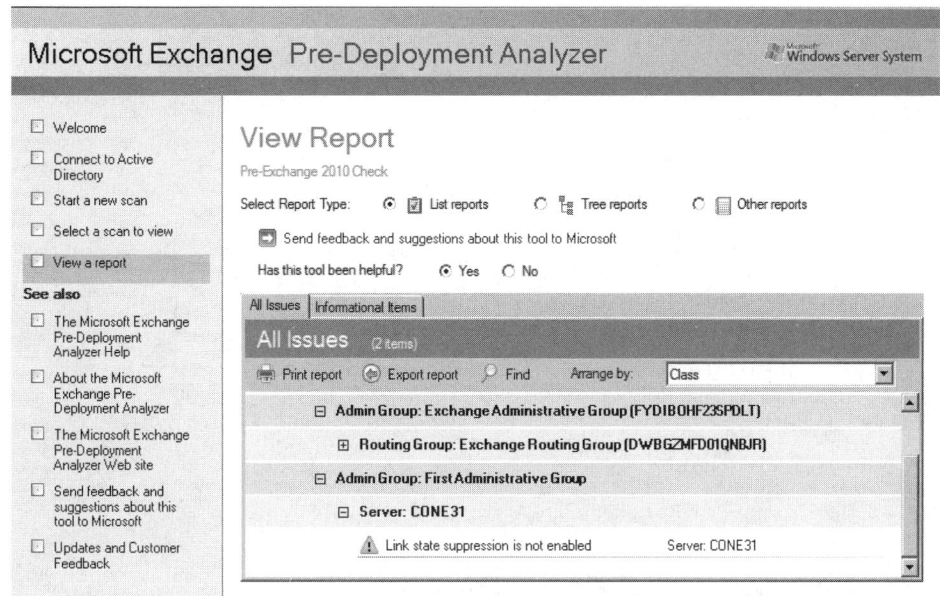

FIGURE 14-5 Viewing a Pre-Deployment Analyzer Report

Exchange Server Remote Connectivity Analyzer

Another online tool available for use before, during, and after your upgrade to Exchange Server 2010 is the Microsoft Exchange Server Remote Connectivity Analyzer, available at *https://www.testexchangeconnectivity.com*. This tool provides you the means to verify your Internet-facing client services and SMTP configurations, including:

- ActiveSync and ActiveSync Autodiscover
- Exchange Web Services
  - Synchronization, Notification, Availability, and OOF
  - Service Account Access
- Outlook Tests
  - Outlook Anywhere
  - Outlook AutoDiscover
- Inbound and Outbound SMTP

The various tests available through the Exchange Remote Connectivity Analyzer are shown in Figure 14-6.

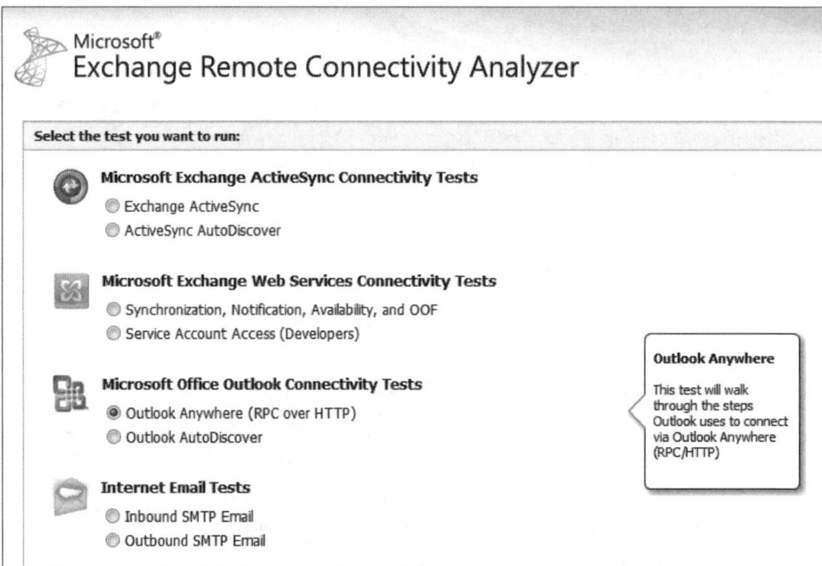

FIGURE 14-6 The Exchange Remote Connectivity Analyzer

Upgrading from and Coexisting with Exchange Server 2003

Because many organizations have not yet implemented Exchange Server 2007, upgrading from Exchange Server 2003 to Exchange Server 2010 is a very common upgrade scenario. As in any upgrade, unless you have a user base that you can move in a single, acceptable period of downtime, there will be a period of coexistence with the legacy (Exchange Server 2003) environment until all resources are upgraded to Exchange Server 2010. This section discusses the factors to consider when planning your coexistence strategy.

This section builds on the scenarios presented in Chapter 2, "Exchange Deployment Projects." Contoso is a company of 750 users running an Exchange Server 2003 environment centralized in Seattle. A logical view of their environment is illustrated in Figure 14-7.

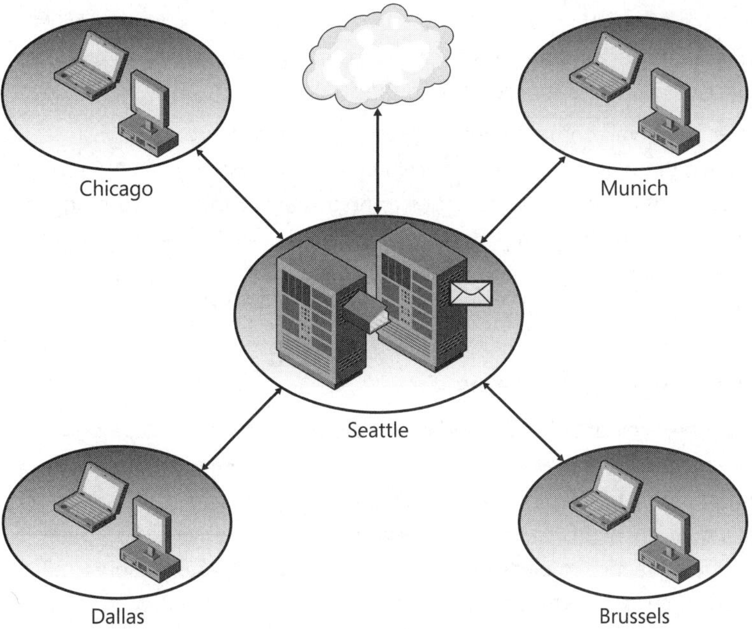

FIGURE 14-7 Logical view of Contoso's Exchange Server 2003 environment

Preparing the Environment

Before you install the first Exchange Server 2010 computer, you must take numerous steps to prepare the environment and to ensure proper coexistence between Exchange Server 2010 and Exchange Server 2003.

Link State vs. Least Cost Routing

When Exchange Server 2003 detects that a connector is down, it communicates minor link state updates throughout the organization and determines another route based on link state routing. Starting in Exchange Server 2007 and continuing in Exchange Server 2010, however, least cost routing is now used and Exchange does not refer to the link state tables maintained and used by Exchange Server 2003. Message routing and transport is covered in more detail in Chapter 5.

In the case of an environment with a single routing group connector between Exchange Server 2003 and Exchange Server 2010, you do not need to make any changes to link state routing in Exchange Server 2003. However, if additional routing-group connectors are configured between Exchange Server 2003 and Exchange Server 2010 (for example, to accommodate message routing in a multiple site coexistence scenario) the potential of routing loops exists. Because link state routing is not used in Exchange Server 2010, the potential exists to direct a message back through a path that Exchange Server 2003 is trying to route around, resulting in a possible routing loop. To avoid this, minor link state updates can be suppressed in Exchange Server 2003, which causes Exchange Server 2003 to use least cost routing and removes the potential for message routing loops.

In an Exchange Server 2003 environment containing multiple routing groups, link state updates should be suppressed on all Exchange Server 2003 servers in the organization to ensure consistent message routing. It is a best practice to do this in any multiple routing groups scenario—even with a single Exchange Server 2003 to Exchange Server 2010 routing group connector—to avoid issues if an additional Exchange Server 2003 to Exchange Server 2010 routing-group connector should be configured later in the project.

Suppressing Minor Link State Updates

It is a best practice to suppress minor link state updates as a precautionary measure prior to deploying Exchange Server 2010 in an Exchange Server 2003 environment with multiple routing groups. This is done on a per-server (Exchange Server 2003 computer) basis. Although strictly speaking it only needs to be performed on Exchange Server 2003 servers hosting connectors, it is best practice to perform the procedure on *all* Exchange Server 2003 servers to maintain a consistent configuration. In the Contoso case, although they have a centralized Exchange Server 2003 environment, they may decide to add another routing group connector for redundancy purposes, so they have opted to suppress minor link state updates as a precautionary measure.

The suppression of minor link state updates is performed as follows:

1. On the Exchange Server 2003 computer, create the following registry entry:

   ```
   HKEY_LOCAL_MACHINE\SYSTEM\CurrentControlSet\Services\RESvc\Parameters
   Value Name: SuppressStateChanges
   Data Type: REG_DWORD
   Data: 1
   Radix: Decimal
   ```

2. On the Exchange Server 2003 computer, restart the following services:
   - Microsoft Exchange Routing Engine (RESvc)
   - SMTP Service (SMTPSVC)
   - Microsoft Exchange MTA Stacks (MSExchangeMTA)
3. Repeat Steps 1 and 2 on each Exchange Server 2003 computer in the environment.

Upgrading Exchange Server 2003 Computers to SP2

Before introducing the first Exchange Server 2010 computer into your Exchange Server 2003 organization, you must upgrade all servers running Exchange Server 2003 to SP2.

Preparing Legacy Exchange Permissions

The first step in preparing your Exchange Server 2003 organization for Exchange Server 2010 is to grant specific Exchange permissions in each domain Exchange Server 2003 computer. This is required to allow the Recipient Update Service in Exchange Server 2003 to function correctly after the schema changes for Exchange Server 2010 are applied to your Active Directory forest.

The legacy Exchange permissions are prepared by running the following command from a command prompt from the directory containing the Exchange Server 2010 setup files:

```
Setup /PrepareLegacyExchangePermissions
```

To prepare every domain in the forest, you must be a member of the Enterprise Admins group to run this command successfully. Otherwise, for a specific domain, or if the forest has only one domain, you must be an Exchange Full Administrator in the Exchange Server 2003 organization and a member of the Domain Admins group in the domain being prepared.

Extending the Active Directory Schema

The next step in preparing your environment for Exchange Server 2010 is extending the Active Directory schema. Exchange Server 2010 modifies a great number of the existing classes and attributes as well as adding many new attributes and classes to the schema. If the legacy Exchange permissions have not been prepared as outlined in the "Preparing Legacy Exchange Permissions" section of this chapter, extending the schema will perform the *Prepare LegacyExchangePermissions* step as well as extend the Active Directory schema.

The following command extends the schema for Exchange Server 2010; run this from a command prompt from the Exchange Server 2010 setup directory:

```
Setup /PrepareSchema
```

To run this command successfully, you must have Schema Admins and Enterprise Admins privileges in the forest.

Exchange Server 2010 also marks numerous attributes for inclusion in the global catalog, which can impact your global catalog database size as well as Active Directory replication in your environment.

Preparing Active Directory for Exchange Server 2010

The final step in getting your Active Directory environment ready for Exchange Server 2010 is to run the *setup /PrepareAD* command to prepare Active Directory. This command performs the following steps:

- Verifies the Exchange Server 2010 schema updates.
- Configures the Active Directory global Exchange objects

- Creates the Exchange universal security groups (USGs) in the root domain.
- Sets permissions on the Exchange configuration objects.
- Prepares the current domain.
- An Exchange Server 2003 administrative group called Exchange Administrative Group (FYDIBOHF23SPDLT) and an Exchange Server 2003 routing group called Exchange Routing Group (DWBGZMFD01QNBJR) are created.

Another potential issue surrounding *PrepareAD* that should be considered is when, in Exchange Server 2003, an SMTP address is ambiguously non-authoritative—that is, the address space has been marked authoritative in one policy but non-authoritative in another. This configuration is illustrated in Figure 14-8; Contoso's primary address space (contoso.com) has been set as authoritative in the Sales recipient policy, but is set as non-authoritative in the Engineering policy.

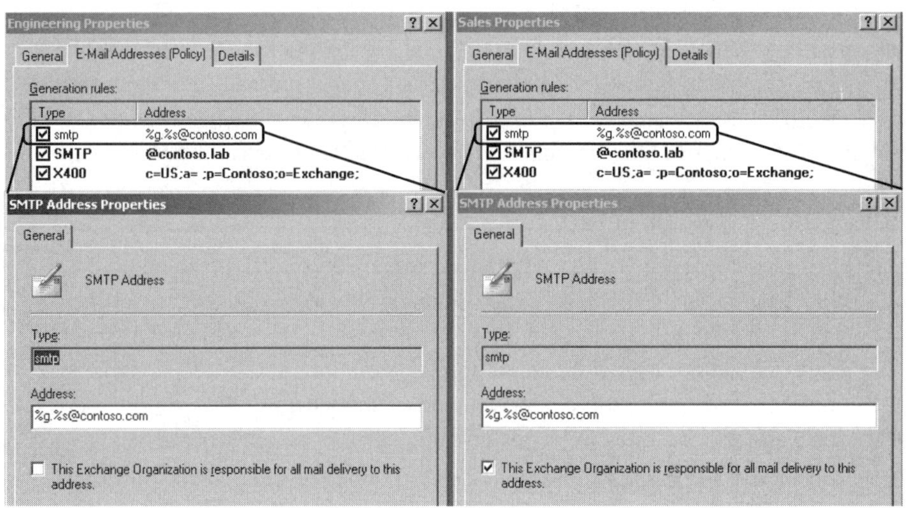

FIGURE 14-8 Ambiguously non-authoritative recipient policies

If this is not detected and corrected before you run *PrepareAD* for Exchange Server 2010, mail flow issues within your Exchange Server 2003 environment may result because the *PrepareAD* process attempts to "correct" the ambiguity by making the address space in question consistently non-authoritative on all recipient policies. The mail flow symptoms can include messages accumulating in deferred delivery queues on bridgeheads and not being delivered, and messages looping a small number of times between mailbox servers and these same bridgeheads. The Microsoft Exchange Team has produced a Windows PowerShell script that can detect these issues, although the corrective steps are a manual process. The script and a more detailed explanation of this issue can be found at *http://msexchangeteam.com/archive/2008/09/05/449764.aspx*.

If the issue is detected before Exchange Server 2010 *PrepareAD* is run, you simply need to correct the offending recipient polices to be either all authoritative or all non-authoritative prior to running *PrepareAD*. If *PrepareAD* has already been run, however, editing the offending recipient policies and restarting IIS on *all* Exchange Server 2003 computers is necessary to cause the IIS metabase to recognize the routing changes and resume normal mail flow.

Running the following command from the Exchange Server 2010 setup directory prepares Active Directory for Exchange Server 2010:

```
Setup /PrepareAD
```

If the *Setup /PrepareLegacyExchangePermissions* and *Setup /PrepareSchema* commands have not yet been run, *PrepareAD* will perform those steps as well. You need Enterprise Admins privileges to run this command, and the computer this command is run from must be able to contact all domains in the forest on port 389. You must also be an Exchange Full Administrator if you have Exchange Server 2003 servers in your organization, and the computer this command is run from must be in the same Active Directory site and domain as the schema master.

Deploying Exchange Server 2010 Computers

The nuts and bolts of installing Exchange Server 2010 are covered in Chapter 15, "Preparing for and Deploying Exchange Server 2010," but when planning your upgrade you need to consider a number of points:

- All Exchange servers in your organization must be Exchange Server 2003 SP2 or later.
- Your Exchange Server 2003 organization must be set to Native Mode.
- The Active Directory forest mode must *not* be Windows Server 2008.
- The computers Exchange Server 2010 will be installed on must be Windows Server 2008 SP2 or later or Windows Server 2008 R2.
- The Exchange Server 2010 computers require all the necessary prerequisites installed on them before installing Exchange Server 2010. The prerequisites and the actual installation of Exchange Server 2010 are covered in Chapter 15.

Finally, unless you install all roles (Mailbox, Client Access, and Hub Transport; Unified messaging is not supported for co-location) on the first Exchange Server 2010 computer in your environment, the Exchange Server 2010 server roles should be deployed in the following order:

1. Client Access server role
2. Hub Transport server role

   The Edge Transport server role, if it is deployed, should be implemented after the Hub Transport server role.
3. Unified Messaging (UM) Server role
4. Mailbox server role

Upgrading Outlook and Remote Access Functionality

The Client Access services you should take into account during an upgrade to Exchange Server 2010 includes multiple services and functionalities, not all of which are immediately obvious:

- Free/busy functionality
- Offline Address Books
- Outlook Web App
- Digital Certificates
- Outlook functionality
- ActiveSync

Table 14-8 outlines the various Exchange Server 2010 Client Access services and how they are presented to Exchange Server 2003 and Exchange Server 2007 mailboxes.

TABLE 14-8 Exchange Server 2010 Client Access Services

EXCHANGE SERVER 2010 CLIENT ACCESS SERVICE	EXCHANGE SERVER 2003 OR EXCHANGE SERVER 2007 MAILBOX TREATMENT
OWA	Exchange Server 2003 mailbox: Single Sign-On (silent redirect to Exchange Server 2003 using legacy URL). Exchange Server 2007 mailbox in the same Active Directory site: Single Sign-On (silent redirect to Exchange Server 2007 using legacy URL). Exchange Server 2007 mailbox in a separate non-Internet facing Active Directory site is proxied.
Exchange ActiveSync	Exchange Server 2007 mailbox: Autodiscover and redirect for Windows Mobile 6.1 and newer, Windows Mobile 6 and older and all non-Microsoft ActiveSync clients are proxied to Exchange Server 2007 Client Access). Exchange Server 2003 mailboxes: Exchange Server 2010 Client Access supports direct access to the Exchange Server 2003 mailbox, provided Integrated Windows authentication is enabled on the Microsoft-Server-ActiveSync virtual directory on the Exchange Server 2003 computer for Kerberos authentication between Exchange Server 2010 CAS and the Exchange Server 2003 back-end server. Any clients that use new Exchange ActiveSync features need to re-sync.
Outlook Anywhere & OAB	Direct Exchange Server 2010 Client Access support.

EXCHANGE SERVER 2010 CLIENT ACCESS SERVICE	EXCHANGE SERVER 2003 OR EXCHANGE SERVER 2007 MAILBOX TREATMENT
Autodiscover	Direct Exchange Server 2010 Client Access support.
Exchange Web Services	Autodiscover.
POP/IMAP	Exchange Server 2007: Connect to a Client Access server in the same Active Directory site as the Mailbox server. Exchange Server 2003: Direct Exchange Server 2010 Client Access support.

INSIDE TRACK

Seamless Coexistence with the Legacy URL

Kristian Andaker
Group Program Manager of OWA, EAS, ExUM, and EWS
Microsoft, Redmond, WA

If you can't migrate all your users from Exchange Server 2003 or 2007 to Exchange Server 2010 over a weekend, you'll probably want to have the two versions of Exchange running alongside one another for a while. To make this coexistence run seamlessly for your users, and to ensure that your users don't need to manually reconfigure their e-mail clients or learn a new OWA URL, you should use a *legacy namespace*.

The legacy namespace (such as *legacy.contoso.com*) should be set up to work exactly the same way as your main external Exchange namespace (*owa.contoso.com*) works today. Before you start migrating anybody, you should ensure that the legacy namespace can be used to access your Exchange Server 2003 or 2007 mailboxes through all the protocols in exactly the same way your main external Exchange namespace works. This means you need to update your SSL certificates (use of a "Subject Alternative Name," or SAN, certificate is recommended) to include the legacy namespace, and that you need to configure reverse proxies, firewalls, and so on to let through the legacy namespace in exactly the same way your main external Exchange namespace is already set up.

When the legacy namespace is set up and works, you're ready to switch over your main external Exchange namespace (*owa.contoso.com*) to point to your new Exchange Server 2010 computers. When you do this, all clients using this namespace in their configuration, and all users who remember an OWA URL that includes this namespace, will start accessing your Exchange Server 2010 computers.

For users who still have their mailboxes on Exchange Server 2003 or 2007, the only thing Exchange Server 2010 will do is authentication. After that their requests will be redirected or proxied to the Exchange Server 2003 or 2007 computers. For the redirection and proxying to work correctly for Exchange 2003 access, you need to configure the *Exchange2003Url* parameter on the Exchange 2010 OWA virtual directory. For Exchange ActiveSync (EAS) to be proxied correctly to Exchange Server 2003, you need to configure the Exchange 2003 EAS virtual directory to allow Windows Integrated authentication. Other Exchange services rely on the Exchange Server 2007 *internalURL* and *externalURL* parameters on virtual directories to redirect and proxy traffic as appropriate for each service. For more information on this, see the TechNet documentation on Exchange Server 2010 migration at *http://technet.microsoft.com/en-us/library/ee332348.aspx* for Exchange Server 2003 and *http://technet.microsoft.com/en-us/library/dd351133.aspx* for Exchange Server 2007.

In coexistence between Exchange Server 2003 or 2007 with Exchange Server 2010, your end users should never have to reconfigure their e-mail clients manually, or learn a different OWA URL. When the Exchange servers are configured correctly and the legacy namespace is deployed, all of the client configuration your users use, and the OWA URL they already know, should continue to work seamlessly.

At the time of this writing, a few mobile phones implementing Exchange ActiveSync (EAS) have a bug preventing them from following EAS redirections correctly. Until these device bugs are fixed, users of these devices will need to manually change the configuration on the phone to use the legacy namespace. By the time you read this, I hope there will be fixes for all mobile devices that have this problem from the device manufacturers.

Free/Busy Functionality

In your Exchange Server 2003 environment, both free/busy functionality and offline address book distribution are provided by public folders—in particular, system folders. The Availability service in Exchange Server 2010 replaces or supplements the free/busy system folders in Exchange Server 2003, depending on the version of Outlook deployed.

In many enterprise environments, the version of Microsoft Office, and in particular Microsoft Outlook, deployed and supported to end users is managed by an IT group separate from the messaging team—usually an enterprise desktop deployment team—who must test the new version of Office extensively against the organization's standard desktop build and applications to ensure compatibility. This means that the deployment of Outlook 2007 or Outlook 2010 can be in a project plan separate from the upgrade of the messaging infrastructure to Exchange Server 2010, and users may receive the new version of Outlook before or after their mailboxes have been moved to Exchange Server 2010. So coexistence of Outlook 2003 with Exchange Server 2010 could be a major factor in your implementation.

Because the Exchange Server 2010 Availability service cannot be used by Outlook 2003, you will need to maintain system folders in your environment as long as Outlook 2003 is in use. The free/busy retrieval methodology for various clients and mailboxes is shown in Table 14-9.

TABLE 14-9 Free/Busy Retrieval in Exchange 2010

CLIENT	MAILBOX RETRIEVING FREE/BUSY INFORMATION	TARGET MAILBOX	FREE/BUSY ACCESS METHOD
Outlook 2007	Exchange 2010 or Exchange 2007	Exchange 2010 or Exchange 2007	Availability service reads free/busy information from the target mailbox.
Outlook 2007	Exchange 2010 or Exchange 2007	Exchange 2003	Availability service makes HTTP connections to the /public virtual directory of the Exchange 2003 mailbox.
Outlook 2003	Exchange 2010 or Exchange 2007	Exchange 2010 or Exchange 2007	Free/busy information is published in public folders.
Outlook 2003	Exchange 2010 or Exchange 2007	Exchange 2003	Free/busy information is published in public folders.
Outlook Web App	Exchange 2010 or Exchange 2007	Exchange 2010 or Exchange 2007	Availability service reads free/busy information from the target mailbox.
Outlook Web App	Exchange 2010 or Exchange 2007	Exchange 2003	Availability service makes HTTP connections to the /public virtual directory of the Exchange 2003 mailbox.
Any	Exchange 2003	Exchange 2010 or Exchange 2007	Free/busy information is published in public folders.

To maintain coexistence and pave the way for a smooth upgrade to Exchange Server 2010, you need to maintain public folders, and system folders in particular, until at least all mailboxes have been moved to Exchange 2010 and all Outlook clients have been upgraded to at least Outlook 2007. In addition, if you have any custom applications that query free/busy information, ensure that these applications will be able to use the Availability service API; otherwise, you will need to maintain system folders in your environment as long as these applications are in use. Public folders coexistence and migration are discussed in more detail in the "Planning Public Folder Access and Migration" section of this chapter.

OWA Coexistence

If OWA is deployed in your Exchange 2003 environment for Internet users, you must take additional steps to ensure interoperability with Outlook Web App and Exchange 2010. Exchange Server 2010 Client Access does not support accessing mailboxes from Exchange Server 2003; all legacy mailbox access is accomplished by redirecting the session to a predefined Exchange 2003 URL (typically an Exchange Server 2003 front-end server). Overall, the recommended implementation process for Exchange 2010 Client Access is as follows:

1. Installing Exchange 2010 within your organization on new hardware
2. Configuring Exchange 2010 Client Access for coexistence
3. Creating the legacy namespace and associating the namespace with your Exchange 2003 infrastructure
4. Obtaining a digital certificate with the names you'll be using during the coexistence period and installing it on your Exchange 2010 Client Access servers and Exchange 2003 front-end servers
5. Associating the namespace you currently use for your Exchange 2003 infrastructure with your newly installed Exchange 2010 infrastructure
6. Moving mailboxes from Exchange 2003 to Exchange 2010
7. Decommissioning your Exchange 2003 infrastructure

Of these steps, we will focus on configuring Exchange 2010 Client Access, managing your legacy (Exchange 2003) OWA host names, and configuring and managing digital (PKI x.509) certificates for coexistence. Planning and configuring of Exchange 2010 Client Access is covered in detail in Chapter 4.

To support a seamless coexistence with and upgrade from Exchange 2003 OWA, an OWA virtual directory property named *Exchange2003URL* was introduced in Exchange 2010 Client Access. This property is assigned on each OWA virtual directory that will be performing redirection to an Exchange 2003 front-end server. This is necessary because Exchange 2003 is not Active Directory–site aware, and does not publish settings in Active Directory—so Exchange 2010 Client Access has no means of determining which server running Exchange Server 2003 a user should be redirected to.

The following cmdlet sets the Exchange 2010 Client Access external URL for Contoso to owa.contoso.com, and sets the Exchange 2003 URL to legacy.contoso.com:

```
Set-OWAVirtualDirectory Seattle-EX10\OWA* -ExternalURL https://mail.contoso.com/OWA
-Exchange2003URL https://legacy.contoso.com/exchange
```

Seattle-EX10 is the server name of the Exchange Server 2010 server hosting the Client Access role.

It is recommended that a new namespace, such as *legacy.contoso.com*, be established for the Exchange 2003 front-end server, and the existing namespace, such as *owa.contoso.com*, be associated with the Exchange 2010 infrastructure. In this way, Contoso users with Exchange Server 2003 mailboxes continue to use the existing URL of *https://owa.contoso.com/exchange* (which now points to the Exchange Server 2010 infrastructure), and are silently redirected to *https://legacy.contoso.com/exchange* (the computer running Exchange Server 2003).

Digital Certificates and Exchange 2010 Client Access

Digital, or X.509, certificates are used to create the SSL-encrypted channel used by Exchange 2010 Client Access services. In addition to protecting data in transit from theft or tampering through encryption, these certificates also authenticate the server running Exchange Server 2010, providing assurance to the end user that the server is indeed the server it claims to be. This assurance is provided by the certificate in question being issued by a certification authority (CA) that the end user either chooses to trust (in the case of a Windows or other internally managed CAs), or that the user trusts because it is issued by a trusted third-party CA.

Exchange 2010 also generates a self-signed certificate automatically, but you should replace this with a certificate issued by a trusted CA. Otherwise, this certificate needs to be manually trusted by every client by manually copying it to the trusted root certificate store on each client computer or mobile device, which is generally not feasible. For Internet-facing Client Access services, the best practice is to use a SAN certificate from a trusted third-party CA. Digital certificates and SAN versus wildcard certificates are covered in detail in Chapter 4.

When requesting your SAN certificate, it is best practice to minimize the number of host names requested, to minimize cost and reduce the certificate management complexity. Examples of recommended host names for Contoso are listed in Table 14-10.

TABLE 14-10 Contoso's SAN Certificate Recommended Host Names

HOST NAME	USE
Mail.contoso.com	Covers most connections to Exchange, including Outlook Web App, Outlook Anywhere, Offline Address Book, Exchange Web Services, POP3, IMAP4, SMTP, Exchange Control Panel, and ActiveSync
Autodiscover.contoso.com	Used by Autodiscover-supported clients, including Outlook 2007 and later; ActiveSync; and Exchange Web Services clients
Legacy.contoso.com	Used for coexistence with Exchange Server 2003 and/or Exchange Server 2007

OWA Customizations

It is quite common for organizations to have modified OWA in Exchange Server 2003 to meet their organization's needs, and you will want to reflect these modifications in your Exchange Server 2010 deployment as well.

Outlook Web App 2010 has a single theme whose graphic elements, colors, and other elements can be modified to accommodate your organization's branding—logos, color scheme, graphic elements, and so on. OWA 2007 supported multiple themes, but Exchange Server 2010 Outlook Web App has one theme for all users, although multiple theme support will be included with Exchange Server 2010 SP1. Any modifications are overwritten when you deploy an Exchange service pack or rollup, so you need to make backups of any changes and reapply them after applying the service pack or rollup.

Another element that is frequently customized is the OWA sign-in and sign-out pages. Outlook Web App can be customized in this manner as well; the sign-in, language selection, and sign-out pages are created based on the graphics and logon.css files. These files are located in the base theme folder in the Exchange installation directory at <Exchange Server>\V14\Client Access\OWA\<version number>\themes\base. Again, any modifications are overwritten when you deploy an Exchange service pack or rollup, so you need to make backups of any changes and reapply them after applying the service pack or rollup.

If you have multiple Client Access servers in your environment, you must copy any changes made to each Client Access server to ensure a consistent user experience.

Outlook Interoperability

In Exchange 2010, the Client Access server role now handles the RPC connectivity from MAPI clients such as Microsoft Office Outlook for connections to mailbox databases; connections to public folder databases are still made directly to the RPC Client Access service on the Mailbox role. In Exchange 2007 and earlier, Outlook clients connecting to an Exchange server from inside an organization's firewall would connect directly to the Exchange 2007 Information Store. This RPC Client Access functionality is explained in detail in Chapter 4.

For the purposes of coexistence, however, it is important to note that RPC Client Access requires RPC encryption by default. Outlook 2007 and later use encryption by default, but Outlook 2003 is not configured for RPC encryption by default. RPC encryption can be turned off on the Client Access server, but best practice is to enable encryption for Outlook 2003 users either manually or through Active Directory group policy to ensure that these users can connect to their mailboxes when they are moved to Exchange 2010. Detailed instructions for configuring RPC encryption for Outlook are available at *http://support.microsoft.com/kb/2006508*.

In addition, as mentioned in the "Free/Busy Functionality" section of this chapter, if Outlook 2003 is in use in the environment, public folders will also need to be maintained to provide free/busy functionality to Outlook 2003 users.

Exchange ActiveSync Coexistence

When Exchange Server 2010 Client Access is deployed, it provides direct support for Exchange Server 2003 mailboxes. Exchange ActiveSync is discussed in detail in Chapter 4, but we will discuss one of the primary considerations here with respect to coexistence with Exchange Server 2003.

You must enable Integrated Windows authentication on the Microsoft-Server-ActiveSync virtual directory on the Exchange 2003 back-end server. This allows the Exchange 2010

Client Access server and the Exchange 2003 back-end server to communicate using Kerberos authentication to provide for seamless coexistence for Exchange Server 2003 mailboxes access via Exchange Server 2010 ActiveSync. IIS Manager cannot be used to change the authentication settings on the ActiveSync virtual directory, because the DS2MB process within the Exchange 2003 System Attendant will overwrite the settings that are configured. Integrated Windows authentication can be configured in one of two ways:

- Install the hotfix located at *http://support.microsoft.com/?kbid=937031*, then use Exchange System Manager to adjust the authentication settings of the Exchange ActiveSync virtual directory.
- Set the *msExchAuthenticationFlags* attribute to a value of 6 on the *Microsoft-Server-ActiveSync* object within the configuration container on each Exchange Server 2003 Mailbox server. An example script is provided at *http://technet.microsoft.com/en-us/library/cc785437(EXCHG.80).aspx*.

Upgrading Message Connectivity From Exchange Server 2003

This section will cover the issues and best practices surrounding upgrading your messaging connectivity to Exchange Server 2010, including internal and external message routing.

Internal Message Routing

You'll find significant differences in message routing between Exchange Server 2003 and Exchange Server 2010. This section describes these changes and outlines the actions necessary to ensure successful coexistence.

NOTES FROM THE FIELD

Optimizing Message Routing in an Exchange Server 2003 and Exchange Server 2010 Environment

Markus Bellmann
Senior Solutions Architect, Siemens, Germany

When deploying Exchange Server 2010 into an Exchange Server 2003 environment with multiple routing groups, I've found that it's best to configure additional routing group connectors between Exchange Server 2003 and Exchange Server 2010. These additional connectors can optimize your message flow for remote routing groups so that messages between user mailboxes upgraded to Exchange Server 2007 and those still on Exchange Server 2003 don't go across the WAN links. Additional connectors can also provide redundancy so that message routing between Exchange Server 2003 and Exchange Server 2010 does not have a single point of failure.

In an Exchange Server 2003 environment consisting of multiple routing groups, it is best practice to create additional routing group connectors to optimize message routing and provide redundancy between Exchange Server 2003 routing groups and Exchange Server 2010. These connectors are created using the *New-RoutingGroupConnector* cmdlet in the Exchange Management Shell (EMS) and not the Exchange System Manager in Exchange Server 2003. In this way, the membership of the ExchangeLegacyInterop universal security group is then automatically updated with the Exchange Server 2003 servers specified so they have the necessary permissions to send and receive mail from the Exchange Server 2010 Hub Transport servers.

An example of creating a new routing group connector is shown here, where the Exchange Server 2010 source transport server is Seattle-EX10.contoso.com, the Exchange Server 2003 bridgehead server is Seattle-EX03.contoso.com, and the routing group connector is a two-way connector with a cost of 100:

```
New-RoutingGroupConnector -Name "Interop RGC" -SourceTransportServers "Seattle-EX10.
contoso.com" -TargetTransportServers "Seattle-EX03.contoso.com" -Cost 100
-Bidirectional $true
```

Exchange Server 2010 Send and Receive Connectors

The Hub Transport server role provides SMTP transport for an Exchange Server 2010 infrastructure. Unlike Exchange Server 2003, where messaging connectivity between locations is provided by routing-group connectors, the Hub Transport role routes messages between Active Directory sites using an inherent connector called the *intra-organization Send connector*. Additionally, during the Hub Transport server role installation two explicit Receive connectors are created. SMTP traffic from all sources on port 25 is received by the first connector, whereas SMTP traffic from non-MAPI clients is received on port 587 by the second Receive connector.

External Message Routing

In some environments, the Exchange Server 2010 Edge Transport role is not deployed and Internet mail is either received directly on the Hub Transport servers or a third-party SMTP smart host is deployed in the perimeter network. Both of the default Exchange Server 2010 Hub Transport Receive connectors (outlined in the "Exchange Server 2010 Send and Receive Connectors" section of this chapter) require authentication by default, so to allow for this scenario the receive connector accepting SMTP connections from the Internet or the smart host must be configured to allow anonymous access to accept SMTP messages from the Internet.

To route messages to the Internet, a Send connector must be configured. In an upgrade where the Exchange Server 2010 Edge Transport server role is deployed in a perimeter network to route messages to remote domains, when the Edge Transport server is subscribed to the Exchange organization the necessary connectors are created automatically. However, if the Exchange Server 2010 Hub Transport servers will be sending SMTP traffic directly, or a third-party SMTP smart host is deployed in the perimeter network, you will need to manually create and configure Send connectors.

You can manually create and configure Send connectors either through the Exchange Management Console or using Windows PowerShell via the EMS. The following is an EMS example of creating an Internet send connector with a cost of 10, where the source Hub Transport server is Seattle-EX10 and all outbound SMTP is routed via a smart host named smtp.contoso.com:

```
New-SendConnector -Name 'Internet Outbound' -Usage 'Custom' -AddressSpaces
'SMTP:*;10' -IsScopedConnector $false -DNSRoutingEnabled $false -SmartHosts
'smtp.contoso.com' -SmartHostAuthMechanism 'None' -UseExternalDNSServersEnabled $false
-SourceTransportServers 'Seattle-EX10'
```

Coexistence for Management

Coexistence for management includes managing mailboxes on Exchange Server 2003 and Exchange Server 2010, configuring and managing Exchange servers, and organization parameters and message tracking.

Numerous complexities are involved in managing Exchange in a coexistence environment. This is why the final goal of your Exchange Server 2010 upgrade should be to upgrade to a native Exchange Server 2010 environment as soon as possible, including decommissioning the Exchange Server 2003 computers. Lowering the Total Cost of Ownership (TCO), including administration costs, is usually a primary goal of the upgrade, and managing a mixed environment presents many opportunities for human error. Managing multiple versions of Exchange will add to your TCO, so it is recommended that you complete your upgrade to Exchange Server 2010 as soon as possible, rather than manage a coexistence environment for an extended period of time.

Managing Mailboxes

Exchange Server 2010 mailboxes are managed with Windows PowerShell via the EMS or the Exchange Management Console (EMC), whereas Exchange Server 2003 mailboxes must be managed using the Active Directory Users and Computers (ADUC) snap-in extension for Exchange.

> ***IMPORTANT*** **Exchange Server 2010 mailboxes cannot be managed using the Exchange Server 2003 tools. Exchange Server 2010 mailboxes modified in this fashion will not be fully functional, although the Exchange Server 2003 tools do not actually block this from happening.**
>
> **In addition, the Exchange Server 2003 Move Mailbox Task Wizard can't be used for any mailbox moves where the source or destination is Exchange Server 2010. Mailbox moves between Exchange Server 2003 and Exchange Server 2010 can be performed with the Exchange Server 2010 tools, with Exchange Server 2003 as either source or destination. You can't create mailboxes on Exchange Server 2003 using the Exchange Server 2010 tools, although you can modify and remove Exchange Server 2003 mailboxes with the Exchange Server 2010 tools; you must use the ADUC Exchange snap-in to create Exchange Server 2003 mailboxes.**

Apart from managing recipients, you need to be aware of several other issues when managing your Exchange organization in a coexistence environment with Exchange Server 2003.

Exchange Server 2003 Administrative Groups

The concept of administrative groups was used in Exchange Server 2003 to allow for administrative delegation of portions of the Exchange organization to different administrators. Although this model provided a basic delegation model, it was not as flexible as it could have been. For example, after an Exchange Server 2003 computer was deployed into a particular administrative group it could not be moved into a different administrative group without removing and re-installing Exchange Server 2003.

As discussed in the "Preparing Active Directory for Exchange Server 2010" section of this chapter, when your Active Directory environment is prepared for Exchange Server 2010, a new administrative group called *Exchange Administrative Group (FYDIBOHF23SPDLT)* is created that holds all Exchange Server 2010 servers. This administrative group is strictly for coexistence purposes; however, all Exchange Server 2010 computers are installed in this administrative group. Servers running Exchange Server 2010 cannot be moved from this administrative group, and Exchange Server 2003 servers cannot be added to it. In addition, this administrative group cannot be renamed.

In Exchange Server 2010, administrative groups have been replaced with a Role-Based Access Control (RBAC) delegation model that allows for much greater granularity. Previously, the delegation model applied only to the administrators who managed the Exchange infrastructure and recipients. In Exchange Server 2010, however, RBAC controls not only administrative tasks but also delegates to users the ability to administer their own mailbox and distribution groups. RBAC is discussed in more detail in Chapter 16, "Managing Exchange."

Managing Exchange Server, Database, and Organizational Settings

All organizational-level settings must be managed with the Exchange Server 2010 administration tools after Exchange Server 2010 has been introduced into the environment. At a more granular level, Exchange Server 2010 computers and mailboxes are managed with the Exchange Server 2010 management tools, whereas Exchange Server 2003 computers must be administered using the Exchange Server 2003 Exchange System Manager. In addition, as mentioned in the "Managing Mailboxes" section of this chapter, Exchange Server 2003 mailboxes must be managed using the Active Directory Users and Computers Exchange snap-in.

Message Tracking

You'll notice significant differences in the message-tracking schemas and tools between Exchange Server 2003 and Exchange Server 2010. This means that messages sent and received by Exchange Server 2010 can only be tracked with the Exchange Server 2010 management tools—Exchange Server 2010 does not have the Windows Management Instrumentation (WMI) support required by the Exchange Server 2003 Message Tracking Center. In addition, the Exchange Server 2003 Message Tracking Center cannot parse the Exchange Server 2010 message tracking logs.

> **NOTE** A message crossing both Exchange Server 2010 and Exchange Server 2003 must be tracked with a combination of the Exchange Server 2003 and Exchange Server 2010 utilities; it can't be tracked with the same tools.

Planning and Implementing Mailbox Moves and Coexistence

This section examines the issues, recommendations, and requirements around migrating mailboxes to Exchange Server 2010 and coexisting with Exchange Server 2003 mailboxes.

Address List and E-mail Address Policy Filters

In Exchange Server 2003, filters for address lists and e-mail address policies were based on LDAP syntax; Exchange Server 2010 uses OPATH filtering syntax. Although LDAP syntax filters are supported in Exchange Server 2010, they must be upgraded to OPATH syntax if you want to edit them in Exchange Server 2010, and LDAP filters can't be created in Exchange Server 2010. In addition, LDAP filters cannot be upgraded to OPATH syntax with the EMC; they must be upgraded using the EMS.

DEFAULT ADDRESS LIST FILTERS

Although upgrading custom filters is essentially a manual process, the following cmdlets upgrade the default address lists from LDAP to OPATH filters:

- All Users default address list:

  ```
  Set-AddressList "All Users" -IncludedRecipients MailboxUsers
  ```

- All Groups default address list:

  ```
  Set-AddressList "All Groups" -IncludedRecipients MailGroups
  ```

- All Contacts default address list:

  ```
  Set-AddressList "All Contacts" -IncludedRecipients MailContacts
  ```

- Public Folders default address list:

  ```
  Set-AddressList "Public Folders" -RecipientFilter { RecipientType -eq
  'PublicFolder' }
  ```

- The Default Global Address List:

  ```
  Set-GlobalAddressList "Default Global Address List" -RecipientFilter {(Alias -ne
  $null -and (ObjectClass -eq 'user' -or ObjectClass -eq 'contact' -or ObjectClass
  -eq 'msExchSystemMailbox' -or ObjectClass -eq 'msExchDynamicDistributionList' -or
  ObjectClass -eq 'group' -or ObjectClass -eq 'publicFolder'))}
  ```

CUSTOM ADDRESS LIST AND E-MAIL POLICY FILTERS

Custom filters for address lists, e-mail address policies, and dynamic distribution groups are a little more complicated to upgrade. Custom filters require you to determine what they are filtering for, and then translate the filter into OPATH syntax. The Microsoft Exchange Team has produced a script that will aid in converting most custom filters from LDAP to OPATH syntax; this script is available at *http://msexchangeteam.com/archive/2007/03/12/436983.aspx*. For any filters that must be upgraded manually, follow these steps:

1. Copy the existing filter into Notepad or another text editor.
2. Write a statement explaining what the filter accomplishes.
3. Construct the filter in OPATH syntax based on the statement created in Step 2.

This process is explained in more detail in the Exchange Server 2010 online help at *http://technet.microsoft.com/en-us/library/cc164375.aspx*.

Moving Offline Address Books

In Exchange Server 2003 and earlier, offline address books (OABs) were stored in and distributed from public folders—system folders in particular—but Exchange Server 2010 (similar to Exchange Server 2007) can distribute OABs by means of a Web-based distribution method that uses HTTP (or HTTPS) and BITS. This new distribution method supports more concurrent clients, reduces bandwidth consumption, and provides more flexibility for distribution points. It does, however, require that clients be running Outlook 2007 or higher, or that they be using OWA.

Exchange Server 2010, similar to Exchange Server 2003, can generate the offline address book in three versions to support various clients, as Table 14-11 outlines. OAB versions prior to version 4 require you to retain public folder distribution.

TABLE 14-11 Offline Address Book Versions

OAB VERSION	CLIENT SUPPORT
Version 2	Outlook 98 SP1 or earlier
Version 3	Outlook 98 SP2 or later
Version 4	Outlook 2003 SP2 or later

When you introduce Exchange Server 2010 into an existing Exchange Server 2003 organization, the offline address book remains hosted on Exchange Server 2003, and Web-based distribution is unavailable. After all mailboxes have been moved to Exchange Server 2010, Web-based distribution can be enabled and public folder distribution can be disabled, provided that clients are using Outlook 2007 or later. If Outlook 2003 or earlier is still in use after mailboxes have been moved, you will need to maintain public folder distribution for OABs.

However, to enable Web-based distribution, you need to move the OAB to an Exchange Server 2010 computer because Exchange Server 2003 only supports public folder distribution for OABs.

Moving OABs to Exchange Server 2010 can be accomplished through the EMC or the EMS. The move task in EMC is accomplished by navigating to the Offline Address Book tab in the Mailbox node beneath the Organization Configuration container, and then clicking Move from the Actions pane as shown in Figure 14-9 (or by right-clicking the OAB and selecting Move).

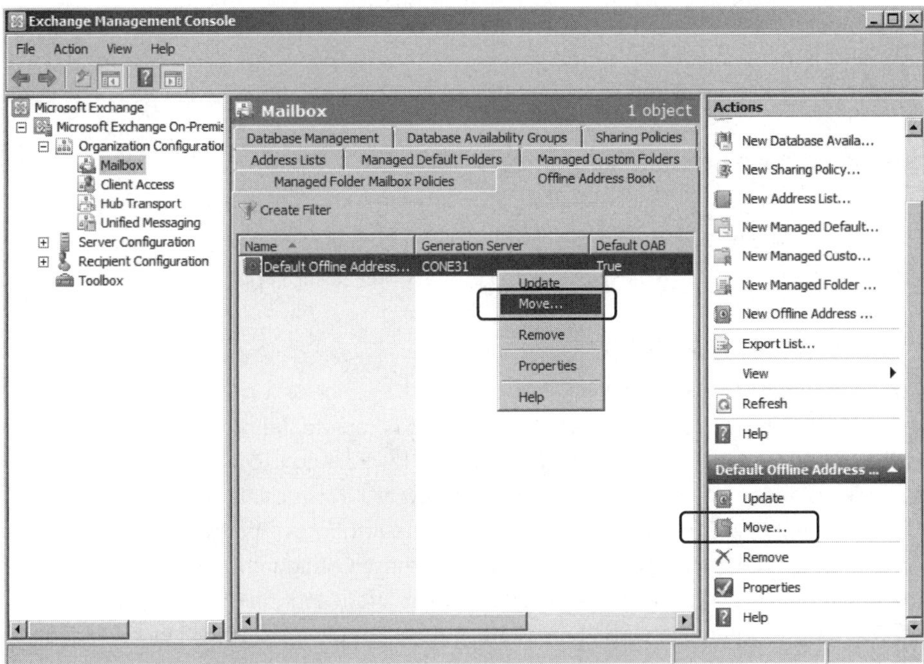

FIGURE 14-9 Moving OABs from EMC

To perform the operation via the EMS, the cmdlet to move all the OABs to an Exchange Server 2010 computer called Seattle-EX10 from an Exchange Server 2003 computer called Seattle-EX03 is:

```
Get-OfflineAddressBook -Server Seattle-EX03 | Move-OfflineAddressBook -Server
Seattle-EX10
```

The GUID of the OAB to be moved is required for the *Move-OfflineAddressBook* cmdlet. The OABs from the source server are retrieved with *Get-OfflineAddressBook*, and piping this output to *Move-OfflineAddressBook* provides the necessary GUIDs to the cmdlet for the move.

To enable Web-based distribution for the address books after they have been moved to Exchange Server 2010 you need to either create a new virtual directory for a distribution point or determine which existing one is to be used for the purpose. To set the distribution point for the Default Offline Address List to an Exchange Server 2010 Client Access server named Seattle-EX10, the following cmdlets will retrieve the OAB virtual directory on Seattle-EX10, and then configure that virtual directory as the distribution point for the OAB:

```
$a=Get-OabVirtualDirectory -Server Seattle-EX10
Set-OfflineAddressBook "Default Offline Address List" -VirtualDirectories $a
```

Client Considerations

Outlook versions earlier than Outlook 2003 are not supported with Exchange Server 2010 mailboxes. As outlined in the "Outlook Interoperability" section of this chapter, if Outlook 2003 is in use, one of the primary considerations for planning mailbox moves is that RPC connectivity for MAPI clients requires RPC encryption by default in Exchange Server 2010.

Recipient Update Service Migration

In addition to considering the Outlook version or versions deployed in the environment, you need to consider how recipients are provisioned in Exchange Server 2010 compared to Exchange Server 2003 as well as how e-mail address policies are applied.

RUS AND EXCHANGE SERVER 2003

The Recipient Update Service (RUS) was introduced in Exchange Server 2000 and used in Exchange Server 2003 as well. Its job was to locate and complete the provisioning process for newly created recipient objects in Active Directory by creating Exchange-specific attribute values on the objects. The RUS was also responsible for updating existing objects by modifying the Active Directory's object's appropriate attributes. The two types of the RUS in an Exchange Server 2003 organization are the Enterprise Configuration Recipient Update Service (one instance per Exchange Server 2003 organization) and the domain Recipient Update Service. As its name implies, there is one instance of the domain RUS for each domain that contains mail or mailbox-enabled users.

When you created an Exchange Server 2003 mail or mailbox-enabled user or mail-enabled group using the Active Directory Users and Computers (ADUC) console, a few key attributes were set immediately when the object was created. These attributes allowed the RUS to discover the object and complete the provisioning process by backfilling the remaining Exchange-specific attributes asynchronously.

RECIPIENT CREATION IN EXCHANGE SERVER 2010

In Exchange Server 2007 and higher, including Exchange Server 2010, recipient objects are now fully provisioned as they are created in the EMS or the EMC GUI; the RUS background process to discover and update objects has been removed. This means that mailboxes can be used immediately after being created in Exchange Server 2010; with the RUS, the asynchronous process had to stamp the user object before the recipient or mailbox was usable. This meant that if problems arose they could be complicated to troubleshoot; the RUS was an asynchronous process and it could be difficult to determine whether it wasn't working or was just delayed.

Another role of the RUS was to apply recipient policies in Exchange 2000 Server and Exchange Server 2003, and to update recipients when recipient policies were modified. Because the RUS is not present in Exchange Server 2007, you need to implement various processes to update recipients due to changes in policies; this will be covered in the next section.

Although the RUS is not present in Exchange Server 2010, you do need to provide RUS functionality in a mixed environment for the duration of your migration. You also need to understand the new recipient update process that occurs when your mailboxes are moved to Exchange Server 2010.

RUS MIGRATION CONSIDERATIONS

In a mixed environment, removing the RUS process from Exchange Server 2010 has implications. One issue is that if you configure an existing RUS instance to use an Exchange Server 2010 computer through the Exchange System Manager GUI, that RUS instance will cease functioning. The RUS functionality must be maintained on an Exchange Server 2003 computer until all mailboxes have been moved to Exchange Server 2010, even for domains containing only servers running Exchange Server 2010.

In addition, you should examine your user-provisioning tools or processes during the Exchange Server 2010 planning process. Some tools or processes designed for Exchange Server 2003 may partially provision users expecting the RUS to complete the provisioning process. Also, changes to E-mail Address Policies in Exchange Server 2007 may have to be applied to existing users because the RUS process no longer exists. Applying E-mail Address Policy changes can easily be accomplished using the *Update-EmailAddressPolicy* and *Update-AddressList* PowerShell cmdlets. Run the *Update-EmailAddressPolicy* cmdlet first because it updates recipients based on the organization's E-mail Address Policies. The *Update-AddressList* cmdlet updates your address lists with changes to recipients, so you should run it after the *Update-EmailAddressPolicy* cmdlet; always run these two cmdlets together. You can combine them with their corresponding *get* cmdlets as follows, to update the entire organization in a single script:

```
Get-EmailAddressPolicy | Update-EmailAddressPolicy
Get-AddressList | Update-AddressList
```

You can also use this approach to update the Global Address Lists in your organization as follows:

```
Get-GlobalAddressList | Update-GlobalAddressList
```

E-mail Address Policies

You need to keep a couple of issues to keep in mind when it comes to e-mail address policies. In Exchange Server 2003, e-mail address policies could be created, but not immediately applied, although this was not desired behavior. In Exchange Server 2010, e-mail address policies are applied synchronously anytime you write recipient objects in Exchange Server 2010, including mailbox moves from Exchange Server 2003 to Exchange Server 2010. What this means is that you may have a number of mailboxes that have been configured with new e-mail proxy addresses or even a different primary SMTP address because the mailbox has been moved; this can lead to confusion and increased support calls. To avoid this, you should evaluate your e-mail address policies prior to implementing mailbox moves to Exchange Server 2010. In the case of mailboxes whose e-mail addresses you don't want to change, clear the Automatically Update E-Mail Addresses Based On E-Mail Address Policy check box on those mailboxes through the ADUC Exchange Server 2003 snap-in as shown in Figure 14-10 before the mailbox is moved to Exchange Server 2010.

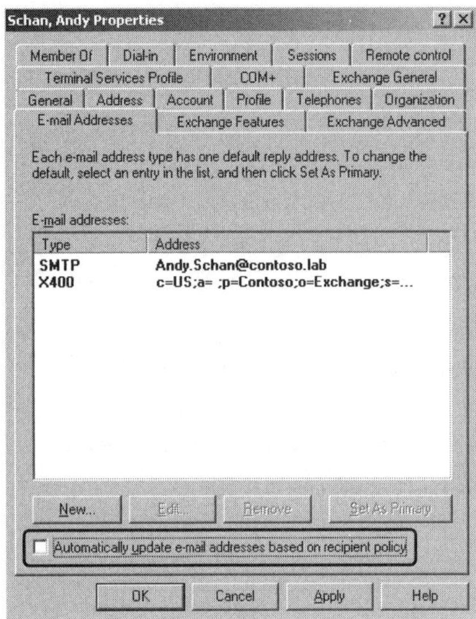

FIGURE 14-10 Preventing e-mail address policies from applying to an Exchange Server 2003 mailbox

A second issue to be considered with respect to e-mail address policies is whether any SMTP address spaces in your Exchange Server 2003 organization are ambiguously non-authoritative—that is, the address space has been marked authoritative in one policy but non-authoritative in another. Any SMTP address spaces configured in this way should be resolved before you run Exchange Server 2010 *PrepareAD* in your environment to avoid potential mail flow interruptions. This issue and its effects, along with the recommended preventative measure, is discussed in detail in the "Preparing Active Directory for Exchange Server 2010" section earlier in this chapter.

Moving Mailboxes from Exchange Server 2003 to Exchange Server 2010

Mailboxes are moved to Exchange Server 2010 using the *Move Request* cmdlets or the Exchange Server 2010 Exchange Management Console; mailbox moves cannot be performed using the Exchange Server 2003 Exchange System Manager (ESM). In addition, the Exchange Server 2003 Mailbox server must be Exchange Server 2003 SP2.

In Exchange Server 2003, mailbox moves were synchronous; this meant that if the ESM console was closed before the move completed, the mailbox move was cancelled. Additionally, all of the mailbox's data was moved through the ESM instance performing the move, so if the move was initiated on an administrative computer other than the source and destination mailbox server, all data flowed through the administrative computer rather than from source to destination mailbox server.

In Exchange Server 2010, mailbox moves are now asynchronous and initiated with move requests. The new *Move Request* cmdlets perform an asynchronous move because they send a request to the Microsoft Exchange Mailbox Replication Service (MRS), a service running on all Exchange Server 2010 Client Access servers in your organization; the mailbox move itself is performed by the MRS. The MRS enables you to manage mailbox moves from anywhere within the organization after the move request is placed, and the console or script initiating it does not need to remain open during the move.

In summary, the new move request functionality in Exchange Server 2010 has the following the benefits:

- Mailbox moves are asynchronous and are carried out by the MRS.
- Mailboxes are kept online during asynchronous moves (Exchange Server 2007 SP2 or Exchange Server 2010 to Exchange Server 2010 only).
- The mailbox's Recoverable Items are moved with the mailbox (Exchange Server 2010 to Exchange Server 2010 only).
- As soon as the mailbox begins to move, content indexing starts to scan the mailbox so that fast searching is available upon completion of the move.
- Throttling can be configured for each MRS instance, each mailbox database, or each mailbox server.
- Move requests can be initiated between forests; these are referred to as *remote move requests*.
- Mailbox moves can be managed from anywhere within the organization.
- Mailbox data content does not travel through an administrative computer.
- The move history of the mailbox is preserved in the mailbox.

NOTES FROM THE FIELD

Moving Mailboxes from Exchange Server 2003 to Exchange Server 2010

Nicolai Wagner
System Manager, Exchange Operations, Axel Springer AG, Germany

We are currently migrating from Exchange Server 2003 to Exchange Server 2010 using Outlook 2003 for clients, and we have found the following factors need to be considered when determining which mailboxes should be moved at the same time when migrating to Exchange Server 2010 in order to reduce user impact:

When moving mailboxes to Exchange Server 2010, any delegates should be moved at the same time—for example, managers and their administrative assistants—as a user

in Exchange Server 2010 can manage calendars on Exchange Server 2003, but not vice versa. When the mailbox of a delegate is on Exchange Server 2003 and the mailbox they are accessing is on Exchange Server 2010, the manager's calendar appears to be empty when the delegate opens it with Outlook 2003 or OWA. An administrative assistant that is based on Exchange 2003 can only open one additional calendar; when trying to open more calendars, Outlook 2003 shows an error message.

We also determined that conference rooms should be moved early in the upgrade to Exchange Server 2010, prior to moving users who book or otherwise manage the conference rooms. Otherwise, users booking the conference rooms are able to book the Exchange Server 2003 conference room mailbox as an attendee but not as a resource. Resolving this requires moving the conference room mailbox to Exchange Server 2010, and then converting the mailbox to a room mailbox using the *Set-Mailbox* cmdlet with the *Type parameter*—for example, *Set-Mailbox* <MailboxID> *-Type Room.*

Planning Public Folder Access and Migration

This section discusses the considerations for coexistence and migration of public folders in your Exchange Server 2003 environment.

Public Folder Access via OWA

Although public folder servers can be replicated to Exchange Server 2010 at the same time as the rest of the Exchange Server 2010 infrastructure is implemented, you should retain public folder replicas on Exchange Server 2003 until all mailboxes have been migrated to Exchange Server 2010. This is to allow for access to public folders via Exchange Server 2003 OWA as well as Exchange Server 2010 Outlook Web App. The behavior for accessing public folders via various combinations of mailbox and public folder server versions is outlined in Table 14-12.

TABLE 14-12 Accessing Public Folders via OWA

MAILBOX LOCATION	PF LOCATION	OWA ACCESS TO PF FROM EXCHANGE SERVER 2010 CAS?	OWA ACCESS TO PF FROM EXCHANGE SERVER 2003 OWA?
Exchange Server 2003	Exchange Server 2003	Yes	Yes
Exchange Server 2003	Exchange Server 2010	No	No
Exchange Server 2010	Exchange Server 2003	Yes (redirected to Exchange Server 2003 OWA)	N/A
Exchange Server 2010	Exchange Server 2010	Yes	N/A

Migrating Public Folders

As mentioned in the previous section, you should retain public folder content on Exchange Server 2003 servers until all mailboxes have been moved to Exchange Server 2010, to ensure access to the content by Exchange Server 2003 OWA users. To replicate public folder content to Exchange Server 2010, it is recommended that you use the AddReplicaToPFRecursive.ps1 Windows PowerShell script, located in the <*Exchange_Installation_Path*>\Scripts directory on the Exchange Server 2010 computer. After all mailboxes have been moved to Exchange Server 2010, the public folder replicas can be removed by using the RemoveReplicaFromPFRecursive.ps1 script.

LESSONS LEARNED

Invalid Categories Set on Public Folder Items

Markus Bellmann
Senior Solutions Architect, Siemens, Germany

I recently worked with a client who was migrating from Exchange Server 2003 to Exchange Server 2010. They use public folders extensively; they have 200 GB of data in almost 18,000 folders, with a total item count of more than 2,000,000 items; one folder alone had more than 125,000 items in it, and there is a significant amount of data that is more than 5 years old. As cleaning up their public folder infrastructure would involve working with multiple business units and persuading them to archive, and the many discussions about what can or can't be archived, this would have taken a considerable amount of time and delayed the Exchange Server 2010 project significantly, so they opted to replicate all the data to Exchange Server 2010 and undertake a public folder cleanup as an ongoing project at a later date. However, when we began replicating the public folders from Exchange Server 2003, we discovered that a significant amount of the content would not replicate; the Exchange Server 2003 information store was sending out folder content backfill messages, but these messages were failing on the store driver on the Exchange Server 2010 Hub Transport server. The cause was invalid Outlook Categories being set on the items in public folders; Exchange Server 2010 (as well as Exchange Server 2007) performs a significant amount of property validation to keep bad data from getting into the public folder store, so data that is accepted by Exchange Server 2003 is rejected by Exchange Server 2010. The invalid categories issue in particular is indicated by the following event logged on the Hub Transport Server:

```
Log Name:      Application
Source:        MSExchange Store Driver
Event ID:      1020
Task Category: MSExchangeStoreDriver
Level:         Error
```

```
Keywords:       Classic
User:           N/A
Description:
The store driver couldn't deliver the public folder replication message
"Folder Content Backfill Response" because the following error occurred:
Property validation failed. Property = [{00020329-0000-0000-c000-
000000000046}:'Keywords'] Categories
Error = Element 0 in the multivalue property is invalid...
```

This issue is documented on the Microsoft Exchange Team Blog at *http://msexchangeteam.com/archive/2008/01/10/447843.aspx*, and the solution is to simply clear the Category on all of the items using Outlook; the invalid Categories usually display in Outlook as "None" and you will see items arranged in two different "None" Categories. You may have to set them to some other category and then set them back to None to clear the Categories successfully. Once the Categories property is truly clear, you'll only have one set of items that show a Category of "None," and the items will replicate successfully. Now, the above works in theory, but when you're dealing with 200 GB of public folder content finding and correcting the items with invalid Categories through Outlook is simply not feasible. Some automated approaches were taken using scripting, but creating, validating and running these scripts took a considerable amount of time and effort that had to be diverted from the rest of the upgrade project. The lesson learned in this case was that public folders need to be managed on an ongoing basis to avoid having them get out of control, and that you're much better off cleaning up your public folders before attempting to replicate them to the new system.

Removing Legacy Exchange Servers

The ultimate milestone in your upgrade to Exchange Server 2010 is the decommissioning of your last legacy Exchange servers. Before you reformat the hard drives on the final legacy server, however, you have numerous items to confirm:

1. To uninstall the last Exchange Server 2003 computer you require Exchange Full Administrator permissions in Exchange Server 2003, as well as the Organization Management role in Exchange Server 2010.
2. Confirm that all legacy Exchange features are decommissioned or replaced, as outlined in the "Discontinued and Deemphasized Functionality in Exchange Server 2010" section of this chapter.
3. Confirm that all mailboxes and public folders are migrated to Exchange Server 2010, as outlined in the "Planning Mailbox Moves and Coexistence" and "Planning Public Folder Access and Migration" sections of this chapter.

4. Move the public folder hierarchy to the Exchange Server 2010 administrative group from the legacy Exchange Server 2003 administrative group by following these steps:
   a. Open the Exchange System Manager console for Exchange Server 2003.
   b. Within Exchange System Manager, expand Administrative Groups, right-click Exchange Administrative Group (FYDIBOHF23SPDLT), select New, and then select Public Folders Container.
   c. Expand the legacy Exchange administrative group that contains the public-folder tree, expand Folders, and then drag Public Folders to Folders under the Exchange 2007 administrative group.
5. Ensure that all offline address books have been moved to Exchange Server 2010, as outlined in the "Moving Offline Address Books" section of this chapter, before you remove the last Exchange Server 2003 computer.
6. Verify that Send and Receive connectors have been created and configured on Exchange Server 2010, and inbound and outbound Internet SMTP traffic has been moved to Exchange Server 2010, as discussed in the "Upgrading Message Connectivity from Exchange Server 2003" section of this chapter. Also verify your DNS MX records have been modified to resolve to Exchange Server 2010 Edge Transport or Hub Transport servers, and verify in Exchange Server 2010 that no Exchange Server 2003 computers are listed as smart hosts for any Send connectors.
7. Check internal and external DNS records to verify that the following protocol services are resolving to Exchange Server 2010 Client Access servers. Confirm as well that all clients are using Exchange Server 2010 for these services and protocols.
   - ActiveSync
   - Outlook Web App
   - Outlook Anywhere
   - POP3
   - IMAP4
   - Autodiscover service
   - Other Exchange Web services
8. Remove public folder stores from Exchange Server 2003 by using the Exchange System Manager. The Exchange Server 2003 SP2 Exchange System Manager console blocks removing a public folder store until all replicas are removed, but best practice dictates confirming all public folders have been moved before removing the public folder store.
9. Delete any routing group connectors connecting Exchange Server 2010 to the Exchange Server 2003 routing groups using either the legacy Exchange System Manager console or the *Remove-RoutingGroupConnector* cmdlet in the EMS.
10. Remove any legacy Exchange recipient policies that don't contain E-mail Address policies using the legacy Exchange System Manager console. If any of the legacy Exchange recipient policies should contain both Mailbox Manager and E-mail Address

policies, remove the mailbox manager policies as follows. (Don't delete any policies that have e-mail address definitions that are still in use because Exchange Server 2010 will use these policies when new mailboxes are created.)

   a. In Exchange System Manager, expand Recipients and then select Recipient Policies.
   b. Right-click the policy and select Change Property Pages.
   c. Clear the Mailbox Manager Settings check box, and then click OK.

11. Delete the Recipient Update Services domain instance for each domain using the Exchange System Manager console.
12. Uninstall Exchange Server 2003 from the last server.
13. Delete the Recipient Update Services (Enterprise Configuration) instance. Because you do this after the last Exchange Server 2003 computer is removed, the Exchange System Manager console can't be used; you must use ADSI Edit (AdsiEdit.msc). Delete the RUS instance by following these steps:

   a. Open ADSI Edit, expand Configuration, expand CN=Configuration, DC=<domain>, DC=<top_level_domain>, expand CN=Services, expand CN=Microsoft Exchange, expand CN=<Exchange organization name>, expand CN=Address Lists Container, and then select CN=Recipient Update Services.
   b. In the Results pane, right-click Recipient Update Service (Enterprise Configuration), click Delete, and then click Yes to confirm the deletion.

IMPORTANT As a final note on decommissioning Exchange Server 2003 in your environment, it is important to point out that Exchange Server 2003 administrative groups that contained mailboxes at any time should *not* be deleted. This is because the *LegacyExchangeDN* attribute on mailboxes moved to Exchange Server 2010 from Exchange Server 2003 continues to reference the legacy administrative group. This attribute is used by Outlook 2003 and earlier to retrieve free/busy information, and is used by all versions of Outlook for delegate access. Outlook will be unable to find the delegated user if the Exchange Server 2003 administrative group is deleted.

Upgrading from and Coexisting with Exchange Server 2007

As you may recall from Chapter 2, "Exchange Deployment Projects," the two example environments running Exchange Server 2007 are Fabrikam and Litware. Fabrikam is composed of 7,000 users and is currently running Exchange Server 2007 in a semi-distributed model; a logical view of their Exchange Server 2007 environment is illustrated in Figure 14-11.

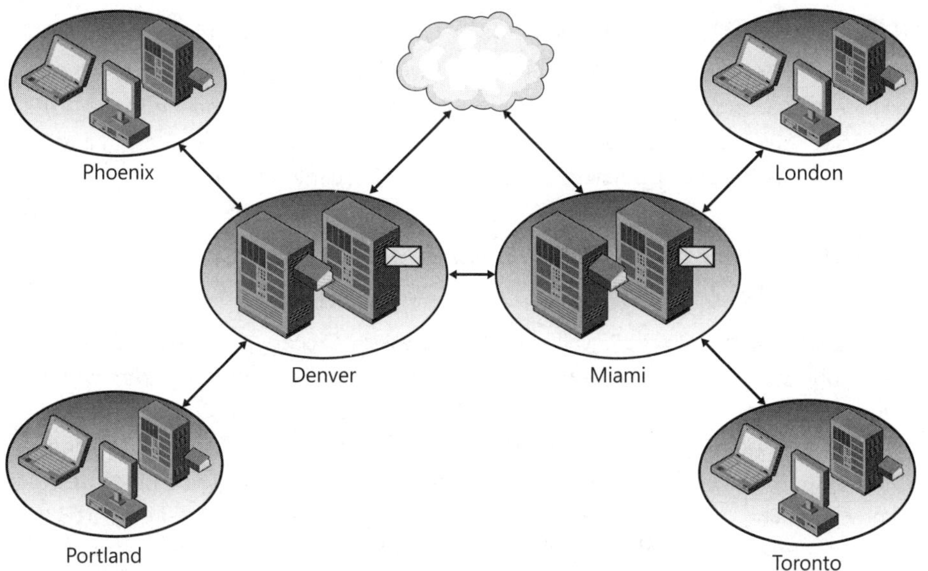

FIGURE 14-11 Logical view of Fabrikam's Exchange Server 2007 environment

Litware, our second example Exchange Server 2007 environment, has 50,000 users in a regionally distributed environment; a logical view of their Exchange Server 2007 environment is shown in Figure 14-12.

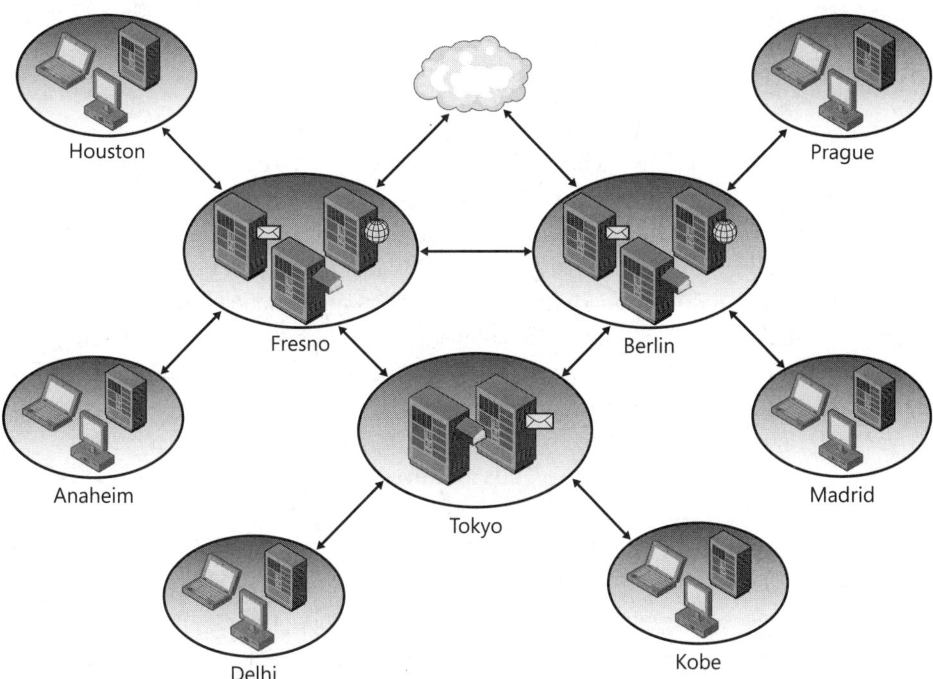

FIGURE 14-12 Logical view of Litware's Exchange Server 2007 environment

Upgrading Exchange Server 2007 Computers to SP2

You need to apply Exchange Server 2007 SP2 to all Exchange Server 2007 CA and UM servers in your organization prior to installing the first server running Exchange Server 2010. Exchange Server 2007 SP2 is also required on all Exchange Server 2007 computers in any Active Directory site before introducing Exchange Server 2010 into that site.

Preparing Active Directory After Applying Exchange Server 2007 SP2

Although Exchange Server 2007 SP2 will apply the necessary Exchange Server 2010 schema changes to your Active Directory forest, you will still need to perform the *setup /PrepareAD* step in your environment prior to performing your first Exchange Server 2010 installation. Otherwise, */PrepareAD* will be done automatically when the first server running Exchange Server 2010 is installed, assuming the account performing the installation has Enterprise Admins privileges and the computer is able to contact all domains in the forest on port 389. The effects of */PrepareAD* were discussed in detail earlier in this chapter in the "Upgrading from and Coexisting with Exchange Server 2003" section.

Deploying Exchange Server 2010 Computers

Deploying your Exchange Server 2010 computers for an upgrade from Exchange Server 2007 involves the same points to consider as discussed in the "Upgrading from and Coexisting with Exchange Server 2003" section of this chapter.

Upgrading Client Access Services

The Client Access issues unique to upgrading from Exchange Server 2007 to Exchange Server 2010 are OWA and Exchange ActiveSync, which this section covers. Outlook Web App coexistence with Exchange Server 2007 OWA is similar to that discussed in the "OWA Coexistence" section under "Upgrading from and Coexisting with Exchange Server 2003." OWA access is a redirect from the Exchange Server 2010 CA server to an Exchange Server 2007 CA server using the legacy host names configuration mentioned in the "Upgrading Outlook and Remote Access Functionality" section of this chapter if the Exchange Server 2007 mailbox is in an Internet-facing site. If the Exchange Server 2007 mailbox is in a non-Internet-facing site, the OWA session will be proxied from the Exchange Server 2010 CA server in the Internet-facing site to an Exchange Server 2007 Client Access server in the mailbox's site. Unlike Exchange Server 2003, however, Exchange Server 2007 is Active Directory site–aware, so you don't need to configure any OWA virtual directory properties for Exchange Server 2010 Client Access to locate the proper Exchange Server 2007 CA server. This OWA coexistence and proxy/redirect behavior for Litware is illustrated in Figure 14-13.

Although Exchange Server 2010 ActiveSync provides direct support for Exchange Server 2003 mailboxes, an Autodiscover and redirect to Exchange Server 2007 Client Access occurs for Exchange Server 2007 mailboxes with Windows Mobile 6.1 and higher. Windows Mobile 6.0 and lower, and all other ActiveSync clients, are proxied to Exchange Server 2007 CA servers.

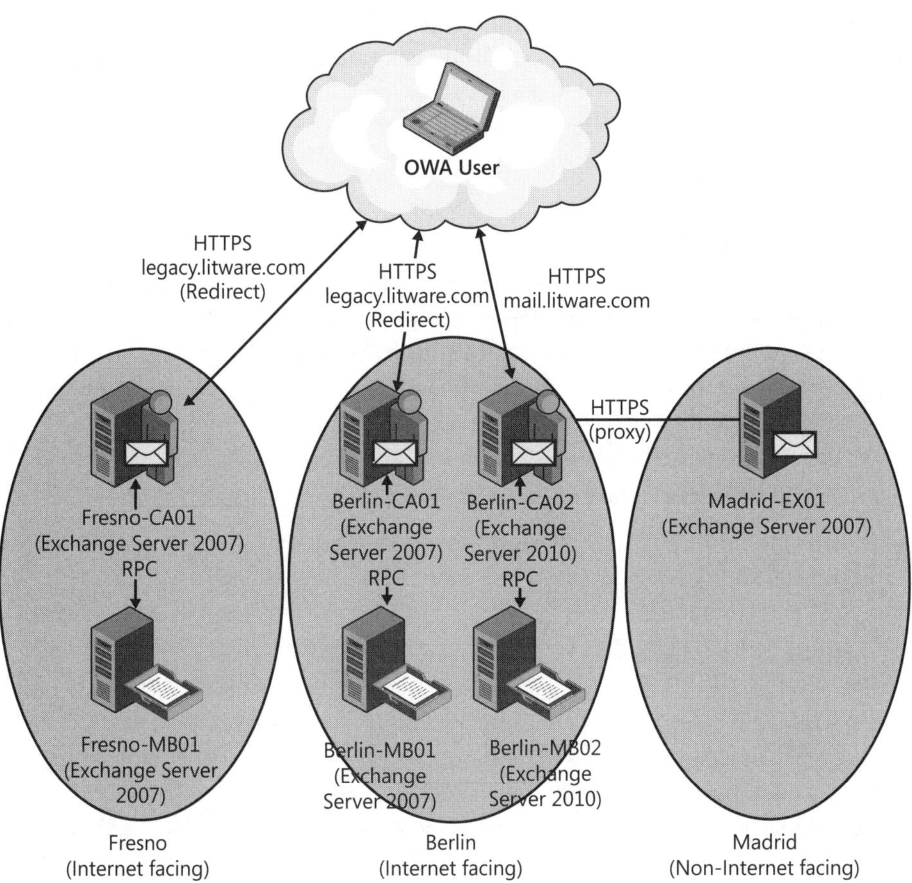

FIGURE 14-13 Exchange Server 2010 and Exchange Server 2007 Client Access coexistence

Upgrading Message Connectivity From Exchange Server 2007

Although both Exchange Server 2007 and Exchange Server 2010 use least cost routing, and use Active Directory sites for internal message routing, there are considerations for upgrading to Exchange Server 2010.

Because of the Exchange Server Object (XSO) model changes in Exchange Server 2010, Exchange Server 2007 Mailbox servers can't communicate with Exchange Server 2010 Hub Transport servers. Conversely, Exchange Server 2010 Mailbox servers can't pick up messages from or deliver messages to Exchange Server 2007 Hub Transport servers. Thus you must maintain both versions of Hub Transport servers in any site with both Exchange Server 2007 and Exchange Server 2010 mailboxes. Between sites, SMTP traffic is the same as it was in Exchange Server 2007; the Hub Transport server simply relays the messages to a Hub Transport server in the remote site.

A feature called *versioned routing* has been introduced in Exchange 2010 to support message flow between Exchange Server 2007 and Exchange Server 2010. Versioned routing enables the routing engine to check the version of a mailbox's home server, along with its Active Directory site. Messages are then transferred to a Hub Transport server matching the version of the mailbox server. In a mixed Exchange Server 2007 and Exchange Server 2010 environment, routing is now dependent on both Active Directory sites and the Exchange versions in play.

Transport Rule Migration

Transport rules are saved in a different Active Directory location for Exchange Server 2010 than in Exchange Server 2007. Exchange Server 2007 stored rules in CN=Transport, CN=Rules, CN=Transport Settings, CN=<org name>, CN=Microsoft Exchange, CN=Services. In Exchange Server 2010 they are stored at CN=TransportVersioned, CN=Rules, CN=Transport Settings, CN=<org name>, CN=Microsoft Exchange, CN=Services.

AUTOMATIC TRANSPORT RULE MIGRATION

When the Exchange Server 2010 Hub Transport role is installed, the Exchange Server 2007 transport rules are automatically exported and imported to the Exchange Server 2010 transport rule container, provided that there are no existing Exchange Server 2007 transport rules (this is what typically happens when the first Exchange Server 2010 Hub Transport computer is introduced). Exchange setup performs the following procedure:

1. Exchange setup queries Active Directory for existing Exchange Server 2010 transport rules by looking for the TransportVersioned container. This is done because the exporting of Exchange Server 2007 rules and subsequent import to Exchange Server 2010 will overwrite existing Exchange Server 2010 rules. If Exchange Server 2010 transport rules exist, Exchange Setup does nothing further with transport rules.
2. If there are no Exchange Server 2010 transport rules, Exchange setup queries Active Directory for Exchange Server 2007 transport rules (checking for the transport container).
3. If there are existing Exchange Server 2007 transport rules, Exchange setup migrates all Exchange Server 2007 transport rules to Exchange Server 2010 (assuming no Exchange Server 2010 transport rules exist) as follows:
    a. The legacy transport rules are exported from the Transport container in Active Directory to a temporary XML file (temp.xml) with the *Export-TransportRuleCollection* cmdlet.
    b. The legacy transport rules are then imported from the temporary XML file to the Active Directory TransportVersioned container with the *Import-TransportRuleCollection* cmdlet.
    c. After the import completes successfully, Exchange setup deletes the temp.xml file.

MANUAL TRANSPORT RULE MIGRATION

After transport rules have been created with Exchange Server 2010, they must be migrated to and from Exchange Server 2007 manually with the *Export-TransportRuleCollection* and *Import-TransportRuleCollection* cmdlets. Importing the Exchange Server 2010 transport rule set to Exchange Server 2007 will overwrite any existing Exchange Server 2007 rules. Importing Exchange Server 2007 transport rules to Exchange Server 2010 will also overwrite any existing Exchange Server 2010 rules, unless a rule has any Exchange Server 2010–specific predicates or actions, in which case the rule will be left untouched.

These cmdlets must be run from Exchange Server 2010. When running the *Export-TransportRuleCollection* cmdlet to export Exchange Server 2010 rules for import to Exchange Server 2007, you must use the *–ExportLegacyRules* parameter. Any Exchange Server 2010–specific predicates or actions that have been defined on the Exchange Server 2010 rules will then be stripped out of the export file automatically.

Upgrading Edge Transport

One of the improvements of the Exchange Server 2010 Edge Transport role in Exchange Server 2010 over Exchange Server 2007 is the introduction of incremental EdgeSync synchronization. The Edge Transport role is discussed in detail in Chapter 7, "Edge Transport and Messaging Security," but we will cover the considerations for upgrading Edge Transport from Exchange Server 2007 to Exchange Server 2010 here.

If you have Exchange Server 2007 Edge Transport servers, you should introduce Exchange Server 2010 Hub Transport into your environment before adding Exchange Server 2010 Edge Transport. As soon as the Exchange Server 2010 Hub Transport server is introduced to the Internet-facing site, it will take over edge synchronization. However, because the Edge Transport server is still running Exchange 2007 SP2, the Exchange 2010 Hub Transport server won't perform incremental EdgeSync synchronization, but instead will replicate the full EdgeSync data on each cycle, similar to an Exchange Server 2007 Hub Transport server. SMTP message flow will continue through the Exchange Server 2007 Hub Transport server, as shown in Figure 14-14.

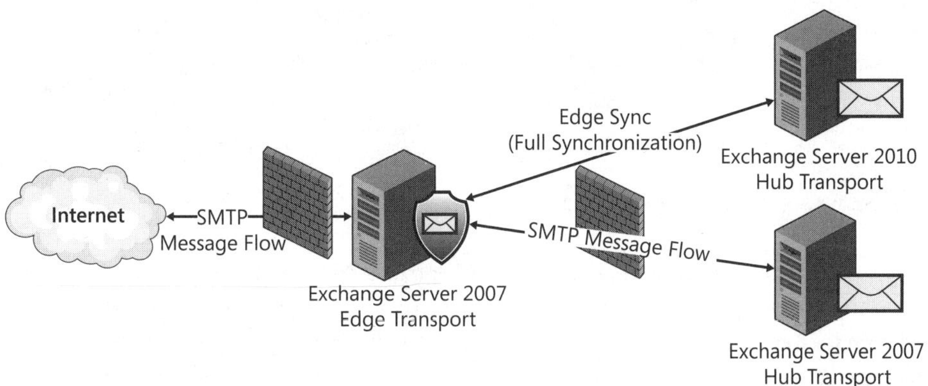

FIGURE 14-14 Exchange Server 2007 Edge Transport with Exchange Server 2007 and Exchange Server 2010 Hub Transport computers

After all your Exchange Server 2010 Hub Transport servers have been introduced, re-subscribe your Exchange 2007 Edge Transport server to your Active Directory site. This adds your Exchange 2010 Hub Transport servers to the Edge Subscription as source servers, as shown in Figure 14-15.

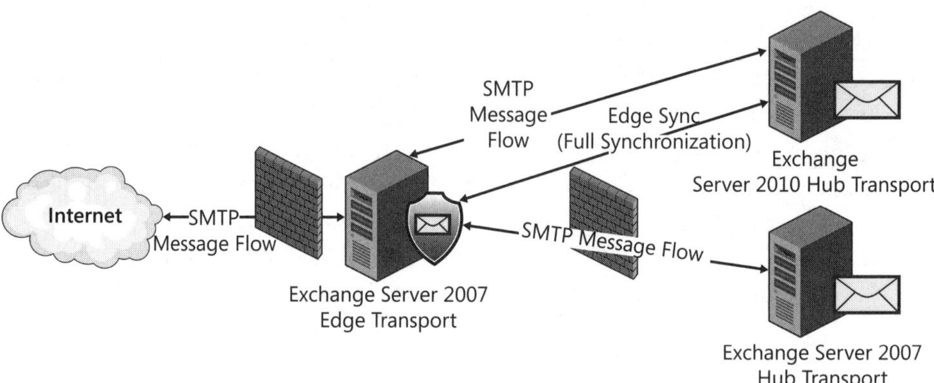

FIGURE 14-15 Re-subscribing Exchange Server 2007 EdgeSync to add Exchange Server 2010 Hub Transport servers

Next, you introduce your first Exchange Server 2010 Edge Transport server to the perimeter network and subscribe it to your Active Directory site. The Exchange Server 2010 Hub Transport server will then begin incremental updates to the Exchange Server 2010 Edge Transport server, as shown in Figure 14-16.

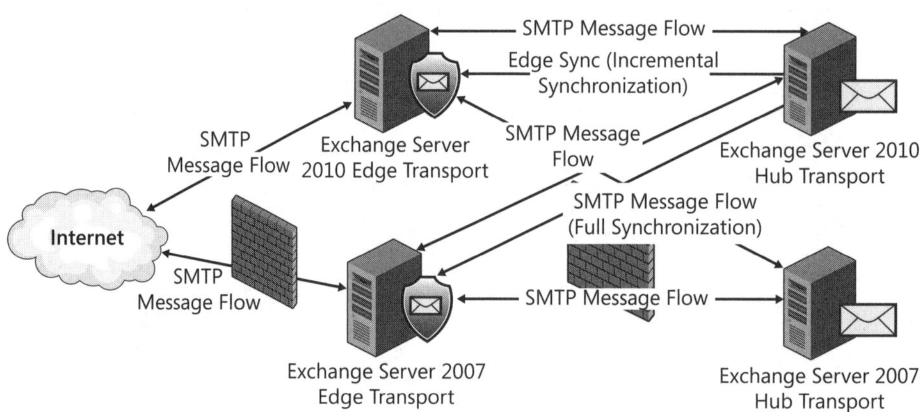

FIGURE 14-16 Introducing Exchange Server 2010 Edge Transport

Finally, you remove the Exchange Server 2007 Edge Subscription, and then decommission your Exchange Server 2007 Edge Transport server as shown in Figure 14-17. When all mailboxes have been moved to Exchange Server 2010, your Exchange Server 2007 Hub Transports can then be removed.

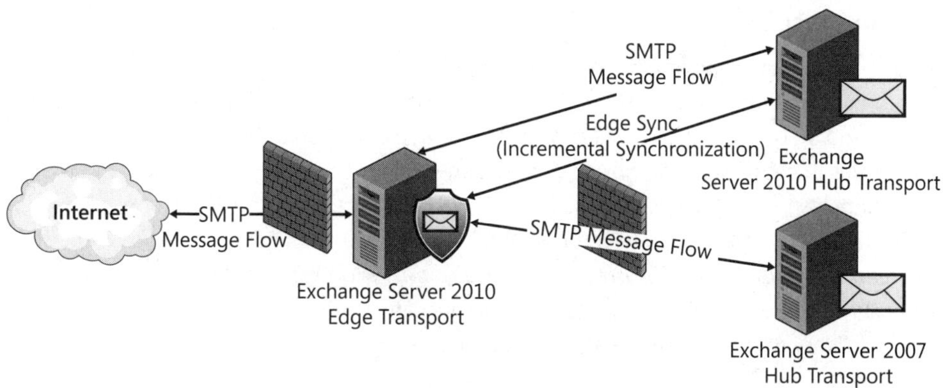

FIGURE 14-17 Decommissioning your Exchange Server 2007 Edge Transport servers

Maintaining DSN Settings in a Mixed Environment

In Exchange Server 2007, Delivery Status Notification (DSN) settings were configured on a per-server basis; in Exchange Server 2010 DSN settings are configured for your entire Exchange organization. As a result, like transport rules, these settings are stored in different locations in Active Directory for Exchange Server 2007 as opposed to Exchange Server 2010 and need to be managed separately in a coexistence scenario.

The following settings are now configured using the *Set-TransportConfig* cmdlet in Exchange Server 2010; in Exchange Server 2007, these were set using the *Set-TransportServer* cmdlet:

- *ExternalDelayDsnEnabled*
- *ExternalDsnDefaultLanguage*
- *ExternalDsnLanguageDetectionEnabled*
- *ExternalDsnMaxMessageAttachSize*
- *ExternalDsnReportingAuthority*
- *ExternalDsnSendHtml*
- *ExternalPostmasterAddress*
- *InternalDelayDsnEnabled*
- *InternalDsnDefaultLanguage*
- *InternalDsnLanguageDetectionEnabled*
- *InternalDsnMaxMessageAttachSize*
- *InternalDsnReportingAuthority*
- *InternalDsnSendHtml*

To maintain these settings in a mixed Exchange Server 2007 and Exchange Server 2010 environment, you must set them once in Exchange Server 2010 with the *Set-TransportConfig* cmdlet and then set them on each Exchange Server 2007 Hub Transport server using the *Set-TransportServer* cmdlet.

Message Tracking

Message tracking has been improved in Exchange Server 2010; these improvements are discussed in more detail in Chapter 17. For the purposes of coexistence, however, this means that—depending on the Exchange version of the source and destination mailboxes—different tracking tools may be used. For messages between Exchange Server 2010 mailboxes, the Delivery Reports tool in the Exchange Control Panel or the Tracking Log Explorer can be used. For messages delivered between Exchange Server 2010 and Exchange Server 2007, or between Exchange Server 2007 mailboxes, the Tracking Log Explorer tool in Exchange Server 2010 must be used. The Delivery Reports tool cannot report on any portion of the message delivery that involves Exchange Server 2007.

Planning Mailbox Moves and Coexistence

To move mailboxes from Exchange Server 2007 to Exchange Server 2010, the Exchange Server 2007 Mailbox server must be running Exchange Server 2007 SP2. As explained in detail in the "Moving Mailboxes from Exchange Server 2003 to Exchange Server 2010" section of this chapter, mailboxes are moved to Exchange Server 2010 using *Move Requests* through the Exchange Server 2010 EMC or EMS. However, when moving mailboxes from Exchange Server 2007 to Exchange Server 2010 these move processes are performed online, meaning end users can access their mailboxes during the move. This is different behavior than when moving mailboxes from Exchange Server 2003, where users are unable to access their mailboxes during the move.

Planning Continuous Replication Migration

The Exchange Server 2007 high-availability solutions for mailboxes have been replaced in Exchange Server 2010 with a single high-availability model: database mobility. Database mobility is composed of database availability groups and database copies. These are covered in detail in Chapter 6,"Mailbox Services," including the concepts surrounding database mobility and the designing of database availability groups and database copies.

In a nutshell, database mobility has the following characteristics:

- Is a combination of database availability groups and database copies
- Abstracts databases from Exchange Server 2010 Mailbox servers; databases are now managed at the organization level
- Provides high availability and site resilience
- Provides 30-second switchover/failover with simplified administrative experience compared to Exchange Server 2007
- Allows for more storage choices, such as Serial ATA (SATA) disks and JBOD (Just a Bunch of Disks) configurations

- In combination with other features, makes deployments without database backups possible
- Replaces Standby Continuous Replication (SCR), Local Continuous Replication (LCR), Single Copy Cluster (SCC), and Cluster Continuous Replication (CCR) from Exchange Server 2007

The Exchange Server 2007 mailbox high-availability concepts do not exist in Exchange Server 2010; mailbox high-availability migration consists of creating DAGs and database copies in Exchange Server 2010 and moving mailboxes from Exchange Server 2007 to Exchange Server 2010.

Planning Unified Messaging Migration

Chapter 9, "Unified Messaging," covers Unified Messaging (UM) in Exchange Server 2010 in detail. Here we will cover the migration of UM from Exchange Server 2007 to Exchange Server 2010. Typically, Exchange Server 2010 UM servers are deployed after the Exchange Server 2010 Client Access and Hub Transport servers but before Exchange Server 2010 mailboxes are implemented.

UM is migrated from Exchange Server 2007 as follows:

1. Verify that you have deployed the Exchange Server 2010 Client Access, Mailbox, and Hub Transport server roles in your organization.
2. Install Exchange Server 2007 SP2 on all existing Exchange Server 2007 UM servers in your organization.
3. Install the Exchange Server 2010 UM server role, including any required language packs.
4. If you will have Exchange Server 2007 UM servers and UM-enabled mailboxes on Exchange Server 2007 in your Exchange Server 2010 organization, you need additional dial plans and UM hunt groups with new pilot numbers.
   - If you're integrating with Office Communications Server (OCS) 2007, you will need to create a new UM Session Initiation Protocol (SIP) Uniform Resource Identifier (URI) dial plan configured with a new pilot identifier. You then have to disable Unified Messaging for your users and then re-enable these users with the new SIP URI dial plan.

> **NOTE** A separate dial plan is required if you are using versions of OCS prior to OCS 2007 R2 with Cumulative Update (CU) 5. OSC 2007 and OCS 2007 R2 do not distinguish between Exchange Server 2007 and Exchange Server 2010 UM servers, and round-robin all calls across both Exchange Server 2007 and Exchange Server 2010 UM servers regardless of the version of the recipient's mailbox. OCS 2007 R2 CU5 is version-aware, so if CU5 is deployed an additional dial plan is not required.

5. Add the Exchange Server 2010 UM servers to the Exchange Server 2007 UM dial plan.

6. Import to Exchange Server 2010 UM any custom prompts created for Exchange Server 2007 auto attendants or UM dial plans.
7. Send incoming calls to the Exchange Server 2010 UM servers by configuring all IP gateways or IP PBXs.
   - Exchange Server 2010 UM determines if the call is for an Exchange Server 2007 or Exchange Server 2010 mailbox and routes the call accordingly. If the call is for an Exchange Server 2007 mailbox, Exchange Server 2010 UM routes the call to an Exchange Server 2007 UM server in the same dial plan using round robin.
8. Move Exchange Server 2007 UM-enabled mailboxes to Exchange Server 2010.
9. After all Exchange Server 2007 UM-enabled mailboxes have been moved to Exchange Server 2010, remove the Exchange Server 2007 UM servers from the UM dial plan.
10. Remove the Exchange Server 2007 UM servers from the environment.

Removing Exchange Server 2007 Computers

Removing the last server running Exchange Server 2007 from your Exchange Server 2010 organization has some similarities to removing Exchange Server 2003. The removal is done by following these steps:

1. To uninstall the last Exchange Server 2007 computer you require Exchange Organization Administrator permissions in Exchange Server 2007, as well as the Organization Management role in Exchange Server 2010.
2. Confirm that all legacy Exchange features are decommissioned or replaced, as outlined in the "Discontinued and De-emphasized Functionality in Exchange Server 2010" section of this chapter.
3. Confirm that all mailboxes and public folders are migrated to Exchange Server 2010, as outlined in the "Planning Mailbox Moves and Coexistence" and "Planning Public Folder Access and Migration" sections of this chapter.
4. Ensure that all OABs have been moved to Exchange Server 2010.
5. Verify that Send and Receive connectors have been created and configured on Exchange Server 2010, and inbound and outbound Internet SMTP traffic has been moved to Exchange Server 2010, as discussed in the "Upgrading Message Connectivity" section of this chapter. Also verify that your DNS MX records have been modified to resolve to Exchange Server 2010 Edge Transport or Hub Transport servers, and verify in Exchange Server 2010 that no Exchange Server 2007 computers are listed as smart hosts for any Send connectors.
6. Check internal and external DNS records to verify that the following protocol services are resolving to Exchange Server 2010 Client Access servers. (Confirm as well that all clients are using Exchange Server 2010 for these services and protocols.)
   - ActiveSync
   - Outlook Web App

- Outlook Anywhere
- POP3
- IMAP4
- Autodiscover service
- Other Exchange Web services

7. Remove public folder stores from Exchange Server 2007 by using the EMC.
8. Uninstall Exchange Server 2007 from the last server.

Additional Resources

- Exchange Server Deployment Assistant: *http://technet.microsoft.com/en-ca/exdeploy2010/default.aspx* and *http://msexchangeteam.com/archive/2009/11/11/453172.aspx*
- Remote Connectivity Analyzer: *https://www.testexchangeconnectivity.com/*
- Ambiguously Nonauthoritative Namespaces: *http://msexchangeteam.com/archive/2008/09/05/449764.aspx* and *http://technet.microsoft.com/en-us/library/ee428168(EXCHG.80).aspx*
- Discontinued Features and De-emphasized Functionality: *http://technet.microsoft.com/en-us/library/aa998911.aspx*
- Exchange 2003: Planning Roadmap for Upgrade and Coexistence: *http://technet.microsoft.com/en-us/library/aa998186.aspx?wt.svl=upgrademigrate*
- Removing the Last Exchange 2003 Server ...: *http://theessentialexchange.com/blogs/michael/archive/2009/05/04/removing-the-last-exchange-2003-server.aspx*
- How to Remove the Last Legacy Exchange Server from an Organization: *http://technet.microsoft.com/en-us/library/bb288905(EXCHG.80).aspx*
- Transitioning Client Access to Exchange Server 2010: *http://msexchangeteam.com/archive/2009/11/20/453272.aspx*
- Upgrade from Exchange 2007 Mailbox: *http://technet.microsoft.com/en-us/library/ee332345.aspx*
- Need Help Converting Your LDAP Filters to OPATH?: *http://msexchangeteam.com/archive/2007/03/12/436983.aspx*

PART IV

Deploying and Managing Exchange Server 2010

CHAPTER 15

Preparing for and Deploying Exchange Server 2010

Successfully deploying Microsoft Exchange Server 2010 often relies on two major factors: preparation and technical ability. If you have ever had the pleasure, or pain, of embarking on a large painting project, such as an automobile or a house, you may have received a common bit of advice. No matter the skill of the painter or the expense of the equipment and paint, a good paint job is all in the preparation. Just as it is in painting, preparation for deploying Exchange Server is essential.

After estimating and buying the equipment and paint for the project, the first step is to ensure that the entire area is protected and the floor and any furniture are covered with a tarp. If the taping is not done accurately, paint will drip onto the exposed surfaces or an area will not be painted because tape is covering the area. The next step is to wash the surface, removing any oils, grease, or dirt that would keep the paint from adhering to the surface. After cleaning the surface, any holes, rough areas, dimples, or imperfections are filled in or sanded down to provide a nice, smooth surface that will look good when painted. In some instances, the surface needs to be primed. Much like a painting project, preparing for deploying Exchange Server starts with the following:

- Surveying the environment
- Understanding what needs to be protected
- Properly scoping and documenting the project
- Gathering the right resources and equipment
- Identify and mitigating the disruption points, including:
  - Third-party applications
  - Previously scheduled outages that overlap with business critical services

Once you've taken these steps, you need to prepare the environment for deploying Exchange. The first part of preparing the environment is to identify any problems with the current messaging environment or Active Directory Domain Services and then fix them. Finally, before deploying Exchange you might need to make some changes to make the transition smooth. This might include upgrading current Exchange Servers to the appropriate service pack level, or other drastic changes. This illustration may be a little over the top, but it is important to underscore the need for preparation. Taking the time to properly prepare will improve the chances that Exchange will be deployed successfully, and you won't end up having to redo the work later.

The second major factor in properly deploying Exchange Server is technical ability. By reading the chapter, following the guidance set forth in Chapter 2, "Exchange Deployment Projects," and by testing your technical abilities in a lab environment ahead of time you can greatly improve the deployment process. This chapter will cover the preparation and deployment of Exchange 2010. Information about coexistence and transition from other messaging platforms is covered fully in Chapter 14, "Upgrading from Exchange Server 2003 and Exchange Server 2007."

The Exchange Server 2010 Deployment Process

The Exchange Server 2010 deployment process can involve many different departments within an IT organization. The departments that manage Active Directory Domain Services, DNS, storage, security, networking, and others may need to be consulted and appeased to make changes or get approval to make changes.

> ***IMPORTANT*** **It is always important to follow good change management practice when deploying Exchange Server.**

Each version of Exchange Server since Exchange 2000 Server has been reliant on Active Directory Domain Services (AD DS) to function. All of the user accounts, mailboxes, distribution groups, and the configuration for the services are stored within AD DS. Anytime information is needed about a mail-enabled object or configuration information is needed for any of the Exchange services, AD DS must be queried. If AD DS is not available, Exchange will fail to work properly. To better understand how tightly Exchange integrates with AD DS and to underscore the importance of properly configuring and preparing AD DS for deployment, it is good to understand the basics.

Exchange and Active Directory Domain Services

As discussed in detail in Chapter 3, "Exchange Environment Considerations," AD DS stores information in three partitions: the configuration partition, the schema partition, and the domain partition. Each of these partitions provides essential services and information for the

Exchange servers in the forest. Because Exchange relies so heavily on Active Directory, proper sizing guidelines for the number and configuration for domain controllers are discussed in Chapter 13, "Hardware Planning for Exchange 2010."

The Configuration Partition

The configuration partition contains information about the configuration of the entire Exchange organization. The same configuration partition is replicated to all of the domain controllers in an AD DS forest. The Exchange configuration is stored within a container in the Services container, as shown in Figure 15-1.

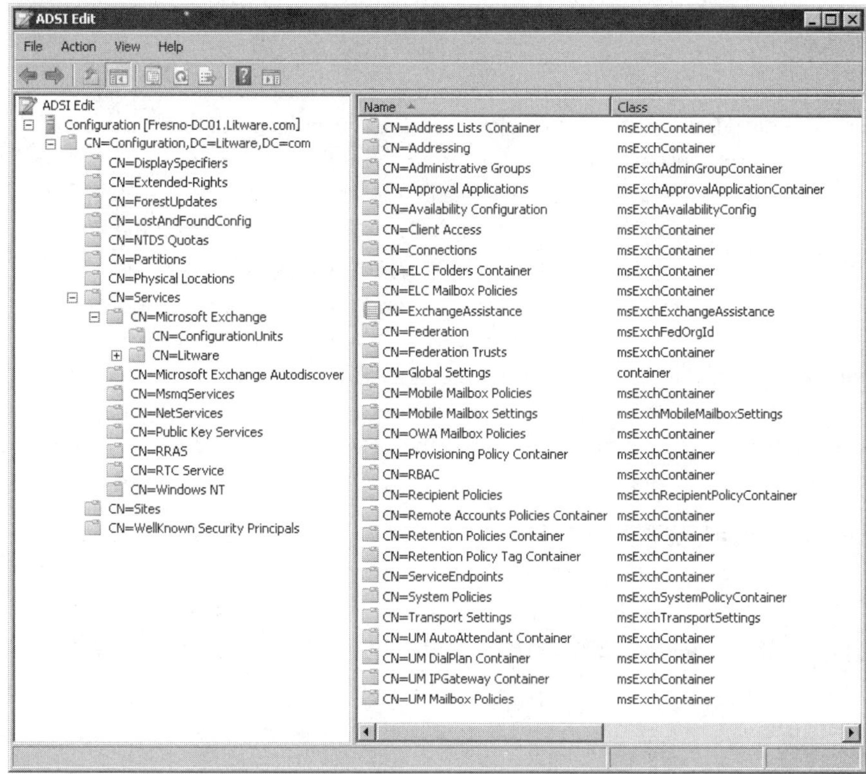

FIGURE 15-1 The Exchange Configuration as stored in the AD DS configuration partition

A number of Exchange configuration objects are stored in this container, including:

- Address lists
- Address policies
- Client access settings
- Messaging records management, mobile, and UM mailbox policies
- Federation settings

- Global settings
- System policies
- Transport settings

Although the Exchange configuration is stored in the configuration container, you should never adjust settings directly unless specifically directed to by Microsoft support personnel. You should always use the Exchange management tools such as the Exchange Management Console or Exchange Management Shell to make any configuration settings.

The Schema Partition

The schema partition stores classes and attributes. Classes are the types of objects that can be created in AD DS and attributes are properties for these objects. The schema partition can be likened to a recipe book, which describes the ingredients and processes that should be followed to make a dish. This is just how the schema defines the objects that are created in the other AD DS partitions. Just as it would seem absurd to eat the recipe book, the schema partition only defines the objects but does not actually store those objects. Unlike other partitions, the schema partition is not multi-master. A single domain controller in the forest acts as a schema master and is the only domain controller with a writeable copy of the schema.

The Exchange installation extends the schema by adding many classes and attributes into it, including mail-enabled users, mail-enabled groups, databases, servers, and connectors. Each of these classes has a number of properties that are used to describe the objects. When a mailbox object is created in domain partition, as seen in Figure 15-2, a number of attributes can be seen using ADSI Edit. These attributes include homeMDB, e-mail address, RBAC role assignment, and a number of others.

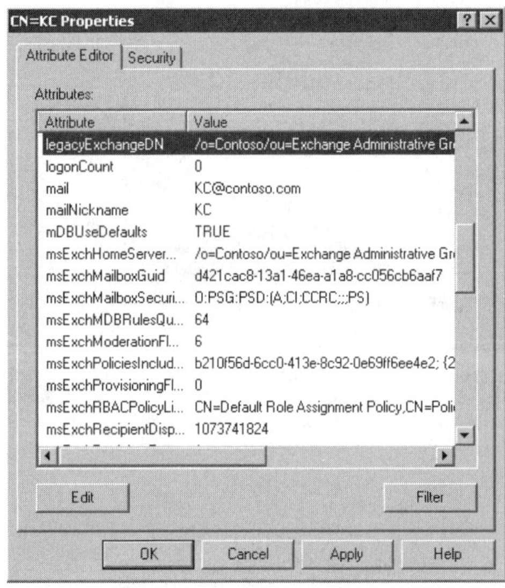

FIGURE 15-2 Mailbox object schema attributes

The Domain Partition

Each domain in a forest has a domain partition. The domain partition is only replicated to the domain controllers that are members of that domain. The domain partition contains information about users, computers, and groups. When users, mailboxes, and distribution groups are created in AD DS they are stored in a domain partition using the class and attributes defined in the schema partition.

How Exchange Uses Active Directory

Each of the Exchange server roles is dependent on the Active Directory Topology service, which is the service that gathers information from each of the Active Directory partitions. As mentioned previously, data about the Active Directory site, where domain controllers and global catalog servers are located, as well as information about the other Exchange servers in the organization is read and cached from Active Directory. When the Active Directory Topology service starts, it binds itself to a random domain controller and global catalog server in the local Active Directory site. After binding and retrieving information from any of the local writeable domain controllers, the service continually evaluates the performance of each Active Directory server in the site to ensure that all available servers are identified and to remove any servers that are no longer suitable for use. A static list of domain controllers can be specified for each Exchange Server computer to use; however, because of the dynamic nature of AD DS you should allow Exchange to build this list dynamically to ensure that all available domain controllers are used. Many organizations with larger Exchange deployments may choose to put the Exchange Server computers in a separate site with dedicated domain controllers so as to segregate any desktop user authentication from any Exchange-related lookups, which could resource completion servicing Exchange and desktop requests. The following list shows how each Exchange role relies on AD DS to function.

> **_NOTE_ Although Exchange 2010 can be deployed in a site with read-only domain controllers, these servers are ignored for use by Exchange. At least one writeable global catalog server is required in each Active Directory site that hosts an Exchange 2010 computer. Two or more writeable domain controllers are recommended for redundancy.**

- **Client Access Server Role** Users connecting to the Client Access Server via: MAPI, Outlook Web App, Exchange Web Services, Exchange Control Panel, Post Office Protocol version 3 (POP3), Internet Message Access Protocol Version 4rev1 (IMAP4), or Microsoft Exchange ActiveSync. AD DS is used to authenticate the user and to determine the user's mailbox database. If the mailbox is located in another directory the connection may be redirected.
- **Edge Transport Server Role** The Edge Transport servers are not to be members of one of domains in the Exchange forest; each Edge Transport server employs a local, lightweight version of an AD DS database within Active Directory Lightweight Directory Services (AD LDS), which stores configuration information for each Edge

Transport server. The Edge Transport server retrieves configuration information including recipient lookup and safe list aggregation through an edge subscription to an Active Directory site. The Hub Transport servers in a subscribed site use the Microsoft Exchange EdgeSync service to synchronize AD DS information into the AD LDS instance on each Edge Transport server.

- **Hub Transport Server Role** The Hub Transport server role queries AD DS when it performs recipient lookup and routing resolution during message categorization. The categorizer also retrieves information about the recipient's mailbox such as the, restrictions, and permissions that apply. The categorizer must also query AD DS to obtain the members and restrictions for distribution lists. To calculate routing information, the categorizer uses the information that is retrieved and cached by the Active Directory Topology service.
- **Mailbox Server Role** The Mailbox server role uses information about mailboxes, agents, global settings, and address lists in AD DS.
- **Unified Messaging Server Role** The Unified Messaging servers query AD DS for configuration information such as dial plans, hunt groups, and gateways. The UM servers also use AD DS to match a destination telephone number to a recipient address to submit the message to a Hub Transport server in the local Active Directory site.

Preparing for an Exchange Deployment

The Microsoft UA team has created a tool called the *Exchange 2010 Deployment Assistant* that provides customized assistance through a wizard drive interface. This tool is available online at *http://technet.microsoft.com/en-us/exdeploy2010*. The tool requires Microsoft Silverlight 3 or higher to be installed; therefore, it might not be suitable to access the tool directly from an Exchange server to minimize any extraneous software from being installed.

The Exchange Deployment Assistant is a wizard-driven interface that asks just a couple of questions and then creates customized deployment instructions. To start the configuration you select one of the available deployment scenarios:

- Upgrade From Exchange 2003
- Upgrade From Exchange 2007
- Upgrade From Exchange 2003 & 2007
- New Installation Of Exchange 2010

After you choose a scenario, a couple of questions are asked about the deployment to further tailor the instruction, and then a customized checklist is created as shown in Figure 15-3. The checklist can be used interactively within the tool or it can be printed, e-mailed, or downloaded for offline use.

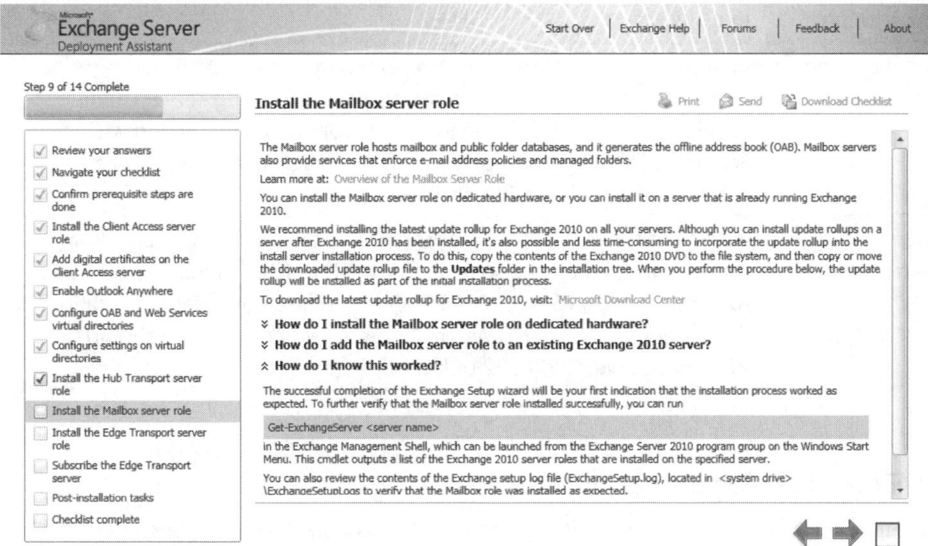

FIGURE 15-3 Exchange Server Deployment Assistant

Prepare AD DS and Domains

A number of prerequisites need to be in place before Active Directory can be prepared for an Exchange 2010 installation. Table 15-1 summarizes the Active Directory requirements. The following list summarizes the AD DS requirements for deploying Exchange 2010:

- The domains and the domain controllers must meet the system requirements.
- Each domain where Exchange Server 2010 will be installed must have at least one writeable domain controller running at least Windows Server 2003 Service Pack 1 (SP1). Because Windows Server 2003 SP1 is no longer in mainstream support, you should be deploying at least Windows Server 2003 SP2 or Windows Server 2008 domain controllers.

TABLE 15-1 Active Directory Requirements for Exchange Server 2010

COMPONENT	REQUIREMENT
Active Directory forest	The AD DS forest must be at least in Windows Server 2003 forest functionality mode. If Exchange Server 2003 is still in place, the domain functional level supported cannot be higher than Windows Server 2003 until after Exchange Server 2003 has been removed from the environment.
Domain controller	In every Active Directory site that Exchange Server 2010 will be deployed, you must have at least one writeable domain controller running Windows Server 2003 Standard edition or Enterprise edition with Service Pack 1 (SP1) or higher. As a best practice you should use Windows Server 2008 SP2 or higher.

COMPONENT	REQUIREMENT
Global catalog server	In every Active Directory site that Exchange Server 2010 will be deployed, you must have at least one global catalog server running Windows Server 2003 Standard edition or Enterprise edition with Service Pack 1 (SP1) or higher. As a best practice you should use Windows Server 2008 SP2 or higher.
Schema master	By default the first domain controller created in an Active Directory forest is designated the schema master. The schema master must be running Windows Server 2003 Standard edition or Enterprise edition with Service Pack 1 (SP1) or higher. As a best practice you should use Windows Server 2008 SP2 or higher.

Installing Exchange Server on Domain Controllers

For security and performance reasons, it is recommended to install Exchange Server 2010 only on member servers and not on domain controllers. In some instances, such as small organizations or offices that do not need the performance of separate servers, it might seem logical to install Exchange Server on a domain controller. However, a server that already has Exchange Server 2010 installed cannot be promoted to become a domain controller or demoted if it already is a domain controller. Additionally, it is critical that Exchange 2010 not be placed on any domain controller within the environment if separation of Exchange and Active Directory permissions or administration is required.

Exchange Organization requirements

Not only will you have requirements that must be met by Active Directory, but you will also have requirements that must be met by the Exchange Servers in your Exchange organization. For example, all Exchange Server 5.5 and Exchange 2000 Server computers must have been properly removed from the organization and the Exchange organization must be set to Exchange 2003 native mode. Any Exchange Server 2003 computers—and computers with the Exchange 2003 management tools installed—must have Service Pack 2 applied. Any Exchange 2007 Hub Transport servers that are located in the same site that Exchange 2010 will be deployed into must have Exchange Server 2007 SP2 installed. All of the Client Access and Unified Messaging servers must also have Exchange Server 2007 SP2 installed. As a best practice all of the Mailbox and Hub Transport servers should also have SP2 applied. Chapter 14 provides details of the upgrade process.

If you are considering performing a domain rename, you must do so before deploying Exchange Server 2010 because Exchange Server 2007 and higher does not support renaming of the Active Directory domain.

One of the key ideas discussed in Chapter 2 is to perform validation and testing of all applications that interact with Exchange. These include backup, file-level and Exchange integrated antivirus, anti-spam services, third-party mobile messaging, and alert monitoring systems that will support Exchange 2010. Often these existing applications will need to be upgraded or replaced with versions that support Exchange 2010. Therefore, you need to budget time and other resources for completing these upgrades.

Checking Exchange Environment Health

Exchange Server relies heavily on AD DS and Domain Name Services (DNS). Therefore, these requirements must be verified to be configured and working optimally; failing to do so before deployment begins will cause problems that are often difficult to trace and fix later. Rather than leaving configuration to chance and assuming that the rest of the environment is working as expected, it is also important to test and verify that they are working. To do this, it is important to systematically verify the health of each environment. To start with it is important to test the health of the domain controllers in the local site. The DcDiag utility is provided to perform a number of tests. More information on using DcDiag can be found at *http://technet.microsoft.com/en-us/library/cc758753(WS.10).aspx.*

The *dcdiag* command performs the following types of checks:

- Connectivity to verify proper DNS records and LDAP/RPC connectivity
- DNS to verify proper operation and health of DNS services
- KCCEvent to verify that the Knowledge Consistency Checker (KCC) is functional and error-free
- NetLogon to verify that the proper permissions exist to allow for replication
- Replication to check for replication errors
- RIDManager to verify that the RID master is accessible and functional
- Topology to verify that an accurate and functional replication topology has been generated by the KCC

To test all of the domain controllers on the site containing the Exchange Servers, you should run DcDiag.exe /a from a domain controller in that site, as shown in the Figure 15-4. All of the information that DcDiag reports should be reviewed and all errors addressed.

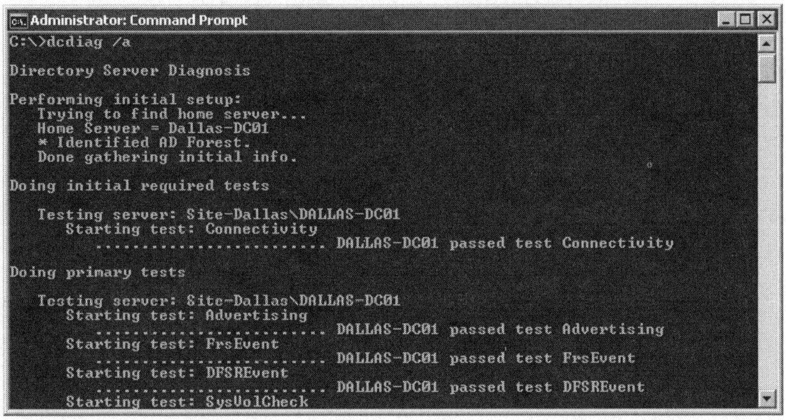

```
Administrator: Command Prompt
C:\>dcdiag /a

Directory Server Diagnosis

Performing initial setup:
   Trying to find home server...
   Home Server = Dallas-DC01
   * Identified AD Forest.
   Done gathering initial info.

Doing initial required tests

   Testing server: Site-Dallas\DALLAS-DC01
      Starting test: Connectivity
         ......................... DALLAS-DC01 passed test Connectivity

Doing primary tests

   Testing server: Site-Dallas\DALLAS-DC01
      Starting test: Advertising
         ......................... DALLAS-DC01 passed test Advertising
      Starting test: FrsEvent
         ......................... DALLAS-DC01 passed test FrsEvent
      Starting test: DFSREvent
         ......................... DALLAS-DC01 passed test DFSREvent
      Starting test: SysVolCheck
```

FIGURE 15-4 Running DcDiag

If the local domain controllers are healthy, you should use DcDiag to scan the remaining domain controllers in the enterprise by running *DcDiag /e*. To ensure that all of the problems have been addressed and what the steady state of the domain is after addressing all issues, it's a good idea to capture the output of the DcDiag report by using *DcDiag /e > DcDiagBeforeDeployment.txt*. With that report, any future problems or issues can be compared to see when they occurred. If additional information is needed or in the event of replications issues, use the repadmin tool. To gather a quick list of replication issues for a forest run, *repadmin /replsummary ** and review the output, as shown in Figure 15-5.

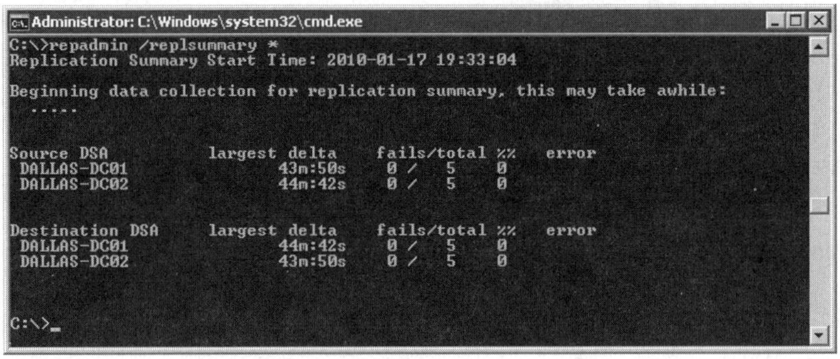

```
Administrator: C:\Windows\system32\cmd.exe
C:\>repadmin /replsummary *
Replication Summary Start Time: 2010-01-17 19:33:04

Beginning data collection for replication summary, this may take awhile:
  .....

Source DSA          largest delta    fails/total %%   error
 DALLAS-DC01              43m:50s    0 /   5    0
 DALLAS-DC02              44m:42s    0 /   5    0

Destination DSA     largest delta    fails/total %%   error
 DALLAS-DC01              44m:42s    0 /   5    0
 DALLAS-DC02              43m:50s    0 /   5    0

C:\>_
```

FIGURE 15-5 Output of using *repadmin /replsummary*

You should resolve any issues noted with either of these tests before installing and configuring Exchange Server 2010.

If you need to identify DNS issues, you can use the DNSLint utility. This tool is used to diagnose DNS delegation issues, DNS record lookups, and Active Directory–related records. To verify that a specific DNS server has the appropriate records to support Active Directory, you run *DNSLint /ad /s <DNS Server>* as shown in Figure 15-6 when run from the DNS server.

If you already have an Exchange environment in place, you should run the Exchange Best Practices Analyzer (ExBPA) using the Health Check feature to gather information about the Exchange organization and verify that it is operating properly before any changes are introduced into the environment. You can download the latest version of ExBPA at *http://www.microsoft.com/downloads/details.aspx?familyid=dbab201f-4bee-4943-ac22-e2ddbd258df3&displaylang=en*.

After installing ExBPA on a server in your forest, you can run a health check on the forest that you will be installing Exchange Server 2010 into. The health check will create a report similar to the one shown in Figure 15-7. Each issue identified by ExBPA should be researched and addressed appropriately to create a healthy baseline configuration to begin an upgrade.

```
Administrator: Command Prompt
C:\dnslint>dnslint.exe /ad /s localhost /v

DNSLint will attempt to verify the
DNS entries used in AD replication

Using 127.0.0.1 for LDAP
DNSLint will check if the local system can
resolve the CNAME and glue (A) records
used for Active Directory forest replication
using its locally configured DNS server(s)

This process may take several minutes to complete...

Finding the name of the root of the AD forest...found

AD forest root is called:
    DC=contoso,DC=com

Attempting to get a list of GUIDs for the forest...

DC: DALLAS-DC01
GUID: 2a029b55-0eae-4cee-aeff-2c3ac29c1752

1 GUIDs found

Querying locally configured DNS server(s)
to check them for records related to forest GUIDs...


querying for CNAME record data...

querying CNAME record for:
   2a029b55-0eae-4cee-aeff-2c3ac29c1752._msdcs.contoso.com...found

dallas-dc01.contoso.com

finding the glue record...found

IP address: 10.112.33.92

=============================

CNAME records found on this DNS server: 1

Creating report called dnslint.htm in current directory
```

FIGURE 15-6 Using DNSLint to troubleshoot DNS issues

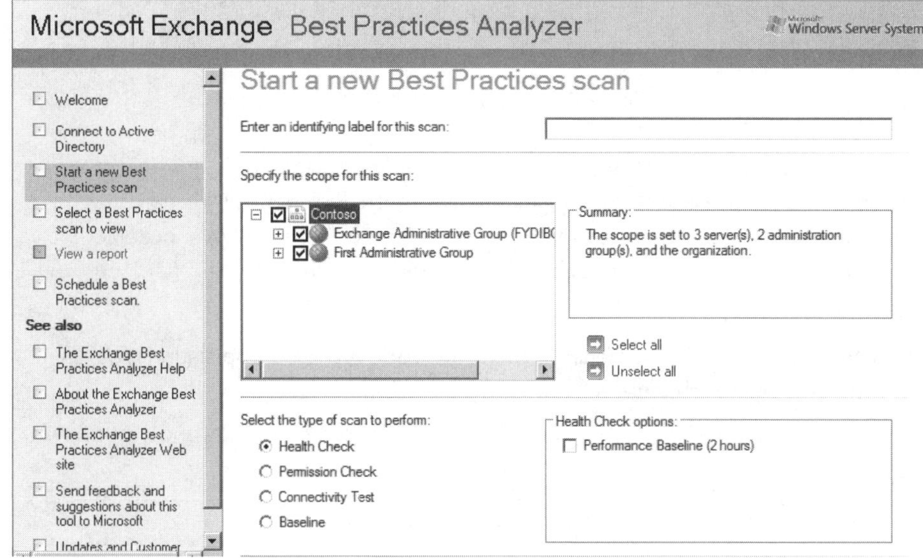

FIGURE 15-7 ExBPA Health Check report

After establishing a healthy Exchange environment—or if no Exchange servers are already deployed—you should use the Exchange Pre-Deployment Analyzer (ExPDA) to generate an Exchange 2010 Readiness Check report, as shown in Figure 15-8. When a Readiness Check is run, a detailed analysis of your existing Exchange organization is performed, and a comprehensive report is generated detailing the preparedness of your organization for the introduction of Exchange 2010 as well as providing the appropriate corrective measures to take, as shown in Figure 15-8.

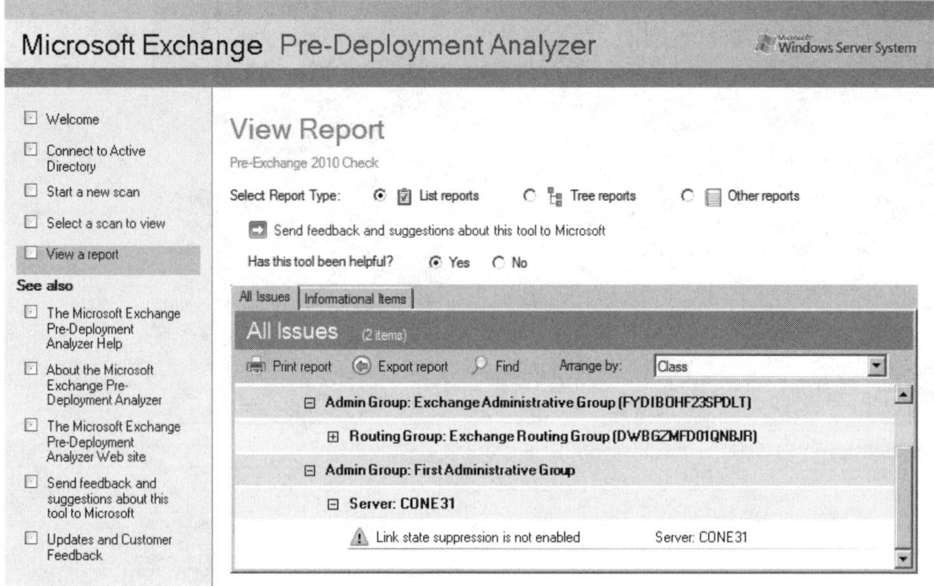

FIGURE 15-8 Viewing a Pre-Deployment Analyzer report

Other than just relying on tools to report problems, it is advisable to do a review of the configuration of the Active Directory domain, domain controllers, Active Directory sites, and DNS when possible to make sure simple configuration errors are not overlooked. The following common mistakes can cause problems with deployment:

Active Directory Forest

- Functionality level is not at the appropriate level and a specific application requires a lower level than Exchange Server does.
- Default and built-in permissions were changed on built-in containers and groups.

Active Directory Sites

- Some subnets are not defined in Active Directory Domain Services.
- Some site links are missing.
- Some domain controllers are listed in the wrong sites.
- Site links do not have the correct costs assigned to them.

Domain controllers

- The local domain controllers are not using a common set of DNS servers.
- The domain controllers are not being backed up regularly.
- Domain controllers that can be promoted to global catalog servers have not been.

DNS

- DNS does not have all of the reverse zones created for each of the available subnets.
- DNS servers are not replicating all required zones either by Active Directory replication or there are missing secondary zones.

Prepare Active Directory and Domains

Now that the health and the configuration of the forest have been verified, it is time to prepare the forest for the first Exchange Server 2010. Exchange Server 2010 requires that new attributes be added to AD DS schema and modifications be made to existing classes and attributes. If Exchange Server 2007 SP2 has already been installed in the forest no additional schema changes will be needed because Exchange 2007 uses the same schema as Exchange Server 2010. However, you need to make other changes to permissions and create additional groups to support Exchange Server 2010.

To prepare the Active Directory schema, a computer running a 64-bit edition of Windows Server 2008 with the Active Directory management tools installed and in the same site as the schema master is required. The schema can be extended directly from the schema master if it is running a 64-bit version of Windows Server 2003 SP2 or higher. If you are using a second server installed in the same site running Windows Server 2008 or higher you must install the AD DS remote server administrator tools feature. To install these tools, run the following command from a command prompt with administrator permissions:

```
ServerManagerCmd -i RSAT-ADDS
```

If you are using Windows Server 2008 R2 you can add the management tools by using Windows PowerShell running as an Administrator after running *Import-Module ServerManager*. The following cmdlet needs to be run to add these tools:

```
Add-WindowsFeature RSAT-ADDS
```

To do this in a simple environment, simply start the Exchange installation GUI or command line with an account with the appropriate permissions. The setup program will then perform all required schema and Active Directory preparation automatically. In more complicated environments, where the Exchange deployment group will not have schema modification permissions, you'll need to run the command-line version of Exchange 2010 setup to prepare the domain. The next few sections explain the process of running the preparation steps manually. Although it is possible to run these steps automatically—in most cases through the GUI—running each step on the command line gives the administrator control over how and when each step is run, thus providing the ability to isolate each change and to be able to test functionality at each step, essentially giving the administrator greater control over the installation. These steps make significant changes in Active Directory and the existing Exchange organization, so additionally they will cause a large amount of replications traffic. Therefore, you should complete these steps during a change management window outside of business hours. This time period should allow enough time for replication to complete as well as perform any user acceptance testing and subsequent remediation if a failure occurs.

Manually preparing the Active Directory forest consists of the following steps:

1. If Exchange Server 2003 is still present in the environment, run */PrepareLegacyExchange Permissions* to ensure that Exchange Server 2003 computers continue to function.
2. Run */PrepareSchema* once in the forest to extend the Active Directory schema with the objects necessary to run Exchange Server 2010.
3. Run */PrepareAD* in the forest root to create the global Exchange objects and configuration.
4. Run */PrepareDomain* in each of the other domains in the forest where Exchange 2010 will be installed or domains where Exchange recipients will exist. Alternatively, */PrepareAllDomains* can be run to effectively run the */PrepareDomain* command against each of the domains in the forest.

Preparing Legacy Permissions

As mentioned in Chapter 14, if the Exchange organization has any Exchange Server 2003 computers, the first step to preparing the forest is to run the Exchange Server 2010 command-line setup (setup.com) with the option to prepare legacy permissions. Running this option ensures that the Exchange Server 2003 services such as the Recipient Update Service can still function during the coexistence period with Exchange Server 2010.

The command should be run from the Exchange Server 2010 installation files on a 64-bit Windows Server 2003 SP2 computer within the same domain and Active Directory site as the schema master. The command that should be run is *setup.com /PrepareLegacyExchangePermissions* or *setup.com /pl*, as shown in Figure 15-9. However, if just a single domain needs to be prepared with legacy permissions, run *setup.com /PrepareLegacyExchangePermissions:<domain name>*. For example, to prepare only the na.litware.com domain you would run *setup.com /pl:na.litware.com.*

> **NOTE** You do not have to manually run */PrepareLegacyPermissions*. Setup will automatically complete these actions when any of the subsequent steps are run if older Exchange versions have been installed in the organization. The benefit of running this separately is that it allows each portion of setup to be replicated and validated individually.

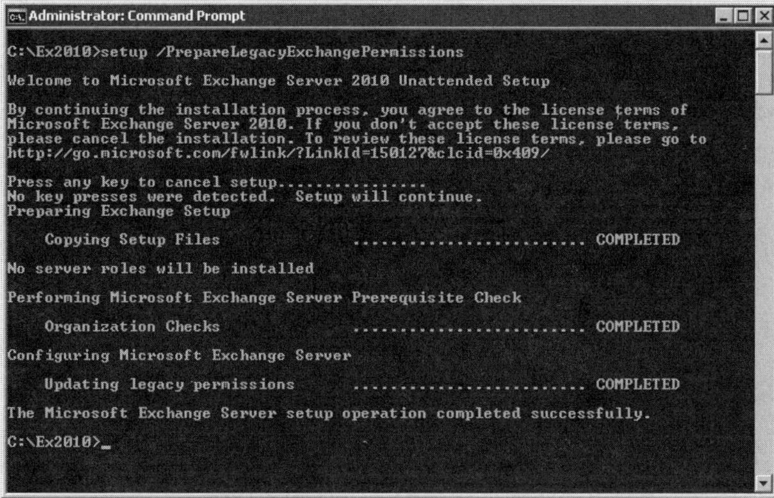

FIGURE 15-9 Preparing Exchange legacy permissions

To successfully run Prepare Legacy Permissions, the user account must be a member of the Enterprise Admins group or in a single domain forest the user must have the Exchange Organization Management role and be a member of the Domain Admins groups of the domain. By running Prepare Legacy Permissions manually before making other changes, you minimize the possibility of causing any problems in the current Exchange environment.

Upon successfully running this command you must allow for replication to complete across the Exchange organization before continuing to the next step. Failure to wait for replication before moving to the next installation step may cause the Recipient Update Service on the Exchange Server 2003 computers to fail.

Preparing the Schema

As mentioned in Chapter 3, schema changes cannot be undone and affect all objects in the forest; therefore, you must take care when preparing the schema for Exchange. Before beginning the schema change you should perform a full system state backup to capture the state of the domain. Modifying the schema is an irreversible change and it affects all objects in the entire Active Directory forest. To minimize the effect of a failed schema change, it is a best practice to keep the schema master from replicating to the rest of the forest until the change is successful. To disable outbound replication from the schema master run *repadmin /options <domain controller> +DISABLE_OUTBOUND_REPL*, as shown in Figure 15-10.

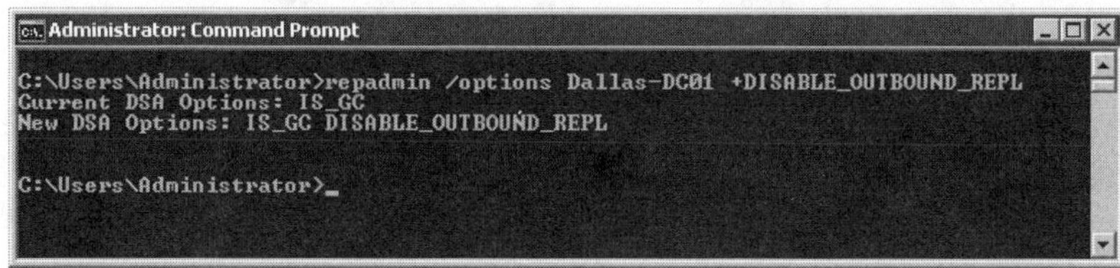

FIGURE 15-10 Disabling outbound replication on schema master

After replication has been stopped on the schema master, the schema can be prepared by running setup from the Exchange 2010 installation media. The schema preparation must be run from the Exchange 2010 installation files on a 64-bit Windows Server 2003 SP2 or higher computer in the same domain and Active Directory site as the schema master. The account that is used to prepare the schema must be a member of the Schema Admins and the Enterprise Admins Active Directory groups. From a command prompt in the Administrative permissions window, run *setup /PrepareSchema* or *setup /ps* as shown in Figure 15-11. Although it might be tempting to manually update the schema by using the LDIF Directory Exchange (LDIFDE) tool to import the LDAP Data Interchange Format (LDIF) files on the Exchange 2010 install media, this is not supported.

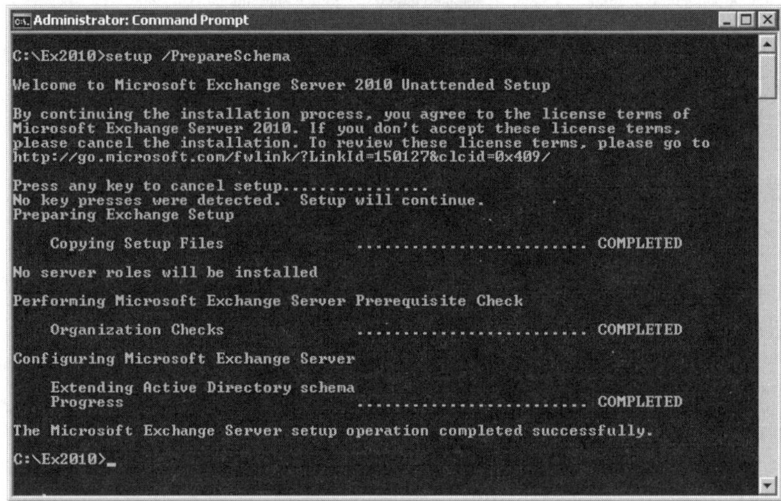

FIGURE 15-11 Running *PrepareSchema*

The *PrepareSchema* process completes the following tasks:

1. Imports the LDIF files to update the AD DS schema with the Exchange Server 2010 specific attributes and classes.
2. If not already completed, also completes the *PrepareLegacyExchangePermissions* process.

After this process has completed successfully and you review the event logs on the schema master server for any errors, you can re-enable replication outbound to the other domain controllers in the domain. To re-enable replication, run *repadmin /options <domain controller> -DISABLE_OUTBOUND_REPL* as shown in Figure 15-12. After enabling replication, use repadmin to verify replication completes before moving on to the next step.

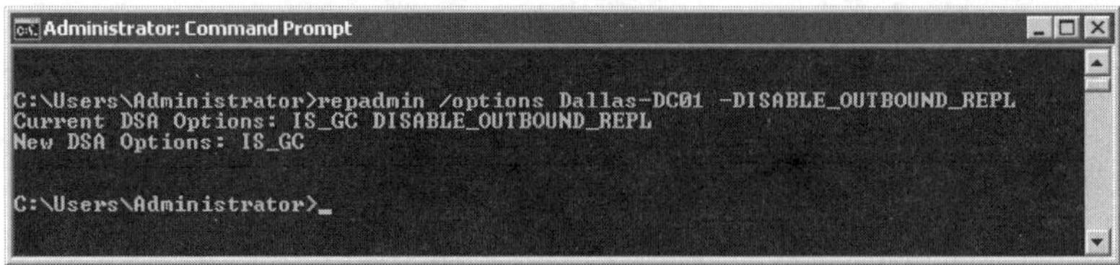

FIGURE 15-12 Re-enabling outbound replication on the schema master

Running Prepare AD

After replication completes, the next part of the preparation is to run Prepare AD. This is run to create the needed objects in the configuration and domain partitions. The Prepare AD process creates a number of containers and objects in the configuration partition. In the Contoso environment these are under CN=Contoso,CN=Microsoft Exchange,CN=Services, CN=Configuration,DC=Contoso,DC=com. These objects and containers are as follows:

CN=Address Lists Container,CN=Contoso,CN=Microsoft Exchange,CN=Services, CN=Configuration,DC=Contoso,DC=Com

CN=Addressing,CN=Contoso,CN=Microsoft Exchange,CN=Services,CN=Configuration, DC=Contoso,DC=Com

CN=Administrative Groups,CN=Contoso,CN=Microsoft Exchange,CN=Services, CN=Configuration,DC=Contoso,DC=Com

CN=Client Access,CN=Contoso,CN=Microsoft Exchange,CN=Services, CN=Configuration,DC=Contoso,DC=Com

CN=Connections,CN=Contoso,CN=Microsoft Exchange,CN=Services, CN=Configuration,DC=Contoso,DC=Com

CN=ELC Folders Container,CN=Contoso,CN=Microsoft Exchange,CN=Services, CN=Configuration,DC=Contoso,DC=Com

CN=ELC Mailbox Policies,CN=Contoso,CN=Microsoft Exchange,CN=Services, CN=Configuration,DC=Contoso,DC=Com

CN=Global Settings,CN=Contoso,CN=Microsoft Exchange,CN=Services, CN=Configuration,DC=Contoso,DC=Com

CN=Mobile Mailbox Policies,CN=Contoso,CN=Microsoft Exchange,CN=Services, CN=Configuration,DC=Contoso,DC=Com

CN=Recipient Policies,CN=Contoso,CN=Microsoft Exchange,CN=Services, CN=Configuration,DC=Contoso,DC=Com

CN=System Policies,CN=Contoso,CN=Microsoft Exchange,CN=Services, CN=Configuration,DC=Contoso,DC=Com

CN=Transport Settings,CN=Contoso,CN=Microsoft Exchange,CN=Services, CN=Configuration,DC=Contoso,DC=Com

CN=UM AutoAttendant,CN=Contoso,CN=Microsoft Exchange,CN=Services, CN=Configuration,DC=Contoso,DC=Com

CN=UM DialPlan,CN=Contoso,CN=Microsoft Exchange,CN=Services, CN=Configuration,DC=Contoso,DC=Com

CN=UM IPGateway Container,CN=Contoso,CN=Microsoft Exchange,CN=Services, CN=Configuration,DC=Contoso,DC=Com

CN=UM Mailbox Policies,CN=Contoso,CN=Microsoft Exchange,CN=Services, CN=Configuration,DC=Contoso,DC=Com

The setup process now verifies the schema has been updated and that the Exchange organization is up to date by checking the *objectVersion* property of the Exchange organization container in the Configuration partition. The *objectVersion* value for the RTM version of Exchange Server 2010 is 12640. Then, if a default accepted domains does not exist, one is created based on the forest root name. Next, the setup process imports the Rights.ldf file to add the extended rights in AD DS. Following this, setup creates the Unified Messaging Voice Originator contact in the Microsoft Exchange System Objects container of the root domain. Then setup creates the Microsoft Exchange Security Groups organizational unit (OU) in the root domain and assigns specific permissions. In that OU, the following universal security groups (USGs) are created and added to the *otherWellKnownObjects* attribute in the Exchange configuration container:

- Delegated Setup
- Discovery Management
- Exchange All Hosted Organizations
- Exchange Servers
- Exchange Trusted Subsystem
- Exchange Windows Permissions
- ExchangeLegacyInterop
- Help Desk
- Hygiene Management
- Organization Management
- Public Folder Management
- Recipient Management
- Records Management
- Server Management
- UM Management
- View-Only Organization Management

Many large organizations are required to minimize the permissions that administrators have. This includes keeping messaging administrators from changing settings in Active Directory as well as keeping Active Directory administrators from changing settings in Exchange. A new option provided in SP1 setup is the ability to enable Active Directory split permissions. To do this you must specify */ActiveDirectorySplitPermissions:true* when you run Prepare AD, or by selecting the option from within the Setup GUI. When this is specified Prepare AD will do the following:

- Create a new OU named Microsoft Exchange Protected Groups
- Create or move the Exchange Windows Permissions group into the Microsoft Exchange Protected Groups OU
- Remove Exchange Trusted Subsystem from the Exchange Windows Permissions group

- Not create or remove any non-delegated RBAC Role Assignments to Roles with Role types of *MailRecipientCreation*, *ActiveDirectoryPermissions*, and *SecurityGroupCreationAndMembership*.

  If */ActiveDirectorySplitPermissions:false* is specified, these changes are undone and the typical permissions are set. More information about RBAC and Active Directory split permissions can be found in Chapter 16, "Managing Exchange."

To run Prepare AD, you must be logged in as a member of the Enterprise Administrators groups, open a command prompt with an Administrative permissions window, and run *setup /PrepareAD /OrganizationName: <organization name>* or *setup /p /on:<organization name>* as shown in Figure 15-13.

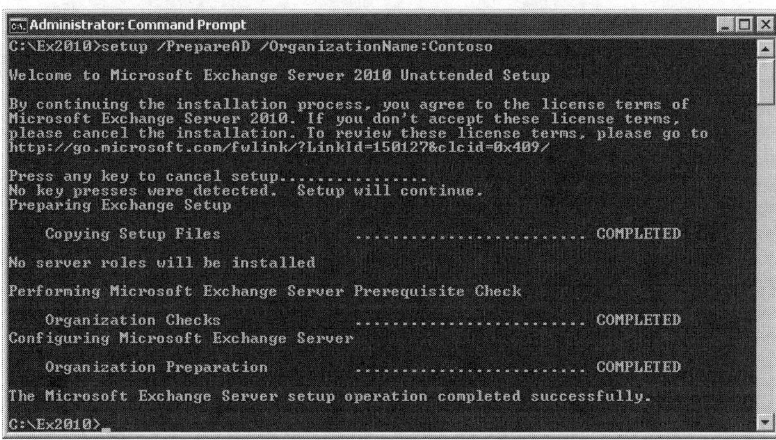

FIGURE 15-13 Running *setup /PrepareAD*

If no Exchange organization container exists, the organization name must be specified by using the */OrganizationName* setup parameter in order to create the container. The organization name must have the following attributes:

- Cannot contain more than 64 characters.
- Cannot be blank.
- If the name contains spaces it must be enclosed in quotation marks.
- Can only use the following characters:
  - A through Z or a through z
  - 0 through 9
  - Space (not leading or trailing)
  - Hyphen or dash

You must keep a number of things in mind when running Prepare AD. The computer running Prepare AD must be able to contact all domains controllers in the forest on port 389. As with previous steps, this command must be run on a computer in the same domain and in the same Active Directory site as the schema master. Setup will make all configuration changes to the schema master to avoid conflicts because of replication latency.

If Prepare Legacy Exchange Permissions and Prepare Schema have not already been completed and Prepare AD is run by a user with the appropriate permission, Prepare AD will also perform those steps. The permission and other requirements for these previous steps are also required when allowing Prepare AD to complete these tasks.

Your change management process will no doubt require that you verify that this step completed successfully. To do this, ensure that a new OU in the root domain called Microsoft Exchange Security Groups has been created and contains the new security groups shown in Figure 15-14.

FIGURE 15-14 Verifying security group creation

Prepare Domain

In single-domain forests, as with the Contoso examples, you don't need to run the Prepare Domain command because the local domain is prepared during the Prepare AD process. In an environment like the Fabrikam and Litware examples, which have multiple domains, you need to execute Prepare Domain executed for each domain that will contain an Exchange 2010 computer or have Exchange recipients. To prepare these additional domains, you run the Prepare Domain or the Prepare All Domains process. This process completes the following tasks:

1. Sets permissions on the domain container for the Exchange Servers, Exchange Organization Administrators, Authenticated Users, and Exchange Mailbox Administrators.
2. Creates a new domain global group in the current domain called Exchange Install Domain Servers, stored in the Microsoft Exchange System Objects container.
3. Assigns permissions at the domain level for the Exchange Servers security group and the Recipient Management security group.

Log on as a member of the Enterprise Administrators groups, open a command prompt with Administrative permissions window, and run *setup /PrepareDomain* or *setup /pd* to prepare the local domain. To run Prepare Domain for another domain you can run *setup /PrepareDomain: <FQDN of domain you want to prepare>*, as shown in Figure 15-15. To run Prepare Domain in a domain that existed before Prepare AD was run, the account must be a member of the Domain Admins group in the domain. If the domain was created after Prepare AD was run, the account must be a member of the Exchange Organization Administrators group and the Domain Admins group in that domain. To prepare all domains in the forest, the logged-in user must also be a member of the Enterprise Admins groups and then run *setup /PrepareAllDomains* or *setup /pad*.

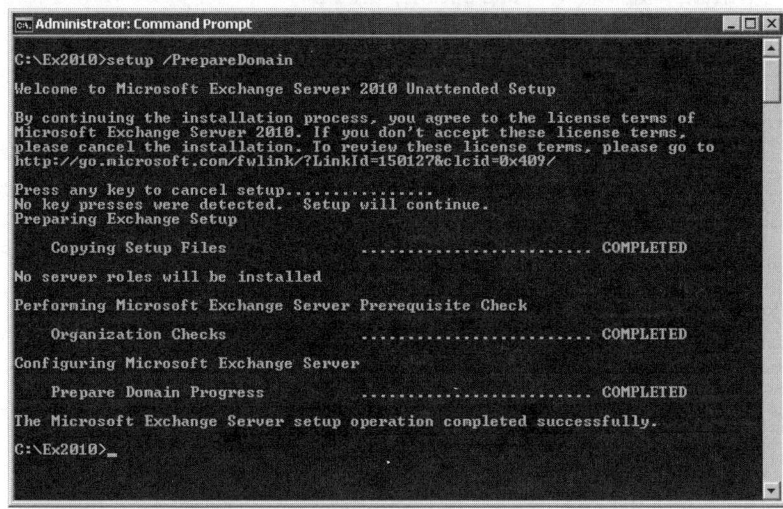

FIGURE 15-15 Running *setup /PrepareDomain*

If replication has not been completed when you attempt to prepare other domains in another Active Directory site, Prepare Domain might fail with the following messages:

```
"PrepareDomain for domain na.litwareinc.com has partially completed. Because of the
Active Directory site configuration, you must wait at least 15 minutes for replication
to occur, and run PrepareDomain for na.litwareinc.com again."

"Active Directory operation failed on Fresno-DC01.na.litwareinc.com. This error is not
retriable. Additional information: The specified group type is invalid.

Active Directory response: 00002141: SvcErr: DSID-031A0FC0, problem 5003 (WILL_NOT_
PERFORM), data 0

The server cannot handle directory requests."
```

To overcome these errors, wait for replication to complete to the other sites before again attempting the Prepare Domain process. If replication does not complete in a timely fashion, there may be replication problems.

Your change management process will no doubt require that you verify that the Prepare Domain process completed successfully. To do this, confirm the following in each prepared domain:

1. A global group in the Microsoft Exchange System Objects container has been created named Exchange Install Domain Servers.
2. The Exchange Install Domain Servers group is a member of the Exchange Servers security group in the root domain.
3. On each domain controller in the prepared domain, the Exchange Servers security group has permissions on the Domain Controller Security Policy\Local Policies\User Rights Assignment\Manage Auditing and Security Log policy.

Checklist for Preparing Active Directory

To prepare Active Directory, you need to complete the following tasks:

1. Create and review a deployment plan.
2. Review AD DS requirements and verify that the requirements are met.
3. Verify environment health using dcdiag, repadmin, DNSLint, ExBPA, and ExPDA.
4. Review and remediate any of the following common problems:

   Active Directory Forest

   - Functionality level is not at the appropriate level and a specific application requires a lower level than Exchange Server does.
   - Default and built-in permissions were changed on built-in containers and groups.

   Active Directory Sites

   - Some subnets are not defined in Active Directory Domain Services.
   - Some site links are missing.
   - Some domain controllers are listed in the wrong sites.
   - Site links do not have the correct costs assigned to them.

   Domain controllers

   - The local domain controllers are not using a common set of DNS servers.
   - The domain controllers are not being backed up regularly.
   - Domain controllers that can be promoted to global catalog servers have not been.

   DNS

   - DNS does not have all of the reverse zones created for each of the available subnets.
   - DNS servers are not replicating all required zones by Active Directory replication or secondary zones are missing.
5. Verify that appropriate permissions are identified and assigned.
6. Install prerequisite components and run *Setup* with the */PrepareLegacyExchangePermissions, /PrepareSchema, /PrepareAD,* and */PrepareDomain* switches.

Deploying Exchange 2010

After Active Directory has been prepared for Exchange 2010, the Exchange Server roles can start to be deployed; however, before beginning the Exchange installation some prerequisites must be met.

Preparing the Exchange 2010 Server Hardware

Although the hardware needs to be properly sized for the needed role, which is covered in more detail in Chapter 13, it is worth mentioning the minimum requirements for installing Exchange, as detailed in Table 15-2.

TABLE 15-2 Minimum Exchange Server Hardware Requirements

COMPONENT	REQUIREMENT
Disk space	To install Exchange 2010, there must be at least 1.2 gigabytes (GB) on the drive on which you install Exchange. An additional 500 MB of available disk space is required for each Unified Messaging (UM) language pack that you plan to install. No matter which drive Exchange Server is installed on, a minimum of 200 MB of available disk space is required on the system drive. For Exchange Servers with the Edge Transport or Hub Transport role installed, at least 500 MB of free space is recommended for the drive that stores the message queue database.
File format	The system partition and partitions that store Exchange binary files, transaction log files, database files, and any other Exchange files should be formatted with the NTFS file system.
Memory	The amount of memory varies depending on the Exchange features that are installed; however, a minimum of 2 GB of RAM is recommended. Additional guidance for hardware configuration can be found in Chapter 13.
Processor	Must have x64 architecture–based computer with Intel processor that supports Intel 64 architecture (formerly known as Intel EM64T) or AMD processor that supports the AMD64 platform. Intel Itanium IA64 processors are not supported.
Screen resolution	The screen resolution used to perform the installation should be at least 800 x 600 pixels to be able to properly view the installation and management tools.

As for the software requirements for the Exchange Server computers, they again depend on the role that will be installed on the server. However, a number of common requirements must be met. The common requirements for any Exchange role are as follows:

- A 64-bit version of Windows Server 2008, Standard edition with Service Pack 2 or higher including Windows Server 2008 R2, Standard edition. The Enterprise edition of Windows is required when the server is a member of a database availability group.

- Microsoft .NET Framework 3.5
- Windows Management Framework Core (Includes Windows PowerShell 2.0 and Windows Remote Management)

Installing Exchange Server Prerequisites

Before installing Exchange it is important to ensure that the operating system has all critical updates applied. This should coincide with the updating standards set through your change management process. To be sure all updates have been applied, run the Microsoft Baseline Security Analyzer. To obtain a list of all applicable updates that may not be considered vulnerability updates you can also run Microsoft Update. Finally, make sure to run the current version of the Malicious Software Removal Tool. This tool is updated each month and is distributed via Microsoft Update to scan, clean, and report any known malicious software installed on the computer.

NOTES FROM THE FIELD

Installing Only Minimum Prerequisites

Andy Schan
Owner, Schan Consulting

On one migration, I had specified that only the minimum prerequisites for the specific role be installed on the servers. Rather than having servers with inconsistent versions of components installed, the customer felt that management would be easier if the basic prerequisites were installed on all servers. The trade-off with this approach is consistency and ease of deployment over a reduction in the number of components that must be maintained with periodic updates. In some cases you may want to install all prerequisites on all servers for consistency, or install the minimum for the roles—the choice depends on the environments.

Also, rather than deploying the minimum versions of components such as the Microsoft .NET Framework, it is usually advisable to install the latest supported version of the components. Updates to each of the components usually provide security enhancements and are more likely to include fixes to known problems that could affect your Exchange deployment.

It is recommended to use Windows Server 2008 R2 for all Exchange 2010 deployments, which reduces the number of prerequisites that need to be installed. Using Windows Server 2008 R2 also provides better processor and power utilization than Windows Server 2008; both of these translate into operational cost savings. Exchange 2010 Service Pack 1 introduced the ability for setup to install any prerequisite Windows Roles and Features. The next several sections review manually installing the prerequisites on both Windows Server 2008 and Windows Server 2008 R2.

INSTALL THE WINDOWS SERVER 2008 SP2 OPERATING SYSTEM PREREQUISITES

To get a Windows Server 2008 server ready for Exchange 2010 installation, first you must install the Microsoft .NET Framework 3.5 Service Pack 1 (SP1) with the first family update or higher. Then install the Windows Management Framework, which includes both Windows Remote Management (WinRM) 2.0 and Windows PowerShell V2. On servers that will host the Hub Transport or Mailbox server role, install the Microsoft Filter Pack (*http://go.microsoft.com/fwlink/?LinkId=123380*).

After downloading and installing the required software, you need to make a number of configuration changes to be ready for installing Exchange 2010. The Exchange 2010 media includes XML-based files that specify the required roles and features that need to be installed. To use these to install the prerequisites, first open an elevated command prompt, navigate to the Scripts folder in the root folder of the Exchange 2010 installation media, and use one of the following commands on servers that will host multiple roles to install the necessary operating system components:

- Client Access, Hub Transport, and the Mailbox role:

  ```
  sc config NetTcpPortSharing start=auto

  ServerManagerCmd -ip Exchange-Typical.xml -Restart
  ```

- Client Access, Hub Transport, Mailbox, and Unified Messaging server roles. (This configuration is not recommended.)

  ```
  sc config NetTcpPortSharing start= auto

  ServerManagerCmd -i Desktop-Experience

  ServerManagerCmd -ip Exchange-Typical.xml -Restart
  ```

- Client Access and Hub Transport or Client Access and Mailbox server roles:

  ```
  sc config NetTcpPortSharing start= auto

  ServerManagerCmd -ip Exchange-Typical.xml -Restart
  ```

- Hub Transport and Mailbox server roles:

  ```
  ServerManagerCmd -ip Exchange-Typical.xml -Restart
  ```

For single role servers, complete the following:

- Client Access role:

  ```
  sc config NetTcpPortSharing start= auto

  ServerManagerCmd -ip Exchange-CAS.xml -Restart
  ```

- Hub Transport role:

  ```
  ServerManagerCmd -ip Exchange-Hub.xml -Restart
  ```

- Mailbox role:

```
ServerManagerCmd -ip Exchange-MBX.xml -Restart
```

- Unified Messaging role:

```
ServerManagerCmd -ip Exchange-UM.xml -Restart
```

- Edge Transport role:

```
ServerManagerCmd -ip Exchange-Edge.xml -Restart
```

After installing the required roles and features, allow the server to reboot and then again use Windows Update or the Security Baseline Analyzer to ensure that all critical updates have been applied to the newly installed components.

> **IMPORTANT** If you intend to allow Exchange setup to install the required Windows Roles and Features, you do not need to run the *ServerManagerCmd* commands. You must, however, manually enable the automatic start of the NetTcpPortSharing service.

INSTALL THE WINDOWS SERVER 2008 R2 OPERATING SYSTEM PREREQUISITES

The Exchange 2010 media does not include scripts to install the prerequisite roles and features on Windows Server 2008 R2 computers using the preferred *Add-WindowsFeature* cmdlet. In addition to using the */InstallWindowsComponents* switch introduced in SP1, you have a number of easy-to-copy commands to use. For servers that will host the Hub Transport or Mailbox server role, install the Microsoft Filter Pack either manually or using a software deployment solution. After that completes, open an elevated Windows PowerShell window and run the following command:

```
Import-Module ServerManager
```

After the Server Manager PowerShell module is imported, the *Add-WindowsFeature* cmdlet is available. To install the roles and features for a server that will have multiple roles installed, run the appropriate cmdlet.

- Client Access, Hub Transport, and the Mailbox role:

```
Add-WindowsFeature NET-Framework,RSAT-ADDS,Web-Server,Web-Basic-Auth,
Web-Windows-Auth,Web-Metabase,Web-Net-Ext,Web-Lgcy-Mgmt-Console,
WAS-Process-Model,RSAT-Web-Server,Web-ISAPI-Ext,Web-Digest-Auth,
Web-Dyn-Compression,NET-HTTP-Activation,RPC-Over-HTTP-Proxy -Restart
```

- Client Access, Hub Transport, Mailbox, and Unified Messaging server roles. (Installing Unified Messaging on a server with other roles is not recommended.)

```
Add-WindowsFeature NET-Framework,RSAT-ADDS,Web-Server,Web-Basic-Auth,
Web-Windows-Auth,Web-Metabase,Web-Net-Ext,Web-Lgcy-Mgmt-Console,WAS-Process-Model,
```

```
RSAT-Web-Server,Web-ISAPI-Ext,Web-Digest-Auth,Web-Dyn-Compression,
NET-HTTP-Activation,RPC-Over-HTTP-Proxy,Desktop-Experience -Restart
```

- Client Access and Hub Transport server roles:

```
Add-WindowsFeature NET-Framework,RSAT-ADDS,Web-Server,Web-Basic-Auth,
Web-Windows-Auth,Web-Metabase,Web-Net-Ext,Web-Lgcy-Mgmt-Console,
WAS-Process-Model,RSAT-Web-Server,Web-ISAPI-Ext,Web-Digest-Auth,
Web-Dyn-Compression,NET-HTTP-Activation,RPC-Over-HTTP-Proxy -Restart
```

- Hub Transport and Mailbox server roles:

```
Add-WindowsFeature NET-Framework,RSAT-ADDS,Web-Server,Web-Basic-Auth,
Web-Windows-Auth,Web-Metabase,Web-Net-Ext,Web-Lgcy-Mgmt-Console,
WAS-Process-Model,RSAT-Web-Server -Restart
```

- Client Access and Mailbox server roles:

```
Add-WindowsFeature NET-Framework,RSAT-ADDS,Web-Server,Web-Basic-Auth,
Web-Windows-Auth,Web-Metabase,Web-Net-Ext,Web-Lgcy-Mgmt-Console,
WAS-Process-Model,RSAT-Web-Server,Web-ISAPI-Ext,Web-Digest-Auth,
Web-Dyn-Compression,NET-HTTP-Activation,RPC-Over-HTTP-Proxy -Restart
```

For single role servers, complete the following:

- Client Access role:

```
Add-WindowsFeature NET-Framework,RSAT-ADDS,Web-Server,Web-Basic-Auth,
Web-Windows-Auth,Web-Metabase,Web-Net-Ext,Web-Lgcy-Mgmt-Console,
WAS-Process-Model,RSAT-Web-Server,Web-ISAPI-Ext,Web-Digest-Auth,
Web-Dyn-Compression,NET-HTTP-Activation,RPC-Over-HTTP-Proxy -Restart
```

- Hub Transport or the Mailbox role:

```
Add-WindowsFeature NET-Framework,RSAT-ADDS,Web-Server,Web-Basic-Auth,
Web-Windows-Auth,Web-Metabase,Web-Net-Ext,Web-Lgcy-Mgmt-Console,
WAS-Process-Model,RSAT-Web-Server -Restart
```

- Unified Messaging role:

```
Add-WindowsFeature NET-Framework,RSAT-ADDS,Web-Server,Web-Basic-Auth,
Web-Windows-Auth,Web-Metabase,Web-Net-Ext,Web-Lgcy-Mgmt-Console,
WAS-Process-Model,RSAT-Web-Server,Desktop-Experience -Restart
```

- Edge Transport role:

```
Add-WindowsFeature NET-Framework,RSAT-ADDS,ADLDS -Restart
```

For all servers on which the Client Access server role is installed you must reboot the server and set the Net.Tcp Port Sharing Service for Automatic startup. To do this, log on as an administrator, open an elevated Windows PowerShell console, and configure by running the following command:

```
Set-Service NetTcpPortSharing -StartupType Automatic
```

After installing the required roles and features, allow the server to reboot and then use Windows Update or the Security Baseline Analyzer to ensure that all critical updates have been applied to the newly installed components.

IMPORTANT If you intend to use the */InstallWindowsComponents* setup option to automatically install the required Windows Roles and Features, you do not need to run the *Add-WindowsFeature* cmdlet. However, you still must manually enable the automatic start of the NetTcpPortSharing service for servers where you install the Client Access server role.

INSTALL THE WINDOWS VISTA SP2 OPERATING SYSTEM PREREQUISITES FOR THE EXCHANGE MANAGEMENT TOOLS

To prepare a Windows Vista computer for installing the Exchange 2010 management tools, you must install the Microsoft .NET Framework 3.5 Service Pack 1 (SP1) with the first family update or higher. Then install the Windows Management Framework, which includes both Windows Remote Management (WinRM) 2.0 and Windows PowerShell V2. Once that is completed, install the IIS 6 Management Console.

INSTALL THE WINDOWS 7 OPERATING SYSTEM PREREQUISITES FOR THE EXCHANGE MANAGEMENT TOOLS

To get a Windows Vista server ready for the Exchange 2010 management tools installation, first you must install Microsoft .NET Framework 3.5.1 and the IIS 6 Management Console.

INSIDE TRACK

Exchange Server 2010 Install Differences

Paul Wimmer

Senior Program Manager, Microsoft Corporation

Automating and reducing the complexity during the deployment should be considered early in the process. With Exchange Server 2010, there are differences between installing the first Exchange Server 2010 server and subsequent Exchange 2010 servers. The Setup UI and unattended experience will change depending on your specific scenario. In addition, the level of permissions required will be different.

The following are some common install scenarios, along with their differences.

First Exchange 2010 Server: any role in a new organization

- The Active Directory schema will be updated and the domain will be prepared—you must have Schema Admin and Enterprise Admin rights in Active Directory.
- The Setup UI will require that you enter an organization name.
- The Setup UI will prompt for whether you want to use split permissions.
- Unattended Setup will require that you use the */OrganizationName* switch.
- The Setup UI will prompt for whether you wish to participate in the Customer Experience Improvement Program.
- The Setup UI will display an option to install required Windows Roles and Feature depending on role selection.

First Exchange 2010 Server: any role in an existing organization

- The Active Directory schema will be updated and the domain will be prepared—you must have Schema Admin and Enterprise Admin rights in Active Directory.
- The Setup UI will prompt for whether you wish to participate in the Customer Experience Improvement Program.
- The client settings decision means choosing whether your organization will support Outlook 2003 or Entourage. If you don't use these clients, select No. If you change your mind later, you will need to manually run a command to introduce a public folder database.
- The Setup UI will display an option to install required Windows roles and feature depending on role selection.
- If the organization has Exchange 2003 and you are installing the Hub Transport role, you will be prompted to choose a Legacy Bridgehead server. This will create a Routing Group connector between Exchange Server 2010 and 2003. Failure to choose this will result in no mail flow between the versions.

Additional Exchange 2010 Server in a new or existing organization

If this is the first Exchange role of a particular type, additional permissions may be required because of Active Directory updates (object creation).

Add/Remove Exchange 2010 Server roles on an existing server (Exchange maintenance)

- Use Add/Remove Programs in Control Panel for maintenance.
- No EULA is displayed because it has already been accepted.
- You may require additional prerequisites depending on the Exchange role being added.

Delegated Setup: granting particular user permissions to install Exchange

This is a common scenario for Enterprises that have separate teams managing Active Directory and Exchange.

- Exchange Admin can only use unattended setup switch to provision a new server object: setup.com */NewProvisionedServer.*
- The user must be a member of the Delegated Setup Role group to install the server associated with the newly provisioned server object.

Installing the Exchange Server Roles

Now that the server is prepared for installation, the individual roles can be installed. As mentioned in Chapter 14, a migration or an upgrade requires that specific installation order is followed. In a Greenfield, or a new deployment, each site first needs a Hub Transport server and a Client Access server. If you are not deploying all of the roles on the same server, a Mailbox role can deployed after the Hub Transport and Client Access server roles.

The Exchange 2010 setup process is very customizable and can be controlled from the command line. To install an Exchange role, the */mode:Install* switch is used and then either the role or roles are specified with the */roles* (also: */roles* or */r*) switch. Multiple roles can be installed at the same time by specifying multiple roles separated by a comma.

The valid options roles are:

- ClientAccess, CA, C
- EdgeTransport, ET, E
- HubTransport, HT, H
- Mailbox, MB, M
- ManagementTools, MT, T
- UnifiedMessaging, UM, U

Also, customization can be done from the command line with the following switches:

- */OrganizationName, /on*

  This parameter is required to specify the Exchange organization name if it hasn't already been created. Only one Exchange organization can be created in an AD DS forest.

- */TargetDir, /t*

  This specifies the location to install Exchange Server 2010 files. The default path is %ProgramFiles%\Microsoft\Exchange Server.

- */SourceDir, /s*

  This specifies the path to the Exchange DVD.

- */UpdatesDir, /u*

  This specifies the directory that contains the updates that will be installed during setup.

- */DomainController, /dc*

  This specifies the domain controller that setup will use to read and to write to Active Directory. The NetBIOS or the FQDN name formats can be used. You would use this switch if there are multiple domain controllers on a site and a specific one needs to be used for setup.

- */InstallWindowsComponents*

  This option was introduced in Service Pack 1, when specified setup will install any required Windows Roles and features to support the install type specified.

Advanced options can also be specified:

- */AnswerFile /af*

  This specifies the location of an answer file that contains advanced parameters for setup. The format for the answer file is *<Key>=<Value>*. Only the advanced parameters are valid for the answer file. Use the */AnswerFile* parameter to specify the location of a file that contains parameters for setup. You can use this file to install multiple computers with the same parameters. You can use the following parameters in the answer file: *EnableLegacyOutlook, LegacyRoutingServer, ServerAdmin, ForeignForestFQDN, OrganizationName, DoNotStartTransport, UpdatesDir, EnableErrorReporting, NoSelfSignedCertificates, AdamLdapPort*, and *AdamSslPort*.

- */DoNotStartTransport*

  This switch configures the Transport Service to not start during setup. This only applies when installing either the Hub Transport or Edge Transport roles.

- */EnableLegacyOutlook*

  This switch specifies that legacy Outlook clients can connect to the Exchange 2010 servers. This can only be specified during the installation of the first Exchange 2010 Mailbox role installation in an organization.

- */LegacyRoutingServer*

  This specifies the name of a legacy Exchange server that will be used to route messages to. This only applies when installing the first Exchange 2010 Hub Transport role in the organization.

- */EnableErrorReporting*

  This enables the Exchange server to automatically submit critical error reports. Microsoft uses this information to diagnose problems and provide solutions.

- */CustomerFeedbackEnabled*

  This specifies whether to participate in the Customer Experience Improvement Program. The value can either be True or False.

- */Industry*

  When specifying whether to join the Customer Experience Program, additional information can be specified to help categorize the telemetry information sent to Microsoft.
- */Mdbname*

  An initial database is created when the Mailbox role is installed; to control the name of this mailbox database, specify this parameter. This applies only when installing the Mailbox role.
- */DbFilePath*

  The full path and filename of the database file. This applies only when installing the Mailbox role.
- */LogFolderPath*

  The folder path to the directory where logs should be placed. This applies only when installing the Mailbox role.
- */ExternalCASServerDomain*

  Specify the external domain for Client Access server to configure the external URL for the OWA/ActiveSync/Web Services/OAB virtual directory. This applies only when installing the Client Access role.
- */NoSelfSignedCertificates*

  Specifies that setup should skip creating self-signed certificates if no other valid certificate is found for use in SSL/TLS sessions. This applies only when installing the Client Access and Unified Messaging roles.
- */AdamLdapPort*

  LDAP Port to use for Edge Transport server role AD/AM instance. This applies only when installing the Edge Transport role. The default value is 50389.
- */AdamSslPort*

  SSL Port to use for Edge Transport server role AD/AM instance. This applies only when installing the Edge Transport role. The default value is 50636.

In Exchange 2007, the */RecoverCMS* option was used to recover clustered mailbox servers. Exchange 2010 no longer has clustered mailbox servers, and therefore no longer has that option. A failed DAG member must be removed from the DAG and then the */m:RecoverServer* switch can then be used. After the server has been recovered, it can be added back to the DAG.

During installation of the Exchange Server roles, the setup process adds the Organization Management USG to the administrator security group on the local computer so that members of the management role group named Organization Management can manage the server. Permissions are also added to the server object in the configuration partition of the domain. Table 15-3 shows the Access Control Entries (ACEs) or the permissions set when you install one of the Exchange Server roles. The permissions are set on the server object.

For example, the distinguished name of the Dallas-EX01 server object would be CN=DALLAS-EX01,CN=Servers,CN=Exchange Administrative Group (FYDIBOHF23SPDLT), CN=Administrative Groups,CN=Contoso,CN=Microsoft Exchange,CN=Services, CN=Configuration,DC=Contoso,DC=Com.

TABLE 15-3 Permissions Set on the Server Object

ACCOUNT	ACE TYPE	INHERITANCE	PERMISSIONS
Server Computer Object	Allow	All	Read
Server Computer Object	Allow	None	Write Property on *msExchServerSite* and *msExchEdgeSyncCredential*
Exchange Servers	Allow	All	Store Constrained Delegation Store Read Only Access Store Read and Write Access Store Transport Access
NETWORK SERVICE	Allow	All	Exchange Web Services Token Serialization (Only server objects that have the Client Access server role installed).
NETWORK SERVICE	Allow	All	Read (Only server objects that have the Hub Transport server role installed).
Delegated Setup	Allow	All	Full Control, Create Child, Delete Child
Delegated Setup	Deny	All	Send As, Receive As, Create/Delete *msExchangePublicMDB* objects
Authenticated Users	Allow	All	Read All Properties

USING THE UPDATES FOLDER

The root of the Exchange 2010 installation media has an Updates folder. This folder is used to apply a Windows Installer update (.msp file) to a fresh install of Exchange 2010. For example, when you're performing a new Exchange 2010 install, and you need to also apply Exchange 2010 RTM rollup update 3, you could place the rollup .msp file in the Updates folder and it would be applied during the install process.

The updates folder is not designed to apply services packs or multiple .msp files—this is also untested and unsupported. If you need to install Exchange 2010 SP1 with rollup update 1, do a clean install of SP1 with the rollup .msp file in the Updates folder. Exchange 2010 service packs include the basic installation, so you don't need to install the RTM version of Exchange 2010.

PROVISIONING SERVERS

In large environments permissions are usually restricted to a privileged few accounts. Therefore silos of responsibility are given out. For example although the third-tier Exchange personnel might be involved in the initial preparation, the subsequent server installation will likely be delegated to other people. The Exchange 2010 installation provides the ability for this. After having at least one other Exchange Server installed you can provision a server for delegated setup. This allows an account to be delegated the ability to install a single Exchange Server computer, without needing to be a member of the Organization Management group. To delegate an account these permissions, first you must provision the new server with an account in the Organization Management group running *Setup.com /NewProvisionedServer: ServerName.*

Similar to the setup process, the New Provisioned Server process creates the server object within the Active Directory configuration partition and then adds the following ACEs to the server object within for the Delegated Setup role group:

- Deny access control entry for the Receive As extended right
- Deny access control entry for the Send As extended right
- Deny CreateChild and DeleteChild permissions for Exchange public folder objects
- Full Control on the server object and its children

To provide the administrator who will perform the installation for the software the appropriate permissions, the account used must have local administrator permissions on the server and also be a member of the domain Delegated Setup security group.

Creating a DAG cannot be completed by an Exchange administrator who does not have access to create computer accounts in Active Directory because this process creates a cluster network object (CNO) for each DAG. If this is the case, an administrator with permissions will need to prestage the Exchange server computer objects and cluster network objects before the setup begins. Prestaging these computer accounts involves an administrator with the appropriate permissions manually creating the objects in Active Directory and then assigning permissions. To prestage the cluster network object, create a computer object with the name of the DAG in the desired OU. Then disable the account and assign it the Create Computer Objects permission for the CNO on the default container for computer accounts. Finally, assign either the first node that will be added to the DAG or the Exchange Trusted Subsystem Group to have full permissions on the CNO. For more information on prestaging cluster network objects, see *http://technet.microsoft.com/en-us/library/ff367878.aspx.*

EXCHANGE SETUP LOGS

Anytime Exchange Setup is run, a folder named ExchangeSetupLogs is created in the root of the system drive. A number of files are created in this folder that chronicle the setup process. Anytime you encounter problems during installation these files will prove invaluable to you and the support professional if you need to call them. The two files that contain the most information are the ExchangeSetup.log and the ExchangeSetup.msilog. The ExchangeSetup.log contains a log of all the actions that the setup process has taken, as shown in Figure 15-16. This file should be consulted first to determine at what point the error occurred during the setup process. The ExchangeSetup.msilog contains a log of all the actions taken by the Microsoft Installer and can be used to troubleshoot issues with the Microsoft Installer packages. The PreReqs subfolder contains the results of the prerequisites check that setup does before installing any new Exchange Server roles. A number of other files are also created in the ExchangeSetupLogs folder. These files detail the exact steps taken during the setup process. If you pinpoint a problem in the ExchangeSetup.log file, you can view these other files to dig further into the problem. In addition, when calling Microsoft for support, the support engineer may want to review the entire contents of the ExchangeSetupLogs folder.

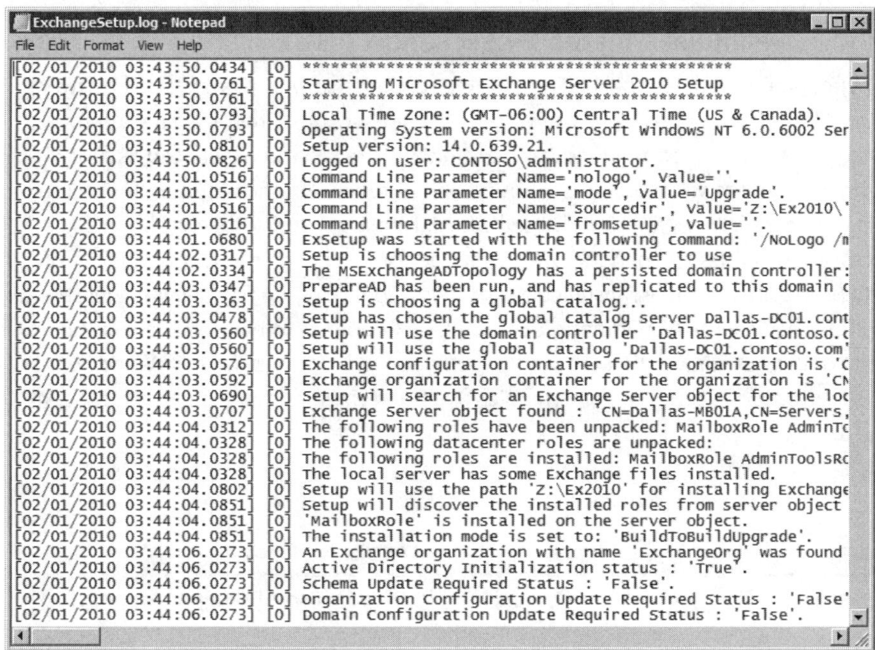

FIGURE 15-16 ExchangeSetup.log

These files are appended every time setup is run, keeping a full history for the server. As a best practice these files should be reviewed after setup is run to verify that no errors or warnings were logged.

Setup Checklist

Use the following checklist when installing Exchange Server roles:

1. Review Exchange 2010 prerequisites for each server role.
2. Define deployment standards.
3. Install prerequisites (if not using the SP1 */InstallWindowsComponents* switch).
4. Install any applicable software updates.
5. For Client Access Server roles enable the automatic start of the NetTcpPortSharing service.
6. Install Exchange Server roles.
7. Review Exchange Setup logs.

Windows Firewall Rules Created by Exchange 2010

In many environments, IT personnel having previous experience with client firewall software may want to disable the Windows Firewall with Advanced Security rather than having to deal with the extra hassle of configuring it. The Windows Firewall with Advanced Security is a stateful, host-based firewall that filters inbound and outbound traffic based on firewall rules. To ease the configuration of Windows Firewall with Advanced Security, the Exchange 2010 setup process creates rules to open the ports required for server and client communication based on the server roles that are installed. To properly configure the firewall when installing Exchange 2007, the Security Configuration Wizard (SCW) tool has to be used. Having this done as part of the installation discourages the lazy approach of disabling the Windows Firewall with Advanced Security. When any role is installed three rules are created, as shown in Table 15-4.

TABLE 15-4 All Roles Windows Firewall Rules

RULE NAME	PORT	PROGRAM
MSExchangeServiceHost - RPC (TCP-In)	Dynamic RPC	Bin\Microsoft.Exchange.ServiceHost .exe
MSExchangeServiceHost - RPCEP-Map (TCP-In)	RPC-EPMap	Bin\Microsoft.Exchange.Service.Host
MSExchangeRPCEPMap (GFW) (TCP-In)	RPC-EPMap	Any

When the Client Access Server role is installed, 18 rules are created to support the client access functionality as listed in Table 15-5.

TABLE 15-5 Client Access Messaging Windows Firewall Rules

RULE NAME	PORT	PROGRAM
MSExchange - IMAP4 (GFW) (TCP-In)	143, 993 (TCP)	All
MSExchangeIMAP4 (TCP-In)	143, 993 (TCP)	ClientAccess\PopImap\Microsoft .Exchange.Imap4Service.exe
MSExchange - POP3 (FGW) (TCP-In)	110, 995 (TCP)	All
MSExchange - POP3 (TCP-In)	110, 995 (TCP)	ClientAccess\PopImap\Microsoft .Exchange.Pop3Service.exe
MSExchange - OWA (GFW) (TCP-In)	5075, 5076, 5077 (TCP)	All
MSExchangeOWAAppPool (TCP-In)	5075, 5076, 5077 (TCP)	Inetsrv\w3wp.exe
MSExchangeAB-RPC (TCP-In)	Dynamic RPC	Bin\Microsoft.Exchange.AddressBook .Service.exe
MSExchangeAB-RPCEPMap (TCP-In)	RPC-EPMap	Bin\Microsoft.Exchange.AddressBook .Service.exe
MSExchangeAB-RpcHttp (TCP-In)	6002, 6004 (TCP)	Bin\Microsoft.Exchange.AddressBook .Service.exe
RpcHttpLBS (TCP-In)	Dynamic RPC	System32\Svchost.exe
MSExchangeMailboxReplication (GFW) (TCP-In)	808 (TCP)	Any
MSExchangeADTopology - RPC (TCP-In)	Dynamic RPC	Bin\MSExchangeADTopologyService .exe
MSExchangeMailboxReplication (TCP-In)	808 (TCP)	Bin\MSExchangeMailboxReplication .exe
MSExchangeMonitoring - RPC (TCP-In)	Dynamic RPC	Bin\Microsoft.Exchange.Management .Monitoring.exe
MSExchangeRPC (GFW) (TCP-In)	Dynamic RPC	Any
MSExchangeRPC - RPC (TCP-In)	Dynamic RPC	Bin\Microsoft.Exchange.RpcClientAccess .Service.exe
MSExchangeRPC - PRCEPMap (TCP-In)	RPC-EPMap	Bin\Microsoft.Exchange.RpcClientAccess .Service.exe
MSExchangeRPC (TCP-In)	6001 (TCP)	Bin\Microsoft.Exchange.RpcClientAccess .Service.exe

When the Mailbox server role is installed, 23 rules are created to support the mailbox functionality as shown in Table 15-6.

TABLE 15-6 Mailbox Windows Firewall Rules

RULE NAME	PORT	PROGRAM
MSExchangeIS - RPC (TCP-In)	Dynamic RPC	Bin\Store.exe
MSExchangeIS RPCEPMap (TCP-In)	RPC-EPMap	Bin\Store.exe
MSExchangeIS (GFW) (TCP-In)	6001, 6002, 6003, 6004 (TCP)	Any
MSExchangeIS (TCP-In)	6001 (TCP)	Bin\Store.exe
MSExchangeMailboxAssistants - RPC (TCP-In)	Dynamic RPC	Bin\MSExchangeMailboxAssistants .exe
MSExchangeMailboxAssistants - RPCEPMap (TCP-In)	RPC-EPMap	Bin\MSExchangeMailboxAssistants .exe
MSExchangeMailSubmission - RPC (TCP-In)	Dynamic RPC	Bin\MSExchangeMailSubmission.exe
MSExchangeMailSubmission - RPCEPMap (TCP-In)	RPC-EPMap	Bin\MSExchangeMailSubmission.exe
MSExchangeMigration - RPC (TCP-In)	Dynamic RPC	Bin\MSExchangeMigration.exe
MSExchangeMigration - RPCEPMap (TCP-In)	RPC-EPMap	Bin\MSExchangeMigration.exe
MSExchangerepl - Log Copier (TCP-In)	64327 (TCP)	Bin\MSExchangeRepl.exe
MSExchangerepl - RPC (TCP-In)	Dynamic RPC	Bin\MSExchangeRepl.exe
MSExchangerepl - RPC-EPMap (TCP-In)	RPC-EPMap	Bin\MSExchangeRepl.exe
MSExchangeSearch - RPC (TCP-In)	Dynamic RPC	Bin\Microsoft.Exchange.Search .ExSearch.exe
MSExchangeThrottling - RPC (TCP-In)	Dynamic RPC	Bin\MSExchangeThrottling.exe
MSExchangeThrottling - RPCEPMap (TCP-In)	RPC-EPMap	Bin\MSExchangeThrottling.exe

RULE NAME	PORT	PROGRAM
MSFTED - RPC (TCP-In)	Dynamic RPC	Bin\MSFTED.exe
MSFTED - RPCEPMap (TCP-In)	RPC-EPMap	Bin\MSFTED.exe
MSExchangeADTopology - RPC (TCP-In)	Dynamic RPC	Bin\MSExchangeADTopologyService .exe
MSExchangeRPC (GFW) (TCP-In)	Dynamic RPC	Any
MSExchangeRPC - RPC (TCP-In)	Dynamic RPC	Bin\Microsoft.Exchange .RpcClientAccess.Service.exe
MSExchangeRPC - PRCEPMap (TCP-In)	RPC-EPMap	Bin\Microsoft.Exchange .RpcClientAccess.Service.exe
MSExchangeRPC (TCP-In)	6001 (TCP)	Bin\Microsoft.Exchange .RpcClientAccess.Service.exe

When the Hub Transport server role is installed, eight rules are created to support the mailbox functionality as shown in Table 15-7.

TABLE 15-7 Windows Firewall Rules for Hub Transport Server Roles

RULE NAME	PORT	PROGRAM
MSExchangeEdgeSync - RPC (TCP-In)	Dynamic RPC	Bin\Microsoft.Exchange .EdgeSyncSvc.exe
MSExchangeEdgeSync - RPCEPMap (TCP-In)	RPC-EPMap	Bin\Microsoft.Exchange .EdgeSyncSvc.exe
MSExchangeTransportWorker - RPC (TCP-In)	Dynamic RPC	Bin\edgetransport.exe
MSExchangeTransportWorker - RPCEPMap (TCP-In)	RPC-EPMap	Bin\edgetransport.exe
MSExchangeTransportWorker (GFW) (TCP-In)	25, 587 (TCP)	Any
MSExchangeTransportWorker (TCP-In)	25, 587 (TCP)	Bin\edgetransport.exe
MSExchangeADTopology - RPC (TCP-In)	Dynamic RPC	Bin\MSExchangeADTopologyService .exe
MSExchangeRPC (GFW) (TCP-In)	Dynamic RPC	Any

When the Hub Transport or the Edge Transport server roles are installed, three rules are created to support the mailbox functionality as shown in Table 15-8.

TABLE 15-8 Hub Transport and Edge Transport Windows Firewall Rules

RULE NAME	PORT	PROGRAM
MSExchangeTransportLogSearch - RPC (TCP-In)	Dynamic RPC	Bin\MSExchangeTransportLogSearch.exe
MSExchangeTransportLogSearch - RPCEPMap (TCP-In)	RPC-EPMap	Bin\MSExchangeTransportLogSearch.exe
MSExchangeMonitoring - RPC (TCP-In)	Dynamic RPC	Bin\Microsoft.Exchange.Management.Monitoring.exe

When the Unified Messaging server role is installed, 10 rules are created to support the mailbox functionality as shown in Table 15-9.

TABLE 15-9 Unified Messaging Windows Firewall Rules

RULE NAME	PORT	PROGRAM
SESWorker (GFW) (TCP-In)	Any	Any
SESWorker (TCP-In)	Any	UnifiedMessaging\SESWorker.exe
UMService (GFW) (TCP-In)	5060, 5061	Any
UMService (TCP-In)	5060, 5061	Bin\UMService.exe
UMWorkerProcess (GFW) (TCP-In)	5065, 5066, 5067, 5068	Any
UMWorkerProcess (TCP-In)	5065, 5066, 5067, 5068	Bin\UMWorkerProcess.exe
UMWorkerProcess - RPC (TCP-In)	Dynamic RPC	Bin\UMWorkerProcess.exe
MSExchangeADTopology - RPC (TCP-In)	Dynamic RPC	Bin\MSExchangeADTopologyService.exe
MSExchangeMonitoring - RPC (TCP-In)	Dynamic RPC	Bin\Microsoft.Exchange.Management.Monitoring.exe
MSExchangeRPC (GFW) (TCP-In)	Dynamic RPC	Any

When you install Internet Information Services, Windows will automatically open the HTTP (port 80, TCP) and HTTPS (port 443, TCP) ports. Exchange 2010 setup does not need to open these ports—they are already available.

NOTES FROM THE FIELD

Considerations for Local Security of Exchange Servers

Erik Szewczyk, MCM
Dell Global Infrastructure Consulting Services

When designing and deploying Exchange in a dispersed environment with split permissions, it's important to consider the functionality of Role Based Access Control (RBAC) within Exchange and the function of the Exchange Trusted Subsystem. This is directly applicable to how local administrators are defined for all Exchange Servers within the environment.

As you'll find, all commands that are executed in either the Exchange Management Shell or the Exchange Management Console are not executed under the security context of your user account. Instead, the RBAC components of Exchange take the commands and evaluate them against the Role Group or Role Groups that the account has been assigned and any policies that have been granted. If authorized to do so, the commands are then executed against Windows, Active Directory, or Exchange under the security context of the Exchange server, a member of the *Exchange Trusted Subsystem*.

The Exchange Trusted Subsystem is a highly privileged universal security group that has access to read or modify all Exchange-related objects and attributes within Active Directory, effectively making the Exchange Trusted Subsystem an organization-wide Exchange superuser. Therefore, access to modify this group should be restricted to only the most trusted administrators in your organization.

Effectively speaking, this means that anyone that has Local Administration privileges over a single Exchange server within your organization should be considered, by extension, a full Exchange Organization Administrator as well as a Local Administrator against all other Exchange servers.

In both Windows Server 2008 and Windows Server 2008 R2, Windows Firewall with Advanced Security allows a process or service to be specified in a rule. Exchange setup creates firewall rules scoped to the process name; however, some rules are created twice, with one being unrestricted to the process for compatibility. It is best practice to disable or remove the rules not restricted to processes and keep the process-restricted rules, if possible. Rules with names that include "(GFW)" are not restricted by a process. It is not possible to modify Windows Firewall rules created by Exchange 2010 setup. To make changes, you could create custom rules based on them and then disable or delete the original rule.

A number of Exchange Server services use Remote Procedure Calls (RPCs) for communication. Server processes that use RPCs register those endpoints in the Endpoint Mapper database. RPC clients contact the remote RPC Endpoint Mapper to determine the endpoints used by the server process. Exchange 2010 setup creates two firewall rules for a process that require RPCs. One of the rules allows communication with the RPC Endpoint Mapper, and the second rule allows communication with the dynamically assigned endpoint.

Automating Exchange Server Installations

In large Exchange deployments, providing automation for the installation and testing will go a long way to improve the accuracy of the deployment and reduce administrator stress. Unfortunately, each deployment will have its own requirements and schedule; therefore, there isn't a one-size-fits-all script that will install Exchange through an enterprise. The focus of this section is to provide some ideas on what portions might easily be automated and provide a few example scripts that you might be able to adapt for your environment.

NOTES FROM THE FIELD

Performing Exchange 2010 Unattended Deployments

Paul Wimmer
Senior Program Manager, Microsoft

To ensure consistent and reproducible deployments, many companies prefer to install Exchange Server 2010 without having to click through a UI to do the installation. This also can speed up the installation process because it requires less interaction when the Exchange deployment specialist deploys the pilot and production servers. Exchange Server 2010 offers a fully unattended experience using the command line. This experience can be scripted and can also include Post-Installation steps to even further reduce the number of manual changes that need to be completed.

Reasons to consider using an unattended deployment:

- **You have many servers to install.**
- **Servers need manual configuration after setup has completed.**
- **You can avoid manual errors caused by user interaction with setup.**
- **You are installing servers remotely.**

Full coverage for all unattended switches can be found on Microsoft TechNet (*http://technet.microsoft.com/en-us/library/aa997281.aspx*). Search for Exchange 2010 Unattended topics.

The following sample script can be used to install Exchange Server 2010 in unattended mode. In this sample, the server being deployed is the first server in a new Exchange organization. To use this sample, create a file called *ProvisionServer.ps1* and put the following code into the file.

Prior to running the script, you must allow scripts to be run by setting the Execution Policy in Windows PowerShell to a value that allows scripts to be executed and you must be using Exchange 2010 SP1. By default, this policy is restricted, which doesn't allow any scripts to run.

```
//Start script sample
#   ProvisionServer.ps1
#   This script is used to demonstrate how to easily provision an
Exchange 2010 Server
param($DVDPath=$(write-error "Enter the location of the Exchange
Server 2010 installation files: provisionserver D:\amd64"))

&"$DVDPath\Setup.com" "/r:H" "/OrganizationName:TestOrg"
#Use E2010 techniques to get connected to remote PowerShell
$exchangeBinPath = (Get-ItemProperty HKLM:\SOFTWARE\Microsoft\
ExchangeServer\v14\Setup).MsiInstallPath + "bin\"
$scriptPath = join-path $exchangeBinPath "RemoteExchange.ps1"
. $scriptPath
Connect-ExchangeServer -auto
//End script sample
```

1. Create the script.
2. Open an elevated Windows PowerShell command shell (Run As Administrator).
3. Enable the Windows PowerShell Execution Policy to allow running scripts (*Set-ExecutionPolicy*).
4. Run the script.

If you want to perform tasks following setup, you can add code after the "Connect-ExchangeServer -auto" command has been executed. That will enable you to run a specific configuration to your environment. You are not restricted in what you can do—if it is an Exchange PowerShell task, it can be run to change settings, or make decisions based on existing settings.

One of the more common portions of the installation that is automated is the basic installation. Earlier in the chapter the command-line options were covered. Because we are using a standard naming convention for different types of servers, we can automate the Exchange installation based on the server name. To automate which roles are installed based on the name of the server, you can use the following script:

```
//Script InstallExchangeRoles.ps1 (Requires Service Pack 1 or higher)
$ServerName=hostname
If ($ServerName -like "*EX*") {$roles="MB,CA,HT"} else
```

```
{If ($ServerName -like "*MB*") {$roles="MB"} else
{If ($ServerName -like "*HT*") {$roles="HT"} else
 {If ($ServerName -like "*ET*") {$roles="ET"} else
  {If ($ServerName -like "*CA*") {$roles="CA"} else
    {If ($ServerName -like "*UM*") {$roles="UM"} else
      {$roles="MT"}
    }
  }
}
}
}
Write-Host "Installing these roles: " $roles
Setup /mode:install /InstallWindowsComponents /roles:$roles
Set-Service NetTcpPortSharing -StartupType Automatic
```

The naming convention used in conjunction with the *InstallExchangeRoles.ps1* script is as follows:

- **SiteName-EX01** All of the basic Exchange Server roles are installed: Mailbox, Client Access, Hub Transport, and the management tools.
- **SiteName-MB01** Just the Exchange Mailbox server role and management tools are installed.
- **SiteName-HT01** Just the Hub Transport server role and management tools are installed.
- **SiteName-ET01** Just the Edge Transport server role and management tools are installed.
- **SiteName-CA01** Just the Client Access server role and management tools are installed.
- **SiteName-UM01** Just the Unified Messaging server role and management tools are installed.
- If the server name does not match any of these, just the management tools will be installed.

You can modify this script to additional steps needed for your environment, such as configuring Client Access URLs, installing certificates, and running configuration tests.

A number of other components of the setup process can be automated. One of the best ways to discover steps that can be automated in your environment is to review your installation documentation. Sections in the documentation with little or standardized information can often be automated with Windows PowerShell scripts or by using a software deployment tool.

Additional Resources

- Microsoft .NET Framework 3.5 Service Pack 1 (SP1): *http://www.microsoft.com/downloads/details.aspx?familyid=AB99342F-5D1A-413D-8319-81DA479AB0D7&displaylang=en*
- Microsoft .NET Framework 3.5 SP1 Family Update for Windows Vista x64, and Windows Server 2008 x64: *http://www.microsoft.com/downloads/details.aspx?FamilyID=98E83614-C30A-4B75-9E05-0A9C3FBDD20D&displaylang=en*
- Windows Management Framework (Windows6.0-KB968930.msu) download: *http://support.microsoft.com/kb/968930/en-us*
- Microsoft Filter Pack download: *http://go.microsoft.com/fwlink/?LinkId=123380*
- How to Configure a Firewall for Domains and Trusts: *http://support.microsoft.com/kb/179442*
- Exchange Supportability Matrix: *http://technet.microsoft.com/en-us/library/ee338574.aspx*
- Description of the DNSLint Utility: *http://support.microsoft.com/kb/321045*
- Using Repadmin.exe to Troubleshoot Active Directory Replication: *http://support.microsoft.com/kb/229896*
- Pre-stage the Cluster Network Object for a DAG: *http://technet.microsoft.com/en-us/library/ff367878.aspx*

CHAPTER 16

Managing Exchange

This chapter provides guidance and best practices on managing an Exchange environment. It will first offer a high-level look at each topic and then provide the guidelines needed to produce a properly managed Exchange environment.

Exchange 2010 Permissions Model

Exchange 2010 adds a new permission management called *role-based access control* (RBAC) that allows you to delegate object creation or modification permission even on an attribute level. The introduction of the RBAC permissions model means that the way that administrators controlled access directly through the assignment of Active Directory permissions in Exchange 2007 also must change.

Active Directory Groups of Exchange

During Exchange Setup, Exchange creates a set of groups in the Microsoft Exchange Security Groups OU of your root domain in Active Directory that are used for assigning permissions to the Exchange system. Table 16-1 describes these groups and their respective functionality. The table only describes Exchange system groups, not the Default Management Role Groups that are used to assign RBAC permissions; those are described later in this section.

TABLE 16-1 Exchange Security Groups

EXCHANGE GROUP	DESCRIPTION
Exchange Servers	This group is used in the same way as it is used in Exchange 2007: to assign permissions to Exchange servers. It automatically includes all Exchange 2007 and 2010 computer objects so that they can authenticate against each other. By default, all Exchange 2007 and 2010 servers and the Domain Install Servers groups of all Exchange-prepared domains in your forest are part of this group.
Exchange Trusted Subsystem	This group is used to perform all RBAC-controlled operation in Exchange to manage existing objects in Active Directory and to create Exchange-related objects such as connectors. It is a highly privileged group and has read/write access to every Exchange-related object in all Exchange-prepared domains in the forest. It's also automatically a member of the local Administrators group on every Exchange 2010 server. If Split Permissions is not enabled, this group is also a member of the Exchange Windows Permissions group.
Exchange Windows Permissions	This group is used to create and modify permissions to all Active Directory objects in all domains. When Split Permissions is not enabled, the Exchange Trusted Subsystem group is automatically added to this group.
ExchangeLegacyInterop	This group is used to assign permissions to Exchange 2003 servers. You need to add your Exchange 2003 computer objects to this group so that they can communicate with Exchange 2010.
Exchange All Hosted Organizations	This group includes all the hosted organization mailboxes groups in a hosted environment and is used for applying password-setting objects to hosted mailboxes.

The Role-Based Access Control Permission Model

RBAC is the new permissions model in Exchange Server 2010. Unlike working with previous versions of Exchange, such as Exchange 2007, you no longer need to manage permissions using access control lists (ACLs) in Active Directory. RBAC allows you to configure and control administrative tasks that administrators or users can perform in a very granular way. It's important that you understand that with RBAC, it doesn't matter what Active Directory permissions you have when using Exchange management tools—everything is authorized and controlled via RBAC. You can define precisely which cmdlets and parameters a user can run or modify.

NOTE RBAC will also filter which cmdlets and functionality in Exchange Management Console (EMC), Exchange Control Panel (ECP), or Exchange Management Shell (EMS) and only display the options available to you. For example, if you do not have the Mailbox Import Export permission, you won't see the *Export-Mailbox* cmdlet and thus cannot use it.

The RBAC permission model applies to all Exchange management tools—EMC, ECP, and EMS and all Exchange server roles that are part of your Exchange organization except for the Edge Transport role. The Edge Transport role is managed using the local built-in Windows groups on the computer and not by RBAC.

RBAC assigns permission in two primary ways, depending on whether the user is an administrator or an end user:

- **Management role groups** Role groups are used to assign permissions to administrators. These administrators may require permissions to manage the Exchange Server organization or some part of it. Some administrators may require limited permissions to manage specific Exchange Server features, such as compliance or specific recipients. To use management role groups, add users to the appropriate built-in management role group or to a custom management role group as described later in this section.
- **Management role assignment policies** Management role assignment policies are used to assign end-user management roles. Role assignment policies consist of roles that control what users can do with their mailboxes or distribution groups. These roles do not allow management of features with which users are not associated directly.

NOTES FROM THE FIELD

Noticeable Improvements with RBAC

Brian Day
Senior Systems Administrator, Commonwealth of Massachusetts

With the implementation of Exchange 2010 we were very excited about RBAC being able to granularly control administrative permissions. The IT shop I work for is essentially a decentralized organization with a centralized e-mail system that makes our administration model interesting. Our database design is based on mailbox quotas, with a set number of mailboxes per database. Each database contains mailboxes from a specific government agency. To maintain order we limit administrators to creating new mailboxes in their assigned databases.

To do this in Exchange 2003 we suffered from *ACL Spray,* or the unmanageable proliferation of ACLs. We required more than 10,000 Deny ACLs across around 200 databases to enforce our permission requirements. Exchange 2007 did not provide enough relief for this problem. Even though Exchange 2007 has a better split-permissions model that helped us more easily control which mailboxes administrators could modify based on Active Directory OUs, it still requires numerous ACLs to prevent administrators from incorrectly placing mailboxes. With Exchange 2010, we have found we can more easily control which recipient accounts administrators are able to modify and create mailboxes; however, we still had no way to prevent which databases they could place new mailboxes into without some customization.

When the ability to control the RBAC scope to specific database was added in Exchange 2010 SP1, we finally received the solution to our problem. We can now control exactly which databases administrators can create mailboxes in, as well as which OUs they can modify.

How are we able to do this? First, we created a new management scope containing the databases that will be assigned to one of the administrative groups. This can be a list of known database names or an OPATH filter. Here is an example of a known list, and then a display name filter:

```
New-ManagementScope ExecDBs -DatabaseList ExecDB-01, ExecDB-02
New-ManagementScope ExecDBs -DatabaseRestrictionFilter {Name -like
"ExecDB-*"}
```

The next step is to create a new role group based on the pre-canned Recipient Management role group using the newly created management scope along with the recipient OU scope:

```
$RG = Get-RoleGroup "Recipient Management"
New-RoleGroup "Executive Recipient Management" -Roles $RG.Roles -
CustomConfigWriteScope ExecDBs -RecipientOrganizationalUnitScope
contoso.com/Executives
```

Now any administrator who is a member of the ExecutiveRecipientManagement role group can only perform recipient modifications on recipients in or below the Executives OU. These administrators can only perform actions on mailboxes within the Executive databases listed via the ExecDBs management scope.

When you combine these two items you isolate an administrator group to a handful of databases where they can create/modify/remove mailboxes and only for users in the specified OU(s)! The administrators don't even need to know the names of the databases they have permissions over because Exchange will filter to only those they have permissions for if the administrator does not specify a database name when creating a new mailbox.

For our organization, we now see the following benefits:

- The Exchange Organization administrators know that agencies can only create and work with mailboxes inside databases they have assigned. Hurray!
- Smaller agencies that share a database with other smaller agencies have peace of mind knowing administrators from the other agencies sharing their database cannot modify or work with the mailboxes of their users even though they share a database. Hurray!
- No more "ACL spray" of tens of thousands of ACLs! Hurray x 10,000!

In addition to EMS, you can manage RBAC settings in the ECP. Management role groups can be found on the Administrator Roles tab and Management role assignment policies can be found on the User Roles tab, as shown in Figure 16-1.

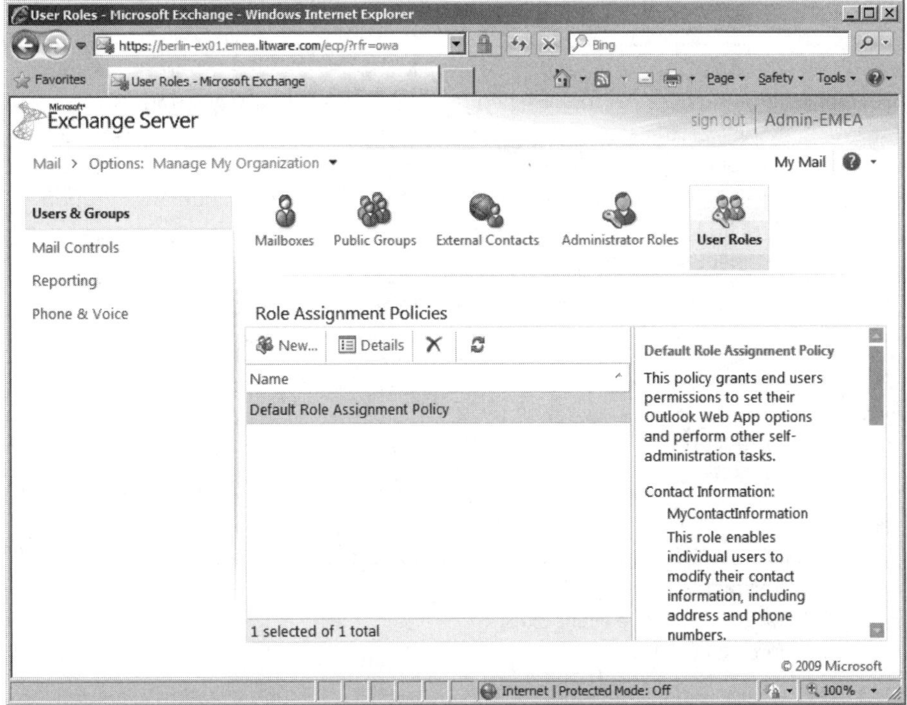

FIGURE 16-1 Managing RBAC roles in ECP

NOTE Exchange 2010 SP1 enhances the RBAC management functionality in ECP to allow you to create new role groups and modify existing role groups to add a write scope and modify roles. In User Roles you are also able to create new management role assignment policies and modify existing ones in more detail than before.

Management Role Groups

Exchange Server 2010 includes several built-in role groups that you can use to provide varying levels of administrative permissions to user groups. RBAC assigns each role group one or more management roles that define the precise permissions that RBAC grants to the group. You can add users to or remove users from any built-in role group. For most companies, the default management role groups shown in Table 16-2 should be sufficient to manage Exchange permissions in the environment.

TABLE 16-2 Default Management Role Groups

ROLE GROUP	ASSIGNED ROLES	DESCRIPTION
Organization Management	Has all roles but the following: Recipient policies, Mailbox Search, Support Diagnostics, ApplicationImpersonation, Mailbox Import Export, UnScoped Role Management	Provides access to the entire Exchange Server 2010 organization and can perform almost any task against any Exchange Server object, including delegating permissions to others.
Server Management	Database Copies, Databases, Exchange Connectors, Exchange Server Certificates, Exchange Servers, Exchange Virtual Directories, Monitoring, POP3 And IMAP4 Protocols, Receive Connectors, Transport Queues	Manages all Exchange servers within the Exchange organization, but members don't have permission to perform operations that have global impact in the Exchange organization.
Delegated Setup	View-Only Configuration	Used to install and uninstall Exchange on provisioned servers.
View-Only Organization Management	Monitoring, View-Only Configuration, View-Only Recipients	View recipient and configuration objects and their properties in the Exchange organization.
Recipient Management	Distribution Groups, Mail Enabled Public Folders, Mail Recipient Creation, Mail Recipients, Message Tracking, Migration, Move Mailboxes, Recipient Policies	Create, manage, and remove Exchange recipient objects in the Exchange organization.
Help Desk	User Options, View-Only Recipients	View and manage the configuration for individual recipients and view recipients in an Exchange organization. Members of this role group can only manage the configuration each user can manage on his or her own mailbox. Additional permissions can be added by assigning additional management roles to this role group.

ROLE GROUP	ASSIGNED ROLES	DESCRIPTION
Discovery Management	Legal Hold, Mailbox Search	Create and run discovery searches of mailboxes.
Public Folder Management	Mail Enabled Public Folders, Public Folders	Manage public folders. Members can create and delete public folders and manage public folder settings such as replicas, quotas, age limits, and permissions as well as mail-enable and mail-disable public folders.
Hygiene Management	ApplicationImpersonation, Receive Connectors, Transport Agents, Transport Hygiene, View-Only Configuration, View-Only Recipients	Manage Exchange anti-spam features and grant permissions for antivirus products to integrate with Exchange.
Records Management	Audit Logs, Journaling, Message Tracking, Retention Management, Transport Rules	Configure compliance features such as retention policy tags, message classifications, transport rules, and more.
UM Management	UM Mailboxes, UM Prompts, Unified Messaging	Manage Unified Messaging organization, server, prompts, and recipient configuration.

MANAGEMENT ROLE GROUP COMPONENTS

Use management role groups to assign administrator permissions to groups of users. To understand how management role groups work, you need to understand their components. Figure 16-2 provides an overview of all the components that are part of a management role group.

The management role groups use the following components to define how RBAC assigns permissions:

- **Management role entries** Defines a cmdlet, including its parameters, which you add to a management role. For example, if you want to see which management role entries are included in the Move Mailboxes management role, you can use the *Get-ManagementRoleEntry "Move Mailboxes*"* cmdlet.
- **Management role** A role is a collection of one or more management role entries. These entries define the tasks that users can perform if RBAC assigns them the role using management role assignments. It is best practice to copy existing roles using the *New-ManagementRole* cmdlet and modify them by removing the unneeded role entries with the *Remove-ManagementRoleEntry* cmdlet.

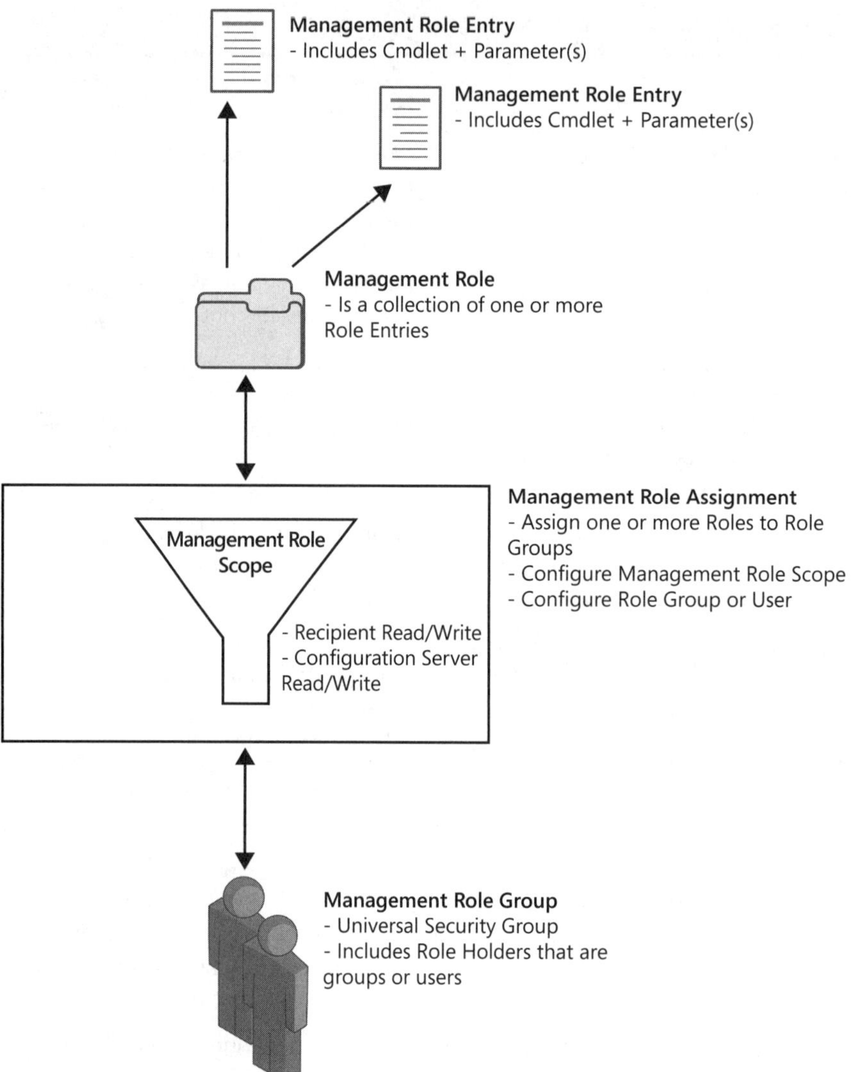

Management Role Entry
- Includes Cmdlet + Parameter(s)
Management Role Entry
- Includes Cmdlet + Parameter(s)
Management Role
- Is a collection of one or more
Role Entries
Management Role Assignment
- Assign one or more Roles to Role
Groups
- Configure Management Role Scope
- Configure Role Group or User
Management Role
Scope
- Recipient Read/Write
- Configuration Server
Read/Write
Management Role Group
- Universal Security Group
- Includes Role Holders that are
groups or users

FIGURE 16-2 Management role group components

- **Management role scope** A management role scope is the scope of influence or impact that the role holder has after RBAC assigns a management role. When assigning a management role, use management scopes to target which objects that role controls. Scopes can include servers, organizational units, recipient objects, and more.

> ***NOTE*** Exchange 2010 SP1 adds the mailbox database as an available scope. This allows you to create role assignments with database scope, but they will apply only on servers running SP1 or later. When you use the database scope together with the *New-MoveRequest* cmdlet, the scope is only checked on the target database.

- **Management role assignment** A management role assignment assigns a management role to a role group. When you create a management role, you must assign it to a role group so that the role holders use it. Assigning a management role to a role group grants the role holders the ability to use the cmdlets that the management role defines.
- **Role holder** A role holder is a user or security group that you can add to a management role group. When a user becomes a management role group member, RBAC grants it all of the permissions that the management roles provide. You can either add user accounts to the group or use the *Add-RoleGroupMember* cmdlet.
- **Management role group** The management role group is a universal security group that contains users or groups that are role group members. Management role groups are assigned to management roles. The combination of all the roles assigned to a role group defines everything that users added to a role group can manage in the Exchange Server organization.

CONFIGURING CUSTOM ROLE GROUPS

In addition to the built-in role groups, you also can create custom role groups to delegate specific permissions within the Exchange Server organization. Use this option when your ability to limit permissions is beyond the scope of the built-in role groups.

RBAC enables complete flexibility in how you assign permissions in an Exchange Server 2010 environment. For example, let's consider the Fabrikam scenario where you have regional offices that are managing their recipients and Exchange servers on their own. To develop your RBAC permission model, you need to consider the following steps:

1. Identify what roles are required by the administrators. To delegate permissions to a custom role group, you can use one or more of the default built-in management roles, or you can create a custom management role that is based on one of the built-in management roles. To view a complete list of all available management roles, use the *Get-ManagementRole* cmdlet.
2. Define the management scope. You should consider what servers or recipients the administrators can manage. You can create a management scope based on a server list, a filter, or a domain. New with Exchange 2010 SP1 is that you can create a scope based on a database.
3. Create a new management role group using the information that you collected. Use the *New-RoleGroup* cmdlet to create the link between the role group, the management roles you want to assign to the group, and the management scope.
4. Add members to your role group to assign permissions. This task basically adds user accounts to the role group's universal security group that is located in the root domain's Microsoft Exchange Security Groups OU.

NOTES FROM THE FIELD

Restricting Permissions Using Custom Role Groups

Ulf Hansen
Principal Systems Administrator, Central Administration Exchange, Siemens AG (Germany)

The company I work for is spread over many countries and has multiple administrative departments that manage their Exchange servers independently. Their servers are located in their own domains. Of course, these departments should only manage their own servers and users and not interfere with the other Exchange servers.

The default role groups would provide them with too many rights because they automatically grant permissions on every server and every user in all domains. Nor can you scope the default role groups. So the only solution was to create new role groups and scope them in a way that meets my company's requirements.

I decided to create one set of scopes for server administration and another for recipients to be more flexible in reusing them in the future. Usually the server scopes are based on a server list, and recipients on domains and OUs. The following cmdlets accomplish this:

```
New-ManagementScope <ServerScope> -ServerList <Server1>,<Server2>
New-ManagementScope <RecipientScope> -RecipientRoot <Domain>
-RecipientRestrictionFilter '(objectclass -like "*")'
```

Then I created two role groups and assigned the respective roles to them: one for user management and one for server management. The roles you add to the role group depend on your individual situation, and in my situation I found that quite a few were important, as you can see in the following cmdlets:

```
New-RoleGroup <UserManagement> -Roles "Mail Recipients","Distribution
Groups", "Move Mailboxes","Migration","Mail Recipient Creation"
-CustomRecipientWriteScope <RecipientScope>
New-RoleGroup <ServerManagement> -Roles "Exchange Servers","Database
Availability Groups","Database Copies","Databases","Exchange Virtual
Directories" -CustomConfigWriteScope <ServerScope>
```

I only used default roles because creating role entries would add a lot of complexity to my design; thus I decided not to go down to the level of creating custom role entries. The existing roles were sufficient for all tasks.

Finally, I added users to the two created role groups so that they received the required permissions:

```
Add-RoleGroupMember <UserManagment> -Member <UserAccount>
Add-RoleGroupMember <ServerManagement> -Member <UserAccount>
```

Of course, I did not complete this in a single day; it evolved over time. If you're planning to customize your role groups, always consider the following tip: The more roles you define, the more confusing it is to manage them. Thus you should always keep your role groups, roles, and role entries as simple as possible.

Management Role Assignment Policies

Management role assignment policies are a collection of one or more end-user management roles that are associated with user accounts. You do not configure administrative permissions with management role assignment policies. Rather, you use management role assignment policies to configure what changes users can make to their mailbox settings and to distribution groups that they own. Every user with an Exchange Server 2010 mailbox receives by default a role assignment policy. You can define the assignment policy as follows:

1. Decide which role assignment policy to assign by default.
2. Choose what to include in the default role assignment policy.
3. Override the default policy for specific mailboxes.
4. Choose not to assign role assignment policies by default.

ROLE ASSIGNMENT COMPONENTS

Role assignment policies consist of the following components that define what users can do with their mailboxes:

- **Mailbox** Mailboxes are assigned a single role assignment policy. When a mailbox is assigned a role assignment policy, the policy is applied to the mailbox. This grants the mailbox all of the permissions that the management roles provide.
- **Management role assignment policy** The management role assignment policy is an object in Exchange Server 2010. Users are associated with a role assignment policy when you create their mailboxes or change the role assignment policy on their mailboxes. The combination of all the roles included in a role assignment policy defines everything that associated users can manage on their mailboxes or distribution groups.
- **Management role assignment** Management role assignments link management roles and role assignment policies. Assigning a management role to a role assignment policy grants users the ability to use the cmdlets in the management role. When you create a role assignment, you cannot specify a scope. The scope that the assignment applies is based on the management role and is either Self or MyGAL.
- **Management role** A management role is a container for a group of management role entries. Roles define the specific tasks that users can do with their mailboxes or distribution groups.
- **Management role entry** A management role entry is a cmdlet, script, or special permission that enables users to perform a specific task. Each role entry consists of a single cmdlet and the parameters that the management role can access.

WORKING WITH MANAGEMENT ROLE ASSIGNMENT POLICIES

Exchange Server 2010 includes a default role assignment policy that provides end users with the most commonly used permissions. For most organizations, you do not need to modify the configuration. However, you can change the management role assignment policy if your organization has specific requirements regarding how users can interact with their mailboxes or groups.

To view the default management role assignment policy configuration, use the *Get-ManagementRoleAssignment –RoleAssignee "Default Role Assignment Policy"* cmdlet. This cmdlet lists all the management roles that are assigned to the default role assignment policy. To view the details of each management role, use the *Get-ManagementRole <rolename> | FL* cmdlet.

WORKING WITH ASSIGNMENT POLICIES

You can modify the default role assignment configuration in some ways:

- Change the default permissions on the default role assignment policy by adding or removing management roles. For example, if you want to enable users to perform additional tasks on their mailboxes, you can identify the management role that grants them the necessary permissions and add the role to the Default Role Assignment Policy.
- Define a new role assignment, and then configure that role assignment to be the default for all mailboxes. Use the *Set-RoleAssignmentPolicy* cmdlet to replace the built-in default role assignment policy with your own. When you do this, RBAC assigns the role assignment policy that you specify to new mailboxes by default.

> ***NOTE*** **When you create an additional role assignment policy, RBAC does not assign the new default role assignment policy automatically. The cmdlets and parameters covered by the roles included in this management policy are not implemented by RBAC until the policy is assigned to mailboxes. For example, you will need to use the *Set-Mailbox* cmdlet to update previously created mailboxes to the new default role assignment policy.**

- Configure additional role assignment policies and assign the policies to a mailbox manually by using the *RoleAssignmentPolicy* parameter on the *New-Mailbox*, *Set-Mailbox*, or *Enable-Mailbox* cmdlets. When you assign an explicit role assignment policy, the new policy takes effect immediately and replaces the previously assigned explicit role assignment policy. If you have many different user groups with special needs, you can create role assignment policies for each group.

Active Directory Split Permissions

Because RBAC is based on Active Directory groups, if you have permissions to change these groups you can grant more permissions than you might have currently in Active Directory. For example, if you can add your user account to the Exchange Trusted Subsystem group, you gain access to powerful permissions over objects in the entire forest.

To prevent this from happening, a change was introduced in Exchange Server 2010 Service Pack 1 (SP1) that allows administrators to separate the Exchange role groups from the security groups such as Exchange Trusted Subsystem.

> ***NOTE*** **Implementing a split permissions model is probably not of interest to you if your Exchange administrators are also Enterprise or Domain administrators.**

Separating control over these groups is especially important when you want to make sure that Exchange administrators only have limited access to recipient objects in Active Directory, such as when they can only manage recipient objects in a specific OU in a domain. This design enables two separate sets of users—such as Active Directory administrators and Microsoft Exchange Server 2010 administrators—to manage their respective services, objects, and attributes separately. The authorization model for account creation is performed by your Active Directory administrators, not the Exchange administrators.

The split permissions model does not replace the RBAC authorization model; RBAC is still used within the Exchange management tools and will prevent Exchange administrators from creating objects such as user accounts. Active Directory administrators will retain control of the Exchange Windows Permissions group, and thus retain control of which Exchange administrators, if any, are allowed to create objects within Active Directory. For your root domain, Domain Admins and Enterprise Admins still own the forest and therefore own any object placed within the root domain and your Active Directory configuration container.

When enabling Active Directory Split Permissions, the following changes are made in the root domain of your forest:

- The Microsoft Exchange Protected Groups OU will be created, which includes the Exchange Windows Permissions group. Microsoft recommends moving this group out of this OU and into an OU that is controlled by the Active Directory administrators.
- The Exchange Windows Permissions group will not include the Exchange Trusted Subsystem group.
- Remove any non-delegating RBAC role assignments to the MailRecipientCreation, ActiveDirectoryPermissions, and SecurityGroupCreationAndMembership roles.

You can enable or disable Active Directory Split Permissions as required. To enable it, run the following commands at a command prompt:

```
Setup /PrepareAD /ActiveDirectorySplitPermissions:true
Setup /PrepareAllDomains
```

If you want to change back to the model used with the release version, run the *Setup /PrepareAD /ActiveDirectorySplitPermissions:false* command.

Managing Exchange Recipients

Exchange has several options with which an administrator can successfully manage the environment. These options are through the EMC, EMS, and ECP. The EMC is where a lot of administrators traditionally start to manage Exchange. However, if you want to perform many tasks or have greater control over the Exchange environment it is important that you become familiar with the EMS, especially when performing bulk administration.

EMS has been designed to allow automation of repetitive administrative tasks and it's a best practice to become very familiar with how EMS can be utilized in your Exchange organization. EMS is used to manage your Exchange Recipients and provide detailed control over these objects.

In addition to the EMS and the EMC, Exchange 2010 now includes the ECP as mentioned earlier in this chapter. The ECP gives both administrators and end users the ability to perform a variety of management tasks through a Web-based interface. Administrative tasks that can be completed in ECP include managing mailboxes, contacts, groups, and User and Administrator roles.

Exchange 2010 SP1 provides a number of improvements in ECP for both users and administrators. The user improvements include:

- Users can modify calendar sharing permissions management.
- Users can better identify their POP/IMAP/SMTP server names.

The ECP improvements for administrators include:

- Support for administrators that do not have a mailbox-enabled account to log on to ECP
- Additional RBAC features, including being able to create, assign, and modify user roles
- Exchange ActiveSync policy, reporting, and device management
- Per-User Mailbox settings
- Improvements to the Message Records Management retention tagging
- Ability to define a group-naming policy

What are Exchange Recipients? In any messaging system, some Active Directory objects are mailbox-enabled or mail-enabled. These objects are referred to as Exchange Recipients. Exchange Recipients include:

- **User mailboxes** A user mailbox is a mailbox assigned to an Active Directory object that can represent a person who uses the network. Each user in Active Directory can be mailbox-enabled, mail-enabled, or neither. Each user's mailbox is a private area that allows an individual user to send, receive, and store messages.
- **Room mailboxes** A room mailbox is an Active Directory object that can be used to manage meeting rooms such as conference rooms, training rooms, or any location where you want scheduling to occur so as to prevent double booking.

- **Equipment mailboxes** These types of mailboxes are also Active Directory objects. Equipment accounts have the user account disabled and are used for items such as company cars for travel, projectors, or loaner laptops.
- **Linked mailboxes** This type of mailbox is accessed by an external account. This comes in handy if an organization has many resources and needs to consolidate them into a resource forest for a simplified management solution.
- **Contacts** These are Active Directory objects that contain information about a person or an organization outside of your Exchange organization. These objects can appear in distribution groups and the Global Address List (GAL).
- **Mail-enabled distribution and security groups** A mail-enabled Active Directory security group object can be used to grant access permissions to Active Directory resources as well as to distribute messages to multiple recipients. You can use a mail-enabled Active Directory distribution group object to distribute messages to a group of recipients.
- **Dynamic distribution groups** A dynamic distribution group uses a recipient filter and conditions to determine its membership at the time messages are sent.

Managing Mail-Enabled Users and Mailboxes

Mailboxes and mail-enabled users are Active Directory objects that contain information about users and also provide credentials to log on to the organization and access resources. Being able to use the credentials to access resources is one of the major differences between a mail-enabled user and a mail-enabled contact. Many tasks are performed when managing user mailboxes, including the following:

- Creating mailboxes
- Adding an e-mail address for a user mailbox
- Creating a linked mailbox
- Connecting a mailbox
- Configuring anti-spam
- Deleting mailboxes
- Disabling mailboxes
- Configuring mail forwarding
- Configuring message size limits
- Configuring storage quotas
- Updating recipient's information

Many of these tasks are fairly straightforward and often control what best practices should be—such as using the New Mailbox Wizard—some attention should be given when managing and designing an Exchange organization. The next several sections touch on a few of the major tasks that are performed on a regular basis.

Creating Mailboxes

The New Mailbox wizard guides and prompts you through the entire process of creating a new mailbox or mail user. However, thought must be given to naming conventions and also to the database where the mailbox will reside.

When determining user and display name, best practice is to use a convention that occurs if you have several users that have the same first name or last name. Often a naming convention that includes a combination of first initial and last name or first initial, middle initial, and last name will help avoid many possible user name issues when users have the same first or last name. A mailbox alias should follow the same standards because these can be used with Outlook and OWA to find user information. In Exchange 2010 SP1, the New Mailbox Wizard no longer requires a mailbox alias to be typed in manually. The wizard will derive the alias from the other information you have entered. In large companies, numerous people have the same last name, such as Smith. If the naming convention is to use the first initial and the last name, both Jeff Smith and John Smith might assume their user name and alias to be jsmith. One solution is to use the first two letters of the first name so that the aliases in this case would be jesmith and josmith. Again, a large organization might have many employees whose names start with the same two letters. To alleviate this potential problem, some companies use numbers. Thus the first alias in our example would be jsmith01 and the second would be jsmith02. This convention allows up to 99 people with the same first-name initial and last name. In companies that support multiple languages or have employees in multiple countries, consideration must also be given to extended character sets, local naming customs, and the likelihood of users having similar names.

Some companies even choose to not have a standard naming convention; instead, aliases are based on some combination of the first, middle, and last name. This would mean that Jeff Smith might be jeffs, jeffsmith, jesmith, or jeffsmi depending on which alias is available. There are a couple of very good reasons to use this method. One reason is that an outside user cannot assume that Jeff Smith's alias is jsmith and try to send an e-mail to jsmith@contoso .com to get in touch with him. This also provides a fair way to distribute aliases.

Choosing a database for the mailbox to reside on also requires some thought. For additional information about sizing and creating databases see Chapter 6, "Mailbox Services." Separating mailboxes into multiple databases is a recommended practice that provides the following benefits:

- Decreases the time to restore a database from backup because each database is smaller
- Reduces impact on the Exchange environment if a database goes offline because each database has fewer mailboxes
- Allows you to separate your users based on conditions such as mailbox size, organization divisions, or titles
- Allows for simpler mailbox limit and deleted item retention management when all users in the same database share the same configuration

Creating separate databases will reduce the time needed to restore because you will have more and smaller databases: The smaller the database, the quicker the restore will be. This can allow an organization to return the affected users to service more quickly. It will also reduce the impact on the organization if you lose a single database because it will only affect those users in the offline database instead of the entire organization.

All Exchange environments see a mix of users when it comes to mailbox sizes. Separating mailboxes based on size, service levels, or user location into different databases is the way many organizations choose to handle mailboxes. This usually makes capacity planning easier and helps to ensure that varying SLAs can be met. For example, Fabrikam has 100 mailboxes with 5-GB limits that have an SLA that only allows for 1 hour of downtime each year, whereas all of the other mailboxes have an SLA that allows for up to 4 hours of downtime a month. To help meet the higher SLA, the Fabrikam IT department decided to create 10 mailbox databases, each with 3 current mailbox database copies and 1 lagged database within the DAG. All of the other mailboxes are deployed with only two additional copies and are backed up using backup software. This has allowed Fabrikam to provide two levels of services that require significantly different functionality.

Another way to approach this problem is to randomly assign the different-sized mailboxes and those with different SLAs across the available mailboxes. This way fewer of the same users are affected.

In a perfect world the mailbox sizes would remain less than 1 GB and thus ease administrative efforts; however, this is not realistic. It is very hard to convince an organization's vice president that she must delete her e-mails and attachments to remain under a mailbox limit, and she would be equally annoyed to receive an e-mail alert every day telling her to do so. Creating a separate database for executives will allow for a different policy set to apply. Each organization is different and some will only need a few databases. Other organizations will require more. Carefully plan how these mailbox databases will be divided.

Managing Mailbox Permissions

In some instances you may need to grant permissions to a mailbox. The user can do this by assigning a delegate within Outlook using the Delegates feature. This will allow a user to give another user access to his mailbox resources. This is done to the manager's mailbox to allow an assistant to manage e-mail and appointments. Delegate access also gives the delegate the ability to send e-mail messages on behalf of the mailbox holder. Delegation can also be configured to allow access to specific folders within the mailbox, as shown in Figure 16-3. Administrators can also set permissions within a mailbox by using the *Set-MailboxFolderPermission* cmdlet. This is especially helpful for users that may not have access to Outlook, or that may rely on assistance from the Exchange administrator.

An administrator can also modify permissions by granting Send On Behalf, Send As, Receive As, or full mailbox permissions to an entire mailbox. This allows users other than the mailbox owner to send or receive messages as if they were sent by the mailbox owner. Setting these permissions may be necessary to support a third-party application that sends

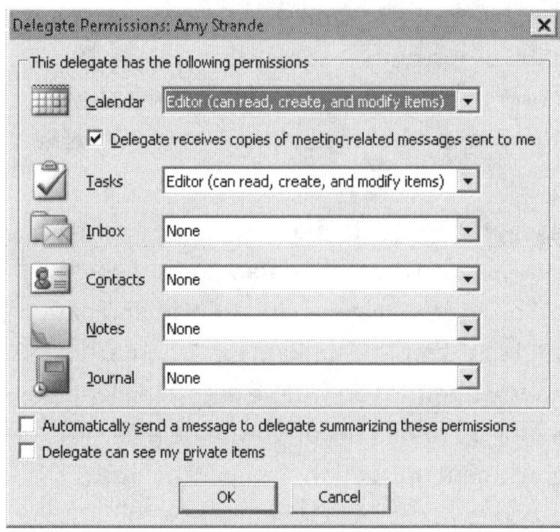

FIGURE 16-3 Adding delegate permissions

or receives e-mail messages to and from users. Keep in mind that it can take up to 120 minutes for permission changes to be loaded into the cache Exchange uses to control mailbox permissions. If the mailbox is hidden from the address list the user will not be able to select the hidden mailbox to send from within the GAL. To manage the Send As permission with the EMS you can run the *Add-MailboxPermission* cmdlet. For example, to give Joe permissions to send as Ed, you would run *Add-MailboxPermission "Ed" -User Joe -Extendedrights "Send-As"*. The Send As right gives the user access to send e-mail as if he was sending it from the mailbox they have the permissions on. Additional rights, including Receive As, can be assigned using the *Add-MailboxPermission* cmdlet. For more information, see *http://technet.microsoft.com/en-us/library/bb124097.aspx.*

You can also set permissions on Exchange objects using *Add-AdPermission* to provide broader permissions. For example, you can give permissions to an entire database. This is especially helpful when granting permissions to a service account. To give ServiceAccount rights to all mailboxes in the DAG01DB1 database, you would run *Add-AdPermission -Identity DAG01DB1 -User ServiceAccount -ExtendedRights Receive-As*. It is important to remember that the EMC does not provide an option to manage Receive As rights or to assign permissions to an entire database. In these cases you need to use the EMS. The Receive As permission allows a user to be able to read all e-mail items in the mailboxes that the permission is assigned to. For more information on how to use *Add-AdPermission*, see *http://technet.microsoft.com/en-us/library/bb124403.aspx.*

You can also assign full access permissions, which allow a user to be able to open and modify mailbox contents as well as send e-mail on behalf of the mailbox. Full access rights are applied to the mailbox and not to a database; therefore, you use the *Add-MailboxPermission* cmdlet or the EMC Manage Full Access Permission Wizard. For example, to grant Ed full access to Joe's mailbox you can run *Add-MailboxPermission Joe -User Ed -AccessRights FullAccess.*

Deleting Mailboxes

At some point a user will leave the company and her mailbox will be disconnected or deleted. Plan ahead of time how you will handle disconnected mailboxes so that they are neither deleted too soon nor remain too long. Getting rid of these mailboxes too soon can lead to the accidental destruction of needed information; keeping mailboxes too long can eat up disk space unnecessarily.

Deleting or removing a mailbox differs from disabling a mailbox in that deleting it disconnects the mailbox from its associated user account and removes the user from Active Directory. Exchange has a default retention of a deleted mailbox of 30 days, which allows for the user to be reconnected to the mailbox. This is useful in case the user decides not to leave or the company decides to retain him. If you determine that the mailbox is no longer needed but you wish to retain the user's Active Directory account, the mailbox should be disabled. Disabling a mailbox might be necessary if an employee goes to different position in the company where company e-mail is not required but the employee still needs to log on to the network each day to fill out reports or other organization-related tasks. To use the EMS to disable mail for a mail-enabled user, run the following cmdlet:

Disable-MailUser Alex@contoso.com

It is recommended that you leave the default 30-day retention period. Choosing not to reduce this retention period can result in having to restore the entire database to recover the mailbox. Any mailbox that is deleted is only marked for deletion during the retention period. This is similar to the Windows Recycle Bin, in which the items are not actually deleted until the Recycle Bin is emptied. A deleted Exchange mailbox is automatically deleted or emptied after the retention period. If you want to permanently remove the mailbox immediately, you can do so using the EMS by running the cmdlet *Remove-Mailbox Kelly -Permanent.*

Disconnected Mailbox Management

After deleting a mailbox you might determine that the mailbox or data within it is still needed. During the deleted mailbox retention period the mailbox can be reconnected to an Active Directory user account that does not already have a mailbox associated with it. Both the EMS and the EMC can be utilized to reconnect a disconnected mailbox. Under the Recipient Configuration node in the Console tree of EMC, the Disconnected Mailbox folder allows an administrator to connect to the Mailbox server and run a wizard to reconnect the mailbox.

You can also use the EMS to reconnect a disconnected mailbox. To retrieve a list of disconnected mailboxes on Fresno-EX01 run *Get-MailboxStatistics -Server Fresno-EX01 | where { $_.DisconnectDate -ne $null } | select DisplayName,DisconnectDate.* You can then reconnect the mailbox using the mailbox GUID while running *Connect-Mailbox -Identity DeletedMailboxGuid -Database MailboxDatabase1 -User NewUserName.*

Note that if the mailbox retention period has passed or you have used *Remove-Mailbox* with the *Permanent* switch, you will not be able to reconnect the mailbox. In this case you might have to restore the mailbox from a backup before you can access the deleted mailbox data.

Managing Contacts

Mail contacts are mail-enabled Active Directory contacts that contain information about recipients that exist outside your Exchange Server organization. Mail contacts are visible in the GAL, and can be added as members to distribution groups. Each contact has an internal e-mail alias and an external e-mail address. All e-mail messages to a contact are automatically forwarded to the external e-mail address.

If multiple people within your organization regularly communicate with a trusted external person, you can create a mail contact with the person's e-mail address. This way the contact will show up in the GAL and allow people send the person e-mail without first having to look up contact information. Mail contacts are often used when contract employees frequently communicate with full-time employees but the contract employee has a separate e-mail system. The contact will allow the company's users to send e-mail to the contract employee using the GAL and the contractor will continue to receive e-mail messages in his primary mailbox.

Mail users are similar to mail contacts because both have external e-mail addresses and can contain information about people outside your Exchange Server organization. You can also display them in the GAL and other address lists. However, unlike a mail contact, mail users have Active Directory logon credentials and can be assigned access to resources. If a contract employee or other external person requires access to network resources and will continue to use her primary e-mail system, you should create a mail user instead of a mail contact.

Another situation in which mail users and mail contacts can be valuable is during migrations or long-term coexistence between Exchange organizations or between mail systems. This allows you to provide a consolidated GAL by creating contacts in both Exchange organizations that forward e-mail to users in the other organization. For example, Litware, Inc., acquired Proseware, Inc., a smaller niche publishing company. Both companies will be working closely together but don't have plans to establish network connectivity between the companies and migrate all users and mailboxes into the same Active Directory forest until the end of the next fiscal year. In the interim they created Mail Users for employees that will require access to the other company's information through a client VPN connection. They created Mail Contacts for all other users, which allows them to use the GAL to look up contact information as well as send e-mail to people in the other company.

Creating a new mail contact is straightforward using both the EMC and the EMS. One example of how to create a contact using the EMS is by running the following cmdlet: *New-MailContact -Name "Kamil Amireh" -ExternalEmailAddress Kamil@proseware.com -OrganizationalUnit ProsewareContacts*

To mail-enable an existing contact using the EMS, you could use a cmdlet like this: run *Enable-MailContact -Identity "Terry Adams" -ExternalEmailAddress Terry@contoso.com*. At times you will need to remove a mail contact from Active Directory. You can do this in the EMS by running *Remove-MailContact -Identity "Terry Adams"*.

Managing Groups

Mail-enabled groups are used to send e-mail to multiple recipients and to assign permissions to multiple users for Exchange objects. These Exchange objects include private mailboxes and public folders. In Exchange 2010, mail-enabled groups belong to one of the following four categories:

- **Distribution groups** These mail-enabled groups can only be assigned Exchange object permissions for things such as Public Folders. Distribution groups can be either static or dynamic. The membership of static distribution groups are defined with a list of members, whereas the membership of a dynamic group is defined by an OPATH filter that provides Exchange with the search criteria to locate the members of the group when e-mail messages are sent to the group. Distribution groups can be used to assign Exchange client permissions for objects such as public folders and mailbox folders; however, they cannot be used to assign permissions outside of Exchange for files or Active Directory.
- **Public groups** A new feature of Exchange 2010 that allows end users to manage the distribution groups that they own through the ECP. Within the ECP, the end user can add or remove group members, moderate the group, or even request access to other public groups.
- **Moderated groups** These allow the distribution group manager to moderate messages sent to the group. This includes approving and rejecting all messages sent to the group or from specific users. Moderated groups can be used to restrict the conversations that occur between group members. These restrictions should be used for large groups or groups that deal with sensitive information that needs to be controlled.
- **Universal Security groups** Security groups are used to assign permissions to groups of users; however, they can also be mail-enabled and used as distribution groups. These security groups can be used to assign permissions both for Exchange and non-Exchange objects.

When creating distribution groups it is important to consider following a naming convention. Doing so allows users to more easily identify distribution groups with their e-mail client. Some organizations like to prepend text or information about who owns the distribution group to the name of the distribution group. For example, the Contoso IT department decided that all distribution groups should be prepended with the ^ character. This helps arrange all distribution lists to the top of the GAL, allowing users to quickly find the groups. Fabrikam chose to prepend all groups with the name of the department—for example, *Sales Engineers* and *Marketing Events*.

Exchange 2010 SP1 adds the ability to require groups to follow a specified naming convention. The naming convention can require a specific suffix or prefix to the group name. The required text could be a specific text string, such as the ^ character that Contoso uses. This required text could also include information included in the following attributes of the group:

- Department
- Company
- Office
- City
- State or Province
- Country or Region
- Country Code
- Title
- *CustomAttribute1* through *CustomAttribute15*

The policy can also include a combination of these rules. This policy can be set using the *Set-OrganizationConfig* cmdlet or by using the ECP, as shown in Figure 16-4. This feature can also block specific words from being used in group names as well as set the default OU that all distribution groups should be created in.

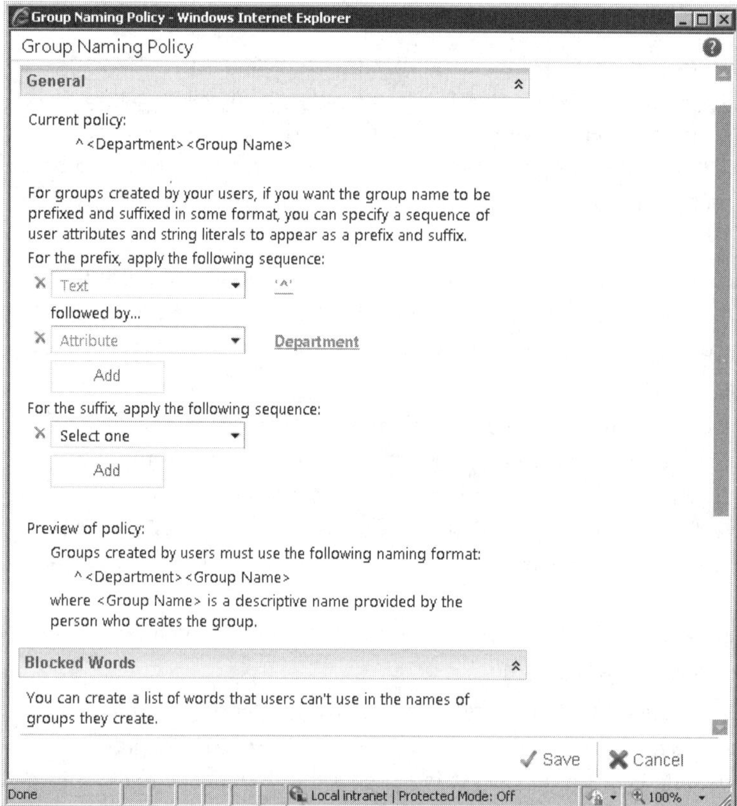

FIGURE 16-4 Setting the Group Naming Policy in the ECP

Moderated Groups

Moderated groups is a new feature in Exchange 2010 that allows messages to be sent to a mail-enabled group. Before the message is delivered to all recipients of the group, it must be approved. A moderator of the group is determined and then given rights to approve or deny a message. This feature helps to detain or remove any messages that might be inappropriate for the group. You can see the Message Moderation properties of a moderated group in Figure 16-5. These properties provide you with the ability to assign multiple administrators, exempt users from moderation, and adjust how unapproved messages are handled.

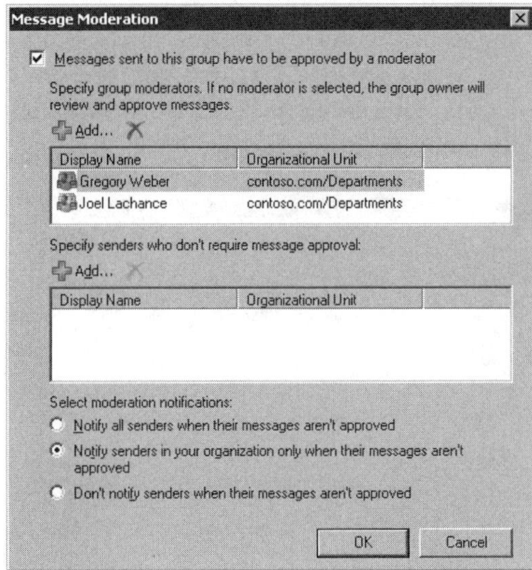

FIGURE 16-5 Distribution group message moderation

Public Groups

Public groups is a new feature in Exchange 2010 that allows users to be able to join and leave groups as needed without having to call the help desk. Users can use the functionality in the ECP to do this. Administrators can also configure a group to allow open membership from within the ECP, EMS, and EMC. Although administrators can use Active Directory Users And Computers to manage membership of these groups, they do not have access to any of the Exchange-specific settings. You should always use the Exchange management tools to manage public groups.

A public group by definition is a distribution group that has been configured to allow users to join the group by using the ECP. To set a mail-enabled group to be a public group using the EMS you can run *Set-DistributionGroup GroupName -MemberJoinRestriction Open -MemberDepartRestriction Open*. Using the ECP, EMS, or EMC the public group can be configured to require owner approval to join the group. If the group is set to be Open, users can join this distribution group without the approval of the distribution group owners. If the group is configured as Closed, only distribution group owners can add members to the group and any requests to join the distribution group will be rejected automatically. If the groups are set for owner approval, users can request membership on this distribution group, and the distribution group owner must approve or reject the request.

A public group can also be configured to require approval for leaving the group. If the *MemberDepartRestriction* property of the group is set to Open, users can leave the distribution group without the approval of the distribution group owners. If the group is set to Closed, only distribution group owners can remove members from this distribution group and any requests to leave this distribution group will be rejected automatically.

A user can view the list of the groups he is currently a member of as well as look for other groups to join within ECP, as shown in Figure 16-6. The Public Groups management section in the ECP is also where a user who is the administrator for a group can modify membership, hide the group from the GAL, modify the MailTip, and make other changes.

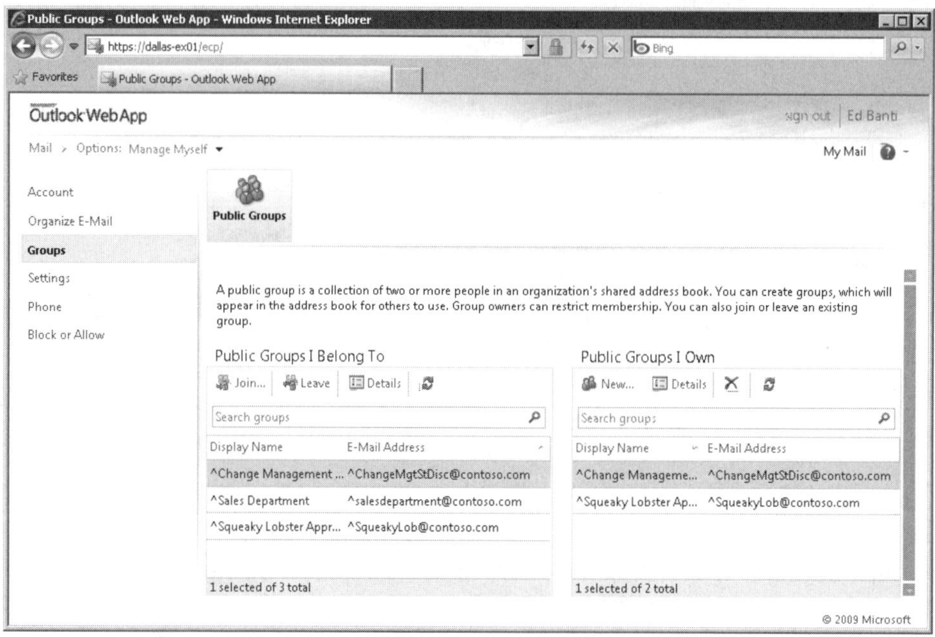

FIGURE 16-6 Managing groups within the ECP

Dynamic Groups

One of the first decisions that you need to make when it comes to distribution groups is deciding whether they will be static or dynamic distribution groups. Static groups are just that, static; you must manually remove or add members. Dynamic groups can be automatically maintained based on user attributes of Active Directory. Wherever possible, it's best practice to use dynamic distribution groups because of the reduced administrative effort required to maintain the group membership over time. Using static groups can lead to distribution groups with no defined purpose and can result in members being in a group that they no longer qualify for or users being left out of essential distribution groups.

Dynamic distribution groups were introduced along with Exchange 2003 and provide an easy way to automatically create groups without manually adding users. To create a dynamic distribution group for a list of all users in the Sales OU, you can run *New-DynamicDistributionGroup -Name "SalesGroup" -IncludedRecipients MailboxUsers -OrganizationalUnit Sales*.

Dynamic groups have drawbacks also. Membership in a dynamic distribution group can be controlled by the user if you base the criteria on a user attribute that the user can modify using the ECP, such as city or state. A user may be able gain membership to a group by changing a user attribute. The filter that controls a dynamic group should be based on user attributes that are secured if sensitive information is being sent to that distribution group. Auditing these groups on a regular basis is recommended to ensure the integrity of the Exchange organization distribution groups. It's important to determine ahead of time whether you need a dynamic or a static group—you can't convert a static group to a dynamic group or vice versa. You can, however, re-create the group and manually configure it as needed.

Managing Resources

Exchange 2010 resource mailboxes will be familiar to any administrator that has spent time with a previous version of Exchange. Exchange 2010 has some improvements that will make the Exchange administrator's job a little easier. In Exchange 2007 an administrator had to use the EMS to create and manage a resource mailbox. This left some administrators asking for another way to manage these mailboxes. One of the changes in Exchange 2010 now allows a majority of the resource mailbox settings to be managed using the EMC. You can use four tabs in the EMC to configure resources: Resource Policy, Resource Information, Resource Out-of-Policy Request, and Resource In-Policy Requests. The Resource General tab is shown in Figure 16-7.

Notice the Resource Capacity field in Figure 16-7. A resource can have a capacity defined in this field to denote the capacity of the resource. For example, you could list the number of chairs available in a conference room. If a conference room has room for five people and this is specified in this field, this information will be displayed within Outlook; however, this field is not used in determining a suitable conference room based on the number of attendees. This information is also not used by Exchange to determine if a meeting request is acceptable. There is also a space to add custom properties to better describe the resource. For example, you may want to identify conference rooms that have a projector, whiteboard, video conferencing equipment, or other features. By default, no custom properties are defined—you must define the custom resource properties for your Exchange organization. For more information on creating customer resource properties, see the help topic "Create or Remove Customer Resource Properties" at *http://technet.microsoft.com/en-us/library/bb124948.aspx*.

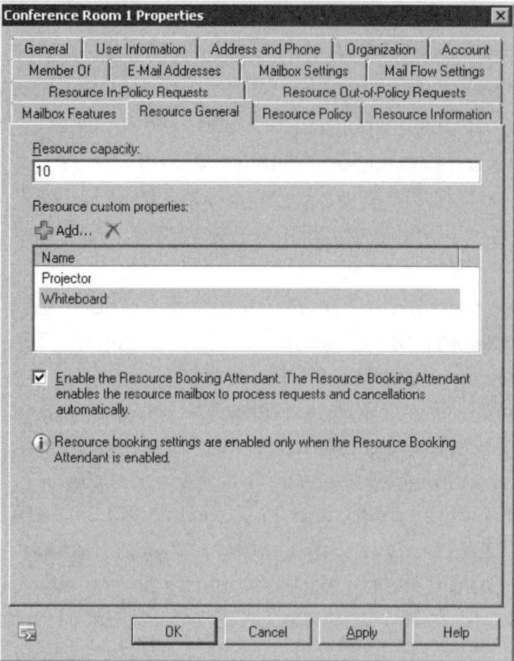

FIGURE 16-7 Resource General tab

Exchange Server 2010 provides several options for configuring resource mailbox settings. Automating calendar processing has three options:

- Automated processing can be disabled (using the *Set-CalendarProcessing* cmdlet with the- *AutomateProcessing None* option).
- Resource booking attendant can be enabled (using the *Set-CalendarProcessing* cmdlet with the - *AutomateProcessing AutoAccept* option).
- Calendar Attendant can be enabled (using the *Set-CalendarProcessing* cmdlet with the *–AutomateProcessing AutoUpdate* option).

By default, the Calendar Attendant is enabled on each resource mailbox. For the resource mailbox to process and accept meeting requests, you must enable the Booking Attendant. In Exchange Server 2010, both the EMC and the EMS can be used to configure resource mailboxes.

Most companies have three common scheduling scenarios: automatic booking, manual approval by delegates, and manual approval from the resources.

- To enable automatic booking, the resource booking attendant should be enabled and the policy should be configured.
- To enable manual approval by delegates, the resource booking attendant should be enabled and then All Book In Policy should be disabled. The All Request In Policy should also be enabled and the delegates should be specified.
- To enable manual approval from the mailbox, the resource booking attendant should be left disabled.

The *Set-CalendarProcessing* command in the EMS has a number of settings that will help you to fully customize the behavior of the resource mailbox. Table 16-3 summarizes the settings that can be configured.

TABLE 16-3 *Set-CalendarProcessing* Settings

SETTING	DESCRIPTION
AllowConflicts	Specifies whether to allow conflicting meeting requests. By default this is set to false, which prevents overlapping appointments for a resource.
AllowRecurringMeetings	Specifies whether to allow meetings to be scheduled with multiple occurrences. By default this is set to true.
AllRequestInPolicy	Specifies whether to allow all users to submit in-policy requests. By default this is set to true, which allows all users to request appointments with the resource if the request meets all specified requirements, such as no conflicts. A resource mail delegate still must approve all requests, unless *AllBookInPolicy* is set to true.
AllBookInPolicy	Specifies whether to approve in-policy requests automatically from all users. By default this is set to true, which allows all users to book appointments with the resource if the request meets all specified requirements, such as no conflicts.
AllRequestOutOfPolicy	Specifies whether to allow all users to submit out-of-policy requests. By default this is set to false, which prevents users from requesting appointments that do not meet specified requirements.
BookInPolicy	Specifies a list of users for whom requests that meet the specified requirements are booked automatically without approval from a resource mailbox delegate.
ConflictPercentageAllowed	Specifies the maximum percentage of meeting conflicts to allow for new recurring meeting requests.
DeleteAttachments	Specifies whether to remove attachments from all incoming messages.
EnableResponseDetails	Specifies whether to include the reasons for accepting or declining a meeting request in the response e-mail message.
ForwardRequestsToDelegates	Specifies whether to forward meeting requests to the resource delegates.
MaximumConflictInstances	Specifies the maximum number of conflicts for new recurring meeting requests.

SETTING	DESCRIPTION
RemoveOldMeetingMessages	Specifies whether to remove old updates and responses.
RemovePrivateProperty	Specifies whether to remove the private flag on meeting requests.
RequestInPolicy	Specifies a list of users who are allowed to submit in-policy meeting requests. By default all users are able to submit in-policy requests.
RequestOutOfPolicy	Specifies a list of users who are allowed to submit appointment requests that do not meet specified requirements. A resource mailbox delegate still must approve all requests.
ResourceDelegates	Specifies a list of users who are resource delegates.
ScheduleOnlyDuringWorkHours	Specifies whether to allow meetings to be scheduled outside of work hours.
TentativePendingApproval	Specifies whether to mark pending requests as tentative on the calendar. The default is true, which marks appointment requests as tentative until they are approved. When this value is false, pending appointments are not displayed on the calendar.
MaximumDurationInMinutes	Specifies the maximum length of the appointment that the resource will accept.

When defining the resource booking policy, you must consider who should be able to schedule a resource and whether all users should be able to book a resource for a meeting. The default settings may work for most resources in the organization, but consider restricting who can book important resources.

You might want to use resources in a number of ways. For example, if you have a large conference room you may want to restrict who can book meetings in it. You may also want to consider what times the resource can be scheduled and thus you may want to set restrictions on the time of day when meetings can be booked. To allow more people to use the resource you may want to restrict the length of meetings. Finally you should also consider the automatic acceptance policy for the meeting resource.

Equipment mailboxes and room mailboxes have similar features and are basically handled the same way. The main difference between the two is that a room mailbox is location-specific, such as a conference room training room or even an auditorium. An equipment mailbox is non-location specific and is used to provide a simple and effective way of managing resources for your users. Some examples of equipment mailboxes are shared portable computers, projectors, or even company vehicles.

One of the challenges in resource mailboxes and user calendars is that inconsistencies can occur because of improperly booked and cancelled meetings, user error, or software error. This can cause users to either miss a meeting announcement or have unreliable or outdated meeting information. Exchange 2010 utilizes Calendar Repair Assistant (CRA) to address this issue. CRA is a mailbox assistant that runs within the Microsoft Exchange Mailbox Assistance service on any Exchange server with the Mailbox server role installed. CRA will automatically detect and correct any inconsistencies that occur in single and reoccurring meeting items. CRA also detects and corrects the following issues:

- Attendee's calendar item has wrong time.
- Attendee's calendar item has wrong location.
- Attendee's calendar item is missing.
- Attendee's calendar item tracking status does not match the organizers tracking status.
- Attendee isn't on the organizers attendee list.
- Attendees and the organizer's reoccurring meetings do not match.
- Organizer and attendees have multiple calendar items that appear the same.
- Organizer's calendar items are missing.

By default CRA is enabled on all mailboxes. At times an administrator might disable CRA with the purpose of pinpointing the cause of recurring issues repaired by CRA. The EMC cannot be used to disable CRA. To disable CRA, run *Set-Mailbox -Identity Kelly@contoso.com -CalendarRepairDisabled:$true*.

Moving Mailboxes

Even with the best intentions, you will most likely need to move mailboxes on a regular basis. Some of the more common reasons for moving mailboxes are:

- **Corrupted mailboxes** If you encounter corrupted mailboxes, you can move the mailboxes to a different server or database to fix the corruption. Often, moving a corrupted mailbox to another database will salvage any of the uncorrupted data in the mailbox.
- **Load Balancing** Because of the dynamic nature of many companies, users change positions or seasonal workers are hired for a short period of time, leaving mailbox databases with uneven numbers of active mailboxes. You may move mailboxes to even out the number of mailboxes in each database.
- **Migration** When you migrate from an existing Exchange Server 2007 or Exchange Server 2003 organization to Exchange Server 2010, you need to move mailboxes from the existing Exchange servers to an Exchange Server 2010 Mailbox server.
- **Physical location changes** You can move mailboxes to a server that is in a different Active Directory site. For example, if a user moves to a different physical location, you can move that user's mailbox to a server that is in a site closer to the new location.

- **Outsourcing e-mail administration** A company may want to outsource the administration of e-mail and retain the administration of Windows user accounts. To do this, you can move mailboxes from a single forest into a resource forest scenario, in which the Microsoft Exchange mailboxes reside in one forest and their associated Windows user accounts reside in a separate forest.
- **Policy Adjustments** In cases where the mailbox databases are used to set the deleted item retention and mailbox limits, you may move mailboxes between databases to move a mailbox to a database with different settings.
- **Reducing Database size** In cases where data has been removed from a database and a lot of white space remains, rather than performing an offline defragmentation on the database, you can move the contained mailboxes online to a new database and delete the original database.
- **Troubleshooting an issue** If you need to investigate an issue with a mailbox, you can move that mailbox to a different server or different mailbox database. In some cases moving a mailbox that is having issues will help to determine whether the problem is with the server, the mailbox, or the mailbox database.

A local move is where a mailbox is moved from one database to another database within the same Exchange organization. At times you many need to move a mailbox to investigate an issue with that mailbox. If you encounter corrupted mailboxes you could move those mailboxes to another server because the corrupted messages will not be moved. In addition, you might want to perform a local mailbox move for load balancing and physical server location changes.

A remote move of a mailbox may be necessary if you are migrating to or from an outsourced Exchange deployment. In previous versions of Exchange, a mailbox wizard would run the mailbox move from the management tool. In Exchange 2010, the management tool is used to create a new move request. The new move request process resembles the move mailbox process in Exchange 2007, as shown in Figure 16-8. However, Exchange 2010 processes the request a bit differently.

A mailbox move is asynchronous in Exchange 2010, meaning that users are still able to access their mailboxes while they are being moved. After finishing the Move Mailbox Wizard, Exchange will only schedule the move by submitting a mailbox move request. This is the one major difference from Exchange 2007, where the wizard would not complete until the mailbox had been moved. With Exchange 2010, mailbox moves are run by the Mailbox Replication Service (MRS) in the background rather than within the Exchange management tools. The new model—in which mailbox moves are controlled by the MRS running on Client Access servers—has a number of advantages:

- Mailboxes are kept online during the asynchronous moves. The larger mailboxes become the longer it takes to move them around. Having online mailbox moves enables support of larger mailboxes.
- Moving the mailboxes is asynchronous, and the MRS performs the move.

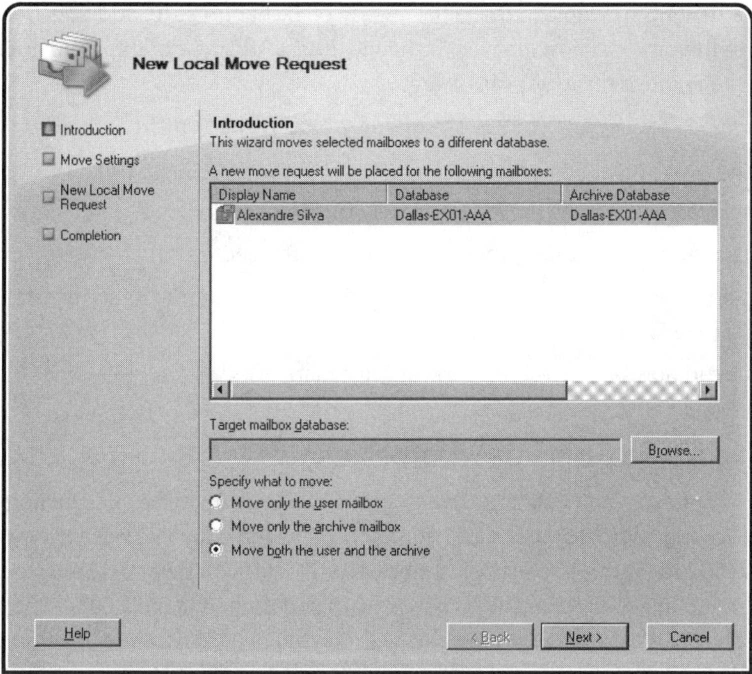

FIGURE 16-8 Move Mailbox Wizard

- The mailbox's dumpster now moves with the mailbox when you move it between Exchange Server 2010 Mailbox servers.
- Fast search is available upon completion. As soon as the mailbox begins to move, content indexing starts to scan the mailbox so that fast searching is available upon the move's completion.
- Each MRS instance, each mailbox database, or each mailbox server can be throttled.
- Mailbox moves now work over the Internet, and you can manage them from anywhere within the organization.
- A mailbox's move history is preserved.

To find out the status of a move request, run the *Get-MoveRequest* cmdlet using the EMS. For example, to move Matt's mailbox to DB100 using the EMS you would run *New-MoveRequest –identity Matt –TargetDatabase DB100*. After the mailbox move is initialized, you can check the status by running *Get-MoveRequest UserName*. The request can have one of the following statuses:

- Completing
- Queued for move
- Move in progress
- Ready to complete

Even with the benefits available in the initial release of Exchange 2010, additional improvements to the process were made in Exchange 2010 SP1. Some of the more notable improvements to the move mailbox process are:

- Outlook no longer needs to be restarted after a local mailbox move.
- A mailbox can be moved to and from a linked mailbox.
- The mailbox archive can be moved separately from the mailbox.
- The mailbox archive can be moved to an online hosted service.
- MRS can now import and export e-mail with PST files without the need to install Outlook on the Exchange server.
- A mailbox can now be moved to a new UM dial plan.

Importing and Exporting Mailboxes

Moving mailbox content to and from PSTs by using the ExMerge utility has been a normal function of an Exchange administrator's job. Although Exchange 2007 was released without a supported method to import and export mailboxes to PST files, this was promptly rectified in Service Pack 1 and again improved in Exchange 2010 and Exchange 2010 SP1. Importing or exporting a mailbox can be done using the EMS with the *Import-Mailbox* and *Export-Mailbox* cmdlets or if SP1 is installed the *New-MailboxExportRequest* and *New-MailboxImportRequest* cmdlets.

> **NOTE** The *Import-Mailbox* and *Export-Mailbox* cmdlets are available in the initial release of Exchange 2010; however, they've been replaced with the *New-MailboxExportRequest* and *New-MailboxImportRequest* cmdlets.

By default no roles have rights to use any of the import or export cmdlets. You will have to add the rights to a role or user before these cmdlets are available. For example, to assign these rights to Alex, run *New-ManagementRoleAssignment –Role "Mailbox Import Export" –User Alex*. Or to assign the roles to an entire group named Import Export Group, run *New-ManagementRoleAssignment –Role "Mailbox Import Export" –Group "Import Export Group"*.

After you assign the proper rights, a few additional prerequisites must be met before you can use *Import-Mailbox* or *Export-Mailbox*:

- When exporting data to a PST file, only one mailbox at a time can be exported.
- Importing or exporting data must be performed on a 64-bit computer with the Exchange Server 2010 role installed and the 64-bit version of Microsoft Outlook 2010. It is recommended that this be a computer dedicated for the purpose of importing and exporting mailbox data.
- The *Import-Mailbox* cmdlet cannot be used on servers running Exchange 2003 or Exchange 2007. You must use ExMerge on those servers and import data to a PST file.
- Public folder data can't be imported.

When you use the *Import-Mailbox* cmdlet, the mailboxes do not have to match. For example, you can import data from a mailbox named kelly@contoso.com to a mailbox named alex@contoso.com. All messages from the transport dumpster are imported, and even hidden data, if it exists in the .pst, will be imported. When data is merged into the existing mailbox it will not import duplicated messages. By default, the *Import-Mailbox* cmdlet will empty all folders and subfolders. When using this cmdlet you have the option of including or excluding special folders, such as the following:

- Inbox
- Deleted Items
- Drafts
- Junk E-mail
- Outbox
- Sent Items
- Calendar
- Notes
- Journal
- Tasks
- Contacts

You export mailbox data by using the *Export-Mailbox* cmdlet in the EMS. Although the cmdlet has a limitation of only being able to export a single mailbox at a time, it does have nice features that allow you to delete associated messages or use filters to filter out messages based on recipients and senders. To filter on senders, use the *SenderKeywords* parameter. To filter on recipients, use the *RecipientKeywords* parameter. You can remove one or even multiple messages using the *Export-Mailbox* cmdlet. You might want to do this when a message is accidently sent to the wrong mailbox or when you need to process a mailbox for legal reasons.

Exchange 2010 SP1 replaces initial release cmdlets for importing and exporting mailboxes that use the MRS to perform the work. This new method has several benefits. One benefit is that Outlook no longer needs to be installed on the management workstation—all of the work is done by the MRS. The second benefit is that the import and export process can access both the primary and archive mailboxes.

After assigning permissions to the account that will be creating the import or export requests, you also need a file share accessible by the MRS to either import from or export to. The MRS server must have permissions to read and write to the file share. To ensure that all MRS instances have permissions to write to the share, you can assign permissions using the Exchange Trusted Subsystem group.

Exchange ActiveSync and Device Management

The last few years have seen a proliferation of devices that support Exchange ActiveSync. This allows users to choose devices that meet their needs and preferences, but at the same time increases the support burden on IT staff, who are needed to help support these devices.

These devices also support different types of policies, making it difficult to enforce a uniform policy across the board. And many companies like to control the devices that are allowed to store company data so as to better control security—in effect not allowing users to provide their own devices. Exchange 2010 improved the administrative control over which devices are allowed to connect with Exchange ActiveSync.

Exchange 2010 provides the ability for administrators and users to remotely wipe the stored information off of a mobile device that is connected with Exchange ActiveSync. This feature is particularly useful when a mobile device is lost or stolen because it will remove any personal information from the device.

Exchange 2010 SP1 provides additional help for administrators in ECP:

- Configure the access level granted to all devices by default.
- Set up e-mail alerts that will enable administrators to take action when a device is being quarantined.
- Personalize the message that is sent to users when their devices are being recognized or get quarantined.
- List quarantined devices.
- Create and manage ActiveSync Device Access Rules, permitting administrators to allow, block, or quarantine certain listed devices.
- Allow or block a device for a particular user.
- For each mailbox the Administrator will be able to:
  - Enumerate a user's devices.
  - Wipe device information wirelessly.
  - Remove old device partnerships.
  - Allow or block the given device for a particular user.

These new features allow administrators to quarantine unknown mobile devices and then approve or block them upon review. The devices can be allowed, quarantined, or blocked based on device type. If your company has standardized a specific mobile device, you can block all devices and then add a Device Access Rule that allows the specific device type.

When a device is quarantined or blocked an e-mail message is sent to the device that informs the user the status of the device. Alternatively, the policy can be configured to send an e-mail message to an administrator with information about the device, so that she can take action to allow the device if she chooses to do so.

Automating Administration

Although the Exchange 2010 management tools are easy to use and make quick work of most management tasks, common management tasks can be time-consuming. When administrators make manual changes, these are also prone to error. Many larger companies have adopted an integrated approach for creating mailboxes, public folders, and other Exchange objects. They do this by tying together core business systems such as payroll, security access systems, and Active Directory to ensure that one system feeds the other systems. This can ensure that when an employee is hired, all the necessary accounts and processes are completed to ensure that the employee gets paid and has access to the building and all of the computing systems. This type of automation is usually done with a meta-directory system such as Microsoft Forefront Identity Manager 2010. These systems take a lot of planning and usually some custom integration development to work in a large business. These systems can significantly reduce administrative burden by reducing manual effort in adding, creating, modifying, and deleting objects. They also reduce effort because less time is spent auditing to ensure that the manual processes are followed.

On a smaller scale, one way to automate some administration tasks is to create EMS scripts, which can provide a number of features that you can use to perform bulk recipient management. For simple tasks, you can pipe output between cmdlets to retrieve a list of appropriate objects, and then you can modify them. You can also use scripting for complex tasks, such as creating users from a .csv file. To review the basic functionality of Windows PowerShell, including using a PowerShell pipeline, review the Windows PowerShell basics section of Chapter 1, "Introducing Exchange Server 2010."

One of the more advanced abilities of PowerShell is the ability to filter large sets of data. For example, you can specify a filter string to search for a subset of mailboxes when you run *Get-User*. To specify the custom filer you must use the *Filter* parameter or the *RecipientFilter* parameter. The filter must be specified in the OPATH querying language. The syntax of an OPATH filter is *{(attribute operation 'value')}*. The following cmdlet selects users with the *Company* attribute defined as Litware users:

```
Get-User -Filter {(Company -eq 'Litware')}
```

Additional parameters can be added to the filter. The following cmdlet selects users with the *Company* attribute defined as *Litware* and the *Department* attribute defined as *Accounting*:

```
Get-User -Filter {(Company -eq 'Litware') -and (Department -eq 'Accounting')}
```

The results of both of these examples are shown in Figure 16-9.

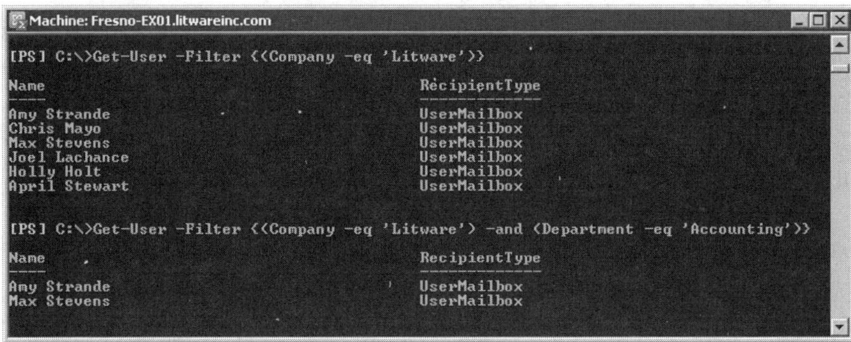

FIGURE 16-9 Using PowerShell filters

The common operators in an OPATH filter are:

- *-and*
- *-eq* (equals)
- *-gt* (greater than)

- *-like* (compares strings)
- *-lt* (less than)
- *-ne* (does not equal)
- *-not*
- *-notlike* (compares strings)
- *-or*

PowerShell has a comprehensive scripting engine. You can create scripts to perform advanced bulk-management tasks that are not possible with simple pipelining. Scripts can create more complex structures and consequently enable you to perform more complex tasks. Scripts can use loops, variables, reading and writing files, and more. If you are interested in learning more about PowerShell scripting see "Scripting with Windows PowerShell" at *http://technet.microsoft.com/en-us/scriptcenter/dd742419.aspx*. If you plan on extensively using Windows PowerShell you may also want to take the Microsoft Official Curriculum Course 6434, "Automating Windows Server 2008 Administration with Windows PowerShell." More information about this course can be found at *http://www.microsoft.com/learning/en/us/course.aspx?ID=6434A*.

Because Windows PowerShell is based on Microsoft .NET technologies, it can be used within other applications to automate administrative tasks. For example, you can run PowerShell commands from within a Web page that returns information about backup status, mailbox size, or other information. More information about developing applications that use Windows PowerShell can be found in a number of locations such as "Programmatic Access via Remote PowerShell in Exchange Server 2010" at *http://msexchangeteam.com/archive/2009/11/02/453016.aspx*.

In addition, a software development kit (SDK) is available for Exchange Web Services (EWS). EWS provides an API to develop applications that work with data within users' mailboxes.

NOTES FROM THE FIELD

User and Mailbox Provisioning

Andy Schan
Principal Consultant, Schan Consulting

In many larger organizations, user provisioning (the creation, management, and deletion/disabling of recipients) is managed by a central group that creates and updates the recipients and mailboxes in Active Directory, Exchange, Human Resources, Customer Relationship management systems, the phone system, and more. If this is the case in your organization, you need to work with these other groups to ensure that the provisioning process works correctly with Exchange Server 2010. For example, many provisioning systems were created to work with Exchange 2003 and thus assume that the Recipient Update Service is present to complete the creation process for the mailbox/mail user/contact once the object has been created in Active Directory.

Many commercial off-the-shelf (COTS) provisioning systems have Exchange 2010 modules available, but for in-house or custom applications the recommended approach for creating and managing Exchange recipients is to invoke the PowerShell cmdlets from .NET.

Managing Other Exchange Objects

You can manage a number of other Exchange objects. The following sections will cover address policies, address lists, and details templates.

Managing Address Policies

For an Exchange recipient to send or receive e-mail messages, the recipient must have an e-mail address. In Exchange, e-mail address policies are defined to generate e-mail addresses for recipients. Before you can create an address policy, you must first create an accepted domain. An accepted domain is an SMTP namespace Exchange servers use to send messages to, or from which they can receive messages. For more information about accepted domains please see Chapter 5, "Routing and Transport."

By default, an Exchange organization contains one e-mail address policy for every mail-enabled user. This default policy specifies the recipient's alias as the local part of the e-mail address and uses the default accepted domain. The local part of an e-mail address is the name that appears before the at (@) symbol. However, you can create a new policy or configure the default policy to customize the recipients' e-mail addresses. To specify additional e-mail addresses for all recipients, or just a subset, you can modify the default policy or create additional e-mail address policies. Although you can adjust the default policy, it is recommended that you add additional addresses to a new address policy.

Creating an E-mail Address Policy

An e-mail address policy is applied to recipients based upon an OPATH filter. The OPATH filter defines the search scope in the Active Directory forest and the attributes to match to define the recipients that the policy will apply to. You may need to create multiple address policies for different divisions of the company. For example, when Litware, Inc., acquired Proseware, Inc., the company migrated all users into the same Exchange organizaton. However, Proseware employees still needed to maintain proseware.com e-mail addresses. To accomplish this, they created a second e-mail address policy that applied only to Proseware employees.

To selectively apply an address policy, you can choose from a number of standard recipient scope filters available when creating a new address policy:

- **All Recipient Types** This will apply to all recipient types and overrides any of the other options.

- **Users With Exchange Mailboxes** This will apply to users in the Exchange organization that have Exchange Server 2010, Exchange Server 2007, and Exchange Server 2003 mailboxes.
- **Users With External E-Mail Addresses** This applies to users who have external e-mail addresses. Users with external e-mail accounts have user domain accounts in Active Directory, but use e-mail accounts that are external to the organization.
- **Resource Mailboxes** This applies to Exchange resource mailboxes.
- **Contacts With External E-Mail Addresses** This applies to contacts with external e-mail addresses.
- **Mail-Enabled Groups** This applies to security groups or distribution groups that have been mail-enabled.

The second part of the E-mail Address Policy filter allows you to specify conditions for the filter in one of the following categories:

- **Recipient Is In A State Or Province** This will set the policy to include only recipients from specific states or provinces. The Address and Phone tabs in the recipient's properties contain this information.
- **Recipient Is In A Department** This will set the policy to include only recipients in specific departments. The Organization tab in the recipient's properties contains this information.
- **Recipient Is In A Company** This will set the policy to include only recipients in specific companies. The Organization tab in the recipient's properties contains this information.
- **Custom Attribute Equals Value** This will set the policy to include only recipients that have a specific value set for one of the 15 custom attributes. Select the check box that corresponds to that custom attribute.

After defining the filter criteria for the address policy, you must also define the e-mail address policy. The three e-mail address types are:

- **Precanned SMTP e-mail address** Precanned SMTP e-mail addresses are commonly used e-mail addresses. These include first initial and last name and first name and last name separated by a period.
- **Custom SMTP e-mail address** If you do not want to use one of the precanned SMTP e-mail addresses, you can specify a custom SMTP e-mail address. When creating a custom SMTP e-mail address, you can use the variables listed in Table 16-4 to specify alternate values for the local part of the e-mail address.
- **Non-SMTP e-mail address** Exchange Server 2010 supports a number of non-SMTP address types. These addresses could be for third-party applications such as Exchange-integrated faxing software.

TABLE 16-4 Custom SMTP E-mail Address Variables

VARIABLE	VALUE
%d	Display name.
%g	Given name (first name).
%i	Middle initial.
%m	Exchange alias.
%s	Surname (last name).
%xg	Uses the *x* number of letters of the given name. For example, if *x* = 2, the first two letters of the given name are used.
%xs	Uses the *x* number of letters of the surname. For example if *x* = 2, the first two letters of the surname are used.

Managing Address Lists

Address lists show recipient objects grouped together based on a query. Address lists are a compilation of Active Directory objects and recipients. An address list might contain many different types of objects, such as Public Folders, contacts, users, and other resources. You can use address lists to sort the GAL into multiple views, which can make it easier to locate recipients in large or highly segmented organizations.

The process for creating an address list is similar to configuring e-mail address policies: you configure address lists with recipient filters that determine which objects will be included. Address lists are evaluated every time a mail-enabled account is modified to determine in which address lists it will appear.

Several lists are created by default when you install Exchange and will satisfy the needs of many organizations without making any custom changes. Note the default address in Figure 16-10.

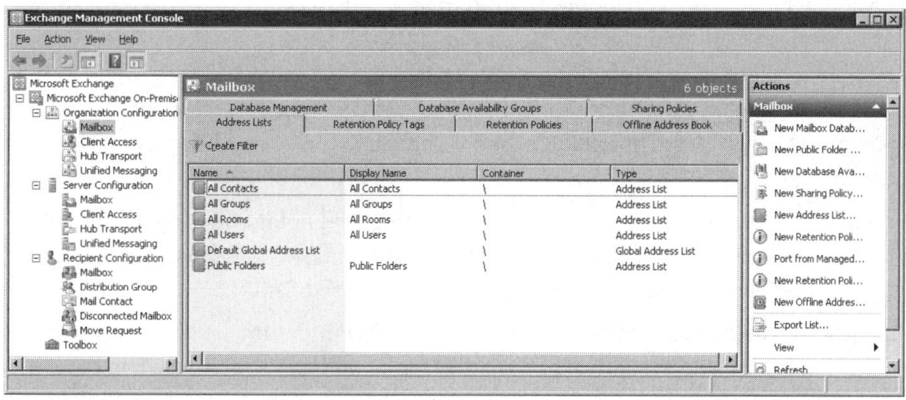

FIGURE 16-10 Default address lists

- **All Rooms** This list contains all resources that are designated as rooms.
- **All Contacts** If a contact is mail-enabled, it appears in the All Contacts list.
- **All Groups** Any mail-enabled group in your organization is shown in this list.
- **All Users** If a user account is mail-enabled it appears in the All Users list.
- **Public Folders** This list contains any Public Folders in your organization.
- **Default Global Address List** This list contains all mail-enabled users, contacts, rooms, or groups. All recipients in the Exchange organization appear here.

Organizations with thousands of objects can result in large and unmanageable default address lists. Take care when modifying address lists. Often an organization might create more lists than are necessary and thus make it difficult for users to find what they are looking for. It is a best practice to create as few address lists as possible to reduce user confusion and management overhead. In addition you should name the address list in such a way that users will know right away which recipients are contained in the list. For example, if they are looking for vendor contacts, name the list *Vendors*. If you find that users are having a difficult time with the naming convention you might have to make adjustments.

For several reasons, you may want to create multiple address lists. For example, if your organization has multiple physical locations, you could base address lists on country, state, city, or building. A large company may want to create separate address lists for departments such as accounting, marketing, or sales.

You can create a new address list in both the EMS and the EMC. The EMC has a New Address List Wizard that will walk you through all the steps of creating a new list and is created for entry-level Exchange administrators. The EMS can also be utilized to create a new address list using the following cmdlet:

```
New-AddressList -Name AdressListName -RecipientFilter {((RecipientType -eq
'UserMailbox')}
```

Offline Address Lists

An offline address list—more commonly referred to as an offline address book (OAB)—is a copy of an address list that can be downloaded by Outlook so users can access the information list locally. This is helpful for employees that travel and need access to this information—for example, if the user is on an airplane with no Internet access. An OAB is also used when Outlook is configured in Cached Exchange mode, even while Outlook is connected to the server.

The default OAB contains a copy of the entire GAL, but does not include any additional GALs that have been created. If you have created a customized GAL, you must either create a new OAB or modify the default OAB to include the customized GAL.

Exchange 2010 can generate three different versions of OAB to support different versions of Outlook, as listed in Table 16-5. This is especially helpful during a migration when older versions of Outlook are being used against the older Exchange servers in the organization.

TABLE 16-5 OAB Versions

OAB VERSION NUMBER	OUTLOOK VERSIONS
2	Outlook 98 SP1 and earlier
3	Outlook 98 SP2 and later
4	Outlook 2003 SP2 and later

The two methods for distributing OABs to the clients are Web-based and Public Folder. Outlook 2003 and earlier clients can only retrieve the OAB from a Public Folder. Outlook 2007 and later clients can retrieve the OAB from either a Public Folder or via Web-based distribution. If you have a mixture of clients you may choose to enable both Web-based and Public Folder distribution.

Regardless of the distribution type, you should consider where the OAB is stored in relation to the users. When using Public Folder distribution in a geographically dispersed environment, it may make sense to replicate the corresponding system public folder to each location using older versions of Outlook.

When using Web-based deployment, you must choose Client Access servers to replicate the OAB. If your Client Access servers are load-balanced, you should copy the OAB to each server to provide redundancy for the OAB distribution. To configure the URL for Outlook 2007 and later clients to use Web-based distribution, you must configure the *InternalURL* and *ExternalURL* attributes for each Client Access server. You can configure the Client Access servers using the EMC or by running the *Set-OABVirtualDirectory* cmdlet.

By default, the default OAB is generated only once each day. So any additions, deletions, or changes made to mail-enabled recipients are updated in the OAB once each day unless you modify the update schedule to generate the OAB more often. Particularly in environments that use Outlook in Cached Exchange mode, users will notice that changes are not visible in the GAL until the following workday. In most environments, you want to modify the OAB update schedule to accommodate the rate of change in your organization. For example, if your environment is constantly changing, you may need to schedule updates every few hours during the workday. In environments with fewer changes, you may be able to schedule an update just once during the day. To reduce the amount of data that needs to be downloaded, Exchange will generate a differential OAB download so that the client only needs to download the changes made since it last downloaded the OAB. The number of times you generate the OAB during the day should also reflect the following considerations:

- The size of each OAB in your organization and the impact on downloading the OAB on the client and the client network.
- The number of OAB downloads. How many clients will you need to download the OAB? How will this affect the OAB generation server and the OAB distribution points?
- The overall number of changes made to the directory. If a large number of changes are made, the size of the differential OAB downloads also will be large, putting a higher load on the clients and servers.

OAB sizes can vary from just a few MBs to hundreds of MBs. The following factors can affect the size of the OAB:

- Usage of client certificates The more public key infrastructure (PKI) certificates that are stored for users, the larger the size of the OAB. PKI certificates range from 1 KB to 3 KB. They are the single largest contributor to the OAB size.
- The number of Active Directory mail recipients and distribution groups.
- Other information included for each mailbox-enabled or mail-enabled object For example, some organizations will populate all of the address properties for each user. The OAB size increases as the number of attributes used increases.

For more information about managing OABs see Dan Goldman's blog at *http://blogs.msdn.com/dgoldman/default.aspx* and "Web-based vs. Public Folder–based OAB Distribution" at *http://technet.microsoft.com/en-us/library/cc535193.aspx*.

Managing Details Templates

Some companies need to change the information users see for users, groups, public folders, mailbox agents, and contacts in the address list. At times an organization might not want users to see certain data when viewing a contact. For example, Contoso has decided to not allow a user's title to be shown in the address book. The Contoso IT department was able to remove the Title label and Title fields by using the Details Templates Editor to edit the US English User template, as shown in Figure 16-11.

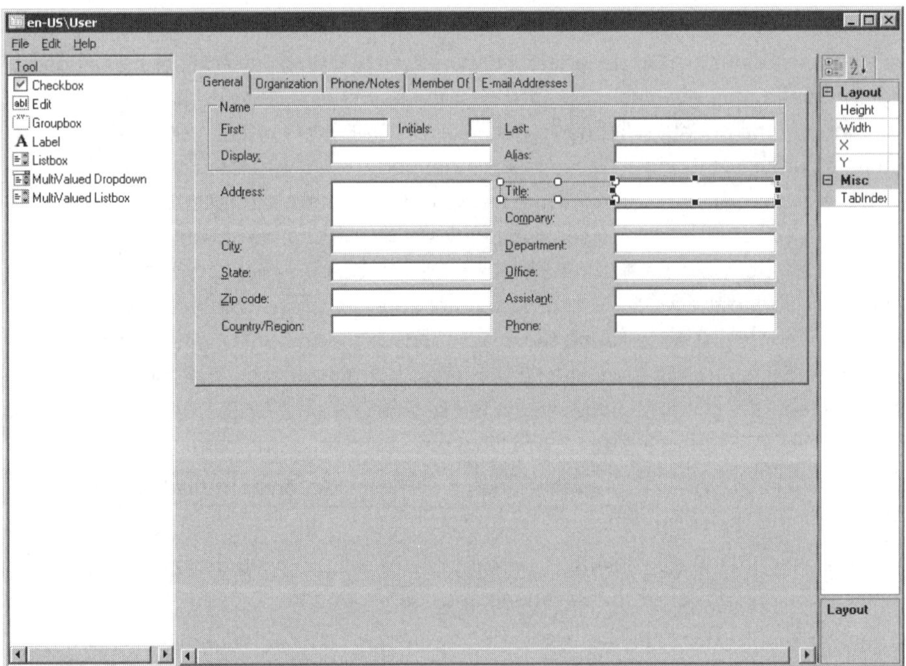

FIGURE 16-11 Editing the Contact template

Keep in mind that the Details Templates Editor does not have an Undo key, so if you make a change by accident or change your mind, you must exit without saving the changes; otherwise, you will need to restore the template. If you perform a restore, all customization is lost and the template is restored to its original configuration. Most changes or customizations can be done via drag and drop, which makes this a simple task for even an entry-level Exchange administrator. Keep in mind that the Details template must be modified for each language that any user may view the address list in.

The Details Template Editor will allow customization on the client-side GUI and allows for the editing of the following Outlook objects:

- Public Folders
- Groups
- Contacts
- Users
- Mailbox agents
- Search dialog boxes

Before users or groups can use the Details Template Editor, they must be assigned Organization Management permissions. For more information about using the Details Template Editor, see *http://technet.microsoft.com/en-us/library/bb124525.aspx.*

Managing Outlook Web App Themes

Outlook Web App Themes provide a way to allow the users to customize the look and feel of OWA. Exchange 2010 SP1 has expanded on those options to provide 27 different theme options. For users, changing the theme is a simple task and can be accessed through the options menu in OWA, as shown in Figure 16-12.

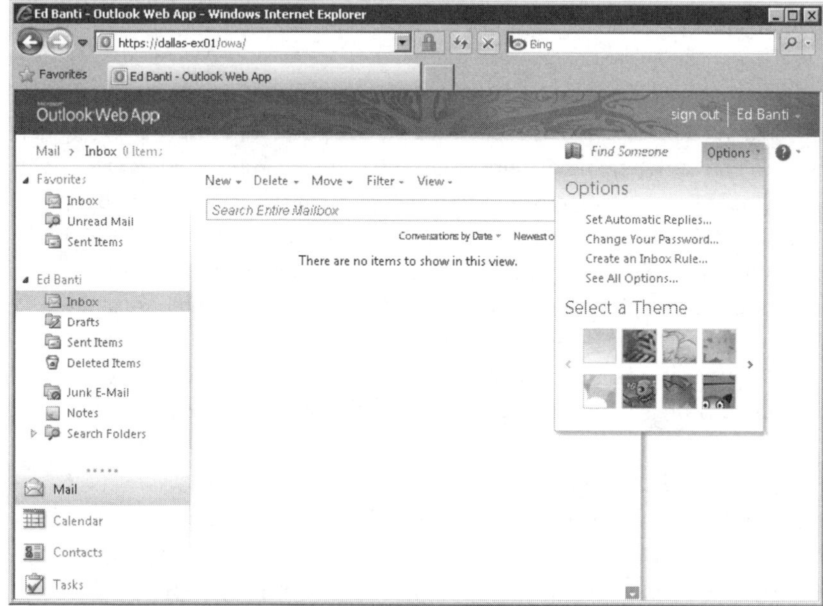

FIGURE 16-12 Outlook Web App Themes

Letting users set their custom themes is a matter each organization has to decide for itself. Some organizations prefer uniformity when it comes to the OWA look and feel, which leads them to setting the default theme and not allowing customization. This might be something to consider if you are concerned, for example, that a sales user could access his e-mail during a client meeting, only to display a less-than-professional image with regards to his choice of Outlook Web App Theme. If you want to set the Base theme as the default theme, you can do this by running *Set-OwaVirtualDirectory "owa (default web site)" -DefaultTheme Base* for each Client Access server used for OWA access. Alternatively, themes can be disabled by running *Set-OwaVirtualDirectory "owa (default web site)" -DefaultTheme base -ThemeSelectionEnabled:$False*.

Many companies like to customize the OWA interface to provide an interface that reflects company branding. Although many have done this in the past, starting with Exchange 2010 SP1, customizing the sign-in and sign-out pages is now supported. For more information on customizing these pages, see "Customize the Outlook Web App Sign-In and Sign-Out Pages" in the Exchange 2010 SP1 help file.

Managing Public Folders

Starting with the very first version of Exchange, Public Folders have been a way to access shared data. Public Folders do have their limits and are not designed to archive data or as a document collaboration solution. Public Folders is an optional feature with no dependencies for features such as free and busy time or OAB downloads if all clients are using Outlook 2007 or 2010. Until your organization is running Outlook 2010 or Outlook 2007, Public Folders should be used and thus are a part of this chapter. However, any proactive Exchange administrator should understand that although Public Folders are supported, Microsoft SharePoint may be a better long-term fit for your business going forward with new content. For more information about designing Public Folders and when to choose SharePoint over Public Folders, see Chapter 6, "Mailbox Services."

When the time comes to start planning for Public Folders, you want to keep in mind a few things about creating Public Folder databases. First, it is important to size your Exchange deployment accurately and to determine the amount of use that your Public Folders will receive. If you determine that Public Folders will be heavily used in your environment, best practice is to deploy a dedicated Public Folder server that will allow you to dedicate CPU and disk space to just the Public Folder function. Second, keep the number of databases to a minimum. This will allow for simplified management of the Public Folders database and will reduce the time required to restore a database. A balance should be met when determining the number of public folder databases so that you have enough databases to meet the organization's requirements while at the same time reducing the management of the databases.

Public Folder content is replicated with an e-mail-based process. When a Public Folder or its contents is modified, the Public Folder database the sends an e-mail message to the other Public Folder databases that host a replica of the Public Folder that describes the changes. If possible, multiple changes are contained within one e-mail message up to the message size limit. If the changes exceed the single message limit, multiple messages are sent.

The Transport servers route the replication messages the same way other e-mail messages are routed. By default, Public Folder content replicates every 15 minutes, and cannot be configured to replicate more than every minute.

> ***IMPORTANT*** **The Public Folder configuration information is stored in Active Directory. To optimize Public Folder replication, Active Directory replication must also be working correctly and efficiently.**

When you create a Public Folder, by default only one replica of that Public Folder exists within the Exchange Server organization. Creating replicas allows you to replicate Public Folder data between Mailbox servers. Just by adding multiple replicas for a Public Folder, the contents will be automatically replicated. Because each mailbox server only has one Public Folder database, it is recommended you install and configure at least two mailbox servers in the Exchange organization so that automatic Public Folder replication will occur. Basic replication can be configured within the EMC by right-clicking the Public Folder database and selecting Properties.

Public Folder replication is not only for redundancy—it also allows you to have Public Folder content in strategic locations, close to where the users are located. This can result in faster access to Public Folder content and reduced communication across wide area network (WAN) links.

You can create Public Folder databases using either the EMC or the EMS. The proper rights must be granted to the user account that will create Public Folders; those rights are organization management and server management. The EMC utilizes a simple wizard to create Public Folder databases; the EMS uses the *New-PublicFolderDatabase* cmdlet. After you have created the Public Folder database you will need to run the *Mount-Database* cmdlet to mount the database.

If you must remove a Public Folder database you should consider the following factors:

- If the Public Folder database contains data it cannot be removed. You must delete or migrate the data to another Public Folder database.
- If a Public Folder database has a mailbox database associated with it you must associate the mailbox database with another Public Folder database before it can be removed.
- If any users are utilizing Outlook 2003 or previous versions, the last Public Folder cannot be removed.

Although either the EMC or the EMS can be used to remove a Public Folder database, you will receive a warning to inform you that it will not remove the actual database files. These database files must be removed manually.

You can create Public Folders using the EMC, EMS, Outlook, and OWA. The Public Folder Management Console is a simplified way for the creation, configuration, and management of Public Folders. The Public Folder Management Console can be found in the Toolbox node in the EMC. Tasks that can be performed using the Public Folder management console include:

- Updating the Public Folder hierarchy
- Updating Public Folder content

- Adding or removing Public Folders
- Viewing and modifying Public Folder properties and replicas
- Managing Send As permissions for mail-enabled Public Folders

For example, to use the EMS to create the Project folder under the Sales top-level Public Folder on the Fresno-EX01 server, run the following cmdlet:

New-PublicFolder -Name "\Sales\Project" -Server Fresno-EX01

The *Remove-PublicFolder* cmdlet works similarly to the *New-PublicFolder* cmdlet; however, it deletes the Public Folder and all replicas.

Public Folders have two types of permissions: administrative and client. Administrative permissions control functions such as configuring replicas, setting deleted item retention, creating new Public Folders, and mail-enabling Public Folders. You can set these permissions using the EMS with the following three cmdlets: *Get-PublicFolderAdministrativePermission*, *Add-PublicFolderAdministrativePermission*, and *Remove-PublicFolderAdministrativePermission*.

Client permissions control functions such as creating, reading, editing, and deleting Public Folders and the items within the folders. You can configure client permissions using the Outlook client, EMS, and the Public Folder Management Console. When assigning client permissions keep in mind the Default and Anonymous special user accounts. These users are shown in the properties of the Sales Public Folder from within Outlook in Figure 16-13. The Default special user represents all users who are not explicitly defined access. By default, the Default special user inherits its permissions from the parent folder. When managing Public Folder permissions, this group is often overlooked, allowing more people access to the folder than the administrator expects. The anonymous special user represents all users who do not have a specific permissions set and users that are not logged in. The Anonymous special user is particularly important when a Public Folder is mail-enabled. E-mail messages sent from the Internet would be submitted anonymously. For a Public Folder to be able to receive messages from the Internet, the anonymous special user requires the Create Items permission. If you do not want your mail-enabled Public Folder to receive e-mail from the Internet, this permission should be removed.

The provided cmdlets are able to fully administer public folders and can be used to automate a variety of administrative tasks. Also included in the Scripts directory of the Exchange installation are a number of valuable pre-created Public Folder management scripts:

- **AddReplicaToPFRecursive.ps1** This script adds the specified server to the replica list for a given Public Folder and all folders underneath it.
- **AddUsersToPFRecursive.ps1** This script allows you to grant user permissions to a folder and all folders beneath it.
- **MoveAllReplicas.ps1** This script finds and replaces a server in the replica list of all Public Folders, including system folders for a given Public Folder database.
- **RemoveReplicaFromPFRecursive.ps1** This script removes the specified server from the replica list for a given Public Folder and all folders underneath it.
- **RemoveUserFromPFRecursive.ps1** This script removes the given user's access permissions from the given public folder and all its subfolders.

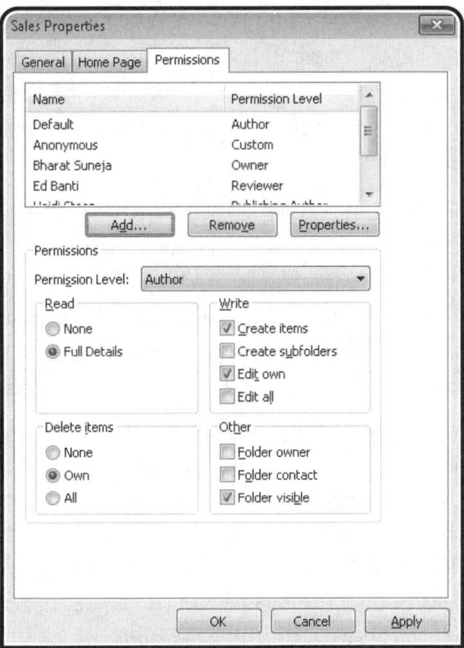

FIGURE 16-13 The Default and Anonymous special users

- **ReplaceReplicaOnPFRecursive.ps1** This script finds and replaces a server in the replica list of a given Public Folder as well as all subfolders.
- **ReplaceUserPermissionOnPFRecursive.ps1** This script finds and replaces one user in the permissions on a given Public Folder and all its subfolders with a second user; the original user permissions are not retained.
- **ReplaceUserWithUserOnPFRecursive.ps1** This script copies one user's access permissions on a given Public Folder and all its subfolders to a second user while retaining permissions for the first user.

Exchange 2010 SP1 added a few important features for Public Folders. For example, it enabled an administrator to set client permissions, override settings, and replicate information recursively, similar to how Exchange 2003 administrators were able to do this. Also introduced in Exchange 2010 SP1 is the repair Public Folder database cmdlet, *Repair-PublicFolderDatabase*, which is used to detect and fix the Public Folder corruptions in the replication state, view verification, and physical corruption.

Managing and Using Public Folders in a Mixed Environment

When you have a mixed Exchange 2003, Exchange 2007, and Exchange 2010 organization, you can still use the Exchange 2003 Exchange System Manager to manage Public Folders, which provide some features that are not present in the other management tools. Be sure, however, to follow the supported scenarios when performing Public Folder management:

- Exchange System Manager can be used to connect to, administer, and configure Exchange 2003 Public Folder databases for administration. Any changes will replicate to both Exchange 2007 and Exchange 2010.
- In an Exchange 2010-only or a mixed Exchange 2010 and Exchange 2007 organization, you can't install or use Exchange System Manager to manage Public Folders. In this case you must use the EMS.
- When verifying hierarchy replication or when viewing the Local Replica Age Limit value on a folder, use Exchange System Manager for Public Folders that exist on an Exchange 2003 server and the EMS for Public Folders that exist on an Exchange 2010 or Exchange 2007 server.

A migration from an older version of Exchange to Exchange 2010 is a good time to groom and maintain your Public Folders. Public Folders are easy to set up and use. Unfortunately, they are also easily abandoned. To ensure that the resources are not wasted, a periodic audit is recommended. One way to do this is to check the *LastAccessTime* property of the Public Folders. Folders that have not been accessed in a number of months or years usually can be archived and deleted. To create an ordered list of the last time each Public Folder has been accessed run *Get-PublicFolderStatistics | Sort-Object LastAccessTime | Format-Table.*

More information about Public Folders and options for deploying them can be found in Chapter 6.

Additional Resources

- Create or Remove Customer Resource Properties: *http://technet.microsoft.com/en-us/library/bb124948.aspx*
- Add-MailboxPermission Documentation: *http://technet.microsoft.com/en-us/library/bb124097.aspx*
- *Add-ADPermission* Documentation: *http://technet.microsoft.com/en-us/library/bb124403.aspx*
- Dan Goldman's OAB blog: *http://blogs.msdn.com/dgoldman/default.aspx*
- Web-based vs. Public Folder–based OAB Distribution: *http://technet.microsoft.com/en-us/library/cc535193.aspx*
- Customizing Details Templates: *http://technet.microsoft.com/en-us/library/bb124525.aspx*
- Scripting with Windows PowerShell: *http://technet.microsoft.com/en-us/scriptcenter/dd742419.aspx*
- Microsoft Official Curriculum Course 6434A: Automating Windows Server 2008 Administration with Windows PowerShell: *http://www.microsoft.com/learning/en/us/course.aspx?ID=6434A*

CHAPTER 17

Operating and Troubleshooting Exchange Server 2010

Monitoring and reacting to conditions in the production environment are essential activities for following best practices. This chapter discusses common best practices for this operational phase.

Microsoft Operations Framework

Chapter 2, "Exchange Deployment Projects," described the three Microsoft Operations Framework (MOF) phases: Plan, Deliver, and Operate. The focus in that chapter was primarily on the Plan and Deliver phases; this chapter continues with the Operate phase. The Operate phase includes operations, service monitoring and control, customer service, and problem management. Examples of specific tasks include proactive maintenance, trend analysis, and capacity planning. Figure 17-1 shows the different activities that are part of the Operate phase.

The goal of the Operate phase is to ensure that the systems are operating within the defined service-level agreements (SLAs) established with the business. You should define your SLAs during the planning phase because the system should be designed to support business requirements. If you don't do this, one outcome is that needless money is spent building overly complex solutions that are difficult to operate (and can potentially result in lower-than-expected uptime).

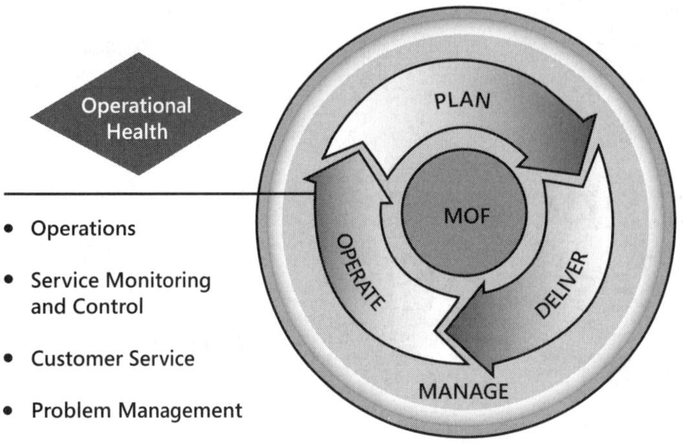

FIGURE 17-1 The Operate phase

Problem vs. Incident Management

Problem management and incident management are sometimes confused. *Incident management* means to troubleshoot an issue to restore service as quickly as possible. *Problem management* seeks to determine root causes to prevent an issue from occurring in the future. These two activities are often at odds with each other. For example, let's say a server is experiencing trouble. From an incident management perspective, rebooting the server may be the quickest way to correct the problem. However, from a problem management perspective a reboot may destroy relevant diagnostic information needed to fully analyze the issue. As a compromise between restoring the service as quickly as possible and collecting useful information, a well-documented troubleshooting plan should be implemented. This plan should include items such as what information to collect and how long to allow for collecting data.

Trending and Capacity Planning

Trend analysis and capacity planning are closely related to performance and problem management. Trend analysis takes a longer view of performance data and problem management records to predict and prevent issues. For example, collecting data related to CPU utilization can show over time that a server is reaching a predetermined threshold and will eventually be unable to meet an SLA. Another example is correlating a rise in the number of helpdesk tickets related to group management to help justify the implementation of a self-service solution. As you can see, trend analysis on its own does not solve problems, but can have a large impact on keeping operations running smoothly over time.

Trending begins with taking a baseline. It is important to establish a baseline that lasts for a full business cycle. This time period will vary between companies, but should include enough time to account for peak busy and slow times. For example, a business cycle may coincide with regular product promotions. This time is considered as peak system usage. Figure 17-2 illustrates the iterative process used for trending systems.

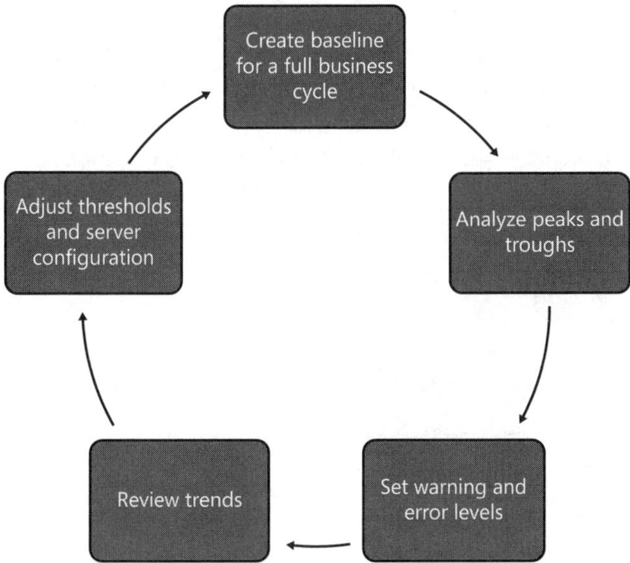

FIGURE 17-2 The trending process

It is important to repeat the process to make sure that the systems stay aligned with changes in the business or even after applying updates to the products.

For example, a new service pack for Exchange is released and changes to the product may affect server performance. The Exchange administrator has periodically taken basic performance monitoring snapshots during peak and non-peak times. She has done this throughout the year, and she has a good idea of what the typical server load should be. Today, she tracks processor utilization for both high thresholds (85 percent) and low thresholds (40 percent). She tracks low CPU usage because it is another indicator of trouble with the server—the server runs on average 50 percent utilized. After applying the new service pack, the administrator now occasionally gets alerts that the CPU is lower than the minimum threshold. Finding that the server is operating normally, she discovers that the service pack re-architected some processes, and the CPU requirements were reduced. She now needs to readjust her normal thresholds by establishing a new baseline. This is just one example of how monitoring and trending need to be performed periodically. It is also an example of the problems that can be caused by rushing a service pack into production without understanding the full impact of the new software.

Another classic example is that servers are often designed to meet a specific load—in this case around RIM BlackBerry devices. To accommodate the additional I/O on the mailbox storage generated by these devices, an administrator must estimate the number of devices when doing storage calculations. If the anticipated demand for mobile devices was inaccurate, and twice the number of users carry these mobile devices, this will have significant impact on the mailbox server storage, but many companies fail to go back and either change the storage configuration or add additional capacity before performance becomes an issue that end users notice. Trending over time will help predict the impact of changes before they become issues.

Troubleshooting Methodology

Troubleshooting is part art and part science. This section presents one possible method to troubleshoot issues, but it is not necessarily the only approach you can take. The goal of troubleshooting is to quickly resolve the issue and find the root cause whenever possible. A feedback loop should be in place for making changes to the environment or processes and prevent the issue from happening again. Figure 17-3 outlines the troubleshooting process.

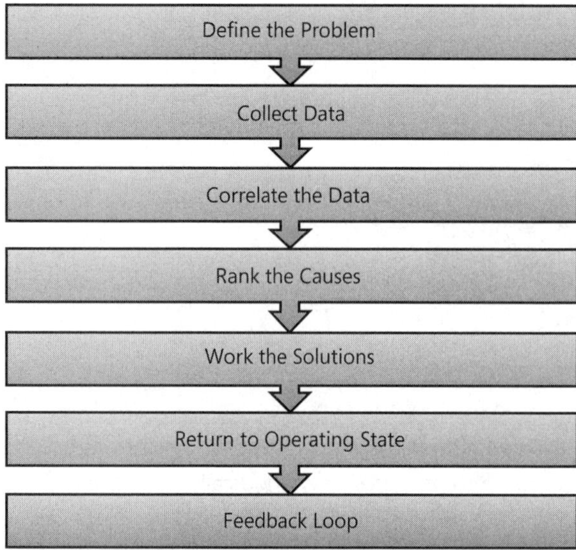

FIGURE 17-3 The troubleshooting process

Define the Scope

It sounds obvious, but defining the scope is a critical step in the troubleshooting process. Without clearly scoping and defining the problem, it's easy to get sidetracked or not have everybody working to solve the same problem. Verifying and recording as much information about the problem as possible is very important. You must also record the initial state of the environment before changes take place and that information is lost forever.

Collect the Data

This step involves collecting data from sources such as event logs, log files, and performance information. If possible, record the steps to reproduce the problem. Sometimes it helps to capture data from ancillary servers. For example, when troubleshooting performance issues with Exchange, you can get a complete picture by coordinating data captured from a client and server at the same time. On both the client and server use perfmon, network tracing, memory dumps, and other tools, and record the exact time that the issue occurs. This way you can look at the problem from several different sources to get a complete picture.

Correlate the Data

With the problem statement and the collected data, make a list of potential causes for the problem. It is also important in this step to pay attention to the problem details and error codes.

One helpful tool with this step is a dependency map. An example of a dependency map is shown in Figure 17-4.

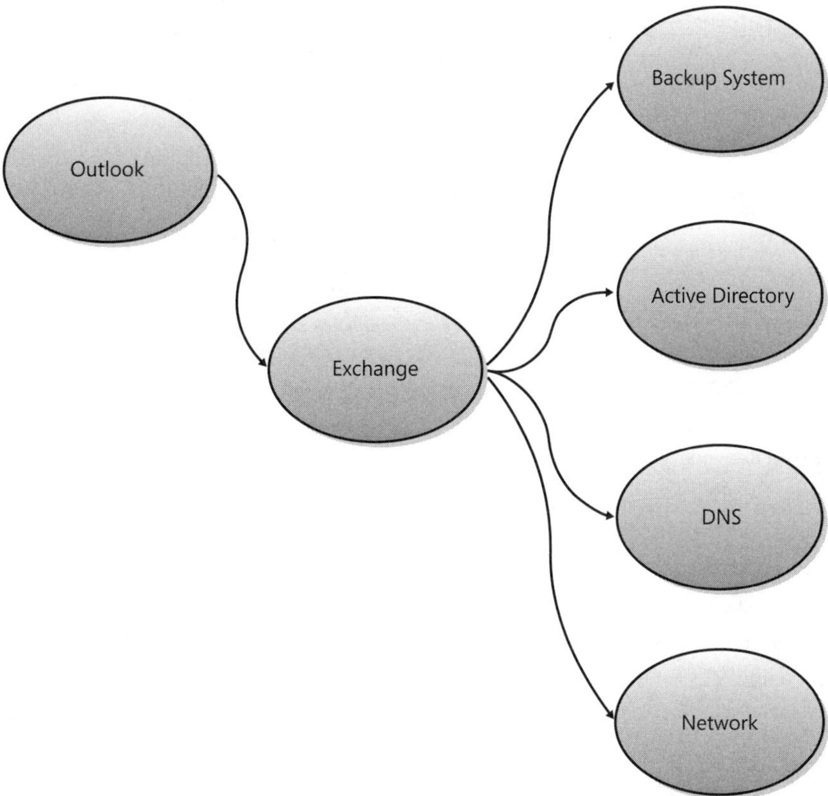

FIGURE 17-4 High-level dependency map

From the high-level example in Figure 17-4, you can pull out an element and create a dependency map for it. For example, Figure 17-5 expands the Exchange service by specifically creating a map for the Exchange Mailbox role. It is possible to continue this process and pick another element, such as direct attached storage, and create a dependency map for it.

Creating these dependency maps helps quickly determine dependencies and can help focus the areas to troubleshoot.

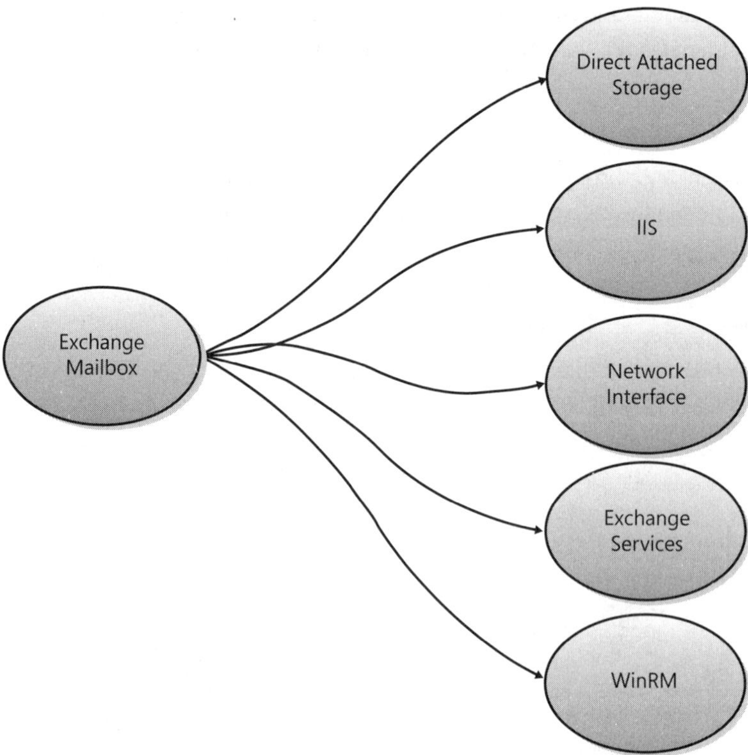

FIGURE 17-5 Low-level dependency map

Rank the Causes

The next step is to make a list of the possible causes, adding additional emphasis on characteristics such as ease of implementation of solution, probability of cause, risk, and so on. This step will help focus on the most likely, easiest, or lowest-risk test solutions.

Work the Solutions

When it's time to work the solutions, start with whichever solution ranked highest from the previous step. Be careful not to make multiple changes at once, and record the changes made and any observations on the change's impact. Continue working the solutions until the problem is resolved.

Return to Operating State

It is important to undo any changes made while troubleshooting from the previous step. Logging, tracing, and other tools may have an impact on server performance, so removing any unnecessary settings is important.

Feedback Loop

Document the root cause and any details learned from troubleshooting and resolving the issue. If the problem resurfaces in the future, it's possible that a different group of people may be troubleshooting the issue. Good documentation preserves institutional knowledge that would be otherwise lost.

Monitoring Exchange Server 2010

With many Exchange projects, monitoring comes late in the project, or even worse, after the project completes. Having a robust monitoring solution and processes can greatly improve your ability to identify, troubleshoot, and repair issues before impacting end users. Designing a carefully thought out and comprehensive monitoring solution is worth the time it saves by reducing services outages that can translate into hard dollar costs. A complete solution should do the following:

- **Identify performance issues** The faster the solution helps an administrator determine cause, the quicker the time to problem resolution will be. Many organizations rely on their end users to alert them to issues. This causes end-user dissatisfaction and drives up help desk calls.
- **Identify growth trends** Over time, usage patterns change, business needs change, and hardware modifications may be needed to satisfy these changes. Trending helps forecast these changes and can proactively fix an environment before it becomes an issue.
- **Track performance against established service level agreements** It is important to work with the business and management to report on how Exchange is meeting the metrics that have been defined. This can help quantify the value Exchange server administrators are providing, and may help with upgrades and other areas that need cost justifications.
- **Track configuration changes** Some Exchange environments can have hundreds of servers, all of which need ongoing maintenance. Even in smaller organizations, ensuring that settings remain consistent across servers can be challenging. Reviewing changes against known best practices also keeps service running smoothly.

Monitoring Exchange 2010 also requires a monitoring solution that can gather information from dependent services, such as Active Directory or DNS. Many enterprise environments have some form of a monitoring solution across their IT infrastructure. In cases where a comprehensive solution does not exist, or companies would like to integrate a best of breed solution for Exchange 2010, System Center Operations Manager 2007 R2 (SCOM) is an enterprise-class monitoring solution. Fundamentally, tools such as SCCM build upon the freely available tools that are part of Windows and Exchange. So although you can use the tools independently, using a comprehensive solution makes it easier to manage midsized or large environments.

Performance Monitor

When monitoring Exchange Server 2010, administrators should know which aspects of server performance are the most important. Performance counters and threshold values can identify potential issues, as well as identify the root cause of issues when troubleshooting. This section highlights some of the most important counters for each role. It is important to know that sometimes these thresholds need to be adjusted to work in a specific environment. One exercise is to create a baseline measurement of server performance during normal operations. After the baseline has been established, set thresholds to let administrators know when performance metrics are not met.

Performance Data for the Mailbox Server

Many performance counters are available for the Mailbox server; the storage-based counters listed in Table 17-1 are a good starting place when collecting performance data.

TABLE 17-1 Storage-Based Counters

COUNTER	DESCRIPTION	EXPECTED VALUE
MSExchange Database\I/O Database Reads (Attached) Average Latency	Shows the average time for reading data from the active database file.	The active copy on average should be below 20 ms. Spikes should not exceed 100 ms.
MSExchange Database\I/O Database Reads (Recovery) Average Latency	Shows the average time for reading data from passive database file.	Passive copies on average should be below 200 ms. Spikes should not exceed 1,000 ms.
Database\Database Page Fault Stalls\sec	Shows the rate of page faults that cannot be serviced because no pages are available for allocation from the database cache.	Should be 0. Values above 0 indicate database write average latency is too high.

When collecting performance data for the Mailbox server, the focus is generally on storage response times. Slow response times will directly impact the user experience and passive copy replay. If the disk subsystem is not meeting demand, fixing the problem may require additional disks, faster disks, or modifying the disk configuration.

Table 17-2 shows the Information Store RPC processing counters. If RPC counters indicate a problem, several causes are possible.

- **Storage Subsystem** Ensure that I/O read/write latencies are not excessive. Correlate the storage-based counters with RPC counters to see whether they align.
- **Network components** Check network card settings for errors, dropped packets, network speed, and duplex settings.

- **CPU Processor** Identify whether the CPU is running near capacity. If the CPU is taxed, it will not be able to process RPC calls.
- **Applications** Identify applications that cause high amounts of RPC calls. Use Client Throttling Policies to prevent an application from consuming excessive server resources.

TABLE 17-2 RPC-Based Counters

COUNTER	DESCRIPTION	EXPECTED VALUE
MSExchangeIS\RPC Requests	Indicated the overall RPC requests that are currently executing within the store process.	Should be below 70 at all times.
MSExchangeIS\RPC Averaged Latency	Shows the RPC latency, in milliseconds, averaged for all operations in the last 1,024 packets.	Should not exceed 10 ms on average.
MSExchangeIS Client (*)\RPC Averaged Latency	Shows a server RPC latency in milliseconds averaged for the past 1,024 packets for a specific client protocol. The value of *Other* is used for MAPI clients.	Should not exceed 10 ms on average.

Performance Data for the Transport and Edge Server

The key counters for transport center on queues. Monitoring transport queues ensures timely message delivery.

TABLE 17-3 Transport- and Edge-Based Counters

COUNTER	DESCRIPTION	EXPECTED VALUE
MSExchangeTransport Queues(_total)\Aggregate Delivery Queue Length (All Queues)	The number of messages from all queues waiting for delivery.	Should be less than 3,000 and not more than 5,000.
MSExchangeTransport Queues(_total)\Active Remote Delivery Queue Length	The number of messages in the active remote delivery queues.	Should be less than 250 at all times.
MSExchangeTransport Queues(_total)\Submission Queue Length	The number of messages in the submission queue.	Should not exceed 100. Sustained high values indicate Active Directory or Mailbox server bottlenecks.

COUNTER	DESCRIPTION	EXPECTED VALUE
MSExchangeTransport Queues(_total)\Retry Remote Delivery Queue Length	The number of messages in a retry state in the remote delivery queues.	Should not exceed 100. Investigate the next hop to determine the causes for queuing.
MSExchangeTransport Queues(_total)\Poison Queue Length	The number of messages in the poison message queue.	Should be 0 at all times.

Performance Data for the Client Access Server

The Client Access Server key counters center on client services such as Outlook Web App and Exchange Web Services.

TABLE 17-4 Client Access Server—Based Counters

COUNTER	DESCRIPTION	EXPECTED VALUE
ASP.Net\application restarts	The number of times the application has been restarted during the Web server's lifetime.	Should be 0 at all times.
ASP.Net\Request Wait Time	The number of milliseconds the most recent request was waiting in the queue.	Should be 0 at all times.
ASP.Net Applications(*)\Requests in Application Queue	The number of requests in the application request queue.	Should be 0 at all times.
MSExchange OWA\Average Search Time	The average time that elapsed while waiting for search to complete.	Should be less than 5,000 ms at all times.
MSExchange Control Panel\Requests – Average Response Time	The average time in milliseconds ECP took to respond to a request during the sampling period.	Should be under 6,000 ms.

Performance Data for the Unified Messaging Server

Unified Messaging key counters monitor UM availability.

TABLE 17-5 Unified Messaging—Based Counters

COUNTER	DESCRIPTION	EXPECTED VALUE
MSExchangeUMAvailability\% of Failed Mailbox Connection Attempts Over the last hour	The percentage of mailbox connection attempts that failed in the last hour.	Should be less than 5 percent.
MSExchangeUMAvailability\% of Messages Successfully Processed Over the Last Hour	The percentage of messages that were successfully processed by UM in the last hour.	Should be greater or equal to 95 percent.
MSExchangeUMAvailability\Direct Access Failures	The number of times that attempts to access Active Directory failed.	Should be 0 at all times.

NOTES FROM THE FIELD

Exchange Perfmon

Andy Schan
Senior Consultant, Schan Consulting, Inc., Canada

For several of my clients, I've been asked a question along the lines of "We're having performance issues—which Exchange Performance Monitor counters should we look at?" My first response is to suggest that they look at it like any other Windows server and check the "big 4" first: CPU, memory, disk, and network. For example, if the network is saturated or the server is memory-starved, any Exchange-specific counters, such as RPC latency or message queues, are very likely to be only symptoms of the fundamental problem. You can't overlook the Exchange metrics you should be monitoring, but don't forget the fundamentals, either.

Another question I've been asked is, "The performance has degraded since we first deployed the servers; what has changed?" I then ask how the current performance compares to their baselines; that is the point when some people feel sheepish and say that gathering baselines has been on the to-do list for quite a while, but they've never had time to do it. Baselines are a crucial component of your monitoring and reporting strategy, and gathering and maintaining them should be made part of your deployment project plan, and should be on the critical path so that they are done before the project is closed off. It can be challenging and time-consuming to gather baselines at the appropriate time; it does no good to baseline your Exchange Server 2010 environment when only 100 of your 50,000 users have been migrated to Exchange Server 2010. On the other hand, if you leave it until the very end of the project, you may find yourself under pressure to simply close off the project and hand it over to the operational support group, who may not have the time or the skill sets required to gather comprehensive baseline metrics.

Windows Server and Active Directory

When troubleshooting Exchange, an administrator often needs to also troubleshoot related services. Active Directory and the underlying operating system are intimately tied together with Exchange. In many companies the Exchange administrators are separated from the network, DNS, and Active Directory infrastructure. Conversely, these other administrators are often not aware of how dependent Exchange is on these related infrastructure services. More mature organizations that are aware of the inter-relationships often create operational-level agreements (OLAs). OLAs are similar to SLAs—the key difference is that the agreements are between internal groups working to support an SLA, and the SLA is the agreement with a business group. To state it a different way, OLAs are created to ensure that core activities performed by different support teams are clearly aligned to meet the agreed-upon business SLAs. This is a fundamental piece of service-level management. As such, Exchange administrators should have enough knowledge to assist other support groups and know where the interdependencies are.

Windows Server 2003 introduced the Server Performance Advisor (SPA) to assist in identifying performance-related issues. Unfortunately, this tool is not compatible with Windows Server 2008/R2, but much of the SPA functionality was built directly into Windows 2008 in the performance monitor tool. The addition of data collector sets allows for collections of monitor counters and system traces that are all related to a specific purpose. Windows 2008 comes with a number of predefined collections: Active Directory Diagnostics, System Diagnostics, System Performance, and LAN diagnostics. Frequently when troubleshooting Active Directory, the first things to look at are search performance and LDAP performance. Using data collection sets, as shown in Figure 17-6, makes this easy to do.

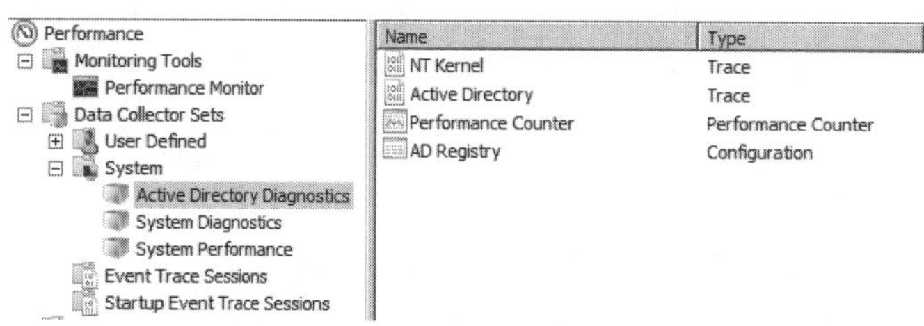

FIGURE 17-6 Performance monitor data collector sets

After the data has been collected, reports can be generated. Some of the more interesting items are the LDAP client with the most CPU, and the searches with the most CPU. Figure 17-7 shows an example of a report.

You can quickly identify any clients consuming large amounts of the server's resources. Additionally, the full search query terms are displayed. Custom applications frequently perform inefficient LDAP searches and might require the use of a Network sniffer to troubleshoot. That typically requires involving groups outside of infrastructure, or deep knowledge of how to read and understand network traces. DNS information can be retrieved with the System Performance data collection.

Keep in mind that the report only shows the symptoms of an issue, and the art of troubleshooting is working through a process to determine the root cause.

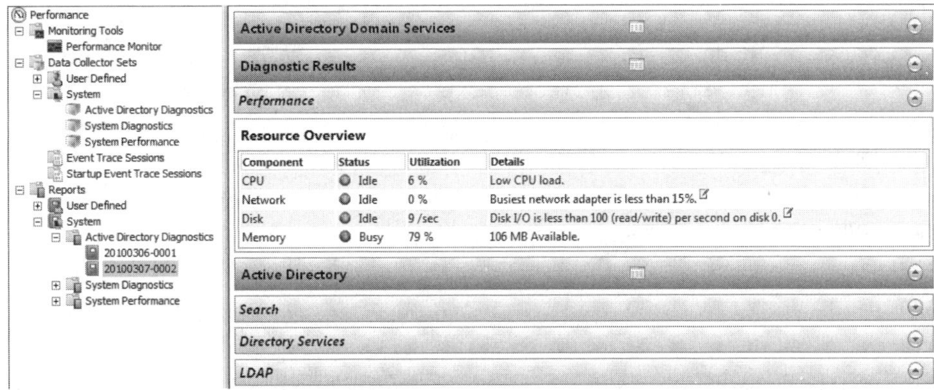

FIGURE 17-7 Performance Monitor report

You may notice that no pre-built data collector sets are specific to Exchange Server. The Exchange team posted role-based XML files that you can use to create a user-defined data collector set. The XML files are at *http://blogs.technet.com/mikelag/archive/2010/01/11/perfwiz-for-exchange-2010.aspx*. XML files are currently available for the Mailbox role, and one with all counters.

NOTES FROM THE FIELD

Creating a Report of Performance Data

Alessandro Goncalves
Senior Support Engineer, Microsoft Corporation, USA

When you need to create a report of performance file, there is a very useful tool called PAL—available at *http://pal.codeplex.com/Wikipage*—that enables you to quickly create a report full of information that can speed up the process of discovering a performance issue and help you with performance troubleshooting.

You can also use it to help determine your own thresholds for a specific environment—the numbers are just a suggestion that works for the majority of scenarios, but might apply to your particular case. Analyze it carefully and trace back issues with the performance monitor numbers.

Always remember to stop performance monitoring collection after you have completed gathering the data you require—the data collecting itself may cause performance impact on normal operations.

These data collection sets make it easy to capture key performance counters, but it is important to know which performance aspects are the most important. There is a tense relationship between running servers to maximize utilization while not crossing the threshold into impacting server performance. Underutilized servers cost money (power, hardware, and options), and can possibly be consolidated. Knowing the key indicators can help an administrator determine when more capacity is needed or excess capacity can be reduced.

PROCESSOR

The processor is one of the core components that need monitoring to ensure server health. Standard counters include the total percentage of processor time, the percentage of user-mode processor time, and the percentage of privilege-mode processor time. Another key counter is the processor queue length. If this length is outside of the operating threshold, the processor may have more work than it can handle. This may be a good indicator that a server could use a faster processor or additional cores.

NOTES FROM THE FIELD

Exchange and Hyper-V CPU Utilization Troubleshooting

Alessandro Goncalves
Senior Support Engineer, Microsoft Corporation, USA

When dealing with a Virtualized Exchange Server 2010, it is very important to select the correct counters to accurately measure CPU performance as well as any other object.

When we have Exchange Server 2010 as a guest in a Hyper-V environment, the counters in the GUEST Virtual Machine do not show the actual physical processor utilization. Instead, we need to use Hyper-V Hypervisor Performance Counters in the root partition to determine the real CPU load. We also need to keep in mind that the host hardware is sharing its resources among other loads and virtual machines and it is important to identify whether another virtual machine is creating the bottleneck in the host and thus affecting Exchange.

Therefore, as far as collecting data for performance is concerned, a more precise picture is obtained by collecting it in the root partition, or in the host itself. As far as the CPU is concerned, a CPU spinner program inside the guest can lead the CPU in the guest operating system to be at 100 percent level, but it has little effect on the host and other virtual machines running. Thus one very important thing to recognize is which virtual machine you are measuring, and %Guest Run Time will match the instance name with the virtual machine you need to measure. It is very likely to be misled by an Exchange server running in a virtual environment and its CPU usage, because the guest could be spinning the CPU and task manager in the virtual machine, showing it is at 100 percent CPU utilization, whereas in the root partition the overall CPU utilization is nowhere near that number. It is critical to realize that in a virtual environment, the accurate measure more often than not comes from the root partition. Please use the additional resources at the end of the chapter for more information.

MEMORY

Exchange 2010 benefits by using the 64-bit processor's ability to address large amounts of memory efficiently. Monitoring the page file can reveal performance impact if the server has to constantly swap pages to slower disk storage. Increasing memory or reducing the server's load are ways to improve performance.

ACTIVE DIRECTORY ACCESS

Exchange heavily relies on Active Directory for everything from configuration information to user property information. Therefore, it is critical to monitor response times for searches and reads. Ensure that you have a good ratio of Exchange server cores to Active Directory cores. If the Global Catalog servers are running on a 32-bit platform, the recommended ratio of Active Directory server cores to Exchange Mailbox Server cores is 1:4. If the Global Catalog servers are running on a 64-bit platform, the recommended ratio of Active Directory server cores to Exchange Mailbox Server cores is 1:8 (assuming the Active Directory server has enough memory to cache the entire Active Directory database in memory). Upgrading Active Directory servers to 64 bit may be a way to get more performance without scaling out with new hardware.

DISK STORAGE

Finally, Exchange is a very demanding database application that requires consistent and fast disk access. When I/O counters fall outside of normal range, client performance is directly impacted. For example, Outlook and Outlook Web App (OWA) users will report "Outlook is slow" when opening mail or moving between folders. Faster disks, more disks, or redesigning existing disk arrays are all ways to mitigate storage issues.

NOTES FROM THE FIELD

Consider Active Directory Replication Delays in Exchange 2010 Troubleshooting

Markus Bellmann
Senior Solution Architect, Siemens AG, Germany

With one customer, we ran into the issue that newly created databases did not mount immediately. The error was "Active Directory operation failed on <servername>. This error is not retriable. Additional information: The name reference is invalid". The reason for that behavior is that Remote PowerShell connects to a Client Access server, not to a Mailbox server. The good news is that Exchange will try to mount the database repeatedly, so when the information is replicated to the configuration domain controller responsible for the Mailbox server, the database will be automatically made available.

The bottom line is that when creating mailbox databases using Remote PowerShell, you may want to make sure that the Mailbox server and the corresponding Client Access servers use the same domain controller for configuration. You can verify this with the *Get-ADServerSettings |fl* cmdlet, and configure the domain controller that is used by PowerShell with the *Set-ADServerSettings* cmdlet.

System Center Operations Manager 2007 R2

System Center Operations Manager 2007 R2 (SCOM) is the platform monitoring and reporting solution from Microsoft. SCOM provides end-to-end service management that includes monitoring, troubleshooting, and reporting tools. SCOM uses the concept of management packs to extend the base framework for specific applications, such as Exchange 2010. A management pack includes all of the rules, knowledge, reports, and tasks needed to monitor a product. SCOM has management packs for all of Microsoft's server products, and even sub-components such as DNS. The Exchange 2010 management pack has a complete health model and diagnostic alerts, and service-level reports needed to smoothly operate Exchange. Although SCOM itself requires licensing, the management Microsoft management pack for Exchange 2010 is free. The latest management pack includes several new features, described in the following sections.

Alert Correlation

A Windows service called the *Correlation Engine* finds dependencies encoded in the health model to determine root cause. It uses the class hierarchy defined in the Exchange MP to understand dependencies. For example, if Active Directory goes offline, it will also report that Exchange is not fully functional. This significantly reduces the noise that was an issue in earlier versions of SCOM.

It is recommended that you install the Correlation Engine on the SCOM Root Management Server (RMS). There is a performance impact to the RMS, because much of the information must be held in memory to determine the related monitors and alerts. It is estimated that the engine requires about 5 MB per Exchange instance that is being monitored.

Alert Classification

Alerts are put into three categories:

- **Key Health indicator** Important, service-impacting issues. Most alerts fall under this category.
- **Non-Service Impacting Issues** Issues that affect specific mailboxes but do not impact the larger system.
- **Forensic** Monitors diagnostics that do not represent a specific problem. These do not create alerts, but may be useful while diagnosing an issue.

Full Protocol Synthetic Transaction Coverage

SCOM uses the native Exchange diagnostic cmdlets to simulate user transactions or protocol tests. Table 17-6 shows the synthetic transactions available in the Exchange 2010 management pack. These cmdlets can also be called directly from PowerShell and do not require SCOM.

TABLE 17-6 Synthetic Transactions

ACTION	CMDLET
Unified Messaging – Remote Voice	*Test-UMConnectivity -UMIPgateway*
Unified Messaging – Local Voice	*Test-UMConnectivity*
Database Replication	*Test-ReplicationHealth*
Search	*Test-ExchangeSearch*
Remote PowerShell – External	*Test-PowerShellConnectivity –TestType:External*
Remote PowerShell – Internal	*Test-PowerShellConnectivity –TestType:Internal*
Mailbox Replication Service	*Test-MRSHealth*
Outlook (MAPI) – Internal	*Test-OutlookConnectivity –RPCTestType:Server*
Outlook – Autodiscover	*Test-OutlookConnectivity –GetDefaultsFromAutoDiscover $True*
Web Services	*Test-WebServicesConnectivity*
POP3	*Test-PopConnectivity*
Exchange Control Panel – External	*Test-EXPConnectivity –TestType:External*
Exchange Control Panel – Internal	*Test-EXPConnectivity –TestType:Internal*
Outlook Web Application – External	*Test-OwaConnectivity –TestType:External*
Outlook Web Application – Internal	*Test-OwaConnectivity –TestType:Internal*
IMAP4	*Test-ImapConnectivity*
Outlook Web Services	*Test-OutlookWebServices*
ActiveSync	*Test-ActiveSyncConnectivity*
EdgeSync	*Test-EdgeSynchronization*

Reporting

The Exchange MP now includes mail flow statistics based on the message tracking logs. Figure 17-8 shows a sample report for mail flow statistics.

Server Hourly Mailflow Statistics Summary

3/29/2010 12:24:40 PM

12:00:00 AM to 11:00:00 PM

End To End Latency Target = 90 Local Latency Target = 30

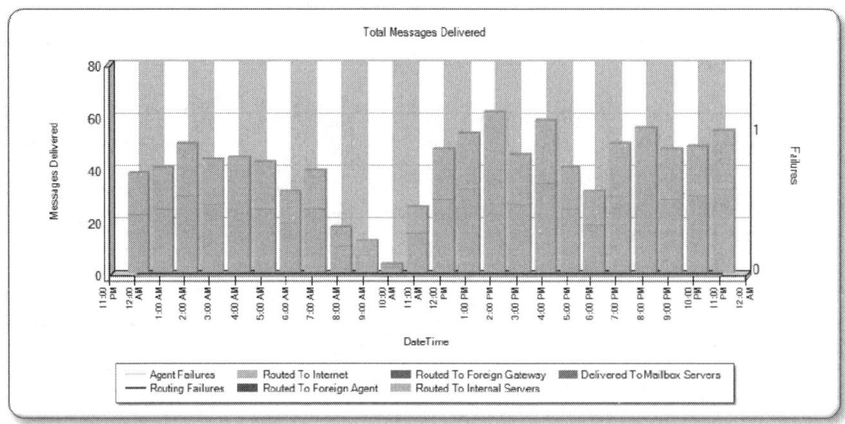

FIGURE 17-8 Sample SCOM mail flow report

Service-oriented reporting is for measuring applications or features, not just the host. It is interesting to note how SCOM calculates availability information. Figure 17-9 shows a sample availability report.

Availability Report

Report time : 3/29/2010 12:24 PM

Data aggregation : Daily

Report duration : 3/22/2010 - 3/28/2010

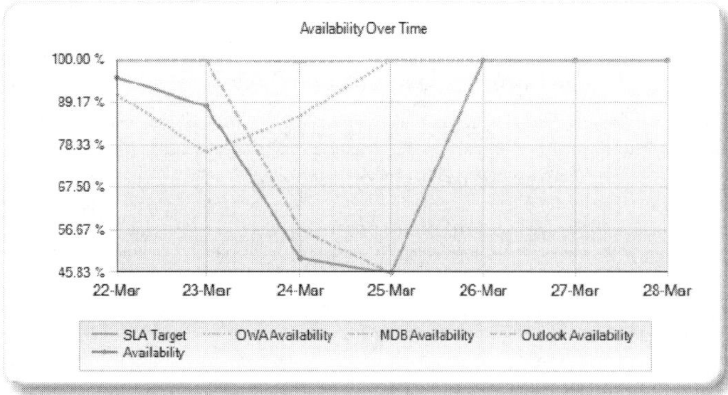

FIGURE 17-9 Sample SCOM availability report

Table 17-7 shows how System Center calculates availability information.

TABLE 17-7 SCOM Availability Information

MEASURMENT	DESCRIPTION
Mailbox Database – Daily Availability	A database is available when one of its copies is mounted. The daily availability is the percent of the day that the database is available.
Outlook Web App – Daily Availability	Both server- and site-level OWA states are reported. The service class is considered available when at least one OWA server is available.
Outlook – Daily Availability	Both server- and site-level Outlook states are reported. The service class is considered available when at least one Outlook server is available.
Site Mailbox Database – Daily Availability	A site's mailbox database availability is an average of mailbox database availabilities.
Site – Daily Availability	A site's availability is its mailbox database availability minus the average of its OWA service class and Outlook service class unavailability.
Datacenter – Daily Ability	A datacenter's availability is an average of site availabilities.
Monthly Availability	The sum of the daily availabilities divided by the number of days in the month.
Raw Uptime	1 – Downtime
Availability	Raw Uptime + Planed Maintenance Planned maintenance is considered uptime in the availability calculation.

NOTES FROM THE FIELD

Exchange and SCOM: Better Together

I had an interesting experience with the Exchange Management Pack in my last customer project. After planning and implementing Exchange Server in their environment, they also wanted a monitoring and reporting solution, so we decided to use System Center Operations Manager for that job.

The installation of the Exchange Management Pack (MP) was very easy, and shortly after we installed the pack it started to bring up alerts on specific items such as large queues and delivery notifications. Because of the fact that the alert also included information on how to solve the issue, it was quite easy to get rid of the alerts.

Every Exchange administrator wants a smooth-running Exchange deployment. We did our best to make sure that our deployment was well-tuned by running ExBPA and other tools. An important lesson I learned from this experience was that SCOM revealed a whole new level of detail about Exchange, and pointed out things that we needed to take care of to achieve a better operating environment. SCOM and the Exchange MP really proved their value to me in this respect.

Troubleshooting Tools

Even a well-designed and operated Exchange system will eventually experience problems that you need to identify and repair. The previous section explained the troubleshooting methodology. This section highlights some of the top tools available for troubleshooting.

Identifying and Resolving Performance Problems

The Exchange Management Console (EMC) ships with a collection of troubleshooting and diagnostic tools. A number of the tools are hosted within the EMC, whereas some, such as the Best Practices Analyzer, are separate executables that can be launched from within the toolbox or have to be installed separately.

This section discusses a few of the top tools in more detail. You can also use a number of additional tools. Table 17-8 lists these tools and their functions.

TABLE 17-8 Troubleshooting Tools

TOOL	DESCRIPTION
DNSLint	DNSLint can be used to help diagnose common DNS configuration errors across multiple DNS servers. DNSLint is useful for identifying connectivity issues.
Error Code Lookup (Err.exe)	Use for Error Code Lookup to determine error values from decimal and hexadecimal error codes. Use in conjunction with error codes.
Event Viewer (eventvwr.msc)	An MMC snap-in to view logged events. Use Event Viewer in any case as a starting point.
LDP (ldp.exe)	A GUI tool used to perform LDAP operations (connect, bind, search, modify, add, delete) against Active Directory or LDAP compatible directory. LDP can display all property information about objects in the directory. LDP can help identify user configuration issues.

TOOL	DESCRIPTION
Process Monitor	A monitoring tool for Windows that shows real-time information from the file system, registry, and process/threads. Process Monitor is helpful for diagnosing performance issues.
Microsoft Product Support Reports	The Microsoft Product Support Reports tool gathers critical system and logging information useful for troubleshooting support issues. This tool is useful for general data gathering. Under most circumstances Microsoft PSS will send the customer a link to run the tool.

Microsoft Exchange Best Practices Analyzer

The Microsoft Exchange Best Practices Analyzer (ExBPA) is a tool to help administrators assess the health of their servers and topology. The tool scans the live environment and compares the results against a vast list of best practices defined by Microsoft. It pulls information from Active Directory, the registry, WMI, the IIS metabase, and Performance Monitor. Additionally, it collects useful information about the Exchange organization. Because it is a stand-alone tool, it has its own help file and is not integrated into the standard Exchange help. You have a lot of flexibility when running the tool. In most cases ExBPA will also display information on how to correct the identified issue. You can scan the entire Exchange organization or scope it down to a single server. Several types of scans are available, as shown in Table 17-9.

TABLE 17-9 ExBPA Scan Types

SCAN TYPE	SCAN ACTIONS	WHEN TO USE
Health Check	Performs a full scan checking for errors, warning, non-default configurations, and configuration changes. Optionally, it can take samples of performance counters over a two-hour period.	Use this scan type to check the health of the organization or to troubleshoot a specific problem.
Permissions Check	Scans Active Directory domain naming context and the Exchange configuration naming context.	Run this scan if you suspect a permissions access issue.
Connectivity Check	This scan tries to validate all network connectivity and Active Directory access.	This scan helps troubleshoot network connectivity issues. It can be very useful if you have firewalls in the topology.
Baseline	The Baseline check allows an administrator to set threshold values that will be checked against the server's actual configuration.	Useful to report on deviations from baseline values.

One interesting way to use ExBPA is to compare information between multiple runs to see what configuration items have changed. If an issue arises, it is easy to compare a new report against a known good baseline and quickly spot any differences.

Microsoft Exchange Performance Troubleshooter

The Microsoft Exchange Performance Troubleshooter (ExPTA) helps locate performance related issues. As you can see in Figure 17-10, an administrator selects the type of performance symptoms he is seeing. RPC issues generally affect client performance, so RPC issues can be a common area administrators need to troubleshoot.

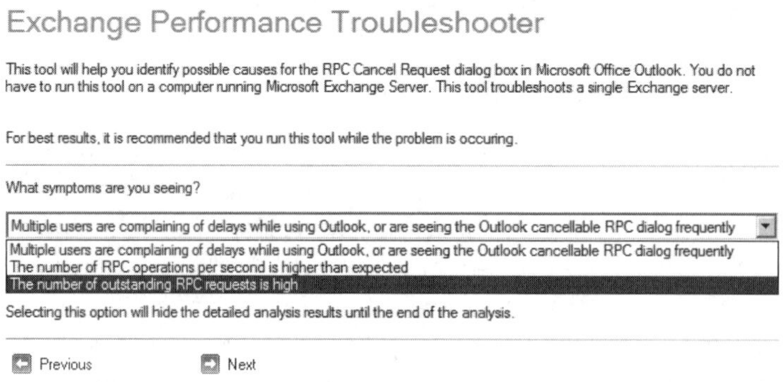

Exchange Performance Troubleshooter

This tool will help you identify possible causes for the RPC Cancel Request dialog box in Microsoft Office Outlook. You do not have to run this tool on a computer running Microsoft Exchange Server. This tool troubleshoots a single Exchange server.

For best results, it is recommended that you run this tool while the problem is occuring.

What symptoms are you seeing?

Multiple users are complaining of delays while using Outlook, or are seeing the Outlook cancellable RPC dialog frequently

Multiple users are complaining of delays while using Outlook, or are seeing the Outlook cancellable RPC dialog frequently
The number of RPC operations per second is higher than expected
The number of outstanding RPC requests is high

Selecting this option will hide the detailed analysis results until the end of the analysis.

Previous Next

FIGURE 17-10 ExPTA

The ExPTA collects configuration information and live performance counter information to analyze each subsystem to determine bottlenecks that can affect RPC calls. For example, it collects disk, memory, LDAP, and event viewer data in its analysis. Like the ExBPA tool, the ExPTA also makes recommendations on how to correct any issues it identifies. Keep in mind that it is best to run this tool while experiencing performance issues. Although you can check all of the performance counters manually, this tool greatly speeds up the troubleshooting process.

Exchange Profile Analyzer

The Exchange Profile Analyzer (ExPA) collects statistical information from a single- or multiple-mailbox database across the Exchange organization. The reports include detailed information such as the average message size, how large mailboxes are, message counts, and recipient information. This tool mainly helps with capacity planning. For example, when planning an Exchange Server 2010 Mailbox server, the tool can gather information that can be later used to complete the Exchange Mailbox Role Calculator spreadsheet. It is also useful for trending information. Chapter 13, "Hardware Planning for Exchange 2010," includes more detail on using ExPA for sizing and planning hardware.

Also included in the installation package is the OWA Profile Analyzer. This tool reports on information such as logon/logoffs and detailed mail operations. Again, this is useful for reporting on trending information and capacity planning. Instead of guessing how many users actually use OWA, you can get solid numbers for reporting.

Client-Side Issues

Service Pack 1 introduces a new cmdlet for fixing mailbox issues named *repair-mailbox*. This cmdlet can be used to detect and fix the following types of mailbox corruptions:

- Search folder corruptions
- Aggregate counts on folders not reflecting correct values
- Views on folders not returning correct contents
- Provisioned folders incorrectly pointing into unprovisioned parents or vice versa

When running this task with the database online, mailbox access will be disrupted only for the mailbox that is being repaired. All other mailboxes on the database or server will still be operational.

Another useful pair of troubleshooting tools are built right into Outlook 2007 and 2010. The Connection Status dialog box shows the client's current connection status and useful information such as the response time and request failures. Occasionally when the network status changes, Outlook fails to reconnect automatically. This sometimes occurs when switching between a wired and wireless connection or enabling a connection to a corporate VPN. If Outlook does not automatically reconnect, a user can click the Reconnect button forcing Outlook to attempt to restore the client's server connection. The second tool is the Test E-mail AutoConfiguration tool. This is useful for diagnosing issues with AutoDiscover or the services that AutoDiscover returns.

Identifying and Resolving Mail Flow Issues

A number of tools are available to help you troubleshoot mail flow issues. The queue viewer, mail flow troubleshooter, and transport logs all help identify the problem.

Transport Logs

Sometimes the administrator needs detailed information to troubleshoot mail flow issues. Fortunately, Exchange provides multiple ways to get behind-the-scenes information to troubleshoot root cause. Table 17-10 shows a summary of the different logs available within Exchange.

TABLE 17-10 Transport Log Summary

LOG	DETAIL	USED FOR
Connectivity Logs	Records connection activity of outbound message delivery queues.	Troubleshooting problems with messages reaching their destination Mailbox server, Send connector, or domain.
Protocol Logs	Tracks SMTP communication between Exchange servers as part of message routing and delivery. Other protocols can be enabled, such as POP, IMAP, and HTTP.	Troubleshooting message delivery from Send and Receive connectors.
Routing Table Log	A snapshot of the message routing table used by the Hub Transport or Edge Servers.	Troubleshooting internal message delivery.
Message Tracking Logs	Track the flow of messages between servers.	Troubleshooting message delivery and determining the status of a message.
Agent Logs	Records actions performed on messages by specific anti-spam agents on Edge or Hub Transport servers.	Troubleshooting messages that have been acted upon by anti-spam agents.

CONNECTIVITY LOGS

The connectivity logs can be used to get connectivity information from the Hub Transport servers and Edge servers with their destination servers. The information in the log is detailed with connection information and is helpful in troubleshooting outbound mail flow issues. The connectivity logs do not contain message information, only information from the mail flow process.

PROTOCOL LOGS

The protocol logs are disabled by default, and can be enabled or disabled on a per-connector basis. A number of settings are configured on the connector and some are set on the server and apply across connectors.

Protocol logs should only be enabled when you are troubleshooting because they can impact the performance of the server. By default, the logs will only consume 250 MB of disk space, but this may need to be increased because the logs can grow quickly. Microsoft IT notes that they capture between 5 and 15 GB of protocol logs per day on their Edge servers.

ROUTING TABLE LOG

The Routing Table Log is enabled by default. The table is recalculated and logged after a routing change or every 12 hours by default. The Microsoft Exchange Transport Service is responsible for this log, and runs on every Hub Transport or Edge server. The Routing Table Log viewer is located in the EMC toolbox, and can be used to read local or remote logs. The routing log can be used to validate Active Directory's configuration information. Within the log is information on site and routing groups, servers, Send connectors, and address spaces.

AGENT LOGS

The agent logs can be useful for an administrator who wants to understand why an action was taken on a message because of the anti-virus agents running on the Edge or Hub Transport servers. The following agents can write information to this log:

- Connection Filter Agent
- Content Filter Agent
- Edge Rules Agent
- Recipient Filter Agent
- Sender Filter Agent
- Sender ID Agent

The information written to the log depends upon which agent and action was performed.

MESSAGE TRACKING LOGS

A very common scenario for administrators is tracking down message delivery. Users report that they sent a message and it was never received, or that they were expecting a message and it never arrived. Exchange 2010 provides a new feature called *Delivery Reports* that allows users and administrators to easily retrieve transport information about messages. Delivery reports will help answer questions about whether or when messages were delivered by providing the following information based on role-based access security. The information is listed in Table 17-11. This table shows how security rights affect what information is available in a report or even what report is available.

TABLE 17-11 Delivery Report Information

EVENT	MANAGEMENT ROLE (ROLE GROUP)
E-mail Submission from the Sender's Mailbox	MyBaseOptions (Default) Message Tracking (Organization Management) View-Only Recipients (Help Desk)
Group Expansion	MyBaseOptions (Default) Message Tracking (Organization Management) View-Only Recipients (Help Desk)

EVENT	MANAGEMENT ROLE (ROLE GROUP)
Delivery Success	MyBaseOptions (Default) Message Tracking (Organization Management) View-Only Recipients (Help Desk)
Delivery Failure	MyBaseOptions (Default) Message Tracking (Organization Management) View-Only Recipients (Help Desk)
Inbox Rules	Message Tracking (Recipient Management) Message Tracking (Organization Management) View-Only Recipients (Help Desk)
Transport Rules	Message Tracking (Organization Management) View-Only Recipients (Help Desk)
Message was read (if enabled)	MyBaseOptions (Default) Message Tracking (Organization Management) View-Only Recipients (Help Desk)
Hub Transfers	Message Tracking (Organization Management) View-Only Recipients (Help Desk)
Transfer to External Servers	MyBaseOptions (Default) Message Tracking (Organization Management) View-Only Recipients (Help Desk)
Transfer to Older Versions	MyBaseOptions (Default) Message Tracking (Organization Management) View-Only Recipients (Help Desk)
Moderation	MyBaseOptions (Default) Message Tracking (Organization Management) View-Only Recipients (Help Desk)

Users can access delivery reports from OWA by clicking the Options button, opening the Exchange control panel, clicking the Organize E-Mail tab and then selecting the Delivery Reports option. Additionally, right-clicking any message in OWA will display the Open Delivery Report option. Administrators can access Delivery Reports from the Exchange Control Panel on the Reporting tab, with PowerShell cmdlets, or within the Exchange Management Console in the Toolbox Message Tracking application. An example of a delivery report is shown in Figure 17-11.

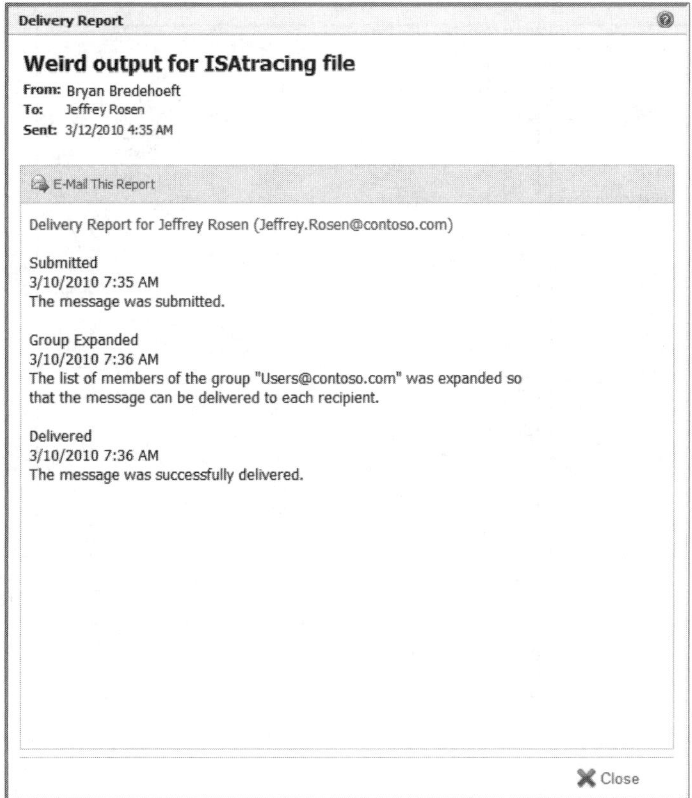

FIGURE 17-11 Delivery report

The Delivery Report tool uses data from the message tracking logs, which by default keep this data for two weeks. It is important to configure Message Tracking to match the log file data for the same length of time—tracking depends on the log data being available at each hop. If a mailbox is moved to a different server, message tracking can no longer follow the path of the message and may fail. Thus, Delivery Reports are only available for the messages in a mailbox that was generated on the server where it is currently located. The Delivery Report tracking works by the method illustrated in Figure 17-12 and the following steps.

1. ECP calls the *Search-MessageTrackingReport* task with the parameters of the search.
2. The *Search-MessageTrackingReport* task locates the sender's Mailbox server.
3. The Log Search Service on Mailbox Server1 is queried to determine the message's next hop.
4. The Log Search Service on Hub Transport1 is queried to determine the message's next hop.

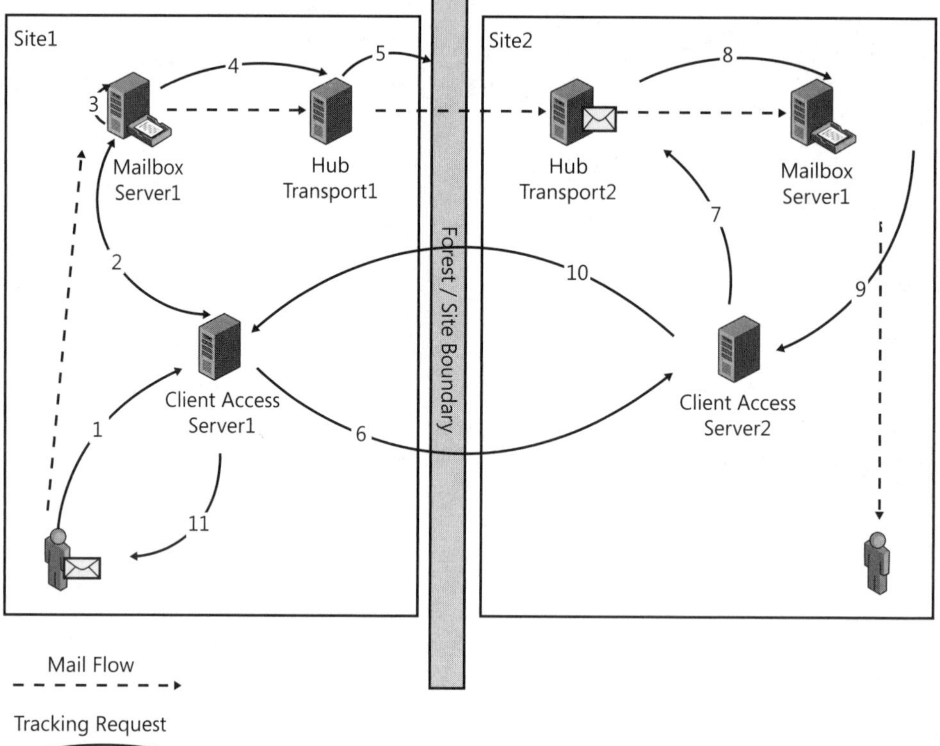

FIGURE 17-12 Message tracking

5. Tracking determines that the message crossed the forest/site boundary.
6. Tracking next contacts Client Access Server2 via EWS in the remote site.
7. Client Access Server2 queries the Log Search Service on Hub Transport2.
8. The Log Search Service on Mailbox Server2 is queried.
9. Delivery status information is returned to Client Access Server2.
10. Client Access Server2 returns delivery status information to Client Access Server1.
11. The task merges all of the results and returns them to the user.

Service Pack 1 also provides the ability to track a message after it has been queued for delivery. Users and Exchange Server Administrators can now be informed in case of a delay that a message will not meet a delivery SLA.

Managing Queues

Queues are a necessary part of transport. Queues allow organizations to not necessarily architect solutions around peak traffic, which can be costly. For example, if traffic spikes once a month during regular business cycles, it may not make sense to build a platform that during non-peak periods is severely underutilized. Queues also help with taking the responsibility of redelivery when the remote server is not responding. In any case, it is important to monitor the queues for unexpected activity, which may indicate a problem. The Exchange Management Shell (EMS) and Exchange Management Console (EMC) have interfaces to view the status and contents of these queues, and also the ability to perform actions on the messages or queues.

Exchange actually uses several queues during normal mail transport. The transport and queue architecture was discussed in more detail in Chapter 5, "Routing and Transport." Like the other troubleshooting tools, the Queue Viewer is located in the EMC in the toolbox. Figure 17-13 shows the Queue Viewer Console.

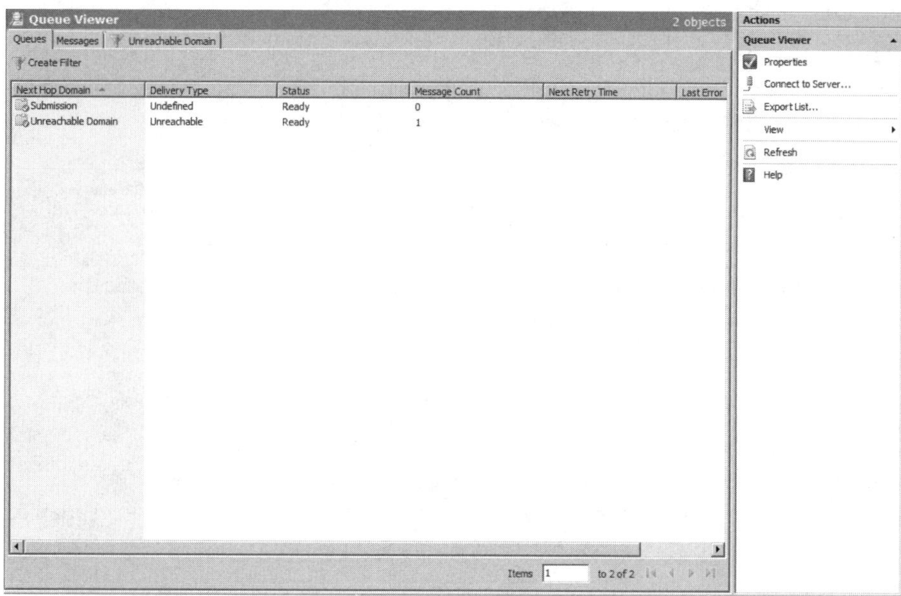

FIGURE 17-13 Queue Viewer

The Queue Viewer will open the local transport database if one is available, but it can connect to any Hub transport database. Edge Transport servers, on the other hand, can only view their local transport database. The console is fairly basic and has tabs that display the available queues, or the messages contained within that queue. Clicking the Create Filter button allows an administrator to view only queues that match the filter conditions. For example, Figure 17-14 shows a filter that when applied will only show queues in a suspended state. This is very helpful when there are many queues and it is difficult to find the information you are looking for.

FIGURE 17-14 Queue Viewer filter

Selecting a queue in the main window will create another tab where filters can be applied. You can also apply filters to the Messages tab. The filter for messages includes the ability to filter out subjects, specific source IP addresses, and even filters based on SCL value. The message view also shows the current status of the message. The status can be one of the following:

- **Active** If in the delivery queue, the message is being delivered to the next hop. If in the submission queue, the categorizer is processing the message.
- **Pending Remove** An administrator has removed the message—it is already in the delivery queue. The message will be deleted if it reenters the queue because of an error, but will be delivered otherwise.
- **Pending Suspend** An administrator has suspended the message, but it is already in the delivery queue. The message will be suspended if it reenters the queue because of an error, but will be delivered otherwise.
- **Ready** The message is waiting to be processed.
- **Retry** The message could not be delivered during the last attempt. Transport will attempt redelivery of the message.
- **Suspended** The processing of the message has been suspended and no further actions will be taken on the message until an administrator resumes the message.

Message Latency

A frequent question when message tracking is "Why did the message take so long to be delivered?" For example, a user reports a message took over an hour to be delivered. The scripts directory includes a script that converts raw latency information into human-readable form. From within the scripts directory, run the following cmdlet:

```
Get-messagetrackinglog -messageid:"<7590C0B7CDB495033BF129504CE4859002394BCB831210
E@BL2SDF0101MB003.Hub01.contoso.com>" | ? {$_.MessageLatencyType -eq 'EndToEnd'} |
ConvertTo-MessageLatency | FT -a ComponentServerFqdn,ComponentCode,ComponentLatency
```

The preceding command produces the following output:

```
ComponentServerFqdn  ComponentCode         ComponentLatency
-------------------  -------------         ----------------
MBX01.contoso.com        TOTAL            00:00:01
MBX01.contoso.com        MSSN             00:00:01
HUB01.contoso.com        TOTAL            00:00:09
HUB01.contoso.com        SDS              00:00:05
HUB01.contoso.com        CAT              00:00:01
HUB01.contoso.com        SDD              00:00:01
```

This shows that the Hub Transport and Mailbox servers handled delivery with a latency of about 9 milliseconds. In this case, the latency exists outside of the Exchange organization. This data is exposed for monitoring purposes through the MSExchange Transport Component

Latency performance counter. This counter provides the latency attributed to specific instances of the object, such as the submission queue, delivery queue, and the categorizer. The object provides latency information according to fiftieth, eightieth, ninetieth, ninety-fifth, and ninety-ninth percentile of messages processed over the last 5-minute intervals. For example, if 99 percent of 100 messages processed in the last 5 minutes had a latency of 50 seconds or less, the Percentile 99 counter for the Total Server Latency instance would be 50.

In this example, SMTP servers are inside the organization, but not part of the Exchange organization. It is possible to include non-Exchange servers in the latency calculations. Add the IP range to the *InternalSMTPServers* property using the *Set-TransportConfig* cmdlet. The External Servers instance is also included on the perfmon object.

Mail Flow Troubleshooter Tool

Another tool available to Administrators for troubleshooting mail flow related issues is the Mail Flow Troubleshooter. The troubleshooter can be found with the other troubleshooting utilities in the Toolbox in the EMC. The tool can help with a wide variety of scenarios. Figure 17-15 shows the tool's initial page. Depending on which symptoms you see, the tool will require different information to automatically diagnose the data. The tool will present an analysis of the possible root causes and suggests corrective actions.

Exchange Mail Flow Troubleshooter
Enter an identifying label for this analysis:
mail delay
What symptoms are you seeing?
Users are receiving unexpected non-delivery reports when sending messages
Users are receiving unexpected non-delivery reports when sending messages
Expected messages from senders are delayed or are not received by some recipients
Messages destined to recipients are delayed or are not received by some recipients
Messages are backing up in one or more queues on a server
Messages sent by user(s) are pending submission on their mailbox server(s) (for Exchange Server 2007 only)
Problems with Edge Server synchronization with Active Directory (for Exchange Server 2007 only)
Next

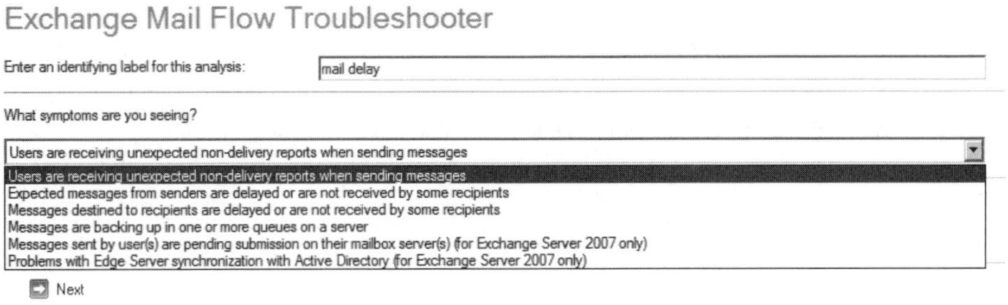

FIGURE 17-15 Mail Flow Troubleshooter

Identifying and Resolving Exchange Server Issues

The event logs are one of the most valuable resources available to administrators for identifying issues. Windows 2008 introduces some changes to the familiar tool. The legacy Windows logs category still exists, and there is a new category for Applications and Services. The Windows logs category adds two new logs: the Setup log and the ForwardedEvents log. These are intended to contain events that apply across the entire system.

The Applications and Services logs store events from a single application or sub-component. This new channel is code-named the application's *crimson channel* and is part of the new event logging API. The Application and Services logs have four sub-types, shown in Table 17-12.

TABLE 17-12 Application and Service Logs Channels

TYPE	DESCRIPTION
Admin	Events that are primarily targeted at administrators and support personnel. Events in the Admin log should provide clear remediation steps that an administrator can perform.
Operational	Operational events are used for analyzing and diagnosing a problem. Events in the Operational log may require more interpretation than events in the Admin log.
Analytic	The events in the Analytic log are not meant to be handled by user intervention. This log is mainly used for tracing information and can generate a high volume of data. By default the analytic logs are hidden and disabled.
Debug	The Debug log is used by developers troubleshooting application issues.

Exchange 2010 utilizes the Application and Service logs channels for HighAvailability and MailboxDatabaseFailureItems. These logs are located on a mailbox server by performing the following steps:

1. Open the Event Viewer MMC.
2. In the console tree, select and expand Applications And Services Logs, then Microsoft, and then Exchange.
3. Select the HighAvailability or MailboxDatabaseFailureItems channel.

If you follow these steps your Event Viewer MMC will resemble Figure 17-16.

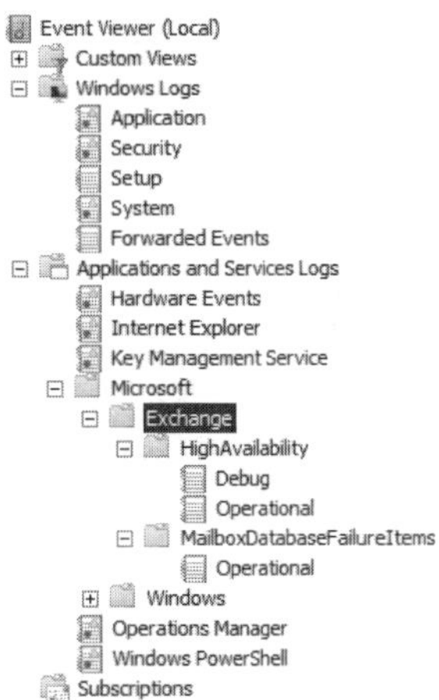

FIGURE 17-16 Applications and Service logs

The HighAvailability channel contains information from the Microsoft Exchange Replication service. The Active Manager logs events related to mounting/dismounting, reseeding, and other database operations. The Volume Shadow Copy Service (VSS), Cluster service, and TCP listener will also log events here.

The MailboxDatabaseFailureItems channel logs events associated with any failures that affect a replication mailbox database.

DAGs and Mailbox Copies

Exchange 2010 ships with a number of scripts that help collect and report on database metrics. These in-box tools are an easy way to show whether the Exchange system is meeting the defined service levels. Additionally, these reports can help an administrator tune the environment if not meeting the SLAs. The scripts are located in the [Exchange install path]\scripts directory. They must be run from an EMS.

The first script is named CollectOverMetrics.ps1. It will collect and report on information related to fail and switchover statistics. Microsoft refers to these database moves as **overs;* a generic way to refer to any time the database moves between hosts. A number of parameters are available for customizing the script, but most useful is the ability for the script to output an HTML report. The following command will collect all of the metrics and generate a report:

```
./CollectOverMetrics.ps1 -GenerateHTMLReport
```

The script was rewritten for Service Pack 1, and shows considerably more output—more than 40 metrics. Table 17-13 lists some of the information that is returned in the HTML report.

TABLE 17-13 Statistics from the CollectOverMetrics Script

PROPERTY	DESCRIPTION
DatabaseName	The name of the DAG
TimeRecoveryStarted	The start time and date of the *over
ActionType	The cause of the *over (move, mount, or dismount)
ActionTrigger	Actions may be initiated automatically or by an administrator
ActionReason	Why the *over occurred
Under 30s, Over 30s	The number of operations taking more or less than 30 seconds
DurationOutage	The total time service was unavailable
DurationDismount, DurationAcll, DurationMount	The amount of time spent at each stage of the operation
NumberOfAttempts	How many times the *over was attempted
LostLogs	The number of logs lost during the *over operation

The second script is CollectReplicationMetrics.ps1. This is useful for troubleshooting because it collects metrics in real time. The output statistics are shown in Table 17-14.

TABLE 17-14 Statistics from the CollectReplicationMetrics Script

PROPERTY	DESCRIPTION
DATABASE REPORT	
DatabaseName	The name of the DAG
ServerName	The name of the Server hosting a DAG
HoursMounted	The length of time the active DAG has been mounted on a given host
MinutesUnavailable	
MinutesResynchronizing	The length of time the mailbox database copy and its log files are being compared with the active copy of the database to check for any divergence between the two copies
MinutesFailed	The length of time the mailbox database copy is in a Failed state because it isn't suspended and it isn't able to copy or replay log files
MinutesSuspended	The length of time the mailbox database copy is in a Suspended state as a result of an administrator manually suspending the database copy
MinutesFailedSuspended	The length of time the Failed and Suspended states have been set simultaneously by the system because a failure was detected and because resolution of the failure explicitly requires administrator intervention
MinutesDisconnected	The length of time the mailbox database copy is no longer connected to the active database copy
AverageLogGenerationRate	The rate at which new logs are being generated
SERVER REPORT	
HoursMeasured	The length of time the script collected performance data
HoursUnavailable	The length of time the server was unreachable
AverageMountedMinutes	The average length of time the server
AverageLogReplayRate	The average rate for log replay
PeakLogReplayRate	The peak rate for log replay

Public Folder Troubleshooting

When it came to public folder management, Exchange 2010 seemed to take a step backward with public folder management with the EMC. Fortunately, Service Pack 1 brings back the ability to manage public folder settings. Because many companies still have public folders deployed, this will make administration easier for administrators not proficient with PowerShell and the **-PublicFolderClientPermission* cmdlets.

Another addition in Service Pack 1 is a new *Repair-PublicFolderDatabase* cmdlet. This cmdlet can be used to detect and fix the following public folder corruptions:

- Public folder replication state
- Public folder view verification
- Public folder physical corruption

NOTES FROM THE FIELD

PowerShell Scripts

Joe Cirillo
Senior Engineer, MCA:M, Horizons Consulting, Inc., USA

One of the most useful but overlooked items regarding the operation and support of Exchange 2010 are the preconfigured scripts that are made available following installation. These preconfigured scripts can be found at the following data path:

<Install Drive>\Program Files\Microsoft\Exchange Server\V14\Scripts

There are 49 out-of-the-box scripts available to assist you with daily operational tasks, one-time configuration changes, and report generation. The following is an example of how these scripts can be used.

Many companies have Public Folder infrastructures that have grown unabated over the years. One of the most challenging aspects of managing Public Folders is determining which Public Folders are no longer being accessed by users. Armed with this information, an administrator can perform some needed housecleaning. The AggregatePFData.ps1 script can assist with this daunting task.

The AggregatePFData.ps1 script aggregates and captures information collected from the following cmdlets:

- *Get-PublicFolderItemStatistics*
- *Get-PublicFolderStatistics*
- *Get-PublicFolder*

This script has been updated in Service Pack 1 to deliver real aggregate information collected from all replicas.

Then, the following information is aggregated at the public folder level:

- Last user access and last user modification times
- Owner of the public folder
- Other properties such as *MailEnabled, HasRules, ItemCount, FolderType, HasModerator,* and *TotalItemSize*

After this report is generated, the administrator can begin the cleanup process. What I like to do with Public Folders I deem unnecessary is to first simply hide the Public Folder from the user's view. Hiding the public folder for a period of time allows you to await any calls from users stating that their Public Folders are missing. After an allotted amount of time passes with no user complaints, you can perform a backup of the Public Folder database for archival and then safely remove the hidden, unused Public Folders from the database.

Client Access Server Troubleshooting

Of course, not everything will always run as smoothly as planned. This section describes some techniques to handle common issues or check on your Client Access Server's health.

CLIENT ACCESS SERVER TEST CMDLETS

You can use a number of PowerShell cmdlets to test Client Access Server health. Table 17-15 lists the relevant PowerShell cmdlets with a description. Many of the cmdlets can target a specific user as a parameter. The New-TestCASConnectivityUser.ps1 script located in the scripts directory will create a test user that you can use with these cmdlets.

TABLE 17-15 CAS PowerShell Test Cmdlets

CMDLET	DESCRIPTION
Test-MapiConnectivity	Tests the RPC Client Access service. Indirectly, this cmdlet also tests the directory service and mailbox store.
Test-OutlookConnectivity	Used to verify that OWA is running. It can be used to test all virtual directories or an individual virtual directory. It can also be used to test all mailboxes running in the same Active Directory site. It is recommended that you run *test-MapiConnectivity* first to ensure that the mailbox is available.
Test-OutlookWebServices	Verifies that the service information returned by AutoDiscover for the Availability Service, Outlook Anywhere, Offline Address Book, and Unified Messaging.
Test-WebServicesConnectivity	Tests the functionality of Exchange Web Services by running *GetFolder*, *CreateItem*, *DeleteItem*, and *SyncFolderItems* operations over Outlook Anywhere.
Test-EcpConnectivity	Verifies Exchange Control Panel Connectivity for all mailboxes on Exchange servers in the same site, or an individual ECP URL.
Test-ActiveSyncConnectivity	Performs a full mailbox synchronization to verify the health of ActiveSync.

CMDLET	DESCRIPTION
Test-ImapConnectivity	Tests IMAP4 connectivity by creating and sending a special message to a mailbox. The cmdlet then logs on to the mailbox to check for the test message. If you use the *LightMode* parameter, only the logon is performed.
Test-PopConnectivity	Tests POP3 connectivity by creating and sending a special message to a mailbox. The cmdlet then logs on to the mailbox to check for the test message. If you use the *LightMode* parameter, only the logon is performed.
Test-PowerShellConnectivity	Used to test whether PowerShell remoting on the target Client Access server is healthy.
Test-ServiceHealth	Tests to ensure that all Windows services required for the Client Access Server role are running.
Test-SystemHealth	Runs a check of the Exchange environment against Microsoft best practices. To write to a file use the following two commands: `$temp=Test-SystemHealth -OutData` `Set-Content -Value $temp.FileData -Path c:\temp\SystemHealthOutData.xml -Encoding Byte` You can then import this XML file into the Best Practices Analyzer tool found in the EMC Toolbox.

AUTODISCOVER

AutoDiscover can be complex to configure correctly when you have a variety of clients coming in from both inside and outside the corporate network. Fortunately, Microsoft has given you a number of tools to help troubleshoot AutoDiscover. The first thing to check is a tool built into Microsoft Outlook. After launching Outlook, press and hold the Ctrl key and right-click the Outlook icon in the system tray. A hidden menu item will appear named Test Email AutoConfiguration. Simply type in an e-mail address and password and run the test. This will return all of the Autodiscover information that it discovers. From the protocol property, you can see the queries to find an SCP object or the queries via DNS as well as the configuration returned for internal (RPC or EXCH) and external (HTTPS or EXPR) connectivity. If it cannot locate Autodiscover information, check the Log tab. This tab shows all of the different methods Autodiscover uses to establish a connection. This can help narrow down which methods are failing. Make sure from the client you can resolve the DNS name correctly using a common tool, such as nslookup.

Another method for troubleshooting Autodiscover is using Windows PowerShell from an Exchange server. The *Test-OutlookWebServices* cmdlet tests Autodiscover and also the service settings Autodiscover returns. Simply run the *Test-OutlookWebServices* cmdlet with the *–Identity* parameter set to a user's e-mail address; for example, *Test-OutlookWebServices –Identity Bryan.Bredehoeft@litwareinc.com.*

REMOTE CONNECTIVITY ANALYZER

The newest of the analyzers, the Remote Connectivity Analyzer, is not included in the EMC Toolbox. This Web-based tool is located at *https://www.testexchangeconnectivity.com.* Figure 17-17 shows the home page and the various tests an administrator can perform with this Web site.

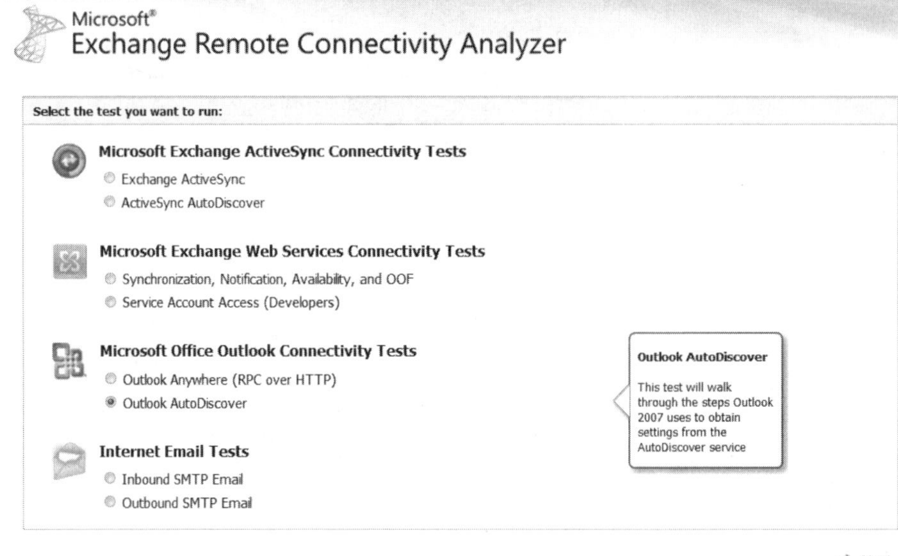

FIGURE 17-17 Remote Connectivity Analyzer

Table 17-16 explains the various tests and how they can be used for troubleshooting.

TABLE 17-16 Remote Connectivity Analyzer tests

TEST TYPE	TEST DETAILS	USED FOR
Exchange ActiveSync	Test simulates a mobile device connecting using EAS.	Identify configuration or connectivity issues with ActiveSync.
ActiveSync AutoDiscover	Test simulates an ActiveSync device obtaining its settings with AutoDiscover.	Identify configuration errors with AutoDiscover.
Exchange Web Services General Test	Tests basic EWS tasks.	Useful for simulating EWS clients, such as Entourage, as well as for identifying configuration or connectivity issues with EWS.

TEST TYPE	TEST DETAILS	USED FOR
Exchange Web Services Service Account Access	Tests a service account's ability to access a specified mailbox and perform basic EWS tasks.	Primarily used by application developers to test the ability to access mailboxes with alternate credentials (Exchange impersonation).
Outlook Anywhere	Tests the steps Outlook uses to connect with Outlook Anywhere.	Test Outlook Anywhere's configuration and connectivity.
Outlook AutoDiscover	Tests the steps used by Outlook 2007 to obtain settings from AutoDiscover.	Identify configuration errors with AutoDiscover.
Inbound SMTP Email	Tests inbound mail to a specified mailbox. This will check DNS MX record configuration and TCP Port 25 connectivity.	Validate your Exchange organization's ability to receive mail.
Outbound SMTP Email	Checks outbound SMTP for connectivity and other issues, including Reverse DNS, Sender ID, and RBL checks.	Validates your Exchange organization's ability to send mail. This is useful when users are reporting that messages are not being delivered because they are marked as spam.

The Remote Connectivity Analyzer provides step-by-step detail to pinpoint where exactly in the test any failures occurred. Of course these tests are all run from the Internet, so they will not help troubleshoot issues from inside the corporate network perspective.

CERTIFICATES

Troubleshooting certificates can be challenging. Even though the certificate management MMC may import a certificate and not report any issues, Exchange may fail to import the certificate. This is because the MMC snap-in only requires basic hierarchy validation and does not perform additional checks. Exchange requires a much more vigorous validation checking, including a certificate revocation check. You can check the certificate status with the *get-ExchangeCertificate* cmdlet. If the import fails or there is an issue, the status field will report invalid. Another symptom is the services using SSL or TLS will fail to start, resulting in the following error:

> ***DESCRIPTION*** **The IMAP4 service failed to connect using SSL or TLS encryption. A valid certificate is not configured to respond to SSL/TLS connections. Check the configured hostname as well as which certificates are installed in the Personal Certificates store of the computer.**

One way to troubleshoot these types of errors is to export the certificate and run the certutil utility to verify the certificate. The syntax is:

```
Certutil -verify filename
```

Examine the output and see whether the error relates to the ability to check the certificate's revocation status. The Exchange server might be unable to connect to the revocation point because of a server proxy configuration error or Internet connection problem.

IIS VIRTUAL DIRECTORY TROUBLESHOOTING

Occasionally an administrator may need to re-create the IIS virtual directories, such as OWA. Maybe the configuration was changed inappropriately, or the Web site was damaged. In Exchange 2010 RTM, this was only achievable with PowerShell cmdlets such as *New-OWAVirtualDirectory*. In Service Pack 1, this ability was added to the EMC. When an administrator selects a Client Access Server in the EMC, there is a new action called *Reset Virtual Directory*. This action will guide the administrator through a process that will delete and re-create a virtual directory back to the initial default settings.

PowerShell Troubleshooting

A frequent request from Exchange administrators in the past was the ability to determine who performed an operation and what was changed. With the change in PowerShell's architecture using the new remoting design, this allows for this auditing to be configured. Cmdlets will now be audited no matter where they are run when they are correctly configured.

PowerShell auditing works by calling an Admin Audit Log Agent when a cmdlet runs. The agent is one of seven available default management shell extension agents. The agent is called when a cmdlet is run, and the agent evaluates the configuration against the configured rules to determine whether the cmdlet or parameters require logging. The agent is enabled by default, and this setting should never need to be changed. For audit logging to work, several parameters must be set first.

The audit logs are sent to a specified auditing mailbox. This is configured with the *Set-AdminAuditLogConfig* cmdlet. For example, to send all of the logs to a mailbox called auditlogs@contoso.com, run the following cmdlet:

```
Set-AdminAuditLogConfig -AdminAuditLogMailbox auditlogs@contoso.com
```

Ensure that only authorized users have access to the mailbox specified. Sensitive information may be included in the log. Also, make sure the mailbox is being monitored so that it does not run out of space.

Next, configure the cmdlets and parameters that should be audited. These can be specific cmdlets or cmdlets with wildcards. For example, to audit the *Set-Mailbox* cmdlet, any cmdlet starting with *Set-Database*, and any cmdlet with the word *rule* in it (*Disable-InboxRule* and *Disable-JournalRule* would both match), use the following syntax:

```
Set-AdminAuditLogConfig -AdminAuditLogCmdlets "Set-Mailbox, Set-Database*, *rule*"
```

Again, you can fine-tune this by specifying specific parameters to enable auditing on. This follows the same conventions as the cmdlet auditing:

```
Set-AdminAuditLogConfig -AdminAuditLogParameters "Database, *mailbox*"
```

Finally, to enable the logging, set the *AdminAuditLogEnabled* parameter to true:

```
Set-AdminAuditLogConfig -AdminAuditLogEnabled $True
```

The combination of enabling the Agent and setting *AdminAuditLogEnabled* to true starts the logging. The following is an example of output when auditing the *Set-Mailbox* cmdlet was configured:

```
Cmdlet Name: Set-Mailbox
Object Modified: Contoso.com/users/Jeffrey Rosen
Parameter: Identity = jrosen
Parameter: CustomAttribute1 = Testing
Property Modified: CustomAttribute1 = Testing
Property Modified: ObjectState = Changed
Caller: Contoso\administrator
Succeeded: True
Error: None
Run Date: 3/5/2010 6:20:57 PM UTC
```

Additional Resources

- Microsoft Exchange Analyzers Portal: *http://technet.microsoft.com/en-us/exchange/bb288481.aspx*
- Monitoring High Availability and Site Resilience: *http://technet.microsoft.com/en-us/library/dd351258.aspx*
- Performance Counter Data Collection Sets for Exchange 2010: *http://blogs.technet.com/mikelag/archive/2010/01/11/perfwiz-for-exchange-2010.aspx*
- Hub Transport Architecture Poster: *http://download.microsoft.com/download/A/1/1/A114432B-84B7-4EF6-8671-7DE62D9EC8AA/Exchange2010_HubTransportRoleArchitecture.pdf*
- How to Use DNSLint to Troubleshoot Active Directory Replication Issues: *http://support.microsoft.com/kb/321046*
- Virtualization Counters: *http://technet.microsoft.com/en-us/library/ff367892.aspx*
- Monitoring Hyper-V Performance: *http://blogs.msdn.com/tvoellm/archive/2009/04/23/monitoring-hyper-v-performance.aspx*

Index

Symbols and Numbers

A

B

C

D

E

F

G

H

I

J

K

L

M

N

O

P

Q

R

S

T

U

V

W

X

Z

About the Authors

SIEGFRIED JAGOTT works as a Principal Consultant and Team Lead for the Microsoft Messaging and Collaboration team at Siemens AG, located in Munich, Germany. He is part of the Siemens central architecture team that works closely with Microsoft to plan future enhancements of not only Windows and Exchange but also other products such as System Center Virtual Machine Manager (SC VMM). He has been involved in Microsoft technology adoption programs since Exchange 2000 and has been working with Microsoft Exchange since Exchange Server 4.0. In the past 15 years he has been involved in planning, designing, and implementing some of the world's largest Windows and Exchange infrastructures for various international customers, including Siemens itself.

Besides this, Siegfried is a frequent writer for various international magazines such as the *Windows IT Pro Magazine* and speaks at conferences about Windows- and Exchange-related topics. He is coauthor of *MCITP: Microsoft Exchange Server 2007 Messaging Design and Deployment Study Guide: Exams 70-237 and 70-238* (Sybex, 2008), *MCTS: Windows Server 2008 Applications Infrastructure Configuration Study Guide: Exam 70-643* (Sybex, 2008) and the Microsoft course MOC 10135: Configuring, Managing, and Troubleshooting Microsoft Exchange Server 2010. In his spare time he likes to go skiing in the Alps and travel around the world to scuba dive. Siegfried lives in a small town called Rednitzhembach in southern Germany, where he is currently building a new house. He holds an MBA and a Diploma in Management from Open University in England and has been a Microsoft Certified Systems Engineer (MCSE) since 1997.

JOEL STIDLEY has been working in the IT field for 15 years, and he has been a computer fanatic for much longer. Joel has been working with Microsoft Exchange since the initial Exchange Server 5.0 beta release. He has also led an engineering team to create a shared Exchange 2000 hosting platform before Microsoft released guidance on how to do so. Since the release of Exchange 2000 Server Service Pack 3, he has participated in the Microsoft Exchange JDP and TAP programs. Currently, he is the Principal

Systems Architect at Terremark Worldwide, where he works with a variety of existing and future technologies related to virtualization, directory services, storage, and messaging. In his 10 years with Terremark, he has filled a number of key roles, including technical lead for creating and operationalizing the company's Infinistructure virtualization platform. He also is a Microsoft MVP, blogger, and author or coauthor of several other technical books, including *Professional Windows PowerShell for Exchange Server 2007 Service Pack 1* (Wrox, 2008), *MCTS: Microsoft Exchange Server 2007 Configuration Study Guide: Exam 70-236* (Sybex, 2009), *MCTS: Windows Server 2008 Applications Infrastructure Configuration Study Guide: Exam 70-643* (Sybex, 2008), and the Microsoft course MOC 10135: Configuring, Managing, and Troubleshooting Microsoft Exchange Server 2010. Joel started an Exchange community and blog Web site called *ExchangeExchange.com* in 2004 to provide a place for others interested in Exchange to share information.

Contributing Authors

ANDY SCHAN started out as an electronics technologist, working on ground aviation systems and radar installations, including the Distant Early Warning System in the high arctic; from there he moved to the installation, care, and feeding of linear electron accelerators for physics research and cancer treatment. Andy's IT career began more than 12 years ago with migrating MS Mail to Exchange 4.0 for an international software company spanning 30 Exchange sites worldwide. Since then, he has worked with every major Exchange release and was the team lead for EDS Canada's Messaging and Active Directory Engineering team. He also drove the first Canadian federal government migration of Exchange 5.5 to Exchange Server 2003, where he experienced the joys of synchronizing a 275,000-object directory between Exchange 5.5, Active Directory and Novell. In addition to numerous large-scale migration projects he has participated in the Exchange Server 2007 and Exchange Server 2010 TAP programs, contributed to an Exchange Server 2007 book, and deployed a message classification and policy solution to 125,000 users in a large military environment. He has also worked on a number of identity management projects, including Active Directory migrations, federation implementations, and digital rights management for environments as large as 525,000 seats, and has spoken at NetPro's Directory Experts Conference and Quest's The Experts Conference. He is currently working as Senior Consultant for Titus International in Ottawa, Canada. In his downtime, Andy can be found on Xbox Live.

JEFFREY ROSEN has a Master of Business Administration from Case Western Reserve Weatherhead School of Management specializing in Information Systems. He is a Microsoft Certified Architect and Microsoft Certified Master, and holds a MCSE specializing in messaging and security. He began his career working with Microsoft Mail and Novell Netware. Jeffrey has been working for Microsoft Consulting Services for 11 years, working on large and complex Exchange deployments. He is a coauthor of *Professional Windows PowerShell for Exchange Server 2007 Service Pack 1* (Wrox, 2008) and *Microsoft PowerShell, VBScript & JScript Bible* (Wiley, 2009). In his spare time, you may catch him on Xbox Live.

Get Certified—Windows Server 2008

Ace your preparation for the skills measured by the Microsoft® certification exams—and on the job. With 2-in-1 *Self-Paced Training Kits*, you get an official exam-prep guide + practice tests. Work at your own pace through lessons and real-world case scenarios that cover the exam objectives. Then, assess your skills using practice tests with multiple testing modes—and get a customized learning plan based on your results.

EXAMS 70-640, 70-642, 70-646

MCITP Self-Paced Training Kit: Windows Server® 2008 Server Administrator Core Requirements

ISBN 9780735625082

EXAM 70-640

MCTS Self-Paced Training Kit: Configuring Windows Server 2008 Active Directory®

Dan Holme, Nelson Ruest, and Danielle Ruest

ISBN 9780735625136

EXAM 70-642

MCTS Self-Paced Training Kit: Configuring Windows Server 2008 Network Infrastructure

Tony Northrup, J.C. Mackin

ISBN 9780735625129

EXAM 70-643

MCTS Self-Paced Training Kit: Configuring Windows Server 2008 Applications Infrastructure

J.C. Mackin, Anil Desai

ISBN 9780735625112

EXAM 70-646

MCITP Self-Paced Training Kit: Windows Server Administration

Ian McLean, Orin Thomas

ISBN 9780735625105

EXAMS 70-640, 70-642, 70-643, 70-647

MCITP Self-Paced Training Kit: Windows Server 2008 Enterprise Administrator Core Requirements

ISBN 9780735625723

EXAM 70-647

MCITP Self-Paced Training Kit: Windows® Enterprise Administration

Orin Thomas, et al.

ISBN 9780735625099

ALSO SEE

Windows Server 2008 Administrator's Pocket Consultant

William R. Stanek

ISBN 9780735624375

Windows Server 2008 Administrator's Companion

Charlie Russel, Sharon Crawford

ISBN 9780735625051

Windows Server 2008 Resource Kit

Microsoft MVPs with Windows Server Team

ISBN 9780735623613

microsoft.com/mspress